Komm mit!

Your passport to proficiency

Dein Pass zur Welt!

Plan your itinerary for success

What's your Destination?

Communication!

Komm mit! takes your classroom there.

It's even possible that "What's next?" will become your students' favorite question!

Communication and culture in context

The clear structure of each chapter makes it easy to present, practice, and apply language skills—all in the context of the location where the chapter takes place!

Grammar support and practice in every lesson

Komm mit! builds a proven communicative approach on a solid foundation of grammar and vocabulary so students become proficient readers, writers, and speakers of German. With the Grammatikheft, Grammar Tutor, and CD-ROM Tutor, students can practice the way they learn best.

Technology that takes you there

Bring the world into your classroom with integrated technology: CD-ROM, DVD and Internet resources including an Online Student Edition.

Assessment for state and national standards

Every chapter features a variety of writing activities, including process writing strategies. To help you incorporate standardized test practice, the Lies mit mir! Reader and Reading Strategies and Skills Handbook offer additional reading practice and reading skills development.

Easy lesson planning for all learning styles

Planning lessons has never been easier with a Lesson Planner with Differentiated Instruction, an editable One-Stop Planner® CD-ROM, and a Student Make-Up Assignments with Alternative Quizzes resource.

Travel a balanced program that's easy to navigate.

Die Welt erwartet dich!

Komm mit!

Program components

Texts
- Pupil's Edition
- Teacher's Edition

Middle School Resources
- Exploratory Guide
- TPR Storytelling Book

Planning and Presenting
- One-Stop Planner CD-ROM with ExamView® Test Generator
- Lesson Planner with Differentiated Instruction
- Student Make-Up Assignments with Alternative Quizzes
- Teaching Transparencies

Grammar
- Grammatikheft
- Grammar Tutor for Students of German

Reading and Writing
- Reading Strategies and Skills Handbook
- Lies mit mir! Reader
- Übungsheft

Listening and Speaking
- Audio CD Program
- Listening Activities
- Activities for Communication
- TPR Storytelling Book (Levels 1 and 2)

Assessment
- Testing Program
- Alternative Assessment Guide
- Student Make-Up Assignments with Alternative Quizzes

Technology
- One-Stop Planner CD-ROM with ExamView Test Generator
- Audio CD Program
- Interactive CD-ROM Tutor (Levels 1 and 2)
- Video Program
- Video Guide
- DVD Tutor (Levels 1 and 2)
- Online Edition (Levels 1 and 2)

Internet
- go.hrw.com
- www.hrw.com

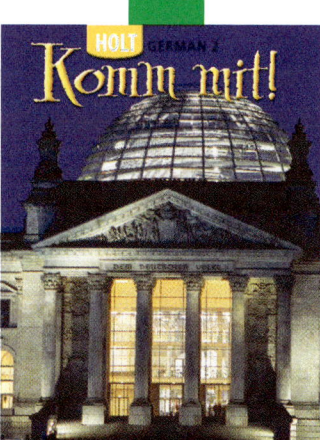
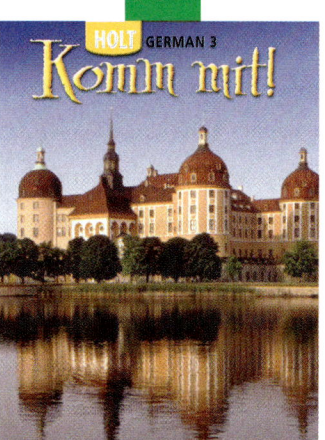

Destination: Communication

Teacher's Edition

HOLT GERMAN 2
Komm mit!

HOLT, RINEHART AND WINSTON
A Harcourt Education Company

Orlando • **Austin** • New York • San Diego • Toronto • London

Copyright © 2006 by Holt, Rinehart and Winston

All rights reserved. No part of this publication may be reproduced or transmitted in any form or by any means, electronic or mechanical, including photocopy, recording, or any information storage and retrieval system, without permission in writing from the publisher.

Requests for permission to make copies of any part of the work should be mailed to the following address: Permissions Department, Holt, Rinehart and Winston, 10801 N. MoPac Expressway, Building 3, Austin, Texas 78759.

KOMM MIT! is a trademark licensed to Holt, Rinehart and Winston, registered in the United States of America and/or other jurisdictions.

ONE-STOP PLANNER is a trademark licensed to Holt, Rinehart and Winston, registered in the United States of America and/or other jurisdictions.

For permission to reprint copyrighted material in the Teacher's Edition, grateful acknowledgment is made to the following sources:
National Standards in Foreign Language Education Project: "National Standards Report" from **Standards for Foreign Language Learning:** Preparing for the 21st Century. Copyright © 1996 by National Standards in Foreign Language Education Project.

For permission to reprint copyrighted material in the Pupil's Edition and the Teacher's Edition, grateful acknowledgment is made to the following sources:
Baedeker Verlag Karl Baedeker GmbH: "Baden–Baden" from *Baedeker Allianz Reiseführer Deutschland,* 2. Copyright © 1992 by Verlag Karl Baedeker GmbH.
Berlin Programm Rimbach Verlag GmbH: "Oper & Theater" from *Berlin Programm,* September 1993. Reviews of "Blau–Rot," "Britzer Mühle," "Istambul," "Restaurant El Pharaoh," "Restaurant Hardtke," "Restaurant Pferdestall," and "Restaurant Seaside" from *Berlin Programm,* September 1993.

Printed in the United States of America

ISBN 0-03-037259-3

3 4 5 6 7 8 9 048 09 08 07 06 05

ACKNOWLEDGMENTS

Front Cover and Title Page: Bryan Reinhart/Masterfile
Back Cover: © AFP/CORBIS; (frame) © 2006 Image Farm, Inc.

All photos by George Winkler/Holt, Rinehart and Winston, Inc. except:

Master element icons: Community Link: HBJ Photo; CD-Rom tutor: Courtesy Neel Heisel; Internet Connection computers: Digital imagery® © 2003 PhotoDisc, Inc.; Jupiter page: Digital imagery® © 2003 PhotoDisc, Inc.; Chess piece: Digital imagery® © 2003 PhotoDisc, Inc.; Clock: Digital imagery® © 2003 PhotoDisc, Inc.; Globes: Mountain High Maps® Copyright © 1997 Digital Wisdom, Inc.; Euros: © European Communities; Recipe border fabric: Victoria Smith/HRW Photo; All Teacher to Teacher photos supplied by the teachers themselves.

Front Matter: (sunflowers, mill, clock tower), Image Copyright (©)2003 Photodisc, Inc., (boy on bike), (c) Digital Vision; (band, girl with textbook, group of girls), HRW Photo; (girl writing, statue at sunset), Creatas; (tulips, man with globe), Corbis Images; T9 (l), Victoria Smith/HRW Photo. Chapter One: 3D (cr), Victoria Smith/HRW Photo. Chapter Three: 59D (cr), Victoria Smith/HRW Photo. Chapter Five: 121E (t), Victoria Smith/HRW Photo. Chapter Seven: 181D (r), Victoria Smith/HRW Photo. Chapter Eight: 209D (br), Victoria Smith/HRW Photo. Chapter Eleven: 297D (cr), Hans H. Alex/HRW Photo.

Art Credits

All art, unless otherwise noted, by Holt, Rinehart & Winston.

Chapter Two: Page 41O, Eduard Böhm; 41X, Holly Cooper. Chapter Three: Page 65S, George McLeod. Chapter Five: Page 127T, Tomm Rummonds. Chapter Six: Page 155U, Eduard Böhm. Chapter Seven: Page 187Q, Holly Cooper. Chapter Nine: Page 243W, Holly Cooper. Chapter Eleven: Page 303S, Mike Krone.

ACKNOWLEDGMENTS continued on page R83, which is an extension of the copyright page.

Komm mit! Level 2 Teacher's Edition

CONTRIBUTING WRITERS
Ulrike Puryear
Austin, TX
Mrs. Puryear wrote background information, activities, and teacher suggestions for all chapters of the *Teacher's Edition*.

CONSULTANTS
The consultants conferred on a regular basis with the editorial staff and reviewed all the chapters of the Level 2 *Teacher's Edition*.

Dorothea Bruschke, retired
Parkway School District
Chesterfield, MO

Diane E. Laumer
San Marcos High School
San Marcos, TX

REVIEWERS
The following educators reviewed one or more chapters of the *Teacher's Edition*.

Inge Atkins
Arvada High School
Arvada, CO

Nancy Butt
Washington and Lee High School
Arlington, VA

Kathleen Cooper
Burnsville High School
Burnsville, MN

Frank Dietz
The University of Texas at Austin
Austin, TX

Connie Frank
John F. Kennedy High School
Sacramento, CA

Gerlind Jenkner
Medina High School
Medina, OH

Patrick T. Raven
National Consultant
Holt, Rinehart and Winston

John Scanlan
Arlington High School
Arlington, OR

Ralph M. Schwägermann
Stuyvesant High School
New York, NY

Jim Witt
Grand Junction High School
Grand Junction, CO

TEACHER-TO-TEACHER CONTRIBUTORS

Chapter 1
Teresa Karrels
Central High School
West Allis, WI

Chapter 2
Jan Haverty
Blue Valley North High School
Overland Park, KS

Chapter 3
Tanya Stevenson
Terrill Middle School
Scotch Plains, NJ

Chapter 4
Haley Crittenden
Herndon High School
Herndon, VA

Chapter 5
Laura Grable
Riverhead Middle School
Riverhead, NY

Chapter 6
Nicole Mitescu
Claremont High School
Claremont, CA

Chapter 7
Gertraud Irwin
Morgantown High School
Morgantown, WV

Chapter 8
Pamela Taborsky
Leander High School
Leander, TX

Chapter 9
Paula Bernard
Sandy Creek High School
Fayette County, GA

Chapter 10
Alisa Glick
Greenwich Country Day School
Greenwich, CT

Chapter 11
Judy Pyne
Homewood-Flossmoor High School
Flossmoor, IL

Chapter 12
Jim Garland
Henry Clay High School
Lexington, KY

PROFESSIONAL ESSAYS

Bringing Standards into the Classroom
Paul Sandrock
Foreign Language Education
Department of Public Instruction
Madison, WI

Reading Strategies and Skills
Nancy A. Humbach
Miami University
Oxford, OH

Technology in the Language Classroom
Cindy A. Kendall
Williamston High School
Williamston, MI

Using Portfolios in the Language Classroom
Jo Anne S. Wilson
J. Wilson Associates
Glen Arbor, MI

Teaching Culture
Nancy A. Humbach
Miami University
Oxford, OH

Dorothea Bruschke, retired
Parkway School District
Chesterfield, MO

Multi-Level Classrooms
Joan H. Manley
University of Texas at El Paso, TX

Learning Styles and Multi-Modality Teaching
Mary B. McGehee
Louisiana State University
Laboratory School
Baton Rouge, LA

To the Teacher

Principles and Practices

As nations become increasingly interdependent, the need for effective communication and sensitivity to other cultures becomes more important. Today's youth must be culturally and linguistically prepared to participate in a global society. At Holt, Rinehart and Winston, we believe that proficiency in more than one language is essential to meeting this need.

The primary goal of the Holt, Rinehart and Winston World Languages programs is to help students develop linguistic proficiency and cultural sensitivity. By interweaving language and culture, our programs seek to broaden students' communication skills while at the same time deepening their appreciation of other cultures.

We believe that all students can benefit from foreign language instruction. We recognize that not everyone learns at the same rate or in the same way; nevertheless, we believe that all students should have the opportunity to acquire language proficiency to a degree commensurate with their individual abilities.

Holt, Rinehart and Winston's World Languages programs are designed to accommodate all students by appealing to a variety of learning styles.

We believe that effective language programs should motivate students. Students deserve an answer to the question they often ask: "Why are we doing this?" They need to have goals that are interesting, practical, clearly stated, and attainable.

Holt, Rinehart and Winston's World Languages programs promote success. They present relevant content in manageable increments that encourage students to attain achievable functional objectives.

We believe that proficiency in another language is best nurtured by programs that encourage students to think critically and to take risks when expressing themselves in the language. We also recognize that students should strive for accuracy in communication. While it is imperative that students have a knowledge of the basic structures of the language, it is also important that they go beyond the simple manipulation of forms.

Holt, Rinehart and Winston's World Languages programs reflect a careful progression of activities that guide students from comprehensible input of authentic language through structured practice to creative, personalized expression. This progression, accompanied by consistent re-entry and spiraling of functions, vocabulary, and structures, provides students with the tools and the confidence to express themselves in their new language.

Finally, we believe that a complete program of language instruction should take into account the needs of teachers in today's increasingly demanding classrooms.

At Holt, Rinehart and Winston, we have designed programs that offer practical teacher support and provide resources to meet individual learning and teaching styles.

We have seen significant advances in modern language curriculum practices:

1. a redefinition of the objectives of foreign language study involving a commitment to the development of proficiency in the four skills and in cultural awareness;
2. a recognition of the need for longer sequences of study;
3. a new student-centered approach that redefines the role of the teacher as facilitator and encourages students to take a more active role in their learning;
4. the inclusion of students of all learning abilities.

The new Holt, Rinehart and Winston World Languages programs take into account not only these advances in the field of foreign language education but also the input of teachers and students around the country.

Teacher's Edition
Contents

TO THE TEACHER	T8
TABLE OF CONTENTS	T9
PACING GUIDE AND ARTICULATION CHART	T10
SCOPE AND SEQUENCE, HOLT GERMAN, LEVEL 2	T12
USING *KOMM MIT!*, LEVEL 2	T24

PUPIL'S EDITION
- Location Opener ... T25
- Chapter Opener ... T25
- Los geht's! ... T26
- Stufen ... T26
- Landeskunde ... T27
- Zum Lesen ... T27
- Mehr Grammatikübungen ... T28
- Anwendung ... T28
- Kann ich's wirklich? ... T28
- Wortschatz ... T28

TECHNOLOGY ... T29

ANCILLARY PROGRAM ... T30

TEACHER'S EDITION ... T32

PROFESSIONAL ESSAYS
- Standards for Foreign Language Learning ... T36
- Reading ... T38
- Using Portfolios in the Language Classroom ... T40
- Multi-Level Classrooms ... T42
- Teaching Culture ... T44
- Learning Styles and Multi-Modality Teaching ... T46

PROFESSIONAL REFERENCES ... T48

A BIBLIOGRAPHY FOR THE GERMAN TEACHER ... T50

TABLE OF CONTENTS, CHAPTERS 1–12 ... T57

INDEX OF CULTURAL REFERENCES, TEACHER'S EDITION ... T70

MAPS ... T76

Pacing and Planning

Traditional Schedule

Days of instruction: 180

Location Opener	2 days per Location Opener x 6 Location Openers	12 days
Chapter	13 days per chapter x 12 chapters	156 days
		168 days

If you are teaching on a traditional schedule, we suggest following the plan above and spending 13 days per chapter. A complete set of lesson plans in the interleaf provides detailed suggestions for each chapter. For more suggestions, see the **Lesson Planner with Substitute Teacher Lesson Plans.**

Block Schedule

Blocks of instruction: 90

Location Opener	1/2 block per Location Opener x 6 Location Openers	3 blocks
Chapter	7 blocks per chapter x 12 chapters	84 blocks
		87 blocks

If you are teaching on a block schedule, we suggest following the plan above and spending seven blocks per chapter. A complete set of lesson plans in the interleaf provides detailed suggestions for each chapter. For more suggestions, see the **Lesson Planner with Substitute Teacher Lesson Plans.**

One-Stop Planner CD-ROM

Use the **One-Stop Planner CD-ROM with Test Generator** to aid in lesson planning and pacing.

- Editable lesson plans with direct links to teaching resources
- Printable worksheets from resource books
- Direct launches to the HRW Internet activities
- Video and audio segments
- Test Generator
- Clip Art for vocabulary items

Pacing Tips

At the beginning of each chapter, you will find a Pacing Tip to help you plan your lessons.

Articulation Across Levels

The following chart shows how topics are repeated across levels in *Komm mit!* from the end of Level 1 to the beginning of Level 3.

- In each level, the last chapter is a review chapter.
- In Levels 2 and 3, the first two chapters review the previous level.

LEVEL 1

CHAPTER 12
Review of Level 1

- The **möchte**-forms; **noch ein** and **kein**
- Nominative and accusative pronouns; definite and indefinite articles
- Possessive pronouns
- The verb **können**; **für**; accusative pronouns; **du**-commands
- The verb **wissen**; word order; formal commands
- The verbs **wollen** and **müssen**; word order
- Asking where something is and giving directions

LEVEL 2

CHAPTER 1
Review of Level 1

- **Haben** and **sein**
- **Mein, dein, sein,** and **ihr**
- The **möchte**-forms and **wollen**
- The nominative and accusative forms of indefinite and definite articles
- Regular and stem-changing verbs
- Third person pronouns
- Asking for and giving information
- Describing people
- Expressing likes and dislikes
- Giving and responding to compliments; expressing wishes

CHAPTER 2

- Clauses with **weil** and **denn**
- Dative case of **mein, dein, sein,** and **ihr**
- **Du**-commands
- The interrogative **warum**
- **Kein**
- **Müssen, können, sollen,** and **mögen**
- **Noch ein**
- Personal pronouns
- Possessives
- Past tense of **sein**
- Asking and telling what to do
- Discussing gift ideas
- Expressing obligations

CHAPTER 12
Review of Level 2

- Adjective endings
- Command forms of strong verbs
- Comparative forms of adjectives
- The past tense
- Prepositions
- Questions and statements
- **Sollen; würde** forms
- Asking for and giving advice
- Asking for, making, and responding to suggestions
- Expressing hearsay; regret

LEVEL 3

CHAPTER 1
Review of Level 2

- Dative-case forms
- **Dieser** and **welcher**
- Past tense
- Prepositions followed by dative-case forms
- Reflexive and object pronouns
- Asking and telling what you may or may not do
- Asking for information
- Asking how someone liked something; expressing enthusiasm, disappointment
- Expressing hope
- Inquiring about someone's health

CHAPTER 2

- Reporting past events
- Adjective endings
- Two-way prepositions
- The verb **hatte**
- Word order in **dass-** and **ob**-clauses
- Asking for and making suggestions
- Asking for, making, and responding to suggestions
- Expressing doubt, conviction, and resignation
- Expressing hearsay
- Expressing preference and giving a reason
- Expressing wishes

CHAPTER 12
Review of Level 3

- Direct and indirect object pronouns
- Infinitive forms of verbs
- The narrative past (imperfect)
- Subjunctive
- The **würde**-forms
- Reporting past events
- Agreeing; agreeing with reservations
- Expressing determination or indecision
- Expressing surprise and disappointment
- Giving advice; reasons
- Hypothesizing

Komm mit! German Level 1
Scope and Sequence

FUNCTIONS	GRAMMAR	VOCABULARY	CULTURE	RE-ENTRY

VORSCHAU, Pages 1–11

		• Das Alphabet • Wie heißt du? • Im Klassenzimmer • Die Zahlen von 0 bis 20		

KAPITEL 1 Wer bist du?, Pages 16–41

FUNCTIONS	GRAMMAR	VOCABULARY	CULTURE	RE-ENTRY
• Saying hello and goodbye • Asking someone's name and giving yours • Asking who someone is • Asking someone's age and giving yours • Talking about places of origin • Talking about getting to school	• Forming questions • Definite articles **der, die, das** • Subject pronouns and **sein**	• Numbers 0-20 • Words to describe how students get to school	• Greetings • Using **der** and **die** in front of people's names • Map of German states and capitals • **Wie kommst du zur Schule?**	• Asking someone's name • Numbers 0–20 • Geography of German-speaking countries

KAPITEL 2 Spiel und Spaß, Pages 42–67

FUNCTIONS	GRAMMAR	VOCABULARY	CULTURE	RE-ENTRY
• Talking about interests • Expressing likes and dislikes • Saying when you do various activities • Asking for an opinion and expressing yours • Agreeing and disagreeing	• The singular subject pronouns and present tense verb endings • The plural subject pronouns and verb endings • Present tense of verbs • Word order • Verbs with stems ending in **d, t,** or **n**	• Sports, instruments, and games you play • Leisure activities and hobbies • Seasons of the year	• Formal and informal address • **Was machst du gern?** • German weekly planner	• Question formation • Greetings • Expressions **stimmt/ stimmt nicht** used in a new context

KAPITEL 3 Komm mit nach Hause!, Pages 68–95

FUNCTIONS	GRAMMAR	VOCABULARY	CULTURE	RE-ENTRY
• Talking about where you and others live • Offering something to eat and drink and responding to an offer • Saying please, thank you, you're welcome • Describing a room • Describing the family • Describing people	• The **möchte**-forms • Indefinite articles **ein, eine** • The pronouns **er, sie, es,** and **sie** • The possessive adjectives **mein, dein, sein,** and **ihr**	• Words to describe where you live • Food and drink items • Words to describe a room • Members of the family	• The German preference for **Mineralwasser** • **Wo wohnst du?**	• Definite articles **der, die, das** • Asking someone's name and age • Asking who someone is • Talking about interests

Brandenburg

FUNCTIONS	GRAMMAR	VOCABULARY	CULTURE	RE-ENTRY
KAPITEL 4 Alles für die Schule!, *Pages 100–127*				
• Talking about class schedules • Using a schedule to talk about time • Sequencing events • Expressing likes, dislikes, and favorites • Responding to good news and bad news • Talking about prices • Pointing things out	• The verb **haben** • Using **Lieblings-** • Noun plurals	• Classes at school • School supplies	• The German school day • 24-hour time system • The German grading system • **Was sind deine Lieblingsfächer?** • German currency	• Numbers • Likes and dislikes: **gern** • Degrees of enthusiasm • The pronouns **er, sie, es,** and **sie** (pl)
KAPITEL 5 Klamotten kaufen, *Pages 128–155*				
• Expressing wishes when shopping • Commenting on and describing clothes • Giving compliments and responding to them • Talking about trying on clothes	• Definite and indefinite articles in the accusative case • The verb **gefallen** • Direct object pronouns • Separable-prefix verbs • Stem-changing verbs **nehmen** and **aussehen**	• Clothing items • Colors • Words to describe clothing	• Exchange rates • German store hours • German clothing sizes • **Welche Klamotten sind „in"?**	• Numbers and prices • Colors • Pointing things out • Expressing likes and dislikes • Asking for and expressing opinions • The verb **aussehen**
KAPITEL 6 Pläne machen, *Pages 156–183*				
• Starting a conversation • Telling time and talking about when you do things • Making plans • Ordering food and beverages • Talking about how something tastes • Paying the check	• The verb **wollen** • The stem-changing verb **essen**	• Telling time • Words used to make plans • Food and drink items in a café	• Clocks on public buildings • **Was machst du in deiner Freizeit?** • Tipping in Germany	• Expressing time when referring to schedules • Vocabulary: School and free-time activities • Inversion of time elements • Sequencing events • Accusative case • The verb **nehmen** • Using **möchte** to order food

Schleswig-Holstein

FUNCTIONS	GRAMMAR	VOCABULARY	CULTURE	RE-ENTRY
KAPITEL 7 Zu Hause helfen, Pages 188–215				
• Extending and responding to an invitation • Expressing obligations • Talking about how often you do things • Offering help and explaining what to do • Talking about the weather	• The modals **müssen** and **können** • The separable-prefix verb **aufräumen** • The accusative pronouns • Using present tense to refer to the future	• Household chores • Words describing how often you have to do things • Words to describe the weather • Months	• **Was tust du für die Umwelt?** • German weather map and weather report • Weather in German-speaking countries	• Separable-prefix verbs • The verb **wollen** • Time expressions • Vocabulary: Free-time activities • Vocabulary: School supplies • Using numbers in a new context, temperature
KAPITEL 8 Einkaufen gehen, Pages 216–243				
• Asking what you should do • Telling someone what to do • Talking about quantities • Saying you want something else • Giving reasons • Saying where you were and what you bought	• The modal **sollen** • The **du-** and **ihr-** commands • The conjunctions **weil** and **denn** • The past tense of **sein**	• Groceries • Weights • Time expressions	• Specialty shops and markets • **Was machst du für andere Leute?** • Weights and measures • German advertisements	• The **möchte**-forms and **können** • Numbers used in a new context, weights and measures • Expressing wishes when shopping • Responding to invitations • Vocabulary: Activities • Vocabulary: Household chores • Sequencing words • Vocabulary: Clothing
KAPITEL 9 Amerikaner in München, Pages 244–271				
• Talking about where something is located • Asking for and giving directions • Talking about what there is to eat and drink • Saying you do/don't want more • Expressing opinions	• The verb **wissen** • The verb **fahren** • The formal commands with **Sie** • The phrase **es gibt** • Using **kein** • The conjunction **dass**	• Places in a city • Words used to give directions • Food and appetite	• The German **Innenstadt** • **Was isst du gern?** • Map of a German neighborhood • **Imbissstube** menu • **Leberkäs**	• Vocabulary: Stores and food items • **Du-**commands, **möchte,** and **zu** • Saying you want something else • Indefinite articles: accusative case • Expressing opinions • Subordinate-clause word order

Stuttgart

FUNCTIONS	GRAMMAR	VOCABULARY	CULTURE	RE-ENTRY

KAPITEL 10   Kino und Konzerte, *Pages 276–303*

• Expressing likes and dislikes • Expressing familiarity • Expressing preferences and favorites • Talking about what you did in your free time	• **Mögen, kennen, sehen, lesen** • **Sprechen** and **sprechen über** • **Lieber, am liebsten, gern**	• Film genres • Words describing how much you do or don't like something • Entertainers and forms of entertainment • Words used to describe films • Book genres	• The German movie rating system • German movie ads • A German pop chart • **Welche kulturellen Veranstaltungen besuchst du?** • German upcoming events poster • German best-seller lists • German video hits list • Popular German novels	• Expressing likes and dislikes • Expressing opinions; giving reasons • Describing people • **Aussehen, nehmen, wissen, essen, können** • Vocabulary: Activities • Talking about when and how often you do things

KAPITEL 11   Der Geburtstag, *Pages 304–331*

• Using the telephone in Germany • Inviting someone to a party • Talking about birthdays and expressing good wishes • Discussing gift ideas	• Introduction to the dative case • Word order in the dative case	• Telephone vocabulary • Dates of the year • Holidays and holiday greetings • Gift ideas	• Using the telephone • Saints' days • German good luck symbols • **Was schenkst du zum Geburtstag?** • German gift ideas	• Numbers 0–20 • Time and days of the week • Months • Accusative case • Vocabulary: Family members

KAPITEL 12   Die Fete, *Pages 332–359*   *Review Chapter*

• Offering help and explaining what to do • Asking where something is located and giving directions • Making plans and inviting someone to come along • Talking about clothing • Discussing gift ideas • Describing people and places • Saying what you would like and whether you do or don't want more • Talking about what you did	• The verb **können**; the preposition **für**; accusative pronouns; **du**-commands • The verb **wissen** and word order following **wissen**; formal commands • The verbs **wollen** and **müssen**; word order • Nominative and accusative pronouns; definite and indefinite articles • The nominative pronouns **er, sie, es,** and **sie** (pl); possessive pronouns • The **möchte**-forms; **noch ein** and **kein**	• Ingredients • Freetime activities • Words used to describe clothing • Furniture and appliances	• **Spätzle** and **Apfelküchle** • **Musst du zu Hause helfen?** • German gift ideas • Photos from furniture ads • Menu from an **Imbissstube**	

Berlin

Komm mit! German Level 2
Scope and Sequence

FUNCTIONS	GRAMMAR	VOCABULARY	CULTURE	RE-ENTRY

KAPITEL 1 Bei den Baumanns, Pages 4–31 — *Review Chapter*

FUNCTIONS	GRAMMAR	VOCABULARY	CULTURE	RE-ENTRY
• Asking for and giving information about yourself and others; describing yourself and others; expressing likes and dislikes • Identifying people and places • Giving and responding to compliments; expressing wishes when buying things • Making plans; ordering food; talking about how something tastes	• Present tense forms of **haben** and **sein** • **Mein, dein, sein,** and **ihr** (nom.) • The nominative and accusative forms of the definite and indefinite articles • The third person pronouns • Regular and stem-changing verbs • The **möchte**-forms and **wollen**	• Personal characteristics • Sports and hobbies • Clothing accessories	• Questionnaire: **Was für eine Person bist du?** • Article: **Sebastian über seine Familie** • Article: **Popstars machen Mode** • **Und was hast du am liebsten?** • Advertisements	• Chapters 1 and 2 are a global review of *Komm mit!*, Level 1.

KAPITEL 2 Bastis Plan, Pages 32–59 — *Review Chapter*

FUNCTIONS	GRAMMAR	VOCABULARY	CULTURE	RE-ENTRY
• Expressing obligations; extending and responding to an invitation; offering help and telling what to do • Asking and telling what to do; telling that you need something else; telling where you were and what you bought • Discussing gift ideas; expressing likes and dislikes; expressing likes, preferences, and favorites; saying you do or don't want more	• **Müssen, können, sollen,** and **mögen** • **Warum** • **Weil** and **denn** • Personal pronouns (acc.) • The possessives **mein, dein, sein, ihr** (acc.) • The **du**-commands • **Sein:** past tense • The dative case of **mein, dein, sein, ihr** • **Noch ein** (nom./acc.) • **Kein** (nom./acc.)	• Words useful for traveling • Things to take on a picnic	• **Was nimmst du mit, wenn du irgendwo eingeladen bist?** • Grocery advertisements • German gift ideas	• Chapters 1 and 2 are a global review of *Komm mit!*, Level 1.

KAPITEL 3 Wo warst du in den Ferien?, Pages 60–89

FUNCTIONS	GRAMMAR	VOCABULARY	CULTURE	RE-ENTRY
• Reporting past events, talking about activities • Reporting past events, talking about places • Asking how someone liked something; expressing enthusiasm or disappointment; responding enthusiastically or sympathetically	• Conversational past • Past tense of **haben** and **sein** • **An** and **in** with dative-case forms to express location • The definite article, dative plural • Personal pronouns, dative case • The dative-case forms of **ein**	• Film media • Places in Frankfurt a.M. • Time expressions • Places to eat or spend the night	• Information on Dresden and **Frankfurt am Main** • **Was hast du in den letzten Ferien gemacht?**	• Expressions of time/frequency • **Weil**-clauses • Expressing likes and dislikes (For additional Re-entry, see Ch. 3, p. 59A.)

Bayern

FUNCTIONS	GRAMMAR	VOCABULARY	CULTURE	RE-ENTRY

KAPITEL 4 Gesund leben, Pages 94–121

• Expressing approval and disapproval • Asking for information and responding emphatically or agreeing, with reservations • Asking and telling what you may or may not do	• The verb **schlafen (schläft)** • **Für** + accusative • Reflexive verbs (accusative) • **Jeder, jede, jedes** (nominative) • The accusative forms of **kein** • The verb **dürfen**	• Words describing healthy habits • Words for how you feel where • Fruits, vegetables, fish, meat	• Interviews of German teenagers • **Was tust du, um gesund zu leben?** • Survey on health habits • **Bioläden** and **Reformhäuser**	• **Essen, sollen** and **müssen** • **Dass**-clauses; **für**; **kein** • Conjunctions **weil** and **denn** • Expressions of place, time, frequency, and quantity • Giving reasons • Responding to an invitation (For additional Re-entry, see Ch. 4, p. 93A.)

KAPITEL 5 Gesund essen, Pages 122–149

• Expressing regret and downplaying; expressing skepticism and making certain • Calling someone's attention to something and responding • Expressing preference and strong preference	• **Dieser, diese, dieses** • The possessives (Summary) • Verbs used with dative case • **Welcher, welche, welches; zu**	• **Schulpause** foods • Things to put on bread • Foods from the supermarket	• **Was isst du, was nicht?** • Nutritious snacks for **Gymnasiasten** • German meals	• Talking about quantities • The possessives • Talking about how food tastes • Comparatives and superlatives • Saying you want more • The interrogative **was für** (For additional Re-entry, see Ch. 5, p. 121A.)

KAPITEL 6 Gute Besserung!, Pages 150–177

• Inquiring about someone's health and responding; making suggestions • Asking about and expressing pain • Asking for and giving advice; expressing hope	• Reflexive pronouns in dative • The inclusive command • Verbs used with dative case • The verbs **brechen, waschen, messen,** and **wehtun** • The dative case to express the idea of something too expensive, too large, too small for you	• Aches and pains • Body parts and injuries • Healthy habits • Toiletries	• **Was machst du, wenn dir nicht gut ist?** • **Apotheke** and **Drogerie** • Article about sun exposure	• The verb **sich fühlen** • The accusative reflexive pronouns • Expressing obligations • The conversational past • **Dass**-clauses (For additional Re-entry, see Ch. 6, p. 149A.)

Hamburg

FUNCTIONS	GRAMMAR	VOCABULARY	CULTURE	RE-ENTRY

KAPITEL 7 Stadt oder Land?, Pages 182–209

FUNCTIONS	GRAMMAR	VOCABULARY	CULTURE	RE-ENTRY
• Expressing preference and giving a reason • Expressing wishes • Agreeing, with reservations; justifying your answers	• Comparative forms of adjectives • The verb **sich wünschen** • Adjective endings following **ein**-words • Adjective endings of comparatives	• Places to live • Advantages and disadvantages of city and country life • Parts of a house • Wishes for the future • Noisy things	• **Wo wohnst du lieber? Auf dem Land? In der Stadt?** • **Schule im Garten** • Letter from a German pen pal	• Talking about where something is located • Reflexive dative verbs • Expressing opinions • Dative verb **gefallen** (For additional Re-entry, see Ch. 7, p. 181A.)

KAPITEL 8 Mode? Ja oder nein?, Pages 210–237

FUNCTIONS	GRAMMAR	VOCABULARY	CULTURE	RE-ENTRY
• Describing clothes • Expressing interest, disinterest, and indifference; making and accepting compliments • Persuading and dissuading	• Adjective endings following **der** and **dieser**-words • **Passen (zu), stehen, tragen**, and **sich interessieren** • The conjunction **wenn** • **Kaufen** with dative	• Clothing • Words to describe clothing • Fabrics	• **Was trägst du am liebsten?** • Clothes typically worn by German-speaking youths • Interviews about fashion	• Talking about what you bought • Accusative reflexive verbs • **Für** + accusative • Giving reasons • Word order with subordinate conjunctions (For additional Re-entry, see Ch. 8, p. 209A.)

KAPITEL 9 Wohin in die Ferien?, Pages 238–265

FUNCTIONS	GRAMMAR	VOCABULARY	CULTURE	RE-ENTRY
• Expressing indecision; asking for and making suggestions • Expressing doubt, conviction, and resignation • Asking for and giving directions	• Articles/names for mountains • **Nach, in, an,** and **auf; ob**-clauses • Expressing direction and location (Summary) • Prepositions followed by dative • **Durch, um, vor, neben,** and **zwischen**	• Means of transportation • Vacation activities • Words for giving directions in a city	• **Wohin fährst du in den nächsten Ferien?** • **Urlaub in letzter Minute** • Statistics on transportation • Students talk about vacations • **Stadtrundgang durch Bietigheim**	• Inclusive commands • **Können, fahren,** and **wissen** • Giving directions • Inviting someone and responding to an invitation (For additional Re-entry, see Ch. 9, p. 237A.)

Stuttgart

FUNCTIONS	GRAMMAR	VOCABULARY	CULTURE	RE-ENTRY

KAPITEL 10 Viele Interessen!, Pages 270–297

FUNCTIONS	GRAMMAR	VOCABULARY	CULTURE	RE-ENTRY
• Asking about and expressing interest • Asking for and giving permission; asking for information and expressing an assumption • Expressing surprise, agreement, and disagreement; talking about plans	• Verbs with prepositions • **Wo**-compounds and **da**-compounds • The verbs **lassen** and **laufen** • The use of **kein** to negate a noun • The future tense with **werden**	• TV programs • TV accessories • Standard and optional car equipment	• Television channels • **Was machst du, um zu relaxen?** • Statistics on television programs • Getting a driver's license in Germany • Statistics on cars	• **Weil** and **dass**, and **was für** • Word order with modals • Time expressions • Expressing future events with present tense • Making plans • Expressing interest • **Können, dürfen,** and **sich freuen** (For additional Re-entry, see Ch. 10, p. 269A.)

KAPITEL 11 Mit Oma ins Restaurant, Pages 298–325

FUNCTIONS	GRAMMAR	VOCABULARY	CULTURE	RE-ENTRY
• Asking for, making, and responding to suggestions • Expressing hearsay • Ordering in a restaurant; expressing good wishes	• The **würde**-forms • Unpreceded adjectives • The **hätte**-forms	• Cultural activities • Cuisine of Germany and other countries • Words to describe food • Things to order in a restaurant	• **Für welche kulturellen Veranstaltungen interessierst du dich?** • State-supported art in Germany • International cuisine • Menu	• Cultural activities and sights • The impersonal pronoun **man** • Talking about favorites • The modal **sollen** • Saying what's available • Ordering and asking for the bill (For additional Re-entry, see Ch. 11, p. 297A.)

KAPITEL 12 Die Reinickendorfer Clique, Pages 326–353   *Review Chapter*

FUNCTIONS	GRAMMAR	VOCABULARY	CULTURE	RE-ENTRY
• Reporting past events; asking for, making, and responding to suggestions • Ordering food; expressing hearsay and regret; persuading and dissuading • Asking for and giving advice; expressing preference, interest, disinterest, and indifference	• The past tense • **Sollen** and the **würde**-forms • Questions and statements • Prepositions • The command forms of strong verbs • Adjective endings • Comparative forms of adjectives	• Places near water • Sport sites • International cuisine • Clothing	• **Welche ausländische Küche hast du gern?** • Article on travel habits • Etiquette in German restaurants • Franziska van Almsick	• Chapter 12 is a global review of Chapters 1–11, Level 2.

Berlin

Komm mit! German Level 3
Scope and Sequence

FUNCTIONS	GRAMMAR	VOCABULARY	CULTURE	RE-ENTRY

KAPITEL 1 Das Land am Meer, Pages 4–31 — *Review Chapter*

Die neuen Bundesländer

FUNCTIONS	GRAMMAR	VOCABULARY	CULTURE	RE-ENTRY
• Reporting past events • Asking how someone liked something; expressing enthusiasm, disappointment, and sympathy • Asking and telling what you may or may not do • Asking for information • Inquiring about someone's health and responding; expressing pain • Expressing hope	• Prepositions followed by dative-case forms • Past tense • Dative-case forms • Forms of **dieser** and **welcher** • Reflexive and object pronouns	• Time expressions • Errands • Produce and cuts of meat • Things to put on bread • Body parts and injuries	• **Insel Rügen** • **Fit ohne Fleisch** • **Währungen und Geld wechseln**	• Chapters 1 and 2 are a global review of *Komm mit!*, Levels 1 and 2.

KAPITEL 2 Auf in die Jugendherberge!, Pages 32–59 — *Review Chapter*

FUNCTIONS	GRAMMAR	VOCABULARY	CULTURE	RE-ENTRY
• Asking for and making suggestions • Expressing preference and giving a reason • Expressing wishes • Expressing doubt, conviction, resignation • Asking for information, expressing assumptions • Expressing hearsay • Asking for, making, and responding to suggestions • Expressing wishes when shopping	• Two-way prepositions • Word order in **dass**- and **ob**-clauses • Adjective endings • The verb **hätte**	• Words useful for traveling • Things to take on a picnic	• **Jugendherbergen** • **Einkaufsliste** • **Programm für eine 6-Tage-Reise nach Weimar** • **Weimar im Blickpunkt** • Poems	• Chapters 1 and 2 are a global review of *Komm mit!*, Levels 1 and 2.

KAPITEL 3 Aussehen: wichtig oder nicht?, Pages 60–87

FUNCTIONS	GRAMMAR	VOCABULARY	CULTURE	RE-ENTRY
• Asking for and expressing opinions; expressing sympathy and resignation • Giving advice; giving a reason • Admitting something and expressing regret	• **Da** and **wo**-compounds (Summary) • Infinitive clauses	• Words teens use in conversation • Phrases used to express sympathy, resignation, and to give advice	• **Die deutsche Subkultur** • Teenagers talking about what they do to feel better	• Expressing interest • Sequencing events • Expressing opinions • Verbs requiring prepositional phrases • Hobby and clothing vocabulary • **Wo-** and **da-**compounds • Responding sympathetically • Asking for and giving advice • Making suggestions • Giving reasons • Infinitives • **Weil**-clauses

FUNCTIONS	GRAMMAR	VOCABULARY	CULTURE	RE-ENTRY
KAPITEL 4 Verhältnis zu anderen, *Pages 92–119*				
• Agreeing; giving advice • Introducing another point of view; hypothesizing	• Ordinal numbers • Relative clauses • **Hätte** and **wäre** • The genitive case	• Words used for describing relationships • Words used for getting along with others	• Importance of **Cliquen** • Die verschiedenen Bildungswege in Deutschland	• Agreeing • **Wenn-, weil-,** and **dass-**clauses • Cardinal numbers • Pronouns (nom., acc., and dat.) • Giving advice • **Wenn-**phrases • Subjunctive (**würde-, hätte-, wäre-**forms) • The preposition **von** + dative
KAPITEL 5 Rechte und Pflichten, *Pages 120–147*				
• Talking about what is possible • Saying what you would have liked to do • Saying that something is going on right now • Reporting past events • Expressing surprise, relief, and resignation	• The **könnte-**forms • Further uses of **wäre** and **hätte** • Verbs used as neuter nouns • The past tense of modals (the imperfect)	• Words to describe rights and responsibilities • Military terms • Time expressions	• Artikel 38/2. Absatz des Grundgesetzes • Artikel 12a des Grundgesetzes • Cartoon • Gleichberechtigung im deutschen Militär? • Wehrpflicht	• **Hätte-**forms and **wäre-**forms • **Weil-**clauses • Giving reasons • The modals **können, wollen,** and **müssen** • Reporting past events • Expressing surprise • Expressing resignation • Expressing hearsay
KAPITEL 6 Medien: stets gut informiert?, *Pages 148–175*				
• Asking someone to take a position; asking for reasons; expressing opinions • Reporting past events • Agreeing or disagreeing; changing the subject; interrupting • Expressing surprise or annoyance	• Narrative past (imperfect) • Superlative forms of adjectives	• Terms used in discussions • Words related to media • Words of quantity	• Die TV-Kids • Die Schülerzeitung • Leserbriefe an die Redaktion der Pepo	• Talking about favorites • Leisure-time activities • Expressing opinions • The conversational past • Agreeing and disagreeing • Television vocabulary • Expressing surprise • The comparative forms of adjectives • Time expressions • Words of quantity

Würzburg

FUNCTIONS	GRAMMAR	VOCABULARY	CULTURE	RE-ENTRY

KAPITEL 7   Ohne Reklame geht es nicht!, *Pages 180–207*

FUNCTIONS	GRAMMAR	VOCABULARY	CULTURE	RE-ENTRY
• Expressing annoyance • Comparing • Eliciting agreement and agreeing • Expressing conviction, uncertainty, and what seems to be true	• **Derselbe, der gleiche** • Adjective endings following determiners of quantity • Introducing relative clauses with **was** and **wo** • **Irgendein** and **irgendwelche**	• Words used in advertising • Words preceded by **irgend**	• Werbung—pro und contra • Warum so wenig Unterbrecherwerbung? • Excerpt from *Frankfurter Allgemeine* • Cartoon	• Expressing annoyance • The conjunctions **wenn** and **dass** • Comparative and superlative • Adjective endings • Agreeing • Relative pronouns • Word order in dependent clauses • Expressing conviction • Expressing uncertainty

KAPITEL 8   Weg mit den Vorurteilen!, *Pages 208–235*

FUNCTIONS	GRAMMAR	VOCABULARY	CULTURE	RE-ENTRY
• Expressing surprise, disappointment, and annoyance • Expressing an assumption • Making suggestions and recommendations • Giving advice	• The conjunction **als** • Coordinating conjunctions (Summary) • Verbs with prefixes (Summary)	• Words used to express prejudices and clichés • Personal characteristics	• Cartoon • Verständnis für Ausländer? • Der sympathische Deutsche	• Expressing surprise • Expressing disappointment • **Dass**-clauses • Narrative past • Conversational past • Coordinating conjunctions • Expressing an assumption • Prepositions followed by dative • Separable-prefix verbs • Making suggestions • Giving advice

KAPITEL 9   Aktiv für die Umwelt!, *Pages 236–263*

FUNCTIONS	GRAMMAR	VOCABULARY	CULTURE	RE-ENTRY
• Expressing concern • Making accusations • Offering solutions • Making polite requests • Saying what is being done about a problem • Hypothesizing	• Subjunctive forms of **können, müssen, dürfen, sollen,** and **sein** • The passive voice, present tense • Use of a conjugated modal verb in the passive • Conditional sentences	• Words describing pollution and the environment	• Environmental concerns • Ein umweltfreundlicher Einkauf	• Adjective endings • **Dass-, wenn-** and **weil-**clauses • **Hätte-, würde-,** and **könnte-**forms • **Werden** and **sollen** • Environment vocabulary • Subjunctive forms

Frankfurt

FUNCTIONS	GRAMMAR	VOCABULARY	CULTURE	RE-ENTRY

KAPITEL 10   Die Kunst zu leben, *Pages 268–295*

FUNCTIONS	GRAMMAR	VOCABULARY	CULTURE	RE-ENTRY
• Expressing preference, given certain possibilities • Expressing envy and admiration • Expressing happiness and sadness • Saying that something is or was being done	• Prepositions with genitive • The passive voice (Summary)	• Words used in the arts and in theaters	• Film critiques • Aphorismen • Kultur findet man überall!	• Expressing preference • **Würde**-forms • Genitive case forms • Prepositions • **Da-** and **wo-** compounds • Past participles • Subjunctive forms of modals • **Von** + dative case

KAPITEL 11   Deine Welt ist deine Sache!, *Pages 296–323*

FUNCTIONS	GRAMMAR	VOCABULARY	CULTURE	RE-ENTRY
• Expressing determination or indecision • Talking about whether something is important or not important • Expressing wishes • Expressing certainty and refusing or accepting with certainty • Talking about goals for the future • Expressing relief	• The use of **wo-** compounds to ask questions • Two ways of expressing the future tense • The perfect infinitive with modals and **werden**	• Careers and occupations • Words used to talk about the future	• German universities • Wie findet man eine Arbeitsstelle in Deutschland? • Umfragen und Tests	• Reflexive verbs • Expressing indecision • Conversational past and conditional • **Ob-** and **dass-**clauses • **Um ... zu** • **Wo-**compounds • Expressing wishes • **Wäre** • Determiners of quantity • Negation with **kein** • Future tense formation

Dresden

KAPITEL 12   Die Zukunft liegt in deiner Hand!, *Pages 324–351*   *Review Chapter*

FUNCTIONS	GRAMMAR	VOCABULARY	CULTURE	RE-ENTRY
• Reporting past events • Expressing surprise and disappointment • Agreeing; agreeing, with reservations • Giving advice; giving reasons • Expressing determination or indecision • Talking about what is important or not important • Hypothesizing	• The narrative past (imperfect) • The **würde**-forms • Infinitive forms of verbs • Direct and indirect object pronouns • Subjunctive	• Careers and occupations • Words used to talk about the future	• Kummerkasten • Pauken allein reicht nicht • Claudias Pläne für die Zukunft • Textbilder	• Chapter 12 is a global review of Chapters 1–11, Level 3.

LEVEL 3   SCOPE AND SEQUENCE

Pupil's Edition

Proficiency is the goal of language instruction in **Komm mit!** *Every chapter begins with authentic situations that model communicative needs common among young people: ordering in a restaurant, expressing wishes, describing clothes. In the ensuing situations, students learn the functions, vocabulary, and grammar that support natural expression. They also become interested, involved, and responsive—in short, they answer the invitation to* **Komm mit!** *and to communicate.*

Komm mit! Level 2

The **Komm mit!** *Pupil's Edition* opens with a two-chapter review of the functions, vocabulary, and grammar learned in Level 1. Following this comprehensive review, Chapters 3–11 provide a carefully sequenced program of balanced skills instruction in the four areas of listening, speaking, reading, and writing. In addition, every chapter is rich in authentic culture and language and additional grammar practice activities in the **Mehr Grammatikübungen.** Most chapter photographs were taken on location and reflect the characters and settings featured in the videos that accompany **Komm mit!**

Chapter 12 is a review of the second year's study of German. It provides an opportunity to reinforce skills and remediate deficiencies before the end of the school year. This opportunity to pause and reflect on what has been learned provides closure and gives students a sense of accomplishment and renewed purpose.

At the end of the *Pupil's Edition*, a Reference Section summarizes functions and grammar rules for quick reference. It also provides a list of Additional Vocabulary as well as German>English and English>German glossaries. The Additional Grammar Practice includes various activities, divided by chapter and **Stufe,** that strengthen students' understanding of the grammar points presented in each chapter. These activities can also be used for review and reinforcement. Throughout the year, students are encouraged to consult the Reference Section to review, expand their choices, and further practice functional expressions, vocabulary, and structures.

Activity-Based Instruction

In **Komm mit!,** language acquisition is an active process. From the first day, students are using German. Within each lesson, a progression of activities moves students from discrete point use of language to completely open-ended activities that promote personalized, meaningful expression. This sequence allows students to practice receptive skills before moving on to language production. It is this carefully articulated sequence that ensures success.

A Guided Tour

On the next several pages, you will find a guided tour of **Komm mit!** On these pages, we have identified for you the essential elements of the textbook and the various resources available. If, as you are using **Komm mit!,** you encounter any particular problems, please contact your regional office for information or assistance.

Starting Out...

Location Opener In *Komm mit!* chapters are arranged in groups of three, with each group set in a different German-speaking location. Each new location is introduced by four pages of colorful photos and information of the city or region presented.

Chapter Opener These pages are a visual introduction to the theme of the chapter and include a list of objectives students will be expected to achieve.

Setting The Scene...

Los geht's! Language instruction begins with this comprehensible input that models language in a culturally authentic setting. Presented also on video, audio, CD and DVD, the highly visual presentation allows students to practice their receptive skills and begin to recognize some of the new functions and vocabulary they will encounter in the chapter.

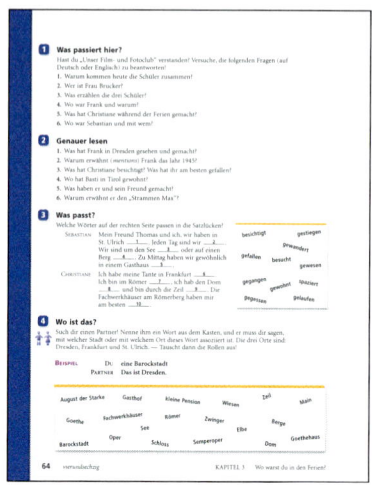

Following **Los geht's!** is a series of activities to check comprehension.

Building Proficiency Step By Step...

Erste, Zweite, and **Dritte Stufe** are the core instructional sections where language acquisition will take place. The communicative goals in each chapter center on the functional expressions presented in **So sagt man das!** boxes. These expressions are supported by material in the **Wortschatz, Grammatik,** and **Ein wenig Grammatik** sections.

Activities following the above features are designed to practice recognition or to provide closed-ended practice. Activities then progress from controlled to open-ended practice where students are able to express themselves in meaningful communication.

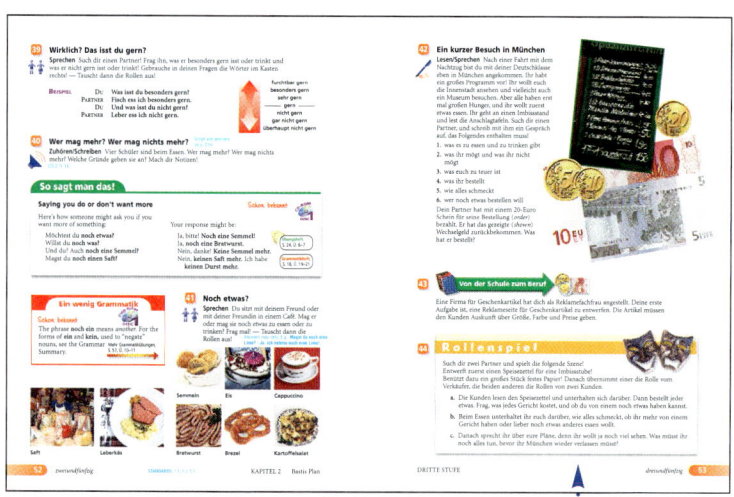

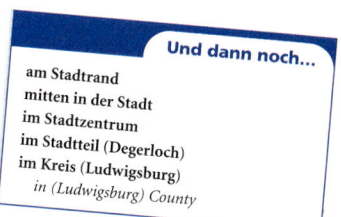

Targeting Students' Needs...

Several special features may be used to enhance language learning.

Sprachtipp provides students with tips for speaking more natural-sounding German.

Und dann noch presents additional useful vocabulary to help students with the theme of the chapter.

Discovering the People and the Culture...

There are two major cultural features to help students develop an appreciation and understanding of the cultures of German-speaking countries.

Landeskunde presents interviews conducted throughout Germany on a topic related to the chapter theme. The interviews may be presented on video, DVD, or done as a reading supplemented by the Audio CD recording. Culminating activities on this page verify comprehension and encourage students to think critically about the target culture as well as their own.

Ein wenig Landeskunde helps students gain knowledge and understanding of the other culture and can be used to enrich and enliven activities and presentations at various places throughout each chapter.

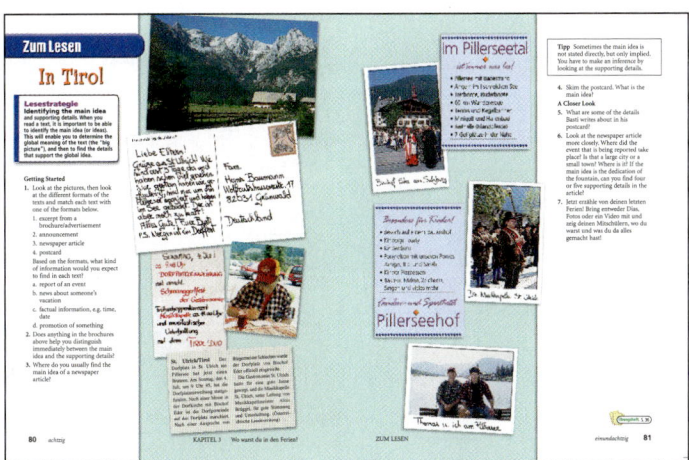

Understanding Authentic Documents...

Zum Lesen presents reading strategies that help students understand authentic German documents and literature presented in each chapter. The reading selections vary from advertisements to letters to short stories or poems in order to accommodate different interests and familiarize the students with different styles and formats. The accompanying prereading, reading, and postreading activities develop students' overall reading skills and challenge their critical thinking abilities. A **Lesestrategie** provides effective ways to enhance students' reading comprehension.

T27

Wrapping It All Up...

Mehr Grammatikübungen provide additional practice on the grammar concepts presented in the chapter. These activities are divided by **Stufe** and may be assigned as homework or as a review for quizzes and tests.

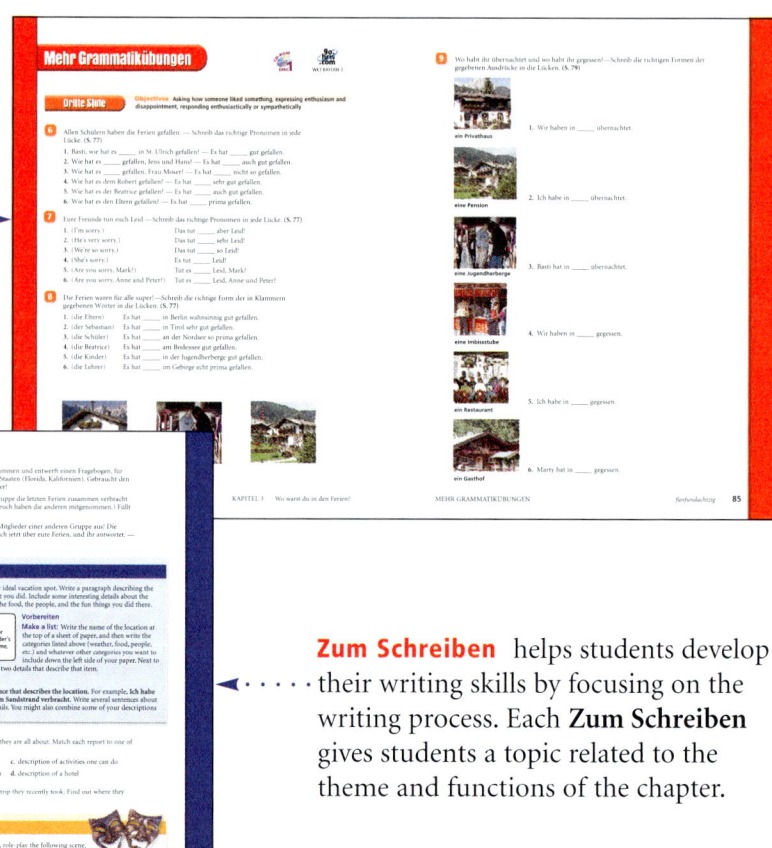

Zum Schreiben helps students develop their writing skills by focusing on the writing process. Each **Zum Schreiben** gives students a topic related to the theme and functions of the chapter.

Anwendung gives students the opportunity to review what they have learned and to apply their skills in new communicative contexts. Focusing on all four language skills as well as cultural awareness, the **Anwendung** can help you determine whether students are ready for the Chapter Test.

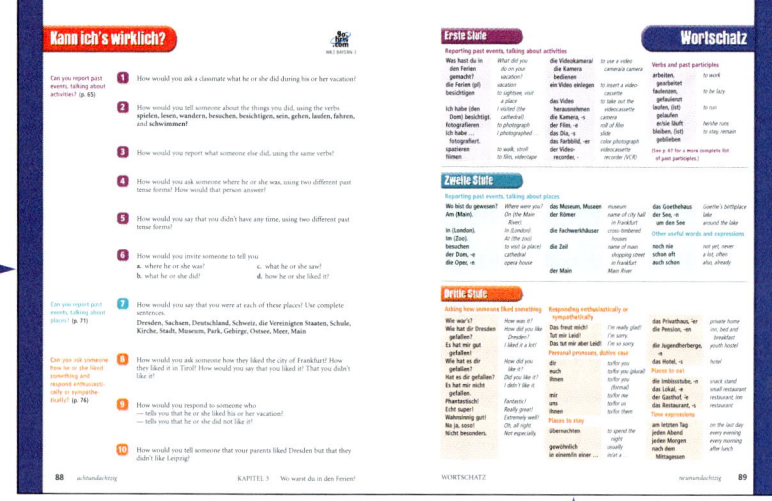

Kann ich's wirklich? is a checklist that students can use on their own to see if they have achieved the goals stated on the Chapter Opener page. Each communicative function is paired with one or more activities for students to use as a self-check.

Wortschatz presents the chapter vocabulary grouped by **Stufe** and arranged according to function or theme.

T28

Technology Resources

Go.Online!

- The **Premier Online Edition** presents the *Pupil's Edition* in an interactive format that allows students to listen to audio at point of use and to complete activities online.

The online edition features the full *Video Program* and a Student Notebook (**E-Notizbuch**)

 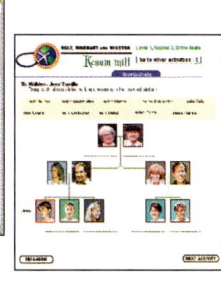 

Keywords in the *Pupil's Edition* provide access to two types of online activities:

- **Interaktive Spiele** are directly correlated to the instructional material in the textbook. They can be used as homework, extra practice or assessment.

- **Internet Aktivitäten** provide students with selected Web sites in German-speaking countries and printable worksheets that guide students through their research.

Interactive CD-ROM Tutor

The *Interactive CD-ROM Tutor* offers:

- a variety of supporting activities correlated to the core curriculum of **Komm mit!** and targeting all five skills

- a Teacher Management System (TMS) that allows teachers to view and assess students' work, manage passwords and records, track students' progress as they complete the activities, and activate English translations

- features such as a grammar reference section and a glossary to help students complete the activities

The Video and DVD Tutor Program

The *Video Program and DVD Tutor* provide the following video support:

- **Location Opener** documentaries
- **Los geht's!** and **Fortsetzung** dramatic episodes
- **Landeskunde** interviews on a variety of cultural topics
- **Videoclips** which present authentic footage from target cultures

The *Video Guide* contains background information, suggestions for presentation, and activities for all portions of the *Video Program*.

One-Stop Planner CD-ROM with ExamView Test Generator

The *One-Stop Planner CD-ROM* is a convenient tool to aid in lesson planning and pacing.

Easy navigation through menus or through lesson plans allows for a quick overview of available resources. For each chapter the *One-Stop Planner* includes:

- Editable lesson plans with direct links to teaching resources
- Printable worksheets from resource books
- Direct launches to the HRW Internet activities
- Video and audio segments
- Test Generator
- Clip Art for vocabulary items

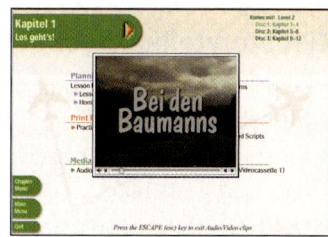

Ancillaries

The *Komm mit!* German program offers a comprehensive ancillary package that addresses the concerns of today's teachers and is relevant to students' lives.

Lesson Planning

One-Stop Planner with Test Generator

- editable lesson plans
- printable worksheets from resource books
- direct link to HRW Internet activities
- entire video and audio programs
- ExamView Test Generator
- Clip Art

Lesson Planner with Substitute Teacher Lesson Plans
- complete lesson plans for every chapter
- block scheduling suggestions
- correlations to Standards for Foreign Language Learning
- a homework calendar
- chapter by chapter lesson plans for substitute teachers
- lesson plan forms for customizing lesson plans

Student Make-Up Assignments
- diagnostic information for students who are behind in their work
- copying masters for make-up assignments

Listening and Speaking

TPR Storytelling Book
- step-by-step explanation of the TPR Storytelling method
- illustrated stories for each **Stufe** with vocabulary lists and gestures
- teaching suggestions
- a final story for each chapter

Listening Activities
- print material associated with the *Audio Program*
- Student Response Forms for all *Pupil's Edition* listening activities
- Additonal Listening Activities
- scripts, answers
- lyrics to each chapter's song

Audio Compact Discs
Listening activities for the *Pupil's Edition*, the Additional Listening Activities, and the *Testing Program*

Activities for Communication
- Communicative Activities for partner work based on an information gap
- Situation Cards to practice interviews and role-plays
- Realia: reproductions of authentic documents

Grammar

Grammatikheft
- re-presentations of major grammar points
- additional focused practice
- *Teacher's Edition* with overprinted answers

Grammar Tutor for Students of German
- presentations of grammar concepts in English
- re-presentations of German grammar concepts
- discovery and application activities

Assessment

Testing Program
- Grammar and Vocabulary quizzes
- **Stufe** quizzes that test the skills
- Chapter Tests
- Speaking Tests
- Midterm and Final Exams
- Score sheets, scripts, answers

Alternative Assessment Guide
- Suggestions for oral and written Portfolio Assessment
- Performance Assessment
- CD-ROM Assessment
- rubrics, portfolio checklists, and evaluation forms

Student Make-Up Assignments
Alternative Grammar and Vocabulary quizzes for students who missed class and have to make up the quiz

Reading and Writing

Reading Strategies and Skills Handbook
- explanations of reading strategies
- copying masters for application of strategies

Lies mit mir!
- readings on familiar topics
- cultural information
- additional vocabulary
- interesting and engaging activities

Übungsheft
- activities for practice
- *Teacher's Edition* with overprinted answers

Teaching Transparencies
Colorful transparencies that help present and practice vocabulary, grammar, culture, and a variety of communicative functions

- Los geht's!
- Mehr Gramatikübungen
- Grammatikheft

Teacher's Edition

Using the Chapter Interleaf

Each chapter of the **Komm mit!** *Teacher's Edition* includes the following interleaf pages to help you plan, teach, and expand your lessons.

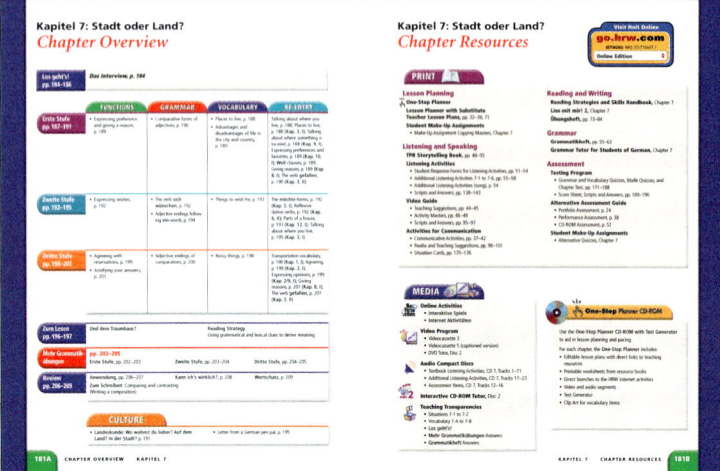

Chapter Overview

The Chapter Overview chart outlines at a glance the functions, grammar, vocabulary, re-entry, and culture featured in the chapter. You will also find a list of corresponding print and audiovisual resources organized by listening, speaking, reading, and writing skills, grammar, and assessment.

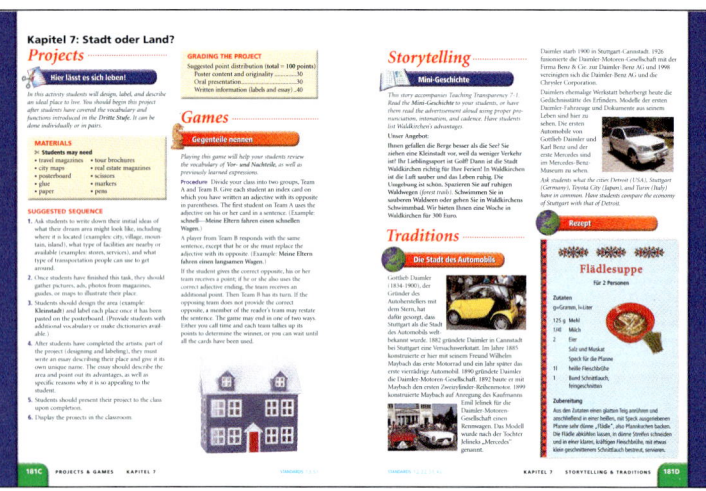

Projects/Games/ Storytelling/Traditions

Projects allow students to personalize and expand on the information from the chapter. Games reinforce the chapter content. In the Storytelling feature, you will find a story related to a *Teaching Transparency*. The Traditions feature concentrates on a unique aspect of the culture of the region. An activity accompanies each of these features. A recipe typical for the region follows at the end.

Technology

These pages assist you in integrating technology into your lesson plans. The Technology page provides a detailed list of video, CD-ROM, and Internet resources for your lesson. You will also find an Internet research project in each chapter.

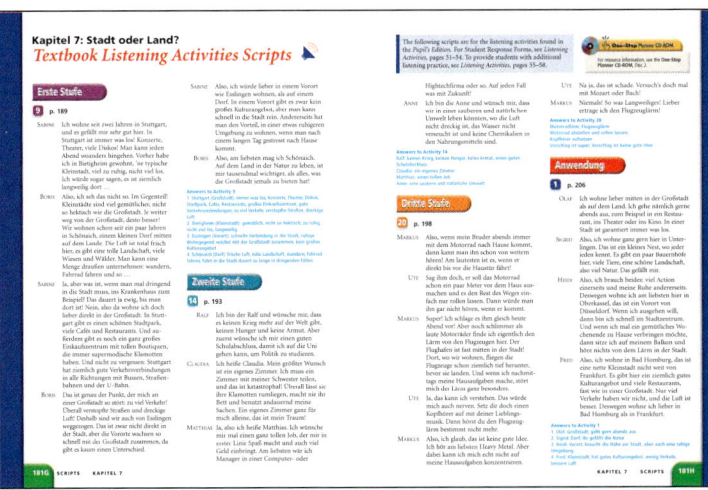
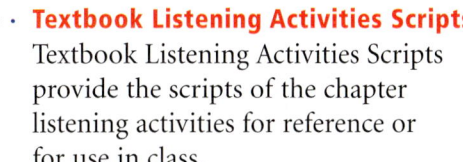

Textbook Listening Activities Scripts

Textbook Listening Activities Scripts provide the scripts of the chapter listening activities for reference or for use in class.

Suggested Lesson Plans—50-Minute Schedule

This lesson plan is used for classes with 50-minute schedules. Each lesson plan provides a logical sequence of instruction along with homework suggestions.

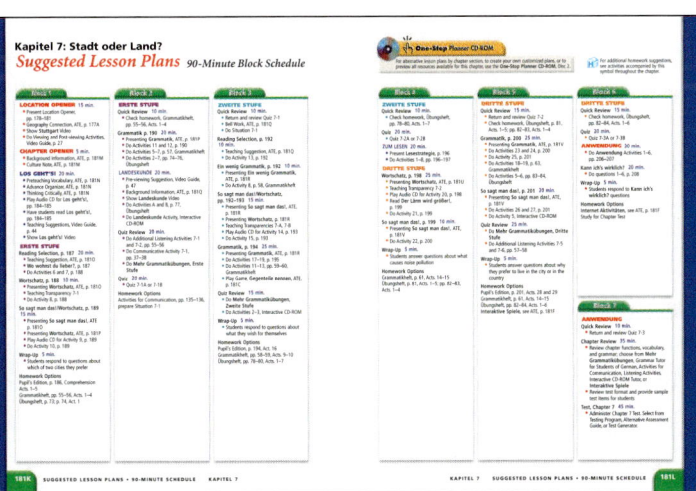

Suggested Lesson Plans—90-Minute Schedule

This lesson plan is used for classes with 90-minute schedules. Each lesson plan provides a logical sequence of instruction along with homework suggestions.

The Annotated Teacher's Edition
Using the Interleaf Teacher Text

Cultures and Communities
Under this head you will find helpful cultural information and suggestions that relate the content to students' families and communities.

Resource Boxes provide a quick list of all the resources you can use for each chapter section.

Connections and Comparisons
Under this head you will find connections and comparisons with other languages, cultures, and disciplines.

ERSTE STUFE

Teaching Resources
pp. 65–69

PRINT
- Lesson Planner, p. 13
- TPR Storytelling Book, pp. 16–17
- Listening Activities, pp. 19, 23–24
- Activities for Communication, pp. 13–14, 82, 85, 127–128
- Grammatikheft, pp. 19–21
- Grammar Tutor for Students of German, Chapter 3
- Übungsheft, pp. 26–28
- Testing Program, pp. 53–56
- Alternative Assessment Guide, p. 34
- Student Make-Up Assignments, Chapter 3

MEDIA
- One-Stop Planner
- Audio Compact Discs, CD3, Trs. 3, 14, 20–21
- Teaching Transparencies
  Situation 3-1
  Vocabulary 3-A
  Mehr Grammatikübungen Answers
  Grammatikheft Answers
- Interactive CD-ROM Tutor, Disc 1
- DVD Tutor, Disc 1

PAGE 65

🔔 **Bell Work**
Make a chart on a transparency on which you write names of vacation places on one side and a typical gift idea from each place in random order on the other side.
Examples:
Schwarzwald	Lebkuchen
Lübeck	eine Freiheitsstatue aus Plastik
New York	Marzipan
Nürnberg	eine Kuckucksuhr

Cultures and Communities

Culture Note
Planning their vacation is generally very important to Germans. They like to share future vacation plans and past experiences with friends. As part of this, they tend to write many postcards to relatives and friends from their vacation spots.

PRESENTING: So sagt man das!
After reading the questions and phrases in **So sagt man das!**, ask students what they notice about the verbs. How many parts do they have? Which part changes to agree with the subject? Can students point out where the second part of the verb is located in the sentences?

Connections and Comparisons

Language-to-Language
You may want to explain the concept of collective nouns (nouns that are singular in form but plural in meaning because they denote a collection of individuals or items, such as the word *army*.) Show that what is a collective singular noun in one language might be a regular plural noun in another.

Examples:

English: *hair*   English: *people* (pl)
(collective singular)   German: **die Leute** (pl)
German: (**die**) **Haare** (pl)   French: **les gens** (pl)
French: **les cheveux** (pl)   Spanish: **la gente**
Spanish: **el pelo** (sg)   (collective singular)

Ask students if they can think of more nouns that are singular in form in English but plural in form in German, French, or Spanish.

Examples:

English: *vacation,* German: **die Ferien,** French: **les vacances,** Spanish: **las vacaciones**

PRESENTING: Wortschatz
Introduce the new vocabulary by acting out the phrases. Use props if available. Then give commands to the class or individual students.
Examples:
Helen, leg das Video bitte ein!
Travis, nimm das Video heraus!
Hier Patty, nimm die Kamera und fotografiere unsere Klasse!
Gib Gary bitte diesen Film!

STANDARDS: 2.1, 4.1

KAPITEL 3

Presenting Features offer useful suggestions for presenting new material.

Correlations to the Standards for Foreign Language Learning are provided for your reference.

T34

Teaching Suggestion

31 Ask students to use several adverbial expressions from the Wortschatz beside the activity in their Notizbuch entry.

Communication for All Students

Auditory Learners

32 To involve the listening student actively in this activity, ask him or her to put the pictures in the order they are described by the partner. At the end, the listening student verifies the sequence with his or her partner. You may also want to call on several students to repeat their reports and have the rest of the class listen to see if the order of the pictures matches the description that students gave.

COMMUNITY LINK

Suggest that students videotape or interview local celebrities or feature local merchants or organizations in their reports. Tell students that they can get information from the Chamber of Commerce to help them with their projects.

Game

In this activity students review and practice in German the places and points of interest that they have learned up to this point. Begin the game by making the following statement:

Im Sommer reisen wir nach Frankfurt, denn wir wollen den Dom besichtigen.

The first student repeats your sentence and reason for visiting and adds another location. The next stu-

Teaching Suggestion

In pairs, have students create a small dialog between two friends. One of them just came back from a trip to Munchen and the other one wants to know everything about it.
Example questions and answers:
 Wie hat es dir/euch dort gefallen? Wahnsinnig gut!
 Wo hast du/habt ihr übernachtet? In einer Pension.

Von der Schule zum Beruf

33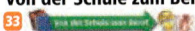

You might want to have students complete the Webprojekt on p. 59F, before doing this activity.

Teacher to Teacher

Tanya Stevenson
Terrill Middle School
Scotch Plains, New Jersey

Tanya uses this idea to present and practice the past tense.

"I model the past by showing students pictures of myself and tell them what I was doing and where I was. Students then show pictures of themselves—perhaps a yearbook or other photo—doing an activity. They tell the class what they did and where they were. I have also taken pictures of students in class and given them the pictures to report what they and other students were doing in German class."

Assess

▶ Testing Program, pp. 61–64
 Quiz 3-3A, Quiz 3-3B
 Audio CD3, Tr. 16

▶ Student Make-Up Assignments
 Chapter 3, Alternative Quiz

▶ Alternative Assessment Guide, p. 34

KAPITEL 3 · DRITTE STUFE 59V

Communication for All Students
Under this head you will find helpful suggestions for students with different learning styles and abilities. Another way to address these differences is the Online Student Edition.

Teaching Suggestions
offer helpful suggestions and information at point-of-use. You will also find references to other ancillaries.

Assessment
At the end of every **Stufe** and again at the end of the chapter, you will find references to assessment material available for that section of the chapter.

T35

Bringing Standards into the Classroom

by Paul Sandrock, Foreign Language Consultant, Wisconsin Department of Public Education

The core question that guided the development of the National Standards and their accompanying goals was simply: what matters in instruction?

Each proposed standard was evaluated. Did the standard target material that will have application beyond the classroom? Was the standard too specific or not specific enough? Teachers should be able to teach the standard and assess it in multiple ways. A standard needs to provide a target for instruction and learning throughout a student's K–12 education.

In the development of standards, foreign languages faced other unique challenges. The writers could not assume a K–12 sequence available to all students. In fact, unlike other disciplines, they could not guarantee that all students would experience even any common sequence.

From this context, the National Standards in Foreign Language Education Project's task force generated the five C's, five goals for learning languages: communication, cultures, connections, comparisons, and communities. First presented in 1995, the standards quickly became familiar to foreign language educators across the US, representing our professional consensus and capturing a broad view of the purposes for learning another language.

To implement the standards, however, requires a shift from emphasizing the means to focusing on the ends. It isn't a matter of grammar versus communication, but rather how much grammar is needed to communicate. Instead of teaching to a grammatical sequence, teaching decisions become based on what students need to know to achieve the communicative goal.

The Focus on Communication

The first standard redefined communication, making its purpose **interpersonal, interpretive,** and **presentational** communication. Teaching to the purpose of interpersonal communication takes us away from memorized dialogues to spontaneous, interactive conversation, where the message is most important and where meaning needs to be negotiated between the speakers. Interpretive communication is not an exercise in translation, but asks beginners to tell the gist of an authentic selection that is heard, read, or viewed, while increasingly advanced learners tell deeper and deeper levels of detail and can interpret based on their knowledge of the target culture. In the presentational mode of communication, the emphasis is on the audience, requiring the speaker or writer to adapt language to fit the situation and to allow for comprehension without any interactive negotiation of the meaning.

Standards challenge us to refocus many of the things we've been doing all along. The requirements of speaking and our expectation of how well students need to speak change when speaking is for a different purpose. This focus on the purpose of the communication changes the way we teach and test the skills of listening, speaking, reading, and writing.

Standards help us think about how to help students put the pieces of language to work in meaningful ways. Our

Standards for Foreign Language Learning

Communication Communicate in Languages Other than English	**Standard 1.1**	Students engage in conversations, provide and obtain information, express feelings and emotions, and exchange opinions.
	Standard 1.2	Students understand and interpret written and spoken language on a variety of topics.
	Standard 1.3	Students present information, concepts, and ideas to an audience of listeners or readers on a variety of topics.
Cultures Gain Knowledge and Understanding of Other Cultures	**Standard 2.1**	Students demonstrate an understanding of the relationship between the practices and perspectives of the culture studied.
	Standard 2.2	Students demonstrate an understanding of the relationship between the products and perspectives of the culture studied.
Connections Connect with Other Disciplines and Acquire Information	**Standard 3.1**	Students reinforce and further their knowledge of other disciplines through the foreign language.
	Standard 3.2	Students acquire information and recognize the distinctive viewpoints that are only available through the foreign language and its cultures.
Comparisons Develop Insight into the Nature of Language and Culture	**Standard 4.1**	Students demonstrate understanding of the nature of language through comparisons of the language studied and their own.
	Standard 4.2	Students demonstrate understanding of the concept of culture through comparisons of the cultures studied and their own.
Communities Participate in Multilingual Communities at Home and Around the World	**Standard 5.1**	Students use the language both within and beyond the school setting.
	Standard 5.2	Students show evidence of becoming life-long learners by using the language for personal enjoyment and enrichment.

standards answer *why* we are teaching various components of language, and we select *what* we teach in order to achieve those very standards.

The 5 C's

Originally the five C's were presented as five equal circles. During the years since the national standards were printed, teachers implementing and using the standards to write curriculum, texts, and lesson plans have come to see that communication is at the core, surrounded by four C's that influence the context for teaching and assessing.

The four C's surrounding our core goal of **Communication** change our classrooms by bringing in real-life applications for the language learned:

- **Cultures:** Beyond art and literature, learning occurs in the context of the way of life, patterns of behavior, and contributions of the people speaking the language being taught.

- **Connections:** Beyond content limited to the culture of the people speaking the target language, teachers go out to other disciplines to find topics and ideas to form the context for language learning.

- **Comparisons:** Foreign language study is a great way for students to learn more about native language and universal principles of language and culture by comparing and contrasting their own to the target language and culture.

- **Communities:** This goal of the standards adds a broader motivation to the context for language learning. The teacher makes sure students use their new language beyond the class hour, seeking ways to experience the target culture.

Implementation at the Classroom Level: Assessment and Instruction

After the publication of the standards, states developed more specific performance standards that would provide evidence of the application of the national content standards. Standards provide the organizing principle for teaching and assessing. The standards-oriented teacher, when asked what she's teaching, cites the standard "students will sustain a conversation." With that clear goal in mind, she creates lessons to teach various strategies to ask for clarification and to practice asking follow-up questions that explore a topic in more depth.

Textbook writers and materials providers are responding to this shift. Standards provide our goals; the useful textbooks and materials give us an organization and a context. Standards provide the ends; textbooks and materials can help us practice the means. Textbooks can bring authentic materials into the classroom, real cultural examples that avoid stereotypes, and a broader exposure to the variety of people who speak the language being studied. Textbooks can model the kind of instruction that will lead students to successful demonstration of the knowledge and skill described in the standards.

To really know that standards are the focus, look at the assessment. If standards are the target, assessment won't consist only of evaluation of the means (grammatical structures and vocabulary) in isolation. If standards are the focus, teachers will assess students' use of the second language in context. The summative assessment of our target needs to go beyond the specific and include open-ended, personalized tasks. Regardless of how the students show what they can do, the teacher will be able to gauge each student's progress toward the goal.

Assessment is like a jigsaw puzzle. If we test students only on the means, we just keep collecting random puzzle pieces. We have to test, and students have to practice, putting the pieces together in meaningful and purposeful ways. In order to learn vocabulary that will help students "describe themselves," for example, students may have a quiz on Friday with an expectation of close to 100% accuracy. But if that is all we ever do with those ten words, they will quickly be gone from students' memory, and we will only have collected a puzzle piece from each student. It is absolutely essential to have students use those puzzle pieces to complete the puzzle to provide evidence of what they "can do" with the language.

During this period of implementing our standards, we've learned that the standards provide a global picture, the essence of our goals. But they are not curriculum, nor are they lesson plans. The standards influence how we teach, but do not dictate one content nor one methodology. How can we implement the standards in our classrooms? Think about the targets; think about how students will show achievement of those targets through our evaluation measures; then think about what we need to teach and how that will occur in our classrooms. Make it happen in your classroom to get the results we've always wanted: students who can communicate in a language other than English.

Komm mit!

supports the Standards for Foreign Language Learning in the following ways:

THE PUPIL'S EDITION

▸ Encourages students to take responsibility for their learning by providing clearly defined objectives at the beginning of each chapter.

▸ Provides a variety of pair- and group-work activities to give students an opportunity to use the target language in print or via the Online Student Edition.

▸ Offers culture-related activities and poses questions that develop students' insight and encourage them to develop observational and analytical skills.

THE TEACHER'S EDITION

▸ Provides a broad framework for developing a foreign language program and offers specific classroom suggestions for reaching students with various learning styles.

▸ Offers ideas for multicultural and multidisciplinary projects as well as community and family links that encourage students to gain access to information both at school and in the community.

THE ANCILLARY PROGRAM

▸ Provides students with on-location video footage of native speakers interacting in their own cultural and geographic context.

▸ Includes multiple options for practicing new skills and assessing performance.

▸ Familiarizes students with the types of tasks they will be expected to perform on exit exams.

Reading Strategies and Skills

by Nancy Humbach, Miami University, Oxford, Ohio

Reading is the most enduring of the language skills. Long after a student ceases to study the language, the ability to read will continue to provide a springboard to the renewal of the other skills. We must consider all the ways in which our students will read and address the skills needed for those tasks.

How can we accomplish this goal? How can we, as teachers, present materials, encourage students to read, and at the same time foster understanding and build the student's confidence and interest in reading?

Selection of Materials

Reading material in the foreign language classroom should be relevant to students' backgrounds and at an accessible level of difficulty, i.e., at a level of difficulty only slightly above the reading ability of the student.

Authentic materials are generally a good choice. They provide cultural context and linguistic authenticity seldom found in materials created for students, and the authentic nature of the language provides a window on a new world. The problem inherent in the selection of authentic materials at early levels is obvious: the level of difficulty is frequently beyond the skill of the student. At the same time, however, readers are inspired by the fact that they can understand materials designed to be read by native speakers.

Presenting a Selection/Reading Strategies

We assume that students of a second language already have a reading knowledge in their first language and that many of the skills they learned in their "reading readiness" days will serve them well. Too often, however, students have forgotten such skills as activating background knowledge, skimming, scanning, and guessing content based on context clues. Helping student to reactivate these skills is part of helping them become better readers.

Teachers should not assume their students' ability to transfer a knowledge set from one reading to another. Students use these skills on a regular basis, but often do not even realize they are doing so. To help students become aware of these processes, they need to be given strategies for reading. These strategies offer students a framework for the higher level skills they need to apply when reading. Strategies also address learners of different learning styles and needs.

Advance Organizers

One way to activate the student's background knowledge is through advance organizers. They also serve to address the student's initial frustrations at encountering an unfamiliar text.

Advance organizers call up pertinent background knowledge, feelings, and experiences that can serve to focus the attention of the entire group on a given topic. In addition, they provide for a sharing of information among the students. Background information that includes cultural references and cultural information can reactivate in students skills that will help them with a text and provide for them clues to the meaning of the material.

A good advance organizer will provide some information and guide students to think about the scenarios being presented. An advance organizer might include photographs, drawings, quotations, maps, or information about the area where the story takes place. It might also be posed as a question, for example, "What would you do if you found yourself in….?" Having students brainstorm in advance, either as a whole class or in small groups, allows them to construct a scenario which they can verify as they read.

Prereading Activities

Prereading activities remind students of how much they really know and can prepare students in a number of ways to experience the language with less frustration. While we know that we must choose a reading selection that is not far beyond students' experience and skill level, we also know that no group of students reads at the same level. In the interest of assisting students to become better language learners, we can provide them with opportunities to work with unfamiliar structures and vocabulary ahead of time.

Preparing students for a reading selection can include a number of strategies that may anticipate but not dwell on potential problems to be encountered by students. Various aspects of grammar, such as differences in the past tenses and the meanings conveyed, can also cause problems. Alerting students to some of the aspects of the language allows them to struggle less, understand more quickly, and enjoy a reading selection to a greater degree.

Grouping vocabulary by category or simply choosing a short list of critical words for a section of reading is helpful. Providing an entire list of vocabulary items at one time can be overwhelming. With a bit of organization, the task becomes manageable to the point where students begin to master words they will find repeated throughout the selection.

Teaching students to skim for a particular piece of information or to scan for words, phrases, indicators of place, time, name, and then asking them to write a sentence or two about the gist of a paragraph or story, allows them to gain a sense of independence and success before they begin to read.

Getting into the Assignment

Teachers can recount the times they have assigned a piece of reading for homework, only to find that few students even attempted the work. Therefore, many teachers choose to complete the reading in class. Homework assignments should then be structured to have the student return to the selection and complete a assignment that requires critical thinking and imagination.

During class, several techniques assist students in maintaining interest and attention to the task. By varying these techniques, the teacher can provide for a lively class, during which students realize they *are* able to read. Partners can read passages to each other or students can take turns reading in small groups. The teacher might pose a question to be answered during that reading. Groups might also begin to act out short scenes, reading only the dialogue. Student might read a description of a setting and then draw what they imagine it to be. Of course, some selections might be silent reading with a specific amount of time announced for completion.

Reading aloud for comprehension and reading aloud for pronunciation practice are two entirely unrelated tasks. We can all recount classes where someone read aloud to us from weary lecture notes. Active engagement of the readers, on the other hand, forces them to work for comprehension, for the development of thought processes, and for improvement of language skills.

Postreading Activities

It is important to provide students with an opportunity to expand the knowledge they have gained from the reading selection. Students should apply what they have learned to their own personal experiences. How we structure activities can provide students more opportunities to reflect on their reading and learn how much they have understood. We often consider a written test the best way to ensure comprehension; however, many other strategies allow students to keep oral skills active. These might include acting out impromptu scenes from the story and creating dialogues that do not exist in a story, but might be imagined, based on other information. Consider the possibility of debates, interviews, TV talk show formats, telephone dialogues, or a monologue in which the audience hears only one side of the conversation.

Written assignments are also valid assessment tools, allowing students to incorporate the vocabulary and structures they have learned in the reading. Students might be encouraged to write journal entries for a character, create a new ending, or retell the story from another point of view. Newspaper articles, advertisements, and other creations can also be a means of following up. Comparisons with other readings require students to keep active vocabulary and structures they have studied previously. Encourage students to read their creations aloud to a partner, to a group, or to the class.

Conclusion

Reading can be exciting. The combination of a good selection that is relevant and rates high on the interest scale, along with good preparation, guidance, and post-reading activities that demonstrate to the students the level of success attained, can encourage them to continue to read. These assignments also allow for the incorporation of other aspects of language learning, and incorporate the Five C's of the National Standards. Communication and culture are obvious links, but so are connections (advance organizers, settings, and so on), comparisons (with other works in the heritage or target language), and communities (learning why a type of writing is important in a culture).

Komm mit!

offers reading practice and develops reading skills and strategies in the following ways:

THE PUPIL'S EDITION

▶ Provides an extensive reading section in each chapter called **Zum Lesen**. Each **Zum Lesen** section offers a strategy students apply to an authentic text, as well as activities to guide understanding and exploration of the text in print or via the Online Student Edition.

THE TEACHER'S EDITION

▶ Provides teachers with additional activities and information in every **Zum Lesen** section. Additional suggestions are provided for Prereading, Reading, and Postreading activities.

THE ANCILLARY PROGRAM

▶ *Lies mit mir!* This component offers reading selections of various formats and difficulty levels. Each chapter has a prereading feature, a reading selection with comprehension questions, and two pages of activities.

▶ The *Reading Skills and Strategies Handbook* offers useful strategies that can be applied to reading selections in the *Pupil's Edition, Lies mit mir!,* or a selection of your choosing.

▶ The *Übungsheft* contains a reading selection, tied to the chapter theme, and reading activities for each chapter in *Komm mit!*

Using Portfolios in the Language Classroom

by Jo Anne S. Wilson, J. Wilson Associates

Portfolios offer a more realistic and accurate way to assess the process of language teaching and learning.

The communicative, whole-language approach of today's language instruction requires assessment methods that parallel the teaching and learning strategies in the proficiency-oriented classroom. We know that language acquisition is a process. Portfolios are designed to assess the steps in that process.

What Is a Portfolio?

A portfolio is a purposeful, systematic collection of a student's work. A useful tool in developing a student profile, the portfolio shows the student's efforts, progress, and achievements for a given period of time. It may be used for periodic evaluation, as the basis for overall evaluation, or for placement. It may also be used to enhance or provide alternatives to traditional assessment measures, such as formal tests, quizzes, class participation, and homework.

Why Use Portfolios?

Portfolios benefit both students and teachers because they:

- **Are ongoing and systematic.** A portfolio reflects the real-world process of production, assessment, revision, and reassessment. It parallels the natural rhythm of learning.

- **Offer an incentive to learn.** Students have a vested interest in creating the portfolios, through which they can showcase their ongoing efforts and tangible achievements. Students select the works to be included and have a chance to revise, improve, evaluate, and explain the contents.

- **Are sensitive to individual needs.** Language learners bring varied abilities to the classroom and do not acquire skills in a uniformly neat and orderly fashion. The personalized, individualized assessment offered by portfolios responds to this diversity.

- **Provide documentation of language development.** The material in a portfolio is evidence of student progress in the language learning process. The contents of the portfolio make it easier to discuss their progress with the students as well as with parents and others.

- **Offer multiple sources of information.** A portfolio presents a way to collect and analyze information from multiple sources that reflects a student's efforts, progress, and achievements in the language.

Portfolio Components

The language portfolio should include both oral and written work, student self-evaluation, and teacher observation, usually in the form of brief, nonevaluative comments about various aspects of the student's performance.

The Oral Component

The oral component of a portfolio might be an audio- or videocassette. It may contain both rehearsed and extemporaneous monologues and conversations. For a rehearsed speaking activity, give a specific communicative task that students can personalize according to their individual interests (for example, ordering a favorite meal in a restaurant). If the speaking activity is extemporaneous, first acquaint students with possible topics for discussion or even the specific task they will be expected to perform. (For example, tell them they will be asked to discuss a picture showing a sports activity or a restaurant scene.)

The Written Component

Portfolios are excellent tools for incorporating process writing strategies into the language classroom. Documentation of various stages of the writing process—brainstorming, multiple drafts, and peer comments—may be included with the finished product.

Involve students in selecting writing tasks for the portfolio. At the beginning levels, the tasks might include some structured writing, such as labeling or listing. As students become more proficient, journals, letters, and other more complicated writing tasks are valuable ways for them to monitor their progress in using the written language.

Student Self-Evaluation

Students should be actively involved in critiquing and evaluating their portfolios and monitoring their own progress.

The process and procedure for student self-evaluation should be considered in planning the contents of the portfolio. Students should work with you and their peers to design the exact format. Self-evaluation encourages them to think about what they are learning (content), how they learn (process), why they are learning (purpose), and where they are going in their learning (goals).

Teacher Observation

Systematic, regular, and ongoing observations should be placed in the portfolio after they have been discussed with the student. These observations provide feedback on the student's progress in the language learning process.

Teacher observations should be based on an established set of criteria that has been developed earlier with input from the student. Observation techniques may include the following:

- Jotting notes in a journal to be discussed with the student and then placed in the portfolio
- Using a checklist of observable behaviors, such as the willingness to take risks when using the target language or staying on task during the lesson
- Making observations on adhesive notes that can be placed in folders
- Recording anecdotal comments, during or after class, using a cassette recorder

Knowledge of the criteria you use in your observations gives students a framework for their performance.

Electronic Portfolios

Technology can provide help with managing student portfolios. Digital or computer-based portfolios offer a means of saving portfolios in an electronic format. Students can save text, drawings, photographs, graphics, audio or video recordings, or any combination of multimedia information. Teachers can create their own portfolio templates or consult one of the many commercial software programs available to create digital portfolios. Portfolios saved on videotapes or compact discs provide a convenient way to access and store students' work. By employing technology, this means of alternative assessment addresses the learning styles and abilities of individual students. Additionally, electronic portfolios can be shared among teachers, and parents have the ability to easily see the students' progress.

Logistically, the hypermedia equipment and software available for students' use determine what types of entries will be included in the portfolios. The teacher or a team of teachers and students may provide the computer support.

How Are Portfolios Evaluated?

The portfolio should reflect the process of student learning over a specific period of time. At the beginning of that time period, determine the criteria by which you will assess the final product and convey them to the students. Make this evaluation a collaborative effort by seeking students' input as you formulate these criteria and your instructional goals.

Students need to understand that evaluation based on a predetermined standard is but one phase of the assessment process; demonstrated effort and growth are just as important. As you consider correctness and accuracy in both oral and written work, also consider the organization, creativity, and improvement revealed by the student's portfolio over the time period. The portfolio provides a way to monitor the growth of a student's knowledge, skills, and attitudes and shows the student's efforts, progress, and achievements.

How to Implement Portfolios

Teacher-teacher collaboration is as important to the implementation of portfolios as teacher-student collaboration. Confer with your colleagues to determine, for example, what kinds of information you want to see in the student portfolio, how the information will be presented, the purpose of the portfolio, the intended purposes (grading, placement, or a combination of the two), and criteria for evaluating the portfolio. Conferring among colleagues helps foster a departmental cohesiveness and consistency that will ultimately benefit the students.

The Promise of Portfolios

The high degree of student involvement in developing portfolios and deciding how they will be used generally results in renewed student enthusiasm for learning and improved achievement. As students compare portfolio pieces done early in the year with work produced later, they can take pride in their progress as well as reassess their motivation and work habits.

Komm mit!

supports the use of portfolios in the following ways:

THE PUPIL'S EDITION

▸ Includes numerous oral and written activities that can be easily adapted for student portfolios, such as **Notizbuch, Zum Schreiben,** and **Rollenspiel.**

THE TEACHER'S EDITION

▸ Suggests activities in the Portfolio Assessment feature that may serve as portfolio items.

THE ANCILLARY PROGRAM

▸ Includes criteria in the *Alternative Assessment Guide* for evaluating portfolios.

▸ Provides Speaking Tests in the *Testing Program* for each chapter that can be adapted for use as portfolio assessment items.

▸ Offers several oral and written scenarios on the *Interactive CD-ROM Tutor* that students can develop and include in their portfolios.

▸ The *DVD* Tutor offers additional practice for the Location Opener, **Landeskunde, Los geht's! Fortsetzung,** and offers an alternative way to present grammar.

Multi-Level Classrooms

by Joan H. Manley, University of Texas at El Paso

There are positive ways, both psychological and pedagogical, to make this situation work for you and your students.

So you have just heard that your third-period class is going to include both Levels 2 and 3! While this is never the best news for a foreign language teacher, there are positive ways, both psychological and pedagogical, to make the multi-level classroom work for you and your students.

Relieving student anxieties

Initially, in a multi-level class environment, it is important to relieve students' anxiety by orienting them to their new situation. From the outset, let all students know that just because they "did" things the previous year, such as learn how to conjugate certain verbs, they may not yet be able to use them in a meaningful way. Students should not feel that it is demeaning or a waste of time to recycle activities or to share knowledge and skills with fellow students. Second-year students need to know they are not second-class citizens and that they can benefit from their classmates' greater experience with the language. Third-year students may achieve a great deal of satisfaction and become more confident in their own language skills when they have opportunities to help or teach their second-year classmates. It is important to reassure third-year students that you will devote time to them and challenge them with different assignments.

Easing your own apprehension

When you are faced with both Levels 2 and 3 in your classroom, remind yourself that you teach students of different levels in the same classroom every year, although not officially. After one year of classroom instruction, your Level 2 class will never be a truly homogeneous group. Despite being made up of students with the same amount of "seat time," the class comprises multiple layers of language skills, knowledge, motivation, and ability. Therefore, you are constantly called upon to make a positive experience out of a potentially negative one. Your apprehension will gradually diminish to the extent that you are able to …

- make students less dependent on you for the successful completion of their activities.
- place more responsibility for learning on the students.
- implement creative group, pair, and individual activities.

How can you do this? Good organization will help. Lessons will need to be especially well-planned for the multi-level class. The following lesson plan is an example of how to treat the same topic with students of two different levels.

Teaching a lesson in a multi-level classroom

Lesson objectives:
Relate an incident in the past that you regret.

- Level 2: Express surprise and sympathy.
- Level 3: Offer encouragement and make suggestions.

Lesson plan

1. **Review and/or teach the past tense.**
   Present the formation of the past tense. Model its use for the entire class or call upon Level 3 students to give examples.

2. **Practice the past tense.**
   Have Level 3 students who have mastered the past tense teach it to Level 2 students in pairs or small groups. Provide the Level 3 student instructors with several drill and practice activities they may use for this purpose.

3. **Relate your own regrettable past experience.**
   Recount a personal regrettable incident—real or imaginary—to the entire class as a model. For example, you may have left your automobile lights on, and when you came out of school, the battery was dead and you couldn't start your car. Or you may have scolded a student for not doing the homework and later discovered the student had a legitimate reason for not completing the assignment.

4. **Prepare and practice written and oral narratives.**

   Have Level 2 students pair off with Level 3 students. Each individual writes about his or her experience, the Level 3 partner serving as a resource for the Level 2 student. Partners then edit each other's work and listen to each other's oral delivery. You might choose to have students record their oral narratives.

5. **Present communicative functions.**
   A. Ask for a volunteer to recount his or her own regrettable incident for the entire class.
   B. Model reactions to the volunteer's narrative.
      (1) Express surprise and sympathy (for Level 2): "Really! That's too bad!"
      (2) Offer encouragement and make suggestions (for Level 3): "Don't worry!" "You can still…."

6. **Read narratives and practice communicative functions.**

   Have Level 2 students work together in one group or in small groups, listening to classmates' stories and reacting with the prescribed communicative function. Have Level 3 students do the same among themselves. Circulate among the groups, listening, helping, and assessing.

7. **Assess progress.**

   Repeat your personal account for the entire class and elicit reactions from students according to their level. Challenge students to respond with communicative functions expected of the other level if they can.

Every part of the above lesson plan is important. Both levels have been accommodated. The teacher has not dominated the lesson. Students have worked together in pairs and small groups, while Level 3 students have helped their Level 2 classmates. Individual groups still feel accountable, both within their level and across levels.

Any lesson can be adapted in this way. It takes time and effort, but the result is a student-centered classroom where students share and grow, and the teacher is the facilitator.

Komm mit!

addresses the *multi-level classroom* in the following ways:

THE PUPIL'S EDITION

▸ Provides creative activities for pair and group work that allow students at different levels to work together and learn form one another.

THE TEACHER'S EDITION

▸ Offers practical suggestions for *Projects* and *Cooperative Learning* that engage students of different levels.

▸ Provides a clear, comprehensive outline of the functions, vocabulary, and grammar that are recycled in each chapter. The *Chapter Overview* of each chapter is especially helpful to the teacher who is planning integrated or varied lessons in the multi-level classroom.

THE ANCILLARY PROGRAM

▸ Provides a variety of materials and activities to accommodate different levels in a multi-level classroom.

Teaching Culture

by Nancy A. Humbach, Miami University, and Dorothea Bruschke, Parkway School District

We must integrate culture and language in a way that encourages curiosity, stimulates analysis, and teaches students to hypothesize.

The teaching of culture has undergone some important and welcome changes in recent years. Instead of teaching the standard notions of cultures, language and regions, we now stress the teaching of analysis and the critical thinking skills required to evaluate a culture, not by comparing it to one's own, but within its own setting. The setting includes the geography, climate, history, and influences of peoples who have interacted within that cultural group.

The National Standards for the Teaching of Foreign Languages suggests organizing the teaching of culture into three categories: products, practices, and perspectives. Through the presentation of these aspects of culture, students should gain the skill to analyze the culture, evaluate it within its context, compare it to their culture and develop the ability to function comfortably in that culture.

Skill and practice in the analysis of cultural phenomena equip students to enter a cultural situation, assess it, create strategies for dealing with it and accepting it as a natural part of the people. The ultimate goal of this philosophy is to reduce the "we vs. they" approach to culture. If students are encouraged to accept and appreciate the diversity of other cultures, they will be more willing and better able to develop the risk-taking strategies necessary to learn a language and to interact with people of different cultures.

There are many ways to help students become culturally knowledgeable and to assist them in developing an awareness of differences and similarities between the target culture and their own. Two of these approaches involve critical thinking, that is, trying to find reasons for a certain behavior through observation and analysis, and putting individual observations into larger cultural patterns. We must integrate culture and language in a way that encourages curiosity, stimulates analysis, and teaches students to hypothesize.

First Approach: Questioning

The first approach involves *questioning* as the key strategy. At the earliest stages of language learning, students learn ways to greet peers, elders, strangers, as well as the use of **du, ihr,** and **Sie.** Students need to consider questions such as: How do German-speaking people greet each other? Are there different levels of formality? Who initiates a handshake? What's considered a good handshake? Each of these questions leads students to think about the values that are expressed through words and gestures. They start to "feel" the other culture, and at the same time, understand how much of their own behavior is rooted in their cultural background.

Magazines, newspapers, advertisements, and television commercials are all excellent sources of cultural material. For example, browsing through a German magazine, one finds an extraordinary number of advertisements for health-related products. Could this indicate a great interest in staying healthy? To learn about customs involving health, reading advertisements can be followed up with viewing videos and films, or by interviewing native speakers or people who have lived in German-speaking countries. Students might want to find answers to questions such as: "How do Germans treat a cold? What is their attitude toward fresh air? Toward exercise?" This type of questioning might lead students to discover that some of the popular leisure-time activities, such as **einen Spaziergang machen** or **eine Wanderung machen,** are related to health consciousness.

An advertisement for a refrigerator or a picture of a German kitchen can provide an insight into practices of shopping for food. Students first need to think about the refrigerator at home, take an inventory of what is kept in it, and consider when and where their family shops. Next, students should look closely at a German refrigerator. What is its size? What could that mean? (Smaller refrigerators might mean that shopping takes place more often, stores are within walking distance, and people eat more fresh foods.)

Food wrappers and containers also provide cultural insight. For example, in German-speaking countries, bottled water is preferred to tap water even though tap water is safe to drink in most places. Why, then, is the rather expensive bottled water still preferred? Is it a tradition stemming from a time when tap water was not pure? Does it relate to the Germans' fondness of "taking the waters," i.e., drinking fresh spring water at a spa?

Second Approach: Associating Words with Images

The second approach for developing cultural understanding involves *forming associations of words with the cultural images they suggest.* Language and culture are so closely related that one might actually say that language is culture. Most words, especially nouns, carry a cultural connotation. Knowing the literal equivalent of a word in another language is of little use to students in understanding this connotation. For example, **Freund** cannot be translated simply as *friend,* **Brot** as *bread,* or **Straße** as *street.* The German word **Straße,** for instance, carries with it such images as people walking, sitting in a sidewalk café, riding bicycles, or shopping in specialty stores, and cars parked partly over the curb amid dense traffic. There is also the image of **Fußgängerzone,** a street for pedestrians only.

When students have acquired some sense of the cultural connotation of words—not only through explanations but, more importantly, through observation of visual images—they start to discover the larger underlying cultural themes, or what is often called deep culture.

These larger cultural themes serve as organizing categories into which individual cultural phenomena fit to form a pattern. Students might discover, for example, that Germans, because they live in much more crowded conditions, have a great need for privacy (cultural theme), as reflected in such phenomena as closed doors, fences or walls around property, and shutters on windows. Students might also discover that love of nature and the outdoors is an important cultural theme as indicated by such phenomena as flower boxes and planters in public places, well-kept public parks in every town, and people going for a walk or hiking.

As we teach culture, students learn to recognize elements not only of the target culture but also of their American cultural heritage. They see how elements of culture reflect larger themes or patterns. Learning what makes us Americans and how that information relates to other people throughout the world can be an exciting discovery for a young person.

As language teachers, we are able to facilitate this discovery of our similarities with others as well as our differences. We do not encourage value judgments about others and their culture, nor do we recommend adopting other ways. We simply say to students, "Other ways exist. They exist, just as our ways exist, due to our history, geography, and what our ancestors have passed on to us through traditions and values."

Komm mit!
develops *cultural understanding and cultural awareness* in the following ways:

THE PUPIL'S EDITION

▸ Informs students about daily life in German-speaking countries through culture notes.

▸ Provides deeper insight into cultural phenomena through personal interviews in the **Landeskunde** section.

▸ Helps students associate language and its cultural connotations through authentic art and photos.

THE TEACHER'S EDITION

▸ Provides additional cultural and language notes and background information.

▸ Suggests critical thinking strategies that encourage students to hypothesize, analyze, and discover larger underlying cultural themes.

THE ANCILLARY PROGRAM

▸ Includes realia to develop cultural insight by serving as catalyst for questioning and discovery.

▸ Offers activities that require students to compare and contrast cultures.

▸ Provides songs, short readings, and poems, as well as many opportunities for students to experience regional variation and idioms in the video, DVD, audio, and CD-ROM programs.

Learning Styles and Multi-Modality Teaching

by Mary B. McGehee, Louisiana State University

Incorporating a greater variety of activities to accommodate the learning styles of all students can make the difference between struggle and pleasure in the foreign language classroom.

The larger and broader population of students who are enrolling in foreign language classes brings a new challenge to foreign language educators, calling forth an evolution in teaching methods to enhance learning for all our students. Educational experts now recognize that every student has a preferred sense for learning and retrieving information: visual, auditory, or kinesthetic. Incorporating a greater variety of activities to accommodate the learning styles of all students can make the difference between struggle and pleasure in the foreign language classroom.

Accommodating Different Learning Styles

A modified arrangement of the classroom is one way to provide more effective and enjoyable learning for all students. Rows of chairs and desks must give way at times to circles, semicircles, or small clusters. Students may be grouped in fours or in pairs for cooperative work or peer teaching. It is important to find a balance of arrangements, thereby providing the most comfort in varied situations.

Since visual, auditory, and kinesthetic learners will be in the class, and because every student's learning will be enhanced by a multi-sensory approach, lessons must be directed toward all three learning styles. Any language lesson content may be presented visually, aurally, or kinesthetically.

Visual presentations and practice may include the chalkboard, charts, posters, television, overhead projectors, books, magazines, picture diagrams, flash cards, bulletin boards, films, slides, or videos. Visual learners need to see what they are to learn. Lest the teacher think he or she will never have the time to prepare all those visuals, Dickel and Slak (1983) found that visual aids generated by students are more effective than ready-made ones.

Auditory presentations and practice may include stating aloud the requirements of the lesson, oral questions and answers, paired or group work on a progression of oral exercises from repetition to communication, tapes, CDs, dialogues, and role-playing. Jingles, catchy stories, and memory devices using songs and rhymes are good learning aids. Having students record themselves and then listen as they play back the cassette allows them to practice in the auditory mode.

Kinesthetic presentations entail the students' use of manipulatives, chart materials, gestures, signals, typing, songs, games, and role-playing. These lead the students to associate sentence constructions with meaningful movements.

A Sample Lesson Using Multi-Modality Teaching

A multi-sensory presentation on greetings might proceed as follows:

For Visual Learners

As the teacher begins oral presentation of greetings and introductions, he or she simultaneously shows the written forms on transparencies, with the formal expressions marked with an adult's hat, and the informal expressions marked with a baseball cap.

The teacher then distributes cards with the hat and cap symbols representing the formal and informal expressions. As the students hear taped mini-dialogues, they hold up the appropriate card to indicate whether the dialogues are formal or informal. On the next listening, the students repeat the sentences they hear.

For Auditory Learners

A longer taped dialogue follows, allowing the students to hear the new expressions a number of times. They write from dictation several sentences containing the new expressions. They may work in pairs, correcting each other's work as they "test" their own understanding of the lesson at hand. Finally, students respond to simple questions using the appropriate formal and informal responses cued by the cards they hold.

For Kinesthetic Learners

For additional kinesthetic input, members of the class come to the front of the room, each holding a hat or cap symbol. As the teacher calls out situations, the students play the roles, using gestures and props appropriate to the age group they are portraying. Non-cued, communicative role-playing with props further enables the students to "feel" the differences between formal and informal expressions.

Helping Students Learn How to Use Their Preferred Mode

Since we require all students to perform in all language skills, part of the assistance we must render is to help them develop strategies within their preferred learning modes to carry out an assignment in another mode. For example, visual students hear the teacher assign an oral exercise and visualize what they must do. They must see themselves carrying out the assignment, in effect watching themselves as if there were a movie going on in their heads. Only then can they also hear themselves saying the right things. Thus, this assignment will be much easier for the visual learners who have been taught this process, if they have not already figured it out for themselves. Likewise, true auditory students, confronted with a reading/writing assignment, must talk themselves through it, converting the entire process into sound as they plan and prepare their work. Kinesthetic students presented with a visual or auditory task must first break the assignment into tasks and then work their way through them.

Students who experience difficulty because of a strong preference for one mode of learning are often unaware of the degree of preference. In working with these students, I prefer the simple and direct assessment of learning styles offered by Richard Bandler and John Grinder in their book *Frogs into Princes*, which allows the teacher and student to quickly determine how the student learns. In an interview with the student, I follow the assessment with certain specific recommendations of techniques to make the student's study time more effective.

It is important to note here that teaching students to maximize their study does not require that the teacher give each student an individualized assignment. It does require that each student who needs it be taught how to prepare the assignment using his or her own talents and strengths. This communication between teacher and student, combined with teaching techniques that reinforce learning in all modes, can only maximize pleasure and success in learning a foreign language.

References

Dickel, M.J. and S. Slak. "Imaging Vividness and Memory for Verbal Material." *Journal of Mental Imagery* 7, i (1983):121–126.

Bandler, Richard, and John Grinder. *Frogs into Princes*. Real People Press, Moab, UT. 1978.

Komm mit!
accommodates different learning styles in the following ways:

THE PUPIL'S EDITION
- Presents basic material in audio, video, print, and online formats.
- Includes role-playing activities and a variety of multi-modal activities, including an extensive listening strand and many art-based activities.

THE TEACHER'S EDITION
- Provides suggested activities for visual, auditory, and kinesthetic learners as well as suggestions for slower-paced learning and challenge activities.
- Includes Total Physical Response activities.

THE ANCILLARY PROGRAM
- Provides additional reinforcement activities for a variety of learning styles.
- Presents a rich blend of audiovisual input through the video program, audio program, CD-ROM Tutor, transparencies, blackline masters and Internet activities.

Professional References

The Professional References section provides you with information about many resources that can enrich your German class. Included are addresses of German government and tourist offices, pen pal organizations, subscription agencies, and many others. Since addresses change frequently, you may want to verify them before you send your requests.

PEN PAL ORGANIZATIONS

The Student Letter Exchange will arrange pen pals for your students. For the names of other pen pal groups, contact your local chapter of AATG. There are fees involved, so be sure to write for information.

Student Letter Exchange (League of Friendship)
211 Broadway, Suite 201
Lynbrook, NY 11563
(516) 887-8628

EMBASSIES AND CONSULATES

Embassy of the Federal Republic of Germany
4645 Reservoir Rd. N.W.
Washington, D.C. 20007-1998
(202) 298-4000

Consulate General of the Federal Republic of Germany
460 Park Avenue
New York, NY 10022-1971
(212) 308-8700
(also in Atlanta, Boston, Chicago, Detroit, Houston, Los Angeles, San Francisco, Seattle)

Embassy of Austria
3524 International Court N.W.
Washington, D.C. 20008
(202) 895-6700

Austrian Consulate General
31 East 69th Street
New York, NY 10021
(212) 737-6400
(also in Los Angeles and Chicago)

Embassy of Switzerland
2900 Cathedral Ave. NW
Washington, DC 20008
(202) 745-7900

Consulate General of Switzerland
665 5th Av. 8th Floor
New York, NY 10022
(212) 758-2560
(also in San Francisco, Los Angeles, Atlanta, Houston, Chicago)

CULTURAL AGENCIES

For historic and tourist information and audiovisual materials relating to Austria, contact:

Austrian Cultural Institute
950 Third Avenue
New York, NY 10022
(212) 759-5165

Material on political matters is available from **Bundeszentrale für politische Bildung,** a German federal agency.

Bundeszentrale für politische Bildung
Berliner Freiheit 7
53111 Bonn, GERMANY
(0228) 5150

For free political, cultural, and statistical information, films, and videos, contact:

German Information Center
871 United Nations Plaza
New York, NY 10017
(212) 610-9800

For various materials and information about special events your classes might attend, contact the **Goethe Institut** nearest you. For regional locations, contact:

Goethe Haus, German Cultural Center
1014 Fifth Avenue
New York, NY 10028
(212) 439-8700

The **Institut für Auslandsbeziehungen** provides cultural information to foreigners. The institute offers books and periodicals on a limited basis as well as a variety of two- and three-week professional seminars which allow educators to learn about the people, education, history, and culture of German-speaking countries.

Institut für Auslandsbeziehungen
Charlottenplatz 17
70173 Stuttgart, GERMANY
(0711) 2225-147

Inter Nationes, a nonprofit German organization for promoting international relations, supplies material on all aspects of life in Germany (literature, posters, magazines, press releases, films, slides, audio and video tapes) to educational institutions and organizations abroad.

Inter Nationes
Kennedyallee 91-103
53175 Bonn, GERMANY
(0228) 8800

TOURIST BUREAUS

Write to the following tourist offices for travel information and brochures.

German National Tourist Office
122 East 42nd St. 52nd Floor
New York, NY 10168
(212) 661-7200
(also in Chicago and San Francisco)

Deutsche Zentrale für Tourismus e.V.
Beethovenstraße 69
60325 Frankfurt GERMANY
(609) 974840

Switzerland Tourism
608 Fifth Avenue
New York, NY 10020
(212) 757-5944

PROFESSIONAL ORGANIZATIONS

The two major organizations for German teachers at the secondary school level are:

American Council on the Teaching of Foreign Languages (ACTFL)
6 Executive Plaza
Yonkers, NY 10701
(914) 963-8830

American Association of Teachers of German (AATG)
112 Haddontowne Court
Suite 104
Cherry Hill, NJ 08034
(609) 795-5553

PERIODICALS

Following are some periodicals published in German. For the names of other German magazines and periodicals contact a subscription agency.

Deutschland Nachrichten, a weekly newsletter available in both German and English, is published by the German Information Center *(see address under Cultural Agencies).*

Goethe Haus *(see address under Cultural Agencies)* publishes **Treffpunkt Deutsch,** a magazine of information, bibliographies, and ideas for teachers.

Bundeszentrale für politische Bildung *(see address under Cultural Agencies)* publishes **Politische Zeitung (PZ),** a quarterly magazine covering issues of social interest.

The Austrian Press and Information Service publishes a monthly newsletter. Write to:

Austrian Information
3524 International Court N.W.
Washington, D.C. 20008

Juma classroom magazine is a free publication to which you can subscribe. You can order multiple copies by writing to:

Redaktion Juma
Frankfurter Straße 40
51065 Köln, GERMANY
(0221) 962513-0

SUBSCRIPTION SERVICES

German magazines can be obtained through subscription agencies in the United States. The following companies are among the many which can provide you with subscriptions:

EBSCO Subscription Services
P.O. Box 1943
Birmingham, AL 35201-1943
(205) 991-6600

Continental Book Company
8000 Cooper Ave. Bldg. 29
Glendale, NY 11385
(718) 326-0572

EXCHANGE PROGRAMS

German American Partnership Program (GAPP)
c/o Goethe-Institut New York
1014 Fifth Avenue
New York, NY 10028
(212) 439-8715

Experiment in International Living
World Learning
Kipling Road, P.O. Box 676
Brattleboro, VT 05302-0676
(802) 257-7751 or
(800) 345-2929

MISCELLANEOUS

(ADAC) Allgemeiner Deutscher Automobil Club
Am Westpark 8
81373 München, GERMANY
(089) 76760

For students who want to find a summer job in Germany, write to:

Zentralstelle für Arbeitsvermittlung (ZAV)
Dienststelle 08100
Postfach 170545
60079 Frankfurt, GERMANY
(069) 71110
(Applicants must have a good knowledge of German.)

For international student passes and other student services contact:

CIEE Student Travel Services
205 E. 42nd Street
New York, NY 10017-5706
(212) 822-2700
(has branch offices in several other large cities)

A Bibliography for the German Teacher

This bibliography is a compilation of several resources available for professional enrichment.

SELECTED AND ANNOTATED LIST OF READINGS

I. Methods and Approaches

Cohen, A. (1994). *Assessing language ability in the classroom* (2nd ed.). Boston: Heinle and Heinle.
- An introduction to assessing students' foreign language ability. Discussions of various assessment techniques including role-playing activities, portfolios, and oral interviews provide instructors with alternatives to more traditional testing techniques. Computer-based testing is also examined.

Lafayette, R. (Ed.). (1996). *National standards: A catalyst for reform.* Lincolnwood, IL: National Textbook Co.
- Provides an outline of the National Standards movement and its implications for the modern foreign language classroom. Issues such as technology, teacher training, materials development, and the changing learning environment are each addressed in terms of the national standards.

Lee, J., & VanPatten, B. (1995). *Making communicative language teaching happen.* New York: McGraw-Hill.
- Discussion of communicative language teaching centered on a task-based approach to second language education. The authors provide both a theoretical and a practical framework for teaching the four skills (reading, writing, listening, speaking). The book includes some two hundred activities as well as test sections to help instructors encourage communicative interaction in their classrooms.

Omaggio Hadley, A. (1993). *Teaching language in context* (2nd ed.). Boston: Heinle and Heinle Publishers.
- Overview of the proficiency movement as well as a survey of past foreign language teaching methods and approaches. The author briefly presents the theory and history of the proficiency movement and then applies these concepts to each of the five skills in foreign language education. Includes sample activities, teaching suggestions, summaries, and references for further reading.

II. Second-Language Theory

Brown, H. D. (1994). *Principles of language learning and teaching* (3rd ed.). Englewood Cliffs, NJ: Prentice Hall Regents
- Addresses the cognitive, psychological, and sociocultural factors influencing the language learning process. Also includes theories of learning, styles and strategies, motivation, and culture; as well as an introduction to assessment, error analysis, communicative competence, and theories of acquisition along with practical vignettes describing classroom applications.

Ellis, R. (1994). *The study of second language acquisition.* Oxford: Oxford University Press.
- Provides an overview of second language acquisition: error analysis, acquisition orders, social factors, affective variables, individual differences, and the advantages and disadvantages of classroom instruction.

Krashen, S. (1987). *Principles and practice in second language acquisition.* New York: Prentice-Hall.
- Summary and discussion of Krashen's Monitor Model and its implications for foreign language instruction. Krashen discusses each of his five hypotheses regarding second language acquisition and their implications for the foreign language classroom.

III. Technology Enhanced Language Learning

Bush, M., & Terry, R. (Eds.). (1997). *Technology enhanced language learning.* Lincolnwood, IL: National Textbook Co.

Muyskens, J. (Ed.). (1997). *New ways of learning and teaching: Focus on technology and foreign language education.* Boston: Heinle and Heinle.
- Both works include articles on application of technology in the modern foreign language classroom. Topics include: multimedia, electronic discussions and computer-mediated communication, the WWW, videos, hypermedia, and the Internet. The authors describe techniques for applying these tools to all aspects of foreign language learning including reading, writing, listening, speaking, and culture. Questions of implementation, teacher training, and language laboratories are also discussed.

IV. Professional Journals

Calico
(Published by the Computer Assisted Language Instruction Consortium)
- Emphasizes applications of technology to foreign language learning. Articles include research on computer assisted language learning, videos and television in the classroom, and the use of the Internet and the WWW for learning and instruction.

Foreign Language Annals
(Published by the American Council on the Teaching of Foreign Languages)
- Publishes both research-based and practical articles on foreign language instruction and learning. In addition to learning and teaching strategies and methods, the journal also features articles on curriculum development and recent trends in foreign language pedagogy.

The IALL Journal of Language Learning Technologies
(Published by the International Association for Learning Laboratories)
- Practical and theoretical articles on technology and language instruction with emphasis on the effective use of media centers for language teaching, learning, and research.

The Modern Language Journal
- Features articles on the most recent research in the fields of language learning and second language acquisition.

Die Unterrichtspraxis
(Published by the American Association of Teachers of German)
- Emphasizes practical reports of successful pedagogical methods and strategies. Ideas for the German language classroom can be found in every issue along with reports on the current state of German studies in the United States.

HOLT GERMAN 2
Komm mit!

HOLT, RINEHART AND WINSTON

A Harcourt Education Company

Orlando • **Austin** • New York • San Diego • Toronto • London

EXECUTIVE EDITOR
George Winkler

SENIOR EDITOR
Konstanze Alex Brown

MANAGING EDITOR
Amber Martin

EDITORIAL STAFF
Sara Anbari

EDITORIAL PERMISSIONS
Janet Harrington, *Permissions Editor*

ART, DESIGN, & PHOTO
BOOK DESIGN
Richard Metzger, *Design Director*
Marta L. Kimball, *Design Manager*

IMAGE SERVICES
Joe London, *Director*
Tim Taylor, *Photo Research Supervisor*
Stephanie Friedman
Michelle Rumpf, *Art Buyer Supervisor*
Coco Weir

DESIGN NEW MEDIA
Kimberly Cammerata, *Design Manager*
Czeslaw Sornat, *Senior Designer*
Grant Davidson

MEDIA DESIGN
Curtis Riker, *Design Director*
Richard Chavez

COVER DESIGN
Richard Metzger, *Design Director*
Candace Moore, *Senior Designer*

PRODUCTION
Gene Rumann, *Production Manager*

MANUFACTURING
Shirley Cantrell, *Supervisor, Inventory & Manufacturing*
Deborah Wisdom, *Senior Inventory Analyst*

NEW MEDIA
Jessica Bega, *Senior Project Manager*
Lydia Doty, *Senior Project Manager*
Elizabeth Kline, *Senior Project Manager*

VIDEO PRODUCTION
Video materials produced by Edge Productions, Inc., Aiken, S.C.

Copyright © 2006 by Holt, Rinehart and Winston

All rights reserved. No part of this publication may be reproduced or transmitted in any form or by any means, electronic or mechanical, including photocopy, recording, or any information storage and retrieval system, without permission in writing from the publisher.

Requests for permission to make copies of any part of the work should be mailed to the following address: Permissions Department, Holt, Rinehart and Winston, 10801 N. MoPac Expressway, Building 3, Austin, Texas 78759.

ACKNOWLEDGMENTS

Front Cover and Title Page: Bryan Reinhart/Masterfile
Back Cover: © AFP/CORBIS; (frame) © 2006 Image Farm, Inc.

For permission to reprint copyrighted material, grateful acknowledgment is made to the following sources:

Baedeker Verlag Karl Baedeker GmbH: "Baden-Baden" from *Baedeker Allianz Reiseführer Deutschland, 2.* Copyright © 1992 by Verlag Karl Baedeker GmbH.

Berlin Programm Rimbach Verlag GmbH: "Oper & Theater" from Berlin Programm, September 1993. Reviews of "Blau-Rot," "Britzer Mühle," "Istanbul," "Restaurant El Pharaoh," "Restaurant Hardtke," "Restaurant Pferdestall," and "Restaurant Seaside" from Berlin *Programm,* September 1993.

Acknowledgments continued on page R83, which is an extension of the copyright page

KOMM MIT! is a trademark licensed to Holt, Rinehart and Winston, registered in the United States of America and/or other jurisdictions.

Printed in the United States of America

ISBN 0-03-037256-9

1 2 3 4 5 6 7 8 9 048 09 08 07 06 05 04

AUTHOR

George Winkler
Austin, TX

Mr. Winkler developed the scope and sequence and framework for the chapters, created the basic material, selected realia, and wrote activities.

CONTRIBUTING WRITERS

Margrit Meinel Diehl
Syracuse, NY

Mrs. Diehl wrote activities to practice basic material, functions, grammar, and vocabulary.

Carolyn Roberts Thompson
Abilene Christian University
Abilene, TX

Mrs. Thompson was responsible for the selection of realia for readings and for developing reading activities.

CONSULTANTS

The consultants conferred on a regular basis with the editorial staff and reviewed all the chapters of the Level 2 textbook.

Dorothea Bruschke, retired
Parkway School District
Chesterfield, MO

Diane E. Laumer
San Marcos High School
San Marcos, TX

Phyllis Manning
Vancouver, WA

Ingeborg H. McCoy
Southwest Texas State University
San Marcos, TX

REVIEWERS

Nancy Butt
Washington and Lee High School
Arlington, VA

Connie Frank
John F. Kennedy High School
Sacramento, CA

Rolf M. Schwägermann
Stuyvesant High School
New York, NY

Scott G. Williams
Language Acquisition Center
University of Texas, Arlington

Linda Wiencken-Williams
Austin, Texas

Jim Witt
Grand Junction High School
Grand Junction, CO

FIELD TEST PARTICIPANTS

We express our appreciation to the teachers and students who participated in the field test. Their comments were instrumental in the development of the entire **Komm mit!** program.

Eva-Maria Adolphi
Indian Hills Middle School
Sandy, UT

Connie Allison
MacArthur High School
Lawton, OK

Linda Brummett
Redmond High School
Redmond, WA

Beatrice Brusstar
Lincoln Northeast High School
Lincoln, NE

Jane Bungartz
Southwest High School
Forth Worth, TX

Devora D. Diller
Lovejoy High School
Lovejoy, GA

Margaret S. Draheim
Wilson Middle School
Appleton, WI

Kay DuBois
Kennewick High School
Kennewick, WA

Petra A. Hansen
Redmond High School
Redmond, WA

Christa Hary
Brien McMahon High School
Norwalk, CT

Ingrid S. Kinner
Weaver Education Center
Greensboro, NC

Diane E. Laumer
San Marcos High School
San Marcos, TX

J. Lewinsohn
Redmond High School
Redmond, WA

Judith A. Lidicker
Central High School
West Allis, WI

Linnea Maulding
Fife High School
Tacoma, WA

Jane Reinkordt
Lincoln Southeast High School
Lincoln, NE

Elizabeth A. Smith
Plano Senior High School
Plano, TX

Elizabeth L. Webb
Sandy Creek High School
Tyrone, GA

TO THE STUDENT

Some people have the opportunity to learn a new language by living in another country. Most of us, however, begin learning another language and getting acquainted with a foreign culture in a classroom with the help of a teacher, classmates, and a textbook. To use your book effectively, you need to know how it works.

Komm mit! (*Come along*) is organized to help you learn German and become familiar with the culture of the people who speak German. The book consists of four Location Openers and twelve chapters.

Location Opener Four four-page photo essays called Location Openers introduce different states or cities in Germany.

Chapter Opener The Chapter Opener pages tell you the chapter theme and goals.

Los geht's! (*Getting started*) This illustrated story, which is also on video, shows you German-speaking people in real-life situations, using the language you'll learn in the chapter.

Erste, Zweite, and Dritte Stufe (*First, Second, and Third Step*) After **Los geht's!**, the chapter is divided into three sections called **Stufen**. Within the **Stufe** are **So sagt man das!** (*Here's how you say it*) boxes that contain the German expressions you'll need to communicate, and **Wortschatz** and **Grammatik / Ein wenig Grammatik** boxes that give you the German words and grammar structures you'll need to know. Activities in each **Stufe** enable you to develop your skills in listening, speaking, reading, and writing.

Landeskunde (*Culture*) On this page are interviews with German-speaking people. You can watch these interviews on video or listen to them on the *Interactive CD-ROM Tutor*, then check to see how well you understood by answering some questions about what the people say.

Ein wenig Landeskunde (*Culture Note*) In each chapter, there are notes with more information about the culture in German-speaking countries.

Zum Lesen (*For reading*) The reading selections in each chapter are related to the chapter themes and will help you develop your reading skills in German.

Mehr Grammatikübungen (*Additional grammar practice*) This section begins the chapter review. You will find four pages of activities that provide additional practice for the grammar concepts you learned in the chapter.

Anwendung (*Review*) The activities on these pages practice what you've learned in the chapter and help you improve your listening, reading, and comprehension skills. You'll also review what you've learned about culture. A section called **Zum Schreiben** (*Let's Write*) in chapters 3–12 will develop your writing skills.

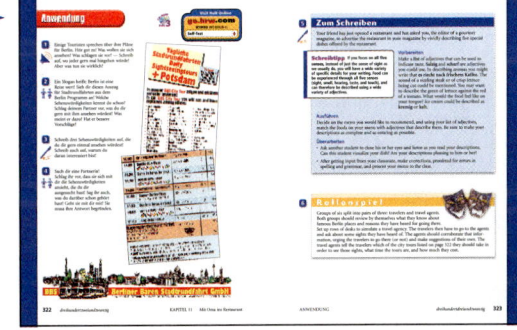

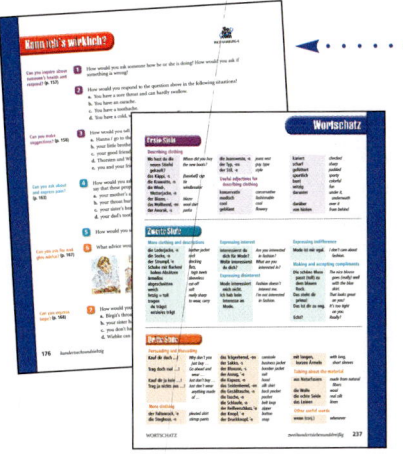

Kann ich's wirklich? (*Can I really do it? . . .*) This page at the end of each chapter contains a series of questions and short activities to help you see if you've achieved the chapter goals.

Wortschatz (*Vocabulary*) On the German-English vocabulary list on the last page of the chapter, the words are grouped by **Stufe**. These words and expressions will appear on quizzes and tests.

T55

You'll also find special features in each chapter that provide extra tips and reminders.

Sprachtipp (*Language tip*) gives you additional insight into the language to add more color to your speech.

Und dann noch . . . (*And then*) lists extra words you might find helpful. These words will not appear on quizzes and tests unless your teacher chooses to include them.

You'll also find German-English and English-German vocabulary lists at the end of the textbook. The words you'll need to know for the quizzes and tests are in boldface type.

At the end of your textbook, you'll find more helpful material, such as:
- a summary of the expressions you'll learn in the **So sagt man das!** boxes
- a summary of the grammar you'll study
- additional vocabulary words that you might want to use
- a grammar index to help you find where grammar is presented

Komm mit! Come along on an exciting trip to a new culture and a new language!

Gute Reise!

Explanation of Icons in *Komm mit!*

Throughout **Komm mit!** *you'll see these symbols, or icons, next to activities. They'll tell you what you'll probably do with that activity. Here's a key to help you understand the icons.*

 **Video** Whenever this icon appears, you'll know there is a related segment in the *Komm mit! Video Program*, and on the *DVD Tutor*.

 Listening Activities This icon indicates a listening activity.

  Pair Work/Group Work Activities

 Writing Activities

 CD-ROM Activities Whenever this icon appears, you'll know there is a related activity on the *Komm mit! Interactive CD-ROM Tutor*.

 DVD Tutor Whenever this icon appears, you'll know there is a related Grammar Presentation on the *Komm mit! DVD Tutor*.

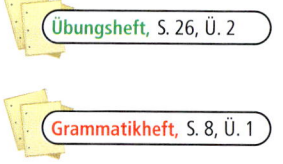 **Practice Activities** These icons tell you which activities from the *Übungsheft* and the *Grammatikheft* practice the material presented.

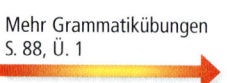 **Mehr Grammatikübungen** This reference tells you where you can find related additional grammar practice in the review section of the chapter.

 **Internet Activities** This icon provides the keyword you'll need to access related online activities at **go.hrw.com**.

Komm mit!

Contents

*Come along—
to a world of new experiences!*

Komm mit! *offers you the opportunity to learn the language spoken by millions of people in several European countries and around the world. Let's find out about these people and their culture.*

KOMM MIT NACH
Bayern!

LOCATION FOR KAPITEL 1, 2, 3 1
LOCATION OPENER T78–T79

KAPITEL 1

CHAPTER OVERVIEW 3A	TECHNOLOGY 3E–3F
CHAPTER RESOURCES 3B	LISTENING SCRIPTS 3G–3H
PROJECTS & GAMES 3C	50 MINUTE LESSON PLAN 3I–3J
STORYTELLING & TRADITIONS 3D	90 MINUTE LESSON PLAN 3K–3L

TEACHING SUGGESTIONS 3M–3X

WIEDERHOLUNGSKAPITEL
Bei den Baumanns 4

Los geht's! 6

Erste Stufe 9

So sagt man das! (Review)
- Asking for and giving information about yourself and others
- Describing yourself and others
- Expressing likes and dislikes
- Identifying people and places

Wortschatz (review)
- Characteristics, hobbies, and sports

Grammatik (review)
- The verb **sein**
- The verb **haben**
- Regular and stem-changing verbs
- Possessive adjectives

Zweite Stufe 16

So sagt man das! (Review)
- Giving and responding to compliments
- Expressing wishes when buying things

Wortschatz
- Clothing accessories

Grammatik (Review)
- The **möchte**-forms

ZUM LESEN: COUSIN UND KUSINE VERSTÄNDIGEN SICH, ODER? 20
Reading personal correspondence
Reading Strategy: Using prereading strategies

LANDESKUNDE 22
Und was hast du am liebsten?

Dritte Stufe 23

So sagt man das! (Review)
- Making plans
- Ordering food and beverages
- Talking about how something tastes

Grammatik (Review)
- The verb **wollen**
- The **möchte**-forms

MEHR GRAMMATIKÜBUNGEN 26

KANN ICH'S WIRKLICH? 30

WORTSCHATZ 31

KAPITEL 2

CHAPTER OVERVIEW	...31A	TECHNOLOGY	...31E–31F
CHAPTER RESOURCES	...31B	LISTENING SCRIPTS	...31G–31H
PROJECTS & GAMES	...31C	50 MINUTE LESSON PLAN	...31I–31J
STORYTELLING & TRADITIONS	...31D	90 MINUTE LESSON PLAN	...31K–31L

TEACHING SUGGESTIONS 31M–31X

WIEDERHOLUNGSKAPITEL

Bastis Plan.....32

LOS GEHT'S! 34

Erste Stufe 37

So sagt man das! (Review)
- Expressing obligations
- Extending and responding to an invitation
- Offering help and telling what to do

Wortschatz
- Things to do around the house

Grammatik (Review)
- The verb **müssen**
- The interrogative **warum?**
- The conjunctions **weil** and **denn**

ZUM LESEN:
MACHT SCHULE SPASS? 42
Reading about what students think of school

Reading Strategy: Using context to derive meaning

Zweite Stufe 44

So sagt man das! (Review)
- Asking and telling what to do
- Telling that you need something else
- Telling where you were and what you bought

Wortschatz
- Fruits and vegetables

Grammatik (Review)
- The verb **sollen**
- The past tense of **sein**

LANDESKUNDE 48
Was nimmst du mit, wenn du irgendwo eingeladen bist?

Dritte Stufe 49

So sagt man das! (Review)
- Discussing gift ideas
- Expressing likes and dislikes
- Expressing likes, preferences, and favorites
- Saying you do or don't want more

Wortschatz
- Gift ideas

Grammatik (Review)
- Dative forms of **mein, dein**
- The verb **mögen**
- Using **noch ein** and **kein**

MEHR GRAMMATIKÜBUNGEN 54

KANN ICH'S WIRKLICH? 58

WORTSCHATZ 59

T59

KAPITEL 3

CHAPTER OVERVIEW 59A	TECHNOLOGY 59E–59F
CHAPTER RESOURCES 59B	LISTENING SCRIPTS 59G–59H
PROJECTS & GAMES 59C	50 MINUTE LESSON PLAN 59I–59J
STORYTELLING & TRADITIONS 59D	90 MINUTE LESSON PLAN 59K–59L

TEACHING SUGGESTIONS 59M–59X

Wo warst du in den Ferien? 60

LOS GEHT'S! 62

Erste Stufe 65

So sagt man das!
- Reporting past events
- Talking about activities

Wortschatz
- Film media

Grammatik
- The conversational past

Zweite Stufe 70

So sagt man das!
- Reporting past events
- Talking about places

Wortschatz
- Sights in Frankfurt a.M.
- Expressions of frequency

Grammatik
- The past tense of **haben** and **sein**
- The dative case with the prepositions **in** and **an**

LANDESKUNDE 75
Was hast du in den letzten Ferien gemacht?

Dritte Stufe 76

So sagt man das!
- Asking how someone liked something
- Expressing enthusiasm or disappointment
- Responding enthusiastically or sympathetically

Wortschatz
- Places to eat and spend the night

Grammatik
- Personal pronouns, dative case (summary)
- Definite article, dative plural

ZUM LESEN: IN TIROL 80
Analyzing different types of texts about events in Tirol

Reading strategy: Identifying the main idea and supporting details

MEHR GRAMMATIKÜBUNGEN 82

ANWENDUNG 86
Zum Schreiben: Finding good details
Spending a month in your ideal vacation spot

KANN ICH'S WIRKLICH? 88

WORTSCHATZ 89

KOMM MIT NACH Hamburg!

LOCATION • KAPITEL 4, 5, 6 90
LOCATION OPENER 89A–89B

KAPITEL 4

CHAPTER OVERVIEW 93A	TECHNOLOGY 93E–93F
CHAPTER RESOURCES 93B	LISTENING SCRIPTS 93G–93H
PROJECTS & GAMES 93C	50 MINUTE LESSON PLAN 93I–93J
STORYTELLING & TRADITIONS 93D	90 MINUTE LESSON PLAN 93K–93L

TEACHING SUGGESTIONS 15M–15X

Gesund leben 94

LOS GEHT'S! 96

Erste Stufe 99
So sagt man das!
• Expressing approval and disapproval

Wortschatz
• Health tips
• Feeling healthy
• How you feel at certain locations

Grammatik
• The stem-changing verb **schlafen**
• Review of the preposition **für**
• Review of word order in **dass**-clauses
• Reflexive verbs

LANDESKUNDE 104
Was tust du, um gesund zu leben?

Zweite Stufe 105
So sagt man das!
• Asking for information and responding emphatically or agreeing, with reservations

Wortschatz
• Expressions of frequency

Grammatik
• The determiner **jeder**

Dritte Stufe 109
So sagt man das!
• Asking and telling what you may or may not do

Wortschatz
• Fruits, vegetables, fish, meat
• Reasons not to eat certain foods

Grammatik
• The verb **dürfen**, present tense

ZUM LESEN:
BLEIBT FIT UND GESUND! 112
Reading health tips and other articles related to health

Reading strategy: Activating your background knowledge

MEHR GRAMMATIKÜBUNGEN 114

ANWENDUNG 118
Zum Schreiben: Doing Research
Writing a health column for a newspaper

KANN ICH'S WIRKLICH? 120

WORTSCHATZ 121

T61

Kapitel 5

Chapter Overview 121A	Technology 121E–121F
Chapter Resources 121B	Listening Scripts 121G–121H
Projects & Games 121C	50 Minute Lesson Plan 121I–121J
Storytelling & Traditions 121D	90 Minute Lesson Plan 121K–121L

Teaching Suggestions 121M–121X

Gesund essen.....122

Los geht's! 124

Landeskunde 127
Was isst du, was nicht?

Erste Stufe 128

So sagt man das!
- Expressing regrets and downplaying
- Expressing skepticism and making certain

Wortschatz
- **Pause** snacks and prices

Grammatik
- The demonstrative **dieser**

Zum Lesen:
Wo ruht ihr euch aus? 132
Reading student essays on their favorite places
Reading strategy: Understanding the tone of a text

Zweite Stufe 134

So sagt man das!
- Calling someone's attention to something and responding

Wortschatz
- Things to put on bread

Grammatik
- The possessives (summary)

Dritte Stufe 138

So sagt man das!
- Expressing preference and strong preference

Wortschatz
- Groceries

Grammatik
- The interrogative **welcher**
- The preposition **zu**

Mehr Grammatikübungen 142

Anwendung 146
Zum Schreiben: Sequencing
Writing a newspaper story

Kann ich's wirklich? 148

Wortschatz 149

Kapitel 6

Chapter Overview 149A	Technology 149E–149F
Chapter Resources 149B	Listening Scripts 149G–149H
Projects & Games 149C	50 Minute Lesson Plan 149I–149J
Storytelling & Traditions 149D	90 Minute Lesson Plan 149K–149L

Teaching Suggestions 149M–149X

Gute Besserung! 150

Los geht's! 152

Landeskunde 155
Was machst du, wenn dir nicht gut ist?

Erste Stufe 156

So sagt man das!
- Inquiring about someone's health and responding
- Making suggestions

Wortschatz
- Aches, pains, and symptoms

Grammatik
- The inclusive command

Zum Lesen:
Viel los unter der Sonne! 160
Analyzing survey results and reading ads for popular **Kurorte**

Reading Strategy: Deciphering charts and graphs

Zweite Stufe 162

So sagt man das!
- Asking about and expressing pain

Wortschatz
- Body parts, pain, and injuries
- Reflexive and non-reflexive verb expressions

Grammatik
- Verbs used with dative case forms
- Reflexive verbs used with dative forms

Dritte Stufe 166

So sagt man das!
- Asking for and giving advice
- Expressing hope

Wortschatz
- Healthy habits
- Body temperature
- Toiletries

Mehr Grammatikübungen 170

Anwendung 174
Zum Schreiben: Peer evaluation
Writing a realistic dialogue

Kann ich's wirklich? 176

Wortschatz 177

KOMM MIT NACH Stuttgart!

LOCATION • KAPITEL 7, 8, 9 178
LOCATION OPENER 177A–177B

KAPITEL 7

CHAPTER OVERVIEW 181A
CHAPTER RESOURCES 181B
PROJECTS & GAMES 181C
STORYTELLING & TRADITIONS 181D
TECHNOLOGY 181E–181F
LISTENING SCRIPTS 181G–181H
50 MINUTE LESSON PLAN 181I–181J
90 MINUTE LESSON PLAN 181K–181L
TEACHING SUGGESTIONS 181M–181X

Stadt oder Land? 182

LOS GEHT'S! 184

Erste Stufe 187
So sagt man das!
• Expressing preference and giving a reason

Wortschatz
• Places to live
• Advantages and disadvantages of city and country life

Grammatik
• Comparative forms of adjectives

LANDESKUNDE 191
Wo wohnst du lieber? Auf dem Land? In der Stadt?

Zweite Stufe 192
So sagt man das!
• Expressing wishes

Wortschatz
• Wishes for my dream house and the future

Grammatik
• Adjective endings following **ein**-words

ZUM LESEN: UND DEIN TRAUMHAUS? 196
Analyzing a questionnaire and reading a poem about a dream house

Reading strategy: Using grammatical and lexical clues to derive meaning

Dritte Stufe 198
So sagt man das!
• Agreeing, with reservations
• Justifying your answers

Wortschatz
• Sources of noise pollution

Grammatik
• Adjective endings of comparatives

MEHR GRAMMATIKÜBUNGEN 202

ANWENDUNG 206
Zum Schreiben: Comparing and contrasting
Writing a composition

KANN ICH'S WIRKLICH? 208

WORTSCHATZ 209

Kapitel 8

Chapter Overview 209A	Technology 209E–209F
Chapter Resources 209B	Listening Scripts 209G–209H
Projects & Games 209C	50 Minute Lesson Plan 209I–209J
Storytelling & Traditions 209D	90 Minute Lesson Plan 209K–209L

Teaching Suggestions 209M–209X

Mode? Ja oder nein? 210

Los geht's! 212

Landeskunde 215
   Was trägst du am liebsten?

Erste Stufe 216
So sagt man das!
• Describing clothes

Wortschatz
• Fashion

Grammatik
• Adjectives following **der-** and **dieser-**words

Zweite Stufe 220
So sagt man das!
• Expressing interest, disinterest, and indifference
• Making and accepting compliments

Wortschatz
• Clothing and words to describe clothing

Grammatik
• Further uses of the dative case

Dritte Stufe 224
So sagt man das!
• Persuading and dissuading

Wortschatz
• Clothing and fabrics

Grammatik
• The conjunction **wenn**

Zum Lesen: Was bedeutet "reich und schön sein" 228
   Reading about a model's day-to-day life; reading students' ideas of what it means to be "rich"

   Reading strategy: Understanding relationships between and within sentences

Mehr Grammatikübungen 230

Anwendung 234
   Zum Schreiben: Tone and word choice
   Writing an interview dialogue

Kann ich's wirklich? 236

Wortschatz 237

Kapitel 9

Chapter Overview 237A	Technology 237E–237F
Chapter Resources 237B	Listening Scripts 237G–237H
Projects & Games 237C	50 Minute Lesson Plan 237I–237J
Storytelling & Traditions 237D	90 Minute Lesson Plan ...237K–237L

Teaching Suggestions 237M–237X

Wohin in die Ferien? 238

Los geht's! 240

Landeskunde 243
Wohin fährst du in den nächsten Ferien?

Erste Stufe 244

So sagt man das!
- Expressing indecision, asking for and making suggestions

Wortschatz
- Transportation and vacation activities

Grammatik
- Expressing directions: the prepositions **nach, an, in,** and **auf**

Zweite Stufe 248

So sagt man das!
- Expressing doubt, conviction, and resignation

Wortschatz
- Vacation activities

Grammatik
- Expressing direction and location

Dritte Stufe 252

So sagt man das!
- Asking for and giving directions

Wortschatz
- Expressions for giving directions in a city

Grammatik
- Prepositions followed by dative case forms
- The prepositions **durch** and **um**
- The prepositions **vor, neben, zwischen**

Zum Lesen: Was ist dein Lieblingsreiseziel? 256
Reading survey results about favorite vacations

Reading strategy: Distinguishing between fact and opinion

Mehr Grammatikübungen 258

Anwendung 262
Zum Schreiben: Organizing around a main idea

Writing an informative newspaper article

Kann ich's wirklich? 264

Wortschatz 265

T66

KOMM MIT NACH Berlin!

LOCATION FOR KAPITEL 10, 11, 12 266
LOCATION OPENER 265A–265B

KAPITEL 10

CHAPTER OVERVIEW 269A	TECHNOLOGY 269E–269F
CHAPTER RESOURCES 269B	LISTENING SCRIPTS 269G–269H
PROJECTS & GAMES 269C	50 MINUTE LESSON PLAN 269I–269J
STORYTELLING & TRADITIONS 269D	90 MINUTE LESSON PLAN ... 269K–269L

TEACHING SUGGESTIONS 269M–269X

Viele Interessen! 270

LOS GEHT'S! 272

Erste Stufe 275

So sagt man das!
- Asking about and expressing interest

Wortschatz
- TV programs

Grammatik
- Verbs with prepositions; **wo-** and **da-**compounds

LANDESKUNDE 279
Was machst du, um zu relaxen?

ZUM LESEN:
WAS LÄUFT IM FERNSEHEN? 280
Analyzing TV program excerpts and highlights

Reading Strategy: Predicting the content of a text

Zweite Stufe 282

So sagt man das!
- Asking for and giving permission
- Asking for information and expressing an assumption

Wortschatz
- TV equipment
- Days of the week

Dritte Stufe 286

So sagt man das!
- Expressing surprise, agreement, and disagreement
- Talking about plans

Wortschatz
- Standard and optional car equipment

Grammatik
- Review of **kein**
- The future tense with **werden**

MEHR GRAMMATIKÜBUNGEN 290

ANWENDUNG 294
Zum Schreiben: Backing up opinions with facts
Writing a persuasive letter

KANN ICH'S WIRKLICH? 296

WORTSCHATZ 297

KAPITEL 11

CHAPTER OVERVIEW 297A	TECHNOLOGY 297E–297F
CHAPTER RESOURCES 297B	LISTENING SCRIPTS 297G–297H
PROJECTS & GAMES 297C	50 MINUTE LESSON PLAN 297I–297J
STORYTELLING & TRADITIONS 297D	90 MINUTE LESSON PLAN ...297K–297L

TEACHING SUGGESTIONS 297M–297X

Mit Oma ins Restaurant 298

LOS GEHT'S! 300

LANDESKUNDE 303
Für welche kulturellen Veranstaltungen interessierst du dich?

Erste Stufe 304
So sagt man das!
• Asking for, making, and responding to suggestions

Wortschatz
• Attractions in Berlin

Grammatik
• The **würde**-forms

Zweite Stufe 308
So sagt man das!
• Expressing hearsay

Wortschatz
• Cuisine of Germany and other countries
• Words to describe food

Grammatik
• Unpreceded adjectives

Dritte Stufe 312
So sagt man das!
• Ordering in a restaurant
• Expressing good wishes

Wortschatz
• Things to order in a restaurant

Grammatik
• The **hätte**-forms

ZUM LESEN: DAS LEBEN IM FREMDEN LAND 316
Reading ethnic literature
Reading Strategy: Reading for comprehension

MEHR GRAMMATIKÜBUNGEN 318

ANWENDUNG 322
Zum Schreiben: Using all five senses
Writing an advertisement for a restaurant

KANN ICH'S WIRKLICH? 324

WORTSCHATZ 325

KAPITEL 12
WIEDERHOLUNGSKAPITEL

CHAPTER OVERVIEW 325A	TECHNOLOGY 325E–325F
CHAPTER RESOURCES 325B	LISTENING SCRIPTS 325G–325H
PROJECTS & GAMES 325C	50 MINUTE LESSON PLAN 325I–325J
STORYTELLING & TRADITIONS 325D	90 MINUTE LESSON PLAN ...325K–325L

TEACHING SUGGESTIONS 325M–325X

Die Reinickendorfer Clique 326

LOS GEHT'S! 328

LANDESKUNDE 331
Welche ausländische Küche hast du gern?

Erste Stufe 332
So sagt man das! (review)
- Reporting past events
- Asking for, making, and responding to suggestions

Wortschatz
- Places near water, sports terms, sports venues

Grammatik (review)
- The present perfect
- Two-way prepositions
- **Sollen;** the **würde**-forms

Zweite Stufe 337
So sagt man das! (review)
- Ordering food, expressing hearsay and regret
- Persuading and dissuading

Wortschatz
- International cuisine

Grammatik (review)
- Command forms

Dritte Stufe 341
So sagt man das! (review)
- Asking for and giving advice
- Expressing preference
- Expressing interest, disinterest, and indifference

Wortschatz
- Casual and formal clothing

Grammatik (review)
- Adjective endings
- Comparisons

ZUM LESEN: NACH DEM KRIEG 346
Reading modern German literature
Reading Strategy: Note-taking

MEHR GRAMMATIKÜBUNGEN 348

KANN ICH'S WIRKLICH? 352

WORTSCHATZ 353

REFERENCE SECTION
SUMMARY OF FUNCTIONS R2
ADDITIONAL VOCABULARY R12
GRAMMAR SUMMARY R20
VOCABULARY: GERMAN — ENGLISH R38
VOCABULARY: ENGLISH — GERMAN R64
GRAMMAR INDEX R78
ACKNOWLEDGMENTS AND CREDITS R83

Cultural References

Page numbers referring to material in the Pupil's Edition appear in regular type. When the material referenced is located in the Teacher's Edition, page numbers appear in boldface type.

ADVERTISEMENTS
Realia: Clothing and school supplies 19
Realia: **Geschenke für jede Gelegenheit** 49
Realia: **Kaufmanns** 138
Realia: **Supermarkt Bausinger** 44

ARCHITECTURE
Bürgerhaus **237M**
Fachwerk. **59R**
German Renaissance. **89B**
Giebelhäuser **59R**
Lüftlmalerei **T79**
Posthalterei **237U**
Zwiebeltürme. **T79**

CASTLES
Neues Schloss, Stuttgart 181, **177B**, **181M**
Schloss Charlottenburg, Berlin. **265A**
Schloss Kranzbach, Bavaria 1, **T78**
Schloss Linderhof, Bavaria. 2

CHURCHES AND TEMPLES
Dom, Frankfurt 63, 70, 71, **59R**
Kaiser-Wilhelm-Gedächtniskirche,
   Berlin. 268, **265B**
Marienkirche, Dresden. 69
Paulskirche, Frankfurt 70
Stiftskirche, Stuttgart. **177A**
St. Michaelis Kirche, Hamburg. **89A**
St. Peter und Paul, Mittenwald 3, **T79**
Synagoge, Berlin 305, **297P**

CLOTHING
see also Advertisements
Fashion. 219
Interview: **Hast du Interesse
   an Mode?**. 220
Realia: **Ich bin kein Wunderkind!** 341
Realia: **Popstars machen Mode** 16
Realia: **Tina—Das Mädchen aus dem Katalog** . . 229
Interview: **Und was hast du am
   liebsten?** 22
Realia: **Was ist heute „in"?** 216
Interview: **Was trägst du am
   liebsten?**. 215

COATS OF ARMS
Bavaria. **T78**
Berlin. 267, **265A**
Hamburg. 91, **89A**
Stuttgart. 179, **177A**

ECONOMY
Automobilindustrie **177B**
Elektrotechnik **177B**
Hamburger Hafen **89B**
Verlage **89A**, **177B**

ENTERTAINMENT
*see also Advertisements, Music and Theater, Sports and
   Activities and Television*
Interview: **Für welche kulturellen
Veranstaltungen interessierst du
   dich?** 303

Public support of the arts 307

ENVIRONMENT
Realia: **Der Lärm wird größer** 199

FOOD
see also Advertisements and Restaurants

Äbbewoi **59R**
Realia: **Andreas Elsholz präsentiert sein bestes Spaghettirezept** 337
Apfelwein **59R**
Berliner Pfannkuchen 266, **265B**
Bratkartoffeln **297U**
Brötchen **121M**
Buletten 266, **265B**
Eisbein 266, **265B**
Flädlesuppe 178, **177B**
Gekochte Eier **121M**
Grüner Aal 266
Hamburger Aalsuppe 90, **89A**
Realia: **Her mit dem Salat!** 113
Käsekuchen **121N**
Kalbshaxe **T79, T80**
Karpfen **T80**
Kartoffelkroketten 313
Klöße 313
Knödel **T80**
Leberkäs **T80**
Matjeshering 90
Maultaschen 178
Meals and mealtimes 135, 140
Nutella® **121M**
Radi **T79, T80**
Scholle 90
Schweinerückensteak 313
Schweinshaxe **T80**
Spätzle 178
Spezi 313
Interview: **Und was hast du am liebsten?** 22
Interview: **Was isst du, was nicht?** 127
Interview: **Welche ausländische Küche hast du gern?** 331
Realia: **Wenn Kinder feiern** 146
Zwetschgenkuchen **T80**

Zwiebelkuchen **59R**

GEOGRAPHY
Population density 191

HEALTH
Realia: **Bleich ist beautiful** 161
Emergency numbers **149M**
German health care system 155
Realia: **Gesundheitstips** 99
Realia: **50 Euro für Nichtraucher** 113
Apotheke 159
Kuren **149S**
Realia: **Kuren und Bäder** 160
Realia: Medical form 118
Realia: **Schmerzen** 174
Realia: **Sechs Tips, die für Sie so wichtig sind wie für Boris** 112
Realia: **Vorsicht vor Sonnenstrahlen!** 166
Interview: **Was machst du, wenn dir nicht gut ist?** 155
Interview: **Was tust du, um gesund zu leben?** 104

HISTORY
Deutsche Nationalversammlung 70
Dresden 62, 69
Francono Furd **59R**
Frankfurt 63, 70, **59R**
Hammaburg **89A**
Hanseatic League **89A, 89B**
Nuremberg Trials **T78**
Railroad **T78**
Stuotgarte **177A**
World War II **89A, 89B, 177A, 265A, 181M**

HOME AND FAMILY LIFE
Realia: **Hier habe ich meine Ruhe** 132
Housing **181M**
Schrebergarten **181M**
Realia: **Sebastian über seine Familie** 14
Realia: **Stadt** vs. **Land** 187
Realia: **Mein Traumhaus** 196
Realia: **Wochenplan** 34
Realia: **Wo ruht ihr euch aus?** 132
Interview: **Wo wohnst du lieber?** 191

T71

MAPS

Bavaria **T80**
Berlin 267
Bietigheim 252
Federal Republic of Germany **T76**
Hamburg 90
Liechtenstein, Switzerland, and
   Austria **T77**
Stuttgart 178

MONEY

Realia: "**Reich ist, wer nix mehr lernen
   muß**" 228

MUSEUMS

Grünes Gewölbe, Dresden 69
Neue Staatsgalerie, Stuttgart **177B**
Pergamonmuseum, Berlin **265A, 297O**
Staatsgalerie, Stuttgart 180, **177A**
Zwinger, Dresden 69

MUSIC

Berlin Philharmonie **297P**
Berliner Dom 304
Berliner Oper **297P**
Berliner Symphoniker 304
Realia: Concert schedule 304
Realia: Opera and Theater schedule 304
Semperoper, Dresden 62
Stuttgarter Liederhalle 180

PEOPLE

August der Starke 62, 69
Wolfgang Borchert **325W**
Robert Bosch **177B**
Bertolt Brecht **T79**
Marlene Dietrich **265A**
Johann Wolfgang von Goethe 70, **59P**
Karl der Große 70, **89B**
Wilhelm Hauff **177B**
G.W. Hegel **177B**
Jürgen Hingsen **325P**
Alexander von Humboldt **265A**
Wilhelm von Humboldt **265A**
Matthias Klotz **T79**
Guido Kratschmer **325P**
Ludwig der Bayer **T79**
Ludwig der Fromme **89A**
Ulrike Meyfarth **325P**
Felix Mendelssohn-Bartholdy **89A**
Wilhelm Münker **59U**
Carl von Ossietzky **89A**
Richard Schirrmann **59U**
Werner von Siemens **265B**
Richard Strauss **T79**

POINTS OF INTEREST

*see also Castles, Churches, Museums, Parks, Statues,
  and Theaters*

Alte Kanzlei, Stuttgart **177B**
Bad Wurzach **149R**
Baden-Baden **149R**
Berlin **297O, 297R**
Berlin Wall, Berlin 268, **265B**
Bietigheim, Baden-Württemberg 252
Binnenalster, Hamburg 90, **89B**
Black Forest **149R**
Blankenese, Hamburg 92, **89B**
Bopser, Stuttgart **177A**
Brandenburger Tor, Berlin 268, **265B**
Café Kranzler, Berlin **265B**
Dresden 62, 69
Fernsehturm, Stuttgart **177A**
Frankfurt am Main 63, 70, **59R**
Frankfurt an der Oder **59R**
Friedenstor, Berlin **265B**
Gaggenau-Bad Rotenfels **149R**
Goethehaus, Frankfurt 63, **59R**
Hamburger Rathaus, Hamburg 92, **89B**
Innsbruck **59M**
Jubiläumssäule **181M**
Jungfernstieg **89A**
Karwendel Mountains **T78**
Kennedy-Brücke **89A**
Kloster Ettal, Bavaria 2
Lombardsbrücke **89A**
Lüneburger Heide **237W**
**Mahnmal für die Opfer der
   Berliner Mauer** **265B**
Main **59R**
Museumsinsel, Berlin **297O**

Neptunbrunnen	T79
Nordtiroler Kalkalpen	T78
Nürnberg	T78
Övelgönne, Hamburg	92, **89B**
Platz der Republik, Berlin	**265A**
Reichstagsgebäude, Berlin	**265A**
Rhein-Main-Donau-Kanal	T78, **59R**
Rhein-Main-Flughafen, Frankfurt	70
Rickmer Rickmers, Hamburg	93, **89B**
Römerberg, Frankfurt	63, **59R**
Schillerplatz, Stuttgart	181
Schwangau	**149R**
Speicherstadt, Hamburg	93, **89B**
Staatstheater, Stuttgart	**177B**
Starnberger See	T78
St. Ulrich, Austria	63
Stuttgart	**177A**
Tirol, Austria	**59M**
Todtmoos	**149R**
Wallfahrtskirche	**149R**
Weißenhofsiedlung, Stuttgart	**177A**
Zugspitze, Bavaria	T78

PROVERBS

Die Glücklichen sind reich, die Reichen nicht immer glücklich	**209V**
Geld regiert die Welt	**209V**
Geld verdirbt den Charakter	**209V**

RECIPES

Beefsteak mit Zwiebeln	**149D**
Berliner Buletten	**269D**
Bollenfleisch	**325D**
Eisbein mit Sauerkraut	**297D**
Flädlesuppe	**181D**
Guglhupf	**59D**
Hennenknödel-Suppe	**31D**
Kartoffelsalat	**209D**
Krautsalat	**3D**
Matjes mit Specksauce	**121D**
Rote Grütze	**93D**
Spargel	**237D**

RESTAURANTS

Realia: **Berliner und ausländische Küche**	308
Foreign cuisine	309, 310
Imbissstand	57
Realia: **Reservation card**	313
Social customs	339
Realia: **Speisekarte Hotel Dannenberg**	312
Types of restaurants	331

SCHOOL LIFE

After-school activities	**269M**
Apprentice system	**181O**
Entschuldigung	**149O**
German school system	**31R**
Klassenbuch	**149O**
Pausenbrot	124, 128
Realia: **Das Pausenklingeln ist die schönste Musik!**	42
Photo club	62
Realia: **Schule im Garten**	206
Schulhofaufsicht	**121M**
Vacation	243, **59M**

SHOPPING

Realia: **Bestellkarte**	234
Bioläden	108
Drogerie	159
Realia: **Einkaufszettel**	45
Realia: **Modekatalog Berger**	224
Stiftung Warentest	**209Q**

SHORT STORIES

Borchert, Wolfgang: *Das Brot*	346
Kip, Cengiz: *Seltsamer Deutscher, komischer Türke*	316

SOCIAL CUSTOMS

German-American Day	**297Q**
Giving and responding to compliments	18
Host/Hostess gifts	**31M**
Kaffeezeit	**121N**
Table manners	127
Interview: **Was nimmst du mit, wenn du irgendwo eingeladen bist?**	48

SPORTS AND ACTIVITIES

German Sports Federation	**93R**
Realia: **Tischkalender**	68

Trimmdichpfad **93M**
Interview: **Und was hast du am liebsten?** 22
Volksmarsch **93R**
Interview: **Was machst du, um zu relaxen?** 279

STATUES
August I., Dresden 69
Matthias-Klotz-Denkmal, Bavaria 2, **T79**
Friedrich von Schiller **177B**

STREETS
Königstraße, Stuttgart 180, **177B**
Ku'damm, Berlin 269, **265B**
Zeil, Frankfurt 63, **59Q**

TELEVISION
ARD **269R**
Realia: **Die erfolgreichsten Sendungen** 282
Realia: **Fernsehprogramm** 278, 280, 281
Realia: **Hitparade der jüngsten TV-Sender** 282
Public and private TV 278
RTL **269R**
Realia: **TV-Hits der Deutschen** 275
Realia: **Wer guckt was?** 275

TRADITIONS
Alsterschwäne **93D**
Altenrieter Brezelmark **209D**
Berliner Bär **325D**
Bürgeroper **149D**
Hamburger Fischmarkt **121D**
Hotel Adlon **269D**
Königsgemüse Spargel **237D**
Maibaum in Bayern **3D**
Märchenkönig **59D**

Münchner Oktoberfest **31D**
Rosinenbomber **297D**
Stadt des Automobils **181D**

TRANSPORTATION
Realia: **Autofahren kostet viel Geld** 286
Driver's license 288
Hamburger Hafenrundfahrt 92

VACATIONS
Realia: **Das Ausland steht an erster Stelle** 262
Realia: **Berliner Stadtrundfahrt** 322
Bezahlter Urlaub **237O**
Realia: **Die Deutschen machen gerne Urlaub** 247
Realia: **Die Deutschen—die Weltmeister im Reisen** 332
Realia: **Dorfplatzeinweihung** 80
Realia: **Fragebogen von St. Ulrich,** Austria 86
Realia: **Gesucht: Bauernhof zum Ausschlafen** 256
Hotels and restaurants 78
Jugendherbergen **59U**
Pension **237M**
Realia: **Pillerseehof,** Austria 81
Realia: Postcard 80
Realia: **Reisetips** 244
Realia: **Stadtrundgang durch Bietigheim** 252
Realia: Tour schedules 322
Interview: **Was has du in den letzten Ferien gemacht?** 75
Realia: **Weißt du schon, wo du die Ferien verbringst?** 248
Interview: **Wohin fährst du in den nächsten Ferien?** 243

Map of the Federal Republic of Germany

Map of Germany

Map of Liechtenstein, Switzerland, and Austria

 Map of Austria and Switzerland

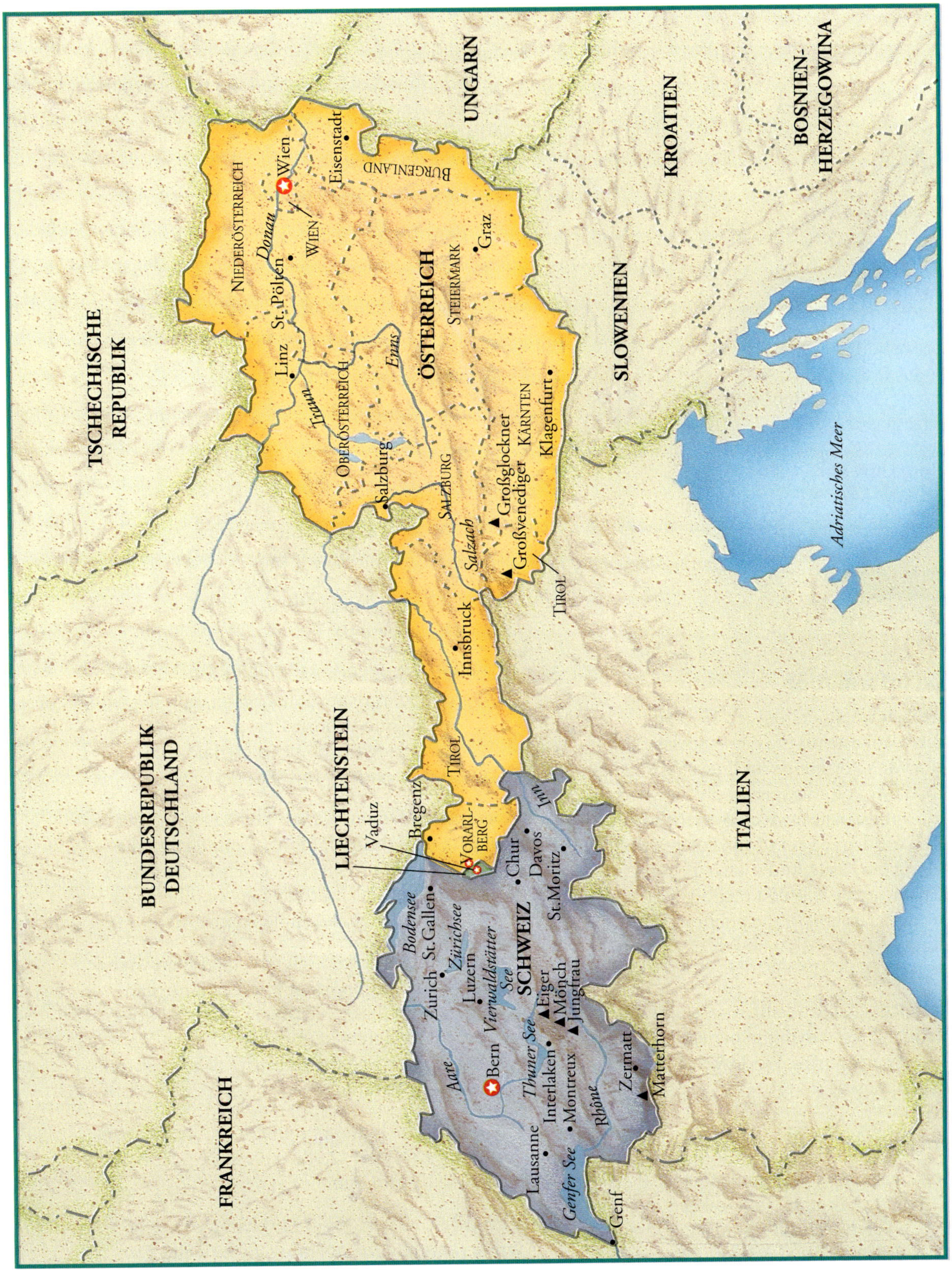

KAPITEL 1, 2, 3

Bayern

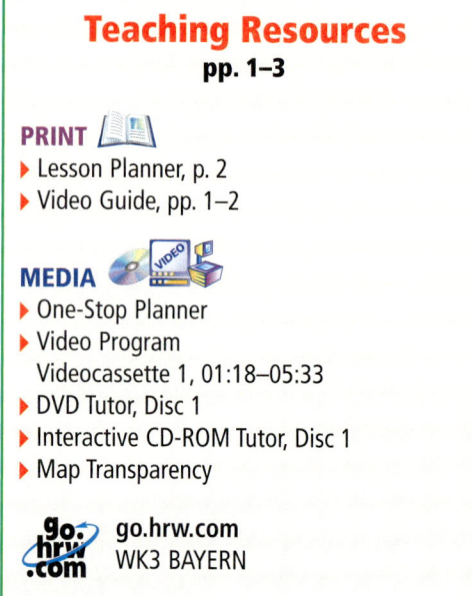

PAGE 1

THE PHOTOGRAPH
Background Information
Schloss Kranzbach was built between 1913 and 1915 near the Kranz brook (hence the name **Schloss Kranzbach**) for Miss Portmann, an Englishwoman. A hall with an orchestra pit was specifically designed for performances by musicians from all over the world. Unfortunately, World War I kept Miss Portmann from ever visiting her castle, and it stayed empty for 18 years. Today the estate is used for church retreats and is also open year-round to the public as a resort.

Thinking Critically
Drawing Inferences Ask students why World War I kept Miss Portmann from living in her estate. (The conflict with Germany during World War I put England on the opposing side.)

Teacher Notes
- You may want to point out to students that although Germany has many state-owned castles of historical and architectural significance, many more, such as **Schloss Kranzbach,** are privately owned. In order to maintain such enormous castles financially, many owners allow some or all of their estates to become museums or resorts.

- The Karwendel Mountains (9,040 ft/2,756 m) in the background of the photo are a national park. They are located between the Isar and Inn rivers and are part of a chain of mountains called the **Nordtiroler Kalkalpen.**

THE ALMANAC AND MAP

 The Bavarian coat of arms was originally the crest of the powerful Duke of Bogen on the Danube. The diagonal rows of blue and white diamonds symbolize the unity of the Free State of Bavaria and the colors of the sky over Bavaria—blue and white.

Terms in the Almanac
- **Nürnberg** (496,000 inhabitants): the second largest city of Bavaria (after Munich), dating back to the Middle Ages. **Nürnberg** is known for being the originating point of the first German railroad in 1835. Between 1945 and 1949 the city was the site of the Nuremberg trials.

- **Starnberger See:** Located south of Munich, this lake is a popular recreational destination for swimming, sailing, and windsurfing. A cross stands in the lake, marking the point where Ludwig II drowned mysteriously in 1886.

- **Rhein-Main-Donau-Kanal:** Also called the **Europa-Kanal,** it runs through Bavaria, connecting the Danube with the Main. This extensive system of waterways is an inland route between the Black Sea and North Sea. It was completed in 1993.

- **Synthesizing** Ask students why the **Rhein-Main-Donau-Kanal** is important to other European countries as well as to Germany. (This waterway facilitates the increased transport of goods between western Europe and the countries of central and southeastern Europe.)

- **Zugspitze:** The highest mountain in the German Alps, it is 9,719 feet (2,962 meters) high. It is easily accessible by cable car.

- **Richard Strauss** (1864–1949): composer who wrote such famous operas as *Elektra* and *Der Rosenkavalier.* He was born in Munich and died in Garmisch.

KAPITEL 1, 2, 3

- **Bertolt Brecht** (1898–1956): considered one of the most influential playwrights of the twentieth century. Brecht is known for his socially critical writings such as *Mutter Courage und ihre Kinder* and *Die Dreigroschenoper.*

- **Radi:** Bavarian term for **Rettich. Radi** is a white vegetable that resembles a long radish or a carrot and tastes like a radish. This vegetable was originally brought to central Europe by Roman soldiers.

- **Kalbshaxe:** This is a veal shank cooked in water, browned, and often served with tomatoes and dumplings.

Teaching Suggestion

Ask students if they know the name of Ludwig II's most famous castle. (**Neuschwanstein**)

Map Activities

- Have students use the map on p. T76 (student page xxiv) to identify the German states that border Bavaria. (**Hessen, Thüringen,** and **Sachsen** to the north; **Baden-Württemberg** to the west) You may also want to use *Map Transparency* 1.

- Have students identify the countries that share a border with Bavaria. (**Österreich** to the south, the **Tschechische Republik** to the east)

- Have students locate the Danube and the Main, and then trace the **Rhein-Main-Donau-Kanal.**

PAGES 2–3

THE PHOTO ESSAY

- **Group Work** Have students work in small groups to study the pictures. They should come up with features that they think might be unique to this area.

1 This memorial is located in front of the **Pfarrkirche St. Peter und Paul** and is a monument to the violin maker Matthias Klotz. After learning his trade under Stradivari in Italy, Klotz returned to his native Mittenwald to continue his work. To this day, this town is known for the outstanding craftsmanship of the violins produced there.

2 This castle was built for **König Ludwig II. von Bayern,** who chose the style of the French King Louis XIV's Versailles as a model. Behind the castle is a beautiful park with many monuments. In the front is the **Neptunbrunnen,** which has a fountain that is 105 feet (32 meters) high. The **Wasserspiele** in the park fountain can be seen every hour.

3 In 1330 Emperor **Ludwig der Bayer** founded this monastery. It was modeled after the Church of the Holy Sepulcher in Jerusalem. The dome was added between 1745 and 1752. The main entrance hall to the church is considered one of the masterpieces of the German rococo style.

4 **Zwiebeltürme,** onion shaped towers, are also called **Zwiebelhauben** (*onion shaped caps*). **Lüftlmalerei** is common in the southern parts of Germany where the facades of houses and churches are often painted with brightly colored scenes. **Lüftlmalerei** is also known as **Freskomalerei,** a term coming from the Italian *al fresco,* which means *on fresh,* because paint is applied to fresh plaster on walls before the plaster hardens.

5 Robert, Christiane, and Sebastian were born in Bavaria; their Bavarian accents attest to it. Thomas is from Poland.

6 The **Pfarrkirche St. Peter und Paul** in Mittenwald was built in the baroque style by Joseph Schmuzer between 1738 and 1740 and was dedicated in 1749. The ceiling painting, as well as the painting at the high altar, was done by Matthäus Günther (1705–1788), a well-known painter who decorated the interior of many churches in southern Germany. Günther was trained by the famous baroque artist Cosmas Damian Asam, and his work marks the transition from the baroque to the rococo style.

LOCATION OPENER

KAPITEL 1, 2, 3

Komm mit nach Bayern!

Einwohner: 12 Millionen

Fläche: 70 500 Quadratkilometer (27 200 Quadratmeilen; halb so groß wie Iowa)

Landeshauptstadt: München

Große Städte: Nürnberg, Regensburg, Augsburg, Würzburg, Fürth, Passau

Flüsse: Donau, Main, Iller, Lech, Isar, Inn

Seen: Bodensee, Ammersee, Starnberger See, Chiemsee

Kanäle: Rhein-Main-Donau-Kanal

Berge: Zugspitze (2962 m), Watzmann (2713 m)

Bedeutende Bayern:
Richard Strauss (1864-1949, Komponist),
Ludwig Thoma (1867-1921, Schriftsteller),
Bertolt Brecht (1898-1956, Schriftsteller),
Carl Orff (1895-1982, Komponist),
Luise Rinser (1911-, Schriftstellerin)

Industrie: Maschinenbau, Elektroindustrie, Automobilindustrie, Textilindustrie, Tourismus

Beliebte Gerichte: Schweinshaxe, Kalbshaxe, Knödel, Leberkäs, Radi

Map of Germany

WK3 BAYERN

STANDARDS: 2.2, 3.1

▶ Schloss Kranzbach bei Mittenwald. Im Hintergrund das Karwendelgebirge

Bayern

Bayern, das größte Land der Bundesrepublik Deutschland, ist das beliebteste Reiseziel Deutschlands. Jedes Jahr besuchen Millionen von Touristen die zahlreichen Attraktionen Bayerns, von den barocken Städten Frankens bis zu den malerischen Bergen und Schlössern Oberbayerns. Land- und Forstwirtschaft sind immer noch sehr wichtig in Bayern, doch spielen moderne Industrien eine zunehmend größere Rolle.

Visit Holt Online
go.hrw.com
KEYWORD: WK3 BAYERN
Internet Aktivitäten

1 Der Geigenbau in Mittenwald
Dieses Denkmal ist dem Begründer des Geigenbaus in Mittenwald gewidmet: Matthias Klotz (1653 - 1743).

2 Schloss Linderhof
Der Bayernkönig Ludwig II. ließ dieses Schloss 1870 bis 1878 im Stil des französischen Rokoko errichten.

3 Kloster Ettal
Die alte gotische Klosterkirche wurde in den Jahren 1710 bis 1753 im Barockstil restauriert. Die Fassade wurde vom Münchner Hofbaumeister Enrico Zuccalli geschaffen.

4 Ein bayrisches Dorf
Typisch für ein oberbayrisches Dorf sind die Kirche mit einem Zwiebelturm und Häuser mit Lüftlmalerei, wie dieses Gasthaus hier in Egling.

Kapitel 1, 2, 3

Die ersten zwei Kapitel spielen in Grünwald, einer Vorstadt von München, wo die Baumanns wohnen. Im dritten Kapitel erzählt Sebastian von seiner Reise nach Österreich, und zwei seiner Freunde berichten über Frankfurt und Dresden. Die Schüler in diesen Kapiteln gehen aufs Gymnasium in Grünwald.

6 Mittenwald
Die barocke Pfarrkirche St. Peter und Paul in Mittenwald, einem Ort am Fuße des Karwendelgebirges gelegen, wurde in den Jahren 1738 bis 1740 errichtet.

5 Robert, Thomas, Sebastian und Christiane

drei 3

Kapitel 1: Bei den Baumanns

Review Chapter

Chapter Overview

Los geht's! pp. 6–8	Sebastian stellt seine Familie vor, p. 6			
	FUNCTIONS	**GRAMMAR**	**VOCABULARY**	**RE-ENTRY**
Erste Stufe pp. 9–15	• Asking for and giving information about yourself and others; describing yourself and others; expressing likes and dislikes, p. 11 • Identifying people and places, p. 13	• The verbs **sein** and **haben**, p. 11 • Regular and stem-changing verbs, p. 12 • The singular possessive adjectives, p. 13	• Characteristics, hobbies, and sports, p. 10	• Chapter 1 is a global review of *Komm mit!* Level 1
Zweite Stufe pp. 16–19	• Giving and responding to compliments, p. 18 • Expressing wishes when buying things, p. 18	• The **möchte**-forms, p. 19 • The nominative and accusative forms of the definite and the indefinite articles, p. 19 • The third person pronouns, p. 19	• Accessories, p. 17	• Chapter 1 is a global review of *Komm mit!* Level 1
Dritte Stufe pp. 23–25	• Making plans, p. 23 • Ordering food and beverages, p. 25 • Talking about how something tastes, p. 25	• The verb **wollen**, p. 23 • The **möchte**-forms, p. 23		• Chapter 1 is a global review of *Komm mit!* Level 1

Zum Lesen pp. 20–21	Cousin und Kusine verständigen sich, oder? Reading Strategy: Using prereading strategies (looking for visual clues, reading the title and subtitles, looking for cognates and other familiar words while skimming)

Mehr Grammatikübungen	**pp. 26–29** Erste Stufe, pp. 26–28 Zweite Stufe, pp. 28–29 Dritte Stufe, p. 29

Review pp. 30–31	Kann ich's wirklich?, p. 30 Wortschatz, p. 31

CULTURE

- Questionnaire: **Was für eine Person bist du?** p. 9
- Article: **Sebastian über seine Familie,** p. 14
- Article: **Popstars machen Mode,** p. 16
- Department store ad, p. 19
- **Landeskunde: Und was hast du am liebsten?** p. 22
- Advertisements, p. 24

Kapitel 1: Bei den Baumanns
Chapter Resources

Review Chapter

Lesson Planning
One-Stop Planner
Lesson Planner with Substitute Teacher Lesson Plans, pp. 2–6, 65
Student Make-Up Assignments
- Make-Up Assignment Copying Masters, Chapter 1

Listening and Speaking
TPR Storytelling Book, pp. x–7
Listening Activities
- Student Response Forms for Listening Activities, pp. 3–6
- Additional Listening Activities 1-1 to 1-6, pp. 7–10
- Additional Listening Activities (songs), p. 6
- Scripts and Answers, pp. 100–105

Video Guide
- Teaching Suggestions, pp. 4–5
- Activity Masters, pp. 6–8
- Scripts and Answers, pp. 81–83, 111

Activities for Communication
- Communicative Activities, pp. 1–6
- Realia and Teaching Suggestions, pp. 74–77
- Situation Cards, pp. 123–124

Reading and Writing
Reading Strategies and Skills Handbook, Chapter 1
Lies mit mir! 2, Chapter 1
Übungsheft, pp. 1–12

Grammar
Grammatikheft, pp. 1–9
Grammar Tutor for Students of German, Chapter 1

Assessment
Testing Program
- Grammar and Vocabulary Quizzes, **Stufe** Quizzes, and Chapter Test, pp. 1–18
- Score Sheets, Scripts and Answers, pp. 19–26

Alternative Assessment Guide
- Portfolio Assessment, p. 18
- Performance Assessment, p. 32
- CD-ROM Assessment, p. 46

Student Make-Up Assignments
- Alternative Quizzes, Chapter 1

Online Activities
- Interaktive Spiele
- Internet Aktivitäten

Video Program
- Videocassette 1
- Videocassette 5 (captioned version)
- DVD Tutor, Disc 1

Audio Compact Discs
- Textbook Listening Activities, CD 1, Tracks 1–14
- Additional Listening Activities, CD 1, Tracks 21–28
- Assessment Items, CD 1, Tracks 15–20

Interactive CD-ROM Tutor, Disc 1

Teaching Transparencies
- Situations 1-1 to 1-2
- Vocabulary 1-A to 1-B
- Los geht's!
- Mehr Grammatikübungen Answers
- Grammatikheft Answers

One-Stop Planner CD-ROM

Use the **One-Stop Planner CD-ROM** with Test Generator to aid in lesson planning and pacing.

For each chapter, the **One-Stop Planner** includes:
- Editable lesson plans with direct links to teaching resources
- Printable worksheets from resource books
- Direct launches to the HRW Internet activities
- Video and audio segments
- Test Generator
- Clip Art for vocabulary items

Kapitel 1: Bei den Baumanns

Review Chapter

Projects

Mein Lebenslauf

Students will write an autobiographical sketch called **Mein Lebenslauf.** Begin this project after students have reviewed and practiced the vocabulary and functions in the **Erste Stufe** and have done Activity 19 (**Beatrices Steckbrief**) on p. 15. This project is a great way for students to learn about one another at the beginning of the new school year.

MATERIALS
✂ **Students may need**
- posterboard or a large sheet of paper
- glue
- photographs of themselves

SUGGESTED SEQUENCE

1. Begin by brainstorming with students as to what kind of information should be included in their **Lebenslauf.** (Examples: first, middle, and last name; date of birth; place of birth; names of parents; siblings; schools attended; address; hobbies) Remind students to use the vocabulary on pp. 9 and 10.
2. Ask students to make an outline of the facts to be included in their autobiographical sketch.
3. Have students write their **Lebenslauf** on posterboard or on a sheet of paper and attach a photograph of themselves.
4. Have students present their project and read their **Lebenslauf** to the classroom.
5. Display all **Lebensläufe** in your classroom.

GRADING THE PROJECT
Suggested point distribution (**total = 100 points**)
Written work..60
Originality, Neatness, Appearance........40

TEACHER NOTE

When giving assignments that entail the disclosure of personal information, keep in mind that some students and their families may consider family matters private. In some cases, you may want to give an alternate assignment in which students discuss a make-believe family.

Games

Das treffende Wort suchen

This game will help your students develop the skill of circumlocution.

Preparation Create a list of words in English related to the vocabulary presented in the chapter/**Stufe.** Write each vocabulary word from the list you created on an index card. Arrange four desks at the front of the room in such a way so that two partners from each team can face each other. Place the cards face down where they can easily be reached by the players from any of the desks. On the board or on a transparency, write the following key phrases:

Aussehen:

Es ist ein Ding / eine Person . . . Das Ding ist aus Metall / Glas / Papier. Es ist . . . klein / groß / alt / neu. Es hat . . . Es sieht aus wie . . .

Funktion:

Man benutzt das Ding für . . . Das Gegenteil ist . . . Man kann es . . . essen, trinken . . .

Ort:

Man kann dort . . . Man findet es . . .

Procedure Divide the class into two teams. Have two players from each team sit at the four desks. A player from Team A selects a card and shows it to one of the players from Team B. Using circumlocution phrases, the Team A player attempts to describe the vocabulary word to his or her partner without saying the word itself. (For example, one could say about an elephant: **Das ist ein Tier. Es ist groß und grau.**) If the partner in Team A guesses the word, Team A receives five points. If not, the Team B player in turn gives a clue to his or her partner. If the partner guesses correctly, Team B receives four points.

Play alternates between the two teams, with the points earned dropping by one each time someone guesses incorrectly. If a player is unable to give a clue within thirty seconds, that team loses its turn and the opposing team gives another clue. If no team scores a point after five clues, any student on Team A may make a guess. If the guess is correct, Team A receives one point. If not, any student from Team B is given the same opportunity. If this guess is also incorrect, announce the correct answer.

Storytelling

Mini-Geschichte

*This story accompanies Teaching Transparency 1-2. Read the **Mini-Geschichte** to your students, or have them role-play the conversation using appropriate gestures and facial expressions. Ask students to add one suitable sentence at the end of the story.*

Was wollen wir jetzt machen?

„Du, Sabine, dein Stirnband sieht klasse aus. Und die Jogging-Hose, ist die neu? Sie sieht fesch aus." „Wirklich, Sandra? Die Hose war ein Geburtstagsgeschenk." „Möchtest du etwas trinken, Sabine?" „Ja, ich nehme Apfelsaft. Und du?" „Also, ich … ich möchte lieber einen Eisbecher." „Wie schmeckt der Eisbecher, Sandra?" „Sehr gut! Er hat leider zu viele Kalorien *(calories)*." „Wollen wir joggen oder lieber einen Langstreckenlauf machen?" „Sehr lustig, Sabine! Aber ich will lieber faulenzen." „Willst du vielleicht ins Kino gehen?" „Das ist eine prima Idee, Sabine!"

Traditions

Der Maibaum in Bayern

Das Aufstellen eines Maibaums ist ein alter bayrischer Brauch. Wenn ein neuer Maibaum aufgestellt wird, ist er zunächst ungeschmückt und unbemalt. Er trägt noch die obersten Äste der Baumkrone, als Zeichen dafür, dass er im folgenden Jahr zum Maibaum geschmückt wird.

Dann wird die Baumkrone entfernt und der Stamm erhält die typischen blauen und weißen Streifen, sowie weitere Ornamente und Zunfttafeln der ansässigen Handwerksberufe. Sobald der Baum geschmückt ist, darf er ‚gestohlen' werden. Das Team, das den Maibaum aufgestellt und geschmückt hat, stellt darum Wachen auf. Wenn der Maibaum trotzdem gestohlen wird, muss er ausgelöst werden, damit er am 1. Mai auch wieder an seinem Platz steht. Dies geschieht oft durch eine kräftige Brotzeit für die ‚Diebe'.

Have students research in the library or on the Internet the significance of May 1. Ask students if they know of a similar holiday in their own culture.

Rezept

Krautsalat
Für 15 Personen

Zutaten
kg=Kilogramm, EL=Esslöffel

2 kg Weißkraut
Salz
Zucker
Pfeffer
2 Zwiebeln
6-8 EL Weinessig
6 EL Öl

Zubereitung
Das geputzte Kraut in Stücke schneiden und fein hobeln. Mit Salz bestreuen und mit dem Kartoffelstampfer oder den Händen so lange stampfen, bis sich etwas Saft bildet. Den Saft abgießen. Das Kraut mit Salz, Zucker, Pfeffer, den fein gewürfelten Zwiebeln und Essig würzen. Zum Schluss das Öl zugießen. Den Salat gut durchziehen lassen. Vor dem Servieren eventuell nachwürzen.

Kapitel 1: Bei den Baumanns
Technology

Review Chapter

Videocassette 1, 5 (captioned version)
DVD Tutor, Disc 1
See Video Guide, pages 3–8

DVD/Video

Los geht's! • Sebastian stellt seine Familie vor
Sebastian shows us his house and introduces us to his brother Robert who isn't thrilled about the interruption by Sebastian.

Landeskunde
Und was hast du am liebsten?
Students from different cities in Germany tell us about their favorite things: school subjects, activities, foods, and clothes.

Fortsetzung
On his way to find his sister Beatrice, Sebastian stops and buys a bandana. Then, he joins Beatrice and her friend Christiane at a café, where Beatrice invites him to have something to eat and drink with them.

Videoclips
- Bad Pyrmonter Mineralwasser® (mineral water)
- Dr. Koch's Trink 10® (multi-vitamin fruit juice)
- Granini Orangensaft® (orange juice)
- Captain Iglo Fischstäbchen® (fish sticks)
- Milka Schokolade® (chocolate)

Interactive CD-ROM Tutor

Activity	Activity Type	Pupil's Edition Reference
1. Wortschatz	Wort und Bild Erfahren/Wählen	p. 10
2. So sagt man das!	Was ist richtig?	pp. 11, 13
3. Wortschatz	Merkspiel	p. 17
4. So sagt man das!	Wozu gehört's?	p. 18
5. Grammatik	Was fehlt?	pp. 12, 23
6. So sagt man das! Landeskunde	Wozu gehört's? Und was hast du am liebsten? Was ist richtig?	pp. 23, 25 p. 22
Zum Sprechen	Guided recording	p. 30
Zum Schreiben	Guided writing	p. 30

Teacher Management System
Launch the program, type "admin" in the password area, and press RETURN. Log on to **www.hrw.com/CDROMTUTOR** for a detailed explanation of the Teacher Management System.

DVD Tutor

The *DVD Tutor* contains all material from the *Video Program* as described above. German captions are available for use at your discretion for all sections of the video. The *DVD Tutor* also provides a variety of video-based activities that assess students' understanding of **Los geht's!**, **Fortsetzung**, and **Landeskunde**, as well as the new **Grammatik im Kontext** presentations.

The *DVD Tutor* may be used on any DVD video player connected to a television or video monitor.

One-Stop Planner CD-ROM

To preview all resources available for this chapter, use the **One-Stop Planner CD-ROM**, Disc 1.

Visit Holt Online
go.hrw.com
KEYWORD: WK3 BAYERN-1
Online Edition

Go.Online!

Premier Online Edition

The Premier Online Edition for *Komm mit!* allows students access to their textbooks anytime, anywhere.

- Audio at point of use
- Additional practice activities
- Self-test activities
- Online reference tools
- Entire Video Program
- Interactive Notebook

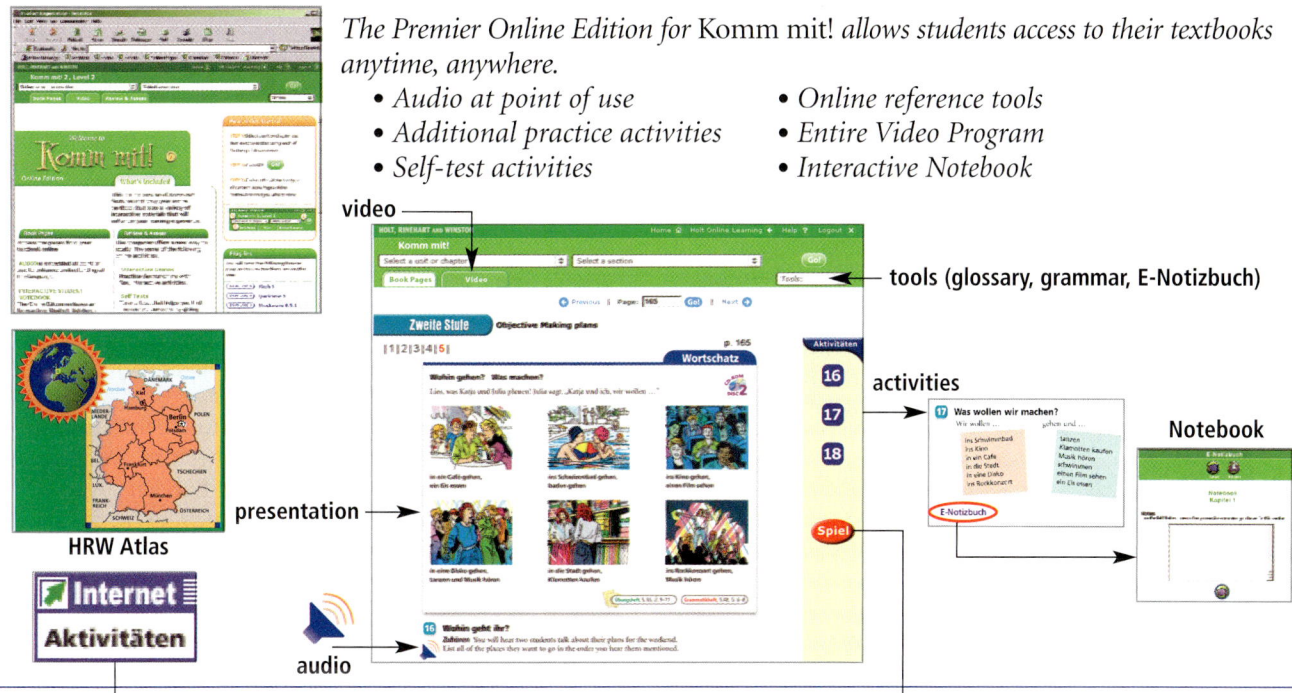

HRW Atlas — presentation — audio — video — tools (glossary, grammar, E-Notizbuch) — activities — Notebook

Internet Aktivitäten

These guided internet activities include a worksheet and pre-selected and pre-screened authentic web sites from the German-speaking countries. You can use these activities

- to help students develop research skills in the target language
- to introduce students to authentic cultural information
- as a project

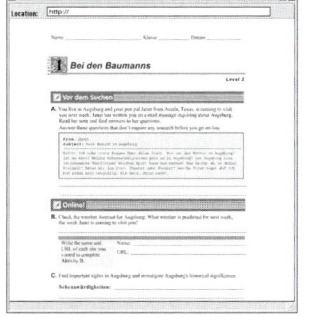

Interaktive Spiele

You can use the interactive activities in this chapter

- to practice grammar, vocabulary, and chapter functions
- as homework
- as an assessment option
- as a self-test
- to prepare for the Chapter Test

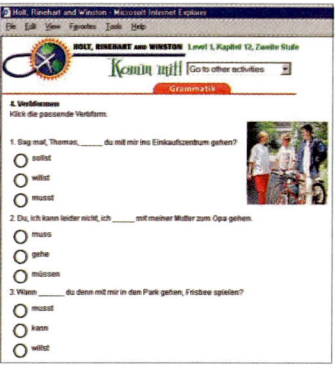

Webprojekt Have students find a picture of and information about any famous person (actor/actress, author, composer, scientist, singer, sports figure, etc.) in a German-speaking country. Students should describe his/her looks, characteristics, likes and dislikes, and hobbies. You may want to have students present the profile of their famous person to the class. Encourage students to exchange useful Web sites with their classmates. Have students document their sources by referencing the names and URLs of all the sites they consulted.

STANDARDS: 1.3, 2.1, 3.1, 3.2, 5.1   KAPITEL 1   TECHNOLOGY   **3F**

Kapitel 1: Bei den Baumanns

Review Chapter

Textbook Listening Activities Scripts

Erste Stufe

6 p. 9

1. Immer freundlich, sehr sympathisch und vor allem immer gut gekleidet. Liebt vor allem bunte Sachen; geht sehr gern aus.
2. Nicht sehr groß, blond, sehr ruhig und vor allem sehr tierlieb. Reitet furchtbar gern und hat sogar ein eigenes Pferd.
3. Nett und freundlich. Steht auf Jeanskleidung. Alle lieben die blonden Locken. Hilft anderen Leuten furchtbar gern; repariert die Fahrräder von Familie und Freunden.
4. Schlank und sehr attraktiv, immer lächelnd, braune Haare, die gewöhnlich mit einem Stirnband zusammengehalten werden. Liebt schicke Sachen, vor allem Lederklamotten.
5. Superschlank und sportlich. Ein Stirnband hält beim Skilaufen die dunklen Haare zusammen — hier natürlich beim Grasskilaufen.

Answers to Activity 6
1. e; 2. d; 3. b; 4. a; 5. c

10 p. 11

1. Also, ich heiße Johannes, bin 16 Jahre alt, 1,70 groß, schlank, und ich habe braune Haare. Ich spiele Squash … ja, was noch? Mein Hobby ist, ja, das hört sich vielleicht komisch an: ich sammle Ansichtskarten. Ich habe schon so viele Karten, Karten aus der ganzen Welt. Das Hobby ist toll: ich lerne sehr viel über Geographie und wie es in der Welt aussieht.
2. Mein Name ist Monika. Ich bin 15, werde aber im nächsten Monat 16. Ja, wie sehe ich aus? Blonde, lockige Haare hab ich, ich trag eine Brille. Meine Klassenkameraden sagen, ich bin furchtbar intelligent. Warum, das weiß ich auch nicht. Vielleicht, weil ich gut in Mathe bin und eigentlich immer eine Eins schreibe.
3. Heike ist mein Name, und ich bin 17 Jahre alt. Ich bin nicht sehr groß, nur 1,55, aber vielleicht wachse ich noch. Ich habe schwarze Haare, ja, was soll ich noch über mich sagen? Ach ja, ich sehe schlecht, sehr schlecht sogar, und ich muss Kontaktlinsen tragen. Mein Hobby ist Kochen — ich koche sogar sehr gern. Das hab ich von meinem Vater; er ist Chefkoch in einem großen, noblen Restaurant. Ja, und wie sieht's mit Sport aus? Radfahren, und ab und zu spiele ich auch Tennis.
4. Ich heiße Dieter Maier — Maier mit *a i* — ich bin 16 Jahre alt. Wie ich aussehe? Meine Freunde sagen: blöd! Na ja, ich hab lange, blonde Haare, die ich mir hinten zusammenbinde. Ich habe braune Augen, sehe sehr gut; dann bin ich ein guter Basketballspieler und spiele in unserer Schulmannschaft. Hobbys? Ich lese sehr gern, alles über Tiere. Tiergeschichten aus Afrika, Indien und so — ja, das ist es wohl. Tja!

Answers to Activity 10
1. Johannes: 16; 1,70 groß; braune Haare; schlank; spielt Squash; sammelt Ansichtskarten. 2. Monika: 15; blond; trägt eine Brille; furchtbar intelligent; gut in Mathe. 3. Heike: 17; nicht sehr groß; 1,55; schwarze Haare; trägt Kontaktlinsen; kocht sehr gerne; fährt sehr gerne Rad; spielt Tennis. 4. Dieter: 16; sieht blöd aus; lange, blonde Haare; braune Augen; guter Basketballspieler in Schulmannschaft; liest gern Tiergeschichten.

20 p. 15

1. Mein Name ist Erika. Ich bin 16 und gehe aufs Gymnasium. Meine Lieblingsfächer sind Deutsch und Englisch, ja auch Biologie. In Bio hab ich sogar 'ne Eins. Physik hab ich überhaupt nicht gern, das Fach interessiert mich nicht.
2. Ich heiße Walter Neumann und bin 17 Jahre alt. Was ich in der Schule gern hab? Ja, das sind zuerst einmal die beiden Pausen, weil ich da … da kann ich mit meinen Klassenkameraden im Schulhof Tischtennis spielen. Na ja, Mathe hab ich schon gern, auch Geschichte, aber Biologie ist absolut furchtbar.
3. Ich bin der Jörg, bin 16 Jahre alt und gehe hier auf die Realschule. Meine Lieblingsfächer sind Musik, weil ich später mal in einer Band spielen möchte. Andere Fächer? Deutsch ist so so, und Englisch geht gerade noch. Aber Mathe — furchtbar! Ich bekomme immer 'ne Fünf!

Answers to Activity 20
1. Erika: 16; Gymnasium; Lieblingsfächer Deutsch, Englisch und Biologie; hat eine Eins in Bio; interessiert sich nicht für Physik. 2. Walter: 17; hat die beiden Pausen gern; Tischtennis; mag Mathe und Geschichte, aber nicht Bio. 3. Jörg: 16; Realschule; Lieblingsfach Musik; will mal in einer Band spielen; mag Deutsch und Englisch ein bisschen; hat eine 5 in Mathe.

24 p. 15

JÖRG Mein Zimmer ist sehr nett. Es ist groß, hat zwei große Fenster. Ich hab also viel Sonne im Zimmer. Meine Möbel sind okay, Bett, Schrank, der Sessel ist ganz neu, hab ich zum Geburtstag bekommen. Jetzt kann ich also ganz bequem im Sessel sitzen und Video schauen, wenn ich nicht selbst Musik mache.

The following scripts are for the listening activities found in the *Pupil's Edition*. For Student Response Forms, see *Listening Activities*, pages 3–6. To provide students with additional listening practice, see *Listening Activities*, pages 7–10.

For resource information, see the **One-Stop Planner CD-ROM**, Disc 1.

ERIKA Ja, ich habe ein schönes Zimmer, klein, aber sehr gemütlich. Ich habe einen super Schrank, ganz alt, den hab ich von meiner Oma. Dann hab ich noch einen kleinen Schreibtisch im Zimmer, zwei Stühle und eine Couch — das ist mein Bett. Muss ich jeden Abend aufmachen, damit ich schlafen gehen kann.

Answers to Activity 24
Jörg: Bett, Schrank, Sessel; Erika: Schrank, Schreibtisch, Stühle, Couch

Zweite Stufe

34 p. 19

Der Sommerschlussverkauf beginnt offiziell nächsten Montag, aber wir haben schon jetzt unsere Preise reduziert — für Sie, liebe Kunden — damit Sie jetzt schon in Ruhe bei uns einkaufen können. Unser Angebot ist groß: T-Shirts in allen Größen und Farben und schon ab 6 Euro. Die Sensation in unserer Jugendabteilung sind Polohemden aus reiner Baumwolle, mit halbem Ärmel, ideal für die heißen Sommertage. Und auch der Preis ist heiß: nur 9 Euro 50! In der Jeansabteilung finden Sie alle Marken und Größen — aber zu kleinen Preisen. Jeans schon ab 18 Euro! Eine Sensation im Junior-Shop: Pullover für die kühlen Herbsttage. Aus Polyacryl. Leider nur in drei Farben: Blau, Grün und Rot. Aber dafür zum einmaligen Preis von nur 10 Euro! Und noch ein ganz heißer Tipp: Cowboystiefel — die Sensation — in Braun und in Schwarz. Viele Größen und schon ab 60 Euro! Sie fühlen sich wie im Westen Amerikas! Also, nichts wie zum Sport-Bauer, das moderne Sportgeschäft, das Ihre Wünsche erfüllt!

Dritte Stufe

36 p. 23

PETRA Also, meistens gehe ich am Samstagnachmittag schwimmen. Wenn das Wetter schön ist, zum Beispiel im Sommer, dann gehen wir ins Freibad, sonst ins Hallenbad. Danach gehen wir meistens in die Stadt zum Bummeln oder Eis essen.

SVEN Ich hab jeden Samstag Fußballtraining von drei bis halb fünf. Entweder fahre ich mit dem Rad oder ich jogge dorthin, als Aufwärmtraining, bevor wir mit dem Spiel anfangen. Nach dem Training gehen wir meistens was trinken.

MARTINA Also, ich geh samstags immer mit meiner Freundin in die Nachmittagsvorstellung ins Kino. Vorher lese ich immer die Wochenendausgabe der Zeitung. Da sind auch alle Kinoprogramme drin.

Answers to Activity 36
Petra: schwimmen; bummeln; Eis essen. Sven: Fußballtraining; Rad fahren; joggen; etwas trinken gehen. Martina: Kino, Zeitung lesen.

42 p. 24

1. A: Worauf hast du denn Appetit?
   B: Du, ich weiß nicht! Ich hab aber großen Hunger.
   A: Also, ich möchte heute mal was Italienisches, eine Pizza vielleicht. Ich glaube, ich nehme die zu acht fünfzig.

2. A: Wo kann ich nur einen Spitzer und einen Radiergummi kaufen?
   B: Komm mit! Da an der Ecke ist ein Schreibwarengeschäft. Da kriegst du alles, was du brauchst.

3. A: Ich brauch unbedingt etwas, was zu meiner Jeans passt, eine Bluse oder ein T-Shirt vielleicht.
   B: Geh doch zum Sport-Bauer! Der hat diese Woche tolle Sonderangebote. Die Ware ist echt gut, und die Preise sind stark reduziert.

4. A: Wie spät ist es denn?
   B: Du weißt doch, meine Uhr ist kaputt.
   A: Dann kauf dir halt eine neue! Ich weiß, wo du sogar eine Solaruhr für 12 Euro bekommst.

5. A: Ich sitz gern in diesem Café. Der Kaffee riecht hier immer so gut.
   B: Stimmt! — Hm, ich glaub, dass ich heute einen Eiskaffee trinke. Es ist so heiß draußen, und ich möchte unbedingt etwas Kaltes.

Answers to Activity 42
1. d; 2. e; 3. a; 4. b; 5. c

Answers to Activity 43, p. 25
Ich möchte heute mal … ; ich glaube, ich nehme … ; wo kann ich … kaufen?; ich brauch unbedingt … ; ich möchte unbedingt …

Kapitel 1: Bei den Baumanns

Review Chapter

Suggested Lesson Plans — 50-Minute Schedule

Day 1

LOCATION OPENER 15 min.
- Present **Location Opener**, pp. 1–3
- Show **Bayern** Video
- Do Viewing and Post-viewing Activities, Video Guide, p. 2

CHAPTER OPENER 10 min.
- Reviewing Vocabulary, ATE, p. 3M
- Reviewing Grammar and Functions, ATE, p. 3M

LOS GEHT'S! 20 min.
- Preteaching Vocabulary, ATE, p. 3N
- Have students read **Los geht's!**, pp. 6–7
- Teaching Suggestions, Video Guide, p. 4
- Show **Los geht's!** Video

Wrap-Up 5 min.
- Students respond to **Los geht's!** questions

Homework Options
- Pupil's Edition, p. 8, Comprehension Acts.
Übungsheft, p. 1, Act. 1
Internet Aktivitäten (see ATE, p. 3F)

Day 2

ERSTE STUFE

Quick Review 15 min.
- Check homework, p. 8, Comprehension Acts.
- Bell Work, ATE, p. 3O

Was für eine Person bist du?, p. 9 10 min.
- Do Activity **Was für eine Person bist du?**, p. 9
- Play Audio CD for Activity 6, p. 9

Wortschatz, p. 10 5 min.
- Presenting **Wortschatz**, ATE, p. 3O
- Teaching Transparencies 1-1, 1-A

So sagt man das!, p. 11 15 min.
- Presenting **So sagt man das!**, ATE, p. 3P
- Do Activities 7–8, pp. 10–11
- Do Communicative Activity 1-1, pp. 1–2

Wrap-Up 5 min.
- Students respond to questions about feelings and sports

Homework Options
Grammatikheft, pp. 1–2, Acts. 1–5
Übungsheft, p. 2, Acts. 1–3

Day 3

ERSTE STUFE

Quick Review 10 min.
- Check homework, Grammatikheft, pp. 1–2, Acts. 1–5

Ein wenig Grammatik, p. 11 10 min.
- Presenting **Ein wenig Grammatik**, ATE, p. 3P
- Do Activity 9, p. 11
- Play Audio CD for Activity 10, p. 11

Ein wenig Grammatik, p. 12 15 min.
- Presenting **Ein wenig Grammatik**, ATE, p. 3P
- Do Activities 11, 12, and 13, p. 12
- Do Activity 14, p. 13

So sagt man das!, p. 13 10 min.
- Presenting **So sagt man das!**, ATE, p. 3P
- Do Activities 15 and 16, p. 13

Wrap-Up 5 min.
- Students respond to questions about Sebastian's family

Homework Options
Grammatikheft, p. 3, Act. 6
Übungsheft, p. 3, Acts. 4–5

Day 4

ERSTE STUFE

Quick Review 10 min.
- Check homework, Übungsheft, p. 3, Act. 4

Ein wenig Grammatik, p. 13 20 min.
- Presenting **Ein wenig Grammatik**, ATE, p. 3P
- Language-to-Language, ATE, p. 3Q
- Read articles about Sebastian, p. 14
- Do Activities 17 and 18, p. 14
- Do Activity 19, p. 15
- Play Audio CD for Activity 20, p. 15
- Do Activities 21, 22, and 25, p. 15
- Play Audio CD for Activity 24, p. 15
- Do Activities 6–7, p. 4, Übungsheft

Quiz Review 15 min.
- Play game, **Das treffende Wort suchen**, ATE, p. 3C

Wrap-Up 5 min.
- Students respond to questions about describing other students

Homework Options
Mehr Grammatikübungen, Erste Stufe
Pupil's Edition, p. 15, Acts. 23, 26

Day 5

ZWEITE STUFE

Quick Review 10 min.
- Check homework, **Mehr Grammatikübungen, Erste Stufe**

Quiz 20 min.
- Quiz 1-1A or 1-1B

Wortschatz, p. 17 15 min.
- Presenting **Wortschatz**, ATE, p. 3S
- Teaching Transparency 1-B
- Do Activities 27–29, p. 16
- Do Activity 30, p. 17
- Do Activity 31, p. 18

Wrap-Up 5 min.
- Students respond to questions about articles of clothing

Homework Options
Grammatikheft, p. 4, Act. 7
Übungsheft, p. 5, Act. 1

Day 6

ZWEITE STUFE

Quick Review 10 min.
- Check homework, Grammatikheft, p. 4, Act. 7

So sagt man das!, p. 18 10 min.
- Presenting **So sagt man das!**, ATE, p. 3S
- TPR Activity, ATE, p. 3S
- Do Activity 32, p. 18

So sagt man das!, p. 18 10 min.
- Presenting **So sagt man das!**, ATE, p. 3S
- Do Activity 33, p. 19

Ein wenig Grammatik, p. 19 15 min.
- Present **Ein wenig Grammatik**, p. 19
- Play Audio CD for Activity 34, p. 19
- Do Activity 35, p. 19

Wrap-Up 5 min.
- Students respond to questions about needing articles of clothing and school supplies

Homework Options
Grammatikheft, pp. 4–6, Acts. 8–11
Übungsheft, pp. 5–7, Acts. 2–6

One-Stop Planner CD-ROM

For alternative lesson plans by chapter section, to create your own customized plans, or to preview all resources available for this chapter, use the **One-Stop Planner CD-ROM**, Disc 1.

 For additional homework suggestions, see activities accompanied by this symbol throughout the chapter.

Day 7

ZWEITE STUFE

Quick Review 10 min.
- Check homework, Übungsheft, pp. 5–7, Acts. 1–6

ZUM LESEN 20 min.
- Present **Lesestrategie**, p. 20
- Do Activities 1–8, pp. 20–21

LANDESKUNDE 15 min.
- Pre-viewing Suggestion, Video Guide, p. 5
- Teacher Notes, ATE, p. 3V
- Show **Landeskunde** Video
- Do Activities A and B, p. 22
- Do **Landeskunde** Activity, Interactive CD-ROM

Wrap-Up 5 min.
- Students respond to questions about the reading selection

Homework Options
Activities for Communication, pp. 3–4, prepare Communicative Activity 1–2
Übungsheft, p. 8, Acts. 1–4; p. 9, Acts. 1–2

Day 8

ZWEITE STUFE

Quick Review 15 min.
- Do Communicative Activity 1–2, pp. 3–4

Quiz Review 15 min.
- Do **Mehr Grammatikübungen, Zweite Stufe**
- Play game, **Ich packe meinen Koffer und nehme ..... mit,** ATE, p. 3T

Quiz 20 min.
- Quiz 1-2A or 1-2B

Homework Options
Activities for Communication, p. 75, fill out Realia 1-2 and underline cognates

Day 9

DRITTE STUFE

Quick Review 15 min.
- Return and review Quiz 1-2
- Bell Work, ATE, p. 3V
- Check homework, Realia 1-2

So sagt man das!, p. 23 15 min.
- Presenting **So sagt man das!,** ATE, p. 3W
- Play Audio CD for Activity 36, p. 23
- Do Activities 37 and 38, p. 23

Ein wenig Grammatik, p. 23 15 min.
- Presenting **Ein wenig Grammatik,** ATE, p. 3W
- Do Activities 39 and 40, p. 23
- Do Activity 41, p. 24
- Play Audio CD for Activity 42, p. 24

Wrap-Up 5 min.
- Students respond to questions about making plans for the weekend

Homework Options
Grammatikheft, p. 7, Activities 12–13
Übungsheft, pp. 10–11, Acts. 1–5

Day 10

DRITTE STUFE

Quick Review 10 min.
- Check homework, Übungsheft, pp. 10–11, Acts. 1–5

So sagt man das!, p. 25 15 min.
- Presenting **So sagt man das!,** ATE, p. 3W
- Play Audio CD for Activity 43, p. 25
- Do Activity 44, p. 25

So sagt man das!, p. 25 20 min.
- Presenting **So sagt man das!,** ATE, p. 3W
- Do Activities 45 and 46, p. 25
- Do Activities 17–18, p. 9, Grammatikheft

Wrap-up 5 min.
- Students respond to questions about ordering food and how food tastes

Homework Options
Grammatikheft, p. 8, Acts. 14–16
Übungsheft, p. 12, Acts. 6–7
Interaktive Spiele (see ATE, p. 3F)

Day 11

DRITTE STUFE

Quick Review 15 min.
- Check homework, Grammatikheft, p. 8, Acts. 14–16

Quiz Review 15 min.
- Show **Fortsetzung** Video
- Do **Mehr Grammatikübungen, Dritte Stufe**

Quiz 20 min.
- Quiz 1-3A or 1-3B

Homework Options
Pupil's Edition, p. 30, **Kann ich's wirklich?**
Activities for Communication, pp. 5–6, prepare Communicative Activity 1–3

Day 12

REVIEW

Quick Review 20 min.
- Check homework, p. 30, **Kann ich's wirklich?**
- Do Communicative Activity 1–3, pp. 5–6

Chapter Review 30 min.
- Review chapter functions, vocabulary, and grammar; choose from **Mehr Grammatikübungen,** Grammar Tutor for Students of German, Activities for Communication, Listening Activities, Interactive CD-ROM Tutor, or **Interaktive Spiele**
- Review test format and provide sample test items for students

Homework Options
Study for Chapter Test

Assessment

Test, Chapter 1 45 min.
- Administer Chapter 1 Test. Select from Testing Program, Alternative Assessment Guide or Test Generator.

Kapitel 1: Bei den Baumanns

Review Chapter

Suggested Lesson Plans — 90-Minute Schedule

Block 1

LOCATION OPENER 15 min.
- Present **Location Opener,** pp. 1–3
- Show **Bayern** Video
- Do Viewing and Post-viewing Activities, Video Guide, p. 2

CHAPTER OPENER 10 min.
- Reviewing Vocabulary, ATE, p. 3M
- Reviewing Grammar and Functions, ATE, p. 3M

LOS GEHT'S! 20 min.
- Preteaching Vocabulary, ATE, p. 3N
- Have students read **Los geht's!,** pp. 6–7
- Teaching Suggestions, Video Guide, p. 4
- Show **Los geht's!** Video

ERSTE STUFE

Was für eine Person bist du?, p. 9 10 min.
- Do Activity **Was für eine Person bist du?,** p. 9
- Play Audio CD for Activity 6, p. 9

Wortschatz, p. 10 5 min.
- Presenting **Wortschatz,** ATE, p. 3O
- Teaching Transparencies 1-1, 1-A

So sagt man das!, p. 11 10 min.
- Presenting **So sagt man das!,** ATE, p. 3P
- Do Activities 7–8, pp. 10–11

Ein wenig Grammatik, p. 11 15 min.
- Presenting **Ein wenig Grammatik,** ATE, p. 3P
- Do Activity 9, p. 11
- Play Audio CD for Activity 10, p. 11

Wrap-Up 5 min.
- Students respond to questions about Sebastian's family

Homework Options
Pupil's Edition, p. 8, Comprehension Acts.
Grammatikheft, pp. 1–2, Acts. 1–5
Übungsheft, p. 1, Act. 1; p. 2, Acts. 1–3
Internet Aktivitäten (see ATE, p. 3F)

Block 2

ERSTE STUFE

Quick Review 10 min.
- Check homework, Grammatikheft, pp. 1–2, Acts. 1–5

Ein wenig Grammatik, p. 12 15 min.
- Presenting **Ein wenig Grammatik,** ATE, p. 3P
- Do Activities 11, 12, and 13, p. 12
- Do Activity 14, p. 13
- Do Act. 6, p. 3, Grammatikheft

So sagt man das!, p. 13 15 min.
- Presenting **So sagt man das!,** ATE, p. 3P
- Do Activities 15 and 16, p. 13

Ein wenig Grammatik, p. 13 30 min.
- Presenting **Ein wenig Grammatik,** ATE, p. 3P
- Language-to-Language, ATE, p. 3Q
- Read articles about Sebastian, p. 14
- Do Activities 17 and 18, p. 14
- Do Activity 19, p. 15
- Play Audio CD for Activity 20, p. 15
- Do Activities 21, 22, 23, and 25, p. 15
- Play Audio CD for Activity 24, p. 15
- Do Activities 6–7, p. 4, Übungsheft

Quiz Review 15 min.
- Play game, **Das treffende Wort suchen,** ATE, p. 3C

Wrap-Up 5 min.
- Students respond to questions about describing other students

Homework Options
Mehr Grammatikübungen, Erste Stufe
Pupil's Edition, p. 15, Act. 26
Übungsheft, p. 3, Acts. 4–5

Block 3

ZWEITE STUFE

Quick Review 10 min.
- Check homework, **Mehr Grammatikübungen,** Erste Stufe

Quiz 20 min.
- Quiz 1-1A or 1-1B

Wortschatz, p. 17 20 min.
- Presenting **Wortschatz,** ATE, p. 3S
- Teaching Transparency 1-B
- Do Activities 27, 28, and 29, p. 16
- Do Activity 30, p. 17
- Do Activity 31, p. 18

So sagt man das!, p. 18 10 min.
- Presenting **So sagt man das!,** ATE, p. 3S
- TPR Activity, ATE, p. 3S
- Do Activity 32, p. 18

So sagt man das!, p. 18 10 min.
- Presenting **So sagt man das!,** ATE, p. 3S
- Do Activity 33, p. 19

Ein wenig Grammatik, p. 19 15 min.
- Present **Ein wenig Grammatik,** p. 19
- Play Audio CD for Activity 34, p. 19
- Do Activity 35, p. 19

Wrap-Up 5 min.
- Students respond to questions about needing articles of clothing and school supplies

Homework Options
Grammatikheft, pp. 4–6, Acts. 7–11
Übungsheft, pp. 5–7, Acts. 1–6

For alternative lesson plans by chapter section, to create your own customized plans, or to preview all resources available for this chapter, use the **One-Stop Planner CD-ROM**, Disc 1.

 For additional homework suggestions, see activities accompanied by this symbol throughout the chapter.

Block 4

ZWEITE STUFE

Quick Review 10 min.
- Check homework, Grammatikheft, pp. 4–6, Acts. 7–11

ZUM LESEN 20 min.
- Present **Lesestrategie**, p. 20
- Do Activities 1-8, pp. 20–21

LANDESKUNDE 25 min.
- Pre-viewing Suggestion, Video Guide, p. 5
- Teacher Notes, ATE, p. 3V
- Show **Landeskunde** Video
- Do Activities A and B, p. 22
- Do **Landeskunde** Activity, Interactive CD-ROM

Quiz Review 15 min.
- Do **Mehr Grammatikübungen, Zweite Stufe**
- Play game, **Ich packe meinen Koffer und nehme ….. mit**, ATE, p. 3T

Quiz 20 min.
- Quiz 1-2A or 1-2B

Homework Options
Übungsheft, p. 8, Acts 1–4; p. 9, Acts. 1–2
Activities for Communication, p. 75, fill out Realia 1-2 and underline cognates

Block 5

DRITTE STUFE

Quick Review 15 min.
- Return and review Quiz 1-2
- Bellwork, ATE, p. 3V
- Check homework, Realia 1-2

So sagt man das!, p. 23 15 min.
- Presenting **So sagt man das!**, ATE, p. 3W
- Play Audio CD for Activity 36, p. 23
- Do Activities 37 and 38, p. 23

Ein wenig Grammatik, p. 23 20 min.
- Presenting **Ein wenig Grammatik**, ATE, p. 3W
- Do Activities 39 and 40, p. 23
- Do Activity 41, p. 24
- Play Audio CD for Activity 42, p. 24

So sagt man das!, p. 25 15 min.
- Presenting **So sagt man das!**, ATE, p. 3W
- Play Audio CD for Activity 43, p. 25
- Do Activity 44, p. 25

So sagt man das!, p. 25 20 min.
- Presenting **So sagt man das!**, ATE, p. 3W
- Do Activities 45 and 46, p. 25
- Do Activities 17–18, p. 9, Grammatikheft

Wrap-Up 5 min.
- Students respond to questions about ordering food and about how food tastes

Homework Options
Grammatikheft, pp. 7–8, Acts. 12–16
Übungsheft, pp. 10–12, Acts. 1–7

Block 6

DRITTE STUFE

Quick Review 20 min.
- Check homework, Grammatikheft, pp. 7–8, Acts. 12–16

Quiz Review 25 min.
- Show **Fortsetzung** Video
- Do **Mehr Grammatikübungen, Dritte Stufe**
- Do Additional Listening Activities 1–5 and 1–6, pp. 9–10

Quiz 20 min.
- Quiz 1-3A or 1-3B

REVIEW

Kann ich's wirklich?, p. 30 20 min.
- Presenting **Kann ich's wirklich?**, ATE, p. 3X
- Do Activities 1–10 (written)

Wrap-Up 5 min.
- Students respond orally to **Kann ich's wirklich?** questions

Homework Options
Interaktive Spiele, see ATE, p. 3F

Block 7

REVIEW

Quick Review 15 min.
- Return and review Quiz 1-3
- Do Communicative Activity 1–3, pp. 5–6

Chapter Review 30 min.
- Review chapter functions, vocabulary, and grammar; choose from **Mehr Grammatikübungen**, Grammar Tutor for Students of German, Activities for Communication, Listening Activities, Interactive CD-ROM Tutor, or **Interaktive Spiele**
- Review test format and provide sample test items for students

Test, Chapter 1 45 min.
- Administer Chapter 1 Test. Select from Testing Program, Alternative Assessment Guide or Test Generator.

Kapitel 1: Bei den Baumanns
Review Chapter
Teaching Suggestions, pages 4–31

Teacher Notes
- Chapter 1 is a review chapter that reintroduces functions, grammar, and vocabulary from *Komm mit!* Level 1.
- Some activities suggested in the *Teacher's Edition* ask students to contact various people, businesses, and organizations in the community. Before assigning these activities, it is advisable to request permission from parents and contactees.

In *Komm mit!* Level 2, most pieces that reflect the traditional spelling are **Zum Lesen** selections and pieces of realia. These are permissioned documents that cannot be altered.

PAGES 4–5

CHAPTER OPENER

Pacing Tips
Chapter 1 is a review chapter. In the **Erste Stufe,** students review the functions of 'asking for and giving information about yourself and others,' 'describing yourself and others,' 'expressing likes and dislikes,' and 'identifying people and places.' Functions reviewed in the **Zweite Stufe** are 'giving and responding to compliments' and 'expressing wishes when buying things.' The **Dritte Stufe** centers around 'making plans,' 'ordering food and beverages,' and 'talking about how something tastes.' You might want to spend more time teaching the **Zweite Stufe** since it also contains the **Landeskunde.** For Lesson Plans and timing suggestions, see pages 3I–3L.

Meeting the Standards
Communication
- Asking for and giving information about yourself and others, p. 11
- Describing yourself and others, p. 11
- Expressing likes and dislikes, p. 11
- Identifying people and places, p. 13
- Giving and responding to compliments, p. 18
- Expressing wishes when buying things, p. 18
- Making plans, p. 23
- Ordering food and beverages, p. 25
- Talking about how something tastes, p. 25

Cultures
- Landeskunde, p. 22
- Teaching Suggestion, p. 3W

For resource information, see the **One-Stop Planner CD-ROM,** Disc 1.

Connections
- Culture Note, p. 3O
- Physical Education Connection, p. 3O

Comparisons
- Language-to-Language, p. 3Q

Communities
- Career Path, p. 3P

Reviewing Vocabulary
Divide the class into six groups with one designated writer. On six index cards write the following categories: clothing, places in Germany, foods, adjectives (characteristics), family members, and sports and activities. Have one member of each group draw one card. Groups try to come up with as many German words as they can for the category listed on their card. The writer records the words. Set a time limit of two minutes. Then ask the groups to name their category and read the words they listed.

Reviewing Grammar and Functions
To reacquaint students with one another as well as to introduce new students, ask students to walk around the classroom asking the following five questions, which you have written on the board:

Wie heißt du?, Wo wohnst du?
Was machst du gern in deiner Freizeit?
Was hast du diesen Sommer gemacht?
Was isst du gern / nicht gern?

After students have returned to their seats, call on several students to share at least three items of information about a classmate.

Chapter Sequence
Los geht's! . . . . .p. 6
Erste Stufe . . . . .p. 9
Zweite Stufe . . . . .p. 16
Zum Lesen . . . . .p. 20
Landeskunde . . . . .p. 22
Dritte Stufe . . . . .p. 23
Mehr Grammatikübungen . . . . .p. 26
Kann ich's wirklich? . . . . .p. 30
Wortschatz . . . . .p. 31

LOS GEHT'S!

Teaching Resources
pp. 6–8

PRINT
- Lesson Planner, p. 2
- Video Guide, pp. 3–4, 6
- Übungsheft, p. 1

MEDIA
- One-Stop Planner
- Video Program
  Los geht's!
  Videocassette 1, 06:09–09:05
  Videocassette 5 (captioned version), 01:22–04:16
  Fortsetzung
  Videocassette 1, 09:07–11:00
  Videocassette 5 (captioned version), 04:19–06:11
- DVD Tutor, Disc 1
- Audio Compact Discs, CD1, Trs. 1–2
- Los geht's! Transparencies

PAGES 6–7

Los geht's! Transparencies

Preteaching Vocabulary

Activating Prior Knowledge
Point out that the setting for this **Los geht's!** is Sebastian Baumann's home and that he is giving a tour of his house and introducing himself. As a review, have students list vocabulary for family members and hobbies or interests mentioned in the photo spread. Can they find any new words in these categories? Then ask students to look for sentences that contain forms of the verb **sein**, listing them as they are found. Finally, ask students to identify sentences that contain modals.

 **Fortsetzung**
You may choose to continue with the
Fortsetzung of *Sebastian stellt seine Familie vor* now or wait until later in chapter. For a synopsis of the **Los geht's!** and **Fortsetzung** episodes, see p. 3E.

STANDARDS: 1.1, 1.2

Advance Organizer
Ask students to introduce themselves to one other student in the class and talk about themselves, their family, and where they live.

Using the Captioned Video/DVD

German captions for every **Los geht's!** and **Fortsetzung** are available on Videocassette 5. Target-language captions give students another opportunity to comprehend the language in the story and offer teachers further possibilities for presenting the new material in class.
Note: The *DVD Tutor* contains captions for all sections of the *Video Program*.

PAGE 8

Using the Captioned Video/DVD

1 An alternate way to complete Activity 1 would be to play the captioned version of *Sebastian stellt seine Familie vor* on Videocassette 5.
Note: The *DVD Tutor* contains captions for all sections of the *Video Program*.

Comprehension Check

Teaching Suggestion
1 Ask students to work with a partner as they go over **Los geht's!** on p. 6 again and answer Questions 1–8 in writing. Have students report their answers. Ask two or three students to give their responses to questions that can have more than one answer.

Auditory Learners
3 Write the names of possible speakers in random order on the board (**Frau Baumann, Herr Baumann, Beatrice, Großvater, Robert, Basti, Artus**). Have students close their books as you read each statement. Ask students to identify the speaker of each statement from the choices on the board.

Teaching Suggestions
4 Have students work with a partner and come up with a different response to each of the stimuli. Then have students reverse roles and again respond differently.

5 You may want to assign this activity as homework.

KAPITEL 1 LOS GEHT'S!

ERSTE STUFE

Teaching Resources
pp. 9–15

PRINT
- Lesson Planner, p. 3
- TPR Storytelling Book, pp. x–1
- Listening Activities, pp. 3–4, 7–8
- Activities for Communication, pp. 1–2, 74–75, 77, 123–124
- Grammatikheft, pp. 1–3
- Grammar Tutor for Students of German, Chapter 1
- Übungsheft, pp. 2–4
- Testing Program, pp. 1–4
- Alternative Assessment Guide, p. 32
- Student Make-Up Assignments, Chapter 1

MEDIA
- One-Stop Planner
- Audio Compact Discs, CD1, Trs. 3–6, 15, 21–22
- Teaching Transparencies
  Situation 1-1
  Vocabulary 1-A
  Mehr Grammatikübungen Answers
  Grammatikheft Answers
- Interactive CD-ROM Tutor, Disc 1
- DVD Tutor, Disc 1

▶ PAGE 9

Bell Work

Have students make a list of several people from the sports and entertainment world. Then ask students to describe these people.

Teaching Suggestion

To present the vocabulary in **Was für eine Person bist du?**

A. Read vocabulary in each category.
   Have students repeat after you.
   Stress new words and cognates, which are always hard to pronounce.

B. Ask either/or and open-ended questions.

Examples:
Bist du sportlich oder unsportlich?
Wer in der Klasse hat kurzes Haar?
Was für Hobbys hast du?

Teacher to Teacher

Teresa Karrels
Central High School
West Allis, Wisconsin

Teresa begins the Erste Stufe with this idea.

"The students choose a classmate to describe using the vocabulary on pages 9 and 31. The students write descriptions ending with the phrase **"Wer ist das?"** Students then take turns reading their descriptions aloud so that everyone can listen and respond with the name of the described person. This activity makes a good icebreaker at the beginning of the year, as well as being good for review."

▶ PAGE 10

PRESENTING: Wortschatz

Ask students to give one situation in which the adjectives **neugierig, lustig, gut gelaunt,** and **schlecht gelaunt** would apply to them.
(Example: **Ich bin gut gelaunt, wenn ich gute Noten in Mathe bekomme.**)

Ask students:
1. Which of the three hobbies shown is a hobby that someone they know would enjoy?
2. Which of the eight featured track-and-field events are they good at, enjoy, or do not like?

Connections and Comparisons

Culture Note

Leichtathletik, soccer, and tennis are the most popular sports in Germany.

Physical Education Connection

Do students know of any famous American track-and-field athletes? Can they name the events these athletes compete(d) in?

Examples:
1. Michael Johnson — 200m-Lauf
2. Jackie Joyner-Kersee — Weitsprung, Hürdenlauf, Speerwerfen
3. Mike Powell — Weitsprung
4. Randy Barnes — Kugelstoßen
5. Dick Fosbury — Hochsprung

Cultures and Communities

Career Path

Have students work together in groups to think of situations in which a competitive athlete would find it helpful to know German. (Suggestions: Many sports competitions are held in German-speaking countries, and the athletes could handle themselves more competently if they knew the language of their hosts; conversely, many German-speaking athletes travel in order to compete in other countries, including the United States.)

> **PAGE 11**

PRESENTING: So sagt man das!

Ask students to work with a partner to review the questions presented in **So sagt man das!** Allow students time to find out about each other and their siblings. Call on several students and ask them to recall what they found out about their partner.

Teacher Note

9 The **Notizbuch** is a personal diary in which students will be asked to write in German. There will be at least one **Notizbuch** activity per chapter.

PRESENTING: Ein wenig Grammatik

The verbs haben and sein Write the conjugated verb forms of **haben** and **sein** in random order on a transparency. Ask students to create sentences using the forms listed. Write several of the students' sentences on the transparency.

> **PAGE 12**

Communication for All Students

Challenge

11 After students have completed their description of the student, ask them to add at least two additional questions they would like to ask that student to find out more about him or her.

PRESENTING: Ein wenig Grammatik

Stem-changing verbs Divide the class into two groups and ask the groups to take turns giving examples of regular and stem-changing verbs. Write the verbs on large sheets of butcher paper as students call them out. Give a sheet to each group and have them write sentences with the verbs listed. Afterwards hang the papers up to display.

Teaching Suggestion

12 You may want to limit the questions (to 5 for example) or the time (not to exceed 30 seconds). If the team cannot guess, it must give up, and the other team gets a turn.

Communication for All Students

A Slower Pace

13 Review the vocabulary on p. 9 to help students with their questions and answers. Give them some examples as to how the vocabulary should be used.

> **PAGE 13**

PRESENTING: So sagt man das!

On a transparency, reintroduce family members by constructing a family tree for a fictitious family or for a popular TV family. Begin by explaining the relationship between the members, then ask several students how certain members of the family are related.

PRESENTING: Ein wenig Grammatik

Possessive Adjectives Help students to refamiliarize themselves with the possessive adjectives through question-answer practice using objects that students have or that are near them.
Examples:
—Michael, ist das deine Sportuhr?
—Ja, das ist meine Uhr. or Nein, das ist nicht meine Uhr.
—Wem gehören die zwei Deutschbücher?
—Das sind unsere Bücher!
—Ist das sein Taschenrechner oder ihr Taschenrechner?
—Das ist sein Taschenrechner.

Connections and Comparisons

Language-to-Language

You may want to tell your students that as in German, the endings of possessives in French and Spanish are often determined by the gender of the noun to which they refer.
Examples:
German: *meine* (f) Schwester, *mein* (m) Bruder, *mein* (n) Kind
French: *ma* (f) sœur, *mon* (m) frère
Spanish: *nuestra* (f) hermana, *nuestro* (m) hermano

Ask your students if they know of other word groups whose forms are determined by the noun to which they refer. (Examples: definite article, indefinite article, adjectives)

Game

Give students additional practice with possessive adjectives by playing *Pass the Buck*. The goal is to pass ownership to another person and to keep the exchange going for several turns.

Examples:
A   Das ist dein Geld, nicht wahr?
B   Nein, das ist sein Geld. (Pointing to a boy)
A   Harold, ist das dein Geld?
C   Nein, das ist ihr Geld. (Pointing to a girl)
A   Tracy, ist das dein Geld?
D   Ja, das ist mein Geld. Danke!

A   Sind das eure Bücher, Alan und Michelle?
B + C Nein, das sind ihre Bücher. (Pointing to two other students)
A   Susan und Barbara, sind das eure Bücher?

Communication for All Students

Challenge

After reading *Sebastian über seine Familie,* ask students to bring a family portrait which shows as many members of their family as possible. They could also make up a family portrait with cutouts from magazines. Students then introduce and explain the relationships among their family members to their group.

A Slower Pace

Have students identify all the family members in the picture, giving their relationship to the other people pictured.

PAGE 14

Communication for All Students

Auditory Learners

17 As an additional activity, students could bring two pictures of the same person taken many years apart. They could then elaborate on the contrast, using the vocabulary from p. 9.
Example: **meine Mutter als Dreijährige**
          meine Mutter heute

Challenge

After reading *Sebastian über seinen Bruder,* ask students to describe a sibling, a parent, or someone they admire in as much detail as possible, emphasizing physical appearance, attributes, and interests. This can be done orally or in writing.

PAGE 15

Teaching Suggestion

19 Ask students to write their own **Steckbrief**. If possible they can include a small school picture. After students have read their **Steckbrief** to the class, display them on the bulletin board under the title **SUCHE BRIEFFREUND/IN**.

Communication for All Students

A Slower Pace

22 Before students proceed with this activity, you may want to (a) review time-telling, using a clock with movable hands and stressing especially the starting times of class periods in your school; and (b) ask students to brainstorm and name all the school subjects that are offered at their school. Write these on the board or on a transparency.

Tactile Learners

25 Ask pairs of students to come up with a sketch to resemble one of the rooms described in the listening activity. Students should also label all furniture and then compare their drawings with others in the class.

Teaching Suggestion

Put the following two incomplete statements on the board or on a transparency. Ask students to choose one statement and complete it.

Ein(e) beste(r) Freund(in) muss … sein.
Ich mag Leute nicht, die …

Performance Assessment

For each **Stufe**, you will find an activity designed for performance assessment in the *Alternative Assessment Guide*. You will find the following activity on p. 32, *Alternative Assessment Guide*. Ask students to describe in writing:

  a. their best friend
     or
  b. their favorite relative.

Students should include physical attributes, interests, and at least one interesting or unusual fact about the person being described.

You may wish to evaluate students' written work using the following rubric.

Writing Rubric

	Points			
	4	3	2	1
Content (Complete – Incomplete)				
Comprehensibility (Comprehensible – Seldom comprehensible)				
Accuracy (Accurate – Seldom accurate)				
Organization (Well-organized – Poorly organized)				
Effort (Excellent – Minimal)				

18–20: A   16–17: B   14–15: C   12–13: D   Under 12: F

Assess

- Testing Program, pp. 1–4
  Quiz 1-1A, Quiz 1-1B
  Audio CD1, Tr. 15
- Student Make-Up Assignments
  Chapter 1, Alternative Quiz
- Alternative Assessment Guide, p. 32

ZWEITE STUFE

Teaching Resources
pp. 16–19

PRINT
- Lesson Planner, p. 4
- TPR Storytelling Book, pp. 2–3
- Listening Activities, pp. 4, 8–9
- Activities for Communication, pp. 3–4, 76, 77, 123–124
- Grammatikheft, pp. 4–6
- Grammar Tutor for Students of German, Chapter 1
- Übungsheft, pp. 5–7
- Testing Program, pp. 5–8
- Alternative Assessment Guide, p. 32
- Student Make-Up Assignments, Chapter 1

MEDIA
- One-Stop Planner
- Audio Compact Discs, CD1, Trs. 7, 16, 23–24
- Teaching Transparencies
  Vocabulary 1-B
  Mehr Grammatikübungen Answers
  Grammatikheft Answers
- Interactive CD-ROM Tutor, Disc 1
- DVD Tutor, Disc 1

PAGE 16

Bell Work

In pairs, have students ask each other if they bought new clothes at the beginning of the school year. What did they buy? What would they still like to buy? What types of clothes are "in" at the moment?

STANDARDS: 1.3

Building on Previous Skills

Collect some cut-out pictures of stars, fashion models, and teenagers from teen magazines and show them to the class. Ask students to describe what the people in the pictures are wearing. At the end, have students vote on the best and worst dressed. Have students put them in order from *like* to *dislike*.

Teaching Suggestion

Ask students to recall at least one item of clothing for each of the five stars mentioned in the reading selection *Popstars machen Mode*.

Group Work

29 Ask students to work with a partner or in groups of three and have them answer the questions in writing. Then ask all groups to share their answers and discuss them.

> PAGE 17

PRESENTING: Wortschatz

Bring a bag full of items of clothing and accessories including the ones featured in this **Wortschatz**. Begin by pulling out one item at a time and telling the class what it is. Once the bag has been emptied, continue with several other teacher-guided activities to help students practice the vocabulary. Ask yes/no, either/or, and open-ended questions. To encourage students to use all new items, ask them to tell you in which order to place the items back into the bag. Tell students to use sequencing words such as **zuerst, dann, nun, danach, jetzt,** and **zum Schluss.** You may want to have those words on the board or on a transparency.

TPR Total Physical Response

Use the bag of accessories you used to present the **Wortschatz**. Give commands to the class or to individual students. These commands should include the vocabulary students have just learned, words from previous chapters, and verbs such as **nehmen, geben, anprobieren, anziehen, aufsetzen,** and **umbinden.**
Examples:
Carol, nimm einen Hut!
Ben, setz die Mütze auf!

> PAGE 18

Communication for All Students

Challenge

31 After students have read the conversation *Wer ist Christiane?* on p. 17 and completed Activity 31, ask them to work with a partner to come up with a dialogue that is based on the one given here but has a different twist. The new dialogue could, for example, be about Sebastian wearing a shirt he just bought and telling Christiane where he got it and how much he paid for it.

PRESENTING: So sagt man das!

After reading the first **So sagt man das!** on p. 18 with the class, ask students to turn to their neighbors and comment on their clothing using the expressions in **So sagt man das!** as models. Partners should respond accordingly. Students alternate giving compliments and responding to compliments.

PRESENTING: So sagt man das!

Bring to class various items or pictures representing vocabulary that students learned in Level 1 and spread these out at the front of the room. (Examples: school supplies, clothes, furniture) Then hand each student an index card on which has been written, in English, the name of one of these objects. Have students come one at a time to the front of the class, pretending that they are customers searching for the items on their cards. You will play the role of the salesclerk, asking them questions from the second **So sagt man das!** on p. 18. They should respond by asking for the appropriate object, holding up the item/picture as they do so. Whenever possible, ask a follow-up question as well. (Example: Was bekommen Sie? — Ich brauche ein Hemd in Blau. — Aus Baumwolle oder aus Seide? — Aus Baumwolle, bitte.)

> PAGE 19

Building on Previous Skills

33 Before students proceed with the role-playing activity, you may want to review fabrics. (Examples: aus Wolle, Baumwolle, Seide, Polyester)

Communication for All Students

Challenge

35 Ask students to create their own short **Radioreklame**, similar to the one in Activity 34. Ask several students to tape their radio commercials and then play them for the class.

Reteaching: Clothing

Ask students to name the types of clothing they would wear during different seasons for occasions such as a party, a dance, a family reunion, or the theater.

Game

Begin this game by making the following statement: **Ich packe meinen Koffer und nehme eine Sonnenbrille mit.** The student closest to you repeats your statement and must add his or her own item. That student then turns to the next student, who must repeat all that was said previously and then add a new item, and so on. If a student makes a mistake, he or she is out of the game. The winner is the student who can remember all the items that were packed in the correct order.

Reviewing: The command form

To prepare for this activity, have pictures of fruit and vegetables on hand. Give students commands using verbs such as **kaufen, holen, einkaufen gehen.**
Examples:
Gena, kauf bitte 1 kg Bananen. Jim, hol bitte den Spinat und die Gurken.

Assess

- Testing Program, pp. 5–8
  Quiz 1-2A, Quiz 1-2B
  Audio CD1, Tr. 16
- Student Make-Up Assignments
  Chapter 1, Alternative Quiz
- Alternative Assessment Guide, p. 32

PAGES 20–21

ZUM LESEN

Teaching Resources
pp. 20–21

PRINT
- Lesson Planner, p. 6
- Übungsheft, p. 8
- Reading Strategies and Skills, Chapter 1
- Lies mit mir! 2, Chapter 1

MEDIA
- One-Stop Planner

Prereading
Building Context

Ask students to name different ways to communicate and get in touch with friends. After you have made a list of these different means of communication, ask students which of these they like and why. (Examples: letters, phone calls, faxes, e-mail)

Teacher Note

Activities 1 and 2 are prereading activities.

Reading
Skimming and Scanning

After students have completed Activity 3, put the words they recognized on the board or on a transparency as a visual aid. Quickly go over the list to familiarize everybody with the meanings, using synonyms and paraphrasing rather than translations.

Cooperative Learning

Divide students into groups of three. Each group should have a writer, a reporter, and a discussion leader. Set a time limit for this assignment of approximately 30 minutes. Ask each group to do Activities 5 and 6. Once students have completed the activities, ask two or three group reporters to share their groups' answers with the rest of the class.

Thinking Critically

5 6 Drawing Inferences Draw two columns on the board, one for each of Questions 5 and 6. Ask students to reread the letters and elicit specific words or phrases that would help answer each of the questions. What types of words helped them out with their answers?

Post-Reading
Teacher Note

Activity 8 is a post-reading task that will show whether students can apply what they have learned.

 Game

This game will help students practice the vocabulary in the reading section. On a transparency, write several nouns that could be part of a compound that you feel students could recognize. In addition, write the three definite articles on top of the transparency.

```
            Rad            Garten
Fuß
                Stadt           Turnier
            Tennis         Farbe
Hof
                Haus            Zentrum
            Training       Ball
Fußball
                Freizeit        Fahrrad
            Haar            Bummel
                Clique
Tour
                            Aufgaben
```

Students work in teams of two or three with a sheet of paper and a pencil in front of them. Within a given amount of time (1-2 minutes), teams write down as many compounds as they can build, using the nouns on the transparency. When time is called, pencils must be put away, and teams read out the words they came up with. You are the final judge as to the authenticity of the word. The team that builds the most correct compound nouns wins.

Zum Lesen Answers
Answers to Activity 1   letters
Answers to Activity 2   title indicates who is writing (two cousins)
Answers to Activity 3   b
Answers to Activity 4   Benjamin is writing because Andrea is coming to Munich. He informs her of his busy weekend schedule. Andrea responds by listing her plans for the weekend.
Answers to Activity 5   Their schedules do not match.
Answers to Activity 6   It does not seem that Benjamin is very excited to see his cousin. He does not try to change his plans for the weekend because of Andrea's visit. She should not count on seeing him.
Answers to Activity 7   Answers will vary.

▶ PAGE 22

LANDESKUNDE

Teaching Resources
p. 22

PRINT
- Video Guide, pp. 3, 5–7
- Übungsheft, p. 9

MEDIA
- One-Stop Planner
- Video Program
  Videocassette 1, 11:37–16:20
- DVD Tutor, Disc 1
- Audio Compact Discs, CD1, Trs. 8–11
- Interactive CD-ROM Tutor, Disc 1

Teacher Notes

- The **Landeskunde** interviews are recorded on compact disc and videocassette. Before doing the activities on this page, go over the prereading activity with your students. Then play the compact disc or have students watch the interviews on the video.

- Before students read the interviews, you may want to tell them that **der Sakko** (**das Sakko** in southern Germany and Austria) means *sports coat*.

Communication for All Students

Group Work

Have students work in groups of four. Students take turns reading the interviews and then answer Questions 1 through 3 of Activity A. Have two or three groups share their information with the rest of the class, using as much German as possible.

Thinking Critically

Drawing Inferences Do Activity B with the whole class. Ask students to go over the three interviews again, scanning the interviews for connectors, sequencing words, and phrases that express reasoning. Make a list on the board or on a transparency as students call these words and phrases out.

Teacher Note

Mention to your students that the **Landeskunde** will also be included in Quiz 1-2B and Quiz 1-3B.

STANDARDS: 1.2

DRITTE STUFE

Teaching Resources
pp. 23–25

PRINT
- Lesson Planner, p. 5
- TPR Storytelling Book, pp. 4–5
- Listening Activities, pp. 5, 9–10
- Activities for Communication, pp. 5–6, 123–124
- Grammatikheft, pp. 7–9
- Grammar Tutor for Students of German, Chapter 1
- Übungsheft, pp. 10–12
- Testing Program, pp. 9–12
- Alternative Assessment Guide, p. 32
- Student Make-Up Assignments, Chapter 1

MEDIA
- One-Stop Planner
- Audio Compact Discs, CD1, Trs. 12–14, 17, 25–26
- Teaching Transparencies
  Situation 1-2
  Mehr Grammatikübungen Answers
  Grammatikheft Answers
- Interactive CD-ROM Tutor, Disc 1
- DVD Tutor, Disc 1

▶ PAGE 23

 Bell Work

Ask students what their favorite weekend activities are. Remind them to use expressions such as **gern** and **Lieblings-**, as well as sequencing words.

Building on Previous Skills

37 Before students make their lists, review sequencing words and discuss their usefulness. You should emphasize to your class the importance of such words and how they enhance the quality of language.

Portfolio Assessment

37 You may want to suggest this activity as a written portfolio item for your students. See *Alternative Assessment Guide*, p. 18.

KAPITEL 1 DRITTE STUFE

PRESENTING: So sagt man das!

After reading **So sagt man das!**, give students the opportunity to practice the expressions with a partner. Have some expressions on the board or on a transparency, such as the following:
wenn es regnet
am Donnerstag
am 4. Juli
zu deinem Geburtstag
Students can use these phrases when asking each other about making plans.

PRESENTING: Ein wenig Grammatik

The verbs wollen and möchte To review the forms of **wollen** and **möchte**, prepare a *Tic Tac Toe* grid on a transparency, using several conjugated forms of the verbs. Divide the class into two groups and ask students to come up with correct sentences using the verb forms shown.

PAGE 24

Communication for All Students

Group Work

41 Ask students to work in groups of three to practice reading the two conversations above Activity 41. After several readings, have the groups answer the questions in Activity 41.

Challenge

41 After students have worked through Activity 41 in groups, ask each group to create a new dialogue to accompany the two pictures. To complete the activity, each group has to come up with two questions about their new dialogue, which the rest of the class should be able to answer.

PAGE 25

PRESENTING: So sagt man das!

To practice the expressions for ordering food, have students role-play the conversation with a partner. Ask students to read with expression and switch roles for additional practice.

📁 Portfolio Assessment

44 You might want to suggest this activity as an oral portfolio item for your students. See *Alternative Assessment Guide*, p. 18.

PRESENTING: So sagt man das!

After reviewing the expressions used to talk about how something tastes, reinforce this vocabulary by asking students to share their likes and dislikes of certain foods. Most students should be familiar with the USDA Food Guide Pyramid. Ask the home economics teacher to lend you a large poster. Ask students about their likes and dislikes as you point to different foods.

Cultures and Communities

Teaching Suggestion

To prepare for this activity, make a number of flashcards on which you write types of foods from the four categories listed below. Write one food item on each card.
Examples:

Vorspeisen:	Käse, Tomatensalat, Gurkensalat, Hühnersuppe, Gemüsesuppe
Getränke:	Limo, Mineralwasser, Kaffee, Tee, Milch
Hauptspeisen:	Bratwurst, gegrilltes Hähnchen, Spaghetti, Pizza, Leberkäs
Nachspeisen:	Kuchen, Obst, Obstsalat, Eis, Pudding

Distribute the cards among students (one per student). Students are then asked to walk around the class and find a student who has a food from the same category on his or her card.
Example:

—Hast du auch eine Vorspeise?
—Nein, tut mir Leid, ich habe eine Nachspeise.

Have the four categories written on the board. Once all students have found the other students who belong to their food category, they share the names of those students with the rest of the class.

Von der Schule zum Beruf

46

You may wish to set aside some class time to have students present their role plays to the class.

Teacher Note

For additional open-ended activities, see the **Zum Sprechen** and **Zum Schreiben** suggestions for Chapter 1 in the *Komm mit! Interactive CD-ROM Tutor* and the *Alternative Assessment Guide*, p. 46.

Video Wrap-up

Videocassette 1, 06:09–19:00
Videocassette 5 (captioned version, 01:22–06:11)
DVD Tutor, Disc 1

At this time, you might want to use the video resources for additional review and enrichment. These resources are also available via the Enhanced Online Student Edition.

See *Video Guide* for suggestions regarding:

- **Sebastian stellt seine Familie vor.** Dramatic episode
- **Landeskunde** Interviews
- **Videoclips** Authentic footage

Assess

▸ Testing Program, pp. 9–12
  Quiz 1-3A, Quiz 1-3B
  Audio CD1, Tr. 17

▸ Student Make-Up Assignments
  Chapter 1, Alternative Quiz

▸ Alternative Assessment Guide, p. 32

> **PAGES 26–29**

MEHR GRAMMATIKÜBUNGEN

The **Mehr Grammatikübungen** activities are designed as supplemental activities for the grammatical concepts presented in the chapter. You might use them as additional practice, for review, or for assessment.

For more grammar presentations, review, and practice, refer to the following:
- Grammatikheft
- Grammar Tutor for Students of German
- Grammar Summary on pp. R20–R36
- Übungsheft
- Grammar and Vocabulary quizzes (Testing Program)
- Test Generator
- Interactive CD-ROM Tutor
- **Interaktive Spiele** at **go.hrw.com**

> **PAGE 30**

KANN ICH'S WIRKLICH?

This page helps students prepare for the test. It is a brief checklist of the major points covered in the chapter. The students should be reminded that it is only a checklist and not necessarily everything that will appear on the test.

For additional self check options, refer students to the *Grammar Tutor,* the *Interactive CD-ROM Tutor,* and the Online self-test for this chapter.

> **PAGE 31**

WORTSCHATZ

Review and Assess

Teaching Suggestions

- At this level you should try to give definitions in German whenever possible to help build vocabulary through synonyms and definitions. Playing the Circumlocution game, **Das treffende Wort suchen,** is an excellent way to help students think in terms of synonyms and definitions. See the description of the Circumlocution game on p. 3C.

- To review family members, students could write the definition of each word in the form of a riddle. Have each student read his or her riddle to the rest of the class and have them guess who that person is.
  Example: Vater—Diese Person ist der Onkel von meinem Cousin.

- Arrange all the adjectives of the **Erste Stufe** randomly on a transparency. Give students a predetermined amount of time to categorize the words under certain headings. (Examples: Größe, Haarfarbe, Interessen)

Circumlocution

To review, play **Das treffende Wort suchen** with the different sports from the **Erste Stufe** vocabulary or with the articles of clothing and accessories from the **Zweite Stufe** vocabulary. Both categories lend themselves well to circumlocution because the nouns in these categories can be easily described. See p. 3C for procedures.

Teacher Note

Give the **Kapitel 1** Chapter Test: *Testing Program,* pp. 13–18
Audio CD 1, Trs. 18–20.

KAPITEL

1
Bei den Baumanns

Objectives

In this chapter you will review and practice how to

Erste Stufe

- ask for and give information about yourself and others
- describe yourself and others
- express likes and dislikes
- identify people and places

Zweite Stufe

- give and respond to compliments
- express wishes when buying things

Dritte Stufe

- make plans
- order food and beverages
- talk about how something tastes

Visit Holt Online
go.hrw.com
KEYWORD: WK3 BAYERN-1
Online Edition

◂ Basti, seine Geschwister, Eltern und Großeltern

Los geht's! · *Sebastian stellt seine Familie vor*

Strategie Verstehen
Look at the images for this story. Where do you think Sebastian is? What do you think he is probably talking about?

Sebastian   Robert

Los geht's! is an abridged version of the video episode.

Sebastian: Hallo! Ich heiße Sebastian Baumann. Ich bin fünfzehn Jahre alt und wohne hier in Grünwald; das ist ein Vorort von München. In diesem Haus haben wir eine schöne Wohnung, hier oben im zweiten Stock.

❶

❷ Das ist unser Wohnzimmer. Wie ihr seht ist es ziemlich groß, aber es ist doch ganz gemütlich. Schaut mal, die vielen Bücher! Meine Eltern lesen gern. Sie lesen eigentlich alles, von Grass bis Goethe.

❸ Und sie hören gern Musik. Hier: die vielen Platten und CDs. Hören wir mal, was aufliegt! — Ich hab's gewusst: etwas Klassisches!

❹ Und hier unsere Familienfotos. Meine Großeltern, meine Eltern, meine Geschwister: mein Bruder Robert, das hier bin ich, und meine Schwester, Beatrice. Und Artus, unser ... nein, Vatis Hund.

sechs   STANDARDS: 1.2   KAPITEL 1   Bei den Baumanns

5
Sebastian: Hallo, altes Haus!
Robert: Ja, was gibt's? Was willst du? Brauchst du wieder Geld?
Sebastian: Nein, ich möchte nur „Grüß Gott" sagen.
Robert: Na ja, sag's schon! Dann kannst du wieder gehen.
Sebastian: Ich geh ja gleich.

6
Sebastian: Mein Bruder Robert ist immer fleißig. Er ist gut in der Schule, bekommt gute Noten. Der Robert ist auch gut in Sport. Ein super Tennisspieler!
Robert: Super? Na ja, das stimmt nicht, aber ganz gut. So, noch was?
Sebastian: Nein, nein, wir lassen dich jetzt in Ruhe. Tschau!

7
Sebastian: Das ist mein Reich. Nicht sehr groß, aber mir gefällt's. Bett, Tisch, Schrank … Entschuldigt bitte, ich hab mein Zimmer nicht aufgeräumt!—
Wie gefallen euch meine Pokale? Tennis, Fußball …
Und Hobbys hab ich auch: ich spiele Gitarre, nicht sehr gut, aber es geht. Und in Schach bin ich auch nicht schlecht. Und ich lese auch ganz gerne, besonders Action.

Note: Have students guess the meaning of **"Hallo, altes Haus!"** (Hello, old pal!)

LOS GEHT'S! STANDARDS: 1.2 *sieben* 7

1 Was passiert hier?

These activities check for global comprehension only. Students should not yet be expected to produce language modeled in Los geht's!

Verstehst du alles, was Basti und Robert sagen? Beantworte die Fragen!
1. Wo wohnen die Baumanns? **1. In Grünwald, München**
2. Haben sie ihr eigenes Haus oder eine Wohnung?
3. Wie groß ist die Familie? **3. Sieben Personen, ein Hund.**
4. Was erzählt Basti von seinen Eltern? **4. Hören gern Musik und lesen viel**
5. Sieht Robert seinen Bruder gern? Was meinst du? **5. Nein.**
6. Was für ein Schüler ist Robert? **6. Fleißig.**
7. Sebastian sagt: „Das ist mein Reich". Was meint er damit? **7. Er hat ein eigenes Zimmer.**
8. Welche Hobbys und Interessen hat Basti? **8. Gitarre, Schach, Lesen, Tennis, Fußball**

2 Genauer lesen

Lies den Text noch einmal und beantworte diese Fragen! **1. Groß, gemütlich; nicht sehr groß, gemütlich.**
1. Mit welchen Wörtern beschreibt Basti das Wohnzimmer und sein Zimmer?
2. Mit welchen Wörtern beschreibt er seine Familie? **2. Eltern: lesen, Musik; Robert: fleißig, gut in Schule u. Sport.**
3. Robert hat es nicht gern, dass Basti in sein Zimmer kommt. Was sagt er, damit (*so that*) Basti wieder geht? **3. „Dann kannst du wieder gehen."**
4. Wie beschreibt Basti seinen Bruder? **4. Fleißig, gut in Schule, Sport besonders Tennis.**
5. Was sagt Basti über sein Zimmer, seine Pokale und seine Hobbys?
   5. Mein Reich; Pokale: Tennis, Fußball; Hobbys: Gitarre, Schach, lese gern Action.

3 Wer ist das?

Lies die Personenbeschreibungen und rate, wer das ist!
1. Ich wohne in einer ziemlich großen Wohnung in Grünwald. Mein Mann und ich hören gern klassische Musik und lesen gern. Wir lesen alles — von Grass bis Goethe! Ich habe drei Kinder: zwei Söhne und eine Tochter. Wer bin ich? **1. Frau Baumann (Bastis Mutter).**
2. Ich wohne mit meiner Familie in einem Vorort von München. Meine Eltern sind sehr nett, und ich habe auch zwei Brüder, Sebastian und Robert. Wer bin ich? **2. Beatrice (Bastis Schwester).**
3. Mein Sohn und seine Familie wohnen in Grünwald, also nicht weit von hier. Ab und zu besuchen sie uns, und das macht viel Spaß. Meine Frau und ich haben die drei Kinder — Sebastian, Robert und Beatrice — sehr gern. Wer bin ich? **3. Bastis Großvater.**
4. Ich wohne bei einer sehr netten Familie in Grünwald. Wir haben eine große Wohnung, und das gefällt mir. Die Kinder in der Familie sind sehr nett und spielen oft mit mir, aber eigentlich liebe ich den Vater der Familie! Wer bin ich? **4. Artus, der Hund.**

4 Was passt zusammen?

Welche Sätze passen zusammen?
1. Die vielen Bücher! **c**
2. Hört mal, was aufliegt! **e**
3. Was gibt's? **d**
4. Der Robert ist ein super Tennisspieler. **a**
5. Das ist mein Zimmer. **b**

a. Super nicht, aber ganz gut.
b. Nicht groß, aber es gefällt mir.
c. Meine Eltern lesen gern.
d. Ich will nur „Grüß Gott" sagen.
e. Etwas Klassisches!

5 Und du?

Schreib Folgendes auf eine Liste! *Answers may vary.*
1. wo du wohnst
2. wie groß deine Familie ist
3. welche Hobbys deine Familie hat
4. wie dein Zimmer aussieht

Erste Stufe

Objectives Asking for and giving information about yourself and others; describing yourself and others; expressing likes and dislikes; identifying people and places

Was für eine Person bist du?

Aussehen
- ☐ groß
- ☐ klein
- ☐ schlank
- ☐ vollschlank
- ☐ attraktiv
- ☐ nicht sehr attraktiv
- ☐ hübsch

Haarfarbe
- ☐ schwarz   ☐ blond
- ☐ hellbraun
- ☐ dunkelbraun
- ☐ rötlich

Haarlänge
- ☐ kurz   ☐ lang
- ☐ mittellang

Augenfarbe
- ☐ braun   ☐ blau
- ☐ grün   ☐ grau

Brille
- ☐ habe eine Brille
- ☐ trage Kontaktlinsen

Eigenschaften
- ☐ nett
- ☐ nicht nett
- ☐ freundlich
- ☐ unfreundlich
- ☐ intelligent
- ☐ sympathisch
- ☐ unsympathisch
- ☐ ruhig   ☐ nervös
- ☐ kinderlieb
- ☐ tierlieb
- ☐ langweilig
- ☐ sportlich
- ☐ unsportlich
- ☐ faul   ☐ fleißig

Sport
- ☐ Fußball   ☐ Football
- ☐ Volleyball
- ☐ Basketball
- ☐ Tennis
- ☐ Skilaufen
- ☐ Schwimmen
- ☐ Golf   ☐ Radfahren
- ☐ Schlittschuhlaufen
- ☐ Rollschuhlaufen

Interessen
- ☐ ausgehen
- ☐ tanzen
- ☐ lesen
- ☐ reisen
- ☐ Musik hören
- ☐ kochen
- ☐ fotografieren
- ☐ Musik machen
- ☐ basteln
- ☐ zeichnen
- ☐ malen
- ☐ (Briefmarken) sammeln

Lies den Text! Welche Wörter und Ausdrücke kennst du schon? Welche sind neu? Kannst du raten, was die neuen Wörter und Ausdrücke bedeuten? Wie beschreibst du dich?

6 Welche Beschreibung passt zu welchem Foto?

Zuhören Welche Beschreibung (*description*) passt zu welchem Foto? — Schreib die Zahlen 1-5 auf ein Blatt Papier und daneben den Buchstaben (a., b., c., d., e.) des Fotos, das zur Beschreibung passt!

a.

b.

c.

d.

e.

Wortschatz

Wie charakterisierst du diese Leute? Er/Sie ist...

 neugierig
 lustig
 sympathisch
 unsympathisch
 gut gelaunt
 schlecht gelaunt

Welche Hobbys haben diese Leute? Was machen sie?

 Er rodelt.
 Sie macht Bogenschießen.
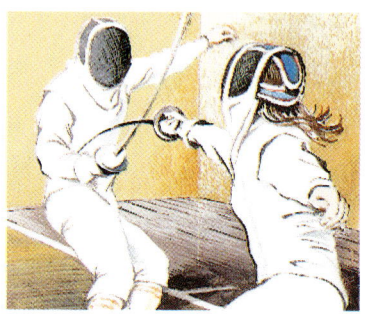 Die beiden fechten.

Diese Leute machen Leichtathletik. Was machen sie?

 Kugelstoßen
 Speerwerfen
 Diskuswerfen
 Langstreckenlauf

 100-Meter-Lauf
 Weitsprung
 Hürdenlauf
 Stabhochsprung

 Übungsheft, S. 2, Ü. 1–3
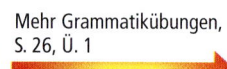 Grammatikheft, S. 1, Ü. 1–3

Mehr Grammatikübungen, S. 26, Ü. 1

7 Und du? Answers may vary. E.g.: **Ich mache ... ; sie macht ...**

Sprechen Sag deiner Partnerin, welche Hobbys du hast und welchen Sport du machst! Was macht deine Partnerin?

So sagt man das!

Asking for and giving information about yourself and others; describing yourself and others; expressing likes and dislikes

Schon bekannt

When talking about yourself and others, you have used a number of words and expressions.

If someone asks:

Wer ist das?
Wie alt ist sie?
Du hast auch einen Bruder. Wie sieht er aus?

Macht er Sport?
Beschreibe deine Schwester!

Und du? Was machst du gern, was machst du nicht gern?

Your response might be:

Das ist meine Schwester.
Sie ist 19 Jahre alt.
Er ist groß und ziemlich schlank und hat braune Haare und dunkle Augen.
Nein, er ist faul.
Sie ist intelligent, freundlich und sehr fleißig.
Ich lese gern und höre gern Musik. Aber ich koche nicht gern.

Remember: you don't always have to answer with a complete sentence. How might you answer these questions more informally, using phrases?

 Grammatikheft, S. 2, Ü. 4–5

8 Wer ist das? Rate mal!

Sprechen Beschreibe einen Klassenkameraden oder eine Klassenkameradin! Erwähne Alter, Aussehen, Haarfarbe, Augenfarbe, Eigenschaften und Sport und Hobbys! Deine Mitschüler sollen dann erraten, wer das ist. *Answers may vary.*

9 Für mein Notizbuch *Answers may vary.*

Schreiben Beschreibe dich selbst! Erwähne alle Eigenschaften, die du hast, und erwähne alle Sportarten und Hobbys, die du hast! *Answers may vary.*

10 Wer ist das? *Script and answers on p. 3G*

CD 1
Tr. 4

Zuhören/Schreiben Vier deutsche Schüler und Schülerinnen erzählen über sich selbst. Mach dir Notizen, damit du über einen Schüler berichten kannst! Verwende die folgenden Kategorien, um deine Notizen zu organisieren: Augen, Haare, Eigenschaften, Interessen, usw.!

Ein wenig Grammatik

Schon bekannt

When you describe yourself or someone else, you use the verb **sein**. To talk about what you have or someone else has, you need the present tense forms of **haben**. To review the forms of **sein** and **haben**, see the Grammar Summary.

 Mehr Grammatikübungen, S. 27, Ü. 2

ERSTE STUFE

11 Über einen Schüler berichten

Sprechen Such dir einen von den vier Schülern von Übung 10 aus und berichte über ihn oder sie! Deine Mitschüler erraten, wen du beschreibst. Answers may vary.

12 Ratespiel

Sprechen Bildet zwei Gruppen! Gruppe A sieht zur Tafel hin, Gruppe B sieht auf die Wand hinten in der Klasse. Gruppe A wählt eine Schülerin aus. Alle Schüler von Gruppe B stellen jetzt Fragen, um die Schülerin aus der Gruppe A zu identifizieren. Tauscht dann die Rollen aus!

Gruppe B	Gruppe A
Schüler 1 Ist das ein Junge?	Schüler 1 Nein.
Schüler 2 Hat sie blonde Haare?	Schüler 2 Ja.
Schüler 3 Hat sie lange Haare?	Schüler 3 Ja.
Schüler 4 Hat sie graue Augen?	Schüler 4 Nein.
Schüler 5 Ist sie …	…
Schüler 6 …	…
Schüler 7 …	…
Schüler 8 Ist das die (Jessica)?	Schüler 8 Ja!

Ein wenig Grammatik

Schon bekannt

In order to talk about your interests, you will have to use verbs, such as **spielen** or **machen**. These verbs are regular and always have the same endings. You can review these endings in the Grammar Summary. Some of the verbs you will use are *stem-changing verbs,* that is, verbs whose stem vowel changes in the **du-** and **er/sie**-forms. Two examples are **lesen** and **essen**. The stem-changing verbs are reviewed in the Grammar Summary.

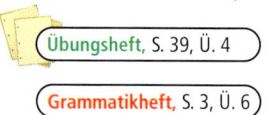

Übungsheft, S. 39, Ü. 4

Grammatikheft, S. 3, Ü. 6

Mehr Grammatikübungen, S. 27, Ü. 3

13 Was wollt ihr von den Zwillingen wissen?

Sprechen Zwei Klassenkameraden übernehmen die Rollen von Herbert und Günther. Fragt die „Zwillinge", was ihr von ihnen wissen wollt! Einer antwortet für die beiden. Tauscht die Rollen aus! Questions and answers may vary.

Kennst du auch Zwillinge?

Wie sehen sie aus?

Herbert und Günther sind Zwillinge. Sie sind gleich alt, und sie sehen sich sehr ähnlich. Zwillinge haben oft auch die gleichen Eigenschaften und die gleichen Interessen.

BEISPIEL
DU Zuerst einmal, wer ist wer?
GÜNTHER Also, ich bin der Günther.
HERBERT Und ich der Herbert.
DU Günther, wie alt sind Sie?
GÜNTHER Ich … wir …

14 Jetzt spielt ihr Zwillinge

Sprechen Bildet Gruppen zu dritt! Zwei von euch sind „Zwillinge", und der dritte fragt die beiden nach Aussehen, Haarfarbe, Augenfarbe, Eigenschaften und Interessen. Tauscht dann die Rollen aus! Questions and answers may vary.

So sagt man das!

Identifying people and places

Schon bekannt

When you want to know who someone ist, you might ask:

Wer ist das, Sebastian?
Und wer ist das Mädchen?
Ist das dein Großvater?
Und das ist deine Mutter, ja?
Und wo ist dein Zimmer?

The response might be:

Das ist mein Bruder, der Robert.
Meine Schwester, die Beatrice.
Ja, das ist mein Großvater.
Stimmt!
Hier! Das ist mein Zimmer.

15 Die Familie Baumann

Sprechen Schau dir die Fotos der Familie Baumann an! Dann beantworte die Fragen mit mehreren Sätzen!

die Kinder

Beatrice
Tochter
Schwester

Sebastian
Sohn
Bruder

Robert
Sohn
Bruder

die Eltern

Hans Baumann, Vater
Elfriede Baumann, Mutter

1. Wer sind Hans und Elfriede Baumann?
   1. Die Eltern von Sebastian, Beatrice und Robert.
2. Wer ist Beatrice?
   2. Die Tochter von … ; die Schwester von …
3. Wer ist Robert?
4. Beschreibe zwei Familienmitglieder!
   3. Der Sohn von … ; der Bruder von …   4. Answers may vary.

16 Klamotten beschreiben

Sprechen Sag deinem Partner, was die Baumanns in diesen Fotos anhaben! Tauscht die Rollen aus! E.g.: Beatrice hat eine Jeansjacke an.

> **Ein wenig Grammatik**
>
> *Schon bekannt*
>
> When you want to identify *whose* father, mother, etc. someone is, you use the possessive adjectives **mein, dein, sein,** and **ihr.** Remember that the ending of the possessive adjective is determined by the noun to which it refers. You can review the singular possessive adjectives in the Grammar Summary.
>
>
> Übungsheft, S. 3, Ü. 5   Mehr Grammatikübungen, S. 28, Ü. 4

Sebastian über seine Familie

Das hier ist meine Familie, meine Eltern, meine Geschwister und meine Großeltern. Die Oma und der Opa sitzen hier in der ersten Reihe. Neben dem Opa kniet mein Vater, und neben ihm liegt Artus, unser… nein, Vatis Hund! Hinter meinem Vater steht meine Mutter und neben ihr der Robert und die Beatrice. Und der da ganz links in der zweiten Reihe, das bin ich!

Erzähle, was Sebastian über seine Familie sagt!

17 Meine Familie und Freunde

1. **Sprechen** Bring Fotos von zwei Familienmitgliedern mit in die Klasse und beschreibe sie! Zeig deiner Partnerin ein Foto und sag ihr, wer diese Person ist, wie alt sie ist, wie sie aussieht und welche Interessen sie hat! 1. E.g.: **Das ist mein Bruder. Er ist 10 Jahre alt.**
2. **Sprechen** Jetzt zeigst du deinem Partner das zweite Foto. Dein Partner stellt Fragen über diese Person, und du beantwortest sie. Tauscht dann die Rollen aus! 2. E.g.: **Wer ist das Mädchen?**
3. **Sprechen** Erzähle jetzt einem Partner, was du über die Familie eines anderen Partners weißt! 3. E.g.: **Er/sie hat zwei Brüder. Die Familie hat einen Hund.**

18 Für mein Notizbuch

Schreiben Beschreibe einen Freund oder jemanden aus deiner Familie! Schreib, wer die Person ist und erwähne Alter, Aussehen, Eigenschaften, Sport und Hobbys! Answers may vary.

Sebastian über seinen Bruder

Mein Bruder, der Robert, ist immer fleißig. Er ist gut in der Schule, bekommt immer gute Noten. Er ist auch gut in Sport. Ein super Tennisspieler!

Erzähle, was Sebastian über seinen Bruder sagt!

19 Beatrices Steckbrief

Lesen/Sprechen Lies zuerst diesen Steckbrief, und beantworte die folgenden Fragen auf Deutsch.

1. Wo wohnt Beatrice? 1. **Sie wohnt in Grünwald.**
2. Was sind ihre Lieblingsfächer? 2. **Musik, Deutsch u. Physik.**
3. Welches Fach hat sie nicht gern? 3. **Geschichte.**

Dann erzähle einem Partner, was du über Beatrice gelesen hast!

Name: Beatrice Baumann, 17
Wohnort: Grünwald
Schule: Gymnasium in Grünwald
Lieblingsfächer: Musik, Deutsch, Physik
nicht gern: Geschichte
Sport: Tennis

20 Wir über uns Script and answers on p. 3G

Zuhören Hör zu, was diese Schüler über sich sagen! Mach dir Notizen!
CD 1 Tr. 5

21 Über wen sprichst du?

Sprechen Such dir einen Schüler aus, über den du dir Notizen gemacht hast, und erzähle deinem Partner über diesen Schüler! Dein Partner verbessert dich, wenn du etwas sagst, was nicht stimmt. Tauscht dann die Rollen aus!

22 Mein Stundenplan

Lesen/Sprechen Such dir einen anderen Partner! Jeder nimmt seinen Stundenplan in die Hand. Fragt euch jetzt gegenseitig (*in turns*), welche Fächer ihr in welcher Stunde habt! Fragt euch auch, welche Fächer ihr gern und welche ihr nicht gern habt!

BEISPIEL Was hast du um (8 Uhr 10)?

23 Für mein Notizbuch

 Übungsheft, S. 4, Ü. 6–7

Schreiben Schreib in dein Notizbuch, auf welche Schule du gehst, welche Fächer du gern hast und welche nicht! Bist du gut in Sport? Bist du vielleicht ein(e) super Volleyballspieler(in)?

24 Unsere Zimmer Scripts and answers on p. 3G

Zuhören/Schreiben Zwei Schüler beschreiben ihr Zimmer. Schreib auf, welche Möbel jeder in seinem Zimmer hat!
CD 1 Tr. 6

25 Wie sieht das Zimmer aus?

Lesen/Sprechen Such dir eine Partnerin! Nimm deine Notizen von Übung 24, und beschreibe eins von den beiden Zimmern! Deine Partnerin muss raten, welches Zimmer du beschrieben hast.

26 Für mein Notizbuch

Schreiben Schreib, wie dein Zimmer aussieht! Welche Möbel hast du? Sind sie alt oder neu? Gefallen sie dir?

Storytelling Book pp. 2–3

Zweite Stufe

Objectives Giving and responding to compliments; expressing wishes when buying things

WK3 BAYERN-1

POPSTARS MACHEN MODE

Bei Popstars spielt der Look eine wichtige Rolle — und du kannst die Styling-Ideen deiner Idole leicht kopieren.

Pop-Superstar Madonna hat immer wieder einen neuen Look. Durch Styling und Klamotten macht sie ihr Image. Ihre Fans sind begeistert! Typisch: Hot Pants, geknotetes Hemd und ganz viele Metallketten.

Bist du ein Prince-Fan? Na, dann sollst du unbedingt seine Lieblingsfarbe Lila tragen. Und sonst? Viel Glitter, hohe Stiefel, Satinmäntel und Rüschenhemden.

Die Beatles — eine Legende wird wieder modern! Mit dem Beatle-Revival sind die bunten Paradejacken von „Sergeant Pepper's Lonely Hearts Club Band" heute in.

Magst du das Outfit von Ex-Punker Billy Idol, oder findest du vielleicht das Minikleid der sensationellen Rock-Lady Tina Turner gut? Den Look kannst du haben — und oft viel billiger als bei den Stars! Mach mal einen Bummel durch den Flohmarkt oder schau mal in einen Secondhand-Laden rein!

27 Über Popstars

Lesen/Sprechen Was ist der Hauptgedanke (*main idea*) dieses Artikels? Welche Wörter kennst du?

1. Many pop stars like to wear bizarre, flashy clothes.
2. If you dress like the pop stars you admire, you will be more like them.
3. It is relatively easy to imitate the look of many pop stars.

28 Wer ist das?

Lesen/Sprechen Lies den Artikel noch einmal. Welche Beschreibung (*description*) passt zu welcher Person?

1. Madonna c.
2. Prince d.
3. Beatles b.
4. Billy Idol e.
5. Tina Turner a.

a. sensationelle Rock-Lady
b. eine Legende, die wieder modern wird
c. trägt Hot Pants, geknotetes Hemd und ganz viele Metallketten.
d. viel Glitter, hohe Stiefel, Satinmäntel
e. Ex-Punker

29 Beantworte die Fragen!

1. Sie hat immer wieder einen neuen Look.
2. Lila tragen; viel Glitter; hohe Stiefel; Satinmäntel u. Rüschenhemden.
3. Bummel durch den Flohmarkt oder in einen Secondhand-Laden reinschauen.

Lesen/Sprechen Lies den Artikel noch einmal, und beantworte dann diese Fragen.

1. How does Madonna create her image?
2. What would you need to wear in order to look like Prince?
3. What is a good way to find what you need in order to look like your favorite pop star?

Wortschatz

Was brauchst du? — Ich brauche ...

ein Stirnband · einen Schal · eine Mütze · einen Hut

eine Halskette · ein Paar Ohrringe · ein Armband · eine Handtasche

Grammatikheft, S. 4, Ü. 7

 30 Was trägst du, wenn du ausgehst? Questions and answers may vary.

Sprechen Frag einen Partner, was er trägt, wenn er ausgeht! Du sagst ihm dann, was du trägst.

WER IST CHRISTIANE?

Sebastian weiß, wo er heute seine Schwester finden kann, denn die Beatrice sitzt an diesem Tag immer mit Freunden in einem Café.

CHRISTIANE   Basti, du siehst heute so fesch aus! Das Tuch da, das ist echt schick!
SEBASTIAN   Wirklich?
CHRISTIANE   Wirklich! Ist das neu?
SEBASTIAN   Das hab ich schon lange.
CHRISTIANE   Wirklich?
SEBASTIAN   Ja, das ist schon alt.

31 Was ist passiert?

Lesen/Sprechen Beantworte diese Fragen auf Englisch oder auf Deutsch!
1. Wie begrüßt Christiane den Sebastian? Was bedeutet das? 1. „Basti, du siehst heute so …" Ein Kompliment.
2. Freut sich der Basti über das Kompliment? Was sagt er? 2. „Wirklich?"
3. Warum fragt Christiane, ob das Tuch neu ist? 3. Sie kennt es nicht. Sie sieht das Preisschild.
4. Was antwortet Sebastian? Warum sagt er wohl das? 4. „Ja, das ist schon alt." Er hat es gerade gekauft.

So sagt man das!

Giving and responding to compliments   Schon bekannt

When you want to compliment someone you might say:

    Du siehst heute so fesch aus!
    Das Tuch da, das ist echt schick!
    Es gefällt mir.

Your friend might respond:

    Meinst du?
    Wirklich?
    Ehrlich?

Übungsheft, S. 5, Ü. 1–2

Grammatikheft, S. 4, Ü. 8

How might you respond after your friend asks **Wirklich?** or **Meinst du?**

32 Komplimente machen   Answers may vary. E.g.: Die Jeans gefällt mir. — Ehrlich?

Sprechen Such dir an deinem Partner etwas aus, was dir gefällt, und mach ihm oder ihr ein Kompliment! Dein Partner reagiert auf dein Kompliment und macht dir dann auch ein Kompliment. — Die Wörter im Kasten sind nur zur Anregung da.

    die Jeans   der Schal   das Kleid   das T-Shirt   die Weste
    das Tuch   die Halskette   der Hut   der Rock   die Stiefel   das Stirnband
    die Jacke   die Handtasche   die Mütze   die Ohrringe   das Armband

So sagt man das!

Expressing wishes when buying things   Schon bekannt

When you want to buy new clothes, there are a number of expressions you have already learned to use.

The salesclerk might ask you:

    Was möchten Sie bitte?
    Was bekommen Sie?
    Haben Sie einen Wunsch?

    Ja sicher. Welche Größe brauchen Sie?

Your response might be:

    Ich brauche einen Schal.
    Den Taschenrechner da.
    Ja, ich suche eine Mütze. Haben
        Sie diese Mütze in Schwarz?
    Größe L.

Übungsheft, S. 6, Ü. 3–4

Grammatikheft, S. 5, Ü. 9–10

33 Im Warenhaus Möller

Lesen/Sprechen Lies zuerst die Reklame für das Warenhaus Möller! Welche Wörter kennst du? Welche sind dir neu? Dann such dir zwei Sachen aus, die du brauchst! Spiel mit einem Partner die Rollen von Verkäufer und Kunde! Führt ein Verkaufsgespräch! Dann tauscht die Rollen aus! Nicht vergessen: Fragt nach Farbe, Größe und Eigenschaft (z.B., aus Wolle), wenn ihr Kleidungsstücke kauft, und fragt immer nach dem Preis! *Answers may vary.*

Grammatikheft, S. 6, Ü. 11

IM ANGEBOT
In unserer Bekleidungsabteilung

Gürtel, echt Leder, circa 3 cm breit, in Braun und in Schwarz
EUR 8,00

Polohemden, 6 aktuelle Farben, mit halbem Ärmel, alle Größen, 100% Baumwolle
EUR 14,25

Ein heißer Tipp: Sweatshirts mit Aufdruck, viele Motive, Größen: S, M, L, XL und XXL
EUR 9,95

Im Junior-Shop: Pullis für Jungen und Mädchen, 100% Polyacryl, Farben: blau, weiß, rot, pink
EUR 12,45

IN UNSERER SCHULABTEILUNG

Taschenwörterbücher	**EUR 10,00**
Taschenrechner	**ab EUR 12,95**
Schultaschen	**ab EUR 7,50**
Etuis	**ab EUR 3,40**
Kugelschreiber	**EUR 0,75**
Filzstifte	**EUR 0,60**
Bleistifte, 6 Stück	**EUR 1,10**

Nur diese Woche! Warenhaus G. Möller

34 Reklame im Radio *Script and answers on p. 3H*

Zuhören/Schreiben Du brauchst ein paar Klamotten. Da hörst du zufällig eine Reklame im Radio für Sachen, die du gern haben möchtest. Schreib dir vier Dinge auf, die du dir gern kaufen möchtest!

35 Was brauchst du? *Answers may vary.*

Sprechen Such dir eine Partnerin! Beschreibe ihr zwei Sachen, die du in der Reklame gehört hast und die du gern kaufen möchtest! Sag ihr auch, warum du diese Sachen haben möchtest!

Ein wenig Grammatik

Schon bekannt

For the **möchte**-forms, for nominative and accusative forms of the definite and the indefinite articles, and for third person pronouns, see the Grammar Summary.

Übungsheft, S. 7, Ü. 5–6

Mehr Grammatikübungen, S. 28–29, Ü. 5–6

ZWEITE STUFE STANDARDS: 1.1, 1.2, 5.1 *neunzehn* **19**

Zum Lesen

Cousin und Kusine verständigen sich, oder?

Lesestrategie Using prereading strategies There are several things you can do before you begin to read a new text in order to get an idea of what the reading is about. You do these things all the time when reading texts in English without even thinking about it. First, look for visual clues, such as format. Next, read the title and any subtitles. Then skim the text once, looking for cognates and other words you already know. These strategies should give you a good idea of what the reading is about and the kinds of information you can expect to find.

Getting Started

1. Based on the format of the readings, what kind of texts are these?
2. Now read the title. What two pieces of information does the title provide that will help you understand the content of the faxes?

Tipp As in English, German uses many compound nouns. The difference is that in German these compound nouns are written as one word: **Tennisturnier**, *tennis tournament*; **Fußballspiel**, *soccer game*. Remember: the gender of the compound noun is that of the last noun in the compound: **das Spiel: das Fußballspiel**. If you understand one or more words within a compound noun, you can usually guess the meaning of the new word.

For answers, see p. 3U.

20, FEB. 02   12:15   5.002

Liebe Andrea,

Mutti sagt, du kommst nach München. Prima! Ich möchte dich gern sehen, nur habe ich dieses Wochenende so viel vor. Lies: Am Samstag von 10 bis 12 Fußballtraining. Von halb zwei bis 4 Uhr ist unser Fußballspiel. Danach fahren wir an den Starnberger See. Dort wollen wir segeln, denn das Wetter wird ideal sein! Dann komm ich erst um 9 Uhr zurück.

Am Sonntagvormittag, von 9 bis 12 Uhr, will ich mit meiner Fahrradclique eine kleine Radtour machen. Zu Mittag bin ich dann wieder zu Hause! So gegen 3 Uhr treff ich mich aber mit meiner Schulclique im Café am Hofgarten. Dort bleib ich bis halb 6. Dann muss ich nach Hause und Hausaufgaben machen.

Ich hoffe, dass ich dich doch irgendwie sehen kann. Ruf doch mal an, wenn du in München bist!

Dein Benjamin

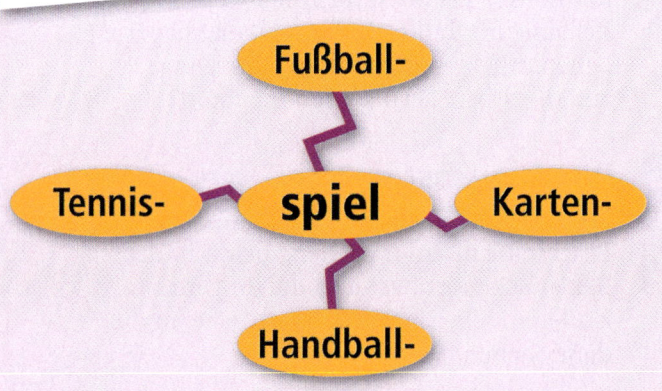

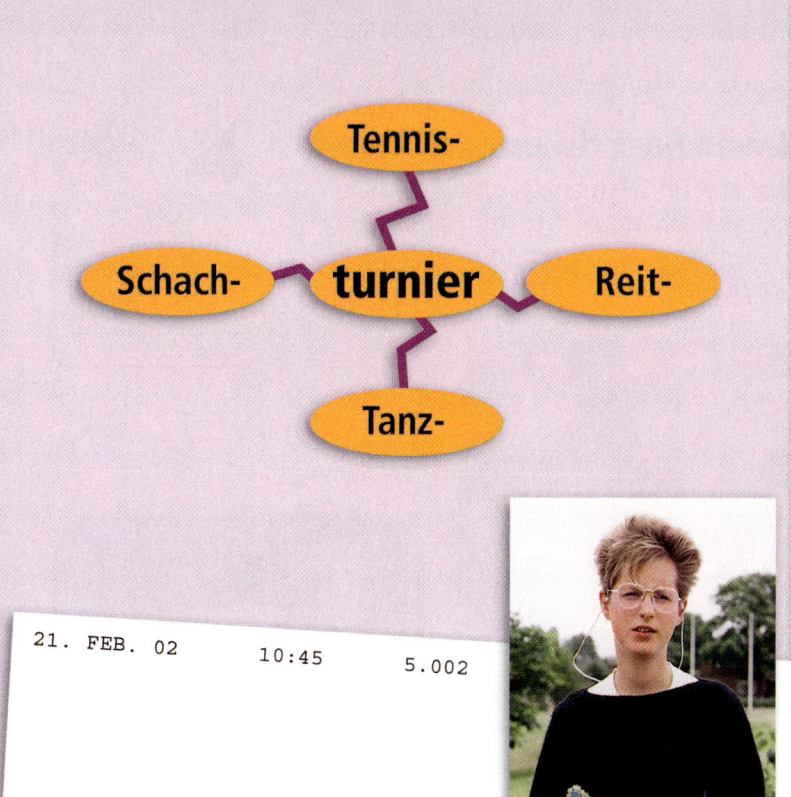

21. FEB. 02   10:45   5.002

Lieber Benjamin!

Danke für dein Fax! Schade, dass du dieses Wochenende so viel zu tun hast. Ist das immer so bei dir?

Meine Freundin und ich, wir wollen auch viel unternehmen. Vielleicht willst du irgendwohin mitgehen?

Hier sind unsere Pläne: Am Samstag komm ich so gegen 10 Uhr 30 an. Dann geh ich gleich mit Renate zum Tennisturnier, bis so um 2 Uhr. Um 3 Uhr wollen wir ins Kino gehen, und um 6 Uhr gehen wir ins Freizeitzentrum. Dort bleiben wir bis halb 10.

Am Sonntag, so zwischen 11 und 12 Uhr, wollen wir einen kleinen Stadtbummel machen. Dann gehen wir in ein Café, etwas essen. Von halb vier bis 5 Uhr sind wir dann zu Hause beim Kaffeetrinken. Um halb 7 Uhr geht mein Zug.

Also, was meinst du, können wir uns sehen?

Deine Kusine Andrea

3. Skim both texts quickly, using cognates or other words you already know to help you get the gist of each letter. Place a piece of paper over the readings and, with a partner, try to remember all the words you saw that meant something to you. Based on this information, the most likely topic of this fax exchange is
   a. eine Einladung
   b. Pläne fürs Wochenende
   c. was man in den Ferien gemacht hat
   d. Schule und neue Freunde

A Closer Look

4. Reread each letter. Together with your partner, try to answer the following questions. Why is Benjamin writing to Andrea? What kind of information is Benjamin giving to Andrea? With what kind of information does Andrea respond?

5. Make a weekend calendar page for Benjamin and another for Andrea. List the times mentioned and next to each, the activity planned. What is the problem?

6. Do you think that Benjamin is very excited about his cousin coming to visit? Why or why not? On what are you basing this inference? Should Andrea count on seeing him?

7. If you received this letter from your cousin, how would you interpret it?

8. Write a letter to a relative of yours who wants to visit you on a busy weekend. Detail all of your plans for him or her. In your letter, you must state whether you plan to see your relative or not. Think of a way to express the following clearly, but politely: a) you do not want to see your relative, b) you do want to get together with him or her. Choose one of these options and write your letter.

Übungsheft, S. 8

ZUM LESEN   STANDARDS: 1.2, 1.3, 3.1   einundzwanzig   21

Und was hast du am liebsten?

We asked several German-speaking students about some of their favorite things in a number of categories. First listen to their interviews, then read the texts. CD 1 Tr. 8

Übungsheft, S. 9, Ü. 1–2

Tim, Berlin CD 1 Tr. 10

„Mein Lieblingssport ist Fitness und Jiu-Jitsu, das ist eine Selbstverteidigung, Vollkontakt, macht mir sehr viel Spaß. Ich…meine Lieblingsfächer sind Deutsch, Sport und Physik. Biologie mag ich nicht so. Ja, meine Lieblingsbücher stammen zum größten Teil von Stephen King. Die sind recht spannend und, also, hab ich fast alle von. Ja, meine Lieblingskleidung sind also T-Shirts, Jeans, Turnschuhe, außer wenn ich halt ein bisschen besser weggehe, dann halt Lederschuhe und mal 'ne Krawatte mit 'nem schönen Hemd oder 'n Sakko."

Sandra, Berlin CD 1 Tr. 9

„Volleyball ist mein Lieblingssport, und ich spiel's so gern, weil man da nicht mit dem Gegner zusammentrifft und es deswegen also auch keine Fouls und so gibt wie im Fußball; und ja, deswegen find ich das ganz gut. Hm, ich ess gern Spaghetti und Pizza, alles, was richtig schön viel Kalorien hat, Schokolade auch, und ja, Kaugummi kau ich auch ab und zu, nur so süßsaure chinesische Gerichte esse ich nicht sehr gern."

Eva, Bietigheim CD 1 Tr. 11

„Also, ich reite, und ich spiel Handball. Und Lieblingsessen, alles, was italienisch ist, so Nudeln, Spaghetti und so was. Und Lieblingskleidung: Es muss gemütlich sein und bequem."

A. 1. Under which five categories do these students' favorites fall? What questions might the interviewer have asked each student to get these responses? Make a grid with the names of the students interviewed and the different categories. Fill in the grid for each student. Identify the phrases in each interview in which a reason is given and add these to your grid.

  2. Interview your partner to find out what his or her favorites are in each category and why. Continue the chart. Then switch roles.

  3. Are there any students who mentioned the same things as you or your partner? Are the things mentioned very similar to or different from things teenagers in the United States might say?   1. Sport; Essen; Kleidung; Schulfächer; Bücher. Possible question: **Was isst du gern?**

B. Choose one of the students above who is most like you. Use this interview as a framework and rewrite it for yourself, changing the information to fit you. Use the words and phrases from the chart your partner made about you.

STANDARDS: 1.2, 2.2, 3.2, 4.2

Storytelling Book
pp. 4–5

Dritte Stufe

Objectives Making plans; ordering food and beverages; talking about how something tastes

WK3 BAYERN-1

36 **Was wir am Samstag tun.** Script and answers on p. 3H

Zuhören/Schreiben Drei Schüler erzählen, was sie alles am Samstag tun. Schreib auf, was jeder zwischen drei Uhr und fünf Uhr macht!
CD 1 Tr. 12

37 **Was willst du am Wochenende machen?**

Schreiben Mach eine Liste und schreib auf, was du am Wochenende machen willst! Schreib auf, wann du das alles machst!

38 **Was machst du gewöhnlich am Samstag?**

Sprechen Such dir einen Partner und sag ihm, was du gewöhnlich am Samstag zwischen drei und sechs Uhr machst — oder am Sonntag, zwischen sechs Uhr und neun Uhr abends!

So sagt man das!

Making plans

Schon bekannt

When you make plans to do something with your friends, you might ask your friend:

    Was möchtest du machen?
or **Und was willst du machen?**

Your friend might respond:

    Ins Kino gehen.
    Du, ich will mal echt faulenzen!

What do you think **faulenzen** means?

39 **Mein Wochenende**

Sprechen Such dir zwei Aktivitäten aus, die du gern machen willst. Frag deinen Partner, ob er mitmachen will! Er fragt dich wann. Tauscht dann die Rollen aus! Dann erzählt euern Mitschülern eure Pläne fürs Wochenende!

Wann?

am Nachmittag	am Abend
von 14 bis 16 Uhr	
am Sonntag	um 15 Uhr

Was?

joggen   100-Meter-Lauf   Schach
   Bogenschießen   wandern
Leichtathletik   Tennis   Klavier

Ein wenig Grammatik

Schon bekannt

When you make plans, you need to know the forms of the verbs **wollen** and **möchte**. To review these forms, see the Grammar Summary.

Übungsheft, S. 10–11, Ü. 1–5   Mehr Grammatikübungen, S. 29, Ü. 7

Grammatikheft, S. 7, Ü. 12–13

40 **Für mein Notizbuch**

Schreiben Schick deinem Freund ein Fax! Berichte, was du am Wochenende alles machen willst! Du hast bestimmt so viele Pläne wie Benjamin und Andrea (siehe Zum Lesen)!

Bestell was, Basti!

Sebastian sitzt da und weiß nicht recht, was er tun soll. Lies den Text!

BEATRICE Bestell was zu trinken, Basti!
SEBASTIAN Hallo!
BEDIENUNG Ja, bitte?
SEBASTIAN Eine Limo, bitte!
BEDIENUNG Alles?
SEBASTIAN Ja.

BEATRICE Etwas zu essen, Basti?
SEBASTIAN N … nein.
BEATRICE Komm, iss doch etwas! Ich zahl's dir. Ich lade dich ein.
SEBASTIAN Na gut! — Ein Stück Torte, Himbeertorte für mich.

41 Wer bezahlt?

Lesen/Sprechen Lies den Text und beantworte diese Fragen!

1. Was bestellt Basti zu trinken? Was sagt er? — Welche Ausdrücke könnte (*could*) er auch gebrauchen? 1. Eine Limo; e.g.: Ich möchte …
2. Dann bestellt er etwas zu essen. Was sagt er? — Was könnte er auch sagen?
3. Warum, glaubst du, will Basti zuerst gar nichts essen?

2. Ein Stück Torte; e.g.: Ich nehme … 3. Possible answer: Er hat nicht genug Geld mit.

42 Welcher Text passt zu welcher Illustration? Script and answers on p. 3H

Zuhören/Schreiben Zwei Schüler sprechen über Dinge, die in den Fotos abgebildet sind. — Schreib die Zahlen 1- 5 auf ein Blatt Papier und daneben den Buchstaben (a. b. c. d. e.) des Fotos, das zu dem Gespräch passt! CD 1 Tr. 13

a.

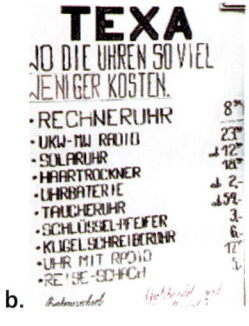
b.

c.

d.

e.

So sagt man das!

Ordering food and beverages

Schon bekannt

When ordering at a café or restaurant, the waiter might ask:

> Was bekommen Sie?
> Und Sie? Was essen Sie?
> Und was möchten Sie?

You might ask a friend:

> Was nimmst du?
> Und du? Was bestellst du?

Your response might be:

> Ich möchte eine Suppe, bitte!
> Für mich ein Wurstbrot, bitte!
> Ich esse ein Käsebrot.

And the response might be:

> Ja, ich nehme den Eisbecher.
> Ich will im Moment gar nichts.

Mehr Grammatikübungen, S. 29, Ü. 8

Grammatikheft, S. 8, Ü. 14–16

43 Was sagen die Schüler? *Script and answers on p. 3H*

Zuhören Hör dir noch einmal die Schüler von Übung 42 an! Schreib jetzt auf, was jeder sagt, wenn er etwas bestellt (*orders*) oder kauft!
CD 1 Tr. 14

44 Was möchtest du essen und trinken?

Sprechen Such dir einen Partner! Einer von euch ist die Bedienung (*waiter* or *waitress*), der andere bestellt etwas zu essen und zu trinken. Gebraucht bei euerm Gespräch die Reklame (*advertisements*) auf Seite 24! Die Bedienung macht dann die Rechnung fertig. *Answers may vary.*
E.g.: **Was bekommen Sie? — Ich möchte eine Pizza, bitte!**

So sagt man das!

Talking about how something tastes

Schon bekannt

Wie schmeckt's?	Lecker! Gut! Echt prima! *oder*
	Es schmeckt nicht, weil es zu salzig ist.
	Der Kaffee schmeckt nicht, weil er zu bitter ist.
Schmeckt's?	Ja, gut! Ausgezeichnet. Sagenhaft! *oder*
	Nicht besonders.

Mehr Grammatikübungen, S. 29, Ü. 9

Übungsheft, S. 12, Ü. 6–7   Grammatikheft, S. 9, Ü. 17–18

45 Wie schmeckt's?

Sprechen Such dir einen Partner! Seht euch die Reklame auf Seite 24 an! Dein Partner fragt dich, was du da isst. Du sagst es ihm. Dann fragt er dich, wie es schmeckt, und du sagst es ihm auch. Tauscht dann die Rollen aus!

46 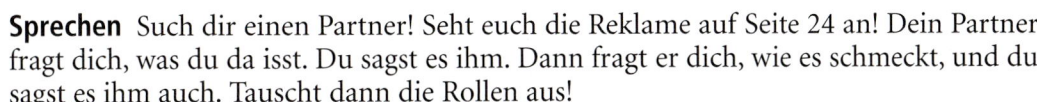 Von der Schule zum Beruf

Du bist ein junger Schriftsteller (*writer*) und willst einen lustigen Sketch über eine Szene in einen Café schreiben. Die Schauspieler sind zwei Kunden und eine Bedienung. (Einige Anregungen: **a.** Bestelle etwas, was nicht so leicht zu haben ist. **b.** Die Bedienung bringt etwas, was du nicht bestellt hast. **c.** Du hast kein Geld dabei.)

DRITTE STUFE   STANDARDS: 1.1, 1.2, 5.1, 5.2   *fünfundzwanzig*   **25**

Mehr Grammatikübungen

Answers

Erste Stufe

Objectives Asking for and giving information about yourself and others; describing yourself and others; expressing likes and dislikes; identifying people and places

1 In welchem Sport sind deine Freunde gut?—Schreib die richtige Sportart auf die entsprechende Zeile. (**S. 10**)

Der Jacob ist gut im _____. Kugelstoßen

Michelle ist die Beste im _____. Speerwerfen

Mark ist im _____ der Beste in der Klasse. Diskuswerfen

Ich halte den Rekord im _____. Langstreckenlauf

10,8 Sek. im _____ ist nicht schlecht! 100-Meter-Lauf

Dirk ist der beste im _____. Weitsprung

Unsere Cindy liebt den _____. Hürdenlauf

Wer ist der beste im _____? Stabhochsprung

26 sechsundzwanzig STANDARDS: 1.2 KAPITEL 1 Bei den Baumanns

2

Du siehst dir mit Freunden ein Fotoalbum an, in dem Bilder von Freunden, Cousins und Kusinen sind. Wer ist wer? Du beschreibst deinen Freunden die Fotos.—Vervollständige die folgenden Sätze mit der richtigen Verbform von **sein** oder **haben**. (S. 11)

1. Das _____ meine Kusine; sie _____ 19 Jahre alt. Meine Kusine _____ braune Haare und grüne Augen. Katja _____ sehr intelligent. Sie _____ sehr gut in der Schule und sie _____ Mathe und Physik besonders gern.   *ist; ist; hat; ist; ist; hat*

2. Wer _____ der Junge da? _____ das dein Cousin? — Ja, das _____ mein Cousin. Roger heißt er. Roger _____ 16, er _____ blonde Haare, und er _____ auch eine Brille. Roger _____ auch einen Hund; er heißt Hasso.   *ist; Ist; ist; ist; hat; hat; hat*

3. Und wer _____ die Kinder da? _____ das deine Geschwister? — Nein, das _____ die Kinder von einer Freundin von meiner Mutter. Die beiden Kinder _____ sehr intelligent. In der Schule _____ sie nur gute Noten.   *sind; Sind; sind; sind; haben*

4. Ja, und das _____ du. Aber hier _____ du doch blaue Augen, nicht? Und deine Augen _____ jetzt braun. — Ganz einfach! Ich _____ jetzt braune Augen, weil meine Kontaktlinsen braun _____ . Und meine Haare _____ blond.   *bist; hast; sind; habe; sind; sind*

5. John und Frank, ihr seht lustig aus! Was _____ ihr denn nur in der Hand? — Ja, der John _____ eine Kugel, zum Kugelstoßen, und der Frank _____ einen Speer, zum Speerwerfen. Ja, die beiden _____ immer lustig.   *habt; hat; hat; sind*

3

Was machst du und was machen deine Freunde in der Freizeit?—Schreib die richtigen Verbformen in die Lücken. (S. 12)

1. Sag mal, was _____ du in deiner Freizeit? _____ du viel Sport? _____ du Hobbys? _____ du ein Instrument? _____ du gern Musik? _____ du gern tanzen? _____ du oft Rad? Und _____ du denn Bücher?   *machst; Machst; Hast; Spielst; Hörst; Gehst; Fährst; liest*

2. Also, ich _____ viel Tennis, ich _____ oft ins Kino, ich _____ jeden Tag die Zeitung, ja, was noch? Ja, ich _____ gern Rad, und wenn ich Zeit _____ , _____ ich meine Freunde. Sie haben viele CDs und wir _____ Musik.   *spiele; gehe; lese; fahre; habe; besuche; hören*

3. Und was _____ ihr gern, Katja und Sabine? _____ ihr gern ins Kino oder _____ ihr lieber Freunde? _____ ihr ein Instrument oder _____ ihr Musik gern? Und _____ ihr Sport? Ich möchte gern wissen, was ihr _____.   *macht; Geht; besucht; Spielt; hört; macht; macht*

4. Ja, wir _____ gern Sport. Die Katja _____ Volleyball und ich _____ Hürdenlauf. Ja, und dann _____ wir beide ein Instrument. Die Katja _____ furchtbar gern Bücher und ich _____ Rad, und ich _____ gern in unserm Pool.
   machen; spielt; mache; spielen; liest; fahre; schwimme

MEHR GRAMMATIKÜBUNGEN   STANDARDS: 1.2   *siebenundzwanzig*   **27**

Mehr Grammatikübungen

WK3 BAYERN-1

4 Du sprichst mit deinen Freunden über Geschenke, die ihr Freunden und Verwandten geben wollt. – Schreib die richtigen Possessivpronomen in die Lücken. (S. 13)

a. use a form of **mein**

1. Kennst du _____ Bruder? Schau, das ist _____ Bruder. Ich habe _____ Bruder sehr gern. Zum Geburtstag schenke ich _____ Bruder immer ein Buch.   meinen; mein; meinen; meinem

2. Was soll ich nur _____ Freundin schenken? Du kennst doch _____ Freundin, die Beate, nicht? _____ Freundin hört Musik gern, also eine CD?   meiner; meine; Meine

b. use a form of **dein**

1. Was gibst du denn _____ Opa? Hast du schon ein Geschenk für _____ Opa? _____ Opa ist so lieb! Ich möchte _____ Opa auch etwas schenken.   deinem; deinen; Dein; deinem

2. Was schenkst du _____ Kusine? Ich weiß, dass _____ Kusine viele Interessen hat. Hat _____ Kusine Bücher gern oder CDs?   deiner; deine; deine

c. use **sein** or **ihr**

1. Ich weiß, was der Basti _____ Schwester schenkt. Eine CD, denn _____ Schwester hört Musik furchtbar gern. Und _____ Bruder gibt er einen Fußball, ganz neu, denn _____ Bruder spielt gern Fußball.   seiner; seine; seinem; sein

2. Die Beatrice schenkt _____ Mutter einen Roman und _____ Vater eine Armbanduhr. _____ Vater sammelt Uhren und _____ Mutter Romane.   ihrer; ihrem; Ihr; ihre

Zweite Stufe

Objectives Giving and responding to compliments; expressing wishes when buying things

5 Frag deine Freunde, was sie als Geschenk haben möchten oder was sie essen möchten. – Schreib die richtigen **möchte**-Formen oder eine Form von **ein** in die Lücken. (S. 19)

1. Was _____ du zum Geburtstag? _____ Taschenrechner oder _____ Taschenwörterbuch? Oder _____ du _____ Rock oder _____ Bluse? Ich _____ dir gern _____ Handtasche schenken oder _____ Armband.   möchtest; Einen; ein; möchtest; einen; eine; möchte; eine; ein

2. Was _____ ihr zu Weihnachten? Habt ihr _____ Idee? _____ ihr _____ CD oder _____ Sachbuch oder vielleicht _____ Kalender?   möchtet; eine; Möchtet; eine; ein; einen

3. Wir wissen, was wir essen _____. Ich _____ _____ Eisbecher, und die Katja _____ _____ Stück Kuchen und _____ Eis.   möchten; möchte; einen; möchte; ein; ein

28 achtundzwanzig   STANDARDS: 1.2   KAPITEL 1   Bei den Baumanns

6 Du sagst einem Verkäufer, was du mit deinen Freunden kaufen möchtest, und du fragst ihn, ob es diesen Artikel auch in einer anderen Farbe gibt.—Schreib in jede erste Lücke die richtige **möchte**-Form, in jede zweite Lücke, die richtige Form des bestimmten Artikels (**der**) und in jede dritte Lücke die richtige Form des Pronomens. (S. 19)

1. Ich _____ _____ Rock da. Haben Sie _____ auch in Blau?   möchte; den; ihn
2. Die Katja _____ _____ Stirnband. Haben Sie _____ auch in Rot?   möchte; das; es
3. Wir _____ _____ T-Shirt da. Haben Sie _____ auch in Blau?   möchten; das; es
4. Der Basti _____ _____ Hut da. Haben Sie _____ auch in Schwarz?   möchte; den; ihn
5. Sabine _____ _____ Bluse da. Haben Sie _____ auch in Braun?   möchte; die; sie
6. Ich _____ _____ Gürtel da. Haben Sie _____ auch in Schwarz?   möchte; den; ihn

Dritte Stufe

Objectives Making plans; ordering food and beverages; talking about how something tastes

7 Bei den Baumanns will jeder etwas anderes tun.—Schreib in jede erste Lücke eine Form von **wollen,** und in jede zweite Lücke einen passenden Infinitiv. (S. 23)

1. Der Basti _____ heute den Rasen _____ .   will; mähen
2. Sein Bruder, der Robert, _____ heute Tennis _____ .   will; spielen
3. Herr und Frau Baumann _____ am Abend ins Kino _____ .   wollen; gehen
4. Basti, _____ du auch den Müll _____ ?   willst; sortieren
5. Basti und Robert, _____ ihr im Garten die Blumen _____ ?   wollt; gießen
6. Nein, ich _____ heute nichts tun, ich _____ einmal _____ .   will; will; faulenzen

8 Du fragst deine Freunde im Lokal, was sie bestellen möchten.—Schreib in jede Lücke die richtige Form des gegebenen Infinitivs. (S. 25)

1. (bekommen)   Was _____ du? — Ich _____ ein Käsebrot.   bekommst; bekomme
2. (essen)   Was _____ du? — Ich _____ ein Stück Pizza.   isst; esse
3. (nehmen)   Und was _____ du? — Ich _____ einen Eisbecher.   nimmst; nehme
4. (wollen)   Was _____ du? — Ich _____ im Moment nichts.   willst; will
5. (möchten)   Was _____ du? — Ich _____ eine Suppe, bitte.   möchtest; möchte
6. (trinken)   Was _____ du? — Ich _____ ein Mineralwasser.   trinkst; trinke

9 Du magst heute überhaupt nichts, und du sagst auch warum du das nicht magst. Vervollständige jeden **weil**-Satz mit dem Ausdruck in Klammern. (S. 25)

BEISPIEL (zu teuer)   Ich bestelle das Fleisch nicht, weil _____ .
   Ich bestelle das Fleisch nicht, weil **es zu teuer ist**.

1. (zu salzig)   Ich esse die Suppe nicht, weil _____ .   sie zu salzig ist
2. (zu kalt)   Ich esse das Eis nicht, weil _____ .   es zu kalt ist
3. (zu bitter)   Ich trinke den Kaffee nicht, weil _____ .   er zu bitter ist
4. (zu sauer)   Ich mag den Joghurt nicht, weil _____ .   er zu sauer ist
5. (zu heiß)   Ich trinke den Tee nicht, weil _____ .   er zu heiß ist
6. (zu teuer)   Ich nehme das Schnitzel nicht, weil _____ .   es zu teuer ist

TPR Storytelling Book pp. 6–7

Kann ich's wirklich?

WK3 BAYERN-1

Can you ask for and give information about yourself and others? (p. 11)

1 How would you say what your name is, how old you are, and where you live?   1. E.g.: Ich heiße Tom. Ich bin sechzehn Jahre alt und wohne in Austin, Texas.

2 How would you ask someone what his or her friend's name, age, and place of residence are?   2. E.g.: Wie heißt deine Freundin? Wie alt ist sie? Wo wohnt sie?

Can you describe yourself and others? (p. 11)

3 How would you ask a friend what a member of his or her family looks like? What would your friend answer if that person is tall and thin, has brown hair and dark eyes, and is very intelligent?
3. E.g.: Wie sieht dein Bruder aus? - Er ist groß und schlank, hat braune Haare und dunkle Augen. Er ist sehr intelligent.

Can you express likes and dislikes? (p. 11)

4 How would you ask someone what he or she likes and doesn't like to do? What would you answer if someone asked you that question?
4. E.g.: Was machst du gern, was machst du nicht gern? - Ich lese gern. Ich koche nicht gern.

Can you identify people and places? (p. 13)

5 How would you ask a friend who someone is? Where his or her room is? What might your friend's answers be?
5. E.g.: Wer ist das Mädchen? Wo ist dein Zimmer? - Das ist meine Schwester. Mein Zimmer ist neben dem Wohnzimmer.

Can you give and respond to compliments? (p. 18)

6 How would you say to someone that he or she looks elegant? How would you respond if someone gave you the same compliment?
6. E.g.: Du siehst heute fesch aus. - Wirklich? Vielen Dank!

Can you express wishes when buying things? (p. 18)

7 How would you tell a salesclerk you would like to buy a hat and a scarf?
7. E.g.: Ich möchte einen Hut und einen Schal kaufen.

Can you make plans? (p. 23)

8 How would you ask a friend what his or her plans are? What might your friend answer?
8. E.g.: Was möchtest du am Wochenende machen? - Ins Kino gehen.

Can you order food and beverages? (p. 25)

9 How would you order soup, a sandwich, ice cream, and a lemon-flavored drink? What would you tell the waiter if you didn't want anything?
9. E.g.: Ich möchte eine Suppe, ein Sandwich, Eis und eine Limo. Ich will im Moment gar nichts.

Can you talk about how something tastes? (p. 25)

10 How would you ask someone if his or her food tastes good? How would he or she respond if it did? If it didn't? What reasons might he or she give?
10. E.g.: Schmeckt's? - Echt prima! / Es schmeckt nicht, weil es zu salzig ist.

30 *dreißig*   STANDARDS: 1.2   KAPITEL 1   Bei den Baumanns

Wortschatz

Erste Stufe

Asking for and giving information about yourself and others

faul	lazy
fleißig	hard-working
intelligent	intelligent
neugierig	curious
lustig	funny
sympathisch	nice, pleasant
unsympathisch	unfriendly, unpleasant
gut gelaunt	in a good mood
schlecht gelaunt	in a bad mood
schlank	slender
dunkel	dark

Family members

beschreiben	to describe
der Sohn, ¨-e	son
die Tochter, ¨-	daughter
der Zwilling, -e	twin
das Kind, -er	child

Expressing likes and dislikes

das Hobby, Hobbys	hobby
rodeln	sledding
fechten	fencing
kochen	cooking
Bogenschießen	archery
die Leichtathletik	track and field
der Sport	sports
Kugelstoßen	shot put
Speerwerfen	javelin throw
Diskuswerfen	discus throw
Langstreckenlauf	long-distance run
100-Meter-Lauf	100-yard dash
Weitsprung	long jump
Hürdenlauf	hurdling
Stabhochsprung	pole vault

Zweite Stufe

Describing and commenting on clothes

das Stirnband, ¨-er	headband
der Schal, -s	scarf
die Mütze, -n	cap
der Hut, ¨-e	hat
die Halskette, -n	necklace
der Ohrring, -e	earring
ein (das) Paar Ohrringe	pair of earrings
das Armband, ¨-er	bracelet
die Handtasche, -n	handbag
das Tuch, ¨-er	scarf

Dritte Stufe

Making plans

Was willst du machen?	What do you want to do?
Ich will faulenzen!	I want to be lazy!

Talking about how something tastes

Wie schmeckt's?	How does it taste?
ausgezeichnet	excellent
zu bitter	too bitter
zu salzig	too salty
die Suppe, -n	soup

Other useful words and expressions

echt	really
bestellen	to order

Kapitel 2: Bastis Plan

Review Chapter

Chapter Overview

Los geht's! pp. 34–36	*Basti, das Schlitzohr!* p. 34			
	FUNCTIONS	**GRAMMAR**	**VOCABULARY**	**RE-ENTRY**
Erste Stufe pp. 37–41	• Expressing obligations, p. 37 • Extending and responding to an invitation, p. 38 • Offering help and telling what to do, p. 40	• The forms of **müssen**, p. 37 • The interrogative **warum** and the conjunctions **weil** and **denn**, p. 39 • The forms of **können**, p. 40 • The accusative forms of the personal pronouns and of the possessives, p. 41	• Things to do around the house, p. 37	• Chapter 2 is a global review of *Komm mit!* Level 1
Zweite Stufe pp. 44–48	• Asking and telling what to do, p. 45 • Telling that you need something else, p. 46 • Telling where you were and what you bought, p. 46	• The forms of **sollen** and the **du**-commands, p. 45 • The past tense forms of **sein**, the **war**-forms, p. 47	• Fruits and vegetables, p. 44	• Chapter 2 is a global review of *Komm mit!* Level 1
Dritte Stufe pp. 49–53	• Discussing gift ideas, p. 50 • Expressing likes and dislikes, p. 50 • Expressing likes, preferences, and favorites, p. 51 • Saying you do or don't want more, p. 52	• The dative forms of **mein** and **dein**, and the dative personal pronouns, p. 50 • The forms of **mögen**, p. 51 • The phrase **noch ein-** and the forms of **ein** and **kein**, p. 52	• Gifts, p. 49	• Chapter 2 is a global review of *Komm mit!* Level 1

Zum Lesen pp. 42–43	Macht Schule Spaß?	**Reading Strategy** Using context to derive meaning

Mehr Grammatikübungen	**pp. 54–57** Erste Stufe, pp. 54–55	Zweite Stufe, p. 56	Dritte Stufe, pp. 56–57

Review pp. 58–59	Kann ich's wirklich? p. 58	Wortschatz, p. 59

CULTURE

• Teenagers doing chores, p. 41
• Grocery advertisement, p. 44
• Landeskunde: Was nimmst du mit, wenn du irgendwo eingeladen bist? p. 48
• German gift ideas, p. 49

Kapitel 2: Bastis Plan
Chapter Resources

Review Chapter

PRINT

Lesson Planning
- One-Stop Planner
- Lesson Planner with Substitute Teacher Lesson Plans, pp. 7–11, 66
- Student Make-Up Assignments
  • Make-Up Assignment Copying Masters, Chapter 2

Listening and Speaking
- TPR Storytelling Book, pp. 8–15
- Listening Activities
  • Student Response Forms for Listening Activities, pp. 11–14
  • Additional Listening Activities 2-1 to 2-6, pp. 15–18
  • Additional Listening Activities (song), p. 14
  • Scripts and Answers, pp. 106–112
- Video Guide
  • Teaching Suggestions, pp. 10–11
  • Activity Masters, pp. 12–14
  • Scripts and Answers, pp. 84–85, 111
- Activities for Communication
  • Communicative Activities, pp. 7–12
  • Realia and Teaching Suggestions, pp. 78–81
  • Situation Cards, pp. 125–126

Reading and Writing
- Reading Strategies and Skills Handbook, Chapter 2
- Lies mit mir! 2, Chapter 2
- Übungsheft, pp. 13–24

Grammar
- Grammatikheft, pp. 10–18
- Grammar Tutor for Students of German, Chapter 2

Assessment
- Testing Program
  • Grammar and Vocabulary Quizzes, Stufe Quizzes, and Chapter Test, pp. 27–44
  • Score Sheet, Scripts and Answers, pp. 45–52
- Alternative Assessment Guide
  • Portfolio Assessment, p. 19
  • Performance Assessment, p. 33
  • CD-ROM Assessment, p. 47
- Student Make-Up Assignments
  • Alternative Quizzes, Chapter 2

MEDIA

 Online Activities
- Interaktive Spiele
- Internet Aktivitäten

 Video Program
- Videocassette 1
- Videocassette 5 (captioned version)
- DVD Tutor, Disc 1

 Audio Compact Discs
- Textbook Listening Activities, CD 2, Tracks 1–16
- Additional Listening Activities, CD 2, Tracks 22–28
- Assessment Items, CD 2, Tracks 17–21

 Interactive CD-ROM Tutor, Disc 1

 Teaching Transparencies
- Situations 2-1 to 2-2
- Vocabulary 2-A to 2-B
- Los geht's!
- Mehr Grammatikübungen Answers
- Grammatikheft Answers

 **One-Stop Planner CD-ROM**

Use the **One-Stop Planner CD-ROM** with Test Generator to aid in lesson planning and pacing.

For each chapter, the **One-Stop Planner** includes:
- Editable lesson plans with direct links to teaching resources
- Printable worksheets from resource books
- Direct launches to the HRW Internet activities
- Video and audio segments
- Test Generator
- Clip Art for vocabulary items

Kapitel 2: Bastis Plan

Projects

Review Chapter

Games

Eine Interessenumfrage

Students will produce a magazine of a survey on topics of interest to teenagers. Start this project after *Zum Lesen* on pp. 42–43.

MATERIALS
Students may need
- a small tape recorder
- magazine pictures
- posterboard
- glue
- scissors
- markers

SUGGESTED TOPICS
Wie schmeckt das Essen in unserer Schule?
Soll unsere Schule Schuluniformen haben?
Wie verbringen Teenager ihre Freizeit?
Sollen Teenager Taschengeld bekommen?
Sollen Teenager für ihre Hilfe zu Hause bezahlt werden?

SUGGESTED SEQUENCE
1. Students choose a topic from the list of suggestions and make an outline of the questions they feel should be part of their survey.
2. Students interview other students throughout the school during lunch and before or after school.
3. Once students have sufficient data, they organize and evaluate the information.
4. Have students draft their surveys and turn them in for suggestions.
5. Students complete their surveys by writing or typing them and placing them onto the posterboard. They should include visuals to resemble an authentic magazine layout.
6. Students present their projects to the class and explain the results of their surveys.

GRADING THE PROJECT
Suggested point distribution (**total = 100 points**)
- Originality and design............................30
- Written assignment 40
- Oral presentation..................................30

Das tut mir Leid

This game will help students review and practice nouns at the end of the *Dritte Stufe.*

Preparation Make a list of categories of all the nouns or expressions learned so far. (Examples: foods, gift ideas, chores, school subjects, family members, hobbies)

Procedure Have students form a line. Ask each of them to name a word that belongs in the category that you announce. Write the words on the board or on a transparency. Once a student has given a word from the category, he or she goes to the end of the line. If a student makes a mistake or waits more than five seconds to give an answer, he or she is dismissed, and you say **Das tut mir Leid.** That student returns to his or her seat. Keep the game going depending on the number of categories and vocabulary you plan to practice. The three remaining students are the winners.

Fang den Ball!

This game will help students review the verbs that have been introduced so far.

Preparation Decide on the verbs you would like to review and write the infinitives on the board. (Examples: **sollen, können, mögen, müssen,** and the past tense of **sein**)

Procedure Ask students to stand up. Use a foam ball or any other soft ball and throw it to one of the students. Name the infinitive of one of the verbs listed and tell the student the conjugated form that you want him or her to say. (Example: **sollen—du**) The student says the verb in its correct form and then throws the ball to another student. This student must give the correct form of the verb called by the student who threw the ball. If a student says the incorrect verb form, he or she drops out of the game and sits down. The last student standing wins.

Storytelling

Mini-Geschichte

*This story accompanies Teaching Transparency 2-1. Read the **Mini-Geschichte** to your students, or have them role-play the conversation using proper pronunciation and intonation and appropriate body language. Have students list Markus's chores.*

Mathehausaufgaben oder Gartenarbeit?

„Hallo, Markus! Kommst du mit ins Schwimmbad?" „Hallo, Sina! Du, ich kann leider nicht, denn ich muss im Haus und im Garten helfen." „Was musst du im Haus helfen, Markus?" „Ich muss die Wäsche waschen, trocknen und bügeln." „Du und die Wäsche, Markus?" „Ja, leider. Meine Mutter ist auf einer Geschäftsreise *(business trip)* und meine Schwester weiß nicht einmal, dass wir eine Waschmaschine haben." „Was musst du im Garten tun, Markus?" „Ich muss den Rasen mähen." „Markus, also ich mäh für dich den Rasen und du hilfst mir bei den Mathehausaufgaben?" „Ich weiß nicht, Sina. Rasenmähen ist leicht, aber deine Mathehausaufgaben sind schwer *(difficult)*."

Traditions

Das Münchner Oktoberfest

Am 12. Oktober 1810 feierte Kronprinz Ludwig, der spätere König Ludwig I, seine Vermählung mit Prinzessin Therese von Sachsen-Hildburghausen. Die Festlichkeiten, zu denen auch die Münchner Bürger eingeladen waren, fanden vor den Toren Münchens auf einer Wiese statt, die später der Braut zu Ehren „Theresienwiese" getauft wurde. Zum Abschluss der Feierlichkeiten fand ein Pferderennen statt, das im folgenden Jahr wiederholt werden sollte. Das erste Karussel wurde 1818 auf der Theresienwiese aufgestellt.

1881 wurde die erste Hühnerbraterei der Welt auf dem Oktoberfest eröffnet. Heute ist das Münchner Oktoberfest das größte Volksfest der Welt, mit über 6 Millionen Besuchern im Jahr 2000. Und weil es immer noch auf der Theresienwiese stattfindet, sagt man einfach: „Willkommen auf der Wiesn".

Ask students to research German communities in their hometown or state. Do these communities have festivals similar to the Oktoberfest?

Rezept

Hennenknödel-Suppe
Für 4 Personen

Zutaten

g=Gramm, l=Liter

6-8	Brötchen, altbacken (trocken)
1/4 l	heiße Milch
1/2	Zwiebel, gehackt
2	Eier
250g	rohes Hühnerfleisch, durchgedreht
	Salz
	Pfeffer
	Muskat
	abgeriebene Schale von 1 Zitrone
1	Bund Petersilie, gehackt
2 l	Fleischbrühe

Zubereitung

Die Brötchen zerbröseln und mit der heißen Milch übergießen. Wenn sie richtig vollgesogen sind, Zwiebeln, Eier und Hühnerfleisch zugeben, einen Teig daraus kneten. Mit Salz, Pfeffer und Muskat kräftig würzen. Die Zitronenschale und die gehackte Petersilie mit einarbeiten. Den Teig weiterkneten, bis er glatt ist. Dann mit nassen Händen Knödel formen. Die Knödel in der heißen Brühe in 15 bis 20 Minuten gar ziehen, aber nicht kochen lassen. Dann in eine vorgewärmte Terrine umfüllen und servieren.

Kapitel 2: Bastis Plan
Technology

Review Chapter

DVD/Video

Videocassette 1, 5 (captioned version)
DVD Tutor, Disc 1
See Video Guide, pages 9–14

Los geht's! • Basti, das Schlitzohr!

The Baumanns are at the breakfast table discussing the children's chores for the day. Sebastian offers to switch chores with his brother Robert, who was supposed to help his grandparents. Later, they discover that Sebastian's grandparents didn't need any help.

Landeskunde
Was nimmst du mit, wenn du irgendwo eingeladen bist?

People of various ages from various parts of Germany tell us what they take with them when they are invited to someone's house.

Fortsetzung

Basti, while lounging on a park lawn, imagines what work everybody else is doing. Later, the rest of the family arrives at Oma's and they ask where Basti is. Beatrice shows her grandmother pictures she took on vacation in the former East Germany. Basti finally shows up and goes to the movies with Robert and Beatrice.

Videoclips
- **Köllnflakes**® (corn flakes)
- **Kölln Müsli**® (muesli cereal)
- **Christ Schmuck**® (jewelry)
- **Neudorff Düngen mit System**® (gardening products)

Interactive CD-ROM Tutor

Activity	Activity Type	Pupil's Edition Reference
1. Wortschatz	Wort und Bild Erfahren/Wählen	p. 37
2. Grammatik	Was fehlt?	pp. 37, 40, 41
3. So sagt man das!	Was ist richtig?	pp. 37, 38, 40, 45, 46
4. Grammatik	Wozu gehört's?	pp. 45, 47
5. Wortschatz	Merkspiel	p. 49
6. Grammatik	Was ist richtig?	pp. 39, 50, 51, 52
Landeskunde	Was nimmst du mit, wenn du irgendwo eingeladen bist? Was ist richtig?	p. 48
Zum Sprechen	Guided recording	p. 58
Zum Schreiben	Guided writing	p. 58

Teacher Management System

Launch the program, type "admin" in the password area, and press RETURN. Log on to **www.hrw.com/CDROMTUTOR** for a detailed explanation of the Teacher Management System.

DVD Tutor

The *DVD Tutor* contains all material from the *Video Program* as described above. German captions are available for use at your discretion for all sections of the video. The *DVD Tutor* also provides a variety of video-based activities that assess students' understanding of **Los geht's!, Fortsetzung,** and **Landeskunde,** as well as the new **Grammatik im Kontext** presentations.

> The *DVD Tutor* may be used on any DVD video player connected to a television or video monitor.

One-Stop Planner CD-ROM

To preview all resources available for this chapter, use the **One-Stop Planner CD-ROM**, Disc 1.

Visit Holt Online
go.hrw.com
KEYWORD: WK3 BAYERN-2
Online Edition

Go.Online!

Premier Online Edition

The Premier Online Edition for *Komm mit!* allows students access to their textbooks anytime, anywhere.
- *Audio at point of use*
- *Additional practice activities*
- *Self-test activities*
- *Online reference tools*
- *Entire Video Program*
- *Interactive Notebook*

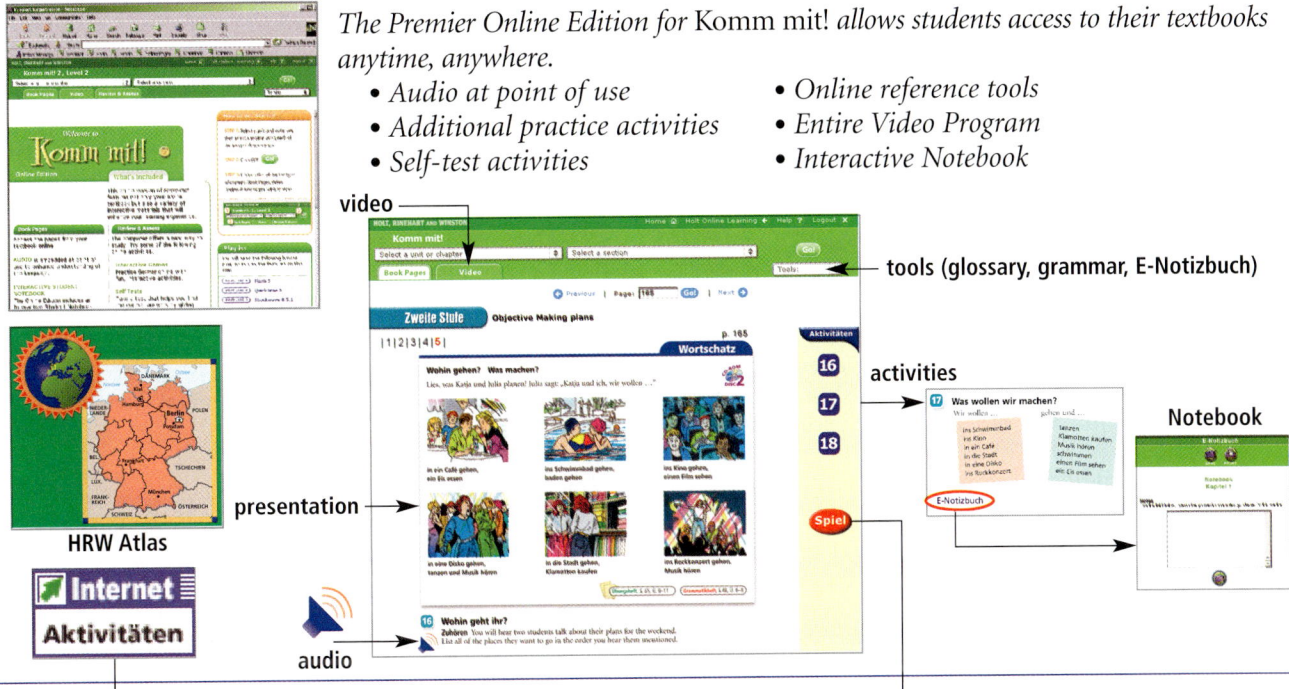

Internet Aktivitäten

These guided internet activities include a worksheet and pre-selected and pre-screened authentic web sites from the German-speaking countries. You can use these activities

- to help students develop research skills in the target language
- to introduce students to authentic cultural information
- as a project

Interaktive Spiele

You can use the interactive activities in this chapter
- to practice grammar, vocabulary, and chapter functions
- as homework
- as an assessment option
- as a self-test
- to prepare for the Chapter Test

Webprojekt Have students visit an online gift shop in Germany. They should find a birthday present for their mother or father that does not cost more than 50 euros. Have students report on the item they chose. How much does it cost and why did they choose this particular item? Encourage students to exchange useful Web sites with their classmates. Have students document their sources by referencing the names and URLs of all the sites they consulted.

STANDARDS: 1.2, 1.3, 3.2, 5.1   KAPITEL 2   TECHNOLOGY   **31F**

Kapitel 2: Bastis Plan
Textbook Listening Activities Scripts
Review Chapter

Erste Stufe

5   p. 37

1. Jutta   Ja, ich muss zu Hause schon was helfen. Also, ich putze das Badezimmer ein- oder zweimal in der Woche. Dann gehe ich nachmittags auch einkaufen oder zur Post, je nach dem, was so anfällt. Außerdem sortiere ich den Müll und bringe die Glasflaschen zum Container. Das geht nur bis 18 Uhr, danach darf man's nicht mehr, wegen Lärmschutz!

2. Rolf   Ja, also ich hab noch zwei Geschwister, und bei uns muss jeder was zu Hause machen. Diese Woche bin ich mit der Küche dran, das heißt Tisch decken, Geschirr spülen, abtrocknen und so. Besonders Spaß macht das nicht, aber ich find's okay, damit meine Eltern nach ihrem Job auch mal relaxen können und nicht direkt zu Hause weiterarbeiten müssen.

3. Franz   Helfen? Ja, direkt helfen muss ich eigentlich nicht so viel. Wir haben nämlich eine Putzfrau. Die kommt zweimal pro Woche und macht eigentlich alles sauber. Meine Eltern wollen lieber, dass ich für die Schule lerne. Aber ab und zu mache ich schon etwas zu Hause, zum Beispiel den Rasen mähen und die Garage aufräumen.

4. Christiane   Ja, ich muss 'ne ganze Menge zu Hause machen. Das find ich echt nicht fair, denn von meinen Freundinnen muss niemand so viel zu Hause machen wie ich! Ich muss mein Zimmer aufräumen, das versteh ich ja noch, aber dann muss ich auch Staub wischen, Staub saugen, den Geschirrspülautomaten leer machen, die Wäsche zusammenfalten und manchmal auch bügeln. Andauernd gibt es was zu tun. Das nervt mich ehrlich!

Answers to Activity 5:   1. Badezimmer putzen; einkaufen; zur Post gehen; Müll sortieren; Glasflaschen zum Container bringen   2. Tisch decken, Geschirr spülen, abtrocknen.   3. Rasen mähen; Garage aufräumen   4. Zimmer aufräumen; Staub wischen; Staub saugen; Geschirrspülautomaten leer machen; Wäsche falten; bügeln

11   p. 38

1. Daniela   Hast du Lust, am Samstagabend ins Kino zu gehen? Der neue Steven-Spielberg-Film läuft im Roxi.

Ilse   Du, ich kann leider nicht, ich bin auf eine Fete eingeladen.

2. Peter   Hallo Martin! Am Sonntag fahr ich nach Garmisch zum Skilaufen. Du kannst mitfahren, wenn du willst.

Martin   Super! Danke für die Einladung!

3. Klaus   He, wir wollen am Wochenende mit der Clique segeln gehen. Willst du mitkommen?

Max   Oh Mann, ich kann überhaupt nicht segeln! Aber ich komm doch mit, okay?

4. Christine   Ich hab gehört, dass Guns 'N' Roses bald auf Konzerttour gehen. Die kommen auch nach München. Ich geh auf jeden Fall hin. Kommst du mit?

Annette   Nein, ganz bestimmt nicht! Ich find die Musik schrecklich.

Answers to Activity 11:   1. declines; 2. accepts; 3. accepts; 4. declines

18   p. 40

Sag mal, wie kann ich dir helfen? Was kann ich für dich tun?

1. Cordula   Du kannst mir beim Einkaufen helfen. Meine Mutter hat hier eine Liste gemacht von allem, was sie braucht. Hol das Brot und den Kuchen beim Bäcker und geh auch zum Metzger, wenn du noch Zeit hast! Den Rest besorg ich dann im Supermarkt.

2. Ulrich   Kannst du meinen kleinen Bruder für mich aus dem Kindergarten holen? Ich habe nämlich heute einen Termin beim Friseur und schaffe es einfach nicht rechtzeitig.

3. Lutz   Weißt du, was du tun kannst? Du kannst mir bei meinen Hausaufgaben helfen! Die Matheaufgaben sind mir viel zu kompliziert. Und wenn du damit fertig bist, kannst du mir helfen, meine Englischvokabeln zu lernen. Danach können wir dann zusammen den Tisch für das Abendessen decken.

Answers to Activity 18
1. Beim Bäcker und Metzger einkaufen   2. Bruder aus dem Kindergarten holen   3. bei Matheaufgaben helfen; bei Englischvokabeln helfen; Tisch decken

Zweite Stufe

24   p. 44

1. Bruno   Ja, also heute hab ich Küchendienst und muss was zu essen kochen. Wir haben zu Hause nur noch zwei oder drei Kartoffeln. Das reicht nicht. Also muss ich einen 3-Kilo-Beutel Kartoffeln besorgen und noch etwas anderes Gemüse dazu, am liebsten mag ich grüne Bohnen. Und dann brauch ich noch ein Hähnchen. Ich glaub, ich hol außerdem noch Tomaten und ein Bund Radieschen. Das Gemüse kaufe ich im Gemüseladen, und das Hähnchen hole ich beim Supermarkt um die Ecke.

2. Heidi   Also, ich kaufe heute nur das ein, was der Supermarkt Bausinger im Sonderangebot hat! Heute sind die Erdbeeren billig, die hol ich ganz bestimmt. Außerdem gibt es dort den Kopfsalat für nur 49 Cent! Ja, und dann nehme ich noch das Hackfleisch und die Butter aus dem Angebot. Eigentlich brauch ich auch noch ein Brot, aber das hol ich lieber beim Bäcker!

Answers to Activity 24
1. Kartoffeln, grüne Bohnen, Tomaten, Radieschen: im Gemüseladen; Hähnchen: im Supermarkt   2. Erdbeeren, Kopfsalat, Hackfleisch, Butter: im Supermarkt Bausinger; Brot: beim Bäcker

27   p. 46

Frische Radieschen, ein Bund nur 49 Cent! Knackfrischer Kopfsalat! Garantiert ohne Pestizide! Zwei Köpfe für einen Euro! Neue Kartoffeln, frisch aus der Erde! Pro Beutel nur 1,49! Holländische Treibhaustomaten! Ein halbes Pfund für 80 Cent! Junge Zucchinis! Direkt vom Gemüsebauer! Vier Stück für nur 2 Euro 10! Zwiebeln und Karotten im 5-Kilo-Beutel für jeweils einen Euro 50!

Answers to Activity 27:   Radieschen; Kopfsalat; Kartoffeln; Tomaten; Zucchinis; Zwiebeln; Karotten

The following scripts are for the listening activities found in the *Pupil's Edition*. For Student Response Forms, see *Listening Activities*, pages 11–14. To provide students with additional listening practice, see *Listening Activities*, pages 15–18.

For resource information, see the **One-Stop Planner** CD-ROM, Disc 1.

29 p. 46

1. GABI Also, ich habe mir gerade ein halbes Pfund süße italienische Trauben auf dem Markt am Rathausplatz gekauft. Dort ist das Obst immer frisch, und man kann es vorher auch probieren!

2. WOLFGANG Die Kirschtorte hier ist von der Bäckerei am Stadttor. Die haben die leckersten Backwaren der ganzen Stadt! Jeder sagt, dass sie dort am besten schmecken.

3. UDO Ich war heute beim Metzger Gutmann und habe einen Haufen Aufschnitt gekauft, also Salami, Kalbsleberwurst, gekochten Schinken und Corned Beef. Ich kaufe Wurst lieber beim Metzger als im Supermarkt, weil der Metzger viele verschiedene Sachen hat.

4. URSULA Heute bin ich für meine Mutter einkaufen gegangen, lauter Konservendosen, als Vorrat für die Speisekammer! Also, Pilze, grüne Bohnen, Tomatenpüree, Mais, alles in Dosen. Ich hab das ganze Zeug bei Aldo-Discount geholt. Dort ist es am billigsten!

Answers to Activity 29   a. 1: Markt am Rathausplatz; 2: Bäckerei am Stadttor; 3: Metzger Gutmann; 4: Supermarkt Aldo-Discount   b. 1: Obst frisch und man kann es probieren; 2: schmeckt lecker; 3: viele verschiedene Sachen; 4: billig

Dritte Stufe

31 p. 49

1. VOLKER Meine Schwester hat nächste Woche Geburtstag. Ich hol ihr einen Tennisschläger. Den wünscht sie sich schon lange, damit sie mit ihrer Freundin Tennis spielen kann.

2. RÜDIGER Meine Oma und mein Opa feiern heute ihren 40-jährigen Hochzeitstag. Wir schenken ihnen ein Gemälde, das total gut in ihr Wohnzimmer passt.

3. ANJA Ich bin am Samstag auf 'ne Fete beim Jürgen, 'nem Schulkameraden, eingeladen, aber ich kenn den Typ leider überhaupt nicht so gut. Ich glaub, ich schenke ihm nichts, ich bring einfach nur Cola und Kartoffelchips oder Salzstangen mit!

4. CHRISTA Zu Weihnachten schenken meine Geschwister und ich meinen Eltern einen neuen Radiowecker. Der alte funktioniert nämlich manchmal nicht mehr!

Answers to Activity 31:   1. Tennisschläger für die Schwester;   2. Gemälde für Oma und Opa;   3. nichts;   4. Radiowecker für Eltern.

34 p. 50

1. RENATE Also, zum Geburtstag mag ich als Geschenk zum Beispiel eine CD, oder ein Abonnement für 'ne Zeitschrift, die ich gut finde. Was ich überhaupt nicht mag, sind so traditionelle Sachen wie Blumen oder Pralinen.

2. TANJA Ich mag Blumen unheimlich gern. Mein ganzes Zimmer ist voll von Pflanzen und Blumen, und ich freue mich immer, wenn ich welche zum Geburtstag kriege. Aber zum Beispiel neue Klamotten als Geschenk, mag ich überhaupt nicht. Mode ist mir nämlich total egal.

3. KONRAD Ich mag es gern, wenn es zu meinem Geburtstag eine Torte gibt, eine Schwarzwälder Kirschtorte genauer gesagt. So einen normalen Kuchen, wie zum Beispiel Nusskuchen, mag ich nicht. Es muss schon eine richtige Torte sein!

Answers to Activity 34:   1. mag: CD, Abonnement für Zeitschrift; mag nicht: Blumen und Pralinen   2. mag: Blumen und Pflanzen; mag nicht: Klamotten   3. mag: Torte; mag nicht: Nusskuchen

37 p. 51

1. OTTO Also, ich hab zum Geburtstag drei CDs geschenkt bekommen. Die mit der Country-Musik mag ich lieber als die von der Techno-Gruppe. Aber am liebsten hör ich die Heavy Metal CD.

2. HANS Wenn ich ins Kino gehe, seh ich mir normalerweise nur Actionfilme an. Die mag ich am liebsten. Aber wenn gerade keiner läuft, guck ich schon mal Slapstick-Komödien. Die mag ich auf jeden Fall lieber als so'n kitschiges romantisches Zeug wie *Bodyguard!*

3. INGE Also, wenn mir jemand Bücher oder CDs zum Geburtstag schenken will, dann würde ich lieber Bücher haben. Mein Musikgeschmack ändert sich so schnell, aber wenn ich ein Buch gut finde, dann mag ich es eigentlich für längere Zeit. Am liebsten lese ich Sciencefictionromane.

4. MONIKA In der Pause hol ich mir am liebsten 'ne Pizza vom Imbiss. Aber wenn ich mir was von zu Hause mitbringe, dann nehm ich lieber Brezeln als ein langweiliges Butterbrot.

Answers to Activity 37:   1. Country lieber als Techno; Heavy Metal am liebsten   2. Slapstick-Komödien lieber als Romanzen; Actionfilme am liebsten   3. Bücher lieber als CDs; Sciencefictionromane am liebsten   4. Brezeln lieber als Butterbrot; Pizza am liebsten

40 p. 52

1. SABINE Hm, die Schokoladentorte ist wahnsinnig lecker! Ich glaub, ich nehme noch ein Stück!

2. THOMAS Also, dieser Hamburger war echt gigantisch! Ich bin total satt und mag meinen Joghurt nicht mehr!

3. SILKE Ich habe gerade fast eine ganze Flasche Mineralwasser ausgetrunken. Jetzt habe ich keinen Durst mehr!

4. MARKUS Ich nehme noch ein Brötchen mit Ei. Heute bin ich tierisch hungrig!

Answers to Activity 40:   1. mehr = ist lecker; 2. nichts mehr = ist satt; 3. nichts mehr = viel getrunken; 4. mehr = ist sehr hungrig

KAPITEL 2   SCRIPTS   31H

Kapitel 2: Bastis Plan

Review Chapter

Suggested Lesson Plans — 50-Minute Schedule

Day 1

CHAPTER OPENER 10 min.
- Teaching Suggestion, ATE, p. 31M
- Culture Note, ATE, p. 31M
- Challenge, ATE, p. 3M

LOS GEHT'S! 25 min.
- Preteaching Vocabulary, ATE, p. 31N
- Have students read **Los geht's!**, pp. 34–35
- Teaching Suggestions, Video Guide, p. 10
- Language Note, ATE, p. 31N
- Show **Los geht's!** Video
- Begin Comprehension Activities, p. 36

ERSTE STUFE 10 min.
- Play Audio CD for Activity 5, p. 37
- Do Activity 6, p. 37

Wrap-Up 5 min.
- Students respond to questions about chores they must do

Homework Options
Pupil's Edition, p. 36, Comprehension Acts.
Übungsheft, p. 13, Act. 1

Day 2

ERSTE STUFE
Quick Review 10 min.
- Check homework, p. 36, Comprehension Activities

So sagt man das!, p. 37 10 min.
- Presenting **So sagt man das!**, ATE, p. 31O
- Do Activity 7, p. 37

Ein wenig Grammatik/Wortschatz, p. 37 15 min.
- Presenting **Ein wenig Grammatik**, ATE, p. 31O
- Presenting **Wortschatz**, ATE, p. 31O
- Do Activity 8, p. 37
- Do Activities 9 and 10, p. 38
- Play Audio CD for Activity 11, p. 38

So sagt man das!, p. 38 10 min.
- Presenting **So sagt man das!**, ATE, p. 31O
- Do Activities 12, 13, and 14, p. 39

Wrap-Up 5 min.
- Students respond to invitations to go to various places

Homework Options
Grammatikheft, pp. 10–11, Acts. 1–4
Übungsheft, pp. 14–16, Acts. 1–5

Day 3

ERSTE STUFE
Quick Review 10 min.
- Check homework, Grammatikheft, pp. 10–11, Acts. 1–4

Ein wenig Grammatik, p. 39 10 min.
- Presenting **Ein wenig Grammatik**, ATE, p. 31P
- Do Activities 15 and 16, p. 39
- Do Activity 17, p. 40
- Play Audio CD for Activity 18, p. 40

So sagt man das!/Ein wenig Grammatik, p. 40 10 min.
- Presenting **So sagt man das!**, ATE, p. 31P
- Presenting **Ein wenig Grammatik**, ATE, p. 31P
- Do Activities 19 and 20, pp. 40–41

Ein wenig Grammatik, p. 41 15 min.
- Reteaching, ATE, p. 31P
- Do Activities 21, 22, and 23, p. 41

Wrap-Up 5 min.
- Students respond to questions about whom they can help

Homework Options
Grammatikheft, p. 12, Acts. 5–6
Übungsheft, p. 16, Acts. 6–7

Day 4

ERSTE STUFE
Quick Review 10 min.
- Check homework, Grammatikheft, p. 12, Acts. 5–6

ZUM LESEN 20 min.
- Present **Lesestrategie**, p. 42
- Do Activities 1–8, pp. 42–43

Quiz Review 15 min.
- Do **Mehr Grammatikübungen, Erste Stufe**
- Do Additional Listening Activities 2-1 and 2-2, pp. 15–16

Wrap-Up 5 min.
- Students respond to questions about what is good and bad about school

Homework Options
Übungsheft, p. 17, Acts. 1–3
Activities for Communication, p. 78, fill out Realia 2-1
Interactive CD-ROM, Acts. 1–2

Day 5

ERSTE STUFE
Quick Review 10 min.
- Check homework, Realia 2-1

Quiz 20 min.
- Quiz 2-1A or 2-1B

Project 20 min.
- Begin Project, ATE, p. 31C

Homework Options
Project Surveys (see ATE, p. 31C)

Day 6

ZWEITE STUFE
Quick Review 15 min.
- Return and review Quiz 2-1
- Bell Work, ATE, p. 31S
- Preliminary Project Reports

Wortschatz, p. 44 15 min.
- Play Audio CD for Activity 24, p. 44
- Presenting **Wortschatz**, ATE, p. 31S
- Teaching Transparency 2-B
- Do Activity 25, p. 45

So sagt man das!/ Ein wenig Grammatik, p. 45 15 min.
- Presenting **So sagt man das!**, ATE, p. 31S
- Presenting **Ein wenig Grammatik**, ATE, p. 31S
- Do Activity 26, p. 45
- Play Audio CD for Activity 27, p. 46

Wrap-Up 5 min.
- Students respond to questions about what they should buy and where they should buy it

Homework Options
Grammatikheft, p. 13, Acts. 7–9
Übungsheft, p. 18, Act. 1

One-Stop Planner CD-ROM

For alternative lesson plans by chapter section, to create your own customized plans, or to preview all resources available for this chapter, use the **One-Stop Planner CD-ROM**, Disc 1.

 For additional homework suggestions, see activities accompanied by this symbol throughout the chapter.

Day 7

ZWEITE STUFE

Quick Review 10 min.
- Check homework, Grammatikheft, p. 13, Acts. 7–9

So sagt man das!, p. 46 15 min.
- Presenting **So sagt man das!**, ATE, p. 31T
- Do Activity 28, p. 46
- Play Audio CD for Activity 29, p. 46

So sagt man das!/Ein wenig Grammatik, pp. 46–47 15 min.
- Presenting **So sagt man das!**, ATE, p. 31T
- Presenting **Ein wenig Grammatik**, ATE, p. 31T
- Do Activity 30, p. 47
- Do Activities 5–7, p. 20, Übungsheft

Quiz Review 10 min.
- Do **Mehr Grammatikübungen**, Zweite Stufe

Homework Options
Grammatikheft, p. 14, Acts. 10–11
Übungsheft, p. 19, Acts. 2–4

Day 8

ZWEITE STUFE

Quick Review 10 min.
- Check homework, Übungsheft, p. 19, Acts. 2–4

LANDESKUNDE 20 min.
- Pre-viewing Suggestion, Video Guide, p. 10
- Teaching Suggestion, ATE, p. 31U
- Show **Landeskunde** Video
- Do Activities A and B, p. 48
- Do Activities 1–3, p. 21, Übungsheft

Quiz 20 min.
- Quiz 2-2A or 2-2B

Homework Options
Activities for Communication, p. 79, Realia 2-2: plan a menu, make a shopping list, and figure out how much the groceries cost

Day 9

DRITTE STUFE

Quick Review 10 min.
- Return and review Quiz 2-2
- Bell Work, ATE, p. 31V
- Check homework, Realia 2-2
- Play Audio CD for Activity 31, p. 49

Wortschatz/So sagt man das!, pp. 49–50 15 min.
- Presenting **So sagt man das!**, ATE, p. 31V
- Teaching Transparency 2-2
- Do Activities 32 and 33, p. 50

Ein wenig Grammatik/So sagt man das!, p. 50 20 min.
- Presenting **Ein wenig Grammatik**, ATE, p. 31V
- Presenting **So sagt man das!**, ATE, p. 31W
- Play Audio CD for Activity 34, p. 50
- Do Activities 35 and 36, p. 51
- Play Audio CD for Activity 37, p. 51

Wrap-Up 5 min.
- Students respond to questions about giving gifts to relatives

Homework Options
Grammatikheft, p. 15, Acts. 12–13

Day 10

DRITTE STUFE

Quick Review 10 min.
- Check homework, Grammatikheft, p. 15, Acts. 12–13

So sagt man das!, p. 51 15 min.
- Presenting **So sagt man das!**, ATE, p. 31W
- Do Activity 38, p. 51
- Do Activity 39, p. 52
- Do Activities 6–7, p. 24, Übungsheft
- Play Audio CD for Activity 40, p. 52

So sagt man das!/Ein wenig Grammatik, p. 52 20 min.
- Presenting **So sagt man das!/Ein wenig Grammatik**, ATE, p. 31W
- Culture Notes, ATE, p. 31W
- Do Activity 41, p. 52
- Do Activities 42 and 44, p. 53

Wrap-Up 5 min.
- Students respond to questions about things they like, prefer and like the most

Homework Options
Pupil's Edition, p. 53, Activity 43
Grammatikheft, pp. 16–17, Acts. 14–18
Übungsheft, pp. 22–23, Acts. 1–5

Day 11

DRITTE STUFE

Quick Review 15 min.
- Check homework, Übungsheft, pp. 22–23, Acts. 1–5

Quiz Review 15 min.
- Do **Mehr Grammatikübungen**, Dritte Stufe
- Do Acts. 19–21, p. 18, Grammatikheft

Quiz 20 min.
- Quiz 2-3A or 2-3B

Homework Options
Pupil's Edition, p. 58, **Kann ich's wirklich?**
Interaktive Spiele, see ATE, p. 31F
Complete Projects

Day 12

REVIEW

Quick Review 10 min.
- Return and review Quiz 2-3
- Check homework, p. 58, **Kann ich's wirklich?**

Final Project Reports 15 min.

Chapter Review 25 min.
- Review chapter functions, vocabulary, and grammar; choose from **Mehr Grammatikübungen**, Grammar Tutor for Students of German, Activities for Communication, Listening Activities, Interactive CD-ROM Tutor, or **Interaktive Spiele**
- Review test format and provide sample test items for students

Homework Options
Study for Chapter Test

Assessment

Test, Chapter 2 45 min.
- Administer Chapter 2 Test. Select from Testing Program, Alternative Assessment Guide, or Test Generator.

KAPITEL 2 • SUGGESTED LESSON PLANS • 50-MINUTE SCHEDULE 31J

Kapitel 2: Bastis Plan

Review Chapter

Suggested Lesson Plans 90-Minute Schedule

Block 1

CHAPTER OPENER 10 min.
- Teaching Suggestion, ATE, p. 31M
- Culture Note, ATE, p. 31M
- Challenge, ATE, p. 3M

LOS GEHT'S! 25 min.
- Preteaching Vocabulary, ATE, p. 31N
- Have students read **Los geht's!**, pp. 34–35
- Teaching Suggestions, Video Guide, p. 10
- Language Note, ATE, p. 31N
- Show **Los geht's!** Video
- Begin Comprehension Activities, p. 36

ERSTE STUFE 10 min.
- Play Audio CD for Activity 5, p. 37
- Do Activity 6, p. 37

So sagt man das!, p. 37 10 min.
- Presenting **So sagt man das!**, ATE, p. 31O
- Do Activity 7, p. 37

Ein wenig Grammatik/Wortschatz, p. 37 20 min.
- Presenting **Ein wenig Grammatik**, ATE, p. 31O
- Presenting **Wortschatz**, ATE, p. 31O
- Teaching Transparencies 2-1, 2-A
- Do Activity 8, p. 37
- Do Activities 9 and 10, p. 38
- Play Audio CD for Activity 11, p. 38

So sagt man das!, p. 38 10 min.
- Presenting **So sagt man das!**, ATE, p. 31O
- Do Activities 12, 13, and 14, p. 39

Wrap-Up 5 min.
- Students respond to invitations to go to various places

Homework Options
Pupil's Edition, p. 36, Comprehension Acts.
Grammatikheft, pp. 10–11, Acts. 1–4
Übungsheft, p. 13, Act. 1; pp. 14–16, Acts. 1–5

Block 2

ERSTE STUFE
Quick Review 10 min.
- Check homework, Grammatikheft, pp. 10–11, Acts. 1–4

Ein wenig Grammatik, p. 39 20 min.
- Presenting **Ein wenig Grammatik**, ATE, p. 31P
- Do Activities 15 and 16, p. 39
- Do Activity 17, p. 40
- Play Audio CD for Activity 18, p. 40

So sagt man das!/Ein wenig Grammatik, p. 40 20 min.
- Presenting **So sagt man das!**, ATE, p. 31P
- Presenting **Ein wenig Grammatik**, ATE, p. 31P
- Do Activity 19, p. 40
- Do Activity 20, p. 41

Ein wenig Grammatik, p. 41 15 min.
- Reteaching: Accusative Pronouns, ATE, p. 31P
- Do Activities 21, 22, and 23, p. 41

ZUM LESEN 20 min.
- Present **Lesestrategie**, p. 42
- Do Activities 1–8, pp. 42–43

Wrap-Up 5 min.
- Students respond to questions about what is good and bad about school

Homework Options
Grammatikheft, p. 12, Acts. 5–6
Übungsheft, p. 16, Acts. 6–7; p. 17, Acts. 1–3
Interactive CD-ROM, Acts. 1–2

Block 3

ZWEITE STUFE
Quick Review 10 min.
- Check homework, Grammatikheft, p. 12, Acts. 5–6

Quiz Review 10 min.
- Do **Mehr Grammatikübungen, Erste Stufe**

Quiz 20 min.
- Quiz 2-1A or 2-1B

Wortschatz, p. 44 10 min.
- Play Audio CD for Activity 24, p. 44
- Presenting **Wortschatz**, ATE, p. 31S
- Teaching Transparency 2-B
- Do Activity 25, p. 45

So sagt man das!/ Ein wenig Grammatik, p. 45 20 min.
- Presenting **So sagt man das!**, ATE, p. 31S
- Presenting **Ein wenig Grammatik**, ATE, p. 31S
- Do Activity 1, p. 18, Übungsheft
- Do Activity 26, p. 45
- Play Audio CD for Activity 27, p. 46

So sagt man das!, p. 46 15 min.
- Presenting **So sagt man das!**, ATE, p. 31T
- Do Activity 28, p. 46
- Play Audio CD for Activity 29, p. 46

Wrap-Up 5 min.
- Students respond to questions about what they should buy and where they should buy it

Homework Options
Grammatikheft, p. 13, Acts. 7–9
Übungsheft, p. 19, Acts. 2–4

One-Stop Planner CD-ROM

For alternative lesson plans by chapter section, to create your own customized plans, or to preview all resources available for this chapter, use the **One-Stop Planner CD-ROM**, Disc 1.

 For additional homework suggestions, see activities accompanied by this symbol throughout the chapter.

Block 4

ZWEITE STUFE

Quick Review 10 min.
- Check homework Grammatikheft, p. 13, Acts. 7–9

So sagt man das!/Ein wenig Grammatik, pp. 46–47 25 min.
- Presenting **So sagt man das!**, ATE, p. 31T
- Presenting **Ein wenig Grammatik**, ATE, p. 31T
- Do Activity 30, p. 47
- Do Activities 5–7, p. 20, Übungsheft
- Do Activities 10–11, p. 14, Grammatikheft

LANDESKUNDE 20 min.
- Pre-viewing Suggestion, Video Guide, p. 10
- Teaching Suggestion, ATE, p. 31U
- Show **Landeskunde** Video
- Do Activities A and B, p. 48
- Do Activities 1–3, p. 21, Übungsheft

Quiz Review 15 min.
- Do **Mehr Grammatikübungen**, Zweite Stufe

Quiz 20 min.
- Quiz 2-2A or 2-2B

Homework Options
Activities for Communication, p. 79, Realia 2-2: plan a menu, make a shopping list, and figure out how much the groceries cost

Block 5

DRITTE STUFE

Quick Review 15 min.
- Return and review Quiz 2-2
- Bell Work, ATE, p. 31V
- Check homework, Realia 2-2
- Play Audio CD for Activity 31, p. 49

Wortschatz/So sagt man das!, pp. 49–50 15 min.
- Presenting **So sagt man das!**, ATE, p. 31V
- Teaching Transparency 2-2
- Do Activities 32 and 33, p. 50

Ein wenig Grammatik/So sagt man das!, p. 50 20 min.
- Presenting **Ein wenig Grammatik**, ATE, p. 31V
- Presenting **So sagt man das!**, ATE, p. 31W
- Play Audio CD for Activity 34, p. 50
- Do Activities 35 and 36, p. 51
- Play Audio CD for Activity 37, p. 51

So sagt man das!, p. 51 15 min.
- Presenting **So sagt man das!**, ATE, p. 31W
- Do Activity 38, p. 51
- Do Activity 39, p. 52
- Play Audio CD for Activity 40, p. 52

So sagt man das!/Ein wenig Grammatik, p. 52 20 min.
- Presenting **So sagt man das!/Ein wenig Grammatik**, ATE, p. 31W
- Culture Notes, ATE, p. 31W
- Do Activity 41, p. 52
- Do Activities 42 and 44, p. 53

Wrap-Up 5 min.
- Students answer questions about wanting something else to eat

Homework Options
Pupil's Edition, p. 53, Activity 43
Grammatikheft, pp. 15–18, Acts. 12–21
Übungsheft, pp. 22–24, Acts. 1–7

Block 6

DRITTE STUFE

Quick Review 15 min.
- Check homework, Grammatikheft, pp. 15–18, Acts. 12–21

Quiz Review 25 min.
- Do **Mehr Grammatikübungen**, Dritte Stufe
- Play **Das tut mir Leid**, ATE, p. 31C

Quiz 20 min.
- Quiz 2-3A or 2-3B

Kann ich's wirklich? 25 min.
- Do Activities 1–11, p. 58

Wrap-Up 5 min.
- Students respond to questions about giving gifts to relatives

Homework Options
Interaktive Spiele, see ATE, p. 31F

Block 7

REVIEW

Quick Review 10 min.
- Return and review Quiz 2-3

Chapter Review 35 min.
- Review chapter functions, vocabulary, and grammar; choose from **Mehr Grammatikübungen,** Grammar Tutor for Students of German, Activities for Communication, Listening Activities, Interactive CD-ROM Tutor, or **Interaktive Spiele**
- Review test format and provide sample test items for students

Test, Chapter 2 45 min.
- Administer Chapter 2 Test. Select from Testing Program, Alternative Assessment Guide, or Test Generator.

Kapitel 2: Bastis Plan
Teaching Suggestions, pages 32–59

Review Chapter

Teacher Note
Chapter 2 is a review chapter that reintroduces functions, grammar, and vocabulary from Komm mit! Level 1.

PAGES 32–33

CHAPTER OPENER

Pacing Tips
Chapter 2 is a review chapter. In the **Erste Stufe** students review the functions of 'expressing obligations,' 'extending and responding to an invitation,' and 'offering help and telling what to do.' The **Zweite Stufe** centers around groceries and the functions of 'asking and telling what to do,' 'telling that you need something else,' and 'telling where you were and what you bought.' In the **Dritte Stufe**, gifts and food are presented alongside the review functions. Because the **Zweite Stufe** is shorter than the other two **Stufen** and has fewer words in the **Wortschatz**, you might spend slightly less time teaching it. For Lesson Plans and timing suggestions, see pages 31I–31L.

Meeting the Standards
Communication
- Expressing obligations, p. 37
- Extending and responding to an invitation, p. 38
- Offering help and telling what to do, p. 40
- Asking and telling what to do, p. 45
- Telling that you need something else, p. 46
- Telling where you were and what you bought, p. 46
- Discussing gift ideas, p. 50
- Expressing likes and dislikes, p. 50
- Expressing likes, preferences, and favorites, p. 51
- Saying you do or don't want more, p. 52

Cultures
- **Landeskunde,** p. 48
- Language Note, p. 31N
- Culture Note, p. 31R
- Culture Notes, p. 31W

Connections
- Thinking Critically, p. 31T
- Multicultural Connection, p. 31U

Comparisons
- Thinking Critically, p. 31Q
- Teaching Suggestions, p. 31S
- Language Note, p. 31T
- Language-to-Language, p. 31W

One-Stop Planner CD-ROM

For resource information, see the **One-Stop Planner CD-ROM,** Disc 1.

Communities
- Culture Note, p. 31M

Teaching Suggestion
Ask students how they have to help around the house and how the work is divided up among family members. Which chores do they not mind and which ones do they dislike?

Cultures and Communities
Culture Note
In the German-speaking countries, it is common to bring a small gift when visiting friends or relatives. Ask students what they take when visiting relatives or friends.

Communication for All Students
Challenge
Have students work with a partner and write a brief dialogue that could accompany the photo. Give a time limit of five minutes, then call on several pairs to read their conversations.

Chapter Sequence
Los geht's!	p. 34
Erste Stufe	p. 37
Zum Lesen	p. 42
Zweite Stufe	p. 44
Landeskunde	p. 48
Dritte Stufe	p. 49
Mehr Grammatikübungen	p. 54
Kann ich's wirklich?	p. 58
Wortschatz	p. 59

STANDARDS: 1.3, 2.1

LOS GEHT'S!

Teaching Resources
pp. 34–36

PRINT
- Lesson Planner, p. 7
- Video Guide, pp. 9–10, 12
- Übungsheft, p. 13

MEDIA
- One-Stop Planner
- Video Program
  Los geht's!
  Videocassette 1, 19:52–22:27
  Videocassette 5 (captioned version), 06:51–09:25
  Fortsetzung
  Videocassette 1, 22:30–27:25
  Videocassette 5 (captioned version), 09:28–14:23
- DVD Tutor, Disc 1
- Audio Compact Discs, CD2, Trs. 1–2
- Los geht's! Transparencies

PAGES 34–35

Los geht's! Transparencies

Preteaching Vocabulary

Activating Prior Knowledge

Point out that the setting for this **Los geht's!** is the Baumann's kitchen and that everyone in the family is home. As a review, have students list time expressions mentioned in the photo spread. Can they identify words referring to the past, present, and future? Then ask students to look for the two sentences that are in the past tense
❸ **Das hab ich schon gestern gehört.**
❼ **Deshalb hat er so schnell mit dem Robert getauscht.** Finally, ask students to categorize the remaining sentences according to the verb. Possible categories are modals, commands, present tense, and no verb (sentence fragment or exclamation).

Fortsetzung

You may choose to continue with the **Fortsetzung** of **Basti, das Schlitzohr!** now or wait until later in the chapter. For a synopsis of the **Los geht's!** and **Fortsetzung** episodes, see p. 31E.

STANDARDS: 1.1

Advance Organizer

Ask students if and how they have tried to get out of doing chores around the house. What excuses have worked for them? Which ones haven't?

Cultures and Communities

Language Note

Schlitzohr means *rascal*. The word originated years ago when swindlers were punished by having their ears slit.

Building on Previous Skills

Ask students to briefly look at the **Wochenplan.** Whose chores would they prefer to do and why? Encourage students to use **denn** or **weil** in their responses.

PAGE 36

Using the Captioned Video/DVD

❷ As an alternative to reading the conversations in the book, you might want to show the captioned version of *Basti, das Schlitzohr!* available on Videocassette 5.
Note: The *DVD Tutor* contains captions for all sections of the *Video Program*.

Comprehension Check

Challenge

❸ After students have completed Activity 3, have them extend their answers for both the **Stimmt** and **Stimmt nicht** categories.
Examples:
Heute will Sebastian in der Küche helfen.
Stimmt nicht! Er will nicht helfen. Er will mit Robert tauschen und zum Opa gehen.

Heute Nachmittag gibt es keinen Regen.
Stimmt! Das Wetter ist gut. Die Familie kann bei den Großeltern im Garten sitzen.

Auditory Learners

❹ Put the eight words in the box on a transparency or the board. Then ask students to close their books as you read each sentence to the class. After each sentence, students choose the word that best completes the statement. Repeat, but this time take groups of sentences and not necessarily in sequence.
Example: 6., 7., 8.; then 1., 2., 3.; then 4., 5.

KAPITEL 2   LOS GEHT'S!   **31N**

ERSTE STUFE

> ### Teaching Resources
> pp. 37–41
>
> **PRINT**
> - Lesson Planner, p. 8
> - TPR Storytelling Book, pp. 8–9
> - Listening Activities, pp. 11, 15–16
> - Activities for Communication, pp. 7–8, 78, 81, 125–126
> - Grammatikheft, pp. 10–12
> - Grammar Tutor for Students of German, Chapter 2
> - Übungsheft, pp. 14–16
> - Testing Program, pp. 27–30
> - Alternative Assessment Guide, p. 33
> - Student Make-Up Assignments, Chapter 2
>
> **MEDIA**
> - One-Stop Planner
> - Audio Compact Discs, CD2, Trs. 3–5, 17, 22–23
> - Teaching Transparencies
>   Situation 2-1
>   Vocabulary 2-A
>   **Mehr Grammatikübungen** Answers
>   Grammatikheft Answers
> - Interactive CD-ROM Tutor, Disc 1
> - DVD Tutor, Disc 1

PAGE 37

Bell Work
Have students list in German at least three things that they have to do this week. (Examples: chores, activities, appointments)

> **Communication for All Students**
>
> **Comparing and Contrasting**
> **5** After students have listened to the activity, ask them whose chores resemble their own the most. What are the things they also have to do?

PRESENTING: So sagt man das!
After reading **So sagt man das!** with the class, ask students for information, using sentences that contain the verb **müssen**.
Examples:
Was müsst ihr heute im Sportunterricht machen?
Was muss dein Bruder zu Hause alles tun?

PRESENTING: Ein wenig Grammatik
Forms of müssen Review the forms of **müssen** with a fast-paced question-answer practice that focuses on form but is still communicative. Using the same phrase through several exchanges, point to students to signal second or third person. Nod or shake your head to indicate a positive or a negative response.
Examples:
Ich muss jetzt gehen.
Musst du auch gehen?   Ja, ich muss auch gehen.
Und er, muss er gehen?   Nein, er muss nicht gehen.
Ihr beide, müsst ihr jetzt gehen?   Ja, wir müssen jetzt gehen.

PRESENTING: Wortschatz
Divide students into groups of three or four. Allow them five minutes to brainstorm and write down as many German phrases as they can remember that relate to household chores (introduced in Chapter 7 of Level 1). When they have finished, review this vocabulary with them. As they name the chores in the **Wortschatz**, write down the German equivalents on the board. When all the new vocabulary has been presented, take a straw poll of the class to find out how many students must do each of these newly introduced chores.

PAGE 38

Teaching Suggestion
10 Remind students to use sequencing words in their answers. (Examples: **zuerst, dann, danach**)

PRESENTING: So sagt man das!
To practice the expressions, make many suggestions for which students may either choose an accepting or declining phrase from **So sagt man das!**
Example:
—Hannah, willst du heute mit deiner Schwester ins Einkaufszentrum gehen?
—Ich geh gern mit!

PAGE 39

Reteaching: 24-Hour Time
14 Using a clock with moveable hands, review 24-hour time. Show several different times and indicate whether it is **nachts, morgens, mittags, nachmittags,** or **abends.** Ask students to give the time accordingly.

PRESENTING: Ein wenig Grammatik

The interrogative warum On the left side of a transparency or work sheet, write several questions that begin with the interrogative **warum**. On the right side, write possible answers for each of the questions in random order. Ask students to combine the sentences first using **weil**, then using **denn**.
Examples:
Warum schenkst du Dieter einen Fußball zum Geburtstag?
Fußball ist sein Lieblingssport.
Ich schenke Dieter einen Fußball, weil Fußball sein Lieblingssport ist.

Warum lernst du Deutsch?
Wir reisen im Sommer nach Deutschland.
Ich lerne Deutsch, denn wir reisen im Sommer nach Deutschland.

Communication for All Students

Thinking Critically

Analyzing Ask students to compare the word order before and after the changes they made. What can they conclude about the word order of dependent clauses?

Cultures and Communities

Career Path

Have students think of reasons Americans employed by multinational corporations based in the United States might benefit from a solid knowledge of German. (Suggestions: They could handle communications with the German branch of the company, and even transfer to Germany to live and work; if the company didn't already have a branch in a German-speaking country and wanted to expand, they could assist in establishing the company in the new location.)

> **PAGE 40**

PRESENTING: So sagt man das!

After reading the expressions introduced in **So sagt man das!** tell students to imagine that their best friend owes them a favor. What would the students like their friends to do for them?

PRESENTING: Ein wenig Grammatik

Forms of können Review the forms of **können** with fast-paced question-answer practice involving the whole class. Use the same phrase so that attention is on producing the right form. Point to students to signal second or third person. Nod or shake your head to signal positive or negative responses.
Examples:
Ich mache am Samstag eine Party.
Kannst du kommen?   Ja, ich kann kommen.
Könnt ihr kommen?   Nein, wir können nicht kommen.
Kann (Jill) kommen?   Ja, sie kann kommen.

> **PAGE 41**

Reteaching: Accusative Pronouns

Review the accusative pronouns with fast-paced substitution practice. Use the same phrase for a number of substitutions so that attention is on form. Point to students to signal to which person(s) the statement is directed.
Examples:
Ich habe hier viele schöne Geschenke.
Das ist für Peter.   Das ist für *ihn*.
Das ist für Ann.   Das ist für *sie*.
Das ist für Mary und dich. Das ist für *euch*.
Das ist für Gene und mich. Das ist für *uns*.
Das ist für Patty und Jeff. Das ist für *sie*.

Next, do a similar pronoun practice using questions. This forces students to respond rather than merely substitute. Use pictures of foods or actual foods as you offer them to students.
Examples:
Ist das für dich?   Ja, das ist für *mich*.
Ist das für euch?   Ja, das ist für *uns*.
Ist das für die Barbara?   Ja, das ist für *sie*.
Ist das für den George?   Ja, das ist für *ihn*.
Ist das für die beiden?   Ja, das ist für *sie*.

Game

Divide the class into two teams. Team A sends a student to the front of the class to act out a vocabulary word that you show him or her on an index card (Example: chores for the **Erste Stufe**). A student from Team B tries to guess the word or expression correctly. Only German can be used. Teams receive one point for each correct guess.

Assess

▸ Testing Program, pp. 27–30
  Quiz 2-1A, Quiz 2-1B
  Audio CD2, Tr. 17

▸ Student Make-Up Assignments
  Chapter 2, Alternative Quiz

▸ Alternative Assessment Guide, p. 33

PAGES 42–43

ZUM LESEN

> **Teaching Resources**
> pp. 42–43
>
> **PRINT**
> - Lesson Planner, p. 11
> - Übungsheft, p. 17
> - Reading Strategies and Skills, Chapter 2
> - Lies mit mir! 2, Chapter 2
>
> **MEDIA**
> - One-Stop Planner

Prereading
Building Context
Go around the classroom and ask several students to talk about what they really like about being at school.

Building on Previous Skills
In Chapter 5 of Level 1, on p. 137, students learned to use the word **gefallen** when describing clothing. Help students infer the meaning of **missfallen** based on this knowledge.

Thinking Critically
Drawing Inferences Ask students where this type of text could be found. Can they determine the title of the magazine and who this text is intended for? (*Eltern;* intended for parents)

Teacher Note
Activities 1 and 2 are prereading activities.

Reading
Teaching Suggestion
3 Before doing the reading activities, ask students what facts or information are given about the participants of the survey. (type of school and age) How many are boys and how many are girls? (7/5) How were students able to tell? (**-in** ending for female)

Thinking Critically
Drawing Inferences Have students do Activity 7 in pairs. Then ask them to think of synonyms for the words **ausquatschen, Heimfahrt,** and **aufdrehen.** Students can also describe each word by paraphrasing. (Examples: **ausquats**chen → reden, sprechen; Heimfahrt → nach Hause fahren; aufdrehen → lauter machen). Do students know what **db** stands for? (Dezibel)

Give students other unknown words from the interviews that they should be able to infer from context. Have students work in pairs and try to find synonyms or other words and phrases to explain the new words.

Klaus: das Mieseste; Tim: das Schwitzen; Dieter: scharf denken, sich leicht vertun; Sara: Dreck abladen; Nicole: saumäßig, abgestandene (Buttermilch), (alte) Pantoffeln

> **Connections and Comparisons**
>
> ### Thinking Critically
> **Comparing and Contrasting** Ask students how most school systems in the United States are structured. Make a chart on the board or transparency. Have students tell the corresponding age for each school. (elementary, middle school or junior high, and senior high school) Then introduce the German school system. Use the Culture Note on p. 31R as a transparency or make a handout for students. Explain to students that, in Germany, at the end of the 4th or 6th grade (depending on the **Bundesland** they live in), parents and teachers decide which of the three secondary schools a student should attend (based on academic performance). Discuss how these three schools differ. Please note that the Culture Note on p. 31R is not a comprehensive description but rather a general overview of the German school system.

Cultures and Communities

Culture Note

The **Grundschule** is the first school that German students attend (after **Kindergarten** and **Vorschule**). After completing four or six years in the **Grundschule**, students (together with their teachers and parents) must decide which of several possible secondary schools they will attend:

1. the **Hauptschule,** which prepares students mainly for blue-collar jobs;
2. the **Realschule,** which concludes with the **Mittlere Reife** at the end of 10th grade and prepares students for work in clerical and administrative jobs; or
3. the **Gymnasium,** which is a nine-year program that ends with a rigorous exam called the **Abitur,** successful completion of which qualifies students to attend an **Universität.**

For those who choose the **Hauptschule,** the next step (at age 16) is the **Berufsschule,** which is a state-sponsored vocational school. The **Berufsschule** offers students training in their chosen craft or trade, as well as general clerical training. Students also must undergo practical on-the-job training.

Successful completion of the **Realschule** program (ending with the acquisition of the **Mittlere Reife** diploma) qualifies students either to become employed in a clerical or administrative position, to begin an apprenticeship, or to attend a **Fachgymnasium** (called **Fachoberschule** in some areas). After graduating from a **Fachgymnasium,** students can choose to attend a **Fachhochschule.**

The **Gymnasium** has the highest academic standards of the German secondary schools. Students attend the **Gymnasium** for nine years and receive a diploma called **Abitur** ("**Abi**"), which entitles them to enter an **Universität.** At the **Universität,** German students do not take general courses, but concentrate solely on their major.

In the 1980s, a new type of school was introduced in Germany: the **Gesamtschule.** The **Gesamtschule** has all the above mentioned types of schools in one complex, and students who attend these schools have a better chance of changing from one track to another. Students who start out in the **Hauptschule** program or track and do very well have the opportunity to switch either to a **Gymnasium** or to a **Realschule** track.

Post-Reading
Teacher Note
Activity 8 is a post-reading task that will show whether students can apply what they have learned.

Connections and Comparisons
Teaching Suggestion
Ask students about their overall impression of German students' attitudes toward school. Is it similar or different from the way American students feel about school?

ZWEITE STUFE

Teaching Resources
pp. 44–48

PRINT
- Lesson Planner, p. 9
- TPR Storytelling Book, pp. 10–11
- Listening Activities, pp. 12–13, 16–17
- Activities for Communication, pp. 79, 81, 125–126
- Grammatikheft, pp. 13–14
- Grammar Tutor for Students of German, Chapter 2
- Übungsheft, pp. 18–20
- Testing Program, pp. 31–34
- Alternative Assessment Guide, p. 33
- Student Make-Up Assignments, Chapter 2

MEDIA
- One-Stop Planner
- Audio Compact Discs, CD2, Trs. 6–8, 18, 24–25
- Teaching Transparencies Vocabulary 2-B
  Mehr Grammatikübungen Answers
  Grammatikheft Answers
- Interactive CD-ROM Tutor, Disc 1
- DVD Tutor, Disc 1

PAGE 44

Bell Work
In pairs, have students ask each other in German to recall what foods and beverages are in their refrigerator and pantry at home.

Communication for All Students

A Slower Pace
 Have students listen to the activity twice. The first time, have them record where the two students plan to do their shopping. The second time, have students list the foods they need to buy underneath the names of the stores or places they plan to go to.

Connections and Comparisons

Teaching Suggestions
The ads on p. 44 are a good source of cultural information. Here are several suggestions on how to present them.
1) Have students scan the ads for weights and liquid measurements. (**g** = **Gramm**; **kg** = **Kilogramm; Liter**)
2) Have students scan the ads for quality indicators or descriptors. (**Kl. I** = **Klasse I; Kl. II** = **Klasse II; Spitzenqualität; täglich frisch; ohne Knochen**)
3) Have students find references to the countries or regions of origin of certain products. What do these references imply? (**aus Italien; aus Holland; aus dem Allgäu; deutscher Schnittkäse;** References imply that the products are of good quality.)
4) Have students find references to amounts other than weight and infer the meaning of these words. (**Stück, Bund, Schale, Becher, Beutel**)
5) Have students compare the store hours in German supermarkets to the hours in American stores. Have them look at opening and closing times, lunch time, and Saturday hours.
6) Have students discuss how their family's shopping habits would have to be changed if they lived in Germany. What responsibilities would they as teenagers have?

PRESENTING: Wortschatz
Introduce the new fruits and vegetables by modeling them and having students repeat. Some are difficult to pronounce (P̲firsiche, Z̲wetschgen, E̲rbsen, S̲pinat). Next, ask questions about *likes* and *dislikes*. Examples:
Welches Obst von den drei Obstarten isst du gern?
Welches Gemüse von den drei Gemüsearten isst du gern? nicht gern?

PAGE 45

PRESENTING: So sagt man das!/Ein wenig Grammatik
Sollen/du-commands Have students work together in pairs to formulate a list of five commands or recommendations using **sollen**. They should then convert each of these into a sentence that utilizes a **du**-command. Encourage them to be as creative as possible. When they have finished, have each student read aloud his or her favorite pair of statements.

PAGE 46

Connections and Comparisons

Language Note
A **Kombi** (**Kombiwagen**) is a station wagon or a delivery truck.

PRESENTING: So sagt man das!

Using the lists the students made in Activity 27, ask a student **Was bekommen Sie?** then **Was bekommen Sie noch? Haben Sie noch einen Wunsch? Sonst noch etwas?**, working through students' lists. Ask these questions to one more student. Then have students ask each other similar questions, using **So sagt man das!** as a model.

Teaching Suggestion

28 After students have completed their dialogues, ask for volunteer pairs to act out their skits in front of the class. As a follow-up activity, ask the audience one or two questions per skit to check for comprehension.
Example:
Wie viel Pfund Erdbeeren will Mark kaufen?

Speaking Assessment

28 You may choose to ask pairs to come to your desk and evaluate their dialogues using the following rubric.

Speaking Rubric	Points			
	4	3	2	1
Content (Complete – Incomplete)				
Comprehension (Total – Little)				
Comprehensibility (Comprehensible – Incomprehensible)				
Accuracy (Accurate – Seldom accurate)				
Fluency (Fluent – Not fluent)				

18–20: A   16–17: B   14–15: C   12–13: D   Under 12: F

Portfolio Assessment

29 You might want to use this activity as an oral portfolio item for your students. See *Alternative Assessment Guide*, p. 19.

PRESENTING: So sagt man das!

After reading the examples in **So sagt man das!**, ask students questions based on their skits from Activity 28. Students should respond using the past tense.
Examples:
Sag mal Robin, wo warst du?
Was hast du vom Christopher gekauft?

PAGE 47

Connections and Comparisons

Thinking Critically
30 **Synthesizing** Once students have completed the activity, ask them to name advantages and disadvantages of buying at specialty stores versus large supermarkets. Make a chart on the board or on a transparency. Expand the activity by asking students why it is more popular in Germany to patronize specialty stores than supermarkets.

PRESENTING: Ein wenig Grammatik

Past tense of sein Have the following sentences listed on a transparency. Ask students to restate the sentences in the past tense using the adverbial phrases in parentheses.
Examples:
Jetzt bist du 15 Jahre alt. (Letztes Jahr)
Michael ist durstig. (Nach dem Tennisspiel)
Ich bin so müde. (Vorgestern)
Angela und Rüdiger sind mit Freunden im Kino. (Gestern)
Diane und du, ihr seid oft im Schwimmbad. (Im Sommer)

> **PAGE 48**

 # LANDESKUNDE

Teaching Resources
p. 48

PRINT
- Video Guide, pp. 9–10, 12–13
- Übungsheft, p. 21

MEDIA
- One-Stop Planner
- Video Program
  Videocassette 1, 28:05–29:39
- DVD Tutor, Disc 1
- Audio Compact Discs, CD2, Trs. 9–12
- Interactive CD-ROM Tutor, Disc 1

Teaching Suggestion

Begin **Landeskunde** by having students do the prereading activity. Then play the compact disc or have students watch the video. Before putting students in groups of three and having them practice reading the interviews, practice some of the more difficult passages with the class.

Group Work

Divide students into groups of three or four and have each group work on Activities A1 and A2. Then have each group share the information with the rest of the class, using as much German as possible.

Teaching Suggestions

- Ask students to look at the interviews again. What word often appears following a **wenn**-clause? What do they notice about the word order in these sentences? Write the sentences on a transparency or on the board. Ask students to infer a rule about the word order of **wenn**-clauses.

- Ask students to think of three occasions, such as a birthday or an invitation to someone's house for dinner, and to list what they would bring (or not bring) if they were invited on each of these occasions. Ask students to use these elements to create their own sentences, joining them together with **wenn** and **dann** and giving their own answers to the interview question. Students should then switch papers with their partners and correct each other's answers. Ask students how similar their answers are to what the people interviewed said.

Connections and Comparisons

Multicultural Connection

Ask students from other countries to share when and what they typically exchange or bring for gifts. Students in class could get information about other countries' customs from exchange students, other foreign language students, or other foreign language teachers.

Teacher Note

Mention to your students that the **Landeskunde** will also be included in Quiz 2-2B given at the end of the **Zweite Stufe** and in the test given at the end of Chapter 2.

Teaching Suggestion

Present students with the following situation: Their doctor has informed them that they need to improve their diet. Ask students to imagine suggestions that the doctor might make based on the major food groups of a balanced diet.
Example:
Du sollst täglich Obst essen!

Cultures and Communities

Teaching Suggestion

Ask students to create a chart with 2 columns. The first column should contain the names of the stores listed below. Into the second column they should paste pictures of items that can be bought at each store. Encourage students to do research on the Internet, using the store names as keywords for their search. The charts could be displayed in the classroom or along the hallways.

beim Metzger
in der Bäckerei
im Reformhaus
im Obst- und Gemüseladen
im Kaufhaus
in der Buchhandlung
im Geschenkladen

Assess

- Testing Program, pp. 31–34
  Quiz 2-2A, Quiz 2-2B
  Audio CD2, Tr. 18

- Student Make-Up Assignments
  Chapter 2, Alternative Quiz

- Alternative Assessment Guide, p. 33

DRITTE STUFE

Teaching Resources
pp. 49–53

PRINT
- Lesson Planner, p. 10
- TPR Storytelling Book, pp. 12–13
- Listening Activities, pp. 13–14, 17–18
- Activities for Communication, pp. 9–12, 80, 81, 125–126
- Grammatikheft, pp. 15–18
- Grammar Tutor for Students of German, Chapter 2
- Übungsheft, pp. 22–24
- Testing Program, pp. 35–38
- Alternative Assessment Guide, p. 33
- Student Make-Up Assignments, Chapter 2

MEDIA
- One-Stop Planner
- Audio Compact Discs, CD2, Trs. 13–16, 19, 26–27
- Teaching Transparencies
  Situation 2-2
  Mehr Grammatikübungen Answers
  Grammatikheft Answers
- Interactive CD-ROM Tutor, Disc 1
- DVD Tutor, Disc 1

PAGE 49

 Bell Work
Ask students to name some of the gifts they received for their last birthday. Which ones did they like and what were they?

 Total Physical Response
To get students warmed up, give students the commands using verbs such as **geben, nehmen, reichen, einpacken, auspacken,** and **aufmachen.**
Examples:
Pam, reich Kimberly bitte die Bücher!
Melanie, pack die Bücher in Papier ein!
John, mach den Kalender auf Seite dreißig auf und schreib deinen Namen und deine Adresse rein!

PRESENTING: Wortschatz
Divide students into eight groups and assign each group one of the **Geschenke** pictured in the **Wortschatz.** Have students describe in German the gift assigned to them, without actually using the word for the item. The other groups should try to guess in English which gift is being referred to; when they have done this successfully, model the pronunciation of the corresponding German word for the class. You might also want to follow up with each group by asking the members questions, such as **Gefällt euch (das Gemälde)?**

PAGE 50

PRESENTING: So sagt man das!
Ask students to read the questions and answers in class. Then help students identify the indirect object in the questions and answers and the changes that occur.

Group Work
32 Ask students to work in small groups and set a time limit of three minutes in which groups build as many sentences or questions as they can. One member in each group is the writer who lists all sentences. Ask students to read some of their sentences to the class.

PRESENTING: Ein wenig Grammatik
Dative possessives and pronouns Go down the rows, asking each student in your class a question, such as **Wem gibst du (den Wecker)?** Have students answer by specifying a friend or family member and using the possessive **mein.** (Example: **Ich gebe meiner Schwester / meiner Freundin Heidi den Wecker.**) Follow up on this statement with a second question, to which the student should respond with a statement utilizing a dative personal pronoun: **Was gibst du (deiner Schwester)? — Ich gebe ihr den Wecker.** You may want to write a model of this exchange on the board for students to use as a reference.

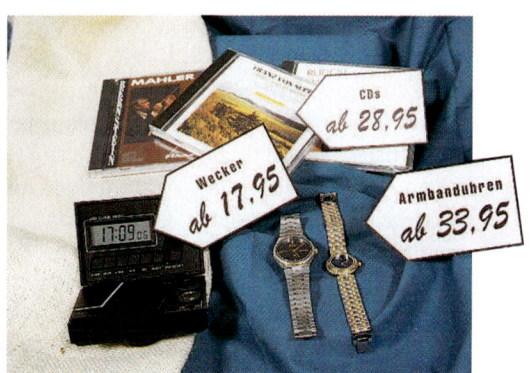

STANDARDS: 1.2

Connections and Comparisons

Language-to-Language

You may want to stress that German possessives (unlike those in French and Spanish) also reflect the case of the noun they accompany. Examples:
nominative: *Mein* Bruder heißt Peter.
accusative: Ich sehe *meinen* Bruder.
dative: Ich gebe *meinem* Bruder ein Buch.

Ask students how these cases are indicated in English. (through word order and use of prepositions)

PRESENTING: So sagt man das!

After reading the expressions in the second So sagt man das! on p. 50, ask students to work with a partner, using the questions as listed but giving their own responses. Then call on several students to tell the class what their partner likes and dislikes.

PAGE 51

PRESENTING: Ein wenig Grammatik

Forms of mögen Practice the forms of **mögen** by providing students with patterned sentences. Examples:

Zum Geburtstag	form of mögen	du	nicht so gern Klamotten
Zum Muttertag		er	
Zum Vatertag		ich	gern Bücher
		sie	lieber Rosen als Pralinen

Communication for All Students

A Slower Pace

36 Before students work with their partners, work with students on a list of possible reasons they would use in this activity. Write these suggestions on a transparency to help students with the interview. Monitor students' work as you walk around the class.

PRESENTING: So sagt man das!

Ask students to read So sagt man das! with a partner and then to further practice the expressions by talking about music, clothing, and sports.

Communication for All Students

Challenge

38 Once students have completed their lists, take a survey of the entire class and record the findings on the board or on a transparency. Help students elicit information from each other, using ordinal numbers. (Example: **Auf dem ersten Platz steht…**) Have students make a general conclusion based on the information. (Example: **Was haben viele Schüler am liebsten? nicht so gern?**)

PAGE 52

PRESENTING: So sagt man das!/Ein wenig Grammatik

To review the functions and the grammar in these boxes, use props or show pictures of foods and ads from grocery stores. Then ask students if they would like more of the foods pictured.

PAGE 53

Cultures and Communities

Culture Notes

- You may want to tell your students what the different types of **Wurst** shown on the menu are made of. **Schweinswurst** is pork sausage; **Currywurst** is curried sausage; **Münchner Weißwurst** is sausage made from veal.

- The design of the euro was a lengthy process that required the cooperation of all of the member countries of the European Union in order to have a currency that would appeal to citizens of many cultures. Have students do a search on the Internet using the keywords "euro currency" for the most recent information on the European Union and the exchange rate of the euro.

Teaching Suggestion

Make a class set of the weekly school cafeteria menu. Ask students to express their likes and dislikes for the foods offered using the scale at the top of p. 52.

Von der Schule zum Beruf

Before starting this activity, have students complete the **Webprojekt** suggested on p. 31F.

Teacher Note

For additional open-ended activities, see the **Zum Sprechen** and **Zum Schreiben** suggestions in the *Alternative Assessment Guide*, p. 47.

 Video Wrap-up

Videocassette 1, 19:52–31:17
Videocassette 5 (captioned version), 06:51–14:23
DVD Tutor, Disc 1

At this time, you might want to use the video resources for additional review and enrichment. These resources are also available via the Enhanced Online Student Edition.

See *Video Guide* for suggestions regarding:
- *Basti, das Schlitzohr!* Dramatic episode
- **Landeskunde** Interviews
- **Videoclips** Authentic footage

Assess
▶ Testing Program, pp. 35–38
  Quiz 2-3A, Quiz 2-3B
  Audio CD2, Tr. 19
▶ Student Make-Up Assignments
  Chapter 2, Alternative Quiz
▶ Alternative Assessment Guide, p. 33

PAGES 54–57

MEHR GRAMMATIKÜBUNGEN

The **Mehr Grammatikübungen** activities are designed as supplemental activities for the grammatical concepts presented in the chapter. You might use them as additional practice, for review, or for assessment.

For more grammar presentations, review, and practice, refer to the following:
- Grammatikheft
- Grammar Tutor for Students of German
- Grammar Summary on pp. R20–R36
- Übungsheft
- Grammar and Vocabulary quizzes (Testing Program)
- Test Generator
- Interactive CD-ROM Tutor
- **Interaktive Spiele** at go.hrw.com

Teacher to Teacher

Jan Haverty
Blue Valley North High School
Overland Park, Kansas

Jan uses this activity before giving the chapter test.

"I always offer bonus points to my students before the chapter test by allowing them to write out the answers in complete sentences to the **Kann ich's wirklich?** questions. We have already answered these questions orally in the course of the chapter, so I consider this to be a valuable way to strengthen their written language prior to assessment. Most students choose to take advantage of this option and improve their test performance, as well."

PAGE 58

KANN ICH'S WIRKLICH?

This page helps students prepare for the test. It is a brief checklist of the major points covered in the chapter. The students should be reminded that it is only a checklist and not necessarily everything that will appear on the test.

For additional self check options, refer students to the *Grammar Tutor*, the *Interactive CD-ROM Tutor*, and the Online self-test for this chapter.

PAGE 59

WORTSCHATZ

Review and Assess

 Circumlocution
- To review, play the circumlocution game, **Das treffende Wort suchen**, with the **Zweite Stufe** vocabulary. Foods can be described according to color, texture, taste, and shape and lend themselves well to circumlocution. Additional food words, cited on p. 44 under activity 24, can be used to enrich this vocabulary game. See p. 3C for procedures.

- Ask students to work in groups of four or five. Using the vocabulary of the **Dritte Stufe,** one student describes to the others in his or her group the item he or she has misplaced or lost. The others have to guess the name of the item. Students can also include gift items from the **Landeskunde.**

 Teacher Note
Give the **Kapitel 2** Chapter Test: *Testing Program*, pp. 39–44
Audio CD 2, Trs. 20–21.

KAPITEL 2
Bastis Plan

Objectives

In this chapter you will review and practice how to

Erste Stufe

- express obligation
- extend and respond to an invitation
- offer help and tell what to do

Zweite Stufe

- ask and tell what to do
- tell that you need something else
- tell where you were and what you bought

Dritte Stufe

- discuss gift ideas
- express likes and dislikes
- express likes, preferences, and favorites
- say you do or don't want more

Visit Holt Online
go.hrw.com
KEYWORD: WK3 BAYERN-2
Online Edition

◀ Wohin gehst du, Basti?

Los geht's! · *Basti, das Schlitzohr!*

CD 2
Trs. 1–2

Strategie Verstehen
Look at the images for this story. Where does the action take place? What do you think the characters are talking about? What might Basti be talking about?

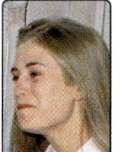  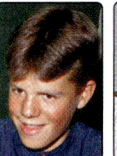  

Beatrice **Robert** **Sebastian** **Vater** **Mutter**

Los geht's! is an abridged version of the video episode.

1
Vater: Iss, iss, mein Sohn! Du musst heute noch viel arbeiten.
Robert: Was muss ich denn heute machen?

2
Beatrice: Nun, schau halt mal auf den Plan drauf!
Sebastian: Wenn du willst, können wir tauschen! Du kannst für mich in der Küche helfen, und ich gehe für dich zum Opa.
Robert: He, prima! Danke dir.

Wochenplan

	Robert	Beatrice	Basti
Mo.		Oma, Opa	
Di.	einkaufen		
Mi.	Küchendienst		Garage
Do.		einkaufen	
Fr.	Oma/Opa	Küchendienst	einkaufen
Sa.	Rasen	Fenster!	Küchendienst
So.			Müll

3
Sebastian: Wie soll das Wetter sein?
Beatrice: Schön. Das hab ich schon gestern gehört.

Mutter: Kein Regen! Das passt prima. Da können wir uns bei den Großeltern in den Garten setzen.
Robert: Was? Wir gehen zur Oma?
Mutter: Wir sind zum Kaffee eingeladen.

Sebastian: Okay, wir sehen uns dann heute Nachmittag bei Oma und Opa.
Mutter: Ja, aber mach dich nicht schmutzig bei der Arbeit!
Sebastian: Aber Mama, kein Problem! Tschau!

Vater: Ja, stimmt! Nein, nein. Ich weiß, um drei Uhr. Was sagst du? Das musst du noch mal wiederholen! Der Basti? So ein Schlitzohr! Na, warte! Ja, bis später! Tschüs!

Vater: Der Basti! Man kann es nicht glauben, so ein Schlitzohr! Er ist gar nicht beim Opa. Der Opa kann ihn heute gar nicht brauchen, er hat gar nichts zu tun. Aber unser Sohn geht zu den Großeltern zum Mittagessen!
Mutter: Jetzt weiß ich's! Deshalb hat er so schnell mit dem Robert getauscht.

LOS GEHT'S!   STANDARDS: 1.2   *fünfunddreißig* **35**

1 Was passiert hier?

These activities check for global comprehension only. Students should not yet be expected to produce language modeled in Los geht's!

Verstehst du alles, was die Leute in Los geht's! sagen? Beantworte die Fragen!

1. Worüber sprechen die Baumanns? 1. Über das, was sie heute alles machen müssen.
2. Was muss Robert heute tun? 2. Oma u. Opa helfen.
3. Was sagt Sebastian zu Robert? 3. „Wenn du willst, können wir tauschen! …"
4. Was sagt Beatrice über das Wetter? 4. Schön.
5. Was meint die Mutter über das Wetter? 5. Passt prima.
6. Wohin gehen die Baumanns am Nachmittag? Warum? 6. zu den Großeltern; zum Kaffee eingeladen.
7. Warum ist Basti nicht beim Opa? 7. Opa braucht ihn nicht.
8. Welche Aufgaben haben Beatrice, Robert und Basti in dieser Woche?
   8. Bea.: Oma u. Opa helfen, einkaufen, Küchendienst, Fenster putzen. Robert: einkaufen, Küchendienst, Oma u. Opa helfen, Rasen. Basti: Garage, einkaufen, Küchendienst, Müll.

2 Genauer lesen

Lies den Text noch einmal und beantworte die Fragen!

1. Warum soll Robert viel essen? 1. Er muss noch viel arbeiten.
2. Welche Aufgaben haben die drei Geschwister heute? 2. Oma u. Opa helfen; Fenster putzen; Küchendienst.
3. Was möchte Basti heute lieber tun? 3. Oma u. Opa helfen.
4. Warum gehen die Baumanns heute Nachmittag zur Oma? 4. Sie sind eingeladen.
5. Wo können sie heute bei den Großeltern sitzen? Warum? 5. im Garten; das Wetter ist schön.
6. Warum nennt Herr Baumann seinen Sohn ein Schlitzohr? 6. Weil Basti gefaulenzt hat.
7. Was bedeutet der Ausdruck „Schlitzohr"? Was meinst du? 7. rascal

3 Stimmt oder stimmt nicht?

Stimmen diese Sätze? Wenn nicht, musst du die richtige Antwort geben.

1. Heute will Sebastian in der Küche helfen. 1. Stimmt nicht; er will den Großeltern helfen.
2. Heute Nachmittag gibt es keinen Regen. 2. Stimmt.
3. Die Baumanns haben die Großeltern zum Kaffee eingeladen. 3. Stimmt nicht; (the other way around).
4. Der Opa ruft Herrn Baumann an. 4. Stimmt.
5. Der Sebastian ist beim Opa und hilft ihm. 5. Stimmt nicht; er faulenzt.

4 Welches Wort passt?

Welche Wörter auf der rechten Seite passen in die Satzlücken?

1. Basti will mit Robert ═══. 1. tauschen
2. Er möchte für Robert zum Opa ═══. 2. gehen
3. Robert muss jetzt in der Küche ═══. 3. helfen
4. Die Baumanns sind zum Kaffee ═══. 4. eingeladen
5. Alle können heute im Garten ═══. 5. sitzen
6. Aber Basti ist nicht beim Opa. Herr Baumann kann es nicht ═══. 6. glauben
7. Der Opa hat für Basti nichts zu ═══. 7. tun
8. Deshalb hat Basti mit Robert ═══. 8. getauscht

eingeladen   getauscht   gehen
tun   helfen
sitzen   glauben   tauschen

Storytelling Book pp. 8–9

Erste Stufe

Objectives Expressing obligations; extending and responding to an invitation; offering help and telling what to do

WK3 BAYERN-2

5 Wer macht was? Script and answers on p. 31G

Zuhören/Schreiben Schüler erzählen, was sie so zu Hause alles machen müssen. Mach dir Notizen! (Schreib auf, wer was macht!)

CD 2 Tr. 3

6 Was müssen die Schüler tun?

Lesen/Sprechen Ordne jetzt deine Notizen nach drei Gruppen von Arbeiten: Küchendienst, Gartenarbeiten und Persönliches! Dann vergleiche mit einem Partner, was ihr beide aufgeschrieben habt!

So sagt man das!

Expressing obligations   *Schon bekannt*

Was musst du heute tun?	Ich muss heute den Rasen mähen.
Und dein Bruder, der Robert?	Er muss in der Küche helfen.

7 Was müssen die Schüler tun?

Sprechen Nimm die Liste, die du für Übung 6 gemacht hast, in die Hand, und berichte vor der Klasse, welche Arbeiten die Schüler von Übung 5 machen müssen! Fang mit den Gartenarbeiten an!

Ein wenig Grammatik

Schon bekannt

To review the forms of **müssen,** see the Grammar Summary.

Übungsheft, S. 14, Ü. 1   Mehr Grammatikübungen, S. 54, Ü. 1

8 Basti sagt, er hat so viel zu tun!

Sprechen Christiane ruft Basti an. Sie möchte irgendwohin gehen, vielleicht ins Kino. Aber der Basti kann heute nicht mitgehen. Er sagt, er hat heute so viel zu tun. Was muss er alles machen? — Such dir einen Partner und spielt die Rollen von Christiane und Basti!

ins Kino	ins Café Fröhlich	zu (Monika)
ins Kaufhaus		in die Stadt

Wortschatz

Things to do around the house

putzen	to clean
in der Küche helfen	to help in the kitchen
die Garage aufräumen	to clean the garage
das Auto polieren	to polish the car
den Müll wegtragen	to take out the garbage
Staub wischen	to dust
die Wäsche waschen	to wash clothes
die Wäsche trocknen	to dry clothes
die Wäsche bügeln	to iron clothes

Übungsheft, S. 15, Ü. 2–4   Grammatikheft, S. 10, Ü. 1–2

9 Was macht der Basti? Und die anderen?

Lesen/Sprechen Lies, was Sebastian sagt, und beantworte die Fragen!

1. Was macht Sebastian? Warum?
2. Warum kann der Basti faulenzen?
3. Was müssen seine Geschwister und sein Vater tun?

1. Faulenzen; Opa hat nichts für ihn zu tun.
2. Er hat mit Robert getauscht.
3. Staub saugen, Fenster putzen, Tisch abräumen

10 Was musst du zu Hause alles tun? 　Übungsheft, S. 16, Ü. 5

Schreiben/Sprechen Mach eine Liste von Arbeiten, die du zu Hause machen musst! Erzähle dann deiner Klasse, was du alles machen musst!

11 Ja, gern! oder Das geht nicht. 　Script and answers on p. 31G

Zuhören You will hear four brief conversations. In each one, someone is being invited somewhere. Determine who accepts and who declines the invitation.
CD 2 Tr. 4

So sagt man das!

Extending and responding to an invitation　　　　　Schon bekannt

When extending an invitation, you might say:

　Ich gehe heute Abend ins Kino. Kommst du mit?

When accepting you might say:

　Ja, gern!
　Ich gehe gern mit!

　Na, klar!

When declining you might say:

　Das geht nicht.
　Das geht leider nicht, weil (ich so viele Hausaufgaben hab.)
　Ich kann leider nicht, denn (ich muss in die Stadt.)

Grammatikheft, S. 11, Ü. 3–4

12 Wohin gehst du?

Schreiben Schreib zwei Orte auf, wo du heute hingehen möchtest! Rechts im Kasten stehen ein paar Ideen.
Answers may vary. E. g.: **Ich möchte heute gern ins Kino gehen.**

> ins Kino
> zum Tennisplatz
> ins Museum
> in die Disko
> ins Schwimmbad
> in ein Café
> in ein Konzert
> ins Einkaufszentrum

13 Kommst du mit?

Such dir einen Partner! Lade ihn ein! Dein Partner geht mit oder nicht.

a. **Sprechen** Wenn dein Partner mitgeht, muss er einen Grund angeben.

b. **Sprechen** Wenn dein Partner nicht mitgeht, muss er drei Gründe angeben. Er muss sagen, was er zuerst tun muss, dann und danach!

14 Für mein Notizbuch

Schreiben Mach einen Stundenplan für jeden Nachmittag in der Woche und für das ganze Wochenende! Trag ein, was du wirklich an jedem Tag und zu welcher Zeit tust!

	Montag	Dienstag	Mittwoch	Donnerstag
14–15	—	—		
15–16	Klavier			
16–17	—	Rasenmähen		
17–18	Tennis	Hausaufgaben		
18–19	Küchend.	Fußball		
19–20				

> Wann geht's?
>
> Geht's am Montag?
>
> Geht's zwischen 17 und 18 Uhr?
>
> Geht's am Abend?

15 Wann geht's?

Sprechen Du möchtest nächste Woche an irgendeinem Tag etwas unternehmen, aber nicht allein. Du möchtest, dass ein Klassenkamerad oder eine Klassenkameradin mitgeht. — Such dir also einen Partner! Nimm dein Notizbuch zur Hand und frag deinen Partner, wann er mitkommen kann! Wenn es nicht geht, muss dein Partner einen Grund angeben. Tauscht dann die Rollen aus!

16 Wann geht's jetzt?

Sprechen Wiederhol Übung 15 noch einmal! Jetzt musst du aber deine Ausreden mit einem weil-Satz begründen.
E.g.: **..., weil ein neuer Film läuft.**

Ein wenig Grammatik

Schon bekannt

The interrogative **warum?** asks for reasons. When giving reasons, the conjunctions **weil** or **denn** can be used. For word order after **weil** and **denn**, see the Grammar Summary.

Übungsheft, S. 16, Ü. 6–7   Mehr Grammatikübungen, S. 54, Ü. 2

ERSTE STUFE   STANDARDS: 1.1, 1.3   neununddreißig **39**

17 Wie oft musst du helfen?

Sprechen Such dir eine Partnerin! Frag sie, wie oft sie bestimmte Tätigkeiten machen muss! Sie sagt es dir. Tauscht dann die Rollen! — Im Kasten stehen einige „wie oft" Antworten.

einmal
zweimal
in der Woche
im Monat
am Tag

oft
nie
manchmal
jeden Tag

Staub saugen
den Rasen mähen
den Großeltern helfen
Staub wischen
den Tisch decken
einkaufen gehen
die Katze füttern
das Geschirr spülen

18 Was kann ich für dich tun? Script and answers on p. 31G

Zuhören Drei Schüler beantworten die Frage: Sag mal, wie kann ich dir helfen, oder was kann ich für dich tun? — Schreib auf, was jeder Schüler tun kann und für wen!
CD 2 Tr. 5

So sagt man das!

Offering help and telling what to do *Schon bekannt*

When someone wants to help you, he or she might ask:

Kann ich etwas für dich tun?
Was kann ich für dich tun?
Für wen kann ich etwas tun?

Your response might be:

Ja, du kannst in der Küche helfen.
Du kannst für mich Staub saugen.
Du kannst für die Oma einkaufen gehen.

Grammatikheft, S. 12, Ü. 5–6

Ein wenig Grammatik

Schon bekannt
For the forms of **können**, see the Grammar Summary.

Mehr Grammatikübungen, S. 54, Ü. 3

19 Grammatik im Kontext

a. **Sprechen** Wie viele Sätze kannst du bauen? Für wen kannst du etwas tun?

b. **Schreiben** Schreib fünf Sätze mit den Wörtern in den Kästen.

Wer?		Für wen?	Was?
ihr	können	Opa	einkaufen gehen
du	könnt	Oma	Staub wischen
ich	kann	Eltern	Müll wegtragen
wir	kannst	mich	Tisch decken
Basti		Christiane	Geschirr spülen
			Fenster putzen
			Wäsche bügeln

Various possibilities.
E.g.: **Basti kann für den Opa Staub wischen.**

vierzig — STANDARDS: 1.2, 1.3 — KAPITEL 2 Bastis Plan

20 **Alle möchten helfen.**

Sprechen Setzt euch in Gruppen von vier oder fünf Personen zusammen! Einer von euch hat sehr viel zu tun, und ihr anderen fragt, was ihr für diese Person tun könnt. Hier sind ein paar Ideen:

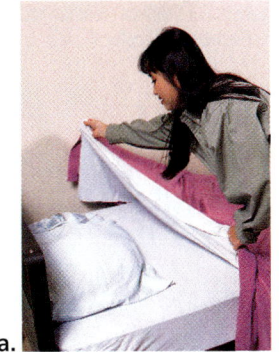
a.
Kann ich für dich das Bett machen?

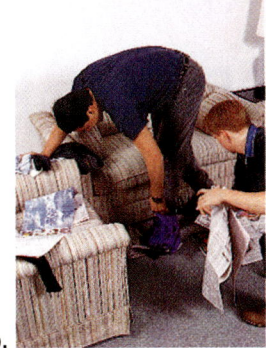
b.
…die Klamotten aufräumen?

c.
…das Geschirr spülen?

d.
…die Blumen gießen?

 21 **Was könnt ihr für andere tun?**

 **Sprechen** Bildet eine neue Gruppe von vier oder fünf Personen! Jeder fragt einmal, einer antwortet! Die Frage ist: „Was tun wir für andere?" — Tauscht dann die Rollen aus!

Ich geh für meine Mutter einkaufen.

Für wen?

für dich? für deine Oma? für euch?
Kusine? Opa?

Ein wenig Grammatik

Schon bekannt
For the accusative forms of the personal pronouns and of the possessives, see the Grammar Summary.

Mehr Grammatikübungen, S. 55, Ü. 4–5

 22 **Viel zu tun!**

Sprechen Frag deine Partnerin, was sie für andere Leute tut! Sie muss dir drei Dinge nennen, und sie muss sagen, wann sie etwas für andere tut und warum. — Tauscht dann die Rollen aus!

23 **Für mein Notizbuch**

Schreiben Schreib in dein Notizbuch, was du für andere Leute tust und warum!

Wann?

einmal im Monat

einmal in der Woche

am Montag

am Dienstag

nach der Schule

nach den Hausaufgaben

Warum?

hat keine Zeit

arbeitet den ganzen Tag

kann das nicht mehr tun

ist schon sehr alt

ERSTE STUFE

Zum Lesen

Macht Schule Spaß?

Lesestrategie Using context to derive meaning
You can often make an intelligent guess about the meaning of new words by looking at the context (the surrounding words). Read the following sentence. **Im Restaurant schmeckt das Essen köstlich, nicht wie das Essen im Café, das schmeckt scheußlich. Köstlich** is probably a new word to you. Notice it is describing the food at a restaurant. Reading on, you find the speaker says it doesn't taste like the food at the café, which is described as **scheußlich**. Any adjective that means the opposite of **scheußlich** would be a good guess for the meaning of **köstlich**, which means *tasty*.

Getting Started

1. Use the prereading strategies you reviewed in Chapter 1 to find out what kind of text this is and what it is about. Try to state in your own words (in German) the two-part question that is the focus of the article.

2. Together with your classmates, brainstorm for words and phrases that you know in German that you might expect to find in the student responses.

3. Now skim the interviews and note whether each student mentions what he or she likes, dislikes, or if he or she mentions both. Write each student's name under the correct heading:
MENTIONS LIKES
MENTIONS DISLIKES
MENTIONS BOTH

Eltern — UMFRAGE

Many *Zum Lesen* selections are permissioned documents that cannot be altered. They therefore do not reflect the changes enacted by the **Rechtschreibreform**.

Das Pausenklingeln ist die schönste Musik!

Was Schülern an der Schule gefällt und mißfällt — das zeigt die neue **ELTERN**-Umfrage

Prima ist der Musikraum unserer Schule, weil man dort die Stereo-Anlage auf 100 db aufdrehen kann.
Tanja, Gymnasiastin, 14 Jahre

Im Schulbus bekommen wir immer viel Spaß. Besonders die Heimfahrt ist gut. Da ist man froh, daß wieder so ein doofer Schultag vorüber ist und ein freier Nachmittag beginnt.
Rolf, Realschüler, 12 Jahre

Schön sind nur die Ferien. Morgens wacht man auf und denkt: Schule und Lehrer, gibt es die überhaupt noch?
Eva, Realschülerin, 14 Jahre

Das Schönste: daß man in der Pause so laut sein darf, wie man will, und sich mit seinen Freunden ausquatschen kann. Das Mieseste: im Unterricht stundenlang still sein müssen, nur antworten, aber sich nicht unterhalten dürfen.
Klaus, Realschüler, 13 Jahre

Es geht nichts über einen fröhlichen, lachenden Lehrer, der nur das Gute für seine Schüler will. Wir haben Herrn Jansen. Wenn er in die Klasse kommt, lacht er gleich. Er hat immer Verständnis, wenn einer einen Fehler macht. Strafe ist für ihn ein Fremdwort.
Christa, Realschülerin, 13 Jahre

Meine Mutter macht mir immer ein Super-Pausenbrot. Zum Beispiel ein Dreikörnerbrot mit Zungenwurst und ganz zarten Gurkenscheiben darunter. Das schmeckt so gut, daß ich den sonstigen Mist in der Schule vergesse.
  Bernd, Grundschüler, 10 Jahre

Das Beste an der Schule ist, daß man morgens etwas zu tun hat. Sonst müßte man zu Hause bei der Hausarbeit helfen. Das wäre noch schlimmer.
  Volker, Realschüler, 13 Jahre

Am besten: die Getränkeautomaten. Am schlechtesten: das Diktatschreiben.
  Werner, Grundschüler, 9 Jahre

Für mich könnte der ganze Lehrplan nur aus Sport bestehen: Badminton, Handball, Fußball, Schwimmen, Turnen, Leichtathletik. Beim Sport fühle ich mich gut. Das Schwitzen dabei ist sogar gesund. Das Schwitzen bei einer Klassenarbeit dagegen macht krank.
  Tim, Gymnasiast, 14 Jahre

Am besten ist Biologie, weil man da so viel über Tiere und Pflanzen erfährt. Am schlechtesten ist Mathematik, weil man da so scharf denken muß, nichts versteht und sich so leicht vertut.
  Dieter, Gymnasiast, 14 Jahre

Das Schlimmste ist für mich der Müllhaufen auf dem Schulhof, wenn viele Mitschüler ihren ganzen Dreck abladen: Dosen von Joghurt und Pudding, Papier von Schokolade und Tüteneis.
  Sara, Realschülerin, 14 Jahre

Saumäßig ist die Luft in unserem Klassenzimmer. Es riecht immer nach faulen Eiern, nach abgestandener Buttermilch oder alten Pantoffeln. Schön ist, wenn unsere Deutschlehrerin reinkommt und einen herrlichen Duft verbreitet. Sie steht nämlich auf Chanel.™
  Nicole, Realschülerin, 14 Jahre

4. For those who mention both likes and dislikes, find out which sentence(s) expresses the negative and which the positive aspects of school. Cognates and words you already know should give you enough information.

A Closer Look

5. What does Tanja like best at school? Notice she says one can do something with the stereo. What might **aufdrehen** mean?   5. Musikraum; to turn up the volume

6. Rolf mentions riding the school bus and says the **Heimfahrt** is especially good. He can either be referring to the ride to school or home again. Read the next sentence and try to determine the meaning of **Heimfahrt**.   6. drive home

7. Read the interviews more closely and use context and the chart you made to help you determine the meaning of the following words:
   Klaus: **ausquatschen**   to talk one's heart out
   Christa: **Verständnis**   understanding
   Volker: **Hausarbeit**   housework
   Tim: **Schwitzen**   sweating
   Dieter: **Pflanzen**   plants

8. During **Austauschwoche**, a group of Austrian students will be paired up with the students interviewed here. You've been given information about the Austrian students, and you must pair each person below with one of the students interviewed.

   BEATE: very athletic   Tim
   HANS: an understanding teacher is the best thing   Christa
   ULRIKE: dislikes doing housework   Volker
   MARIO: interested in zoology, botany   Dieter
   NORBERT: enjoys talking with friends   Klaus
   SONJA: likes to listen to loud music   Tanja

Übungsheft, S. 17

Zweite Stufe

Objectives Asking and telling what to do; telling that you need something else; telling where you were and what you bought

WK3 BAYERN-2

24 **Was wir kaufen und wo** Script and answers on p. 31G

Zuhören Zwei Schüler haben Küchendienst. Sie sagen, was sie heute einkaufen müssen und wo sie alles kaufen!

CD 2 Tr. 6

Bausinger

SUPERANGEBOT:

Trauben blau, Kl. I, 1 kg	**1,40**
Erdbeeren aus Italien, 250g	**−,99**
Himbeeren 200g Schale	**1,59**
Äpfel Jonathan, 1kg	**1,49**
Bananen 1kg	**1,19**
Hackfleisch täglich frisch!, 100g	**−,79**
Aufschnitt Spitzenqualität!, 100g	**−,75**
Hähnchen 1kg	**3,49**
Schweinebraten ohne Knochen, 1 kg	**4,59**

STARK IM PREIS!

Kartoffeln 3 kg-Beutel	**1,19**
Tomaten aus Holland 500g	**1,09**
Kopfsalat Klasse I Stück	**−,49**
Radieschen Bund	**−,49**
Zwiebeln Klasse II 1kg	**−,59**

Tilsiter deutscher Schnittkäse 100g	**−,59**
Frische Milch 3,8% Fett 1 Liter	**−,69**
Markenbutter Kl. I, aus dem Allgäu 250g	**1,09**
Sahnejoghurt verschiedene Sorten 150g-Becher	**−,29**
Diätmargarine 250g-Becher	**−,49**

Unsere Öffnungszeiten:

| Mo – Fr. | 9.00 – 12.30 14.00 – 20.00 | Samstag | 8.30 – 16.00 |

Für Druckfehler keine Haftung!

Wortschatz

Obst und Gemüse

Bananen Zwetschgen Pfirsiche Spinat grüne Bohnen Erbsen

25 Was gibt's im Angebot?

Sprechen Such dir einen Partner! Du bewunderst verschiedene Angebote bei Bausinger. Dein Partner stimmt zu und sagt, dass die Ware auch gar nicht so teuer ist. Tauscht dann die Rollen aus!

Beispiel
— Die Pfirsiche sehen lecker aus!
— Stimmt! Und sie sind sehr preiswert. Nur eins zwanzig das halbe Kilo!

So sagt man das!

Asking and telling what to do

Schon bekannt

Someone who wants to help you might ask:

Was soll ich jetzt tun?
Wo soll ich das Brot kaufen?

Your response might be:

Geh bitte für mich einkaufen!
Kauf es doch beim Bäcker!

26 Was soll ich kaufen?

Lesen/Sprechen Du musst einkaufen gehen. Deine Mutter gibt dir einen Einkaufszettel. Du liest, was du alles kaufen sollst, und du willst wissen, wo du alles kaufen sollst. — Such dir einen Partner und spielt diese Rollen! Tauscht dann die Rollen aus!

Wo?

- beim Bäcker?
- im Supermarkt?
- im Obst- und Gemüseladen?
- beim Metzger?

Ein wenig Grammatik

Schon bekannt

For the forms of **sollen** and the **du**-commands, see the Grammar Summary.

Mehr Grammatikübungen, S. 56, Ü. 6

Übungsheft, S. 18, Ü. 1
Grammatikheft, S. 13, Ü. 8–9

1/2 Pfd. Butter
1 kg Trauben
250 g Erdbeeren
100 g Aufschnitt
1 kg Zwiebeln
1 Liter Milch

ZWEITE STUFE

27 Der Gemüsemann ist da! Script and answers on p. 31G

Zuhören Der Gemüsemann kommt auch heute noch mit seinem Kombi in viele Wohngegenden und ruft mit lauter Stimme seine Ware und die Preise aus. — Schreib fünf Artikel auf, die du kaufen willst!

CD 2 Tr. 7

So sagt man das!

Telling that you need something else Schon bekannt

To ask if someone needs something else, you might ask:

  Was bekommen Sie noch?

  Haben Sie noch einen Wunsch?
  Sonst noch etwas?

Your response might be:

  Ein Kilo Tomaten, und dann
    bekomme ich noch eine Gurke.
  Nein, danke!
  Danke, das ist alles.

Übungsheft, S. 19, Ü. 2–4

Grammatikheft, S. 14, Ü. 10

28 Sonst noch etwas?

Sprechen Such dir einen Partner! Dein Partner spielt den Gemüsemann oder die Gemüsefrau, und du kaufst die Artikel, die du auf den Zettel geschrieben hast. Tauscht dann die Rollen aus!

29 Was, wo und warum? Script and answers on p. 31H

Zuhören Vier Schüler sagen, was sie gekauft haben, in welchen Geschäften sie waren und warum sie dort eingekauft haben. Mach dir Notizen!

CD 2 Tr. 8

a. Schreiben Schreib auf, in welchen Geschäften jeder war!

b. Schreiben Schreib auf, warum sie dort eingekauft haben!

So sagt man das!

Telling where you were and what you bought Schon bekannt

To ask a friend where he was and what he did, you might ask:

  Wo warst du?
  Was hast du im Supermarkt
    gekauft?
  Warst du auch beim Metzger?

His response might be:

  Beim Bäcker und im Supermarkt.
  Die Milch und die Eier.

  Ja, dort hab ich das Fleisch
    gekauft.

Grammatikheft, S. 14, Ü. 11

46 sechsundvierzig   STANDARDS: 1.1, 1.2   KAPITEL 2   Bastis Plan

30 Grammatik im Kontext

a. Sprechen Du kommst vom Einkaufen zurück und hast die Lebensmittel, die unten abgebildet sind, gekauft. Wo warst du? Warst du im Supermarkt? Im Obst- und Gemüseladen? Beim Metzger? Deine Mutter will es wissen. Wenn du die Artikel woanders gekauft hast, dann sag warum! — Such dir einen Partner und spielt diese Rollen!

MUTTER **Wo hast du das Brot gekauft? Im Supermarkt?**
DU **Nein, ich war beim Bäcker.**
MUTTER **Du warst beim Bäcker?**
DU **Dort ist das Brot immer frisch!**

b. Schreiben Schreib drei Gespräche wie im Beispiel.

Warum?

Dort ist alles nicht so teuer!

Dort ist (das Brot) immer frisch!

Dort muss ich nicht lange warten.

Die Verkäufer sind so nett.

Der (Bäcker) ist nicht so weit von hier.

Ein wenig Grammatik

Schon bekannt

For the past tense forms of **sein**, the **war**-forms, see the Grammar Summary.

Übungsheft, S. 20, Ü. 5–7

Mehr Grammatikübungen, S. 56, Ü. 7

ZWEITE STUFE   STANDARDS: 1.1   *siebenundvierzig* **47**

Was nimmst du mit, wenn du irgendwo eingeladen bist?

We asked people from around Germany what they bring with them when they are invited somewhere. First listen to the interviews, then read the texts. CD 2 Tr. 9

Übungsheft, S. 21, Ü. 1–3

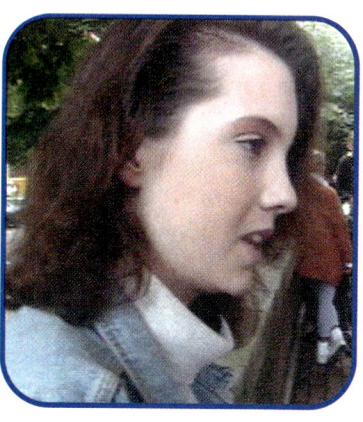

Sandra, Stuttgart CD 2 Tr. 10

„Also, wenn ich zu 'ner Geburtstagsfete eingeladen bin, dann nehm ich meistens ein Geschenk mit, zum Beispiel 'ne CD, also grad' von 'ner Lieblingsgruppe, oder 'ne Single einfach. Oder wenn die Person halt gerne was liest, dann ein Buch. Und wenn es 'ne ganz normale Party ist, dann nimmt man irgendwas zum Knabbern, oder 'nen Salat, oder irgendwelche Snacks halt mit."

Martina, München CD 2 Tr. 11

„Also, wenn ich zu 'ner Fete eingeladen bin und ein Geschenk mitbringe, dann richte ich mich eigentlich immer nach dem Gastgeber und versuche dann, also irgendwie schon so seinen …Dings …zu entsprechen, dass das für ihn was Schönes ist. Also nicht nur 'nen Blumenstrauß oder 'ne Flasche Wein, das sollte dann schon irgendwie passen."

Julia, Hamburg CD 2 Tr. 12

„Also, wenn es ein Geburtstag ist, dann überlege ich mir ein Geschenk, was zu der Person passt. Und wenn es einfach so 'ne Einladung ist zu 'ner Feier, dann nehm ich eigentlich gar nichts mit, also nur für mich dann, wenn ich irgendwas mitnehme, brauche oder so. Sonst eigentlich nur zum Geburtstag oder zu irgendeinem Anlass."

1. Gifts are underlined in interviews. Occasions: **Geburtstag u. normale Party/Fete/Feier**

A. 1. Skim over the interviews again and find as many words as you can that are mentioned as possible gifts. Julia and Sandra mention two different types of occasions that would influence what they would bring. What are the two kinds of occasions? (*Hint:* they state under what conditions they would bring certain gifts. Do you remember the conjunction that signals a condition?) What gifts would they bring for each kind of occasion?

2. Although social customs are always changing, many long-held traditions are still important in German-speaking countries today, especially those concerning social courtesies. In general, when one is invited to someone's home, it is customary to bring flowers for the host or hostess. Read Martina's interview again. What does she say she would not give as a present? Why does she say this? How well do you think she knows the people she has in mind?

B. Think about how you would answer the interview question. Are there any particular customs where you live or where your family is from? How do these customs compare to German customs? 2. **Blumenstrauß oder Flasche Wein.** She knows people well enough to bring a personalized gift.

STANDARDS: 1.2, 2.2, 3.2, 4.2

Storytelling Book pp. 12–13

Dritte Stufe

Objectives Discussing gift ideas; expressing likes and dislikes; expressing likes, preferences, and favorites; saying you do or don't want more

WK3 BAYERN-2

31 **Welche Geschenke und für wen?** Script and answers on p. 31H

Zuhören Vier Schüler brauchen Geschenke. Sie sagen, was sie schenken möchten und wem. Mach dir Notizen! Schreib auf, was für ein Geschenk jeder Schüler kauft und wem er es schenkt!

CD 2 Tr. 13

Wortschatz

Geschenkideen

  2–2

 Grammatikheft, S. 15, Ü. 3

DRITTE STUFE — STANDARDS: 1.2 — neunundvierzig 49

So sagt man das!

Discussing gift ideas *Schon bekannt*

To find out what someone is giving as a gift, you might ask:

Your response might be:

Was schenkst du deiner Mutter zum Geburtstag?
Ich schenke **ihr** Schokolade.

Was kaufst du **deinem Vater?**
Ich kauf **ihm** ein Gemälde.

Wem gibst du den Blumenstrauß?
Meiner Oma.

Was schenkst du **deinem Opa?**
Ich weiß noch nicht. Hast du eine Idee?

Grammatikheft, S. 15, Ü. 13

32 Grammatik im Kontext
Various possibilities.
E.g.: **Ich gebe meinem Opa ein Buch.**

a. Sprechen Wie viele Sätze kannst du bauen?

Wer?		Wem?	Was?
meine Schwester ich mein Bruder wir	schenken kaufen geben	meine Mutter mein Freund meine Oma meine Freundin mein Vater meine Kusine mein Opa	Buch Tennisschläger Wecker Klamotten Ring aus Silber Blumenstrauß Armbanduhr Gemälde

b. Schreiben Schreib vier Sätze mit den Wörtern in den Kästen.

33 Was schenkst du?

Schreiben/Sprechen Schreib deine eigene Geschenkliste! Wem schenkst du was? — Dann such dir einen Partner! Frag ihn, was er schenkt und wem! Tauscht dann die Rollen aus!

34 Was wir mögen und was wir nicht mögen
Script and answers on p. 31H

Zuhören Drei Schüler sagen, was sie mögen und was sie nicht mögen. Mach dir Notizen!
CD 2 Tr. 14

Ein wenig Grammatik

Schon bekannt

For the dative forms of **mein** and **dein,** and the dative personal pronouns, see the Grammar Summary.

Übungsheft, S. 22–23, Ü. 1–3

Mehr Grammatikübungen, S. 56, Ü. 8

So sagt man das!

Expressing likes and dislikes *Schon bekannt*

You might ask someone what he or she likes or does not like by saying:

His or her response might be:

Was für Geschenke **magst du?**
Ich **mag** alles: Bücher, CDs, Klamotten und so.

Was **magst du nicht?**
Pralinen **mag** ich **nicht.**

Magst du Horrorfilme?
Und wie!

35 Eine Umfrage in der Klasse

Setzt euch in einer großen Gruppe zusammen! Das Thema lautet: „Wer mag was für Geschenke?"

a. Sprechen Einer von euch fragt alle anderen Mitschüler, und ein anderer schreibt das Ergebnis auf.

b. Lesen/Sprechen Ein Dritter liest dann das Ergebnis der Klasse vor. Zum Beispiel: Drei mögen …

Ein wenig Grammatik

Schon bekannt

For the forms of **mögen,** see the Grammar Summary.

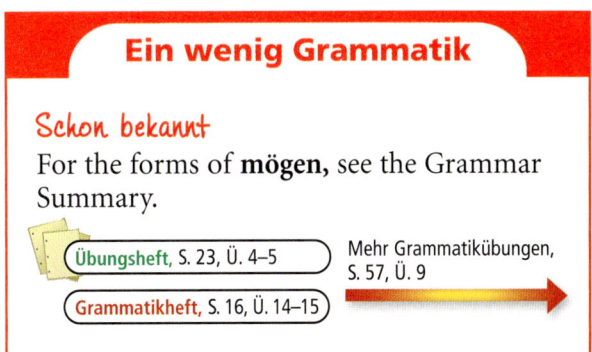

36 Was magst du?

Sprechen Such dir einen Partner! Frag ihn, was er alles mag und warum! Er muss einen Grund angeben.

BEISPIEL
DU Was magst du zum Geburtstag?
PARTNER Eine CD mit Country, denn das hör ich gern. Oder ja, ein Buch, weil ich gern lese und Bücher sammle.

37 Was wir lieber mögen und was wir am liebsten mögen   Script and answers on p. 31H

Zuhören/Schreiben Vier Schüler sagen, was sie lieber mögen und was sie am liebsten mögen. Mach dir Notizen! Vergleiche dann deine Notizen mit den Notizen von deinem Partner!

CD 2 Tr. 15

So sagt man das!

Expressing likes, preferences, and favorites   **Schon bekannt**

To find out what someone likes or prefers, you might ask:

Was für Filme **siehst** du **gern**?
Magst du zum Geburtstag **lieber** eine CD oder ein Buch?
Welche CDs **magst** du **am liebsten**?

The response might be:

Ich **sehe gern** Actionfilme.
Lieber ein Buch.

Am liebsten mag ich die CDs von Matthias Reim.

38 Was magst du gern? Nicht gern?

Schreiben/Lesen Schreib auf eine Liste die Dinge, die du gern und nicht gern isst oder trinkst! Dann ordne die einzelnen Posten (*items*) auf deiner Liste! Was steht ganz oben? Was steht ganz unten?

Cola   Kaffee   Kuchen   Spinat
Pizza   Fleisch   Pralinen   Leber
Fisch   Milch   Äpfel   Brokkoli

DRITTE STUFE   STANDARDS: 1.1, 1.2, 1.3   einundfünfzig   51

39 **Wirklich? Das isst du gern?**

 Sprechen Such dir einen Partner! Frag ihn, was er besonders gern isst oder trinkt und was er nicht gern isst oder trinkt! Gebrauche in deinen Fragen die Wörter im Kasten rechts! — Tauscht dann die Rollen aus!

Beispiel	Du	Was isst du besonders gern?
	Partner	Fisch ess ich besonders gern.
	Du	Und was isst du nicht gern?
	Partner	Leber ess ich nicht gern.

furchtbar gern
besonders gern
sehr gern
— gern —
nicht gern
gar nicht gern
überhaupt nicht gern

40 **Wer mag mehr? Wer mag nichts mehr?** Script and answers on p. 31H

 Zuhören/Schreiben Vier Schüler sind beim Essen. Wer mag mehr? Wer mag nichts mehr? Welche Gründe geben sie an? Mach dir Notizen!
CD 2 Tr. 16

So sagt man das!

Saying you do or don't want more

Here's how someone might ask you if you want more of something:

Möchtest du **noch etwas**?
Willst du **noch was**?
Und du? Auch **noch eine Semmel**?
Magst du **noch einen Saft**?

Your response might be:

Ja, bitte! **Noch eine Semmel**!
Ja, **noch eine Bratwurst**.
Nein, danke! **Keine Semmel mehr**.
Nein, **keinen Saft mehr**. Ich habe **keinen Durst mehr**.

Schon bekannt

Ein wenig Grammatik

Schon bekannt

The phrase **noch ein** means *another*. For the forms of **ein** and **kein,** used to "negate" nouns, see the Grammar Summary.

Mehr Grammatikübungen, S. 57, Ü. 10–11

41 **Noch etwas?**

  Sprechen Du sitzt mit deinem Freund oder mit deiner Freundin in einem Café. Mag er oder mag sie noch etwas zu essen oder zu trinken? Frag mal! — Tauscht dann die Rollen aus!

Answers may vary. E.g.: **Magst du noch eine Limo? - Ja, ich nehme noch eine Limo!**

Semmeln   Eis   Cappuccino

Saft   Leberkäs   Bratwurst   Brezel   Kartoffelsalat

52 *zweiundfünfzig*   STANDARDS: 1.1, 1.2, 5.1   KAPITEL 2   Bastis Plan

42 Ein kurzer Besuch in München

Lesen/Sprechen Nach einer Fahrt mit dem Nachtzug bist du mit deiner Deutschklasse eben in München angekommen. Ihr habt ein großes Programm vor! Ihr wollt euch die Innenstadt ansehen und vielleicht auch ein Museum besuchen. Aber alle haben erst mal großen Hunger, und ihr wollt zuerst etwas essen. Ihr geht an einen Imbissstand und lest die Anschlagtafeln. Such dir einen Partner, und schreib mit ihm ein Gespräch auf, das Folgendes enthalten muss!

1. was es zu essen und zu trinken gibt
2. was ihr mögt und was ihr nicht mögt
3. was euch zu teuer ist
4. was ihr bestellt
5. wie alles schmeckt
6. wer noch etwas bestellen will

Dein Partner hat mit einem 20-Euro Schein für seine Bestellung (*order*) bezahlt. Er hat das gezeigte (*shown*) Wechselgeld zurückbekommen. Was hat er bestellt?
2 Paar Wiener oder 2 Weißwürste

43 Von der Schule zum Beruf

Eine Firma für Geschenkartikel hat dich als Reklamefachfrau angestellt. Deine erste Aufgabe ist, eine Reklameseite für Geschenkartikel zu entwerfen. Die Artikel müssen den Kunden Auskunft über Größe, Farbe und Preise geben.

44 Rollenspiel

Such dir zwei Partner und spielt die folgende Szene!
Entwerft zuerst einen Speisezettel für eine Imbissstube!
Benützt dazu ein großes Stück festes Papier! Danach übernimmt einer die Rolle vom Verkäufer, die beiden anderen die Rollen von zwei Kunden.

a. Die Kunden lesen den Speisezettel und unterhalten sich darüber. Dann bestellt jeder etwas. Frag, was jedes Gericht kostet, und ob du von einem noch etwas haben kannst.

b. Beim Essen unterhaltet ihr euch darüber, wie alles schmeckt, ob ihr mehr von einem Gericht haben oder lieber noch etwas anderes essen wollt.

c. Danach sprecht ihr über eure Pläne, denn ihr wollt ja noch viel sehen. Was müsst ihr noch alles tun, bevor ihr München wieder verlassen müsst?

Mehr Grammatikübungen

Erste Stufe

Objectives Expressing obligations; extending and responding to an invitation; offering help and telling what to do

1 Wer muss zu Hause helfen? – Schreib eine Antwort zu den folgenden Fragen, und schreib dabei in jede Lücke eine Form von **müssen** und die Information, die in der Frage enthalten ist. (S. 37)

BEISPIEL   Wer wischt heute Staub? Der Basti?
– Ja, er <u>muss heute Staub wischen</u>.

1. Wer fährt heute in die Stadt? Der Basti? — Ja, er _____ .   muss heute in die Stadt fahren
2. Wer mäht den Rasen? Ihr beiden? — Ja, wir _____ .   müssen den Rasen mähen
3. Wer räumt die Garage auf? Du? — Ja, ich _____ .   muss die Garage aufräumen
4. Wer trägt den Müll weg? Jens und Moni? — Ja, sie _____ .   müssen den Müll wegtragen
5. Wer gießt die Blumen? Die Anja? — Ja, sie _____ .   muss die Blumen gießen
6. Wer wäscht die Wäsche? Die Mutti? — Ja, sie _____ .   muss die Wäsche waschen

2 Du und deine Freunde, ihr habt heute viel zu tun. Du schreibst, warum ihr das nicht tun könnt. – Schreib in jede Lücke die Information, die in Klammern steht. (S. 39)

1. (keine Zeit haben)   Du, ich kann leider die Garage heute nicht aufräumen, weil ich wirklich _____ .   keine Zeit habe
2. (in die Stadt müssen)   Der Basti kann leider nicht mit euch Fußball spielen, weil er heute um 15 Uhr _____ .   in die Stadt muss
3. (14 Jahre alt sein)   Ich kann diesen super Film leider nicht mit euch im Kino sehen, weil ich erst _____ .   14 Jahre alt bin
4. (kein Geld haben)   Wir können unserer Mutti diesen Schmuck leider nicht zum Geburtstag kaufen, denn wir _____ .   haben kein Geld
5. (helfen müssen)   Die Beatrice kann leider nicht mit ihren Freundinnen in die Stadt fahren, denn sie _____ .   muss helfen
6. (in Berlin sein)   Wir können leider nicht am Wochenende zu eurer Fete kommen, denn wir _____ .   sind in Berlin

3 Alle wollen dir helfen. – Schreib eine Form von **können** in jede Lücke. (S. 40)

Sag, was _____ wir für dich tun? — Ja, ihr _____ für mich einkaufen gehen. Ja, zuerst _____ du, lieber Basti, der Mutti helfen. Du _____ für sie Staub saugen, und die Beatrice _____ der Mutti in der Küche helfen. Wir _____ dann den Müll sortieren, und ich _____ den Müll zum Container bringen. Danach _____ ihr den Rasen mähen, der Basti _____ die Blumen gießen, und ich _____ danach Fußball spielen.

können; könnt
kannst; kannst
kann; können
kann; könnt
kann; kann

4 Was kannst du für deine Freunde tun? Und für ihre Verwandten? – Schreib in jede Lücke ein passendes Personalpronomen (*personal pronoun* - mich, dich, etc.) oder ein passendes Possessivpronomen (*possessive pronoun* - mein, dein, etc.) **(S. 41)**

1. Basti, was kann ich für _____ tun? Kann ich für _____ Staub saugen? — Ja, du kannst für _____ Staub saugen und die Fenster putzen. dich; dich; mich

2. Basti, was kann ich für _____ Opa tun? Kann ich für _____ den Rasen mähen? — Prima! Ja, du kannst für _____ Opa den Rasen mähen. deinen; ihn; meinen

3. Basti, was kann ich für _____ Oma tun? Kann ich für _____ einkaufen gehen? — Das ist eine gute Idee. Geh für _____ Oma einkaufen! deine; sie; meine

4. Was kann ich für _____ tun, Herr Müller? Kann ich für _____ oder für _____ Großeltern etwas tun? — Ja, du kannst für _____ zur Post gehen. Sie; Sie; Ihre; mich/sie

5. Was kann ich für _____ Schwester tun, Basti? Kann ich für _____ zur Post gehen, oder soll ich für _____ einkaufen gehen? — Geh für _____ Schwester zur Post! deine; sie; sie; meine

Zweite Stufe

Objectives Asking and telling what to do; telling that you need something else; telling where you were and what you bought

5 Schreib, was diese Schüler kaufen sollen. – Gebrauche (*use*) eine Form von **sollen** in der ersten Lücke und den Artikel in der Illustration in der zweiten Lücke. **(S. 45)**

Der Basti _____ ein Kilo _____ kaufen.   soll; Bananen

Du _____ mir nur ein Pfund _____ bringen.   sollst; Zwetschgen

Ihr _____ Mutti nur zwei _____ kaufen.   sollt; Pfirsiche

Wir _____ viel _____ essen. Er ist gesund!   sollen; Spinat

Kinder _____ auch _____ essen.   sollen; grüne Bohnen

Mehr Grammatikübungen

Answers

WK3 BAYERN-2

Und ich _____ auch 250 Gramm _____ kaufen.   soll; Erbsen

6 Zuerst sagst du einem Freund, was er tun soll, und dann sagst du dasselbe mehreren Freunden. – Schreib die Imperative der gegebenen Verben in die Lücken. (S. 45)

1. (fahren; gehen)   _____ in die Stadt und _____ ins Kino!   Fahr; geh   Fahrt; geht
2. (gehen; essen)   _____ in eine Imbissstube und _____ eine Pizza!   Geh; iss   Geht; esst
3. (nehmen; trinken)   _____ ein Käsebrot und _____ eine Limo!   Nimm; trink   Nehmt; trinkt
4. (geben; kaufen)   _____ der Oma ein Geschenk; _____ ihr eine CD!   Gib; kauf   Gebt; kauft
5. (suchen; spielen)   _____ dir einen Partner und _____ diese Rolle!   Such; spiel   Sucht; spielt

7 Deine ganze Familie war irgendwo in der Stadt. – Schreib die richtigen Formen von **war** in die Lücken der Fragen und Antworten. (S. 47)

1. Wo _____ du denn? _____ du schon beim Metzger?   warst; Warst
2. Ich _____ beim Bäcker, aber der Basti _____ beim Metzger.   war; war
3. Und wo _____ ihr? _____ ihr schon im Supermarkt?   wart; Wart
4. Ja, wir _____ im Supermarkt und wir _____ auch beim Bäcker.   waren; waren
5. Und wo _____ deine Geschwister? _____ sie auch in der Stadt?   waren; Waren
6. Ja, der Robert _____ im Kino und der Basti _____ in einem Café.   war; war

Dritte Stufe

Objectives Discussing gift ideas; expressing likes and dislikes; expressing likes, preferences, and favorites; saying you do or don't want more

8 Zwei Freunde sprechen über Geschenke, die sie für Freunde und Verwandte kaufen wollen. – Schreib die richtige Form des Possessivpronomens in jede Lücke. (S. 50)

1. Was schenkst du _____ Mutter, Basti? — Ja, _____ Mutter mag Bücher und CDs; ich glaube, ich schenke _____ Mutter einen Roman.   deiner; meine; meiner
2. Was schenkst du _____ Opa zum Namenstag? — Hm, _____ Opa mag gern Schokolade. Ich gebe _____ Opa also eine Schachtel Pralinen.   deinem; mein; meinem
3. Was gibst du _____ Kusine zum Geburtstag? — Ja, ich gebe _____ Kusine eine CD. _____ Kusine hört Musik gern, also ein gutes Geschenk für sie.   deiner; meiner; Meine
4. Was kaufst du _____ Bruder? _____ Bruder hat doch bald Geburtstag, nicht? — Ja, _____ Bruder hat am Sonntag Geburtstag. Ja, was schenke ich ihm?   deinem; Dein; mein

9 Du sprichst mit einer Freundin über Geschenke. – Schreib die richtige Form von **mögen** in die Lücken. (S. 51)

1. Was _____ du zum Geburtstag? — Ich _____ Bücher und CDs.   magst; mag
2. Wer _____ die CD? — Du, der Basti _____ die CD.   mag; mag
3. Was _____ ihr denn? — Wir _____ Geld!   mögt; mögen
4. Was _____ deine Geschwister? — Sie _____ Klamotten.   mögen; mögen
5. Was _____ der Robert? — Er _____ ein super Video!   mag; mag

10 Du bist in verschiedenen Geschäften und du möchtest in jedem Geschäft noch zwei Dinge kaufen. Schreib die richtige Form von **noch ein**, *another*, in jede Lücke. (S. 52)

1. Haben Sie _____ Wunsch?   noch einen
2. Ich möchte _____ Stück Pizza und _____ Limonade.   noch ein; noch eine
3. Ich möchte _____ Eisbecher und danach _____ Mineralwasser.   noch einen; noch ein
4. Ja, ich nehme _____ Eibrötchen und dann _____ Kaffee.   noch ein; noch einen
5. Ich nehme _____ Pfund Aufschnitt und _____ Kilo Hackfleisch.   noch ein; noch ein
6. Ich bekomme _____ Kartoffel und _____ Stück Brot.   noch eine; noch ein

11 Du bist mit einer Freundin in einem Restaurant. Sie fragt dich, ob du noch etwas essen oder trinken möchtest (siehe Bild), und du sagst ihr, dass du nichts mehr möchtest. – Schreib eine Form von **noch ein** und den abgebildeten Artikel in die erste Lücke und eine Form von **kein** und den abgebildeten Artikel in die zweite Lücke. (S. 52)

BEISPIEL

Möchtest du _____ ?   Möchtest du **noch eine Semmel?**
Nein, danke, _____ mehr.   Nein, danke, **keine Semmel** mehr.

Möchtest du _____ ?   noch einen Leberkäs
Nein, danke, _____ mehr.   keinen Leberkäs

Möchtest du _____ ?   noch ein Eis
Nein, danke, _____ mehr.   kein Eis

Möchtest du _____ ?   noch einen Cappuccino
Nein, danke, _____ mehr.   keinen Cappuccino

Möchtest du _____ ?   noch einen Pfirsich
Nein, danke, _____ mehr.   keinen Pfirsich

MEHR GRAMMATIKÜBUNGEN   STANDARDS: 1.2

TPR Storytelling Book pp. 14–15

Kann ich's wirklich?

WK3 BAYERN-2

Can you express obligations? (p. 37)

1 How would you ask a friend what he or she has to do at home? How would your friend say he or she has to help in the kitchen, wash clothes, and take out the garbage? 1. E.g.: Was musst du heute zu Hause tun? - Ich muss in der Küche helfen, die Wäsche waschen und den Müll wegtragen.

Can you extend and respond to an invitation? (p. 38)

2 How would you tell someone you are going to the movies, and ask that person if he or she is coming along? How would that person

a. accept your invitation?

b. decline your invitation and give a reason? 2. E.g.: Ich gehe heute ins Kino. Kommst du mit? - a. Ja, gern.; b. Das geht leider nicht, weil ich zu Hause helfen muss.

Can you offer help and tell what to do? (p. 40)

3 How would you ask your mother what you can do for her? How would she say you can polish her car and go grocery shopping?
3. E.g.: Was kann ich für dich tun? - Du kannst für mich das Auto polieren und einkaufen gehen.

Can you ask and tell what to do? (p. 45)

4 How would you ask your grandmother where you are supposed to buy the bread? How would she tell you to buy it at the baker's?
4. E.g.: Wo soll ich das Brot kaufen? - Kauf es doch beim Bäcker!

Can you tell that you need something else? (p. 46)

5 How would a salesperson ask you if you want something else? How would you say

a. that you need one kilo of plums?   b. that "that will be it"?
5. E.g.: Sonst noch was? - a. Ja, ich bekomme noch ein Kilo Pflaumen.; b. Danke, das ist alles.

Can you tell where you were and what you bought? (p. 46)

6 How would your grandmother ask you where you were and what you bought there? How would you answer that you bought meat at the butcher's and beans and peaches at the supermarket?
6. E.g.: Wo warst du? - Ich habe das Fleisch beim Metzger gekauft und die Bohnen und Pfirsiche im Supermarkt.

Can you discuss gift ideas? (p. 50)

7 How would you ask a friend what he or she is giving

a. his father?   b. her mother?   c. his grandparents?
7. E.g.: a. Was schenkst du deinem Vater?; b. Was kaufst du deiner Mutter?; c. Was gibst du deinen Großeltern?

8 How would your friend answer that she is giving

a. a radio to her father? 8. E.g.: a. Ich schenke meinem Vater ein Radio.;

b. a silver ring to her mother? b. Ich kaufe meiner Mutter einen Ring aus Silber.; c. Ich schenke meinen Großeltern Tennisschläger.

c. tennis rackets to her grandparents?

Can you express likes and dislikes? (p. 50)

9 How would you ask someone what kind of movies he or she likes? How would that person say he or she likes action movies but doesn't like horror movies?
9. E.g.: Was für Filme siehst du gern? - Ich sehe gern Actionfilme, aber Horrorfilme mag ich nicht.

Can you express likes, preferences, and favorites? (p. 51)

10 How would you say you like reading books but you like listening to CDs the best? 10. E.g.: Ich lese gerne Bücher, aber am liebsten höre ich CDs.

Can you say you do or don't want more? (p. 52)

11 How would you ask a friend if he or she wants another banana? How would your friend answer that he or she 11. E.g.: Möchtest du noch eine Banane? - a. Ja, ich möchte noch eine Banane!; b. Nein danke! Keine Banane mehr.

a. wants another one?   b. doesn't want another one?

58   achtundfünfzig   STANDARDS: 1.2   KAPITEL 2   Bastis Plan

Wortschatz

Erste Stufe

Things to do around the house

putzen	to clean	das Auto polieren	to polish the car	die Wäsche waschen	to wash clothes
in der Küche helfen	to help in the kitchen	den Müll wegtragen	to take out the garbage	die Wäsche trocknen	to dry clothes
die Garage aufräumen	to clean the garage	Staub wischen	to dust	die Wäsche bügeln	to iron clothes

Zweite Stufe

 p. 31X

Food items

die Zwetschge, -n	plum	die Erbse, -n	pea	
die Banane, -n	banana	der Spinat	spinach	
der Pfirsich, -e	peach	die Gurke, -n	cucumber	
die (grüne) Bohne, -n	(green) bean			

Telling you need something else

Sonst noch etwas?   Anything else?

Dritte Stufe

Gift ideas

das Gemälde, -	painting
der Ring, -e	ring
aus Silber	made of silver
aus Gold	made of gold

Other words and expressions

der Durst	thirst	die Schokolade	chocolate
Durst haben	to be thirsty	das Radio, -s	radio
Willst du noch was?	Do you want anything else?	der Tennisschläger, -	tennis racket
		der Wecker, -	alarm clock

Kapitel 3: Wo warst du in den Ferien?
Chapter Overview

Los geht's! pp. 62–64	Unser Film- und Fotoclub, p. 62			
	FUNCTIONS	**GRAMMAR**	**VOCABULARY**	**RE-ENTRY**
Erste Stufe pp. 65–69	• Reporting past events, talking about activities, p. 65	• The conversational past, pp. 66–67	• Film and videos, p. 65	Past participles, pp. 65, 66 (**Kap. 10, I**); Activity vocabulary, p. 66 (**Kap. 2/6, I**); Talking about when you do things, p. 68 (**Kap. 6, I**); Using a schedule to talk about time, p. 68 (**Kap. 6, I**); Sequencing events, p. 68 (**Kap. 4, I**)
Zweite Stufe pp. 70–75	• Reporting past events, talking about places, p. 71	• The past tense of **haben** and **sein**, p. 72 • The dative case with the prepositions **in** and **an**, p. 73	• Things to see in Frankfurt a.M., p. 71 • Expressions of frequency, p. 72	Accusative case, p. 70 (**Kap. 5, I**); Past tense of **sein**, pp. 71, 72 (**Kap. 8, I**); The **möchte**-forms, p. 72 (**Kap. 3, I**); **Weil**-clauses, p. 72 (**Kap. 8, I**); City vocabulary, pp. 73, 74 (**Kap. 6/9, I**)
Dritte Stufe pp. 76–79	• Asking how someone liked something, expressing enthusiasm or disappointment, responding enthusiastically or sympathetically, p. 76	• The personal pronouns, dative case, p. 77 (Summary) • The definite article, dative plural, p. 77 • The dative case forms of **ein**, p. 79	• Places to eat and spend the night, p. 78 • Time expressions, p. 79	Talking about likes and dislikes, p. 76 (**Kap. 2/10, I**); Dative pronouns, p. 77 (**Kap. 11, I**); The verb **gefallen**, p. 77 (**Kap. 5, I**); Time expressions, p. 79 (**Kap. 7, I**)

Zum Lesen pp. 80–81	In Tirol	Reading Strategy Identifying the main idea and supporting details

Mehr Grammatikübungen	pp. 82–85		
	Erste Stufe, p. 82	Zweite Stufe, p. 83	Dritte Stufe, pp. 84–85

Review pp. 86–89	Anwendung, pp. 86–87	Kann ich's wirklich?, p. 88	Wortschatz, p. 89
	Zum Schreiben: Finding good details (Spending a month in your ideal vacation spot) Assessment Options		

CULTURE

- Information on Dresden, p. 69
- Information on **Frankfurt am Main**, p. 70
- **Landeskunde:** Was hast du in den letzten Ferien gemacht?, p. 75

Kapitel 3: Wo warst du in den Ferien?
Chapter Resources

Lesson Planning
One-Stop Planner
Lesson Planner with Substitute Teacher Lesson Plans, pp. 12–16, 67
Student Make-Up Assignments
- Make-Up Assignment Copying Masters, Chapter 3

Listening and Speaking
TPR Storytelling Book, pp. 16–23
Listening Activities
- Student Response Forms for Listening Activities, pp. 19–22
- Additional Listening Activities 3-1 to 3-6, pp. 23–26
- Additional Listening Activities (song), p. 22
- Scripts and Answers, pp. 113–118

Video Guide
- Teaching Suggestions, pp. 16–17
- Activity Masters, pp. 18–20
- Scripts and Answers, pp. 86–88, 112

Activities for Communication
- Communicative Activities, pp. 13–18
- Realia and Teaching Suggestions, pp. 82–85
- Situation Cards, pp. 127–128

Reading and Writing
Reading Strategies and Skills Handbook, Chapter 3
Lies mit mir! 2, Chapter 3
Übungsheft, pp. 25–36

Grammar
Grammatikheft, pp. 19–27
Grammar Tutor for Students of German, Chapter 3

Assessment
Testing Program
- Grammar and Vocabulary Quizzes, **Stufe** Quizzes, and Chapter Test, pp. 53–70
- Score Sheet, Scripts and Answers, pp. 71–78

Alternative Assessment Guide
- Portfolio Assessment, p. 20
- Performance Assessment, p. 34
- CD-ROM Assessment, p. 48

Student Make-Up Assignments
- Alternative Quizzes, Chapter 3

Online Activities
- Interaktive Spiele
- Internet Aktivitäten

Video Program
- Videocassette 1
- Videocassette 5 (captioned version)
- DVD Tutor, Disc 1

Audio Compact Discs
- Textbook Listening Activities, CD 3, Tracks 1–13
- Additional Listening Activities, CD 3, Tracks 20–26
- Assessment Items, CD 3, Tracks 14–19

Interactive CD-ROM Tutor, Disc 1

Teaching Transparencies
- Situations 3-1 to 3-2
- Vocabulary 3-A to 3-B
- Los geht's!
- Mehr Grammatikübungen Answers
- Grammatikheft Answers

Use the **One-Stop Planner CD-ROM with Test Generator** to aid in lesson planning and pacing.

For each chapter, the **One-Stop Planner** includes:
- Editable lesson plans with direct links to teaching resources
- Printable worksheets from resource books
- Direct launches to the HRW Internet activities
- Video and audio segments
- Test Generator
- Clip Art for vocabulary items

Kapitel 3: Wo warst du in den Ferien?

Projects

Meine Traumreise

In this activity students will describe their dream vacation (**Meine Traumreise**). It should be started after completion of the **Zum Lesen** section of this chapter. Students will create a poster that includes visual and written information. They will also give a brief oral presentation.

MATERIALS
Students may need
- brochures from travel agencies
- maps
- magazine ads
- scissors
- posterboard
- paper
- glue or tape

SUGGESTED SEQUENCE

1. Students choose the destination of their dream vacation.
2. Students look for sources and materials. (Examples: library books, old magazines, travel agency brochures)
3. Once all materials have been gathered, each student should make an outline of the information and realia he or she wants to include in the report.
4. Students begin the layout of their poster, leaving space for the paper they write about their **Traumreise**. The realia and other visuals should support and illustrate the written part of the assignment.
5. Students present their **Traumreise** to the class.
6. Optional: At the end of all presentations, the class votes via secret ballot for the best **Traumreise**, the place they have been convinced would be the best place to visit.

GRADING THE PROJECT
Suggested point distribution (**total = 100 points**)
- Oral presentation....................30
- Appearance of project/Originality.......40
- Accuracy of language 30

Games

Mal doch schnell!

This game will help tactile learners review the vocabulary learned in the chapter.

Procedure Make a list of the words from the **Wortschatz** of this chapter that are suitable for illustrating. Write the words on small pieces of paper and put them all in a hat. Have students take turns coming to the board or to the overhead projector. Ask students to take a piece of paper from the hat. Give them a few seconds to think about how to draw the word. Then give the signal for the student to begin drawing. The rest of the class tries to guess what is being drawn using German only. The student who first says the word or phrase correctly wins a point.

Stadt, Land, Fluss

This game is popular among German teenagers and can be adapted to a variety of teaching needs.

MATERIALS
Students will need
- ruler
- paper
- pen

Procedure Ask each student to make a chart like the one below:

Stadt Land Fluss Substantiv Verb Adjektiv | Punkte

Go through the alphabet, beginning by saying "A" aloud and then continuing silently. A designated student says "**Halt!**", and the letter that you are thinking of becomes the beginning letter for the words. If, for example, the letter is **F**, students must write a word that begins with the letter **F** in each category. The student who completes his or her chart first says "**Fertig!**", and all students stop writing and mark their empty spaces with a zero. Then students share their words and get one point per correct entry. The total points per game are added to the far right. Continue the game as time permits. At the end, students total their points under the heading "**Punkte**", and the student with the highest score wins.

Storytelling

Mini-Geschichte

*This story accompanies Teaching Transparency 3-B. Read the **Mini-Geschichte** to your students, or have them read the letter aloud using proper pronunciation and intonation. Ask students which animal they think is the most dangerous animal in the world. Students should explain their answer.*

Liebe Franziska!

Viele Grüße aus Frankfurt am Main. Es gefällt mir hier sehr gut. Gestern war ich in der Alten Oper. Ich habe das Märchen *(fairy tale)* „Die Schöne und das Biest" gesehen. Ich habe auch schon das Goethehaus besucht. Hier wurde Johann Wolfgang von Goethe 1749 geboren. In der Zeil war ich auch schon. Ich habe aber nichts gekauft, denn die Geschäfte sind sehr teuer. Morgen besuchen wir den Zoo und beobachten *(watch)* das gefährlichste *(most dangerous)* Tier der Welt. Weißt du, wie es heißt?

Deine Manuela

Traditions

Der Märchenkönig

König Ludwig II. (1845–1886), der Mäzen Richard Wagners und Erbauer märchenhafter Schlösser trat mit 18 Jahren die Thronfolge in Bayern an. In den ersten Regierungsjahren versuchte er die ideale Vorstellung eines Königtums der Kunst und der Kultur zu verwirklichen. Er begriff sein Königtum im Sinne einer absoluten Monarchie, die die Wünsche der Minister nicht berücksichtigte—eine Auffassung, die ihm später zum Verhängnis werden sollte. Das einfache Volk sah ihn als Märchenkönig, seine Familie und die Minister hingegen beklagten sich bitterlich über die verschwenderischen Kosten seiner Prachtbauten.

Seine drei Schlösser, Neuschwanstein, Linderhof (siehe Foto) und Herrenchiemsee, verschlangen in einem Jahr mehr als sechs Millionen Mark. Die in Ungnade gefallenen Minister beschlossen, den König für geisteskrank zu erklären und entmündigen zu lassen. Am 8. Juni 1886 wurde der König von Ärzten, die ihn niemals untersucht hatten, für geisteskrank erklärt. Am 12. Juni wurde er festgenommen und nach Schloss Berg gebracht. Am nächsten Tag fand man ihn tot im Starnberger See. Die Ursache seines Todes ist bis heute ein Rätsel.

Have students research in the library or on the Internet the life and accomplishments of Ludwig II. Students should report their research to the class.

Rezept

Gugelhupf

Zutaten

g=Gramm, l=Liter

500g	Mehl
60g	Zucker
1	Prise Salz
40g	Hefe
¼l	lauwarme Milch
60g	Butter
2	Eier
100g	Rosinen
	Mehl für die Arbeitsfläche
	Fett für die Form
	Puderzucker zum Bestäuben

Zubereitung

Aus Mehl, Zucker, Milch, Salz, Hefe, Butter und Eiern einen Hefeteig herstellen und zu doppeltem Volumen aufgehen lassen. Auf einer bemehlten Arbeitsfläche nochmals kurz durchkneten. Den Teig in eine gefettete Gugelhupfform geben und zugedeckt 20 Minuten gehen lassen. Dann im vorgeheizten Backofen bei 200 Grad Celsius circa 1 Stunde backen. Den fertigen Gugelhupf aus der Form auf ein Kuchengitter stürzen, abkühlen lassen und vor dem Servieren mit Puderzucker bestäuben.

Kapitel 3: Wo warst du in den Ferien?
Technology

Videocassette 1, 5 (captioned version)
DVD Tutor, Disc 1
See Video Guide, pages 15–20

DVD/Video

Los geht's! • Unser Film- und Fotoclub
Members of the **Film- und Fotoclub** are meeting for the first time after the summer break. The club members talk about the places they visited during their vacation. Frank, Christiane, and Basti share the photos and videos they took on their vacations. In the middle of Basti's video, the tape breaks.

Landeskunde
Was hast du in den letzten Ferien gemacht?
People from different cities in Germany and Austria describe their most recent vacation.

Fortsetzung
Basti returns with another video and continues to show his vacation highlights. Unfortunately, there is a power failure, and his video gets cut off again. The three students who talked about their vacations display photos on the wall for the club to decide which one they like the best.

Videoclips
- **Grundig Lifecam Cameras**® (video cameras)
- **TUI Ferienhäuser**® (vacation houses)
- **Metro Ferienclub Gründelsee**® (vacation housing)
- **Katjes**® (candies)

Interactive CD-ROM Tutor

Activity	Activity Type	Pupil's Edition Reference
1. Grammatik	Wozu gehört's?	pp. 66, 67
2. Grammatik	Was fehlt?	pp. 66, 67
3. Wortschatz	Merkspiel	p. 71
4. Grammatik	Was fehlt?	p. 72
5. Wortschatz	Wort und Bild Erfahren/Wählen	p. 78
6. So sagt man das!	Was ist richtig?	pp. 73, 76
Landeskunde	Was hast du in den letzten Ferien gemacht? Was ist richtig?	p. 75
Zum Sprechen	Guided recording	pp. 86–87
Zum Schreiben	Guided writing	pp. 86–87

Teacher Management System
Launch the program, type "admin" in the password area, and press RETURN. Log on to **www.hrw.com/CDROMTUTOR** for a detailed explanation of the Teacher Management System.

DVD Tutor

The *DVD Tutor* contains all material from the *Video Program* as described above. German captions are available for use at your discretion for all sections of the video. The *DVD Tutor* also provides a variety of video-based activities that assess students' understanding of **Los geht's!, Fortsetzung,** and **Landeskunde,** as well as the new **Grammatik im Kontext** presentations.

The *DVD Tutor* may be used on any DVD video player connected to a television or video monitor.

One-Stop Planner CD-ROM

To preview all resources available for this chapter, use the **One-Stop Planner CD-ROM**, Disc 1.

Visit Holt Online
go.hrw.com
KEYWORD: WK3 BAYERN-3
Online Edition

Go.Online!

Premier Online Edition

The Premier Online Edition for *Komm mit!* allows students access to their textbooks anytime, anywhere.

- Audio at point of use
- Additional practice activities
- Self-test activities
- Online reference tools
- Entire Video Program
- Interactive Notebook

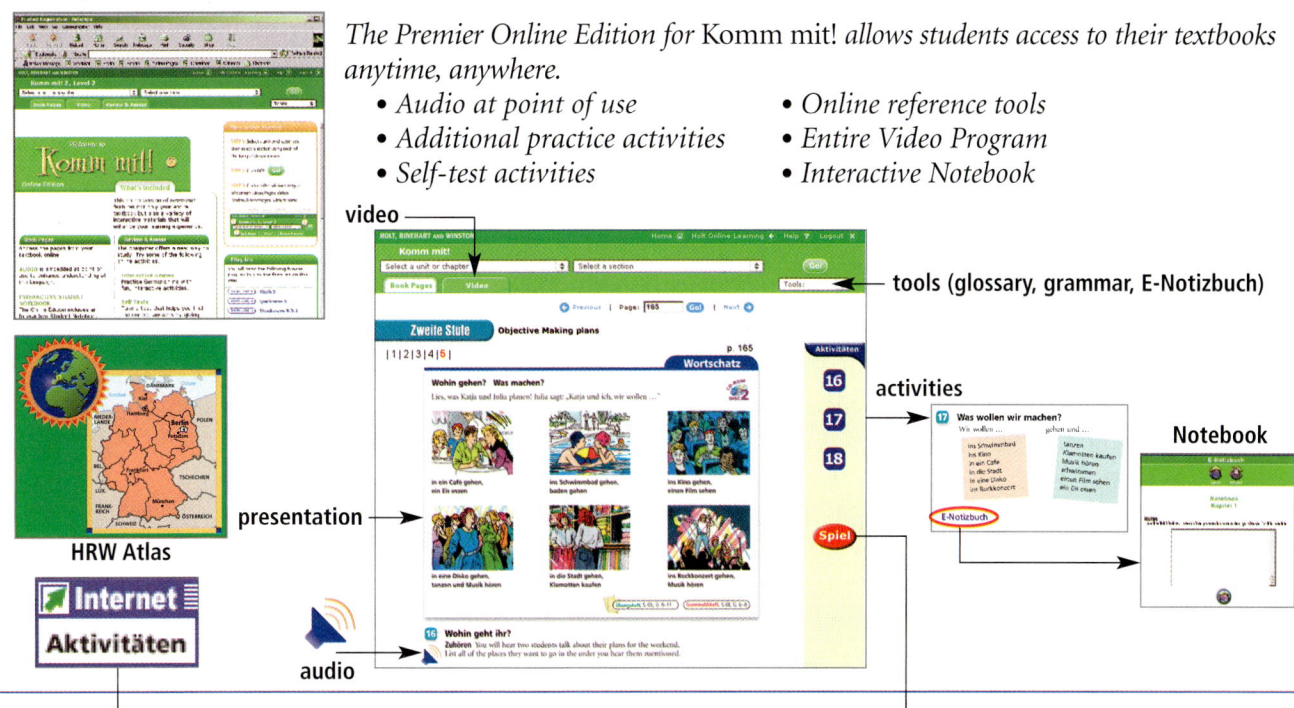

HRW Atlas

Internet Aktivitäten

These guided internet activities include a worksheet and pre-selected and pre-screened authentic web sites from the German-speaking countries. You can use these activities

- to help students develop research skills in the target language
- to introduce students to authentic cultural information
- as a project

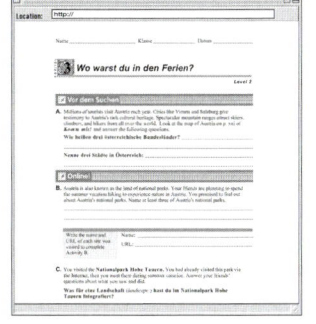

Interaktive Spiele

You can use the interactive activities in this chapter

- to practice grammar, vocabulary, and chapter functions
- as homework
- as an assessment option
- as a self-test
- to prepare for the Chapter Test

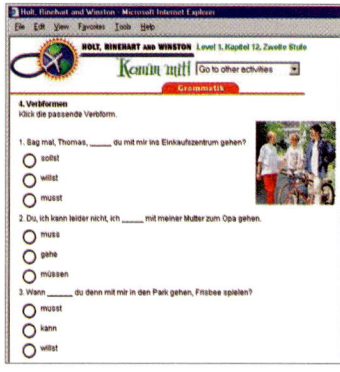

Webprojekt Have students go sightseeing in Frankfurt a. M. They should visit at least three sights. They should report on which sights they visited, describe each sight, and provide a brief history or other pertinent information. Encourage students to exchange useful Web sites with their classmates. Have students document their sources by referencing the names and URLs of all the sites they consulted.

STANDARDS: 1.3, 3.2, 5.1   KAPITEL 3   TECHNOLOGY   **59F**

Kapitel 3: Wo warst du in den Ferien?
Textbook Listening Activities Scripts

Erste Stufe

5 p. 65

JAN Was ich in den Ferien so gemacht habe? Also ich bin mit zwei Freunden nach Südtirol gefahren, mit dem Zug natürlich. Wir haben bei Verwandten von uns auf 'nem Bauernhof gewohnt, mitten in den Bergen. Tagsüber sind wir meistens gewandert und abends dann runter ins Dorf. Da gab es 'ne Disko, da sind wir dann immer zum Tanzen hingegangen. Wir waren die Hälfte der Sommerferien dort, also drei Wochen lang. Die anderen drei Wochen war ich zu Hause und hab meistens im Jugendzentrum rumgehangen.

ANJA Ja, also ich war mit meiner Volleyballmannschaft im Schwarzwald. Da waren auch andere Mannschaften aus Bayern, und wir haben ein paar Wettbewerbsspiele gemacht, aber nur so zum Spaß. Zweimal sind wir auch nach Freiburg gefahren, alle zusammen mit dem Reisebus. Dort haben wir uns die Stadt angesehen und den Dom, also ich meine das Freiburger Münster. Und dann sind wir fast jeden Tag schwimmen gegangen. In der Nähe von der Jugendherberge gab es nämlich ein riesiges Freibad.

UDO Ich war in den Ferien das erste Mal in Amerika, mit meinen Eltern. Wir sind nach Washington geflogen und haben uns da 'ne ganze Menge angeschaut. Ich war sogar im Weißen Haus und auch im Pentagon! Dann sind wir weiter nach Virginia gefahren mit einem Mietwagen. Wir waren da in einem Hotel am Strand, um ein paar Tage zu relaxen, weil wir den totalen Jetlag hatten! Ja, und als ich dann wieder zu Hause war, habe ich noch 'ne kurze Radtour mit meiner Freundin gemacht am letzten Wochenende in den Ferien.

JÖRG Wir waren diesmal nicht weg, weil mein Vater zur Zeit arbeitslos ist. Also war ich die ganzen Ferien lang zu Hause. Das war aber nicht schlecht, denn wir haben ziemlich viel im Garten gemacht und einen Fischteich angelegt. Aber nicht nur einfach ein normales Plastikbecken, sondern einen Teich mit Ökosystem, also mit Wasserpflanzen, Insekten, Fröschen und so. Das hat echt Spaß gemacht. Ja, und sonst war ich mit 'nem Klassenkameraden, der auch zu Hause geblieben ist, ab und zu im Kino, oder wir haben uns ein Video ausgeliehen.

Answers to Activity 5
JAN: gewandert; in die Disko gegangen; im Jugendzentrum rumgehangen
ANJA: Volleyball gespielt; die Stadt Freiburg u. den Dom angesehen; schwimmen gegangen
UDO: das Weiße Haus u. Pentagon besichtigt; am Strand relaxt; eine Radtour gemacht
JÖRG: einen Fischteich im Garten angelegt; ins Kino gegangen; ein Video ausgeliehen

Zweite Stufe

15 p. 71

LISA Ja, also ich war mit meinen Eltern in Lindau am Bodensee. Wir haben den ganzen Tag Wassersport gemacht, also schwimmen, segeln, tauchen und so. War echt super!

EVA Ich bin in Paris gewesen, und hab so einen Französischkurs mitgemacht. Ich glaub, ich hab eine ganze Menge neue Vokabeln gelernt, aber eigentlich war ich immer froh, wenn der Unterricht zu Ende war und wir uns die Stadt ansehen konnten.

KURT Ich bin mit einer Jugendgruppe in Holland gewesen, in so einem kleinen Nest in der Nähe von Rotterdam, direkt am Meer. Wir haben alle auf dem Campingplatz gezeltet. Am letzten Abend haben wir ein riesiges Lagerfeuer gemacht, Lieder gesungen, und ein paar Leute haben Gitarre gespielt. Das hat mir echt gut gefallen.

INGE Ich war in den Ferien zu Hause. Ich bin aus Trier, das liegt an der Mosel. Die Landschaft ist echt toll hier. Jedes Jahr kommen Tausende von Touristen an die Mosel, um hier ihren Urlaub oder die Ferien zu verbringen. Also, warum soll ich irgendwo anders hinfahren?

The following scripts are for the listening activities found in the *Pupil's Edition.* For Student Response Forms, see *Listening Activities,* pages 19–22. To provide students with additional listening practice, see *Listening Activities,* pages 23–26.

For resource information, see the **One-Stop Planner CD-ROM**, Disc 1.

Answers to Activity 15
LISA: Lindau am Bodensee; EVA: Paris;
KURT: in der Nähe von Rotterdam, in Holland; INGE: zu Hause in Trier an der Mosel

Dritte Stufe

25 p. 76

GRETE Mir hat es wahnsinnig gut in den Ferien gefallen. Ich habe so viele neue Leute kennen gelernt. Es war echt super!

LUTZ Also, mir hat's leider überhaupt nicht gefallen. Wir hatten die meiste Zeit nur Regen und konnten gar nichts unternehmen. Das war furchtbar!

ELKE Ach, das tut mir Leid. Aber bei mir war es fast genauso. Wir haben in den Ferien nur so ein langweiliges Zeug gemacht. Es hat mir nicht besonders gefallen.

UTE Meine Ferien waren phantastisch! Ich war mit einer ganz tollen Jugendgruppe im Schwarzwald. Nächstes Jahr möchte ich auch wieder mit denen zusammen in die Ferien fahren.

ERIK Mir hat es auch ziemlich gut in den Ferien gefallen! Ich habe zwar nichts Besonderes gemacht, nur gefaulenzt, aber das war ja gerade das Gute daran!

Answers to Activity 25
GRETE: gefallen (viele Leute kennen gelernt); LUTZ: nicht gefallen (Regen); ELKE: nicht gefallen (war langweilig); UTE: gefallen (tolle Jugendgruppe); ERIK: gefallen (hat gefaulenzt)

Anwendung

5 p. 87

1. In der Nähe gibt es einen großen, modernen Freizeitpark mit einem Schwimmbad, Tennisplätzen und einer Minigolf-Anlage. In der Stadt gibt es mehrere Kinos, ein Schauspielhaus und die Oper. Wer gerne wandert, kann raus aufs Land fahren. Dort gibt es mehrere Wanderwege, oder man kann eine Bootstour auf dem See machen.

2. Die Stadt ist ziemlich klein, so ungefähr 50 000 Einwohner. Aber nur etwa 3 Kilometer von hier gibt es ein riesiges Waldgebiet. Und etwas außerhalb liegt der Kaarster See. Ganz in der Nähe von der Stadt sind ein paar Bauernhöfe. Die Felder reichen bis zum Stadtrand.

3. Das größte Hotel der Stadt ist das Seehotel. Es gibt dort über 200 Zimmer, mehrere Konferenzräume, einen großen Speisesaal, ein Schwimmbad und vieles mehr. Es ist fast immer ausgebucht, besonders im Sommer, wenn alle Touristen kommen, um Ferien zu machen.

4. Hier in der Stadt gibt es viele Sehenswürdigkeiten. Man kann sich zum Beispiel die so genannte Altstadt ansehen. Sie fängt am Marktplatz an und geht weiter durch die kleinen Gassen bis hin zur Dominikanerkirche. Direkt hinter der Kirche ist das Archäologische Museum, mit Funden, die hier aus der Gegend stammen. Und wenn man sich für Kunst interessiert, dann muss man sich unbedingt die Engelskulptur im Rokokostil auf dem Stadtbrunnen ansehen!

Answers to Activity 5
1. c   2. a   3. d   4. b

6 p. 87

1. Wir waren zum Camping am Burger See. Das Wetter war echt toll, und wir haben ein Boot gemietet. Dann sind wir angeln gewesen. Am Abend haben wir dann die Fische gegrillt. Es hat uns wirklich gut gefallen.

2. Wir sind nach Paris geflogen. Es hat das ganze Wochenende geregnet, und wir haben uns ein Museum nach dem anderen angesehen. Echt langweilig. Vom Eiffelturm aus konnte man gar nichts sehen, es war total nebelig und verregnet. Es hat mir überhaupt nicht gefallen.

3. Ich bin zu meiner Tante nach Hamburg gefahren. Schon im Zug habe ich echt nette Leute kennen gelernt. Und wir haben uns dann verabredet, zusammen ins Kino zu gehen, uns die Stadt anzusehen und so. Ich war fast kaum zu Hause. Meine Tante fand es nicht so gut, aber mir hat es gefallen.

4. Ich war zum Skilaufen in der Schweiz. Es gab kaum Schnee, viel zu viel Sonne und steigende Temperaturen. Ich habe kein einziges Mal Ski laufen können. Ich war echt sauer. Es hat mir gar nicht gefallen.

Answers to Activity 6
1. Burger See; gefallen; 2. Paris; nicht gefallen; 3. Hamburg; gefallen; 4. Schweiz; nicht gefallen

Kapitel 3: Wo warst du in den Ferien?
Suggested Lesson Plans 50-Minute Schedule

Day 1

CHAPTER OPENER 10 min.
- Culture Note, ATE, p. 59M
- Geography Connection, ATE, p. 59M
- Thinking Critically, ATE, p. 59M

LOS GEHT'S! 20 min.
- Preteaching Vocabulary, ATE, p. 59N
- Have students read **Los geht's!**, pp. 62–63
- Teaching Suggestions, Video Guide, p. 16
- Show **Los geht's!** Video

ERSTE STUFE
So sagt man das!/Wortschatz, p. 65 15 min.
- Do Activity 5, p. 65
- Presenting **So sagt man das!**, ATE, p. 59O
- Do Activity 1, p. 19, Grammatikheft
- Presenting **Wortschatz**, ATE, p. 59O
- Teaching Transparency 3-A

Wrap-Up 5 min.
- Students respond to questions about activities they have done in the past

Homework Options
Pupil's Edition, p. 64, Comprehension Acts.
Grammatikheft, p. 19, Act. 2
Übungsheft, p. 25, Act. 1

Day 2

ERSTE STUFE
Quick Review 15 min.
- Check homework, p. 64, Comprehension Acts.
- Do Activities 6, 7, and 8, p. 66

Grammatik, pp. 66–67 30 min.
- Presenting **Grammatik**, ATE, p. 59P
- Do Activity 9, p. 67
- Do Activity 10, p. 68
- Do Activities 3-6, pp. 20–21, Grammatikheft
- Do Activity 1, **Mehr Grammatikübungen**

Wrap-Up 5 min.
- Students respond to questions about what they did during their vacations

Homework Options
Pupil's Edition, p. 68, Act. 11
Übungsheft, pp. 26–28, Acts. 1–7

Day 3

ERSTE STUFE
Quick Review 15 min.
- Check homework, Übungsheft, pp. 26–28, Acts. 1–7

Reading Selection, p. 69 15 min.
- Read **Dresden, Hauptstadt von Sachsen**, p. 69
- Do Activity 12, p. 69

Quiz Review 15 min.
- Do Communicative Activity 3-1, pp. 13–14

Wrap-Up 5 min.
- Students respond to questions about what they did last weekend

Homework Options
Do **Mehr Grammatikübungen, Erste Stufe**
Interactive CD-ROM, Acts. 1–2

Day 4

ERSTE STUFE
Quick Review 10 min.
- Check homework, **Mehr Grammatikübungen, Erste Stufe**

Quiz 20 min.
- Quiz 3-1A or 3-1B

ZWEITE STUFE
Reading Selection, p. 70 15 min.
- Read **Frankfurt a. M.**, p. 70
- Do Activity 13, p. 70

Wrap-Up 5 min.
- Students respond to questions about where they were in Frankfurt and what they did there

Homework Options
Pupil's Edition, p. 70, Act. 14, prepare lists

Day 5

ZWEITE STUFE
Quick Review 15 min.
- Return and review Quiz 3-1
- Do Activity 14, p. 70
- Play Audio CD for Activity 15, p. 71
- Do Activity 16, p. 71

So sagt man das!/Wortschatz, p. 71 15 min.
- Presenting **So sagt man das!**, ATE, p. 59R
- Presenting **Wortschatz**, ATE, p. 59R
- Background Information, ATE, p. 59R
- Teaching Transparencies 3-B, 3-1
- Do Activity 17, p. 72

Grammatik/Wortschatz, p. 72 15 min.
- Presenting **Grammatik**, ATE, p. 59S
- Presenting **Wortschatz**, ATE, p. 59S
- Do Activities 18 and 19, p. 72

Wrap-Up 5 min.
- Students respond to questions about why they were not in various places

Homework Options
Grammatikheft, p. 22, Acts. 7–8
Activities for Communication, p. 83, Realia 3-2, write "Geheimtips" for your own city

Day 6

ZWEITE STUFE
Quick Review 10 min.
- Check homework, Grammatikheft, p. 22, Acts. 7–8

Grammatik, p. 73 15 min.
- Presenting **Grammatik**, ATE, p. 59S
- Do Activities 20 and 21, p. 73
- Do Activity 22, p. 74
- Present **Sprachtipp**, p. 74
- Do Activity 23, p. 74

LANDESKUNDE 20 min.
- Pre-viewing Suggestion, Video Guide, p. 16
- Language Note, ATE, p. 59T
- Show **Landeskunde** Video
- Do Activities A and B, p. 75
- Do Activities 1–3, p. 32, Übungsheft

Wrap-Up 5 min.
- Students respond to questions about where they were and what they saw and did during the last vacation

Homework Options
Pupil's Edition, p. 74, Act. 24
Grammatikheft, pp. 23–24, Acts. 9–11
Übungsheft, pp. 29–31, Acts. 1–7

 One-Stop Planner CD-ROM

For alternative lesson plans by chapter section, to create your own customized plans, or to preview all resources available for this chapter, use the **One-Stop Planner CD-ROM**, Disc 1.

 For additional homework suggestions, see activities accompanied by this symbol throughout the chapter.

Day 7

ZWEITE STUFE

Quick Review 10 min.
- Check homework, Übungsheft, pp. 29–31, Acts. 1–7

Quiz Review 20 min.
- Do **Mehr Grammatikübungen, Zweite Stufe**
- Do Situation 3-2, pp. 127–128

Quiz 20 min.
- Quiz 3-2A or 3-2B

Homework Options
Activities for Communication, pp. 15–16, prepare Communicative Activity 3-2

Day 8

DRITTE STUFE

Quick Review 15 min.
- Return and review Quiz 3-2
- Bell Work, ATE, p. 59T
- Do Communicative Activity 3-2, pp. 15–16

So sagt man das!, p. 76 10 min.
- Play Audio CD for Activity 25, p. 76
- Presenting **So sagt man das!**, ATE, p. 59U
- Do Activity 26, p. 76

Grammatik, p. 77 20 min.
- Presenting **Grammatik**, ATE, p. 59U
- Do Activities 27 and 28, p. 77
- Do Activities 1–3, pp. 33–34, Übungsheft

Wrap-Up 5 min.
- Students respond to questions about how they liked something

Homework Options
Grammatikheft, p. 25, Act. 12

Day 9

DRITTE STUFE

Quick Review 10 min.
- Check homework, Grammatikheft, p. 25, Act. 12

Grammatik, p. 77 15 min.
- Presenting **Grammatik**, ATE, p. 59U
- Do Activity 29, p. 78
- Do Activities 13–14, p. 26, Grammatikheft

Wortschatz, p. 78 10 min.
- Presenting **Wortschatz**, ATE, p. 59U
- Teaching Transparency 3-2
- Do Activity 30, p. 79

Ein wenig Grammatik/Wortschatz, p. 79 10 min.
- Present **Ein wenig Grammatik**, p. 79
- Presenting **Wortschatz**, ATE, p. 59U
- Do Activities 31 and 32, p. 79

Wrap-Up 5 min.
- Students respond to questions about how they and their parents liked various cities

Homework Options
Grammatikheft, p. 27, Acts. 15–17
Übungsheft, pp. 34–35, Acts. 4–7

Day 10

DRITTE STUFE

Quick Review 15 min.
- Check homework, Übungsheft, pp. 34–35, Acts. 4–7

ZUM LESEN 20 min.
- Present **Lesestrategie**, p. 80
- Do Activities 1–7, pp. 80–81

Quiz Review 15 min.
- Do **Mehr Grammatikübungen, Dritte Stufe**

Homework Options
Pupil's Edition, p. 79, Act. 33
Übungsheft, p. 36, Acts. 1–4
Interaktive Spiele, see ATE, p. 59F

Day 11

DRITTE STUFE

Quick Review 10 min.
- Reports on Activity 33, p. 79

Quiz 20 min.
- Quiz 3-3A or 3-3B

ANWENDUNG 15 min.
- Do **Anwendung** Activities 1–3, pp. 86–87

Wrap-Up 5 min.
- Students respond to questions about vacation activities

Homework Options
Pupil's Edition, p. 88, **Kann ich's wirklich?**
Pupil's Edition, p. 87, Act. 4, **Zum Schreiben**

Day 12

ANWENDUNG

Quick Review 20 min.
- Return Quiz 3-3
- Check homework, p. 88, **Kann ich's wirklich?**
- Do **Anwendung** Activities 5–7, p. 87

Chapter Review 30 min.
- Review chapter functions, vocabulary, and grammar; choose from **Mehr Grammatikübungen**, Grammar Tutor for Students of German, Activities for Communication, Listening Activities, Interactive CD-ROM Tutor, or **Interaktive Spiele**
- Review test format and provide sample test items for students

Homework Options
Study for Chapter Test

Assessment

Test, Chapter 3 45 min.
- Administer Chapter 3 Test. Select from Testing Program, Alternative Assessment Guide or Test Generator.

KAPITEL 3 • SUGGESTED LESSON PLANS • 50-MINUTE SCHEDULE

Kapitel 3: Wo warst du in den Ferien?
Suggested Lesson Plans 90-Minute Schedule

Block 1

CHAPTER OPENER 10 min.
- Culture Note, ATE, p. 59M
- Geography Connection, ATE, p. 59M
- Thinking Critically, ATE, p. 59M

LOS GEHT'S! 25 min.
- Preteaching Vocabulary, ATE, p. 59N
- Have students read **Los geht's!**, pp. 62–63
- Teaching Suggestions, Video Guide, p. 16
- Show **Los geht's!** Video
- Do Comprehension Activities, p. 64

ERSTE STUFE

So sagt man das!/Wortschatz, p. 65 25 min.
- Do Activity 5, p. 65
- Presenting **So sagt man das!**, ATE, p. 59O
- Do Activity 1, p. 19, Grammatikheft
- Presenting **Wortschatz**, ATE, p. 59O
- Teaching Transparency 3-A
- Do Activity 2, p. 19, Grammatikheft

Grammatik, p. 66–67 25 min.
- Presenting **Grammatik**, ATE, p. 59P
- Do Activity 9, p. 67
- Do Activity 10, p. 68
- Do Activities 3–6, pp. 20–21, Grammatikheft
- Do Activity 1, **Mehr Grammatikübungen**

Wrap-Up 5 min.
- Students respond to questions about activities they have done in the past

Homework Options
Pupil's Edition, p. 68, Act. 11
Übungsheft, p. 25, Act. 1; pp. 26–28, Acts. 1–7

Block 2

ERSTE STUFE
Quick Review 10 min.
- Check homework, Übungsheft, pp. 26–28, Acts. 1–7

Reading Selection, p. 69 20 min.
- Read **Dresden, Hauptstadt von Sachsen**, p. 69
- Do Activity 12, p. 69

Quiz Review 10 min.
- Do Communicative Activity 3-1, pp. 13–14

Quiz 20 min.
- Quiz 3-1A or 3-1B

ZWEITE STUFE
Reading Selection, p. 70 25 min.
- Read **Frankfurt a. M.**, p. 70
- Do Activity 13, p. 70
- Do Activity 14, p. 70
- Play Audio CD for Activity 15, p. 71
- Do Activity 16, p. 71

Wrap-Up 5 min.
- Students respond to questions about where they were in Frankfurt and what they did there

Homework Options
Activities for Communication, p. 83, Realia 3-2, write "Geheimtips" for your own city

Block 3

ZWEITE STUFE
Quick Review 10 min.
- Return and review Quiz 3-1
- Check homework, Realia 3-2

So sagt man das!/Wortschatz, p. 71 20 min.
- Presenting **So sagt man das!**, ATE, p. 59R
- Presenting **Wortschatz**, ATE, p. 59R
- Background Information, ATE, p. 59R
- Teaching Transparencies 3-B, 3-1
- Do Activity 17, p. 72
- Play Circumlocution Game, ATE, p. 59X

Grammatik/Wortschatz, p. 72 15 min.
- Presenting **Grammatik**, ATE, p. 59S
- Presenting **Wortschatz**, ATE, p. 59S
- Do Activities 18 and 19, p. 72

Grammatik, p. 73 20 min.
- Presenting **Grammatik**, ATE, p. 59S
- Do Activities 20 and 21, p. 73
- Do Activity 22, p. 74
- Present **Sprachtipp**, p. 74
- Do Activity 23, p. 74

LANDESKUNDE 20 min.
- Pre-viewing Suggestion, Video Guide, p. 16
- Language Note, ATE, p. 59T
- Show **Landeskunde** Video
- Do Activities A and B, p. 75
- Do Activities 1–3, p. 32, Übungsheft

Wrap-Up 5 min.
- Students respond to questions about where they were and what they saw and did during the last vacation

Homework Options
Pupil's Edition, p. 74, Act. 24
Grammatikheft, pp. 22–24, Acts. 7–11
Übungsheft, pp. 29–31, Acts. 1–7
Interactive CD-ROM, Acts. 3–4

 **One-Stop Planner CD-ROM**

For alternative lesson plans by chapter section, to create your own customized plans, or to preview all resources available for this chapter, use the **One-Stop Planner CD-ROM**, Disc 1.

 For additional homework suggestions, see activities accompanied by this symbol throughout the chapter.

Block 4

DRITTE STUFE

Quick Review 10 min.
- Check homework Übungsheft, pp. 29–31, Acts. 1–7

Quiz Review 20 min.
- Do **Mehr Grammatikübungen, Zweite Stufe**
- Do Situation 3-2, pp. 127–128

Quiz 20 min.
- Quiz 3-2A or 3-2B

So sagt man das!, p. 76 20 min.
- Play Audio CD for Activity 25, p. 76
- Presenting **So sagt man das!**, ATE, p. 59U
- Do Activity 26, p. 76

Grammatik, p. 77 15 min.
- Presenting **Grammatik,** ATE, p. 59U
- Do Activities 27 and 28, p. 77

Wrap-Up 5 min.
- Students respond to questions about how they liked something

Homework Options
Grammatikheft, p. 25, Act. 12
Übungsheft, pp. 33–34, Acts. 1–3

Block 5

DRITTE STUFE

Quick Review 15 min.
- Return and review Quiz 3-2
- Check homework, Übungsheft, pp. 33–34, Acts. 1–3

Grammatik, p. 77 15 min.
- Presenting **Grammatik**, ATE, p. 59U
- Do Activity 29, p. 78
- Do Activities 13–14, p. 26, Grammatikheft

Wortschatz, p. 78 10 min.
- Presenting **Wortschatz**, ATE, p. 59U
- Teaching Transparency 3-2
- Do Activity 30, p. 79

Ein wenig Grammatik/Wortschatz, p. 79 20 min.
- Present **Ein wenig Grammatik**, p. 79
- Presenting **Wortschatz,** ATE, p. 59U
- Do Activities 31 and 32, p. 79

ZUM LESEN 25 min.
- Present **Lesestrategie**, p. 80
- Do Activities 1–7, pp. 80–81
- Do Acts. 1–4, p. 36, Übungsheft

Wrap-Up 5 min.
- Students respond to questions about how they and their parents liked various cities

Homework Options
Pupil's Edition, p. 79, Act. 33
Grammatikheft, p. 27, Acts. 15–17
Übungsheft, pp. 34–35, Acts. 4–7

Block 6

DRITTE STUFE

Quick Review 20 min.
- Check homework, Übungsheft, pp. 34–35, Acts. 4–7
- Reports on Activity 33, p. 79

Quiz Review 20 min.
- Do **Mehr Grammatikübungen, Dritte Stufe**

Quiz 20 min.
- Quiz 3-3A or 3-3B

ANWENDUNG 25 min.
- Do **Anwendung** Activities 1–7, pp. 86–87

Wrap-Up 5 min.
- Students respond to questions about vacation activities

Homework Options
Pupil's Edition, p. 88, **Kann ich's wirklich?**
Interaktive Spiele, see ATE, p. 59F

Block 7

ANWENDUNG

Quick Review 15 min.
- Return and review Quiz 3-3
- Check homework, p. 88, **Kann ich's wirklich?**

Chapter Review 30 min.
- Review chapter functions, vocabulary, and grammar; choose from **Mehr Grammatikübungen,** Grammar Tutor for Students of German, Activities for Communication, Listening Activities, Interactive CD-ROM Tutor, or **Interaktive Spiele**
- Review test format and provide sample test items for students

Test, Chapter 3 45 min.
- Administer Chapter 3 Test. Select from Testing Program, Alternative Assessment Guide or Test Generator.

Kapitel 3: Wo warst du in den Ferien?
Teaching Suggestions, pages 60–89

PAGES 60–61

CHAPTER OPENER

Pacing Tips
The **Erste Stufe** centers around the conversational past with a complete grammar presentation on pp. 66–67. A reading about Dresden occurs on p. 69. The **Zweite Stufe** begins with a reading about **Frankfurt am Main**. The **hatte**- and **war**-forms are presented on p. 72. Students also learn about the dative case with the prepositions **in** and **an**. The dative case is continued in the **Dritte Stufe** with the verb **gefallen** and dative personal pronouns. You will probably spend less time teaching the **Dritte Stufe** than the **Erste Stufe** or the **Zweite Stufe**. For Lesson Plans and timing suggestions, see pages 59I–59L.

Meeting the Standards

Communication
- Reporting past events, talking about activities, p. 65
- Reporting past events, talking about places, p. 71
- Asking how someone liked something, expressing enthusiasm or disappointment, responding enthusiastically or sympathetically, p. 76

Cultures
- Culture Note, p. 59M
- Thinking Critically, p. 59M
- Background Information, p. 59R
- Language Note, p. 59T
- Culture Note, p. 59U

Connections
- Geography Connection, p. 59M
- Art and Media Connection, p. 59N
- Music Connection, p. 59P
- Geography Connection, p. 59Q
- Thinking Critically, p. 59R
- Language Note, p. 59U
- Geography Connection, p. 59W

Comparisons
- Language-to-Language, p. 59O
- Language-to-Language, p. 59R
- Background Information, p. 59W

Communities
- Career Path, p. 59Q
- Community Link, p. 59V

Teaching Suggestion
Ask students where they would like to go on vacation if they had unlimited time and the money to do so.

For resource information, see the **One-Stop Planner CD-ROM**, Disc 1.

Cultures and Communities

Culture Note
German students generally get six weeks of vacation in the summer (**Sommerferien**), two weeks in the fall (**Herbstferien**), two weeks at Christmas (**Weihnachtsferien**), and two weeks around Easter (**Osterferien**). Holidays vary slightly throughout the **Bundesländer**.

Connections and Comparisons

Thinking Critically
Drawing Inferences German students can participate in many after-school activities as can students in the United States. Can students tell from the photograph what club or organization these German teenagers belong to? (Film and Photo Club)

Geography Connection
Ask students to scan the maps of Germany, Austria, and Switzerland for towns with the suffix **-berg**. Students should notice that these towns and cities are often located in mountainous areas.

Language Note
The suffix **-berg** should not be confused with **-burg**, which means *castle*. (Examples: Würzburg, Hamburg vs. Heidelberg, Nürnberg)

Chapter Sequence

Los geht's!	p. 62
Erste Stufe	p. 65
Zweite Stufe	p. 70
Landeskunde	p. 75
Dritte Stufe	p. 76
Zum Lesen	p. 80
Mehr Grammatikübungen	p. 82
Anwendung	p. 86
Kann ich's wirklich?	p. 88
Wortschatz	p. 89

LOS GEHT'S!

Teaching Resources
pp. 62–64

PRINT
- Lesson Planner, p. 12
- Video Guide, pp. 15–16, 18
- Übungsheft, p. 25

MEDIA
- One-Stop Planner
- Video Program
  Los geht's!
  Videocassette 1, 32:10–36:14
  Videocassette 5 (captioned version), 15:03–19:07
  Fortsetzung
  Videocassette 1, 36:17–38:15
  Videocassette 5 (captioned version), 19:10–21:07
- DVD Tutor, Disc 1
- Audio Compact Discs, CD3, Trs. 1–2
- Los geht's! Transparencies

▶ **PAGES 62–63**

Los geht's! Transparencies

Preteaching Vocabulary

Guessing Words from Context
Ask students what types of functions they would expect in a conversation during the **Film- und Fotoclub** (describing pictures, telling where you were, expressing likes and dislikes, etc.). Students should scan **Los geht's!** for German phrases that match the functions they listed. Then have students use contextual clues in Frank's discussion to guess the meanings of these words: ❸ ❹ den **Zwinger**, *Fidelio*, and **zerstört**. What kind of work is *Fidelio*? Where did the performance take place? Finally, have students list the places that Frank, Christiane, and Sebastian saw or visited in Dresden, Frankfurt, and St. Ulrich.

 ### Fortsetzung

You may choose to continue with the **Fortsetzung** of *Unser Film- und Fotoclub* now or wait until later in the chapter. For a synopsis of the **Los geht's!** and **Fortsetzung** episodes, see p. 59E.

STANDARDS: 1.2, 3.1

Advance Organizer
As an advance organizer to **Los geht's!**, do the prereading activity at the top of p. 62 with the class. Then have students scan the text and the pictures, looking for visual clues and cognates to help them anticipate what they are going to hear and see.

Connections and Comparisons

Art and Media Connection
If your school has a photography club, ask a member of the club to tell the class what the club does, where, and when members meet. The speaker could also bring some of the equipment and samples of the club's work to show students.

Geography Connection
Ask students to look in an atlas and locate Dresden, Frankfurt, and St. Ulrich.

▶ **PAGE 64**

Using the Captioned Video/DVD

As an alternative to reading the conversations in the book, you might want to show the captioned version of *Unser Film- und Fotoclub* available on Videocassette 5.
Note: The *DVD Tutor* contains captions for all sections of the *Video Program*.

Comprehension Check

Auditory Learners
❶ Have students read Questions 1 through 6. Replay the video or the compact disc of *Unser Film- und Fotoclub* and have students answer the questions while they listen to the story. Suggest that students take notes. You might want to tell them that their answers do not have to be in complete sentences.

Teaching Suggestions
❷ Ask students to work with a partner. Students go over the text and answer the questions in German in writing. Remind students to use the reading strategies they have learned so far to help them complete the assignment.

Challenge
❸ Ask students to rewrite the paragraphs as if Sebastian and Christiane were planning trips to Tyrol and Frankfurt and are telling someone what they are going to do.

ERSTE STUFE

Teaching Resources
pp. 65–69

PRINT
- Lesson Planner, p. 13
- TPR Storytelling Book, pp. 16–17
- Listening Activities, pp. 19, 23–24
- Activities for Communication, pp. 13–14, 82, 85, 127–128
- Grammatikheft, pp. 19–21
- Grammar Tutor for Students of German, Chapter 3
- Übungsheft, pp. 26–28
- Testing Program, pp. 53–56
- Alternative Assessment Guide, p. 34
- Student Make-Up Assignments, Chapter 3

MEDIA
- One-Stop Planner
- Audio Compact Discs, CD3, Trs. 3, 14, 20–21
- Teaching Transparencies
  Situation 3-1
  Vocabulary 3-A
  Mehr Grammatikübungen Answers
  Grammatikheft Answers
- Interactive CD-ROM Tutor, Disc 1
- DVD Tutor, Disc 1

PAGE 65

Bell Work
Make a chart on a transparency on which you write names of vacation places on one side and a typical gift idea from each place in random order on the other side.
Examples:

Schwarzwald	Lebkuchen
Lübeck	eine Freiheitsstatue aus Plastik
New York	Marzipan
Nürnberg	eine Kuckucksuhr

Have students make up as many sentences as they can.
Example:
In den Ferien war ich in … und habe … gekauft.

Building on Previous Skills
Ask students which words or phrases they used in the Bell Work activity to express past events. (**war** and **habe gekauft**)

Cultures and Communities

Culture Note
Planning their vacation is generally very important to Germans. They like to share future vacation plans and past experiences with friends. As part of this, they tend to write many postcards to relatives and friends from their vacation spots.

PRESENTING: So sagt man das!
After reading the questions and phrases in **So sagt man das!**, ask students what they notice about the verbs. How many parts do they have? Which part changes to agree with the subject? Can students point out where the second part of the verb is located in the sentences?

Connections and Comparisons

Language-to-Language
You may want to explain the concept of collective nouns (nouns that are singular in form but plural in meaning because they denote a collection of individuals or items, such as the word *army*.) Show that what is a collective singular noun in one language might be a regular plural noun in another.

Examples:

English: *hair* (collective singular)
German: (**die**) **Haare** (pl)
French: **les cheveux** (pl)
Spanish: **el pelo** (sg)

English: *people* (pl)
German: **die Leute** (pl)
French: **les gens** (pl)
Spanish: **la gente** (collective singular)

Ask students if they can think of more nouns that are singular in form in English but plural in form in German, French, or Spanish.

Examples:

English: *vacation*, German: **die Ferien**, French: **les vacances**, Spanish: **las vacaciones**

PRESENTING: Wortschatz
Introduce the new vocabulary by acting out the phrases. Use props if available. Then give commands to the class or individual students.
Examples:
Helen, leg das Video bitte ein!
Travis, nimm das Video heraus!
Hier Patty, nimm die Kamera und fotografiere unsere Klasse!
Gib Gary bitte diesen Film!

PAGES 66–67

Communication for All Students

Teaching Suggestion

6 Ask students to take the key ideas from their answers to the six questions and write a brief report about
- the kind of camera they have,
- the kind of pictures they usually take,
- their favorite photo subjects, and
- the last photos they took.

Challenge

7 Ask a student what he or she did during summer vacation. Then call on another student to restate what that student did using the third person.

Teaching Suggestion

8 After students have found all the sentences, ask them to group the sentences, naming all the phrases that use **sein** and the ones that use **haben**.

PRESENTING: Grammatik

The conversational past Before introducing the **Grammatik,** ask students how they express past events in English. Write students' responses on the board. Since they will probably come up with several different ways, ask them to point out the one that most resembles the German conversational past.

Ask students to explain the function of a past participle (expressing a completed action), then underline the past participle in the sample phrases. Ask students to name several regular and several irregular past participles used in English.

After going over the conversational past with students, take time to practice saying the verb phrases in Activity 9.

- Go from present to past, using different pronouns. Focus especially on the irregular or strong verbs.

- Have students find the common denominator in most of the verbs in the box that take **sein** as an auxiliary in the conversational past. (All but **sein** and **bleiben** are verbs of motion, showing motion towards a place.)

- Go from past to present. Say a complete sentence in the past, such as **Er ist nach Hause gegangen,** and ask students to give the same sentence in the present.

- Ask students to identify all the strong verbs in the box that do <u>not</u> have a vowel change in the past participle. (Example: **geben - gegeben**) Then have them identify the strong verbs that <u>do</u> have a vowel change. (Example: **bleiben - geblieben**)

Connections and Comparisons

Music Connection

For additional reading, refer students to the song *Kein schöner Land* (lyrics and music by Anton Wilhelm von Zuccalmaglio), Level 2 *Listening Activities,* p. 14. Can they find the verb in the conversational past tense? (**haben … gesessen**) Why is the helping verb **haben** instead of **sein?** (**Sein** tends to be used with intransitive verbs that indicate change of condition or location; there is no such change involved here, so **haben** is used.) You may also want to play the song, Level 2 CD 7, Tr. 23.

PAGE 68

Communication for All Students

Challenge

10 Once students have completed Activities a through c, ask them to add one additional activity to Sebastian's daily calendar.

Example:
Was hat der Sebastian noch am Montag gemacht?

PAGE 69

12 Teaching Suggestion

Have students preview Questions 1–5 before they read about Dresden. If you find the text too challenging for your students, you may want to read each paragraph aloud, using various strategies to establish meaning when necessary. (Examples: giving definitions and examples, stressing key concepts, paraphrasing, and simplifying sentence structures)

STANDARDS: 1.3, 4.1

Cultures and Communities

Career Path
Have students pair up to brainstorm scenarios in which a travel agent (or anyone working in the tourism industry) would find it advantageous to possess a knowledge of German. (Suggestions: America is a popular vacation destination for German tourists, and an agent who spoke the language could work with German agencies to help arrange activities and accommodations for their clients; such an agent could also specialize in arranging the trips of Americans who want to travel to German-speaking countries.)

Teaching Suggestion
Ask students to share with the class in German how they or their family documented their last trip and vacation. Did they take photographs, buy postcards, or make movies with video cameras? What were some of the souvenirs they brought back from their trip?

Performance Assessment
For performance assessment activities for each **Stufe**, see the *Alternative Assessment Guide*.

Assess
- Testing Program, pp. 53–56
  Quiz 3-1A, Quiz 3-1B
  Audio CD3, Tr. 14
- Student Make-Up Assignments
  Chapter 3, Alternative Quiz
- Alternative Assessment Guide, p. 34

ZWEITE STUFE

Teaching Resources
pp. 70–75

PRINT
- Lesson Planner, p. 14
- TPR Storytelling Book, pp. 18–19
- Listening Activities, pp. 19, 24–25
- Activities for Communication, pp. 15–16, 83, 85, 127–128
- Grammatikheft, pp. 22–24
- Grammar Tutor for Students of German, Chapter 3
- Übungsheft, pp. 29–31
- Testing Program, pp. 57–60
- Alternative Assessment Guide, p. 34
- Student Make-Up Assignments, Chapter 3

MEDIA
- One-Stop Planner
- Audio Compact Discs, CD3, Trs. 4, 15, 22–23
- Teaching Transparencies
  Vocabulary 3-B
  Mehr Grammatikübungen Answers
  Grammatikheft Answers
- Interactive CD-ROM Tutor, Disc 1
- DVD Tutor, Disc 1

PAGE 70

Bell Work
Ask students to write down as many German cities as they can, including those introduced in Level 1. If they had to pick one, which would they choose to visit and what would they like to do and see there?

Connections and Comparisons

Geography Connection
Ask students to look in an atlas for towns named Frankfurt in the United States. (Examples: Frankfurt, Michigan and Frankfort, Kentucky) Ask students to research the heritage and the background of one of those American cities. This could be done as a brief written assignment or for extra credit.

Connections and Comparisons

Thinking Critically

Drawing Inferences Ask students why **a.M. (am Main)** follows the name **Frankfurt**. Remind students that there is another city named Frankfurt in Germany (**Frankfurt an der Oder**). Have students look up these two cities on a map.

Cultures and Communities

Background Information

- **Frankfurt am Main** dates back to 794, which makes it over 1200 years old. Its original name was **Francono Furd**. The city is located in Hessen, and its population is around 651,000. **Frankfurt an der Oder** was founded in 1226 and has a population of 83,850 people. It is located in Brandenburg.

- Students might be interested in the two specialties mentioned in the reading. **Zwiebelkuchen** resembles quiche. It is made of puff pastry, browned onions, bacon, eggs, sour cream, salt, and cumin. It is baked and traditionally served with wine and beer. (**Der**) **Äbbewoi** is the name in the Hessian dialect for **Apfelwein,** a hard cider. For a **Zwiebelkuchen** recipe, see Level 1 *Teacher's Edition*, p. 331D.

▶ **PAGE 71**

PRESENTING: So sagt man das!

Ask students in English how they would ask a person where he or she was last weekend. Since students might give two versions (Where were you? and Where have you been?), mention to students that those two ways of expressing this question are also used in the German language. Then read the expressions in **So sagt man das!** with the students.

PRESENTING: Wortschatz

As you go over the photos, give simple and brief facts about each one in German (see Background Information below). Then practice the words.

Cultures and Communities

Background Information

Fachwerk is a building style consisting of a framework of straight and crosstimbered beams in which the area between the beams is filled in with clay or bricks. This style of architecture reached its high point in the 16th and 17th centuries.

STANDARDS: 2.2, 3.1, 4.1

Cultures and Communities

Background Information

Die Alte Oper This Neorenaissance building, reconstructed in 1981, is a conference and concert center. It features a restaurant, a bistro, a café, and exhibition and meeting rooms as well as several conference rooms, the largest of which holds 2,500 people.

Der Römer (das Rathaus) got its name for being the oldest in the set of 11 **Giebelhäuser** on the **Römerberg**. It is actually a group of three buildings whose steep step gables are a symbol of Frankfurt. The upper floor of the **Römer** was used for banquets following the coronation of kings. Today the **Römer** is Frankfurt's city hall.

Der Dom Dating back to 1356, this is where the coronation of German kings took place.

Die Zeil is a modern pedestrian zone that houses many large department stores and smaller shops. This is Germany's busiest shopping area.

Der Main This river should be familiar to students from p. 1. It is part of the **Rhein-Main-Donau-Kanal.** The **Main** is 524 kilometers (325.4 miles) long.

Das Goethehaus is the famous writer's birthplace and childhood home. It was destroyed in World War II and rebuilt between 1946 and 1951. It features the workroom where Goethe wrote *Werther, Götz von Berlichingen,* and parts of *Faust.* The house is connected to the Goethe-Museum.

Der Zoo The German TV show "Ein Platz für Tiere," directed by Prof. Dr. Grzimek, made the **Zoo** famous. Built in 1873, the zoo's main attraction is the Grzimek Haus, which converts day into night, thus allowing visitors to observe nocturnal animals.

▶ **PAGE 72**

Connections and Comparisons

Language-to-Language

You may want to mention to your students that French, like German, uses the equivalents of *to be* and *to have* as helping verbs to build the perfect tenses. English and Spanish only use the equivalent of *to have.*

Examples:
English: *You* have *gone* / *You* have *done*
German: **Du** *bist* **gegangen** / **Du** *hast* **gemacht**
French: **Tu** *es* **allé** / **Tu** *as* **fait**
Spanish: **Tú** *te has* **ido** / **Tú** *has* **hecho**

KAPITEL 3   ZWEITE STUFE   59R

PRESENTING: Grammatik

Past tense of haben and sein Read the explanations and go over the verb forms with students. Prepare a transparency with many possible ways to create meaningful sentences. Have students practice the forms.

Ich	haben	in Frankfurt
Wir	sein	nur zwei Tage Zeit
Der Dom		interessant
Die Fachwerk-		sehr schön
häuser		nicht viel Geld mit
Die Zeil		auch im Goethehaus
		keine Karten für die Oper
		toll zum Einkaufen

PRESENTING: Wortschatz

Go down the rows, making statements about various things that you have done and asking students about their own experiences. Students should respond with complete sentences, using one of the three phrases from the **Wortschatz**. (Example: Ich bin letztes Jahr nach Kalifornien gefahren. Und du? — Ich bin schon oft nach Kalifornien gefahren.)

Communication for All Students

Challenge

18 Ask students to react to what their partner says, using the phrases **noch nie, schon oft,** and **auch schon** presented in the **Wortschatz**.

Example: — Wo warst du in den Ferien?
— Ich war in Kalifornien.
— Ja? Ich war noch nie da! Wie war es?

PAGE 73

PRESENTING: Grammatik

Dative Case: in and an It will take much practice before students can easily respond to questions involving prepositions of place. To practice the four different uses featured, use visual aids such as posters, photographs, large wall maps, and postcards. This is also a good way to review names of **Bundesländer**, rivers, cities, and other points of interest from Level 1.

Speaking Assessment

20 For assessment you may have pairs come to your desk. You might wish to evaluate students' conversations using the following rubric.

Speaking Rubric

	Points			
	4	3	2	1
Content (Complete – Incomplete)				
Comprehension (Total – Little)				
Comprehensibility (Comprehensible – Incomprehensible)				
Accuracy (Accurate – Seldom accurate)				
Fluency (Fluent – Not fluent)				

18–20: A   16–17: B   14–15: C   12–13: D   Under 12: F

PAGE 74

Communication for All Students

Visual Learners

22 If possible, use photographs and realia representing places and points of interest in each of the listed cities. Talk about the pictures with students. Then hang them up so students can see them as they work on the activity.

PAGE 75

LANDESKUNDE

Teaching Resources
p. 75

PRINT
▸ Video Guide, pp. 15–16, 18–19
▸ Übungsheft, p. 32

MEDIA
▸ One-Stop Planner
▸ Video Program
  Videocassette 1, 38:52–45:05
▸ DVD Tutor, Disc 1
▸ Audio Compact Discs, CD3, Trs. 5–10
▸ Interactive CD-ROM Tutor, Disc 1

Teaching Suggestion

Begin the presentation of **Landeskunde** by doing the prereading activity with your class. Then have students listen to the compact disc or watch the video segment of the interviews.

STANDARDS: 1.1, 1.2

Communication for All Students

A Slower Pace

Make a chart on the board with the following heads:

Wer?   Woher?   Wohin?   Was?

Then ask students to scan each interview and note the name of each person interviewed, where he or she is from, where that person spent his or her vacation, and the activities that person took part in.

Cultures and Communities

Language Note

The word **Ferien** is used when talking about vacations for **Schüler** and **Studenten.** The word **Urlaub** applies when talking about vacations for people in the working world (**arbeitstätige oder berufstätige Leute**). You may want to explain these terms in German.

Teaching Suggestion

Ask students if they can recall any mishaps they had (**Pech haben**) while they were on a trip. Where were they and what happened? Have them try to tell the story in German. You could also ask students about times when they got lucky (**Schwein haben**) on one of their trips.

Teacher Note

Mention to your students that the **Landeskunde** will also be included in Quiz 3-2B given at the end of the **Zweite Stufe.**

Game

Play the game **Stadt, Land, Fluss.** See p. 59C for the procedure.

Assess

- Testing Program, pp. 57–60
  Quiz 3-2A, Quiz 3-2B
  Audio CD3, Tr. 15
- Student Make-Up Assignments
  Chapter 3, Alternative Quiz
- Alternative Assessment Guide, p. 34

STANDARDS: 1.2, 4.1

DRITTE STUFE

Teaching Resources
pp. 76–79

PRINT
- Lesson Planner, p. 15
- TPR Storytelling Book, pp. 20–21
- Listening Activities, pp. 20, 25–26
- Activities for Communication, pp. 17–18, 84, 85, 127–128
- Grammatikheft, pp. 25–27
- Grammar Tutor for Students of German, Chapter 3
- Übungsheft, pp. 33–35
- Testing Program, pp. 61–64
- Alternative Assessment Guide, p. 34
- Student Make-Up Assignments, Chapter 3

MEDIA
- One-Stop Planner
- Audio Compact Discs, CD3, Trs. 11, 16, 24–25
- Teaching Transparencies
  Situation 3-2
  Mehr Grammatikübungen Answers
  Grammatikheft Answers
- Interactive CD-ROM Tutor, Disc 1
- DVD Tutor, Disc 1

PAGE 76

Bell Work

Ask students to list as many expressions in English as they can to describe their last summer break (last birthday, last concert they attended).

Building on Previous Skills

25 In the **Zum Lesen** section of Chapter 2, students were introduced to the verbs **gefallen** and **missfallen.** To help students prepare for the listening activity, ask them for synonyms of **gefallen** and make a list of the words and phrases that students suggest. (Examples: **mögen, gern haben**)

PRESENTING: So sagt man das!

After you have read the expressions, give the students several situations to practice these new functions. Ask them to respond to questions about:

- a movie they saw,
- a book they read,
- a sports event they attended,
- a party they attended.

Connections and Comparisons

Language Note

You might want to give students the literal meaning of **Es hat mir gefallen.** *(It was pleasing to me.)* You may also want to mention that **gefallen** is one of the many verbs that require an object in the dative case.

PAGE 77

PRESENTING: Grammatik

Dative pronouns After introducing the first- and second-person dative pronouns, have students practice these pronouns, as well as the third-person pronouns. Ask students, for example, how they liked books they have read, movies or concerts they have attended, or a party they went to.

For Additional Practice

28 After students have completed the activity, have them ask an additional question. (Example: **Und was habt ihr da gemacht?**)

PRESENTING: Grammatik

Definite article, dative plural Read the explanations with students. Give additional examples of nominative plurals ending in **-n** such as **Studenten, Jungen,** and **Mädchen.** Ask students to use these nouns to create sentences.

PAGE 78

Communication for All Students

Challenge

29 Give students three to four minutes to do this activity. Encourage them to add any words or phrases they feel would make their sentences sound as natural as possible. Ask four or five students to read their sentences in class.

PRESENTING: Wortschatz

Present the new vocabulary, then write open-ended phrases on a transparency. Ask students to complete the sentences using the new vocabulary. Examples:
Wenn wir nach Frankfurt reisen, übernachten wir gern …
Wenn ihr in Dresden esst, esst ihr oft …
Wenn ich in London bin, wohne ich immer …

Cultures and Communities

Culture Note

Jugendherbergen originated in Germany, the first being the youth hostel in Altena, founded in 1909 by Richard Schirrmann and Wilhelm Münker. In 1910, the German Youth Hostel Association came into being. Since 1925, youth hostels also have been established in other countries, and in 1932 the International Youth Hostel Federation was founded. Today there are over 5,000 youth hostels worldwide.

PAGE 79

Communication for All Students

Challenge

30 Have students imagine that they are taking a survey for a travel magazine to find out people's lodging preferences. Students should take notes and then report their findings to the class.

PRESENTING: Wortschatz

Divide the class into groups of three or four. Give each group of students an envelope that contains eighteen small slips of paper; on nine should appear the terms from the **Wortschatz,** and on the other nine should be written various vacation activities. (Examples: **schwimmen, in die Disko gehen, in einer Pension übernachten**) Ask students in each group to write a short report about an imaginary vacation they took together, using all the words and phrases in their envelope. Encourage them to be as creative as possible. When all groups have finished, students should read their reports aloud to the rest of the class.

Teaching Suggestion

31 Ask students to use several adverbial expressions from the **Wortschatz** beside the activity in their **Notizbuch** entry.

Communication for All Students

Auditory Learners

32 To involve the listening student actively in this activity, ask him or her to put the pictures in the order they are described by the partner. At the end, the listening student verifies the sequence with his or her partner. You may also want to call on several students to repeat their reports and have the rest of the class listen to see if the order of the pictures matches the description that students gave.

COMMUNITY LINK

Suggest that students videotape or interview local celebrities or feature local merchants or organizations in their reports. Tell students that they can get information from the Chamber of Commerce to help them with their projects.

 **Game**

In this activity students review and practice in German the places and points of interest that they have learned up to this point. Begin the game by making the following statement:

Im Sommer reisen wir nach Frankfurt, denn wir wollen den Dom besichtigen.

The first student repeats your sentence and reason for visiting and adds another location. The next student must remember both places with the reasons given and then add his or her own, and so on. If students make a mistake or forget a place, they drop out of the game. The student who can repeat the most places wins.

Teaching Suggestion

In pairs, have students create a small dialog between two friends. One of them just came back from a trip to **München** and the other one wants to know everything about it.
Example questions and answers:
  Wie hat es dir/euch dort gefallen? Wahnsinnig gut!
  Wo hast du/habt ihr übernachtet? In einer Pension.

Von der Schule zum Beruf

33

You might want to have students complete the **Webprojekt** on p. 59F, before doing this activity.

Teacher to Teacher

Tanya Stevenson
Terrill Middle School
Scotch Plains, New Jersey

Tanya uses this idea to present and practice the past tense.

"I model the past by showing students pictures of myself and tell them what I was doing and where I was. Students then show pictures of themselves—perhaps a yearbook or other photo—doing an activity. They tell the class what they did and where they were. I have also taken pictures of students in class and given them the pictures to report what they and other students were doing in German class."

Assess

▸ Testing Program, pp. 61–64
  Quiz 3-3A, Quiz 3-3B
  Audio CD3, Tr. 16

▸ Student Make-Up Assignments
  Chapter 3, Alternative Quiz

▸ Alternative Assessment Guide, p. 34

PAGES 80–81

ZUM LESEN

> **Teaching Resources**
> pp. 80–81
>
> **PRINT**
> ▸ Lesson Planner, p. 16
> ▸ Übungsheft, p. 36
> ▸ Reading Strategies and Skills, Chapter 3
> ▸ Lies mit mir! 2, Chapter 3
>
> **MEDIA**
> ▸ One-Stop Planner

Prereading
Building Context
Get several brochures from a travel agency. Ask students to work in pairs or in small groups. Each group receives one brochure. Give groups about two minutes to skim their brochures, then call on two or three groups to tell the class in German why they think their vacation destinations would appeal to travelers. Allow students to keep the brochures until they have done the additional activities suggested for Activity 1.

Teacher Note
Activities 1–3 are prereading activities.

Making Connections
1 Before starting the activity, ask students about postcards and announcements. What types of information do the writers of postcards usually give? What information is usually contained in a public announcement?

1 After doing Activity 1, ask students to look again at the travel brochure they used for the Building Context activity. Ask them to compare the format of the brochure with the format of the brochure for the **Pillersee**.

Reading
Skimming and Scanning
Give students three minutes to skim over each text. Then give them three more minutes to scan for words or phrases they think are some of the main points of the readings. Write students' ideas on the board or on a transparency.

Connections and Comparisons

Geography Connection
Have students locate **Tirol** and St. Ulrich and the **Pillersee.**

Geography Connection
Ask students to look at a map of Europe and have them locate **Tirol.** Based on what they see in the photograph, where should students look? (mountains such as the Alps) What types of activities could they expect to be offered in that area? (Examples: skiing, hiking)

Background Information
Tirol is one of Austria's **Bundesländer** (4,882 square miles or 12,648 square kilometers, comparable in size to the state of Connecticut). Its state capital is Innsbruck. It is a mountainous area and is known as a great winter sport region. Many resorts are located in this alpine state. The mountains in the background are called the Tyrolean Alps.

Cooperative Learning
5 **6** Divide students into groups of three. Each group should have a reader, a writer, and a reporter. The reader reads Questions 5 and 6 aloud, then all group members answer the questions together while the writer takes notes. Give groups ten minutes to finish their assignments. Encourage students to discuss their findings in German. Once groups have completed their assignments, call on two or three reporters to present their answers to the class.

Post-Reading

Communication for All Students

Challenge
Tell students that they have been invited to St. Ulrich. Based on what students have learned about this town and its surrounding area, what would they like to do there and why?

Teacher Note
Activity 7 is a post-reading task that will show whether students can apply what they have learned.

Answers to Activity 5 They have seen a lot in three days; Yesterday they were being lazy; They walked around the Pillersee; They swam in the lake; Tomorrow there is a town festival.
Answers to Activity 6 The event took place in St. Ulrich; It is a small town (village); located at the Pillersee in Tirol, Austria; supporting details for main event: e.g. day, time, people attending, food, music

STANDARDS: 1.3, 3.1

PAGES 82–85

MEHR GRAMMATIKÜBUNGEN

The **Mehr Grammatikübungen** activities are designed as supplemental activities for the grammatical concepts presented in the chapter. You might use them as additional practice, for review, or for assessment.

For more grammar presentations, review, and practice, refer to the following:
- Grammatikheft
- Grammar Tutor for Students of German
- Grammar Summary on pp. R20–R36
- Übungsheft
- Grammar and Vocabulary quizzes (Testing Program)
- Test Generator
- Interactive CD-ROM Tutor
- **Interaktive Spiele** at go.hrw.com

PAGES 86–87

ANWENDUNG

Video Wrap-up
Videocassette 1, 32:10–47:20
Videocassette 5 (captioned version), 15:03–21:07
DVD Tutor, Disc 1

At this time, you might want to use the video resources for additional review and enrichment. These resources are also available via the Enhanced Online Student Edition.
See *Video Guide* for suggestions regarding:
- *Unser Film- und Fotoclub* Dramatic episode
- *Landeskunde* Interviews
- *Videoclips* Authentic footage

Apply and Assess

Thinking Critically
1 Drawing Inferences Based on what the Stegmüllers have checked off, can students describe the family's interests?

 Portfolio Assessment
3 You might want to suggest this activity as a written and oral portfolio item for your students. See *Alternative Assessment Guide*, p. 20.

Process Writing
4 Before students begin writing, draw their attention to the list of verbs whose conversational past forms they have learned. Have them get together in pairs to brainstorm various activities that go together with these verbs (Examples: **meine Tante an der Nordsee / habe besucht; viele Actionfilme / habe gesehen**). You may want to supply them with additional past forms that will aid them in their writing, such as **hat geregnet, hat gut (gut) geschmeckt**.

Apply and Assess

Visual Learners
5 Before students listen to the script, ask them what words or phrases they would expect to hear in each one of the summaries. Then make a list and leave it on the transparency or board for students to see as they listen to the activity. After students have listened to the summaries, ask them which of the listed phrases they actually heard.

PAGE 88

KANN ICH'S WIRKLICH?

This page helps students prepare for the test. It is a brief checklist of the major points covered in the chapter. The students should be reminded that it is only a checklist and not necessarily everything that will appear on the test.

For additional self check options, refer students to the *Grammar Tutor*, the *Interactive CD-ROM Tutor*, and the Online self-test for this chapter.

PAGE 89

WORTSCHATZ

Review and Assess

 Game
Play the game **Mal doch schnell!** See p. 59C for the procedure.

Group Work
Divide students into groups of three or four. Give students a list of interesting headlines from newspapers from German-speaking countries. (Examples: *Frankfurter Allgemeine, Dresdener Rundschau, Süddeutsche Zeitung, Neue Züricher Zeitung, Liechtensteiner Vaterland, Der Standard*) Students should use the vocabulary of the *Zweite Stufe* to write brief, humorous stories to fit the headlines.

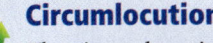 **Circumlocution**
The circumlocution game, **Das treffende Wort suchen,** can be played with the nouns from the *Zweite Stufe* (places to visit) and with nouns from the *Dritte Stufe* vocabulary (places to stay and places to eat). See p. 3C for procedures.

Teacher Note
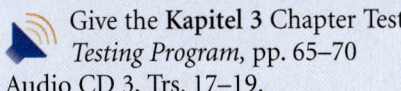 Give the **Kapitel 3** Chapter Test: *Testing Program,* pp. 65–70
Audio CD 3, Trs. 17–19.

STANDARDS: 1.1

KAPITEL

3

Wo warst du in den Ferien?

Objectives

In this chapter you will learn to

Erste Stufe
- report past events
- talk about activities

Zweite Stufe
- report past events
- talk about places

Dritte Stufe
- ask how someone liked something
- express enthusiasm and disappointment
- respond enthusiastically or sympathetically

Visit Holt Online
go.hrw.com
KEYWORD: WK3 BAYERN-3
Online Edition

◀ Wir haben viel Zeit auf dem Wasser verbracht.

Los geht's! · Unser Film- und Fotoclub

Los geht's! is an abridged version of the video episode.

CD 3
Trs. 1–2

Strategie Verstehen
Look at the images for this story. Where does the story take place? Who is there? What do you think these young people are talking about?

  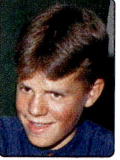 

Lehrerin   **Frank**   **Sebastian**   **Christiane**

1 An Sebastians Gymnasium gibt es einen Film- und Fotoclub. Frau Sabine Brucker, die Biologie- und Sportlehrerin, leitet den Klub. Die langen Sommerferien sind vorüber, und heute sind die Klubmitglieder zum ersten Mal im neuen Schuljahr zusammengekommen. Die Schüler unterhalten sich angeregt: heute können sie nämlich zeigen, was sie in den Ferien gefilmt oder fotografiert haben. Drei Leute haben sogar ein Video mitgebracht.

2 **Lehrerin:** Na, wie hat es euch in den Ferien gefallen? Habt ihr viel gesehen? Habt ihr viel fotografiert und gefilmt?

3 **Frank:** Mein Vater hatte in Dresden zu tun, und ich bin mitgefahren.
Lehrerin: Wie hat dir Dresden gefallen?
Frank: Phantastisch!
Lehrerin: Dann erzähl uns einmal etwas über Dresden!

4 **Dresden**
Frank: August der Starke hat Dresden im 18. Jahrhundert zu einer der schönsten deutschen Barockstädte gemacht. Ich hab das Schloss gesehen, den Zwinger – das ist ein phantastisches Kunstmuseum, weltbekannt! Ich bin in Dresden mit meinem Vater in die Oper gegangen, in die berühmte Semperoper. Wir haben Beethovens „Fidelio" gehört. Überall baut man in Dresden, denn die Stadt wurde 1945 fast total zerstört. Über 35 000 Menschen verloren in einer Nacht das Leben.

Christiane erzählt, wo sie war.

Frankfurt

Christiane: Ich habe meine Tante in Frankfurt besucht. Ich bin oft im Römer gewesen; meine Tante arbeitet dort. Ich hab natürlich den Dom besichtigt, und ich bin oft durch die Zeil spaziert. In der Oper war ich auch einmal. Ach ja, ich bin natürlich auch im Goethehaus und im Goethemuseum gewesen. Was mir am besten gefallen hat, das sind die Fachwerkhäuser auf dem Römerberg.

St. Ulrich

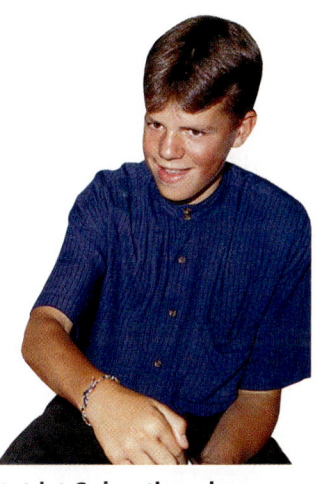

**Jetzt ist Sebastian dran.
Er legt seine Kassette ein.**

Sebastian: Ich war mit meinem Freund Thomas in Tirol. Wir haben in St. Ulrich gewohnt, in einer netten Pension für junge Leute. Jeden Tag sind wir gewandert, durch die Wälder, durch die Wiesen. Wir sind auch oft um den See gegangen oder sind auf einen Berg gestiegen. Zu Mittag haben wir gewöhnlich in einem Gasthof gegessen, irgendeine Tiroler Spezialität, wie zum Beispiel einen „Strammen Max", das ist Schinken mit Spiegelei.

1 Was passiert hier?

These activities check for global comprehension only. Students should not yet be expected to produce language modeled in Los geht's!

Hast du „Unser Film- und Fotoclub" verstanden? Versuche, die folgenden Fragen (auf Deutsch oder Englisch) zu beantworten!

1. Warum kommen heute die Schüler zusammen? 1. Zeigen, was sie in den Ferien gefilmt/fotografiert haben.
2. Wer ist Frau Brucker? 2. Biologie- und Sportlehrerin; leitet den Klub.
3. Was erzählen die drei Schüler? 3. Was sie in den Ferien gemacht haben.
4. Wo war Frank und warum? 4. Dresden; sein Vater hatte dort zu tun.
5. Was hat Christiane während der Ferien gemacht? 5. Tante in Frankfurt besucht.
6. Wo war Sebastian und mit wem? 6. Tirol; mit seinem Freund.

2 Genauer lesen

1. Was hat Frank in Dresden gesehen und gemacht? 1. Schloss u. Zwinger gesehen; in die Oper gegangen.
2. Warum erwähnt (*mentions*) Frank das Jahr 1945? 2. Zerstörung der Stadt im Zweiten Weltkrieg.
3. Was hat Christiane besichtigt? Was hat ihr am besten gefallen? 3. Dom; Fachwerkhäuser auf dem Römerberg.
4. Wo hat Basti in Tirol gewohnt? 4. Pension für junge Leute in St. Ulrich.
5. Was haben er und sein Freund gemacht? 5. Gewandert, um den See gegangen, auf Berg gestiegen.
6. Warum erwähnt er den „Strammen Max"? 6. Tiroler Spezialität.

3 Was passt?

Welche Wörter auf der rechten Seite passen in die Satzlücken?

SEBASTIAN Mein Freund Thomas und ich, wir haben in St. Ulrich ——1——. Jeden Tag sind wir ——2——. Wir sind um den See ——3—— oder auf einen Berg ——4——. Zu Mittag haben wir gewöhnlich in einem Gasthaus ——5——.

CHRISTIANE Ich habe meine Tante in Frankfurt ——6——. Ich bin im Römer ——7——, ich hab den Dom ——8—— und bin durch die Zeil ——9——. Die Fachwerkhäuser am Römerberg haben mir am besten ——10——.

besichtigt   gestiegen
gefallen   gewandert
    besucht
gegangen   gewesen
    spaziert
gegessen   gewohnt
    gelaufen

1. gewohnt; 2. gewandert; 3. gegangen/gelaufen/spaziert; 4. gestiegen; 5. gegessen; 6. besucht; 7. gewesen; 8. besichtigt; 9. spaziert/gelaufen/gegangen; 10. gefallen.

4 Wo ist das?

Such dir einen Partner! Nenne ihm ein Wort aus dem Kasten, und er muss dir sagen, mit welcher Stadt oder mit welchem Ort dieses Wort assoziiert ist. Die drei Orte sind: Dresden, Frankfurt und St. Ulrich. — Tauscht dann die Rollen aus!

BEISPIEL DU eine Barockstadt
PARTNER Das ist Dresden.

August der Starke   Gasthof   kleine Pension   Wiesen   Zeil   Main
Goethe   Fachwerkhäuser   Römer   Zwinger   Berge
    See   Elbe
Barockstadt   Oper   Schloss   Semperoper   Dom   Goethehaus

KAPITEL 3 Wo warst du in den Ferien?

 Storytelling Book pp. 16–17

Erste Stufe

Objectives Reporting past events, talking about activities

WK3 BAYERN-3

5 **Was wir in den Ferien gemacht haben** Script and answers on p. 59G

 Zuhören/Schreiben Vier Schüler haben sehr aktive Ferien gehabt und berichten darüber. Schreib von jedem Schüler drei Dinge auf, die er gemacht hat!
CD 3 Tr. 3

So sagt man das!

Reporting past events, talking about activities

Grammatikheft, S. 19, Ü. 1

When asking someone about something in the past, you ask:

  Was hast du in den Ferien gemacht?
  Was hat Sebastian in Tirol gemacht?

And the response might be:

  Ich habe meine Tante in Frankfurt besucht. Ich habe den Dom besichtigt und bin oft durch die Stadt spaziert.
  Er hat in St. Ulrich gewohnt. Er ist dort viel gewandert, und er hat gefilmt und fotografiert.

Wortschatz

Was macht ihr im Filmclub?

 3–A

Grammatikheft, S. 19, Ü. 2

 **Wir sprechen über:**

Wir fotografieren mit einer Kamera.

Ich filme mit einer Videokamera.

Videos

CD-ROMs und DVDs

Ich bediene den Videorecorder/die Kamera.

Dias

Filme

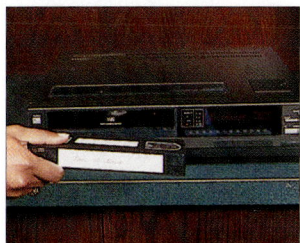
Ich lege ein Video ein.

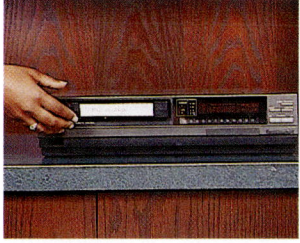
Ich nehme das Video heraus.

Farbbilder

6 Und du?

Sprechen Such dir einen Partner! Stellt euch diese Fragen und beantwortet sie!
1. Was filmst du oder fotografierst du gewöhnlich?
2. Was für eine Kamera hast du? War das ein Geschenk, oder hast du die Kamera selbst gekauft?
3. Kaufst du einen Film für Dias oder für Farbbilder?
4. Hast du einen Videorecorder? Was für einen?
5. Was sind deine Lieblingsmotive, wenn du fotografierst?
6. Wann hast du die letzten Fotos gemacht? Was hast du fotografiert?

7 Was hast du in den Ferien gemacht?

Sprechen Sag vier Dinge, die du in den Ferien gemacht hast! Im Kasten sind ein paar Ideen.

ICH HABE …	ICH BIN …
☐ Freunde besucht	☐ viel geschwommen
☐ viel gearbeitet	☐ zu Hause geblieben
☐ eine große Fete gemacht	☐ viel gewandert
☐ viel Tennis gespielt	☐ oft ins Kino gegangen
☐ viel gelesen	☐ nach (Denver) gefahren
☐ viele Videos geschaut	☐ Wasserski gelaufen
☐ sehr oft gefaulenzt	☐ in (Kalifornien) gewesen
☐ eine Reise gemacht	☐ viel schwimmen gegangen
☐ (Orlando) besichtigt	
☐ einen Sommerkurs besucht	

8 Was war los?

Lesen/Schreiben Lies den Text **Los geht's!** noch einmal! Welche Sätze erkennst du, die die Vergangenheit (*past*) ausdrücken? Schreib die Sätze in gekürzter Form auf einen Zettel!

BEISPIEL Die Klubmitglieder sind zusammengekommen.
Sie haben in den Ferien gefilmt.
Ich bin in die Oper gegangen.

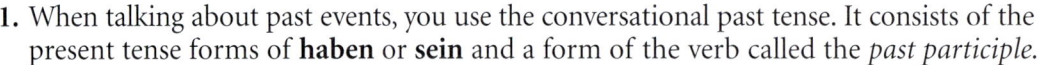

Grammatik

The conversational past

1. When talking about past events, you use the conversational past tense. It consists of the present tense forms of **haben** or **sein** and a form of the verb called the *past participle*.

    Ich **habe** meine Tante **besucht**.
    Ich **bin** um den See **gegangen**.

2. Most past participles have the prefix **ge-**: gemacht, gelesen.
3. The past participles of so-called regular or weak verbs end in **-t**: machen, er macht, er hat (Ferien) gemacht.
4. The past participles of so-called irregular or strong verbs end in **-en**, like the infinitive: lesen, liest, er hat (Zeitung) gelesen. Some have other changes: gehen, geht, er ist gegangen; bleiben, bleibt, sie ist geblieben.

continued on page 67

Grammatik

5. The past participles of verbs ending in **-ieren** do not have the prefix **ge-**: **fotografieren, er fotografiert, er hat (viel) fotografiert.**

6. The past participles of verbs that already have an inseparable prefix do not add the prefix **ge-**: **besuchen, er besucht, er hat besucht; gefallen, es gefällt mir, es hat mir gefallen.**

7. The past participles of verbs that have a separable prefix keep the **ge-**: **mitkommen, er kommt mit, er ist mitgekommen; aussehen, sie sieht (nett) aus, sie hat (nett) ausgesehen.**

8. Most verbs in German are regular or weak. Therefore, unless you have learned otherwise, form the past participle with **-t,** the prefix **ge-,** and the auxiliary **haben.**

9. Here are some past participles of verbs that you should know.

WEAK VERBS	STRONG VERBS	VERBS WITH sein
hat gearbeitet	hat gegeben	ist gekommen
hat gefaulenzt	hat gegessen	ist gefahren
hat gefilmt	hat gelesen	
hat gehabt	hat gesehen	ist gelaufen
hat gehört	hat geholfen	ist geblieben
hat gekauft	hat getrunken	ist geschwommen
hat gemacht		ist gewesen
hat gemäht		ist gegangen
hat geschenkt		
hat gespielt		ist gewandert
hat gewohnt		ist spaziert
hat fotografiert		
hat besucht		
hat besichtigt		

Mehr Grammatikübungen, S. 82, Ü. 1–2

Übungsheft, S. 26–28, Ü. 1–7

Grammatikheft, S. 20–21, Ü. 3–6

9 Grammatik im Kontext

a. Sprechen Such dir einen Partner! Frag ihn, was er in den Ferien gemacht hat! Er sagt es dir. Dann fragt er dich. Benutzt die Ausdrücke im Kasten als Anregung (*as suggestions*)!

viel schwimmen gehen	viel wandern	die Natur fotografieren	gar nicht arbeiten
meine Oma besuchen	viel Musik hören	Klamotten kaufen	Volleyball spielen
nach (Kanada) fahren	in Mexiko sein	viel lesen	
		viel essen und trinken	ziemlich viel faulenzen

b. Schreiben Schreib jetzt zehn Sätze über deine Ferien, wo du warst und was du alles in den Ferien gemacht hast.

Answers may vary. E.g.: **Was hast du … ?**
— **Ich habe meine Oma besucht.**

10 Grammatik im Kontext

Hier ist ein Blatt aus Sebastians Tischkalender vom Juli.

a. **Lesen** Lies, was er alles gemacht hat!

b. **Sprechen** Such dir dann einen Partner! Sag ihm, was Sebastian am Montag gemacht hat! Dein Partner sagt dir dann, was Sebastian am Dienstag gemacht hat und so weiter.

c. **Sprechen** Zur Abwechslung (*for variety*) nennt jetzt mal nicht die Uhrzeit, sondern gebraucht die Reihenwörter wie: zuerst, dann, danach und zuletzt!

d. **Schreiben** Schreib auf, was Sebastian an zwei Tagen in der letzten Juliwoche gemacht hat.

JULI — 30. Woche

23 MONTAG
- 10.00–12.00 mit Robert schwimmen gehen
- 13.30–16.00 Volleyball
- 17.00 Rasen mähen

24 DIENSTAG
- 9.00–11.00 einen Stadtbummel machen — Neue Jeans!

25 MITTWOCH
- 9.00 zum Frisör!
- 10.00–12.00 Thomas besuchen
- 14.00–15.30 Fußball

26 DONNERSTAG
- 8.00 mit Vati nach Tirol, wandern, schwimmen, gut essen
- 20.30 nach Hause fahren

27 FREITAG
- 10.00–12.00 dem Opa im Garten helfen, dort zu Mittag essen
- 14.30–15.30 Flöte spielen
- 16.00 Freunde besuchen

28 SAMSTAG
- 9.00–12.00 Stadtbummel mit Christiane, zu Mittag essen
- 14.00–16.30 lesen, Musik hören, faulenzen
- ab 19.00 Rockkonzert besuchen

29 SONNTAG
- 7.00–8.00 Tennis
- 10.00–11.00 mit Rad zum See
- 14.00–16.00 Großeltern besuchen
- ab 19.00 Fernsehen (Krimi)

11 Für mein Notizbuch

Schreiben Schreib in dein Notizbuch, was du letztes Wochenende (am Samstag und am Sonntag) gemacht hast! Schreib mindestens fünf Sätze. Verwende dabei auch Zeitausdrücke wie: am Nachmittag, am Abend, zuerst, zuletzt, und so weiter.

Marienkirche (im Aufbau)

Zwinger

Dresden, Hauptstadt von Sachsen

Dresden, Kunst- und Kulturstadt an der oberen Elbe, war bis zur Zerstörung im Jahre 1945 eine der schönsten Städte Europas. Dresden war — und ist — weithin als „Elbflorenz" bekannt, weil die Stadt mit ihrer wundervollen Architektur an Florenz erinnert.

Kurfürst Friedrich August I. (August der Starke) war Landesfürst von Sachsen. Als konvertierter Katholik war er auch König von Polen. Unter seiner Herrschaft wurde Dresden in die schönste Barockstadt seiner Epoche verwandelt.

Der Zwinger, ein Meisterstück des Barocks, beherbergt die berühmte Gemäldegalerie „Alte Meister" (Raffael, Giorgione, Tizian, Tintoretto, u.a.). Die „Neuen Meister" hängen in einem anderen Museum, im Albertinum. Dort, im sogenannten Grünen Gewölbe, ist auch die königliche Sammlung ausgestellt: Gefäße, Schmuck und Waffen.

Zur Zeit wird Dresden renoviert. Die total zerstörte Marienkirche wird wieder aufgebaut. Bis zur 800-Jahr-Feier im Jahre 2006 soll Dresden völlig renoviert sein und wieder in alter Pracht glänzen.

August I.

Blick auf die Elbe

12 Und du? Was weißt du über Dresden?

Lesen/Sprechen Lies den Bericht über Dresden! Dann such dir einen Partner, stellt euch abwechselnd diese Fragen und beantwortet sie!

1. Was für eine Stadt ist Dresden, und wo liegt sie? 1. Kunst- und Kulturstadt; an der oberen Elbe.
2. Warum wird Dresden auch „Elbflorenz" genannt? 2. Wundervolle Architektur erinnert an Florenz.
3. Wer war August der Starke? Was hat er gemacht? 3. Landesfürst von Sachsen und König von Polen; machte aus Dresden die schönste Barockstadt seiner Epoche.
4. Wo hängen die „Alten Meister"? Und die „Neuen Meister"? 4. Im Zwinger; im Albertinum.
5. Wie sieht Dresdens Zukunft (future) aus? 5. Dresden wird renoviert.

Zweite Stufe

Objectives Reporting past events, talking about places

Frankfurt a. M.

Frankfurt am Main ist Deutschlands Finanzmetropole und seit 1993 auch Sitz der Zentralbank der Europäischen Gemeinschaft. In Frankfurts Skyline sitzen nicht nur deutsche Banken, sondern viele ausländische Firmen, die in Deutschlands fünftgrößter Stadt ihre Büros haben. Der Rhein-Main-Flughafen außerhalb Frankfurts ist einer der größten Europas.

Frankfurt ist eine alte Stadt und wird 794 zum ersten Mal als einer der Sitze Karls des Großen erwähnt. Seit 1356 wurden hier im Dom der deutsche Kaiser und die deutschen Könige gewählt und zwischen 1562 und 1792 auch hier gekrönt.

In den Jahren 1848/49 war die Paulskirche in Frankfurt auch der Tagungsort der ersten deutschen Nationalversammlung.

In Frankfurt wurde am 28. August 1749 Johann Wolfgang von Goethe geboren. Der große Dichter, auf den die Frankfurter besonders stolz sind, hat hier seine Kindheit und Jugend verbracht.

Frankfurt hat auch eine sehr freundliche Seite: hier gibt es viele gemütliche Lokale, wo man sich nach einem vollen Arbeitstag mit Freunden treffen kann, bei leckerem Zwiebelkuchen und Äbbewoi, zwei Frankfurter Spezialitäten.

Frankfurts Skyline

Der Dom

1. Sitz der Zentralbank der EG; viele ausländische Firmen; internationaler Flughafen.
2. Sitz Karls des Großen; im Dom Wahl und Krönung deutscher Kaiser und Könige; in der Paulskirche Tagung der ersten deutschen Nationalversammlung.

13 Und du? — Was weißt du über Frankfurt?

Lesen Lies den Bericht über Frankfurt! Dann such dir eine Partnerin! Stellt euch abwechselnd diese Fragen und beantwortet sie!

1. **Sprechen** Warum nennt man die Stadt Frankfurt „Deutschlands Finanzmetropole"? Was gibt es dort?
2. **Sprechen** Was sind die Hauptpunkte in der langen Geschichte Frankfurts? Gib die Antwort in Stichwörtern (*by mentioning keywords*)!
3. **Sprechen** Was interessiert dich am meisten an Frankfurt?

Goethe (1749–1832)

14 Ich war in Frankfurt

Schreiben/Sprechen Du warst in Frankfurt! Schreib auf eine Liste, was du gesehen hast, welche Gebäude du besichtigt hast, wo und was du gegessen hast und was du gefilmt oder fotografiert hast! Erzähl einem Partner über deinen Besuch in Frankfurt! Tauscht dann die Rollen aus!

Auf dem Römerberg

15 Wo waren die Schüler? Script and answers on pp. 59G

Zuhören/Schreiben Schüler erzählen, wo sie in den Ferien waren. Schreib dir auf, wo sie waren! Wer ist am meisten gereist? Hör dann noch einmal zu und schreib auf, was du hörst!
CD 3 Tr. 4

16 Wo waren die Schüler?

Lesen/Sprechen Such dir einen Partner! Vergleicht (*compare*) eure Notizen! Du fragst: „Wo war …?" Dein Partner antwortet dir. Dann fragt er dich, und du antwortest ihm.

So sagt man das!

Reporting past events, talking about places

When asking someone where he or she was, you ask:

> Wo bist du gewesen?
>
> Und wo warst du?

And the answer may be:

> Ich bin in Frankfurt gewesen.
>   Ich war dort im Römer — das ist das Rathaus.
>
> Ja, zuerst war ich in der Stadt. Ich war mit
>   Robert im Kino. Danach waren wir im Café Mozart
>   und haben dort Eis gegessen.

Wortschatz

Sehenswürdigkeiten in Frankfurt

LEHRERIN Sag mir mal, was du alles in Frankfurt gesehen hast!
CHRISTIANE Ich hab … gesehen.

die Fachwerkhäuser
(am Römerberg)

die Alte Oper

das Rathaus
(den Römer)

den Dom

die Zeil

den Main

das Goethehaus

den Zoo

ZWEITE STUFE   STANDARDS: 1.1, 1.2   einundsiebzig   71

17 **Und du?**

Sprechen Was möchtest du sehen, wenn *du* nach Frankfurt kommst?

Grammatik

The past tense of haben and sein

For the conversational past tense of **haben** or **sein**, the forms of the **Imperfekt** or simple past tense are often preferred, especially in northern Germany. These forms are shorter. They are:

Singular		Plural		Singular		Plural	
ich	hatte	wir	hatten	ich	war	wir	waren
du	hattest	ihr	hattet	du	warst	ihr	wart
er/sie/es	hatte	sie, Sie	hatten	er, sie, es	war	sie, Sie	waren

you may say: Ich **habe** keine Zeit **gehabt**.
or Ich **hatte** keine Zeit.
Ich **bin** in der Stadt **gewesen**.
or Ich **war** in der Stadt.

Mehr Grammatikübungen, S. 83, Ü. 3

Grammatikheft, S. 22, Ü. 7–8

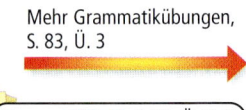

18 **Grammatik im Kontext**

Answers may vary. E.g.: **Wo warst du in den Ferien? — Ich war in Kalifornien. Dort war ich schon oft.**

 a. Sprechen Such dir eine Partnerin und frag sie, wo sie in den Ferien war! Dann fragt sie dich. Ihr könnt die Ausdrücke im Kasten gebrauchen, wenn ihr wollt.

im Gebirge   am Michigansee   am Meer
in den Rockies   an der (Ost)küste
in Kalifornien   in (Virginia) bei (meiner Tante)

Wortschatz

noch nie	*never, not yet*
schon oft	*often, a lot*
auch schon	*already, also*

 b. Schreiben Schreib jetzt ein Gespräch, das du mit deiner Partnerin gehabt hast.

19 **Grammatik im Kontext**

 a. Sprechen Dein Partner war nicht dort und sagt dir warum.

Du   **Du warst nicht (im Kino). Warum nicht?**
Partner   **Ich war nicht im Kino, weil ich (zu viel zu tun hatte).**

Wo?

im Schülercafé   im Einkaufszentrum
im Kino
im Klub   in der Schule

Warum nicht?

Karten fürs Fußballspiel haben   keinen Hunger haben
zu viel zu tun haben   kein Geld haben
das Wetter schlecht sein   keine Zeit haben

 b. Schreiben Schreib jetzt drei kurze Gespräche, die du mit deinem Partner zu diesem Thema gehabt hast.

72 *zweiundsiebzig*   STANDARDS: 1.1, 4.1   KAPITEL 3   Wo warst du in den Ferien?

Grammatik

The dative case with the prepositions **in** and **an**

In answer to a question beginning with **wo,** the prepositions **in** and **an** (and some others) indicate location and are followed by dative case forms.

1. The preposition **in** can be followed by the name of a city or town, state or country.

   Wo warst du? { Ich war **in** Dresden.   (city)
                    Ich war **in** Sachsen.   (state)
                    Ich war **in** Deutschland.   (country)

2. When the name of the country is feminine or used in the plural, the noun phrase is in the dative case.

   Wo warst du? { Ich war **in der** Schweiz.
                    Ich war **in der** Türkei.
                    Ich war **in den** Vereinigten Staaten.

3. The preposition **in** is followed by dative case forms with all specific locations, such as areas, buildings, rooms. Note that **im** is a contraction of **in** + **dem**.

   Wo warst du? { Ich war **im** Gebirge, **in den** Bergen …
                    Ich war **im** Museum, **im** Rathaus, **in der** Oper …
                    Ich war **im** Garten, **in der** Küche …

Mehr Grammatikübungen, S. 83, Ü. 4–5

4. The preposition **an,** *at,* is followed by dative case forms when indicating location. Note that **am** is a contraction of **an** + **dem**.

   Wo liegt das? { **Am** See, **am** Meer, **an der** Nordsee
                     Am Main, **an der** Elbe

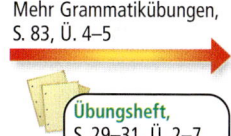

Übungsheft, S. 29–31, Ü. 2–7

Grammatikheft, S. 23–24, Ü. 9–11

---

20 **Sag mal, wo warst du denn?**

Sprechen Ihr hattet ein besonders langes Wochenende, vier Tage! — Such dir einen Partner! Frag ihn, wo er am letzten Wochenende war und was er dort alles gemacht hat! Danach fragt er dich, und du sagst es ihm. Ihr könnt die Wörter im Kasten in euren Antworten gebrauchen.

New York	Stadt	Schweiz
Café (Mozart)	Eriesee	Museum
		Oper
	Gebirge	
Restaurant (Koch)		Kino

Answers may vary. E.g.: **Sag mal, wo …?** — Ich bin in New York gewesen. — Was hast du dort alles gemacht? — Ich war in der Oper.

21  **Für mein Notizbuch**

Schreiben Schreib in dein Notizbuch, wo du letzte Woche warst und was du dort alles gemacht hast!

ZWEITE STUFE   STANDARDS: 1.1, 1.3, 4.1   *dreiundsiebzig* 73

22 Grammatik im Kontext

Stell dir vor, du warst zwei Tage zu Besuch in einer deutschen Stadt, in Berlin, Dresden, Frankfurt, Hamburg oder München!

a. **Schreiben** Schreib auf, was du alles gesehen oder besichtigt hast. Du musst mindestens *(at least)* fünf Dinge erwähnen.

b. **Sprechen/Schreiben** Such dir einen Partner und frag ihn, wo er war und was er da alles gesehen hat. Dann fragt dein Partner dich, wo du warst. Schreib danach ein Gespräch auf.

c. **Sprechen/Schreiben** Such dir einen anderen Partner! Diesmal wart ihr beiden in derselben Stadt, aber ihr habt nicht dasselbe gesehen oder gemacht. Einer von euch ist sehr kulturell interessiert, der andere geht lieber einkaufen, liebt die Natur und Tiere. Was habt ihr euch angesehen?—Schreib danach ein Gespräch auf.

Was habt ihr euch in der Stadt angesehen?

das Rathaus, die Universität, den Zoo, den Dom, den Marktplatz, den … Park, die Innenstadt, das … Stadion, den Botanischen Garten, die Einkaufsstraße, die …kirche, das Einkaufszentrum, das …Museum, die Oper

SPRACHTIPP

When talking about sightseeing, one can use the verbs **besichtigen, besuchen,** and **sehen.**

Besichtigen is used for sightseeing of buildings, where one takes a close view of the inside (churches, museums). **Besuchen** is used for performances that one attends (opera, theater, concert). **Sehen** is used in general with everything, but implies that one sees it without close inspection.

Übungsheft, S. 29, Ü. 1

23 Ich war so beschäftigt!

Deine Eltern sind ärgerlich, dass du am Wochenende nur selten zu Hause warst. Aber du hattest so viel zu tun, für die Schule, für deinen Job und mit deinen Freunden.

a. **Schreiben** Schreib auf eine Liste, was du alles am Wochenende gemacht hast!

b. **Sprechen** Spiel mit einem Partner die Rollen von Vater/Mutter und Sohn/Tochter! Zeig deinem Vater/deiner Mutter die Liste und erzähle, was du alles gemacht hast! Es gibt viele Fragen, die du beantworten musst, aber am Ende sind deine Eltern stolz auf dich.

c. **Lesen/Sprechen** Vergleiche deine Liste mit der Liste deines Partners! Was habt ihr beide gemacht? Was hat nur einer von euch gemacht?

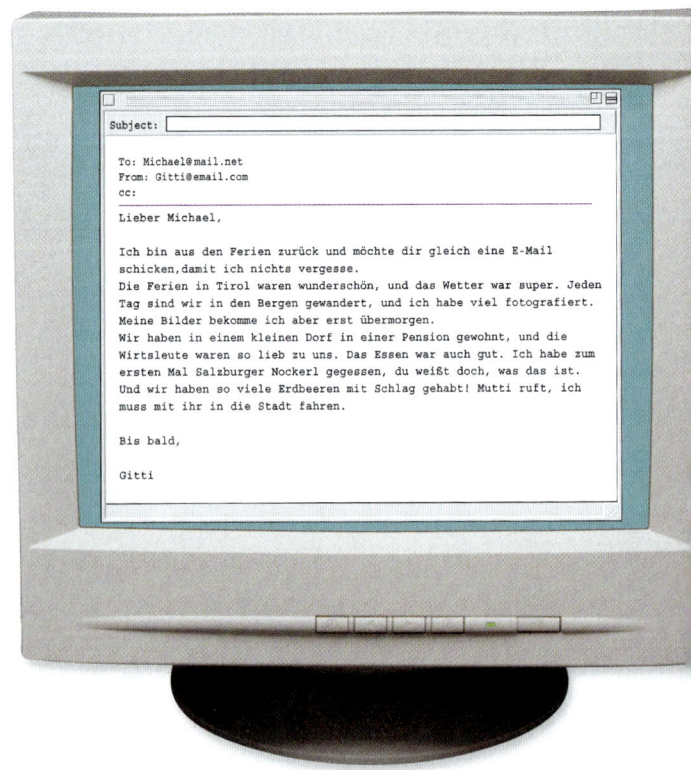

Subject:
To: Michael@mail.net
From: Gitti@email.com
cc:

Lieber Michael,

Ich bin aus den Ferien zurück und möchte dir gleich eine E-Mail schicken, damit ich nichts vergesse.
Die Ferien in Tirol waren wunderschön, und das Wetter war super. Jeden Tag sind wir in den Bergen gewandert, und ich habe viel fotografiert. Meine Bilder bekomme ich aber erst übermorgen.
Wir haben in einem kleinen Dorf in einer Pension gewohnt, und die Wirtsleute waren so lieb zu uns. Das Essen war auch gut. Ich habe zum ersten Mal Salzburger Nockerl gegessen, du weißt doch, was das ist. Und wir haben so viele Erdbeeren mit Schlag gehabt! Mutti ruft, ich muss mit ihr in die Stadt fahren.

Bis bald,

Gitti

24 Meine Ferien

Schreiben Schick eine E-Mail an einen Freund. Schreib ihm, wo du in den letzten Ferien warst und was du alles gesehen und gemacht hast!

Was hast du in den letzten Ferien gemacht? CD 3 Tr. 5

We asked several German-speaking people where they spent their last vacation and what they did. Listen. Before you read the interviews, write down your last vacation spot and the activities in which you participated during your vacation.

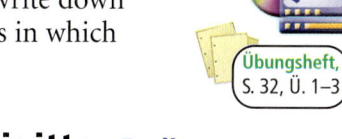

Hans, Hamburg CD 3 Tr. 6

„Hab hier gearbeitet, hab ja … trainiert auch, Volleyball trainiert, und ja … mehr eigentlich nicht."

Brigitte, Berlin CD 3 Tr. 9

„Wir waren, wann war das? … im März … drei Wochen in Midwest City, das ist ein Stadtteil von Oklahoma City, weil wir von unserer Schule aus, von unserem Gymnasium, alle zwei Jahre einen Schüleraustausch machen."

Monika, Hamburg CD 3 Tr. 7

„Ich war in den Ferien in Kanada, und … hab einen Sprachkurs gemacht, in Englisch. Ich bin nach Montreal gefahren und hab Toronto und die Niagarafälle auch gesehen. Hm, ja, und was war noch? Ja, ich wollte nach New York, weil … das ist nur sechs Stunden von Montreal entfernt, wo ich gewohnt habe, und das ging dann leider nicht."

Herr Troger, St. Ulrich, Österreich CD 3 Tr. 10

„Letzten Urlaub waren wir auf Mallorca; da haben wir uns bei einer Radfahrgruppe angeschlossen und sind da eine Woche Rad gefahren. Es war aber eigentlich ein schlechtes Wetter, und trotzdem war das Wetter für uns nicht so schlecht, weil wir mit den Rädern ziemlich nach oben gefahren sind und wieder runter, und wir waren also eher froh, wenn es nicht zu heiß war, nicht wahr …"

Sandra, Berlin CD 3 Tr. 8

„Also, ich war in Spanien, und ich hab da auch Granada besucht, und ansonsten lag ich eigentlich meistens am Strand und hab also die Sonne genossen. Aber ich hatte leider dummerweise 'ne Sonnenallergie: da ging das dann auch nicht mehr so gut. Na ja, also, ich hab viel Spaß mit meiner Freundin gehabt. Dann waren die Ferien auch schon vorbei."

A1. Monika: Montreal, Kanada - Sprachkurs. Sandra: Granada, Spanien - Strand und Sonne. Brigitte: Midwest City, USA - Schüleraustausch. Herr Troger: Mallorca, Spanien - Radfahren.

A. 1. On a map, locate the places where these people went on vacation. Jot these places down on a list along with the reason each gives for his or her trip.

2. Which two different words do Monika and Herr Troger use for "vacation"? Can you figure out the difference between these two words based on who uses them? A2. Ferien - Schule; Urlaub - Arbeit.

3. Three interviewees had some bad luck on their vacation. What happened to each?

B. What do all these vacations have in common? Sandra's and Herr Troger's trips are typical vacation goals for Germans. Why do you think that is?

A3. Monika: wollte nach N.Y. - es ging nicht. Sandra: hatte Sonnenallergie. Herr Troger: es war schlechtes Wetter.
B. Urlaub/Ferien im Ausland; schlechtes Wetter in Deutschland.

STANDARDS: 1.2, 2.2, 3.2, 4.2

Storytelling Book pp. 20–21

Dritte Stufe

Objectives Asking how someone liked something, expressing enthusiasm or disappointment, responding enthusiastically or sympathetically

WK3 BAYERN-3

25 **Wo waren die Schüler, und wie hat es ihnen gefallen?** Script and answers on p. 59H

Zuhören/Schreiben Fünf Schüler sprechen über ihre Ferien. Wo waren sie? Wem hat es gefallen? Wem hat es nicht gefallen? Warum wohl? Mach dir Notizen! Vergleiche dann deine Notizen mit den Notizen eines Partners!

CD 3 Tr. 11

So sagt man das!

Asking how someone liked something, expressing enthusiasm or disappointment, responding enthusiastically or sympathetically

Here are some ways to ask how someone liked something or some place:

> Wie war's?
> Wie hat dir Dresden gefallen?
> Wie hat es dir gefallen?
> Hat es dir gefallen?

If you liked it, you may say:

> Phantastisch!
> Es war echt super!
> Es hat mir gut gefallen.
> Wahnsinnig gut!

If you didn't like it, you may say:

> Na ja, soso!
> Nicht besonders.
> Es hat mir nicht gefallen.
> Es war furchtbar!

The other person asking may respond enthusiastically:

> Na, prima!
> Ja, Spitze!
> Das freut mich!

Or sympathetically:

> Schade!
> Tut mir Leid!
> Das tut mir aber Leid!

Grammatikheft, S. 25, Ü. 12

26 **Na, wie war's?**

Sprechen Such dir einen Partner! Stell dir vor, du warst an den Orten, die hier rechts im Kasten stehen! Dein Partner fragt dich, wie es war. Du antwortest, und dein Partner reagiert darauf. — Tauscht dann die Rollen aus!

PARTNER Wo warst du in den Ferien?
DU Ich war in/an …
PARTNER Wie war's?
DU …
PARTNER …

San Francisco
in den Alleghenies
Meer
Ostküste
Minnesota
Michigansee
Disneyland
Swamps von Florida
Key West
Mojave Wüste

Grammatik

Personal pronouns, dative case (Summary)

You already know the third-person dative pronouns **ihm** and **ihr.** Here are the others. With the verb **gefallen,** you always use dative case forms for the person.

Mehr Grammatikübungen, S. 84, Ü. 6–7

Übungsheft, S. 33–34, Ü. 1–3

Second Person		First Person	
Wie hat es **dir** gefallen?		Es hat **mir** gut gefallen.	
Wie hat es **euch** gefallen?		Es hat **uns** echt prima gefallen.	
Wie hat es **Ihnen** gefallen?		Es hat **mir** nicht gefallen.	

Third Person	
Wie hat es **dem Sebastian** gefallen?	Es hat **ihm** gut gefallen.
Wie hat es **der Beatrice** gefallen?	Es hat **ihr** echt prima gefallen.
Wie hat es **den Baumanns** gefallen?	Es hat **ihnen** nicht gefallen.

27 **Wie hat es ihnen gefallen?**

 Sprechen Such dir einen Partner! Du weißt, wo die Baumanns in den Ferien waren. (Das steht hier rechts!) Dein Partner fragt dich, wo sie waren. Du antwortest und sagst ihm, wie es ihnen gefallen hat. —Tauscht dann die Rollen aus!

Sebastian war mit einem Freund in Österreich.

Beatrice war in den Bergen, in den Alpen.

Die Großeltern waren am Rhein und an der Mosel.

Robert war an der Ostsee, auf der Insel Rügen.

Bastis Eltern waren in den USA, in Minnesota.

28 **Grammatik im Kontext**

a. Sprechen Such dir jetzt zwei Partner. Frag sie, wo sie in den Ferien waren. Einer antwortet für beide. Frag sie auch, wie es ihnen gefallen hat.

b. Schreiben Schreib jetzt drei Gespräche darüber, was du von deinen Partnern gehört hast.

        Du   **Wo wart ihr denn in den Ferien?**
  Ein Partner **Wir waren …**
        Du   **Wie hat es …**

Grammatik

Definite article, dative plural

1. The dative plural form of the definite article is **den.**

        Es hat **den** Eltern in Amerika echt gut gefallen.

2. The dative plural of almost all nouns ends in **-n.** If the nominative plural form already ends in **-n,** the dative plural form is the same.

Mehr Grammatikübungen, S. 84, Ü. 8

Nominative plural	Dative plural
die Eltern	Es hat **den** Eltern gut gefallen.
die Schüler	Es hat **den** Schüler**n** gut gefallen.
die Kinder	Es hat **den** Kinder**n** gut gefallen.

Übungsheft, S. 34–35, Ü. 4–7

Grammatikheft, S. 26, Ü. 13–14

DRITTE STUFE   STANDARDS: 1.1, 1.3, 4.1, 5.1   *siebenundsiebzig*

29 Grammatik im Kontext

 Various answers possible. E.g.: **Amerika hat den Baumanns sehr gut gefallen.**

Schreiben Schreib Sätze mit den Wörtern in den Kästen.

der Stadtbummel		Baumanns	echt gut	
die Berge		Beatrice	besonders gut	
Amerika	hat	Opa	sehr gut	
Dresden	haben	Sebastian	ganz gut	gefallen
Tirol		Kinder	nicht besonders	
das Meer		Geschwister	nicht so gut	
der Film		Großmutter	überhaupt nicht	
		Schüler		
		ich		

Wortschatz

Übernachten und essen

Basti war mit einem Freund, dem Thomas, in Tirol. Die beiden haben in einer Pension gewohnt und haben oft in einem Café gegessen, im Café Troger.

Wo übernachtet man gewöhnlich?

in einem Privathaus | in einer Pension | in einer Jugendherberge | in einem Hotel

Wo isst man gewöhnlich?

in einer Imbissstube | in einem Lokal | in einem Gasthof | in einem Restaurant

30 Grammatik im Kontext

a. **Sprechen** Such dir einen Partner! Frag ihn, wo er gewöhnlich übernachtet und wo er gewöhnlich isst, wenn er mit (seinen Eltern) unterwegs ist!

b. **Schreiben** Schick deinem Freund eine E-Mail mit denselben Fragen.

31 Für mein Notizbuch

Schreiben Schreib in dein Notizbuch etwas über deine Ferien! Wo bist du gewesen? Was hast du alles gemacht? Wie hat es dir gefallen und warum? Wo hast du übernachtet? Wo hast du gegessen?

32 Bastis Ferien

Sprechen Sebastian hat einige Fotos von seinen Ferien ausgesucht, die er seinen Klassenkameraden im Film- und Fotoclub zeigen möchte. Spiel die Rolle von Basti und erzähle, wo du warst, was du gemacht hast und wie es dir gefallen hat! Dein Bericht muss zu den Fotos passen. Gebrauche auch die Wörter im Kasten oben rechts.

Ein wenig Grammatik

The dative case forms of **ein** are:

Masculine/Neuter	Feminine
einem	einer

Mehr Grammatikübungen, S. 85, Ü. 9

Wortschatz

Schon bekannt	Neu
jeden Tag	am letzten Tag
oft	jeden Abend
einmal	nach dem
dreimal	Mittagessen
am Wochenende	jeden Morgen

Grammatikheft, S. 27, Ü. 17

1.

2.

3.

4.

5.

33 Von der Schule zum Beruf

Schreiben Du arbeitest in der Tourismus-Abteilung für die Zeitung in deiner Stadt. Für die nächste Ausgabe sollst du einen Artikel schreiben mit dem Titel: Unsere Stadt, ein Paradies für Touristen.

Zum Lesen

In Tirol

Lesestrategie
Identifying the main idea and supporting details. When you read a text, it is important to be able to identify the main idea (or ideas). This will enable you to determine the global meaning of the text (the "big picture"), and then to find the details that support the global idea.

Getting Started

1. Look at the pictures, then look at the different formats of the texts and match each text with one of the formats below.
   1. excerpt from a brochure/advertisement
   2. announcement
   3. newspaper article
   4. postcard

   Based on the formats, what kind of information would you expect to find in each text?
   a. report of an event   3.
   b. news about someone's vacation   4.
   c. factual information, e.g. time, date   2.
   d. promotion of something   1.

2. Does anything in the brochures above help you distinguish immediately between the main idea and the supporting details?

3. Where do you usually find the main idea of a newspaper article?   3. headline

---

Loferer Steinberge St. Ulrich a.P.

Liebe Eltern!
Grüße aus St. Ulrich! Wir sind erst 3 Tage da und haben schon viel gesehen. Nur gestern haben wir gefaulenzt, sind nur um den Pillersee spaziert und haben im See gebadet. Der ist aber noch zu kalt!
Alles Gute! Euer Basti
P.S. Morgen ist ein Dorffest

Fam.
Hans Baumann
Wolfratshauserstr. 17
82031 Grünwald

Deutschland

SONNTAG, 4. JULI
ca. 9.45 Uhr
DORFPLATZEINWEIHUNG
mit anschl.
Schmanggerlfest
der Gastronomie
Frühschoppenkonzert
Musikkapelle ca. 11.00 Uhr
und musikalischer
Unterhaltung
mit dem TIROL DUO

St. Ulrich/Tirol Der Dorfplatz in St. Ulrich am Pillersee hat jetzt einen Brunnen. Am Sonntag, den 4. Juli, um 9 Uhr 45, hat die Dorfplatzeinweihung stattgefunden. Nach einer Messe in der Dorfkirche mit Bischof Eder ist die Dorfgemeinde auf den Dorfplatz marschiert. Nach einer Ansprache von Bürgermeister Schlechter wurde der Dorfplatz von Bischof Eder offiziell eingeweiht.

Die Gastronomie St. Ulrich hatte für eine gute Jause gesorgt, und die Musikkapelle St. Ulrich, unter Leitung von Musikkapellmeister Alois Brüggel, für gute Stimmung und Unterhaltung. (Österreichische Landeszeitung)

STANDARDS: 1.2, 3.1   KAPITEL 3   Wo warst du in den Ferien?

Im Pillerseetal

ist immer was los!

- Pillersee mit Badestrand
- Angeln im fischreichen See
- Tretboote, Ruderboote
- 60 km Wanderwege
- Tennis und Kegelbahnen
- Minigolf und Hallenbad
- Reithalle (Islandpferde)
- 7 Golfplätze in der Nähe

Bischof Eder aus Salzburg

Besonders für Kinder!

- Besuch auf einem Bauernhof
- Kindergrillparty
- Kinderdisco
- Ponyreiten mit unseren Ponies Amigo, Bibi und Sarah
- Kinder-Pizzaessen
- Basteln, Malen, Zeichnen, Singen und vieles mehr

Familien- und Sporthotel

Pillerseehof

Die Musikkapelle St. Ulrich

Thomas u. ich am Pillersee

Tipp Sometimes the main idea is not stated directly, but only implied. You have to make an inference by looking at the supporting details.

4. Skim the postcard. What is the main idea?

A Closer Look

5. What are some of the details Basti writes about in his postcard?

6. Look at the newspaper article more closely. Where did the event that is being reported take place? Is that a large city or a small town? Where is it? If the main idea is the dedication of the fountain, can you find four or five supporting details in the article?

7. Jetzt erzähle von deinen letzten Ferien! Bring entweder Dias, Fotos oder ein Video mit und zeig deinen Mitschülern, wo du warst und was du da alles gemacht hast!

5. They have seen a lot in three days; Yesterday they were being lazy; They walked around the Pillersee; They swam in the lake; Tomorrow there is a town festival.
6. The event took place in St. Ulrich; It is a small town (village); located at the Pillersee in Tirol, Austria; supporting details for main event: e.g. day, time, people attending, food, music

Übungsheft, S. 36

Mehr Grammatikübungen

Answers

Erste Stufe

Objectives Reporting past events, talking about activities

1 Du erzählst einer Schulfreundin, was du alles am Wochenende gemacht hast.—Such dir aus dem Kasten das richtige Partizip *(past participle)* aus und schreib es in die Lücken. (S. 66–67)

gearbeitet	gelesen	geschenkt
gegangen	gemacht	gesehen
geholfen	gemäht	gespielt

1. Ich habe am Wochenende viel _____ .   gemacht
2. Ich habe mit meinem Vater Tennis _____ .   gespielt
3. Ich bin mit meiner Freundin ins Kino _____ .   gegangen
4. Wir haben einen tollen Film _____ .   gesehen
5. Am Samstag habe ich meinem Opa _____ .   geholfen
6. Ich habe mit ihm im Garten _____ .   gearbeitet
7. Ich habe für ihn den Rasen _____ .   gemäht
8. Der Opa hat mir ein tolles Buch _____ .   geschenkt
9. Ich habe sofort ein Kapitel _____ .   gelesen

2 Du berichtest, was du in den Ferien gemacht hast.—Schreib eine Form von **haben** oder **sein** und das Partizip der gegebenen Verben in die Lücken. (S. 66–67)

1. (arbeiten) Ja, zuerst _____ ich zwei Wochen für den Opa _____ .   habe; gearbeitet
   (fahren) Danach _____ ich mit den Eltern an die Nordsee _____ .   bin; gefahren
   (schwimmen) Dort _____ wir sehr oft im Meer _____ ; und wenn das   sind; geschwommen
   (hören; lesen) Wetter schlecht war, _____ wir unsere CDs _____ und   haben; gehört
   Bücher _____ .   gelesen

2. (sehen) Wir _____ in den Sommerferien furchtbar viel _____ .   haben; gesehen
   (besuchen) Wir _____ unsere Tante in Frankfurt _____ , und wir   haben; besucht
   (bleiben) _____ zehn Tage bei ihr _____ . Frankfurt ist sehr   sind; geblieben
   (gehen) schön. Wir _____ durch die Zeil _____ , und wir _____   sind; gegangen; haben
   (essen; trinken) in tollen Cafés _____ und Limo _____ .   gegessen; getrunken

3. (machen) Sagt mal, was _____ ihr denn in den Ferien _____ ?   habt; gemacht
   (sein) _____ ihr mit euren Großeltern am Rhein _____ , und   Seid; gewesen
   (besichtigen) _____ ihr in Köln den Kölner Dom _____ ? Ja, und   habt; besichtigt
   (spazieren) ihr _____ bestimmt oft am Rhein entlang _____ , und   seid; spaziert
   (wandern) ihr _____ doch auch viel _____ . Und ich weiß auch,   seid; gewandert
   (fotografieren) dass ihr wieder viel _____ _____ .   fotografiert; habt

4. (fahren) Und der Basti _____ mit Thomas nach Tirol _____ .   ist; gefahren
   (wohnen) Die Jungen _____ dort in einer Pension _____ , und   haben; gewohnt
   (filmen) sie _____ in den Bergen _____ . Das Wetter war toll,   haben; gefilmt
   (faulenzen) und sie _____ oft am See _____ .   haben; gefaulenzt

Zweite Stufe

Objectives Reporting past events, talking about places

3 Du fragst deine Freunde über ihre Ferien.—Schreib eine Vergangenheitsform *(past tense form)* von **haben** oder **sein** in die Lücken. (S. 72)

1. Wo _____ du denn in den Ferien? — Ich _____ an der Nordsee.   *warst; war*
2. Sag, _____ du prima Wetter? — Wir _____ nur Sonne, keinen Regen!   *hattest; hatten*
3. Und wo _____ ihr, Anna und Ria? — Ja, wir _____ in den Bergen.   *wart; waren*
4. Ja, _____ ihr Regen? — Nein, wir _____ immer nur Sonnenschein.   *hattet; hatten*
5. Wer _____ denn an der Ostsee? — Ich _____ dort mit meinen Eltern.   *war; war*
6. Mein Vater _____ drei Wochen Urlaub, und wir _____ auf Rügen.   *hatte; waren*

4 Deine Freunde haben in den Ferien viele Städte besucht. Sie sagen dir, wo sie waren und wo diese Städte liegen. Such dir eine Präposition oder eine Präposition mit Artikel aus dem Kasten aus und schreib sie in die Lücken. (S. 73)

in	im	an der	in der
am	in der	in den	

1. Erik: Ich war _____ Aspen, und Aspen liegt _____ Gebirge.   *in; im*
2. Steffi: Ich war _____ Frankfurt, und Frankfurt liegt _____ Main.   *in; am*
3. Mark: Ich war _____ Istanbul, und Istanbul liegt _____ Türkei.   *in; in der*
4. Sandra: Ich war _____ Hamburg, und Hamburg liegt _____ Elbe.   *in; an der*
5. Max: Ich war _____ Miami, und Miami liegt _____ Vereinigten Staaten.   *in; in den*
6. Tamara: Ich war _____ Rostock, und Rostock liegt _____ Ostsee.   *in; an der*
7. Bruce: Ich war _____ New York, und New York liegt _____ Meer.   *in; am*
8. Bettina: Ich war _____ Zürich, und Zürich liegt _____ Schweiz.   *in; in der*

5 Du erzählst, wo du mit deiner Schwester in den Ferien warst.—Schreib in jede Lücke die richtige Präposition und den richtigen Artikel, wenn nötig *(if necessary)*. (S. 73)

1. Ja, ich war mit den Eltern _____ Schweiz. Zuerst waren wir _____ Gebirge. Jeden Tag sind wir _____ Bergen gewandert. Und _____ Bodensee waren wir auch. Dann waren wir _____ Rhein und _____ Schwarzwald.   *in der; im* / *in den; am* / *am; im*

2. Meine Schwester, die Anne, war _____ Nordsee, _____ Ostfriesland. Sie war dort den ganzen Tag _____ Meer, und am Abend _____ Kino, denn dort ist nichts los. Ach ja, dann war sie _____ Frankfurt; sie hat dort viel gesehen. Sie war _____ Museum, _____ Alten Rathaus, und einmal war sie auch _____ Oper!   *an der; in* / *am; im* / *in* / *im; im* / *in der*

MEHR GRAMMATIKÜBUNGEN

Mehr Grammatikübungen

Answers

WK3 BAYERN-3

Dritte Stufe

Objectives Asking how someone liked something, expressing enthusiasm and disappointment, responding enthusiastically or sympathetically

6 Allen Schülern haben die Ferien gefallen. — Schreib das richtige Pronomen in jede Lücke. (S. 77)

1. Basti, wie hat es _____ in St. Ulrich gefallen? — Es hat _____ gut gefallen. dir; mir
2. Wie hat es _____ gefallen, Jens und Hans? — Es hat _____ auch gut gefallen. euch; uns
3. Wie hat es _____ gefallen, Frau Moser? — Es hat _____ nicht so gefallen. Ihnen; mir
4. Wie hat es dem Robert gefallen? — Es hat _____ sehr gut gefallen. ihm
5. Wie hat es der Beatrice gefallen? — Es hat _____ auch gut gefallen. ihr
6. Wie hat es den Eltern gefallen? — Es hat _____ prima gefallen. ihnen

7 Eure Freunde tun euch Leid.—Schreib das richtige Pronomen in jede Lücke. (S. 77)

1. (I'm sorry.)   Das tut _____ aber Leid!   mir
2. (He's very sorry.)   Das tut _____ sehr Leid!   ihm
3. (We're so sorry.)   Das tut _____ so Leid!   uns
4. (She's sorry.)   Es tut _____ Leid!   ihr
5. (Are you sorry, Mark?)   Tut es _____ Leid, Mark?   dir
6. (Are you sorry, Anne and Peter?) Tut es _____ Leid, Anne und Peter? euch

8 Die Ferien waren für alle super!—Schreib die richtige Form der in Klammern gegebenen Wörter in die Lücken. (S. 77)

1. (die Eltern)   Es hat _____ in Berlin wahnsinnig gut gefallen.   den Eltern
2. (der Sebastian)   Es hat _____ in Tirol sehr gut gefallen.   dem Sebastian
3. (die Schüler)   Es hat _____ an der Nordsee so prima gefallen.   den Schülern
4. (die Beatrice)   Es hat _____ am Bodensee gut gefallen.   der Beatrice
5. (die Kinder)   Es hat _____ in der Jugendherberge gut gefallen.   den Kindern
6. (die Lehrer)   Es hat _____ im Gebirge echt prima gefallen.   den Lehrern

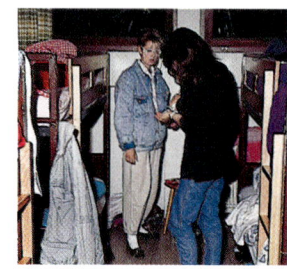

9 Wo habt ihr übernachtet und wo habt ihr gegessen?—Schreib die richtigen Formen der gegebenen Ausdrücke in die Lücken. (S. 79)

ein Privathaus

1. Wir haben in _____ übernachtet.   einem Privathaus

eine Pension

2. Ich habe in _____ übernachtet.   einer Pension

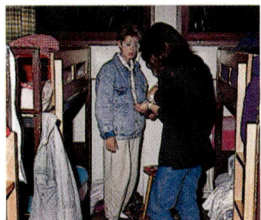
eine Jugendherberge

3. Basti hat in _____ übernachtet.   einer Jugendherberge

eine Imbissstube

4. Wir haben in _____ gegessen.   einer Imbissstube

ein Restaurant

5. Ich habe in _____ gegessen.   einem Restaurant

ein Gasthof

6. Marty hat in _____ gegessen.   einem Gasthof

MEHR GRAMMATIKÜBUNGEN STANDARDS: 1.2 *fünfundachtzig* **85**

TPR Storytelling Book pp. 22–23

Anwendung

The *CD-ROM Tutor* offers guided recording and writing activities to accompany the **Anwendung.** These activities are designed to practice students' oral and written communication skills and to review material from each chapter.

1 Die Stegmüllers aus Düsseldorf haben mit ihren Kindern Melissa (7) und Jochen (9) den Sommerurlaub in St. Ulrich am Pillersee verbracht. Am Ende ihres Urlaubs haben sie den Fragebogen des Fremdenverkehrsvereins ausgefüllt. Lies diesen Fragebogen! Was haben die Stegmüllers abgehakt?

FRAGEBOGEN
Fremdenverkehrsverein St. Ulrich am Pillersee in Tirol

1. Wo haben Sie gewohnt?
   ☐ Hotel   ☐ Gasthof   ☑ Pension   ☐ Privatquartier

2. Wie hat Ihnen die Unterkunft gefallen?
   ☐ ausgezeichnet   ☑ sehr gut   ☐ gut   ☐ nicht gut   ☐ nicht besonders

3. Wo haben Sie gewöhnlich gegessen?
   ☐ Hotel   ☑ Gasthaus   ☐ Café   ☐ Restaurant   ☐ selbst gekocht

4. Wie war die Qualität des Essens in unseren Lokalen?
   ☐ ausgezeichnet   ☑ sehr gut   ☐ gut   ☐ nicht gut

5. Wie haben Sie Ihren Urlaub verbracht? Kreuzen Sie bitte die Dinge an, die Sie am meisten gemacht haben!
   ☑ wandern   ☐ angeln   ☑ Minigolf   ☑ baden gehen
   ☐ bergsteigen   ☑ Boot fahren   ☐ Tennis   ☐ reiten
   ☐ spazierengehen ☐ Rad fahren   ☑ Tischtennis ☐ kegeln

6. Was hat den Kindern am meisten Spaß gemacht?
   a. _Ponyreiten_   c. _____
   b. _Grillparty_

7. Welche Unterhaltungsprogramme haben Ihnen am besten gefallen? Kreuzen Sie bitte nur drei Programme an!
   ☑ Musikabende   ☐ Tanzveranstaltungen   ☐ Vorträge
   ☑ Theateraufführungen ☐ Dia-Vorführungen

8. Wie lange waren Sie bei uns?
   ☐ eine Woche   ☑ zwei Wochen   _____

2 Such dir einen Partner! Diskutiert gemeinsam die folgenden Fragen!

1. Hat es den Stegmüllers in St. Ulrich gefallen? Wenn ja, warum? Wenn nein, warum nicht?

2. Warum, glaubt ihr, hat die Familie in einer Pension gewohnt? In einem Gasthaus gegessen?

3. Warum, glaubt ihr, sind die Stegmüllers nicht bergsteigen gegangen?

4. Was meint ihr: Welche Freizeitbeschäftigungen kosten Geld? Welche nicht?

3
a. Setzt euch in kleinen Gruppen zusammen und entwerft einen Fragebogen, für einen Ferienort in den Vereinigten Staaten (Florida, Kalifornien). Gebraucht den Fragebogen von St. Ulrich als Muster!

b. Stellt euch vor, dass alle in eurer Gruppe die letzten Ferien zusammen verbracht haben! (Die Eltern von einem von euch haben die anderen mitgenommen.) Füllt gemeinsam euern Fragebogen aus!

c. Teilt jetzt leere Fragebögen an die Mitglieder einer anderen Gruppe aus! Die Mitglieder dieser Gruppe fragen euch jetzt über eure Ferien, und ihr antwortet. — Tauscht dann die Rollen aus!

4 Zum Schreiben

Imagine you spent a month in your ideal vacation spot. Write a paragraph describing the place. Say where you went and what you did. Include some interesting details about the weather, the recreational facilities, the food, the people, and the fun things you did there.

Schreibtipp Finding good **details** makes writing more exciting. For example, sharp details will grab your reader's interest immediately. Include details of time, place, sight, sound, or smell.

Vorbereiten

Make a list: Write the name of the location at the top of a sheet of paper, and then write the categories listed above (weather, food, people, etc.) and whatever other categories you want to include down the left side of your paper. Next to each item on your list, write at least two details that describe that item.

Ausführen

Begin your paragraph with **a sentence that describes the location.** For example, **Ich habe die Ferien auf einer Insel mit einem Sandstrand verbracht.** Write several sentences about what you did, using descriptive details. You might also combine some of your descriptions with connecting words.

5 Listen to the reports and decide what they are all about. Match each report to one of these summaries: Script and answers on p. 59H

CD 3 Tr. 12
a. description of a town or area
b. description of sightseeing in a town
c. description of activities one can do
d. description of a hotel

6 Listen to these people talking about a trip they recently took. Find out where they were and how they liked it. Script and answers on p. 59H
CD 3 Tr. 13

7 Rollenspiel

Together with two other classmates, role-play the following scene.

You are working in a travel agency and have a customer who wants suggestions from you about where he could spend his vacation. As you make your suggestions, another customer joins in and tells of his experiences at a particular vacation spot. Have some brochures at your disposal, either from German vacation spots or vacation spots in the United States.

ANWENDUNG STANDARDS: 1.1, 1.2, 1.3, 3.1, 5.1, 5.2 *siebenundachtzig*

Kann ich's wirklich?

Can you report past events, talking about activities? (p. 65)

1 How would you ask a classmate what he or she did during his or her vacation?
1. E.g.: Was hast du in den Ferien gemacht?

2 How would you tell someone about the things you did, using the verbs **spielen, lesen, wandern, besuchen, besichtigen, sein, gehen, laufen, fahren,** and **schwimmen?** 2. E.g.: Ich habe meine Tante in Tirol besucht und bin dort viel gewandert.

3 How would you report what someone else did, using the same verbs?
3. E.g.: Er/sie hat den Dom in Frankfurt besichtigt.

4 How would you ask someone where he or she was, using two different past tense forms? How would that person answer?
4. a. Wo bist du gewesen? — Ich bin … gewesen. b. Wo warst du? — Ich war …

5 How would you say that you didn't have any time, using two different past tense forms? 5. a. Ich habe keine Zeit gehabt. b. Ich hatte keine Zeit.

6 How would you invite someone to tell you
a. where he or she was?
b. what he or she did?
c. what he or she saw?
d. how he or she liked it?

a. E.g.: Wo bist du gewesen?
b. E.g.: Was hast du alles gemacht?
c. E.g.: Was hast du dort alles gesehen?
d. E.g.: Wie hat es dir gefallen?

Can you report past events, talking about places? (p. 71)

7 How would you say that you were at each of these places? Use complete sentences. 7. Ich war … ; Ich bin … gewesen.
in | in | in | in der | in den | in der
Dresden, Sachsen, Deutschland, Schweiz, die Vereinigten Staaten, Schule, Kirche, Stadt, Museum, Park, Gebirge, Ostsee, Meer, Main
in der | in der | im | im | im | an der | am | am

Can you ask someone how he or she liked something and respond enthusiastically or sympathetically? (p. 76)

8 How would you ask someone how they liked the city of Frankfurt? How they liked it in Tirol? How would you say that you liked it? That you didn't like it? 8. E.g.: Wie hat dir Frankfurt gefallen? Wie hat es dir in Tirol gefallen? Es war echt super! Es hat mir nicht gefallen.

9 How would you respond to someone who
— tells you that he or she liked his or her vacation? E.g.: Das freut mich!
— tells you that he or she did not like it? E.g.: Tut mir Leid!

10 How would you tell someone that your parents liked Dresden but that they didn't like Leipzig?
10. E.g.: Meinen Eltern hat Dresden gut gefallen, aber Leipzig hat ihnen überhaupt nicht gefallen.

Wortschatz

Erste Stufe

Reporting past events, talking about activities

Was hast du in den Ferien gemacht?	What did you do on your vacation?	die Videokamera/ die Kamera bedienen	to use a video camera/a camera	**Verbs and past participles**	
die Ferien (pl)	vacation	ein Video einlegen	to insert a videocassette	arbeiten, gearbeitet	to work
besichtigen	to sightsee, visit a place	das Video herausnehmen	to take out the videocassette	faulenzen, gefaulenzt	to be lazy
Ich habe (den Dom) besichtigt.	I visited (the cathedral).	die Kamera, -s	camera	laufen, (ist) gelaufen	to run
fotografieren	to photograph	der Film, -e	roll of film	er/sie läuft	he/she runs
Ich habe … fotografiert.	I photographed …	das Dia, -s	slide	bleiben, (ist) geblieben	to stay, remain
spazieren	to walk, stroll	das Farbbild, -er	color photograph		
filmen	to film, videotape	der Videorecorder, -	videocassette recorder (VCR)	(See p. 67 for a more complete list of past participles.)	

Zweite Stufe

 p. 59X

Reporting past events, talking about places

Wo bist du gewesen?	Where were you?	das Museum, Museen	museum	das Goethehaus	Goethe's birthplace
Am (Main).	On (the Main River).	der Römer	name of city hall in Frankfurt	der See, -n	lake
In (London).	In (London).	die Fachwerkhäuser	cross-timbered houses	um den See	around the lake
Im (Zoo).	At (the zoo).	die Zeil	name of main shopping street in Frankfurt	**Other useful words and expressions**	
besuchen	to visit (a place)			noch nie	not yet, never
der Dom, -e	cathedral			schon oft	a lot, often
die Oper, -n	opera house	der Main	Main River	auch schon	also, already

Dritte Stufe

Asking how someone liked something

Wie war's?	How was it?
Wie hat dir Dresden gefallen?	How did you like Dresden?
Es hat mir gut gefallen!	I liked it a lot!
Wie hat es dir gefallen?	How did you like it?
Hat es dir gefallen?	Did you like it?
Es hat mir nicht gefallen.	I didn't like it.
Phantastisch!	Fantastic!
Echt super!	Really great!
Wahnsinnig gut!	Extremely well!
Na ja, soso!	Oh, all right.
Nicht besonders.	Not especially.

Responding enthusiastically or sympathetically

Das freut mich!	I'm really glad!
Tut mir Leid!	I'm sorry.
Das tut mir aber Leid!	I'm so sorry.

Personal pronouns, dative case

dir	to/for you
euch	to/for you (plural)
Ihnen	to/for you (formal)
mir	to/for me
uns	to/for us
ihnen	to/for them

Places to stay

übernachten	to spend the night
gewöhnlich	usually
in einem/in einer …	in/at a …
das Privathaus, ¨-er	private home
die Pension, -en	inn, bed and breakfast
die Jugendherberge, -n	youth hostel
das Hotel, -s	hotel

Places to eat

die Imbissstube, -n	snack stand
das Lokal, -e	small restaurant
der Gasthof, ¨-e	restaurant, inn
das Restaurant, -s	restaurant

Time expressions

am letzten Tag	on the last day
jeden Abend	every evening
jeden Morgen	every morning
nach dem Mittagessen	after lunch

KAPITEL 4, 5, 6

Hamburg

Teaching Resources
pp. 90–93

PRINT
- Lesson Planner, p. 17
- Video Guide, pp. 21–22

MEDIA
- One-Stop Planner
- Video Program
  Videocassette 2, 01:20–04:30
- DVD Tutor, Disc 1
- Interactive CD-ROM Tutor, Disc 1
- Map Transparency

 go.hrw.com
WK3 HAMBURG

PAGES 90–91

THE PHOTOGRAPH
Background Information
The **Binnenalster** is an artificial lake in the shape of a trapezoid. It is located in the heart of Hamburg and encompasses an area of **18 Hektar** (44 acres). Its four banks make it unique. The **Jungfernstieg** on one side is the main boulevard of the city and houses many famous stores and hotels. The picture was taken from the bridge that was once known as the **Lombardsbrücke.** Parallel to this bridge runs the **Kennedy-Brücke** named in memory of the late U.S. president.

Thinking Critically
Comparing and Contrasting Ask students to compare the architecture of the buildings alongside the **Binnenalster.** (They are very similar in style and size.) Tell students that the uniform look is no accident. Street building codes required architects and builders to aim for a very connected and unified appearance.

THE ALMANAC AND MAP

 Hamburg's coat of arms dates back to the 12th and 13th centuries and depicts a silver gate tower with two silver stars above the outer towers, all on a red background. The crest represents the port of Hamburg's historical role as gateway to the world.

Terms in the Almanac
- **St. Michaelis-Kirche:** Better known as **der Michel,** the church is one of the symbols of Hamburg. It was built between 1751 and 1762 and stands 132 meters (433 feet) tall. It burned down in 1906, was rebuilt, then was destroyed during World War II. It was rebuilt the second time using the original plans of architects J.L. Prey and E.G. Sonnin.

- **Felix Mendelssohn-Bartholdy:** Famous German pianist and composer who founded the Leipzig conservatory. He was the grandson of Moses Mendelssohn, a well-known German philosopher.

- **Carl von Ossietzky:** German writer who was imprisoned by the Nazis in 1933 and then received the Nobel Peace Prize in 1935. He published the **Weltbühne,** a famous cultural and political newspaper. Since 1962, **Carl-von-Ossietzky-Medaillen** have been given annually to outstanding artists and writers who contribute to human rights awareness.

- **Verlage:** The city is home to many publishers and printing businesses. Many of the country's magazines and newspapers, such as *Bild, Die Zeit, Deutsches Allgemeines Sonntagsblatt,* and *Der Spiegel* are published in Hamburg.

- **Hamburger Aalsuppe:** This is a soup made of fresh eel, potatoes, soup greens, onions, lemon juice, and various herbs and spices.

- **Matjeshering:** Salted filet of young herring that is considered a great delicacy in northern Germany. It is often eaten on pumpernickel bread.

Map Activities
- Have students use a map to identify the German states that border on the Free Hanseatic City of Hamburg. (**Schleswig-Holstein** and **Niedersachsen**) You may also want to use *Map Transparency* 1.

- Have students locate and trace the Elbe and Alster rivers in an atlas.

Background Information
Originally named **Hammaburg,** the city was founded in the 9th century by the son of **Karl der Große,**

Emperor **Ludwig der Fromme.** Hamburg is called the *Free Hanseatic City*. It received this status in the 13th century when Hamburg, together with Lübeck, founded the Hanseatic League. Bremen later joined the League in 1358. The Hanseatic League was a collective union of merchants from dozens of cities from Norway to Russia. The merchants formed the League to strengthen their economic position. Hamburg was almost completely destroyed during World War II and rebuilt in the postwar years. Today the city is still called **Hansestadt Hamburg** and is a state in its own right. It is Germany's second largest city after Berlin.

PAGES 92–93

THE PHOTO ESSAY

① Hamburg is Germany's largest seaport. The port is one of the city's main attractions. Tourists as well as locals enjoy informative trips on tour boats as they cruise around small and large ships. Since harsh winters can freeze the port, icebreakers must be used during part of the year to keep the port and its shipping channels open.

② **Blankenese** is an exclusive residential area that is considered by many the most beautiful neighborhood in Hamburg. Homes are built on slopes and are surrounded and concealed by trees. Sea captains, ship owners, and heads of trading firms make up a good part of the residents of the area.

③ The community of **Övelgönne** attracts many visitors interested in seeing its many small houses with small windows and large wooden shutters. Most of the homes are those of retired river pilots, sea captains, and sailors. They are located along the banks of the Elbe river, and it is said that these retirees spend most of their time behind large telescopes viewing passing ships.

④ This spectacular city hall is located in the center of the city and is the seat of the state government as well as the senate of the city. The senate occupies the right side of the building, and the state parliament has its chamber and workrooms on the other side. A group of nine architects under the direction of **Baumeister Haller** built the **Rathaus** between 1886 and 1897 in the German Renaissance style. The front facade features 18 statues of German emperors.

COMMUNITY LINK

Ask students about the city hall in their community. Have them find out when it was built and by whom.

⑤ The **Speicherstadt** was designed and built at the end of the 19th century by 42 architects and 15 engineers. It is architecturally unique in that it is a city within a city. It is a 10 km² (3.86 square miles) large free port and storage facility in which goods are stored without customs clearance. Goods such as coffee, tea, tobacco, or spices are kept in huge, gothic-style brick buildings that form one big warehouse facility, the largest of its kind in the world. Today the **Speicherstadt** is also a historical landmark.

⑥ The **SS Rickmer Rickmers** is a sailing ship that was built in Bremerhaven in 1896. It was named after the grandchild of the shipyard's founder. It is 97 meters (318 feet) long and 12.20 meters (40 feet) wide. On its maiden voyage, it sailed to Hong Kong and returned loaded with rice and bamboo. During its history, it has relied on three major sources of power: it began with wind power, then added steam engines, and was finally converted to diesel engines. The **SS Rickmer Rickmers** was retired in 1987. It is now docked in Hamburg and is open to the public for tours.

⑦ Maike, Thorsten, Wiebke, and David were born in Hamburg. Nicolas' parents are French. They both work for French companies in Hamburg. David's father is a Nigerian official who works in Hamburg. David went to school in Nigeria for five years, but he has been back in Hamburg for several years.

KAPITEL 4, 5, 6

Komm mit nach Hamburg!

Einwohner: 1,6 Millionen

Fläche: 755 Quadratkilometer (292 Quadratmeilen; etwa viermal so groß wie der District of Columbia)

Flüsse: Alster, Elbe

Berühmte Gebäude: Rathaus, St. Michaelis-Kirche, Chilehaus

Bedeutende Hamburger: Johannes Brahms (1833-1897, Komponist), Felix Mendelssohn-Bartholdy (1809-1847, Komponist), Carl von Ossietzky (1888-1938, Schriftsteller), Wolfgang Borchert (1921-1947, Schriftsteller), Helene Lange (1848-1930, Frauenrechtlerin)

Industrie: Handel, Verlage, Nahrungsmittel, Chemie

Beliebte Gerichte: Hamburger Aalsuppe, Matjeshering, Scholle

Map of Germany

WK3 HAMBURG

STANDARDS: 2.2, 3.1

▶ Blick auf Hamburg, von der Lombardsbrücke aus gesehen

Hamburg

Die Freie und Hansestadt Hamburg, nach Berlin die größte Stadt Deutschlands, ist auch ein Bundesland. Schon im Mittelalter war die Stadt an der Elbe ein wichtiger Handelsplatz. Heute ist Hamburg, das „Tor zur Welt", Deutschlands bedeutendster Hafen. Die Konzentration von Zeitungen, Verlagen, Rundfunk- und Fernsehanstalten macht Hamburg zum kulturellen Zentrum Norddeutschlands.

Visit Holt Online
go.hrw.com
KEYWORD: WK3 HAMBURG
Internet Aktivitäten

❶ Hafenrundfahrt auf der Elbe
Der Hamburger Hafen ist einer der größten Häfen der Welt. Hafenrundfahrten an den großen Schiffen vorbei sind sehr beliebt.

❷ Blankenese
Blankenese ist ein reicher Vorort von Hamburg, wo viele Geschäftsleute ihre Villen haben.

❸ Övelgönne
Övelgönne, direkt an der Elbe gelegen, ist die Heimat vieler ehemaliger Schiffskapitäne. Haustüren wie diese hier schmücken jedes Haus.

❹ Rathaus
Das Hamburger Rathaus, 1866 bis 1897 im Stil der deutschen Renaissance erbaut, ist Mittelpunkt dieser geschäftigen internationalen Stadt.

5 Speicherstadt
Die Speicherstadt befindet sich an der Einfahrt zum Freihafen wo große Frachtschiffe zollfrei ihre Güter auf kleinere Schiffe umschlagen, welche die Güter dann auf anderen Wasserwegen an ihr Ziel bringen.

6 Im Hafen von Hamburg
Die „Rickmer Rickmers", ein Segelschiff mit einer großen Vergangenheit, ist heute ein Museum.

Kapitel 4, 5, 6
Die folgenden drei Kapitel führen uns nach Hamburg, in die Wirtschafts- und Kulturmetropole an der Elbe. Die Schüler in diesen Kapiteln gehen auf eine zweisprachige Schule, das Helene-Lange-Gymnasium.

7 Maike, Nicolas, Thorsten, Wiebke und David

dreiundneunzig

Kapitel 4: Gesund leben
Chapter Overview

Los geht's! pp. 96–98	*Wie fühlst du dich?*, p. 96			

	FUNCTIONS	**GRAMMAR**	**VOCABULARY**	**RE-ENTRY**
Erste Stufe pp. 99–104	• Expressing approval and disapproval, p. 100	• The verb **schlafen**, p. 100 • The accusative-case forms after the preposition **für**, p. 101 • The reflexive verbs, p. 102	• Health tips, pp. 99, 101 • How you feel in certain locations, p. 103	The modals **sollen** and **müssen**, p. 99 **(Kap. 7/8, I)**; Saying how often you do things, p. 100 **(Kap. 7, I)**; **Dass**-clauses, pp. 100, 101 **(Kap. 9, I)**; Expressing opinions, p. 101 **(Kap. 9, I)**; Responding to good and bad news, p. 101 **(Kap. 4, I)**; Greeting someone, p. 103 **(Kap. 1, I)**; **Weil** and **denn**; giving reasons, p. 103 **(Kap. 8, I)**
Zweite Stufe pp. 105–108	• Asking for information and responding emphatically or agreeing, with reservations, p. 107	• The determiner **jeder**, p. 106	• Expressions of frequency, p. 108	Saying how often you do things, p. 105 **(Kap. 7, I)**; Telling someone what to do, p. 106 **(Kap. 8, I)**; **Aber**, p. 107 **(Kap. 3, I)**; **Sie**-form; agreeing, p. 107 **(Kap. 2, I)**
Dritte Stufe pp. 109–111	• Asking and telling what you may or may not do, p. 110	• The accusative forms of **kein**, p. 110 • The verb **dürfen**, p. 111	• Fruits, vegetables, fish, and meat, p. 109 • Reasons not to eat certain foods, p. 110	Expressing likes and dislikes, p. 109 **(Kap. 10, I)**; **Essen**, p. 109 **(Kap. 6, I)**; Saying how often you do things, p. 109 **(Kap. 7, I)**; **Weil** and **denn**, p. 110 **(Kap. 8, I)**; Talking about how things taste, p. 110 **(Kap. 6, I)**; Giv-ing reasons, p. 110 **(Kap. 8, I)**; **Kein**, p. 110 **(Kap. 9, I)**; **Man**, p. 111 **(Kap. 9, I)**

Zum Lesen pp. 112–113	Bleibt fit und gesund!	**Reading Strategy** Activating your background knowledge	
Mehr Grammatikübungen	**pp. 114–117** Erste Stufe, pp. 114–115	Zweite Stufe, p. 116	Dritte Stufe, pp. 116–117
Review pp. 118–121	Anwendung, pp. 118–119 Zum Schreiben: Doing research (Writing a health column for a newspaper)	Kann ich's wirklich?, p. 120	Wortschatz, p. 121

CULTURE

- Interviews of German teenagers, p. 99
- Landeskunde: Was tust du, um gesund zu leben? p. 104
- Survey on health habits, p. 105
- Ein wenig Landeskunde: Bioläden and Reformhäuser, p. 108

Kapitel 4: Gesund leben
Chapter Resources

Lesson Planning
One-Stop Planner
Lesson Planner with Substitute Teacher Lesson Plans, pp. 17–21, 68
Student Make-Up Assignments
- Make-Up Assignment Copying Masters, Chapter 4

Listening and Speaking
TPR Storytelling Book, pp. 24–31
Listening Activities
- Student Response Forms for Listening Activities, pp. 27–30
- Additional Listening Activities 4-1 to 4-6, pp. 31–34
- Additional Listening Activities (song), p. 30
- Scripts and Answers, pp. 119–124

Video Guide
- Teaching Suggestions, pp. 24–25
- Activity Masters, pp. 26–28
- Scripts and Answers, pp. 89–90, 112

Activities for Communication
- Communicative Activities, pp. 19–24
- Realia and Teaching Suggestions, pp. 86–89
- Situation Cards, pp. 129–130

Reading and Writing
Reading Strategies and Skills Handbook, Chapter 4
Lies mit mir! 2, Chapter 4
Übungsheft, pp. 37–48

Grammar
Grammatikheft, pp. 28–36
Grammar Tutor for Students of German, Chapter 4

Assessment
Testing Program
- Grammar and Vocabulary Quizzes, **Stufe** Quizzes, and Chapter Test, pp. 79–96
- Score Sheet, Scripts and Answers, pp. 97–104

Alternative Assessment Guide
- Portfolio Assessment, p. 21
- Performance Assessment, p. 35
- CD-ROM Assessment, p. 49

Student Make-Up Assignments
- Alternative Quizzes, Chapter 4

Online Activities
- Interaktive Spiele
- Internet Aktivitäten

Video Program
- Videocassette 2
- Videocassette 5 (captioned version)
- DVD Tutor, Disc 1

Audio Compact Discs
- Textbook Listening Activities, CD 4, Tracks 1–15
- Additional Listening Activities, CD 4, Tracks 21–27
- Assessment Items, CD 4, Tracks 16–20

Interactive CD-ROM Tutor, Disc 1

Teaching Transparencies
- Situations 4-1 to 4-2
- Vocabulary 4-A to 4-B
- Los geht's!
- Mehr Grammatikübungen Answers
- Grammatikheft Answers

 **One-Stop Planner CD-ROM**

Use the **One-Stop Planner CD-ROM with Test Generator** to aid in lesson planning and pacing.

For each chapter, the **One-Stop Planner** includes:
- Editable lesson plans with direct links to teaching resources
- Printable worksheets from resource books
- Direct launches to the HRW Internet activities
- Video and audio segments
- Test Generator
- Clip Art for vocabulary items

Kapitel 4: Gesund leben

Projects

Ein super Fitnessprogramm

In this project students will create a fitness program advertised by a fictional health center.

MATERIALS
✂ Students may need
- large piece of construction paper
- ads from fitness magazines and health food stores
- scissors
- glue or tape
- markers

OUTLINE

Students' programs should include the following information:

- Introduction to new members
- Outline for an exercise program
- Nutritional information and program
- At least 2 seminars that are offered. Include a topic and a brief (2-3 sentences) summary of the lecture.

SUGGESTED SEQUENCE

1. In pairs or individually, students begin by making an outline of what they plan to include in the various parts of their program. They should look at several magazines and ads for ideas.
2. Students then gather all information to make their program appealing to potential members. Encourage students to use some realia in each part of their program.
3. Students do the actual layout and write-up of their program and glue or tape it on the construction paper.
4. Students present their final project to the class in a short oral presentation.
5. Optional: Ask students to vote on whose program provided the best overall choices for improving their physical fitness.

GRADING THE PROJECT
Suggested point distribution (total = 100 points)
- Originality and design............................30
- Written assignment 40
- Oral presentation..................................30

Games

Ratet mal, was ich bin!

This game will help students review the food and health vocabulary presented in this chapter.

Preparation Write the names of food items from this chapter and previous chapters on index cards.

Procedure Ask one of the students to come to the front of the class and pick a card. He or she "becomes" the food item on that card and tells the class **Ratet mal, was ich bin!** The other students then ask **ja/nein** questions in order to determine what food item he or she is.

Examples:

Hast du viele Kalorien?

Bist du gesund?

Isst man dich zum Mittagessen?

Kann man dich beim Bäcker kaufen?

Bist du eine Obstsorte?

Bist du eine Gemüsesorte?

The student who guesses the correct food item comes to the front of the class, and the game begins again.

Storytelling

Mini-Geschichte

This story accompanies Teaching Transparency 4-2. Read the Mini-Geschichte to your students or have them role-play the conversation using appropriate gestures and facial expressions. Ask students to complete the reply of the salesperson at the end of the conversation.

Gratis einkaufen – gibt's das?

VERKÄUFERIN:	Guten Morgen! Was darf es sein?
FRAU SPARGUT:	Guten Morgen! Was haben Sie heute im Angebot?
VERKÄUFERIN:	Wir haben Pilze und Blumenkohl im Angebot. Die Butter kostet nur 1,10. Wir haben auch gegrilltes Hähnchen für 4,50 Euro das Stück.
FRAU SPARGUT:	Die Pilze sind viel zu teuer. Leider bin ich allergisch gegen Blumenkohl. Butter macht dick und gegrilltes Hähnchen schmeckt mir nicht.
VERKÄUFERIN:	Tja, dann …
FRAU SPARGUT:	Geben Sie mir drei Kirschen! Wie viel macht das?
VERKÄUFERIN:	Die Kirschen sind gratis.
FRAU SPARGUT:	Prima. Dann nehm ich ein Kilo.
VERKÄUFERIN:	Aber …

Traditions

Die Alsterschwäne

Die Alsterschwäne sind mit der Tradition Hamburgs eng verbunden. Schon im 11. Jahrhundert zierte ein Schwan das Wappen der Schauenburger Grafen.

Eine Mühlenabrechnung von 1591 belegt, dass die Hansestadt schon damals Gerste, Hafer und anderes Getreide zur Fütterung der Schwäne gekauft hat. 1664 wurden die Tiere unter besonderen Schutz gestellt. Es war fortan bei Strafe verboten, die Tiere zu verletzen oder zu töten. Zur Internationalen Gartenbauausstellung 1953 ließ Königin Elizabeth II. zwei Schwäne als Geschenk mit British Airways einfliegen. Seit 1818 sorgt ein von der Stadt bezahlter „Schwanenvater" für die Schwäne. Er füttert sie, kümmert sich um verletzte Tiere und bringt die ungefähr 120 Schwäne im Winter auf den eigens für sie eisfrei gehaltenen Mühlenteich.

Have students research in the library or on the Internet coats of arms. What animals are commonly depicted and why? Have students present their research to the class.

Rezept

Rote Grütze
Für 4 Personen

Zutaten

kg=Kilogramm, g=Gramm, l=Liter

1kg	Beeren in beliebiger Mischung (Himbeeren, rote und schwarze Johannisbeeren, Erdbeeren)
250g	Zucker
80g	Speisestärke

Zubereitung

Gewaschene Beeren mit 1/4 l Wasser und Zucker zum Kochen bringen. Ein Sieb mit einem feuchten Tuch auslegen und die Früchte hineinschütten. Den Saft ohne Druck durch das Tuch in einen Topf laufen lassen. Wenn nötig, mit Wasser auf 1 l Flüssigkeit ergänzen. Saft aufkochen. Speisestärke mit etwas kaltem Wasser anrühren, unter den Saft rühren und mehrfach aufkochen lassen. In eine Schüssel gießen und im Kühlschrank kalt werden lassen. Vor dem Servieren auf einen Teller stürzen. Bei Tisch füllt sich jeder Rote Grütze und Milch, Sahne oder Vanillesauce auf seinen Teller.

Kapitel 4: Gesund leben
Technology

Videocassette 2, 5 (captioned version)
DVD Tutor, Disc 1
See Video Guide, pages 23–28

DVD/Video

Los geht's! • Wie fühlst du dich?
Renate Sprick, the athletics teacher at the **Helene-Lange-Gymnasium** in Hamburg, interviews Nicolas and his friends, asking them what they do to lead a healthy life.

Landeskunde
Was tust du, um gesund zu leben?
People from Germany discuss their eating and exercising habits and philosophies.

Fortsetzung
The teacher interviews one more student.

Videoclips
- **Balance**® (nutritional products)
- **Livio**® (cooking oil)
- **Frosta Mahlzeit**® (frozen dinners)
- **Creme Mouson**® (facial cream)

Interactive CD-ROM Tutor

Activity	Activity Type	Pupil's Edition Reference
1. Wortschatz	Wort und Bild Erfahren/Wählen	p. 99
2. Grammatik	Was kommt dann?	pp. 101, 102
3. Grammatik	Was fehlt?	p. 106
4. Wortschatz	Merkspiel	p. 109
5. So sagt man das!	Was ist richtig?	pp. 100, 103, 107, 108, 110
6. Grammatik	Was fehlt?	p. 111
Landeskunde gesund zu leben? Was ist richtig?	Was tust du, um	p. 104
Zum Sprechen	*Guided recording*	pp. 118–119
Zum Schreiben	*Guided writing*	pp. 118–119

Teacher Management System
Launch the program, type "admin" in the password area, and press RETURN. Log on to **www.hrw.com/CDROMTUTOR** for a detailed explanation of the Teacher Management System.

DVD Tutor

The *DVD Tutor* contains all material from the *Video Program* as described above. German captions are available for use at your discretion for all sections of the video. The *DVD Tutor* also provides a variety of video-based activities that assess students' understanding of **Los geht's!, Fortsetzung,** and **Landeskunde,** as well as the new **Grammatik im Kontext** presentations.

The *DVD Tutor* may be used on any DVD video player connected to a television or video monitor.

One-Stop Planner CD-ROM

To preview all resources available for this chapter, use the **One-Stop Planner CD-ROM**, Disc 1.

Visit Holt Online
go.hrw.com
KEYWORD: WK3 HAMBURG-4
Online Edition

Go.Online!

Premier Online Edition

The Premier Online Edition for Komm mit! *allows students access to their textbooks anytime, anywhere.*

- Audio at point of use
- Additional practice activities
- Self-test activities
- Online reference tools
- Entire Video Program
- Interactive Notebook

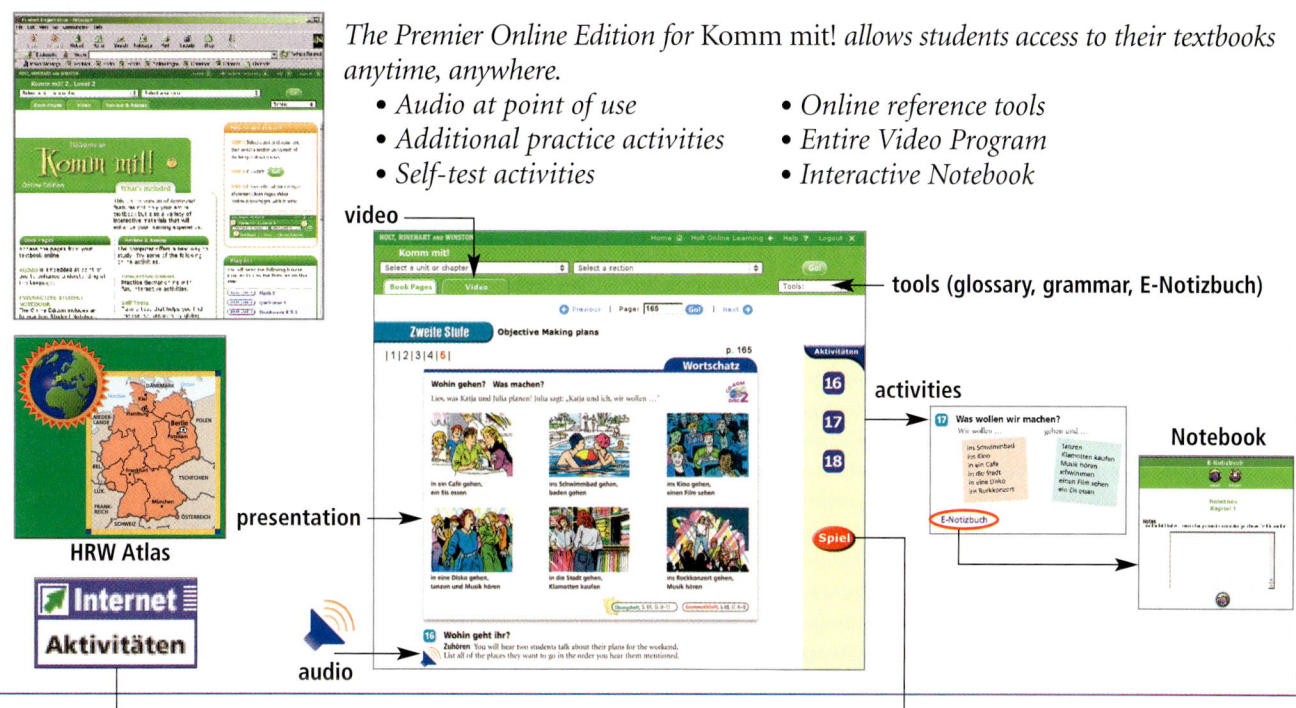

Internet Aktivitäten

These guided internet activities include a worksheet and pre-selected and pre-screened authentic web sites from the German-speaking countries. You can use these activities

- to help students develop research skills in the target language
- to introduce students to authentic cultural information
- as a project

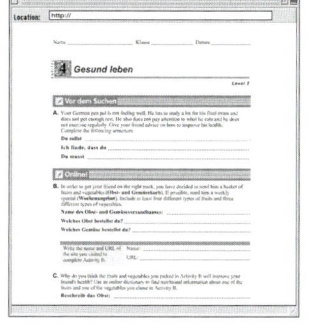

Interaktive Spiele

You can use the interactive activities in this chapter

- to practice grammar, vocabulary, and chapter functions
- as homework
- as an assessment option
- as a self-test
- to prepare for the Chapter Test

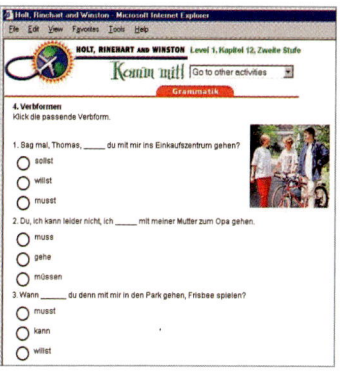

Webprojekt Have students find information about a **Gesundheitsurlaub** or a **Gesundheitskur** in a German-speaking country. Students should provide the name of the place they chose and its location. They should report on the activities that are offered, the food that is served, and the health benefits that are promised. Encourage students to exchange useful Web sites with their classmates. Have students document their sources by referencing the names and URLs of all the sites they consulted.

STANDARDS: 1.2, 2.2, 3.1, 3.2, 5.1   KAPITEL 4   TECHNOLOGY   93F

Kapitel 4: Gesund leben
Textbook Listening Activities Scripts

Erste Stufe

8 p. 100

Der Gesundheitsmuffel! Ja, ich kenne einen. Er treibt selbst überhaupt keinen Sport. Na ja, Fußball liebt er heiß und innig, aber nur als Zuschauer. Er schaut den ganzen Tag Fernsehen. Dabei raucht er eine Zigarette nach der anderen. Wenn er müde wird, trinkt er literweise Kaffee. Er mag am liebsten Schweinefleisch. Außer Kartoffeln isst er kein Gemüse, und Obst schmeckt ihm nur mit viel Zucker und Schlagsahne obendrauf. Kennst du auch so einen Gesundheitsmuffel?

Answers to Activity 8
Treibt keinen Sport; schaut den ganzen Tag Fernsehen; raucht; trinkt Kaffee; mag Schweinefleisch am liebsten; isst kein Gemüse außer Kartoffeln; isst viel Zucker und Schlagsahne.

12 p. 101

1. JASMIN   Ich bin sehr sportlich! Dreimal pro Woche geh ich direkt nach der Schule schwimmen. Und wenn das Wetter schön ist, mache ich oft am Wochenende eine Fahrradtour mit Freunden.
   KLAUS   Spitze! Darf ich nächstes Wochenende mitfahren?

2. ELKE   Ich esse fast kein Fleisch, eigentlich nur Gemüse, Obst, Käse, Brot, und so weiter. Alkohol trinke ich nicht gern, schmeckt mir normalerweise nicht. Ich tanze sehr gern und mache zweimal die Woche Gymnastik.
   KLAUS   Das finde ich toll, Elke! Du siehst auch ziemlich fit aus.

3. PETER   Eigentlich brauche ich jeden Tag meine acht Stunden Schlaf, sonst fühle ich mich nicht wohl. Meistens aber schlafe ich nur sechs Stunden oder so. Normalerweise trainiere ich zweimal pro Woche morgens in einer Fußballmannschaft, aber ich bin oft zu müde dazu.
   KLAUS   Das ist schade! Mensch, geh doch früher ins Bett!

Answers to Activity 12
1. positiv 2. positiv 3. negativ

16 p. 102

Ich schlafe immer genügend und halte mich sehr fit. Jeden Morgen laufe ich zwei Kilometer. Dann esse ich frisches Obst und Müsli zum Frühstück. Man soll sich schließlich richtig ernähren. Bei der Arbeit trinke ich keinen Kaffee mehr, nur Saft und Wasser. Ich esse sehr viel Gemüse und Fisch, und selten auch mal Rindfleisch. Ich bin zwar gern draußen, aber ich vermeide die Sonne.

Answers to Activity 16
schläft genügend; läuft jeden Morgen; isst Obst und Müsli; trinkt nur Saft und Wasser; isst viel Gemüse und Fisch; selten Rindfleisch; vermeidet die Sonne

Zweite Stufe

23 p. 105

Guten Abend, meine Damen und Herren! Unsere heutige Sendung informiert Sie über die Sportgewohnheiten der deutschen Bevölkerung. Bei den Männern steht dabei Fußball an erster Stelle. 43% aller sporttreibenden deutschen Männer spielen mindestens einmal pro Woche Fußball, aber nur 4% aller sporttreibenden Frauen! Aber 50% der Frauen machen wöchentlich Aerobik und Jazztanz; die Männer sind hier nur mit 2% repräsentiert. Dafür liegt die Zahl der Teilnehmer am Bodybuilding am höchsten! 80% der gesamten sporttreibenden deutschen Bevölkerung sind Mitglied in einem Klub; Männer und Frauen sind mit jeweils 40% dabei. Sie trainieren im Durchschnitt zweimal die Woche.

Answers to Activity 23
Fußball: 43% Männer; 4% Frauen; (mind. einmal pro Woche)
Aerobik/Jazztanz: 50% Frauen; 2% Männer; (wöchentlich)
Bodybuilding: 40% Männer; 40% Frauen; (zweimal pro Woche)

27 p. 107

Im Vergleich zu den Amerikanern gehen die meisten Deutschen ziemlich oft zu Fuß, weil sie es gesund finden, viel an der frischen Luft zu sein. Der Sonntagsspaziergang nach dem Mittagessen ist nach wie vor sehr beliebt. Außerdem spielen die Deutschen auch gerne Squash und Tennis, weil es einen fit hält. An den Schulen gibt es normalerweise

The following scripts are for the listening activities found in the *Pupil's Edition*. For Student Response Forms, see *Listening Activities*, pages 27–30. To provide students with additional listening practice, see *Listening Activities*, pages 31–34.

For resource information, see the **One-Stop Planner** CD-ROM, Disc 1.

keine Mannschaften. Deshalb sind viele Deutsche Mitglieder in einem Fitnessklub oder Sportverein. Heutzutage vermeiden die Deutschen es auch, so viel zu rauchen, denn es ist total ungesund!

Answers to Activity 27
1. walk
2. squash; tennis; it keeps you fit.
3. have school teams; members in a sport club
4. smoking; it is unhealthy.

Dritte Stufe

31 p. 109

BETTINA   Mein Lieblingsessen ist Fisch. Fisch schmeckt toll, und hier in Hamburg kriegt man die Salzwasserfische ganz frisch. Am liebsten mag ich Krabben!

ROLAND   Ich mag keine Grapefruit! Die sind meistens viel zu sauer. Aber dafür esse ich Kirschen unheimlich gern! Die sind viel süßer.

RICHARD   Blumenkohl finde ich gar nicht lecker. Er schmeckt mir nicht, aber sonst esse ich alle Gemüsesorten gern. Ja, und dann Fleisch, besonders Rind- und Schweinefleisch mag ich überhaupt nicht. Ich will Kühe und Schweine nicht essen, weil sie nette Tiere sind!

Answers to Activity 31
Bettina: mag Fisch und Krabben, weil sie frisch sind.
Roland: mag Grapefruit nicht, weil sie sauer sind; mag Kirschen, weil sie süß sind.
Richard: mag Blumenkohl nicht, weil er nicht schmeckt; mag Fleisch nicht, weil Tiere nett sind und er sie nicht essen will.

34 p. 110

ANNELIESE   Ich darf noch gar nicht mit dem Auto fahren, weil ich noch nicht 18 bin!

ULRIKE   Ich darf nicht so spät abends ausgehen und soll schon um 10 Uhr wieder zu Hause sein!

NORBERT   Ich darf kein Fleisch essen.

JÖRG   In der Klasse darf ich meine Lieblingszeitschrift nicht lesen.

Answers to Activity 34
Anneliese b; Ulrike d; Norbert c; Jörg a

Anwendung

1 p. 118

1. Der Gesundheitsminister appelliert an die Raucher: Aus gesundheitlichen Gründen vermeiden Sie es bitte, in Zimmern zu rauchen, in denen sich auch Nichtraucher aufhalten!

2. Tanzen Sie sich fit! Das City-Sportstudio lädt zu einer kostenlosen Stunde im Jazztanz oder Jitterbug ein! Machen Sie mit! Unsere Kurse laufen täglich! Schauen Sie noch heute bei uns herein!

3. Guten Abend, liebe Zuhörer! Hier ist Ihr Sender WDR-Y mit dem 9-Uhr-Abendprogramm. Relaxen Sie heute eine Stunde lang bei Mozarts Kleiner Nachtmusik bevor Sie ins Bett gehen, damit Sie morgen früh um sechs frisch und ausgeschlafen den Tag beginnen können!

4. Haben Sie heute schon Ihre Vitamine bekommen? Wenn nicht, dann auf zum Aldo-Markt! Wir haben für Sie eine große Auswahl von gartenfrischem Obst und Gemüse. Täglich neue Sonderangebote!

Answers to Activity 1
1. d; 2. a; 3. c; 4. b

5 Activity 5, p. 118

Hallo! Hier ist Peter Buschmann. Ich rufe an, weil ich ein Problem habe. Es geht mir nämlich gar nicht gut. Mir ist total schlecht geworden, nachdem ich eine große Tüte Kartoffelchips gegessen habe. Vorher habe ich mir, wie auch sonst jeden Tag, eine Portion Pommes frites mit Mayonnaise vom Imbiss geholt. Ich weiß echt nicht, warum mir schlecht ist, denn ich habe sonst nichts gegessen. Ich war den ganzen Tag in der Wohnung und habe nur Fernsehen geschaut! Wir haben nämlich Schulferien. Also, hoffentlich habe ich nichts Schlimmes! Ich bin doch erst 14 Jahre alt!

Answers to Activity 5
Peter Buschmann; 14 Jahre alt; Schüler; ihm ist schlecht; hat sich ungesund ernährt; soll Sport machen und frisches Obst und Gemüse essen

Kapitel 4: Gesund leben
Suggested Lesson Plans 50-Minute Schedule

Day 1

LOCATION OPENER 15 min.
- Present **Location Opener**, pp. 90–93
- Show **Hamburg** Video
- Do Viewing and Post-viewing Activities, Video Guide, p. 22

CHAPTER OPENER 10 min.
- Culture Note, ATE, p. 93M
- Building on Previous Skills, ATE, p. 93M

LOS GEHT'S! 20 min.
- Preteaching Vocabulary, ATE, p. 93N
- Have students read **Los geht's!**, pp. 96–97
- Teaching Suggestions, Video Guide, p. 24
- Show **Los geht's!** Video

Wrap-Up 5 min.
- Students respond to questions about how they keep themselves fit

Homework Options
Pupil's Edition, p. 98, Comprehension Acts.
Übungsheft, p. 37, Act. 1
Internet Aktivitäten, see ATE, p. 93F

Day 2

ERSTE STUFE
Quick Review 10 min.
- Bell Work, ATE, p. 93O
- Check homework, p. 98, Comprehension Acts.

Wortschatz, p. 99 15 min.
- Read **Gesundheitstips**, p. 99
- Presenting **Wortschatz**, ATE, p. 93O
- Teaching Transparency 4-1
- Do Activity 7, p. 99
- Play Audio CD for Activity 8, p. 100

Ein wenig Grammatik, p. 100 10 min.
- Presenting **Ein wenig Grammatik**, ATE, p. 93O
- Do Activity 9, p. 100

So sagt man das!, p. 100 10 min.
- Presenting **So sagt man das!**, ATE, p. 93O
- Do Activity 11, p. 100
- Play Audio CD for Activity 12, p. 101

Wrap-Up 5 min.
- Students respond to questions about what German teens do to stay healthy

Homework Options
Pupil's Edition, p. 100, Act. 10
Grammatikheft, pp. 28–29, Acts. 1–4
Übungsheft, pp. 38–39, Acts. 1–3

Day 3

ERSTE STUFE
Quick Review 10 min.
- Check homework, Grammatikheft, pp. 28–29, Acts. 1–4

Ein wenig Grammatik/Wortschatz, p. 101 10 min.
- Presenting **Ein wenig Grammatik**, ATE, p. 93P
- Do Activity 13, p. 101
- Present **Wortschatz**, p. 101
- Do Activity 14, p. 101

Grammatik, p. 102 25 min.
- Presenting **Grammatik**, ATE, p. 93Q
- Do Activity 15, p. 102
- Play Audio CD for Activity 16, p. 102
- Do Activity 17, p. 102
- Do Activities 6 and 7, p. 40, Übungsheft

Wrap-Up 5 min.
- Students respond to questions about how they feel and how others feel

Homework Options
Grammatikheft, p. 30, Act. 5
Übungsheft, pp. 39–40, Acts. 4–5

Day 4

ERSTE STUFE
Quick Review 10 min.
- Check homework, Übungsheft, pp. 39–40, Acts. 4–5

Wortschatz, p. 103 15 min.
- Presenting **Wortschatz**, ATE, p. 93Q
- Do Activities 18, 19, 20, 21, and 22, p. 103

LANDESKUNDE 20 min.
- Pre-viewing Suggestion, Video Guide, p. 24
- Culture Notes, ATE, p. 93R
- Language Note, ATE, p. 93R
- Show **Landeskunde** Video
- Do Activities A and B, p. 104
- Do **Landeskunde** Activity, Interactive CD-ROM

Wrap-Up 5 min.
- Students respond to questions about where they feel comfortable

Homework Options
Grammatikheft, p. 30, Act. 6
Übungsheft, p. 41, Acts. 1–3

Day 5

ERSTE STUFE
Quick Review 15 min.
- Check homework, Grammatikheft, p. 30, Act. 6

Quiz Review 15 min.
- Do **Mehr Grammatikübungen, Erste Stufe**

Quiz 20 min.
- Quiz 4-1A or 4-1B

Homework Options
Activities for Communication, p. 86, read and fill out Realia 4-1

Day 6

ZWEITE STUFE
Quick Review and PE Activities 25 min.
- Return and review Quiz 4-1
- Check homework, Realia 4-1
- Bell Work, ATE, p. 93S
- Play Audio CD for Activity 23, p. 105
- Do Activity 24, p. 105

Grammatik, p. 106 20 min.
- Presenting **Grammatik**, ATE, p. 93T
- Present **Sprachtipp**, p. 106
- Do Activities 25 and 26, p. 106

Wrap-Up 5 min.
- Students respond to questions about how often they do various sports

Homework Options
Grammatikheft, p. 31, Act. 7
Übungsheft, pp. 42–43, Acts. 1–4

One-Stop Planner CD-ROM

For alternative lesson plans by chapter section, to create your own customized plans, or to preview all resources available for this chapter, use the **One-Stop Planner CD-ROM**, Disc 1.

 For additional homework suggestions, see activities accompanied by this symbol throughout the chapter.

Day 7

ZWEITE STUFE

Quick Review 10 min.
- Check homework, Übungsheft, pp. 42–43, Acts. 1–4

So sagt man das!, p. 107 15 min.
- Presenting **So sagt man das!**, ATE, p. 93T
- Play Audio CD for Activity 27, p. 107
- Do Activities 28 and 29, p. 107

Ein wenig Landeskunde, p. 108 10 min.
- Presenting **Ein wenig Landeskunde**, ATE, p. 93T
- Do Activity 30, p. 108

Wortschatz, p. 108 10 min.
- Presenting **Wortschatz**, ATE, p. 93T
- Do Activity 9, p. 32, Grammatikheft

Wrap-Up 5 min.
- Students answer questions about how often they do things for their health

Homework Options
Grammatikheft, p. 32, Acts. 8, 10
Übungsheft, pp. 43–44, Acts. 5–7

Day 8

ZWEITE STUFE

Quick Review 15 min.
- Check homework, Grammatikheft, p. 32, Acts. 8–10

Quiz Review 15 min.
- Do **Mehr Grammatikübungen, Zweite Stufe**
- Do Additional Listening Activities 4-3 and 4-4, pp. 32–33

Quiz 20 min.
- Quiz 4-2A or 4-2B

Homework Options
Activities for Communication, pp. 129–130, prepare Situation 4-2

Day 9

DRITTE STUFE

Quick Review 10 min.
- Return and review Quiz 4-2
- Bell Work, ATE, p. 93U
- Do Situation 4-2

Wortschatz, p. 109 15 min.
- Presenting **Wortschatz**, ATE, p. 93U
- Teaching Transparencies 4-2, 4-A, 4-B
- Play Audio CD for Activity 31, p. 109
- Do Activity 32, p. 109

Wortschatz/Ein wenig Grammatik, p. 110 10 min.
- Presenting **Wortschatz**, ATE, p. 93U
- Presenting **Ein wenig Grammatik**, ATE, p. 93U
- Do Activity 33, p. 110

So sagt man das!, p. 110 10 min.
- Presenting **So sagt man das!**, ATE, p. 93V
- Play Audio CD for Activity 34, p. 110
- Do Activity 35, p. 111

Wrap-Up 5 min.
- Students respond to questions about what they like and don't like to eat

Homework Options
Grammatikheft, pp. 33–34, Acts. 11–13
Übungsheft, pp. 45–46, Acts. 1–2

Day 10

DRITTE STUFE

Quick Review 10 min.
- Check homework, Grammatikheft, pp. 33–34, Acts. 11–13

Grammatik, p. 111 15 min.
- Presenting **Grammatik**, ATE, p. 93V
- Do Activities 36, 37, and 38, p. 111

ZUM LESEN 20 min.
- Present **Lesestrategie**, p. 112
- Do Activities 1–8, pp. 112–113

Wrap-Up 5 min.
- Students respond to questions about what they are not allowed to do

Homework Options
Grammatikheft, pp. 35–36, Acts. 14–16
Übungsheft, pp. 46–47, Acts. 3–7; p. 48, Acts. 1–4

Day 11

DRITTE STUFE

Quick Review 15 min.
- Check homework, Übungsheft, pp. 46–47, Acts. 3–7; p. 48, Acts. 1–4

Quiz Review 15 min.
- Show **Fortsetzung** Video
- Do **Mehr Grammatikübungen, Dritte Stufe**

Quiz 20 min.
- Quiz 4-3A or 4-3B

Homework Options
Pupil's Edition, p. 120, **Kann ich's wirklich?**
Interaktive Spiele, see ATE, p. 93F

Day 12

ANWENDUNG

Quick Review 30 min.
- Return and review Quiz 4-3
- Check homework, p. 120, **Kann ich's wirklich?**
- Do Acts. 1–5, p. 118, Act. 7, p. 119

Chapter Review 20 min.
- Review chapter functions, vocabulary, and grammar; choose from **Mehr Grammatikübungen**, Grammar Tutor for Students of German, Activities for Communication, Listening Activities, Interactive CD-ROM Tutor, or **Interaktive Spiele**
- Review test format and provide sample test items for students

Homework Options
Pupil's Edition, p. 119, Act. 6, **Zum Schreiben**
Study for Chapter Test

Assessment

Test, Chapter 4 45 min.
- Administer Chapter Test 4. Select from Testing Program, Alternative Assessment Guide, or Test Generator.

Kapitel 4: Gesund leben
Suggested Lesson Plans 90-Minute Schedule

Block 1

LOCATION OPENER 15 min.
- Present **Location Opener,** pp. 90–93
- Show **Hamburg** Video
- Do Viewing and Post-viewing Activities, Video Guide, p. 22

CHAPTER OPENER 10 min.
- Culture Note, ATE, p. 93M
- Building on Previous Skills, ATE, p. 93M

LOS GEHT'S! 20 min.
- Preteaching Vocabulary, ATE, p. 93N
- Have students read **Los geht's!,** pp. 96–97
- Teaching Suggestions, Video Guide, p. 24
- Show **Los geht's!** Video

ERSTE STUFE
Wortschatz, p. 99 20 min.
- Read **Gesundheitstips,** p. 99
- Presenting **Wortschatz,** ATE, p. 93O
- Teaching Transparency 4-1
- Do Activity 7, p. 99
- Play Audio CD for Activity 8, p. 100

Ein wenig Grammatik, p. 100 10 min.
- Presenting **Ein wenig Grammatik,** ATE, p. 93O
- Do Activity 9, p. 100

So sagt man das!, p. 100 10 min.
- Presenting **So sagt man das!,** ATE, p. 93O
- Do Activity 11, p. 100
- Play Audio CD for Activity 12, p. 101

Wrap-Up 5 min.
- Students respond to questions about what teenagers in Germany do to stay healthy

Homework Options
Pupil's Edition, p. 98, Comprehension Acts.
Grammatikheft, pp. 28–29, Acts. 1–4
Übungsheft, p. 37, Act. 1; pp. 38–39, Acts. 1–3

Block 2

ERSTE STUFE
Quick Review 10 min.
- Check homework, Grammatikheft, pp. 28–29, Acts. 1–4

Ein wenig Grammatik/Wortschatz, p. 101 15 min.
- Presenting **Ein wenig Grammatik,** ATE, p. 93P
- Do Activity 13, p. 101
- Present **Wortschatz,** p. 101
- Do Activity 14, p. 101

Grammatik, p. 102 25 min.
- Presenting **Grammatik,** ATE, p. 93Q
- Do Activity 15, p. 102
- Play Audio CD for Activity 16, p. 102
- Do Activity 17, p. 102
- Do Activities 6 and 7, p. 40, Übungsheft

Wortschatz, p. 103 15 min.
- Presenting **Wortschatz,** ATE, p. 93Q
- Do Activities 18, 19, 20, 21, and 22, p. 103

LANDESKUNDE 20 min.
- Pre-viewing Suggestion, Video Guide, p. 24
- Culture Notes, ATE, p. 93R
- Language Note, ATE, p. 93R
- Show **Landeskunde** Video
- Do Activities A and B, p. 104
- Do **Landeskunde** Activity, Interactive CD-ROM

Wrap-Up 5 min.
- Students respond to questions about where they feel comfortable

Homework Options
Grammatikheft, p. 30, Acts. 5–6
Übungsheft, pp. 39–40, Acts. 4–5; p. 41, Acts. 1–3

Block 3

ERSTE STUFE
Quick Review 10 min.
- Check homework, Übungsheft, pp. 39–40, Acts. 4–5

Quiz Review 15 min.
- Do **Mehr Grammatikübungen, Erste Stufe**

Quiz 20 min.
- Quiz 4-1A or 4-1B

ZWEITE STUFE 20 min.
- Play Audio CD for Activity 23, p. 105
- Do Activity 24, p. 105

Grammatik, p. 106 20 min.
- Presenting **Grammatik,** ATE, p. 93T
- Present **Sprachtipp,** p. 106
- Do Activities 25 and 26, p. 106

Wrap-Up 5 min.
- Students respond to questions about how often they do various sports

Homework Options
Grammatikheft, p. 31, Act. 7
Übungsheft, pp. 42–43, Acts. 1–4

 **One-Stop Planner CD-ROM**

For alternative lesson plans by chapter section, to create your own customized plans, or to preview all resources available for this chapter, use the **One-Stop Planner CD-ROM**, Disc 1.

 For additional homework suggestions, see activities accompanied by this symbol throughout the chapter.

Block 4

ZWEITE STUFE

Quick Review 10 min.
- Check homework, Übungsheft, pp. 42–43, Acts. 1–4

So sagt man das!, p. 107 15 min.
- Presenting **So sagt man das!**, ATE, p. 93T
- Play Audio CD for Activity 27, p. 107
- Do Activities 28 and 29, p. 107

Ein wenig Landeskunde, p. 108 10 min.
- Presenting **Ein wenig Landeskunde**, ATE, p. 93T
- Do Activity 30, p. 108

Wortschatz, p. 108 10 min.
- Presenting **Wortschatz**, ATE, p. 93T
- Do Activity 9, p. 32, Grammatikheft

Quiz Review 25 min.
- Do Additional Listening Activities 4-3 and 4-4, pp. 32–33
- Do Activities 8 and 10, p. 32, Grammatikheft
- Do Activities 5–7, pp. 43–44, Übungsheft

Quiz 20 min.
- Quiz 4-2A or 4-2B

Homework Options
Activities for Communication, pp. 129–130, prepare Situation 4-2
Internet Aktivitäten, see ATE, p. 93F

Block 5

DRITTE STUFE

Quick Review 10 min.
- Return and review Quiz 4-2
- Bell Work, ATE, p. 93U
- Do Situation 4-2

Wortschatz, p. 109 15 min.
- Presenting **Wortschatz**, ATE, p. 93U
- Teaching Transparencies 4-2, 4-A, 4-B
- Play Audio CD for Activity 31, p. 109
- Do Activity 32, p. 109
- Do Circumlocution Activity, p. 93X

Wortschatz/Ein wenig Grammatik, p. 110 10 min.
- Presenting **Wortschatz**, ATE, p. 93U
- Presenting **Ein wenig Grammatik**, ATE, p. 93U
- Do Activity 33, p. 110

So sagt man das!, p. 110 10 min.
- Presenting **So sagt man das!**, ATE, p. 93V
- Play Audio CD for Activity 34, p. 110
- Do Activity 35, p. 111

Grammatik, p. 111 20 min.
- Do Activities 36, 37, and 38, p. 111

ZUM LESEN 20 min.
- Present **Lesestrategie**, p. 112
- Do Activities 1–8, pp. 112–113

Wrap-Up 5 min.
- Students respond to questions about what they are not allowed to do

Homework Options
Grammatikheft, pp. 33–36, Acts. 11–16
Übungsheft, pp. 45–47, Acts. 1–7; p. 48, Acts. 1–4

Block 6

DRITTE STUFE

Quick Review 15 min.
- Check homework, Übungsheft, pp. 45–47, Acts. 1–7; p. 48, Acts. 1–4

Quiz Review 20 min.
- Show **Fortsetzung** Video
- Do Mehr Grammatikübungen, Dritte Stufe

Quiz 20 min.
- Quiz 4-3A or 4-3B

ANWENDUNG 30 min.
- Do Activities 1–7, pp. 118–119

Wrap-Up 5 min.
- Students respond to **Kann ich's wirklich?** questions

Homework Options
Pupil's Edition, p. 120, **Kann ich's wirklich?**
Interaktive Spiele, see ATE, p. 93F
Study for Chapter Test

Block 7

ANWENDUNG

Quick Review 15 min.
- Return and review Quiz 4-3
- Check homework, p. 120, **Kann ich's wirklich?**
- Review Anwendung Activities

Chapter Review 30 min.
- Review chapter functions, vocabulary, and grammar; choose from **Mehr Grammatikübungen,** Grammar Tutor for Students of German, Activities for Communication, Listening Activities, Interactive CD-ROM Tutor, or **Interaktive Spiele**
- Review test format and provide sample test items for students

Test, Chapter 4 45 min.
- Administer Chapter 4 Test. Select from Testing Program, Alternative Assessment Guide or Test Generator.

KAPITEL 4   SUGGESTED LESSON PLANS • 90-MINUTE SCHEDULE   **93L**

Kapitel 4: Gesund leben
Teaching Suggestions, pages 94–121

PAGES 94–95

CHAPTER OPENER

Pacing Tips
In the **Erste Stufe,** students learn phrases about good health. The function of 'expressing approval and disapproval' is introduced alongside reflexive verbs (accusative). The determiner **jeder** occurs on p. 106 of the **Zweite Stufe**. Students read about **Bioläden, Vollwertkost,** and **Reformhäuser** on p. 108. In the **Dritte Stufe,** **kein** is reviewed and the modal verb **dürfen** is presented. Because of the longer **Wortschatz** and the complexity of reflexive verbs, you will probably spend more time teaching the **Erste Stufe** than the **Zweite Stufe** or the **Dritte Stufe**. For Lesson Plans and timing suggestions, see pages 93I–93L.

Meeting the Standards
Communication
- Expressing approval and disapproval, p. 100
- Asking for information and responding emphatically or agreeing, with reservations, p. 107
- Asking and telling what you may or may not do, p. 110

Cultures
- Landeskunde, p. 104
- Ein wenig Landeskunde, p. 108
- Culture Note, p. 93M
- Culture Notes, p. 93R

Connections
- Language Note, p. 93R
- Multicultural Connection, p. 93V
- Family Link, p. 93V
- Thinking Critically, p. 93V

Comparisons
- Language-to-Language, p. 93P
- Thinking Critically, p. 93W

Communities
- Career Path, p. 93Q

Building on Previous Skills
Ask students to describe in German what the girls are doing and what they are wearing. Continue by asking your students what they usually wear when they jog or exercise and where they do this.

One-Stop Planner CD-ROM

For resource information, see the **One-Stop Planner CD-ROM,** Disc 1.

Cultures and Communities

Culture Note
Trimm-dich-Pfade (*trails with suggested fitness activities marked along the path*) are very popular and can be found all over Germany. An English equivalent of **trimm dich** might be *get in shape*.

Connections and Comparisons

Thinking Critically
Comparing and Contrasting Make a transparency of the **Stundenplan** in the Level I *Pupil's Edition* on p. 105. Ask students to look for the physical education classes the German students have each week. How does the number of hours per week compare with their own schedules?

Home Economics Connection
Have students consult the home economics teacher to find out the daily recommended servings for fruits and vegetables. (five to nine servings) Then ask students which of the pictured items they typically eat and how many servings of fruits and vegetables they eat each day.

Chapter Sequence
Los geht's! . . . . .p. 96
Erste Stufe . . . . .p. 99
Landeskunde . . . . .p. 104
Zweite Stufe . . . . .p. 105
Dritte Stufe . . . . .p. 109
Zum Lesen . . . . .p. 112
Mehr Grammatikübungen . . . . .p. 114
Anwendung . . . . .p. 118
Kann ich's wirklich? . . . . .p. 120
Wortschatz . . . . .p. 121

LOS GEHT'S!

> ### Teaching Resources
> pp. 96–98
>
> **PRINT**
> - Lesson Planner, p. 17
> - Video Guide, pp. 23–24, 26
> - Übungsheft, p. 37
>
> **MEDIA**
> - One-Stop Planner
> - Video Program
>   **Los geht's!**
>   Videocassette 2, 05:06–08:00
>   Videocassette 5 (captioned version), 21:46–24:40
>   **Fortsetzung**
>   Videocassette 2, 08:04–09:34
>   Videocassette 5 (captioned version), 24:45–26:15
> - DVD Tutor, Disc 1
> - Audio Compact Discs, CD4, Trs. 1–2
> - Los geht's! Transparencies

Fortsetzung

You may choose to continue with the Fortsetzung of *Wie fühlst du dich?* now or wait until later in the chapter. For a synopsis of the **Los geht's!** and **Fortsetzung** episodes, see p. 93E.

Advance Organizer

Ask students what kinds of things they do to stay healthy. Do any of them exercise, eat special foods, or avoid certain foods? Try to discuss as much as possible in German.

> ### Using the Captioned Video/DVD
>
> As an alternative to reading **Los geht's!** on pp. 96–98, you might want to show the captioned version of *Wie fühlst du dich?* available on Videocassette 5.
> Note: The *DVD Tutor* contains captions for all sections of the *Video Program*.

▶ **PAGES 96–97**

Los geht's! Transparencies

> ### Preteaching Vocabulary
>
> **Identifying Keywords**
> Start by asking students to guess the context of the **Los geht's!** episode (interviews about health and how people feel). Then have students use the German they know and the context of the situation to identify key words and phrases that tell what is happening. Students should first list the topics that occur in the interviews and look for words that seem important or that occur several times. Here are some of the words and phrases they might identify as keywords:
>
> ❷ Heimweh
> ❸ gesund; Gesundheit; Gymnastik; jogge; schlafe
> ❹ Mannschaft
> ❺ trainieren
> ❻ Fleisch
> ❼ allergisch
>
> Can they identify the phrase Maike uses to ask Thorsten what he may not eat? (**Gibt es etwas, was du nicht essen darfst?**) Finally, have students identify which of their keywords are cognates.

▶ **PAGE 98**

> ### Comprehension Check
>
> ❶ After students have seen the video, use the five questions in Activity 1 to check for comprehension. This can be done orally. If some students are insecure about answering the questions, have them look back at **Los geht's!**.
>
> ❷ Ask students to read **Los geht's!** with a partner. Monitor students' pronunciation and intonation and make suggestions when needed. Students then answer the six questions in writing.
>
> **Auditory Learners**
> ❸ Ask students to close their books. Write the names of the students from the video on the board. Read the six statements in Activity 3 to the class in German. After each statement, ask students whom this statement best fits. Students choose one of the names on the board. (geht zu Bett, gewöhnlich um zehn Uhr; isst keine Schokolade; wohnt gern in Hamburg; isst Obst und Gemüse; spielt in der Basketballmannschaft; isst nur mageres Fleisch)

STANDARDS: 1.2   KAPITEL 4   LOS GEHT'S!   **93N**

ERSTE STUFE

Teaching Resources
pp. 99–104

PRINT
- Lesson Planner, p. 18
- TPR Storytelling Book, pp. 24–25
- Listening Activities, pp. 27–28, 31–32
- Activities for Communication, pp. 19–20, 86, 89, 129–130
- Grammatikheft, pp. 28–30
- Grammar Tutor for Students of German, Chapter 4
- Übungsheft, pp. 38–40
- Testing Program, pp. 79–82
- Alternative Assessment Guide, p. 35
- Student Make-Up Assignments, Chapter 4

MEDIA
- One-Stop Planner
- Audio Compact Discs, CD4, Trs. 3–5, 16, 21–22
- Teaching Transparencies Situation 4-1
- **Mehr Grammatikübungen** Answers
- Grammatikheft Answers
- Interactive CD-ROM Tutor, Disc 1
- DVD Tutor, Disc 1

PAGE 99

Bell Work
Ask students what one piece of advice they would give somebody to keep healthy and stay fit.

Teaching Suggestion
Ask four volunteers to read the four interviews. Then ask your students which statement they can most identify with. Ask them to read that statement to their partner, making minor changes or deletions as necessary to fit their own situation.

PRESENTING: Wortschatz
To introduce the new expressions, use visual aids such as the symbols on p. 99, flashcards, magazine cutouts, or other pictures. Hold up each visual and give the corresponding expression from the **Wortschatz**. Repeat the expressions several times. Then ask yes/no and either/or questions to help students practice the new vocabulary.

Building on Previous Skills
7 Before students write the 7 **Gebote**, mention that they can use modal verbs such as **sollen, dürfen**, and **müssen**.
Examples:
Man soll vernünftig essen!
Man muss viel Obst essen!
Man darf nicht rauchen!

Communication for All Students

Visual Learners
7 Ask students to match each of the sentences they have written to accompany the symbols to one of the four interviews in the "Gesundheitstipps" selection, according to how well each sentence fits that German student's tips.

PAGE 100

Communication for All Students

Challenge
8 To expand this activity, ask students what they would suggest to the **Gesundheitsmuffel** to help him overcome his **Laster**. Students should use the new **Wortschatz** expressions introduced on p. 99.

PRESENTING: Ein wenig Grammatik
Stem-vowel changes In Level 1 students learned the words **fahren** and **einladen**, two verbs that have stem-vowel changes: **a** changes to **ä** in the **du-** and **er/sie-**forms. Review those two verbs before introducing **schlafen.**

PRESENTING: So sagt man das!
Ask students about expressions of approval and disapproval they commonly use in English and then write some on the board or on a transparency. Have students look at the examples in **So sagt man das!** and ask them what the expressions mean. Use the familiar phrase **Ich glaube, dass …** to review the verb position in dependent clauses. Can students recall another conjunction that requires the verb to be in final position? (**weil**)

Communication for All Students

Challenge
11 After students have chosen the correct replies to Markus' statements, ask them to restate his statements using the conjunction **dass**. This can be done orally or in writing.
Examples:
Das ist prima, dass du regelmäßig Sport machst!
Das finde ich nicht gut, dass du nicht richtig isst!

Challenge
11 On a transparency, list additional statements that refer to healthy or unhealthy habits. Uncover one statement at a time and have students react to each of them using **dass**-clauses.
Examples:
Ich liege oft in der Sonne, denn ich will braun werden.
Mein Bruder raucht zwanzig Zigaretten am Tag.
In meiner Familie essen wir viel Obst, Gemüse und Salat.
Meine Eltern trinken gar keinen Alkohol.
Meine Mutter trinkt sehr viel Kaffee.

Connections and Comparisons

Language-to-Language
You may want to warn your students about using false cognates, also called false friends (*faux amis*). A false cognate is a term in one language that appears to be similar in form or meaning to a term in another language, but that does not have the same meaning.
Examples:
Gift: a present in English, poison in German
Chef: a cook in English, a boss in German
Boot: a shoe in English, a boat in German

Students may remember many more false cognates they have encountered in their German lessons. (Examples: **das Gymnasium**/*gymnasium*; **das Alter**/*alter*; **die** (definite article)/*to die*; **den** (definite article, accusative)/*den*; **man**/*man*; **das Wetter**/*wetter*; **das Kind**/*kind*; **die Kinder**/*kinder*; **gut**/*gut*; **war** (past tense)/*war*; **der See**/*to see*; **das Bad**/*bad*; **das Ding**/*to ding*; **der Roman**/*Roman*; **die Note**/*note*; **der Rock**/*rock*; **links**/*links* (plural); **die Mutter**/*to mutter*; **die Art**/*art*)

▶ PAGE 101

Teaching Suggestion
12 Have students listen to the recording twice before they write down which remarks are positive and which are negative. Then play each of the monologues again, one at a time. Ask students to summarize what Jasmin said. Do the same for Elke's and Peter's reports.

PRESENTING: Ein wenig Grammatik
Für and accusative Divide the class into small groups. Read aloud ten statements in English, each of whose German equivalents should use the preposition **für** plus accusative or a **dass**-clause. Have students work together to write down translations. When all groups have finished, go over the German sentences in class.

PRESENTING: Wortschatz
Give several examples to complete the phrases.
Ich fühle mich wohl, wenn ich richtig esse.
Ich ernähre mich richtig, wenn ich viel Obst und Gemüse esse.
Ich halte mich fit, indem ich dreimal in der Woche jogge.
Then ask students to practice these new expressions by completing the phrases themselves.

Teaching Suggestion
14 After students have finished Activity 14, ask them to form groups according to the **Laster** they share. Then ask students in each group to design a plan to improve their health. They should make fitness as well as dietary changes.

STANDARDS: 1.3, 4.1

PAGE 102

PRESENTING: Grammatik

Reflexive verbs To present the reflexive verb structures, bring several hand-held mirrors to class. Also prepare flashcards with adhesive tape on the back. Make one flashcard using the same color for each subject pronoun in the nominative and another card for each corresponding reflexive pronoun.

ich   —> mich   (in red)
du   —> dich   (in blue)
er/sie   —> sich   (in green)
wir   —> uns   (in orange)
ihr   —> euch   (in purple)
sie *(pl)* —> sich   (in brown)

Then write the different verb conjugations for the verb **sehen** on six different cards, all in black. Look in the mirror and say **Ich sehe mich.** Then hand the mirror to a student and ask him or her to look into it. Tell the student **Du siehst dich** (**im Spiegel**). Turn to the class and, pointing to the student, say **Er/sie sieht sich** (**im Spiegel**). Hand the mirror to two students, have them look at themselves in the mirror, and tell them **Ihr seht euch** (**im Spiegel**). Turn to the class and, pointing at the two students, say **Sie sehen sich** (**im Spiegel**). Finally, look into the mirror with students and say **Wir sehen uns** (**im Spiegel**). Repeat all the sentences you just introduced, and as you do so, tape the corresponding flashcards onto the board. Have different students come to the board and circle each subject pronoun and draw a line to the corresponding reflexive pronoun. Tell students that **ich** and **mich**, **du** and **dich**, **er** and **sich**, and so on, refer to the same person. Explain that a reflexive verb is a verb whose action is turned back (reflected as in the mirror activity) to the subject of the verb.

Teaching Suggestion

16 Have students number lines from 1 to 7 in their notebooks. Then ask them to listen to Mr. Dingsda's report and jot down any information they can understand. Play the recording at least twice. Then play it again, stopping repeatedly so students can fill in the information they have missed. Next, ask students to write the report in short sentences. Have students compare their versions with their partners' versions and make up a composite report.

Cultures and Communities

Career Path

Have students come up with reasons why Americans involved in the fitness or sports medicine industry might find a knowledge of German helpful. (Suggestions: Health clubs are becoming more popular in the German-speaking countries, and an American fluent in German might find a position as an aerobics instructor or personal trainer; many athletes, especially skiers and those who participate in luge competitions, train in the Alps.)

Communication for All Students

A Slower Pace

17 Have students do Activity 17 with a partner. They should read the dialogue and use the **Grammatik** to complete the sentences. You may also want to keep the flashcards taped to the board so students can refer to them as needed. Partners should then switch roles and go over the conversations again.

PAGE 103

PRESENTING: Wortschatz

When people are asked in English how they feel about something, their answers usually vary greatly; they use different expressions to express their feelings. Go over the expressions under the heading **wie?** and give their meanings through synonyms, if possible. Then ask students:
Wie fühlst du dich in dieser Klasse?
Wie fühlst du dich an dieser Schule?
Wie fühlst du dich in dieser Stadt?
Students should use one of the expressions under the heading **wie?** to answer the questions.

Teaching Suggestion

18 Have partners make a list of all the things they think a health conscious person would do and not do. Then as each pair reports, keep track of their ideas on a transparency or on the board. Each idea mentioned by other groups gets five points, each idea mentioned only once gets ten points. The pair with the most points wins.

Teaching Suggestions

19 After students have completed the basic task, ask them to do it again, expanding on their answers and telling why they feel good or bad.
Examples:
— Wie fühlst du dich in dieser Schule?
— Ich fühle mich sehr wohl. Ich habe viele Freunde und die Lehrer sind nett.

or

— Ich fühle mich sehr wohl, weil ich viele Freunde habe und die Lehrer nett sind.

21 After students have completed the written part of this activity, have them get together with another student to exchange what they have written down. Then call on several students to share with the class what their partners wrote about themselves and where they feel most comfortable.

22 Ask students to conduct this conversation as though one of them is being interviewed for an article on teen fitness. Both students should write down the questions and answers from their interview. For additional practice, students could ask two or three more questions than the activity calls for. Since this is a lengthy assignment, you may want to have students work on it during two class periods. Then call on three or four pairs to read their interviews to the rest of the class. To ensure that all students are listening, each pair should ask the class two questions related to the interview to check comprehension.

PAGE 104

LANDESKUNDE

> ### Teaching Resources
> p. 104
>
> **PRINT**
> ▸ Video Guide, pp. 23–24, 26–28
> ▸ Übungsheft, p. 41
>
> **MEDIA**
> ▸ One-Stop Planner
> ▸ Video Program
>   Videocassette 2, 10:12–15:33
> ▸ DVD Tutor, Disc 1
> ▸ Audio Compact Discs, CD4, Trs. 6–9
> ▸ Interactive CD-ROM Tutor, Disc 1

Teaching Suggestion

Do the prereading activity at the top of p. 104. Then make a chart on the board or on a transparency and write on one side **Fitness in den U.S.A.** and on the other side **Fitness in Deutschland und Österreich**. Have students brainstorm what they think might be popular fitness activities in those countries. This will help students build expectations for the **Landeskunde** interviews.

Cultures and Communities

 Culture Notes

• Physical fitness is made important to Germans early in life. The German Sports Federation (**DSB = Deutscher Sportbund**), for example, challenges people of all ages to try for the gold, silver, and bronze **Sportabzeichen**, sports medals for which participants test and challenge their own level of fitness in a number of disciplines.

• **Volksmarsch**, also called **Volkswanderung**, is also a very popular way for Germans to stay fit, enjoy nature, and meet other people. It is an organized hike that varies in length and time (5, 10, or 20 km) for which participants sign up and receive awards for attending.

Connections and Comparisons

Language Note

Herr Troger is from St. Ulrich, in **Tirol**. Ask students if they can guess what the word **bissel** means. Do they see or hear a resemblance to the word **bisschen**? Regina uses the word **arg** at the end of her interview. It is a synonym for **sehr**.

Teaching Suggestion

Ask students how they can combine staying fit with doing something for the environment. Can students list some of the things they do regularly to help in this matter? (Example: riding bikes) Encourage students to use as much German as possible in their discussion. Many of the phrases and expressions they will need to answer this question were taught in Chapter 7 of Level 1. (Examples: **Rad fahren = keine Abgase in der Luft; Biokost essen = keine Pestizide in der Erde; mindestens acht Stunden am Tag schlafen = Licht aus: weniger Energie verbrauchen**)

Teacher Note

Mention to your students that the **Landeskunde** will also be included in Quiz 4-1B given at the end of the **Erste Stufe**.

Teaching Suggestion

To prepare for this activity, cut out several pictures from magazines that show people involved in physical fitness activities or ads for local health food stores. You may want to paste these on construction paper for future activities. Hold up one picture at a time and ask students in what way these people are staying fit or are taking care of themselves. Encourage students to use expressions of approval or disapproval about the featured activities or ads.

Assess

- Testing Program, pp. 79–82
  Quiz 4-1A, Quiz 4-1B
  Audio CD4, Tr. 16
- Student Make-Up Assignments
  Chapter 4, Alternative Quiz
- Alternative Assessment Guide, p. 35

ZWEITE STUFE

Teaching Resources
pp. 105–108

PRINT
- Lesson Planner, p. 19
- TPR Storytelling Book, pp. 26–27
- Listening Activities, pp. 28–29, 32–33
- Activities for Communication, pp. 87, 89, 129–130
- Grammatikheft, pp. 31–32
- Grammar Tutor for Students of German, Chapter 4
- Übungsheft, pp. 42–44
- Testing Program, pp. 83–86
- Alternative Assessment Guide, p. 35
- Student Make-Up Assignments, Chapter 4

MEDIA
- One-Stop Planner
- Audio Compact Discs, CD4, Trs. 10–11, 17, 23–24
- Teaching Transparencies
  Mehr Grammatikübungen Answers
  Grammatikheft Answers
- Interactive CD-ROM Tutor, Disc 1
- DVD Tutor, Disc 1

PAGE 105

Bell Work

In pairs, have students ask each other how they feel in certain situations.
Example: A Wie fühlst du dich beim Tennis?
         B Großartig!
         B Wie fühlst du dich in der Clique?
         A Super!

TPR Total Physical Response

To get students' attention and increase their awareness of physical fitness, introduce them to the **Fünf-Minuten Herzclub!** Give commands, using reflexive verbs such as **sich setzen, sich drehen, sich stellen, sich kämmen,** and other verbs such as **gehen, laufen, bringen, springen, stampfen, klatschen,** and **aufstehen.** Model each of the commands. Give commands to the class as a whole and to individual students.
Examples:
Stellt euch an die Wand!
Dreht euch um!
Klatscht in die Hände!
Kämm dich!
Spring vorwärts!

At the end you may want to ask a few students:
Und wie fühlst du dich jetzt?

For Additional Practice

24 Ask students to use their answers to the questionnaire to write a short, coherent paragraph. Encourage students to use connectors. This could be assigned for homework. You might want to ask two or three students to read their paragraphs in class the following day.

PAGE 106

PRESENTING: Grammatik

The determiner jeder Write the sentence **Jeden Tag esse ich um 12 Uhr.** Underline the ending **-en.** Ask students a) the gender of the word **Tag,** (masculine) and b) in what case **jeden** is used (accusative). Tell students that **jeder** has ending changes just like definite articles. Give other common examples of expressions with **jeder.**
Examples:
Welche Musik   Ich höre jede
  hörst du gern?   Musik gern.

PAGE 107

PRESENTING: So sagt man das!

Ask students to look back at **Los geht's!** on p. 96 and to list the various ways the interviewer initiates the interviews with Nicolas, Maike, David, and Thorsten. After they have made a list of the different ways she asked questions, ask students to provide English equivalents.

Teaching Suggestion

28 As a follow-up to this activity, students could further research this topic on the Internet using a German search engine. For a related online research project, see the **Webprojekt** on p. 93F.

PAGE 108

PRESENTING: Ein wenig Landeskunde

Students have learned reading strategies to help them determine the meaning of compound words. Put the following words on the board and help students infer the meaning of the words before they read the interviews:
Bioläden, Vollwertkost, Reformhäuser, Umweltbewusstsein

Portfolio Assessment

30 You may want to suggest this activity as an oral portfolio item for your students. See *Alternative Assessment Guide,* p. 21.

PRESENTING: Wortschatz

Go over the new words and phrases and help students practice them by asking them how often they do certain activities.
Examples:
Wie oft liest du Bücher?
Wie oft gehst du schwimmen?

Play the game **Ratet mal, was ich bin!** See p. 93C for the procedure.

Assess
▸ Testing Program, pp. 83–86
  Quiz 4-2A, Quiz 4-2B
  Audio CD4, Tr. 17

▸ Student Make-Up Assignments
  Chapter 4, Alternative Quiz

▸ Alternative Assessment Guide, p. 35

DRITTE STUFE

> **Teaching Resources**
> pp. 109–111
>
> **PRINT**
> - Lesson Planner, p. 20
> - TPR Storytelling Book, pp. 28–29
> - Listening Activities, pp. 29, 34
> - Activities for Communication, pp. 21–24, 88, 89, 129–130
> - Grammatikheft, pp. 33–36
> - Grammar Tutor for Students of German, Chapter 4
> - Übungsheft, pp. 45–47
> - Testing Program, pp. 87–90
> - Alternative Assessment Guide, p. 35
> - Student Make-Up Assignments, Chapter 4
>
> **MEDIA**
> - One-Stop Planner
> - Audio Compact Discs, CD4, Trs. 12–13, 18, 25–26
> - Teaching Transparencies
>   Situation 4-2
>   Vocabulary 4-A, 4-B
>   **Mehr Grammatikübungen** Answers
>   **Grammatikheft** Answers
> - Interactive CD-ROM Tutor, Disc 1
> - DVD Tutor, Disc 1

PAGE 109

Bell Work

As a warm-up for the upcoming activities, put the following incomplete statement on the board and ask students to think about how they would complete it:
Meine Mutter sagt, dass ich kein … essen soll, weil …

PRESENTING: Wortschatz

Introduce the new vocabulary using visual aids or a transparency of the items. Point to the foods and tell students what they are. Then ask yes/no questions and either/or questions. Once you think students feel comfortable with the words, ask open-ended questions such as the following:

Wie isst du die Möhren? Roh oder gekocht?
Wie oft isst du Rindfleisch?
Wie schmeckt dir Forelle?
Trinkst du Magermilch? Warum? or Warum nicht?
Wie viele Eier isst du pro Woche?
Was kommt denn so alles in eine gute Hühnersuppe?

PAGE 110

PRESENTING: Wortschatz

Use props or other visual aids to teach the new phrases. For example, hold up a candy bar and tell students: **Die Schokolade will ich nicht essen, denn sie hat zu viel Fett, zu viel Zucker, zu viele Kalorien.** Checking the information on the wrapper, say: **Lass mal sehen, … 500 Kalorien! Das ist zu viel!** Then hold up a carrot and ask students: **Was hat weniger Kalorien: die Möhre oder die Schokolade?** For each of the new expressions, try to use visual aids and make comparisons with previously learned food items to give students plenty of practice.

PRESENTING: Ein wenig Grammatik

Kein Divide the class into two equal teams. Toss a coin to decide which team gets to go first, and then ask a member of that team a question such as **Magst/Isst du Aprikosen?** The student should use **kein** in his or her answer: **Ich mag/esse keine Aprikosen.** Go down the rows asking similar questions, staying with the same team until a student answers incorrectly. Then switch to the other team and ask the same kind of question of those students. Continue in this manner, always returning to the student who answered his or her last question incorrectly when going back and forth between teams. The first team whose members all answer their questions correctly wins.

PRESENTING: So sagt man das!

As you introduce the verb **dürfen,** you may want to explain the difference between **dürfen** and **können.** Usually **dürfen** implies permission and **können** implies ability. Read through the examples in **So sagt man das!,** then provide practice for students by asking questions such as the following:

Was darf ein Diabetiker essen/nicht essen?
Was darf ein Vegetarier essen/nicht essen?
Jim ist allergisch gegen Orangen. Was darf er nicht essen?

PAGE 111

PRESENTING: Grammatik

Dürfen, present tense To practice the forms of **dürfen,** make index cards with pronouns and nouns and combine them with pictures of foods and beverages or activities to prompt students to produce sentences.

Speaking Assessment

37 You could also assign this activity in pairs and have students prepare a dialogue for assessment. You might wish to evaluate their dialogue using the following rubric.

Speaking Rubric	Points			
	4	3	2	1
Content (Complete – Incomplete)				
Comprehension (Total – Little)				
Comprehensibility (Comprehensible – Incomprehensible)				
Accuracy (Accurate – Seldom accurate)				
Fluency (Fluent – Not fluent)				

18–20: A   16–17: B   14–15: C   12–13: D   Under 12: F

Connections and Comparisons

Multicultural Connection
Ask students to find out from exchange students what types of rules they have in their schools and with individual teachers. Ask a few students to report their findings in German to the class, using the verb **dürfen**.

FAMILY LINK

37 After completing this activity, have students interview their family members or friends about allergies. Or you may choose to have a few students interview the school nurse to find out about common allergies among the students at school. Have the students report back to the class and add their findings to the allergies listed on p. 111.

Thinking Critically

37 **Drawing Inferences** Discuss allergies your students or members of their families might have. Write the following words on the board or on a transparency and see if students can guess their meaning:

   Blütenstaub, Katzenhaare, Wolle,
   Medikamente, synthetische Stoffe

Teaching Suggestion

Divide the class into two groups to play *Tic Tac Toe*. Fill the nine squares of the grid with nine infinitive verbs such as **dürfen, können, sollen, müssen, wollen, sich fühlen, sich fit halten, schlafen,** and **sich freuen**. Teams must form sentences in the present tense, using the verb indicated in the square, in order to get an X or an O in a square. The first team to get three in a row wins.

Teacher to Teacher

Haley Crittenden
Herndon High School
Herndon, Virginia

Haley helps students practice **dürfen** with this idea.

"Distribute butcher paper and markers to each group. Students work with a partner to write school rules. Partner A writes the positive rules, e.g., **Wir dürfen jetzt Pause machen.** Partner B writes the negative rules: **Ich darf nicht rauchen.** Students can compete for the craziest rules, for example, **Ich darf meine Katze nicht mit in die Schule bringen.** I like to display the rules in the classroom."

Assess

▸ Testing Program, pp. 87–90
  Quiz 4-3A, Quiz 4-3B
  Audio CD4, Tr. 18

▸ Student Make-Up Assignments
  Chapter 4, Alternative Quiz

▸ Alternative Assessment Guide, p. 35

STANDARDS: 1.3, 4.2, 5.1

> **PAGES 112–113**

ZUM LESEN

Teaching Resources
pp. 112–113

PRINT
- Lesson Planner, p. 21
- Übungsheft, p. 48
- Reading Strategies and Skills, Chapter 4
- Lies mit mir! 2, Chapter 4

MEDIA
- One-Stop Planner

Prereading
Building Context
Ask students to jot down four things they consider important to staying healthy.

Teacher Note
Activity 1 is a prereading activity.

Reading
Teaching Suggestion
Ask students to scan the pictures and titles. Which article would they read first? Ask them to list the words that caught their eye. What type of words are they?

Connections and Comparisons
Thinking Critically
- **Comparing and Contrasting** Ask students if they know of any companies in the United States that provide incentives for their employees to improve their health or encourage physical activity. Students could call companies in their area and make inquiries about such incentives. (Example: Large companies often help pay for membership dues to health clubs.)

- **Drawing Inferences** Can students think of reasons that might have made the German company owner promise money to his non-smoking employees? (Example: Some employees might have complained about second-hand smoke.)

- **Drawing Inferences** After students read the article about **Salat,** ask them to look for specific words that indicate **Salat** isn't necessarily a choice for Germans.

Post-Reading
Teacher Note
Activity 8 is a post-reading task that will show whether students can apply what they have learned.

Teaching Suggestion
Define in German several of the words that appear in the Zum Lesen selections, and ask students to tell you the term to which you are referring.
Examples:
Leute, die keine Zigaretten rauchen. (Nichtraucher)
Leute, die mit dir zusammenarbeiten. (Mitarbeiter)

Zum Lesen Answers
Answers to Activity 1   Examples: eating healthy, no smoking, exercising
Answers to Activity 2   An employer rewards his employees who quit smoking by giving them € 50.
Answers to Activity 3   a. The offer has been very successful; all but one smoker gave up smoking.
b. One employee uses the extra money to pay for his vacation every year.
Answers to Activity 4   a. no reason given
b. no reason implied or hinted at
c. Examples: Non-smokers are healthier and will, therefore, miss fewer days at work.
Answers to Activity 5   A meal without a salad; it's not important whether we like it or not; eating a healthy salad makes up for guilty feelings after eating a hearty pork roast; in general, it is implied that Germans probably prefer the main course to a salad, but a lot of people tend to choose eating healthy foods such as salads these days.
Answers to Activity 6   1. richtig aufwärmen; 2. richtiges Schuhwerk; 3. richtig essen; 4. richtig laufen; 5. richtig kühlen; 6. richtig sitzen
Answers to Activity 7   gymnastics and stretching (Gymnastik und Stretching); Italian soccer players (italienische Fußballstars); out: ice cubes to cool injuries; in: "hot ice"; water near the freezing point

> **PAGES 114–117**

MEHR GRAMMATIKÜBUNGEN

The **Mehr Grammatikübungen** activities are designed as supplemental activities for the grammatical concepts presented in the chapter. You might use them as additional practice, for review, or for assessment.

For more grammar presentations, review, and practice, refer to the following:
- Grammatikheft
- Grammar Tutor for Students of German
- Grammar Summary on pp. R20–R36
- Übungsheft
- Grammar and Vocabulary quizzes (Testing Program)
- Test Generator
- Interactive CD-ROM Tutor
- **Interaktive Spiele** at **go.hrw.com**

PAGES 118–119

ANWENDUNG

Video Wrap-up

Videocassette 2, 05:06–17:52
Videocassette 5 (captioned version), 21:46–26:15
DVD Tutor, Disc 1

At this time, you might want to use the *Video Resources* for additional review and enrichment. These resources are also available via the Enhanced Online Student Edition.

See *Video Guide* for suggestions regarding:

- *Wie fühlst du dich?* Dramatic episode
- **Landeskunde** Interviews
- **Videoclips** Authentic footage

Apply and Assess

A Slower Pace

1 Ask students to read the four summary statements before listening to the recording. Have students come up with words and phrases they expect to hear.

Teaching Suggestion

3 To help students prepare for this assignment, brainstorm with them a brief outline of what the response letter should entail. Remind them to use words and expressions from the **Gesundheitstipps** on p. 99, from the **Wortschatz** on pp. 109 and 110, and expressions of approval and disapproval on p. 100 to help them write their response letter.

Portfolio Assessment

3 You may want to suggest this activity as a written portfolio item for your students. See *Alternative Assessment Guide,* p. 21.

Process Writing

6 Guide your students through this activity by writing the following chart on the board, and suggesting they use a similar one to organize their ideas:

WAS ESSEN?	WIE VIEL UND WIE OFT?	WARUM?
Brokkoli	wenigstens zwei Portionen *(servings)* pro Woche	… weil er wenige Kalorien hat und gut für die Gesundheit ist

Encourage students to include reasons for their recommendations as often as possible, so that their writing will be more persuasive. Allow students to make recommendations using **kein** as well, such as **Man soll keine Schokolade essen, denn es ist zu viel Zucker darin.**

PAGE 120

KANN ICH'S WIRKLICH?

This page helps students prepare for the test. It is a brief checklist of the major points covered in the chapter. The students should be reminded that it is only a checklist and not necessarily everything that will appear on the test.

For additional self check options, refer students to the *Grammar Tutor,* the *Interactive CD-ROM Tutor,* and the Online self-test for this chapter.

PAGE 121

WORTSCHATZ

Review and Assess

Teaching Suggestion

Since many of the new vocabulary items are expressions and phrases, suggest that students write the new phrases on index cards. They should give a context to each phrase by including it in a sentence.

Circumlocution

To review, ask students to describe the foods in the **Dritte Stufe** according to taste, texture, color, and flavor. **Blumenkohl** might be described as **Es ist etwas, das einen milden Geschmack hat. Es ist etwas, das rund, groß und weiß ist.** These descriptions can be used with the circumlocution game, **Das treffende Wort suchen.** See p. 3C for procedures.

Teacher Note

Give the **Kapitel 4** Chapter Test: *Testing Program,* pp. 91–96 Audio CD4, Trs. 19–20.

KAPITEL 4

Gesund leben

Objectives

In this chapter you will learn to

Erste Stufe
- express approval and disapproval

Zweite Stufe
- ask for information and respond emphatically or agree with reservations

Dritte Stufe
- ask and tell what you may or may not do

Visit Holt Online
go.hrw.com
KEYWORD: WK3 HAMBURG-4
Online Edition

◀ Auf unserm Joggingpfad durch den Wald

Los geht's! · *Wie fühlst du dich?*

Los geht's! is an abridged version of the video episode.

CD 4
Trs. 1–2

Strategie Verstehen
Look at the photos that accompany the story. Who are the students pictured? What do you think they are talking about?

Nicolas · Maike · David · Thorsten

Wir haben junge Hamburger Gymnasiasten interviewt. Nicolas stellt uns seine Freunde vor.

①
Nicolas: Das ist unsere Clique, Thorsten, ich, Wiebke, David und Maike. Wir gehen aufs Helene-Lange-Gymnasium. Das ist ein zweisprachiges Gymnasium.

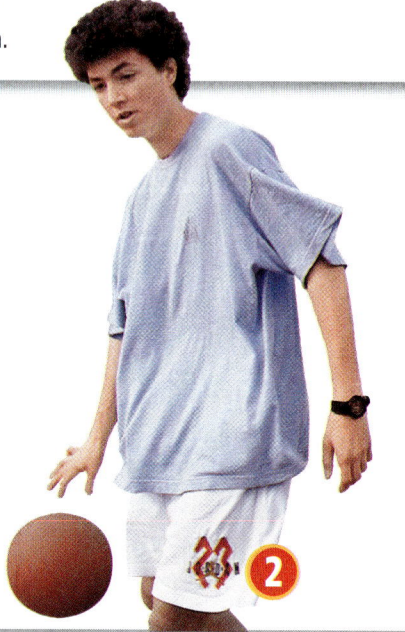

Interviewerin: Kann ich dich mal etwas fragen? Wo kommst du her, und wie fühlst du dich hier in Hamburg?
Nicolas: Ich komme aus Frankreich. Meine Mutter arbeitet für Air France. Ich bin schon sieben Jahre in Hamburg, und ich fühle mich hier sehr wohl.
Interviewerin: Hast du kein Heimweh?
Nicolas: Nein, überhaupt nicht!
Interviewerin: Das freut mich, dass es dir hier so gut gefällt. **②**

96 *sechsundneunzig*   STANDARDS: 1.2   KAPITEL 4   Gesund leben

Interviewerin: Ihr seht alle so gesund aus! Könnt ihr mir mal sagen, was ihr für eure Gesundheit tut?
Maike: Ja, also, ich lebe eigentlich sehr gesund. Ich mache jeden Morgen Gymnastik, und ich jogge, wenn ich Zeit habe. Und ich schlafe auch genug. Jeden Tag gehe ich gewöhnlich um zehn Uhr ins Bett.
Interviewerin: Ich finde es prima, Maike, dass du so gesund lebst.

Interviewerin: Na, David, dann sag uns mal, wie du dich fit hältst!
David: Tja, auch Sport, gesund essen, genügend schlafen. Ich spiele Basketball. Ich freue mich, dass ich auch in der Mannschaft bin. Ich fühle mich sehr wohl in der Mannschaft. Aber leider sind wir dieses Jahr nicht so gut.
Interviewerin: Ach, das wird schon wieder!

Interviewerin: Und Thorsten, wie ist es mit dir? Wie lebst du? Wie hältst du dich fit?
Thorsten: Heute Nachmittag, zum Beispiel, spiele ich Basketball. Ich spiele in unserer Mannschaft. Wir trainieren zweimal die Woche, immer montags und donnerstags. Ja, und dann esse ich vernünftig.

Bei Thorsten in der Küche. Maike ist da.

Maike: Und was isst du so?
Thorsten: Ach, alles, was gesund ist: Obst und Gemüse … und Fisch.
Maike: Und Fleisch? Wie steht es mit Fleisch?
Thorsten: Natürlich esse ich Fleisch! Warum nicht? Aber es muss mager sein!

Maike: Gibt es etwas, was du nicht essen darfst?
Thorsten: Ja, Schokolade.
Maike: Warum nicht?
Thorsten: Ich bin allergisch gegen Schokolade.
Maike: Schade! Ich esse Schokolade gern.
Thorsten: Hier! Kannst du haben!
Maike: Danke schön!

1 Was passiert hier?

These activities check for global comprehension only. Students should not yet be expected to produce language modeled in Los geht's!

Verstehst du alles, was diese Schüler sagen? Beantworte die Fragen!

1. Where is Nicolas from? Why is he living in Hamburg?   1. France. His mother works for Air France in Hamburg.
2. What do Maike, David, and Thorsten do to keep fit?   2. Exercise, eat healthy food, and get plenty of sleep.
3. What kinds of food does Thorsten eat?   3. Fruit, vegetables, fish, and lean meat.
4. What doesn't he eat? Why not?   4. Chocolate. He is allergic to it.
5. Judging by her comments, what do you think the interviewer's attitude towards staying healthy is?   5. Positive.

2

Lies den Text noch einmal und beantworte diese Fragen!

1. Wie heißt die Schule? In welcher Stadt ist sie?   1. Helene-Lange-Gymnasium; in Hamburg.
2. Wie lange wohnt Nicolas schon in Hamburg?   2. Sieben Jahre.
3. Was für einen Sport macht Maike?   3. Gymnastik, joggen.
4. Wann geht sie gewöhnlich zu Bett?   4. Um zehn Uhr.
5. David nennt drei Sachen, die wichtig sind zum Fithalten. Was sind sie?   5. Sport, gesund essen, genügend schlafen.
6. Was spielt Thorsten? Wie oft?   6. Basketball; zweimal die Woche.

3 Wer macht was?

On a piece of paper, mark the statements with the initial of the person to whom they most logically apply: N=Nicolas; M=Maike; D=David; T=Thorsten. (Each statement might apply to more than one person.)

1. __M__ usually goes to bed at 10:00 P.M.
2. __T__ doesn't eat chocolate.
3. __N__ likes living in Hamburg.
4. __T__ eats fruit and vegetables.
5. __D & T__ plays on a basketball team.
6. __T__ eats only lean meat.

4 Stimmt oder stimmt nicht?

Wenn der Satz nicht stimmt, schreib die richtige Antwort!

1. Auf dem Helene-Lange-Gymnasium lernen die Schüler keine Sprachen.   1. Stimmt nicht. Es ist ein zweisprachiges Gymnasium.
2. Nicolas' Mutter arbeitet in Hamburg.   2. Stimmt.
3. Maike geht immer sehr spät zu Bett, um 12 Uhr oder so.   3. Stimmt nicht. Um 10 Uhr.
4. David spielt Basketball und ist in der Mannschaft.   4. Stimmt.
5. Thorsten isst kein Fleisch.   5. Stimmt nicht. Er isst mageres Fleisch.
6. Er darf auch keine Schokolade essen.   6. Stimmt.

5 Wie geht der Satz zu Ende?

1. Ich halte mich   1. b
2. Ich schlafe   2. d
3. Ich gehe um zehn   3. g
4. Ich esse   4. e
5. Ich mache viel   5. f
6. Ich esse auch Fleisch, aber   6. a
7. Ich bin allergisch   7. c

a. es muss mager sein.
b. fit.
c. gegen Schokolade.
d. genug.
e. vernünftig.
f. Sport.
g. zu Bett.

6 Und du?

Welche Sätze passen auch für dich?   Answers will vary.

98 achtundneunzig   STANDARDS: 1.2   KAPITEL 4   Gesund leben

Storytelling Book
pp. 24–25

Erste Stufe

Objective Expressing approval and disapproval

WK3 HAMBURG-4

Gesundheitstipps

"Ich tu eigentlich recht viel für meine Gesundheit. Jeden Morgen mache ich Gymnastik, ich trinke keinen Alkohol, und ich rauche auch nicht."

"Ganz oben steht bei mir: richtige Ernährung, viel Obst, Gemüse und Salat, wenig Fett. Ich schlafe wenigstens acht Stunden, und ich vermeide die Sonne. Die ist schlecht für meine Haut."

"Ich halte mich fit durch Fitnesstraining. Ich trinke keinen Alkohol, ich trinke auch wenig Kaffee. Ich ernähre mich richtig, ja ich esse auch langsam und kaue richtig."

"Nach der Schule relaxe ich erst einmal, ich lese etwas, oder ich fahre Rad. Ich kleide mich auch richtig, nicht zu warm und nicht zu kalt!"

Wortschatz

sehr gesund leben	Gymnastik machen	viel Obst essen
viel für die Gesundheit tun	keinen Alkohol trinken	jeden Morgen joggen
vernünftig essen	die Sonne vermeiden	Rad fahren
genügend schlafen	nicht rauchen	

 4–1
 CD-ROM DISC 1

Übungsheft, S. 38, Ü. 1
Grammatikheft, S. 28, Ü. 1

7 Lebst du gesund?

Lesen Lies, was diese Schüler zum Thema Gesundheit sagen! Dann beantworte die Fragen!

1. **Schreiben** Welche Gesundheitstipps sind dir neu? Schreib die Verben auf, die diese Schüler verwenden, wenn sie über ihre Gesundheit reden! Was bedeuten sie?

2. **Schreiben** Schau die Logos oben an! Was bedeuten sie? Schreib einen Satz für jedes Logo — „Die 7 Gebote (*commands*) der Gesundheit!" Pass auf! Wie drückt man im Deutschen die Idee *one, people in general* aus? Welche zwei Modalverben kannst du hier gebrauchen? 2. E.g.: **Man soll nicht rauchen. Man muss vernünftig essen.**

ERSTE STUFE   STANDARDS: 1.2, 3.1   *neunundneunzig* **99**

8 So ein Muffel! Script and answers on p. 93G

Zuhören Der Gesundheitsmuffel: ein Muffel ist ein Mensch, der sich für nichts interessiert. Ein Gesundheitsmuffel ist also jemand, der sich wenig für seine Gesundheit interessiert. Hör mal zu, wie ein Muffel beschreibt, was er alles gegen seine Gesundheit macht! Schreib eine Liste von seinen Lastern (*vices*)!

> **Ein wenig Grammatik**
>
> The verb **schlafen** has a stem-vowel change in the **du-** and **er/sie-**forms.
>
> Wie lange **schläfst** du?
> Er **schläft** acht Stunden.
>
> Mehr Grammatikübungen, S. 114, Ü. 1
>
> Übungsheft, S. 38–39, Ü. 2–3   Grammatikheft, S. 28, Ü. 2

9 Was tust du für die Gesundheit?

Sprechen Frag deine Partnerin, was sie für ihre Gesundheit tut! Sie erzählt dir mindestens drei Sachen. Dann tauscht die Rollen aus!
E.g.: Ich rauche nicht. Ich schlafe genug. Ich esse viel Obst und Gemüse.

10 Für mein Notizbuch

Schreiben Schreib in dein Notizbuch, was du für deine Gesundheit tust! Schreib auch, wie oft du verschiedene Sportarten machst, und verwende dabei Wörter wie „ansonsten" (*otherwise*) und „auch", um deinen Text interessanter zu machen!

So sagt man das!

Expressing approval and disapproval

When expressing approval of what a friend or family member does, you might say:

> **Es ist prima, dass** du nicht rauchst.
> **Ich finde es toll, dass** du regelmäßig Sport machst.
> **Ich freue mich, dass** du in der Mannschaft bist.
> **Ich bin froh, dass** es dir hier gefällt.

When expressing disapproval, you might say:

> **Es ist schade, dass** du nicht viel Rad fährst.
> **Ich finde es nicht gut, dass** du so wenig schläfst.

Which of these expressions are new to you? What do you notice about the verbs in the **dass**-clauses?

Grammatikheft, S. 29, Ü. 3–4

11 Ich bin froh, dass …

Lesen/Sprechen Markus spricht mit Freunden über seine Gewohnheiten, was er für seine Gesundheit macht und was er nicht macht. Seine Freunde reagieren darauf. Welche Bemerkungen sind logisch?

1. **Markus:** Ich mache regelmäßig Sport!
   a. Ich finde das nicht gut.
   b. Das ist aber schade!
   c. <u>Das ist prima!</u>

2. **Markus:** Ich esse aber nicht richtig.
   a. Ich bin froh, dass du richtig isst!
   b. <u>Das finde ich nicht gut!</u>
   c. Das freut mich!

3. **Markus:** Ich rauche aber nicht!
   a. <u>Du, das ist aber prima!</u>
   b. Das finde ich nicht gut!
   c. Das ist aber wirklich schade!

4. **Markus:** Und ich spiele in einer Mannschaft.
   a. Das finde ich nicht gut.
   b. <u>Das ist toll!</u>
   c. Das ist aber wirklich schade!

12 Und was tust du? Script and answers on p. 93G

CD 4 Tr. 4

Zuhören Hör zu, wie verschiedene Schüler einem Freund erzählen, was sie machen oder nicht machen, um gesund zu bleiben! Schreib für jedes Gespräch auf, ob der Freund positiv oder negativ darauf reagiert!

13 Grammatik im Kontext

a. **Lesen/Sprechen** Denk an einen Freund in der Klasse und sag ihm, was du über seine Gewohnheiten denkst!

b. **Schreiben** Schreib einer Freundin, was du über ihre Gewohnheiten denkst. Schreib mindestens fünf Sätze.

Ein wenig Grammatik

Schon bekannt
Remember that after the preposition **für**, accusative case forms are used:

Einen Cappuccino für **mich**!
Was machst du für **deine Gesundheit**?

And remember that in **dass**-clauses the conjugated verb is in the last position:

Es freut mich, dass du vernünftig lebst.
Es ist schade, dass du dich nicht fit hältst!

Übungsheft, S. 39–40, Ü. 4–5   Mehr Grammatikübungen, S. 114–115, Ü. 2–4

Es ist	nicht gut		rauchen
Ich bin	prima		nicht rauchen
Ich finde es	toll	, dass du …	gesund sein
	schade		regelmäßig Sport machen
	wirklich gut		richtig essen
	wirklich schade		wenig schlafen
	froh		genug schlafen
			in einer Mannschaft sein

Wortschatz

—Wie geht's Ihnen, Herr Dingsda?
—Danke, ich …

ernähre mich richtig

fühle mich wohl

halte mich fit

—Ausgezeichnet, freut mich!

14 Das finde ich …

Sprechen Deine Partnerin erzählt dir, was sie für ihre Gesundheit tut und auch welche Laster sie hat. Reagier darauf entweder positiv oder negativ! Schau auf den **So sagt man das!** Kasten und such dir die richtigen Ausdrücke aus! Tauscht dann die Rollen aus! Berichte danach, was deine Klassenkameradin gesagt hat! Alle Mitschüler dürfen darauf reagieren.

ERSTE STUFE   STANDARDS: 1.1, 1.2

Grammatik

Reflexive verbs

1. Reflexive verbs are verbs that require a reflexive pronoun, such as in the sentence *I cut myself.* or *He enjoys himself.* The reflexive verbs used in this section, **sich fühlen, sich freuen, sich ernähren,** and **sich fit halten,** require a reflexive pronoun in the accusative case.

Ich	fühle	**mich**	hier sehr wohl.
Du	fühlst	**dich**	hier nicht wohl.
Er(Sie, Man)	fühlt	**sich**	großartig.
Wir	fühlen	**uns**	hier wohl.
Ihr	fühlt	**euch**	hier wohl, ja?
Sie(pl), Sie	fühlen	**sich**	hier wohl.

2. In questions, the reflexive pronoun follows the subject pronoun.

   Wie hältst **du dich** fit?
   Wie fühlt **ihr euch** hier in Hamburg?

3. When a reflexive verb is used in a **dass**-clause, the reflexive pronoun also follows the personal pronoun.

   Ich freue mich, dass **du dich** hier wohl fühlst.
   Meine Mutter freut sich, dass **sie sich** fit hält.

Look at the sentences with the verb **sich fit halten.** What do you notice about the **du** and **er/sie**-forms?

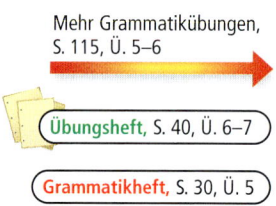

Mehr Grammatikübungen, S. 115, Ü. 5–6

Übungsheft, S. 40, Ü. 6–7

Grammatikheft, S. 30, Ü. 5

---

15 Für mein Notizbuch

Schreiben Schreib alles in dein Notizbuch, was du machst, was für dich ungesund ist! Reagiere entweder positiv oder negativ auf deine eigenen Laster! Findest du sie okay, oder möchtest du anders leben?

16 Herr Dingsda fühlt sich wohl   Script and answers on p. 93G

Zuhören Herr Dingsda erzählt seinen Freunden ganz stolz, was er für seine Gesundheit tut. Hör gut zu und schreib auf, was er macht, dass er sich so wohl fühlt!
CD 4 Tr. 5

17 Grammatik im Kontext

Schreiben As a waiter in the restaurant „Zum Hirschen" you overhear many conversations, but not everything that's said. Complete these conversations by filling in the correct reflexive pronoun.

1. — Fühlt ihr _____ hier wohl?
   — Ich, ja. Aber mein Bruder freut _____ nicht, hier in München zu sein. Und seine Frau fühlt _____ auch nicht wohl. 1. euch / sich / sich

2. — Mensch, wie siehst du aus! Du hältst _____ aber fit!
   — Ja. Mein Mann und ich, wir halten _____ fit, und ich fühle _____ dabei sehr wohl! 2. dich / uns / mich

3. — Fühlen Sie _____ hier in Bayern wohl, Herr Krause?
   — Sehr wohl, danke! Ich freue _____ sehr, hier zu sein. 3. sich / mich

Wortschatz

wo?
an der Schule
in der Klasse
in der Clique
in dieser Stadt
in der (Basketball-)mannschaft
in …

wie?
ganz wohl
nicht wohl
sehr wohl
nicht sehr wohl
großartig
überhaupt nicht wohl
super-toll

Grammatikheft, S. 30, Ü. 6

18 Der Gesundheitsfanatiker

Sprechen Sag deiner Partnerin, was Herr Dingsda wahrscheinlich alles macht, um gesund zu bleiben, zum Beispiel, was er isst, um sich richtig zu ernähren!

19 Wie fühlt ihr euch?

Sprechen Such dir einen Klassenkameraden und fragt euch gegenseitig, wie ihr euch fühlt! Verwendet dabei die Wörter im Wortschatzkasten oben, die beschreiben, wie gut oder schlecht man sich fühlen kann!

20 Was erzählen die Schüler?

Lesen/Schreiben/Sprechen Lest noch einmal, was die Schüler Maike, Thorsten, David und Nicolas über sich sagen! Wählt mit zwei anderen Mitschülern einen von den vieren aus und schreibt eine Zusammenfassung (*synopsis*) von seinen Aussagen! Einer von euch liest dann allen Mitschülern diese Zusammenfassung vor, ohne den Namen des Schülers zu sagen. Die anderen Mitschüler müssen raten, wen ihr beschreibt.

21 Wo fühlst du dich am wohlsten?

a. Schreiben Es gibt verschiedene Plätze, wo man sich am wohlsten fühlt. Füll die Tabelle rechts aus! Wie fühlst du dich an den Orten, die oben im Wortschatzkasten aufgelistet sind? Schreib auch warum!

b. Schreiben Schreib jetzt zwei Sätze in dein Notizbuch und verwende dabei die Information aus deiner Tabelle! Schreib einen Satz darüber, wo du dich am wohlsten fühlst, und einen darüber, wo du dich am unwohlsten fühlst (verwende dabei entweder „weil" oder „denn")!

Wo?	Wie?	Warum?
Schule		
Klasse		
Mannschaft		
Clique		

22 Grüß dich!

Sprechen Grüß deinen Partner und frag ihn, wie er sich fühlt oder fit hält! Er erzählt dir drei Dinge über sich. Reagier auf seine Aussagen! Tauscht dann die Rollen aus!

ERSTE STUFE   STANDARDS: 1.1, 1.3   *hundertdrei* 103

Was tust du, um gesund zu leben?

Health habits play an important role in German-speaking cultures. However, the focus and the trends have changed from one generation to the next. Let's find out what these people do for their health. CD 4 Tr. 6

Herr Troger, St. Ulrich

„Ja, wenn Sie mich fragen, ob ich gesund lebe, muss ich sagen eigentlich schon. Einmal zuallererst darf ich vielleicht sagen, ich rauche nicht, wobei aber nicht unbedingt ein Raucherfeind bin, nicht wahr. Aber ich rauche nicht, und ich trinke auch wenig und mache gerne Sport, ich fahre also sehr gern Rad. Im Winter gehen wir zum Langlauf oder ein bissel Skifahren. Also, muss sagen, ich lebe gesund." CD 4 Tr. 7

Regina, Bietigheim CD 4 Tr. 9

„Also, ich ess am liebsten sehr viel Obst und Gemüse, weil es … weil ich glaub, dass das sehr gesund ist. Ich esse es am liebsten aus dem eigenen Garten, weil ich da weiß, dass es nicht irgendwie gespritzt ist oder mit chemischen Düngemitteln behandelt ist. Fleisch esse ich nicht so gerne, weil ich erstens mal, weil ich mir denk, ich hab oft Filme im Fernsehen gesehen, wie die Tiere behandelt werden und so weiter. Und ich kann, ehrlich gesagt, auch drauf verzichten, das muss echt nicht sein. Ja, so Schnellimbiss und so was, das mag ich auch nicht so arg."

Gerd, Bietigheim CD 4 Tr. 8

„Oh, um gesund zu leben … na, das wird schwer. Na ich ess halt einfach das, was mir Spaß macht. Ich ess halt gerne Obst, und ansonsten viel zum Gesundleben fällt mir eigentlich nicht ein. Also ich fahr halt Skateboard, das bringt auch teilweise Kondition, aber mehr fällt mir eigentlich nicht ein."

A. 1. Which two types of things do these people do to stay healthy? Under each category, list what each person mentions.
2. From where does Regina like to get her food? What does she not like to eat? What reason does she give for this?
3. Does it sound like staying healthy is very important to Gerd? Why or why not?
4. Does Herr Troger do anything different from what the younger interviewees do for their health?

B. A number of America's favorite health pastimes, such as jogging or in-line skating, are becoming increasingly popular among the younger generation in Germany. Eating organic foods is also quite popular. How prevalent are these trends, and the things the interviewees mentioned, among your friends? Do your parents do different kinds of things for their health than you do?

STANDARDS: 1.2, 2.2, 3.2, 4.2

Zweite Stufe

Objective Asking for information and responding emphatically or agreeing, with reservations

23 Wer macht Sport? *Script and answers on p. 93G*

Zuhören/Schreiben Du hörst gerade im Radio eine Sendung über Sport, und es kommen Statistiken darüber, wie oft Deutsche verschiedene Sportarten treiben und wie viel Prozent der Bevölkerung an diesen Sportarten teilnimmt. Mach dir Notizen! Schreib dann mit einer Partnerin die Informationen in eine Tabelle um! Glaubst du, dass diese Tabelle auch für Amerikaner stimmt? Warum? Warum nicht?

	Fußball	Aerobic	Jazztanz	Bodybuilding
Wie oft?				
Wie viel Prozent?				

24 Gesünder leben

a. Lesen/Schreiben Der folgende Ausschnitt stammt aus einer Umfrage mit dem Titel „Gesünder leben", die in einem Gesundheitsmagazin erschienen ist. Lies den Fragebogen und, auf einem Stück Papier, fülle den Fragebogen für dich selbst aus!

FRAGEBOGEN

Machen Sie wirklich genug Sport?

1. **Wie oft machen Sie Sport?**
   - ❏ nie   ❏ oft
   - ❏ fast nie   ❏ sehr oft
   - ❏ selten   ❏ fast immer
   - ❏ manchmal   ❏ immer

2. **Wie oft?**
   - ❏ jeden Tag
   - ❏ jeden zweiten Tag
   - ❏ einmal am Tag
   - ❏ zweimal am Tag
   - ❏ einmal in der Woche
   - ❏ zweimal in der Woche

Ernähren Sie sich richtig?

3. **Ich esse ... Fleisch und Wurst.**
   - ❏ zu viel   ❏ wenig
   - ❏ viel   ❏ ganz wenig
   - ❏ ziemlich viel   ❏ kein

4. **Ich esse ... Obst und Gemüse.**
   - ❏ kein   ❏ viel
   - ❏ wenig   ❏ sehr viel
   - ❏ genug   ❏ nur

b. Sprechen Such dir einen Partner! Fragt euch gegenseitig über eure Antworten in dem Fragebogen! Oder: Einer fragt über Sport, der andere über Ernährung.

Grammatik

The determiner jeder

1. You have seen different forms of the word **jeder** throughout this chapter. What does it mean? What endings does it take? What other words or groups of words have you learned that have the same endings?[1]

	Masculine	Feminine	Neuter	Plural
Nominative	jeder	jede	jedes	alle
Accusative	jeden	jede	jedes	alle
Dative	jedem	jeder	jedem	allen

Ich mache **jeden** Sport.
Ich mag **jedes** Gemüse.
Wir fragen **alle** Klassenkameraden.

Mehr Grammatikübungen, S. 116, Ü. 7

Übungsheft, S. 42–43, Ü. 1–4

Grammatikheft, S. 31, Ü. 7

2. Look at the two sentences below. Which *case* is used when **jeder** is in a time expression, expressing definite time?[2]

Wir schwimmen **jeden** Montag.
Wir wandern **jedes** Wochenende.

25 Grammatik im Kontext

Sprechen/Schreiben Deine Mutter glaubt nicht, dass du alles tust, was du tun sollst. Sag ihr, dass du das doch tust! Verwende die Zeitausdrücke, die mit jedem Satz gegeben sind! (Begin your sentences with **Doch!** where appropriate.)

You have heard and seen the word **doch** used a lot by Germans in everyday conversations. One purpose **doch** serves is to soften the impact of a command: **Geh doch für mich einkaufen!** Doch has other meanings as well. If someone erroneously tells you that you don't do something, you can respond positively using **doch**. Read the following sentences and determine what **doch** means in this context:
  Du räumst nie auf!
  Doch! Ich räume fast jede Woche auf.
How would you respond if someone said to you **Du isst überhaupt kein Obst!** or **Du machst nie Sport!**

BEISPIEL Du isst kein Obst. (Tag)
Doch! Ich esse jeden Tag Obst!

1. Du machst keinen Sport! (Woche)
2. Du isst selten Obst und Gemüse! (Tag)
3. Du gehst nie schwimmen! (Wochenende)
4. Du sollst deine Großmutter besuchen! (Sonntag)
5. Du gehst selten ins Konzert! (Monat)

26 Beschreibungen

Lesen Such dir aus Zeitschriften bunte Fotos von Leuten aus, die Sport machen oder etwas Gesundes essen! Beschreib mit ein paar Sätzen, was jede Person macht, und stell dir vor, wie oft die Person die Aktivität macht! Dann reagiere entweder positiv oder negativ darauf! Danach mach Folgendes:

a. **Sprechen** Zeig deinen Mitschülern dein Foto und beschreibe es ihnen! *oder*
b. **Lesen/Sprechen** Du hängst mit deinen Mitschülern eure Fotos auf. Dann liest einer von euch eine Beschreibung vor, und die andern versuchen, das Foto zu erraten.

---

1. the definite articles; You may also remember seeing **dieser**-words with the same endings.
2. accusative case

So sagt man das!

Asking for information and responding emphatically or agreeing with reservations

You want to find out something specific about some of your friends. There are several ways to initiate your questions. You can say:

Ich habe eine Frage: Isst du Obst und Gemüse?
Sag mal, trinkst du jeden Tag Milch?
Wie steht's mit Fleisch? **Isst du eigentlich** viel Fleisch?
Darf ich dich etwas fragen? Wie hältst du dich fit?

To respond emphatically, your friend might say:

Ja, natürlich! or **Na klar!** or **Aber sicher!**

To agree with your statements, but with reservations, your friend might say:

(Du isst viel Kuchen!)	**Ja, das kann sein, aber** ich esse auch viel Obst!
(Du schaust oft Fernsehen!)	**Das stimmt, aber** ich mache auch Sport!
(Du isst gern Fleisch?)	**Eigentlich schon, aber** ich esse wenig Fleisch.

Übungsheft, S. 43–44, Ü. 5–7

Grammatikheft, S. 32, Ü. 8

How would you begin your questions if you were speaking to two friends? Look at the last three responses. How do we express these same ideas in English?

27 Simone und Fitness

Script and answers on p. 93G

CD 4 Tr. 11

Zuhören Hör gut zu, wenn Simone, eine Studentin in Krefeld, über die Fitnessgewohnheiten der Deutschen redet. Lies zuerst die englische Zusammenfassung unten, dann hör zu und versuche, die Zusammenfassung zu ergänzen!

1. According to Simone, most Germans ▃▃▃ in order to stay healthy.
2. Simone says that Germans also enjoy playing ▃▃▃ and ▃▃▃, because ▃▃▃.
3. Although Germans don't ▃▃▃, they are often ▃▃▃.
4. Today, Germans avoid ▃▃▃ more and more, because ▃▃▃.

28 Was tun die Amerikaner für ihre Gesundheit?

Sprechen Your school newspaper has asked you to interview your peers regarding their health habits. Think of at least six questions in German that you could ask on this topic. Three should be addressed to the group and three to individuals. Get together in groups of four and use your questions to interview your partners, but initiate your questions appropriately (refer to the **So sagt man das!** box). Then prepare similar questions in order to interview your teacher. Take turns with your classmates, finding out his or her health habits.

29 Für mein Notizbuch

Schreiben Using the information from Activity 28, summarize your findings, in German, in a paragraph describing what your friends and teacher do to stay healthy.

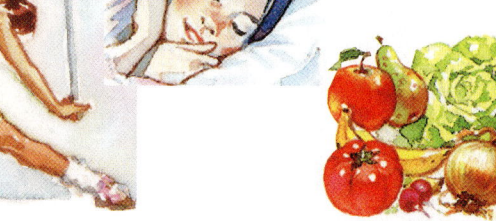

ZWEITE STUFE

Ein wenig Landeskunde

Among the younger generation there are several new trends. For instance, teenagers, far more than their parents, shop and consume foods from **Bioläden,** where they can get everything for **Vollwertkost. Bioläden** specialize in organically grown products, whole-grain foods, and the like. These shops are different from those called **Reformhäuser,** which have been around a lot longer. Usually frequented by older consumers, **Reformhäuser** specialize in products for people with special diets or medical needs. For many people in Germany, healthy eating goes hand in hand with **Umweltbewusstsein.** And don't bother coming to a **Bioladen** without your own bag! Students favor carrying groceries in burlap bags or wicker baskets on the back of their bicycles. They also have to bring their own containers to fill up on bulk products. And you might see a strange sight when shopping at any regular store in Germany: people removing the excess packaging from products they buy and leaving it in a pile at the front of the store. What do you think is going on here?

30 Eigentlich schon, aber ...

Schreiben/Sprechen You and your partner each write down three of your health-related vices on index cards and then trade cards. Your partner should fuss at you about your bad habits, stating what you do or don't do for your health. You have to agree, but with reservations, using statements from the **So sagt man das!** box.

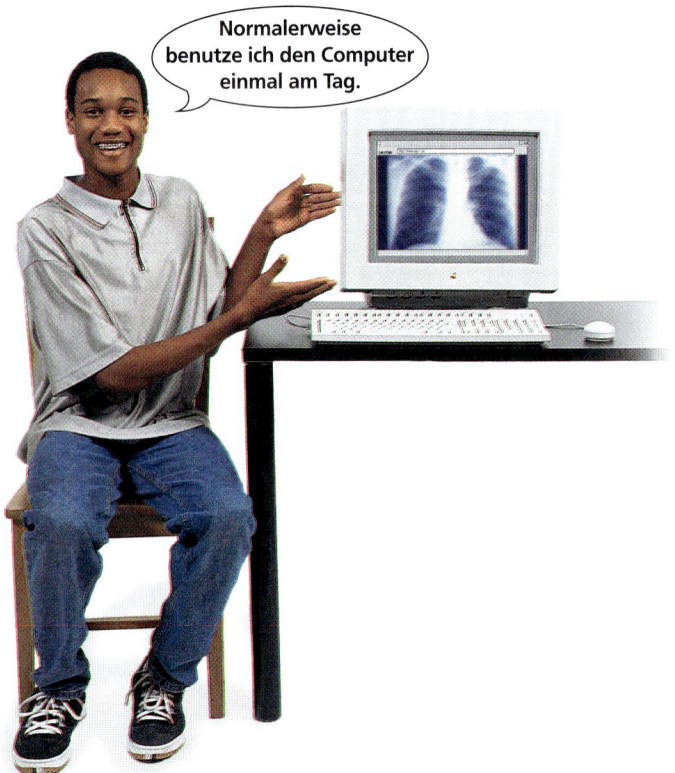

> Normalerweise benutze ich den Computer einmal am Tag.

Wortschatz

Schon bekannt
- oft
- viel
- ziemlich viel
- gewöhnlich
- jeden Tag
- einmal am Tag
- zweimal die Woche
- jede Woche
- jedes Wochenende

Neu
- selten
- meistens
- normalerweise
- wenig

Grammatikheft, S. 32, Ü. 9–10

Storytelling Book pp. 28–29

Dritte Stufe

Objective Asking and telling what you may or may not do

WK3 HAMBURG-4

Wortschatz

Für jeden etwas! Oder?

p. 93X
4–A
4–B
4–2

Gemüse
- Blumenkohl 
- Brokkoli 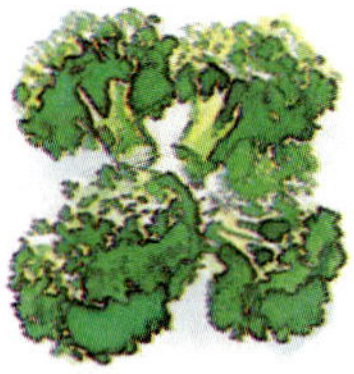
- Möhren 
- Pilze 

Obst
- Kirschen 
- Aprikosen 

Beeren
- Erdbeeren 
- Blaubeeren 

Fisch
- Forelle 

Fleisch
- Rindfleisch 
- Huhn/Hähnchen  
- Suppe: Fisch-Hühner-, Gemüse-Nudel-, Kartoffel-Reis-

Welche von diesen Speisen essen Amerikaner oft? Selten? Gar nicht? Wie steht's mit Hühnersuppe?

Übungsheft, S. 45, Ü. 1   Grammatikheft, S.33, Ü. 11

Script and answers on p. 93H

31 Was essen sie gern? Was nicht?

Schüler erzählen, was sie gern und was sie nicht gern essen und warum. Mach dir Notizen! Vergleiche deine Notizen mit den Notizen eines Partners!

CD 4 Tr. 12

Und dann noch...

Pudding	Magermilch
Vollmilch	Sahne
Joghurt	Eier
Milch	Butter

32 Was isst du?

Schreiben Mach eine Liste von deinen Essgewohnheiten! Ordne deine Liste in drei Gruppen: **1.** Was isst du (sehr) oft? **2.** Was isst du manchmal? **3.** Was isst du nie? — Teil diese Informationen deinen Klassenkameraden mit!

DRITTE STUFE   STANDARDS: 1.2   hundertneun   **109**

Wortschatz

Warum nicht?

Grammatikheft, S. 34, Ü. 13

(ist) allergisch gegen
hat zu viele Kalorien
hat zu viel Zucker
hat zu viel Fett
macht dick
nicht gut für die Gesundheit
schmeckt mir nicht
ungesund

Welche Speisen von Seite 109 passen zu diesen Gründen?

Beispiel Ich esse keinen Blumenkohl, weil er mir nicht schmeckt.

Ein wenig Grammatik

Schon bekannt

Do you remember which case forms go with **kein** when it is a direct object?

Ich esse **keinen** Fisch. (der Fisch)
Ich mag **keine** Suppe. (die Suppe)
Ich esse **kein** Gemüse. (das Gemüse)
Ich mag **keine** Möhren. (plural)

Übungsheft, S. 46, Ü. 2

Mehr Grammatikübungen, S. 116, Ü. 8

Grammatikheft, S. 33, Ü. 12

33 Was isst du nicht?

Sprechen Gibt es etwas, was du nicht gern isst? Such dir einen Partner! Er fragt dich, was du nicht isst und warum. Du sagst es ihm. Tauscht dann die Rollen aus!

So sagt man das!

Asking and telling what you may or may not do

If you want to know what a friend is allowed to eat or to do, you could ask:

    Was darfst du essen?
    Darfst du alles essen?
    Was darfst du tun?

The answer might be:

    Fleisch, Gemüse, …
    Klar! Ich darf alles essen.
    Ich darf Auto fahren.

To find out what your friend is not allowed to eat or to do, you could ask:

    Was darfst du nicht tun?
    Was darfst du nicht essen?

    Ich darf nicht joggen.
    Ich darf keine Schokolade essen.

What do you think the words **darf** and **darfst** mean? What other verbs do they remind you of?

34 Was die Schüler nicht machen dürfen! Script and answers on p. 93H

Zuhören Schüler in Deutschland erzählen, was sie nicht machen dürfen. Hör gut zu! Welche Aussage passt zu welchem Bild?
CD 4 Tr. 13

a.

b.

c.

d.

STANDARDS: 1.1, 1.2   KAPITEL 4   Gesund leben

35 **Klar darf ich das!**

Sprechen Sag deinem Partner, ob du auch die Dinge (von Übung 34) machen darfst oder nicht! Er sagt es dir.

Grammatik

The verb dürfen, present tense

The verb **dürfen**, *to be allowed* or *permitted to*, has these forms in the present tense:

Ich	**darf** alles essen!		Wir	**dürfen** gehen!
Du	**darfst** nicht rauchen!		Ihr	**dürft** alles essen!
Er/Sie/Es/Man	**darf** nicht joggen!	Sie (pl), Sie	**dürfen** keine Schokolade essen!

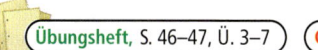

Mehr Grammatikübungen, S. 116–117, Ü. 9–10

 36 **Das darf man nicht machen!**

Schreiben Welche Regeln gibt es in eurem Klassenzimmer? Was darf man nicht machen? Schreib eure Klassenregeln auf Deutsch, damit auch die Austauschschüler sie verstehen können und nicht in Schwierigkeiten geraten (*get into trouble*)!

 37 **Blöde Allergien!**

Sprechen Setz dich mit drei Klassenkameraden zusammen! Unterhaltet euch über Allergien! Wer darf gewisse Lebensmittel nicht essen oder trinken und warum? Wer hat Allergien gegen andere Speisen? —Unten stehen ein paar Dinge, gegen die manche Menschen allergisch sind. Sagt den anderen Gruppen, welche Allergien in eurer Gruppe am meisten vorkommen!

allergisch gegen:

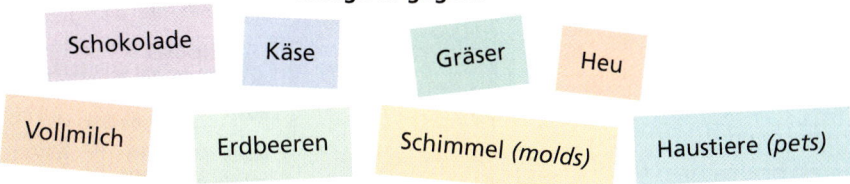

Schokolade, Käse, Gräser, Heu, Vollmilch, Erdbeeren, Schimmel (*molds*), Haustiere (*pets*)

auch gegen die Sonne!

 38 **Was darfst du zu Hause nicht machen?**

a. **Schreiben** Schreib drei Sachen auf, die du zu Hause nicht machen darfst! Frag danach deine Partnerin darüber, und sie fragt dann auch dich.

b. **Sprechen/Schreiben** Macht jetzt eine Umfrage! Einer geht an die Tafel und fragt ein paar Schüler, was ihre Partner gesagt haben und schreibt dann die Ergebnisse auf. Welches Verbot kommt am häufigsten (*the most*) vor?

 39  Von der Schule zum Beruf

Du bist in einem Fitness-Center angestellt, das jeden Monat für die Mitglieder des Centers eine Broschüre herausgibt mit dem Titel: *Wie halte ich mich gesund und fit?* Man hat dir den Auftrag gegeben, etwas für die nächste Ausgabe zu schreiben.

Zum Lesen

Bleibt fit und gesund!

Lesestrategie Activating your background knowledge. Activating your background knowledge (thinking about what you already know) will help you tremendously as you read German. For instance, if someone asked you out of the blue "What does **Am Kanal 24, 96407 Bamberg** mean?," you would probably have a hard time guessing. But if you saw this information in an ad for a pen pal, it would be easier to conclude that it must be an address. Try to activate your background knowledge each time you start reading something in German, even if you are not explicitly told to do so.

Getting Started For answers, see p. 93W.

1. Judging by the pictures and titles of the readings, what do these authors consider important for staying healthy? Which of these concerns were also addressed by the people who were interviewed for this chapter (see p. 104)? With your classmates, brainstorm for German vocabulary or phrases that you would expect to find in texts on these health topics.

Tipp: Some German prefixes carry their own meaning. Whether at the beginning of a noun or verb, they will change the meaning of the word in a certain way. For example, the prefix **auf** at the beginning of a verb often means *up*. You already know the phrases **das Zimmer aufräumen** and **den Hörer auflegen**; if you know the verb **geben,** what do you think the verb **aufgeben** might mean?

Warum ist Dr. Müller-Wohlfahrt nie krank?

Sechs Tips, die für Sie so wichtig sind wie für Boris

1 Richtig aufwärmen. „Nicht gleich loslegen, sondern in jeder Sportart sich vorher gezielt auf Touren bringen" – das rät der „Doc" dringend. Gymnastik und Stretching verhindern Verletzungen. „Am besten einen Sportarzt fragen, was individuell richtig ist."

2 Richtiges Schuhwerk. „Die meisten Sportler brauchen Einlegesohlen nach Maß. Solche Gehhilfen vom orthopädischen Schuhmacher verhindern Zerrungen, Muskelrisse, Ermüdungsbrüche. Eigentlich sollte jeder mit »seiner« Sohle Sport treiben."

3 Richtig essen. „Die italienischen Fußballstars haben die besten Werte, was Spurenelemente, Mineralien, Enzyme betrifft. Die mediterrane Küche ist die ideale Ernährung", schwört der „Doc". „Sie sollten Wert auf ausgewogene und leichte Kost legen".

4 Richtig laufen. „Es kommt auf den Stil an: Mit dem vorderen Mittelfuß aufsetzen, leicht abfedern, den Schritt leicht überlang machen, sich harmonisch nach vorne entwickeln, abrollen. Sie müssen das Gefühl haben, daß Sie vollkommen »rund« und mühelos laufen".

5 Richtig kühlen. Eiswürfel sind out – ideal zum Kühlen von Verletzungen ist „hot ice": Wasser in Gefrierpunktnähe. Verhindert spätere Überwärmung. Besonders effektiv: auf das „hot ice" ein paar Stöße Eisspray. Das garantiert dann dauerhafte Kühlung.

6 Richtig sitzen. Der „Doc" verpaßt seinen Patienten, die viel im Büro sitzen müssen, einen Sitzkeil aus hartem Schaumstoff. „Dadurch ergibt sich von vornherein die richtige Stellung der Wirbelsäule".

50 Euro für Nichtraucher

„50 Euro für jeden, der das Rauchen aufgibt", sagte der Bielefelder Fahrradfabrikant Hans-Werner Schreiber zu seinen Angestellten. Gesagt, getan. Jeden Monat zahlt der Fabrikant 50 Euro an seine Nichtraucher. Das verlockende Angebot wirkte: Zwei Männer und drei Frauen hörten sofort mit dem Rauchen auf. Nach und nach folgten alle anderen Mitarbeiter – bis auf einen. Die Nichtraucher freuen sich natürlich über das zusätzliche Geld. Sven Harter (22 Jahre): „Ich bezahle damit jedes Jahr meinen Urlaub."

Her mit dem Salat!

Eine Mahlzeit ohne Salat, das ist wie Brot ohne Butter oder Tee ohne Zucker, eins gehört zum andern. Das Grün eines Salats erfreut unsere Augen, und ist er noch ganz frisch und knackig, so regt er auch unsern Gaumen an. Ob wir nun den Salat wirklich mögen oder nicht, ist eine andere Frage. Wir essen ihn, ob er uns schmeckt oder nicht. Wir essen ihn, weil er gesund ist. Und wir ziehen den Salat vor, der ohne Pestizide gewachsen ist, denn der ist noch gesünder. Der Salat ist unser gutes Gewissen für den deftigen Schweinsbraten.

2. Read the first sentence of the article about **Nichtraucher.** What is the topic? (*Hint:* What did Hans-Werner promise his employees?)

A Closer Look

3. Before you read the rest of the article on **Nichtraucher,** try to predict: a) how successful the manufacturer's offer has been, and b) what the employees might do with their 50 euros. Then read the article to confirm or correct your predictions.

4. Now think about the following questions: a) Was any reason given explicitly for the manufacturer's offer? b) Was a reason implied or hinted at? c) If not, could you assume, using your background knowledge, what the reason(s) might be?

5. Read the article about **Salat.** What does the author compare to bread without butter and tea without sugar? According to the author, what is not important when eating salad? If you know that **Gewissen** means *conscience,* what might the last sentence mean? How serious do you think the author is about how Germans view salad?

6. What are the six tips that Dr. Müller-Wohlfahrt offers? Read the boldface print after each number.

7. Read the first tip from Dr. Müller-Wohlfahrt. What two things help prevent injuries? Now skim over the third tip. According to the doctor, which athletes have the best diet? Look at the fifth tip. What is "out"? What is "in"? If you know that **Gefrier-** is freezing, what is "hot ice"?

8. Such dir einen Partner. Fragt die Schüler und Lehrer an eurer Schule, wie sie sich fit halten! Schreibt die Resultate auf Deutsch um! Schreibt danach einen Bericht über die Ergebnisse! Entwerft ein Poster mit Tipps dazu.

Übungsheft, S. 48

Mehr Grammatikübungen

Erste Stufe
Objective Expressing approval and disapproval

1 Bekommen deine Freunde genügend Schlaf? – Schreib die richtige Form von **schlafen** in jede Lücke. (S. 100)

1. Ich freue mich, dass du genügend _____ . Ich _____ auch acht Stunden. schläfst; schlafe
2. Toll, dass der David acht Stunden _____ . Wir _____ auch so lange. schläft; schlafen
3. Wie lange _____ die Maike? _____ sie auch acht Stunden? schläft; Schläft
4. Es ist schade, dass ihr nicht genügend _____ . Wie lange _____ ihr? schlaft; schlaft
5. Der Thorsten _____ genügend; nur der Nicolas _____ zu wenig. schläft; schläft

2 Lebt dein Freund gesund oder nicht? – Vervollständige die **dass**-Sätze mit den Ausdrücken in Klammern. (S. 101)

1. (Sport machen)   Ich bin froh, dass du genügend _____ . Sport machst
2. (genügend schlafen)   Es ist nicht gut, dass du nicht _____ . genügend schläfst
3. (Rad fahren)   Ich finde es toll, dass du so viel _____ . Rad fährst
4. (nicht rauchen)   Ich freue mich, dass du _____ . nicht rauchst
5. (gesund leben)   Es ist prima, dass du so _____ . gesund lebst

3 Du sagst, dass es schade ist, dass deine Freundin kein gesundes Leben führt. – Vervollständige die **dass**-Sätze mit den Ausdrücken in Klammern. (S. 101)

1. (nicht genügend schlafen)   Es ist schade, dass du _____ . nicht genügend schläfst
2. (nicht vernünftig essen)   Es ist schade, dass du _____ . nicht vernünftig isst
3. (kein Obst essen)   Es ist schade, dass du _____ . kein Obst isst
4. (nicht die Sonne vermeiden)   Es ist schade, dass du _____ . nicht die Sonne vermeidest
5. (nichts für die Gesundheit tun) Es ist schade, dass du _____ . nichts für die Gesundheit tust

4 Du freust dich darüber, dass deine Freunde gesund leben. – Vervollständige die **dass**-Sätze mit den Ausdrücken, die die Symbole auf der linken Seite repräsentieren. (S. 101)

1. Ich freue mich, dass du _____ .   nicht rauchst
2. Wir freuen uns, dass ihr _____ .   die Sonne vermeidet
3. Ich freue mich, dass Bob _____ .   viel Obst und Gemüse isst
4. Wir freuen uns, dass du _____ .   keinen Alkohol trinkst
5. Oma freut sich, dass Inge _____ .   genügend schläft
6. Mutti freut sich, dass Jenny _____ .   Gymnastik macht

5 Wie fühlen sich diese Leute, und wie halten sie sich fit? – Schreib das richtige Reflexivpronomen in die Lücken. (S. 102)

1. Wie fühlst du _____ ? — Du, ich fühle _____ großartig!   dich; mich
2. Fühlt ihr _____ hier wohl? — Wir fühlen _____ hier sehr wohl.   euch; uns
3. Wie fühlt _____ die Maike? — Ich denke, sie fühlt _____ wohl.   sich; sich
4. Wie fühlen _____ die Schüler? — Sie fühlen _____ großartig.   sich; sich
5. Und hältst du _____ auch fit? — Klar! Ich halte _____ sehr fit.   dich; mich
6. Und ihr beiden? Haltet ihr _____ auch fit? — Klar! Wir halten _____ fit.   euch; uns
7. Herr Sauer, wie halten Sie _____ fit? — Ich halte _____ mit Sport fit.   sich; mich

6 Du bist froh, dass deine Freunde gesund leben. – Vervollständige die Sätze mit den Ausdrücken in Klammern. (S. 102)

1. (s. wohl fühlen)   Es ist prima, dass du _____ .   dich wohl fühlst
2. (s. fit halten)   Es ist gut, dass ihr _____ .   euch fit haltet
3. (s. richtig ernähren) Ich finde es toll, dass ihr _____ .   euch richtig ernährt
4. (s. darüber freuen) Wir sind froh, dass du _____ .   dich darüber freust
5. (s. fit halten)   Ich finde es prima, dass du _____ .   dich fit hältst
6. (s. hier wohl fühlen) Ich freue mich, dass Nicolas _____ .   sich hier wohl fühlt

MEHR GRAMMATIKÜBUNGEN   STANDARDS: 1.2   *hundertfünfzehn* **115**

Mehr Grammatikübungen

 Answers  WK3 HAMBURG-4

Zweite Stufe

Objective Asking for information and responding emphatically or agreeing with reservations

7 Eine Schulkollegin stellt dir viele Fragen. – Beantworte sie und schreib dabei die richtige Form von **jeder** in die Lücken. (S. 106)

1. Du schwimmst nicht gern? — Doch, ich schwimme sogar _____ Tag.   jeden
2. Du spielst nicht gern Fußball? — Doch, ich spiele _____ Woche, _____ Samstag.   jede; jeden
3. Du wanderst nicht gern? — Doch! Ich wandre _____ Wochenende.   jedes
4. Du gehst nicht gern ins Konzert? — Doch, ich gehe _____ Monat ins Konzert.   jeden
5. Du hast keine CDs von Nena? — Du, ich habe sogar _____ CDs von ihr.   alle
6. Du gibst keinem Freund ein Geschenk? — Ich geb _____ Freund etwas.   jedem

Dritte Stufe

Objective Asking and telling what you may or may not do

8 Du und deine Freunde, ihr dürft vieles nicht essen. – Schreib die richtige Form von **kein** in die Lücken. (S. 110)

1. Ja, du, ich darf _____ Fisch essen, _____ Erdbeeren, _____ Joghurt, dann darf ich auch _____ Milch trinken, und ich darf _____ Schokolade essen.   keinen; keine; keinen keine; keine
2. Und ich mag _____ Eier, _____ Butter, ja, auch _____ Blumenkohl, und dann mag ich auch _____ Reis und _____ Spinat.   keine; keine; keinen keinen; keinen
3. Ich glaube, die Maike darf _____ Schweinefleisch essen, _____ Pilze und _____ Bananen, weil sie sehr allergisch dagegen ist.   kein; keine; keine

9 Du erzählst, wer in eurer Familie etwas nicht essen oder trinken darf. – Schreib die richtige Form von **dürfen** in die Lücken. (S. 111)

Du sagst, du _____ alles essen. Das finde ich prima. Ich _____ zum   darfst; darf

Beispiel keine Beeren essen, und meine Schwester _____ keine Milch   darf

trinken. Wir sind allergisch gegen Beeren und Milch. Meine

Großeltern _____ keinen Kaffee trinken, und mein Vater _____ auch   dürfen; darf

keine Schokolade essen. Ja, was _____ ihr nicht essen und trinken?   dürft

10 Sieh dir die Zeichnungen an und schreib in die Lücken, was du und die anderen nicht essen oder trinken dürfen. Gebrauche eine Form von **dürfen,** eine Form von **kein,** und das Wort, das abgebildet ist. (S. 111)

BEISPIEL

1. Ich _____ _____ _____ essen.
   Ich **darf keine Erdbeeren** essen.

2. Max _____ _____ _____ trinken.   darf keine Milch

3. Mutti _____ _____ _____ essen.   darf kein Eis

4. Wir _____ _____ _____ essen.   dürfen keine Kirschen

5. Ihr _____ _____ _____ essen!   dürft keinen Fisch

6. Ich _____ _____ _____ essen.   darf keine Eier

7. Du _____ _____ _____ trinken!   darfst keinen Saft

8. Wir _____ _____ _____ essen!   dürfen keine Butter

Storytelling Book pp. 30–31

Anwendung

The *CD-ROM Tutor* offers guided recording and writing activities to accompany the **Anwendung**. These activities are designed to practice students' oral and written communication skills and to review material from each chapter.

1 You will hear four radio ads trying to persuade you to do different things for your health and fitness. Match each of the summary statements below with one of the ads that you hear. Script and answers on p. 93H

CD 4 Tr. 14

a. Du sollst so oft wie möglich Sport machen!
b. Man soll jeden Tag Obst und Gemüse essen!
c. Du sollst jeden Tag mindestens sieben Stunden schlafen!
d. Rauchen ist nicht gesund!

2 Read this letter to Dr. Müller-Meier, health columnist for the Dietzburger Zeitung. Then answer the questions below.

1. Er weiß nicht, was mit ihm los ist. 2. Kopfschmerzen; Magenschmerzen; keine Energie. 3. Sitzt am Schreibtisch; liest und lernt.

1. Warum schreibt Hans Giecht?
2. Was ist sein Problem?
3. Beschreib sein Leben!

3 As Dr. Müller-Meier's assistant, you often respond to the letters from his readers. Write a response to Hans Giecht, telling him what to do — or what not to do — in order to improve his health and regain his energy. Your response will appear in next Sunday's "Dietzburger Zeitung."

> Lieber Dr. Müller-Meier!
> Ich weiß nicht, was mit mir los ist! Vielleicht können Sie mir helfen. Ich fühle mich nie so richtig wohl — ich habe immer Kopfschmerzen, oder Magenschmerzen oder irgendetwas! Und das Schlimmste ist — ich habe überhaupt keine Energie! Ich bin Student an der Uni (ich studiere Germanistik), und ich muss jeden Tag lange am Schreibtisch sitzen und lesen und lernen. Ich brauche dafür viel Energie! Was soll ich tun? Ich esse genug, glaube ich — ich esse jeden Tag Brot, Nudeln, Fleisch — was es so eben in der Mensa gibt. Und ich rauche und trinke nicht viel. Ich rauche etwa fünf Zigaretten am Tag, und ich trinke ab und zu abends mit Freunden. Was soll ich tun, um meine Energie zurückzubekommen? Hilfe!!!
>
> Mit bestem Dank
> Hans Giecht

4 Your younger siblings look to you for advice. How often would you tell them to do or not to do the following?

Sport machen
Kuchen essen
Obst und Gemüse essen
Milch trinken
rauchen
Alkohol trinken
schwimmen

5 You work as an assistant in a clinic. A student who hasn't been feeling well calls you to seek your advice. As he describes his symptoms, you fill out the following form for your records.
Script and answers on p. 93H

CD 4 Tr. 15

Name: _____ Alter: _____ Beruf: _____
Beschwerden: _____
Diagnose: _____
Empfehlung: _____

KAPITEL 4   Gesund leben

6 Zum Schreiben

You write a health column for the *Salzburger Nockerl Zeitung* and this week you are describing an ideal diet for a teenager. You give advice about what, how much, and how often a teenager should eat.

> **Schreibtipp** **Doing Research**
> In order for your article to be factual, you might want to interview the health or home economics teacher at your school or consult health and nutrition books in your school library. Take brief notes on 3 × 5 cards and include your source on each card.

Vorbereiten
After gathering your information, you need to organize it in a **logical manner**. Decide whether you want to recommend foods as sources of protein, carbohydrates, and fats, or whether you want to concentrate on a good day's or week's diet.

Ausführen
Start your paragraph with a **topic sentence,** which will introduce your subject and focus your writing. For instance, **Schüler müssen sich gut ernähren, denn sie brauchen viel Energie.** In order to convince students that they need to follow your diet, be sure to make it tempting by varying taste, color, and texture.

Überarbeiten
- After writing your paragraph, set it aside for a day and then reread it.
- Assess its strengths and weaknesses.
- Make changes, and then read your paper aloud, listening for confusing statements and awkward wording. Have a peer evaluate strengths and weaknesses of your paragraph.
- Revise, proofread, and submit your paragraph to your teacher.

7 Rollenspiel

Do the following activity with a partner or small group.

You work for a German marketing firm and need some good ideas for health-related advertisements to send to your firm back in Germany. Make a list of commercials you see on American television or hear on American radio that reflect health and fitness consciousness. Write down the ad (or the product being advertised) and, in German, tell what the health problem is and the basic message related to its cure. With your partner or group, select the commercial that you think is most effective, write it in German, and present it to the class. Use props and sound effects to make your commercial more interesting and fun. The rest of the class can serve as the "advisory board" in your German firm and select the commercial that they would most like to show on German television.

Kann ich's wirklich?

Can you express approval? (p. 100)

1 How would you react if your friend told you that he or she
a. lives in a healthy way? a. E.g.: **Es ist prima, dass du gesund lebst.**
b. eats properly? b. E.g.: **Ich bin froh, dass du richtig isst.**
c. exercises regularly? c. E.g.: **Ich finde es toll, dass du regelmäßig Sport machst.**

Can you express disapproval? (p. 100)

2 How would you react if your friend told you that he or she
a. does not live in a healthy manner? a. E.g.: **Es ist schade, dass du nicht gesund lebst.**
b. does not get enough exercise? b. E.g.: **Ich finde es nicht gut, dass du nicht genug Sport machst.**
c. doesn't eat right? c. E.g.: **Es ist schade, dass du nicht richtig isst.**
d. gets too little sleep? d. E.g.: **Es ist nicht gut, dass du so wenig schläfst.**

Can you ask for information and respond to a question emphatically? (p. 107)

3 How would someone ask you if you
a. play sports? a. E.g.: **Machst du Sport?**
b. eat correctly? b. E.g.: **Ernährst du dich richtig?**
c. exercise? c. E.g.: **Machst du Gymnastik?**

4 How would you respond emphatically to the questions in Activity 3 by saying that you
a. play sports every week? a. E.g.: **Ja, natürlich! Ich mache jede Woche Sport.**
b. eat fruit and vegetables every day? b. E.g.: **Na klar! Ich esse jeden Tag Obst und Gemüse.**
c. exercise every morning? c. E.g.: **Aber sicher! Ich mache jeden Morgen Gymnastik.**

Can you agree with reservations? (p. 107)

5 How would you respond in the following situations?
a. Your mom accuses you of eating too much chocolate, but you know that you also eat a lot of fruit. a. E.g.: **Ja, das kann sein, aber ich esse auch viel Obst!**
b. Your friend tells you that you watch too much television, but you also exercise three times a week. b. E.g.: **Das stimmt, aber ich mache auch dreimal die Woche Gymnastik!**
c. Your doctor says that you eat too much meat, but you tell him that you eat only lean meat. c. E.g.: **Ja, das stimmt, aber ich esse nur mageres Fleisch!**

Can you ask and tell what you may and may not do, using dürfen? (p. 110)

6 How would you tell someone that you
a. may not eat meat? a. **Ich darf kein Fleisch essen.**
b. may not drink alcohol? b. **Ich darf keinen Alkohol trinken.**
c. may eat cheese? c. **Ich darf Käse essen.**
d. may not eat chocolate because you are allergic to it?
d. **Ich darf keine Schokolade essen, weil ich allergisch dagegen bin.**

120 hundertzwanzig STANDARDS: 1.2 KAPITEL 4 Gesund leben

Wortschatz

Erste Stufe

Expressing approval

Es ist prima, dass …	It's great that …
Ich finde es toll, dass …	I think it's great that …
Ich bin froh, dass …	I'm happy that …
Ich freue mich, dass …	I'm happy that …

Expressing disapproval

Es ist schade, dass …	It's too bad that …
Ich finde es nicht gut, dass …	I think it's bad that …

For your health

sich fit halten	to keep fit
sehr gesund leben	to live in a very healthy way
sich ernähren richtig	to eat and drink proper(ly)
viel für die Gesundheit tun	to do a lot for your health
vernünftig essen	to eat healthy foods
genügend schlafen er/sie schläft	to get enough sleep he/she sleeps
Gymnastik machen	to exercise
keinen Alkohol trinken	not to drink alcohol
die Sonne vermeiden	to avoid the sun
nicht rauchen	not to smoke
viel Obst essen	to eat lots of fruit
jeden Morgen joggen	to jog every morning
Rad fahren (sep)	to bicycle

Where?

an der Schule	at school
in der Klasse	in class
in der Clique	in the clique
in dieser Stadt	in this city
in der (Basketball-) mannschaft	on the (basketball) team

Talking about how you feel

sich fühlen	to feel
ganz wohl	extremely well
sehr, nicht, nicht sehr wohl	very, not, not very well
überhaupt nicht wohl	not well at all
großartig	wonderful
super-toll	really great

Reflexive pronouns, accusative case

mich	myself
dich	yourself
sich	herself, himself
uns	ourselves
euch	yourselves
sich	themselves, yourself, yourselves

Zweite Stufe

Asking for information

Ich habe eine Frage: …	I have a question: …
Sag mal, …	Tell me, …
(Essen Sie) eigentlich …?	Do you really (eat) …?
Wie steht's mit …?	So what about …?
Darf ich euch etwas fragen?	May I ask you something?

Responding emphatically

Ja, natürlich!	Certainly!
Na klar!	Of course!
Doch!	Yes, I do!

Agreeing with reservations

Ja, das kann sein, aber …	Yes, maybe, but …
Das stimmt, aber …	That's true, but …
Eigentlich schon, aber …	Well yes, but …

When?

selten	seldom
meistens	most of the time
gewöhnlich	usually
normalerweise	normally
wenig	little

p. 93X

Dritte Stufe

Food items

die Speise, -n	food
der Blumenkohl	cauliflower
der Brokkoli	broccoli
die Möhre, -n	carrot
der Pilz, -e	mushroom
die Kirsche, -n	cherry
die Aprikose, -n	apricot
die Erdbeere, -n	strawberry
die Blaubeere, -n	blueberry
die Forelle, -n	trout
das Rindfleisch	beef
das Huhn, ¨-er	chicken
der Reis	rice

Saying why you don't eat something

hat zu viel Fett	has too much fat
hat zu viele Kalorien	has too many calories
macht dick	is fattening
es schmeckt mir nicht	it doesn't taste good
allergisch sein gegen	to be allergic to
nicht gut für die Gesundheit	not good for your health
ungesund	unhealthy
alles	everything

Asking or telling what you may or may not do

dürfen	to be allowed to, may (for the forms of **dürfen**, see page 111.)

Kapitel 5: Gesund essen
Chapter Overview

Los geht's! pp. 124–126

Wiebkes Pausenbrot, p. 124

	FUNCTIONS	GRAMMAR	VOCABULARY	RE-ENTRY
Erste Stufe pp. 127–131	• Expressing regret and downplaying, p. 129 • Expressing skepticism and making certain, p. 130	• The demonstrative **dieser**, p. 130	• **Pause** snacks, p. 128	Talking about prices, p. 128 (**Kap. 4, I**); Saying what you would like to eat or drink, p. 128 (**Kap. 3, I**); Expressing regret, p. 129 (**Kap. 9, I**); Talking about quantities, giving reasons, p. 129 (**Kap. 8, I**); **Sollen**, p. 130 (**Kap. 8, I**); **Essen**, p. 130 (**Kap. 6, I**)
Zweite Stufe pp. 134–137	• Calling someone's attention to something and responding, p. 134	• The preposition **auf**, p. 135 • The possessives (Summary), p. 136	• Things to put on a **Pausenbrot**, p. 134	**Mein, dein, sein,** and **ihr**, p. 135 (**Kap. 3/11, I**); Ordering food, p. 137 (**Kap. 6, I**); **Möchte**, p. 137 (**Kap. 3, I**); **Essen**, p. 137 (**Kap. 6, I**)
Dritte Stufe pp. 138–141	• Expressing preference and strong preference, p. 139	• Verbs used with dative-case forms, p. 139 • The interrogative **welcher**, p. 140 • The preposition **zu**, p. 141	• Food in a supermarket, p. 138	Talking about how food tastes, p. 138 (**Kap. 6, I**); Expressing preferences, p. 138 (**Kap. 10, I**); **Lieber/am liebsten**, p. 138 (**Kap. 10, I**); Saying you want more, p. 138 (**Kap. 9, I**); **Mögen**, p. 138 (**Kap. 10, I**); Food vocabulary, pp. 138, 140 (**Kap. 8, I**); **Was für**, p. 141 (**Kap. 10, I**)

Zum Lesen pp. 132–133

Wo ruht ihr euch aus?

Reading Strategy
Understanding the tone of a text

Mehr Grammatikübungen

pp. 142–145

Erste Stufe, p. 142   Zweite Stufe, p. 143   Dritte Stufe, pp. 144–145

Review pp. 146–149

Anwendung, pp. 146–147   Kann ich's wirklich?, p. 148   Wortschatz, p. 149
Zum Schreiben: Sequencing (Writing a newspaper story)

CULTURE

• **Landeskunde: Was isst du, was nicht?** p. 127
• **Ein wenig Landeskunde:** Students' mothers sell nutritious snacks to **Gymnasiasten**, p. 128

German meals, p. 135

German mealtimes, p. 140

Kapitel 5: Gesund essen
Chapter Resources

Lesson Planning
One-Stop Planner
Lesson Planner with Substitute Teacher Lesson Plans, pp. 22–26, 69
Student Make-Up Assignments
- Make-Up Assignment Copying Masters, Chapter 5

Listening and Speaking
TPR Storytelling Book, pp. 32–39
Listening Activities
- Student Response Forms for Listening Activities, pp. 35–38
- Additional Listening Activities 5-1 to 5-6, pp. 39–42
- Additional Listening Activities (song), p. 38
- Scripts and Answers, pp. 125–131

Video Guide
- Teaching Suggestions, pp. 30–31
- Activity Masters, pp. 32–34
- Scripts and Answers, pp. 91–93, 112–113

Activities for Communication
- Communicative Activities, pp. 25–30
- Realia and Teaching Suggestions, pp. 90–93
- Situation Cards, pp. 131–132

Reading and Writing
Reading Strategies and Skills Handbook, Chapter 5
Lies mit mir! 2, Chapter 5
Übungsheft, pp. 49–60

Grammar
Grammatikheft, pp. 37–45
Grammar Tutor for Students of German, Chapter 5

Assessment
Testing Program
- Grammar and Vocabulary Quizzes, **Stufe** Quizzes, and Chapter Test, pp. 105–122
- Score Sheet, Scripts and Answers, pp. 123–130

Alternative Assessment Guide
- Portfolio Assessment, p. 22
- Performance Assessment, p. 36
- CD-ROM Assessment, p. 50

Student Make-Up Assignments
- Alternative Quizzes, Chapter 5

Online Activities

- Interaktive Spiele
- Internet Aktivitäten

Video Program

- Videocassette 2
- Videocassette 5 (captioned version)
- DVD Tutor, Disc 1

Audio Compact Discs

- Textbook Listening Activities, CD 5, Tracks 1–13
- Additional Listening Activities, CD 5, Tracks 19–26
- Assessment Items, CD 5, Tracks 14–18

Interactive CD-ROM Tutor, Disc 2

Teaching Transparencies

- Situations 5-1 to 5-2
- Vocabulary 5-A
- Los geht's!
- Mehr Grammatikübungen Answers
- Grammatikheft Answers

Use the **One-Stop Planner CD-ROM** with Test Generator to aid in lesson planning and pacing.

For each chapter, the **One-Stop Planner** includes:
- Editable lesson plans with direct links to teaching resources
- Printable worksheets from resource books
- Direct launches to the HRW Internet activities
- Video and audio segments
- Test Generator
- Clip Art for vocabulary items

Kapitel 5: Gesund essen

Projects

Mein Lieblingsplatz

In this activity students write a composition in which they describe the place where they feel safest and most comfortable. This assignment should be started after students have completed the Zum Lesen *section. Students work individually on the project. They may include pictures or drawings to support and illustrate the content of their writing.*

MATERIALS

Students may need
- paper
- pen
- pencil
- some photos or pictures
- ruler

SUGGESTED SEQUENCE

1. During the prewriting stage, help students focus on their writing skills. Have them brainstorm, make lists of words and phrases, and come up with drawings as they plan a rough draft. Students may want to reread some of the articles of the *Zum Lesen* section to help them get started.

2. Students begin to focus on specific ideas and come up with a main idea for their compositions.

3. Students study their notes again to ensure that their ideas are all relevant to the main idea of their composition.

4. Students use their outline to write their compositions in the present tense. They should use connectors and intensifiers such as the ones introduced in the *Zum Lesen* section.

5. Students edit their compositions (encourage peer editing) to identify and correct grammatical or mechanical errors.

6. Students write the final copy of their compositions and add visual aids to accompany their projects.

7. Students turn in the projects for a grade.

GRADING THE PROJECT

Suggested point distribution (total = 100 points)
- Content 25
- Correct language usage 50
- Originality 25

Games

Wörter kreuz und quer

This game will help students review the vocabulary they have learned thus far.

Procedure Divide the class into three or four teams and draw a large grid on the board. Write a word in the grid. The first team sends one member to the board and writes a word in the grid which intersects with the first word. Then the next team adds a word which again has to intersect with an existing word. Give one point per vowel, two points for most consonants, three points for umlauts, and four points for any consonants you consider more difficult. Points are added after each team's turn and are totalled at the end of the game or after a set amount of time has elapsed.

```
      H
      A
A U S G E Z E I C H N E T
      S           U   L
                  N   T
                  D   E
                      R
                      N
```

Entschuldigung, eine Frage bitte!

This game will help students review and practice vocabulary and verb tenses.

Provide each student in your class with a list of 20 items based on the vocabulary or expressions they have previously studied.

Example:

Finde jemanden, der …

  Eier zum Frühstück gegessen hat.

  keinen Joghurt mag.

With the list and a pen or pencil, all students walk around the classroom and try to find someone who can affirmatively answer each of the questions. If a student answers with **ja**, the student who asked the question writes that student's name next to the item. Students may not use their own names for any of the items. The student who first completes his or her list is the winner.

Storytelling

Mini-Geschichte

*This story accompanies Teaching Transparency 5-1. Read the **Mini-Geschichte** to your students, or have them role-play the conversation using proper pronunciation and intonation. Ask students to make conjectures about the aliens.*

Was essen die Erdbewohner *(earthlings)*?

XYNE5   Schau mal, ZYRUS11!

ZYRUS11   Was denn?

XYNE5   Sieh mal! Was tun diese Erdbewohner?

ZYRUS11   Sie essen und trinken. Der Junge mit der Brille trinkt Milch und isst ein belegtes Brötchen. Das Mädchen mit den schwarzen Haaren hat Käse auf ihrem Brötchen. Das Mädchen im roten Pullover trinkt Milch. Ich seh leider nicht, was sie isst.

XYNE5   Hör doch mal, ZYRUS11!

ZYRUS11   Was ist denn jetzt los?

XYNE5   Die Erdbewohner machen Geräusche!

ZYRUS11   Ja, das tun viele Erdbewohner beim Essen und Trinken.

XYNE5   Komisch!

Traditions

Der Hamburger Fischmarkt

Fische, Bananen, Plüschteddybären und sogar Würste fliegen jeden Sonntag zwischen 5 Uhr und 10 Uhr morgens auf dem Hamburger Fischmarkt durch die Luft.

Von den Verkäufern werden schauspielerische Höchstleistungen verlangt, um ihre Ware zu verkaufen. Nachtschwärmer, die auf einem Konzert in der Fischauktionshalle waren, und Frühaufsteher treffen sich dort, um frischen Fisch direkt vom Kutter zu kaufen oder einfach nur, um sich das Spektakel anzusehen. Mittlerweile ist der Markt ebenso internationale Touristenattraktion wie Einkaufsort.

Have students investigate the impact of Hamburg's geographical location on its economy and cuisine. Ask students to discuss cities in the United States whose economies are influenced by their geographical location.

Rezept

Matjes mit Specksauce
Für 4 Personen

Zutaten

g=Gramm, l=Liter, EL=Esslöffel, TL=Teelöffel

8	Matjesfilets *(filets of soused herring)*
1/2 l	Mineralwasser oder Milch
200g	Speck, geräuchert
4	Zwiebeln
20g	Mehl
1/4 l	Wasser
1/4 l	Milch
2 EL	Weinessig
1 TL	Zucker
	Salz
	schwarzer Pfeffer

Zubereitung

Von den Matjesfilets die restlichen Gräten abschneiden. Filets waschen und 2 Stunden in Mineralwasser oder Milch legen. Inzwischen Speck und geschälte Zwiebeln fein würfeln; Speck knusperig braten. Zwiebeln zugeben, Mehl hineinrühren und hellgelb anrösten. Wasser und Milch unter Rühren zugießen und aufkochen. Die Sauce mit Essig, Zucker, Salz und Pfeffer abschmecken. Matjesfilets mit Küchenpapier trockentupfen, auf einer Platte anrichten und gut durchkühlen lassen. Mit der heißen Sauce und Ofenkartoffeln servieren.

Kapitel 5: Gesund essen
Technology

Videocassette 2, 5 (captioned version)
DVD Tutor, Disc 1
See Video Guide, pages 29–34

DVD/Video

Los geht's! • Wiebkes Pausenbrot
In this segment of the video, students buy healthy snacks at school. Wiebke has packed her own snack: a **Brötchen** with tofu and bean sprouts. She tells her friends about the foods she ate for breakfast that morning and about a nutritious meal she once cooked.

Landeskunde
Was isst du, was nicht?
People of various ages from several German and Austrian cities discuss the foods they like and dislike, and explain why they like or dislike them.

Fortsetzung
Nicolas asks if Wiebke will help him cook pizza for everybody. At his house, everybody is helping prepare the things that will go on the pizza. Nicolas explains that he has bought enough dough for two pizzas at a pizzeria. He takes half of the dough and starts to throw it in the traditional way, but fails to catch it.

Videoclips
- Frosta Mahlzeit® (frozen dinners)
- Blou Bajou Käse® (cheese)
- Cremor 0,2 Prozent Cremequark® ("quark")
- Müller Milchreis® (rice pudding)

Interactive CD-ROM Tutor

Activity	Activity Type	Pupil's Edition Reference
1. Grammatik	Was fehlt?	p. 130
2. Wortschatz	Merkspiel	pp. 128, 134
3. So sagt man das!	Wozu gehört's?	pp. 129, 130, 134
4. Grammatik	Was fehlt?	p. 136
5. Wortschatz	Wort und Bild Erfahren/Wählen	p. 138
6. So sagt man das!	Was ist richtig?	pp. 139, 140, 141
Landeskunde	Was isst du, was nicht? Was ist richtig?	p. 127
Zum Sprechen	Guided recording	pp. 146–147
Zum Schreiben	Guided writing	pp. 146–147

Teacher Management System
Launch the program, type "admin" in the password area, and press RETURN. Log on to **www.hrw.com/CDROMTUTOR** for a detailed explanation of the Teacher Management System.

DVD Tutor

The *DVD Tutor* contains all material from the *Video Program* as described above. German captions are available for use at your discretion for all sections of the video. The *DVD Tutor* also provides a variety of video-based activities that assess students' understanding of **Los geht's!, Fortsetzung,** and **Landeskunde,** as well as the new **Grammatik im Kontext** presentations.

The *DVD Tutor* may be used on any DVD video player connected to a television or video monitor.

Visit Holt Online
go.hrw.com
KEYWORD: WK3 HAMBURG-5
Online Edition

Go.Online!

Premier Online Edition

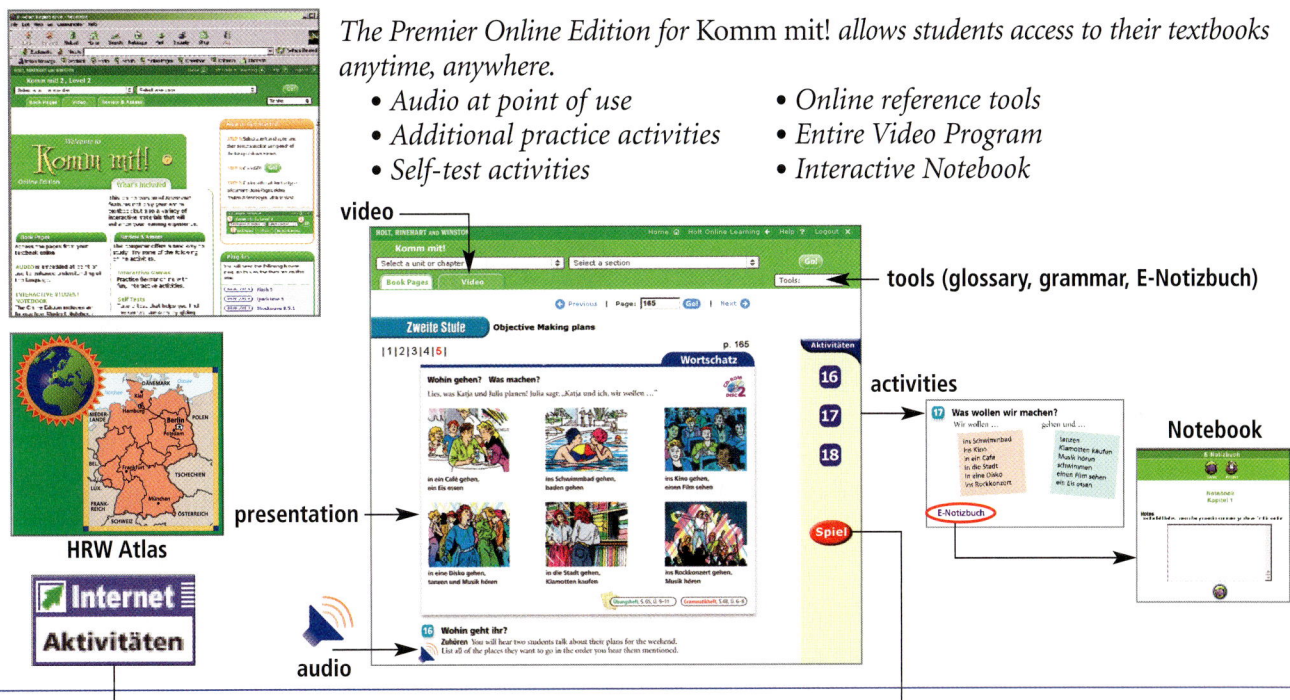

The Premier Online Edition for *Komm mit!* allows students access to their textbooks anytime, anywhere.
- Audio at point of use
- Additional practice activities
- Self-test activities
- Online reference tools
- Entire Video Program
- Interactive Notebook

Internet Aktivitäten

These guided internet activities include a worksheet and pre-selected and pre-screened authentic web sites from the German-speaking countries. You can use these activities

- to help students develop research skills in the target language
- to introduce students to authentic cultural information
- as a project

Interaktive Spiele

You can use the interactive activities in this chapter
- to practice grammar, vocabulary, and chapter functions
- as homework
- as an assessment option
- as a self-test
- to prepare for the Chapter Test

Webprojekt Have students find a vegetarian restaurant in a German-speaking country. Alternatively, students may find a restaurant that serves vegetarian dishes in addition to non-vegetarian specialties. Students should report on the location of the restaurant, its menu, daily specials, and prices. Encourage students to exchange useful Web sites with their classmates. Have students document their sources by referencing the names and URLs of all the sites they consulted.

STANDARDS: 1.2, 1.3, 2.2, 3.2, 5.1   KAPITEL 5   TECHNOLOGY   121F

Kapitel 5: Gesund essen
Textbook Listening Activities Scripts

Erste Stufe

6 p. 128

REGINA Ich nehme einen kleinen Orangensaft, ein Schinkencroissant und einen Vanillejoghurt.

VERKÄUFER Alles klar. Das macht dann zusammen zwei Euro fünfzig.

MAX Ich hätte gern einen Kakao und zwei Eibrötchen. Das ist alles.

VERKÄUFER Gut, also einmal Kakao und zweimal Eibrötchen. Einen Euro vierzig, bitte!

KATJA Für mich bitte eine Banane, einen Müslijoghurt und eine kleine Flasche Milch. Mmmh, die Quarkbrötchen sehen lecker aus. Ich nehme auch noch ein Quarkbrötchen dazu!

VERKÄUFER Also, Banane, Joghurt, Milch und Quarkbrötchen. Da bekomme ich dann genau zwei Euro.

FELIX Ich nehme zwei Äpfel und ein Salamibrötchen. Ist noch ein Bananenjoghurt da?

VERKÄUFER Ja, hier ist noch einer. Der letzte übrigens! Da hast du Glück gehabt. Also, alles zusammen kostet einen Euro sechzig.

Answers to Activity 6
Regina: Orangensaft, Schinkencroissant, Vanillejoghurt; € 2,50
Max: Kakao, zwei Eibrötchen; € 1,40
Katja: Banane, Müslijoghurt, Milch, Quarkbrötchen; € 2,00
Felix: zwei Äpfel, Salamibrötchen, Bananenjoghurt; € 1,60

9 p. 129

1. MICHI Du, Mutti, haben wir etwas Leckeres im Kühlschrank? Ich möchte so gern etwas Süßes essen, ein Eis zum Beispiel!

   MUTTER Schauen wir doch mal nach! Ja, also Eis haben wir nicht, aber hier ist ein Joghurt. Den kannst du haben, wenn du willst. Der ist bestimmt genauso lecker wie ein Eis.

   MICHI Ach nein, einen Joghurt mag ich nicht. Der schmeckt doch ganz anders als Eis!

2. EVI Vati, haben wir noch Cola im Kühlschrank?

   VATER Nein, ich glaube, du hast gestern die letzte Dose ausgetrunken, und der Apfelsaft ist leider auch schon alle. Aber, wie wäre es mit einem Glas Milch?

   EVI Milch? Ach Papa, ich bin doch kein Baby mehr. Nein, also Milch mag ich nicht!

3. GRETCHEN Papa, ist noch etwas von der Schokoladentorte übrig? Deine Geburtstagstorte war so lecker!

   VATER Nein, ich glaube, von der Torte ist nichts mehr übrig. Wir haben gestern alle Stücke aufgegessen. Aber hier sind noch ein paar Schokoladenplätzchen. Willst du die?

   GRETCHEN Ja, danke. Die schmecken zwar nicht genauso gut wie deine Torte, aber ich mag sie trotzdem!

4. ULLI Mama, ich möchte so gern eine Portion Erdbeeren mit Schlagsahne essen. Haben wir welche im Kühlschrank?

   MUTTER Mal sehen! Ja, also Schlagsahne haben wir, aber leider keine Erdbeeren mehr. Tut mir Leid. Aber schau mal, wir haben Milch und wir haben auch Bananen. Du kannst dir einen Bananenmilchshake machen mit Schlagsahne oben drauf! Also, was hältst du davon?

   ULLI Au ja, super! Möchtest du auch einen? Dann mach ich gleich zwei!

   MUTTER Ja, gern!

Answers to Activity 9
Michi: will Eis; mag keinen Joghurt
Evi: will Cola; mag keine Milch
Gretchen: will Schokoladentorte; mag auch Schokoladenplätzchen
Ulli: will Erdbeeren mit Schlagsahne; mag auch Bananenmilchshake

12 p. 131

1. HEINZ Sag mal, Richard, was hast du denn heute auf deinem Pausenbrot?

   RICHARD Ich habe heute Salami drauf!

   HEINZ Du hast immer nur Wurst auf deinem Pausenbrot! Isst du nie was anderes? Käse, zum Beispiel! Oder mal was Süßes wie Marmelade oder so!

   RICHARD Nein, Käse ist nicht mein Fall. Auf meinem Pausenbrot mag ich nun mal gerne Wurst. Salami, Schinken und Leberwurst mag ich am liebsten. Und wenn ich mal was Süßes will, dann nur Eis!

2. ULRIKE Hallo, Claudia! Kommst du in der Pause mit in den Supermarkt? Oder hast du dir was von zu Hause mitgebracht?

   CLAUDIA Nein, du weißt doch, ich bringe mir selten was von zu Hause mit. Aber ich komme trotzdem nicht mit in den Supermarkt. Ich hole mir heute ein Fischbrötchen vom Fischstand. Freitags esse ich nämlich immer Fisch!

3. HEIKE He, Gerhard! Was hast du denn da in der Tragetasche?

   GERHARD Da ist mein Pausensnack drin!

   HEIKE Zeig doch mal, was hast du denn alles mitgebracht?

   GERHARD Ja, also heute habe ich meinen Obsttag. Zwei Bananen, einen Apfel und ein Pfund blaue Trauben. Die sind echt lecker.

   HEIKE Isst du denn heute sonst nichts, nur Obst?

   GERHARD Doch! Ich gehe gleich noch zum Bäcker und hole mir ein Stück Strudel. Aber Obst esse ich jeden Tag, der Vitamine wegen!

Answers to Activity 12
Richard: b, c   Claudia: e   Gerhard: a, d

Zweite Stufe

16 p. 134

UWE Martina, was hast du denn immer so auf deinem Pausenbrot?

MARTINA Also, meistens habe ich irgendeine Wurst drauf, zum Beispiel Salami, oder ich mag auch gerne Corned Beef. Manchmal streiche ich auch Senf oder Mayonnaise auf die Wurst, das schmeckt mir auch gut. Ich hab selten auch mal Marmelade drauf, aber

121G   SCRIPTS   KAPITEL 5

The following scripts are for the listening activities found in the *Pupil's Edition*. For Student Response Forms, see *Listening Activities*, pages 35–38. To provide students with additional listening practice, see *Listening Activities*, pages 39–42.

For resource information, see the **One-Stop Planner CD-ROM**, Disc 2.

normalerweise nicht auf einer Scheibe Brot, sondern nur wenn's ein Brötchen ist.

UWE Angelika, erzähl du uns doch mal, was du so gewöhnlich auf deinem Pausenbrot hast!

ANGELIKA Ja, also ich mag wahnsinnig gerne Tofu mit Sojasprossen, am liebsten auf einem Stück Knäckebrot. Und meistens habe ich auch noch ein paar Radieschen- oder Gurkenscheiben drauf auf dem Tofu. Das ist echt lecker.

UWE Und Klaus, wie sieht denn dein Pausenbrot so aus?

KLAUS Ja, also ich bin der totale Käsefreak! Ich hab jeden Tag eine andere Sorte Käse drauf. Was das Brot anbetrifft, ist es mir eigentlich egal, welche Sorte es ist, also Vollkorn, Weiß- oder Schwarzbrot … esse ich alles gern. Aber auf den Käse kommt es an! Holländischen Edamer mag ich total gern und auch französischen Camembert. Ach ja, Margarine mag ich auf meinem Brot nicht. Butter schmeckt viel besser!

Answers to Activity 16
Martina: Salami und Corned Beef mit Senf und Mayonnaise; Marmelade
Angelika: Tofu mit Sojasprossen, Radieschen- und Gurkenscheiben
Klaus: holländischen Edamer, französischen Camembert, Butter

20 p. 137

1. - Hallo, Frau Becker! Dieser Kugelschreiber hier ist Ihnen gerade aus der Tasche gefallen.
   - Danke, Horst. Das war sehr aufmerksam von dir.

2. - Habt ihr Lust, heute Abend zu mir zu kommen? Wir können uns die neuen CDs anhören, die ich von euch zum Geburtstag bekommen habe!
   - Au ja, Klasse! Wir kommen gern, oder was meinst du, Martin?

3. - Du, Britta, schau mal! Da hinten kommt die neue Biologielehrerin. Sie soll ganz nett sein, hab ich gehört.
   - Ja, das hab ich auch gehört.

4. - Entschuldigung, können Sie mir sagen, wo der Hausmeister ist? In unserer Klasse ist die Tafel kaputtgegangen.
   - Ja, natürlich. Er hat sein Büro gleich hinter dem Lehrerzimmer.

5. - He Frank, ich glaube, dass ich aus Versehen dein Mathebuch eingesteckt habe. Ich habe nämlich zwei in meiner Schultasche. Guck doch mal nach, ob dir deins fehlt!
   - Ja, du hast Recht. Es gehört tatsächlich mir. Danke!

Answers to Activity 20
1. einer älteren Person; 2. zwei Freunden; 3. einem Freund;
4. einer älteren Person; 5. einem Freund

Dritte Stufe

26 p. 139

ILSE Also, wenn ich Obst esse, dann mag ich Bananen lieber als Äpfel. Aber im Sommer mag ich Melonen am liebsten. Am besten schmeckt mir eisgekühlte Wassermelone mit Parmaschinken! Das haben wir zum ersten Mal in Italien gegessen, als wir dort in den Ferien waren. Und jetzt machen wir es auch oft zu Hause, weil es uns so gut geschmeckt hat.

ULF Wir essen sehr viel Gemüse zu Hause. Mein Vater macht eine ganz tolle Gemüsesuppe, mit frischen Kräutern und saurer Sahne und so. Da sind ganz viele verschiedene Gemüsesorten drin, eigentlich alles, was ich gerne mag. Also, Zucchini, Karotten und grüne Bohnen. Die mag ich lieber als zum Beispiel Paprika. Am liebsten mag ich es, wenn auch Tomaten drin sind.

UWE An meinem Geburtstag darf ich mir aussuchen, was es zu essen gibt. Ich weiß noch nicht, ob ich mir lieber ein chinesisches Reisgericht oder italienische Pasta wünschen soll. Ja, eigentlich mag ich die chinesische Küche lieber. Aber, ehrlich gesagt, schmecken mir die deutschen Gerichte am besten, besonders wenn meine Oma kocht.

ANJA Ich esse Obst nicht so gern, aber dafür trinke ich alle Fruchtsäfte, die es so gibt. Also, zum Beispiel, Orangensaft, Apfelsaft und Grapefruitsaft. Am liebsten mag ich Traubensaft. Der schmeckt immer richtig süß und fruchtig. Ja, und sonst, wenn ich total durstig bin oder viel Sport gemacht habe, dann trinke ich am liebsten literweise Wasser, Mineralwasser natürlich! Das löscht den Durst am besten.

Answers to Activity 26
Ilse: mag Bananen lieber als Äpfel; mag Melone am liebsten
Ulf: mag Zucchini, Karotten und grüne Bohnen lieber als Paprika; mag Tomaten am liebsten
Uwe: mag chinesische Küche lieber als italienische; mag deutsche Gerichte am liebsten
Anja: mag Traubensaft lieber als Orangen-, Apfel- und Grapefruitsaft; mag am liebsten Mineralwasser

Anwendung

1 p. 146

MUTTER Also, Bernd, was möchtest du trinken?

BERND Ah, ich freue mich schon auf den leckeren Orangensaft hier. Der schmeckt so gut, weil er immer aus frisch gepressten Apfelsinen ist. Eigentlich mag ich den Apfelsaft ja auch gern, aber der Orangensaft schmeckt mir doch viel besser. Und du, Annette, was trinkst du?

ANNETTE Ach, Bernd! Saft! Saft! Immer trinkst du nur Saft! Nimm doch mal was anderes, eine Cola zum Beispiel, so wie ich! Und dann bestelle ich mir jetzt die Gemüseplatte. Die haben ja sonst hier nicht so viel ohne Fleisch. Entweder Salatbuffet oder Gemüseplatte. Na ja, hoffentlich sind auch meine Lieblingspilze mit dabei. Mutti, nimmst du wieder die Krabben wie letztes Mal?

MUTTER Ja, also, ich nehme wieder die frischen Krabben mit Kräuterbutter und Petersilienkartoffeln. Und dazu noch ein paar Scheiben Baguette. Das habe ich schon lange nicht mehr gehabt. Oder nein, ich glaube, ich lasse mal das Brot weg und nehme lieber nachher noch ein Dessert. Und was nimmst du, Hans-Peter?

VATER Ja also, der Kuchen soll hier ausgezeichnet sein. Schau mal auf die Karte, was die alles haben: Apfeltorte, Kirschstreusel, Rosinennapfkuchen. Mmmh, und alles hausgemacht, ach, und auch noch Zitronencremeschnitten. Schokoladentorte mit Sahne hört sich nun auch gut an! Na ja, aber zuerst nehme ich mal die Aalsuppe, und dann sehen wir weiter!

Answers to Activity 1
1. Annette; 2. Bernd; 3. Nein, sie isst vegetarisch; 4. Ja, denn er liest zuerst, welche Kuchen/Torten es auf der Speisekarte gibt.

Kapitel 5: Gesund essen
Suggested Lesson Plans *50-Minute Schedule*

Day 1

CHAPTER OPENER 10 min.
- Culture Note, ATE, p. 121M
- Background Information, ATE, p. 121M
- Language Note, ATE, p. 121M

LOS GEHT'S! 20 min.
- Preteaching Vocabulary, ATE, p. 121N
- Advance Organizer, ATE, p. 121N
- Culture Notes, ATE, p. 121N
- Play Audio CD for **Los geht's!**, pp. 124–125
- Have students read **Los geht's!**, pp. 124–125
- Teaching Suggestions, Video Guide, p. 30
- Show **Los geht's!** Video

ERSTE STUFE
LANDESKUNDE 15 min.
- Pre-viewing Suggestion, Video Guide, p. 30
- Background Information, ATE, p. 121O
- Show **Landeskunde** Video
- Do Activities A and B, p. 127

Wrap-Up 5 min.
- Students respond to questions about what they like to eat

Homework Options
Pupil's Edition, p. 126, Comprehension Acts.
Übungsheft, p. 50, Act. 1

Day 2

ERSTE STUFE
Quick Review 10 min.
- Check homework, p. 126, Comprehension Acts.

Wortschatz/Ein wenig Landeskunde, p. 128 15 min.
- Presenting **Wortschatz**, ATE, p. 121O
- Teaching Transparency 5-A
- Play Audio CD for Activity 6, p. 128
- Present **Ein wenig Landeskunde**, p. 128
- Do Activity 7, p. 128

So sagt man das!, p. 129 20 min.
- Presenting **So sagt man das!**, ATE, p. 121P
- Do Activity 8, p. 129
- Play Audio CD for Activity 9, p. 129
- Present **Sprachtipp**, p. 129
- Do Activity 10, p. 129
- Do Activity 1, p. 51, Übungsheft

Wrap-Up 5 min.
- Students respond to questions about snack foods and availability

Homework Options
Grammatikheft, p. 37, Acts. 1–2
Übungsheft, p. 49, Act. 1

Day 3

ERSTE STUFE
Quick Review 10 min.
- Check homework, Grammatikheft, p. 37, Acts. 1–2

So sagt man das!, p. 130 15 min.
- Presenting **So sagt man das!**, ATE, p. 121P
- Do Activities 3–4, p. 38, Grammatikheft

Grammatik, p. 130 20 min.
- Presenting **Grammatik**, ATE, p. 121Q
- Do Activity 11, p. 131
- Play Audio CD for Activity 12, p. 131
- Do Activities 13 and 14, p. 131
- Do Activities 2–7, pp. 51–53, Übungsheft

Wrap-Up 5 min.
- Students respond to questions about their eating habits

Homework Options
Pupil's Edition, p. 131, Act. 15
Activities for Communication, pp. 25–26, prepare Communicative Activity 5-1

Day 4

ERSTE STUFE
Quick Review 10 min.
- Do Communicative Activity 5-1, pp. 25–26

ZUM LESEN 25 min.
- Present **Lesestrategie**, p. 132
- Do Activities 1–9, pp. 132–133

Quiz Review 15 min.
- Do Activities 5–7, p. 39, Grammatikheft
- Do Activity 1, Interactive CD-ROM
- Do Additional Listening Activities 5-1 and 5-2, pp. 39–40

Homework Options
Mehr Grammatikübungen, Erste Stufe
Übungsheft, p. 54, Acts. 1–4

Day 5

ZWEITE STUFE
Quick Review 10 min.
- Check homework, **Mehr Grammatikübungen, Erste Stufe**

Quiz 20 min.
- Quiz 5-1A or 5-1B

Wortschatz, p. 134 15 min.
- Presenting **Wortschatz**, ATE, p. 121S
- Present **Und dann noch**, p. 134
- Teaching Transparencies 5-1, 5-A
- Play Audio CD for Activity 16, p. 134
- Do Activity 17, p. 134

Wrap-Up 5 min.
- Students respond to questions about what teenagers in Germany eat on bread

Homework Options
Grammatikheft, p. 40, Act. 8
Übungsheft, p. 55, Acts. 1–2

Day 6

ZWEITE STUFE
Quick Review 10 min.
- Check homework, Übungsheft, p. 55, Acts. 1–2

So sagt man das!, p. 134 10 min.
- Presenting **So sagt man das!**, ATE, p. 121T
- Do Activity 9, p. 40, Grammatikheft

Ein wenig Landeskunde/Ein wenig Grammatik, p. 135 25 min.
- Present **Ein wenig Landeskunde**, p. 135
- Present **Sprachtipp**, p. 135
- Present **Ein wenig Grammatik**, p. 135
- Do Activity 18, p. 135
- Do Activity 3, p. 55, Übungsheft
- Do Situation 5-2, pp. 131–132

Wrap-Up 5 min.
- Students respond to someone calling their attention

Homework Options
Activities for Communication, pp. 27–28, prepare Communicative Activity 5–2

One-Stop Planner CD-ROM

For alternative lesson plans by chapter section, to create your own customized plans, or to preview all resources available for this chapter, use the **One-Stop Planner CD-ROM**, Disc 2.

H For additional homework suggestions, see activities accompanied by this symbol throughout the chapter.

Day 7

ZWEITE STUFE

Quick Review 10 min.
- Check homework, Realia 5-2

Grammatik, p. 136 25 min.
- Presenting **Grammatik**, ATE, p. 121T
- Do Activity 19, p. 136
- Play Audio CD for Activity 20, p. 137
- Do Activities 21, 22, 23, and 24, p. 137
- Do Activities 10–12, pp. 41–42, Grammatikheft

Quiz Review 10 min.
- Do Activities 4–7, pp. 56–57, Übungsheft

Wrap-Up 5 min.
- Students respond to questions about what is on their sandwiches

Homework Options
Mehr Grammatikübungen, Zweite Stufe

Day 8

DRITTE STUFE

Quick Review 10 min.
- Check homework, **Mehr Grammatikübungen, Zweite Stufe**

Quiz 20 min.
- Quiz 5-2A or 5-2B

Wortschatz, p. 138 15 min.
- Presenting **Wortschatz**, ATE, p. 121U
- Teaching Transparency 5-2
- Do Activity 25, p. 138

Wrap-Up 5 min.
- Students respond to questions about how they liked something

Homework Options
Grammatikheft, p. 43, Act. 13

Day 9

DRITTE STUFE

Quick Review 15 min.
- Return and review Quiz 5-2
- Bell Work, ATE, p. 121U
- Check homework, Grammatikheft, p. 43, Act. 13

So sagt man das!, p. 139 15 min.
- Presenting **So sagt man das!**, ATE, p. 121U
- Play Audio CD for Activity 26, p. 139
- Do Activity 27, p. 139

Ein wenig Grammatik, p. 139 15 min.
- Present **Ein wenig Grammatik,** p. 139
- Do Activity 28, p. 139
- Do Activities 1-2, p. 58, Übungsheft

Wrap-Up 5 min.
- Students respond to questions about which foods they like, prefer and like the most

Homework Options
Grammatikheft, pp. 43–44, Acts. 14–17

Day 10

DRITTE STUFE

Quick Review 10 min.
- Check homework, Grammatikheft, pp. 43–44, Acts. 14–17

Grammatik, p. 140 15 min.
- Presenting **Grammatik**, ATE, p. 121V
- Do Activities 29 and 30, p. 140
- Do Activity 18, p. 45, Grammatikheft

Ein wenig Landeskunde/Grammatik, pp. 140–141 20 min.
- Present **Ein wenig Landeskunde,** p. 140
- Presenting **Grammatik**, ATE, p. 121V
- Do Activity 31, p. 141
- Present **Sprachtipp,** p. 141
- Do Activities 32 and 33, p. 141

Wrap-Up 5 min.
- Students respond to questions about what they usually eat for breakfast, lunch, and dinner

Homework Options
Grammatikheft, p. 45, Act. 19
Übungsheft, pp. 58–60, Acts. 3–7
Interaktive Spiele, see ATE, p. 121F

Day 11

DRITTE STUFE

Quick Review 10 min.
- Check homework, Übungsheft, pp. 58–60, Acts. 3–7

Quiz Review 20 min.
- Do **Mehr Grammatikübungen, Dritte Stufe**
- Do Communicative Activity 5-3, pp. 29–30
- Do Activities 5 and 6, Interactive CD-ROM

Quiz 20 min.
- Quiz 5-3A or 5-3B

Homework Options
Pupil's Edition, p. 147, Act. 4, **Zum Schreiben**; p. 148, **Kann ich's wirklich?**

Day 12

ANWENDUNG

Quick Review 30 min.
- Return and review Quiz 5-3
- Students present **Zum Schreiben** paragraphs
- Do **Anwendung** Activities 1–3, pp. 146–147

Chapter Review 20 min.
- Review chapter functions, vocabulary, and grammar; choose from **Mehr Grammatikübungen,** Grammar Tutor for Students of German, Activities for Communication, Listening Activities, Interactive CD-ROM Tutor, or **Interaktive Spiele**
- Review test format and provide sample test items for students

Homework Options
Study for Chapter Test

Assessment

Test, Chapter 5 45 min.
- Administer Chapter 5 Test. Select from Testing Program, Alternative Assessment Guide, or Test Generator.

Kapitel 5: Gesund essen
Suggested Lesson Plans 90-Minute Block Schedule

Block 1

CHAPTER OPENER 10 min.
- Culture Note, ATE, p. 121M
- Background Information, ATE, p. 121M
- Language Note, ATE, p. 121M

LOS GEHT'S! 25 min.
- Preteaching Vocabulary, ATE, p. 121N
- Advance Organizer, ATE, p. 121N
- Culture Notes, ATE, p. 121N
- Play Audio CD for Los geht's!, pp. 124–125
- Have students read Los geht's!, pp. 124–125
- Teaching Suggestions, Video Guide, p. 30
- Show Los geht's! Video
- Do Comprehension Activities, p. 126

ERSTE STUFE
LANDESKUNDE 15 min.
- Pre-viewing Suggestion, Video Guide, p. 30
- Background Information, ATE, p. 121O
- Show Landeskunde Video
- Do Activities A and B, p. 127

Wortschatz/Ein wenig Landeskunde, p. 128 15 min.
- Presenting Wortschatz, ATE, p. 121O
- Teaching Transparency 5-A
- Play Audio CD for Activity 6, p. 128
- Present Ein wenig Landeskunde, p. 128
- Do Activity 7, p. 128

So sagt man das!, p. 129 20 min.
- Presenting So sagt man das!, ATE, p. 121P
- Do Activity 8, p. 129
- Play Audio CD for Activity 9, p. 129
- Present Sprachtipp, p. 129
- Do Activity 10, p. 129

Wrap-Up 5 min.
- Students respond to questions about snack foods and availability

Homework Options
Grammatikheft, p. 37, Acts. 1–2
Übungsheft, p. 49, Act. 1; p. 50, Act. 1; p. 51, Act. 1

Block 2

ERSTE STUFE
Quick Review 10 min.
- Check homework, Grammatikheft, p. 37, Acts. 1–2

So sagt man das! p. 130 15 min.
- Presenting So sagt man das!, ATE, p. 121P
- Do Activities 3-4, p. 38, Grammatikheft

Grammatik, p. 130 25 min.
- Presenting Grammatik, ATE, p. 121Q
- Do Activity 11, p. 131
- Play Audio CD for Activity 12, p. 131
- Do Activities 13 and 14, p. 131
- Do Activities 2-7, pp. 51–53, Übungsheft

Quiz Review 20 min.
- Do Activities 5-7, p. 39, Grammatikheft
- Do Mehr Grammatikübungen, Erste Stufe
- Do Activity 1, Interactive CD-ROM
- Do Communicative Activity 5-1, pp. 25–26

Quiz 20 min.
- Quiz 5-1A or 5-1B

Homework Options
Pupil's Edition, p. 131, Act. 15

Block 3

ZWEITE STUFE
Quick Review 15 min.
- Return and review Quiz 5-1
- Bell Work, ATE, p. 121S
- Check homework, p. 131, Act. 15

ZUM LESEN 25 MIN.
- Present Lesestrategie, p. 132
- Do Activities 1–9, pp. 132–133

Wortschatz, p. 134 20 min.
- Presenting Wortschatz, ATE, p. 121S
- Present Und dann noch, p. 134
- Teaching Transparencies 5-1, 5-A
- Play Audio CD for Activity 16, p. 134
- Do Activity 17, p. 134

So sagt man das!, p. 134 10 min.
- Presenting So sagt man das!, ATE, p. 121T
- Do Activity 9, p. 40, Grammatikheft

Ein wenig Landeskunde/Ein wenig Grammatik, p. 135 15 min.
- Present Ein wenig Landeskunde, p. 135
- Present Sprachtipp, p. 135
- Present Ein wenig Grammatik, p. 135
- Do Activity 18, p. 135

Wrap-Up 5 min.
- Students respond to someone calling their attention

Homework Options
Grammatikheft, p. 40, Act. 8
Übungsheft, p. 55, Acts. 1–3

 **One-Stop Planner CD-ROM**

For alternative lesson plans by chapter section, to create your own customized plans, or to preview all resources available for this chapter, use the **One-Stop Planner CD-ROM**, Disc 2.

 For additional homework suggestions, see activities accompanied by this symbol throughout the chapter.

Block 4

ZWEITE STUFE
Quick Review 10 min.
- Check homework, Übungsheft, p. 55, Acts. 1–3

Grammatik, p. 136 30 min.
- Presenting **Grammatik**, ATE, p. 121T
- Do Activity 19, p. 136
- Play Audio CD for Activity 20, p. 137
- Do Activities 21, 22, 23, and 24, p. 137
- Do Activities 10–12, pp. 41–42, Grammatikheft

Quiz Review 30 min.
- Do **Mehr Grammatikübungen, Zweite Stufe**
- Do Activities 4–7, pp. 56–57, Übungsheft
- Do Activities 2–4, Interactive CD-ROM

Quiz 20 min.
- Quiz 5-2A or 5-2B

Homework Options
Übungsheft, p. 54, Acts. 1–4
Interaktive Spiele, see ATE, p. 121F

Block 5

DRITTE STUFE
Quick Review 15 min.
- Return and review Quiz 5-2
- Bell Work, ATE, p. 121U
- Check homework, Übungsheft, p. 54, Acts. 1–4

Wortschatz, p. 138 15 min.
- Presenting **Wortschatz**, ATE, p. 121U
- Teaching Transparency 5-2
- Do Activity 25, p. 138

So sagt man das!, p. 139 15 min.
- Presenting **So sagt man das!**, ATE, p. 121U
- Play Audio CD for Activity 26, p. 139
- Do Activity 27, p. 139

Ein wenig Grammatik, p. 139 15 min.
- Present **Ein wenig Grammatik**, p. 139
- Do Activity 28, p. 139
- Do Activities 1–2, p. 58, Übungsheft

Grammatik, p. 140 25 min.
- Presenting **Grammatik**, ATE, p. 121V
- Do Activities 29 and 30, p. 140
- Do Activity 18, p. 45, Grammatikheft
- Do Activities 4–7, pp. 59–60, Übungsheft

Wrap-Up 5 min.
- Students respond to questions about which foods and activities they like, prefer and like the most

Homework Options
Grammatikheft, pp. 43–44, Acts. 13–17
Übungsheft, p. 58, Act. 3

Block 6

DRITTE STUFE
Quick Review 15 min.
- Check homework, Grammatikheft, pp. 43–44, Acts. 13–17

Ein wenig Landeskunde/Grammatik, pp. 140–141 25 min.
- Present **Ein wenig Landeskunde**, p. 140
- Presenting **Grammatik**, ATE, p. 121V
- Do Activity 31, p. 141
- Present **Sprachtipp**, p. 141
- Do Activities 32 and 33, p. 141

Quiz Review 15 min.
- Do **Mehr Grammatikübungen, Dritte Stufe**
- Do Activities 5 and 6, Interactive CD-ROM

Quiz 20 min.
- Quiz 5-3A or 5-3B

Kann ich's wirklich?, p. 148 10 min.
- Write answers to questions 1–10, p. 148

Wrap-Up 5 min.
- Students respond to **Kann ich's wirklich?** questions

Homework Options
Pupil's Edition, p. 147, Act. 4, **Zum Schreiben**

Block 7

ANWENDUNG
Quick Review 25 min.
- Return and review Quiz 5-3
- Students present **Zum Schreiben** paragraphs
- Do **Anwendung** Activities 1–3 and 5, pp. 146–147

Chapter Review 20 min.
- Review chapter functions, vocabulary, and grammar; choose from **Mehr Grammatikübungen,** Grammar Tutor for Students of German, Activities for Communication, Listening Activities, Interactive CD-ROM Tutor, or **Interaktive Spiele**
- Review test format and provide sample test items for students

Test, Chapter 5 45 min.
- Administer Chapter 5 Test. Select from Testing Program, Alternative Assessment Guide, or Test Generator.

Kapitel 5: Gesund essen
Teaching Suggestions, pages 122–149

PAGES 122–123

CHAPTER OPENER

Pacing Tips
The **Erste Stufe** centers around the **Pause**. The function of 'expressing regret and downplaying' is introduced, along with the demonstrative **dieser**. In the **Zweite Stufe**, students learn more about the **Pausenbrot**. A complete presentation of all possessive adjectives occurs on p. 136. The interrogative **welcher** and the preposition **zu** are presented in the **Dritte Stufe** in conjunction with 'expressing preference and strong preference.' Because the three **Stufen** are all four pages long and present similar types of material, you will probably spend about the same amount of time teaching each **Stufe**. For Lesson Plans and timing suggestions, see pages 121I–121L.

Meeting the Standards
Communication
- Expressing regret and downplaying, p. 129
- Expressing skepticism and making certain, p. 130
- Calling someone's attention to something and responding, p. 134
- Expressing preference and strong preference, p. 139

Cultures
- Landeskunde, p. 127
- Ein wenig Landeskunde, p. 128
- Culture Note, p. 121M
- Background Information, p. 121M
- Culture Note, p. 121N
- Culture Note, p. 121S

Connections
- Language Note, p. 121M
- Language-to-Language, p. 121X

Comparisons
- Thinking Critically, p. 121O
- Thinking Critically, p. 121Q

Communities
- Career Path, p. 121X

Building Context
Ask students what healthy snack foods and beverages are for sale and about those they would like to see for sale at their school.

For resource information, see the **One-Stop Planner CD-ROM**, Disc 2.

Cultures and Communities

Culture Note
During breaks, German students are encouraged to leave the school building but remain on school grounds. Several teachers are assigned to monitor (**Schulhofaufsicht**) students outside, and, depending on the school size, some teachers have **Aufsicht** *(hall monitor duty)* inside the school.

Background Information
Generally, Germans do not eat waffles, pancakes with syrup, or eggs and bacon for breakfast. They may eat **weich gekochte Eier** *(soft-boiled eggs)* or **hart gekochte Eier** *(hard-boiled eggs)*, especially on Sunday. **Frische Brötchen** are often part of the breakfast meal, and they are served along with butter or margarine, cold cuts, cheese, jam, honey, or **Nutella**® (chocolate and hazelnut spread).

Connections and Comparisons

Language Note
Students have seen the diminutive form **-chen** in words such as **Mädchen** or **Päckchen**. You might want to remind them that this ending denotes something small or young. Can students infer the meaning of **Brötchen**? (literally: *small bread*)

Chapter Sequence
Los geht's!	p. 124
Landeskunde	p. 127
Erste Stufe	p. 128
Zum Lesen	p. 132
Zweite Stufe	p. 134
Dritte Stufe	p. 138
Mehr Grammatikübungen	p. 142
Anwendung	p. 146
Kann ich's wirklich?	p. 148
Wortschatz	p. 149

LOS GEHT'S!

Teaching Resources
pp. 124–126

PRINT
- Lesson Planner, p. 22
- Video Guide, pp. 29–30, 32
- Übungsheft, p. 49

MEDIA
- One-Stop Planner
- Video Program
  Los geht's!
  Videocassette 2, 18:44–22:06
  Videocassette 5 (captioned version), 26:53–30:15
  Fortsetzung
  Videocassette 2, 22:10–24:02
  Videocassette 5 (captioned version), 30:19–32:12
- DVD Tutor, Disc 1
- Audio Compact Discs, CD5, Trs. 1–2
- **Los geht's!** Transparencies

PAGES 124–125

 **Los geht's! Transparencies**

Preteaching Vocabulary

Recognizing Cognates

Los geht's! contains several words that students will be able to recognize as cognates. Some are compound words in which only part of the word is a cognate. Have students find these words and describe what is happening in the story.

- ❷ Pausenbrot
- ❸ Tofu mit Sojasprossen, vegetarisch, Fleisch
- ❹ Honig, Marmelade
- ❻ Hände, Flasche, Schokolade
- ❼ Suppe, Kühlschrank, Spinat
- ❽ Huhn, Nudeln, Reis, Soße

Fortsetzung

You may choose to continue with the Fortsetzung of *Wiebkes Pausenbrot* now or wait until later in the chapter. For a synopsis of the **Los geht's!** and **Fortsetzung** episodes, see p. 121E.

STANDARDS: 2.1, 2.2

Advance Organizer

As an advance organizer to **Los geht's!**, ask students to describe a healthy
a) breakfast,
b) lunch they would pack for school,
c) lunch they would prepare for friends.

Cultures and Communities

Culture Note

- Germans usually do not eat pastries or cake right after lunch. They prefer to wait until around four o'clock to have cake or pastries, which they usually have with coffee. They call this time **die Kaffeezeit**.

- In **Los geht's!**, David requests a **Quarkbrötchen**. **Quark** is a soft, fresh cheese that looks much like yogurt. It is used in the preparation of **Käsekuchen**, dips, or eaten as a spread on bread. It comes in many flavors. **Quark** is hard to find in American stores, but specialty health food stores occasionally carry it.

PAGE 126

Using the Captioned Video/DVD

If students have trouble understanding, you may want to play the captioned version of *Wiebkes Pausenbrot* on Videocassette 5. Ask students to use vocabulary and expressions they know to write two or three sentences in German to describe some of the things the teenagers did in the video episode.
Note: The *DVD Tutor* contains captions for all sections of the *Video Program*.

Comprehension Check

A Slower Pace
❶ To ensure comprehension of the text, go through each frame of **Los geht's!**, eliciting responses to the five questions from students.

Challenge
❹ After students have successfully matched the sentences, have them think of a different response to each of the sentences or questions on the left.
Example:
—Hier sind zehn Euro. —Es tut mir Leid. Ich habe nicht genug Wechselgeld.

KAPITEL 5 LOS GEHT'S! 121N

PAGE 127

LANDESKUNDE

Teaching Resources
p. 127

PRINT
- Video Guide, pp. 29–30, 32–33
- Übungsheft, p. 50

MEDIA
- One-Stop Planner
- Video Program
  Videocassette 2, 24:42–28:36
- DVD Tutor, Disc 1
- Audio Compact Discs, CD5, Trs. 3–6
- Interactive CD-ROM Tutor, Disc 2

Teaching Suggestions
Ask students to help you make a list of foods that are representative of particular areas or regions in the United States. Then ask students if they would eat the foods that were just mentioned by the class, and if not why?

Teacher to Teacher

Laura Grable
Riverhead Middle School
Riverhead, NY

Laura motivates her students with this ongoing activity:

"My students keep a manila envelope entitled **Andere Länder, andere Sitten**. Each time they encounter a custom or tradition that gives them an insight into culture, they jot it down on a 3x5 index card (including the name of the city or region) and put it in the envelope. They look forward to the **Ein wenig Landeskunde** and the **Landeskunde** sections to learn more about specific areas to add to their collections. I keep their envelopes as part of their portfolio throughout their German studies."

Connections and Comparisons

Thinking Critically
Comparing and Contrasting In Activity B, students are introduced to German and Austrian table manners (**Tischmanieren**). Ask students what is considered appropriate in the United States for the hand that is not being used. (Americans generally keep that hand in their laps.)

Total Physical Response
After having discussed some of the rules of table manners, use several of those commands with your students. Here are some examples:

Ruth, nimm den Ellbogen vom Tisch!
Linda, gerade sitzen, bitte!
Scott, wasch deine Hände! (student pretends)

Teacher Note
Mention to your students that the **Landeskunde** will also be included in Quiz 5-1B given at the end of the **Erste Stufe**.

ERSTE STUFE

Teaching Resources
pp. 128–131

PRINT
- Lesson Planner, p. 23
- TPR Storytelling Book, pp. 32–33
- Listening Activities, pp. 35–36, 39–40
- Activities for Communication, pp. 90, 93, 131–132
- Grammatikheft, pp. 37–39
- Grammar Tutor for Students of German, Chapter 5
- Übungsheft, pp. 51–53
- Testing Program, pp. 105–108
- Alternative Assessment Guide, p. 36
- Student Make-Up Assignments, Chapter 5

MEDIA
- One-Stop Planner
- Audio Compact Discs, CD5, Trs. 7–9, 14, 19–20
- Teaching Transparencies
  Mehr Grammatikübungen Answers
  Grammatikheft Answers
- Interactive CD-ROM Tutor, Disc 2
- DVD Tutor, Disc 1

PAGE 128

Bell Work
Have students imagine they need to raise money for a club by selling fresh fruit. Which fruits would sell well? Which would keep well and not require refrigeration? How much would they have to pay for the fruit? What would they charge per piece?

Building on Previous Skills
6 After students have completed their charts, ask them which of the German students' choices they like and why. Remind students to use **denn** or **weil** and the phrases expressing how something tastes. (Chapter 6 of Level 1)

Group Work
7 Students work in groups of three: one student is the **Verkäufer(in)**, and the other two are students going through the line at the snack counter. Ask students to make up a conversation using the **Wortschatz** on p. 128. They may want to ask how much things cost. They could even ask a friend for extra money and explain that an item might be sold out (**alle; ausverkauft**). Ask two or three groups to read or perform their conversations for the class.

STANDARDS: 1.1

PAGE 129

PRESENTING: So sagt man das!

- Go over the new expressions with your students. Then ask them to look at the frames of **Los geht's!** and find examples of the expressions they just learned.

- To provide students with practice using the new expressions, ask students questions to make them use an appropriate phrase from **So sagt man das!** Examples:
  Margaret, wir haben leider keine Milch mehr!
  Al, ich dachte, der Saft kostet nur 25 Cent!

Teaching Suggestion
9 After completing the listening task as suggested in the activity, do a follow-up activity. This time ask students to write down what each of the four children wants and what each is being offered instead. On a transparency, make a simple chart with the names of the four children down the left side and two columns labeled **Was das Kind möchte** and **Was die Eltern anbieten**. After listening to the conversations twice, call on students to help fill in the chart.

Teaching Suggestion
10 Have students help you make a list of things that can be found at markets. Students should use this list as they work on Activity 10.

PAGE 130

PRESENTING: So sagt man das!

- Before introducing the new phrases, ask students how they express skepticism in English about something they see or hear. Ask students how intonation affects these types of remarks.

- Next, ask students how they make certain in English. What expressions do they use? Does intonation play a role? Now practice the expressions in **So sagt man das!** using the given examples and adding more. Reinforce especially the new vocabulary from **Los geht's!** and the **Erste Stufe**. Have students respond affirmatively or negatively using the expressions from the right-hand side of **So sagt man das!** and any others they have learned. (Natürlich! Ja, sehr gern! Nein, absolut nicht! Nein, überhaupt nicht!)

KAPITEL 5 ERSTE STUFE

PRESENTING: Grammatik

The demonstrative dieser On a table, place several familiar items such as foods, classroom objects, and accessories. Tell students that you are a customer in a store. Point to each item and use the phrase **Ich möchte dies(en/e/es) … gern kaufen/haben.** Ask students to listen carefully and repeat what you just said. Have students point out the various endings and compare them to the endings of the definite articles in the accusative. Do a similiar demonstration with the nominative: **Dieser … schmeckt gut (ist teuer, kommt aus …).** Then demonstrate the dative with the location. **Was ist alles in diesem Salat? In dieser Suppe? In diesem Fertiggericht?** Finally, go over the **Grammatik** with the class.

PAGE 131

Teaching Suggestion

13/15 You may want to assign Activities 13 and 15 as homework.

 Game

Play the game **Wörter kreuz und quer.** See page 121C for the procedure.

Teaching Suggestion

Using the food vocabulary presented in the **Erste Stufe,** have students write their own **Lückensätze** in which the demonstrative **dieser** is missing. There should be at least two missing demonstratives for a partner to fill in.

Assess
- Testing Program, pp. 105–108
  Quiz 5-1A, Quiz 5-2B
  Audio CD5, Tr. 14
- Student Make-Up Assignments
  Chapter 5, Alternative Quiz
- Alternative Assessment Guide, p. 36

PAGES 132–133

ZUM LESEN

Teaching Resources
pp. 132–133

PRINT
- Lesson Planner, p. 26
- Übungsheft, p. 54
- Reading Strategies and Skills, Chapter 5
- Lies mit mir! 2, Chapter 5

MEDIA
- One-Stop Planner

Prereading
Building Context

Ask students why people sometimes prefer to be alone, without friends or other family members around them. When or how often does this happen to them?

Connections and Comparisons
Thinking Critically

Comparing and Contrasting After reading the **Lesestrategie,** ask students for examples of intensifiers in English. Can students think of intensifiers their parents or other relatives use and how these vary from generation to generation?

Teacher Note
Activity 2 is a prereading activity.

Reading
Thinking Critically

3 Drawing Inferences Before students scan the texts to find the German students' favorite places, remind them of the reading strategy they learned in Chapter 4: *activating your background knowledge.* To help students build expectations for the text, brainstorm with them places where they would typically like to go to be by themselves. Then do Activity 3.

Cooperative Learning

Divide students into groups of three. Each group should have a writer, a discussion leader, and a reporter. Set a time limit of approximately 20 minutes to complete Activities 5-8. When students have finished, ask each group reporter to share his or her group's discussion outcomes with the class.

Communication for All Students

Challenge

6 Ask students to substitute synonyms for the words in bold in the three sentences. You may help students by providing them with a list of phrases that students should be able to recognize. (Examples: wirklich, sicher, zwei Stunden oder mehr/länger, bestimmt, ziemlich)

Thinking Critically

Drawing Inferences Ask students to skim the four interviews again and then make up an appropriate title for each of them. Titles should reflect the students' choices for a quiet place.

Post-Reading

Teacher Note

Activity 9 is a post-reading task that will show whether students can apply what they have learned.

Teaching Suggestion

Divide the class into groups of three students. Each group should have a recorder and a reporter. Draw a flower like the one below on a transparency or the board and fill in each of the petals with a word from the reading selection. Each group creates a description using the words in the petals. Set a time limit for this activity. Then call on two or three groups and have the reporter read his or her group's story to the class.

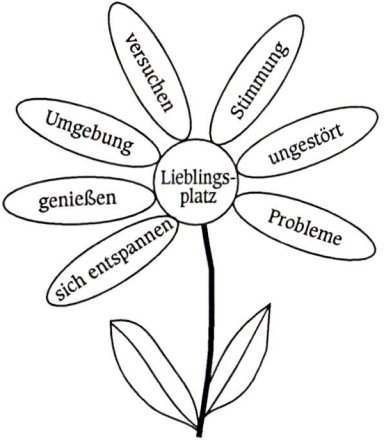

Writing Assessment

You could collect the written work of the previous Teaching Suggestion and use it for assessment. To evaluate the assignments you may wish to use the following rubric.

Writing Rubric

	Points 4	3	2	1
Content (Complete – Incomplete)				
Comprehensibility (Comprehensible – Seldom comprehensible)				
Accuracy (Accurate – Seldom accurate)				
Organization (Well-organized – Poorly organized)				
Effort (Excellent – Minimal)				

18–20: A   16–17: B   14–15: C   12–13: D   Under 12: F

Zum Lesen Answers

Answers to Activity 1
Favorite "get-away-spots" of young people

Answers to Activity 2
Answers will vary.

Answers to Activity 3
Markus: Café; Tanja: eigenes Zimmer; Nicole: Turm; Christian: Schülervertretungsbüro
Answers will vary.

Answers to Activity 4
Markus: abgelegen, nicht viele Leute / trinkt etwas, liest, schreibt Gedichte; Tanja: klein, unterm Dach / liegt im Bett, hört Musik, liest, bummelt herum, schläft lange, sortiert Flaschensammlung, blättert Zeitschriften durch; Nicole: im Stadtwald, es ist ruhig um den Turm, wenige Leute / denkt nach, unterhält sich mit Hund, genießt die Sonne; Christian: in der Schule, ruhig in den Pausen / denkt nach, entspannt sich, liest Briefe, verschönert den Raum

Answers to Activity 5
Answers will vary.

Answers to Activity 6
a. The word **eigentlich** is a filler with various meanings. In this case it conveys the notion of "basically", "actually", or "really", and allows the speaker more time to think.
b. Using **mindestens** (at least) in this case indicates an extension of the time period stated.
c. **Ganz schön** intensifies the adjective **eng**.

Answers to Activity 7
now and then; from time to time

Answers to Activity 8
Crazy as it may sound—sometimes I talk with him then.

ZWEITE STUFE

Teaching Resources
pp. 134–137

PRINT
- Lesson Planner, p. 24
- TPR Storytelling Book, pp. 34–35
- Listening Activities, pp. 36–37, 41
- Activities for Communication, pp. 25–26, 91, 93, 131–132
- Grammatikheft, pp. 40–42
- Grammar Tutor for Students of German, Chapter 5
- Übungsheft, pp. 55–57
- Testing Program, pp. 109–112
- Alternative Assessment Guide, p. 36
- Student Make-Up Assignments, Chapter 5

MEDIA
- One-Stop Planner
- Audio Compact Discs, CD5, Trs. 10–11, 15, 21–22
- Teaching Transparencies
  Situation 5-1
  Vocabulary 5-A
  Mehr Grammatikübungen Answers
  Grammatikheft Answers
- Interactive CD-ROM Tutor, Disc 2
- DVD Tutor, Disc 1

PAGE 134

Bell Work
In groups of three, have students brainstorm all the sandwiches they could make using the many foods they already know. Have them think of meat, cheese, eggs, vegetables, and jam, or honey. How many can they think of?
(Examples: **Wurstbrötchen, Tomatenbrot, Quarkbrötchen**)

PRESENTING: Wortschatz
Ask students to bring the foods from the **Wortschatz** to class. You may also want to bring a small selection of different types of German breads. (Examples: **Schwarzbrot, Mischbrot, Roggenbrot, Bauernbrot**) Label each food with the appropriate German word and display them on a table in front of the class. Introduce the items to the class. Repeat each word several times to ensure comprehension.

Communication for All Students

Kinesthetic Learners
Once you feel that students are familiar with the new words, ask students to make their own sample **Pausenbrot**, using the ingredients available. Students can form a line, preparing their **Pausenbrote**. Once all students have finished, ask several students **Was hast du denn auf dem Brot?**

Cultures and Communities

Culture Note
You might want to remind students that Germans usually eat open-faced sandwiches (except when prepared ahead of time for school or work). They often spread unsalted butter on the bread and then cover it with cold cuts, cheese, or jam. There are many varieties of breads available such as **Mischbrot,** which is made from wheat and rye flour, **Weißbrot,** which Germans generally use to make toast, and **Vollkornbrot,** which is made from coarsely ground rye and wheat grains.

Connections and Comparisons

Thinking Critically
17 Comparing and Contrasting After students have talked to their partners, ask the class to make a list of the typical ingredients used for a **Pausenbrot** in the United States and in Germany. Have students compare the two.

PRESENTING: So sagt man das!

Ask students to look back at **Los geht's!** on p. 124. Have them reread Frames 2 and 6 where the phrases **Guck mal!** and **Schaut mal da!** are first introduced. Can students infer from the context the meaning of those two expressions? Then go over the expressions in **So sagt man das!** with students.

PAGE 135

Communication for All Students

A Slower Pace

18 Write the sentences on the board. To help students see the relationship between the possessive pronoun and the subject, ask several students to come to the board and underline or connect the two elements.
Example:
Was haben _sie_ denn auf _ihrem_ Pausenbrot?

PAGE 136

PRESENTING: Grammatik

The possessives After reviewing the possessives and their endings, ask individual students questions like the example below. Students have to answer using possessive pronouns with their correct endings.
James, wem gehört denn dieses Buch?

PAGE 137

TPR Total Physical Response

23 Once students have correctly identified the owner of the belongings, give commands to individual students, using such verbs as **nehmen, geben, hinlegen, bringen, weitergeben, aufheben, zeigen, reichen, suchen,** or **finden** as well as possessive adjectives.
Examples:
Marie, gib Andrew bitte deinen Kuli!
Hier ist Morgans Buch. Reich ihm bitte sein Buch!

Communication for All Students

Visual Learners
The day you plan to do this activity, ask students to leave one item belonging to them on your desk on their way to their seat. (Examples: watch, pen, book, photo, snack) Hold up one item at a time, and ask students whose item it is. Examples:
Grace, gehört dir dieser Kuli?
Diego, ist dies deine Uhr?
If the item doesn't belong to the student you just asked, that student may know who the owner is and should answer with **Nein, das ist nicht meine Uhr, das ist ihre Uhr.** (pointing to another student). Continue until all items have been returned to their owners.

Teaching Suggestion

Ask students to write a description of how they make their favorite breakfast. Students should include sequencing words.

Assess

▶ Testing Program, pp. 109–112
  Quiz 5-2A, Quiz 5-2B
  Audio CD5, Tr. 15

▶ Student Make-Up Assignments
  Chapter 5, Alternative Quiz

▶ Alternative Assessment Guide, p. 36

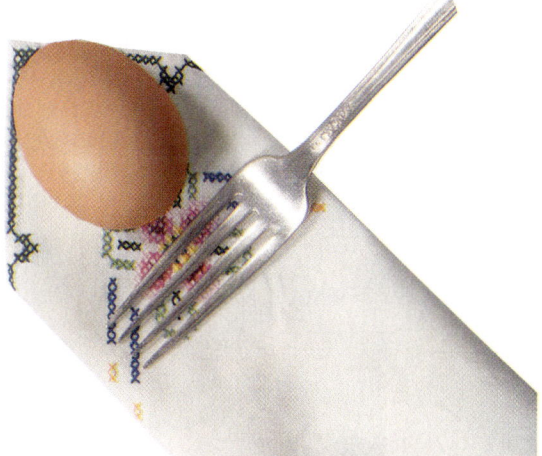

DRITTE STUFE

> **Teaching Resources**
> pp. 138–141
>
> **PRINT**
> - Lesson Planner, p. 25
> - TPR Storytelling Book, pp. 36–37
> - Listening Activities, pp. 37, 42
> - Activities for Communication, pp. 27–30, 92, 93, 131–132
> - Grammatikheft, pp. 43–45
> - Grammar Tutor for Students of German, Chapter 5
> - Übungsheft, pp. 58–60
> - Testing Program, pp. 113–116
> - Alternative Assessment Guide, p. 36
> - Student Make-Up Assignments, Chapter 5
>
> **MEDIA**
> - One-Stop Planner
> - Audio Compact Discs, CD5, Trs. 12, 16, 23–24
> - Teaching Transparencies
>   Situation 5-2
>   **Mehr Grammatikübungen** Answers
>   Grammatikheft Answers
> - Interactive CD-ROM Tutor, Disc 2
> - DVD Tutor, Disc 1

PAGE 138

Bell Work

Tell students that they are going to shop for a family dinner at the local supermarket. They will go to both the meat department and the fish department. What foods can they recall in German that can be found in these two places? Write the two heads **Fleischabteilung** and **Fischabteilung** on a transparency and have small groups of students brainstorm all the items that would fit under either one of the two heads.

PRESENTING: Wortschatz

Ask students to look at the KAUFMANNS advertisement and have them find the imported food items. Can students tell from the abbreviations where the items are from? (grapes/France, bananas/Guatemala, chicken and carrots/Holland, lamb/Australia) In addition to the notations for imports, have students find all the words and phrases in small print that are used as qualifiers for various items. Some of these words should already be familiar to students. Have students first guess at the others and then verify their meaning. (Examples: **aus dem Fass, vom Schwein, Kl. A, gefroren, zart, mager, abgehangen, 1000 g Beutel, 500 g Packung**) Have students work in pairs and present their findings to the class.

PAGE 139

PRESENTING: So sagt man das!

Using visual aids such as realia, transparencies, or photos, introduce the new functions by holding up the visual aid and asking directed questions that incorporate the new expressions. Elicit responses from individual students. This is also a great way to recycle vocabulary from different content areas you feel students need to review.

> ### Communication for All Students
>
> #### A Slower Pace
> **26** Inform students that they will hear the recording twice. The first time, students should try to take notes of the food and drink items mentioned. When students listen the second time, they should make notes on the preferences mentioned by the different students.
>
> #### For Additional Practice
> **27** For extra practice, have students interview each other about the foods they prefer for different occasions. (Examples: **Fete, Grillparty, Picknick**)
>
> #### Challenge
> **27** Have students make up pairs of beverages that could logically be compared. (Examples: **Kaffee/Tee, Milch/Saft, Leitungswasser/Mineralwasser, Cola/Eistee**) Then have students use these choices in practice with their partner.

PAGE 140

PRESENTING: Grammatik

The interrogative welcher To introduce the interrogative **welcher**, recycle such phrases as **gern haben, gut finden, lieber machen, gern sehen,** and **gern hören**. Question students about their interests, tastes, likes, dislikes, and preferences. As you ask some of the questions, write them on a transparency as well. Then ask students to examine the new question word and determine why they think **welch-** has different endings.

Portfolio Assessment

29 You might want to suggest this activity as a written portfolio item for your students. See *Alternative Assessment Guide,* p. 22.

Building on Previous Skills

29 Before students begin with the activity, write the six food categories on the board and have students brainstorm as many items for each of the listed categories as they can remember. Students can later refer to this list as they work with their partners.

Teaching Suggestion

30 Students should use the list you prepared for Activity 29 as they work on Activity 30. Point out to students that they can use the phrases underneath the word **Warum?** to give a reason for selecting a food as their favorite.

PAGE 141

PRESENTING: Grammatik

The preposition zu On a transparency, make a list of phrases that students know. First ask them to shorten each phrase using a contraction.

     zu der Schule —> zur Schule
zu dem Supermarkt —> zum Supermarkt
zu dem Mittagessen —> zum Mittagessen

Then ask students to tell you what **zu der (zur)** and **zu dem (zum)** mean. (*to:* to school, to the supermarket; *for,* with meals: for lunch)

Teaching Suggestion

Tell students that they are all going to visit relatives this weekend. They need to tell you whom they are going to see. Make a list of all suggestions on a transparency. Try to elicit some plurals, too.

Examples:
Ich gehe zu meinem Onkel.
Ich gehe zu meiner Kusine.
Ich gehe zu meinen Großeltern.

Portfolio Assessment

31 You might want to suggest this activity as an oral portfolio item for your students. See *Alternative Assessment Guide,* p. 22.

> ### Communication for All Students
>
> #### For Additional Practice
>
> **32** Ask students to come up with other possible answers beyond those offered in the word boxes. (Examples: **Schokoladeneis, Scholle, Mohnbrötchen, Brokkoli, Erdbeerjoghurt, Gurkensalat**)

Reteaching: Using the interrogative *welcher*

Ask students to look back at the **KAUFMANNS** advertisement on p. 138. Then ask students to imagine that they are the salesclerk at that supermarket. They didn't quite understand what a customer ordered and ask him or her about the order. Examples:
Welchen Fisch möchten Sie, bitte?
Welches Fleisch wünschen Sie?
Welche Äpfel dürfen es sein?

Teaching Suggestion

Play the following skit with students. In German, ask students to join you for an after-school study lesson. Students then try to get out of staying after school by telling you that they already have to go somewhere else. Here are some possible responses students might give you:

Das tut mir Leid, aber ich muss zum Zahnarzt.
Ich bedaure, aber ich muss zum Supermarkt.
Es ist schade, aber ich muss zu meiner Oma.

Have each student try to talk himself or herself out of joining the study session. If possible, you might want to display a variety of pictures depicting reasons for excuses to which students can refer for this activity.

Von der Schule zum Beruf

33 Von der Schule zum Beruf

Have students research the Web sites of various **Reformhäuser** using German search engines.

Assess

▸ Testing Program, pp. 113–116
 Quiz 5-3A, Quiz 5-3B
 Audio CD5, Tr. 16

▸ Student Make-Up Assignments
 Chapter 5, Alternative Quiz

▸ Alternative Assessment Guide, p. 36

PAGES 142–145

MEHR GRAMMATIKÜBUNGEN

The **Mehr Grammatikübungen** activities are designed as supplemental activities for the grammatical concepts presented in the chapter. You might use them as additional practice, for review, or for assessment.

For more grammar presentations, review, and practice, refer to the following:
- Grammatikheft
- Grammar Tutor for Students of German
- Grammar Summary on pp. R20–R36
- Übungsheft
- Grammar and Vocabulary quizzes (Testing Program)
- Test Generator
- Interactive CD-ROM Tutor
- **Interaktive Spiele** at go.hrw.com

PAGES 146–147

ANWENDUNG

Video Wrap-up
Videocassette 2, 18:44–30:46
Videocassette 5 (captioned version), 26:53–32:12
DVD Tutor, Disc 1

At this time, you might want to use the video resources for additional review and enrichment. These resources are also available via the Enhanced Online Student Edition.
See *Video Guide* for suggestions regarding:
- *Wiebkes Pausenbrot* Dramatic episode
- **Landeskunde** Interviews
- **Videoclips** Authentic footage

Apply and Assess

A Slower Pace
1 On a transparency or the board, write in random order all the foods that are mentioned in the listening activity. As students listen to the activity, they can refer to the list to help them complete the chart.

Group Work
2 Read the text with students and go over unfamiliar words or phrases. Then divide the class into groups of three to four students. Ask each group to answer Questions 1–4 within a set amount of time. One student should write down the answers. When students have finished, call on several groups to share their answers with the class.

Process Writing
4 Encourage your students to liven up and add humor to their articles through the use of dialogue. Many of the functional expressions presented in this chapter could be utilized in this manner. Remember to review with students beforehand the proper way to write German quotation marks and the correct placement of associated punctuation.

Cultures and Communities

Language-to-Language
One way languages influence each other is through "loanwords" — words that one language takes from another. For example, "Alcatraz" comes from the Spanish *Isla de Alcatraces* (Island of Pelicans). The Spanish word *alcatraz* (pelican) was adopted, in turn, from the Arabic *al-qatras* (albatross). Names for different types of foods are especially likely to become loanwords. (Example: German has adopted the term **Pommes frites**, *fried potatoes*, from the French.) Have students brainstorm food words that English has borrowed from other languages. (Examples: *escargots, sauerkraut, sushi, pizza, baklava, paella*)

Career Path
Have students work in groups to think of reasons someone in the nutrition industry would benefit from a knowledge of German. (Suggestions: A good deal of research is conducted in German-speaking countries about the benefits and effects of various foods and chemicals on the body, and a nutritionist could increase his or her expertise by staying abreast of the German literature; such a person could also travel to Germany and become involved in the sizable organic food industry, either as a grower or seller.)

> **PAGE 148**

KANN ICH'S WIRKLICH?

This page helps students prepare for the test. It is a brief checklist of the major points covered in the chapter. The students should be reminded that it is only a checklist and not necessarily everything that will appear on the test.

For additional self check options, refer students to the *Grammar Tutor,* the *Interactive CD-ROM Tutor,* and the Online self-test for this chapter.

> **PAGE 149**

WORTSCHATZ

Apply and Assess

Circumlocution
The circumlocution game, **Das treffende Wort suchen,** is especially well suited to review the vocabulary in this chapter. All three **Stufen** contain foods that can easily be described according to taste, texture, color, appearance, and what one eats with a particular food. For instance, for **Marmelade** one could say, **Es ist etwas Süßes, das man auf dem Brot isst.** See p. 3C for procedures.

Tactile Learners
Use sentence strips to practice sentences that include the expressions or phrases from each **Stufe**. Write each sentence on a piece of paper, cutting it into its word components. Put the fragments of each sentence into a numbered envelope. Write the corresponding sentence on a separate sheet of paper beside the number. Give one envelope to each pair of students, who will try to put the sentences back together.

Game
Play the game **Zeichenspiel,** using the food vocabulary from this chapter. See p. 187C in the Level 1 *Teacher's Edition* for the procedure.

Teaching Suggestion
To practice the names of foods, ask students to name foods that can be found in certain sections of a grocery store.
Examples:
Was kann man in der Fischabteilung kaufen?
Welche Sorte Fleisch gibt es in der Fleischabteilung?
Was für Obst findet man gewöhnlich bei dem Obsthändler?
Nenne einige Produkte in der Tiefkühlkostabteilung.

Teacher Note
Give the **Kapitel 5** Chapter Test: *Testing Program,* pp. 117–122
Audio CD 5, Trs. 17–18

STANDARDS: 1.1, 4.1, 5.1

KAPITEL

5
Gesund essen

Objectives

In this chapter you will learn to

Erste Stufe
- express regret and downplay
- express skepticism and make certain

Zweite Stufe
- call someone's attention to something and respond

Dritte Stufe
- express preference and strong preference

Visit Holt Online
go.hrw.com
KEYWORD: WK3 HAMBURG-5
Online Edition

◀ Tofu mit Sojasprossen! Lecker!

Los geht's! · Wiebkes Pausenbrot

Los geht's! is an abridged version of the video episode.

CD 5
Trs. 1–2

Strategie Verstehen
Look at the images for this story. In how many different places does the story take place? What do you think the students are talking about?

Nicolas   Wiebke   David   Thorsten

Am Helene-Lange-Gymnasium in Hamburg können sich die Schüler in der Pause etwas zu essen und zu trinken kaufen. Alles ist gut, gesund und billig. Die „Verkäuferinnen" sind nämlich die Mütter der Schüler. Sie kaufen alles billig ein, sie bereiten die belegten Brötchen vor und stehen dann auch hinter der Theke.

1

Maike: Ein Salamibrötchen, bitte!— Danke!
Nicolas: Ich nehme heute mal einen Joghurt.
Thorsten: Ein Eibrötchen!
Frau: Eibrötchen gibt es heute nicht.
Thorsten: Dann nehm ich eine Banane.
David: Ich möchte eine Milch und ein Quarkbrötchen, bitte.

2

Nicolas: Was isst du denn da, Wiebke?
Wiebke: Das ist mein Pausenbrot. Das hab ich mir mitgebracht.
Nicolas: Und was hast du denn da auf dem Brot?
Wiebke: Guck mal! Lecker, nicht?

3

Nicolas: Und was soll das da sein für ein Gemüse?
Wiebke: Tofu mit Sojasprossen!
Thorsten: Igitt! Du isst wohl vegetarisch, was?
Wiebke: Nö, nicht unbedingt. Manchmal ess ich auch Fleisch.

124   hundertvierundzwanzig   STANDARDS: 1.2   KAPITEL 5   Gesund essen

Heute morgen beim Frühstück

4
- **Mutter:** Ich hab hier noch ein Ei, Wiebke. Willst du es?
- **Wiebke:** Nein, danke! Gib es doch dem Bernie! Aber ich nehme jetzt noch ein Stück Brot mit … hm …
- **Mutter:** Hier ist Honig, Marmelade, Wurst …
- **Wiebke:** Ich nehme mir eine Scheibe Wurst. Der Aufschnitt sieht echt prima aus.

5
- **Wiebke:** Tofu ist gesund, Thorsten! Willst du mal probieren?
- **Thorsten:** Hm, wirklich prima! Fast wie Quark.

6
- **Nicolas:** Schaut mal da, der David! Du, David, wie willst du denn das alles essen? Da brauchst du ja drei Hände!
- **David:** Einfach: Die Flasche in die Tasche; die Schokolade in die andere Tasche, und jetzt hab ich meine Hände frei für mein Quarkbrötchen.

Einmal hat Wiebke für ihre Freunde ein prima Mittagessen gemacht.

7
- **David:** Was ist das für eine Suppe?
- **Wiebke:** Eine Gemüsesuppe. Kommt aus dem Kühlschrank! Es ist ein Fertiggericht, man braucht sie nur noch aufwärmen.
- **David:** Hm, gut! Ich mag Gemüse.
- **Wiebke:** Welches Gemüse magst du am liebsten?
- **David:** Eigentlich alles. Nur Spinat mag ich nicht.
- **Wiebke:** Mensch, da bin ich aber froh, dass ich keinen Spinat gemacht habe.

8
- **Wiebke:** Und dann gibt es Huhn, mit Nudeln oder Reis. Hier ist die Soße. Ach ja, und dann gibt es noch Salat, Kopfsalat mit Tomaten. —Und zum Nachtisch gibt es Obst. Und nun wünsch ich euch einen guten Appetit!

Übungsheft, S. 49

1 Was passiert hier?

These activities check for global comprehension only. Students should not yet be expected to produce language modeled in Los geht's!

Verstehst du alles, was diese Leute sagen? Beantworte die Fragen!   1. during the break; students' mothers
1. When do the students buy something to eat and drink? Who sells it to them?
2. What does Thorsten ask for? What does he buy? Why?   2. egg sandwich; a banana; egg sandwiches are sold out
3. What does Wiebke have on her sandwich?   3. Tofu and bean sprouts
4. What did Wiebke have for breakfast?   4. bread and sausage
5. What did Wiebke serve her friends the day she made lunch for them?
   5. vegetable soup, chicken with noodles or rice, salad and fruit

2 Genauer lesen

Lies den Text noch einmal, und beantworte diese Fragen!
1. Was hat Wiebke von zu Hause mitgebracht?   1. Pausenbrot
2. Was isst Wiebke zum Frühstück?   2. Stück Brot, Scheibe Wurst
3. Wie findet Thorsten den Tofu?   3. prima, fast wie Quark
4. Was isst David alles?   4. Schokolade, Quarkbrötchen
5. Was hat Wiebke für ihre Freunde nicht gemacht?   5. Spinat
6. Welches Gemüse mag David nicht?   6. Spinat

3 Stimmt oder stimmt nicht?

Wenn der Satz nicht stimmt, schreib die richtige Antwort!
1. Thorsten kauft ein Eibrötchen.   1. stimmt nicht; eine Banane
2. Das Eibrötchen kostet zwei Euro.   2. stimmt nicht; Eibrötchen sind alle
3. Wiebke hat Tofu mit Sojasprossen auf ihrem Pausenbrot.   3. stimmt
4. Wiebke isst immer vegetarisch.   4. stimmt nicht; sie isst auch Fleisch
5. Auf ihrem Frühstücksbrot hat sie immer Honig.   5. stimmt nicht; sie isst auch Wurst
6. Thorsten probiert den Tofu.   6. stimmt
7. Wiebke braucht die Gemüsesuppe nur aufwärmen.   7. stimmt
8. David mag jedes Gemüse.   8. stimmt nicht; Spinat mag er nicht

4 Was passt zusammen?

Welche Sätze auf der rechten Seite passen zu den Sätzen auf der linken Seite?
1. Die Eibrötchen sind leider alle.   a
2. Du isst wohl nur vegetarisch?   e
3. Willst du mal den Tofu probieren?   d
4. Die Suppe schmeckt gut!   b
5. Was gibt's heute zum Mittagessen?   c

a. Dann nehme ich eben eine Banane.
b. Das ist ein Fertiggericht, kommt aus dem Kühlschrank.
c. Huhn mit Nudeln und Reis.
d. Hm, lecker! Fast wie Quark.
e. Nein, manchmal esse ich auch Fleisch und Wurst.

5 Und du?

Beantworte die Fragen!   Answers will vary.
1. Kaufst du dein Essen in der Schule, oder bringst du etwas von zu Hause mit?
2. Isst du nur vegetarisch?
3. Hast du schon mal Tofu mit Sojasprossen gegessen? Wie hat er dir geschmeckt?
4. Magst du Spinat?
5. Was kostet die Milch in deiner Schule?

Was isst du, was nicht?

We have asked people from around Germany and Austria what kinds of food they usually eat and why. Before you read the responses, think about the most popular and unpopular foods in the United States. What do most teenagers like? Listen to the interviews, then read the texts. *CD 5 Tr. 3*

CD 5 Trs. 3–6

Übungsheft, S. 50, Ü. 1

Heidemarie, München

„Also, ich mag die italienische Küche und die chinesische Küche, und auch also chinesisch, weil das ist, das ist manchmal sehr interessant, hat 'nen interessanten Geschmack. Und nicht so gern ess ich Meeresfrüchte und so was mit Meeres …Fisch und so zu tun hat." *CD 5 Tr. 5*

Jens und Sabine, Berlin *CD 5 Tr. 4*

Sabine: „Ich esse gerne Nudeln, Gemüse, Obst, besonders in Aufläufen, sehr gern auch Reisgerichte. Risotto schmeckt sehr gut."

Jens: „Ja, und wir haben uns gerade ein Buch gekauft über italienische Nudelgerichte. Und weil wir sehr gerne kochen, vor allem italienisch, wollen wir es mal ausprobieren."

Gerhard, St. Ulrich

„Essen tu ich alles sehr gern, bis auf Innereien, Fisch weniger. Mehlspeisen, die mag ich überhaupt sehr gern. Alles, was so Hausmannskost ist, ist alles gefragt." *CD 5 Tr. 6*

A. 1. Gerhard; predominantly meat and starches with sides of traditional vegetables (e.g. peas, carrots); innards; seafood

A. 1. Which person mentions "home cooking" as his or her favorite? What might a typical home-cooked meal in Germany look like? What do you think **Innereien** are, judging by the sound of it? If **Meer** means *sea* or *ocean,* what do you think **Meeresfrüchte** means? Read the interviews again and make a list of the different kinds of foods mentioned. Which foods do people say they like? Which don't they like?

   2. Make a list of popular and unpopular foods in the United States. Are there any similarities between the two cultures with respect to food?

B. Both in Germany and Austria it is considered good manners to leave your lower arm (the one you're not eating with) on the edge of the table. It is also polite to eat with your fork in your left hand while holding your knife in your right hand. When your host is serving you food or a drink, you should let him or her know when to stop by saying **Danke!** Otherwise your host will keep on pouring!

STANDARDS: 1.2, 2.2, 3.2, 4.2

Storytelling Book pp. 32–33

Erste Stufe

Objectives Expressing regret and downplaying; expressing skepticism and making certain

WK3 HAMBURG-5

Wortschatz

Was gibt es heute in der Pause? Und wie teuer ist es?

p. 121X   5-A

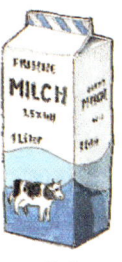
Milch

Kakao

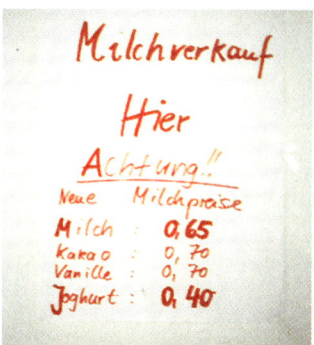

Vanillemilch

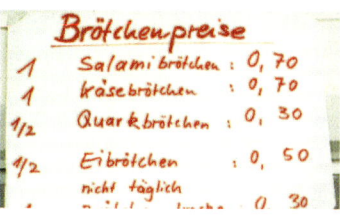
Joghurt

Welche von diesen Speisen und Getränken kannst du an deiner Schule kaufen? Was kosten sie?

Grammatikheft, S. 37, Ü. 1

6 Was kaufen sich die Schüler?

Script and answers on p. 121G

CD 5 Tr. 7

Zuhören/Schreiben Vier Schüler kaufen sich in der Pause etwas zu essen und zu trinken. Schreib auf, was jeder kauft und was das kostet! Wie viel hat jeder Schüler ausgegeben?

Ein wenig Landeskunde

Am Helene-Lange-Gymnasium in Hamburg sorgen die Mütter der Gymnasiasten dafür, dass sich ihre Söhne und Töchter in den beiden Pausen etwas zu essen und zu trinken kaufen können, was gut, nahrhaft und auch billig ist. Und das ist nur möglich, weil die Mütter die Speisen und Getränke preisgünstig einkaufen und die belegten Brötchen selbst vorbereiten. Auch Obst ist immer reichlich vorhanden.

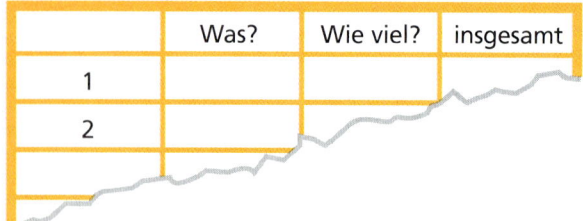

	Was?	Wie viel?	insgesamt
1			
2			

7 Und du? Was möchtest du?

Sprechen Was möchtest du in der Pause essen und trinken? Wähl einige Sachen aus! Du hast nur zwei Euro dabei. Sag deinen Mitschülern, was du möchtest! Wie viel Geld bekommst du zurück?

So sagt man das!

Expressing regret and downplaying

When you need to express regret, you could say:

Ich bedaure, die Eibrötchen sind alle.
Es tut mir Leid, die Milch kostet jetzt 70 Cent.
Was für ein Pech! Kein Joghurt mehr.
Ich hab **leider** nur Quarkbrötchen.

To respond to an expression of regret and to downplay your response, you could say:

Das macht nichts!   or   **Schon gut!**   or   **Nicht so schlimm!**

To indicate you'll do something else instead, use **eben** or **halt.**

Dann nehm ich **eben** ein Salamibrötchen.
Dann trink ich **halt** ein Mineralwasser.

Which of the expressions of regret sounds the most formal? The least formal? How would you express the last two statements in English?

Übungsheft, S. 51, Ü. 1
Grammatikheft, S. 37, Ü. 2

8 Es tut mir Leid!

Sprechen Together with a partner, choose a store that specializes in something, for example, food, clothing, musical instruments, furniture, pets, or gifts. See pages R12–R19 for additional vocabulary. Bring in photos or props of things that your shop sells. Your partner will make a shopping list of things she would like to buy at your store. Your partner asks if you have the things on her list. If you happen to be out of stock, express your regret and give a reason why. Your partner then responds, downplaying her response. Role-play your conversation in front of the class.

9 Was ist im Kühlschrank? Script and answers on p. 121G

CD 5
Tr. 8

Zuhören/Schreiben Listen as four children ask their parents about what there is in the refrigerator to eat. Write down which children are satisfied with the parent's answer (and decide to have something else), and which are not.

Remember that when you ask for certain quantities, you do so by weight: **200 Gramm Wurst, bitte!** How would you ask for two pounds of plums? One kilogram of potatoes?[1]

10 Was für ein Pech!

Sprechen Such dir einen Partner! Stell dir vor, du bist auf einem Marktplatz, wo es gewöhnlich alles zu kaufen gibt! Aber jetzt ist es Samstagnachmittag, so um halb zwei. Vieles ist schon alle, denn die Stände machen um zwei Uhr zu. — Du bist jetzt der Verkäufer, dein Partner kauft bei dir ein. Tauscht dann die Rollen aus! Gebraucht die Wörter im Kasten, wenn ihr wollt!

Brokkoli	Möhren	Aprikosen
Zwetschgen	Blaubeeren	Erdbeeren
	Wurst	Käse
Äpfel	Birnen	Kartoffeln

Answers will vary. E.g.: **Ich möchte 200 g Erdbeeren, bitte. — Ich bedaure, die Erdbeeren sind alle.**

---

1. **Ich möchte bitte zwei Pfund Zwetschgen. Ein Kilo Kartoffeln, bitte!**

So sagt man das!

Expressing skepticism and making certain

Grammatikheft, S. 38, Ü. 3–4

You may be skeptical about something you see or hear. You could say:

Was soll denn das sein, dieser Quark und dieses Gemüse?

You want to make certain and ask:

Du isst wohl vegetarisch, **was?**
Du isst wohl viel Fleisch, **ja?**
Du magst Joghurt, **oder?**
Du magst doch Quark, **nicht wahr?**

An answer may be:

Das ist Tofu, und das sind Sojasprossen.

And the response might be:

Ja! *or* Nein!
Nicht unbedingt!
Na klar!
Sicher!

What do you think the first question means? How would you express this idea in English? What could **dieser** and **dieses** mean? How does adding a question (such as **was?**) at the end of the four statements change their meaning? How is **nicht unbedingt** different from the other responses?[1]

Was soll denn das sein, dieses Gemüse?

Grammatik

The demonstrative **dieser**

1. **Dieser, diese, dieses** *(this)*, and **diese** *(pl) (these)* are called demonstratives. They are used to indicate specific items.

    Was soll denn das sein, **dieses Gemüse?**
    Kann ich bitte **diesen Apfel** haben?

2. **Dieser** has the following forms:

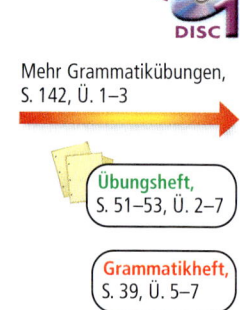

Mehr Grammatikübungen, S. 142, Ü. 1–3

	Masculine	Feminine	Neuter	Plural
Nominative	dieser	diese	dieses	diese
Accusative	diesen	diese	dieses	diese
Dative	diesem	dieser	diesem	diesen

Übungsheft, S. 51–53, Ü. 2–7

Grammatikheft, S. 39, Ü. 5–7

What other group of words that you have learned has similar endings?[2]

---

1. **nicht unbedingt** means *not necessarily* and leaves open the possibility the statement could be true.
2. The definite articles **der, die, das** have the same endings, as well as **jeder**.

11 Grammatik im Kontext

Schreiben Schreib diese Sätze ab, und setz dabei die richtigen Endungen ein! Vergleiche dann deine Sätze mit den Sätzen eines Partners!

A: Dies __1__ Eibrötchen sehen lecker aus! Schau!   1. diese

B: Stimmt! Ich nehme dies __2__ Brötchen, denn auf dies __3__ Brötchen liegt mehr Ei drauf!   2. dieses 3. diesem

A: Hm, dies __4__ Pausenbrot sieht gut aus! Dies __5__ Sojasprossen, prima! Aber was ist denn dies __6__ Pudding da drunter?   4. dieses 5. diese 6. dieser

B: Dies __7__ Pudding ist Tofu!   7. dieser

A: Willst du mal probieren? Dies __8__ Schokolade schmeckt echt prima.   8. diese

B: Nein, danke! Dies __9__ Apfel schmeckt auch sehr gut.   9. dieser

A: Was ist in dies __10__ Flasche, David? Orangensaft? Darf ich mal probieren?   10. dieser

B: Hm, dies __11__ Saft schmeckt lecker. Dies __12__ Orangensaft kauf ich mir auch!   11. dieser 12. diesen

12 Was isst du denn heute?   Script and answers on p. 121G

Zuhören Three students are asking their friends about the snacks they brought to school. Each also asks his or her friends about their eating habits. Match each of the friend's eating habits with the most appropriate photo below.

CD 5 Tr. 9

 a.    b.    c.    d.    e.

13 Schreib mal eine Geschichte!

Schreiben Was sagt Calvin zu seinem Vater? Calvin betrachtet skeptisch, was auf seinem Teller ist. Schreib Sätze, die in die Sprechblasen passen!
Answers may vary. E.g.: **Was soll denn das grüne Ding da sein? — Ach, Calvin, das ist doch dein Rindersteak.**

CALVIN AND HOBBES © Watterson. Reprinted with permission of UNIVERSAL PRESS SYNDICATE. All rights reserved.

14

Sprechen Take a minute and draw on a piece of paper an item of food that you especially like to eat. Your partner, quite skeptical in nature, asks what it could be. After you tell what it is, she can make a general assumption about your eating habits, giving the statement one of the question tags from the **So sagt man das!** box. Switch roles.
Answers may vary. E.g. **Was soll denn das sein? — Das ist Schinken. — Ach, du isst nicht vegetarisch, was?**

15 Für mein Notizbuch

Schreiben Was gibt es in deiner Schule zu essen und zu trinken? Was kaufst du, und was kostet das? Was bringst du von zu Hause mit? Oder isst du nur in der Schulcafeteria?

ERSTE STUFE   STANDARDS: 1.1, 1.2, 1.3, 5.1

Zum Lesen

Wo ruht ihr euch aus?

Lesestrategie
Understanding the tone of a text. When looking at a German text, you can spot the nouns quickly because they are capitalized, and you can locate the verbs in the second and/or last position of a sentence. If you recognize the nouns and verbs (or at least some of them), you've probably got the gist of the text. But sometimes you will also want to look at adjectives, conjunctions, and adverbs in order to understand the "tone", that is, how the author feels about the subject. What is the difference between the following pairs of sentences?

Wie alt ist er?	Das weiß ich nicht.
Wie alt ist er **denn**?	Das weiß ich **gar** nicht.

The words **denn** and **gar** act as intensifiers. **Denn** indicates interest on the part of the speaker, and **gar** shows totality. Look for this type of word in the readings that follow to help you understand more fully the feelings of the writers.

Getting Started For answers, see p. 121R.
1. Read the introduction to this article from JUMA. What and who is the focus of the article?
2. Where do you go when you want to get away? What do you like to do there to relax? Do **Ruhe** and **ungestört sein** play a role in your choice?
3. Scan the articles on these pages to find the favorite place for each student. Which place do you think was the most predictable? And the most unusual?

Hier hab ich meine Ruhe

Mal ganz für sich alleine sein, in Ruhe nachdenken oder lesen. Nicht gestört werden und machen können, was man will. Oder ganz einfach überhaupt nichts tun müssen, herumsitzen und an gar nichts denken. Das alles sind Dinge, die Jugendliche von ihrem Lieblingsplatz erwarten.

Sehr viele verschiedene Aspekte sind ihnen wichtig. Genauso wie jeder von ihnen einen ganz bestimmten Platz hat, wohin er sich am liebsten zurückzieht. Dabei ist erstaunlich, wie unterschiedlich diese sein können: Billardsalon oder Café, ein Baum im Wald, ein Strand am Meer, das eigene Zimmer, der Keller im Elternhaus, der Trainingsraum im Fitneß-Studio, eine Bibliothek, die Garage, das Büro, die Schulaula...JUMA stellt Euch vier Jugendliche und ihre Lieblingsplätze vor.

Markus (18), Student: „Ich mag dieses Café. Es ist etwas abgelegen, und darum kommen nicht so viele Leute hierher. Das ist genau das Richtige für mich – man ist relativ ungestört. Ich komme zwei bis dreimal pro Woche ins Café. Was ich hier liebe, ist die Atmosphäre: Gedämpftes Licht, schöne alte Möbel, ruhige Leute, das Rascheln von Zeitungen.
Ich trinke Tee oder Kaffee, denke nach, lese Zeitungen oder ein Buch. Ich habe hier auch schon mal versucht, Gedichte zu schreiben. Vielleicht probiere ich es noch einmal. Ob ich gut bin, weiß ich nicht, aber es macht Spaß und lenkt ab. Die Umgebung inspiriert mich jedenfalls. Wie lange ich hier durchschnittlich sitze, kann ich eigentlich nicht so genau sagen. Mindestens eine Stunde, manchmal auch zwei Stunden. Am schönsten ist es, wenn ich genau weiß, daß ich am Nachmittag nichts mehr machen muß. Dann genieße ich meine Zeit so richtig."

Nicole (19), Handelsschülerin: „Mein Lieblingsplatz ist ein alter Turm im Stadtwald. Meistens gehe ich nach der Berufsschule dorthin. Am meisten genieße ich die Ruhe rund um den Turm. Nur wenige Leute kommen wochentags hierher.
Ich kann dort ungestört über alles mögliche nachdenken – über mich selbst, meine Freunde oder über Streß in der Schule. Ab und zu nehme ich auch unseren Hund mit. Auch wenn es verrückt klingt – manchmal unterhalte ich mich dann mit ihm. Ich stelle mir halt vor, daß er mir zuhört.
Dann gibt es Tage, da sitze ich hier und denke über gar nichts nach. Ich genieße einfach die Sonne und freue mich, daß es hier im Wald so schön ist.
Am meisten liebe ich den Platz im Frühling, wenn es grün wird und sich der Wald jede Woche verändert."

6 JUMA

Christian (16), Schüler: „Mein Lieblingsplatz ist vielleicht ein bißchen ungewöhnlich. Ich sitze gerne im Schülervertretungs-Büro unserer Schule. Man denkt vielleicht, daß hier viel los ist — ein ständiges Kommen und Gehen von Schülern, deren Interessen wir vertreten sollen — aber das ist gar nicht so. Am liebsten bin ich in den Pausen hier. Draußen toben die Schüler, hier im Büro ist es ruhig. Ich kann nachdenken, mich zwischen den Stunden ein bißchen entspannen. Wenn wir Post von Schülern haben, lese ich deren Briefe. Das lenkt auch von eigenen Problemen ab — man denkt über die Lage seiner Mitschüler nach.
Manchmal verschönere ich auch den Raum ein bißchen, hänge Plakate, Poster und Fotos auf. Auch dabei entspannt man sich, finde ich. Wenn ich hier aus dem Büro komme, habe ich eigentlich immer gute Laune. Und das ist der Zweck eines Lieblingsplatzes, denke ich."

Tanja (19), Auszubildende: „Mein Lieblingsplatz? Ganz einfach: Das ist mein eigenes kleines Zimmer unter dem Dach. Den Raum habe ich seit rund vier Jahren. Davor hatte ich zusammen mit meinen Schwestern ein Zimmer. Das war manchmal ganz schön eng.
In meinem Zimmer bin ich sehr gerne. Besonders dann, wenn ich Ärger an meiner Arbeitsstelle hatte. Ich will dann meine Ruhe haben. Je nach Stimmung liege ich auf meinem Bett, tue gar nichts oder höre Musik per Kopfhörer. Ab und zu lese ich auch, um auf andere Gedanken zu kommen — meistens nichts „Hochgeistiges". Am liebsten so ein paar richtig schöne Liebesromane mit Happy-End.
In den Ferien bummele (herumbummeln: umgangssprachlich für „etwas langsam machen") ich hier oben herum. Lange ausschlafen, meine Flaschensammlung sortieren, alte Zeitschriften durchblättern — das ist richtig schön."

Die interessantesten Lieblingsplätze stellen wir im JUMA vor. Die Gewinner erhalten wertvolle Bücher.
Schreibt an:
**Redaktion JUMA
Stichwort: Lieblingsplatz
Frankfurter Straße 40
51065 Köln**

A Closer Look

4. Read the articles more carefully. For each student jot down key words and phrases that describe the place and his or her favorite activities.

5. Search each article for occurrences of **Ruhe, ruhig,** and **ungestört.** Carefully read the contexts in which these words occur. What, if anything, is the writer seeking peace from? Specific people? Specific situations?

6. Notice the words that express tone in the sentences. Look at the following pairs of sentences and determine how the words in bold print give the second sentence of each pair a slightly different tone.

   a. Das weiß ich nicht.
      Das weiß ich **eigentlich** nicht.

   b. Da sitze ich zwei Stunden.
      Da sitze ich **mindestens** zwei Stunden.

   c. Mein Zimmer war eng.
      Mein Zimmer war **ganz schön** eng.

7. Locate the phrase **ab und zu** in Tanja's statement. What do you think **ab und zu** means?

8. What do you think Nicole means when she says: **Auch wenn es verrückt klingt — manchmal unterhalte ich mich dann mit ihm.**

9. Jeder in der Klasse schreibt an JUMA, aber ohne Namensangabe. Beschreib deinen Lieblingsplatz, und was du da gern tust! Zeichne ein Bild dazu, oder mach ein Foto! Häng die Beschreibung und Zeichnung an die Wand. Die Klasse übernimmt die Rolle von der JUMA Redaktion. Wählt die interessantesten Lieblingsplätze aus!

Übungsheft, S. 54

Storytelling Book pp. 34–35

Zweite Stufe

Objective Calling someone's attention to something and responding

WK3 HAMBURG-5

Wortschatz

Was hast du denn auf dem Brot?

Margarine und Wurst, Aufschnitt

Quark mit Schnittlauch

Tofu mit Sojasprossen

Was für Marmelade? **Was für Käse?**

Erdbeermarmelade
Himbeermarmelade

Schweizer   Tilsiter
Camembert

Und dann noch...

Erdnussbutter   Schinkensalat
saure Gurken   Eiersalat
Thunfischsalat   Mayonnaise

Was hast du gewöhnlich auf deinem Pausenbrot?

Übungsheft, S. 55, Ü. 1–2   Grammatikheft, S. 40, Ü. 8

16 Was ist auf dem Pausenbrot? Scripts and answers on p. 121G

CD 5 Tr. 10

Zuhören/Schreiben Was haben die Schüler gewöhnlich auf ihrem Pausenbrot? — Schreib die Namen von den Schülern auf, und schreib neben den Namen, was jeder Schüler auf seinem Pausenbrot hat!

17 Also, das schmeckt mir!

Sprechen Was hast du gewöhnlich auf deinem Brot oder Sandwich? Sag es einem Mitschüler! Dann frag einen Mitschüler, was er gewöhnlich isst, und so weiter!

So sagt man das!

Calling someone's attention to something and responding

If you want to call someone's attention to something, you may say:

Schau mal!
Guck mal!
Sieh mal!
Hör mal!
Hör mal zu!

And the response may be:

Ja? Was denn?
Ja, was bitte?
Was ist denn los?
Was ist?
Was gibt's?

How would you say these expressions in English? Are there other similar expressions in English? How would you call two friends' attention to something? An adult's?

Grammatikheft, S. 40, Ü. 9

134 hundertvierunddreißig   STANDARDS: 1.1, 1.2, 5.1   KAPITEL 5   Gesund essen

Ein wenig Landeskunde

What Germans eat for a particular meal probably differs somewhat from your own habits. For breakfast, **das Frühstück,** they might eat a grain cereal, **das Müsli,** but you will generally find fresh rolls, **Brötchen,** on every table. Germans like to spread butter on them, adding honey, cheese, or even slices of meat or sausage. A boiled egg is also common. Lunch, **das Mittagessen,** is typically the only warm meal of the day, and usually includes meat or fish, potatoes, and a salad. Closing out the day is **das Abendbrot (das Abendessen),** usually a cold, less heavy meal consisting of bread, cold cuts, cheese, salad, and maybe soup, or even some heated-up leftovers from lunch.

SPRACHTIPP

There are regional differences in many expressions: **Schau mal!** is used more in the South, **Guck mal!** or even **Kuck mal!** in the North of Germany. **Sieh mal!** is standard but also more formal.

Ein wenig Grammatik

You learned in **Kapitel 4** that the prepositions **an** and **in** are followed by the dative case when the phrase indicates location. The same is true for the preposition **auf** (*on, on top of*). To express where something is, you can say:

Wo ist der Käse? Er ist schon auf meinem Brot.

Germans also use **auf** when referring to what is *in* their sandwiches:

Und was willst du auf deinem Sandwich?

Übungsheft, S. 55, Ü. 3

18 **Was haben alle auf ihrem Pausenbrot?**

Die Schüler freuen sich auf die Pause. Sie können miteinander sprechen und auch etwas essen. Lies, was diese Schüler fragen! Achte dabei genau auf die Wörter, die vor dem Wort „Pausenbrot" stehen! Was bedeuten diese Wörter? **euer** = your (pl.); **unser** = our; **sein** = his; **ihr** = her; **ihr** = their

—Ist das euer Pausenbrot? Was habt ihr denn auf euerem Pausenbrot?
—Auf unserem Pausenbrot haben wir Käse, Schweizer Käse.

David isst jetzt sein Pausenbrot. Ich weiß, was er auf seinem Brot hat.

Wiebke isst ihr Pausenbrot. Weißt du, was sie auf ihrem Pausenbrot hat?

Die Schüler essen ihr Pausenbrot. Was haben sie denn auf ihrem Pausenbrot?

Grammatik

The possessives (Summary)

1. You have been using some possessives, such as **mein, dein, sein,** and **ihr.** Here is a summary and the meaning of all of them.

	Singular		Plural
my	mein	our	unser
your	dein	your	euer
his, its	sein	their	ihr
her, its	ihr		
your, formal	Ihr	your, formal	Ihr

2. These are the endings you need when you use the possessives, using **mein** as a model. What other group of words has the same endings?[1]

	Nominative Das ist	Accusative Ich mag	Dative Was ist in
masculine	mein Kakao.	meinen Kakao.	meinem Kakao?
feminine	Das ist meine Milch.	Ich mag meine Milch.	in meiner Milch?
neuter	Das ist mein Brötchen.	Ich mag mein Brötchen.	auf meinem Brötchen?
plural	Das sind meine Brötchen.	Ich mag meine Brötchen.	auf meinen Brötchen?

3. The dative plural of almost all nouns ends in **-n**.

   Was kaufst du deinen Freunde**n**?

4. If the plural form of the noun already ends in **-n,** no further **-n** is added.

   Was ist auf deinen Brötchen? (das Brötchen, die Brötchen)

Mehr Grammatikübungen, S. 143, Ü. 4–5

Übungsheft, S. 56–57, Ü. 4–7   Grammatikheft, S. 41–42, Ü. 10–12

19 Grammatik im Kontext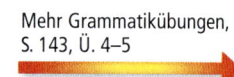

Schreiben Schreib, was alle auf ihren Brötchen haben! Gebrauche dabei die richtige Form des Possessivpronomens!

A: David fragt Wiebke: „Was hast du auf ___1___ Brot?" 1. deinem

B: Wiebke antwortet: „Auf ___2___ Brot? Da hab ich Tofu drauf!" 2. meinem

A: David fragt die Lehrerin: „Was haben Sie auf ___3___ Brötchen, Frau Weber?" 3. Ihrem

B: „Auf ___4___ Brötchen? Nur Käse." 4. meinem

A: Wiebke fragt David: „Was hat Frau Weber auf ___5___ Brot?" 5. ihrem

B: „Auf ___6___ Brot hat sie nur Käse." 6. ihrem

A: David fragt Nicolas und Thorsten: „Was habt ihr auf ___7___ Brötchen?" 7. euren

B: Thorsten antwortet: „Auf ___8___ Brötchen haben wir Quark mit Schnittlauch." 8. unseren

---

1. the indefinite articles **ein, eine, ein**

20 Mit wem sprechen sie?

Zuhören Hör die folgenden Gespräche während der Pause im Schulhof an! Entscheide für jedes Gespräch, ob der Schüler mit einem Freund, zwei Freunden oder einer älteren Person spricht!

CD 5
Tr. 11
Script and answers on p. 121H

	mit: einem Freund	zwei Freunden	einer älteren Person
1			
2			
3			

21 Ist das dein …?

Sprechen Setzt euch in Gruppen von vier oder fünf Personen zusammen! Jeder muss einen oder mehrere Artikel von sich und von anderen Schülern in der Hand haben. Jetzt fragt ihr abwechselnd (*in turns*), wem das gehört.

Heft Radiergummi Spitzer
Deutschbuch Taschenrechner Schultasche
Brille Pausenbrot Volleyball

Ist das dein …?
Nein, das ist ihr …
Ist das euer …?
Das ist nicht mein …

Answers may vary. E.g.: **Ist das deine Brille? — Nein, das ist ihre Brille.**

22 Und auf eurem Sandwich?

Sprechen You and two friends are at an **Imbissstube** and want to order from the vendor. Unfortunately, it's very crowded and you have to order for your friends. Follow these guidelines:

a. the vendor asks for your order
b. you ask your friends for their wishes
c. they decide and one answers for both
d. the other friend asks you what you want
e. you tell the vendor all of your orders
f. the vendor repeats them

Was möchtest du auf deinem Sandwich?

Schinken Käse Quark
mit Tomaten Aufschnitt
Erdnussbutter Mayonnaise Marmelade
Senf Schnittlauch Butter Sojasprossen

23 Klar! Das ist mein …

Schreiben/Sprechen Identify and make a list of several objects you see around you, marking down to whom each belongs. Then describe each item, saying "his/her/their/our … is …" Now go to various students and see if you were right about the ownership: „Das ist doch dein …?"

Answers may vary. E.g.: **Das ist doch dein Heft, oder? — Klar, das ist mein Heft.**

24 Was planst du heute fürs Mittagessen?

Sprechen Fragt euch gegenseitig, ob ihr etwas zum Mittagessen mitgebracht habt oder ob ihr heute in der Cafeteria esst! Wenn du etwas mitgebracht hast, kannst du allen erklären „Schaut mal!" und zeigen, was du hast. Oder wenn du heute in der Cafeteria isst, dann sag ihnen „Hört mal zu!" und erkläre ihnen, was du dort essen willst!

Answers may vary. E.g.: **Hast du etwas von zu Hause mitgebracht? - Ja, schau mal! Ich habe Joghurt und ein Brot mitgebracht. Und du? — Hör mal zu! Ich esse in der Cafeteria. Heute gibt es Fischstäbchen.**

ZWEITE STUFE   STANDARDS: 1.1, 1.2, 1.3, 5.1   *hundertsiebenunddreißig*

Storytelling Book
pp. 36–37

Dritte Stufe

Objective Expressing preference and strong preference

WK3 HAMBURG-5

Wortschatz

KAUFMANNS
Wir garantieren Qualität
Alle Angebote sind gültig ab Montag, den 3. September

TÄGLICH FRISCH		TIEFKÜHLKOST AUS UNSERER FLEISCHABTEILUNG		IN UNSERER FISCHABTEILUNG
Trauben aus Frankr. kg **2.10**	**Fischstäbchen** gefroren 300 g Packung **0.99**	**Rindersteak** zart, abgehangen 100 g **0.79**	**Heilbutt** 100 g **0.70**
frische Bohnen kg **1.45**	**Rindfleisch** mager kg **4.99**	**Holl. Hühner** Kl. A per kg **1.22**	**Forellen** 100 g **0.65**
Bananen aus Guatem. kg **1.49**	**Pommes frites** 1000 g Beutel **0.44**	**Schnitzel** vom Schwein 100 g **0.62**	**Karpfen** 100 g **0.45**
holländ. Möhren kg **0.85**	**Lamm** aus Austral. kg **4.20**	**Spinat** gefroren 500 g Packung **0.89**	Für Druckfehler keine Haftung!
Sauerkraut aus dem Faß kg **1.05**	**Schweinefleisch** kg **3.80**	**Schweinekoteletts** 100 g **0.49**	*Auf zu Kaufmanns!*
Äpfel Schwarzwald kg **1.85**	**Gemüsesuppe** 500 g Packung **1.13**		

Which of these foods do you recognize? Can you guess the meaning of words you don't know? What does **Tiefkühlkost** mean? Which food items confirm that? Which different places have shipped food to Kaufmanns? Which specialty stores would you go to if you didn't want to go to the **Supermarkt**?

 p. 121X 5-2  Grammatikheft, S. 43, Ü. 13

Answers will vary. E.g.: **Ich möchte bitte 200 Gramm Schnitzel. — Tut mir Leid, aber die Schnitzel sind schon alle! — Macht nichts. Dann geben Sie mir …**

25 Abendessen zu viert

a. Sprechen/Schreiben You and your partner are planning to invite two other friends to dinner and want to serve the following: a fish entrée, two vegetables, potatoes or noodles, and a fruit salad for dessert. Have a look at Kaufmanns' specials. With only ten euros, decide what and how much to buy of each thing (enough to feed four people). Make a shopping list.

b. Sprechen Go to Kaufmanns with your list. Your partner is the vendor. Order everything over the counter. Unfortunately, Kaufmanns is out of some things on your list. Downplay your disappointment and ask for a different item. Be polite!

So sagt man das!

Expressing preference and strong preference

Grammatikheft, S. 43, Ü. 14

When asking about someone's preference, you could ask:

Welche Suppe magst du **lieber**?
   Nudelsuppe oder Gemüsesuppe?
Welches Fleisch schmeckt dir **besser**?
   Schwein oder Rind?

Asking for strong preference:

Welches Gemüse magst du **am liebsten**?
Welche Suppe schmeckt dir **am besten**?

And the answer may be:

Nudelsuppe mag ich **lieber**.

Rind schmeckt mir **besser**.

Am liebsten mag ich Spinat.
Nudelsuppe schmeckt mir **am besten**.

---

26 Gespräche im Schulhof Script and answers on p. 121H

Zuhören/Schreiben Im Schulhof sprechen einige Schüler über Essen und Trinken. Schreib auf, wer was lieber oder am liebsten isst, wem was besser oder am besten schmeckt!
CD 5 Tr. 12

27 Was schmeckt dir am besten?

Sprechen Such dir eine Partnerin! Frag sie, was ihr besser schmeckt! Du musst zwei Dinge nennen, und sie muss auswählen. Frag sie dann, was ihr am besten schmeckt! — Tauscht dann die Rollen aus!
Answers will vary. E.g.: **Was schmeckt dir besser: Pudding oder Joghurt? - Mir schmeckt Pudding besser.**

Reis		Nudeln
Äpfel		Birnen
Fisch		Fleisch
Pudding	oder	Joghurt
Tomaten		Möhren
Kuchen		Eis
Schnitzel		Steak
Forelle		Karpfen

28 Eine Umfrage: Was schmeckt euch?

Schreiben/Sprechen Stellt euch vor, ihr müsst einen Brunch für alle Deutschschüler an der Schule organisieren! Was gibt es alles zu essen? Schreibt eure Gerichte auf ein Poster! — Vergleicht eure Poster und sagt, was euch besser und am besten schmeckt! Fragt auch euern Lehrer, was ihm besser schmeckt. Am Ende wählt ihr das schönste Poster aus.

Was schmeckt Ihnen besser, die Bohnen oder das Kraut?

Wem schmeckt das Rindfleisch?

Was schmeckt dir am besten?

Was schmeckt euch nicht?

Ein wenig Grammatik

There are some verbs that are always used with dative case forms, such as **gefallen**.

Dresden hat **mir** gut gefallen.

The verb **schmecken** can be used with or without a dative object.

Die Nudeln schmecken gut.
Die Suppe schmeckt **dem** David.
Die Soße hat **mir** nicht geschmeckt.

Übungsheft, S. 58, Ü. 1–2
Grammatikheft, S. 44, Ü. 15–17

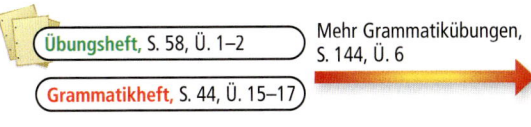
Mehr Grammatikübungen, S. 144, Ü. 6

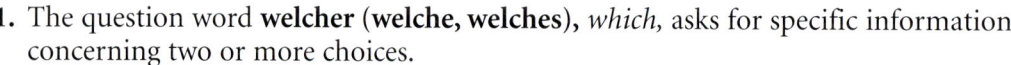

Grammatik

The interrogative **welcher**

1. The question word **welcher** (**welche, welches**), *which,* asks for specific information concerning two or more choices.

   Welche Suppe möchtest du? Die Nudelsuppe oder die Gemüsesuppe?

2. The interrogative **welcher** is used in front of nouns and has these forms:

	Masculine	Feminine	Neuter	Plural
Nominative	welcher	welche	welches	welche
Accusative	welchen	welche	welches	welche
Dative	welchem	welcher	welchem	welchen

Welcher Joghurt schmeckt gut? **Welches Obst** magst du?
Welchen Salat magst du am liebsten? Auf **welche Schule** gehen diese Schüler?
How would you express the last sentence in English? Of which word and forms does **welcher** remind you?[1]

Übungsheft, S. 59–60, Ü. 4–7   Grammatikheft, S. 45, Ü. 18   Mehr Grammatikübungen, S. 144, Ü. 7

29 Welches Obst magst du?

Sprechen Ask your partner which of these general categories of food he likes: **Fleisch, Salat, Fisch, Gemüse, Obst,** or **Wurst.** When your partner says he likes a certain category of food, find out which foods in that category he likes.
Answers will vary. E.g.: **Magst du Gemüse? Welches Gemüse magst du?**

30 Grammatik im Kontext

a. Sprechen Behalte (*keep*) den gleichen Partner von Übung 29 und frag ihn, welche von zwei Speisen er lieber mag oder welche von zwei Speisen ihm besser schmeckt und warum!

Warum?
- schmeckt mir am besten
- ist gesund für mich
- ist nicht so teuer
- hat nicht so viele Kalorien
- ist besser für mich
- geht schnell zu kochen

BEISPIEL
DU   Was magst du lieber, ==== oder ====?
PARTNER   ====
DU   Und welch-==== magst du am liebsten?
PARTNER   ====
DU   Und warum?

b. Schreiben Schreib jetzt drei Gespräche wie im Beispiel.

Für viele Deutsche besteht die Hauptmahlzeit noch immer aus einem warmen Mittagessen, das gewöhnlich zwischen 12 und 13 Uhr serviert wird. In kleineren Orten schließen die meisten Geschäfte zur Mittagszeit, und die Schulkinder kommen zu dieser Zeit von der Schule nach Hause. In größeren Betrieben gibt es Betriebskantinen, die ihren Angestellten eine kleine Auswahl an warmen Gerichten anbieten. Wer zu Mittag kalt essen möchte, der muss lange suchen, denn in Restaurants gibt es zur Mittagszeit keine kalte Küche.

---

1. dieser, jeder

Grammatik

The preposition zu

The preposition **zu** (*to*) is always followed by dative case forms. **Zu** and the definite articles **der** and **dem** contract to **zur** and **zum**.

Ich gehe jetzt **zum Großvater.** (zu + dem = zum)
Jetzt fahr ich immer mit dem Moped **zur Schule.** (zu + der = zur)
Zum Nachtisch ess ich gewöhnlich Obst.
Was gibt's heute **zum Abendessen?**

Zu has other meanings as well. Look at the last two sentences. Can you guess the meaning of **zu** in these sentences? Which other prepositions are always followed by the dative case?[1]

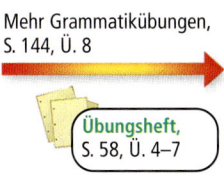

Mehr Grammatikübungen, S. 144, Ü. 8

Übungsheft, S. 58, Ü. 4–7

Grammatikheft, S. 45, Ü. 19

31 Grammatik im Kontext

a. Sprechen Such dir eine Partnerin! Stell ihr diese Fragen! Dann fragt sie dich.

1. Was isst du gewöhnlich zum Frühstück?
2. Und was trinkst du zum Frühstück?
3. Was isst du meistens zum Mittagessen?
4. Was esst ihr gewöhnlich zum Abendessen?
5. Was esst ihr zu Hause zum Nachtisch?
6. Wenn es bei euch Fleisch gibt, was gibt es dazu?

b. Schreiben Schreib jetzt Antworten zu diesen Fragen.

ein Stück Käse   eine Scheibe Wurst   ein Glas Milch   ein Stück Brot

32 Was ist das für ein …?

Sprechen Du gehst mit einem deutschen Schüler durch einen Supermarkt in deiner Stadt. Er sieht sich alles an, weiß aber oft nicht, was das ist, und er hat viele Fragen. Du beantwortest sie. Gebrauch dabei die Wörter in den Kästen!
— Tauscht dann die Rollen aus!

PARTNER   Was ist das für (ein …) …?
DU   Das ist …

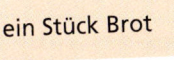

SPRACHTIPP

When asking for a certain kind of information, you have been using the interrogative **was für ein**, as in:

   Was für ein Film ist das?

In colloquial German, the interrogative is often split:

   Was ist das **für ein** Film?
   Was ist das **für eine** Suppe?

Mehr Grammatikübungen, S. 145, Ü. 9

Fragen

Suppe	Fleisch	Gemüse
Kuchen	Eis	Joghurt
Salat	Brötchen	Wurst
Marmelade	Fisch	

Antworten

Vanilleeis	Käsekuchen
Karpfen	Erdbeermarmelade
Vollkornbrötchen	Gemüsesuppe
Salami	Tomatensalat
Schweinefleisch	
Spinat	
Vanillejoghurt	

33 Von der Schule zum Beruf

Du arbeitest in einem Reformhaus *(health food store)*, das Flugblätter *(flyers)* über gesunde Ernährung an seine Kunden verteilt. Du sollst das nächste Flugblatt schreiben.

---

1. bei, mit, nach, von

Mehr Grammatikübungen

Erste Stufe
Objectives Expressing regret and downplaying; expressing skepticism and making certain

1 Du bedauerst, dass dir bestimmte Sachen nicht schmecken. – Schreib die richtige Form von **dieser** in die Lücken. (S. 130)

1. Ich habe leider nur noch _____ Joghurt. — diesen
2. Es tut mir Leid, _____ Joghurt kostet jetzt einen Euro. — dieser
3. Ich bedaure, dass _____ Erdbeeren nicht sehr süß sind. — diese
4. Ich bedaure, _____ Fleisch schmeckt mir nicht. — dieses
5. Was für ein Pech! _____ Apfel ist zu sauer. — Dieser
6. Es tut mir Leid, _____ Wurst ist schlecht. Ich kann sie nicht essen. — diese

2 Du bist nicht sicher, was das ist. – Schreib die richtige Form von **dieser** in die Lücken. (S. 130)

1. Was soll denn das sein, _____ Gemüse da? — Du, _____ Gemüse da ist Spinat. — dieses; dieses
2. Was soll das sein, _____ Käse da? — Ja, _____ Käse da ist Tofu! — dieser; dieser
3. Was soll das sein, _____ Saft da? — Ja, trink mal _____ Saft! Gut, nicht? — dieser; diesen
4. Was soll das sein, _____ Butter da? — Na, _____ Butter da ist keine Butter. — diese; diese
5. Was soll das sein, _____ Wasser da? — Ja, _____ Wasser ist Mineralwasser. — dieses; dieses
6. Was soll das sein, _____ Möhre? — Ha, _____ Möhre ist eine Süßkartoffel! — diese; diese

3 Du bedauerst, dass du viele Dinge nicht essen oder trinken kannst. – Schreib die richtige Form von **dieser** und den Namen des Artikels in die Lücken. (S. 130)

BEISPIEL 1. Ich bedaure, dass ich _____ _____ nicht trinken kann.
Ich bedaure, dass ich <u>diese</u> <u>Milch</u> nicht trinken kann.

2. Ich kann leider _____ _____ nicht essen. — diesen Joghurt

3. Es tut mir Leid, ich kann _____ _____ nicht essen. — dieses Ei

4. Ich bedaure, dass ich _____ _____ nicht essen kann. — diesen Käse

5. Ich kann leider _____ _____ nicht essen. — diese Äpfel

Zweite Stufe

Objective Calling someone's attention to something and responding

4 Was hast du und was haben deine Freunde auf dem Pausenbrot? – Schreib die richtige Form des Possessivpronomens (mein, dein, ihr, usw.) in die Lücken. (S. 136)

1. Schau mal, was ich auf _____ Brot habe! — Ja, sag mir doch, was du auf _____ Brot hast.   meinem / deinem

2. Guck doch mal, was die Wiebke auf _____ Pausenbrot hat! — Ja, sag doch, was sie auf _____ Pausenbrot hat!   ihrem / ihrem

3. Weißt du, was der David auf _____ Pausenbrot hat? — Du, ich denke, er hat Käse auf _____ Pausenbrot.   seinem / seinem

4. Schau mal, was wir auf _____ Pausenbroten haben! — Das interessiert mich nicht, was ihr auf _____ Pausenbroten habt.   uns(e)ren / eu(e)ren

5. Sieh mal, was Wiebke und Thorsten auf _____ Pausenbroten haben! — Du, sie haben Tofu mit Sojasprossen auf _____ Pausenbroten.   ihren / ihren

6. Herr Müller, was haben Sie denn auf _____ Brot? — Ganz einfach, ich habe Quark mit Schnittlauch auf _____ Brot.   Ihrem / meinem

5 Was habt ihr auf euren Pausenbroten? – Schreib was du auf dem Pausenbrot hast in die erste Lücke und die richtige Form des Possessivpronomens in die zweite Lücke. (S. 136)

BEISPIEL

1. Guck mal! Ich habe _____ auf _____ Pausenbrot.
   Guck mal! Ich habe **Käse** auf **meinem** Pausenbrot.

2. Schau! Die Wiebke hat _____ auf _____ Pausenbrot.   Tofu mit Sojasprossen; ihrem

3. Sieh mal! Der Rolf hat _____ auf _____ Pausenbrot.   Quark mit Schnittlauch; seinem

4. Was, du hast _____ auf _____ Pausenbrot?   Marmelade; deinem

5. Guck! Frau Wagner hat _____ auf _____ Brot.   Aufschnitt; ihrem

MEHR GRAMMATIKÜBUNGEN   STANDARDS: 1.2

Mehr Grammatikübungen

WK3 HAMBURG-5

Dritte Stufe
Objective Expressing preference and strong preference

6 Du fragst deine Freunde, was ihnen gut schmeckt. – Schreib das richtige Pronomen oder das richtige Possessivpronomen in die Lücken. (S. 139)

1. Sag mal, Thorsten, was schmeckt _____ besser, Schweinefleisch oder Rindfleisch? — Hm, Rindfleisch schmeckt _____ besser.   dir / mir
2. Welche Suppe schmeckt _____ besser, Maike und David, Kartoffelsuppe oder Fischsuppe? — Kartoffelsuppe schmeckt _____ besser.   euch / uns
3. Und dein Vater, Wiebke? Welcher Käse schmeckt _____ besser, Camembert oder Tilsiter? — Ich denke, Camembert schmeckt _____ besser.   ihm / ihm
4. Und was schmeckt _____ Mutter besser, Brokkoli oder Blumenkohl? — Ich denke, Brokkoli schmeckt _____ Mutter besser.   deiner / meiner

7 Was isst du am liebsten? – Schreib die richtige Form von **welcher** in die Lücken. (S. 140)

1. _____ Gemüse isst du am liebsten? Und _____ Beeren?   Welches; welche
2. _____ Fisch isst du am liebsten? Und _____ Fleisch?   Welchen; welches
3. _____ Joghurt isst du am liebsten? Und _____ Eis?   Welchen; welches
4. _____ Obst magst du am liebsten? Und _____ Gemüse?   Welches; welches
5. _____ Reis magst du am liebsten? Und _____ Nudeln?   Welchen; welche
6. _____ Brot magst du am liebsten? Und _____ Kuchen?   Welches; welchen

8 Welche Beilagen *(side dishes)* isst du zu deinen Gerichten? – Such dir eine passende Präposition (plus Artikel) aus den Kasten aus und schreib sie in die Lücken. (S. 141)

| zu | zum | zur |

1. Schau mal, was es heute _____ Mittagessen gibt!   zum
2. Also, ich esse gewöhnlich Obst _____ Nachtisch.   zum
3. Was isst du _____ Schweinefleisch? Reis oder Kartoffeln?   zum/zu
4. Du, ich brauche ein Stück Brot _____ Suppe.   zur
5. _____ Abendessen gibt es heute Fisch.   Zum
6. Was haben wir _____ Fisch? Nudeln oder Reis?   zum
7. Sag, was gibt es _____ Forelle? Nur Brot?   zur

144   hundertvierundvierzig   STANDARDS: 1.2   KAPITEL 5   Gesund essen

9 Du möchtest wissen, was das alles ist. – Schreib je zwei Sätze für jede Abbildung und gebrauche dabei **was für ein** auf zwei verschiedene Arten, wie im Beispiel. **(S. 141)**

BEISPIEL

_____ _____ _____ _____ ist das?
Was für eine Suppe ist das? *oder*
_____ ist das _____ _____ _____
Was ist das **für eine Suppe?**

1. _____ _____ _____ _____ ist das ?   Was für ein Joghurt ist das?
2. _____ ist das _____ _____ _____ ?   Was ist das für ein Joghurt?

3. _____ ?   Was für ein Käse ist das?
4. _____ ?   Was ist das für ein Käse?

5. _____ ?   Was für eine Milch ist das?
6. _____ ?   Was ist das für eine Milch?

7. _____ ?   Was für ein Eis ist das?
8. _____ ?   Was ist das für ein Eis?

9. _____ ?   Was für Äpfel sind das?
10. _____ ?   Was sind das für Äpfel?

Anwendung

Storytelling Book pp. 38–39

KEYWORD: WK3 HAMBURG-5
Self-Test

The *CD-ROM Tutor* offers guided recording and writing activities to accompany the **Anwendung**. These activities are designed to practice students' oral and written communication skills and to review material from each chapter.

1 Bernd und seine Familie sind heute Abend im **Café an der Elbe** zum Abendessen. Sie haben die Speisekarte gelesen und wollen bestellen. Hör ihrem Gespräch gut zu und schreib auf, was jedes Familienmitglied (Bernd, Vater, Mutter, Bernds Schwester Annette) mag, nicht mag, lieber mag und am liebsten mag! Stell deine eigene Tabelle her, und füll sie dann aus! Dann beantworte die Fragen!

CD 5 Tr. 13

1. Wer mag nur vegetarische Gerichte?
2. Wer trinkt wohl zu Hause am liebsten Saft? Was meinst du?
3. Glaubst du, dass die Annette auch Krabben mag? Warum oder warum nicht?
4. Glaubst du, dass Bernds Vater ein Stück Kuchen mit Sahne zum Nachtisch möchte? Warum oder warum nicht? *Script and answers on p. 121H*

2 Lies diesen Text und beantworte die Fragen!

1. Hier sind einige Tipps für eine Party. Was für eine Party soll das sein? Woher weißt du das? *1. eine Geburtstagsparty; „… wenn sie Geburtstag haben …"*
2. Was soll man nach der Kuchenschlacht (*run for the cake*) tun? *2. essen*
3. Was ist „Fleischsalat"? Was soll man mit dem Fleischsalat tun? *3. Salat aus Wurst oder Aufschnitt; Tomaten füllen*
4. Was empfiehlt man hier zum Trinken? In welcher Jahreszeit soll man das servieren? *4. Eistee; im Sommer*

Wenn Kinder feiern …

hat was los zu sein! Von klein auf wünschen sich Kinder Gäste, wenn sie Geburtstag haben: die Spielfreunde, die Kinder aus der Schule. Da sind Eltern gefordert, zu planen, zu organisieren, sich Spiele auszudenken und für Überraschungen zu sorgen, die eine Kinderparty zu einem richtigen Erlebnis machen.

Nach der Kuchenschlacht und dem Spielprogramm kommt Hunger auf — wetten daß? Gegen den gibt es:

Gefüllte Tomaten

Zutaten: 4 feste, mittelgroße Tomaten, wenig Salz, etwas Pfeffer, 200g Fleischsalat, 4 Scheiben Salatgurken, 4 Scheiben hart gekochte Eier, etwas leichte Mayonnaise, einige Salatblätter.

Zubereitung: Tomaten waschen, abtrocknen, einen Deckel abschneiden und vorsichtig mit einem Teelöffel aushöhlen. Die Innenräume mild würzen und gleichmäßig den Fleischsalat einfüllen. Jede Tomate mit einer Gurken- und Eischeibe belegen, den Tomatendeckel aufsetzen und mit einigen Tupfern Mayonnaise versehen. Eine Platte mit gewaschenen Salatblättern auslegen, und die Tomaten daraufsetzen. Dazu steht aufgeschnittenes Stangenbrot bereit.

Was gibt es hier zu trinken? Kinder haben immer Durst, weil ihr Wasserhaushalt einen viel höheren Pegel hat als der von Erwachsenen. Im Sommer, wenn draußen gefeiert wird, gibt es leicht gekühlten Eistee, der mit Orangen- und Zitronensaft angereichert und mit Süßstoff oder wenig Zucker gesüßt wird. Außerdem empfiehlt sich — weil es irgendwie „erwachsen" wirkt — eine Früchte-Bowle.

Früchte-Bowle

Zutaten und Zubereitung: 200g Erdbeeren (auch aufgetaute Tiefkühlerdbeeren), 4 Kiwis, 1 kleine Melone, 4 Orangen, 4 EL Traubenzucker, 2 Päckchen Vanillezucker, Saft von 4 Zitronen, 1 Orangensaft, 2 Flaschen Mineralwasser.

Erdbeeren putzen und in Stückchen schneiden, das Fruchtfleisch der Melone herauslösen und ebenfalls stückeln, Orangen schälen, die Filets zwischen den Häuten herausschneiden. Alle Früchte in ein Bowle-Gefäß geben, mit den Zuckersorten bestreuen und etwa eine Stunde ziehen lassen. Dann mit Orangensaft und Mineralwasser aufgießen, noch einmal gut verrühren — und „Zum Wohl"!

3 Zwei Klassenkameraden und du, ihr plant eine Geburtstagsparty für kleine Kinder. Ihr macht die gefüllten Tomaten und die Früchte-Bowle. Zuerst müsst ihr einkaufen gehen. Schreibt zuerst eine Einkaufsliste! Dann geht ihr zu verschiedenen Geschäften. In jedem Geschäft spielt einer von euch die Rolle vom Verkäufer. Als Kunden seid ihr ab und zu nicht sicher, was verschiedene Sachen sind. Ihr müsst den Verkäufer danach fragen.
Was soll das sein, dieses Gemüse? — Das sind Tomaten!

4 Zum Schreiben

Write an article for your school newspaper describing the best or worst holiday meal or holiday celebration you ever had.

Schreibtipp Arranging your ideas in a sequence makes your writing easier for the reader to understand. When you write about a series of actions or events, it makes sense to arrange them according to the order in which they happened. Since this was a specific day on which exciting things happened, if you use a sequential arrangement you probably won't leave out notable events.

Vorbereiten
Use a **cluster diagram** to help you organize your memories of your holiday. Clusters might be labeled *People, Food, Activities, Gifts* (if it was a gift-giving occasion), and *Location*(s).

Ausführen
Begin your article with a **topic sentence**. This sentence should let the reader know what type of celebration it was, and how you felt about the day. Then go on to the first thing, second thing, etc. you did on that day. Write a few sentences about each activity and what made this day so special, or so especially bad.

Überarbeiten
- Check your spelling and proofread for errors.
- Print a revised copy of your article.
- Share your writing with your friends and decide who spent the best day.

5 Rollenspiel

Spiel mit drei Klassenkameraden die folgende Szene der Klasse vor!

Du und ein Freund, ihr habt eine kleine Imbissstube. Entwerft eine Speisekarte für alle Speisen, die ihr verkauft! Illustriert die Speisekarte! Die anderen zwei Schüler sind die Kunden bei euch. Sie müssen sich entscheiden (*to decide*), was sie essen und trinken möchten. Dein Partner oder du, ihr sagt, ob ihr diese Speise noch habt oder nicht. Die zwei Kunden sprechen darüber, was sie wollen und was für Speisen sie normalerweise essen.

Kann ich's wirklich?

WK3 HAMBURG-5

Can you express regret and downplay something? (p. 129)

1 How would you tell someone that
  a. you're sorry that there isn't any more milk? a. Es tut mir Leid, die Milch ist alle.
  b. you're sorry that **Salamibrötchen** now cost €1.10? b. Ich bedaure, die Salamibrötchen kosten jetzt ein Euro zehn.
  c. he or she is out of luck — there isn't any more pudding? c. Was für ein Pech! Der Pudding ist alle.
  d. you unfortunately only have trout?
  d. Ich habe leider nur Forelle.

2 How would you respond to the above by saying that it doesn't matter or that it is all right? Das macht nichts!; Schon gut!; Nicht so schlimm!

3 How would you say that you'll just take a **Käsebrot** instead?
3. Dann nehme ich eben nur ein Käsebrot.

4 How would you ask a friend what in the world he has on his sandwich?
Was hast du auf deinem Brot? Was soll denn das sein auf deinem Brot?

Can you express skepticism and make certain? (p. 130)

5 How would you make certain that
  a. your friend is a vegetarian? a. Du isst vegetarisch, nicht wahr?
  b. someone you know likes apples? b. Du magst Äpfel, ja?
  c. someone you know likes chocolate milk? c. Du magst Kakao, was?

6 How might the persons in 5a., 5b., and 5c. above respond to your questions?
E.g.: a. Ja, das stimmt. b. Nein, Äpfel schmecken mir nicht. c. Ja, Kakao mag ich.

Can you call someone's attention to something and respond? (p. 134)

7 How would you point something out to a friend? How would you tell him or her to listen? Schau mal!; Guck mal!; Hör mal zu!

8 How would you respond to the above and ask what is going on?
Ja? Was denn? Was ist?

9 How would you ask someone
  a. what fish he or she eats often? a. Welchen Fisch isst du oft?
  b. what fruit there is? b. Welches Obst gibt es?
  c. what soup costs EUR 1,90? c. Welche Suppe kostet EUR 1,90?

Can you express preference and strong preference? (p. 139)

10 How would you say that
  a. you like grapes? a. Ich mag Trauben.
  b. you prefer apples? b. Ich mag Äpfel lieber.
  c. you like bananas the best? c. Ich mag Bananen am liebsten.

Wortschatz

p. 121X

Erste Stufe

Expressing regret

Ich bedaure, …	I'm sorry, …
bedauern	to be sorry about
Was für ein Pech!	That's too bad!
Ich hab leider nur …	I only have …

Downplaying

(Das) macht nichts!	That's all right!
Schon gut!	It's okay.
Nicht so schlimm!	That's not so bad.

Adjusting

Dann nehm ich eben …	In that case I'll take …

Expressing skepticism and making certain

Was soll denn das sein?	What's that supposed to be?
Du isst wohl vegetarisch, was?	You eat vegetarian, right?
Du isst wohl viel Fleisch, ja?	You eat a lot of meat, right?
Du magst Joghurt, oder?	You like yogurt, don't you?
Du magst doch Quark, nicht wahr?	You like quark, don't you?
Dann trink ich halt …	I'll drink … instead.
Nicht unbedingt!	Not entirely!/ Not necessarily!

Food items

die Milch	milk
der Kakao	chocolate milk
die Vanillemilch	vanilla flavored milk
der Joghurt	yogurt
die Birne	pear

Other useful words and expressions

dies-	this

Zweite Stufe

Calling someone's attention to something and responding

Schau mal!	Look!
Guck mal!	Look!
Sieh mal!	Look!
Hör mal!	Listen!
Hör mal zu!	Listen to this!
Ja? Was denn?	Okay, what is it?
Ja, was bitte?	Yes, what?
Was ist?	What is it?
Was gibt's?	What is it?
Was ist denn los?	What's going on?

Food items

Was hast du denn auf dem Brot?	What do you have on your sandwich?
das Pausenbrot, -e	sandwich for class break
das Sandwich, -es	sandwich
die Margarine	margarine
der Quark	a soft cheese similar to ricotta or cream cheese
der Schnittlauch	chives
der Tofu	tofu
die Sojasprossen (pl)	bean sprouts
die Marmelade	marmalade
die Erdbeermarmelade	strawberry marmalade
die Himbeermarmelade	raspberry marmalade
der Schweizer Käse	Swiss cheese
der Tilsiter Käse	Tilsiter cheese
der Camembert Käse	Camembert cheese

Possessive pronouns

Ihr	your (formal, singular)
Ihr	your (formal, plural)
ihr	their
unser	our
euer	your (informal, plural)

Dritte Stufe

Expressing preferences and strong preferences

Welche Suppe magst du lieber?	Which soup do you prefer?
Rind schmeckt mir besser.	Beef tastes better to me.
Welches Gemüse magst du am liebsten?	Which vegetable is your favorite?
Welche Suppe schmeckt dir am besten?	Which soup tastes the best to you?

Talking about what you eat at meals

Zum Nachtisch ess ich …	For dessert I eat …
Zum Abendessen gibt es …	For dinner there is …
das Frühstück	breakfast

Food items

das Sauerkraut	sauerkraut
die Pommes frites (pl)	french fries
das Fischstäbchen, -	fish stick
der Heilbutt	halibut
das Rindersteak, -s	steak (beef)
das Schnitzel, -	cutlet (pork or veal)
das Schweinekotelett, -s	pork chop
das Schweinefleisch	pork
das Lammfleisch	lamb
die Traube, -n	grape
der Karpfen, -	carp

Kapitel 6: Gute Besserung!
Chapter Overview

Los geht's! pp. 152–154 — *Was fehlt dir?, p. 152*

	FUNCTIONS	GRAMMAR	VOCABULARY	RE-ENTRY
Erste Stufe pp. 155–159	• Inquiring about someone's health and responding, p. 157 • Making suggestions, p. 158	• Reflexive pronouns in dative, p. 157 • **Sollen** used to make suggestions, p. 159 • The inclusive command, p. 159	• Pains and symptoms, p. 156	**Sich fühlen**, p. 156 (**Kap. 4, II**); how often you do something, p. 156 (**Kap. 7, I**); giving reasons, p. 157 (**Kap. 8, I**); accus. refl. pronouns, p. 158 (**Kap. 4, II**); **mal**, p. 158 (**Kap. 6, I**); **sollen** p. 159 (**Kap. 8, I**); responding to an invitation, expressing obligations, p. 159 (**Kap. 7, I**)
Zweite Stufe pp. 162–165	• Asking about and expressing pain, p. 163	• Verbs used with dative-case forms, p. 163 • **Wehtun**, p. 163 • Reflexive verbs used with dative-case forms, p. 164 • **Brechen**, p. 165 • **Waschen**, p. 165	• Body parts and injuries, p. 162 • Washing, combing, and cleaning, p. 165	The dative pronouns, p. 163 (**Kap. 3, II**); time expressions, pp. 163, 165 (**Kap. 7, I**); family members, p. 163 (**Kap. 3, I**); the conversational past, p. 164 (**Kap. 3, II**); accusative reflexive verbs, p. 165 (**Kap. 4, II**); asking what you should do, p. 165 (**Kap. 8, I**)
Dritte Stufe pp. 166–169	• Asking for and giving advice, p. 167 • Expressing hope, p. 168	• **Messen**, p. 168 • The dative case to express the idea of something too expensive, too large, too small, p. 169	• Health tips, p. 167 • More health terms, p. 168 • Things to buy in a **Drogerie**, p. 169	Asking what you should do, p. 167 (**Kap. 8, I**); **du**-commands, p. 168 (**Kap. 8, I**); **dass**-clauses, p. 168 (**Kap. 9, I**); using the telephone, p. 168 (**Kap. 11, I**); talking about likes and dislikes, p. 169 (**Kap. 10, I**)

Zum Lesen pp. 160–161 — Viel los unter der Sonne! — Reading Strategy: Deciphering charts and graphs

Mehr Grammatikübungen pp. 170–173
Erste Stufe, pp. 170–171   Zweite Stufe, pp. 171–172   Dritte Stufe, p. 173

Review pp. 174–177
Anwendung, pp. 174–175   Kann ich's wirklich?, p. 176   Wortschatz, p. 177
Zum Schreiben: Peer evaluation (Writing a realistic dialogue)

CULTURE
• Landeskunde: Was machst du, wenn dir nicht gut ist? p. 155
• Ein wenig Landeskunde: **Apotheke** and **Drogerie**, p. 159
• Article about sun exposure, p. 166

Kapitel 6: Gute Besserung!
Chapter Resources

Visit Holt Online
go.hrw.com
KEYWORD: WK3 HAMBURG-6
Online Edition

Lesson Planning
- One-Stop Planner
- **Lesson Planner with Substitute Teacher Lesson Plans,** pp. 27–31, 70
- **Student Make-Up Assignments**
  - Make-Up Assignment Copying Masters, Chapter 6

Listening and Speaking
- **TPR Storytelling Book,** pp. 40–47
- **Listening Activities**
  - Student Response Forms for Listening Activities, pp. 43–45
  - Additional Listening Activities 6-1 to 6-6, pp. 47–50
  - Additional Listening Activities (song), p. 46
  - Scripts and Answers, pp. 132–137
- **Video Guide**
  - Teaching Suggestions, pp. 36–37
  - Activity Masters, pp. 38–40
  - Scripts and Answers, pp. 93–95, 113
- **Activities for Communication**
  - Communicative Activities, pp. 31–36
  - Realia and Teaching Suggestions, pp. 94–97
  - Situation Cards, pp. 133–134

Reading and Writing
- **Reading Strategies and Skills Handbook,** Chapter 6
- **Lies mit mir! 2,** Chapter 6
- **Übungsheft,** pp. 61–72

Grammar
- **Grammatikheft,** pp. 46–54
- **Grammar Tutor for Students of German,** Chapter 6

Assessment
- **Testing Program**
  - Grammar and Vocabulary Quizzes, **Stufe** Quizzes, and Chapter Test, pp. 131–148
  - Score Sheet, Scripts and Answers, pp. 149–156
  - Midterm Exam, pp. 157–164
  - Midterm Exam Score Sheets, Scripts, and Answers, pp. 165–170
- **Alternative Assessment Guide**
  - Portfolio Assessment, p. 23
  - Performance Assessment, p. 37
  - CD-ROM Assessment, p. 51
- **Student Make-Up Assignments**
  - Alternative Quizzes, Chapter 6

MEDIA

Online Activities
- Interaktive Spiele
- Internet Aktivitäten

Video Program
- Videocassette 2
- Videocassette 5 (captioned version)
- DVD Tutor, Disc 1

Audio Compact Discs
- Textbook Listening Activities, CD 6, Tracks 1–10
- Additional Listening Activities, CD 6, Tracks 19–25
- Assessment Items, CD 6, Tracks 11–18

Interactive CD-ROM Tutor, Disc 2

Teaching Transparencies
- Situations 6-1 to 6-2
- Vocabulary 6-A to 6-C
- Los geht's!
- **Mehr Grammatikübungen** Answers
- **Grammatikheft** Answers

One-Stop Planner CD-ROM

Use the **One-Stop Planner CD-ROM with Test Generator** to aid in lesson planning and pacing.

For each chapter, the **One-Stop Planner** includes:
- Editable lesson plans with direct links to teaching resources
- Printable worksheets from resource books
- Direct launches to the HRW Internet activities
- Video and audio segments
- Test Generator
- Clip Art for vocabulary items

Kapitel 6: Gute Besserung!

Projects

Die Ratgeberspalte

In this activity, students will prepare and write an advice column for a health magazine. After completing the Zum Lesen *section of this chapter, students should begin the projects in pairs.*

MATERIALS
Students may need
- paper
- pen or pencil
- advice columns from health magazines to familiarize themselves with the format

OUTLINE

The project should include two letters in the physician's advice column (**Ratgeberspalte des Doktor Tutgut**): a request for advice and a response.

- The first letter should include complaints about a physical problem, a description of symptoms, and a request for **Doktor Tutgut**'s help and advice.
- The second letter should be a response to the first letter. It should offer advice and solutions for the writer's problems and might include a suggestion for visiting a certain **Kurort**.
- Students should include as much of the vocabulary from Chapter 6 as possible.

SUGGESTED SEQUENCE

1. Pair students up and give them the guidelines explained in the outline above.
2. Have pairs write their letters.
3. Have three or four pairs read their letters to the rest of the class.
4. Prepare a simple handout with one heading on each half of the paper: **Probleme/Lösungen**. As students listen to the presentations, have them jot down key information contained in the letter.

GRADING THE PROJECT

Suggested point distribution (**total = 100 points**)
Completion of
assignment requirements......................40
Correct language usage........................40
Oral presentation....................................20

Games

Wörter bilden

Students will enjoy reviewing vocabulary with the following game.

Procedure Choose several words from the **Wortschatz** section. (Example: **Fieber**) Then ask students to think of one new word that begins with each letter of that word. (Example: FIEBER—Fuß, ich, Ellbogen, Bauch, Eltern, Rücken) The student who finishes first shouts **Halt!**, and all students must put their pens down. The student who called **Halt!** reads out his or her words. If the words are all correct, this round of the game is over. If the student has an incorrect word (or words), the game continues until another student finishes and calls **Halt!** The caller now reads his or her words, one at a time. The rest of the students also give their words for each letter. If a word has been thought of by only one person, it receives ten points. If more than one person thought of the word, it receives five points. The person with the most points wins.

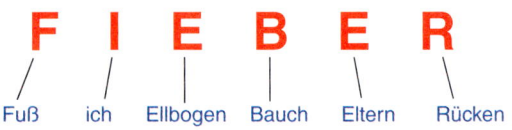

Fuß ich Ellbogen Bauch Eltern Rücken

Storytelling

Mini-Geschichte

*This story accompanies Teaching Transparency 6-A. Read the **Mini-Geschichte** to your students or have them role-play the conversation using appropriate gestures and facial expressions. Ask students to identify the main idea of the story.*

Alles tut weh!

DOKTOR Basti, was fehlt dir?

BASTI Mein Knöchel tut mir weh. Ich kann nicht richtig gehen.

DOKTOR Hmmm, du hast dir den Knöchel nicht gebrochen. Du hast ihn dir auch nicht verstaucht. Er ist überhaupt nicht verletzt. Du kannst bestimmt gehen.

BASTI Ich habe auch Schmerzen in meiner Schulter. Ich kann nicht richtig schreiben.

DOKTOR Hmmm, deine Schulter ist nicht gebrochen oder verletzt. Du kannst bestimmt schreiben.

BASTI Mein Kopf tut mir auch sehr weh. Ich kann nicht richtig denken.

DOKTOR Hmmm, dein Kopf ist auch nicht verletzt. Du kannst bestimmt denken.

BASTI Aber ich kann morgen nicht in die Schule gehen. Wir haben eine Mathearbeit …

Traditions

Die Bürgeroper

Die Geschichte der Oper in Deutschland beginnt in Hamburg. Schon 1678 war am Gänsemarkt das erste ständige Opernhaus Europas, ein lang gestreckter Holzbau, eröffnet worden. Es wurde von den kunstliebenden Bürgern der reichen Hansestadt finanziert. Georg Friedrich Händel wurde 1703 als Geiger engagiert. Als seine Opern aufgeführt wurden, spielte er selbst im Orchester mit. Das Opernhaus wurde 1758 abgerissen und durch ein „Comödienhaus" ersetzt, dessen berühmter Dramaturg, Gotthold Ephraim Lessing, das Theater Europas verändern sollte. Unter seinem Einfluss wurden seine Schauspiele und die von Goethe, Schiller und Shakespeare aufgeführt. Wolfgang Amadeus Mozarts Werke gehörten ab 1781 zum festen Repertoire. Im Jahr 1897 feierte das Opernhaus die 1000. Aufführung der Opern von Richard Wagner. Längst wird die Oper nicht mehr von den Hamburger Bürgern subventioniert, sondern vom Hamburger Senat. Die Hamburger Staatsoper gehört zu den bedeutendsten Opernbühnen der Welt.

*Have students research in the library or on the Internet the history of the **Hamburgische Staatsoper**. Students should report their research to the class.*

Rezept

Beefsteak mit Zwiebeln
Für 4 Personen

Zutaten

g=Gramm, EL=Esslöffel

4	Beefsteaks je 200g
250g	Zwiebeln
2EL	Butter
	Salz
	Pfeffer
1EL	Öl

Zubereitung

Die Beefsteaks mit Pfeffer einreiben und bei Zimmertemperatur liegen lassen. Inzwischen die gepellten Zwiebeln in Streifen oder Ringe schneiden. Butter in einer Pfanne bräunen, die Zwiebeln hineingeben und unter Wenden goldbraun braten, zum Schluss mit etwas Salz bestreuen. Öl in eine schwere Pfanne geben und heiß werden lassen. Das Fleisch hineingeben und von jeder Seite anbraten. Die Temperatur reduzieren und insgesamt 8-10 Minuten braten. Wenden nicht vergessen! Salzen und auf vorgewärmte Teller legen, die Zwiebeln darüber legen. Den Bratfond mit wenig Wasser loskochen, über die Zwiebeln geben. Dazu Gemüse und Salzkartoffeln oder Ofenkartoffeln reichen.

Kapitel 6: Gute Besserung!
Technology

Videocassette 2, 5 (captioned version)
DVD Tutor, Disc 1
See Video Guide, pages 35–40

DVD/Video

Los geht's! • Was fehlt dir?
In this segment of the video, Thorsten and David call Maike to find out why she was not at school. Maike tells them about her ailments and asks them to pick up her medicine at the pharmacy. Meanwhile, Wiebke and Nicolas are at a **Drogerie** buying toiletries for Wiebke.

Landeskunde
Was machst du, wenn dir nicht gut ist?
Two German students describe what they do when they get sick.

Fortsetzung
Wiebke and Nicolas are in the park waiting for David and Thorsten to return. By accident, Wiebke almost puts toothpaste on her face instead of sunscreen, but luckily, Nicolas points out her mistake before any harm is done. When the two start playing ball, Nicolas falls and says he thinks he has sprained or broken his ankle.

Videoclips
- **Signal Tag und Nacht**® (mouthwash)
- **Blend-A-Med**® (toothpaste)
- **Coldastop**® (nose drops)
- **Ilrido**® (sunscreen)

Interactive CD-ROM Tutor

Activity	Activity Type	Pupil's Edition Reference
1. Wortschatz	Merkspiel	p. 156
2. Wortschatz	Wort und Bild Erfahren/Wählen	pp. 156, 162
3. Grammatik	Was fehlt?	pp. 163, 164
4. Grammatik	Was kommt dann?	pp. 164, 165
5. So sagt man das!	Wozu gehört's?	pp. 157, 163, 167
6. Wortschatz	Was ist richtig?	pp. 167, 168, 169
Landeskunde	Was machst du, wenn dir nicht gut ist? Was ist richtig?	p. 155
Zum Sprechen	*Guided recording*	pp. 174–175
Zum Schreiben	*Guided writing*	pp. 174–175

Teacher Management System
Launch the program, type "admin" in the password area, and press RETURN. Log on to **www.hrw.com/CDROMTUTOR** for a detailed explanation of the Teacher Management System.

DVD Tutor

The *DVD Tutor* contains all material from the *Video Program* as described above. German captions are available for use at your discretion for all sections of the video. The *DVD Tutor* also provides a variety of video-based activities that assess students' understanding of **Los geht's!, Fortsetzung,** and **Landeskunde,** as well as the new **Grammatik im Kontext** presentations.

The *DVD Tutor* may be used on any DVD video player connected to a television or video monitor.

Visit Holt Online
go.hrw.com
KEYWORD: WK3 HAMBURG-6
Online Edition

Go.Online!

Premier Online Edition

The Premier Online Edition for *Komm mit!* allows students access to their textbooks anytime, anywhere.

- Audio at point of use
- Additional practice activities
- Self-test activities
- Online reference tools
- Entire Video Program
- Interactive Notebook

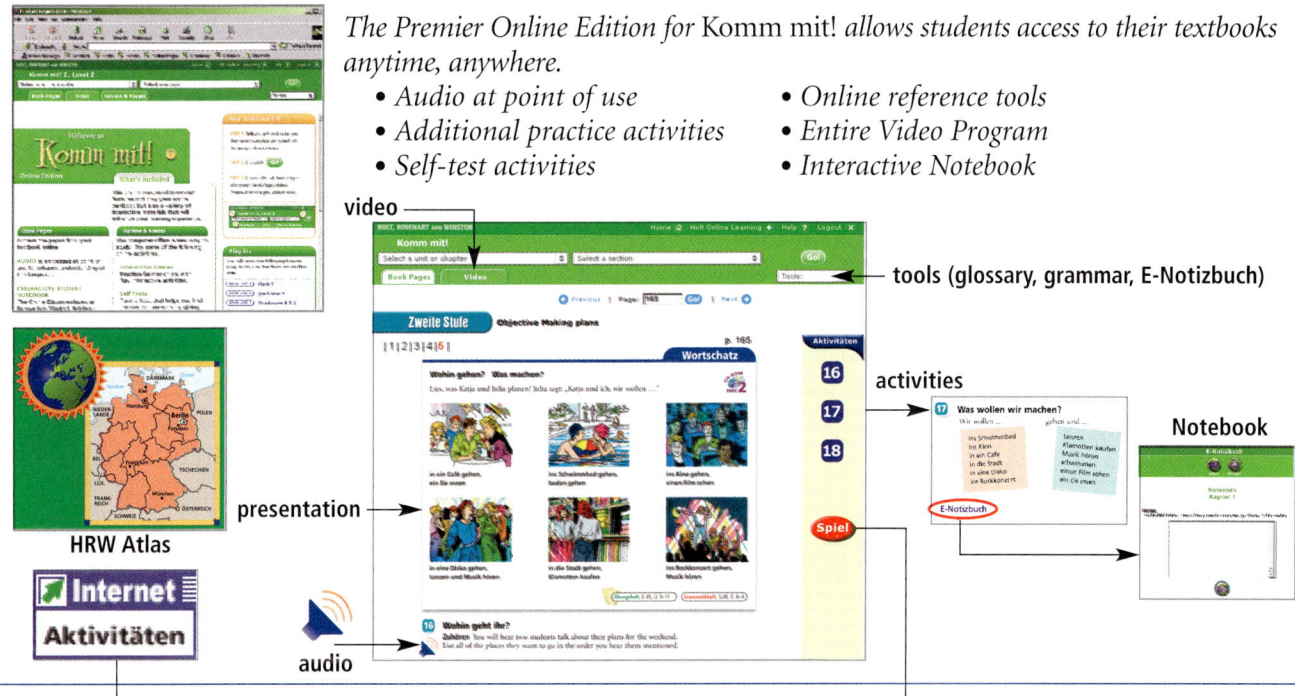

Internet Aktivitäten

These guided internet activities include a worksheet and pre-selected and pre-screened authentic web sites from the German-speaking countries. You can use these activities

- to help students develop research skills in the target language
- to introduce students to authentic cultural information
- as a project

Interaktive Spiele

You can use the interactive activities in this chapter

- to practice grammar, vocabulary, and chapter functions
- as homework
- as an assessment option
- as a self-test
- to prepare for the Chapter Test

Webprojekt Have students find an online pharmacy in a German-speaking country. The pharmacy should suggest a treatment for toothache or earache. Have students report on the suggested treatment.

Encourage students to exchange useful Web sites with their classmates. Have students document their sources by referencing the names and URLs of all the sites they consulted.

STANDARDS: 1.2, 1.3, 3.2, 5.1, 5.2   KAPITEL 6   TECHNOLOGY   149F

Kapitel 6: Gute Besserung!
Textbook Listening Activities Scripts

Erste Stufe

6   p. 156

1. JÜRGEN — Meine Stirn ist so furchtbar heiß! Mir ist schlecht. Ich habe bestimmt Fieber.
2. KARIN — Mir geht es überhaupt nicht gut! Ich habe Bauchschmerzen und gar keinen Appetit! Der Arzt war gerade da und hat mir ein Rezept geschrieben.
3. STEFAN — Ich treffe mich gleich mit ein paar Freunden. Wir gehen zum Fußballtraining. Ich bin heute gut in Form!
4. ULRIKE — Ich fühl mich heute nicht wohl! Ich habe Halsschmerzen und kann kaum schlucken.

Answers to Activity 6
a. 4; b. 1; c. 2; d. 3

Zweite Stufe

15   p. 162

ROSI — Zuerst habe ich in der Nacht angefangen zu husten, weil mein Hals gekratzt hat. Und heute Morgen, als ich aufgewacht bin, konnte ich vor lauter Halsschmerzen gar nicht schlucken.

JAN — Schon seit Tagen tun mir die Zähne weh, wenn ich Schokolade oder Eis esse. Heute ist es besonders schlimm. Ich glaube, ich muss wohl endlich mal zum Zahnarzt gehen. Ich kann die Schmerzen kaum noch aushalten!

SANDRA — Gestern Abend habe ich Fisch gegessen, und heute habe ich starke Bauchschmerzen. Mir ist so übel. Hoffentlich muss ich mich nicht übergeben!

TOBIAS — Ahh, ich habe tierische Kopfschmerzen. Und ausgerechnet heute, wo ich einen Mathetest in der Schule habe. Ich kann mich gar nicht konzentrieren.

Answers to Activity 15
a. Tobias; b. Rosi; c. Sandra; d. Jan

Dritte Stufe

23   p. 167

MARKUS — Markus Weber hier. Hallo?

UWE — Guten Morgen, Markus! Ich bin's, Uwe. Du, ich wollte dich fragen, ob es dir etwas besser geht. Kommst du heute zur Schule? Soll ich dich abholen?

MARKUS — Ach Uwe, nee, ich kann heute nicht zur Schule kommen. Ich hab wirklich schlimme Zahnschmerzen. Meine Wange ist sogar ein bisschen geschwollen. Es hat gestern Nachmittag angefangen.

UWE — Ja, also, das tut mir echt Leid. Ich hab gestern in der Schule schon gemerkt, dass du nicht so gut drauf warst! Gehst du heute denn zum Zahnarzt?

MARKUS — Nein, ich bleibe lieber im Bett. Meine Eltern kommen morgen aus dem Urlaub zurück, bis dahin warte ich noch! Dann kann mich meine Mutter zum Arzt hinfahren.

UWE — Das finde ich aber nicht so gut! Du solltest sofort zum Zahnarzt gehen. Ich hol dich nach der Schule mit meinem Moped ab und fahr dich zu Doktor Dressler, okay?

MARKUS — Also gut, wenn du meinst. Und vielen Dank für deinen Anruf!

UWE — Nichts zu danken. Tschüs dann, bis nachher!

Answers to Activity 23
Markus hat Zahnschmerzen; er soll zum Zahnarzt gehen; Uwe holt ihn ab und bringt ihn hin.

The following scripts are for the listening activities found in the *Pupil's Edition*. For Student Response Forms, see *Listening Activities*, pages 43–46. To provide students with additional listening practice, see *Listening Activities*, pages 47–50.

One-Stop Planner CD-ROM
For resource information, see the **One-Stop Planner CD-ROM**, Disc 2.

27 p. 168

KLAUS Ja also, das Spiel war echt sensationell! Beide Mannschaften waren ziemlich gut in Form! Ich glaube aber, dass es bei uns mehr Verletzungen gegeben hat. Der Lothar zum Beispiel hat sich ganz schön den Knöchel verstaucht, gleich nach den ersten zehn Spielminuten!

THOMAS Ja stimmt! Ich glaube aber, dass es bei ihm nicht so schlimm ist, wie beim Rudi. Der hat sich nämlich in der zweiten Halbzeit das Knie verletzt. Es hat sogar geblutet. Das war ein ziemlich blödes Foul von der anderen Mannschaft! Hoffentlich kann er nächste Woche wieder beim Training mitmachen.

ANDREAS Ach ja, das kann er bestimmt. Der Rudi ist ganz schön „tough"! Mir tut der Marco echt Leid. Ausgerechnet unser bester Spieler muss sich den Fuß brechen! Ich hoffe, dass er in dieser Saison überhaupt wieder spielen kann. Es sieht ziemlich schlecht für ihn aus. Das dauert bestimmt lange, bis der Fuß wieder in Ordnung ist!

Answers to Activity 27
Lothar: Knöchel verstaucht; Rudi: Knie verletzt; Marco: Fuß gebrochen; Thomas und Andreas drücken Hoffnungen aus.

Anwendung

1 p. 174

SONJA Ich fahre in den Ferien ans Meer und brauche unbedingt eine gute Sonnencreme. Am besten mit einem hohen Lichtschutzfaktor, denn ich will auf keinen Fall einen Sonnenbrand bekommen!

MELANIE Ich habe schon seit ein paar Tagen Kopfschmerzen. Mein Arzt hat mir ein Rezept für Tabletten gegeben, aber ich hatte noch keine Zeit, sie abzuholen.

UTE Meine Hustenmedizin ist alle. Ich muss mir neue kaufen.

JÖRG Ich brauche unbedingt eine neue Zahnpasta. Heute Morgen habe ich den letzten Rest verbraucht.

Answers to Activity 1
1: Wenn man Sonnencreme braucht, muss man zur Drogerie.
2: Wenn man Tabletten braucht, muss man zur Apotheke.
3: Wenn man Medizin braucht, muss man zur Apotheke.
4: Wenn man Zahnpasta braucht, muss man zur Drogerie.

Kapitel 6: Gute Besserung!
Suggested Lesson Plans — 50-Minute Schedule

Day 1

CHAPTER OPENER 10 min.
- Background Information, ATE, p. 149M
- Building Context, p. 149M

LOS GEHT'S! 20 min.
- Preteaching Vocabulary, ATE, p. 149N
- Math Connection, ATE, p. 149N
- Play Audio CD for Los geht's!, pp. 152–153
- Have students read Los geht's!, pp. 152–153
- Teaching Suggestions, Video Guide, p. 36
- Show Los geht's! Video

ERSTE STUFE
LANDESKUNDE 15 min.
- Pre-viewing Suggestion, Video Guide, p. 36
- Show Landeskunde Video
- Do Landeskunde Activities, Video Guide, pp. 38–39

Wrap-Up 5 min.
- Students respond to questions about what German teens do when sick

Homework Options
Pupil's Edition, p. 154, Comprehension Acts. 1–5; p. 155, Acts. A, B, and C
Übungsheft, p. 61, Act. 1; p. 62, Acts. 1–3

Day 2

ERSTE STUFE
Quick Review 10 min.
- Check homework, Comprehension Acts. 1–5, p. 154

Wortschatz, p. 156 10 min.
- Presenting Wortschatz, ATE, p. 149O
- Teaching Transparency 6-1
- Play Audio CD for Activity 6, p. 156
- Do Activity 7, p. 156

So sagt man das!, p. 157 10 min.
- Presenting So sagt man das!, ATE, p. 149P
- Do Activity 8, p. 157

Ein wenig Grammatik, p. 157 15 min.
- Presenting Ein wenig Grammatik, ATE, p. 149P
- Do Activity 9, p. 157
- Do Activities 10 and 11, p. 158

Wrap-Up 5 min.
- Students respond to questions about how they feel

Homework Options
Grammatikheft, pp. 46–47, Acts. 1–3
Übungsheft, pp. 63–65, Acts. 1–6

Day 3

ERSTE STUFE
Quick Review 10 min.
- Check homework, Grammatikheft, pp. 46–47, Acts. 1–3

So sagt man das!, p. 158 10 min.
- Presenting So sagt man das!, ATE, p. 149Q
- Do Activity 12, p. 159

Ein wenig Grammatik/Grammatik, p. 159 10 min.
- Presenting Ein wenig Grammatik/Grammatik, ATE, p. 149Q
- Do Activity 4, p. 47, Grammatikheft

Ein wenig Landeskunde, p. 159 15 min.
- Present Ein wenig Landeskunde, p. 159
- Do Activity 13, p. 159

Wrap-Up 5 min.
- Students make suggestions to others about where to go

Homework Options
Pupil's Edition, p. 159, Act. 14
Activities for Communication, p. 94, Realia 6-1, write a letter telling a friend why he should take topfitz®

Day 4

ERSTE STUFE
Quick Review 15 min.
- Check homework, Realia 6-1
- Do Additional Listening Activity 6-1, p. 47

ZUM LESEN 30 min.
- Present Lesestrategie, p. 160
- Do Activities 1–6, pp. 160–161
- Do Activities 1–5, p. 66, Übungsheft

Wrap-Up 5 min.
- Students make suggestions to others about taking a "cure" in Germany

Homework Options
Mehr Grammatikübungen, Erste Stufe

Day 5

ERSTE STUFE
Quick Review 15 min.
- Check homework, Mehr Grammatikübungen, Erste Stufe
- Do Activity 1, Interactive CD-ROM

Quiz Review 15 min.
- Do Additional Listening Activity 6-2, p. 47
- Do Situation 6-1, pp. 133–134

Quiz 20 min.
- Quiz 6-1A or 6-1B

Homework Options
Activities for Communication, pp. 31–32, prepare Communicative Activity 6-1

Day 6

ZWEITE STUFE
Quick Review 15 min.
- Bell Work, ATE, p. 149S
- Do Communicative Activity 6-1

Wortschatz, p. 162 15 min.
- Presenting Wortschatz, ATE, p. 149T
- Teaching Transparencies 6-2, 6-A
- Play Audio CD for Activity 15, p. 162
- Do Activity 16, p. 162

So sagt man das!/Ein wenig Grammatik, p. 163 15 min.
- Presenting So sagt man das!, ATE, p. 149T
- Presenting Ein wenig Grammatik, ATE, p. 149T
- Do Activity 17, p. 163

Wrap-Up 5 min.
- Students respond to questions about what hurts

Homework Options
Grammatikheft, p. 48, Acts. 5–6
Übungsheft, p. 67, Acts. 1–2

One-Stop Planner CD-ROM

For alternative lesson plans by chapter section, to create your own customized plans, or to preview all resources available for this chapter, use the **One-Stop Planner CD-ROM**, Disc 2.

 For additional homework suggestions, see activities accompanied by this symbol throughout the chapter.

Day 7

ZWEITE STUFE

Quick Review 10 min.
- Check homework, Grammatikheft, p. 48, Acts. 5–6

Grammatik/Grammatik, pp. 163–164 20 min.
- Presenting **Grammatik**, ATE, p. 149T
- Presenting **Grammatik**, ATE, p. 149U
- Do Activities 18 and 19, p. 164

Wortschatz/Ein wenig Grammatik, p. 165 15 min.
- Presenting **Wortschatz**, ATE, p. 149U
- Present **Ein wenig Grammatik**, p. 165
- Do Activity 20, p. 165

Wrap-Up 5 min.
- Students answer questions about what hurts or what is injured

Homework Options
Grammatikheft, pp. 49–51, Acts. 7–9, 11
Übungsheft, p. 68, Act. 3
Interaktive Spiele, see ATE, p. 149F

Day 8

ZWEITE STUFE

Quick Review 5 min.
- Check homework, Übungsheft, p. 68, Act. 3

Ein wenig Grammatik, p. 165 10 min.
- Presenting **Ein wenig Grammatik**, ATE, p. 149V
- Do Activity 21, p. 165

Quiz Review 15 min.
- Do Activities 4–7, pp. 68–69, Übungsheft
- Do Activty 10, p. 51, Grammatikheft

Quiz 20 min.
- Quiz 6-2A or 6-2B

Homework Options
Activities for Communication, pp. 133–134, prepare Situation 6-2

Day 9

DRITTE STUFE

Quick Review 10 min.
- Return and review Quiz 6-2
- Bell Work, ATE, p. 149V
- Do Situation 6-2

Reading Selection 15 min.
- Read **Vorsicht vor Sonnenstrahlen!**, p. 166
- Do Activity 22, p. 166
- Play Audio CD for Activity 23, p. 167

Wortschatz, p. 167 10 min.
- Presenting **Wortschatz**, ATE, p. 149W
- Teaching Transparency 6-C
- Do Activity 24, p. 167

So sagt man das!, p. 167 10 min.
- Presenting **So sagt man das!**, ATE, p. 149W
- Do Activity 25, p. 168

Wrap-Up 5 min.
- Students respond to questions about what they should do for their health

Homework Options
Grammatikheft, p. 52, Acts. 12–13
Übungsheft, pp. 70–71, Acts. 1, 3

Day 10

DRITTE STUFE

Quick Review 10 min.
- Check homework, Übungsheft, pp. 70–71, Acts. 1, 3

Wortschatz/Ein wenig Grammatik, p. 168 10 min.
- Presenting **Wortschatz**, ATE, p. 149W
- **Ein wenig Grammatik**, ATE, p. 149W
- Do Activity 26, p. 168

So sagt man das!, p. 168 10 min.
- Presenting **So sagt man das!**, ATE, p. 149W
- Play Audio CD for Activity 27, p. 168
- Do Activity 28, p. 169

Wortschatz/Ein wenig Grammatik, p. 169 15 min.
- Presenting **Wortschatz**, ATE, p. 149W
- Do Activity 2, p. 70, Übungsheft
- Presenting **Ein wenig Grammatik**, ATE, p. 149W
- Do Activities 29, 30, and 31, p. 169

Wrap-Up 5 min.
- Students respond to questions about why they buy certain products

Homework Options
Grammatikheft, pp. 53–54, Acts. 14–18
Übungsheft, pp. 71–72, Acts. 4–7

Day 11

DRITTE STUFE

Quick Review 10 min.
- Check homework, Grammatikheft, pp. 53–54, Acts. 14–18

Quiz Review 20 min.
- Do **Mehr Grammatikübungen, Dritte Stufe**
- Do Communicative Activity 6-3, pp. 35–36

Quiz 20 min.
- Quiz 6-3A or 6-3B

Homework Options
Pupil's Edition, p. 175, Act. 7, **Zum Schreiben;** p. 176, **Kann ich's wirklich?**
Internet Aktivitäten, see ATE, p. 149F

Day 12

ANWENDUNG

Quick Review 30 min.
- Return and review Quiz 6-3
- Check homework, p. 176, **Kann ich's wirklich?**
- Do **Anwendung** Activities 1-6, p. 174

Chapter Review 20 min.
- Review chapter functions, vocabulary, and grammar; choose from **Mehr Grammatikübungen,** Grammar Tutor for Students of German, Activities for Communication, Listening Activities, Interactive CD-ROM Tutor, or **Interaktive Spiele**

Homework Options
Study for Chapter Test

Assessment

Test, Chapter 6 45 min.
- Administer Chapter 6 Test. Select from Testing Program, Alternative Assessment Guide or Test Generator.

Kapitel 6: Gute Besserung!
Suggested Lesson Plans 90-Minute Block Schedule

Block 1

CHAPTER OPENER 5 min.
- Background Information, ATE, p. 149M
- Building Context, ATE, p. 149M

LOS GEHT'S! 20 min.
- Preteaching Vocabulary, ATE, p. 149N
- Math Connection, ATE, p. 149N
- Play Audio CD for **Los geht's!**, pp. 152–153
- Have students read **Los geht's!**, pp. 152–153
- Show **Los geht's!** Video

ERSTE STUFE
LANDESKUNDE 20 min.
- Pre-viewing Suggestion, Video Guide, p. 36
- Background Information, ATE, p. 149O
- Show **Landeskunde** Video
- Do Activities A, B and C, p. 155
- Do **Landeskunde** Activities, Video Guide, pp. 38–39

Wortschatz, p. 156 15 min.
- Presenting **Wortschatz**, ATE, p. 149O
- Play Audio CD for Activity 6, p. 156
- Do Activity 7, p. 156

So sagt man das!, p. 157 15 min.
- Presenting **So sagt man das!**, ATE, p. 149P
- Do Activity 8, p. 157
- Do Activity 3, p. 47, Grammatikheft

Ein wenig Grammatik, p. 157 10 min.
- Presenting **Ein wenig Grammatik**, ATE, p. 149P
- Do Activity 9, p. 157
- Do Activities 10 and 11, p. 158

Wrap-Up 5 min.
- Students respond to questions about how they feel

Homework Options
Pupil's Edition, p. 154, Comprehension Acts. 1–5
Grammatikheft, p. 46, Acts. 1–2
Übungsheft, p. 61, Act. 1; p. 62, Acts. 1–3; pp. 63–65, Acts. 1–6

Block 2

ERSTE STUFE
Quick Review 10 min.
- Check homework, Grammatikheft, p. 46, Acts. 1–2

So sagt man das!, p. 158 10 min.
- Presenting **So sagt man das!**, ATE, p. 149Q
- Do Activity 12, p. 159

Ein wenig Grammatik/Grammatik, p. 159 15 min.
- Presenting **Ein wenig Grammatik**, ATE, p. 149Q
- Presenting **Grammatik**, ATE, p. 149Q
- Do Activity 13, p. 159
- Do Activity 4, p. 47, Grammatikheft

Ein wenig Landeskunde, p. 159 15 min.
- Present **Ein wenig Landeskunde**, p. 159
- Do Activity 14, p. 159

ZUM LESEN 25 min.
- Present **Lesestrategie**, p. 160
- Do Activities 1–6, pp. 160–161
- Do Activities 1–5, p. 66, Übungsheft

Wrap-Up 5 min.
- Students make suggestions to others about where to go

Homework Options
Mehr Grammatikübungen, Erste Stufe
Activities for Communication, pp. 133–134, prepare Situation 6-1

Block 3

ZWEITE STUFE
Quick Review 10 min.
- Check homework, **Mehr Grammatikübungen, Erste Stufe**

Quiz Review 15 min.
- Do Additional Listening Activities 6-1 and 6-2, p. 47
- Do Situation 6-1, pp. 133–134

Quiz 20 min.
- Quiz 6-1A or 6-1B

Wortschatz, p. 162 25 min.
- Presenting **Wortschatz**, ATE, p. 149T
- Teaching Transparencies 6-2, 6-A
- Play Audio CD for Activity 15, p. 162
- Do Activity 16, p. 162
- Do Activities 1–2, p. 67, Übungsheft

So sagt man das!/Ein wenig Grammatik, p. 163 15 min.
- Presenting **So sagt man das!**, ATE, p. 149T
- Presenting **Ein wenig Grammatik**, ATE, p. 149T
- Do Activity 17, p. 163

Wrap-Up 5 min.
- Students respond to questions about what hurts

Homework Options
Grammatikheft, p. 48, Acts. 5–6

One-Stop Planner CD-ROM

For alternative lesson plans by chapter section, to create your own customized plans, or to preview all resources available for this chapter, use the **One-Stop Planner CD-ROM**, Disc 2.

 For additional homework suggestions, see activities accompanied by this symbol throughout the chapter.

Block 4

ZWEITE STUFE

Quick Review 10 min.
Check homework, Grammatikheft, p. 48, Acts. 5–6

Grammatik/Grammatik, pp. 163–164 25 min.
- Presenting **Grammatik**, ATE, p. 149T
- Do Activities 4–6, **Mehr Grammatikübungen, Zweite Stufe**
- Presenting **Grammatik**, ATE, p. 149U
- Do Activities 18 and 19, p. 164

Wortschatz/Ein wenig Grammatik, p. 165 15 min.
- Presenting **Wortschatz**, ATE, p. 149U
- Present **Ein wenig Grammatik**, p. 165
- Do Activity 20, p. 165

Ein wenig Grammatik, p. 165 15 min.
- Presenting **Ein wenig Grammatik**, ATE, p. 149V
- Do Activity 21, p. 165
- Do Activity 8, **Mehr Grammatikübungen, Zweite Stufe**

Quiz Review 20 min.
- Do Activity 7, **Mehr Grammatikübungen, Zweite Stufe**
- Do Additional Listening Activities 6-3 and 6-4, pp. 48–49
- Do Activities 3–4, Interactive CD-ROM

Wrap-Up 5 min.
- Students answer questions about what hurts or what is injured

Homework Options
Grammatikheft, pp. 49–51, Acts. 7–11
Übungsheft, pp. 68–69, Acts. 3–7
Interaktive Spiele, see ATE, p. 149F

Block 5

DRITTE STUFE
Quick Review 15 min.
- Check homework, Grammatikheft, pp. 49–51, Acts. 7–11

Quiz
- Quiz 6-2A or 6-2B 20 min.

Reading Selection 20 min.
- Read **Vorsicht vor Sonnenstrahlen!**, p. 166
- Do Activity 22, p. 166
- Play Audio CD for Activity 23, p. 167

Wortschatz, p. 167 10 min.
- Presenting **Wortschatz**, ATE, p. 149W
- Teaching Transparency 6-C
- Do Activity 24, p. 167

So sagt man das!, p. 167 10 min.
- Presenting **So sagt man das!**, ATE, p. 149W
- Do Activity 25, p. 168

Wortschatz/Ein wenig Grammatik, p. 168 10 min.
- Presenting **Wortschatz**, ATE, p. 149W
- Presenting **Ein wenig Grammatik**, ATE, p. 149W
- Do Activity 26, p. 168

Wrap-Up 5 min.
- Students respond to questions about what they should do for their health

Homework Options
Grammatikheft, pp. 52–53, Acts. 12–15
Übungsheft, pp. 70–72, Acts. 1, 3–7
Interaktive Spiele, see ATE, p. 149F

Block 6

DRITTE STUFE
Quick Review 10 min.
- Return and review Quiz 6-2
- Check homework, Grammatikheft, pp. 52–53, Acts. 12–15

So sagt man das!, p. 168 15 min.
- Presenting **So sagt man das!**, ATE, p. 149W
- Play Audio CD for Activity 27, p. 168
- Do Activity 28, p. 169

Wortschatz/Ein wenig Grammatik, p. 169 10 min.
- Presenting **Wortschatz**, ATE, p. 149W
- Presenting **Ein wenig Grammatik**, ATE, p. 149W
- Do Activities 29, 30, and 31, p. 169

Quiz Review 10 min.
- Do Activity 2, p. 70, Übungsheft
- Do Activities 16–18, pp. 53–54, Grammatikheft

Quiz 20 min.
- Quiz 6-3A or 6-3B

ANWENDUNG 20 min.
- Do **Anwendung** Activities 1–6, p. 174

Wrap-Up 5 min.
- Students respond to questions about aches and pains

Homework Options
Pupil's Edition, p. 175, Act. 7, **Zum Schreiben**

Block 7

ANWENDUNG
Quick Review 15 min.
- Return and review Quiz 6-3
- Check homework, p. 175, **Zum Schreiben**

Kann ich's wirklich?, p. 176 10 min.
- Students respond to **Kann ich's wirklich?** questions

Chapter Review 20 min.
- Review chapter functions, vocabulary, and grammar; choose from **Mehr Grammatikübungen**, Grammar Tutor for Students of German, Activities for Communication, Listening Activities, Interactive CD-ROM Tutor, or **Interaktive Spiele**

Test, Chapter 6 45 min.
- Administer Chapter 6 Test. Select from Testing Program, Alternative Assessment Guide or Test Generator.

Kapitel 6: Gute Besserung!
Teaching Suggestions, pages 150–177

PAGE 150–151

CHAPTER OPENER

Pacing Tips

The **Erste Stufe** centers around the function of 'inquiring about someone's health and responding.' Students learn about various pains and symptoms, study the inclusive (**wir**) command, and discover the difference between an **Apotheke** and a **Drogerie**. The **Zweite Stufe** focuses on 'asking about and expressing pain' of several parts of the body. Reflexive verbs used with dative case forms are presented on p. 164. The **Dritte Stufe** includes the functions of 'asking for and giving advice' and 'expressing hope.' Because the **Dritte Stufe** contains less grammatical or cultural concepts, you might spend less time on it than on the **Erste Stufe** or the **Zweite Stufe**. For Lesson Plans and timing suggestions, see pages 149I–149L.

Meeting the Standards

Communication
- Inquiring about someone's health and responding, p. 157
- Making suggestions, p. 158
- Asking about and expressing pain, p. 163
- Asking for and giving advice, p. 167
- Expressing hope, p. 168

Cultures
- **Landeskunde,** p. 155
- **Ein wenig Landeskunde,** p. 159
- Background Information, p. 149M
- Culture Note, p. 149O
- Background Information, p. 149R
- Background Information, p. 149S
- Language Note, p. 149T

Connections
- Thinking Critically, p. 149M
- Multicultural Connection, p. 149Q
- Geography Connection, p. 149R
- Multicultural Connection, p. 149T

Comparisons
- Thinking Critically, p. 149O
- Language-to-Language, p. 149U

Communities
- Career Path, p. 149V

For resource information, see the **One-Stop Planner CD-ROM**, Disc 2.

Building Context

Ask your students if they have ever had a serious illness or an accident or know someone who has. Ask if any of them are familiar with first aid procedures and what should be done in case of an emergency.

Cultures and Communities

Background Information

In Germany, there are numbers to call in case of emergency that are similar to the 911 number in the United States. Germans can dial 110 to reach the police and 112 to call the local fire department.

Connections and Comparisons

Thinking Critically

Analyzing Ask students to look at the photo and determine where these students might be. Can students guess what might have happened in the photo? (In a park; one of the students fell and hurt himself.)

Drawing Inferences Ask students to imagine they are one of the three students surrounding the injured student. What are some of the questions they could ask him in order to find out what happened or how they might be able to help?

Chapter Sequence

Los geht's!	p. 152
Landeskunde	p. 155
Erste Stufe	p. 156
Zum Lesen	p. 160
Zweite Stufe	p. 162
Dritte Stufe	p. 166
Mehr Grammatikübungen	p. 170
Anwendung	p. 174
Kann ich's wirklich?	p. 176
Wortschatz	p. 177

LOS GEHT'S!

Teaching Resources
pp. 152–154

PRINT
- Lesson Planner, p. 27
- Video Guide, pp. 35–36, 38
- Übungsheft, p. 61

MEDIA
- One-Stop Planner
- Video Program
  Los geht's!
  Videocassette 2, 31:40–36:20
  Videocassette 5 (captioned version), 32:52–37:33
  Fortsetzung
  Videocassette 2, 36:25–37:50
  Videocassette 5 (captioned version), 37:38–39:02
- DVD Tutor, Disc 1
- Audio Compact Discs, CD6, Trs. 1–2
- Los geht's! Transparencies

PAGES 152–153

Los geht's! Transparencies

Preteaching Vocabulary

Guessing words from context

First, ask students to identify where each scene is taking place and what the people are doing there. Then have students use contextual clues to guess the meanings of these words and phrases: **Was meinst du?, Apotheke, Abholschein, Drogerie, Schutzfactor.** Which of these words are cognates? Finally, have students find instances of the word **mir.** Where can **mir** be used in a sentence? How does **mir** add to or slightly alter the meaning of each sentence?

Fortsetzung

You may choose to continue with the Fortsetzung of *Was fehlt dir?* now or wait until later in the chapter. For a synopsis of the Los geht's! and Fortsetzung episodes, see p. 149E.

Advance Organizer

Ask students about the last time they had to stay home from school because they were sick. What was wrong and what did they do to get better? Did friends do something to help?

Connections and Comparisons

Math Connection
The standard German fever thermometer measures degrees in Celsius. Have students determine how high Maike's fever is. To convert Celsius to Fahrenheit, multiply by 9, divide by 5, and add 32. (Maike has a fever of 102° F.)

PAGE 154

Using the Captioned Video/DVD

As an alternative to reading the conversations in the book, you might want to show the captioned version of *Was fehlt dir?* available on Videocassette 5.
Note: The *DVD Tutor* contains captions for all sections of the *Video Program.*

Comprehension Check

Auditory Learners
1 Ask students to look again at the eight frames of **Los geht's!**. Read Questions 1–5 to students while they scan the text for the answers.

A Slower Pace
2 Ask students to do this activity in writing as they refer to **Los geht's!** for the answers. Call on several students to read their sentences to the class.

Challenge
3 After students have completed this activity, have them use the sentences on the left side to come up with a different completion or follow-up sentence for each one.

Thinking Critically
4 Analyzing To expand this activity, ask students to think of another way to describe each of the six people. Their descriptions should not be based on something that is stated explicitly, but rather should reflect an impression they got about that person after having watched the video segment and read **Los geht's!**.

5 This activity could also be done as a written assignment in pairs. Students will need to change the text from direct discourse to a narrative. This will require students to concentrate on the main ideas of the text. Students will have to use connectors, change word order, and replace nouns with pronouns.

STANDARDS: 3.1

▶ **PAGE 155**

LANDESKUNDE

Teaching Resources
p. 155

PRINT
- Video Guide, pp. 35–36, 38–39
- Übungsheft, p. 62

MEDIA
- One-Stop Planner
- Video Program
  Videocassette 2, 38:29–39:20
- DVD Tutor, Disc 1
- Audio Compact Discs, CD6, Trs. 3–5
- Interactive CD-ROM Tutor, Disc 2

Connections and Comparisons

Thinking Critically
Comparing and Contrasting In German, ask students to look at the symbol used to represent pharmacies in Germany. Do students notice a difference between the symbol used in Germany and the one used in the United States? (symbol in the United States: Rx, mortar and pestle)

Teaching Suggestion
In German, ask students what the procedure is at their school when they need to go home early due to illness. Encourage students to give a description using the impersonal pronoun **man**. You might want to introduce the following additional vocabulary to help students understand the interviews:

etwas dabei haben *to have something along or nearby*
der Magen *stomach*
die Tablette *pill*
Tabletten einnehmen *to take pills*

Cultures and Communities

Culture Note
German students who have to go home from school because of illness must inform the teacher of the class that they are leaving. That teacher notes the absence in the **Klassenbuch**. The day the student returns to school, he or she must bring a note from home (**eine Entschuldigung**).

Teaching Suggestion
C You may want to assign Activity C for extra credit and let students present a report to the class.

ERSTE STUFE

Teaching Resources
pp. 156–159

PRINT
- Lesson Planner, p. 28
- TPR Storytelling Book, pp. 40–41
- Listening Activities, pp. 43, 47
- Activities for Communication, pp. 94, 97, 133–134
- Grammatikheft, pp. 46–47
- Grammar Tutor for Students of German, Chapter 6
- Übungsheft, pp. 63–65
- Testing Program, pp. 131–134
- Alternative Assessment Guide, p. 37
- Student Make-Up Assignments, Chapter 6

MEDIA
- One-Stop Planner
- Audio Compact Discs, CD6, Trs. 6, 11, 19–20
- Teaching Transparencies
  Situation 6-1
  Mehr Grammatikübungen Answers
  Grammatikheft Answers
- Interactive CD-ROM Tutor, Disc 2
- DVD Tutor, Disc 1

▶ **PAGE 156**

Bell Work
In pairs, have students tell each other in English how their voice sounds when they are not feeling well.

PRESENTING: Wortschatz

- Teach the new expressions by acting them out. For example, you could cup your hand over your ear, indicating that you have pain, and say **Ich habe Ohrenschmerzen!** Have students repeat after you, also acting out the new phrases and putting much expression into their voices.

- To further practice the new expressions, use pantomime. Act out some kind of pain and have students tell you or ask you what your ailment is. Examples:
Sie haben Zahnschmerzen.
Haben Sie eine Erkältung?

PAGE 157

PRESENTING: So sagt man das!

Ask students what expressions they use in English to inquire about someone's health. Then go over the expressions in So sagt man das!, emphasizing the intonation of each question and response. Have students repeat. Explain that the tone communicates how concerned the speaker is. Ask students to practice these new phrases with a partner, taking turns asking and responding. After students feel comfortable with the new material, the person answering should expand the response by adding what is wrong with him or her in particular, using phrases just learned in the Wortschatz. The person who initiated the exchange should respond to what is being said.

PRESENTING: Ein wenig Grammatik

Reflexive pronouns Review the reflexive pronouns and dative pronouns for persons other than du and ich. Use the pictures and captions in the Wortschatz on p. 156 for the review. Have students respond accordingly.
Examples:
— Wie geht es dem Jungen auf Bild 1?
— Ihm ist nicht gut. Er ist krank.

— Was hat das Mädchen auf Bild 2?
— Sie hat Halsschmerzen. Sie kann kaum schlucken.

Continue with the rest of the pictures. Then ask about the whole group so that students get practice with the third person plural.
Example:
Wie geht es den Jungen und Mädchen auf diesen Fotos? Wie fühlen sie sich?

Teaching Suggestion

9 To expand this activity, gather photographs from magazines featuring teenage idols or other famous people who look unwell in that particular shot (you may want to glue the photo on construction paper for later use). Give each pair of students a picture. Looking at one of the pictures, student A asks questions modeled after those in So sagt man das! but changed to third person. Student B answers accordingly. When a pair finishes with a picture, it should pass it to the next pair. Monitor students' work as you move around the classroom.

PAGE 158

Teaching Suggestion

11 Have students play this situation as a telephone conversation with person A expressing real concern about person B's health, asking several questions, and at the end wishing him or her well. After students have exchanged roles and practiced both conversations, have them record their "telephone conversations." Play some of the conversations in class and use them for third person questions and responses.

Communication for All Students

Challenge

11 Have students play out a similar situation but after the classmate's illness is over, and he or she has returned to school. Person A does not know why person B was absent. This situation will require both partners to use the past tense for at least part of the exchange. Again, an audio or video recording of the exchanges could be made and used for teaching purposes and then become part of the students' portfolios.

Challenge

11 Once students have completed their dialogues, ask several students to tell in German what their partner said. (Example: **Michael hat gesagt, dass er nicht in der Schule war, weil er Zahnschmerzen hatte.**) Since this may be a difficult construction for some students, you may give an example first or put an example on the board.

STANDARDS: 1.1

PRESENTING: So sagt man das!

Before students look at **So sagt man das!**, ask them to look back at the first frame of the **Los geht's!** in which Thorsten and David each make a suggestion. Ask students to point out and compare the two ways suggestions are made. Then go over the expressions in **So sagt man das!**

▶ **PAGE 159**

PRESENTING: Grammatik

The inclusive command Before introducing the inclusive command, review the **du-** and **Sie-** command forms. You can review these commands using TPR. (Examples: **Steve, geh bitte zur Tafel!** or **Fräulein Norwood, gehen Sie bitte zur Tür!**) Ask students how those commands are formed. Then introduce the new forms, giving additional examples using "chore" verbs, such as **das Zimmer aufräumen, den Tisch decken, abwaschen, abtrocknen,** and **Fenster putzen.**

PRESENTING: Ein wenig Grammatik

The verb sollen After students have had ample practice with making suggestions and responding, have them extend their dialogues by at least one more exchange beyond the reply.
Examples:
— Sollen wir mal den Thorsten besuchen?
— Warum nicht?
— Gut, wann gehen wir?
— Heute nach der Schule.
or
— Sollen wir mal den Thorsten besuchen?
— Tut mir Leid. Ich hab keine Zeit.
— Kannst du vielleicht morgen?
— Ja, wie wär's um vier?
— Prima!

Connections and Comparisons

Multicultural Connection
Have students find out whether the distinction between **Apotheke** and **Drogerie** exists in other countries.

Reteaching: The inclusive command

Prepare a chart similar to the one below. Ask students to choose activities from the list to make suggestions about things their partners could do in the Hamburg area.

besuchen	mal	zuerst	eine Hafenrundfahrt
besichtigen	wir	später	den Michel
machen	doch	danach	Matjeshering
essen		zum Schluss	nach Övelgönne
spazieren			das Rathaus
fahren			durch Blankenese
bummeln			an der Binnenalster entlang

 Game

Play the game **Kettenspiel** to review vocabulary for types of stores and items found in stores. Begin by saying: **Ich gehe heute in die Drogerie und kaufe Parfüm.** The first student repeats your sentence and adds another store and one item he or she will buy there, and so on.

Teaching Suggestion

Have students research some **Drogerien** and **Apotheken** Web sites using these two words as keywords in a German search engine. Have them list the differences and similarities found in these Web sites. For a related online research project, see p. 149F.

Assess
▶ Testing Program, pp. 131–134
  Quiz 6-1A, Quiz 6-1B
  Audio CD6, Tr. 11
▶ Student Make-Up Assignments
  Chapter 6, Alternative Quiz
▶ Alternative Assessment Guide, p. 37

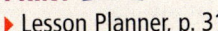

PAGES 160–161

ZUM LESEN

> ### Teaching Resources
> pp. 160–161
>
> **PRINT**
> - Lesson Planner, p. 31
> - Übungsheft, p. 66
> - Reading Strategies and Skills, Chapter 6
> - Lies mit mir! 2, Chapter 6
>
> **MEDIA**
> - One-Stop Planner

Prereading

Building Context
Ask students what Americans do to take care of their health. Then ask them what role concerns for health play when they and their families are planning a vacation. What criteria are taken into consideration as they choose where to go?

Teacher Note
Activity 1 is a prereading activity.

Cultures and Communities

Background Information
- Located in Baden-Württemberg, Baden-Baden is one of the best known spa towns possessing salt-water springs. Over 2,000 years ago, the Romans already knew of Baden-Baden's mild climate and valued the soothing effects of its hot springs.
- Located in the **Voralpen** of Bavaria, Schwangau is a popular climatic health resort as well as ski resort. Schwangau has a population of 3,300. The area surrounding Schwangau is a **Naturschutzgebiet** (national preserve).
- Gaggenau-Bad Rotenfels is a well-known spa town in the romantic Murgtal in the northern part of the Black Forest. It is also popular for its hiking and biking trails.
- Located in the southern part of the Black Forest, Todtmoos attracts many tourists because of its spectacular scenery. Since the second half of the 13th century, it has been a place of pilgrimage. People from many countries pray in its **Wallfahrtskirche** for good health and spiritual support.

STANDARDS: 2.1, 3.1

Cultures and Communities

Background Information
Bad Wurzach is known as the oldest mud-bath resort in Baden-Württemberg and also possesses the largest continuous bog in Central Europe. The bog encompasses an area of 16 km^2 (6.2 square miles).

Connections and Comparisons

Geography Connection
After doing Activity 1, have students look up Baden-Baden, Gaggenau-Bad Rotenfels, Schwangau, Todtmoos, and Bad Wurzach in an atlas. Ask students to give the general location of these towns. (southern Germany)

Thinking Critically

- **Drawing Inferences** Ask students in what ways a health spa such as Schwangau might be beneficial to people.
- **Analyzing** Ask students where they might find the kind of articles and survey found in this **Zum Lesen** section. (Examples: health magazine, health section of a newspaper)

Reading

Communication for All Students

A Slower Pace
3 After students have read the two survey questions, have them brainstorm for the kind of responses they might find. Make a list of students' ideas on butcher paper taped to the board. Use this paper to gather students' input for the other **Zum Lesen** activities.

Teaching Suggestions

3 The task of summarizing the data could be done orally or in writing. Either way, it requires students to draw from previously learned language elements. (Examples: connectors, dependent clauses, paraphrasing) To simplify the activity, you could provide students with a completion paragraph or cloze passage.

5 Treat this as a scanning activity where students look for the information needed under the five headings suggested. You may have to help students find the necessary information in one or two of the articles and see to it that they do not get bogged down in all the detail the articles provide.

5 After students have completed this activity with their partners, use the butcher paper from Activity 3 or a transparency and make an outline of the chart. Have individual students come up to the board and fill in the chart using the information they compiled with their partners. The rest of the class can make suggestions to delete or add information.

Cultures and Communities

Background Information
6 The costs of **Kuren** are paid in part through the health care system if prescribed by a physician. **Kuren** are considered to be therapeutic and part of health maintenance.

Post-Reading
Teacher Note
Activity 6 is a post-reading task that will show whether students can apply what they have learned.

Teaching Suggestion
Ask students which of the featured health spas they would choose to visit, and why. (Example: **Wenn du einen Badekurort besuchen könntest, welchen von diesen hier würdest du wählen und warum?**)

Zum Lesen Answers
Answers to Activity 1
chart: combination of health and fashion; articles: combination of health and leisure
Answers to Activity 2
One will look beautiful when following the new trend; people questioned (male and female, male, female); percentage scale; percentages
Answers to Activity 3
For results, see colored bars in chart.
Answers to Activity 4
Kurstadt; Kochsalzquellen
Answers to Activity 6
Health treatment using natural resources such as saltwater spas, mineral springs, and mud baths under supervision of a physician; healthy diet; exercise. Health spas in the United States are generally much more expensive.

ZWEITE STUFE

Teaching Resources
pp. 162–165

PRINT
- Lesson Planner, p. 29
- TPR Storytelling Book, pp. 42–43
- Listening Activities, pp. 43, 48–49
- Activities for Communication, pp. 31–32, 133–134
- Grammatikheft, pp. 48–51
- Grammar Tutor for Students of German, Chapter 6
- Übungsheft, pp. 67–69
- Testing Program, pp. 135–138
- Alternative Assessment Guide, p. 37
- Student Make-Up Assignments, Chapter 6

MEDIA
- One-Stop Planner
- Audio Compact Discs, CD6, Trs. 7, 12, 21–22
- Teaching Transparencies
  Situation 6-2
  Vocabulary 6-A, 6-B
  Mehr Grammatikübungen Answers
  Grammatikheft Answers
- Interactive CD-ROM Tutor, Disc 2
- DVD Tutor, Disc 1

PAGE 162

Bell Work
Have students prepare for this section by thinking of common pains and injuries (a) they have (b) athletes have (c) older people have. List students' suggestions in German on a transparency.
Examples:
Schmerzen haben/wehtun: der Rücken, die Hüfte, der Kopf
sich etwas brechen: den Fuß, die Hüfte, den Arm
sich etwas verstauchen: den Knöchel, den Finger
sich etwas verletzen: das Knie, die Schulter

PRESENTING: Wortschatz

- To teach the new body parts, introduce them by pointing to them on yourself or on a drawing. Name the body parts as you point to them.

- Teach the new expressions using cause and effect situations as examples.
  Example:
  Ich habe gestern zu viel Chili con carne gegessen, und heute tut mir der Bauch weh.

- Use a doll for practicing the phrases and communicative functions. Act as if the doll were speaking. For example, make her fall and break her leg and say: **Ich habe mir das Bein gebrochen!**

- If students know of athletes who are injured, use their names and the expressions that fit their injury.

Cultures and Communities

Language Note
In German, people often wish others good luck by saying: **Hals- und Beinbruch!** (Break a leg!)

Another expression using a body part is **Lügen haben kurze Beine!** (Lies won't get you anywhere.)

Communication for All Students

Challenge
16 To provide students with further practice, write the following question on the board or on a transparency: **Hast du dich schon mal verletzt?** Have students ask their partners this question and then switch roles.

> **PAGE 163**

PRESENTING: So sagt man das!

Introduce the new expressions to the class, then ask students to think of other ways to answer each of the questions posed in **So sagt man das!**
Examples:
Tut's weh?   Ja, sehr.
               Ja, aber nur ein bisschen.
               Nein, nicht sehr.
Tut dir der
Kopf weh?   Nein, aber der Hals.
               Ja, er tut sehr weh.

PRESENTING: Ein wenig Grammatik

The verb wehtun Give each student a card on which has been written (in German) a part of the body. Have students stand at their desks or go to the front of the classroom and pretend that they have some kind of ache or pain in that part of the body. Other members of the class must guess what is ailing the student, and express their ideas in German. (Example: **Der Arm tut ihr weh.**) When a correct guess has been made, the student must acknowledge it with a statement of his or her own before sitting back down. (Example: **Ja, mir tut der Arm weh.**) Continue until everyone has had a turn.

Connections and Comparisons

  Multicultural Connection
If possible, have students find out about other languages and the expressions people use to communicate pain. Example: When French speakers hurt themselves, they often yell out *aïe!* (pronounced like the English word *eye*).

Communication for All Students

Challenge
17 For each of the sentences students come up with, ask them to add a reason or the cause of the pain. (Example: **Meiner Mutter tun oft die Knie weh, denn sie arbeitet viel im Garten.**) This activity can be done orally or in writing.

PRESENTING: Grammatik

Verbs used with dative case forms Before presenting the verbs that require a direct object in the dative, review verbs from Level 1 that have indirect objects in the dative case. (Examples: **schenken, geben, kaufen, glauben, sagen**) To review the dative case personal pronouns, refer students to the Grammar Summary.

Practice each of the verbs from the **Grammatik** in brief activities. Set up "situations" and ask questions to which students can respond on their own.
Examples:
Ich habe gehört, dass deine Mutter krank war. Wie geht es ihr jetzt?
Du bist immer so nett und hilfst allen Leuten. Wem hast du am letzten Wochenende geholfen?

> **PAGE 164**

PRESENTING: Grammatik

Reflexive verbs and dative case forms Simplify the idea of the dative reflexive pronoun by telling students that the verb's action is turned back on the subject of the verb. Then give examples of previously introduced verbs used reflexively and non-reflexively. Examples:
Er hat seinen Bleistift gebrochen.
Er hat sich das Bein beim Fußballspiel gebrochen.

Connections and Comparisons

Language-to-Language

You may want to explain to your students that, like German, French and Spanish use verbs that require reflexive pronouns.
Examples:
German: *sich* waschen: Ich wasche *mich* (acc).
French: *se* laver: Je *me* lave.
Spanish: *lavarse*: *Me* lavo.

Point out to students that the German, French, and Spanish equivalents of the sentence *I wash my hair* are constructed in a manner quite different from that used in English. English uses a possessive with the noun; German, French, and Spanish use some verbs with a reflexive object pronoun and a definite article.
Example:
English: *I wash* my *hair*.
German: *Ich wasche mir die Haare*.
French: *Je me lave les cheveux*.
Spanish: *Me lavo el pelo*.

Ask students if they can think of other English sentences whose German equivalents are similar to the example above.

Group Work

18 Divide students in groups of three and ask them to imagine that they just returned from their **Klassenfahrt in den Alpen** where they went skiing. Ask them to come up with a creative narrative, using the sentence fragments to tell what happened to students and teachers on that trip. Students can replace the pronouns with proper names for this activity.

Teaching Suggestion

19 Ask students to answer the questions in the form of a narrative in which they describe in chronological order what happened. Call on several students to read their narrative to the class.

Teacher to Teacher

Nicole Mitescu
Claremont High School
Claremont, CA

Nicole uses this idea to practice narrative.

❝This activity requires audio tapes and tape recorders or a language lab. It's fun for one class to record messages for the second German class and then have the students in the other class respond. They can use the tapes to "leave messages" for the second class by describing how they feel, inquiring about whom they are calling, etc. If you don't have a language lab, the students enjoy working on this at home too. I don't grade this assignment, but I do listen to the tapes before giving them to the second class.❞

> **PAGE 165**

PRESENTING: Wortschatz

Waschen, kämmen, and **putzen** are three common verbs that can be used reflexively or non-reflexively. Model them by demonstrating the actions depicted in the pictures and several others, each time contrasting action directed toward another person or thing with action directed toward oneself. Then ask questions about the pictures.
Examples:
Was macht das Mädchen im Rollstuhl?
Was machen die beiden Jungen im Badezimmer?
Wie hilft der Junge seiner Mutter auf Bild 5?

Communication for All Students

Tactile Learners

21 Write the six sentences on the board and ask students to draw lines from the reflexive pronouns to the subject pronouns to emphasize that these people are doing something for themselves.

PRESENTING: Ein wenig Grammatik

Verbs with stem-vowel change Write the verbs **geben, sehen, lesen, essen,** and **nehmen** on the board and remind students that these are stem-vowel changing verbs. Introduce **brechen** and ask students to infer what the stem-vowel change should be. Do the same for **waschen** by reintroducing verbs such as **fahren** and **einladen**.

Total Physical Response

Give commands to the class or to individual students using vocabulary that focuses on body parts. Examples:
Heb den linken Arm!
Zeig auf das rechte Knie!
Stampf mit beiden Füßen!
Leg die Hände auf die Schultern!

Teaching Suggestion

Have students form groups of two to role-play a scene in an **Apotheke.** One of the students plays the pharmacist and the other the customer. The customer is looking for something to cure three different ailments. The pharmacist can help with two of the ailments but regrets not being able to help with the third.

Speaking Assessment

You might choose to have students come to your desk to assess their role play. For evaluation you may wish to use the following rubric.

Speaking Rubric

	Points			
	4	3	2	1
Content (Complete – Incomplete)				
Comprehension (Total – Little)				
Comprehensibility (Comprehensible – Incomprehensible)				
Accuracy (Accurate – Seldom accurate)				
Fluency (Fluent – Not fluent)				

18–20: A   16–17: B   14–15: C   12–13: D   Under 12: F

Assess

- Testing Program, pp. 135–138
  Quiz 6-2A, Quiz 6-2B
  Audio CD6, Tr. 12
- Student Make-Up Assignments
  Chapter 6, Alternative Quiz
- Alternative Assessment Guide, p. 37

DRITTE STUFE

Teaching Resources
pp. 166–169

PRINT
- Lesson Planner, p. 30
- TPR Storytelling Book, pp. 44–45
- Listening Activities, pp. 44, 49–50
- Activities for Communication, pp. 33–36, 95–96, 97, 133–134
- Grammatikheft, pp. 52–54
- Grammar Tutor for Students of German, Chapter 6
- Übungsheft, pp. 70–72
- Testing Program, pp. 139–142
- Alternative Assessment Guide, p. 37
- Student Make-Up Assignments, Chapter 6

MEDIA
- One-Stop Planner
- Audio Compact Discs, CD6, Trs. 8–9, 13, 23–24
- Teaching Transparencies
  Vocabulary 6-C
  Mehr Grammatikübungen Answers
  Grammatikheft Answers
- Interactive CD-ROM Tutor, Disc 2
- DVD Tutor, Disc 1

PAGE 166

Bell Work

Divide the class into three to four large groups. Each of the groups should choose a writer who will have to go to the board once the game is underway. Groups are given one to two minutes to tell their writers the phrases or ideas they come up with for the topic at hand. Here are some sample topics you may want to use:
Gründe, warum man zum Doktor gehen soll;
Was einem alles wehtun kann.

Cultures and Communities

Career Path

Have students formulate scenarios in which an American doctor or nurse might need to know German. (Suggestions: Medical personnel who work for international relief agencies such as **Das Rote Kreuz** sometimes serve in German-speaking countries.)

STANDARDS: 1.2, 5.1

Cooperative Learning

22 Divide students into groups of three. Each group should have a writer, a group leader, and a reporter. Set a time limit of approximately 10–15 minutes for this activity. Ask each group to use the questions and answers from this activity to create a public service announcement warning people about the dangers of frequent exposure to the sun.

PAGE 167

PRESENTING: Wortschatz/ So sagt man das!

Introduce the new expressions by making a transparency of the **Wortschatz** and leaving out the captions. Then ask students what captions they would use if asked **Was soll ich tun?** Based on the pictures, have students complete the phrase **Du musst unbedingt …!** Then show the class a transparency containing the captions from the book. Have students compare their expressions with the expressions in the **Wortschatz**.

PAGE 168

PRESENTING: Wortschatz

Divide the class into two groups. Ask one group to use the terms in the **Wortschatz** to formulate health complaints; the other team should respond with suggestions about what one should do to alleviate or prevent these difficulties. The team giving advice should use the term **das Fieber messen** and phrases from the **Wortschatz** on p. 167.

PRESENTING: Ein wenig Grammatik

Stem-vowel change Tell students that the verb **messen** has a stem-vowel change in the **du-** and **er/sie-**forms, and ask them if they can guess what that change would be. What other verb does **messen** resemble? (**essen**) Once students have noticed this similarity, have them tell you how it should be conjugated and write the forms on the board as they do so. Can they also guess the **du-**command form of this verb? (**miss**)

PRESENTING: So sagt man das!

Lead the students to discover how the following sentences differ in structure but not in meaning:
Ich hoffe, du hast kein Fieber.
Ich hoffe, dass du kein Fieber hast.
Hoffentlich hast du kein Fieber.

PAGE 169

PRESENTING: Wortschatz

To teach the new vocabulary, you may want to bring the actual items to class with price stickers still attached if possible.

PRESENTING: Ein wenig Grammatik

Dative case pronouns Write on a transparency five or ten sentences similar to those that appear in the **Wortschatz** on p. 169, but leave out the dative pronouns. Ask students to fill in the blanks with dative pronouns or proper nouns of their choice, and have some of them read their sentences aloud. Then ask them why it was necessary to use the dative case in those instances. If students have difficulty explaining why, have them give you the English equivalents of a few of the statements. What words did they always have to put before the missing pronouns/proper nouns in their English translations? (*to* or *for*, markers of the dative case)

Game

Each student needs a pen and paper for this game. Give students several minutes to look through the **Dritte Stufe** and pick out a new word or phrase. Tell students to make up a sentence in which that new word is omitted intentionally. The blank space is called **Dingsda**. For example, a student may choose the word **Sonnenschutzmittel** and use it as follows:
Im Sommer benutze ich immer (Sonnenschutzmittel), denn ich habe empfindliche Haut.
Each student gets a turn to call on another classmate to whom he or she reads the sentence, substituting the word **Dingsda** for the new word. The challenged student tries to complete the sentence by identifying the missing word. If that student guesses correctly, he or she challenges another student.

Von der Schule zum Beruf

Have students take a look at various Web sites of **Drogerien** to find out about products typically advertised.

> **Assess**
> ▸ Testing Program, pp. 139–142
>   Quiz 6-3A, Quiz 6-3B
>   Audio CD6, Tr. 13
> ▸ Student Make-Up Assignments
>   Chapter 6, Alternative Quiz
> ▸ Alternative Assessment Guide, p. 37

PAGES 170–173
MEHR GRAMMATIKÜBUNGEN

The **Mehr Grammatikübungen** activities are designed as supplemental activities for the grammatical concepts presented in the chapter. You might use them as additional practice, for review, or for assessment.

For more grammar presentations, review, and practice, refer to the following:
- Grammatikheft
- Grammar Tutor for Students of German
- Grammar Summary on pp. R20–R36
- Übungsheft
- Grammar and Vocabulary quizzes (Testing Program)
- Test Generator
- Interactive CD-ROM Tutor
- **Interaktive Spiele** at go.hrw.com

PAGES 174–175
ANWENDUNG

Video Wrap-up

Videocassette 2, 31:40–41:38
Videocassette 5 (captioned version), 32:52–39:02
DVD Tutor, Disc 1

At this time, you might want to use the video resources for additional review and enrichment. These resources are also available via the Enhanced Online Student Edition.
See *Video Guide* for suggestions regarding:
- **Was fehlt dir?** Dramatic episode
- **Landeskunde** Interviews
- **Videoclips** Authentic footage

> **Apply and Assess**
>
> 📁 **Portfolio Assessment**
> You may want to suggest this activity as a written portfolio item for your students. See *Alternative Assessment Guide*, p. 23.

STANDARDS: 1.1

> **Apply and Assess**
>
> **Process Writing**
> Since these dialogues take place between a doctor and several high school students, which pronouns should the participants employ when speaking to each other? If you intend to have your students present their dialogues orally to the class, suggest that they read their work aloud (or in an undertone) as they go. Encourage them to make the language flow as smoothly as possible.
>
> 📁 **Portfolio Assessment**
> 8 You may want to suggest this activity as an oral portfolio item for your students. See *Alternative Assessment Guide*, p. 23.

PAGE 176
KANN ICH'S WIRKLICH?

This page helps students prepare for the test. It is a brief checklist of the major points covered in the chapter. The students should be reminded that it is only a checklist and not necessarily everything that will appear on the test.

For additional self check options, refer students to the *Grammar Tutor*, the *Interactive CD-ROM Tutor*, and the Online self-test for this chapter.

PAGE 177
WORTSCHATZ

> **Review and Assess**
>
> ❓ **Circumlocution**
> To review names of various body parts, play the circumlocution game **Das treffende Wort suchen**. To describe a foot or a leg, or to explain their function, one could say **Man läuft damit**. The names of the illnesses listed in the **Erste Stufe** also lend themselves well to circumlocution. See p. 3C for procedures.
>
> 🔊 **Teacher Note**
> • Give the **Kapitel 6** Chapter Test: *Testing Program*, pp. 143–148 Audio CD6, Trs. 14–15.
>
> • Give the Midterm Exam: *Testing Program*, pp. 157–164 Audio CD6, Trs. 16–18.

KAPITEL 6
Gute Besserung!

Objectives

In this chapter you will learn to

Erste Stufe
- inquire about someone's health and respond
- make suggestions

Zweite Stufe
- ask about and express pain

Dritte Stufe
- ask for and give advice
- express hope

Visit Holt Online
go.hrw.com
KEYWORD: WK3 HAMBURG-6
Online Edition

◀ Hast du dich verletzt, Nicolas?

hunderteinundfünfzig

Los geht's! · *Was fehlt dir?*

Los geht's! is an abridged version of the video episode.

Strategie Verstehen
Look at the images for this story. Where are the scenes taking place? What do you think is the matter with Maike? What do you think Maike's friends are doing?

Nicolas Maike David Thorsten Wiebke

David und Thorsten sitzen im Alsterpark. Sie lernen zusammen ihre Englischvokabeln für den Englischtest.

①

Thorsten: Wollen wir aufhören?
David: Nie! Aber machen wir mal eine Pause!
Thorsten: Okay! Übrigens, wollen wir mal die Maike anrufen?
David: Klar! Die Maike, die war heute nicht in der Schule. Hoffentlich ist sie nicht krank.

②

Maike: Tag, Thorsten! Was gibt's?
Thorsten: Du warst heute nicht in der Schule. Ist was mit dir?
Maike: Mir ist nicht gut. Mir tut der Hals weh, und ich kann kaum schlucken.

Maike mit ihrer Mutter früh am Morgen

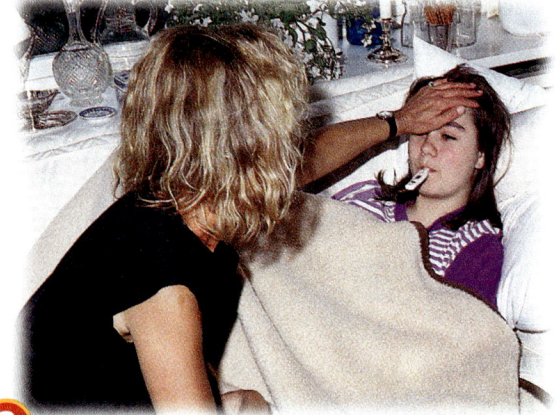

③

Mutter: Ich glaub, du hast Fieber. Du musst heute unbedingt zu Hause bleiben.
Maike: Aber ich hab heute eine Klassenarbeit!
Mutter: Ich mess mal, wie hoch deine Temperatur ist.

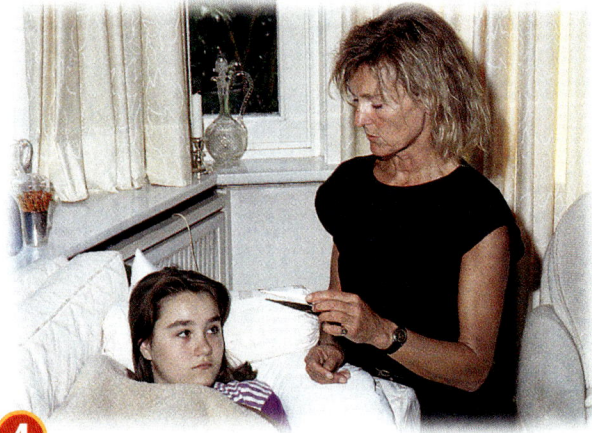

④

Maike: Mir ist so heiß!
Mutter: Mit Fieber kannst du nicht in die Schule gehen. Deine Stirn ist auch ganz schön heiß. 38,9, das ist ganz schön hoch!

Maike weiter am Telefon

Maike: Der Hals tut noch weh, aber es geht mir schon besser. Ich glaube, ich habe kein Fieber mehr.

Thorsten: Können wir etwas für dich tun?

Maike: Ihr könnt mir die Medizin aus der Apotheke holen, aus der Manstein Apotheke. Aber kommt erst vorher hier vorbei! Ihr müsst den Abholschein noch mitnehmen.

In der Apotheke

Apothekerin: Guten Tag! Ja bitte?

Thorsten: Einmal die Medizin für Johannsen, bitte! Hier ist der Abholschein.

Apothekerin: Einen Moment mal!

Thorsten: Danke! Bin ich Ihnen etwas schuldig?

Apothekerin: Nein, es war schon bezahlt. Tschüs!

Zu dieser Zeit sind Wiebke und Nicolas in einer Drogerie. Die beiden wollen sich später mit Maike, David und Thorsten treffen und Ball spielen.

Wiebke: Das ist meine Marke. Die nehme ich.

Nicolas: So eine große Tube?

Wiebke: Ja, nach jeder Mahlzeit putze ich mir meine Zähne. Schau! Da geht so eine Tube schnell weg.

Nicolas: Da, Sonnencreme, Schutzfaktor acht!

Wiebke: Das ist nicht hoch genug für mich. Meine Haut ist sehr empfindlich. Ich nehme gewöhnlich Schutzfaktor zwanzig.

Nicolas: Da, sogar fünfundzwanzig!

Wiebke: Das ist zu teuer.—Die nehme ich.

Verkäufer: Ja, danke schön!

Wiebke: Bitte schön!

Verkäufer: So.

Wiebke: Danke schön!

Verkäufer: Bitte schön! Wiedersehen!

1 Was passiert hier?

These activities check for global comprehension only. Students should not yet be expected to produce language modeled in Los geht's!

Verstehst du alles, was diese Schüler sagen? Beantworte die Fragen!

1. Warum rufen Thorsten und David die Maike an?   1. Sie war heute nicht in der Schule.
2. Warum will Maike heute in die Schule gehen? Warum kann sie nicht gehen?
3. Was machen Thorsten und David für Maike? Was müssen sie zuerst tun?
4. Was braucht Wiebke in der Drogerie? Warum braucht sie jeden Artikel?
5. Warum kauft Wiebke die Sonnenmilch nicht?   2. Hat heute eine Klassenarbeit; hat Fieber.

3. Medizin aus der Apotheke holen; Abholschein von Maike holen.   4. Zahnpasta, weil sie sich nach jeder Mahlzeit die Zähne putzt; Sonnencreme, weil sie eine sehr empfindliche Haut hat.   5. zu teuer

2 Genauer lesen

Lies den Text noch einmal und beantworte diese Fragen!

1. Was tut Maike weh?   der Hals
2. Was kann sie kaum tun?   schlucken
3. Was meint Maikes Mutter, was Maike hat?   Fieber
4. Wo holen Thorsten und David die Medizin?   Apotheke
5. Was macht die Wiebke nach jeder Mahlzeit?   Zähne putzen
6. Welchen Schutzfaktor braucht Wiebke gewöhnlich?   zwanzig

3 Was passt zusammen?

Welche Ausdrücke auf der rechten Seite passen zu den Ausdrücken auf der linken Seite?

1. Maikes Hals tut ihr noch weh, aber   c   a. Hoffentlich ist sie nicht krank.
2. Du hast Fieber.   d   b. Okay!
3. Maike war heute nicht in der Schule.   a   c. es geht ihr schon besser.
4. Schutzfaktor acht!   f   d. Du musst unbedingt zu Hause bleiben.
5. Du kannst mir die Medizin aus   e   e. Aber du brauchst erst den Abholschein.
   der Apotheke holen.   f. Nicht hoch genug für mich.
6. Machen wir mal eine Pause!   b

4 Beschreibungen

Welche Beschreibung passt zu welcher Person?

1. Maike   d   a. braucht eine große Tube Zahnpasta, weil sie sich nach jeder
2. Thorsten   f   Mahlzeit die Zähne putzt.
3. David   b   b. will nicht mit dem Englischlernen aufhören, sondern will nur
4. Nicolas   e   eine Pause machen.
5. Wiebke   a   c. misst Maikes Temperatur und sagt ihr, dass sie zu Hause bleiben muss.
6. Maikes Mutter   c   d. hat heute Halsweh und geht nicht in die Schule.
   e. will wissen, warum Wiebke so viel Zahnpasta braucht.
   f. spricht mit Maike am Telefon und holt dann für sie die Medizin in der
      Apotheke.

5 Nacherzählen

Erzähle einem Partner, was in dieser Fotogeschichte passiert!

Was machst du, wenn dir nicht gut ist?

What do German students do when they don't feel well? Is it that different from what we do in the United States? Let's find out. CD 6 Tr. 3

Übungsheft, S. 62, Ü. 1–3

Birgit, Bietigheim

"Ja, so wenn's mir in der Schule halt schlecht wird, dann geh ich nach Hause, und ja, wenn halt, wenn ich jetzt stark krank bin, dann geh ich zum Arzt." CD 6 Tr. 4

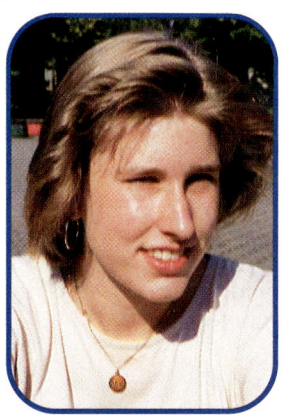
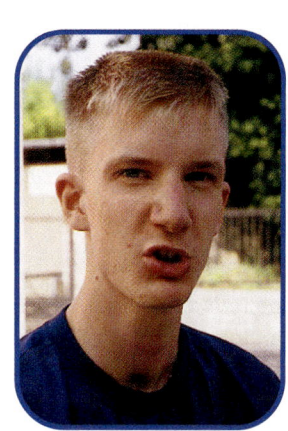

Tim, Berlin CD 6 Tr. 5

"Es kommt öfters vor, dass ich Magenprobleme habe, dass ich Magenkrämpfe habe. Und dagegen hab ich von meinem Arzt ein paar Tabletten bekommen, die ich dann also auch meistens nicht dabeihabe, also so schnell wie möglich nach Hause fahre und die Tabletten einnehme."

A. 1. Where does Birgit go when she is sick? What phrases does she use to describe how she feels? A. 1. home, doctor; **wenn mir schlecht wird … / wenn ich krank bin …**

 2. What kind of problems does Tim describe? What does he do when he has this problem? A. 2. stomachache, stomach cramps; goes home and takes pills

B. You may have heard that Germany has a national health-care system. Did you know that the first health-care system was introduced in Germany in 1883? Because of this long history, Germans have come to expect that every person has some kind of insurance. If you're an exchange student or visit Germany for any length of time, you are required to have insurance in order to stay in the country. For the average German, the amount paid for health insurance is relatively small. The government and employers carry much of the cost in this system.

C. What is the status of health-care reform in the United States? Do you think everyone should be insured? Who should pay for it? The individual, the government, or employers? Do you think America's tradition of individualism has influenced our views on this issue?

STANDARDS: 1.2, 2.1, 2.2, 3.2, 4.2

Storytelling Book
pp. 40–41

Erste Stufe

Objectives Inquiring about someone's health and responding; making suggestions

WK3 HAMBURG-6

Wortschatz

Wie geht's dir denn? Was ist los mit dir?

Mir ist überhaupt nicht gut. Ich glaube, ich bin krank.

Ich habe Halsschmerzen. Ich kann kaum schlucken.

Ich fühl mich nicht wohl. Mir ist nicht gut.

Kopfschmerzen

Zahnschmerzen

Mir ist so schlecht. Ich habe Fieber.

Mir ist gar nicht gut. Ich hab eine Erkältung.

Ich hab Husten und Schnupfen.

Ohrenschmerzen

Bauchschmerzen

Übungsheft, S. 63, Ü. 1   Grammatikheft, S. 46, Ü. 1–2

6 Wie fühlen sich die Schüler? Script and answers on p. 149G

CD 6
Tr. 6

Zuhören Vier Schüler erzählen, wie sie sich fühlen. Mach dir Notizen, dann beantworte die folgenden Fragen!

a. Wer hat Halsschmerzen?
b. Wer hat hohes Fieber?
c. Wer muss in die Apotheke gehen?
d. Wer fühlt sich heute wohl?

7 Was ist los mit dir?

Schreiben/Sprechen Was hast du, wenn du krank bist? Schreib auf, was du gewöhnlich hast und wie oft! Such dir dann einen Partner und fragt euch gegenseitig, was ihr manchmal habt!

oft	gewöhnlich	manchmal
ab und zu		nie

So sagt man das!

Inquiring about someone's health and responding

You have used the expression **Wie geht's?** to ask about general well-being. As a response to this question, you used such expressions as **Danke, gut! Danke, es geht! Nicht gut!** and **Miserabel!**

Here are some specific ways to inquire about someone's health.

You may ask:

  Wie fühlst du dich?
  Wie geht es dir?
  Ist dir nicht gut?
  Ist was mit dir?
  Was fehlt dir?

And the response may be:

  Ich fühl mich wohl!
  Es geht mir nicht gut!
  Mir ist schlecht.
  Mir ist nicht gut. Ich bin krank.
  Nichts!

If someone tells you that he or she is not doing well, you might say:

  Ach schade!
  Gute Besserung!
  Hoffentlich geht es dir bald besser!

How many dative pronouns do you recognize?

Übungsheft, S. 63–65, Ü. 2–6

Grammatikheft, S. 47, Ü. 3

---

8 Wie fühlst du dich?

Sprechen Such dir einen Partner! Frag ihn, wie er sich fühlt! Er sagt es dir. — Tauscht dann die Rollen aus! Dann beschreibt die beiden hier rechts!

9 Was ist mit …?

Sprechen Such dir einen Partner! Dein Partner möchte wissen, was mit jemandem (*someone*) in der Klasse los ist, warum er so schlecht aussieht. Du sagst es ihm. — Tauscht dann die Rollen aus!

Ein wenig Grammatik

Schon bekannt

Remember to use the correct reflexive pronouns with **sich wohl fühlen.** It requires a reflexive pronoun in the accusative case. Can you name these pronouns?[1] How would you ask an older person how he or she feels? And two friends?[2]

Pay attention to the dative forms used with these phrases:

  Ist **dir** nicht gut?
  Nein, **mir** ist schlecht.
  Es geht **mir** nicht gut.

When using an adjective to describe how you feel, you use the dative pronoun **mir** to refer to yourself. When asking a friend or family member, you use **dir**.

Mehr Grammatikübungen, S. 170, Ü. 1–3

---

1. **mich, dich, sich, uns, euch** 2. **Fühlen Sie sich wohl? Fühlt ihr euch wohl?**

Maike speech bubble: Ich fühl ___ nicht wohl. Es geht ___ nicht gut. ___ ist schlecht, ich fühl ___ miserabel!

David speech bubble: Gestern hab ich ___ nicht wohl gefühlt. ___ war furchtbar schlecht, aber heute geht es ___ viel besser!

Saskia und Finn speech bubble: Wir fühlen ___ absolut prima. Es geht ___ echt gut! ___ fehlt nichts!

Maike — David — Saskia und Finn

10 Grammatik im Kontext

a. **Maike:** mich/mir/Mir/mich; **David:** mich/Mir/mir; **Saskia und Finn:** uns/uns/Uns
b. **Maike:** sich/ihr/Ihr/sich; **David:** sich/Ihm/ihm; **Saskia und Finn:** sich/ihnen/Ihnen

Was sagen diese Schüler?

a. **Schreiben** Schreib, was diese Schüler sagen! Welche Pronomen kommen in die Lücken?

b. **Schreiben** Jetzt schreib, was diese Schüler gesagt haben! Fang so an: Maike hat gesagt, sie fühlt …

11 Was hast du?

Sprechen Deine Partnerin war heute nicht in der Schule! Frag sie, warum sie nicht in der Schule war, was sie hat und wie sie sich jetzt fühlt! — Tauscht dann die Rollen aus!

Schnupfen Husten Kopfschmerzen Fieber
Zahnschmerzen eine Erkältung Halsschmerzen

So sagt man das!

Making suggestions

Here are some ways you have learned to make suggestions so far:

Möchtest du ins Kino gehen?   *or*   **Willst du** ins Café Freizeit gehen?
Du kannst für mich Brot **holen.**   *or*   **Kauf** es doch beim Bäcker!

Here are two other ways to make suggestions:

Rufen wir mal die Maike **an!**
Sollen wir mal die Maike **anrufen?**

What are the English equivalents of the last two sentences? What purpose does the word **mal** serve in these suggestions?

12 Sollen wir mal …?

Sprechen Such dir einen Partner! — Du weißt nicht so recht, was du tun sollst, und du fragst deshalb deinen Partner. Gebraucht die Ausdrücke in den Kästen! — Tauscht dann die Rollen aus!

DU **Sollen wir mal …?**
PARTNER **Prima Idee!**

Was tun?
- in den Alsterpark gehen
- die Englischvokabeln lernen
- die … anrufen
- den … besuchen
- zu Hause bleiben
- in die Drogerie gehen
- in die Apotheke gehen

Ja?
- Prima Idee!
- Na klar!
- Ja, gern!
- Warum nicht?
- Machen wir!

Nein?
- Es geht nicht.
- Ich hab keine Zeit.
- Ich muss zu Hause bleiben.
- Ich hab zu viel zu tun.
- Ich …

Grammatik

The inclusive command

1. When making suggestions, the inclusive command can be used. It consists of the **wir-** form of the verb with the verb itself in first position followed by **wir**.

   gehen: wir gehen

   Gehen wir mal ins Kino!
   Let's go to the movies!

2. If a verb has a separable prefix, the prefix is at the end of the command.

   anrufen: wir rufen an

   Rufen wir mal Maike **an**!
   Let's call Maike!

   Grammatikheft, S. 47, Ü. 4   Mehr Grammatikübungen, S. 171, Ü. 4

Ein wenig Grammatik

Schon bekannt

Read the following sentence.

Ich soll einkaufen gehen.

What does the modal verb **sollen** mean here? **Sollen** is often used to express obligation, but it has other meanings as well.

Sollen wir ein Eis essen?

In what way is **sollen** being used in the sentence above?[1]

Ein wenig Landeskunde

Traditionally, the **Apotheke** and the **Drogerie** in German towns and cities serve two different purposes. If you need medicine, whether prescription or over-the-counter, you go to the **Apotheke**. You can also get vitamins, herbal teas, and other health-related items at the **Apotheke**. If you need shampoo, toothpaste, or other such items, you would go to the **Drogerie**. In many larger cities, the **Drogerie** is being replaced by larger stores that sell everything from toiletries to books.

13 Schade, es geht leider nicht!

Sprechen Such dir eine Partnerin! Ruf sie an und lade sie ins Kino oder ins Konzert ein! Sie kann aber leider nicht mitgehen. Sie fühlt sich nicht wohl, ihr ist nicht gut. Du fragst sie, was sie hat, und sie sagt es dir. — Tauscht dann die Rollen aus!

14 Für dein Notizbuch

a. **Schreiben** Schreib in dein Notizbuch, wann du das letzte Mal krank warst, was du gehabt hast, wie du dich gefühlt hast und wie lange du nicht in der Schule warst!

b. **Sprechen** Sag es dann auch einer Partnerin!

---
1. To make a suggestion.

Zum Lesen

Viel los unter der Sonne!

> **Lesestrategie**
> **Deciphering charts and graphs** Charts and graphs can be confusing, even in your native language, but if you follow a few important steps before answering any questions, you can master the information: 1) read titles and subtitles; 2) check for a legend and become familiar with it; 3) understand what the numbers represent (percents, parts per thousand, etc.); and 4) check the source and the way survey questions are worded. Remember, charts and graphs require careful reading—shortcuts won't work.

Getting Started

1. Skim over the headline areas of the chart and the articles. What general concern do these texts all have in common? Is this information about work? fashion? health? leisure? Or some combination of topics?

2. Look at the title area of the chart. Notice that the chart depicts the results of an **Umfrage**. What does the slogan „**Bleich ist beautiful**" tell you to expect of the new trend? Locate the legend. What do the colored bars indicate? And the vertical lines? What do the numbers represent? Make sure you feel comfortable with the organization of information.
   For answers, see p. 149S

Kuren und Bäder

Baden-Baden
Bundesland: Baden-Württemberg
Kfz-Kennzeichen: BAD
Höhe: 183 m ü.d.M. - Einwohnerzahl: 50 000
Postleitzahl: #76530
Telefonvorwahl: 07221
ⓘ Kurdirektion (Gäste-Information), Augustaplatz 1; Tel.: 27 52 00

14 Baden-Baden
Baden-Baden besitzt als Kurstadt Weltruf. Seit zweitausend Jahren werden die heißen Kochsalzquellen genutzt.
Friedrichsbad (→ Marktplatz): Der Renaissancebau ist eines der prächtigsten und traditionsreichsten Badehäuser der Welt. Das „Römisch-Irische Bad" bietet u. a. Heißluft-Dampfbad, Thermal-Vollbad, Sprudelbad und Tauchbad.
Römische Badruinen (unter dem → Römerplatz): Etwa 2000 Jahre alt sind die Reste einer römischen Badeanlage für die Legionäre, ein anschauliches Bild antiker Thermen.

Schwangau
Gesundzeit mit Heubad

Unter dem Motto „Gesundzeit in Bayern" bietet der heilklimatische Kurort Schwangau 2002 Gesundheitsurlaube von einwöchiger Dauer an. Darin enthalten sind: ärztliche Untersuchung mit Gesundzeitplan, drei medizinische Anwendungen (davon ein Heubad aus ungedüngtem Bergwiesenheu, eine Kneippsche Anwendung, eine Massage), zweimal Gymnastik, je eine geführte Wanderung zu den beiden Königsschlössern Hohenschwangau und Neuschwanstein. Außerdem gibt es Tips und Anleitungen vom Gesundheitsberater. Preis pro Person ab 190 Euro. Gültig ist die „Gesundzeit" ganzjährig.
Infos: Kurverwaltung Schwangau, Münchener Str. 2, 87645 Schwangau, Tel. 08362/8198-0

Todtmoos
Schlittenhunde unterwegs

Am Wochenende vom 28. bis 30. Januar 2002 sind in Todtmoos im Südschwarzwald wieder die Hunde los! Bei den schon traditionellen Schlittenhunderennen, die bereits zum 19. Mai in Todtmoos ausgetragen werden, laufen die schnellsten Hunde Europas. Zu diesem Hundespektakel hat die Kurverwaltung Todtmoos ein interessantes Pauschalangebot zusammengestellt: Gültig vom 28. bis 30. Januar ab 48 Euro für Übernachtung mit Frühstück in Privatzimmern mit Dusche und WC. Die Kurtaxe ist im Preis inbegriffen. Das Pauschalpaket enthält außerdem die Eintritte für die Rennen, den großen Countryabend am 29. Januar und den Bustransfer zur Rennstrecke.
Infos: Kurverwaltung, 79682 Todtmoos, Tel. 07674/534

Bad Wurzach
Moor und vieles mehr

Zur Bad Wurzacher Gesundheitswoche lädt das älteste Moorheilbad Baden-Württembergs in der Zeit vom 9. Januar bis 30. April 2002 ein. Dabei werden nicht nur Mooranwendungen, sondern auch Wassergymnastik, Massagen und Gesundheitsvorträge angeboten. Zur Behandlung von rheumatischen Erkrankungen, Bandscheiben- und Wirbelsäulenschäden, Gelenkerkrankungen.
Infos: Städtische Kurverwaltung, Mühltorstr. 1, 88410 Bad Wurzach, Tel. 07564/302150

Bad Rotenfels
Neuer Saunapark lädt ein

Der Thermal-Mineral-Badeort Gaggenau-Bad Rotenfels im romantischen Murgtal präsentiert bis zum 30. April 2002 ein Bade- und Saunavergnügen zum Supersparpreis. Im Mittelpunkt stehen dabei das Thermal-Mineral-Badezentrum Rotherma mit über 600 qm Wasserfläche und der neue Saunapark mit einer Größe von über 3000 qm. Das Sparangebot ab 94 Euro beinhaltet fünf Übernachtungen mit Frühstück in Privat- oder Gästehäusern. Weiter sind vier Thermalbäder und ein Saunabesuch sowie Kurtaxe enthalten.
Infos: Gaggenau-Tourist-Info, Rathausstr. 11, 76571 Gaggenau-Bad Rotenfels, Tel. 07225/62301

A Closer Look

Tipp: If you know how to divide long compound words, you can usually guess their meaning. An **-s** following a masculine or neuter noun belongs with that word. The same is often true of **-n** following feminine nouns, as in **Sonnenbaden**. Also be aware of common prefixes, such as **er-** or **be-**. How would you divide **Alterserscheinungen**?

3. Read the two survey questions. What were the results? Try to summarize the data in two sentences.
4. Read the description of Baden-Baden. Give two reasons why it is world famous.
5. Read the articles from **Kuren und Bäder** and, together with a partner, fill out a chart with the following headings as you read: Place, Main Feature of **Kur**, Other Attractions, Cost, and Number of Days.
6. **Kuren** have long been a part of Germany's health traditions. How would you describe a typical **Kur** based on the information from the four descriptions you read? What are the general characteristics of a **Kur**? Is there anything comparable in the United States?

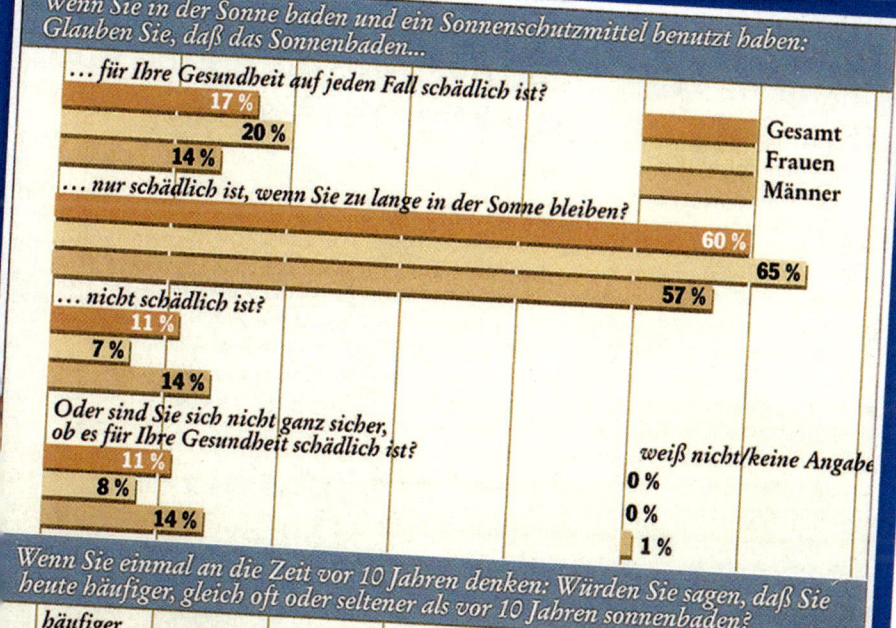

Übungsheft, S. 66

Storytelling Book
pp. 42–43

Zweite Stufe

Objective Asking about and expressing pain

WK3 HAMBURG-6

Wortschatz

Was tut dir weh? — Mir tut / tun ... weh!

p. 149X   6-A, 6-2   CD-ROM DISC 2

Mir tut der Hals weh.

Der Kopf tut mir weh.

Der Bauch tut mir weh.

die Schulter

der Rücken

die Hüfte

Hast du dich verletzt? Hast du dir etwas gebrochen?

die Beine

der Arm

Ich hab mir den Fuß gebrochen.

Ich hab mir den Knöchel verstaucht.

Ich hab mir das Knie verletzt.

Übungsheft, S. 67, Ü. 1–2   Grammatikheft, S. 48, Ü. 5–6

15 Was tut ihnen weh? Script and answers on p. 149G

Zuhören Was ist mit diesen Leuten los? Schau diese Bilder an und hör gleichzeitig die Kassette an! Welches Bild passt zu welcher Beschreibung?

CD 6 Tr. 7

a.

b.

c.

d.

16 Tut dir was weh?

Sprechen Such dir einen Partner! Frag ihn, was ihm manchmal weh tut! Er muss dir zwei Dinge sagen, die ihm weh tun. — Tauscht dann die Rollen aus!

hundertzweiundsechzig   STANDARDS: 1.1, 1.2, 5.1   KAPITEL 6   Gute Besserung!

So sagt man das!

Asking about and expressing pain

To ask a friend if he or she is hurting, you say:

Tut's weh?
Tut es noch weh?

The response might be:

Au! *or* **Aua! Es tut weh!**
Nein, es geht!

To inquire what hurts, you ask:

Was tut dir weh?
Tut dir der Kopf weh?

And the response might be:

Die Ohren tun mir weh.
Ja, ich hab Kopfschmerzen.

Why do you think the verb form **tut** is used sometimes, and sometimes the form **tun**?[1]
What other verb does **wehtun** remind you of?

Ein wenig Grammatik

The verb **wehtun** acts like a separable prefix verb, with the adverb **weh** in last position in a simple statement. **Tun** is an irregular verb, but you need only two forms in this phrase:

Der Hals **tut** mir **weh.**
Die Augen **tun** ihm **weh.**

17 Grammatik im Kontext

Schreiben Wie viele Sätze kannst du schreiben?

Beispiel Meinem Opa tun oft die … weh.

Wem?		Wie oft?	Was?	
(mein) Opa		ab und zu	Arm	Beine
Oma		oft	Schulter	Hals
Mutter	wehtun	sehr oft	Ellbogen	Hüfte
Vater		häufig	Kopf	Hand
Bruder		manchmal	Knöchel	Füße
Schwester		nie	Bauch	Rücken
Eltern			Knie	
ich				

Grammatik

Verbs used with dative case forms

There are verbs that require the direct object to be in the dative case.

wehtun	Was tut **dir** weh? — Der Hals tut **mir** weh.
(gut) gehen	Wie geht es **dir**? — Danke, es geht **mir** gut.
gefallen	Dresden hat **dem Frank** gut gefallen.
helfen	Der Robert hilft **seiner Oma** gern.
schmecken	Die Quarkbrötchen schmecken **den Schülern** gut.
fehlen	Was fehlt **dir**? — **Mir** fehlt nichts.

Name all the direct objects in these questions and statements.
Can you express these sentences in English?

Mehr Grammatikübungen, S. 171, Ü. 5–7

Übungsheft, S. 68, Ü. 3

Grammatikheft, S. 49, Ü. 7

---

1. **Tut** is used with a singular subject, **tun** if the subject is plural.

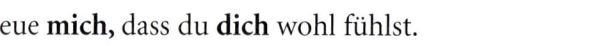

Grammatik

Reflexive verbs used with dative case forms

1. You already know some reflexive verbs that require a reflexive pronoun in the accusative case, such as **sich freuen** and **sich fühlen.**

   Ich freue **mich,** dass du **dich** wohl fühlst.

2. When there is another object, a direct object, in the accusative case, the reflexive pronoun must be in the dative case.

   Ich habe **mir** *das Knie* verletzt.

3. Look at the chart. Are the dative reflexive pronouns the same as the personal pronouns? What difference do you observe?

Ich	habe	**mir**	
Du	hast	**dir**	
Er/ Sie/Es	hat	**sich**	das Bein gebrochen.
Wir	haben	**uns**	
Ihr	habt	**euch**	
Sie (pl)/Sie	haben	**sich**	

4. Also note the use of the definite article with the direct object:

   Ich habe mir **das** Bein gebrochen. *I broke my leg.*
   Er hat sich **den** Fuß verstaucht. *He sprained his ankle.*

What do you notice about the positions of the pronoun and the direct object?[1]

Mehr Grammatikübungen, S. 172, Ü. 8

Grammatikheft, S. 50, Ü. 8–9

18 Grammatik im Kontext

Schreiben Schreib sieben Sätze mit den Wörtern in jedem Kasten.

ich	haben	uns	Ellbogen		
wir	habt	euch	Arm	Knöchel	verletzt
unser Lehrer	habe	sich	Hand	Bein	gebrochen
du	hast	mir	Knie	Finger	verstaucht
meine Oma	hat	dir	Fuß	Auge	
ihr			Daumen	Hüfte	
			Nase		

19 Und du?

Schreiben Lies die folgenden Fragen! Schreib, was für dich zutrifft (*what pertains to you*)!

1. Wie oft verletzt du dich?
2. Was hast du dir schon öfter verletzt?
3. Hast du dir schon einmal etwas verstaucht? Was? Wievielmal?
4. Was hast du dir schon einmal gebrochen?

---

1. The reflexive pronoun precedes the direct object.

20 Hast du dir etwas gebrochen?

Sprechen Frag jetzt einen Partner, ob er sich schon einmal etwas gebrochen, verstaucht oder verletzt hat! — Tauscht dann die Rollen aus! Erzähl danach deinen Mitschülern, was dein Partner gesagt hat!

Ein wenig Grammatik

The verb **waschen** has a stem-vowel change in the **du**-form and the **er/sie**-form of the present tense.

Wann **wäschst** du dir die Hände?
Jeden Tag **wäscht** er sich die Haare.

Mehr Grammatikübungen, S. 172, Ü. 9–10

Ein wenig Grammatik

The verb **brechen** has a stem-vowel change in the **du**-form and the **er/sie**-form of the present tense.

Was **brichst** du dir oft?
Wiebke **bricht** sich nie etwas!

---

21 Grammatik im Kontext

a. Sprechen Such dir einen Partner! Frag ihn:
1. wie oft er sich die Hände wäscht
2. wie oft er sein Auto wäscht
3. wie oft er sich die Haare kämmt
4. wie oft er (seine Katze) kämmt
5. wie oft er sich die Zähne putzt
6. wie oft er sein Fahrrad putzt
Danach fragt er dich.

b. Schreiben Schreib jetzt die Fragen und die Antworten.

wann? und wie oft?

- jeden Tag
- abends
- zweimal am Tag
- vor dem Essen
- morgens
- nach dem Essen
- nach jeder Mahlzeit
- wenn ich (Zeit) habe
- wenn (sie) schmutzig sind

Wortschatz

Er wäscht das T-Shirt. Er wäscht sich die Hände.

Sie kämmt den Hund. Sie kämmt sich.

Er putzt die Fenster. Er putzt sich die Zähne.

Übungsheft, S. 68–69, Ü. 4–7   Grammatikheft, S. 51, Ü. 11

Dritte Stufe

Objectives Asking for and giving advice; expressing hope

Vorsicht vor Sonnenstrahlen!

Ein Sonnenbad kann ein Genuss sein. Aber zu intensive Sonneneinstrahlung schadet nicht nur der Haut, sondern kann einen Sonnenstich oder sogar Hitzschlag verursachen.

Zu viel Sonne! Was passiert?

Die Symptome eines Sonnenstichs treten schon beim Sonnenbaden oder manchmal kurz danach auf. Die Haut ist heiß und trocken, der Kopf hochrot, der Puls läuft schnell. Die Körpertemperatur ist hoch. Es kommt zu Kopfschmerzen, Ohrensausen — der Patient fühlt sich unwohl.

Wann müssen Sie zum Arzt?

Bei erhöhter Temperatur nach einem Sonnenbad und bei eintretenden Kopfschmerzen unbedingt den Arzt anrufen. Nur er kann die Tätigkeit von Herz und Kreislauf stabilisieren.

Wie kann man sich schützen?

- Setzen Sie sich nie zu lange intensiver Sonneneinstrahlung aus!
- Trinken Sie viel Wasser, bis zu vier Liter am Tag, damit Sie genug schwitzen können!
- Vermeiden Sie körperliche Anstrengung in der Hitze!
- Vermeiden Sie Alkohol und essen Sie nur leichte Speisen!

Helfen Sonnenschutzmittel?

Einen absolut sicheren Sonnenschutz gibt es nicht. Wenn Sie unbedingt in der Sonne sein müssen, so schützen Sie Ihre Haut mit einer guten Sonnencreme! Eine Creme mit einem hohen Lichtschutzfaktor schützt die Haut vor schädlichen UV-Strahlen!

22 Was hast du verstanden?

Lesen/Sprechen Lies den Bericht! Dann diskutier die Antworten zu den folgenden Fragen mit deinen Mitschülern!

1. Was kann zu intensive Sonneneinstrahlung verursachen?
2. Was sind die Symptome eines Sonnenstichs?
3. Wann soll man sofort den Arzt anrufen?
4. Wie kann man sich vor einem Sonnenstich schützen?
5. Wie helfen Sonnenschutzmittel?

23 Was fehlt dem Schüler? Script and answers on p. 149G

Zuhören Ein Schüler kann heute nicht zur Schule kommen, weil er krank ist. Hör zu, als ein Freund ihn anruft und fragt, wie es ihm geht! Schreib dann auf, was dem Schüler fehlt, was er machen soll und wie sein Freund ihm helfen will!

Wortschatz

Was soll ich tun? — Du musst unbedingt …!

die Sonne vermeiden

Alkohol vermeiden

viel Wasser trinken

nur Sonnencreme mit hohem Lichtschutzfaktor benutzen

nur leichte Speisen essen

den Arzt anrufen

Übungsheft, S. 70, Ü. 1

Grammatikheft, S. 52, Ü. 12

24 Bist du vorsichtig?

Sprechen Frag deine Partnerin, was sie macht, wenn sie im Sommer in der großen Hitze zu einem Konzert unter freiem Himmel (*open-air concert*) geht! Und was machst du? Wie schützt du dich?

So sagt man das!

Asking for and giving advice

When asking for advice, you say:

   Was soll ich machen?
   Was soll ich bloß tun?

When giving advice, you say:

   Du gehst am besten zum Arzt.
   Geh doch mal zum Arzt!
   Du musst unbedingt zum Arzt gehen!

How does **bloß** affect the meaning of the question?
How would you say the responses in English?

Übungsheft, S. 70–71, Ü. 4–7

Grammatikheft, S. 52, Ü. 13

DRITTE STUFE   STANDARDS: 1.1, 1.2, 5.1   *hundertsiebenundsechzig*   **167**

Wortschatz

das Fieber messen	to measure one's temperature
müde	tired
der Sonnenstich	sunstroke
die Haut	skin
die Temperatur	temperature

Grammatikheft, S. 53, Ü. 14

Ein wenig Grammatik

The verb **messen**, as in **Fieber messen**, has a stem-vowel change in the **du-** and **er/sie-** forms.

Misst du mal mein Fieber?
Er **misst** jetzt sein Fieber.

The **du**-command is **miss!**
Miss doch mal deine Temperatur!

Übungsheft, S. 71–72, Ü. 4–7   Grammatikheft, S. 53, Ü. 15

25 Du musst unbedingt …!

Sprechen Such dir eine Partnerin! — Deine Partnerin hat viele Beschwerden (*complaints*). Du sagst ihr, was sie tun muss. Gebraucht die Ideen in beiden Kästen! Eure Antworten müssen aber stimmen! — Tauscht dann die Rollen aus!

Beschwerden
Was soll ich bloß machen?

Ich bin krank.
Ich brauche Medizin.
Ich glaub, ich hab einen Sonnenstich.
Meine Haut ist ja ganz rot.
Ich fühl mich nicht wohl.
Ich bin so müde.
Ich habe Hunger.
Meine Stirn ist so heiß.

Was tun?
Du musst unbedingt …

die Sonne vermeiden
den Arzt anrufen
eine gute Sonnencreme benutzen
etwas essen
eine Pause machen
in die Apotheke gehen
(dein) Fieber messen
zu Hause bleiben
zum Arzt gehen

26 Geh doch mal zum Arzt!

Sprechen Such dir einen neuen Partner! — Macht jetzt die gleiche Übung noch einmal, aber diesmal mit der **du**-Form des Imperatives!

BEISPIEL   PARTNER   Ich bin so müde.
           DU   Mach doch mal eine Pause!
           PARTNER   Gute Idee!

27 Beim Fußballspielen verletzt

Script and answers on p. 149H

Zuhören Nach dem großen Fußballspiel am Samstag sprechen drei Schüler über das Spiel und die Verletzungen. Hör zu und schreib auf, über wen sie reden und welche Schmerzen diese Personen haben! Welche Personen drücken auch Hoffnung aus?

CD 6 Tr. 9

So sagt man das!

Expressing hope

To express hope, you may say:

Ich hoffe, du hast kein Fieber.
Wir hoffen, dass du dir nichts gebrochen hast.
Hoffentlich hast du dir nur den Fuß verstaucht.

What do you notice about the word order in the **dass**-clause? What do you think **hoffentlich** means?

Grammatikheft, S. 53, Ü. 16   Mehr Grammatikübungen, S. 173, Ü. 11

28 Was hoffst du?

Sprechen Sprich mit einem Partner am Telefon darüber, wie er sich fühlt und was ihm fehlt! Drück Hoffnung aus und sage ihm, wie du ihm helfen kannst! Wenn ihr wollt, könnt ihr die Wörter rechts als Hilfe benutzen.

- kein Fieber mehr haben
- morgen wieder in die Schule gehen können
- wieder besser gehen
- die Medizin nehmen
- der Hals nicht mehr wehtun
- nichts gebrochen haben

Wortschatz

Warum kaufst du dir nicht …?

Sonnencreme	Sonnenmilch	Haarshampoo	Zahnpasta	Seife	Handcreme

   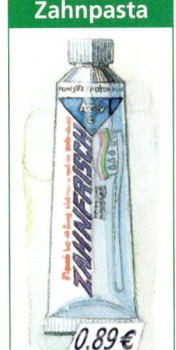  

Die Sonnencreme ist mir zu teuer. | Schutzfaktor 8 ist mir nicht hoch genug. | Das Shampoo ist mir nicht gut genug. | Die Zahnpasta ist mir zu süß. | Die Seife ist mir zu parfümiert. | Die Handcreme ist mir zu fett.

Übungsheft, S. 70, Ü. 2
Grammatikheft, S. 54, Ü. 17

29 Warum kaufst du das nicht?

Sprechen Such dir eine Partnerin! — Ihr seid in einer Drogerie! Sag ihr, dass du hoffst, dass sie sich etwas kauft, was dir gefällt, aber sie hat für alles eine Ausrede (*an excuse*).

Das ist mir zu teuer!

30 In der Drogerie

Sprechen Du bist in einer Drogerie. Dein Partner ist der Drogist. Du brauchst drei ganz bestimmte Artikel. Du fragst, ob er diese Artikel hat und was sie kosten. Wenn es einen Artikel nicht gibt, sag, dass du etwas anderes nimmst!

Ein wenig Grammatik

You also use the dative-case forms to express the idea of something being "too expensive, too large, too small for you."

Die Creme ist **mir** zu teuer.
Die Seife ist **ihr** zu parfümiert.

Grammatikheft, S. 54, Ü. 18

Mehr Grammatikübungen, S. 173, Ü. 12

31 Sie wünschen, bitte?

Schreiben Schreib jetzt mit deinem Partner ein Gespräch, das du mit ihm in der Drogerie gehabt hast! Führt dann dieses Gespräch in der Klasse vor!

32 Von der Schule zum Beruf

Du arbeitest in einer Drogerie und deine Aufgabe ist es, jede Woche eine Werbung mit Sonderangeboten zu entwerfen. Die Werbeblätter bieten gewöhnlich sechs bis acht Produkte an, die für gewisse Krankheiten gut sind.

Mehr Grammatikübungen

Erste Stufe

Objectives Inquiring about someone's health and responding; making suggestions

1 Du fragst deine Freunde, wie es ihnen geht, und sie sagen es dir.—Schreib das richtige Pronomen in die Lücken. (S. 157)

1. Wiebke, wie geht es _____ ? Ist _____ wieder besser? — Ja, _____ geht's gut! *dir; dir; mir*
2. Wie geht's _____ beiden? Ist was mit _____ ? — Du, _____ ist nicht gut. *euch; euch; uns*
3. Ist _____ nicht gut, Herr Müller? Was fehlt _____ ? — Danke, _____ fehlt nichts. *Ihnen; Ihnen; mir*
4. Fehlt _____ etwas, David? Ist _____ nicht gut? — Ja, _____ ist nicht gut. *dir; dir; mir*
5. Maike und Wiebke, was ist mit _____ ? Was fehlt _____ ? — _____ fehlt nichts. *euch; euch; Uns*

2 Du fragst, wie es deinen Freunden geht. Sie sagen es dir.—Schreib die richtigen Pronomen in die Lücken. (S. 157)

1. Wie fühlst du _____ , Maike? Ist _____ nicht gut? — Ich fühl _____ nicht wohl. Ich hab Kopfschmerzen. _____ ist gar nicht gut. *dich; dir; mich Mir*
2. Und was ist mit _____ , David und Thorsten? Fühlt ihr _____ auch nicht wohl? — _____ ist nicht gut, wir fühlen _____ miserabel. *euch; euch Uns; uns*
3. Wie fühlen Sie _____ , Herr Becker? Ist _____ nicht gut? Sagen Sie, was fehlt _____ ? — _____ fehlt nichts, _____ ist wieder besser. *sich; Ihnen Ihnen; Mir; mir*

3 Schau dir die Illustrationen an, und schreib die richtige Information in die Lücken. (S. 157)

1. Die Susanne fühlt _____ nicht wohl. Ich glaube, sie hat _____.
   sich; Halsschmerzen

2. Wie geht es _____ , Sam? — Ich hab eine _____, _____ ist nicht gut.
   dir; Erkältung; mir

3. Ist was mit _____ , Jenny? — Ich fühle _____ nicht wohl; ich habe _____.
   dir; mich; Zahnschmerzen

4. Ist _____ nicht gut, Bruce? — Es geht _____ schlecht. Ich habe furchtbare _____. *dir; mir; Ohrenschmerzen*

5. Wie fühlst du _____ ? Ist _____ nicht gut? — Ich fühle _____ miserabel. Und ich habe _____. *dich; dir; mich; Fieber*

170 hundertsiebzig   STANDARDS: 1.2   KAPITEL 6   Gute Besserung!

4 Du tust, was dein Freund vorschlägt. — Schreib jeden Satz zu Ende und gebrauche dabei den **wir**-Imperativ *(inclusive command form)*. (S. 159)

1. Sollen wir in den Park gehen? — Klar, _____ ! *gehen wir in den Park*
2. Sollen wir die Maike anrufen? — Klar, _____ ! *rufen wir die Maike an*
3. Sollen wir einen Ball mitnehmen? — Klar, _____ ! *nehmen wir einen Ball mit*
4. Sollen wir zuerst zur Apotheke gehen? — Klar, _____ ! *gehen wir zuerst zur Apotheke*
5. Sollen wir uns warm anziehen? — Klar, _____ ! *ziehen wir uns warm an*
6. Sollen wir etwas zum Trinken kaufen? — Klar, _____ ! *kaufen wir etwas zum Trinken*

Zweite Stufe

Objective Asking about and expressing pain

5 Viele Leute sagen dir, was ihnen fehlt. — Schreib die richtige Form des Pronomens in die Lücken. (S. 163)

1. Maike, was tut _____ weh? Tut _____ der Hals weh? — Ja, er tut _____ weh. *dir; dir; mir*
2. Was tut _____ weh, Wiebke und David? — Du, _____ tut der Kopf weh. *euch; uns*
3. Herr Müller, was tut _____ weh? — Ach, _____ tut der Rücken so weh. *Ihnen; mir*
4. Was tut dem Thorsten weh? — Ich glaube, _____ tut der Fuß weh. *ihm*
5. Was tut denn der Antje weh? — Ach, die Schulter tut _____ weh. *ihr*
6. Was tut den Kindern weh? — Ich weiß nicht, was _____ wehtut. *ihnen*

6 Deinen Familienmitgliedern fehlt auch viel. — Schreib die richtige Form des Possessivpronomens in die Lücken. (S. 163)

In meiner Familie sind alle krank. _____ Vater tut die Hüfte weh, *Meinem*
_____ Mutter der Rücken, _____ Geschwistern die Beine; _____ *meiner; meinen; meinem*
Bruder der Fuß und _____ Schwester der Knöchel. Und _____ *meiner; meinen*
Großeltern tut auch immer was weh; _____ Oma tun oft die Beine *meiner*
weh und _____ Opa die Füße. *meinem*

7 Wie fühlen sich diese Leute? — Schreib die richtige Form der unterstrichenen Wörter aus dem ersten Satz in die Lücke im zweiten Satz. (S. 163)

1. Die Schüler essen die Beeren nicht. Die Beeren schmecken ____ nicht. *den Schülern*
2. Meine Oma ist alt und krank. Deshalb helfe ich ____ gern im Garten. *meiner Oma*
3. Mein Bruder hat sich das Knie verletzt. Das Knie tut ____ weh. *meinem Bruder*
4. Die Kinder haben sich verletzt, aber ich weiß nicht, was ____ wehtut. *den Kindern*
5. Meine Geschwister mögen diese CD. Diese CD gefällt ____ sehr gut. *meinen Geschwistern*
6. Der Tim hat immer Bauchweh. Ich weiß nicht, was ____ fehlt. *dem Tim*
7. Mein Cousin schreibt nicht, aber ich glaube, dass es ____ gut geht. *meinem Cousin*

Mehr Grammatikübungen

Answers

WK3 HAMBURG-6

8 Viele Leute verletzen sich beim Sport. — Schreib die richtige Form des Reflexivpronomens in die Lücken. (S. 164)

1. A: Sag, Tim, was hast du ____ beim Fußballspielen gebrochen?   dir
   B: Ich hab ____ nichts gebrochen; ich hab ____ die Hand verstaucht.   mir; mir
2. A: Maike und David, habt ihr ____ beim Tennisspielen den Fuß gebrochen?   euch
   B: Nein, wir haben ____ nur den Knöchel verstaucht.   uns
3. A: Was hat ____ der David beim Radfahren gebrochen?   sich
   B: Ich habe gehört, dass er ____ die Schulter gebrochen hat.   sich
4. A: Weißt du, ob ____ zwei Schüler beim Skifahren etwas gebrochen haben?   sich
   B: Ja, ich habe gehört, dass ____ die beiden überhaupt nichts gebrochen haben.   sich

9 Was kann man tun, um sich frisch und sauber zu fühlen? — Schreib das richtige Pronomen in die Lücken. (S. 165)

1. Nach jeder Mahlzeit wasche ich ____ die Hände, putze ____ die Zähne und kämme   mir; mir
   ____ die Haare. Putzt du ____ auch die Zähne nach jeder Mahlzeit?   mir; dir
2. Maike, wie sehen deine Haare aus? Warum kämmst du ____ nicht? Du, kämm ____   dich dir;
   doch die Haare! Du hast so schöne Haare! — Ich wasche ____ jetzt, ich wasche ____   mich; mir
   auch die Haare, und danach kämme ich ____ .   mich
3. So, wer wäscht ____ zuerst? Also, zuerst wäscht ____ der David, dann der Thorsten,   sich; sich
   und zuletzt wasche ich ____ . Ich muss ____ die Füße waschen; sie sind so schmutzig   mich; mir
   vom Fußballspielen.

10 Was tun diese Leute? — Schreibe ganze Sätze. (S. 165)

1. Der Junge _____ .
   Der Junge wäscht das/sein T-Shirt.

4. _____ .
   Der Junge wäscht sich die Hände.

2. Das Mädchen _____ .
   Das Mädchen kämmt sich.

5. _____ .
   Der Junge putzt sich die Zähne.

3. Der Junge _____ .
   Der Junge putzt das Fenster.

6. _____ .
   Das Mädchen kämmt den Hund.

Dritte Stufe

Objectives Asking for and giving advice; expressing hope

11 Du hoffst, dass es deinem Partner besser geht. — Vervollständige die Sätze und benutze dabei die Wörter in Klammern. (S. 168)

1. (kein Fieber mehr haben)
   Ich hoffe, du _____ .   hast kein Fieber mehr
   Ich hoffe, dass _____ .   du kein Fieber mehr hast
   Hoffentlich _____ .   hast du kein Fieber mehr

2. (s. nichts gebrochen haben)
   Ich hoffe, du _____ .   hast dir nichts gebrochen
   Ich hoffe, dass _____ .   du dir nichts gebrochen hast
   Hoffentlich _____ .   hast du dir nichts gebrochen

3. (s. nicht verletzt haben)
   Ich hoffe, ihr _____ .   habt euch nicht verletzt
   Ich hoffe, dass _____ .   ihr euch nicht verletzt habt
   Hoffentlich _____ .   habt ihr euch nicht verletzt

12 Du schreibst, warum du nicht tun kannst, was man dir vorschlägt. — Schreib das richtige Pronomen in die Lücken. (S. 169)

1. Wiebke, kauf dir doch diese Creme! — Du, diese Creme ist _____ zu fett.   mir
2. Warum kauft sich der David nicht diese Zahnpasta? — Sie ist _____ zu süß.   ihm
3. Kauft euch doch diese Sonnencreme! — Sie ist _____ viel zu teuer.   uns
4. Warum kauft die Maike das Shampoo nicht? — Es ist _____ zu parfümiert.   ihr
5. Warum kaufst du diese Seife nicht? Ist sie _____ auch zu parfümiert?   dir
6. Ich kann diesen Anzug nicht mehr tragen. Er ist _____ viel zu groß!   mir
7. Du kannst den Pulli nicht anziehen, David. Er ist _____ viel zu eng.   dir
8. Wir können uns diese Sachen nicht kaufen. Sie sind _____ einfach zu teuer.   uns

Storytelling Book pp. 46–47

Anwendung

Visit Holt Online
go.hrw.com
KEYWORD: WK3 HAMBURG-6
Self-Test

The *CD-ROM Tutor* offers guided recording and writing activities to accompany the **Anwendung.** These activities are designed to practice students' oral and written communication skills and to review material from each chapter.

1 CD 6 Tr. 10

Einige Leute erzählen, was sie haben, was ihnen fehlt und was sie brauchen. Wo muss jeder hingehen, um das zu bekommen, was er braucht? (Zum Beispiel: Wenn man Brot braucht, muss man zur Bäckerei.) Schreib auf, wo jeder hingehen muss! *Script and answers on p. 149H*

Jetzt ein Eis!

Sie lesen diese Überschrift – und plötzlich können Sie gar nicht anders: Immer wieder denken Sie an ein Eis. Und je mehr Sie versuchen, nicht daran zu denken, desto stärker wird der Gedanke. Forscher der Uni Houston haben dieses Phänomen untersucht und festgestellt: Machen Sie es genau andersrum – denken Sie bewußt an etwas, das Sie verdrängen wollen, und Sie werden es bald vergessen. So lassen sich auch Schmerzen „wegdenken". Je mehr Sie sich auf den Schmerz konzentrieren, desto leichter vergeht er.

2 Ab und zu mal hat jeder Schmerzen und muss etwas dagegen tun. In diesem Artikel von *Bunte* werden Vorschläge gemacht, wie man mit Schmerzen zurechtkommt.
What is this article about? 2. c

  a. If you have pain, think about something like ice cream and the pain won't seem so severe.
  b. If you force yourself to think about something else, your body will forget about the pain and it will go away.
  c. If you concentrate on whatever is causing you pain, it will make it easier for the pain to go away.

3 Was für Schmerzen hast du gehabt? Was machst du, wenn du Schmerzen hast? Schreib mindestens vier Sätze darüber in dein Notizbuch!

4 You are the health official in a new resort opening up soon. It is your responsibility to prepare a pamphlet informing tourists of what they should and should not do in order to stay healthy and safe while they are at the resort, and what they should do in case of sickness or an accident. Work with two other students, your team of health workers, to prepare this document. Use drawings or photos from magazines to illustrate your ideas.

5 Dein Brieffreund in Dresden will wissen, wie dein tägliches (*daily*) Leben in den USA aussieht. Schreib ihm einen Brief und erzähl ihm alles, was du an einem Tag machst — von früh morgens bis abends!

Beispiel Ich stehe um 7 Uhr auf (*get up*). Dann wasche ich mich, putze mir …

6 Tell a friend about several things you are planning to do. Your friend expresses hope that you will take care of yourself so that nothing bad happens. Du willst:

  a. acht Stunden in Kalifornien am Strand liegen
  b. ein hartes Fußballspiel gegen eine College-Mannschaft spielen
  c. eine tolle Party in einer anderen Stadt besuchen
  d. heute Abend gar nicht für den großen Test lernen

  a. — Ich will acht Stunden in Kalifornien am Strand liegen.
     — Hoffentlich bekommst du keinen Sonnenstich.
  b. — Ich werde ein hartes Fußballspiel gegen eine College-Mannschaft spielen. — Ich hoffe, du verletzt dich nicht.
  c. — Ich werde eine tolle Party in einer anderen Stadt besuchen. — Hoffentlich kommst du nicht so spät nach Hause.
  d. — Ich werde heute Abend gar nicht für den großen Test lernen. — Ich hoffe, dass du keine schlechte Note bekommst.

STANDARDS: 1.1, 1.2, 1.3, 5.1   KAPITEL 6   Gute Besserung!

7 Zum Schreiben

Write a dialogue between a doctor and some sick students. You are the doctor on call at a boarding school in Germany and plan on using actual examples in a radio program about health. In order to make the program interesting, you have decided to use dialogues between doctor and patient with several students playing the parts of patients. You sorted through your charts and found a number of students who had complained of various ailments. You gave each advice on how to handle his or her illness and recommendations about staying healthy in the future. You use these charts as a basis for your dialogue.

> **Schreibtipp** Peer evaluation is reading and commenting on someone else's writing. It trains you to read critically and helps you see your writing from someone else's point of view.

Vorbereiten

Brainstorm different ailments, and then write down advice for someone with those problems. Using this as a base, begin your doctor/patient dialogues. Remember also the recommendations for leading a healthy life that are discussed in Chapter 4 as well as in this chapter.

Ausführen

Try to make your dialogue realistic. Make the questions and answers flow logically from one to another. Give logical advice for each ailment and give logical health advice.

Überarbeiten

- Reread your dialogue. For each piece of advice given, ask yourself if an actual doctor would agree with what you advise.
- Trade papers with a partner and read each other's dialogues. Ask questions when necessary, and suggest where your partner might add details or make changes.
- Proofread for spelling and punctuation errors. Rewrite and share your final draft. You might want to present your radio program to the class.

8 Rollenspiel

Work with several students to act out the following situation.

You are an **Apotheker** in a German city. Several people come to you during the day and explain their injuries, aches, or pains. You listen to their explanations, ask questions to get more specific information, then make recommendations about what they can do to remedy the situation. Take turns playing the **Apotheker**. Bring props to make the situation livelier.

ANWENDUNG STANDARDS: 1.3, 5.1, 5.2 *hundertfünfundsiebzig* **175**

Kann ich's wirklich?

Can you inquire about someone's health and respond? (p. 157)

1 How would you ask someone how he or she is doing? How would you ask if something is wrong? E.g.: **Wie fühlst du dich? Fehlt dir etwas?**

2 How would you respond to the question above in the following situations?
  a. You have a sore throat and can hardly swallow. a. **Ich habe Halsschmerzen und kann kaum schlucken.**
  b. You have an earache. b. **Ich habe Ohrenschmerzen.**
  c. You have a toothache. c. **Ich habe Zahnschmerzen.**
  d. You have a cold, with coughing and a stuffy nose. d. **Ich habe eine Erkältung mit Husten und Schnupfen.**

Can you make suggestions? (p. 158)

3 How would you tell the following people what they should do?
  a. Hanna / go to the pharmacy a. **Geh mal zur Apotheke!**
  b. your little brother / not to go to school b. **Geh mal nicht zur Schule!**
  c. your good friend / stay at home c. **Bleib mal zu Hause!**
  d. Thorsten and Wiebke / go to the **Drogerie** d. **Geht mal in die Drogerie!**
  e. you and your friends / go to the movies e. **Gehen wir mal ins Kino!**

Can you ask about and express pain? (p. 163)

4 How would you ask someone what is hurting him or her? How would you say that these people have the following problems? 4. **Was tut dir/Ihnen weh?**
  a. your mother's arm hurts often a. **Meiner Mutter tut oft der Arm weh.**
  b. your throat hurts b. **Der Hals tut mir weh.**
  c. your sister's head hurts sometimes c. **Meiner Schwester tut manchmal der Kopf weh.**
  d. your dad's tooth hurts d. **Meinem Vater tut ein Zahn weh.**

5 How would you say that you are doing great — that nothing hurts?
  E.g.: **Ich fühle mich wohl. Mir tut nichts weh.**

Can you ask for and give advice? (p. 167)

6 What advice would you give to these people? **Du musst unbedingt …** (Answers will vary).

Can you express hope? (p. 168)

7 How would you express hope that
  a. Birgit's throat doesn't hurt anymore a. **Ich hoffe, Birgits Hals tut nicht mehr weh.**
  b. your sister hasn't broken her leg b. **Hoffentlich hat sich meine Schwester das Bein nicht gebrochen.**
  c. you don't have a fever anymore c. **Ich hoffe, dass ich kein Fieber mehr habe.**
  d. Wiebke can go to school tomorrow d. **Hoffentlich kann Wiebke morgen zur Schule gehen.**

Wortschatz

Erste Stufe

p. 149X

Inquiring about someone's health and responding

Wie fühlst du dich?	How do you feel?	Ach schade!	That's too bad.	die Kopfschmerzen, (pl)	headache
Wie geht es dir?	How are you?	Gute Besserung!	Get well soon!	die Zahnschmerzen, (pl)	toothache
Ist dir nicht gut?	Are you not feeling well?	Hoffentlich geht es dir bald besser!	I hope you'll get better soon.	die Ohrenschmerzen, (pl)	earache
Ist was mit dir?	Is something wrong?			die Bauchschmerzen, (pl)	stomachache

Talking about health

Was fehlt dir?	What's wrong with you?
Ich kann kaum schlucken.	I can hardly swallow.
Ich habe Husten und Schnupfen.	I have a cough and stuffy nose.
das Fieber	fever
die Erkältung	cold
die Halsschmerzen, (pl)	sore throat

Ich fühle mich wohl!	I feel great!
Es geht mir (nicht) gut!	I'm (not) doing well.
Mir ist schlecht.	I'm feeling sick.
Ich bin krank.	I'm sick.
Mir ist nicht gut.	I'm not doing well.

What to do when you are sick

zu Hause bleiben	to stay at home
in die Drogerie gehen	to go to the drugstore
in die Apotheke gehen	to go to the pharmacy

Zweite Stufe

Asking about and expressing pain

Tut's weh?	Does it hurt?	das Bein, -e	leg
Au!, Aua!	Ouch!	der Arm, -e	arm
Es tut weh!	It hurts!	der Fuß, ⸚e	foot
Was tut dir weh?	What hurts?	der Knöchel, -	ankle
Tut dir … weh?	Does your … hurt?	das Knie, -	knee
… tut mir weh.	My … hurts.	sich etwas brechen	to break something
der Hals, ⸚e	throat		
der Kopf, ⸚e	head	er/sie/es bricht sich	he/she/it breaks
der Bauch, ⸚e	stomach	sich verstauchen	to sprain something
die Schulter, -n	shoulder		
der Rücken, -	back	sich verletzen	to injure (oneself)
die Hüfte, -n	hip		

Reflexive pronouns, dative case

See p. 164

Verbs that can be both reflexive and non-reflexive

(sich) waschen	to wash
er/sie/es wäscht	he/she/it washes
(sich) kämmen	to comb
(sich) putzen	to clean
sich die Zähne putzen	to brush one's teeth

Dritte Stufe

Talking about health

nur leichte Speisen essen	to only eat light foods
Ich bin so müde.	I am so tired.
der Arzt, ⸚e	doctor
der Lichtschutzfaktor, -en	sun protection factor
der Sonnenstich, -e	sunstroke
die Haut	skin
die Temperatur	temperature
Fieber messen	to take one's temperature
er/sie/es misst	he/she measures

Asking for and giving advice

Was soll ich bloß tun?	What should I do?
Geh doch mal (zum Arzt)!	Go to (the doctor)!
Du musst unbedingt (zum Arzt) gehen!	You have to go to (the doctor)!

Expressing hope

Ich hoffe, (dass) …	I hope that …
hoffentlich …	hopefully …

Other useful words

die Sonnenmilch	suntan lotion
die Sonnencreme	suntan lotion
das Shampoo, -s	shampoo
die Zahnpasta	toothpaste
die Seife, -n	soap
die Handcreme	hand cream
benutzen	to use
süß	sweet
fett	greasy
parfümiert	perfumed

KAPITEL 7, 8, 9

Stuttgart

LOCATION OPENER

Teaching Resources
pp. 178–181

PRINT
- Lesson Planner, p. 32
- Video Guide, pp. 41–42

MEDIA
- One-Stop Planner
- Video Program
  Videocassette 3, 01:30–04:20
- DVD Tutor, Disc 2
- Interactive CD-ROM Tutor, Disc 2
- Map Transparency

 go.hrw.com
WK3 STUTTGART

PAGES 178–179

THE PHOTOGRAPH
Background Information
Stuttgart, the largest city in southwestern Germany, is also the capital of Baden-Württemberg (see Location Opener, Level 1, pp. 272–275). This panoramic view of the city shows modern buildings juxtaposed to wooded hills and vineyards. Economically and culturally, it is the focal point of southwestern Germany because it is home to more than 500 businesses. Numerous technical institutes, agricultural schools, and the Institute of Music and Art indicate the educational and cultural importance of the city as well.

Thinking Critically
Drawing Inferences Point out the tower at the top center of the photograph and ask students what it might be used for. (It is the **Fernsehturm,** *TV tower,* which was built in 1956 on the side of the mountain called **der Bopser**. It measures 217 meters (711 feet), including the antenna, and sends out TV signals for the **Süddeutscher Rundfunk.**)

Geography Connection
To get an idea of the size of the population of Stuttgart, ask students to compare it to a U.S. city of similar size. (Examples: Cleveland, Ohio; Jacksonville, Florida)

THE ALMANAC AND MAP

It is said that the depiction of the horse on the Stuttgart coat of arms emerged around the year 950 when Duke Ludolf of Swabia founded a stud farm in the area that is now Stuttgart. It was then referred to as **stuotgarte** (could be translated as **Stuten-Garten** in modern German), and later became known as Stuttgart around 1250. Today, the emblem of Stuttgart is commonly referred to as **Stuttgarter Rössle.**

Terms in the Almanac

- **Neckar:** A tributary river of the **Rhein** (367 kilometers/223.5 miles), it originates in the Black Forest and ends at the city of Mannheim.

- **Schloss Solitude** was built for Duke Carl Eugen by the French architect La Guépière. It is built in the rococo style and is situated on the edge of a plateau west of the city.

- **Stiftskirche:** The **Evangelische Stiftskirche Heiliges Kreuz** was built between 1433 and 1460 following plans of the builder Aberlin Jörg. The structure emerged from the expansion of a pre-existing tower and basilica, which dates back to 1230. Inside the church are the tombs of the counts of Württemberg. The tombs were sculpted by S. Schlör during the 17th century and are some of the most famous sculptures of that time.

- **Weißenhofsiedlung:** This group of housing complexes was built in 1927 by a group of 16 architects from five European countries under the direction of Mies van der Rohe. Each of the houses showcased new ideas and styles for the home. Ten of these homes were destroyed during World War II.

- **Staatsgalerie:** The **Staatsgalerie** was originally opened in 1843. It contains a large collection of European art from periods ranging from the Middle Ages to the present. They are works of old German masters as well as French, Dutch, Spanish, and Italian artists, including Hals, Rembrandt, Rubens, and Picasso.

KAPITEL 7, 8, 9

- **Georg Wilhelm Friedrich Hegel:** He was one of the major figures in nineteenth-century philosophy. He taught in Heidelberg and Berlin.

- **Wilhelm Hauff:** Hauff, who was born and also died in Stuttgart, was a well-known writer and novelist who created an extensive collection of writing in his short life. He was well known for his fairy tales *Kalif Storch, Zwerg Nase, Der kleine Muck,* and *Das kalte Herz.* He also wrote a historical novel, *Lichtenstein.*

- **Robert Bosch:** Bosch was an electrical engineer who invented the high-tension electric ignition for the **Ottomotor** in 1902. He was the first to design and invent electrical equipment for automobiles.

- **Automobilindustrie:** Stuttgart is especially well known for its high-quality automobile production. It is often referred to as **die Stadt des guten Sterns,** not only because it has the highest per capita income of all German cities, but also because of the silver Mercedes star attached to the hood of every Mercedes manufactured. DaimlerChrysler and Porsche produce cars here, and both companies have museums where visitors can follow the history of early automobile engineering.

- **Elektrotechnik:** IBM Germany in Stuttgart manufactures integrated circuits such as DRAM chips (dynamic random access memory) and logic chips for computers.

- **Verlage:** Publishing companies also make up a large percentage of Stuttgart's industry, with Klett being one of the best known.

- **Flädlesuppe:** **Flädle** is a sweet egg dough that is rolled out and cut into thin strips. The dough strips are then added to a pot of soup stock or bouillon.

Map Activities

Have students locate and trace the path of the Neckar river on the map of Germany. You may also want to use *Map Transparency* 1.

Industrial Arts Connection

Find out from your industrial arts teacher what type of electrical components were used in Bosch's invention and how Bosch's invention improved the automobile. Try to get a diagram or illustration to share with students if possible.

> **PAGES 180–181**

THE PHOTO ESSAY

1. The **Königstraße** is a pedestrian zone similar to the one in Munich that students saw in Level 1.

2. The concert hall houses three music halls: the **Beethovensaal**, which seats 2,000 people, the **Mozartsaal** with a seating capacity of 750, and the **Silchersaal** with 350 seats. The **Konzerthaus** was built in 1955/56.

3. In 1984 the **Staatsgalerie** was expanded, moved into a new building behind the **Staatstheater,** and became known also as the **Neue Staatsgalerie.**

4. In 1746 Duke Carl Alexander and his son Carl Eugen commissioned the building of the **Neues Schloss** based on the plans of the Palace of Versailles. After a fire in 1944, the interior was completely remodeled and refurbished in a more contemporary style between 1958 and 1963.

5. Judith, Roland, Katrin, and Boris attend the same school and are good friends. All of them are interested in other languages, and — when we were filming — they were just about to go on vacations with their parents. Boris was on his way to see parts of the United States, and Katrin was going to Sweden, her mother's native country.

6. This memorial to Friedrich von Schiller, the famous German writer and poet, was erected in 1839. The square is surrounded by significant buildings such as the **Stiftskirche** and the **Alte Kanzlei,** which dates back to the 16th century. Schiller wrote such plays as *Die Räuber* and *Don Carlos.*

7. The city of Stuttgart is also often referred to as **Die Großstadt zwischen Wald und Reben.** Long before the city achieved a leading position in manufacturing goods, its economic foundation was based on wine-making.

LOCATION OPENER

STANDARDS: 2.2, 3.1

KAPITEL 7, 8, 9

Komm mit nach Stuttgart!

Einwohner: 550 000

Flüsse: Neckar

Berühmte Gebäude: Schloss Solitude, Stiftskirche, Weißenhofsiedlung, Staatsgalerie

Bedeutende Stuttgarter: Georg Wilhelm Friedrich Hegel (1770-1831, Philosoph), Wilhelm Hauff (1802-27, Schriftsteller), Robert Bosch (1861-1942, Erfinder), Marcia Haydée (1937-, Choreografin)

Industrie: Automobilindustrie, Elektrotechnik, Maschinenbau, Textilindustrie, Verlage

Beliebte Gerichte: Spätzle, Maultaschen, Flädlesuppe

Map of Germany

WK3 STUTTGART

DISC 2

STANDARDS: 2.2, 3.1

▶ Stuttgart, in einem Talkessel gelegen, ist von Obstgärten und Weinbergen umrahmt

Stuttgart

Stuttgart, die Hauptstadt des südwestdeutschen Bundeslandes Baden-Württemberg, hat viele Attraktionen. Institutionen wie die Staatsgalerie, die Württembergische Landesbibliothek, das Stuttgarter Ballett, sowie der Süddeutsche Rundfunk bezeugen die kulturelle Bedeutung dieser Stadt. Der Großraum Stuttgart ist außerdem ein Industriestandort ersten Ranges. Neben Weltfirmen in der Automobilbranche gibt es hier auch hunderte von hoch spezialisierten kleinen Betrieben in den Bereichen Feinmechanik und Maschinenbau.

Visit Holt Online
go.hrw.com
KEYWORD: WK3 STUTTGART
Internet Aktivitäten

❶ Die Königstraße
Die Königstraße ist eine beliebte Einkaufsstraße in der Stuttgarter Innenstadt.

❷ Liederhalle
Die Stuttgarter Liederhalle ist ein modernes Konzerthaus ersten Ranges.

❸ Staatsgalerie
Die Stuttgarter Staatsgalerie ist eine der größten Kunstsammlungen Deutschlands, mit circa 4000 Gemälden aus der Zeit vom 14. Jahrhundert bis zur Gegenwart. Vor dem Eingang der Galerie ist diese Bronzefigur von Henry Moore.

4 Das Neue Schloss
Dieses Schloss ist im Stil französischer Schlösser erbaut.

Kapitel 7, 8, 9
In den Kapiteln 7, 8 und 9 besuchen wir Stuttgart, die Großstadt zwischen „Wald und Reben". Dort treffen wir Boris, Katrin, Roland und Judith, die auf das Dillmann-Gymnasium gehen.

5 Judith, Roland, Katrin und Boris

6 Schillerplatz mit Schillerdenkmal
Friedrich v. Schiller (1759 - 1805), der große deutsche Dichter, schaut auf den wöchentlichen Blumenmarkt auf dem nach ihm benannten Platz herab.

7 Weinberge am Neckar
Obst- und Weinberge, wie diese am Neckar, sieht man auch in der Stadt Stuttgart.

Kapitel 7: Stadt oder Land?
Chapter Overview

Los geht's! pp. 184–186 — *Das Interview,* p. 184

	FUNCTIONS	GRAMMAR	VOCABULARY	RE-ENTRY
Erste Stufe pp. 187–191	• Expressing preference and giving a reason, p. 189	• Comparative forms of adjectives, p. 190	• Places to live, p. 188 • Advantages and disadvantages of life in the city and country, p. 189	Talking about where you live, p. 188; Places to live, p. 188 (**Kap. 3, I**); Talking about where something is located, p. 188 (**Kap. 9, I**); Expressing preferences and favorites, p. 189 (**Kap. 10, I**); **Weil**-clauses, p. 189; Giving reasons, p. 189 (**Kap. 8, I**); The verb **gefallen**, p. 190 (**Kap. 3, II**)
Zweite Stufe pp. 192–195	• Expressing wishes, p. 192	• The verb **sich wünschen**, p. 192 • Adjective endings following **ein**-words, p. 194	• Things to wish for, p. 193	The **möchte**-forms, p. 192 (**Kap. 3, I**); Reflexive dative verbs, p. 192 (**Kap. 6, II**); Parts of a house, p. 193 (**Kap. 12, I**); Talking about where you live, p. 195 (**Kap. 3, I**)
Dritte Stufe pp. 198–201	• Agreeing with reservations, p. 199 • Justifying your answers, p. 201	• Adjective endings of comparatives, p. 200	• Noisy things, p. 198	Transportation vocabulary, p. 198 (**Kap. 1, I**); Agreeing, p. 199 (**Kap. 2, I**); Expressing opinions, p. 199 (**Kap. 2/9, I**); Giving reasons, p. 201 (**Kap. 8, I**); The verb **gefallen**, p. 201 (**Kap. 3, II**)

Zum Lesen pp. 196–197 — Und dein Traumhaus? — **Reading Strategy** Using grammatical and lexical clues to derive meaning

Mehr Grammatikübungen pp. 202–205
Erste Stufe, pp. 202–203 Zweite Stufe, pp. 203–204 Dritte Stufe, pp. 204–205

Review pp. 206–209
Anwendung, pp. 206–207 Kann ich's wirklich?, p. 208 Wortschatz, p. 209
Zum Schreiben: Comparing and contrasting (Writing a composition)

CULTURE

• Landeskunde: Wo wohnst du lieber? Auf dem Land? In der Stadt? p. 191
• Letter from a German pen pal, p. 195

Kapitel 7: Stadt oder Land?
Chapter Resources

Lesson Planning
One-Stop Planner
Lesson Planner with Substitute Teacher Lesson Plans, pp. 32–36, 71
Student Make-Up Assignments
- Make-Up Assignment Copying Masters, Chapter 7

Listening and Speaking
TPR Storytelling Book, pp. 48–55
Listening Activities
- Student Response Forms for Listening Activities, pp. 51–54
- Additional Listening Activities 7-1 to 7-6, pp. 55–58
- Additional Listening Activities (song), p. 54
- Scripts and Answers, pp. 138–143

Video Guide
- Teaching Suggestions, pp. 44–45
- Activity Masters, pp. 46–48
- Scripts and Answers, pp. 95–97

Activities for Communication
- Communicative Activities, pp. 37–42
- Realia and Teaching Suggestions, pp. 98–101
- Situation Cards, pp. 135–136

Reading and Writing
Reading Strategies and Skills Handbook, Chapter 7
Lies mit mir! 2, Chapter 7
Übungsheft, pp. 73–84

Grammar
Grammatikheft, pp. 55–63
Grammar Tutor for Students of German, Chapter 7

Assessment
Testing Program
- Grammar and Vocabulary Quizzes, **Stufe** Quizzes, and Chapter Test, pp. 171–188
- Score Sheet, Scripts and Answers, pp. 189–196

Alternative Assessment Guide
- Portfolio Assessment, p. 24
- Performance Assessment, p. 38
- CD-ROM Assessment, p. 52

Student Make-Up Assignments
- Alternative Quizzes, Chapter 7

Online Activities
- Interaktive Spiele
- Internet Aktivitäten

Video Program
- Videocassette 3
- Videocassette 5 (captioned version)
- DVD Tutor, Disc 2

Audio Compact Discs
- Textbook Listening Activities, CD 7, Tracks 1–11
- Additional Listening Activities, CD 7, Tracks 17–23
- Assessment Items, CD 7, Tracks 12–16

Interactive CD-ROM Tutor, Disc 2

Teaching Transparencies
- Situations 7-1 to 7-2
- Vocabulary 7-A to 7-B
- **Los geht's!**
- **Mehr Grammatikübungen** Answers
- **Grammatikheft** Answers

One-Stop Planner CD-ROM

Use the **One-Stop Planner CD-ROM with Test Generator** to aid in lesson planning and pacing.

For each chapter, the **One-Stop Planner** includes:
- Editable lesson plans with direct links to teaching resources
- Printable worksheets from resource books
- Direct launches to the HRW Internet activities
- Video and audio segments
- Test Generator
- Clip Art for vocabulary items

Kapitel 7: Stadt oder Land?

Projects

Hier lässt es sich leben!

In this activity students will design, label, and describe an ideal place to live. You should begin this project after students have covered the vocabulary and functions introduced in the **Dritte Stufe**. It can be done individually or in pairs.

MATERIALS
Students may need
- travel magazines
- city maps
- posterboard
- glue
- paper
- tour brochures
- real estate magazines
- scissors
- markers
- pens

SUGGESTED SEQUENCE

1. Ask students to write down their initial ideas of what their dream area might look like, including where it is located (examples: city, village, mountain, island), what type of facilities are nearby or available (examples: stores, services), and what type of transportation people can use to get around.
2. Once students have finished this task, they should gather pictures, ads, photos from magazines, guides, or maps to illustrate their place.
3. Students should design the area (example: **Kleinstadt**) and label each place once it has been pasted on the posterboard. (Provide students with additional vocabulary or make dictionaries available.)
4. After students have completed the artistic part of the project (designing and labeling), they must write an essay describing their place and give it its own unique name. The essay should describe the area and point out its advantages, as well as specific reasons why it is so appealing to the student.
5. Students should present their project to the class upon completion.
6. Display the projects in the classroom.

GRADING THE PROJECT
Suggested point distribution (**total = 100 points**)
- Poster content and originality 30
- Oral presentation..................................30
- Written information (labels and essay) ..40

Games

Gegenteile nennen

Playing this game will help your students review the vocabulary of **Vor- und Nachteile,** *as well as previously learned expressions.*

Procedure Divide your class into two groups, Team A and Team B. Give each student an index card on which you have written an adjective with its opposite in parentheses. The first student on Team A uses the adjective on his or her card in a sentence. (Example: **schnell—Meine Eltern fahren einen schnellen Wagen.**)

A player from Team B responds with the same sentence, except that he or she must replace the adjective with its opposite. (Example: **Meine Eltern fahren einen langsamen Wagen.**)

If the student gives the correct opposite, his or her team receives a point; if he or she also uses the correct adjective ending, the team receives an additional point. Then Team B has its turn. If the opposing team does not provide the correct opposite, a member of the reader's team may restate the sentence. The game may end in one of two ways. Either you call time and each team tallies up its points to determine the winner, or you can wait until all the cards have been used.

Storytelling

Mini-Geschichte

*This story accompanies Teaching Transparency 7-1. Read the **Mini-Geschichte** to your students, or have them read the advertisement aloud using proper pronunciation, intonation, and cadence. Have students list Waldkirchen's advantages.*

Unser Angebot:

Ihnen gefallen die Berge besser als die See? Sie ziehen eine Kleinstadt vor, weil da weniger Verkehr ist? Ihr Lieblingssport ist Golf? Dann ist die Stadt Waldkirchen richtig für Ihre Ferien! In Waldkirchen ist die Luft sauber und das Leben ruhig. Die Umgebung ist schön. Spazieren Sie auf ruhigen Waldwegen *(forest trails)*. Schwimmen Sie in sauberen Waldseen oder gehen Sie in Waldkirchens Schwimmbad. Wir bieten Ihnen eine Woche in Waldkirchen für 300 Euro.

Traditions

Die Stadt des Automobils

Gottlieb Daimler (1834-1900), der Gründer des Autoherstellers mit dem Stern, hat dafür gesorgt, dass Stuttgart als die Stadt des Automobils weltbekannt wurde.  1882 gründete Daimler in Cannstadt bei Stuttgart eine Versuchswerkstatt. Im Jahre 1885 konstruierte er hier mit seinem Freund Wilhelm Maybach das erste Motorrad und ein Jahr später das erste vierrädrige Automobil. 1890 gründete Daimler die Daimler-Motoren-Gesellschaft. 1892 baute er mit Maybach den ersten Zweizylinder-Reihenmotor. 1899 konstruierte Maybach auf Anregung des Kaufmanns Emil Jelinek für die Daimler-Motoren-Gesellschaft einen Rennwagen. Das Modell wurde nach der Tochter Jelineks „Mercedes" genannt.

Daimler starb 1900 in Stuttgart-Cannstadt. 1926 fusionierte die Daimler-Motoren-Gesellschaft mit der Firma Benz & Cie. zur Daimler-Benz AG und 1998 vereinigten sich die Daimler-Benz AG und die Chrysler Corporation.

Daimlers ehemalige Werkstatt beherbergt heute die Gedächnisstätte des Erfinders. Modelle der ersten Daimler-Fahrzeuge und Dokumente aus seinem Leben sind hier zu sehen. Die ersten Automobile von Gottlieb Daimler und Karl Benz und der erste Mercedes sind im Mercedes-Benz-Museum zu sehen.

Ask students what the cities Detroit (USA), Stuttgart (Germany), Toyota City (Japan), and Turin (Italy) have in common. Have students compare the economy of Stuttgart with that of Detroit.

Rezept

Flädlesuppe

Für 2 Personen

Zutaten

g=Gramm, l=Liter

125 g	Mehl
1/4 l	Milch
2	Eier
	Salz und Muskat
	Speck für die Pfanne
1 l	heiße Fleischbrühe
1	Bund Schnittlauch, feingeschnitten

Zubereitung

Aus den Zutaten einen glatten Teig anrühren und anschließend in einer heißen, mit Speck ausgeriebenen Pfanne sehr dünne „Flädle", also Pfannkuchen backen. Die Flädle abkühlen lassen, in dünne Streifen schneiden und in einer klaren, kräftigen Fleischbrühe, mit etwas klein geschnittenem Schnittlauch bestreut, servieren.

Kapitel 7: Stadt oder Land?
Technology

DVD/Video

Videocassette 3, 5 (captioned version)
DVD Tutor, Disc 2
See Video Guide, pages 43–48

Los geht's! • Das Interview

In this segment of the video, Katrin stops two passers-by to interview them for her German class. She asks them if they enjoy living where they are, and if they would prefer to live in the city or the country. Later, Katrin meets her friend Judith at her house and talks about her own home.

Landeskunde
Wo wohnst du lieber? Auf dem Land? In der Stadt?

Several people give their responses to the question **Wohnst du lieber auf dem Land oder in der Stadt?**

Fortsetzung

Katrin's little brother joins Katrin and Judith, and they play with his guinea pig.

Videoclips
- **Schwäbisch Hall®** (savings and loans institution)
- **BUND** (ecological interest group)
- **Verkehrsprojekte deutscher Einheit** (infrastructure development project)
- **Fremde brauchen Freunde** ("Stop the hate" public service announcement)
- **Grundig®** (television sets)

Interactive CD-ROM Tutor

Activity	Activity Type	Pupil's Edition Reference
1. Wortschatz	Wozu gehört's?	pp. 188, 189
2. Wortschatz	Merkspiel	p. 193
3. Grammatik	Was fehlt?	p. 194
4. Wortschatz	Wort und Bild Erfahren/Wählen	p. 198
5. So sagt man das!	Was ist richtig?	pp. 189, 192, 199, 201
6. Grammatik	Was fehlt?	pp. 190, 194, 200
Landeskunde	Wo wohnst du lieber? Auf dem Land? In der Stadt? Was ist richtig?	p. 191
Zum Sprechen	*Guided recording*	pp. 206-207
Zum Schreiben	*Guided writing*	pp. 206-207

Teacher Management System

Launch the program, type "admin" in the password area, and press RETURN. Log on to **www.hrw.com/CDROMTUTOR** for a detailed explanation of the Teacher Management System.

DVD Tutor

The *DVD Tutor* contains all material from the *Video Program* as described above. German captions are available for use at your discretion for all sections of the video. The *DVD Tutor* also provides a variety of video-based activities that assess students' understanding of **Los geht's!, Fortsetzung,** and **Landeskunde,** as well as the new **Grammatik im Kontext** presentations.

The *DVD Tutor* may be used on any DVD video player connected to a television or video monitor.

One-Stop Planner CD-ROM

To preview all resources available for this chapter, use the **One-Stop Planner CD-ROM**, Disc 2.

Visit Holt Online
go.hrw.com
KEYWORD: WK3 STUTTGART-7
Online Edition

Go.Online!

Premier Online Edition

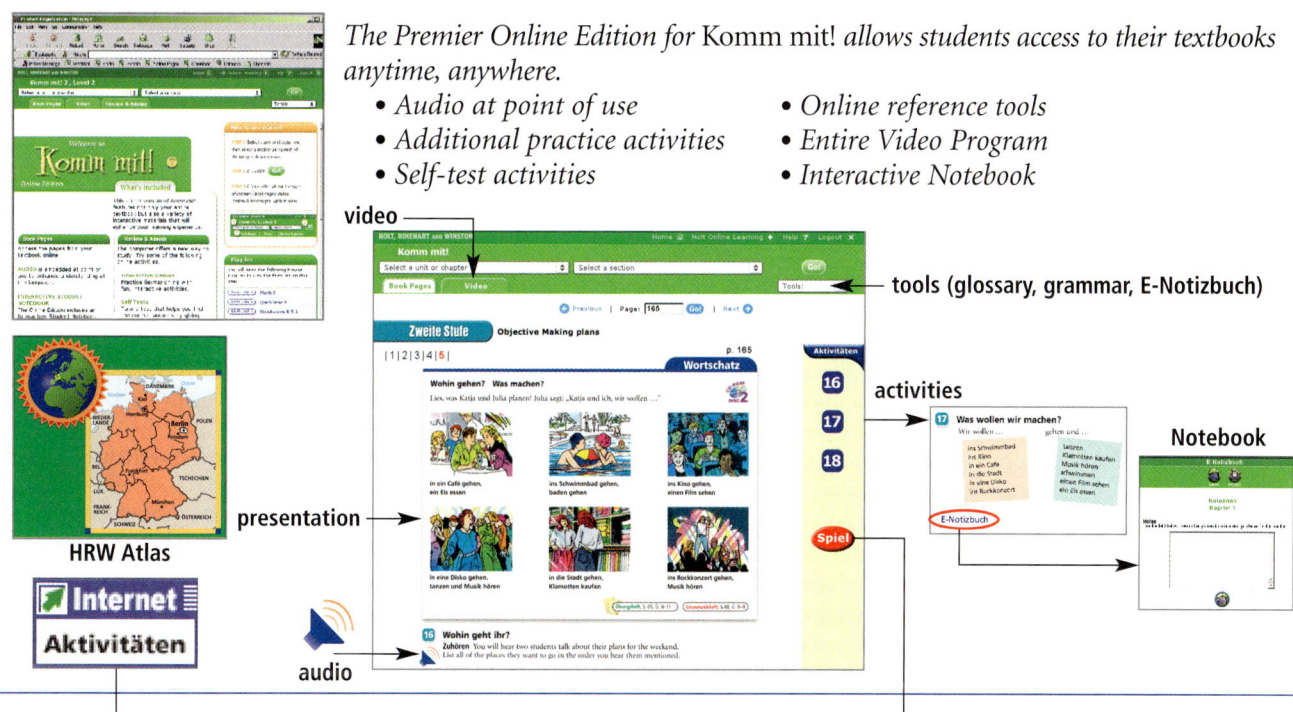

The Premier Online Edition for *Komm mit!* allows students access to their textbooks anytime, anywhere.

- Audio at point of use
- Additional practice activities
- Self-test activities
- Online reference tools
- Entire Video Program
- Interactive Notebook

HRW Atlas

Internet Aktivitäten

presentation
video
audio
tools (glossary, grammar, E-Notizbuch)
activities
Notebook

Internet Aktivitäten

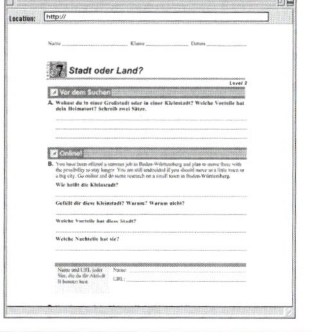

These guided internet activities include a worksheet and pre-selected and pre-screened authentic web sites from the German-speaking countries. You can use these activities

- to help students develop research skills in the target language
- to introduce students to authentic cultural information
- as a project

Interaktive Spiele

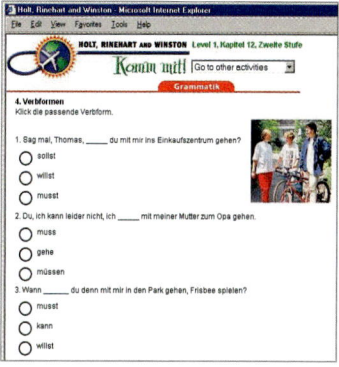

You can use the interactive activities in this chapter

- to practice grammar, vocabulary, and chapter functions
- as homework
- as an assessment option
- as a self-test
- to prepare for the Chapter Test

Webprojekt Have students visit sites for a big city in Austria. They should report on the attractions of the city, as well as on the environmental and health problems the city's inhabitants may be facing. Encourage students to exchange useful Web sites with their classmates. Have students document their sources by referencing the names and URLs of all the sites they consulted.

STANDARDS: 1.2, 1.3, 3.1, 3.2, 5.1   KAPITEL 7   TECHNOLOGY

Kapitel 7: Stadt oder Land?
Textbook Listening Activities Scripts

Erste Stufe

9 p. 189

SABINE Ich wohne seit zwei Jahren in Stuttgart, und es gefällt mir sehr gut hier. In Stuttgart ist immer was los! Konzerte, Theater, viele Diskos! Man kann jeden Abend woanders hingehen. Vorher habe ich in Bietigheim gewohnt, 'ne typische Kleinstadt, viel zu ruhig, nicht viel los. Ich würde sogar sagen, es ist ziemlich langweilig dort …

BORIS Also, ich seh das nicht so. Im Gegenteil! Kleinstädte sind viel gemütlicher, nicht so hektisch wie die Großstadt. Je weiter weg von der Großstadt, desto besser! Wir wohnen schon seit ein paar Jahren in Schönaich, einem kleinen Dorf mitten auf dem Lande. Die Luft ist total frisch hier, es gibt eine tolle Landschaft, viele Wiesen und Wälder. Man kann eine Menge draußen unternehmen: wandern, Fahrrad fahren und so …

SABINE Ja, aber was ist, wenn man mal dringend in die Stadt muss, ins Krankenhaus zum Beispiel? Das dauert ja ewig, bis man dort ist! Nein, also da wohne ich doch lieber direkt in der Großstadt. In Stuttgart gibt es einen schönen Stadtpark, viele Cafés und Restaurants. Und außerdem gibt es noch ein ganz großes Einkaufszentrum mit tollen Boutiquen, die immer supermodische Klamotten haben. Und nicht zu vergessen: Stuttgart hat ziemlich gute Verkehrsverbindungen in alle Richtungen mit Bussen, Straßenbahnen und der U-Bahn.

BORIS Das ist genau der Punkt, der mich an einer Großstadt so stört: zu viel Verkehr! Überall verstopfte Straßen und dreckige Luft! Deshalb sind wir auch von Esslingen weggezogen. Das ist zwar nicht direkt in der Stadt, aber die Vororte wachsen so schnell mit der Großstadt zusammen, da gibt es kaum einen Unterschied.

SABINE Also, ich würde lieber in einem Vorort wie Esslingen wohnen, als auf einem Dorf. In einem Vorort gibt es zwar kein großes Kulturangebot, aber man kann schnell in die Stadt rein. Andererseits hat man den Vorteil, in einer etwas ruhigeren Umgebung zu wohnen, wenn man nach einem langen Tag gestresst nach Hause kommt.

BORIS Also, am liebsten mag ich Schönaich. Auf dem Land in der Natur zu leben, ist mir tausendmal wichtiger, als alles, was die Großstadt jemals zu bieten hat!

Answers to Activity 9
1. Stuttgart (Großstadt): immer was los, Konzerte, Theater, Diskos, Stadtpark, Cafés, Restaurants, großes Einkaufszentrum, gute Verkehrsverbindungen; zu viel Verkehr, verstopfte Straßen, dreckige Luft
2. Bietigheim (Kleinstadt): gemütlich, nicht so hektisch; zu ruhig, nicht viel los, langweilig
3. Esslingen (Vorort): schnelle Verbindung in die Stadt, ruhige Wohngegend; wächst mit der Großstadt zusammen, kein großes Kulturangebot
4. Schönaich (Dorf): frische Luft, tolle Landschaft, wandern, Fahrrad fahren; Fahrt in die Stadt dauert zu lange in dringenden Fällen

Zweite Stufe

14 p. 193

RALF Ich bin der Ralf und wünsche mir, dass es keinen Krieg mehr auf der Welt gibt, keinen Hunger und keine Armut. Aber zuerst wünsche ich mir einen guten Schulabschluss, damit ich auf die Uni gehen kann, um Politik zu studieren.

CLAUDIA Ich heiße Claudia. Mein größter Wunsch ist ein eigenes Zimmer. Ich muss ein Zimmer mit meiner Schwester teilen, und das ist katastrophal! Überall lässt sie ihre Klamotten rumliegen, macht nie ihr Bett und benutzt andauernd meine Sachen. Ein eigenes Zimmer ganz für mich alleine, das ist mein Traum!

MATTHIAS Ja, also ich heiße Matthias. Ich wünsche mir mal einen ganz tollen Job, der mir in erster Linie Spaß macht und auch viel Geld einbringt. Am liebsten wär ich Manager in einer Computer- oder

The following scripts are for the listening activities found in the *Pupil's Edition.* For Student Response Forms, see *Listening Activities,* pages 51–54. To provide students with additional listening practice, see *Listening Activities,* pages 55–58.

For resource information, see the **One-Stop Planner CD-ROM**, Disc 2.

          Hightechfirma oder so. Auf jeden Fall was mit Zukunft!

ANNE   Ich bin die Anne und wünsch mir, dass wir in einer sauberen und natürlichen Umwelt leben könnten, wo die Luft nicht dreckig ist, das Wasser nicht verseucht ist und keine Chemikalien in den Nahrungsmitteln sind.

Answers to Activity 14
Ralf: keinen Krieg, keinen Hunger, keine Armut, einen guten Schulabschluss
Claudia: ein eigenes Zimmer
Matthias: einen tollen Job
Anne: eine saubere und natürliche Umwelt

Dritte Stufe

20 p. 198

MARKUS   Also, wenn mein Bruder abends immer mit dem Motorrad nach Hause kommt, dann kann man ihn schon von weitem hören! Am lautesten ist es, wenn er direkt bis vor die Haustür fährt!

UTE   Sag ihm doch, er soll das Motorrad schon ein paar Meter vor dem Haus ausmachen und es den Rest des Weges einfach nur rollen lassen. Dann würde man ihn gar nicht hören, wenn er kommt.

MARKUS   Super! Ich schlage es ihm gleich heute Abend vor! Aber noch schlimmer als laute Motorräder finde ich eigentlich den Lärm von den Flugzeugen hier. Der Flughafen ist fast mitten in der Stadt! Dort, wo wir wohnen, fliegen die Flugzeuge schon ziemlich tief herunter, bevor sie landen. Und wenn ich nachmittags meine Hausaufgaben mache, stört mich der Lärm ganz besonders.

UTE   Ja, das kann ich verstehen. Das würde mich auch nerven. Setz dir doch einen Kopfhörer auf mit deiner Lieblingsmusik. Dann hörst du den Flugzeuglärm bestimmt nicht mehr.

MARKUS   Also, ich glaub, das ist keine gute Idee. Ich hör am liebsten Heavy Metal. Aber dabei kann ich mich echt nicht auf meine Hausaufgaben konzentrieren.

UTE   Na ja, das ist schade. Versuch's doch mal mit Mozart oder Bach!

MARKUS   Niemals! So was Langweiliges! Lieber ertrage ich den Flugzeuglärm!

Answers to Activity 20
Motorradlärm; Flugzeuglärm
Motorrad abstellen und rollen lassen;
Kopfhörer aufsetzen
Vorschlag ist super; Vorschlag ist keine gute Idee

Anwendung

1 p. 206

OLAF   Ich wohne lieber mitten in der Großstadt als auf dem Land. Ich gehe nämlich gerne abends aus, zum Beispiel in ein Restaurant, ins Theater oder ins Kino. In einer Stadt ist garantiert immer was los.

SIGRID   Also, ich wohne ganz gern hier in Unterlingen. Das ist ein kleines Nest, wo jeder jeden kennt. Es gibt ein paar Bauernhöfe hier, viele Tiere, eine schöne Landschaft, also viel Natur. Das gefällt mir.

HEIDI   Also, ich brauch beides: viel Action einerseits und meine Ruhe andererseits. Deswegen wohne ich am liebsten hier in Oberkassel, das ist ein Vorort von Düsseldorf. Wenn ich ausgehen will, dann bin ich schnell im Stadtzentrum. Und wenn ich mal ein gemütliches Wochenende zu Hause verbringen möchte, dann sitze ich auf meinem Balkon und höre nichts von dem Lärm in der Stadt.

FRED   Also, ich wohne in Bad Homburg, das ist eine nette Kleinstadt nicht weit von Frankfurt. Es gibt hier ein ziemlich gutes Kulturangebot und viele Restaurants, fast wie in einer Großstadt. Nur viel Verkehr haben wir nicht, und die Luft ist besser. Deswegen wohne ich lieber in Bad Homburg als in Frankfurt.

Answers to Activity 1
1. Olaf: Großstadt; geht gern abends aus
2. Sigrid: Dorf; ihr gefällt die Natur
3. Heidi: Vorort; braucht die Nähe zur Stadt, aber auch eine ruhige Umgebung
4. Fred: Kleinstadt; hat gutes Kulturangebot, wenig Verkehr, bessere Luft

KAPITEL 7   SCRIPTS   **181H**

Kapitel 7: Stadt oder Land?
Suggested Lesson Plans 50-Minute Schedule

Day 1

LOCATION OPENER 15 min.
- Present Location Opener, pp. 178–181
- Geography Connection, ATE, p. 177A
- Show **Stuttgart** Video
- Do Viewing and Post-viewing Activities, Video Guide, p. 27

CHAPTER OPENER 5 min.
- Background Information, ATE, p. 181M
- Culture Note, ATE, p. 181M

LOS GEHT'S! 25 min.
- Preteaching Vocabulary, ATE, p. 181N
- Advance Organizer, ATE, p. 181N
- Thinking Critically, ATE, p. 181N
- Play Audio CD for **Los geht's!**, pp. 184–185
- Have students read **Los geht's!**, pp. 184–185
- Teaching Suggestions, Video Guide, p. 44
- Show **Los geht's!** Video

Wrap-Up 5 min.
- Students respond to questions about living in certain places

Homework Options
Pupil's Edition, p. 186, Comprehension Acts. 1–5
Übungsheft, p. 73

Day 2

ERSTE STUFE

Quick Review 5 min.
- Check homework, Übungsheft, p. 73, Act. 1

Reading Selection, p. 187 15 min.
- Teaching Suggestion, ATE, p. 181O
- **Wo wohnst du lieber?**, p. 187
- Do Activities 6 and 7, p. 188

Wortschatz, p. 188 10 min.
- Presenting **Wortschatz**, ATE, p. 181O
- Teaching Transparency 7-1
- Do Activity 8, p. 188

So sagt man das!/Wortschatz, p. 189 15 min.
- Presenting **So sagt man das!**, ATE, p. 181O
- Presenting **Wortschatz**, ATE, p. 181P
- Play Audio CD for Activity 9, p. 189
- Do Activity 10, p. 189

Wrap-Up 5 min.
- Students respond to questions about which of two cities they prefer

Homework Options
Grammatikheft, pp. 55–56, Acts. 1–4
Übungsheft, p. 74, Act. 1

Day 3

ERSTE STUFE

Quick Review 10 min.
- Check homework, **Grammatikheft**, pp. 55–56, Acts. 1–4

Grammatik, p. 190 15 min.
- Presenting **Grammatik**, ATE, p. 181P
- Do Activities 11 and 12, p. 190
- Do Activities 5–7, p. 57, Grammatikheft
- Do Activities 2–7, pp. 74–76, Übungsheft

LANDESKUNDE 15 min.
- Pre-viewing Suggestion, Video Guide, p. 44
- Background Information, ATE, p. 181Q
- Show **Landeskunde** Video
- Do Activities 1–3, p. 77, Übungsheft
- Do **Landeskunde** Activity, Interactive CD-ROM

Wrap-Up 5 min.
- Students respond to questions about where they live and where they prefer to live

Homework Options
Mehr Grammatikübungen, Erste Stufe

Day 4

ERSTE STUFE

Quick Review 15 min.
- Check homework, **Mehr Grammatikübungen, Erste Stufe**

Quiz Review 15 min.
- Do Additional Listening Activities 7-1 and 7-2, pp. 55–56
- Do Communicative Activity 7-1, pp. 37–38

Quiz 20 min.
- Quiz 7-1A or 7-1B

Homework Options
Activities for Communication, pp. 135–136, prepare Situation 7-1

Day 5

ZWEITE STUFE

Quick Review 10 min.
- Return and review Quiz 7-1
- Bell Work, ATE, p. 181Q
- Do Situation 7-1

Reading Selection, p. 192 10 min.
- Teaching Suggestion, ATE, p. 181Q
- Do Activity 13, p. 192

Ein wenig Grammatik, p. 192 10 min.
- Presenting **Ein wenig Grammatik**, ATE, p. 181R
- Do Activity 8, p. 58, Grammatikheft

So sagt man das!/Wortschatz, pp. 192–193 15 min.
- Presenting **So sagt man das!**, ATE, p. 181R
- Presenting **Wortschatz**, p. 181R
- Teaching Transparencies 7-A, 7-B
- Play Audio CD for Activity 14, p. 193
- Do Activity 15, p. 193

Wrap-Up 5 min.
- Students respond to questions about what they wish for themselves

Homework Options
Grammatikheft, pp. 58–59, Acts. 9–10
Übungsheft, pp. 78–79, Acts. 1–3

Day 6

ZWEITE STUFE

Quick Review 10 min.
- Check homework, Grammatikheft, pp. 58–59, Acts. 9–10

Grammatik, p. 194 20 min.
- Presenting **Grammatik**, ATE, p. 181R
- Do Activities 17–19, p. 195
- Do Activities 11–13, pp. 59–60, Grammatikheft
- Play Game, **Gegenteile nennen**, ATE, p. 181C

Quiz Review 20 min.
- Do **Mehr Grammatikübungen, Zweite Stufe**
- Do Activities 2–3, Interactive CD-ROM

Homework Options
Pupil's Edition, p. 194, Act. 16
Übungsheft, pp. 79–80, Acts. 4–7

 **One-Stop Planner CD-ROM**

For alternative lesson plans by chapter section, to create your own customized plans, or to preview all resources available for this chapter, use the **One-Stop Planner CD-ROM**, Disc 2.

 For additional homework suggestions, see activities accompanied by this symbol throughout the chapter.

Day 7

ZWEITE STUFE
Quick Review 10 min.
- Check homework, Übungsheft, pp. 79–80, Acts. 4–7

Quiz 20 min.
- Quiz 7-2A or 7-2B

ZUM LESEN 20 min.
- Present **Lesestrategie**, p. 196
- Do Activities 1–8, pp. 196–197

Wrap-Up 5 min.
- Students compare places to live

Homework Options
Übungsheft, p. 81, Acts. 1–5
Interaktive Spiele, see ATE, p. 181F

Day 8

DRITTE STUFE
Quick Review 10 min.
- Check homework, Übungsheft, p. 81, Acts. 1–5

Wortschatz, p. 198 20 min.
- Presenting **Wortschatz**, ATE, p. 181U
- Teaching Transparency 7-2
- Play Audio CD for Activity 20, p. 198
- Read **Der Lärm wird größer!**, p. 199
- Do Activity 21, p. 199

So sagt man das!, p. 199 15 min.
- Presenting **So sagt man das!**, ATE, p. 181V
- Do Activity 22, p. 200
- Do Activity 4, p. 83, Übungsheft

Wrap-Up 5 min.
- Students respond to questions about what causes noise pollution

Homework Options
Grammatikheft, p. 61, Acts. 14–15
Übungsheft, pp. 82–83, Acts. 1–4

Day 9

DRITTE STUFE
Quick Review 10 min.
- Check homework, Übungsheft, pp. 82–83, Acts. 1–4

Grammatik, p. 200 20 min.
- Presenting **Grammatik**, ATE, p. 181V
- Do Activities 23 and 24, p. 200
- Do Activity 25, p. 201
- Do Activities 18–19, p. 63, Grammatikheft

So sagt man das!, p. 201 15 min.
- Presenting **So sagt man das!**, ATE, p. 181V
- Do Activities 26 and 27, p. 201
- Do Activity 5, Interactive CD-ROM

Wrap-Up 5 min.
- Students respond to questions about why they prefer to live in the city or in the country

Homework Options
Pupil's Edition, p. 201, Acts. 28 and 29
Übungsheft, pp. 83–84, Acts. 5–6

Day 10

DRITTE STUFE
Quick Review 10 min.
- Check homework, Übungsheft, pp. 83–84, Acts. 5–6

Quiz Review 20 min.
- Do **Mehr Grammatikübungen, Dritte Stufe**
- Do Additional Listening Activities 7-5 and 7-6, pp. 57–58

Quiz 20 min.
- Quiz 7-3A or 7-3B

Homework Options
Interaktive Spiele, see ATE, p. 181F
Activities for Communication, pp. 135–136, prepare Situation 7-3

Day 11

DRITTE STUFE
Quick Review 10 min.
- Return and review Quiz 7-3

Project: Hier lässt es sich leben! 35 min.
- Suggested Sequence, ATE, p. 181C
- Students design and label a dream place to live

Wrap-Up 5 min.
- Students briefly report on progress of projects

Homework Options
Complete Project
Pupil's Edition, p. 179, Act. 5, **Zum Schreiben**
Internet Aktivitäten, see ATE, p. 181F

Day 12

ANWENDUNG
Quick Review 25 min.
- Students present **Zum Schreiben** compositions
- Do **Anwendung** Activities 1–4, 6 pp. 206–207

Kann ich's wirklich? 10 min.
- Answer orally questions 1–4 and 6, p. 208

Chapter Review 15 min.
- Review chapter functions, vocabulary, and grammar; choose from **Mehr Grammatikübungen**, Grammar Tutor for Students of German, Activities for Communication, Listening Activities, Interactive CD-ROM Tutor, or **Interaktive Spiele**

Homework Options
Study for Chapter Test

Assessment

Test, Chapter 7 45 min.
- Administer Chapter 7 Test. Select from Testing Program, Alternative Assessment Guide, or Test Generator.

Kapitel 7: Stadt oder Land?
Suggested Lesson Plans — 90-Minute Block Schedule

Block 1

LOCATION OPENER 15 min.
- Present Location Opener, pp. 178–181
- Geography Connection, ATE, p. 177A
- Show **Stuttgart** Video
- Do Viewing and Post-viewing Activities, Video Guide, p. 27

CHAPTER OPENER 5 min.
- Background Information, ATE, p. 181M
- Culture Note, ATE, p. 181M

LOS GEHT'S! 20 min.
- Preteaching Vocabulary, ATE, p. 181N
- Advance Organizer, ATE, p. 181N
- Thinking Critically, ATE, p. 181N
- Play Audio CD for **Los geht's!**, pp. 184–185
- Have students read **Los geht's!**, pp. 184–185
- Teaching Suggestions, Video Guide, p. 44
- Show **Los geht's!** Video

ERSTE STUFE
Reading Selection, p. 187 20 min.
- Teaching Suggestion, ATE, p. 181O
- **Wo wohnst du lieber?**, p. 187
- Do Activities 6 and 7, p. 188

Wortschatz, p. 188 10 min.
- Presenting **Wortschatz**, ATE, p. 181O
- Teaching Transparency 7-1
- Do Activity 8, p. 188

So sagt man das!/Wortschatz, p. 189 15 min.
- Presenting **So sagt man das!**, ATE p. 181O
- Presenting **Wortschatz**, ATE, p. 181P
- Play Audio CD for Activity 9, p. 189
- Do Activity 10, p. 189

Wrap-Up 5 min.
- Students respond to questions about which of two cities they prefer

Homework Options
Pupil's Edition, p. 186, Comprehension Acts. 1–5
Grammatikheft, pp. 55–56, Acts. 1–4
Übungsheft, p. 73; p. 74, Act. 1

Block 2

ERSTE STUFE
Quick Review 10 min.
- Check homework, Grammatikheft, pp. 55–56, Acts. 1–4

Grammatik p. 190 20 min.
- Presenting **Grammatik**, ATE, p. 181P
- Do Activities 11 and 12, p. 190
- Do Activities 5–7, p. 57, Grammatikheft
- Do Activities 2–7, pp. 74–76, Übungsheft

LANDESKUNDE 20 min.
- Pre-viewing Suggestion, Video Guide, p. 47
- Background Information, ATE, p. 181Q
- Show **Landeskunde** Video
- Do Activities A and B, p. 77, Übungsheft
- Do **Landeskunde** Activity, Interactive CD-ROM

Quiz Review 20 min.
- Do Additional Listening Activities 7-1 and 7-2, pp. 55–56
- Do Communicative Activity 7-1, pp. 37–38
- Do **Mehr Grammatikübungen**, Erste Stufe

Quiz 20 min.
- Quiz 7-1A or 7-1B

Homework Options
Activities for Communication, pp. 135–136, prepare Situation 7-1

Block 3

ZWEITE STUFE
Quick Review 10 min.
- Return and review Quiz 7-1
- Bell Work, ATE, p. 181Q
- Do Situation 7-1

Reading Selection, p. 192 10 min.
- Teaching Suggestion, ATE, p. 181Q
- Do Activity 13, p. 192

Ein wenig Grammatik, p. 192 10 min.
- Presenting **Ein wenig Grammatik**, ATE, p. 181R
- Do Activity 8, p. 58, Grammatikheft

So sagt man das!/Wortschatz, pp. 192–193 15 min.
- Presenting **So sagt man das!**, ATE, p. 181R
- Presenting **Wortschatz**, p. 181R
- Teaching Transparencies 7-A, 7-B
- Play Audio CD for Activity 14, p. 193
- Do Activity 15, p. 193

Grammatik, p. 194 25 min.
- Presenting **Grammatik**, ATE, p. 181R
- Do Activities 17–19, p. 195
- Do Activities 11–13, pp. 59–60, Grammatikheft
- Play Game, **Gegenteile nennen**, ATE, p. 181C

Quiz Review 15 min.
- Do **Mehr Grammatikübungen**, Zweite Stufe
- Do Activities 2–3, Interactive CD-ROM

Wrap-Up 5 min.
- Students respond to questions about what they wish for themselves

Homework Options
Pupil's Edition, p. 194, Act. 16
Grammatikheft, pp. 58–59, Acts. 9–10
Übungsheft, pp. 78–80, Acts. 1–7

For alternative lesson plans by chapter section, to create your own customized plans, or to preview all resources available for this chapter, use the **One-Stop Planner CD-ROM**, Disc 2.

 For additional homework suggestions, see activities accompanied by this symbol throughout the chapter.

Block 4

ZWEITE STUFE
Quick Review 10 min.
- Check homework, Übungsheft, pp. 78–80, Acts. 1–7

Quiz 20 min.
- Quiz 7-2A or 7-2B

ZUM LESEN 20 min.
- Present **Lesestrategie**, p. 196
- Do Activities 1–8, pp. 196–197

DRITTE STUFE
Wortschatz, p. 198 25 min.
- Presenting **Wortschatz**, ATE, p. 181U
- Teaching Transparency 7-2
- Play Audio CD for Activity 20, p. 198
- Read **Der Lärm wird größer!**, p. 199
- Do Activity 21, p. 199

So sagt man das!, p. 199 10 min.
- Presenting **So sagt man das!**, ATE, p. 181V
- Do Activity 22, p. 200

Wrap-Up 5 min.
- Students answer questions about what causes noise pollution

Homework Options
Grammatikheft, p. 61, Acts. 14–15
Übungsheft, p. 81, Acts. 1–5; pp. 82–83, Acts. 1–4

Block 5

DRITTE STUFE
Quick Review 15 min.
- Return and review Quiz 7-2
- Check homework, Übungsheft, p. 81, Acts. 1–5; pp. 82–83, Acts. 1–4

Grammatik, p. 200 25 min.
- Presenting **Grammatik**, ATE, p. 181V
- Do Activities 23 and 24, p. 200
- Do Activity 25, p. 201
- Do Activities 18–19, p. 63, Grammatikheft
- Do Activities 5–6, pp. 83–84, Übungsheft

So sagt man das!, p. 201 20 min.
- Presenting **So sagt man das!**, ATE, p. 181V
- Do Activities 26 and 27, p. 201
- Do Activity 5, Interactive CD-ROM

Quiz Review 25 min.
- Do **Mehr Grammatikübungen, Dritte Stufe**
- Do Additional Listening Activities 7-5 and 7-6, pp. 57–58

Wrap-Up 5 min.
- Students answer questions about why they prefer to live in the city or in the country

Homework Options
Pupil's Edition, p. 201, Acts. 28 and 29
Grammatikheft, p. 61, Acts. 14–15
Übungsheft, pp. 82–84, Acts. 1–6
Interaktive Spiele, see ATE, p. 181F

Block 6

DRITTE STUFE
Quick Review 15 min.
- Check homework, Übungsheft, pp. 82–84, Acts. 1–6

Quiz 20 min.
- Quiz 7-3A or 7-3B

ANWENDUNG 30 min.
- Do **Anwendung** Activities 1–6, pp. 206–207

Kann ich's wirklich? 20 min.
- Do questions 1–6, p. 208

Wrap-Up 5 min.
- Students respond to **Kann ich's wirklich?** questions

Homework Options
Internet Aktivitäten, see ATE, p. 181F
Study for Chapter Test

Block 7

ANWENDUNG
Quick Review 10 min.
- Return and review Quiz 7-3

Chapter Review 35 min.
- Review chapter functions, vocabulary, and grammar; choose from **Mehr Grammatikübungen**, Grammar Tutor for Students of German, Activities for Communication, Listening Activities, Interactive CD-ROM Tutor, or **Interaktive Spiele**
- Review test format and provide sample test items for students

Test, Chapter 7 45 min.
- Administer Chapter 7 Test. Select from Testing Program, Alternative Assessment Guide, or Test Generator.

Kapitel 7: Stadt oder Land?
Teaching Suggestions, pages 182–209

PAGES 182–183

CHAPTER OPENER

Pacing Tips
The **Erste Stufe** begins with a reading that leads up to lists of advantages and disadvantages of living in a city or in the country. Students learn how to form the comparative forms of adjectives on p. 190. The **Zweite Stufe** focuses on wishes for a dream house and the future, with a presentation of adjective endings following **ein**-words on p. 194. The adjective endings of comparatives are discussed in the **Dritte Stufe**. Noise pollution is the topic of the **Wortschatz** and a short reading. Because all three **Stufen** present a similar amount of new materials, you will probably spend about an equal amount of time on each **Stufe**. For Lesson Plans and timing suggestions, see pages 181I–181L.

Meeting the Standards
Communication
- Expressing preference and giving a reason, p. 189
- Expressing wishes, p. 192
- Agreeing with reservations, p. 199
- Justifying your answers, p. 201

Cultures
- **Landeskunde**, p. 191
- Background Information, p. 181M
- Culture Note, p. 181M
- Language Note, p. 181O
- Background Information, p. 181O

Connections
- Geography Connection, p. 181P
- Geography Connection, p. 181Q
- Family Link, p. 181W
- Language-to-Language, p. 181X

Comparisons
- Background Information, p. 181Q
- Teaching Suggestion, p. 181T

Communities
- Career Path, p. 181V

For resource information, see the **One-Stop Planner CD-ROM**, Disc 2.

Cultures and Communities

Background Information
Das Neue Schloss was built as a residence for **Herzog Carl Alexander** in the 18th century. The **Jubiläumssäule**, which stands in the middle of the **Schlossplatz**, was added in 1841. The palace was almost completely destroyed during World War II and rebuilt afterward. Today the palace houses two government offices and is used by the **Landesregierung** for official and social purposes.

Culture Note
The cost of housing is extremely high in Germany. Owning or living in a house is a source of great pride to those living there. Germans often keep flowers and potted plants on window sills and balconies. For those who would like a garden but live in an apartment, **Schrebergärten** are a good alternative. People can lease a small plot of land, usually located at the edge of town, and use it for gardening purposes.

Building on Previous Skills
Make an enlarged transparency or a class set of the city map of Stuttgart from p. 356 of Level 1. Ask students to imagine they are students at the university on **Keplerstraße**. Where would they like to have an apartment and why? (You may want to keep the maps for other activities in this chapter.)

Chapter Sequence

Los geht's!	p. 184
Erste Stufe	p. 187
Landeskunde	p. 191
Zweite Stufe	p. 192
Zum Lesen	p. 196
Dritte Stufe	p. 198
Mehr Grammatikübungen	p. 202
Anwendung	p. 206
Kann ich's wirklich?	p. 208
Wortschatz	p. 209

LOS GEHT'S!

Teaching Resources
pp. 184–186

PRINT
- Lesson Planner, p. 32
- Video Guide, pp. 43–44, 46
- Übungsheft, p. 73

MEDIA
- One-Stop Planner
- Video Program
  Los geht's!
  Videocassette 3, 04:55–10:03
  Videocassette 5 (captioned version), 39:40–44:46
  Fortsetzung
  Videocassette 3, 10:06–10:55
  Videocassette 5 (captioned version), 44:51–45:50
- DVD Tutor, Disc 2
- Audio Compact Discs, CD7, Trs. 1–2
- **Los geht's!** Transparencies

PAGES 184–185

Los geht's! Transparencies

Preteaching Vocabulary

Identifying keywords
Start by asking students to guess the context of the **Los geht's!** episode (discussions about where people live). Then have students use the German they know and the context of the situation to identify key words and phrases that tell what is happening. Students should first list the topics that occur in the interviews and look for words that seem important or that occur several times. Here are some of the words and phrases they might identify as keywords: ❷ Umfrage; wohnen; ❸ geschieden; Innenstadt; ❹ Vorteile; Nachteile; Verkehr; Umgebung; Luft; ❻ wünschen; ⓫ eigenes.

Then have students list keywords in the conversation that occurs at Katrin's house. Which of the keywords are cognates? Which of the keywords do they already know?

Fortsetzung
You may choose to continue with the **Fortsetzung** of *Das Interview* now or wait until later in the chapter. For a synopsis of the **Los geht's!** and **Fortsetzung** episodes, see p. 181E.

Advance Organizer
Ask students what type of questions they would ask somebody to find out more about a) the area they live in, b) their home, and c) how they feel about living there. Have students compile a list of possible questions and write them on the board or on a transparency.

Connections and Comparisons

Thinking Critically

Analyzing After students have watched the video, ask them to look at Photo 1 of **Los geht's!**. What can students say about interview etiquette? How do Germans make polite inquiries?

PAGE 186

Using the Captioned Video/DVD

❶ An alternate way to complete Activity 1 would be to play the captioned version of *Das Interview* on Videocassette 5.
Note: The *DVD Tutor* contains captions for all sections of the *Video Program*.

Comprehension Check

Challenge
❶ After students have watched the video or listened to the compact disc, use these eight questions to check for comprehension. Do this orally. If you feel some students are insecure about answering the questions, let them look at the text.

Visual Learners
❷ Make a chart on the board with two columns for the **Vorteile** and **Nachteile** of living in a **Großstadt** and two columns for the **Vorteile** and **Nachteile** of a **Kleinstadt**. Ask students to look for relevant phrases in the text and record them on the chart on the board. Review all expressions with the class.

Teaching Suggestions
❹ Have students work in pairs to answer the questions. Upon completion, call on students to share their answers with the class.

❹ This activity could be assigned for homework. Students could begin an outline in class and then complete the final draft at home.

STANDARDS: 1.2

ERSTE STUFE

Teaching Resources
pp. 187–191

PRINT
- Lesson Planner, p. 33
- TPR Storytelling Book, pp. 48–49
- Listening Activities, pp. 51, 55–56
- Activities for Communication, pp. 37–38, 98, 101, 135–136
- Grammatikheft, pp. 55–57
- Grammar Tutor for Students of German, Chapter 7
- Übungsheft, pp. 74–76
- Testing Program, pp. 171–174
- Alternative Assessment Guide, p. 38
- Student Make-Up Assignments, Chapter 7

MEDIA
- One-Stop Planner
- Audio Compact Discs, CD7, Trs. 3, 12, 17–18
- Teaching Transparencies Situation 7-1
- **Mehr Grammatikübungen** Answers
- Grammatikheft Answers
- Interactive CD-ROM Tutor, Disc 2
- DVD Tutor, Disc 2

Cultures and Communities

Language Note
The adjective **piekfein** is a colloquial expression used to describe immaculate conditions. Britta's tone is somewhat defensive, but she also expresses hope for change by using the adverb **noch**.

Background Information
A **Gesellenprüfung**, which Norbert plans to take in another year, is an examination that follows two to three years of apprenticeship in a professional trade under the guidance of a **Meister**. The apprentice system requires all apprentices to undergo several years of practical on-the-job training, with additional vocational theory classes. Apprentices receive **Ausbildungsgeld**, a minimal salary, while training.

Connections and Comparisons

Thinking Critically
Drawing Inferences Britta compares the homes in the former East to those in the West. Can students tell how she feels by looking at the adverbs and adjectives she uses?

Drawing Inferences After students have read the two interviews, ask them with which of the two German students they can best identify and why.

▶ PAGE 187

Bell Work
In pairs, have students ask each other in German how long they have lived in their present home and ask them to tell one thing they like and one thing they dislike about their home. Survey students as to how often they have moved from one home to another.

Teaching Suggestion
Ask several students to take turns reading the interviews with Britta and Norbert aloud in class. Other students should jot down any words or expressions they do not recognize. Explain new vocabulary, giving German definitions or synonyms when possible.

▶ PAGE 188

PRESENTING: Wortschatz
To introduce the new vocabulary, use names of cities, towns, suburbs, and villages you think students will be familiar with. Once you feel students are comfortable with the new expressions, ask them to give you an example of **ein Dorf, eine Großstadt, eine Kleinstadt,** and so on.

▶ PAGE 189

PRESENTING: So sagt man das!
To practice previously learned material as well as new expressions, ask students to express preferences in a different context, for example, **essen, trinken, spielen, lesen,** or **hören.** Have them use the expressions from **So sagt man das!** in short sentences.
Example:
Ich finde die Musik von Madonna besser als die Musik von den Beatles.

PRESENTING: Wortschatz

On the board or a transparency, set up a table with four columns: 1) **Vorteile in der Stadt,** 2) **Nachteile in der Stadt,** 3) **Vorteile auf dem Land,** and 4) **Nachteile auf dem Land.** Then ask students for their suggestions about what information should go in each column. When they mention an advantage or disadvantage that appears in this **Wortschatz,** add the German equivalent to the table. Continue until all the new vocabulary has been introduced, prompting students if necessary to get the last few terms. Then ask several students in the class **Wo wohnst du lieber, auf dem Land oder in der Stadt?** and have them reply using **denn-** or **weil-**clauses and the new vocabulary.

Connections and Comparisons

Geography Connection

9 Before students begin the listening activity, ask them to locate the four places on a map or in an atlas. (All four places are located in the state of Baden-Württemberg, ranging in size as follows: Stuttgart, Esslingen, Bietigheim, Schönaich.)

PAGE 190

PRESENTING: Grammatik

Comparative forms of adjectives A simple way to teach comparisons is by using concrete examples. Be prepared to bring several items of equal and unequal size and teach the comparatives by contrasting the items.
Example:
Schuhe: kleiner als
länger als
größer als
so groß wie

To provide further practice, ask students to make comparisons using the same items. Encourage them to make comparisons using other objects in the classroom.

TPR Total Physical Response

To further practice the comparative forms of adjectives, give students commands such as:
Kim, zeig auf Schuhe in der Klasse, die größer als deine sind!
Richard, finde einen Schüler, der Schuhe trägt, die kleiner als deine sind!
Kelli, gib Wendy eine Schultasche, die so groß wie deine ist!

Teaching Suggestions

11 After groups have completed the activity, call on each group to share with the rest of the class an advantage and a disadvantage. Write these down as students call them out. Continue discussing and contrasting the points listed on the board with the entire class.

12 To make this activity more realistic, ask students to review the interview in **Los geht's!** on pp. 184–185. Then have students do this activity in a similar way. Students may want to record their interviews on audio- or videocassette.

PAGE 191

LANDESKUNDE

Teaching Resources
p. 191

PRINT
- Video Guide, pp. 43–44, 47
- Übungsheft, p. 77

MEDIA
- One-Stop Planner
- Video Program
  Videocassette 3, 11:34–17:47
- DVD Tutor, Disc 2
- Audio Compact Discs, CD7, Trs. 4–8
- Interactive CD-ROM Tutor, Disc 2

Teaching Suggestion

Begin **Landeskunde** by having students do the prereading activity. Then have students listen to the compact disc or watch the interviews on video.

Building on Previous Skills

Ask students to look at the name of the place where each of the students is from. Can students recall in what general part of Germany each place is located and in what **Bundesland?**

Group Work

Divide the class into groups of three or four students. Have each group member read one of the interviews, then ask the group to work through Activities A1–A2. Have each group share its answers with the rest of the class.

Connections and Comparisons

Thinking Critically

Drawing Inferences Based on what students know of these four locations, have them place each in a category (**Großstadt, Kleinstadt, Dorf**) assuming that a **Großstadt** has a population of at least 100,000, a **Kleinstadt** between 5,000 and 20,000, and a **Dorf** under 5,000. (Berlin: **Großstadt**, Hamburg: **Großstadt**, Wedel: **Kleinstadt**, Bietigheim: **Kleinstadt**)

Background Information

When visitors travel around Germany for the first time, they might be struck by the sight of a typical German city. Visitors will notice that only the very large cities have skyscrapers. Even in cities considered **Großstädte**, the tallest buildings are generally no more than about ten stories high.

Geography Connection

Have students use an atlas, almanac, or encyclopedia to find out the populations of the six largest cities in Germany. Then have students compare the list to cities of similar size in the United States. (1. Berlin: 3,478,000, 2. Hamburg: 1,704,000, 3. Munich: 1,251,000, 4. Cologne: 966,000, 5. Frankfurt a. M: 650,000, 6. Essen: 616,000)

Teacher Note

Mention to your students that the **Landeskunde** will also be included in Quiz 7-1B given at the end of the **Erste Stufe** and in the test given at the end of the chapter.

Play the game **Gegenteile nennen.** See p. 181C for the procedure.

Make copies of the map of Stuttgart on p. 356 of the Level 1 *Pupil's Edition* and hand them out to your class. Ask students to look at the map and choose one or two sites they would like to visit if they were in Stuttgart. They should also give reasons for their choices.

Assess

- Testing Program, pp. 171–174
  Quiz 7-1A, Quiz 7-1B
  Audio CD7, Tr. 12
- Student Make-Up Assignments
  Chapter 7, Alternative Quiz
- Alternative Assessment Guide, p. 38

ZWEITE STUFE

Teaching Resources
pp. 192–195

PRINT
- Lesson Planner, p. 34
- TPR Storytelling Book, pp. 50–51
- Listening Activities, pp. 52, 56–57
- Activities for Communication, pp. 39–40, 99, 101, 135–136
- Grammatikheft, pp. 58-60
- Grammar Tutor for Students of German, Chapter 7
- Übungsheft, pp. 78–80
- Testing Program, pp. 175–178
- Alternative Assessment Guide, p. 38
- Student Make-Up Assignments, Chapter 7

MEDIA
- One-Stop Planner
- Audio Compact Discs, CD7, Trs. 9, 13, 19–20
- Teaching Transparencies
  Vocabulary 7-A, 7-B
  Mehr Grammatikübungen Answers
  Grammatikheft Answers
- Interactive CD-ROM Tutor, Disc 2
- DVD Tutor, Disc 2

PAGE 192

 **Bell Work**
Ask students to think about their room at home. Is there anything they wish they could change to improve the room? Is there anything they would like to get for their room to make it perfect?

Teaching Suggestion

13 Ask six students to read the six bubbles on this page. Then ask students to work with a partner to answer Questions 1 and 2 of Activity 13. Students should then take turns telling a partner with which students they can identify and why.

PRESENTING: Ein wenig Grammatik

Dative reflexive pronoun Tell students that when expressing wishes in German, they should use the reflexive verb **sich wünschen,** with the reflexive pronoun in the dative case. Why must the pronoun take the dative? (It plays the role of an indirect object; one wishes something *for* him- or herself.) Then allow students five minutes to write down a sentence expressing a wish of their own. Encourage them to be as creative and specific as possible. When they have finished, take up their papers and read them aloud to the class, asking students to guess who the author of each wish is.

PRESENTING: So sagt man das!

Students should already be familiar with the **möchte**-forms in the context of saying what they would like to eat (see Chapter 9, Level 1). Ask students to practice the new expressions by telling the class what they would like for their next birthday. Ask students to look back at **Los geht's!** and find what Katrin wished for to improve her room. How were the expressions used in the context of **Los geht's!**?

Teaching Suggestion

Have students look back at the six speech bubbles at the beginning of this section and tell for what each of the speakers wishes.
Examples:
Sven wünscht sich einen guten Wagen, einen tollen Job …
Britta wünscht sich und ihren Mitmenschen eine saubere Umwelt, …

▶ **PAGE 193**

PRESENTING: Wortschatz

The items in this **Wortschatz** provide students with the vocabulary to discuss abstract concepts and ideas. After introducing the vocabulary, have students choose at least two or three non-material things they wish for most. You may also introduce the following additional vocabulary for further practice:
ein Leben
  ohne Krankheit
  ohne Familienkonflikte
  ohne (finanzielle) Probleme.

Communication for All Students

A Slower Pace
15 You may want to offer some specific suggestions to make this activity more concrete for students. (Examples: this school year, your family, the year you graduate, your first job)

Speaking Assessment

15 You might want to have pairs come to your desk to assess their interviews. You may wish to use the following rubric for evaluation.

Speaking Rubric

	Points 4	3	2	1
Content (Complete – Incomplete)				
Comprehension (Total – Little)				
Comprehensibility (Comprehensible – Incomprehensible)				
Accuracy (Accurate – Seldom accurate)				
Fluency (Fluent – Not fluent)				

18–20: A   16–17: B   14–15: C   12–13: D   Under 12: F

▶ **PAGE 194**

PRESENTING: Grammatik

Adjective endings The students will better understand the reason for the different adjective endings if you first show them the change from definite article to indefinite article and adjective:
der Garten —> ein großer Garten
die Wohnung —> eine nette Wohnung
das Zimmer —> ein schönes Zimmer
For practice, ask students to repeat Activity 16, this time adding a second adjective to their wish.

PAGE 195

Communication for All Students

Tactile Learners

18 Along with the letter students write describing where they live, ask them to draw a map of their neighborhood or area that indicates places such as parks, schools, stores, or churches. In addition, students should draw the floor plan of their house or apartment, labeling each room.

Challenge

- Ask all students to give a detailed response to the question: **Sag mal, wo wohnst du denn?** Students should write the longest descriptive sentence they can think of, such as the one below:
Ich wohne in einem netten Haus mit einem schönen Garten in einer ruhigen Straße in einem kleinen Dorf an einem schönen See, nicht weit von einer kleinen Kirche.
Call on a few individual students to read their sentences aloud.

Teaching Suggestion

Tell students to imagine that they will be granted three wishes. Ask them to tell you what their three wishes are.

Assess

- Testing Program, pp. 175–178
  Quiz 7-2A, Quiz 7-2B
  Audio CD7, Tr. 13
- Student Make-Up Assignments
  Chapter 7, Alternative Quiz
- Alternative Assessment Guide, p. 38

ZUM LESEN

Teaching Resources
pp. 196–197

PRINT
- Lesson Planner, p. 36
- Übungsheft, p. 81
- Reading Strategies and Skills, Chapter 7
- Lies mit mir! 2, Chapter 7

MEDIA
- One-Stop Planner

Prereading
Building Context

Where would students build their dream houses if they were millionaires and why?

Teacher Note

Activity 1 is a prereading activity.

Reading
Teacher Note

1 Students who answered Question B in the **Landeskunde** will have done some thinking about overcrowding in Germany and how it might affect personal living space; because of the scarcity of space in some areas, there is no room for many teenagers to have their own room.

Teaching Suggestions

- Tell students that the format of a text clues the reader in on the intent of the writer and should influence how the reader approaches it. When you read a poem, for example, you need to be sensitive to the emotions the images evoke.

- Letting one or more volunteers read the poem *Traumhaus* aloud to the class while the others just listen may help bring out the quality of a child's song (regular rhyme and almost sing-song rhythm).

- Give students the following guidelines to help them read the poem:

Read the poem slowly two or three times. If possible, just listen while someone else reads it aloud. What visual impression does the pattern **X aus Y** (*something made of something*) invoke? Could you sketch the **Traumhaus?** How do the **zwei Türme** (*towers*) fit into your picture? Are they an expected element or do they shift the picture into a slightly different focus?

Thinking Critically

4 Drawing Inferences After students have read the poem, ask them who the author of this poem might be and how old he or she might be. Then ask students on what evidence they based their guesses.

Communication for All Students

Tactile Learners

4 Ask students to use the images created by the author to draw a picture of the **Traumhaus**.

Cooperative Learning

Divide students into groups of three. Each student has a specific role: writer, discussion leader, or reporter. Set a time limit of at least 30 minutes for students to complete Activities 5–7. Ask each group to read the test and then answer each question to find out what **Wohntyp** they are. Encourage students to keep their discussion in the target language. Once students have added up their score and interpreted it using the **Lösung**, the reporter uses the information the writer recorded to share his or her group's test outcomes with the rest of the class.

Thinking Critically

Analyzing Ask students where they might find this type of a quiz.

Teaching Suggestion

Pair students up and ask them to write one new multiple-choice question that could be added to the quiz. Then have pairs share their questions with the class. Write all of the new questions on a transparency and have the class "take the test" by responding to each question orally.

Post-Reading

Teacher Note

Activity 8 is a post-reading task that will show whether students can apply what they have learned.

Connections and Comparisons

Teaching Suggestion

Based on what students have learned in previous chapters and this reading selection, ask students to compare a typical American student's room to that of a German student. Make a list of comparisons on the board or butcher paper. Then discuss advantages and disadvantages of both rooms.

Zum Lesen Answers
Answers to Activity 1 Answers will vary.
Answers to Activity 2 furniture; article, poem, self-test
Answers to Activity 3 approx. 88–132 square feet; answers will vary.
Answers to Activity 4 furnishing a dream house; sweets
Answers to Activity 5 teenagers from Munich; what kind of person you are in regard to living conditions
Answers to Activity 6
sich vorstellen (reflexive verb)—*to imagine*
Himmelbett (noun)—*canopy bed*
Umzug (noun)—*move*
sich verhalten (reflexive verb)—*to behave*
verkaufen (verb)—*to sell*
wählen (verb)—*to choose*
schädlich (adverb)—*harmful*
Answers to Activity 7
Kuschelecke (noun)—*quiet corner*
giftfrei (adjective)—*non-toxic*
anbieten (verb)—*to offer*
vertreiben (verb)—*to drive away*
einschüchtern (verb)—*to intimidate*
Schmuse-Typ (noun)—*cuddly type*
einrichten (verb)—*to furnish*

DRITTE STUFE

Teaching Resources
pp. 198–201

PRINT
- Lesson Planner, p. 35
- TPR Storytelling Book, pp. 52–53
- Listening Activities, pp. 52, 57–58
- Activities for Communication, pp. 41–42, 100, 101, 135–136
- Grammatikheft, pp. 61–63
- Grammar Tutor for Students of German, Chapter 7
- Übungsheft, pp. 82–84
- Testing Program, pp. 179–182
- Alternative Assessment Guide, p. 38
- Student Make-Up Assignments, Chapter 7

MEDIA
- One-Stop Planner
- Audio Compact Discs, CD7, Trs. 10, 14, 21–22
- Teaching Transparencies Situation 7-2
  Mehr Grammatikübungen Answers
  Grammatikheft Answers
- Interactive CD-ROM Tutor, Disc 2
- DVD Tutor, Disc 2

▶ **PAGE 198**

 **Bell Work**

In Chapter 7, Level 1, students were introduced to expressions concerning the environment. Ask students to make a list of what they do to help protect the environment. (Examples: **Müll sortieren; Rad fahren anstatt Auto fahren**)

PRESENTING: Wortschatz

Use realia, such as pictures from magazines or newspapers, to teach various modes of transportation, including new as well as previously learned vocabulary. Ask students if they can think of other sources of undesirable noise. (Examples: **Straßenbau, Heavy-Metal-Musik, Sirenen, Feuerwerk**) If students can't think of a particular word, encourage them to describe it in German.

Communication for All Students

Challenge

After students are familiar with the three sentences in the **Wortschatz**, including the **man**-construction and **wenn**-clauses, have them manipulate the vocabulary in the following ways:

- Change the last three picture captions into the same pattern.
  Example: **Man vermeidet Lärm, wenn man langsam fährt.**

- Make up other sentences using **man** and **wenn**-clauses.
  Example: **Man produziert Lärm, wenn man den Rasen mäht.**

Thinking Critically

20 Drawing Inferences As an advance organizer to the activity, write the opposites **laut** and **leise** on the board. Ask students to think of words and phrases that they associate with each of these adjectives.

▶ **PAGE 199**

Teaching Suggestion

21 After students have read the selection *Der Lärm wird größer!*, ask them to find the various modes of transportation that were mentioned. Make a list. Ask students if they can think of synonyms for the following words from the reading: **Bevölkerung, Personenkraftwagen, Kraftfahrer, zuschlagen,** and **Lärm machen.** Ask students to work with a partner to answer Questions 1–3.

Teacher to Teacher

Gertraud Irwin
Morgantown High School
Morgantown, West Virginia

Gertraud uses "Lebende Sätze" to reinforce adjective endings and word order.

"I make up one long sentence containing several different adjectives and adjective endings. Example: **Unser Haus hat ein großes Wohnzimmer, eine moderne Küche und einen schönen Garten mit einem tollen Pool.** I write each word on a separate index card. As students enter the classroom, they are handed a card. Students are instructed to look at each other's cards and try to recreate the sentence by lining up in front of the class. Students without cards function as 'advisors.' Each student then reads his/her word using correct pronunciation and intonation."

Communication for All Students

A Slower Pace

21 Help students understand the reading selection by giving them German synonyms and definitions for difficult or unknown words and phrases.
Examples:
Der Lärm nimmt zu. —-> Der Lärm wird immer größer.
Lärmminderung —-> Lärmreduzierung

Thinking Critically

Drawing Inferences Ask students if they can think of places where road signs encourage noise reduction. (Examples: hospitals or senior citizen homes)

COMMUNITY LINK

Ask students to contact the local government to ask if the area has a problem with noise pollution and, if so, what measures have been taken so far to decrease or reduce the noise. Have students report to the class what they have learned.

PRESENTING: So sagt man das!

To help students become familiar with the new ways to express reservation, ask them to react to what you say. Repeat the same statement several times in order to get several different responses.
Examples:
Es ist ideal, in einem Vorort zu wohnen.

- Ja schon, aber der Verkehr ist furchtbar.
- Ja, aber es ist so weit in die Stadt.
- Da stimme ich dir zu, aber es ist auch sehr teuer.

Remind students of other phrases they have learned that could be used to agree with reservations.
Examples:
Das finde ich auch, aber …
Ja, ich glaube aber, dass …

To allow students to practice the expressions, ask them to work with a partner, discussing topics such as the latest trends in music, clothing, movies, books, and cars.

Examples:
— Findest du Rock nicht besser als Countrymusik?
— Ja schon, aber Rock geht mir manchmal auf die Nerven!

Cultures and Communities

Career Path

Have students pair up to think of reasons someone working for a US-based human rights organization might find a knowledge of German helpful. (Suggestions: They could keep track of issues pertaining to human rights in the German-speaking countries; if a citizen of another country sought asylum in Germany, they could follow the case and help their organization to intercede, if necessary, on the individual's behalf.)

PAGE 200

PRESENTING: Grammatik

Adjective endings of comparatives Review the adjective endings of all genders and cases the students have learned. Then have them list all the adjectives they know that could be applied to cars.
Examples: sportlich   schön   ruhig
           teuer   neu   bequem
           sicher   schnell

Students then go through the list, using the adjectives in the comparative form (where appropriate) to talk about the topic **Auto**.

For Additional Practice

23 Ask students to express other advantages of living in a city, using comparative forms. This activity will help students recycle previously learned vocabulary, such as places around town and other adjectives.

PAGE 201

PRESENTING: So sagt man das!

After presenting the questions and responses in **So sagt man das!**, have students refer to the Stuttgart Location Opener on pp. 178–181 to find some other reasons why people might like to live in Stuttgart. Students should express these reasons with a statement containing **halt** or **eben**.

FAMILY LINK

Have students interview members of their family about all the places they have lived. Students should ask the relative being interviewed to give a detailed description of the different places he or she has lived, as well as the advantages and disadvantages of each location.

Reteaching: Adjective endings of comparatives

Ask students to imagine that they had a terrible experience on their last vacation. Prepare a chart like the one below and have students say how their next vacation is going to be better than the last one, using the suggested phrases.

| In | unseren meinen unserem meinem | nächsten Ferien nächsten Urlaub | werden wir werde ich | gutes Wetter haben bequeme Betten haben Museen besuchen viel Geld ausgeben kleine Pensionen besuchen |

Ask students to use the fragments to create as many sentences as possible.

Teaching Suggestion

On the day you plan to do this activity, hand each student a blank family tree and give students a few minutes to fill it out. (You can use a tree of your own or the one on p. 84 of the Level 1 *Activities for Communication* ancillary.) When students have finished, have them describe their family (or a fictitious family) in terms of who is older and younger, larger and smaller, and so on.

Example:
Meine Mutter hat eine jüngere Schwester, die Tante Barbara.
Onkel Daniel hat einen größeren Bruder, den Onkel Charles.

Assess

▶ Testing Program, pp. 179–182
  Quiz 7-3A, Quiz 7-3B
  Audio CD7, Tr. 14

▶ Student Make-Up Assignments
  Chapter 7, Alternative Quiz

▶ Alternative Assessment Guide, p. 38

PAGES 202–205

MEHR GRAMMATIKÜBUNGEN

The **Mehr Grammatikübungen** activities are designed as supplemental activities for the grammatical concepts presented in the chapter. You might use them as additional practice, for review, or for assessment.

For more grammar presentations, review, and practice, refer to the following:
- Grammatikheft
- Grammar Tutor for Students of German
- Grammar Summary on pp. R20–R36
- Übungsheft
- Grammar and Vocabulary quizzes (Testing Program)
- Test Generator
- Interactive CD-ROM Tutor
- **Interaktive Spiele** at **go.hrw.com**

PAGES 206–207

ANWENDUNG

Video Wrap-up
Videocassette 3, 04:55–22:09
Videocassette 5 (captioned version), 39:40–45:50
DVD Tutor, Disc 2

At this time, you might want to use the video resources for additional review and enrichment. These resources are also available via the Enhanced Online Student Edition.
See *Video Guide* for suggestions regarding:
- **Das Interview** (Dramatic episode)
- **Landeskunde** Interviews
- **Videoclips** (Authentic footage)

Apply and Assess

A Slower Pace

1 Tell students that they will hear the recording twice. As they listen the first time, they should listen only for information answering the question **wo**. As they listen the second time, students should listen for information answering the question **warum.**

Portfolio Assessment

2 You might want to suggest this activity as an oral portfolio item for your students. See *Alternative Assessment Guide*, p. 24.

4 You might want to suggest this activity as a written portfolio item for your students. See *Alternative Assessment Guide*, p. 24.

Apply and Assess

Process Writing

5 You may want to give your students the option of using their essays to compare and contrast the differences in quality of life between city and country. How has their environment changed since their move? Is their residence in the city at all similar to their home in the country? When students have finished their comparisons, have them wrap up their essays with a sentence summarizing their overall opinion, such as **Ich habe das Leben auf dem Land gern, aber das Leben in der Stadt gefällt mir besser.**

▶ PAGE 208

KANN ICH'S WIRKLICH?

This page helps students prepare for the test. It is a brief checklist of the major points covered in the chapter. The students should be reminded that it is only a checklist and not necessarily everything that will appear on the test.

For additional self check options, refer students to the *Grammar Tutor*, the *Interactive CD-ROM Tutor*, and the Online self-test for this chapter.

▶ PAGE 209

WORTSCHATZ

Connections and Comparisons

Language-to-Language

You may want to mention to your students that the German equivalent of "to like something" uses a construction similar to the one used in Spanish and French. German, French, and Spanish use a verb in the third person singular that requires an indirect object pronoun.
English: *I like it.*
German: **Es gefällt mir.**
Spanish: **Me encanta.**
French: **Ça me plaît.**

Ask students to brainstorm similar German constructions. (Examples: **Es tut mir Leid; Es geht mir gut; Mir ist schlecht; Was fehlt dir?**)

Review and Assess

Teaching Suggestion

To practice talking about where you live, give students an example, such as New York, and ask them: **Was für eine Stadt ist New York?** They should respond with: **New York ist eine Großstadt.** Use locations in Germany, Austria, Switzerland, and Liechtenstein for this activity to increase geography skills.

Circumlocution

Circumlocution can be used to review the German words for the different rooms of the house and areas around the house listed in the **Zweite Stufe.** Play **Das treffende Wort suchen** with the presenter telling what one can do or what one can find in a certain room: **Man kann dort … (schlafen). Man findet in diesem Zimmer … (einen Tisch).** See p. 3C for procedures.

Tactile Learners

- Provide students with a blank copy of a floor plan of a house, including the yard, and ask them to label all rooms and places you have numbered. Time this activity.

Visual Learners

- Show pictures of all the modes of transportation students have studied so far. Ask students to name each, including the articles that accompany the nouns. Write each noun on the board or on a transparency. In addition, you may ask students to describe the vehicles in more detail in order to practice the use of descriptive adjectives and adjectives following **ein**-words.

Teacher Note

Give the **Kapitel 7** Chapter Test: *Testing Program*, pp. 183–188
Audio CD 7, Trs. 15–16.

STANDARDS: 1.1, 4.1

KAPITEL

7
Stadt oder Land?

Objectives

In this chapter you will learn to

Erste Stufe
- express preferences and give a reason

Zweite Stufe
- express wishes

Dritte Stufe
- agree, with reservations
- justify your answers

Visit Holt Online
go.hrw.com
KEYWORD: WK3 STUTTGART-7
Online Edition

◀ Ich wohne gern in einer Stadt.

Los geht's! · *Das Interview*

Los geht's! is an abridged version of the video episode.

CD 7
Trs. 1–2

Strategie Verstehen
Look at the images for the story. Where are the students? What are they doing there? What do you think they are talking about? Who do you think the older people are?

Katrin   Frank   Bettina   Judith

1
Katrin: Hallo! — Hallo, darf ich dich mal etwas fragen? Und dürfen wir dich filmen?
Frank: Ja, schon. Aber erst mal, worum geht's?

2
Katrin: Wir machen eine Umfrage für unsern Deutschunterricht. Ich möchte dich fragen, wo du wohnst, wohnst du gern dort und warum oder warum nicht?

3
Katrin: Aber erst mal, wie heißt du?
Frank: Ja, ich heiße Frank Härtle, und ich wohne hier in Stuttgart — wir, das ist meine Mutter und ich, meine Mutter ist geschieden. Wir haben eine nette Wohnung in der Innenstadt.
Katrin: Und du wohnst gern in der Stadt?
Frank: Ja, eigentlich schon. Alles ist eben in der Nähe, die Geschäfte und so …

4
Frank: Ja, das sind schon Vorteile, wenn man in der Stadt wohnt. Aber leider gibt es auch Nachteile. Es sind oft zu viele Leute in der Stadt. Und der Verkehr ist größer, und damit ist die Luft auch schmutziger als in der Umgebung. Aber, ehrlich gesagt, ich möchte nicht fort von hier, nicht fort von Stuttgart!

5
Katrin: Wo wohnst du, und wie gefällt dir dein Wohnort?
Bettina: Ich heiße Bettina, und ich wohne in der Umgebung von Stuttgart, in Bietigheim. Also, ich möchte nicht in einer großen Stadt wie Stuttgart wohnen. Ich ziehe eine kleine Stadt wie Bietigheim vor. Das Leben ist hier ruhiger, wir haben weniger Verkehr, und die Luft ist hier besser als in einer großen Stadt.

184 *hundertvierundachtzig*   STANDARDS: 1.2   KAPITEL 7   Stadt oder Land?

Bettina: Tja, was wünsche ich mir noch? Was es hier in Bietigheim nicht gibt, gibt es in Stuttgart. Und Stuttgart ist mit der Bahn nur fünfundzwanzig Minuten entfernt.
Katrin: Vielen Dank, Bettina! Das war ein toller Bericht!
Bettina: Das freut mich. Viel Glück! Tschüs!

Bei Katrin zu Hause

Katrin: Hallo! Übrigens, ich bin die Katrin. Und das ist die Judith, eine Klassenkameradin von mir.

Katrin: Hallo, Oma, Opa! Meine Großeltern wohnen auch bei uns. Sie sind gern im Garten, immer aktiv! Ja, hier bin ich zu Hause. Ein schönes Haus, nicht? — Komm! Meine Eltern sind nicht da. Sie arbeiten.

Judith: Wie viele Zimmer habt ihr denn?
Katrin: Ach ja, was haben wir? Eine Küche, ein großes Wohnzimmer, vier Schlafzimmer, ja … ein Badezimmer und zwei Toiletten. — Aber komm! Ich zeig dir mein Zimmer.

Judith: Toll! Ein eigenes Zimmer!
Katrin: Ja, das ist schon prima! Aber ich wünsch mir noch so viele Dinge: einen größeren Schreibtisch, einen bequemeren Sessel und einen größeren Schrank für meine vielen Klamotten.
Judith: Wirklich? Der ist doch groß genug!

1 Was passiert hier?

These activities check for global comprehension only. Students should not yet be expected to produce language modeled in Los geht's!

Verstehst du alles, was diese Leute sagen? Beantworte die Fragen!

1. Wer macht eine Umfrage? *1. Katrin*
2. Wofür ist diese Umfrage? *2. für den Deutschunterricht*
3. Wen hat Katrin interviewt? *3. Frank und Bettina*
4. Woher ist Frank? *4. aus Stuttgart*
5. Wo wohnt Bettina? *5. in Bietigheim*
6. Was hast du über Katrins Familie gehört? *6. Großeltern wohnen im gleichen Haus; Eltern arbeiten*
7. Und über Katrins Haus? *7. großes Haus mit einer Küche, einem Wohnzimmer, vier Schlafzimmern, einem Badezimmer und zwei Toiletten*
8. Was wünscht sich Katrin? *8. größeren Schreibtisch, bequemeren Sessel, größeren Schrank*

2 Genauer lesen

Lies den Text noch einmal und beantworte diese Fragen!

1. Frank wohnt gern in Stuttgart. — Welche Vorteile hat Stuttgart? *1. Alles ist in der Nähe, z.B. Geschäfte.*
2. Er nennt auch drei Nachteile. Was sind diese? *2. zu viele Leute in der Stadt; viel Verkehr; schmutzigere Luft*
3. Bettina zieht das Leben in einer Kleinstadt vor. Welche Vorteile nennt sie? *3. ruhigeres Leben; weniger Verkehr; bessere Luft*
4. Was tut Bettina, wenn sie etwas braucht, was es in ihrer Stadt nicht gibt? *4. Sie fährt mit der Bahn nach Stuttgart.*

3 Was ist richtig?

Ergänze die folgenden Aussagen mit der besten Antwort!

1. Frank wohnt __b__ .
   a. in Bietigheim   b. bei seiner Mutter   c. gern in einer Kleinstadt
2. Es gibt in Stuttgart Nachteile wie __a__ .
   a. viel Verkehr   b. nicht genug Geschäfte   c. bessere Luft
3. Bettina fährt nach Stuttgart __b__ .
   a. …, wenn es viel Lärm in Bietigheim gibt   b. mit der Bahn   c. …, weil es ruhiger ist
4. Katrin wünscht sich __a__ .
   a. einen größeren Schrank   b. immer mehr Klamotten   c. ihr eigenes Zimmer

4 Ein Interview

Beantworte die folgenden Fragen auf Deutsch, bitte!

1. How does Katrin initiate her interview with Frank? What does she say? How does he respond? *1. Hallo! Darf ich dich mal etwas fragen? Und dürfen wir dich filmen? — Ja, schon.*
2. What does Frank want to know first? What does he ask her? *2. Aber erst mal, worum geht's?*
3. What does Katrin give as a reason for the interview? *3. Umfrage für den Deutschunterricht*
4. What does Katrin say to Bettina at the close of the interview? *4. Vielen Dank! Das war ein toller Bericht!*
5. Using your answers to these questions as a guide, write a "framework" for an interview that you will do later in this chapter.

5 Und du?

Das Leben in einer Großstadt hat Vorteile (*advantages*) und Nachteile (*disadvantages*), wie auch das Leben auf dem Land. Wohnst du in der Stadt oder auf dem Land? In einer Großstadt oder in einer Kleinstadt? Welche Vorteile und Nachteile hat dein Wohnort? Schreib sie auf!

Storytelling Book pp. 48–49

Erste Stufe

Objectives Expressing preference and giving a reason

WK3 STUTTGART-7

Wo wohnst du lieber? In der Stadt oder auf dem Land?

Diese Frage haben wir zwei jungen Leuten gestellt. Lies, was sie gesagt haben!

Britta
17 Jahre

„Ich heiße Britta Wegener, bin 17 Jahre alt und gehe hier auf die Oberschule in Weißensee. Weißensee ist ein Stadtteil hier im Osten Berlins, also — ich meine auch im früheren Osten."

Wohnst du gern hier in Weißensee?

„Eigentlich schon, aber… na ja, die Gegend sieht im Moment noch nicht sehr schön aus. Unsere Häuser sind alt, alles sieht halt noch ziemlich grau aus und ist nicht so piekfein wie im Westen."

Möchtest du lieber woanders wohnen?

„Nö. Berlin gefällt mir. Berlin ist eine internationale Stadt; hier ist eben immer was los! Mir gefällt zum Beispiel Berlin besser als Hamburg oder sogar München. Berlin hat so viele Seen und Kanäle. Wir können segeln und Kajak fahren, im Winter können wir sogar Ski laufen auf unserm Teufelsberg.[1] Und es gibt billige öffentliche Verkehrsmittel: U-Bahn, S-Bahn, Busse."

Norbert
17 Jahre

„Ich bin Norbert Seemüller, bin 17 Jahre und lerne Schreiner. Ich bin im zweiten Lehrjahr. Ich wohne auf dem Land außerhalb von Besigheim."

Wo wohnst du? Und bist du dort zufrieden?

„Ja, klar! Ich wohne bei meinen Eltern, und wir haben ein schönes Haus mit einem großen Garten. Ja, und ich habe meine Lehrstelle hier — ich muss noch ein Jahr lernen, bis ich meine Gesellenprüfung machen kann."

Du möchtest also nicht woanders wohnen, zum Beispiel in Stuttgart?

„Nein. Und warum denn? Ich hab hier halt alles, was ich brauche: eine schöne Umgebung, viel mehr Platz als in der Stadt. Ja, was noch? Die Luft ist eben hier viel sauberer als in einer großen Stadt und der Verkehr geringer. Ja, ich bin hier schon sehr zufrieden."

---

1. The **Teufelsberg,** an artificial mountain in the Grunewald section of Berlin, was built after World War II from the rubble of the destroyed city. Now beautifully landscaped, it is the site of many sports events, grass-skiing in the summer, and skiing and sledding in the winter.

6 Ein Fragebogen: Britta und Norbert

Schreiben Nimm ein Blatt Papier zur Hand und mach deinen eigenen Fragebogen! Schreib auf, was du über Britta und Norbert gelesen hast!

1. Nachname 1. Wegener; Seemüller
2. Alter 2. 17; 17
3. Wohnort 3. Weißensee; außerhalb von Besigheim
4. Beschreibung des Wohnorts
5. Vorteile des Wohnorts
6. Nachteile des Wohnorts
   6. Die Gegend sieht nicht sehr schön aus.

	Britta	Norbert
Nachname		
Alter		

4. alte Häuser, alles sieht grau aus, nicht so piekfein; auf dem Land 5. international, immer was los, Seen u. Kanäle, billige Verkehrsmittel; schöne Umgebung, mehr Platz, sauberere Luft, geringerer Verkehr

7 Britta oder Norbert?

Sprechen Such dir einen Partner! — Nimm deinen ausgefüllten Fragebogen zur Hand und sag deinem Partner, was du alles über Britta weißt! — Dann sagt dir dein Partner, was er über Norbert weiß. Stimmt das, was dein Partner sagt?

Wortschatz

Wo wohnst du? Ich wohne ...

in einer Großstadt

in einem Vorort   an einem See
in den Bergen   an einem Fluss

in einem Dorf

in einer Kleinstadt

Und dann noch...

am Stadtrand
mitten in der Stadt
im Stadtzentrum
im Stadtteil (Degerloch)
im Kreis (Ludwigsburg)
  in (Ludwigsburg) County

Übungsheft, S. 74, Ü. 1   Grammatikheft, S. 55, Ü. 1

8 Wo wohnst du?

Sprechen Erzähl deinen Mitschülern möglichst genau (*in as much detail as possible*), wo du wohnst! Gebrauche auch die Wörter rechts, die dir schon bekannt sind!

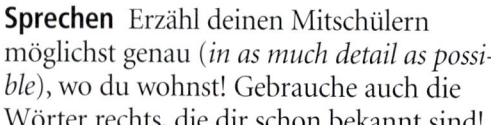

auf dem Land   in der Stadt
in (Chicago)   in der ...straße   in der Innenstadt
(nicht) weit von hier   am ...platz   in der Nähe von ...

So sagt man das!

Expressing preference and giving a reason

You already know some ways to express preference and favorites:

> Ich sehe lieber einen Actionfilm.
> Am liebsten lese ich Sciencefiction.
> Mein Lieblingsstar ist Tom Cruise.

Here are some other ways to express preference:

> Mir gefällt Berlin besser als Hamburg.
> Ich finde die Innenstadt von Hamburg schöner.
> Ich ziehe eine kleine Stadt wie Bietigheim vor.

You may also want to give a reason for your preference:

> Ich wohne lieber in einem Dorf. Da ist die Luft besser.
> Wir ziehen die Stadt vor, weil da einfach mehr los ist.

Which words or phrases help to make a comparison and show preference? What might the verb **vorziehen** mean? Where is the conjugated verb in a **weil**-clause?

 Grammatikheft, S. 55, Ü. 2

Wortschatz

Vorteile

Land:
Wohnungen billiger
Umgebung schöner
weniger Verkehr
weniger Lärm
Luft sauberer
Leben ruhiger

Stadt:
mehr los
mehr zu tun
Geschäfte in der Nähe
Theater, Museen, Oper, Ballett
öffentliche Verkehrsmittel (Bus, U-Bahn)

Nachteile

Stadt:
mehr Menschen
Wohnungen teurer
mehr Verkehr
Lärm größer
Luft schmutziger

Land:
weniger Geschäfte
weniger los
keine Theater, Museen
keine Oper, kein Ballett
keine U-Bahn oder S-Bahn

 Grammatikheft, S. 56, Ü. 3–4

9 Stadt oder Land? Warum? *Script and Answers on p. 181G*

Zuhören In der Radiosendung „Guten Morgen!" diskutieren zwei Zuhörer über das Thema: Stadt oder Land? Vorteile oder Nachteile. Schreib die Vorteile und Nachteile auf, die diese Leute für jeden dieser Orte erwähnen!
1. Stuttgart 2. Bietigheim 3. Esslingen 4. Schönaich

10 Für mein Notizbuch

Schreiben Schreib in dein Notizbuch
a. warum dir dein Wohnort gefällt!
b. warum dir dein Wohnort besser gefällt als dein Nachbarort!

ERSTE STUFE

Grammatik

Comparative forms of adjectives

1. Words such as *larger, cleaner,* and *more beautiful* are called comparatives. In English, most comparatives have the ending *-er*. In German, almost all comparatives end in **-er**.

Positive	Comparative
Die Umgebung ist **schön**.	Die Umgebung hier ist aber **schöner**.
Die Wohnungen sind **billig**.	Die Wohnungen hier sind **billiger**.

2. Most one-syllable adjectives with stem-vowels **a**, **o**, **u** add an umlaut in the comparative:

   alt **älter**   groß **größer**   jung **jünger**

3. As in English, some comparative forms are completely different from the positive forms.

   gern **lieber**   gut **besser**   viel **mehr**

4. To compare two things that are equal, the words **so … wie** are used:

   Die Luft ist hier **so** schlecht **wie** in der Großstadt.

5. To compare two things that are not equal, the comparative form and the word **als** are used.

   Die Luft ist hier **schlechter als** in der Großstadt.

Übungsheft, S. 74–76, Ü. 2–7   Grammatikheft, S. 57, Ü. 5–7   Mehr Grammatikübungen, S. 202–203, Ü. 1–4

11 Grammatik im Kontext

Schreiben/Sprechen Setzt euch in Gruppen von vier oder fünf Personen zusammen! Ihr vergleicht euren Heimatort mit einem Nachbarort.

a. Macht zuerst zusammen eine Liste mit Vor- und Nachteilen von euerm Heimatort! Dann macht eine Liste mit Vor- und Nachteilen von dem Nachbarort! Schreibt dann alle Vor- und Nachteile auf kleine Karteikarten. Legt die Karten in vier Stapel (*piles*)!

b. Ein Partner in der Gruppe fragt dann einen anderen Schüler, welchen Ort er schöner findet. Dieser Schüler gibt eine Antwort und zieht (*draws*) eine Karte von einem der vier Stapel. Er sagt dann seinen Grund dafür.

c. Macht weiter, bis alle ihre Meinung gesagt haben!

BEISPIEL DU Welche Stadt gefällt dir besser, Denver oder Colorado Springs?
PARTNER Colorado Springs (Zieh eine Karte!) **…, weil es dort weniger Verkehr gibt.**

12 Und du? Wo wohnst du lieber?

Sprechen Am Anfang des Kapitels (Übung 6, S. 188) hast du einen Grundriss (*framework*) für ein Interview gemacht. Verwende ihn jetzt, um deine Partnerin zu interviewen. Frag sie, wo sie wohnt, wie es ihr dort gefällt und welche Vor- und Nachteile ihr Wohnort hat! Möchte sie lieber woanders wohnen? Wo und warum?

Wo wohnst du lieber? Auf dem Land? In der Stadt?

Where do teenagers in Germany like to live? In the big cities, in the country, or somewhere in between? We asked many students about their preferences and this is what some of them said. CD 7 Tr. 4

Ilse, Wedel   CD 7 Tr. 5

„Ja, also, ich wohn gerne in Wedel, weil Wedel halt 'ne nette Kleinstadt ist. Es ist nicht allzu dreckig, es ist nicht dieser Stress mit dem vielen Verkehr, und … es ist einfach lustig. Man kann viel unternehmen, dafür, dass es so 'ne Kleinstadt ist. Und … na ja, es ist einfach nett hier."

Iwan, Bietigheim   CD 7 Tr. 6

„Also, ich würde lieber in 'ner Kleinstadt wohnen, so wie hier in Bietigheim, weil hier es doch ruhiger ist. Und es ist besser für … ich mein, besser auch für kleinere Kinder, weil die hier besser aufwachsen können als in 'ner großen Stadt. In 'ner großen Stadt ist halt auch schlecht, dass die Luftverschmutzung dort groß ist. Aber andererseits, in einer großen Stadt kann man natürlich alles bekommen, was in 'ner kleinen Stadt nicht zu haben ist."

Hans, Hamburg   CD 7 Tr. 7

„Ja, Hamburg ist schön, hat viele grüne Flächen, aber ich würde auch eigentlich auch mal gern auf dem Lande leben, für 'ne Weile auf jeden Fall. Ja, weil eben hier viel Verkehr ist eben, stickige Luft auch, eben typische Großstadt, eben."

Heide, Berlin   CD 7 Tr. 8

„Ich leb eigentlich relativ gerne in Berlin, obwohl Berliner, Berlin sowohl Nachteile als auch Vorteile hat. Die Nachteile sind halt, dass immer relativ schlechtes Wetter ist und dann die Luft stickig ist und man Kopfschmerzen hat. Aber dann Vorteil halt ist auch, dass in Berlin immer relativ viel los ist, so konzertmäßig und partymäßig, und von daher ist es ganz schön, hier zu leben."

A.   1. What do you think a **Kleinstadt** is? And a **Großstadt?** In which categories do the places where these students live belong?   A. 1. small town; big city; Ilse and Iwan: **Kleinstadt;** Heide and Hans: **Großstadt**

2. Which advantages and disadvantages does each student mention? What seems to be the big disadvantage to living in a large city, according to most of these students? Did that surprise you?   A. 2. various; air pollution caused by too much traffic; answers will vary

3. Think about where you live and places you've visited in the United States. What would you say are the advantages and disadvantages of living in a) cities, b) small towns, and c) the country? Are they similar to what these students said?

B. Germany's population density is 593 people per square mile compared to seventy-one per square mile in the United States. How do you think Germany's population density might affect Germans' daily lives, their habits, and their concerns? Write a short essay on this question. Be sure to include any facts or first-hand information from Germans that help to illustrate the effects of Germany's dense population.

STANDARDS: 1.2, 2.2, 3.2, 4.2

Zweite Stufe

Objective Expressing wishes

Nicco, 15: „Ich wünsch mir erst mal ein eigenes Zimmer mit neuen Möbeln, eine größere Stereoanlage und vor allem meinen eigenen Fernseher mit einem Videorecorder."

Nadine, 16: „Ich möchte gern mal ein großes aber gemütliches Haus haben mit bequemen Möbeln. Dann wünsch ich mir einen großen Garten mit vielen Blumen und Sträuchern und vielen Bäumen, und ein kleiner Pool wäre auch nicht schlecht."

Sven, 17: „Meine Wünsche? Ja, einen guten Wagen, einen tollen Job, später einmal eine nette Frau, gute Freunde, ja, ich wünsch mir mal ein schönes Leben. Warum nicht?"

André, 16: „Was ich mir wünsche und was ich dringend brauche sind gute Noten in der Schule, damit ich später eine gute Ausbildung bekomme und einmal einen guten Job."

Jeanine, 16: „Mein großer Wunsch ist ein guter Schulabschluss, das heißt bei mir ein gutes Abitur, damit ich einen Platz an der Uni bekomme und studieren kann. Dann wünsch ich mir einen netten Freundeskreis, ein schönes Familienleben und vor allem ein gutes und sicheres Einkommen."

Britta, 16: „Ich wünsche mir und meinen Mitmenschen vor allem eine saubere Umwelt und ein friedliches Leben, ohne Armut, ohne Hunger und ohne Krieg."

13 Wer wünscht sich was?

Lesen/Sprechen Lies, was sich diese Schüler wünschen und beantworte die Fragen!

1. Welche Schüler wünschen sich mehr materielle Dinge? Welche nicht?
2. Mit welchen Schülern kannst du dich identifizieren? Warum?

1. Nicco, Nadine / Sven, André, Jeanine, Britta

Ein wenig Grammatik

Look again at the first interview above. What do you notice about the pronoun that follows the verb **wünschen**? Here, **wünschen** is used reflexively (**sich wünschen**), and the reflexive pronoun is always in the dative case.

Was wünschst du **dir**?
Ich wünsche **mir** einen großen Garten.

Grammatikheft, S. 58, Ü. 8   Mehr Grammatikübungen, S. 203, Ü. 5

So sagt man das!

Expressing wishes

Grammatikheft, S. 58, Ü. 9

When asking someone about his or her wishes, you may ask:

    Was möchtest du gern mal haben?
or Was wünschst du dir mal?
    Und was wünscht ihr euch?

And the answer may be:

Ich möchte gern mal einen tollen Wagen!
Ich wünsche mir mal eine schöne Wohnung!
Wir wünschen uns ein eigenes Zimmer.

Name the noun phrases in the right-hand column. What are the genders of the three nouns? How do you know? To how many people is the third question addressed?

Wortschatz

Für mein Traumhaus wünsch ich mir

einen kleinen Pool

einen Garten mit Blumen, Sträuchern und Bäumen

auch:
eine moderne Küche
ein nettes Wohnzimmer
ein gemütliches Esszimmer
ein hübsches Schlafzimmer
ein eigenes Badezimmer
einen hellen Flur
zwei Toiletten
einen kühlen Keller
eine ruhige Terrasse
mein eigenes Computerzimmer

Ich wünsch mir auch:
eine gute Ausbildung   *a good education*
einen tollen Job   *a great job*
ein friedliches Leben   *a peaceful life*
eine saubere Umwelt   *a clean environment*
ein sicheres Einkommen   *a secure income*
keine Armut   *no poverty*
keinen Hunger   *no hunger*
keinen Krieg   *no war*

Sag deinen Klassenkameraden, was du dir wünschst!

(Übungsheft, S. 78–79, Ü. 1–3)   (Grammatikheft, S. 59, Ü. 10)

---

14 Was wünschen sich die Schüler?   Script and Answers on p. 181G

Zuhören Hör zu, was sich diese Schüler wünschen! Wer wünscht sich was? Schreib zuerst die Namen auf, die du hörst! Dann schreib neben jeden Namen, was sich diese Person wünscht!   CD 7 Tr. 9

15 Was sind deine Wunschträume?

Sprechen Such dir einen Partner! Er fragt dich nach deinen Wunschträumen, und du sagst ihm, was du dir wünschst. Tauscht dann die Rollen aus!

Was du dir wünschst:

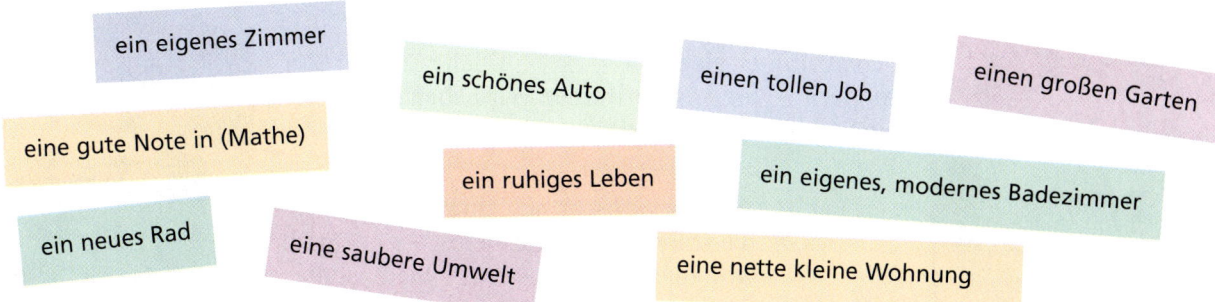

ZWEITE STUFE   STANDARDS: 1.1, 1.2, 5.1   *hundertdreiundneunzig*

Grammatik

Adjective endings following ein-words

1. Adjectives following **ein**-words (**ein, kein,** and the possessives **mein, dein, sein, ihr,** etc.) have these endings:

Nominative	Das ist	ein	groß**er**	Garten.	*masculine nouns*
Accusative	Ich wünsche mir	einen	groß**en**	Garten.	
Nominative	Das ist	eine	nett**e**	Wohnung.	*feminine nouns*
Accusative	Ich wünsche mir	eine	nett**e**	Wohnung.	
Nominative	Das ist	ein	schön**es**	Zimmer.	*neuter nouns*
Accusative	Ich wünsche mir	ein	schön**es**	Zimmer.	
Nominative	Das sind	keine	modern**en**	Möbel.	*plural nouns*
Accusative	Ich möchte	keine	modern**en**	Möbel.	

2. Since **ein** has no plural form itself, the plural adjective ending is **e** in both the nominative and the accusative.

	Singular				Plural			
Nominative	Das ist	ein	toll**er**	Garten!	Das sind		toll**e**	Gärten!
Accusative	Ich habe	eine	neu**e**	Lampe.	Ich habe	zwei	neu**e**	Lampen.

3. In the dative case, the adjective endings are **-en** for nouns of all gender and for plural nouns.

Ich möchte mal in
- einem klein**en** Vorort
- einer groß**en** Stadt
- einem schön**en** Haus
- groß**en** Städten

wohnen.

4. When more than one adjective is used, both have the same ending.

Das ist aber ein schön**es**, klein**es** Haus, nicht?

Übungsheft, S. 79–80, Ü. 4–7   Grammatikheft, S. 59–60, Ü. 11–13   Mehr Grammatikübungen, S. 203–205, Ü. 6–9

16 Grammatik im Kontext

Schreiben Schreib, was sich diese Schüler wünschen und setz dabei die richtigen Endungen ein!

Ich habe alles, was ich brauche. Wir haben eine nett __e__ Wohnung in einem groß __en__ Mietshaus. Die Wohnung hat ein gemütlich __es__ Wohnzimmer, zwei schön __e__ Schlafzimmer, eine groß __e__ Küche und ein modern __es__ Badezimmer. Wir haben sogar einen schön __en__, klein __en__ Garten.

Bettina wünscht sich ein ruhig __es__ Leben; sie zieht eine klein __e__ Stadt vor. In einer klein __en__ Stadt ist die Luft besser, sagt sie.

KAPITEL 7   Stadt oder Land?

17 Ein Briefpartner schreibt

Lesen/Schreiben Stell dir vor, dein Briefpartner aus Deutschland hat dir geschrieben! Lies das Ende seines Briefes! Dann beantworte die Fragen!

1. What is Jochen talking about in the first part of the letter? 1. sports
2. How does Jochen describe where he lives? 2. small suburb, nice house, big garden, modern kitchen, sunny living room, 3 big bedrooms
3. Does he have his own room? 3. yes
4. What is special about the cellar? 4. hobby-room

> immer Tennis spielen.
> Nun, genug über Sport. Jetzt möchte ich deine Fragen beantworten. Also, wir wohnen in einem kleinen Vorort von Stuttgart, in Eßlingen. Dort haben wir ein schönes Haus mit einem großen Garten. Wir haben eine moderne Küche, ein sonniges Wohnzimmer und drei große Schlafzimmer. Mein Bruder und ich, wir haben jeder unser eigenes Schlafzimmer. Ach ja, im Keller haben wir einen schönen Hobbyraum.
> Schreib mal, wie du wohnst!
> Viele Grüße Jochen

18 Lieber Jochen!

Schreiben/Lesen Schreib deinem Briefpartner Jochen, wie du wohnst! Lies danach deinem Partner deinen Brief vor, und er tut das Gleiche (*the same*)!

19 Für mein Notizbuch

Schreiben Überleg dir (*think about*), was du dir wirklich einmal wünschst, und schreib deine Wünsche in dein Notizbuch!

Wo wohnst du?

Stadtrand
Kleinstadt
Vorort
Dorf
Großstadt

Was habt ihr?

Haus
Wohnung
Garten
Schlafzimmer
Wohnzimmer
Küche
Toilette
Bad
Terrasse
Garage

ZWEITE STUFE   STANDARDS: 1.2, 1.3   *hundertfünfundneunzig*

Zum Lesen

Und dein Traumhaus?

Lesestrategie Using grammatical and lexical clues to derive meaning. You can guess the meaning of many words and phrases by looking at cognates, the context, and words you know within compounds. You can also look for variations of root words, for example, the addition of prefixes (**bieten, verbieten**) or suffixes (**Person, persönlich**). And you can look at the part of speech (noun, verb, etc.) to help you guess the meaning.

Getting Started For answers, see p. 181T.

1. Do you think having one's own room might be something German teenagers dream about? Considering what you have learned about the kinds of clothes German teens wear and their lifestyles in general, could you make any predictions about what a **Traumzimmer** would look like? Or would it depend on the individual?

2. Skim quickly over the readings. What theme do they all have in common? What are the different formats? How will you adjust your reading strategy to get the most out of each text?

A Closer Look

3. Read the paragraph about **Kinderzimmer.** Convert the size of the average child's room in Germany from square meters to square feet (1 square meter equals approximately 11 square feet). Do you think the average child's room in the United States

MEIN TRAUMHAUS IST AUS SCHOKOLADE

Kinderzimmer in deutschen Mietwohnungen sind zwischen 8 und 12 Quadratmeter groß. Zieht man die notwendigen Flächen für Bett, Schrank und Tisch ab, bleiben 1,20m x 1,80m für Spiel und Bewegung übrig. In Wohn- und Schlafzimmern, tagsüber meistens leer, dürfen nur wenige Kinder spielen.

Traumhaus

Mein Traumhaus ist aus Schokolade, und im Schwimmbecken fließt Limonade. Aus Marzipan sind die Gardinen, und das Bett ist aus Rosinen. Mein Sofa ist aus Kaubonbons, und daran hängen Luftballons. Die Treppe ist aus Joghurteis, da lauf' ich rauf mit sehr viel Fleiß. Zwei Türme, die sind auch noch dran, worin man sehr gut zeichnen kann.

Test
(von Susi, Anette, Dani und Julie aus München. Alle sind 14 Jahre alt.)

Was bist Du für ein Wohntyp?
1. Stell Dir vor, Du kannst Dein neues Bett selber aussuchen. Was wählst Du?
   a) Ein rosarotes Himmelbett in Herzform.
   b) Eine neonfarbene Couch.
   c) Du würdest am liebsten auf dem Fußboden schlafen, weil das alle tun.
   d) Dir ist das Design egal — Hauptsache bequem.

2. Wie würdest Du Dich bei einem Umzug verhalten?
   a) Der Umzug ist Dir egal. Hauptsache, Dein Teddybär kommt mit.
   b) Du würdest Deinen Hamster mit Punkfrisur mitnehmen. Was sonst!
   c) Du nimmst keine Möbel mit. Du kaufst neue, die gerade „in" sind.
   d) Du nimmst alles Brauchbare mit, was Dir zur Verfügung steht.

3. Du brauchst Geld und mußt etwas verkaufen. Wovon trennst Du Dich als erstes?
   a) Von dem Drahtbett, das Dir ein Freund geschenkt hat.
   b) Von dem braunen Kleiderschrank, den Deine Eltern gekauft haben.
   c) Von Deiner Zahnbürste, weil Zähneputzen „uncool" ist.
   d) Von Deinem Computer, weil er schädlich für Dich ist.

4. Du bist umgezogen. Mit wem freundest Du Dich zuerst an?
   a) Mit Lisa, weil sie eine schöne Kuschelecke hat.
   b) Mit dem Punker von nebenan, weil Du seine Klamotten „cool" findest.
   c) Mit dem Typen, der den Schaukelstuhl (siehe Bild) entworfen hat, weil Du solche Sachen gut findest.
   d) Mit Hannelore, weil sie Dir giftfreie Farbe für Deine Wände geschenkt hat.

5. Du hast nach Deiner dritten Mahnung die Miete noch nicht gezahlt. Nun klingelt der Vermieter. Wie verhältst Du Dich?
   a) Du versuchst, ihn mit echten Tränen einzuschüchtern.
   b) Du vertreibst ihn mit einem Heavy-Metal-Song.
   c) Du sagst: „Mann, ich bin Kick-Boxer. Das schwöre ich Dir!"
   d) Du bietest ihm Deinen selbstgebackenen Bio-Kuchen an.

Lösung

Du hast a) am meisten angekreuzt. Du bist ein verspielter Schmuse-Typ. Dein Zimmer würdest Du am liebsten nur mit Stofftieren einrichten. Du träumst davon, in einem großen Stofftier zu leben.

Du hast b) am meisten angekreuzt. Du liebst grelle Farben und Verrücktes. Sanfte Farben findest Du langweilig. Bist Du vielleicht ein Punker?

Du hast c) am meisten angekreuzt. Du magst moderne Möbel, die nicht unbedingt bequem sein müssen. Man findet bei Dir das Nagelbett eines Fakirs — wenn es gerade modern ist.

Du hast d) am meisten angekreuzt. Du bist der praktische Öko-Typ. Du faßt nichts an, was Du nicht vorher desinfiziert hast. Wer mit Dir reden will, muß sich mindestens fünfmal täglich waschen. Frage: Übertreibst Du da nicht ein bißchen?

ZUM LESEN   STANDARDS: 1.2, 1.3, 3.1

is bigger or smaller? What about your own room?

4. Now read the poem slowly two times. Then listen as a classmate reads it aloud. What is it about? What terms does the writer use in his or her description? Could you sketch the **Traumhaus**?

5. Look at the self-test. Who wrote it, and what is it designed to reveal?

6. Read the first three questions of the test once. Then look back at the individual sentences and try to guess the meanings of the following words from the words on the right. First determine the part of speech, then look for clues to its meaning.

sich vorstellen	to sell
Himmelbett	to choose
Umzug	to imagine
sich verhalten	harmful
verkaufen	move
wählen	to behave
schädlich	canopy bed

7. Reread the questions and answer them for yourself. Follow the same procedure with questions four and five and the solutions. What type are you?

Kuschelecke	non-toxic
giftfrei	to intimidate
anbieten	to offer
vertreiben	to drive away
einschüchtern	quiet corner
Schmuse-Typ	to furnish
einrichten	cuddly type

8. Schreib jetzt nach dem Muster unten dein eigenes, fünfzeiliges Gedicht über dein Traumhaus!

a noun	Apfel
two adjectives	rot, vergiftet
three verbs	essen, schmecken, geben
an idea	Ein schöner Apfel ist nicht immer gut.
a noun	Schein

Übungsheft, S. 81

hundertsiebenundneunzig **197**

Dritte Stufe

Objectives Agreeing, with reservations; justifying your answers

Wortschatz

Was produziert Lärm?

Übungsheft, S. 82–83, Ü. 1–3 Grammatikheft, S. 61, Ü. 14–15

LKWs (Lastkraftwagen)

Flugzeuge

Motorräder

Man produziert auch Lärm, wenn man…

zu schnell in die Kurven fährt

die Autotür oder den Kofferraumdeckel zuschlägt

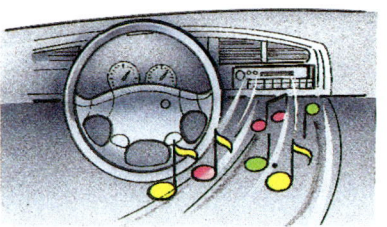
das Autoradio zu laut spielt

Sieh dir die Illustrationen an! Was kann man tun, um Lärm zu vermeiden?

langsam fahren

den Motor abstellen

nicht hupen

20 Probleme mit der Umwelt

Script and Answers on p. 181H

CD 7 Tr. 10

Zuhören Zwei Schüler, Markus und Ute, sprechen über den Lärm in ihrer Stadt. Markus nennt einige Probleme, und Ute macht Vorschläge *(suggestions)*, wie man das Problem lösen *(solve)* kann. Wie reagiert Markus auf Utes Vorschläge? Hör dem Gespräch zweimal zu! Schreib zuerst die Probleme auf, die Markus erwähnt! Dann schreib Utes Vorschläge auf und wie Markus darauf reagiert!

Und dann noch…

PKWs (Personenkraftwagen)
Mofas und Mopeds
Busse
zu viel Verkehr
Motorboote

Der Lärm wird größer!

Der Lärm in unseren größeren Städten nimmt zu.

Mehr als 50 Prozent der Bevölkerung fühlt sich durch Lärm belästigt. Verkehrslärm steht mit 70% an erster Stelle. Lastkraftwagen und Busse verursachen einen größeren Lärm als Personenkraftwagen. Unsere motorisierten Zweiräder, besonders die Leichtkrafträder und Motorräder, machen einen größeren Lärm als zum Beispiel Mofas und Mopeds. Als Kraftfahrer können Sie aber durch ein lärmbewusstes Verhalten zur Lärmminderung beitragen.

Hier sind einige Tipps:
- Vermeiden Sie Kavalierstarts!
- Fahren Sie nicht zu schnell in Kurven!
- Schlagen Sie Ihre offene Autotür und den Kofferraumdeckel nicht zu!
- Drehen Sie Ihr Autoradio auf Normalstärke!
- Machen Sie keine unnötigen Fahrten, vor allem in Wohngebieten!
- Stellen Sie den Motor an Bahnübergängen ab!
- Beachten Sie strikt die Geschwindigkeitsbeschränkungen aus Lärmschutzgründen!

21 Was tun, um Lärm zu beseitigen? *Answers will vary.*

Sprechen/Schreiben Beantworte die folgenden Fragen!

1. Welcher Lärm belästigt die Bevölkerung am meisten?
2. Welche Fahrzeuge machen den größten Lärm? Welche machen weniger Lärm?
3. Bist du ein Lärmmuffel? — Was tust du selbst, um Verkehrslärm zu mindern? Schau dir die Tipps an und nenne zwei Dinge, die du selbst tust!

So sagt man das!

Agreeing, with reservations

If someone wants to know about your preference, he or she might ask:

> **Findest du Boston schöner als New York?**
> **Ich finde die Innenstadt von Baltimore schöner. Du auch?**
> **Wohnst du auch lieber in der Stadt als auf dem Land?**
> **Das Leben auf dem Land ist todlangweilig, nicht wahr?**

In your answer, you may want to express reservations by saying:

> **Ja schon, aber …** (Boston hat im Winter mehr Schnee).
> **Ja, aber …** (New York hat bessere Theater).
> **Eigentlich schon, aber …** (in einer Großstadt gibt es schönere Museen).
> **Ja, ich stimme dir zwar zu, aber …** (es ist viel gesünder).

Which words or phrases show that the speaker has reservations?

Übungsheft, S. 83, Ü. 4
Grammatikheft, S. 62, Ü. 16–17

22 Eigentlich schon, aber…

Schreiben/Sprechen Schreib drei Vorteile deiner Heimatstadt auf einen Zettel. Deine Partnerin schreibt drei Nachteile auf. Sag ihr jetzt, was du über deine Heimatstadt denkst! Sie stimmt dir zwar zu, aber sie hat dazu auch etwas anderes zu sagen. — Tauscht dann die Rollen aus!

Grammatik

Adjective endings of comparatives

Read the following pairs of sentences.

Adjectives before nouns	Comparatives before nouns
Das ist ein **groß er** Garten.	Aber dort ist ein viel **größer er** Garten!
Wir haben einen **groß en** Garten.	Schmitts haben einen **größer en** Garten.
Frank hat ein **klein es** Zimmer.	Sein Bruder hat ein **kleiner es** Zimmer.
Wir wohnen in einer **klein en** Stadt.	Webers wohnen in einer **kleiner en** Stadt!
Meiers haben keine **modern en** Möbel.	Sie wollen keine **moderner en** Möbel.

What do you notice about the endings of the comparative forms of adjectives?[1]

Übungsheft, S. 83–84, Ü. 5–6   Grammatikheft, S. 63, Ü. 18–19   Mehr Grammatikübungen, S. 205, Ü. 10–11

23 Grammatik im Kontext

Schreiben Peter glaubt, in der Stadt ist alles besser. Schreib auf, was er sagt!

1. In der Stadt gibt es modern **ere** Häuser!
2. Ihr wohnt bestimmt in einer bess **eren** Gegend.
3. In der Stadt gibt es immer größ **ere** Wohnungen.
4. Hier gibt es auch ein bess **eres** Theater.
5. Es gibt auch einen schön **eren** Tennisplatz als bei uns.

24 Ich stimme dir zwar zu, aber … !

Sprechen Such dir eine Partnerin! — Du sagst deiner Partnerin etwas über deine Wohnung. Deine Partnerin stimmt dir zuerst zu, aber dann sagt sie, dass bei ihr doch alles besser, schöner oder größer ist! Tauscht dann die Rollen aus!

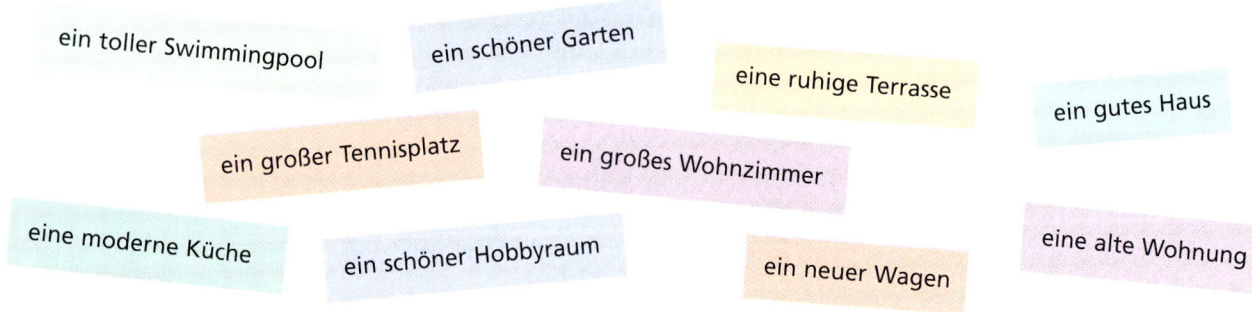

---

[1]. The endings are the same for both comparative and positive adjectives.

25 Nach Gründen suchen

Lesen Lies noch einmal, was Britta und Norbert auf Seite 187 gesagt haben! Such beim Lesen die Gründe heraus, die die Wörter „eben" und „halt" enthalten! Welche Aufgabe, glaubst du, erfüllen diese beiden Wörter?   emphatic confirmation of justification or explanation

So sagt man das!

Justifying your answers

If someone asked you about your preferences, for example:

Warum gefällt es dir in Stuttgart besser als in Bietigheim?

You might answer:

Mir gefällt es in Stuttgart besser, weil da **halt** alles in der Nähe ist. Hier kann man **eben** schnell einmal ins Theater gehen.

Eben and **halt** are often used when giving a reason, justifying something, or giving an explanation.

26 Ein guter Grund?

Lesen/Sprechen Für jede Aussage auf der linken Seite gibt es einen guten Grund auf der rechten Seite. Für jeden Grund gebrauche entweder „eben" oder „halt".

1. Wir wohnen jetzt in einer kleinen Stadt in der Nähe von Stuttgart.   1. e
2. Wir wohnen jetzt in einer schönen Gegend.   2. d
3. Wir haben jetzt viel mehr Platz, und einen Garten. Die Großeltern können jetzt auch bei uns wohnen.   3. c
4. Ich hab jetzt mein eigenes Zimmer.   4. a
5. Und einen kleinen Swimmingpool haben wir auch!   5. b

a. Da hab ich alles, was ich brauche.
b. Da kann ich schnell mal schwimmen gehen.
c. Da können wir alle zusammen sein.
d. Aber da sind die Häuser und die Wohnungen teurer.
e. Die Luft ist da viel besser als in Stuttgart.

27 Bei uns ist alles besser, oder?

a. **Sprechen** Bildet zuerst zwei Gruppen! Eure Aufgabe ist, etwas über eure Gegend zu berichten oder über eine Gegend, in der ihr gern wohnen möchtet. Welche Vor- und Nachteile bietet diese Gegend?

b. **Sprechen** Dann trägt jemand aus der Gruppe den Bericht vor, den ihr gemeinsam erarbeitet habt. Die Mitglieder der anderen Gruppe dürfen sich dabei Notizen machen.

c. **Sprechen** Sprecht eure Vorbehalte (*reservations*) aus!

28 Für mein Notizbuch

Sprechen/Schreiben Frag zuerst deine Eltern (oder andere Verwandte oder Bekannte), ob sie gern oder nicht gern in deiner Gegend wohnen! Welche Vor- und Nachteile erwähnen sie? Schreib danach in dein Notizbuch, was sie gesagt haben!

29

Ein Häusermakler (*realtor*) hat dich in der Werbeabteilung angestellt. Deine Aufgabe ist es, Häuser zu beschreiben, die zum Kauf angeboten werden. Die Beschreibung soll die Häuser und die Umgebung im besten Licht zeigen.

DRITTE STUFE   STANDARDS: 1.2, 1.3, 5.2   *zweihunderteins*   **201**

Mehr Grammatikübungen

Erste Stufe
Objectives Expressing preference and giving a reason

1 Wo wohnst du gern? – Schreib den Komparativ des Wortes in Klammern in die erste Lücke und die deutsche Form von "than" in die zweite Lücke. (S. 190)

1. (gern)   Ich wohne _____ in einer Kleinstadt _____ in einer Großstadt.   lieber; als
2. (schön)   In einem Dorf ist es _____ _____ in einer Kleinstadt.   schöner; als
3. (billig)   Die Wohnungen sind hier _____ _____ in einer Stadt.   billiger; als
4. (alt)   Oft sind in einem Dorf die Häuser _____ _____ in einer Stadt.   älter; als
5. (gut)   Die Luft ist _____ auf dem Land _____ in der Stadt.   besser; als
6. (viel)   Aber in einer Stadt gibt es _____ zu sehen _____ auf dem Land.   mehr; als
7. (groß)   In einer Stadt sind die Häuser _____ _____ auf dem Land.   größer; als

2 Wie oder als? - Schreib die richtigen Komparativformen in die Lücken. (S. 190)

1. Die Luft in Berlin ist _____ gut _____ die Luft in München; aber die Luft im Schwarzwald ist _____ _____ die Luft in Berlin und München.   so; wie   besser; als
2. Die Insel Juist ist _____ groß _____ die Insel Norderney; aber die Insel Rügen ist _____ _____ Juist und Norderney.   so; wie   größer; als
3. Die Stadt Berlin hat _____ viel Verkehr _____ München; aber die Stadt New York hat _____ Verkehr _____ Berlin und München.   so; wie   mehr; als
4. Ich habe die Umgebung von Hamburg _____ gern _____ die Umgebung von Berlin; aber die Umgebung von München habe ich _____ _____ die Umgebungen von Hamburg und Berlin.   so; wie   lieber; als

3 Schau auf die Liste vom Milchverkauf und schreib vier Sätze mit dem Komparativ von „billig" und „teuer". (S. 190)

1. _____
2. _____
3. _____
4. _____

Answers may vary: Suggested answers
Milch ist teurer als Joghurt.
Kakao ist so teuer wie Vanille.
Joghurt ist billiger als Kakao.
Joghurt ist billiger als Milch.

4 Vergleiche die gegebenen Aussagen und drücke die Unterschiede (*differences*) mit dem Komparativ aus. (**S. 190**)

Suggested Answers

Peter ist 1,80 m groß.
Heidi ist 1,85 m groß.

1. _____ . Peter ist kleiner als Heidi.
2. _____ . Heidi ist größer als Peter.

Das T-Shirt kostet € 10,– .
Das Hemd kostet € 14, – .

3. _____ . Das T-Shirt ist billiger als das Hemd.
4. _____ . Das Hemd ist teurer als das T-Shirt.

Meine Oma ist 70 Jahre alt.
Mein Opa ist 72 Jahre alt.

5. _____ . Meine Oma ist jünger als mein Opa.
6. _____ . Mein Opa ist älter als meine Oma.

In Berlin ist es 8 Grad C.
In Prag ist es - 4 Grad C.

7. _____ . In Berlin ist es wärmer als in Prag.
8. _____ . In Prag ist es kälter als in Berlin.

Art läuft die 100 m in 16 Sek.
Kara läuft die 100 m in 14 Sek.

9. _____ . Art läuft langsamer als Kara.
10. _____ . Kara läuft schneller als Art.

Zweite Stufe

Objective Expressing wishes

5 Was wünschen sich diese Schüler? – Schreib das richtige Reflexivpronomen in die Lücken. (**S. 192**)

1. Was wünschst du _____ mal, liebe Katrin? Wünschst du _____ mal ein schönes Haus? — Ich wünsche _____ mal ein tolles Auto.   *dir; dir*
   mir
2. Bettina und Judith, was wünscht ihr _____ mal? Wünscht ihr _____ mal ein tolles Auto? — Ja, wir wünschen _____ mal ein tolles Auto.   *euch; euch*
   uns
3. Was wünscht _____ Frank? Glaubst du, dass er _____ ein Auto wünscht?—Ich glaube, dass er _____ ein Motorrad wünscht.   *sich; sich*
   sich

6 Was sind deine Wünsche für die Zukunft? – Schreib die richtige Form des unbestimmten Artikels (**ein, eine,** etc.) und die richtige Form des Adjektivs in Klammern in jede Lücke. (**S. 194**)

1. Ich wünsche mir mal (schön) _____ Haus mit (groß) _____ Garten und (klein) _____ Swimmingpool.   *ein schönes; einem großen; einem kleinen*
2. Und ich wünsche mir (toll) _____ Job, (sicher) _____ Einkommen und vor allem (sauber) _____ Umwelt.   *einen tollen; ein sicheres; eine saubere*
3. Ich wünsche mir (gut) _____ Ausbildung, (nett) _____ Familie und natürlich auch (friedlich) _____ Leben.   *eine gute; eine nette; ein friedliches*
4. Ich ziehe (klein) _____ Stadt wie Ulm vor. In (klein) _____ Stadt ist die Luft viel besser, denn (klein) _____ Stadt hat wenig Verkehr.   *eine kleine; einer kleinen; eine kleine*
5. Ich möchte mal (modern) _____ Küche, (gemütlich) _____ Wohnzimmer und natürlich auch (groß) _____ Wagen.   *eine moderne; ein gemütliches; einen großen*
6. Ich möchte mal an (klein) _____ See wohnen oder in (klein) _____ Dorf mit (schön) _____ Umgebung.   *einem kleinen; einem kleinen; einer schönen*

Mehr Grammatikübungen

 Answers    WK3 STUTTGART-7

7 Was für Klamotten wünschst du dir? – Schreib die richtige Form des unbestimmten Artikels (**ein, eine,** etc.) und die richtige Form des Adjektivs in Klammern in jede Lücke. (S. 194)

1. Ich wünsche mir (blau) _____ Pulli und (rot) _____ T-Shirt.   einen blauen; ein rotes
2. Ich möchte (weiß) _____ Hemd und (schwarz) _____ Hose.   ein weißes; eine schwarze
3. Ich brauche (grau) _____ Rock und (hellblau) _____ Bluse.   einen grauen; eine hellblaue
4. Ich wünsche mir (rot) _____ Kleid und (weiß) _____ Gürtel.   ein rotes; einen weißen
5. Ich möchte (kurz) _____ Shorts und (leicht) _____ Turnschuhe.   eine kurze; leichte
6. Und ich brauche (braun) _____ Jogging-Anzug.   einen braunen

Dritte Stufe

Objectives Agreeing with reservations; justifying your answers

8 Was ist das?—Schreib die richtige Form des unbestimmten Artikels in die erste Lücke, ein passendes Adjektiv mit der richtigen Endung in die zweite Lücke und den Namen des abgebildeten Artikels in die dritte Lücke. (S. 194)

Suggested Answers

1. Das ist _____ _____ _____.   eine braune Handtasche

2. Das ist _____ _____ _____.   ein bayrischer Kartoffelsalat

3. Das ist _____ _____ _____.   ein warmer Leberkäs

4. Das ist _____ _____ _____.   ein gebratenes Hähnchen

5. Das ist _____ _____ _____.   eine heiße Suppe

6. Das ist _____ _____ _____.   ein frischer Fisch

9 Du sagst, was du mal gern möchtest. – Schreib die richtigen Adjektivendungen in die Lücken. (S. 194)

1. Das ist aber ein groß_____ Garten! Ich möchte auch mal einen groß_____ Garten. Ich finde groß_____ Gärten Spitze. In einem groß_____ Garten fühle ich mich wohl.   er; en
e; en

2. Das ist ein alt_____ Haus. Ich habe mal in einem alt_____ Haus gewohnt. Ich liebe alt_____ Häuser. Ich möchte mal ein alt_____ Haus kaufen. Alt_____ Häuser können aber sehr teuer sein.   es; en
e; es; e

3. Was für eine modern_____ Küche! Ich liebe modern_____ Küchen. Ich möchte mal eine modern_____ Küche. In einer groß_____ , modern_____ Küche koche ich lieber als in einer klein_____ , alt_____ Küche. Aber modern_____ Küchen sind teuer!   e; e
e; en; en
en; en; e

10 Alles ist größer oder besser. – Schreib die richtige Form des unbestimmten Artikels (**ein, eine,** etc.) und die richtige Komparativform des Adjektivs in Klammern in jede Lücke. (S. 200)

1. Ich weiß, ihr habt (groß) _____ Garten, aber wir haben dafür (groß) _____ Haus mit (groß) _____ Swimmingpool.   einen größeren; ein größeres; einem größeren

2. Ja schon, aber wir haben (alt) _____ Haus in (ruhig) _____ Umgebung in (klein) _____ Vorort von Stuttgart.   ein älteres; einer ruhigeren; einem kleineren

3. Du weißt, ich wohne lieber in (klein) _____ Wohnung, aber in (groß) _____ Stadt, wo es (gut) _____ Museum gibt als hier bei uns.   einer kleineren; einer größeren; ein besseres

4. Ich weiß, du hast (neu) _____ Wagen und (gut) _____ Motorrad als ich; aber ich habe (gut) _____ Wagen als du.   einen neueren; ein besseres; einen besseren

11 Schreib, was du mal gern möchtest. – Schreib die richtigen Komparativformen des gegebenen Adjektivs in die Lücken. (S. 200)

1. Ich möchte mal (ein) _____ (groß) _____ Garten haben. Ich finde (groß) _____ Gärten toll. In (groß) _____ Gärten kann man auch (ein) _____ (groß) _____ Party haben.   einen; größeren
größere; größeren
eine; größere

2. Ich möchte auch einmal (ein) _____ (neu) _____ Wagen fahren. Ich liebe (neu) _____ Autos. In (neu) _____ Autos kann man (schnell) _____ fahren.   einen; neueren
neuere; neueren
schneller

3. Ich möchte gern mal (ein) _____ (alt) _____ Haus haben. Ich finde (alt)_____ Häuser Klasse. Ich weiß, (alt) _____ Häuser können Probleme haben, aber ich möchte gern in (ein) _____ (alt) _____ Haus wohnen.   ein; älteres
ältere; ältere
einem; älteren

Storytelling Book pp. 54–55

The *CD-ROM Tutor* offers guided recording and writing activities to accompany the **Anwendung**. These activities are designed to practice students' oral and written communication skills and to review material from each chapter.

1 Ein paar Leute sagen, wo sie lieber wohnen und warum. Mach eine Tabelle wie diese und füll sie dann aus!
Script and answers on p. 181H
CD 7 Tr. 11

Person	wo?	warum?
1		

2 Zeichne dein Traumhaus! Zeichne zuerst das Haus auf ein großes Blatt Papier! Danach beschreibe deinem Partner das Haus! Dein Partner hört dir zu und zeichnet dein Traumhaus. Vergleicht dann die beiden Zeichnungen! Hat dein Partner alles richtig gehört? Dann erzählt dir dein Partner, wie sein Traumhaus aussieht, und du zeichnest sein Traumhaus auf ein Blatt Papier.

3 Lies den Text unten und beantworte die folgenden Fragen!

1. Worüber berichtet der Text?   1. Schüler arbeiten in ihrem eigenen Garten.
2. Wo ist der Garten?   2. in der Schule
3. Was wächst im Garten?   3. Gemüse, Blumen, Kräuter, Obst
4. Wie finden die Schüler den Garten? Warum? Was sagen sie?   4. Es macht ihnen Spaß, weil etwas Eigenes entsteht.
5. Was, meinst du, lernen die Schüler von der „Schule im Garten"?
   5. Sie lernen etwas Praktisches.

SCHULE IM GARTEN

Schüler ziehen mit Spaten, Hacken, Heckenscheren und Schubkarren hinaus ins Freie, um an „ihrer" Oase zu arbeiten. Und wie die blüht und wächst! Es gibt Gemüse- und Blumenbeete sowie einen Kräutergarten. Die Schüler beliefern die Schulküche mit Zwiebeln, Karotten, Tomaten, Kartoffeln und Erdbeeren. Nicht nur der Garten, auch die Klassenzimmer werden immer grüner: Im Sommer gibt es dort jetzt frische Blumensträuße. Die jungen Hobbygärtner sind ganz begeistert. „Die Penne (Schule) macht viel mehr Spaß, weil etwas ganz Eigenes entsteht", meint Lizzy. „Klar kostet das Arbeit, aber dann siehst du etwas wachsen, kannst riechen, es anschauen." Am Ende kann man einiges sogar schmecken, essen und davon satt werden.

4 Die Schüler im Bericht haben einen Garten angelegt, um ihr Schulleben zu bereichern *(enrich)*. Was kannst du tun, um deine Schule oder dein Schulleben zu bereichern? Such dir zwei Klassenkameraden! Ihr macht ein Poster von allem, was ihr wünscht, um die Schule zu verbessern. Auf der linken Seite schreibt die Verbesserungsvorschläge auf, und auf der rechten Seite schreibt Ideen, wie ihr diese Wünsche erfüllen könnt! Dann erzählt euren Klassenkameraden etwas über eure Ideen!

5 Zum Schreiben

You moved from the country to the city six months ago. Write a short composition comparing and contrasting what you used to do when you lived in the country with what you now do in the city.

Schreibtipp Comparing and contrasting helps your reader understand an unfamiliar idea or see something familiar in a new way. Comparing is telling how two things are alike, and contrasting is telling how two things are different.

Vorbereiten

Make three lists: "Things I did in the country," "Things I do in the city," "Things I can do in both places." Then cross the items on the third list off of the first two lists. You will then have one list of similarities and two lists of differences. This will make organizing comparisons and contrasts easy.

Ausführen

Begin with a **topic sentence** that states your purpose in writing. For example, **Das Leben auf dem Land und das Leben in der Stadt sind fast gleich.** Or you could take the opposite viewpoint and say that life in the country and life in the city are not at all alike. Then write six to eight sentences supporting your viewpoint by comparing and contrasting life in both places.

Überarbeiten

- Check for clarity. Have you clearly stated your activities in both places?
- Proofread for spelling and punctuation errors, and then exchange with a partner and use your peer editing skills to help each other.
- Write and share a final draft.

6 Rollenspiel

Using props, role-play the following scene in front of the class.

You and three of your classmates are participants in a television talk show. The topic of the day is "The best place in the world to live." One of you will play the role of the host and ask questions of the others, who will play the guests. Everyone in the class writes the name of a large city anywhere in the world on a slip of paper and puts it in a box. Each guest draws a city from the box. He or she must think of some reasons and justifications for why he or she thinks this city is the best place in the world to live. The host will ask specific questions about the guest's interests to try to find out more information about why each person thinks he or she lives in the best place in the world.

Kann ich's wirklich?

Can you express preference and give a reason? (p. 189)

1 How would you say you prefer to live in the following places and give a reason for it?   Ich wohne lieber …
   a. in a small town   a. in einer Kleinstadt, weil …
   b. in a big city   b. in einer Großstadt, weil …
   c. in the country   c. auf dem Land, weil …
   d. in the mountains   d. in den Bergen, weil …
   e. by a river   e. an einem Fluss, weil …
   f. by a lake   f. an einem See, weil …

2 How would you ask a friend's opinion about different locations, using the following expressions?
   a. lieber   a. E.g.: Wo wohnst du lieber? In der Stadt oder auf dem Land?
   b. gefallen   b. E.g.: Wo gefällt es dir besser? In Bonn oder in Berlin?

Can you express your wishes, and ask others about their own? (p. 192)

3 How would you say you wish for the following things?   Ich wünsche mir …
   a. a television and a VCR   a. einen Fernseher und einen Video-Recorder.
   b. a great job   b. einen guten Job.
   c. a secure income   c. ein sicheres Einkommen.
   d. a peaceful life   d. ein friedliches Leben.
   e. a clean environment   e. eine saubere Umwelt.
   f. no war   f. keinen Krieg.

4 How would you ask someone what he or she wishes for?
E.g.: Was wünschst du dir?

Can you agree, with reservations? (p. 199)

5 How would you say to your friend that you agree that he or she does everything possible to avoid making excessive noise, but that you have the following reservations? He or she …
   a. drives too fast around curves   a. E.g.: Ja schon, aber du fährst zu schnell in die Kurven.
   b. slams the car door   b. E.g.: Ja, aber du schlägst deine Autotür zu.
   c. plays the car radio too loud   c. E.g.: Eigentlich schon, aber du spielst dein Autoradio zu laut.

Can you justify your answers, using halt and eben? (p. 201)

6 How would you now tell your friend he or she actually does make too much noise, and use the same arguments to justify your opinion?
Du machst zu viel Lärm, weil du halt/eben …   … deine Autotür zuschlägst.
… zu schnell in die Kurven fährst.   … dein Autoradio zu laut spielst.

Wortschatz

Erste Stufe

Expressing preference

Mir gefällt … besser als …	I like … better than …
da ist einfach mehr los	there's simply more going on
vorziehen (sep)	to prefer
Ich ziehe …vor	I prefer …
so …wie	as … as
(schlechter) als	(worse) than
älter	older
größer	bigger
jünger	younger

Talking about where you live

in einer Großstadt	in a big city
in einem Vorort	in a suburb
der Vorort, -e	suburb
in einer Kleinstadt	in a town
in einem Dorf	in a village
das Dorf, ¨er	village
in den Bergen	in the mountains
der Berg, -e	mountain
an einem See	on a lake
der See, -n	lake
an einem Fluss	on a river
der Fluss, ¨e	river

Living in your community

der Vorteil, -e	advantage
der Nachteil, -e	disadvantage
mehr Menschen	more people
weniger Geschäfte	fewer stores
öffentliche Verkehrsmittel (pl)	public transportation
die Wohnung, -en	apartment
die Umgebung, -en	surrounding area
der Verkehr	traffic
der Lärm	noise
die Luft	air
das Leben	life
sauber	clean
schmutzig	dirty
ruhig	calm

 p. 181X

Zweite Stufe

Around the house

das Haus, ¨er	house
der Flur, -e	hallway
das Wohnzimmer, -	living room
das Esszimmer, -	dining room
die Küche, -n	kitchen
das Schlafzimmer, -	bedroom
das Badezimmer, -	bathroom
die Toilette, -n	bathroom, toilet
der Keller, -	cellar
die Terrasse, -n	terrace, porch
der Garten, ¨	garden, yard
der Pool, -s	pool
der Strauch, ¨er	bush
der Baum, ¨e	tree

Expressing wishes

sich wünschen	to wish
Was wünschst du dir (mal)?	What would you wish for?
Ich wünsche mir …	I wish for …
die Ausbildung, -en	education
der Job, -s	job

das Einkommen	income
die Umwelt	environment
die Armut	poverty
der Krieg, -e	war

Useful words for describing things

friedlich	peaceful
gemütlich	comfortable, cozy
hell	bright
sicher	secure
eigen	(one's) own

Dritte Stufe

Talking about noise pollution

der Lärm	noise
Was produziert Lärm?	What produces noise?
der Lastkraftwagen (LKW), -	truck
das Flugzeug, -e	airplane
das Motorrad, ¨er	motorcycle
langsam	slow, slowly
abstellen (sep)	to switch off
der Motor, -en	motor
Stellen Sie den Motor ab!	Turn your engine off!
hupen	to honk the horn
Du fährst zu schnell in die Kurve!	You're taking the curve too fast!
Er schlägt die Autotür (den Kofferraumdeckel) zu!	He's slamming the car door (the trunk)!
He, Sie da! Sie spielen das Autoradio zu laut!	Hey you there! You're playing your car radio too loud!

Agreeing, but with reservations

Ja schon, aber …	Well yes, but …
Eigentlich schon, aber …	I suppose so, but …
Ja, ich stimme dir zwar zu, aber … todlangweilig	Yes, I do agree with you, but … extremely boring

Giving reasons or justifications

halt: Die Kleinstadt gefällt mir gut, weil es da halt ruhiger ist.	I like a small town because it's just quieter there.
eben: Man kann eben den Großstadtlärm vermeiden.	You can really avoid big city noise.

Kapitel 8: Mode? Ja oder nein?
Chapter Overview

Los geht's! pp. 212–214 — *Ein starkes Outfit*, p. 212

	FUNCTIONS	GRAMMAR	VOCABULARY	RE-ENTRY
Erste Stufe pp. 215–219	• Describing clothes, p. 217	• Adjectives following **der** and **dieser**-words, p. 217	• Clothes that are "in," p. 216	Clothing vocabulary, pp. 216–217 (**Kap. 5, I**); expressing wishes when buying things, p. 217 (**Kap. 5, I**); commenting on clothes, p. 218 (**Kap. 5, I**); talking about what you bought, p. 219 (**Kap. 8, I**); talking about prices, p. 219 (**Kap. 4, I**)
Zweite Stufe pp. 220–223	• Expressing interest, disinterest, and indifference, p. 221 • Making and accepting compliments, p. 222	• The verb **sich interessieren**, p. 222 • The verb **tragen**, p. 222 • Further uses of the dative case, p. 223	• Clothing and shoes, p. 221	Accusative reflexive verbs, p. 222 (**Kap. 4, II**); **für** + acc., p. 222 (**Kap. 7, I**); giving reasons, p. 222 (**Kap. 8, I**); complimenting someone, p. 222 (**Kap. 5, I**); dative pronouns, p. 223 (**Kap. 3, II**); commenting on clothing, p. 223 (**Kap. 5, I**)
Dritte Stufe pp. 224–227	• Persuading and dissuading, p. 226	• The verb **kaufen** with dative reflexive pronouns, p. 226 • The conjunction **wenn**, p. 227	• Clothing, fabrics, and fasteners, p. 225	Clothing items, pp. 224, 225 (**Kap. 5, I**); **möchte**-forms, pp. 225, 226 (**Kap. 3, I**); giving reasons, p. 225 (**Kap. 8, I**); **gefallen**, p. 225 (**Kap. 3, II**); expressing opinions, p. 226 (**Kap. 2/9, I**); dative reflexive verbs, p. 226 (**Kap. 6, II**); **du**-commands, p. 226 (**Kap. 8, I**); subordinate conjunctions, p. 227 (**Kap. 8/9, I**)

Zum Lesen pp. 228–229 — Was bedeutet „reich und schön sein"?
Reading Strategy Understanding relationships between and within sentences

Mehr Grammatikübungen pp. 230–233
Erste Stufe, pp. 230–231   Zweite Stufe, pp. 231–232   Dritte Stufe, pp. 232–233

Review pp. 234–237
Anwendung, pp. 234–235   Kann ich's wirklich?, p. 236   Wortschatz, p. 237
Zum Schreiben: Tone and word choice (Writing an interview dialogue)

CULTURE

• **Landeskunde:** Was trägst du am liebsten? p. 215
• **Ein wenig Landeskunde:** Clothes typically worn by youths, p. 219
• Interviews with German students about fashion, p. 220
• Excerpt from a clothing catalog, p. 224

Kapitel 8: Mode? Ja oder nein?
Chapter Resources

Lesson Planning
One-Stop Planner
Lesson Planner with Substitute Teacher Lesson Plans, pp. 37–41, 72
Student Make-Up Assignments
- Make-Up Assignment Copying Masters, Chapter 8

Listening and Speaking
TPR Storytelling Book, pp. 56–63
Listening Activities
- Student Response Forms for Listening Activities, pp. 59–62
- Additional Listening Activities 8-1 to 8-6, pp. 63–66
- Additional Listening Activities (song), p. 62
- Scripts and Answers, pp. 144–149

Video Guide
- Teaching Suggestions, pp. 50–51
- Activity Masters, pp. 52–54
- Scripts and Answers, pp. 97–99

Activities for Communication
- Communicative Activities, pp. 43–48
- Realia and Teaching Suggestions, pp. 102–105
- Situation Cards, pp. 137–138

Reading and Writing
Reading Strategies and Skills Handbook, Chapter 8
Lies mit mir! 2, Chapter 8
Übungsheft, pp. 85–96

Grammar
Grammatikheft, pp. 64–72
Grammar Tutor for Students of German, Chapter 8

Assessment
Testing Program
- Grammar and Vocabulary Quizzes, **Stufe** Quizzes, and Chapter Test, pp. 197–214
- Score Sheet, Scripts and Answers, pp. 215–222

Alternative Assessment Guide
- Portfolio Assessment, p. 25
- Performance Assessment, p. 39
- CD-ROM Assessment, p. 53

Student Make-Up Assignments
- Alternative Quizzes, Chapter 8

Online Activities
- Interaktive Spiele
- Internet Aktivitäten

Video Program
- Videocassette 3
- Videocassette 5 (captioned version)
- DVD Tutor, Disc 2

Audio Compact Discs
- Textbook Listening Activities, CD 8, Tracks 1–13
- Additional Listening Activities, CD 8, Tracks 19–25
- Assessment Items, CD 8, Tracks 14–18

Interactive CD-ROM Tutor, Disc 2

Teaching Transparencies
- Situations 8-1 to 8-2
- Vocabulary 8-A to 8-C
- Los geht's!
- Mehr Grammatikübungen Answers
- Grammatikheft Answers

Use the **One-Stop Planner CD-ROM with Test Generator** to aid in lesson planning and pacing.

For each chapter, the **One-Stop Planner** includes:
- Editable lesson plans with direct links to teaching resources
- Printable worksheets from resource books
- Direct launches to the HRW Internet activities
- Video and audio segments
- Test Generator
- Clip Art for vocabulary items

Kapitel 8: Mode? Ja oder nein?

Projects

Modische Klamotten

In this activity each student will design his or her ideal wardrobe by cutting out photos and ads from favorite clothing catalogs or advertisements. Each item or outfit will include a detailed description. Students should begin this project after they are familiar with the new phrases and expressions of all three *Stufen*.

MATERIALS

Students may need
- posterboard
- glue
- advertisements
- pens
- scissors
- old catalogs
- paper

SUGGESTED SEQUENCE

1. After you have discussed the project with students, they should make an outline of what they would like to include in their ideal wardrobe.
2. With their wardrobes in mind, students should search through catalogs and ads to find pictures for their poster project.
3. Once students have collected their materials, they should design the layout and arrange the various outfits on the posterboard.
4. For the writing component of this project, students should incorporate the new phrases and expressions they have learned in this chapter in written descriptions of each of the outfits.
5. Before students write a final description, they should ask a classmate to proofread what they have written.
6. The final descriptions should be placed underneath each outfit.
7. Finally, students present their ideal wardrobe to the rest of the class.

GRADING THE PROJECT

Suggested point distribution (total = 100 points)
Appearance 25
Accurate descriptions and correct
language usage 50
Presentation 25

Games

Auf dem Kostümball

This game gives students an opportunity to use the vocabulary from Chapter 8 in a fun way and to review expressions from previous chapters.

Preparation Prepare a list of possible costumes one might see at a costume ball, including some that are currently popular.

Procedure Divide students into two teams. Have a member of team A come to the front of the class and show him or her the name of a costume. (Example: **ein Clown**) The student then describes the costume to the class in German within a set amount of time. The first team to guess the correct costume wins a point. After the student from team A has finished, a member of team B comes to the front to describe the next costume. The team with the highest score at the end of the game wins. Here are other suggestions for costumes: **Ärztin, Bauer, Cowboy, Hexe**.

Games

Anziehwettbewerb

Play this game to review the clothing vocabulary from this and previous chapters.

Preparation Prepare for this game by filling two bags with clothing articles you would like to review. Each bag should have the same number of clothing items, but the items need not be identical.

Procedure Divide the class into two teams and place the two bags at the front of the classroom. A member of each team comes to the front of the class. When you give the signal, each of the two students should put on all of the clothing in his or her bag while the rest of the team writes down the clothing items in the order he or she puts them on. The first team that writes down all clothing items correctly wins.

Storytelling

Mini-Geschichte

*This story accompanies Teaching Transparency 8-2. Read the **Mini-Geschichte** to your students, or have them role-play the conversation using appropriate body language and gestures. Ask students what criteria Katrin and Ulrike use in their selection of clothes.*

Was soll ich mir kaufen?

KATRIN Schau mal, Ulrike! Dieser gelbe Rock gefällt mir sehr gut!

ULRIKE Ja, er ist fesch, aber er ist aus Polyester und Viskose. Kauf dir ja nichts aus Polyester. Das ist sehr ungesund, weil die Haut darunter nicht atmen *(to breathe)* kann.

KATRIN Schade! Der rote Minirock ist aus Baumwolle, aber er ist viel zu kurz. Was meinst du?

ULRIKE Ja, er sieht kurz aus. Kauf dir doch die grüne Shorts. Die ist aus Baumwolle und sieht echt lässig aus.

KATRIN Gute Idee! Die Shorts ist auch viel billiger als der gelbe Rock.

Traditions

Der Altenrieter Brezelmarkt

Altenriet ist eine kleine Stadt in der Stuttgarter Region, in der Traditionen sehr lebendig sind: Seit Jahrhunderten wird hier am Palmsonntag der Brezelmarkt gehalten. Einige der im Festumzug fahrenden Wagen erzählen die Geschichte von der Entstehung der Brezel. Vor langer Zeit soll in Altenriet ein Bäcker gelebt haben, der sehr geizig war. Er streckte sein Mehl mit gemahlenem Kalk. Als der Burgherr von Neuenriet das merkte, warf er den Bäcker in den Kerker. Auf Bitten der Frau des Bäckers, versprach der Ritter, den Bäcker freizulassen, wenn dieser einen Kuchen backen könnte, durch den die Sonne dreimal hindurchscheine.

Der Bäcker probierte viele verschiedene Formen, bis er schließlich die Idee hatte, eine Brezel zu formen. Das neue Gebäck hatte nicht nur drei Löcher, sondern schmeckte dem Ritter auch vorzüglich! Der Bäcker wurde befreit und die Brezel war geboren.

Have students research in the library or on the Internet the celebrations and customs associated with Palm Sunday. Students should present their research to the class.

Rezept

Kartoffelsalat
Für 4 Personen

Zutaten

kg=Kilogramm, EL=Esslöffel, TL=Teelöffel, l=Liter

1kg	Kartoffeln
1	Knoblauchzehe
3-4EL	Essig
¼l	warme Fleischbrühe
1½TL	Salz
½ TL	weißer Pfeffer
1	kleine Zwiebel, fein gehackt
3-4EL	Öl

Die ungeschälten Kartoffeln kochen, abgießen, abschrecken, pellen und dann in feine Scheiben schneiden. Die Schüssel mit der geschälten, halbierten Knoblauchzehe ausreiben. Die Kartoffelscheiben hineingeben. Den Essig mit der Brühe mischen und über die Kartoffelscheiben gießen. Mit Salz, Pfeffer und der Zwiebel würzen und pikant abschmecken. Dann erst das Öl zugießen und untermischen. Den Salat noch 1 Stunde durchziehen lassen.

Kapitel 8: Mode? Ja oder nein?
Technology

Videocassette 3, 5 (captioned version)
DVD Tutor, Disc 2
See Video Guide, pages 49–54

DVD/Video

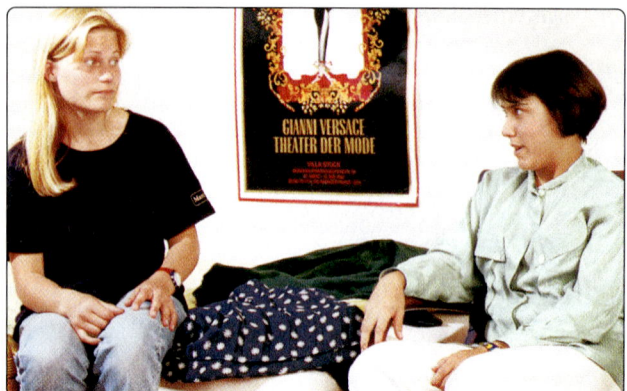

Los geht's! • Ein starkes Outfit

Judith is visiting Katrin. Katrin points out the clothes she needs to wash, take to the cleaners, and give away. They discuss Judith's outfit and their interest in fashion. Then they discuss Roland, and his interest in fashion. Roland then explains his taste in clothes. As Judith and Katrin talk about Boris, the camera moves to Boris and Rolf, who in turn are talking about Katrin.

Landeskunde
Was trägst du am liebsten?
People from various cities in Germany discuss their favorite clothes.

Fortsetzung

Judith and Katrin are on their way to the dry cleaner's, where they bump into Boris, who is dressed up for a party. The girls compliment him on his clothes, and he invites them to come along with him, dressed as they are right now. They protest that they would have to change first, and say they might come later.

Videoclips
- **Quelle Damenmodekatalog**® (mail-order women's fashions)
- **Persil Supra Waschpulver**® (laundry detergent)
- **Dralle Beauty**® (hair care products)

Interactive CD-ROM Tutor

Activity	Activity Type	Pupil's Edition Reference
1. Wortschatz	Merkspiel	p. 216
2. Grammatik	Was fehlt?	p. 217
3. Wortschatz	Merkspiel	p. 221
4. So sagt man das!	Wozu gehört's?	pp. 221, 222
5. Wortschatz	Wort und Bild Erfahren/Wählen	pp. 224, 225
6. So sagt man das!	Was ist richtig?	pp. 217, 221, 222, 223, 226
Landeskunde	Was trägst du am liebsten und warum? Was ist richtig?	p. 215
Zum Sprechen	*Guided recording*	pp. 234–235
Zum Schreiben	*Guided writing*	pp. 234–235

Teacher Management System
Launch the program, type "admin" in the password area, and press RETURN. Log on to **www.hrw.com/CDROMTUTOR** for a detailed explanation of the Teacher Management System.

DVD Tutor

The *DVD Tutor* contains all material from the *Video Program* as described above. German captions are available for use at your discretion for all sections of the video. The *DVD Tutor* also provides a variety of video-based activities that assess students' understanding of **Los geht's!**, **Fortsetzung**, and **Landeskunde**, as well as the new **Grammatik im Kontext** presentations.

The *DVD Tutor* may be used on any DVD video player connected to a television or video monitor.

One-Stop Planner CD-ROM

To preview all resources available for this chapter, use the **One-Stop Planner CD-ROM**, Disc 2.

Visit Holt Online
go.hrw.com
KEYWORD: WK3 STUTTGART-8
Online Edition

Go.Online!

Premier Online Edition

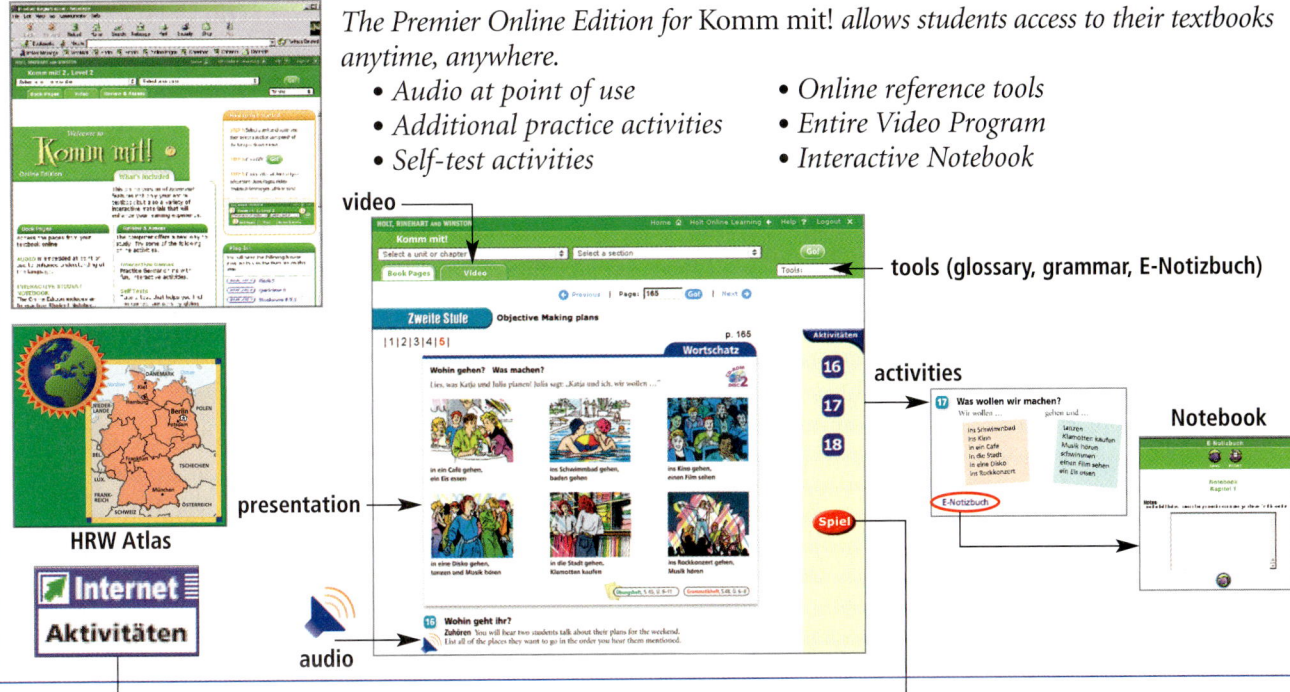

The Premier Online Edition for *Komm mit!* allows students access to their textbooks anytime, anywhere.

- Audio at point of use
- Additional practice activities
- Self-test activities
- Online reference tools
- Entire Video Program
- Interactive Notebook

HRW Atlas

presentation

audio

video

tools (glossary, grammar, E-Notizbuch)

activities

Notebook

Internet Aktivitäten

These guided internet activities include a worksheet and pre-selected and pre-screened authentic web sites from the German-speaking countries. You can use these activities

- to help students develop research skills in the target language
- to introduce students to authentic cultural information
- as a project

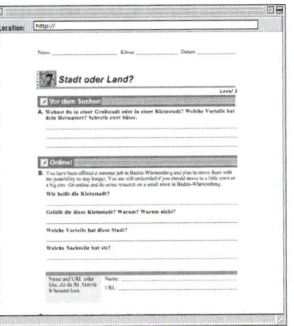

Interaktive Spiele

You can use the interactive activities in this chapter

- to practice grammar, vocabulary, and chapter functions
- as homework
- as an assessment option
- as a self-test
- to prepare for the Chapter Test

Webprojekt Have students visit the site of a theater or an opera house in Germany and choose a play or an opera. Ask students to look at scenes from the play or opera and describe the costumes of two main characters. Encourage students to exchange useful Web sites with their classmates. Have students document their sources by referencing the names and URLs of all the sites they consulted.

STANDARDS: 1.2, 1.3, 3.2, 5.1   KAPITEL 8   TECHNOLOGY

Kapitel 8: Mode? Ja oder nein?
Textbook Listening Activities Scripts

Erste Stufe

7 p. 217

KLAUS Also, der Lutz sieht immer total ordentlich aus: weißes Hemd, schicke Hose, glänzende Lederschuhe. Und wenn er mal 'ne Jeans trägt, dann hat die garantiert 'ne Bügelfalte! Die Katrin hat immer tolle Klamotten an, je nachdem, was gerade so „in" ist. Enger Minirock, „cooles" Lederoutfit und hohe Stöckelschuhe. Sie sieht fast aus wie Claudia Schiffer! Die Silke sieht auch ganz klasse aus. Sie hat zwar nicht immer den neuesten Look, aber dafür zieht sie sich echt originell an! Große, silberne Ohrringe, ein buntes Stirnband, 'ne fetzige Jeans und das geknotete Männerhemd, … eigentlich viel zu weit, steht ihr aber toll! So wie der Udo, lauf ich gerne selber 'rum. Er trägt die bequemsten Klamotten: ausgewaschene Jeans und alte Turnschuhe. Heute sieht er echt lässig aus in dem T-Shirt von seiner Lieblingsfußballmannschaft!

Answers to Activity 7
a. Katrin: toll, eng, „cool", hoch
b. Udo: bequem, verwaschen, alt
c. Silke: groß, silbern, bunt, fetzig, geknotet, weit
d. Lutz: weiß, schick, glänzend
Answers will vary.

11 p. 218

ERIK Also, mein Freund, der Otto, hat immer wahnsinnig witzige Klamotten an. Er kombiniert die unmöglichsten Farben miteinander. Heute hat er zum Beispiel ein oranges Hemd an, drei Nummern zu groß natürlich! Das trägt er ganz lässig über der Hose. Am Kragen steht es offen, und um den Hals hat er locker eine alte Seidenkrawatte von seinem Opa geschlungen, weiß mit großen roten Punkten. Seine fetzigen Jeans sind an den Knien zerrissen und ganz hellblau verwaschen. Dazu trägt er knallgrüne Socken und, typisch Otto, die feinsten Schuhe aus schwarzem Leder! Tja, alle finden Otto supercool!

Zweite Stufe

17 p. 222

MIRIAM Ich interessiere mich für Sprachen. Französisch ist mein Lieblingsfach, und in den Sommerferien fahre ich nach Paris. Es macht mir Spaß, die Sprache eines anderen Landes zu lernen, um die Mentalität und Kultur dieser Menschen besser zu verstehen.

AXEL Mich interessiert klassische Musik. Ich höre Schumann, Bach und Tschaikowsky sehr gern, besonders wenn ich Hausaufgaben mache. Am meisten interessiere ich mich für die Klavierstücke von Chopin. Ich mag klassische Musik, weil ich selber ein klassisches Instrument spiele.

TINA Es gefällt mir, wenn ich Komplimente für mein Aussehen bekomme. Deswegen interessiere ich mich für Mode und Kosmetik. Es macht mir Spaß, mich zu stylen und immer die neuesten Klamotten zu haben. Am liebsten probiere ich verschiedene Frisuren aus. Wenn ich mit der Schule fertig bin, möchte ich irgendwas mit Mode und Design machen.

BEATE Ich interessiere mich für Politik. Ich finde es sehr wichtig, darüber informiert zu sein, was so alles in der Welt los ist. Ich sehe gern die Nachrichten im Fernsehen und lese jeden Morgen die Zeitung.

Answers to Activity 17
a. 1. Miriam: Sprachen, Französisch; 2. Axel: klassische Musik; 3. Tina: Mode und Kosmetik; 4. Beate: Politik
b. 1. Miriam: um Mentalität und Kultur zu verstehen; 2. Axel: weil er selbst ein klassisches Instrument spielt; 3. Tina: weil sie gern Komplimente für ihr Aussehen bekommt; 4. Beate: weil sie es wichtig findet, informiert zu sein

Dritte Stufe

26 p. 225

SYLVIA Hallo, Elke! Du hast es aber eilig. Wo willst du denn hin?

ELKE Ach, hallo, Sylvia! Hallo, Tina! Ich will den Bus um drei Uhr noch bekommen, um in

The following scripts are for the listening activities found in the *Pupil's Edition*. For Student Response Forms, see *Listening Activities*, pages 59–62. To provide students with additional listening practice, see *Listening Activities*, pages 63–66.

For resource information, see the **One-Stop Planner CD-ROM**, Disc 2.

die Stadt zu fahren. Heute kaufe ich mir endlich die schwarze Lederjacke aus der kleinen Boutique neben dem Kaufhaus. Morgen Abend ziehe ich sie an, wenn wir zum Pop-Festival am Brandenburger Tor gehen. Hast du dir schon die fransige Jeansweste geholt, die du so gern haben wolltest, Sylvia?

SYLVIA Nein, und ich werde sie mir auch nicht kaufen. Ich hab sie vor ein paar Tagen mal anprobiert. Die Tina und ich, wir waren letzten Donnerstag zusammen in der Stadt. Die Weste sah schrecklich an mir aus, stimmt's Tina? Viel zu weit und zu lang. Ich war echt enttäuscht.

TINA Ja, das stimmt, leider! Aber ich hatte auch ein ziemliches Pech an diesem Tag. Ich wollte mir so gern dieses gepunktete Outfit aus Seide kaufen, weißt du, so eins, wie die Julia Roberts in *Pretty Woman* anhatte. Im „Mode-Schlösschen" gab es nur noch eins in meiner Größe. Die Sylvia hat gesagt, dass es mir super steht. Aber dann, an der Kasse, haben wir bemerkt, dass es einen großen Fleck auf dem Ärmel hatte. Ich hab mich vielleicht geärgert und war den ganzen Donnerstag lang schlecht gelaunt deswegen!

ELKE Du, Tina, ich hab das gleiche Outfit im Heinemann-Katalog gesehen. Bestell es dir doch einfach dort!

TINA Echt? Das mach ich bestimmt! Ich komm heute Abend mal bei dir vorbei und schau mir den Katalog an, okay?

ELKE Ja, klar. Gern! Aber jetzt muss ich schnell zur Bushaltestelle laufen. Also tschüs dann, bis heute Abend!

TINA Tschüs!

SYLVIA Tschüs, Elke!

Answers to Activity 26
Elke: will Lederjacke kaufen, fürs Pop-Festival
Sylvia: will Jeansweste nicht kaufen, weil sie ihr nicht passt
Tina: will gepunktetes Outfit kaufen, aber es hat einen Fleck; will es dann aus dem Katalog bestellen

32 p. 227

DORO Ich fahr eigentlich nur mit dem Auto zur Schule, wenn mein Fahrrad mal kaputt ist. Das heißt, ich fahr nicht selber, sondern meine Mutter fährt mich natürlich, weil ich noch keinen Führerschein habe.

ROLAND Am Wochenende oder in den Ferien gehe ich gerne segeln, aber nur wenn es sonnig und warm ist. Bei schlechtem Wetter und stürmischer See segeln zu gehen, ist viel zu gefährlich.

ANITA Wenn es draußen regnet, gehe ich meistens ins Jugendzentrum, um Schach zu spielen. Dort sind immer zwei, drei Leute, die auch gern Schach spielen. Ich finde es ziemlich langweilig, an einem regnerischen Tag zu Hause herumzusitzen.

HOLGER Normalerweise muss ich mich bei uns zu Hause nicht um den Einkauf kümmern, das besorgt alles meine Mutter. Ich gehe eigentlich nur Lebensmittel einkaufen, wenn ich meine Oma besuche. Aber das mache ich gern, weil sie nicht so schwere Sachen schleppen kann.

Answers to Activity 32
1. b; 2. d; 3. c; 4. a

Anwendung

1 p. 234

KATRIN Boris, kauf dir doch diese Jacke aus Baumwolle hier! Die ist nicht so teuer wie die Wildlederjacke dort, und außerdem sieht sie echt sportlich aus. Probier sie doch mal an! Also, ich finde, du solltest sie unbedingt nehmen!

BORIS Wirklich? Ja, wenn du meinst, sie steht mir dann, kauf ich sie doch glatt!

KATRIN Du, Judith, gestern wollte ich mir Schuhe in dem neuen Schuhgeschäft am Bahnhof kaufen. Als ich ein Paar Stiefel anprobiert habe, ist ein Absatz kaputtgegangen und die Sohle war auch schon lose. Kauf dir ja keine Schuhe dort! Die haben eine ganz schlechte Qualität.

JUDITH Ja, das habe ich auch schon gehört. Da geh ich bestimmt nichts kaufen.

Answers to Activity 1
Baumwolljacke kaufen; sieht sportlich aus
Keine Schuhe in dem neuen Schuhgeschäft kaufen; schlechte Qualität

Kapitel 8: Mode? Ja oder nein?
Suggested Lesson Plans 50-Minute Schedule

Day 1

CHAPTER OPENER 10 min.
- Building on Previous Skills, ATE, p. 209M
- Thinking Critically, ATE, p. 209M

LOS GEHT'S! 20 min.
- Preteaching Vocabulary, ATE, p. 209N
- Play Audio CD for **Los geht's!**
- Have students read **Los geht's!**, pp. 212–213
- Teaching Suggestions, Video Guide, p. 50
- Show **Los geht's!** Video

LANDESKUNDE 15 min.
- Pre-viewing Suggestion, Video Guide, p. 50
- Teaching Suggestions, ATE, p. 209O
- Show **Landeskunde** Video

Wrap-Up 5 min.
- Students respond to questions about how they would describe their clothing styles

Homework Options
Pupil's Edition, p. 214, Comprehension Acts. 1–5; p. 215, Acts. A and B
Übungsheft, p. 85, Act. 1; p. 86, Act. 1
Interactive CD-ROM, **Landeskunde** Activity

Day 2

ERSTE STUFE
Quick Review 10 min.
- Check homework, Comprehension Acts. 1–5, p. 214

Wortschatz, p. 216 15 min.
- Presenting **Wortschatz**, ATE, p. 209P
- Teaching Transparency 8-1
- Do Activity 6, p. 216
- Play Audio CD for Activity 7, p. 217
- Do Activity 8, p. 217

So sagt man das! / Grammatik, p. 217 20 min.
- Presenting **So sagt man das!**, ATE, p. 209P
- Teaching Transparency 8-A
- Do Activities 9 and 10, p. 218
- Play Audio CD for Activity 11, p. 218
- Do Activity 13, p. 219
- Do Activity 2, p. 65, Grammatikheft

Wrap-Up 5 min.
- Students respond to questions about colors and types of clothing they wear

Homework Options
Pupil's Edition, p. 219, Act. 12
Grammatikheft, p. 64, Act. 1
Übungsheft, pp. 87–89, Acts. 1–7

Day 3

ERSTE STUFE
Quick Review 15 min.
- Check homework, Pupil's Edition, p. 219, Act. 12

Ein wenig Landeskunde, p. 219 15 min.
- Present **Ein wenig Landeskunde**, p. 219
- Present **Lerntrick**, p. 219
- Do Activities 14 and 15, p. 219

Quiz Review 15 min.
- Do Situation 8-1, pp. 137–138, Activities for Communication
- Do Additional Listening Activities 8-1 and 8-2, p. 63
- Do **Erste Stufe** Activities, Interactive CD-ROM

Wrap-Up 5 min.
- Students respond to questions about how they like the outfits of other students

Homework Options
Mehr Grammatikübungen, Erste Stufe

Day 4

ERSTE STUFE
Quick Review 10 min.
- Check homework, **Mehr Grammatikübungen, Erste Stufe**

Quiz 20 min.
- Quiz 8-1A or 8-1B

ZWEITE STUFE
Reading Selection 15 min.
- Total Physical Response, ATE, p. 209R
- Read quotations, p. 220
- Do Activity 16, p. 220

Wrap-Up 5 min.
- Students respond to questions about whether or not they are interested in fashion

Homework Options
Activities for Communication, p. 103, Realia 8-2: create and describe an outfit for a fashion show

Day 5

ZWEITE STUFE
Quick Review 10 min.
- Return and review Quiz 8-1
- Check homework, Realia 8-2

Wortschatz / So sagt man das!, p. 221 10 min.
- Presenting **Wortschatz / So sagt man das!**, ATE, p. 209R
- Teaching Transparency 8-B
- Play Audio CD for Activity 17, p. 222

Ein wenig Grammatik / Ein wenig Grammatik, p. 222 15 min.
- Present **Ein wenig Grammatik**, p. 222
- Do Activities 18 and 19, p. 222
- Present **Ein wenig Grammatik**, p. 222
- Do Activity 20, p. 222

So sagt man das!, p. 222 10 min.
- Presenting **So sagt man das!**, ATE, p. 209S
- Do Activity 7, p. 68, Grammatikheft

Wrap-Up 5 min.
- Students respond to questions about their interests

Homework Options
Grammatikheft, pp. 66–67, Acts. 3–6
Übungsheft, p. 90, Acts. 1–3

Day 6

ZWEITE STUFE
Quick Review 10 min.
- Check homework, Grammatikheft, pp. 66–67, Acts. 3–6

Grammatik, p. 223 15 min.
- Presenting **Grammatik**, ATE, p. 209S
- Do Activities 21, 22, 23, and 24, p. 223

Quiz Review 20 min.
- Do **Mehr Grammatikübungen, Zweite Stufe**
- Do Communicative Activity 8-2, pp. 45–46
- Do Additional Listening Activities 8-3 and 8-4, pp. 64–65

Wrap-Up 5 min.
- Students respond to questions about which clothing pieces go with other clothing

Homework Options
Grammatikheft, p. 68, Act. 8
Übungsheft, pp. 91–92, Acts. 4–6

One-Stop Planner CD-ROM

For alternative lesson plans by chapter section, to create your own customized plans, or to preview all resources available for this chapter, use the **One-Stop Planner CD-ROM**, Disc 2.

 For additional homework suggestions, see activities accompanied by this symbol throughout the chapter.

Day 7

ZWEITE STUFE
Quick Review 10 min.
- Check homework, Übungsheft, pp. 91–92, Acts. 4–6

Quiz 20 min.
- Quiz 8-2A or 8-2B

DRITTE STUFE 15 min.
- Do Activity 25, p. 224
- Teaching Transparency 8-2

Wrap-Up 5 min.
- Students respond to questions about which clothing items they like to wear

Homework Options
Internet Aktivitäten, see ATE, p. 209F

Day 8

DRITTE STUFE
Quick Review 10 min.
- Return and review Quiz 8-2
- Bell Work, ATE, p. 209T

Wortschatz, p. 225 15 min.
- Presenting **Wortschatz**, p. 209T
- Teaching Transparency 8-C
- Play Audio CD for Activity 26, p. 225
- Do Activities 27 and 28, p. 225

So sagt man das!, p. 226 10 min.
- Presenting **So sagt man das!**, ATE, p. 209T
- Do Activity 29, p. 226

Ein wenig Grammatik, p. 226 10 min.
- Presenting **Ein wenig Grammatik**, ATE, p. 209U
- Do Activities 30 and 31, p. 226
- Play Audio CD for Activity 32, p. 227

Wrap-Up 5 min.
Students respond to questions about which fabrics they should buy for themselves

Homework Options
Grammatikheft, pp. 69–71, Acts. 9–14
Übungsheft, pp. 93–94, Acts. 1–3

Day 9

DRITTE STUFE
Quick Review 10 min.
- Check homework, Grammatikheft, pp. 69–71, Acts. 9–14

Ein wenig Grammatik, p. 227 15 min.
- Presenting **Ein wenig Grammatik**, ATE, p. 209U
- Do Activities 33, 34, 35, and 37, p. 227

ZUM LESEN 20 min.
- Present **Lesestrategie**, p. 228
- Do Activities 1–10, pp. 228–229

Wrap-Up 5 min.
- Students respond to questions about the difference between **wenn** and **wann**

Homework Options
Pupil's Edition, p. 227, Act. 36
Grammatikheft, p. 72, Act. 15
Übungsheft, pp. 94–95, Acts. 4–7; p. 96

Day 10

DRITTE STUFE
Quick Review 10 min.
- Check homework, Übungsheft, pp. 94–95, Acts. 4–7

Quiz Review 20 min.
- Do **Mehr Grammatikübungen, Dritte Stufe**
- Do Communicative Activities 8-2 and 8-3, pp. 45–48

Quiz 20 min.
- Quiz 8-3A or 8-3B

Homework Options
Interaktive Spiele, see ATE, p. 209F

Day 11

ANWENDUNG
Quick Review 10 min.
- Return and review Quiz 8-3

ANWENDUNG 35 min.
- Do **Anwendung** Activities 1–6, and 8 pp. 234–235

Wrap-Up 5 min.
- Students respond to questions about what clothing is "in" and what clothing they prefer to wear

Homework Options
Pupil's Edition, p. 235, Act. 7

Day 12

ANWENDUNG
Quick Review 10 min.
- Students present **Zum Schreiben** dialogues

Kann ich's wirklich?, p. 236 20 min.
- Do Activities 1-8, p. 236

Chapter Review 20 min.
- Review chapter functions, vocabulary, and grammar; choose from **Mehr Grammatikübungen**, Grammar Tutor for Students of German, Activities for Communication, Listening Activities, Interactive CD-ROM Tutor, or **Interaktive Spiele**
- Review test format and provide sample test items for students

Homework Options
Study for Chapter Test

Assessment

Test, Chapter 8 45 min.
- Administer Chapter 8 Test. Select from Testing Program, Alternative Assessment Guide, or Test Generator.

Kapitel 8: Mode? Ja oder nein?
Suggested Lesson Plans — 90-Minute Block Schedule

Block 1

CHAPTER OPENER 10 min.
- Building on Previous Skills, ATE, p. 209M
- Thinking Critically, ATE, p. 209M

LOS GEHT'S! 20 min.
- Pre-teaching Vocabulary, ATE, p. 209N
- Play Audio CD for Los geht's!
- Have students read Los geht's!, pp. 212–213
- Teaching Suggestions, Video Guide, p. 50
- Show Los geht's! Video

LANDESKUNDE 20 min.
- Teaching Suggestions, ATE, p. 209O
- Pre-viewing Suggestion, Video Guide, p. 50
- Show Landeskunde Video
- Do Landeskunde Activity, Interactive CD-ROM

ERSTE STUFE
Wortschatz, p. 216 15 min.
- Presenting Wortschatz, ATE, p. 209P
- Teaching Transparency 8-1
- Do Activity 6, p. 216
- Play Audio CD for Activity 7, p. 217
- Do Activity 8, p. 217

So sagt man das! / Grammatik, p. 217 20 min.
- Presenting So sagt man das!, ATE, p. 209P
- Teaching Transparency 8-A
- Do Activities 9 and 10, p. 218
- Play Audio CD for Activity 11, p. 218
- Do Activity 13, p. 219
- Do Activity 2, p. 65, Grammatikheft

Wrap-Up 5 min.
- Students respond to questions about colors and types of clothing they wear

Homework Options
Pupil's Edition, p. 214, Comprehension Acts. 1–5; p. 215, Acts. A and B; p. 219, Act. 12
Grammatikheft, p. 64, Act. 1
Übungsheft, p. 85, Act. 1; p. 86, Act. 1; pp. 87–89, Acts. 1–7

Block 2

ERSTE STUFE
Quick Review 15 min.
- Check homework, Pupil's Edition, p. 219, Act. 12

Ein wenig Landeskunde, p. 219 15 min.
- Present Ein wenig Landeskunde, p. 219
- Present Lerntrick, p. 219
- Do Activities 14 and 15, p. 219

Quiz Review 20 min.
- Do Situation 8-1, pp. 137–138, Activities for Communication
- Do Erste Stufe Activities, Interactive CD-ROM
- Do Mehr Grammatikübungen, Erste Stufe

Quiz 20 min.
- Quiz 8-1A or 8-1B

ZWEITE STUFE
Reading Selection 15 min.
- Total Physical Response, ATE, p. 209R
- Read quotations, p. 220
- Do Activity 16, p. 220

Wrap-Up 5 min.
- Students respond to questions about whether or not they are interested in fashion

Homework Options
Activities for Communication, p. 103, Realia 8-2: create and describe an outfit for a fashion show

Block 3

ZWEITE STUFE
Quick Review 15 min.
- Return and review Quiz 8-1
- Check homework, Realia 8-2

Wortschatz / So sagt man das!, p. 221 10 min.
- Presenting Wortschatz/So sagt man das!, ATE, p. 209R
- Teaching Transparency 8-B
- Play Audio CD for Activity 17, p. 222

Ein wenig Grammatik / Ein wenig Grammatik, p. 222 15 min.
- Present Ein wenig Grammatik, p. 222
- Do Activities 18 and 19, p. 222
- Present Ein wenig Grammatik, p. 222
- Do Activity 20, p. 222

So sagt man das!, p. 222 10 min.
- Presenting So sagt man das!, ATE, p. 209S
- Do Activity 7, p. 68, Grammatikheft

Grammatik, p. 223 15 min.
- Presenting Grammatik, ATE, p. 209S
- Do Activities 21, 22, 23, and 24, p. 223
- Do Activities 4–6, pp. 91-92, Übungsheft

Quiz Review 20 min.
- Do Mehr Grammatikübungen, Zweite Stufe
- Do Communicative Activity 8-2, pp. 45–46
- Do Additional Listening Activities 8-3 and 8-4, pp. 64–65

Wrap-Up 5 min.
- Students respond to questions about their interests

Homework Options
Grammatikheft, pp. 66–67, Acts. 3–6; p. 68, Act. 8
Übungsheft, p. 90, Acts. 1–3

One-Stop Planner CD-ROM

For alternative lesson plans by chapter section, to create your own customized plans, or to preview all resources available for this chapter, use the **One-Stop Planner CD-ROM**, Disc 2.

 For additional homework suggestions, see activities accompanied by this symbol throughout the chapter.

Block 4

ZWEITE STUFE
Quick Review 10 min.
- Check homework, Übungsheft, p. 90, Acts. 1–3

Quiz 20 min.
- Quiz 8-2A or 8-2B

DRITTE STUFE
Reading Selection 15 min.
- Do Activity 25, p. 224
- Teaching Transparency 8-2

Wortschatz, p. 225 15 min.
- Presenting **Wortschatz**, p. 209T
- Teaching Transparency 8-C
- Play Audio CD for Activity 26, p. 225
- Do Activities 27 and 28, p. 225

So sagt man das!, p. 226 10 min.
- Presenting **So sagt man das!**, ATE, p. 209T
- Do Activity 29, p. 226

Ein wenig Grammatik, p. 226 15 min.
- Presenting **Ein wenig Grammatik**, ATE, p. 209U
- Do Activities 30 and 31, p. 226
- Play Audio CD for Activity 32, p. 227

Wrap-Up 5 min.
- Students respond to questions about which clothing items they like to wear

Homework Options
Grammatikheft, pp. 69–71, Acts. 9–14
Übungsheft, pp. 93–94, Acts. 1–3

Block 5

DRITTE STUFE
Quick Review 10 min.
- Return and review Quiz 8-2
- Check homework, Grammatikheft, pp. 69–71, Acts. 9–14

Ein wenig Grammatik, p. 227 25 min.
- Presenting **Ein wenig Grammatik**, ATE, p. 209U
- Do Activities 33, 34, 35, 36, and 37, p. 227
- Do Activity 15, p. 72, Grammatikheft
- Do Activities 4–7, pp. 94–95, Übungsheft

ZUM LESEN 25 min.
- Present **Lesestrategie**, p. 228
- Do Activities 1–10, pp. 228–229

Quiz Review 10 min.
- Do **Mehr Grammatikübungen, Dritte Stufe**

Quiz 20 min.
- Quiz 8-3A or 8-3B

Homework Options
Übungsheft, p. 96
Interaktive Spiele, see ATE, p. 209F

Block 6

ANWENDUNG
Quick Review 10 min.
- Return and review Quiz 8-3

ANWENDUNG 45 min.
- Do **Anwendung** Activities 1–8, pp. 234–235

Kann ich's wirklich?, p. 236 25 min.
- Do Activities 1–8, p. 236

Wrap-Up 10 min.
- Students respond to questions about what clothing is "in" and what clothing they prefer to wear

Homework Options
Complete final draft of **Zum Schreiben** dialogue
Study for Chapter Test

Block 7

ANWENDUNG
Quick Review 20 min.
- Students present **Zum Schreiben** dialogues

Chapter Review 25 min.
- Review chapter functions, vocabulary, and grammar; choose from **Mehr Grammatikübungen**, Grammar Tutor for Students of German, Activities for Communication, Listening Activities, Interactive CD-ROM Tutor, or **Interaktive Spiele**
- Review test format and provide sample test items for students

Test, Chapter 8 45 min.
- Administer Chapter 8 Test. Select from Testing Program, Alternative Assessment Guide, or Test Generator.

Kapitel 8: Mode? Ja oder nein?
Teaching Suggestions, pages 210–237

PAGES 210–211

CHAPTER OPENER

Pacing Tips
The **Erste Stufe** begins with adjectives following **der-** and **dieser-**words. Students describe clothes and learn how young people in Germany dress. The **Zweite Stufe** includes the functions of 'expressing interest, disinterest, and indifference' using the verb **sich interessieren** and clothing vocabulary, along with 'making and accepting compliments' and uses of the dative case. The **Dritte Stufe** also centers around clothing and fabrics. The function of 'persuading and dissuading' is introduced. Since all three **Stufen** are about the same in length and amount of material introduced, you might spend about the same amount of time on each. For Lesson Plans and timing suggestions, see pages 209I–209L.

Meeting the Standards

Communication
- Describing clothes, p. 217
- Expressing interest, disinterest, and indifference, p. 221
- Making and accepting compliments, p. 222
- Persuading and dissuading, p. 226

Cultures
- Landeskunde, p. 215
- Ein wenig Landeskunde, p. 215
- Background Information, p. 209R

Connections
- Multicultural Connection, p. 209O
- Thinking Critically, p. 209Q
- Music Connection, p. 209U

Comparisons
- Language-to-Language, p. 209P
- Language Notes, p. 209V

Communities
- Career Path, p. 209S

For resource information, see the **One-Stop Planner CD-ROM**, Disc 2.

Advance Organizer
Ask students about the latest fashions. What types of clothing are currently fashionable and trendy? How do their parents feel about the clothes students wear?

Connections and Comparisons

Thinking Critically
Drawing Inferences Ask students to look again at the clothes the two girls are wearing and make a guess as to what fabrics their clothes could be made of. Students may be able to recall some of the following vocabulary: **Baumwolle, Seide, Leinen.**

Building on Previous Skills
Recycle some of the words that students learned in Level 1. Put the following words in two columns on the board and ask students to use some of the words on the board in reaction to the clothes they see:

fesch	scheußlich
stark	blöd
schick	furchtbar
lässig	doof
prima	schlecht
toll	hässlich

Chapter Sequence

Los geht's!	p. 212
Landeskunde	p. 215
Erste Stufe	p. 216
Zweite Stufe	p. 220
Dritte Stufe	p. 224
Zum Lesen	p. 228
Mehr Grammatikübungen	p. 230
Anwendung	p. 234
Kann ich's wirklich?	p. 236
Wortschatz	p. 237

LOS GEHT'S!

Teaching Resources
pp. 212–214

PRINT
- Lesson Planner, p. 37
- Video Guide, pp. 49–50, 52
- Übungsheft, p. 85

MEDIA
- One-Stop Planner
- Video Program
  Los geht's!
  Videocassette 3, 22:58–25:52
  Videocassette 5 (captioned version), 46:19–49:10
  Fortsetzung
  Videocassette 3, 25:55–27:18
  Videocassette 5 (captioned version), 49:14–50:37
- DVD Tutor, Disc 2
- Audio Compact Discs, CD8, Trs. 1–2
- **Los geht's!** Transparencies

PAGES 212–213

 Los geht's! Transparencies

Preteaching Vocabulary

Recognizing Cognates

Los geht's! contains several words that students will be able to recognize as cognates. Some are compound words in which only part of the word is a cognate. Have students find these words and describe what is happening in the story. Then have students identify the two meanings of **der Typ** (*type* or *guy, fellow*).

1. Ordnung
3. Acryl, Wolle, Baumwolle
4. Mode-Freak
5. Rollkragenpullover
6. der Typ, Weste
7. allerbesten, natürlich, humorvoll

Fortsetzung

You may choose to continue with the **Fortsetzung** of *Ein starkes Outfit* now or wait until later in the chapter. For a synopsis of the **Los geht's!** and **Fortsetzung** episodes, see p. 209E.

STANDARDS: 1.2

Advance Organizer

Ask students to estimate how much of the clothing in their closet they actually wear. Then ask them to give a reason why they do not wear some of their clothes.

Communication for All Students

Auditory Learners

Have students watch the video segment of **Los geht's!**. Pause the tape after each frame and give students time to write down in English the gist of each conversation. After the last frame, ask students to share their findings. Based on these, have students try to summarize what is going on in **Los geht's!**.

Using the Captioned Video/DVD

 As an alternative to reading the conversations in the book, you might want to show the captioned version of *Ein starkes Outfit* available on Videocassette 5.
Note: The *DVD Tutor* contains captions for all sections of the *Video Program*.

PAGE 214

Comprehension Check

A Slower Pace

1. Ask students to work with a partner to write down the answers to each of the eight questions. Beside each answer students must indicate specifically what led them to that answer. (Example: For Question 4—Ich kaufe mir jetzt auch nur noch Sachen aus Baumwolle oder Wolle.)

Challenge

3. After students have successfully matched the four pairs of sentences, ask them to rephrase each pair of statements by combining them into one. Students should use connectors such as **denn, und, deshalb,** or **weil**.

Teaching Suggestion

5. This activity can be assigned as homework. Students should write at least three sentences and give each sentence a different sentence structure.

Teaching Suggestion

Replay the video segment of *Ein starkes Outfit,* this time without sound. Put students into groups of four and have them assume the roles of Katrin, Judith, Roland, and Boris. As you play the video, have them take turns filling in the dialogue. After each scene, call on one group to perform.

PAGE 215

LANDESKUNDE

Teaching Resources
p. 215

PRINT
- Video Guide, pp. 49–50, 52–53
- Übungsheft, p. 86

MEDIA
- One-Stop Planner
- Video Program
  Videocassette 3, 57:58–33:15
- DVD Tutor, Disc 2
- Audio Compact Discs, CD8, Trs. 3–7
- Interactive CD-ROM Tutor, Disc 2

Teaching Suggestions

- Before students watch the video segment or listen to the Audio CD, ask them to do the prereading activity. Ask students the question that was posed in the interview: "**Was trägst du am liebsten und warum?**" Ask students if they think the answers of the interviewees will be similar to theirs.

- Help students with words and phrases they may not be able to guess from the context of the interviews: **gruftimäßig** *dark; alternative (grunge)* **zeckig; richtig links** *slang terms to describe an alternative or grunge style*

Connections and Comparisons

Thinking Critically

Comparing and Contrasting Monika talks about her interest in clothes from the seventies. You may want to try to get several yearbooks from the seventies from your school library and let students browse through the photo section. Then ask them to describe the clothes and compare them to what students typically wear at school today.

B Drawing Inferences After discussing the questions, ask students how their own parents are involved in their clothing purchases and how their parents feel about the way they dress.

Multicultural Connection
Have students interview foreign exchange students or people they know from other countries. They should try and find out what teenagers in other countries like to wear. What is "in" and what is "out" in different countries?

Teacher Note
Mention to your students that the **Landeskunde** will also be included in Quiz 8-1B given at the end of the Erste Stufe.

ERSTE STUFE

Teaching Resources
pp. 216–219

PRINT
- Lesson Planner, p. 38
- TPR Storytelling Book, pp. 56–57
- Listening Activities, pp. 59, 63
- Activities for Communication, pp. 102, 105, 137–138
- Grammatikheft, pp. 64–65
- Grammar Tutor for Students of German, Chapter 8
- Übungsheft, pp. 87–89
- Testing Program, pp. 197–200
- Alternative Assessment Guide, p. 39
- Student Make-Up Assignments, Chapter 8

MEDIA
- One-Stop Planner
- Audio Compact Discs, CD8, Trs. 8–9, 14, 19–20
- Teaching Transparencies
  Situation 8-1
  Vocabulary 8-A
  Mehr Grammatikübungen Answers
  Grammatikheft Answers
- Interactive CD-ROM Tutor, Disc 2
- DVD Tutor, Disc 2

PAGE 216

Bell Work
Bring a collection of mail-order catalogs, department store advertisements, or fashion magazines and let each student look for an outfit that he or she really likes. Ask students to describe the outfit to a partner, telling him or her in German why they like it.

STANDARDS: 4.2

Cooperative Learning

6 Divide students in groups of four. Instruct each group to choose a discussion leader, a recorder, a proofreader, and a reporter. Give students a specific amount of time in which to complete Activity 6 (20–30 minutes). Groups should begin by reading the questions out loud. The recorder of each group can write his or her group's answers on a piece of paper. Tape the paper on the wall or the blackboard with masking tape. Then call on a few group reporters to read what their groups wrote.

PRESENTING: Wortschatz

Using the nouns and adjectives from the **Wortschatz**, describe the clothing of several students in your class. Have students write down the new terms they hear, and attempt to guess whose outfit you are describing. When someone guesses correctly, have him or her read back to the class the words used in reference to the student's outfit. Alternatively, you may wish to bring in pictures of well-known individuals and describe their clothing instead, following the same procedure.

PAGE 217

Communication for All Students

A Slower Pace

7 As an advance organizer to this activity, write the adjectives **modisch, sportlich, witzig,** and **konservativ** on the blackboard or on a transparency. Ask students what type of clothes or outfits they would label with each of the adjectives. Make a list of students' ideas underneath each adjective.

PRESENTING: So sagt man das!

Go over the functions in So sagt man das! Then remind students of the Bell Work activity they did at the beginning of this **Stufe**. See if any of their descriptions are similar to the German expressions introduced in So sagt man das!

PRESENTING: Grammatik

Adjectives after der and dieser-words In Chapter 7, students learned the adjective endings following **ein**-words (see p. 194). Make transparencies of the two **Grammatik** boxes on pp. 194 and 217. Ask students to compare adjective endings and point out the differences in endings after **der**- and **ein**-words. Remind students that the **-er** and **-es** adjective endings are necessary where the **ein**-word gives no indication of gender. The *Grammar Tutor for Students of German* can be very helpful at this point.

Connections and Comparisons

Language-to-Language

You may want to remind your students that in German, as well as in Spanish and French, the gender of a noun determines the endings of definite articles, indefinite articles, possessives, determiners, interrogatives, and adjectives. Examples:

English: *a brother / a sister; the brother / the sister; this brother / this sister*

German: **ein Bruder / eine Schwester; der Bruder / die Schwester; dieser Bruder / diese Schwester**

French: **un frère / une sœur; le frère / la sœur; ce frère / cette sœur**

Spanish: **un hermano / una hermana; el hermano / la hermana; este hermano / esta hermana**

You might want to ask your students to think of other features of a noun that may influence the endings of articles, possessives, or determiners. (Examples: case, number)

PAGE 218

Building on Previous Skills

Recycle some of the colors by pointing and asking students to describe classroom objects, students' clothing, and photos if necessary. Then introduce the new colors in a similar manner. Reinforce the new colors by asking students to think of other objects that have these colors.

Thinking Critically

10 Drawing Inferences Take a survey asking students if their family takes any clothes or laundry items to the cleaner's. Have them name the items and give reasons why people take certain clothing items to the cleaner's.

STANDARDS: 4.1

KAPITEL 8 ERSTE STUFE

Teaching Suggestion

11 Have students work in pairs to create Otto. One student is the note taker and the other is the artist. Play the recording several times. During the first and second listenings, stop the compact disc after each description so that one student can take notes and the other can draw the item. During the third listening, have students listen for colors. After pairs have finished their drawings, let them listen to the complete description one more time, making sure they included all details.

Cultures and Communities

Background Information
Advertisements for washing machines and similar large appliances indicate that consumers are concerned about water usage, electrical usage, and size. Before purchasing a washing machine, many Germans consult the German equivalent of *Consumer Reports*, which is called *Test* and is published by **Stiftung Warentest**. Most German washing machines are smaller than those in the United States.

Connections and Comparisons

Thinking Critically
Analyzing Ask students to think of some reasons Germans are so concerned about the size and performance of appliances such as washing machines. (Water and electricity are considerably more expensive in Germany than in the United States. Since homes, especially apartments, tend to be smaller in Germany, washing machines are often kept in the bathroom, kitchen, or basement.)

▶ **PAGE 219**

Communication for All Students

Tactile Learners
13 In preparation for this activity, place a suitcase of unusual clothing (you may want to ask the drama teacher if you could borrow some costumes) in front of the class. Encourage each group to take items of clothing for a **verrücktes Outfit** from the suitcase. One of the group members puts on the clothes the other members have picked out for him or her and becomes the **Mode-Freak**.

Connections and Comparisons

Thinking Critically
Synthesizing Can students think of reasons why Germans are more aware of proper attire when they participate in a sport? (If Germans plan to participate in such activities as tennis, golf, or horseback riding, they must often join a club and abide by a dress code.)

Teacher Note
15 After all teams have created their **Reklameseite**, you may want to collect their creations and make a catalog similar to those mailed out by department stores. Display it in your classroom or in the foreign language area.

Reteaching: Adjective endings after *der/dieser*-words and colors

Scatter the items of clothing from your suitcase (see Activity 13) on the floor. Students should request a particular piece of clothing from you.
Examples:
Könnte ich bitte diesen gelben Anorak haben?
or
Bitte geben Sie mir den feuerroten Pulli da!

 **Game**

Play the game **Auf dem Kostümball**. See p. 209C for the procedure.

Teaching Suggestion
Have students give a written description of the contents of a typical grocery bag their parents would come home with.

Assess
▶ Testing Program, pp. 197–200
  Quiz 8-1A, Quiz 8-1B
  Audio CD8, Tr. 14
▶ Student Make-Up Assignments
  Chapter 8, Alternative Quiz
▶ Alternative Assessment Guide, p. 39

ZWEITE STUFE

Teaching Resources
pp. 220–223

PRINT
- Lesson Planner, p. 39
- TPR Storytelling Book, pp. 58–59
- Listening Activities, pp. 60, 64–65
- Activities for Communication, pp. 43–44, 103, 105, 137–138
- Grammatikheft, pp. 66–68
- Grammar Tutor for Students of German, Chapter 8
- Übungsheft, pp. 90–92
- Testing Program, pp. 201–204
- Alternative Assessment Guide, p. 39
- Student Make-Up Assignments, Chapter 8

MEDIA
- One-Stop Planner
- Audio Compact Discs, CD8, Trs. 10, 15, 21–22
- Teaching Transparencies Vocabulary 8-B
  Mehr Grammatikübungen Answers
  Grammatikheft Answers
- Interactive CD-ROM Tutor, Disc 2
- DVD Tutor, Disc 2

PAGE 220

Bell Work
In pairs, have students tell each other how their clothes are cleaned. Are they washed in the machine, by hand, or taken to the cleaner's?

Total Physical Response
To recycle clothing vocabulary, descriptive adjectives, and colors, give commands with the following phrases:

Steht bitte auf, wenn ihr … anhabt!
Komm nach vorne, wenn du … trägst!
Heb die Hand, wenn du heute … anhast!
Zeigt auf einen Schüler in der Klasse, der … anhat!

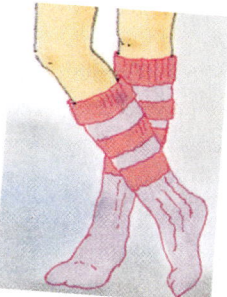

STANDARDS: 1.2

Communication for All Students

Auditory Learners
16 Have students keep their books closed while you read all five interviews. Have the three questions and the names of the interviewees written on the board. Read each interview twice as students take notes to answer questions 1–3. Call on students to check for comprehension.

PAGE 221

PRESENTING: Wortschatz
To teach this new vocabulary, you may want to use realia, such as actual clothing, pictures from catalogs, or ads. Include the adjectives in **Und dann noch …** in your presentation.

PRESENTING: So sagt man das!
Ask students to look back at the five interviews in Activity 16 and identify as many expressions as they can find that indicate interest, disinterest, or indifference. To practice the new expressions, ask students to tell you their level of interest in:

a) klassische Musik
b) Country-Western Musik
c) Sport
d) Autos
e) Kochen

PAGE 222

Communication for All Students

A Slower Pace
17 On a transparency or on the board, list the interests mentioned in random order down one side and the reasons down the other side. As students listen to the reports, they should use the clues on the board to help them complete Activities 1a and 1b.

For Additional Practice
18 If you feel students need further practice, you can brainstorm with them to come up with further topics. Make a list on the board and then conduct a class survey to find out in which topics students are interested or not and reasons for their opinions.

KAPITEL 8 ZWEITE STUFE 209R

Speaking Assessment

19 You may wish to assess the spoken answers in this activity. Have student pairs come to your desk and evaluate one after the other. You may wish to use the following rubric for evaluation.

Speaking Rubric	Points			
	4	3	2	1
Content (Complete – Incomplete)				
Comprehension (Total – Little)				
Comprehensibility (Comprehensible – Incomprehensible)				
Accuracy (Accurate – Seldom accurate)				
Fluency (Fluent – Not fluent)				

18–20: A   16–17: B   14–15: C   12–13: D   Under 12: F

PRESENTING: So sagt man das!

Have students practice these expressions with a partner. One student should read the compliment and the other student the response. Ask students if they can think of other similar expressions that they learned in previous chapters. There are some other expressions students should be familiar with:
Die Jacke sieht lässig aus!   Findest du?
Die Jeans gefällt mir!   Wirklich?

PAGE 223

PRESENTING: Grammatik

Further uses of the dative case To reintroduce previously learned verbs that take the dative case, ask students to respond to questions such as:
Was schenkst du deiner Freundin zum Geburtstag?
Welche Musik gefällt dir am besten?
Was gibst du deinen Eltern gewöhnlich zum Geburtstag?
Wie geht es dir heute?
Use verbs such as
  schenken, geben, helfen, gefallen, schmecken, and gehen.

Communication for All Students

Challenge

22 To expand this activity, hang up large pictures from magazines. Ask students to address compliments to the people in the pictures, observing formal or familiar forms of address. Other students should give appropriate responses.

Kinesthetic Learners Bring to class unusual outfits or costumes borrowed from the drama department. Give students certain items of clothing to try on. Then ask other students to comment on them. (Examples: zu eng, zu klein, zu lang, zu weit, zu groß, zu unpraktisch)

Reteaching: Adjectives after der/dieser-words

In preparation for this activity, use old catalogs. Cut out a class set of pictures of colorful outfits and glue or tape these on construction paper (students can help you with this). Then give each student one picture. They should describe the outfit in detail using phrases such as:
Ich möchte gern …
Ich finde …
Ich kaufe … für …

Cultures and Communities

Career Path

Have students brainstorm scenarios in which an employee of an American clothing company would benefit from a strong background in German. (Suggestions: If the company wanted to start exporting to a German-speaking country, it would need someone who could monitor the fashion trends there and suggest which items might be most popular; they could also act as liaison with whichever German advertising firm was hired to promote the company's products.)

Assess

▸ Testing Program, pp. 201–204
  Quiz 8-2A, Quiz 8-2B
  Audio CD8, Tr. 15

▸ Student Make-Up Assignments
  Chapter 8, Alternative Quiz

▸ Alternative Assessment Guide, p. 39

DRITTE STUFE

Teaching Resources
pp. 224–227

PRINT
- Lesson Planner, p. 40
- TPR Storytelling Book, pp. 60–61
- Listening Activities, pp. 60–61, 65–66
- Activities for Communication, pp. 45–48, 104, 105, 137–138
- Grammatikheft, pp. 69–72
- Grammar Tutor for Students of German, Chapter 8
- Übungsheft, pp. 93–95
- Testing Program, pp. 205–208
- Alternative Assessment Guide, p. 39
- Student Make-Up Assignments, Chapter 8

MEDIA
- One-Stop Planner
- Audio Compact Discs, CD8, Trs. 11–12, 16, 23–24
- Teaching Transparencies
  Situation 8-2
  Vocabulary 8-C
  Mehr Grammatikübungen Answers
  Grammatikheft Answers
- Interactive CD-ROM Tutor, Disc 2
- DVD Tutor, Disc 2

PAGE 224

Bell Work

In pairs, have students ask each other where they and their family members purchase their clothes. Write a list of choices on the board. (Examples: **in Einkaufszentren, in Spezialgeschäften, in Boutiquen, aus Katalogen**) Students should also give an explanation or reason for their preference.

Group Work
25 Divide the class into groups of three. Assign one student in each group to be the writer. The group begins by reading the advertisements from the **Berger-Katalog.** Then the group answers Questions 1 through 3, and the writer records all answers. Set a time limit to complete this activity, then call on groups to share their findings with the rest of the class.

PAGE 225

PRESENTING: Wortschatz
Use real pieces of clothing or pictures from magazines to introduce the new items of clothing pictured. For the details in the bottom row, show a pair of jeans and a jacket. In all cases, model the new word or phrase and have students repeat. Follow up with either/or and open-ended questions. Examples:

Wie macht man diese Jacke zu?
Hat sie einen Reißverschluss oder Knöpfe?
Woher wissen wir, ob man einen Gürtel zu dieser Hose braucht?
Hat diese Hose einen Gürtel?

Communication for All Students

Challenge
27 To expand this activity, you may want to provide each pair of students with pages from a mail-order clothing catalog. Students tell each other what they would purchase with a $1500 shopping allowance. Monitor students' work as you walk from pair to pair. Occasionally ask one partner what the other one has chosen to buy and why.

28 As an alternative, have students bring a magazine picture of a celebrity. One of the partners plays the role of the famous person, while the other partner comments on, compliments, or criticizes his or her style. Though similar in task, this variation avoids students' directly criticizing each other's clothing.

PAGE 226

PRESENTING: So sagt man das!
Model the expressions in **So sagt man das!** by addressing individual students, using the phrases on the left side. Have students respond with the corresponding responses on the right side.

PRESENTING: Ein wenig Grammatik

The verb kaufen Write clothing terms from this chapter on slips of paper and place these in a hat. Go down the rows with the hat, asking students to draw one slip of paper each, and to formulate a sentence using the term they drew and **kaufen** plus a reflexive pronoun. To add some variety to the activity, you may want to stipulate the subject students should use in their sentences. (Example: Have the first student use **ich**, the second **du**, the third **er** or **sie**, and so on.)

Communication for All Students

Tactile Learners

30 Before beginning this activity, let students look at and feel several different swatches of material. (Examples: **Baumwolle, Seide, Wolle, Kunstfasern**) Have students try to guess what each material is.

PAGE 227

PRESENTING: Ein wenig Grammatik

The conjunction wenn Write on a transparency a number of short sentences such as **Es schneit. Ich spiele gern Tennis. Ich gehe um drei Uhr nach Hause. Ich muss die Katze füttern.** Have students assemble in groups of three or four and allow them a few minutes to come up with five new sentences, created by using **wenn**-clauses to combine pairs of statements taken from the transparency. When all groups have finished, have students read their sentences aloud. The class as a whole should then decide whether the resulting statements are **logisch** or **unlogisch**.

Connections and Comparisons

Music Connection

For additional reading, refer students to the first stanza of the folksong *Nun ade, du mein lieb Heimatland* (lyrics by August Dischoff), Level 2 *Listening Activities*, p. 46. Have them underline the **wenn**-clause they find. (**wenn man wandern tut**) Why is **wenn** used here instead of **wann**? (**Wann** is used only in questions; **wenn** must be used in this instance to convey the idea of *whenever*.) You might also want to play the song, Level 2 CD6, Tr. 25.

FAMILY LINK

34 Students can also interview different family members to find out about their clothing preferences. Students can point out and name the clothing that the family member is wearing to teach him or her some German words and phrases.

Communication for All Students

Visual Learners

35 To expand this activity, let students take a look at the outfits they are wearing that day. Give students a minute to discuss their style, making use of any of the suggested words. Then have students volunteer to come to the front to model their outfits and give an ad-lib description of their style.

Teaching Suggestion

Provide students with the following **Lückensatz**, which each one of them should try to complete in an interesting way:
Meine drei Lieblingskleidungsstücke in meinem Schrank sind …, weil …
Students should take a few minutes to write out their sentence. Have several students read their sentence to the class.

Von der Schule zum Beruf

Have students browse German online clothing catalogs to prepare for this activity.

Assess
▸ Testing Program, pp. 205–208
  Quiz 8-3A, Quiz 8-3B
  Audio CD8, Tr. 16
▸ Student Make-Up Assignments
  Chapter 8, Alternative Quiz
▸ Alternative Assessment Guide, p. 39

ZUM LESEN

Teaching Resources
pp. 228–229

PRINT
- Lesson Planner, p. 41
- Übungsheft, p. 96
- Reading Strategies and Skills, Chapter 8
- Lies mit mir! 2, Chapter 8

MEDIA
- One-Stop Planner

Prereading

Building Context
Take a survey asking students how important money is to them now and also for their future.

Language Note
The word **nix** in the title of the first text is colloquial for the pronoun **nichts**.

Thinking Critically
Drawing Inferences Ask students to think about the title "Reich ist, wer nix mehr lernen muß!" Do they agree or disagree with that statement? Have students give at least one reason for their opinion.

Teacher Note
Activity 1 is a prereading activity.

Reading

Communication for All Students

A Slower Pace

3 On the board or a transparency, write the numbers 1 through 7 for each of the survey responses. Then elicit words or phrases from students that sum up each of the responses. Sometimes more than one word or phrase may be suggested. Have students come to a consensus as to which noun or phrase best summarizes the interviewee's opinion.

Challenge
Ask students to reread the students' answers and decide under which category of the survey summary each answer would best fit.

Teaching Suggestion
After students have determined how **sonst**, **damit**, and **besonders** affect the meanings of the responses referred to in Activities 4, 5, and 6, have them identify other transitional words that link thoughts together and indicate relationships within sentences. (Examples: **aber**, **leider**, **wenn**)

Connections and Comparisons

Thinking Critically
Comparing and Contrasting Ask students to take a closer look at the expression the thirteen-year-old **Hauptschüler** used when talking about money. **Mäuse in der Tasche haben.** Can students think of similar colloquial phrases used in English? (Examples: *to have lots of dough; to be loaded*)

Language Notes
- The German language has several proverbs that are related to money. Here are some examples you can share with your class:
  Geld verdirbt den Charakter. *Money spoils character.*
  Die Glücklichen sind reich, die Reichen nicht immer glücklich. *Money can't buy you happiness.*
  Geld regiert die Welt. *Money rules the world.*

- The 11-year-old **Gesamtschüler** uses the expression "Ich fühle mich sauwohl." (*I feel great.*) Although the expression "sauwohl" is used fairly often in German, it is considered colloquial. The German language has many other expressions that include the names of animals. Here are a few examples:
  hundemüde (*very tired*), **hundekalt** (*very cold*), **bärenstark** (*very strong*), **mäuschenstill** (*very quiet*), **vogelfrei** (*outlawed*), **wieselflink** (*quick*)

Thinking Critically
Drawing Inferences Tina considers her work as a model a **Nebenjob**. What do students think **Nebenjob** refers to? Survey your students as to what they consider to be **Nebenjobs**. Do any of them work part-time in addition to going to school? Tina works because she enjoys it. Do the students who do have jobs feel the same?

Post-Reading

Teacher Note
Activity 10 is a post-reading task that will show whether students can apply what they have learned.

Zum Lesen Answers

Answers to Activity 1
a survey; what must one have to be rich?; answers will vary; answers will vary.

Answers to Activity 2
Minister, Fabrik, Personal

Answers to Activity 3
Zufriedenheit, Klamotten/Auto, nichts, Bungalow/Kunst, saubere Umwelt, Computer, Gesundheit

Answers to Activity 4
One must have good health, otherwise money and luxuries are worthless; **sonst** provides the contrast between good health and money and luxuries.

Answers to Activity 5
Damit expresses *for what purpose* the students want to have something.

Answers to Activity 6
He says he doesn't need anything; **besonders** *(especially)* emphasizes *when/on what occasions* he feels really good.

Answers to Activity 7
about 18-year-old student Tina who works as a model; on her beauty

Answers to Activity 8
modeling; yes; parents are happy to see her in pictures, but say that school is more important than looks

Answers to Activity 9
It's probably not so easy; e.g.: **Wenn man gut aussieht, hat man vielleicht nicht so viele Freunde, wie man glaubt.**

PAGES 230–233

MEHR GRAMMATIKÜBUNGEN

The **Mehr Grammatikübungen** activities are designed as supplemental activities for the grammatical concepts presented in the chapter. You might use them as additional practice, for review, or for assessment.

For more grammar presentations, review, and practice, refer to the following:
- Grammatikheft
- Grammar Tutor for Students of German
- Grammar Summary on pp. R20-R36
- Übungsheft
- Grammar and Vocabulary quizzes (Testing Program)
- Test Generator
- Interactive CD-ROM Tutor
- Interaktive Spiele at go.hrw.com

PAGE 234–235

ANWENDUNG

Video Wrap-up
Videocassette 3, 22:58–35:35
Videocassette 5 (captioned version) 46:19–50:37
DVD Tutor, Disc 2

At this time, you might want to use the video resources for additional review and enrichment. These resources are also available via the Enhanced Online Student Edition.
See *Video Guide* for suggestions regarding:
- **Ein starkes Outfit** Dramatic episode
- **Landeskunde** Interviews
- **Videoclips** Authentic footage

Apply and Assess

Challenge
1 After students have completed the activity, ask them to think of another reason Judith and Boris should or should not buy these same items.

Teaching Suggestion
2 Make a copy of the **Bestellkarte** for each student and have them answer Questions 1-5 on a separate piece of paper. Have students compare answers with a partner.

Auditory Learners
3 After students have chosen three items and determined the rest of the information they need, ask them to continue working in pairs. Students take turns reading the information to each other. The student who is listening could pretend to be the catalog operator taking the order over the phone.

Teaching Suggestion
4 This activity could be added to the previous suggestion. Encourage students to act out the phone conversation, using props such as plastic phones and order forms.

Portfolio Assessment
6 You may want to suggest this activity as a written portfolio item for your students. See *Alternative Assessment Guide*, p. 25.

Apply and Assess

Process Writing

7 To help your students get started writing, you may want to provide them with a list of possible questions for the interviewer to ask, such as the following:

Stellen Sie sich bitte vor!
Haben Sie Hobbys? Was für (Bücher) (lesen) Sie gern? (Hören) Sie auch gern (Musik)?
Warum wollen Sie Schauspieler(in) werden? Wollen Sie Geld? Ruhm?
Was wünschen Sie sich? Warum?
Sprechen wir jetzt über Mode! Was haben Sie heute an?
Was ist heutzutage ‚in'?
Vielen Dank fürs Interview!

PAGE 236

KANN ICH'S WIRKLICH?

This page helps students prepare for the test. It is a brief checklist of the major points covered in the chapter. The students should be reminded that it is only a checklist and not necessarily everything that will appear on the test.

For additional self check options, refer students to the *Grammar Tutor*, the *Interactive CD-ROM Tutor*, and the Online self-test for this chapter.

Teacher to Teacher

Pamela Taborsky
Leander High School
Leander, TX

Pam evaluates students' speaking skills with the **Kann ich's wirklich?** activities.
"Several teachers in my school use the **Kann ich's wirklich?** questions as oral tests. Since these questions test all the functions in the chapter, they are perfect for this use. Students may begin the one-on-one orals as soon as we have covered the first concept. All students are required to complete the orals before the chapter test."

PAGE 237

WORTSCHATZ

Review and Assess

Game
Play the game **Wer ist das?** to review the clothing vocabulary as well as the descriptive adjectives from this chapter. Students look around the classroom and secretly choose someone whose outfit they want to describe. They write that student's name on a small piece of paper and turn it face down. As each student names the items a classmate is wearing, the rest of the class tries to guess who it is. The first student to guess correctly wins a point. To verify the answer, you can check the name on the paper. The student who guessed correctly then begins the next round.

Teaching Suggestions

- Ask students to pick at least 10 words or phrases from the **Wortschatz** to use at a fashion show to describe an outfit being modeled.

- Bring in photos or ads of the vocabulary items and ask students to give the word in German.

Circumlocution
To review, play **Das treffende Wort suchen** with nouns that relate to clothing in all three **Stufen. Man trägt es wenn … Man benutzt es für … Es sieht aus wie …** are some phrases that might be used to describe these articles of clothing. See p. 3C for procedures.

Tactile Learners
Each student should have a blank piece of paper and a pen or pencil. Use the vocabulary from the **Wortschatz** to describe an outfit. Students try to draw the outfit as you describe it. When students have finished, have them compare drawings.

Game
Play the game **Anziehwettbewerb.** See p. 209C for the procedure.

Teacher Note
Give the **Kapitel 8** Chapter Test: *Testing Program*, pp. 209–214
Audio CD8, Trs. 17–18.

STANDARDS: 1.1, 1.2

KAPITEL

8
Mode? Ja oder nein?

Objectives
In this chapter you will learn to

Erste Stufe
- describe clothes

Zweite Stufe
- express interest, disinterest, and indifference
- make and accept compliments

Dritte Stufe
- persuade and dissuade

Visit Holt Online
go.hrw.com
KEYWORD: WK3 STUTTGART-8
Online Edition

◀ Diese Klamotten sind nicht mehr in Mode.

zweihundertelf

Los geht's! · *Ein starkes Outfit*

Strategie Verstehen
Look at the photos on this page. What might the topic of the conversation be? Now look at the photos on the next page. What is the topic there? What roles do the two boys play?

Katrin   **Judith**   **Roland**   **Boris**

Los geht's! is an abridged version of the video episode.

1
- **Judith:** Was machst du denn da? Willst du verreisen?
- **Katrin:** Nö! Ich muss mal ein bisschen Ordnung in meine Sachen bringen und sehen, was ich hab.

2
- **Katrin:** Das Zeug da muss ich waschen, und das kommt in die Reinigung. Und das dort möchte ich am liebsten wegwerfen.

3
- **Judith:** Hm! Diesen Pulli willst du wirklich wegwerfen?
- **Katrin:** Ja, schau! Er passt mir nicht. Er ist viel zu weit, und er ist aus Acryl! Kauf dir nie etwas aus Acryl! Ich kaufe mir jetzt auch nur noch Sachen aus Baumwolle oder Wolle.
- **Judith:** Wie findest du meine grüne Bluse?
- **Katrin:** Die ist echt stark, und sie steht dir gut. Sie passt gut zu der weißen Jeans. Das ist ein echt heißes Outfit!
- **Judith:** Meinst du?
- **Katrin:** Ja, wirklich! Du interessierst dich eben mehr für Mode als ich.

4
Katrin: Du bist wie dein Bruder, der Roland.
Judith: Ja, der Roland, das ist ein richtiger Mode-Freak. Wie stolz er auf seine Klamotten ist!

5
Roland: Mode ist für mich ziemlich wichtig. Im Moment trage ich Schwarz. Meine Lieblingsklamotten sind …dieser schwarze Rollkragenpullover, diese schwarze Jeans und leichte Schuhe.

6
Katrin: Dieses schwarze Outfit steht deinem Bruder aber auch gut. Er sieht toll aus.
Judith: Stimmt! Aber der Typ da in der 10b, wie hieß er denn schnell …?
Katrin: Du meinst wohl den Boris?
Judith: Ja, der Boris, der sieht doch immer scharf aus. Hast du ihn heute Morgen gesehen? Das rote Hemd, die grüne Weste und die schwarzweiße Baumwollhose. Er ist ein wirklich lässiger Typ.
Katrin: Gefällt dir der Boris?
Judith: Er sieht gut aus, stimmt! Aber er ist nicht mein Typ. Magst du ihn vielleicht?
Katrin: Hm, vielleicht, ich weiß nicht. Aber der redet bestimmt nicht über uns.
Judith: Bist du so sicher?

7
Boris: Die Katrin ist ein nettes Mädchen, sehr gescheit. Was mir an ihr so gefällt, ist …sie ist einfach, sie interessiert sich nicht für Mode. Sie trägt keine verrückten Sachen, und am allerbesten gefällt mir, dass sie so natürlich und humorvoll ist.

Übungsheft, S. 85

LOS GEHT'S!   STANDARDS: 1.2   *zweihundertdreizehn* **213**

1 Was passiert hier?

These activities check for global comprehension only. Students should not yet be expected to produce language modeled in **Los geht's!**

Verstehst du alles, was diese Leute sagen? Beantworte die Fragen!

1. What is this text about? 1. clothes and fashion
2. Why does Judith think that Katrin is going on a trip? 2. because she is sorting through her clothes
3. What does Katrin intend to do with her clothes? 3. wash some, take some to the cleaners, throw some away
4. What are her favorite materials? What clothes will she never buy again? 4. cotton and wool; acrylic
5. Which one of the two girls is interested in fashion? How does that show? 5. Judith; she dresses stylishly
6. What does Judith's brother like to wear? 6. the color black
7. Whom do the girls seem to like and why? 7. Boris; because he is so stylish
8. What does this person like about Katrin? 8. she is natural, does not care about fashion, has sense of humor

2 Stimmt oder stimmt nicht?

Wenn der Satz nicht stimmt, schreib die richtige Antwort!

1. Katrin möchte verreisen. 1. stimmt nicht; sie muss Ordnung in ihre Sachen bringen
2. Sie möchte den Pulli in die Reinigung geben. 2. stimmt nicht; sie will ihn wegwerfen
3. Sie kauft sich jetzt nur noch Klamotten aus Acryl. 3. stimmt nicht; aus Baumwolle und Wolle
4. Katrin interessiert sich sehr für Mode. 4. stimmt nicht; sie interessiert sich nicht dafür
5. Der Roland trägt am liebsten Schwarz. 5. stimmt
6. Die Katrin mag den Boris nicht. 6. stimmt nicht; er gefällt ihr
7. Der Boris ist ein lässiger Typ. 7. stimmt

3 Welche Sätze passen zusammen?

Welche Sätze auf der rechten Seite passen zu den Sätzen auf der linken Seite?

1. Katrin bringt Ordnung in ihre Klamotten. c
2. Der grüne Pullover passt ihr nicht. d
3. Judiths grüne Bluse passt gut zu der weißen Jeans. a
4. Der Roland ist ein richtiger Mode-Freak. b

a. Das ist ein heißes Outfit.
b. Er ist stolz auf seine Klamotten.
c. Sie möchte sehen, was sie hat.
d. Er ist ihr viel zu weit, und er ist aus Acryl.

4 Welche Wörter passen in die Lücken?

1. Ich muss mal ___1___ in meine Klamotten bringen.
2. Das muss ich waschen, und das muss in die ___2___.
3. Diesen Pullover willst du ___3___?
4. Der Roland ist ein ___4___ Mode-Freak.
5. Er ist ___5___ auf seine Klamotten.
6. Mode ist für ihn ziemlich ___6___.
7. Der Boris ist ein wirklich lässiger ___7___.

1 Ordnung   4 richtiger   2 Reinigung
5 stolz   3 wegwerfen   7 Typ   6 wichtig

5 Und du?

Wie beschreibst du dich selbst? Was ist dein Stil? Gebrauche drei Adjektive aus dem Kasten, um dich zu beschreiben.

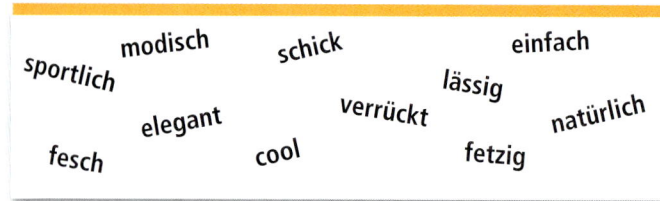

sportlich   modisch   schick   einfach   lässig
elegant   verrückt   natürlich
fesch   cool   fetzig

Was trägst du am liebsten? CD 8 Tr. 3

We asked several teenagers the question **Was trägst du am liebsten und warum?** Based on what you already know about what German students like to wear, think about the kinds of clothing these teenagers might mention. What reasons might they give for wearing certain kinds of clothing? Listen to and then read the interviews.

CD 8 Trs. 3–7

Grammatikheft, S. 86, Ü. 1

Monika, Hamburg CD 8 Tr. 4

„Also, ich wechsle mein Outfit auch je nach Gelegenheit. Entweder zieh ich mich total gruftimäßig an oder im siebziger Jahrestil, wie man das jetzt so sieht. Nicht zu eng. Oder, na ja, ich geh halt ganz normal zeckig, ganz normal richtig links."

Rosi, Berlin CD 8 Tr. 6

„Ich trage am liebsten 'ne Jeans und T-Shirt, also, weil es ist in der Schule so, da zieht keiner schicke Sachen an, also mit Kleidern nur wenige Ausnahmen, und ich fühl mich darin am wohlsten."

Jens, Berlin CD 8 Tr. 5

„Also, was ich gerne anziehe, kann ich nicht sagen. Ich …kleide mich gerne sportlich, weil ich fein nicht so mag, weil das was Besonderes ist. Und meine Lieblingsfarbe ist Dunkelblau."

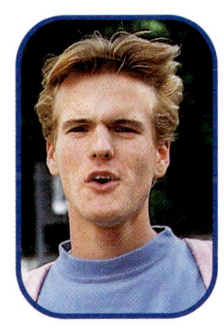

Uli, München CD 8 Tr. 7

„Also, Kleidung muss natürlich bequem sein, in erster Linie, und es unterscheidet sich natürlich, ob ich abends weggehe mit Freunden oder ob ich arbeite. Also, wenn man mich jetzt sieht, das ist eine typisch bequeme Arbeitsklamotte, sag ich mal, die ich anhab, also mit Turnschuhen, in denen ich bequem laufen kann, weil ich doch viel unterwegs bin. Wenn ich abends weggehe, zieh ich mich gerne etwas feiner an, also sprich weg, so dass ich meine, ich sehe besser aus, in dann engen Hosen oder mal ein ausgeschnittenes T-Shirt."

A. 1. Monika: changing; Jens: sporty; Rosi: Jeans and T-shirt; Uli: comfortable clothes. Uli. She wears comfortable clothes during the day and finer clothes in the evening. When going out she thinks she looks better in finer clothes. Comfortable clothes and tennis shoes for work; tight pants and low-cut T-shirt for the evening.

A. 1. What kinds of clothing do each of these people say they like to wear the best? What reasons do they give for their choices? Which person says he or she likes to dress up? Who mentions comfort? The athletic look? Does Uli make a distinction between clothes she wears every day and clothes she wears when she goes out in the evening? What does she say? Describe the two outfits she wears.

2. With a partner choose one of the interviews above and jot down a few notes about what that person said. Then summarize in German (in your own words) the interview. Describe that person to your classmates using the phrase **Diese Person …** to identify him or her. Let your classmates guess which person you are describing.

B. What do these people's statements and their choice of clothes tell you about them? Do you think their parents would make the same choices? How does their taste in clothes compare to yours and your friends'?

STANDARDS: 1.2, 2.1, 2.2, 3.2, 4.2

TPR Storytelling Book pp. 56–57

Erste Stufe

Objective Describing clothes

go.hrw.com WK3 STUTTGART-8

6 Hast du alles verstanden?

Lesen/Sprechen Lies zuerst den Text unten, und dann beantworte die Fragen!

1. Was ist heute in der jungen Mode anders als früher?
2. Die Jugend experimentiert. Wie zeigt sich das?
3. Nenne die Adjektive, die diese Modeartikel beschreiben!

1. Heute geht alles. Früher hat es nur zwei Stile gegeben.
2. Sie kombinieren verschiedene Stile und Farben.
3. cool, schwarz, bunt, lässig, gefüttert, kariert, „in“, klassisch, toll, blau, weit, scharf, witzig

Wortschatz

CD-ROM DISC 2 · 8–1 · p. 209X

Was ist heute „in“?

Früher hat es in der jungen Mode gewöhnlich nur zwei Stile gegeben: konservativ und modisch. Und heute? — Heute geht alles. Die Jugend von heute experimentiert und kombiniert: Hosen aus den 60er Jahren mit geblümten Hemden aus den 70er Jahren. Und farblich? Alles geht! Aber Schwarz ist zur Zeit „in“.

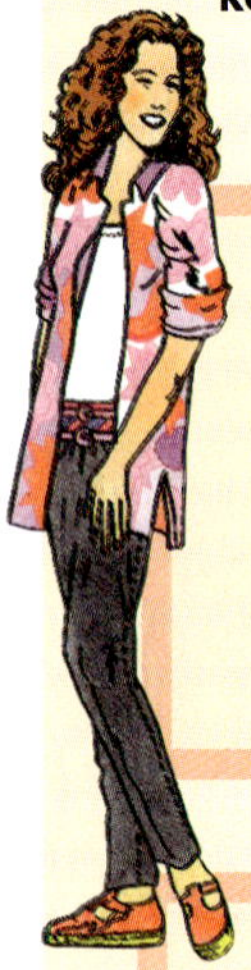

Richtig cool ist die schwarze Jeans und das bunte Shirt darüber, das am besten offen bleibt.

Jeans 63,50
Shirt 40,90

Für jeden sportlichen Typ: Käppis! Am liebsten natürlich von US-Baseball-Mannschaften.

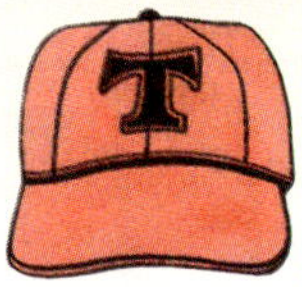

Käppis ab 14,00

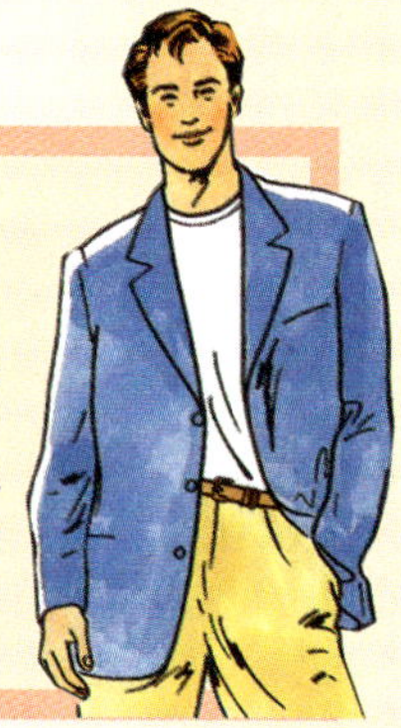

Echt toll ist dieser blaue Blazer und das lässige, weite Hemd darunter.

Blazer 95,00
Hemd 34,50

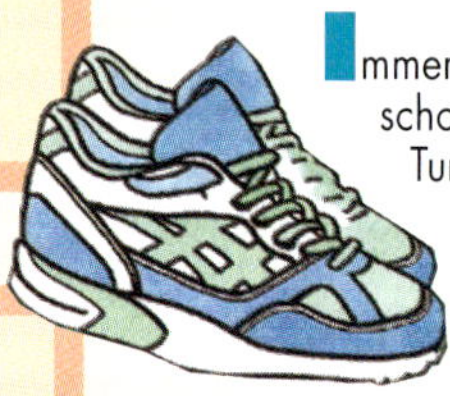

Immer noch „in“: Die schon klassischen Turnschuhe gibt's jetzt in tollen Farben.

Turnschuhe 39,60

Lässig für den kalten Winter: diese gefütterte Wind- und Wetterjacke über der Jeansweste und dem karierten Wollhemd.

Windjacke 93,00
Jeansweste 48,00
Wollhemd 27,50

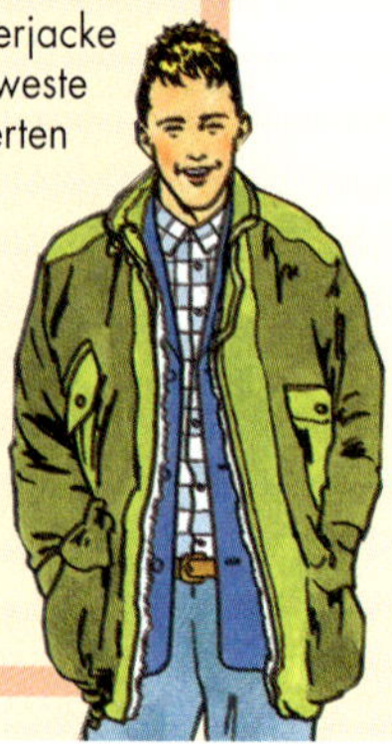

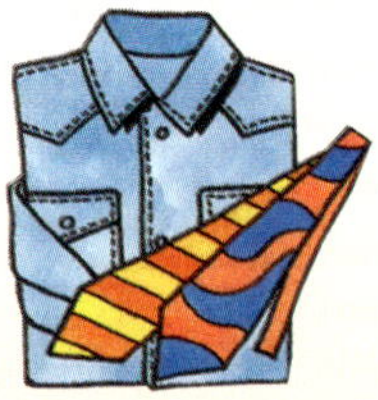

Diese bunten Krawatten passen besonders gut zu dem blauen Jeansshirt.

Krawatten ab 13,00

Dieser bunte Anorak sieht auch von hinten scharf aus – ein Anorak mit Patches! Darunter trägt man, was man will. Dieses witzige T-Shirt vielleicht?

Anorak 54,00
T-Shirt 19,90

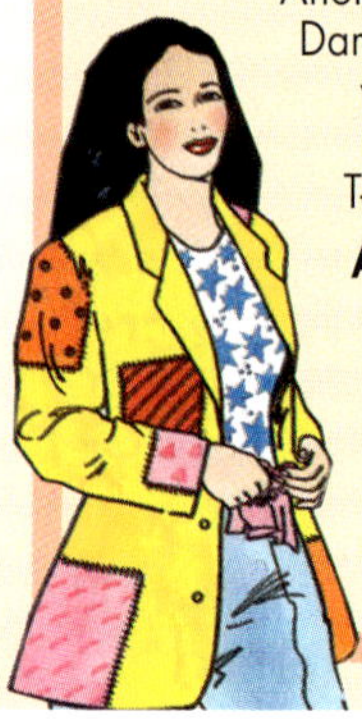

Welche Adjektive beschreiben die Kleidungsstücke von deinen Klassenkameraden?

Übungsheft, S. 87–88, Ü. 1–3   Grammatikheft, S. 64, Ü. 1

7 Wie kleiden sich die Schüler? Script and answers on p. 209G

Zuhören Ein Schüler beschreibt die Kleidung von vier neuen Klassenkameraden. Mach dir Notizen (zum Beispiel Adjektive) über die verschiedenen Kleidungsstile! Wer von den Klassenkameraden kleidet sich a. modisch? b. sportlich? c. witzig? d. konservativ?

8 Du und dein Partner

Lesen/Sprechen Du und dein Partner, ihr müsst euch jeder einen Artikel aus der Reklameseite (Seite 216) heraussuchen. Was gefällt euch? Was nicht? Was kauft sich dann jeder von euch?

So sagt man das!

Describing clothes

When describing clothes, as well as other things, you want to use adjectives in your description.

Diese schwarze Jeans und das bunte Shirt sind echt cool.
Für den kalten Winter bei uns brauch ich diese gefütterte Windjacke.
Dieser bunte Anorak sieht sehr gut aus.

Identify the adjectives in the noun phrases above. Why do you think **schwarze, bunte,** and **gefütterte** have an **-e** ending, but **kalten** an **-en** ending?

Grammatik

Adjectives following der and dieser-words

1. Adjectives following **der** and **dieser**-words (**dieser, jeder, welcher**) have these endings.

Nominative:	Dieser bunt**e**	Anorak sieht toll aus.	} Masculine
Accusative:	Diesen bunt**en**	Anorak kauf ich mir.	
Nominative:	Die schwarz**e**	Jacke ist echt cool.	} Feminine
Accusative:	Die schwarz**e**	Jacke kauf ich mir auch.	
Nominative:	Das weit**e**	Hemd ist lässig.	} Neuter
Accusative:	Das weit**e**	Hemd trag ich gern.	
Nominative:	Diese bunt**en**	Krawatten sehen gut aus.	} Plural
Accusative:	Diese bunt**en**	Krawatten mag ich nicht.	

2. In the dative case, the adjective endings are **-en** for all nouns of all genders, and for the plural.

Dative: Das passt echt gut zu
 diesem grün**en** Anorak.
 dieser weiß**en** Jacke.
 diesem bunt**en** Hemd.
 diesen bunt**en** Turnschuhen.

3. When more than one adjective is used to describe a noun, all adjectives have the same ending: Du willst diese schön**e**, grün**e** Bluse wegwerfen?

ERSTE STUFE STANDARDS: 1.1, 1.2, 4.1, 5.1 zweihundertsiebzehn

9 Grammatik im Kontext

a. Sprechen Setz dich mit einer Partnerin zusammen, und sprecht über die Leute auf den Fotos! Welche Kleidungsstücke gefallen euch? Welche nicht? Sagt, welche Farben diese Kleidungsstücke haben!

b. Schreiben Beschreibe die Kleidungsstücke in jedem Bild. Was gefällt dir, was nicht?

Schon bekannt

rot   blau   grau   grün   gelb
weiß   schwarz   braun

Und dann noch…

Mehr Farben

feuerrot	knallgelb
wollweiß	hellbraun
türkisblau	dunkelgrau
olivgrün	tiefschwarz

10 Waschen? In die Reinigung? Oder wegwerfen?

Sprechen Katrin bringt Ordnung in ihre Klamotten. Aber was soll sie nur mit den vielen Klamotten tun? Welche Stücke soll sie waschen? Welche soll sie in die Reinigung bringen? Welche soll sie wegwerfen? Sag deinen Mitschülern, was Katrin machen soll!

waschen?

wegwerfen?

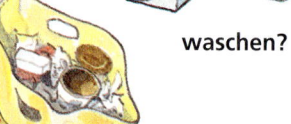

in die Reinigung bringen?

11 Ottos Outfit Script on p. 209G

Zuhören Hör zu, wie Erik ein Outfit von seinem Freund Otto beschreibt! Otto trägt nämlich gern ganz verrückte Klamotten. Mach eine Skizze von Ottos Outfit, in Farbe natürlich! Vergleiche dann deine Skizze mit denen deiner Mitschüler! Wer hat den schönsten Otto gezeichnet?

CD 8 Tr. 9

12 Reklame für Klamotten

Sprechen Jeder in der Klasse muss eine Reklameseite aus einem Katalog mit in die Klasse bringen. Sprecht über die einzelnen Artikel! Was gefällt euch? Was gefällt euch nicht? Wo gibt es diese Sachen? Wie teuer sind sie?

13 Typen wie der Boris?

Sprechen Bildet Gruppen von drei Personen! Jede Gruppe muss einen Mode-Freak haben, der gern „verrückte" Kleidung trägt. Wenn keiner ein Mode-Freak sein will, verwendet die beste Otto-Zeichnung! Sprecht jetzt über euren Mode-Freak oder Otto!

a. Beschreibt das Outfit!
b. Sagt, was euch besonders gefällt oder überhaupt nicht gefällt!
c. Wie passen die Klamotten?

- bei Beck
- bei Karstadt
- zu Weihnachten
- im Kaufhaus
- zum Geburtstag

14 Dieses Hemd gefällt mir!

Sprechen Get together with three other classmates. Find something about each person's outfit that you really like and tell him or her how much you like it. Then find out where each person bought that clothing article. Your classmate will tell you where he or she bought it or if he or she received it as a present. Try to find out how much it costs. The phrases above can help.

BEISPIEL
DU Das Kleid gefällt mir sehr. Wo hast du es gekauft?
PARTNER Ich hab das nicht gekauft, ich hab es zum Geburtstag bekommen.

LERNTRICK

It is important to listen not only for meaning, but also for other clues that may be helpful, such as gender clues. You already know that indefinite articles can clue you in to the gender of a noun:

**Nimmst du einen Saft?
Ja, bitte, der Saft schmeckt wunderbar.**

Dieser-words can also give you clues about a noun's gender. If someone asks: **Wie gefällt dir dieses blaue Hemd?** the ending **-es** on **dieses** tells you that **Hemd** is a neuter noun, and you can begin to think of an appropriate response:

Du, das Hemd gefällt mir gut. Ich finde es stark.

Ein wenig Landeskunde

Heutzutage ist es fast unmöglich, junge Deutsche der Kleidung nach von jungen Amerikanern zu unterscheiden: die Jugend ist in ihrer Freizeit locker und lässig gekleidet.

Beim Sport legen die jungen Deutschen vielleicht ein bisschen mehr Wert auf richtige Kleidung. Man wandert in bequemen Wanderhosen mit den richtigen Schuhen dazu, man reitet in Reithosen und Stiefeln und man spielt Tennis in Weiß — vielleicht auch deshalb, weil man viele Tennisplätze nur im weißen Outfit betreten darf.

In manchen Gegenden, besonders in Bayern und in Österreich, trägt die Jugend auch Tracht, besonders an Sonntagen oder zu Festtagen, wie zum Beispiel beim Besuch von Volksfesten.

15 Der tolle Sommerjob

Lesen/Schreiben Du hast einen Sommerjob in der Reklameabteilung eines Kaufhauses bekommen. Du arbeitest in der Layout-Abteilung. Such dir einen Partner und entwerft *(create)* zusammen eure eigene Reklameseite! Schneidet Artikel aus einem Katalog aus, klebt *(glue)* sie auf ein Blatt Papier und beschreibt die Artikel!

Zweite Stufe

Objectives Expressing interest, disinterest, and indifference; making and accepting compliments

Hast du Interesse an Mode?

Roland
„Mode ist für mich ziemlich wichtig. Ich trag eigentlich schon, was ‚in' ist. Im Moment trage ich Schwarz."

Stefan
„Mode? — Nein. Ich zieh mir auch Klamotten an, die nicht in Mode sind. Ich kauf mir zum Beispiel viele Klamotten auf dem Trödelmarkt, weil sie dort billiger sind."

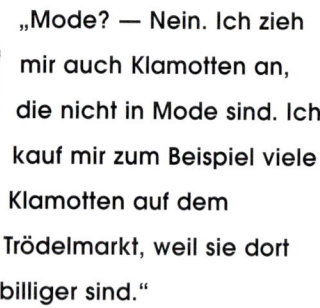

Sandra
„Ich interessier mich schon für Mode. Vor allem müssen die Farben passen. Zum blauen Hemd zum Beispiel passen die grüne Jacke und diese weiße Jeans. Toll! Was?"

Lin
„Es ist mir ziemlich egal, was ich anhab. Es muss nur sauber sein. Ich lieb aber fetzige Klamotten, bedruckte T-Shirts und Jacken mit bunten Prints."

Johanna
„Ja, für Mode interessiere ich mich schon ein bisschen. Die Kleidung muss mir auch gut passen und gut stehen. Ich trag furchtbar gern Kleider. Und zu diesem braunen Kleid trag ich schwarze Strümpfe und schwarze Schuhe mit hohen Hacken."

16 Verschiedene Interessen

Lesen/Sprechen Lies, was diese jungen Leute über Mode sagen! Beantworte die folgenden Fragen! 1. Roland, Sandra, Johanna; Stefan, Lin
1. Wer interessiert sich für Mode? Wer nicht? 2. Mode ist wichtig, sie interessieren sich für Mode; Mode — Nein, ist ihnen egal
2. Wie drücken die Schüler ihr Interesse oder Desinteresse aus? Was sagen sie?
3. Wer ist dir sympathisch? Warum? 3. Answers will vary.

Wortschatz

Was trägst du zu deinen Klamotten? Ich trage …

 Socken

 Schuhe mit flachen Absätzen

 Schuhe mit hohen Absätzen

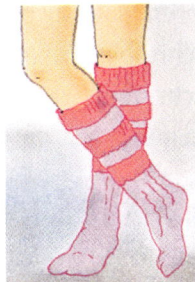 Strümpfe

Was gefällt dir…

diese gepunktete Jeans?
oder gestreifte, abgeschnittene Jeans?

die ärmellose Bluse?

diese weiche Lederjacke?

Und dann noch…

bedruckt	monoton
einfarbig	mehrfarbig
gemustert	locker

Übungsheft, S. 90, Ü. 1–2

Grammatikheft, S. 66, Ü. 3

So sagt man das!

Expressing interest, disinterest, and indifference

When asking about someone's interests, you ask:

Interessierst du dich für Mode?
Wofür interessierst du dich?

When expressing interest, you say:

Mode interessiert mich sehr.
Ich interessiere mich für Mode.

When expressing disinterest, you may answer:

Mode interessiert mich nicht.
Ich hab kein Interesse an Mode.

When expressing indifference, you may say:

Mode ist mir egal.

Which of the two questions is more general? What do you notice about the verb **interessieren**? What case follows the preposition **für**?[1]

Grammatikheft, S. 66, Ü. 4

---

1. **Für** is always followed by accusative-case forms.

ZWEITE STUFE STANDARDS: 1.2 zweihunderteinundzwanzig **221**

17 Viele Interessen Script and answers on p. 209G

 1. **Zuhören** Schüler berichten über ihre Interessen. Hör dir die Berichte zweimal an!
  a. **Schreiben** Schreib zuerst auf, welche Interessen jeder Schüler hat!
  b. **Schreiben** Dann schreib die Gründe neben die Interessen der einzelnen Schüler!
2. **Sprechen** Such dir dann einen Schüler aus und erzähl deinem Partner von ihm!

 18 Man kann sich für vieles interessieren

Schreiben Mach eine Liste mit mindestens drei Dingen, für die du dich interessierst und für die du dich nicht interessierst! Schreib auch Gründe dafür auf! Hier sind einige Ideen:

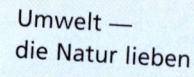 Umwelt — die Natur lieben
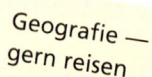 Geografie — gern reisen
Bücher — gern lesen

Kameras — gern fotografieren
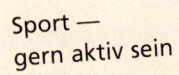 Sport — gern aktiv sein

Ein wenig Grammatik

Sich interessieren (*to be interested*) requires a reflexive pronoun in the accusative case. To talk about your or someone else's interest *in* something, the preposition **für** is used:

Ich interessiere mich für alte Autos.

How would you ask two classmates what they are interested in? How might they respond?[1]

Übungsheft, S. 90, Ü. 3   Mehr Grammatikübungen, S. 231, Ü. 4
Grammatikheft, S. 67, Ü. 5

 19 Wofür interessierst du dich?

Sprechen Such dir eine Partnerin! Frag sie nach ihren Interessen und Desinteressen! In ihrer Antwort muss sie dir auch einen Grund nennen. Verwende dabei die Information von Übung 18! — Tauscht dann die Rollen aus!

 20 Was trägst du gern?

 Sprechen Frag einen Mitschüler, was er gern im Sommer trägt! Er sagt es dir. Dann darf er auch einen Mitschüler fragen, was dieser gern im Sommer, im Winter, usw. trägt. Frag auch, was deine Lehrerin gerne trägt!

Ein wenig Grammatik

The verb **tragen**, *to wear*, has a stem-vowel change in the **du-** and **er/sie/es**-forms:

Was **trägst du** gern?
Und was **trägt** Roland?

There is no umlaut in the **du**-command.

Trag dieses Kleid nicht!

Grammatikheft, S. 67, Ü. 6   Mehr Grammatikübungen, S. 231, Ü. 5

So sagt man das!

Making and accepting compliments

When making a compliment, you could say:

  Deine Jeans steht dir gut.
  Sie passt dir auch echt gut.
  Und diese Jacke passt dir prima!
  Sie passt gut zu deiner blauen Bluse.

And the responses might be:

  Meinst du wirklich?
  Ist sie mir nicht zu eng?
  Ehrlich?
  Echt?

How would you reassure your friend that you really meant it?

 Grammatikheft, S. 68, Ü. 7

---

1. Wofür interessiert ihr euch? Wir interessieren uns für Politik.

Grammatik

Further uses of the dative case

1. In **Kapitel 6** you learned that there are certain verbs that are usually used with dative-case forms, such as **passen,** *to fit,* and **(gut) stehen,** *to look (good).*

   Diese Jeans passt **dir** sehr gut.
   Dieses fetzige Outfit steht **deinem Bruder** gut.

2. Dative-case forms are always used after the preposition **zu.**

   Das grüne Hemd passt gut **zu dieser blauen Jacke.**

3. When expressing personal comfort, dative-case forms are also usually used.

   Diese Jacke ist **mir** viel zu eng.
   Sind **dir** diese Schuhe nicht zu groß?

Mehr Grammatikübungen, S. 232, Ü. 6

Übungsheft, S. 91–92, Ü. 4–6

Grammatikheft, S. 68, Ü. 8

21 Grammatik im Kontext

a. Sprechen Du bist mit deiner Partnerin in der Stadt, und ihr seht diese Leute auf dem Marktplatz. Erzählt euch gegenseitig, was diese Leute tragen und wie ihnen die Kleidung passt! Gefällt euch ihre Kleidung? Ist sie zu konservativ oder zu fetzig?

b. Schreiben Beschreibe alle sechs Leute in dieser Zeichnung.

22 Komplimente machen

Sprechen Such dir einen Partner und bewundere, was er anhat! Mach ihm Komplimente! — Tauscht dann die Rollen aus!

zu kurz	zu lang	zu fetzig
zu eng	zu weit	zu teuer
zu klein	zu groß	zu konservativ
zu monoton	zu bunt	zu unpraktisch

23 Für mein Notizbuch

Schreiben Schreib in dein Notizbuch, ob du dich für Mode interessierst! Schreib, was du gern trägst und warum, und welche von deinen Klamotten besonders gut zusammenpassen oder dir gut stehen!

24 Dein Job: Modefachmann oder Modefachfrau

Sprechen/Schreiben Du arbeitest in einem Modegeschäft. Ein Kunde hat keine Ahnung, was er sich kaufen soll. Er weiß nicht, was ihm gut steht und was nicht, was ihm gut passt und was nicht, und welche Farben er tragen soll. Du berätst (*advise*) ihn. Entwickelt ein Rollenspiel und spielt es der Klasse vor!

ZWEITE STUFE   STANDARDS: 1.1, 1.3, 4.1, 5.1   zweihundertdreiundzwanzig

Storytelling Book
pp. 60–61

Dritte Stufe

Objective Persuading and dissuading

WK3 STUTTGART-8

25 Aus dem Modekatalog 8–2

Lesen/Sprechen Lies die folgende Werbung aus dem Katalog der Firma Berger! Dann beantworte die Fragen!

1. Welche Kleidungsstücke sind für Frauen? Für Männer? Für beide?
2. Welche Kleidungsstücke sind aus Naturfasern? Aus Kunstfasern?
3. Such dir zwei Angebote aus, und sag einem Partner, warum du diese Sachen haben möchtest!

1. Frauen: 21, 31, 41, 43, 47; Männer: 112, 126, 127, 134; Beide: 7, 13, 23, 37, 101, 103, 108, 116
2. Naturfasern: 7, 13, 19, 23, 31, 47, 103, 112, 116, 126; Kunstfasern: 108, 134; Beides: 21, 37, 41, 43, 101, 127

7 Fischerhose. Mit Gummibund. Reine Baumwolle. **37.-**

13 Shorts. Gestreift. Mit Reißverschluss. 100% Baumwolle. **11.50**

19 Minirock. Reine Baumwolle. Mit Gürtelschlaufen. Ohne Gürtel. **12.50**

21 Jeans-Röhre. 5 Taschen. 98% Baumwolle, 2% Elasthan. Ohne Gürtel. **19.50**

23 Jeans-Jacke. Bund verstellbar. Denim. Stone-washed. **34.00**

31 Hemdbluse. Mit 2 Brusttaschen. 100% Viskose. **18.-**

37 Rollkragen-Pullover. Lang. 80% Polyacryl, 20% Wolle. **18.95**

41 Rock. 67% Polyester, 33% Viskose. Ohne Gürtel. **34.95**

43 Steghose. Mit Gürtelschlaufen. 63% Polyester, 30% Wolle, 7% sonstige Fasern. **38.95**

47 Träger-Top. Einfarbig. Mit Knöpfen. Hinten elastisch. 100% Viskose. **7.50**

101 Parka. Mit Brusttaschen. Ärmel mit Gummibund. 65% Polyester, 35% Baumwolle. **35.-**

103 Jeans. Fetzig u. fransig, wie's junge Leute mögen. Denim. Reine Baumwolle, stone-washed. **19.95**

108 Jacke. Mit vielen Taschen. Vorn mit Reißverschluss und Druckknöpfen. 100% Nylon. **24.95**

112 Sakko. Leichte Qualität. 55% Leinen, 45% Baumwolle. **49.-**

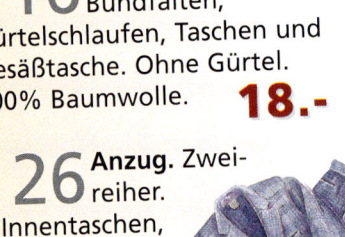

116 Shorts. Mit Bundfalten, Gürtelschlaufen, Taschen und Gesäßtasche. Ohne Gürtel. 100% Baumwolle. **18.-**

126 Anzug. Zweireiher. 2 Innentaschen, 1 Gesäßtasche. 55% Leinen, 45% Baumwolle. Ohne Gürtel. **65.-**

127 Anzug. Einreiher. 4 Innentaschen. 67% Polyester, 33% Viskose. Ohne Gürtel. **104.-**

134 Bundfaltenhose. Vollwaschbar, mit Reißverschluss. 100% Polyester. **29.-**

Wortschatz

p. 209X
8-C
CD-ROM DISC 2

Aus welchem Material?

Aus Naturfasern:

Wolle *wool*
Baumwolle *cotton*
Leinen *linen*
Seide *silk*

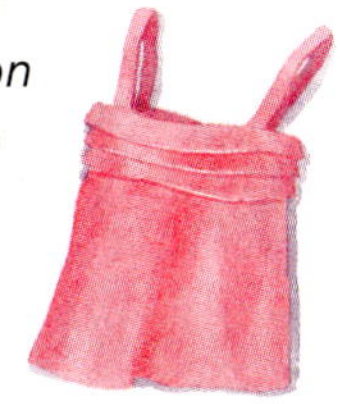

das Trägerhemd

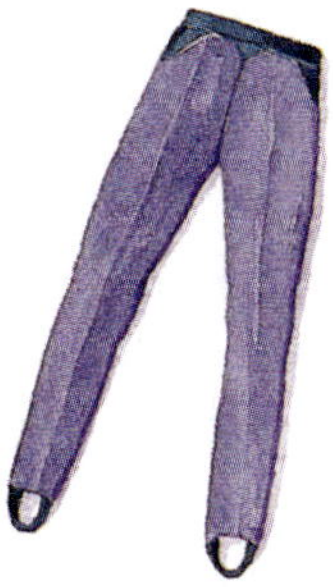

die Steghose

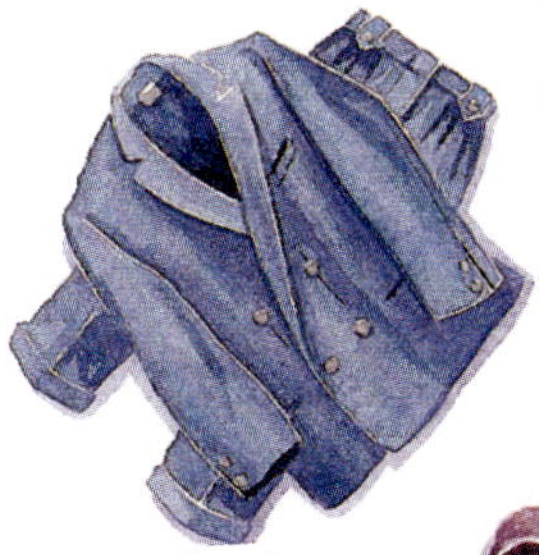

der Anzug

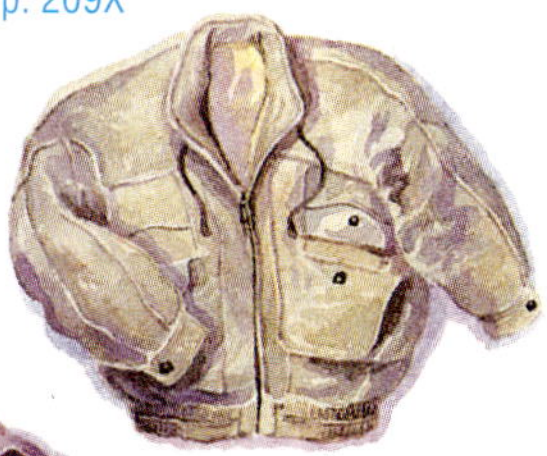

der Blouson

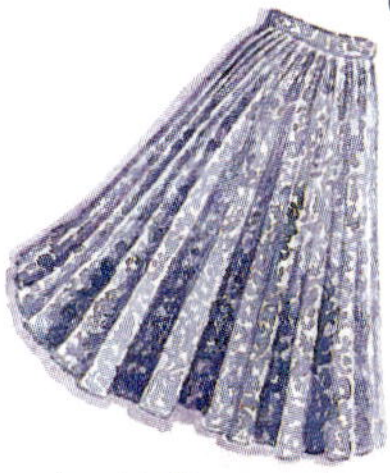

der Faltenrock

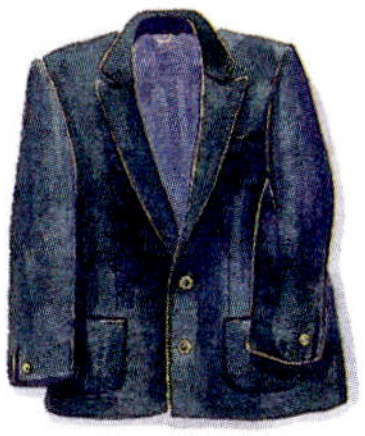

der Sakko

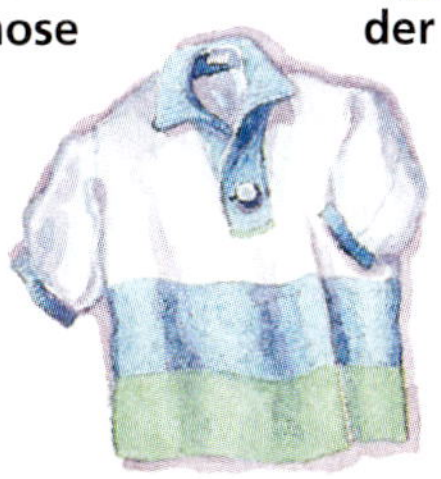

mit kurzen Ärmeln

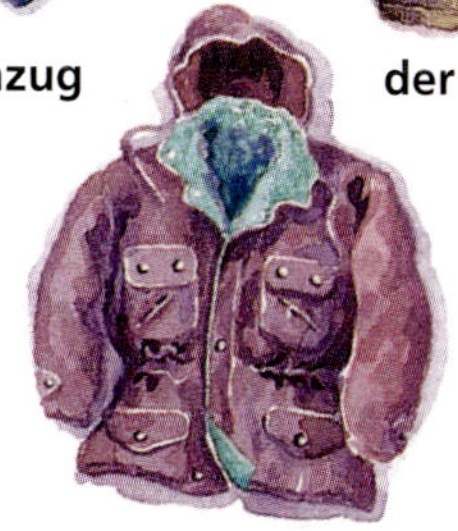

mit Kapuze

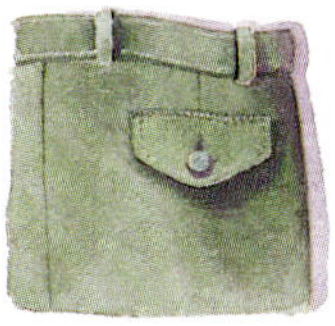

mit Gesäßtasche

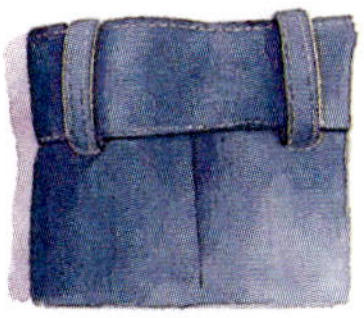

mit Schlaufen

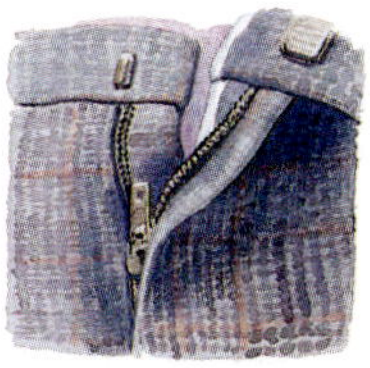

mit Reißverschluss

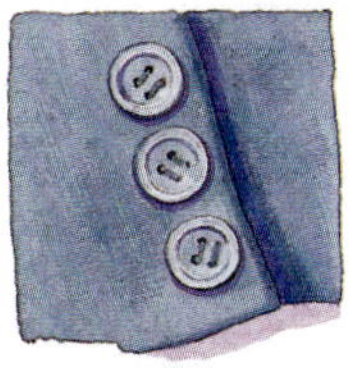

mit Knöpfen

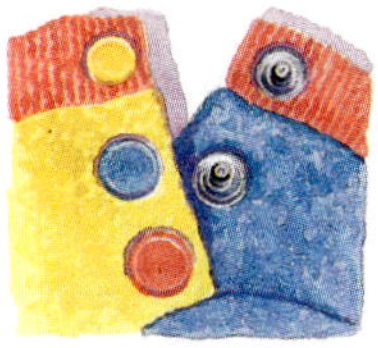

mit Druckknöpfen

Welches von diesen Kleidungsstücken hast du auch? Aus welchem Material ist es? Schau dir die Werbung auf Seite 224 an! Welche Kleidungsstücke haben Reißverschlüsse, Knöpfe oder Taschen?

Und dann noch...

Aus Kunstfasern:

Polyester, Acryl, Polyacryl, Nylon, Kunstseide

Übungsheft, S. 93, Ü. 1–2   Grammatikheft, S. 69, Ü. 9–10

26 Wer kauft sich Klamotten? Script and answers on p. 209G

Zuhören Schüler sprechen über ihre Einkäufe. Wer von diesen Schülern will sich etwas kaufen und wer nicht? Warum? Warum nicht? Mach dir Notizen!
CD 8 Tr. 11

27 Was möchtest du dir kaufen?

Lesen/Sprechen Such dir eine Partnerin! Nenne ihr zwei Angebote aus dem Berger-Katalog und sag ihr, warum du dir diese Sachen kaufen möchtest!

BEISPIEL **Ich möchte mir die Jacke kaufen, die Nummer hundertacht, weil sie viele Taschen hat und auch einen Reißverschluss und Druckknöpfe.**

28 Was trägt dein Klassenkamerad?

Sprechen Such dir einen Partner und beschreibe seine Kleidung! Sag ihm, was dir gefällt und warum, und sag ihm, was dir nicht gefällt und warum nicht! — Tauscht dann die Rollen aus!

So sagt man das!

Persuading and dissuading

When trying to persuade someone, you may want to say:

> Warum kaufst du dir kein Wollhemd?
> Kauf dir doch dieses karierte Hemd!
> Trag doch mal etwas Lustiges!

The response may be:

> Ich mag keine Wollhemden!
> Das ist mir zu teuer.
> Meinst du?

When trying to dissuade someone, you may want to say:

> Kauf dir ja kein Seidenhemd!
> Trag ja nichts aus Polyester!

The response may be:

> Ich finde Seide aber toll!
> Warum nicht?

Which words or phrases are used to persuade someone? And dissuade?

Grammatikheft, S. 70, Ü. 11–12

29 Soll ich das kaufen?

Lesen/Sprechen Such dir einen Kleidungsartikel aus dem Katalog oder aus dem Wortschatz aus, und sag deiner Partnerin, dass du dir diesen Artikel kaufen möchtest! Sie hat ihre eigene Meinung über diesen Artikel. Sie stimmt dir zu oder auch nicht und sagt dir, warum. Versuch, sie zu überzeugen (*convince*)!

Ein wenig Grammatik

The verb **kaufen** is often used with a reflexive pronoun in the dative case.

> Kauf **dir** doch ein Wollhemd!

Do you remember the reflexive pronouns?[1] How would you tell two friends to buy themselves jackets? How would you say you want to buy yourself shoes?[2]

Übungsheft, S. 94, Ü. 3

Grammatikheft, S. 71, Ü. 13–14

Mehr Grammatikübungen, S. 232–233, Ü. 7–8

30 Aus welchem Material ist eure Kleidung?

Sprechen Bildet kleine Gruppen und fragt euch gegenseitig, aus welchem Material eure Kleidungsstücke sind! Sind sie aus Naturfasern? Aus Kunst- oder Mischfasern?

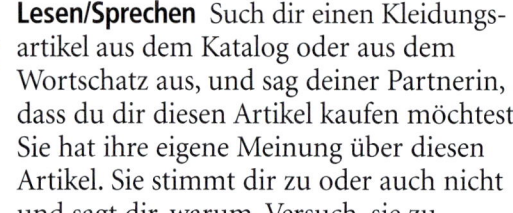

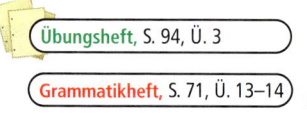

31 Eine Auswahl aus deinem Katalog

Sprechen Such dir zu Hause einen Katalog mit Kleidungsreklame heraus! Dann such dir zwei Kleidungsstücke aus, für die du dich interessierst und zwei, für die du dich nicht interessierst! Bring die Reklame mit in den Deutschunterricht! Sag deiner Gruppe, für welche Klamotten du dich interessierst und warum, und für welche du dich nicht interessierst und warum! Erwähne Farbe, Material und Preis!

---

1. mir, dir, sich, uns, euch, sich.   2. Kauft euch Jacken! Ich kaufe mir Schuhe.

32 Was die Schüler tun Script and answers on p. 209H

Zuhören Listen as four different students talk about what they like to do and under what conditions they usually do this. For each description you hear, match the activity with the condition the student mentions.

CD 8
Tr. 12

1. Mit dem Auto fahren
2. segeln
3. Schach spielen
4. Lebensmittel einkaufen

a. I visit Grandma
b. my bicycle is broken
c. it rains
d. it's warm and sunny

33 Grammatik im Kontext

a. Lesen/Sprechen Finde heraus, welche Satzteile logisch zusammenpassen, und verbinde sie dann mit einem wenn-Satz!

Ich gehe ins Kino.
Wir spielen alle Tennis.
Ich muss mein Zimmer aufräumen.
Wir gehen ins Restaurant.
Ich fahre nach Deutschland.
Ich gehe nicht in die Schule.

Wir haben großen Hunger.
Das Wetter ist wunderbar.
Es ist Weihnachten.
Ich habe genug Geld.
Dort ist Chaos.
Das Wetter ist schlecht.

b. Schreiben Schreib wenn-Sätze, die zusammenpassen.

E.g.: Ich gehe ins Kino, wenn ich genug Geld habe.

Ein wenig Grammatik

Read the following sentences:

**Ich spiele gern Fußball, wenn das Wetter schön ist.
Aber ich bastle zu Hause, wenn es regnet.**

What do you think the conjunction **wenn** means? How would you say these two sentences in English? Here, the conjunction **wenn** has the meaning of *whenever*. Don't confuse this word with the question word **wann**, which asks about specific time. What do you notice about the word order in clauses beginning with **wenn**?[1] What other conjunctions have you seen that have the same word-order rule?[2]

Übungsheft, S. 94–95, Ü. 4–7
Grammatikheft, S. 72, Ü. 15

Mehr Grammatikübungen, S. 233, Ü. 9

---

34 Was trägst du, wenn …?

Sprechen Sag deiner Partnerin, welche Klamotten du gern trägst, wenn du …

Beispiel Ich trage …, wenn ich Sport mache.

a. Sport machst
b. zur Schule gehst
c. arbeitest
d. zu Hause bist
e. in ein Konzert gehst
f. auf eine Fete gehst

35 Wie trägst du deine Sachen gern?

Sprechen Sag deinem Partner, wie du deine Sachen gern trägst!

weiter *oder* enger
länger *oder* kürzer
einfarbig *oder* mehrfarbig
einfach *oder* gemustert

36 Für mein Notizbuch

Schreiben Schreib in dein Notizbuch etwas über deine Kleidung! Deine Beschreibung muss folgende Fragen beantworten:

a. Wofür interessierst du dich und warum?
b. Was für Sachen kaufst du dir gewöhnlich und warum?
c. Wie gut müssen die Sachen passen, und welche Farben magst du gern?
d. Aus welchem Material sind deine Sachen und warum?

37  Von der Schule zum Beruf

Du arbeitest in der Werbeabteilung eines Modehauses. Mit zwei anderen Mitarbeitern musst du eine Damenseite oder eine Herrenseite für den Katalog entwerfen, der die Modeartikel detailliert beschreibt.

---

1. The conjugated verb is in last position.   2. **weil, dass,** and **ob.**

DRITTE STUFE   STANDARDS: 1.1, 1.2, 1.3, 5.1

Zum Lesen

Was bedeutet „reich und schön sein"?

Lesestrategie Understanding relationships between and within sentences. Cohesive devices are words or phrases that help "glue" a text together and show relationships between ideas, such as time sequence or cause and effect. Cohesive devices can be pronouns, conjunctions (**aber, wenn**), or adverbs (**leider, danach**). Read the following sentences: *My mother is a banker. My mother does volunteer work. My mother is a banker, but she also does volunteer work.* Several words in the last sentence help tie the two ideas together. *But* is a conjunction that joins the two sentences, and *she* is a pronoun that refers back to (and thus forms a connection to) the subject of the first sentence.

Getting Started *For answers, see p. 209W*

1. Read the title, subtitle, and introduction to the list of results from the text on the left. What kind of article is this? What question is the focus of the article? Choose a German noun that would sum up your answer to this question. Now answer the question by completing this statement: **Um reich zu sein, muss man …**

2. Look at the survey summary list. With a partner, see how many words you can understand. Can you identify the three false cognates?

3. Skim the survey responses to get the gist of each student's answer. Most answers contain

---

Eltern—UMFRAGE

Reich ist, wer nix mehr lernen muss!
Realschüler, 12 Jahre

Neben Geld gibt es ganz andere Güter, die den Menschen reich machen – das finden unsere Kinder. Nachdenkenswertes Ergebnis der neuesten ELTERN-Umfrage

Großes Herz und volle Kasse
ELTERN fragte 1880 Schülerinnen und Schüler, zehn bis 16 Jahre alt: Was muß man haben, um reich zu sein? Am häufigsten genannt:

1. soziale Einstellung (Hilfsbereitschaft, Großzügigkeit);
2. materieller Besitz (Geld, Aktien, Häuser, Fabriken);
3. Luxusgüter (teuerste Autos, Yachten, Schmuck, Kunstsammlungen);
4. gesunde Umwelt;
5. kluger Steuerberater;
6. Personal (Diener, Köchin, Chauffeur);
7. liebevoller Lebenspartner;
8. gute Freunde;
9. Bescheidenheit und Zufriedenheit;
10. Kinder;
11. Titel (Professor, Doktor, Minister);
12. Gesundheit

Das Wichtigste, was man braucht, um sich reich zu fühlen, ist die Zufriedenheit. Aber leider hat man immer neue Wünsche, die nicht erfüllt werden. Orientierungsstufenschülerin, 12 Jahre

Tolle Klamotten und ein schnelles Auto, damit jeder sieht, daß da einer kommt, der Mäuse in der Tasche hat. Hauptschüler, 13 Jahre

Ich brauche nichts, um reich zu sein. Ich fühl' mich sauwohl, besonders wenn ich mit meinen Eltern in Urlaub fahre. Gesamtschüler, 11 Jahre

Einen tollen Bungalow mit viel Kunst an den Wänden. Möglichst ein Bild von Chagall und eines von Hundertwasser. Gymnasiast, 15 Jahre

Eine saubere Umwelt. Was hab' ich vom Geld, wenn ich in Dreck ersticke? Gymnasiastin, 14 Jahre

Einen Computer, damit ich immer genau ausrechnen kann, wieviel ich noch habe und wieviel ich ausgeben darf. Gesamtschüler, 13 Jahre

Eine gute Gesundheit, sonst hat man nichts von all dem Geld und Luxus. Hauptschülerin, 13 Jahre

Tina
Das Mädchen aus dem Katalog

Zur Zeit arbeitet Tina (18) als Modell für eine Agentur. Was sagen sie, ihre Eltern, und ihre Freunde dazu? Tina meint: „Es macht mir Spaß. Ich mag meinen Nebenjob, denn man kann reisen und lernt viele interessante Leute kennen." Ihre Eltern freuen sich, Tina auf Fotos für Werbung oder Modenschauen zu sehen. Andererseits sagen sie: „Vergiß die Schule nicht. Sie ist wichtiger als gutes Aussehen." Und die Freunde? „Die finden mich ganz normal, auch wenn ich Modell bin. Am Anfang, als ich einen Schönheitswettbewerb gewonnen hatte, gab es sehr viele häßliche Bemerkungen. Viele Mädchen waren neidisch. Ich war darüber sehr geschockt. Denn ich habe doch meine Persönlichkeit nicht verändert. Und ein guter Charakter ist für mich bei Freunden viel wichtiger als Schönheit. Wenn man gut aussieht, hat man vielleicht nicht so viele Freunde, wie man glaubt." Simona (16), Tinas Freundin, sagt: „Ich finde wichtig, daß Tina trotz ihres Erfolgs als Modell genauso nett wie früher ist. Natürlich, sie ist wirklich sehr hübsch, und manche unserer Mitschüler denken: ‚Sie ist bestimmt eingebildet und arrogant.' Aber ich glaube, sehr viele Jugendliche sind neidisch oder haben Vorurteile. Wenn wir zusammen einkaufen gehen, wird Tina von vielen Jungen bewundert. Manchmal ist Schönheit auch lästig. Man fällt überall auf. Vielleicht möchten schöne Menschen viel lieber ganz normal aussehen und in ein Café gehen, ohne angestarrt zu werden."

one noun that sums up the person's opinion. Can you identify these words?

A Closer Look

4. What does the thirteen-year-old girl say about health? How does the word **sonst** affect the meaning of the sentence?

> **Tipp:** If you see a word that looks like a form for *the* (**der, die, das,** etc.), but it is not followed by a noun, it is usually a pronoun. Try translating it as either *who* or *that*.

5. Look at the two 13-year-old boys' responses. What function does **damit** (*so that*) serve in their answers?
6. What does the eleven-year-old boy say about being rich? How does **besonders** affect the meaning of his sentence?
7. Now skim the article *Tina*. Who is the article about? On which characteristic of this person does the article focus?
8. Reread the article. What is Tina's job? Does she like it? What do her parents think about her job?
9. Do you think that Tina has an easy life because she is pretty? Which sentence(s) from the article can support your answer?
10. Together with your classmates, think of ten answers to the *Eltern* survey question. Form groups of four and, using these choices, design your own questionnaire. Be sure to include instructions on how people should fill out your form. Each person will survey four people (including oneself). With your group, tally the results, then do the same with your class as a whole. With the final results each group will design a summary chart like the one from the *Eltern* survey.

Übungsheft, S. 96

Mehr Grammatikübungen

Erste Stufe
Objective Describing clothes

1 Du beschreibst einem Freund verschiedene Klamotten. – Schreib die richtige Form von **dieser** und die richtige Form des Adjektivs in die Lücken. (S. 217)

1. (bunt) _____ Anorak sieht echt toll aus. Darf ich _____ Anorak einmal anprobieren? Ich glaube, ich sehe gut aus in _____ Anorak. *Dieser bunte; diesen bunten; diesem bunten*

2. (weiß) _____ Hemd steht dir gut. Probier doch mal _____ Hemd an! Ja, in _____ Hemd siehst du wirklich fesch aus. *Dieses weiße; dieses weiße; diesem weißen*

3. (grün) _____ Jacke ist echt cool. Probier doch mal _____ Jacke an! Ja, wirklich, in _____ Jacke siehst du sehr fesch aus. *Diese grüne; diese grüne; dieser grünen*

4. (schwarz) _____ Turnschuhe passen gut zu _____ Jeans. *Diese schwarzen; dieser schwarzen*

5. (blau) _____ Hemd passt nicht zu _____ Anorak. *Dieses blaue; diesem blauen*

6. (rot) _____ Krawatte passt nicht zu _____ Hemd. *Diese rote; diesem roten*

2 Was gefällt dir, und was brauchst du? – Schreib die richtige Endung in jede erste Lücke (oder keine Endung, wenn keine Endung nötig ist), die richtige Form des Adjektivs in jede zweite Lücke und den Namen des Kleidungsstücks in jede dritte Lücke. (S. 217)

Beispiel

Dies_____ _____ _____ gefällt mir.
Dies**es blaue Hemd** gefällt mir.
Ich brauche ein_____ _____ _____.
Ich brauche **ein blaues Hemd.**

1. Dies_____ _____ _____ gefällt mir. *er; blaue; Rock*
2. Ich brauche ein_____ _____ _____ . *en; blauen; Rock*

3. Dies_____ _____ _____ gefällt mir. *e; weiße; Bluse*
4. Ich brauche ein_____ _____ _____ . *e; weiße; Bluse*

5. Dies_____ _____ _____ gefällt mir. *er; rote; Pulli*
6. Ich brauche ein_____ _____ _____ . *en; roten; Pulli*

7. Dies_____ _____ _____ gefällt mir. *es; rote; Käppi*
8. Ich brauche ein _____ _____ _____ . *–; rotes; Käppi*

9. Dies_____ _____ _____ gefällt mir. *e; braune; Jacke*
10. Ich möchte ein_____ _____ _____ . *e; braune; Jacke*

3 Du erzählst, was du gern trägst. – Schreib die richtige Adjektivendung in die Lücken. **(S. 217)**

1. Ich möchte ein____ rot____ Krawatte zu dies____ grün____ Hemd.   e; e; em; en
2. Ich möchte ein____ weiß____ Hemd zu dies____ blau____ Jacke.   -; es; er; en
3. Trägst du ein____ gelb____ Pulli zu dies____ weiß____ T-Shirt?   en; en; em; en
4. Trägst du ein____ schwarz____ Käppi zu dies____ grün____ Anorak?   -; es; em; en
5. Ich brauche ein____ braun____ Gürtel für dies____ braun____ Hose.   en; en; e; e
6. Ich brauche ein____ weiß____ T-Shirt für dies____ blau____ Shorts.   -; es; e; e

Zweite Stufe

Objectives Expressing interest, disinterest, and indifference; making and accepting compliments

4 Wofür interessieren sich diese Schüler? – Schreib das richtige Reflexivpronomen in die Lücken. **(S. 222)**

1. Boris, wofür interessierst du _____ ? Interessierst du _____ für Musik oder für Sport?   dich; dich
— Ich interessiere _____ für Musik, Sport und Politik.   mich
2. Weißt du, wofür _____ der Roland interessiert? Interessiert er _____ auch für Musik   sich; sich
und Sport? — Der Roland interessiert _____ nur für Sport.   sich
3. Katrin und Judith, wofür interessiert ihr _____ ? Interessiert ihr _____ für Sport oder   euch; euch
Politik? — Wir interessieren _____ für Bücher und Musik.   uns
4. Ja, viele Schüler interessieren _____ für Sport und Musik, aber viele interessieren   sich
_____ auch für Politik und für die Umwelt.   sich

5 Was für Klamotten tragen die Schüler gern? – Schreib die richtige Form von **tragen**, *to wear*, in die Lücken. **(S. 222)**

Was für Klamotten _____ die Schüler gern? Die Judith _____ gern   tragen; trägt
weiße Outfits, und der Roland _____ alles gern, was schwarz ist. Die   trägt
Katrin _____ nichts aus Acryl, und der Boris _____ lässige Klamotten   trägt; trägt
gern. So, jetzt wissen wir, was unsere vier Schüler gern _____ .   tragen

MEHR GRAMMATIKÜBUNGEN   STANDARDS: 1.2   *zweihunderteinunddreißig*

Mehr Grammatikübungen

6 Du sagst deinen Freunden, dass sie in ihren Klamotten gut aussehen. – Schreib die richtigen Pronomen und die richtigen Endungen in die Lücken. (S. 223)

1. Boris, diese Jacke steht _____ gut. Sie passt gut zu dies_____ blau_____ Hose. *dir; er; en*
2. Judith, diese Bluse passt _____ nicht; sie ist _____ viel zu eng. Die grüne Bluse passt besser zu dein_____ weiß_____ Jeans. *dir; dir er; en*
3. Dieser schwarze Pulli passt d_____ Roland ausgezeichnet; Schwarz steht _____ sehr gut. Die Jeans passt auch gut zu dies_____ schwarz_____ Pulli. *em; ihm em; en*
4. Die Turnschuhe passen d_____ Kindern nicht. Sie sind _____ viel zu eng! *en; ihnen*
5. Dieses Käppi steht dein_____ Schwester gut. Es passt _____ prima, und die Farbe passt auch gut zu ihr_____ grün_____ Bluse. *er; ihr er; en*
6. Frau Meier, dieses Kleid steht _____ gut! *Ihnen*

Dritte Stufe — Objective Persuading and dissuading

7 Was sollen sich diese Leute kaufen? Du sagst es ihnen. – Schreib das richtige Reflexivpronomen in die erste Lücke, die richtige Endung in die zweite Lücke, die richtige Form des Adjektivs in die dritte Lücke und den Namen des Artikels in die vierte Lücke. (S. 226)

BEISPIEL Michelle, kauf _____ doch dies_____ _____ _____ !
Michelle, kauf **dir** doch dies**es rote Trägerhemd**!

1. Katrin, kauf _____ doch dies_____ _____ _____ ! *dir; en; blauen; Faltenrock*
2. Roland und Boris, kauft _____ doch dies_____ _____ _____ ! *euch; e, braunen; Blousons*
3. Herr Meier, kaufen Sie _____ doch dies_____ _____ _____ ! *sich; e; blauen; Turnschuhe*
4. Jack, kauf _____ doch dies_____ _____ _____ ! *dir; en; blauen; Anzug*
5. Katie und Sara, kauft _____ doch dies_____ _____ _____ ! *euch; e; braune; Handtasche*
6. Frau Weiß, kaufen Sie _____ doch dies_____ _____ _____ ! *sich; es; rote; Auto*

8 Schreib das richtige Reflexivpronomen in die erste Lücke, die richtige Endung des Artikels in die zweite Lücke und die richtige Endung des Adjektivs in die dritte Lücke. (**S. 226**)

1. Katrin, kauf _____ doch dies_____ kariert_____ Hemd!   dir; es; e
2. Katrin und Judith, kauft _____ dies_____ braun_____ Schuhe!   euch; e; en
3. Herr Wagner, kaufen Sie _____ doch dies_____ toll_____ T-Shirt!   sich; es; e
4. Judith, kauf _____ ja nicht dies_____ blöd_____ Pulli!   dir; en; en
5. Boris und Roland, kauft _____ ja nicht dies_____ bunt_____ Krawatte!   euch; e, e
6. Frau Moser, kaufen Sie _____ ja nicht dies_____ geblümt_____ Anorak!   sich; en; en

9 Schreib die folgenden **wenn**-Sätze zu Ende und gebrauche dabei die Sätze in den Klammern. (**S. 227**)

1. (Das Wetter ist schlecht.)   Ich bleibe zu Hause, wenn _____ .   das Wetter schlecht ist
2. (Ich habe genug Geld.)   Ich kaufe mir eine CD, wenn _____ .   ich genug Geld habe
3. (Ich gehe ins Kino.)   Ich rufe dich an, wenn _____ .   ich ins Kino gehe
4. (Du hast Geburtstag.)   Ich kaufe dir ein Buch, wenn _____ .   du Geburtstag hast
5. (Wir gehen ins Café.)   Ich hole euch ab, wenn _____ .   wir ins Café gehen
6. (Es regnet nicht.)   Wir spielen Fußball, wenn _____ .   es nicht regnet

MEHR GRAMMATIKÜBUNGEN   STANDARDS: 1.2   *zweihundertdreiunddreißig* **233**

Storytelling Book pp. 62–63

Anwendung

Visit Holt Online
go.hrw.com
KEYWORD: WK3 STUTTGART-8
Self-Test

The *CD-ROM Tutor* offers guided recording and writing activities to accompany the **Anwendung.** These activities are designed to practice students' oral and written communication skills and to review material from each chapter.

1 Katrin sagt ihren Freunden Judith und Boris, was sie kaufen und nicht kaufen sollen. Sie gibt auch Gründe dafür. Hör gut zu und schreib auf, was Judith und Boris kaufen und nicht kaufen sollen, und aus welchen Gründen!   *Script and answers on p. 209H*

CD 8
Tr. 13

2 Auf Seite 224 sind einige Sachen aus einem Modekatalog abgebildet. Schau dir mit einer Freundin diese Sachen an! Jeder von euch möchte zwei Sachen bestellen *(order)*. Schau dir jetzt die Bestellkarte an und beantworte die folgenden Fragen zusammen mit einem Partner!

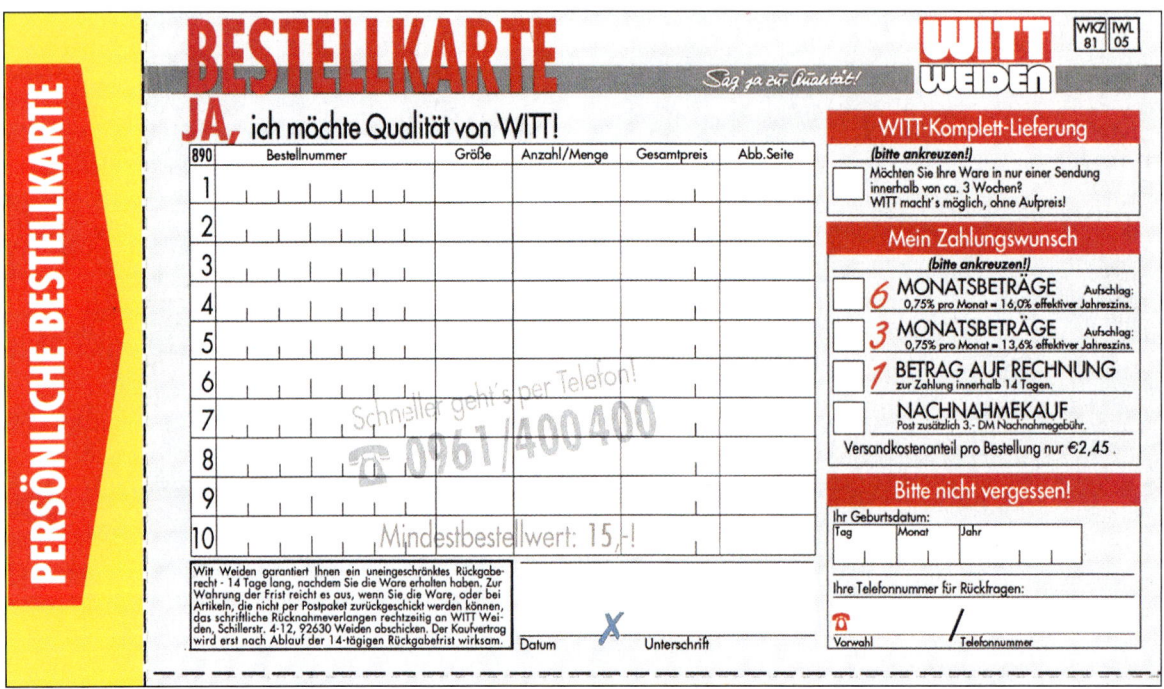

1. What would you write in the columns with these labels: **Bestellnummer? Größe? Anzahl/Menge? Gesamtpreis? Abb. Seite?**
   1. order number/size/quantity/total amount/page number
2. What should you do if you want to receive your order within three weeks?
   2. check the upper right box
3. What are the different possibilities for paying for your merchandise?
   3. 6 installments in 6 months; 3 installments in 3 months; total sum within 14 days; collect on delivery
4. What information should you not forget (**Bitte nicht vergessen!**) to include?
   4. date of birth and telephone number
5. What on the form tells you that you may order the goods more quickly?
   5. telephone number printed crossways over the order form

3 Such dir drei Sachen aus dem Katalog, Seite 224, aus! Schreib die Information auf, die du brauchst, um diese Sachen zu bestellen!

4 Du möchtest die drei Sachen schneller bekommen. Ruf die Nummer an, die auf der Bestellkarte steht, und sag der Verkäuferin (deiner Partnerin), was du bestellen möchtest! Die Verkäuferin stellt Fragen, und du beantwortest sie, um die Bestellkarte auszufüllen.

5 Deine Oma möchte dir etwas kaufen, aber sie weiß nicht genau, was dir gefällt. Schreib ihr einen Brief, und beschreib darin das neue „Outfit", das du gestern im Kaufhaus gesehen hast!

6 Such dir einen Partner für dieses kleine Projekt! Entwerft zusammen eine Reklameseite, auf der ihr eure Lieblingskleidungsstücke zeichnet und genau beschreibt! Gebraucht dabei so viele Details wie nur möglich! — Zeigt eure Reklame den anderen Mitschülern! Wer hat die beste Reklameseite?

7 Zum Schreiben

You are a fashion model who wants to become a movie star, and have been asked for an interview by a fashion magazine. Write a dialogue between yourself and the interviewer in which the interviewer asks questions about what is "in" today, about what clothing you prefer to wear, and about what activities you enjoy doing. Men, as well as women, are fashion models.

Schreibtipp Tone and word choice can influence the effect of your writing on your readers. The tone might be serious, formal, humorous, or cheerful. Decide on the tone that will most interest your readers. Adjectives and adverbs are particularly effective for setting a tone; think about the difference in feeling between the words **gut** and **super**.

Vorbereiten

What general feeling do you want your readers to have about you, and what image do you want to project as a highly visible model who wants to go into the movies? What questions can the interviewer use to grab the reader's interest? How do you want to respond to those questions? You could be humorous or serious, depending on what image you want to project.

Ausführen

Begin with a question that will immediately **grab the reader's attention**. Write the first response to include something rather ingenious in order to focus the reader's interest on you as a person and not as just another nameless model.

Überarbeiten

- Read your dialogue to a partner. Ask your partner if the responses address the questions asked, and if the dialogue will hold the reader's interest. Has the tone you wanted to use actually been conveyed to your partner?
- Change any words or phrases that need improvement. Proofread and make corrections.
- Print a final copy and then present the interview to the class.

8 Rollenspiel

Get together with a classmate and role-play the following scene.

You are a salesperson in the clothing department of a large department store. A customer with really bizarre taste wants to buy certain items of clothing that either do not fit, do not match, or are simply not the right style for this person. Your job is to convince the customer to buy the right clothes, without being offensive.

ANWENDUNG STANDARDS: 1.1, 1.3, 5.1

Kann ich's wirklich?

WK3 STUTTGART-8

Can you describe clothes, using adjectives? (p. 217)

1 How would you ask a friend what he or she likes to wear?
1. Was trägst du gern?

2 How might your friend respond if he or she likes to wear the following clothes? 2. Ich trage gerne …
   a. black jeans and a colorful shirt/blouse   a. eine schwarze Jeans und ein buntes Hemd/eine bunte Bluse.
   b. a red skirt with white stockings and brown shoes   b. einen roten Rock mit weißen Strümpfen und braunen Schuhen.
   c. a striped shirt and a leather bomber jacket   c. ein gestreiftes Hemd und einen Lederblouson.
   d. a blue wool blazer and gray pants
   d. einen blauen Blazer aus Wolle und eine graue Hose.

Can you ask someone about his or her interests and disinterests? Can you express indifference? (p. 221)

3 How would you ask a friend what he or she is interested in?
3. Wofür interessierst du dich?

4 How might your friend respond
   a. that he or she is interested in soccer?   a. Ich interessiere mich für Fußball.
   b. that he or she has no interest in fashion?   b. Ich interessiere mich nicht für Mode.
   c. that he or she is indifferent to sports?   c. Sport ist mir egal.

Can you make and accept compliments? (p. 222)

5 How would you make the following compliments to someone?
   a. this jacket looks great on you   a. Diese Jacke steht dir gut.
   b. these socks go very well with your gray pants   b. Diese Socken passen sehr gut zu deiner grauen Hose.

6 How would that person respond?
6. E.g.: Meinst du wirklich? Echt?

Can you persuade and dissuade? (p. 226)

7 How would you try to persuade someone to buy a silk shirt or blouse?
7. Kauf dir doch ein Seidenhemd oder eine Seidenbluse.

8 How might that person respond   a. Seidenhemden/Seidenblusen sind mir zu teuer.
   a. that silk shirts/blouses are too expensive for him or her?
   b. that he or she doesn't like silk shirts/blouses?   b. Ich mag keine Seidenhemden/Seidenblusen.
   c. that he or she is not sure?   c. Meinst du?

236   zweihundertsechsunddreißig   STANDARDS: 1.2   KAPITEL 8   Mode? Ja oder nein?

Wortschatz

Erste Stufe

 p. 209X

Describing clothing

Wo hast du die neuen Stiefel gekauft?	Where did you buy the new boots?	die Jeansweste, -n	jeans vest	kariert	checked
		der Typ, -en	guy, type	scharf	sharp
das Käppi, -s	(baseball) cap	der Stil, -e	style	gefüttert	padded
die Krawatte, -n	tie			sportlich	sporty
die Wind-, Wetterjacke, -n	windbreaker	**Useful adjectives for describing clothing**		bunt	colorful
				witzig	fun
der Blazer, -	blazer	konservativ	conservative	darunter	under it, underneath
das Wollhemd, -en	wool shirt	modisch	fashionable		
der Anorak, -s	parka	cool	cool	darüber	over it
		geblümt	flowery	von hinten	from behind

Zweite Stufe

More clothing and descriptions

die Lederjacke, -n	leather jacket
die Socke, -n	sock
der Strumpf, ¨-e	stocking
Schuhe mit flachen/ hohen Absätzen	flats, high heels
ärmellos	sleeveless
abgeschnitten	cut-off
weich	soft
fetzig = toll	really sharp
tragen du trägst er/sie/es trägt	to wear, carry

Expressing interest

Interessierst du dich für Mode?	Are you interested in fashion?
Wofür interessierst du dich?	What are you interested in?

Expressing disinterest

Mode interessiert mich nicht.	Fashion doesn't interest me.
Ich hab kein Interesse an Mode.	I'm not interested in fashion.

Expressing indifference

Mode ist mir egal.	I don't care about fashion.

Making and accepting compliments

Die schöne Bluse passt (toll) zu dem blauen Rock.	The nice blouse goes (really) well with the blue skirt.
Das steht dir prima!	That looks great on you!
Das ist dir zu eng.	It's too tight on you.
Echt?	Really?

Dritte Stufe

Persuading and dissuading

Kauf dir doch …!	Why don't you just buy …
Trag doch mal …!	Go ahead and wear …
Kauf dir ja kein …!	Just don't buy …
Trag ja nichts aus …!	Just don't wear anything made of …

More clothing

der Faltenrock, ¨-e	pleated skirt
die Steghose, -n	stirrup pants

das Trägerhemd, -en	camisole
der Sakko, -s	business jacket
der Blouson, -s	bomber jacket
der Anzug, ¨-e	suit
die Kapuze, -n	hood
das Seidenhemd, -en	silk shirt
die Gesäßtasche, -n	back pocket
die Tasche, -n	pocket
die Schlaufe, -n	belt loop
der Reißverschluss, ¨-e	zipper
der Knopf, ¨-e	button
der Druckknopf, ¨-e	snap

mit langen, kurzen Ärmeln	with long, short sleeves

Talking about the material

aus Naturfasern	made from natural fibers
die Wolle	wool
die echte Seide	real silk
das Leinen	linen

Other useful words

wenn (conj.)	whenever

Kapitel 9: Wohin in die Ferien?
Chapter Overview

Los geht's! pp. 240–242	*Verpatzte Ferien,* p. 240			
	FUNCTIONS	**GRAMMAR**	**VOCABULARY**	**RE-ENTRY**
Erste Stufe pp. 243–247	• Expressing indecision, asking for and making suggestions, p. 245	• **-er** endings with place names, p. 245 • The prepositions **nach, in, an,** and **auf,** p. 246	• Places to go on vacation and how to get there, p. 245	Prepositions with location, p. 244 (**Kap. 3, II**); talking about interests, p. 244 (**Kap. 8, II**); asking what to do, p. 245 (**Kap. 8, I**); commands, p. 245 (**Kap. 6, II**); **können,** p. 245 (**Kap. 7, I**); **möchte,** p. 246 (**Kap. 3, I**); **fahren,** p. 246 (**Kap. 9, I**); talking about free-time, p. 247 (**Kap. 2/6, I**)
Zweite Stufe pp. 248–251	• Expressing doubt, conviction, and resignation, p. 249	• The conjunction **ob,** p. 250 • Expressing direction and location (summary), p. 250	• Things to do at a hotel or resort, p. 249	**Dass**-clauses, p. 249 (**Kap. 9, I**); subordinate clauses, pp. 249, 250 (**Kap. 8/9, I**); **wissen** with subord. clauses, p. 249 (**Kap. 9, I**); accusative vs. dative case, p. 250 (**Kap. 3, II**); using the telephone, p. 251 (**Kap. 11, I**); saying where you were on vacation, p. 251 (**Kap. 3, II**); talking about free-time activities, p. 251 (**Kap. 2/6, I**)
Dritte Stufe pp. 252–255	• Asking for and giving directions, p. 254	• Prepositions followed by dative-case forms, p. 254 • The prepositions **durch** and **um,** p. 254 • The prepositions **vor, neben,** and **zwischen,** p. 255	• Places to see in Bietigheim, p. 253	Giving directions, pp. 253, 254 (**Kap. 9, I**); asking where something is, p. 254 (**Kap. 9, I**); two-way prepositions, p. 254 (**Kap. 3, II**); prepositions and accusative, p. 254 (**Kap. 7, I**); inviting someone and responding, p. 255 (**Kap. 11, I**)

Zum Lesen pp. 256–257	Was ist dein Lieblingsreiseziel?	**Reading Strategy** Distinguishing between fact and opinion
Mehr Grammatikübungen	pp. 258–261 Erste Stufe, p. 258 Zweite Stufe, p. 259 Dritte Stufe, p. 261	
Review pp. 262–265	Anwendung, pp. 262–263 Kann ich's wirklich?, p. 264 Wortschatz, p. 265 Zum Schreiben: Organizing around a main idea (Writing an informative magazine article)	

CULTURE

- **Landeskunde:** Wohin fährst du in den nächsten Ferien? p. 243
- **Reisetipps,** p. 244
- **Ein wenig Landeskunde:** Statistics on the means of transportation Germans use to go on vacation, p. 247
- Students talk about vacations, p. 248
- **Stadtrundgang durch Bietigheim,** p. 252

Kapitel 9: Wohin in die Ferien?
Chapter Resources

Lesson Planning
One-Stop Planner
Lesson Planner with Substitute Teacher Lesson Plans, pp. 42–46, 73
Student Make-Up Assignments
- Make-Up Assignment Copying Masters, Chapter 9

Listening and Speaking
TPR Storytelling Book, pp. 64–71
Listening Activities
- Student Response Forms for Listening Activities, pp. 67–70
- Additional Listening Activities 9-1 to 9-6, pp. 71–74
- Additional Listening Activities (song), p. 70
- Scripts and Answers, pp. 150–156

Video Guide
- Teaching Suggestions, pp. 56–57
- Activity Masters, pp. 58–60
- Scripts and Answers, pp. 99–101

Activities for Communication
- Communicative Activities, pp. 49–54
- Realia and Teaching Suggestions, pp. 106–109
- Situation Cards, pp. 139–140

Reading and Writing
Reading Strategies and Skills Handbook, Chapter 9
Lies mit mir! 2, Chapter 9
Übungsheft, pp. 97–108

Grammar
Grammatikheft, pp. 73–81
Grammar Tutor for Students of German, Chapter 9

Assessment
Testing Program
- Grammar and Vocabulary Quizzes, **Stufe** Quizzes, and Chapter Test, pp. 223–240
- Score Sheet, Scripts and Answers, pp. 241–248

Alternative Assessment Guide
- Portfolio Assessment, p. 26
- Performance Assessment, p. 40
- CD-ROM Assessment, p. 54

Student Make-Up Assignments
- Alternative Quizzes, Chapter 9

Online Activities
- Interaktive Spiele
- Internet Aktivitäten

Video Program
- Videocassette 3
- Videocassette 5 (captioned version)
- DVD Tutor, Disc 2

Audio Compact Discs
- Textbook Listening Activities, CD 9, Tracks 1–11
- Additional Listening Activities, CD 9, Tracks 17–23
- Assessment Items, CD 9, Tracks 12–16

Interactive CD-ROM Tutor, Disc 3

Teaching Transparencies
- Situations 9-1 to 9-2
- Vocabulary 9-A to 9-C
- Los geht's!
- Mehr Grammatikübungen Answers
- Grammatikheft Answers

Use the **One-Stop Planner** CD-ROM with Test Generator to aid in lesson planning and pacing.

For each chapter, the **One-Stop Planner** includes:
- Editable lesson plans with direct links to teaching resources
- Printable worksheets from resource books
- Direct launches to the HRW Internet activities
- Video and audio segments
- Test Generator
- Clip Art for vocabulary items

Kapitel 9: Wohin in die Ferien?

Projects

Ein Werbeplakat

In this project each student will create an illustrated advertisement with the title ... **muss man gesehen und erlebt haben!** Students will choose a city for which they will create a convincing advertisement.

MATERIALS
Students may need
- posterboard
- pens
- paper
- travel magazines
- travel sections from newspapers
- encyclopedia for reference

SUGGESTED CITIES
Hamburg, Bietigheim, Munich, Stuttgart, Leipzig, Vienna, Zurich, or any other city that you find appropriate for this project.

SUGGESTED SEQUENCE
1. Each student decides on a city for his or her advertisement and makes an outline showing how he or she plans to organize the project.
2. Students use resources such as travel brochures, reference materials, and travel ads to prepare a convincing visual and written report about their city.
3. The written part of the project should include facts and data. Realia, such as photos or graphs, should be incorporated into a convincing article that would invite people to visit that particular location.
4. As part of the oral component, students should be prepared to give a brief (1 minute) statement to the rest of the class to convince them to visit the city. This oral report should not be read directly from the written advertisement, but instead should be delivered as a sales pitch.

GRADING THE PROJECT
Suggested point distribution (**total = 100 points**)
  Originality and design............................30
  Written assignment (language
     usage and accuracy) 40
  Oral presentation...................................30

Games

Warum denn dahin?

This game tests students' knowledge of German cities and also the grammar structures introduced in this chapter.

Procedure Divide the class into two teams. Each team makes a list of ten to fifteen German cities, mountains, lakes, and so on, that they have learned about. Students may use the book to look for names of cities, mountains, and lakes. The first player on team A chooses the first city on his or her group's list and asks a student on team B: **Warum fährst du denn nach (München)?** The student who was asked then replies by restating the question and also adding an interesting fact or point of interest that made him or her decide to visit the city.

Example:
  Ich fahre nach München, weil ich zum Oktoberfest will.

If the student answers with a correct point of interest or idea, he or she wins a point for the team. Then team B gets to ask the next question. The team with the most points at the end of the game wins.

Storytelling

Mini-Geschichte

This story accompanies Teaching Transparency 9-B. Read the Mini-Geschichte to your students, or have them role-play the conversation using proper pronunciation and intonation. Have students list the advantages of vacationing at the North Sea.

Wohin fahren wir?

„Du, Sabine, wohin fahren wir in den Ferien?" „Ich bin dafür, dass wir ans Meer fahren, vielleicht nach Florida. Dort gibt es schöne Sandstrände. Wir können dort auch segeln und windsurfen." „Ach, Brigitte, wir waren doch erst letztes Jahr in Florida. Fahren wir doch an die Nordsee! Dort können wir tauchen und Boot fahren." „Ich weiß nicht, ob es mir an der Nordsee gefällt. Es ist dort kalt und es regnet oft." „Wenn es regnet, können wir in die Sauna gehen. Viele Hotels haben auch Whirlpools und Fitnessräume. Und an der Nordsee musst du nicht Englisch sprechen." „Also gut."

Traditions

Königsgemüse Spargel

Königsgemüse oder auch Frühlingswonne - so wird der Spargel zur Erntezeit von seinen Genießern liebevoll genannt. Bis ins 19. Jahrhundert war Spargel auch tatsächlich nur auf den Tafeln von Fürsten und Königen zu finden. Die Ernte bedarf auch heute noch viel Sorgfalt und vorallem Handarbeit.

Spargel wird in fast allen Bundesländern angebaut, aber er hat seine historischen Wurzeln in der Gegend um Stuttgart. Der in Deutschland bevorzugte Bleichspargel muss durch kniehohe Erdwälle gegen das Sonnenlicht geschützt werden, denn wenn Licht darauf fällt, verfärben sich die Spitzen. Deshalb wird Spargel auch in der Morgendämmerung geerntet. Der Pflücker legt den Spross mit der Hand frei und schneidet ihn kurz über dem Stock ab. Die Erntezeit hängt ganz von der Temperatur ab und kann sich von April bis Juni erstrecken.

Echte Spargelkenner mögen das Gemüse am liebsten frisch, nach dem Motto: „Morgens gestochen, mittags gegessen."

Why was asparagus once considered the food of royalty and nobility? Have students discuss this question in German.

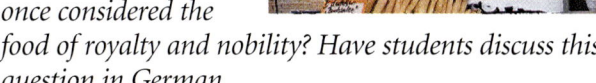

Rezept

Spargel

Der Spargel sollte möglichst frisch sein!

Für 4 Personen

Zutaten

kg=Kilogramm, EL=Esslöffel, TL=Teelöffel, l=Liter

2kg Spargel (weiß)
1EL Butter
     Salz
1 Prise Zucker

Zubereitung

Den Spargel waschen und schälen, dabei immer vom Kopf zum dickeren Ende hin schälen, die Enden abschneiden. In einem großen Topf reichlich Wasser mit der Butter, etwas Salz und Zucker zum Kochen bringen. Den Spargel in das sprudelnde Wasser einlegen und bei kleiner Hitze in 12-15 Minuten gar ziehen lassen. Aus dem Topf heben, abtropfen lassen und auf einer vorgewärmten Platte servieren.

Kapitel 9: Wohin in die Ferien?
Technology

Videocassette 3, 5 (captioned version)
DVD Tutor, Disc 2
See Video Guide, pages 55–60

DVD/Video

Los geht's! • Ein starkes Outfit

Katrin comes in to find her parents watching TV. They tell her they've just seen a weather report on a flood in Austria, and they found out that a bridge on the road to their vacation spot is out, meaning they won't be able to go. The landlord calls to let them know that the bridge will not be repaired before their vacation. Next, Katrin is with her friends trying to decide what to do during their vacation. Several suggestions are made before they decide to play "Tourists in the City."

Landeskunde

Wohin fährst du in den nächsten Ferien?
People talk about their vacation plans.

Fortsetzung

In "Tourists in the City" the friends act like they are tourists in Bietigheim asking random passers-by for directions to various sights. They have lots of fun until they are recognized by an acquaintance of Katrin's father.

Videoclips
- **Wettervorhersage**

Werbung
- **Saalbach Hinterglemm, Österreich** (winter resort)
- **Deutsche Bundesbahn**® (youth discounts on German trains)

Interactive CD-ROM Tutor

Activity	Activity Type	Pupil's Edition Reference
1. Grammatik	Was fehlt?	p. 246
2. Wortschatz	Was ist richtig?	pp. 245, 249
3. Grammatik	Wozu gehört's?	p. 250
4. Wortschatz	Wort und Bild Erfahren/Wählen	p. 253
5. Grammatik	Was fehlt?	pp. 254, 255
6. So sagt man das!	Was kommt dann?	pp. 245, 249, 254
Landeskunde	Wohin fährst du in den nächsten Ferien? Was ist richtig?	p. 243
Zum Sprechen	*Guided recording*	pp. 262–263
Zum Schreiben	*Guided writing*	pp. 262–263

Teacher Management System

Launch the program, type "admin" in the password area, and press RETURN. Log on to **www.hrw.com/CDROMTUTOR** for a detailed explanation of the Teacher Management System.

DVD Tutor

The *DVD Tutor* contains all material from the *Video Program* as described above. German captions are available for use at your discretion for all sections of the video. The *DVD Tutor* also provides a variety of video-based activities that assess students' understanding of **Los geht's!**, **Fortsetzung**, and **Landeskunde**, as well as the new **Grammatik im Kontext** presentations.

The *DVD Tutor* may be used on any DVD video player connected to a television or video monitor.

To preview all resources available for this chapter, use the **One-Stop Planner CD-ROM**, Disc 3.

KEYWORD: WK3 STUTTGART-9
Online Edition

Go.Online!

Premier Online Edition

The Premier Online Edition for *Komm mit!* allows students access to their textbooks anytime, anywhere.
- Audio at point of use
- Additional practice activities
- Self-test activities
- Online reference tools
- Entire Video Program
- Interactive Notebook

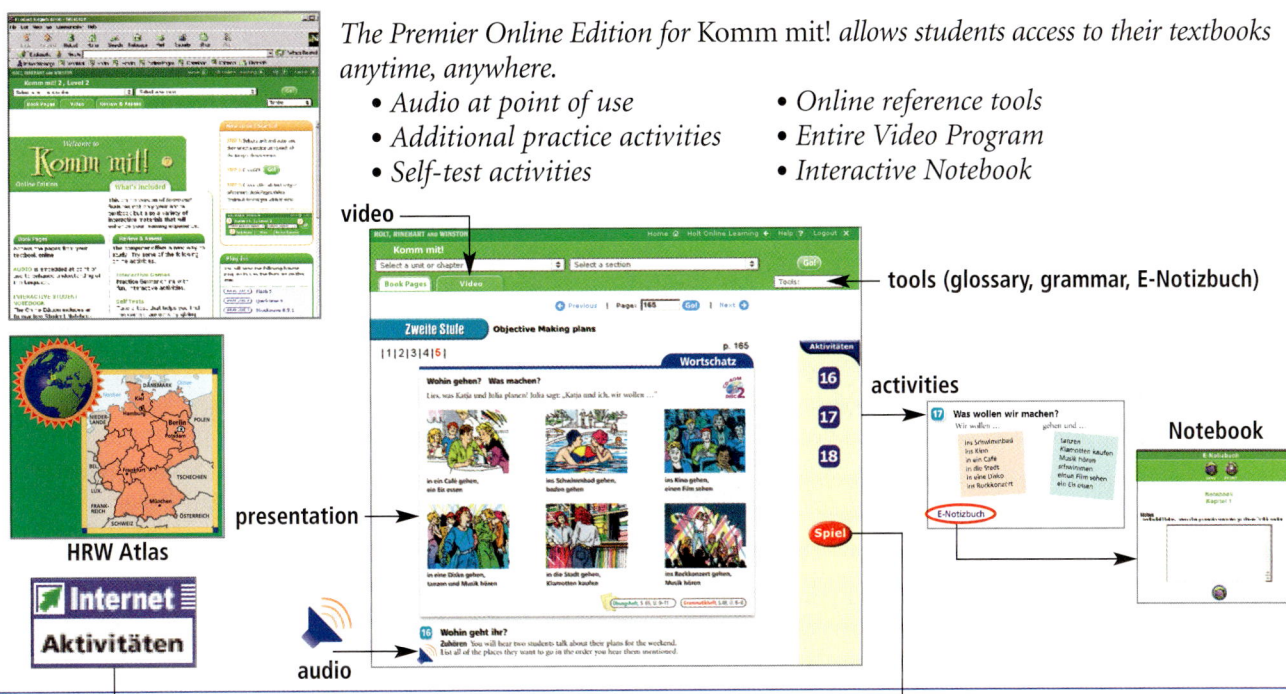

Internet Aktivitäten

These guided internet activities include a worksheet and pre-selected and pre-screened authentic web sites from the German-speaking countries. You can use these activities

- to help students develop research skills in the target language
- to introduce students to authentic cultural information
- as a project

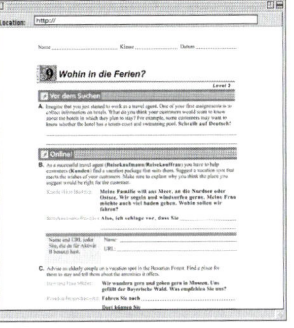

Interaktive Spiele

You can use the interactive activities in this chapter
- to practice grammar, vocabulary, and chapter functions
- as homework
- as an assessment option
- as a self-test
- to prepare for the Chapter Test

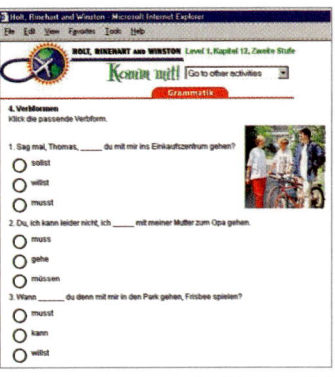

Webprojekt Have students visit a hotel in Austria or Switzerland. Have them report on the location of the hotel and its amenities and prices. Encourage students to exchange useful Web sites with their classmates. Have students document their sources by referencing the names and URLs of all the sites they consulted.

STANDARDS: 1.2, 1.3, 3.2, 5.1   **KAPITEL 9**   **TECHNOLOGY**   **237F**

Kapitel 9: Wohin in die Ferien?
Textbook Listening Activities Scripts

Erste Stufe

6 p. 244

1. **HORST** Mit der Bahn drei Tage an die Nordsee in das kleine Fischerdorf Bensersiel. In diesem Dorf direkt an der Küste sind noch Zimmer frei. Entspannen Sie im Hallenbad, beim Reiten und Stadtwandern. Ein Besuch im Buddelschiffmuseum lohnt sich!

2. **HANNI** Einmalig preiswert! Eine Drei-Tage-Busfahrt nach Dresden und in die Sächsische Schweiz. In Dresden besuchen Sie den berühmten Zwinger, und Sie erleben die einmalig schönen Sandsteinfelsen der Bastei.

3. **HORST** Eine Tagesfahrt an den Bodensee nach Unteruhldingen und weiter mit dem Schiff auf die Insel Mainau, wo Sie unter Palmen spazieren und die Blumenwelt bewundern können. Abfahrt sechs Uhr.

4. **HANNI** Eine Wochenendfahrt (Samstag/Sonntag) in die Schweiz. Übernachtung in Brienz. Am nächsten Vormittag mit der Bergbahn aufs Brienzer Rothorn, die Schweizer Bergwelt genießen. Ein Superangebot!

5. **HORST** Sonderfahrt mit dem Bus nach Ulm zum bekannten Fischerstechen auf der Donau. Am Vormittag Gelegenheit zum Messebesuch im Dom. Mittagessen in einem soliden Gasthaus. Das Fischerstechen beginnt um 14 Uhr. Rückkehr gegen 19 Uhr 30.

6. **HANNI** Drei Tage mit dem Bus durch die schönsten Täler in der Schweiz. Im Emmental Besichtigung eines typischen Bauernhauses und Besuch einer Käserei.

7. **HORST** Drei Tage (von Dienstag bis Donnerstag) mit dem Bus nach Österreich, nach Alpbach in Tirol. Sehr preisgünstig. Ideal für Bergwanderer und solche, die's noch werden wollen!

Answers to Activity 6
1. f; 2. b; 3. d; 4. e; 5. g; 6. c; 7. a

Zweite Stufe

14 p. 249

1. **TANJA** Ich möchte so gern im Sommer nach Südfrankreich, an die Atlantikküste zum Zelten. Es gibt dort ganz tolle Campingplätze, hab ich gehört! Aber in den Sommerferien ist da natürlich Hochsaison. Ich bezweifle, dass es dort noch einen freien Platz für ein 4-Personen-Zelt gibt.

   RUTH Ja also, wir waren letztes Jahr an der französischen Atlantikküste, auch mitten in den großen Ferien. Wir hatten überhaupt nicht im Voraus gebucht und haben trotzdem einen Platz auf einem schönen großen Campingplatz direkt am Meer bekommen. Ich bin sicher, dass du auch etwas findest.

2. **DIRK** Ich habe zum Geburtstag eine neue Taucherausrüstung bekommen. Martin, hast du vielleicht Lust, am Wochenende mit mir an den Strümper See zu fahren? Ich weiß nur nicht genau, ob man dort auch tauchen darf.

   MARTIN Mein Bruder hat mir gesagt, dort gibt es Schilder, auf denen steht, dass man dort weder schwimmen noch angeln darf. Also, das mit dem Tauchen, das kannst du vergessen. Da kann man nichts machen.

3. **MARITA** Wir haben ein Zimmer in einem ganz modernen Sporthotel im Schwarzwald gebucht. Dort gibt es ein Schwimmbad, 'ne Sauna, ein Fitnessstudio und einen Golfplatz nebenan. Ich bin nur nicht sicher, ob es dort auch Tennisplätze gibt.

   OLIVER Also, wenn es ein ganz modernes Sporthotel ist, dann gibt es dort bestimmt auch einen Tennisplatz. Das kannst du mir glauben!

4. **NINA** Ich freu mich schon wahnsinnig auf unseren Urlaub. Wir fahren an die Nordsee, in ein kleines Fischerdorf am Meer. Ich werde jeden Tag an den Strand gehen, um zu schwimmen und ein Sonnenbad zu nehmen. Ich möchte auch gern unseren Hund, den Waldi, mitnehmen. Aber ich weiß nicht, ob er auch mit an den Strand darf.

   BERT Also, ich bin ziemlich sicher, dass man Hunde nicht mit an den Strand nehmen darf. Besonders dann nicht, wenn es ein Badestrand ist und viele Touristen dort sind. Tja, das ist leider so.

Answers to Activity 14
1. ob sie noch einen Zeltplatz bekommen; hat andere Meinung
2. ob man im See tauchen darf; stimmt zu
3. ob es einen Tennisplatz gibt; hat andere Meinung
4. ob der Hund mit an den Strand darf; stimmt zu

16 p. 251

KATJA Ja, hallo Sandra! Katja hier. Du, die Fahrt nach Zürich ist endlos! Wir sind heute Morgen ganz früh von Berlin losgefahren, so um vier Uhr! Jetzt sind wir gerade in Nürnberg und machen eine kleine Pause. Wir haben ungefähr noch fünf Stunden vor uns. Puh! Du kannst dir gar nicht vorstellen, wie froh ich bin, wenn wir endlich ankommen! Also, ich meld mich wieder, wenn wir in Zürich sind. Tschüs!

BERND Hallo Sandra! Hier ist Bernd. Ja, also ich wollte eigentlich nur mal sehen, wie es dir so geht in Berlin. Echt schade, dass du die ganzen Ferien zu Hause bleiben musst. Aber wir können ja was zusammen unternehmen, wenn der Patrick und ich wieder zurückkommen. Also, unser Zug ist gerade erst in Lindau angekommen, so ungefähr vor einer Minute! Wir sind noch auf dem Bahnhof und müssen jetzt erstmal herausfinden, wie wir zum Campingplatz kommen. Also, wir sehen uns dann in zwei Wochen! Tschüs!

PINAR Sandra! Hier ist die Pinar! Du, endlich sind wir in Antalya angekommen! Es ist einfach herrlich hier! Die Sonne, der Strand, traumhaft, sag ich dir! Und ich hab dir ja schon erzählt, dass meine Großeltern ein kleines Häuschen direkt am Meer haben! Einfach sagenhaft! Meine Eltern sind natürlich auch total happy, wieder hier zu sein. Das nächste Mal musst du unbedingt mit in die Türkei kommen! Also, viel Spaß noch in Berlin. Bis nach den Ferien!

The following scripts are for the listening activities found in the *Pupil's Edition*. For Student Response Forms, see *Listening Activities*, pages 67–70. To provide students with additional listening practice, see *Listening Activities*, pages 71–74.

For resource information, see the **One-Stop Planner CD-ROM**, Disc 3.

BORIS He Sandra! Hier ist Boris. Schade, dass du nicht zu Hause bist. Ich wollte dir halt nur schnell schöne Ferien wünschen. Wir haben uns ja gar nicht mehr gesehen, bevor ich losgefahren bin. Ach übrigens, der Enrico und ich, wir sind gerade unterwegs nach Thüringen. Wir wollen uns Weimar, Jena und Eisenach anschauen. Die Hälfte der Strecke haben wir schon hinter uns. Also, na ja, wie gesagt, schöne Ferien dann noch, und bis bald! Ach ja, und viele Grüße auch vom Enrico!

Answers to Activity 16
Katja: auf dem Weg dorthin   **Pinar:** aus dem Ferienort
Bernd: aus dem Ferienort   **Boris:** auf dem Weg dorthin

Dritte Stufe

22 p. 253

1. Beginnen Sie Ihren Rundgang durch das schöne Städtchen Bietigheim am großen Parkplatz an der Holzgartenstraße. Überqueren Sie die Metter und gehen Sie geradeaus, bis Sie auf der linken Seite das Stadttor sehen, ein imposantes Mauerwerk aus dem 14. Jahrhundert. Spazieren Sie durch das Stadttor und biegen Sie dann gleich nach rechts in die Fräuleinstraße ein. Gehen Sie in die zweite Straße links, dann die erste Straße rechts. Dort sehen Sie direkt an der Ecke das Kachelsche Haus aus dem 16. Jahrhundert. Direkt neben dem Kachelschen Haus auf der rechten Seite endet der Rundgang vor einem prächtigen Fachwerkhaus.

2. Treffpunkt für diesen Rundgang ist der Ulrichsbrunnen am Marktplatz. Gehen Sie von dort aus in die Farbstraße hinein, um auch die schönen Seitenfassaden des Bietigheimer Rathauses aus dem 16. Jahrhundert zu besichtigen. Hinter dem Rathaus biegen Sie in die nächste Straße rechts ein, und Sie werden auf der linken Seite eines der ältesten Wohnhäuser Bietigheims sehen, das Hormoldhaus. Gehen Sie nun wieder rechts und dann nach links. Halten Sie sich geradeaus, bis Sie auf der linken Seite ein imposantes Gebäude erblicken. Der Stadtrundgang endet mit einer Innenbesichtigung dieses Gebäudes.

3. Dieser Rundgang beginnt am alten Stadttor auf der Hauptstraße, die in die Innenstadt hineinführt. Gehen Sie hinter dem Stadttor nach rechts in die Fräuleinstraße. Biegen Sie dann in die vierte Straße links. Auf der rechten Seite befindet sich das alte, sehenswürdige Backhaus. Wenn Sie an dem Backhaus vorbei weiter geradeaus gehen, sehen Sie auf der linken Seite das stattliche Bürgerhaus, ein Fachwerkgebäude aus dem 17. Jahrhundert. Gehen Sie weiter die Schieringsbrunnerstraße entlang, bis Sie zum Marktplatz kommen. Dort biegen Sie nach rechts in die Hauptstraße. Biegen Sie die erste Straße rechts ein, gehen Sie am Dom vorbei und überqueren Sie das Schwätzgäßle. Vor dem Fachwerkgebäude auf der rechten Seite endet der Rundgang.

Answers to Activity 22
1. Schieringerstraße, Bürgerhaus
2. Schieringsbrunnerstraße, Evangelische Kirche
3. Pfarrstraße, Kleines Bürgerhaus

Anwendung

1 p. 262

Hi, ich bin's, die Gabi! Stell dir vor, ich war in den Sommerferien drei Wochen lang in Österreich. Es war ganz toll, ich bin gerade vor ein paar Tagen wieder zurückgekommen. Die Moni, das ist meine Freundin, und ich, wir sind zuerst mit dem Zug von München nach Salzburg gefahren. Dort haben wir uns erstmal die Innenstadt angeschaut und, ach ja, auch das Schloss Mirabell haben wir besichtigt! Wunderschön, sag ich dir! Dann sind wir von Salzburg aus mit dem Reisebus nach Tirol gefahren. Auf dem Wolfgangsee haben wir eine super Bootsfahrt gemacht. Ach ja, und hab ich dir schon von den wunderschönen Bergen in Österreich erzählt? Wir wollten so gern eine Bergtour in den Alpen machen, aber stell dir mal vor, Moni und ich hatten leider keine richtigen Wanderschuhe mit, nur unsere Turnschuhe. So was Blödes! Damit kann man natürlich nicht wandern gehen! Na ja, aber dafür haben wir jeden Morgen Tennis gespielt. Wir haben übrigens in einer kleinen Pension gewohnt, die gleich in der Nähe von einer supermodernen Sportanlage war, sogar mit Schwimmbad. Aber Moni und ich sind lieber im See schwimmen gegangen. Das hat viel mehr Spaß gemacht. Und du, erzähl doch mal, was hast du denn alles in den Ferien gemacht?

Answers to Activity 1
Ist mit dem Zug nach Salzburg gefahren; hat die Innenstadt von Salzburg angeschaut; hat Schloss Mirabell besichtigt; ist mit dem Reisebus nach Tirol gefahren; hat eine Bootsfahrt auf dem Wolfgangsee gemacht; hat Tennis gespielt; ist im See schwimmen gegangen

Kapitel 9: Wohin in die Ferien?
Suggested Lesson Plans 50-Minute Schedule

Day 1

CHAPTER OPENER 10 min.
- Background Information, ATE, p. 237M
- Thinking Critically, ATE, p. 237M

LOS GEHT'S! 20 min.
- Preteaching Vocabulary, ATE, p. 237N
- Play Audio CD for Los geht's!
- Have students read Los geht's!, pp. 240–241
- Teaching Suggestions, Video Guide, p. 56
- Show Los geht's! Video

LANDESKUNDE 15 min.
- Pre-viewing Suggestion, Video Guide, p. 56
- Teaching Suggestions, ATE, p. 237O
- Show Landeskunde Video

Wrap-Up 5 min.
- Students respond to questions about where they like to spend their vacations

Homework Options
Pupil's Edition, p. 242, Comprehension Acts. 1–5; p. 243, Acts. A and B
Übungsheft, p. 97, Act. 1; p. 98, Acts. 1–2
Interactive CD-ROM, Landeskunde Activity

Day 2

ERSTE STUFE
Quick Review 10 min.
- Check homework, Comprehension Acts. 1–5, p. 242

Reading Selection, p. 244 15 min.
- Play Audio CD for Activity 6, p. 244
- Do Activity 7, p. 244

Wortschatz / So sagt man das! / Ein wenig Grammatik, p. 245 20 min.
- Presenting Wortschatz, ATE, p. 237P
- Teaching Transparency 9-1
- Do Activity 1, p. 73, Grammatikheft
- Presenting Ein wenig Grammatik / So sagt man das!, ATE, p. 237P
- Do Activity 2, p. 73, Grammatikheft
- Do Activity 8, p. 245

Wrap-Up 5 min.
- Students respond to questions about what they like to do on vacation

Homework Options
Übungsheft, p. 99, Act. 1

Day 3

ERSTE STUFE
Quick Review 10 min.
- Check homework, Übungsheft, p. 99, Act. 1

Grammatik, p. 246 25 min.
- Presenting Grammatik, ATE, p. 237P
- Teaching Transparencies 9-1, 9-A
- Do Activity 9, p. 246
- Do Activities 10, 11, and 12, p. 247
- Do Activities 3–4, p. 74, Grammatikheft

Quiz Review 10 min.
- Do Additional Listening Activities 9-1 and 9-2, p. 71
- Do Erste Stufe Activities, Interactive CD-ROM

Wrap-Up 5 min.
- Students respond to questions about where they plan to spend their summer vacation

Homework Options
Mehr Grammatikübungen, Erste Stufe
Übungsheft, pp. 99–101, Acts. 2–6

Day 4

ERSTE STUFE
Quick Review 10 min.
- Check homework, Mehr Grammatikübungen, Erste Stufe

Quiz 20 min.
- Quiz 9-1A or 9-1B

ZWEITE STUFE
Reading Selection 15 min.
- Do Activity 13, p. 248

Wrap-Up 5 min.
- Students respond to questions about whether they already know where they are spending their vacations

Homework Options
Activities for Communication, p. 107, Realia 9-2: underline cognates, look up words you don't know

Day 5

ZWEITE STUFE
Quick Review 10 min.
- Return and review Quiz 9-1
- Check homework, Realia 9-2
- Bell Work, ATE, p. 237R

Wortschatz / So sagt man das!, p. 249 15 min.
- Presenting Wortschatz / So sagt man das!, ATE, p. 237R
- Teaching Transparencies 9-B, 9-C
- Play Audio CD for Activity 14, p. 249

Ein wenig Grammatik / Grammatik, p. 250 20 min.
- Presenting Ein wenig Grammatik, ATE, p. 237S
- Do Activity 15, p. 250
- Presenting Grammatik, ATE, p. 237S
- Play Audio CD for Activity 16, p. 251
- Do Activities 17, 18, 19, and 20, p. 251

Wrap-Up 5 min.
- Students respond to questions about where they are going and where they have already been on vacation

Homework Options
Grammatikheft, pp. 75–78, Acts. 5–13

Day 6

ZWEITE STUFE
Quick Review 10 min.
- Check homework, Grammatikheft, pp. 75–78, Acts. 5–13

Quiz Review 20 min.
- Do Acts 1–6, pp. 102–104, Übungsheft
- Do Communicative Activity 9-1, pp. 49–50

Quiz
- Quiz 9-2A or 9-2B 20 min.

Homework Options
Internet Aktivitäten, see ATE, p. 237F

 **One-Stop Planner CD-ROM**

For alternative lesson plans by chapter section, to create your own customized plans, or to preview all resources available for this chapter, use the **One-Stop Planner CD-ROM**, Disc 3.

 For additional homework suggestions, see activities accompanied by this symbol throughout the chapter.

Day 7

DRITTE STUFE
Quick Review 15 min.
- Return and review Quiz 9-2
- Bell Work, ATE, p. 237T

Reading Selection 15 min.
- Read **Stadtrundgang durch Bietigheim**, p. 252
- Teaching Transparency 9-2
- Do Activity 21, p. 253

Wortschatz, p. 253 15 min.
- Presenting **Wortschatz**, ATE, p. 237U
- Teaching Transparency 9-2
- Play Audio CD for Activity 22, p. 253

Wrap-Up 5 min.
- Students respond to questions about where one could go in Bietigheim

Homework Options
Grammatikheft, p. 79, Act. 14
Übungsheft, pp. 105–106, Acts. 1–4

Day 8

DRITTE STUFE
Quick Review 10 min.
- Check homework, Grammatikheft, p. 79, Act. 14

Grammatik / Ein wenig Grammatik, p. 254 10 min.
- Presenting **Grammatik**, ATE, p. 237U
- Presenting **Ein wenig Grammatik**, ATE, p. 237V
- Do Activity 23, p. 254

So sagt man das!, p. 254 10 min.
- Presenting **So sagt man das!**, ATE, p. 237V
- Do Activity 24, p. 255

Ein wenig Grammatik, p. 255 15 min.
- Presenting **Ein wenig Grammatik**, ATE, p. 237V
- Do Activities 25, 26, 27, 28, and 29, p. 255

Wrap-Up 5 min.
- Students respond to questions about how to get to various places in Bietigheim

Homework Options
Grammatikheft, pp. 80–81, Acts. 15–18
Übungsheft, p. 107, Acts. 5–6

Day 9

DRITTE STUFE
Quick Review 15 min.
- Check homework, Grammatikheft, pp. 80–81, Acts. 15–18

ZUM LESEN 30 min.
- Present **Lesestrategie**, p. 256
- Do Activities 1–10, pp. 256–257
- Do Activities 1–2, p. 108, Übungsheft

Wrap-Up 5 min.
- Students respond to questions about the best vacation they ever had

Homework Options
Übungsheft, p. 108, Acts. 3–5

Day 10

DRITTE STUFE
Quick Review 10 min.
- Check homework, Übungsheft, p. 108, Acts. 3–5

Quiz Review 20 min.
- Do **Mehr Grammatikübungen, Dritte Stufe**
- Do Communicative Activity 9-2, pp. 51–52
- Do Additional Listening Activities 9-5 and 9-6, pp. 73–74

Quiz 20 min.
- Quiz 9-3A or 9-3B

Homework Options
Interaktive Spiele, see ATE, p. 237F

Day 11

ANWENDUNG
Quick Review 10 min.
- Return and review Quiz 9-3

Anwendung 35 min.
- Do **Anwendung** Activities 1–4 and 6 pp. 262–263

Wrap-Up 5 min.
- Students respond to questions about where they could go on vacation

Homework Options
Pupil's Edition, p. 263, Act. 5

Day 12

ANWENDUNG
Quick Review 15 min.
- Students present **Zum Schreiben** compositions

Kann ich's wirklich?, p. 264 15 min.
- Do Activities 1–9, p. 264

Chapter Review 20 min.
- Review chapter functions, vocabulary, and grammar; choose from **Mehr Grammatikübungen**, Grammar Tutor for Students of German, Activities for Communication, Listening Activities, Interactive CD-ROM Tutor, or **Interaktive Spiele**
- Review test format and provide sample test items for students

Homework Options
Study for Chapter Test

Assessment

Test, Chapter 9 45 min.
- Administer Chapter 9 Test. Select from Testing Program, Alternative Assessment Guide, or Test Generator.

KAPITEL 9 • SUGGESTED LESSON PLANS • 50-MINUTE SCHEDULE

Kapitel 9: Wohin in die Ferien?
Suggested Lesson Plans 90-Minute Schedule

Block 1

CHAPTER OPENER 10 min.
- Background Information, ATE, p. 237M
- Thinking Critically, ATE, p. 237M

LOS GEHT'S! 20 min.
- Pre-teaching Vocabulary, ATE, p. 237N
- Play Audio CD for **Los geht's!**
- Have students read **Los geht's!**, pp. 240–241
- Teaching Suggestions, Video Guide, p. 56
- Show **Los geht's!** Video

LANDESKUNDE 15 min.
- Pre-viewing Suggestion, Video Guide, p. 56
- Teaching Suggestions, ATE, p. 237O
- Show **Landeskunde** Video

ERSTE STUFE
Reading Selection, p. 244 15 min.
- Play Audio CD for Activity 6, p. 244
- Do Activity 7, p. 244

Wortschatz / So sagt man das! / Ein wenig Grammatik, p. 245 25 min.
- Presenting **Wortschatz**, ATE, p. 237P
- Teaching Transparency 9-1
- Do Activity 1, p. 73, Grammatikheft
- Presenting **Ein wenig Grammatik / So sagt man das!**, ATE, p. 237P
- Do Activity 2, p. 73, Grammatikheft
- Do Activity 8, p. 245

Wrap-Up 5 min.
- Students respond to questions about where they like to go and what they like to do on vacation

Homework Options
Pupil's Edition, p. 242, Comprehension Acts. 1–5; p. 243, Acts. A and B
Übungsheft, p. 97, Act. 1; p. 98, Acts. 1–2; p. 99, Act. 1
Interactive CD-ROM, **Landeskunde** Activity

Block 2

ERSTE STUFE
Quick Review 15 min.
- Check homework, Pupil's Edition, p. 242, Comprehension Acts. 1–5; p. 243, Acts. A and B

Grammatik, p. 246 35 min.
- Presenting **Grammatik**, ATE, p. 237P
- Teaching Transparencies 9-1, 9-A
- Do Activity 9, p. 246
- Do Activities 10, 11, and 12, p. 247
- Do Activities 3–4, p. 74, Grammatikheft
- Do Activities 2–6, pp. 99–101, Übungsheft

Quiz Review 20 min.
- Do Additional Listening Activities 9-1 and 9-2, p. 71
- Do **Mehr Grammatikübungen, Erste Stufe**

Quiz 20 min.
- Quiz 9-1A or 9-1B

Homework Options
Activities for Communication, p. 107, Realia 9-2: underline cognates, look up words you don't know

Block 3

ZWEITE STUFE
Quick Review 10 min.
- Return and review Quiz 9-1
- Check homework, Realia 9-2
- Bell Work, ATE, p. 237R

Reading Selection 15 min.
- Do Activity 13, p. 248

Wortschatz / So sagt man das!, p. 249 15 min.
- Presenting **Wortschatz / So sagt man das!**, ATE, p. 237R
- Teaching Transparencies 9-B, 9-C
- Play Audio CD for Activity 14, p. 249

Ein wenig Grammatik / Grammatik, p. 250 30 min.
- Presenting **Ein wenig Grammatik**, ATE, p. 237S
- Do Activitiy 15, p. 250
- Presenting **Grammatik**, ATE, p. 237S
- Play Audio CD for Activity 16, p. 251
- Do Activities 17, 18, 19, and 20, p. 251

Quiz Review 15 min.
- Do **Mehr Grammatikübungen, Zweite Stufe**

Wrap-Up 5 min.
- Students respond to questions about where they are going and where they have already been on vacation

Homework Options
Grammatikheft, pp. 75–78, Acts. 5–13
Übungsheft, pp. 102–104, Acts. 1–6

One-Stop Planner CD-ROM

For alternative lesson plans by chapter section, to create your own customized plans, or to preview all resources available for this chapter, use the **One-Stop Planner CD-ROM**, Disc 3.

 For additional homework suggestions, see activities accompanied by this symbol throughout the chapter.

Block 4

ZWEITE STUFE
Quick Review 10 min.
- Übungsheft, pp. 102–104, Acts. 2–6

Quiz Review 15 min.
- Do Communicative Activity 9-1, pp. 49–50
- Do **Zweite Stufe** Activities, Interactive CD-ROM

Quiz 20 min.
- Quiz 9-2A or 9-2B

DRITTE STUFE
Reading Selection 20 min.
- Read **Stadtrundgang durch Bietigheim**, p. 252
- Teaching Transparency 9-2
- Do Activity 21, p. 253

Wortschatz, p. 253 20 min.
- Presenting **Wortschatz**, ATE, p. 237U
- Teaching Transparency 9-2
- Play Audio CD for Activity 22, p. 253
- Do Activity 14, p. 79, Grammatikheft

Wrap-Up 5 min.
- Students respond to questions about how to get to various places in Bietigheim

Homework Options
Übungsheft, pp. 105–106, Acts. 1–4

Block 5

DRITTE STUFE
Quick Review 15 min.
- Return and review Quiz 9-2
- Check homework, Übungsheft, pp. 105–106, Act. 1–4

Grammatik / Ein wenig Grammatik, p. 254 10 min.
- Presenting **Grammatik**, ATE, p. 237U
- Presenting **Ein wenig Grammatik**, ATE, p. 237V
- Do Activity 23, p. 254

So sagt man das!, p. 254 10 min.
- Presenting **So sagt man das!**, ATE, p. 237V
- Do Activity 24, p. 255

Ein wenig Grammatik, p. 255 20 min.
- Presenting **Ein wenig Grammatik**, ATE, p. 237V
- Do Activities 25, 26, 27, 28, and 29, p. 255

ZUM LESEN 30 min.
- Present **Lesestrategie**, p. 256
- Do Activities 1–10, pp. 256–257
- Do Activities 1–2, p. 108, Übungsheft

Wrap-Up 5 min.
- Students respond to questions about the best vacation they ever had

Homework Options
Grammatikheft, pp. 80–81, Acts. 15–18
Übungsheft, p. 107, Acts. 5–6; p. 108, Acts. 3–5

Block 6

DRITTE STUFE
Quick Review 15 min.
- Check homework, Grammatikheft, pp. 80–81, Acts. 15–18

Quiz Review 20 min.
- Do **Mehr Grammatikübungen, Dritte Stufe**
- Do Communicative Activity 9-2, pp. 51–52
- Do Additional Listening Activities 9-5 and 9-6, pp. 73–74

Quiz 20 min.
- Quiz 9-3A or 9-3B

ANWENDUNG 30 min.
- Do **Anwendung** Activities 1–4 and 6, pp. 262–263

Wrap-Up 5 min.
- Students respond to questions about where they could go on vacation

Homework Options
Pupil's Edition, p. 263, Act. 5

Block 7

ANWENDUNG
Quick Review 15 min.
- Return and review Quiz 9-3
- Students present **Zum Schreiben** compositions

Kann ich's wirklich?, p. 264 10 min.
- Do Activities 1–9, p. 264

Chapter Review 20 min.
- Review chapter functions, vocabulary, and grammar; choose from **Mehr Grammatikübungen,** Grammar Tutor for Students of German, Activities for Communication, Listening Activities, Interactive CD-ROM Tutor, or **Interaktive Spiele**

Test, Chapter 9 45 min.
- Administer Chapter 9 Test. Select from Testing Program, Alternative Assessment Guide, or Test Generator.

Kapitel 9: Wohin in die Ferien?
Teaching Suggestions, pages 238–265

PAGES 238–239

CHAPTER OPENER

Pacing Tips
The **Erste Stufe** centers around vacations and the functions of 'expressing indecision, asking for and making suggestions.' The prepositions **nach**, **in**, **an**, and **auf** are explained. A grammar summary of expressing direction and location occurs in the **Zweite Stufe** alongside the function 'expressing doubt, conviction, and resignation.' Students also use the conjunctions **dass** and **ob**. In the **Dritte Stufe**, prepositions followed by dative case forms are used in 'asking for and giving directions.' Since all three **Stufen** include major grammar concepts, you will probably spend the same amount of time on each. For Lesson Plans and timing suggestions, see pages 237I–237L.

Meeting the Standards
Communication
- Expressing indecision, asking for and making suggestions, p. 245
- Expressing doubt, conviction, and resignation, p. 249
- Asking for and giving directions, p. 254

Cultures
- Landeskunde, p. 243
- Reisetipps, p. 244
- Ein wenig Landeskunde, p. 247
- Stadtrundgang durch Bietigheim, p. 252
- Culture Note, p. 237N
- Culture Note, p. 237O
- Geography Connection, p. 237U

Connections
- Multicultural Connection, p. 237O
- Geography Connection, p. 237Q
- Music Connection, p. 237S
- Music Connection, p. 237U
- Geography Connection, p. 237W

Comparisons
- Language-to-Language, p. 237Q
- Language-to-Language, p. 237U
- Thinking Critically, p. 237V

Communities
- Career Path, p. 237Q

For resource information, see the **One-Stop Planner CD-ROM**, Disc 3.

Building Context
Ask students about their family vacations. How do they generally decide on a vacation destination? What are some of their most memorable vacations? Have there been any that did not turn out as planned?

Cultures and Communities

Background Information
Many Germans prefer to vacation in small villages and towns. Since large resorts or hotels cannot be found there, lodging is typically provided by bed-and-breakfast establishments (**Pension**). At a reasonable price visitors stay in a home, often share bathrooms with other guests, and receive a full breakfast included in the price.

Teacher Note
A **Bürgerhaus** is an old apartment building in the historical part of a town that dates back to the 15th-17th centuries.

Connections and Comparisons

Thinking Critically
Drawing Inferences Have students imagine that they are calling the proprietors of the **Pension** where they will be staying. They are not familiar with the area and need help planning some day trips. Have students come up with a list of questions to ask.

Chapter Sequence
Los geht's!	p. 240
Landeskunde	p. 243
Erste Stufe	p. 244
Zweite Stufe	p. 248
Dritte Stufe	p. 252
Zum Lesen	p. 256
Mehr Grammatikübungen	p. 258
Anwendung	p. 262
Kann ich's wirklich?	p. 264
Wortschatz	p. 265

LOS GEHT'S!

Teaching Resources
pp. 240–242

PRINT
- Lesson Planner, p. 42
- Video Guide, pp. 55–56, 58
- Übungsheft, p. 97

MEDIA
- One-Stop Planner
- Video Program
  Los geht's!
  Videocassette 3, 36:27–38:52
  Videocassette 5 (captioned version), 51:18–53:42
  Fortsetzung
  Videocassette 3, 38:54–40:49
  Videocassette 5 (captioned version), 53:47–55:41
- DVD Tutor, Disc 2
- Audio Compact Discs, CD9, Trs. 1–2
- Los geht's! Transparencies

PAGES 240–241

Los geht's! Transparencies

Preteaching Vocabulary

Guessing Words from Context

First, ask students to identify where each scene is taking place and what the people are doing there. Then, have students use contextual clues to guess the meanings of these words and phrases: **ins Wasser gefallen, Hochwasser, die Brücke, zufällig, enttäuscht, Da kann man nichts machen., Pfingstferien.** Which of these words are cognates? Ask students to consider the literal and figurative meanings of the phrase **ins Wasser gefallen.** Finally, have students guess the meanings of phrases that begin certain sentences: **Ich bezweifle; Ich bin dafür; Dann schlage ich vor.** Do these phrases express fact or opinion? Ask students to observe the use of **dass** and its effect on word order.

 **Fortsetzung**
You may choose to continue with the **Fortsetzung** of *Verpatzte Ferien* now or  wait until later in the chapter. For a synopsis of the **Los geht's!** and **Fortsetzung** episodes, see p. 237E.

Advance Organizer

Ask students if they ever had a trip or vacation cancelled or changed due to unforeseen problems. If so, can they tell the class what happened?

Cultures and Communities

Culture Note

Pfingstferien (*Whitsuntide* or *Pentecost vacation*) usually falls at the end of May and varies in length from **Bundesland** to **Bundesland** from four to seven days. **Pfingsten** is a Christian holiday.

Using the Captioned Video/DVD

 As an alternative to reading the conversations in the book, you might want to show the captioned version of *Verpatzte Ferien* available on Videocassette 5.
Note: The *DVD Tutor* contains captions for all sections of the *Video Program*.

PAGE 242

Comprehension Check

Auditory Learners

1 After students have watched the video segment of *Verpatzte Ferien,* ask the questions in Activity 1. Depending on students' comprehension, you may or may not want to let them keep their books open.

Challenge

1 Ask the questions in German immediately after students have watched the video segment, without having them look at the script.

A Slower Pace

4 Before students scan the story for this activity, ask them to think of phrases they use in English to express each of the ideas listed. Make a list and have students compare it with the German expressions they found in **Los geht's!**.

Teaching Suggestion

Have students choose roles and act out **Los geht's!**. Students should choose to play a member of the Simon family (in groups of three) or a member of Katrin's circle of friends (in groups of four).

PAGE 243

LANDESKUNDE

Teaching Resources
p. 243

PRINT
- Video Guide, pp. 55–56, 58–59
- Übungsheft, p. 98

MEDIA
- One-Stop Planner
- Video Program
  Videocassette 3, 41:28–46:26
- DVD Tutor, Disc 2
- Audio Compact Discs, CD9, Trs. 3–6
- Interactive CD-ROM Tutor, Disc 3

Teaching Suggestions

- After students have done the prereading activity, ask them to close their books. While students watch the video segment or listen to the Audio CD, ask them to take notes about the vacation plans the four interviewees talk about. If necessary, play the interviews two or three times. Then, divide the board into four sections and write the name of each interviewee at the top of each section. Ask students to tell you how these people spend their vacation. Then read the four interviews in the book and have students compare the information on the board with the actual readings.

- You might want to introduce the following definitions to help students better understand the video segment or listening script:
  aufgrund dessen—weil
  'n bissel (southern dialect)—ein bisschen; ein wenig
  der Verstärker—Teil einer Stereoanlage

Cultures and Communities

 **Culture Note**
In Germany, every employee is entitled by law to a minimum of five weeks of paid vacation each year. However, collective agreements with most employers give many employees six weeks or more of paid vacation (**bezahlter Urlaub**).

Connections and Comparisons

Multicultural Connection
Ask students to find information about the length of school vacations in foreign countries. If possible, have students interview foreign exchange students about their favorite vacation spots and the usual length of their stay.

Teacher Note

Mention to your students that the **Landeskunde** will also be included in Quiz 9-1B given at the end of the **Erste Stufe**.

ERSTE STUFE

Teaching Resources
pp. 244–247

PRINT
- Lesson Planner, p. 43
- TPR Storytelling Book, pp. 64–65
- Listening Activities, pp. 67, 71
- Activities for Communication, pp. 106, 109, 139–140
- Grammatikheft, pp. 73–74
- Grammar Tutor for Students of German, Chapter 9
- Übungsheft, pp. 99–101
- Testing Program, pp. 223–226
- Alternative Assessment Guide, p. 40
- Student Make-Up Assignments, Chapter 9

MEDIA
- One-Stop Planner
- Audio Compact Discs, CD9, Trs. 7, 12, 17–18
- Teaching Transparencies
  Vocabulary 9-A
  Mehr Grammatikübungen Answers
  Grammatikheft Answers
- Interactive CD-ROM Tutor, Disc 3
- DVD Tutor, Disc 2

PAGE 244

 **Bell Work**
In pairs, have students ask each other where they would go if they were offered a round-trip ticket to anywhere in the United States for the upcoming weekend. What would they do there?

STANDARDS: 2.1, 4.2

Communication for All Students

Auditory Learners

6 After students have listened to the descriptions and matched them with the corresponding photos, play the descriptions a second time. This time ask students to listen for the particular phrase or word that helped them match the description and photo. Students should write that phrase or word next to the number and its letter. (Example: 3. d; **Insel, Palmen**)

Answers to Activity 7   Questions 1. and 2: **an die Nordsee/nach Bensersiel—drei Tage
nach Dresden—drei Tage
an den Bodensee/auf Mainau—einen Tag (eine Tagesfahrt)
in die Schweiz—zwei Tage (eine Wochenendfahrt)
nach Ulm—einen Tag
in die Schweiz—drei Tage
nach Österreich—drei Tage
Question 3:   Meer/See—1, 3; in die Berge—4, 7; Stadtbesichtigungen—2, 5
Question 4:   Answers will vary.**

▶ PAGE 245

PRESENTING: Wortschatz

Review previously learned means of transportation such as **Auto, Fahrrad, Mofa, Moped, S-Bahn, U-Bahn,** and **Bus** by asking questions such as:
**Wie kommst du gewöhnlich zur Schule?
Wie fährt dein Vater/deine Mutter zur Arbeit?**

Using a world map, introduce the new vocabulary through meaningful context.
Example: **Von New York nach Frankfurt geht es am schnellsten mit dem Flugzeug.**

Practice using the vocabulary by asking students what type of transportation they use:
 a) to go on vacation,
 b) to visit family,
 c) to go into town.

Teaching Suggestion

You may want to introduce the names of some vacation places students have not yet learned:

ins Ferienlager
aufs Land
ins Freibad
ins Wellenbad
auf einen Bauernhof
in den Vergnügungspark

PRESENTING: Ein wenig Grammatik

Mountain names Have students use an atlas or a map of Europe to find other examples of such mountain names.
Examples:

Wildspitze—Österreich
Rheinwaldhorn—Schweiz
Hochalmspitze—Österreich
Stanserhorn—Schweiz
Sustenhorn—Schweiz

PRESENTING: So sagt man das!

Ask your students what other ways of making suggestions they remember. (In Chapter 6 students used modals as well as the inclusive command to make suggestions.) Students can practice the expressions in **So sagt man das!** with a partner as they discuss plans for the afternoon or the weekend. Examples:

**Was machen wir heute Nachmittag?
Ich bin dafür, dass wir mal ins Kino gehen.**

▶ PAGE 246

PRESENTING: Grammatik

The prepositions nach, in, an and auf To demonstrate the use of prepositions to express direction, use pictures of geographic features like the ones used in this **Grammatik.** Then elicit answers to the question "**Wohin fährst du diesen Sommer?**" To emphasize the concept of direction, demonstrate the difference between **in** as a response to **wohin?** and **in** as a response to **wo?** Have one student leave the classroom and then walk back in. Ask the other students: **Wohin geht Thomas?** answer: **In die Klasse.** Then ask: **Und wo ist Thomas?** stressing **ist.** Elicit the answer or answer yourself: **In der Klasse.**

Connections and Comparisons

Language-to-Language

You may want to explain to students that German, like French and Spanish, contracts some prepositions with a following article. Examples:
German: **an + das = ans**
French: **à + le = au**
Spanish: **a + el = al**

Have students make a list of the German prepositions that form contractions with the definite article. (Examples: **ins, ans, aufs, durchs, beim, am, im, vom, vorm, hinterm**) Students should establish linguistic rules explaining when such contractions are possible. (You may want to point out that while **ins** [in+das] is easy to pronounce, "inr" [in+der] is a tongue twister and does not exist.)

Communication for All Students

Challenge

9 To expand this activity, ask students to reuse their notes to compose a series of travel journal entries for an imaginary trip. Students should give an account of their daily activities for a minimum of three days.

PAGE 247

Teacher Note

12 You may want to have a selection of travel brochures available for students to choose from. You can obtain these materials from local travel agencies or order materials from the **Deutsche Zentrale für Tourismus e. V.** or the German National Tourist Office. For addresses, see pp. T48–49 of the *Teacher's Edition* or visit the HRW Web site at http://www.hrw.com.

Connections and Comparisons

Geography Connection

12 As an alternative to having students work on destinations in German-speaking countries, ask students to refer to foreign countries they have studied in Social Studies or Geography and have them incorporate that information into the **Reisebüro** conversation.

Cultures and Communities

Career Path

Have students work in groups to think of situations in which someone specializing in Internet services would find a knowledge of German advantageous. (Suggestions: If a German city or hotel chain wanted to increase its appeal to American tourists by means of the World Wide Web, such a person could design an English-German web site for them; the same would hold true for an American city or hotel chain targeting German tourists.)

Reteaching: Expressing direction

To review the uses of **an, auf, in,** and **nach,** prepare a list of sentences like the following examples. Students receive a handout and are asked to underline all bodies of water in blue, all countries or geographic areas that require an article in green, all countries or geographic areas that do not require an article in red, and all areas referring to height or flat surfaces in brown. Then, have students decide which preposition to use to fill in the blanks.
Wir fahren im Sommer _____ (die Ostsee).
Ihre Familie steigt jedes Jahr _____ (die Zugspitze).
Ich fliege nächste Woche _____ (die Türkei).
Am Wochenende fährt er immer _____ (Ulm).

 Game

Play the game **Warum denn dahin?** See p. 237C for the procedure.

Teaching Suggestion

Ask students to give an account of an excursion or trip that did not turn out as planned. Where did they go and what happened?

Assess

▸ Testing Program, pp. 223–226
Quiz 9-1A, Quiz 9-1B
Audio CD9, Tr. 12

▸ Student Make-Up Assignments
Chapter 9, Alternative Quiz

▸ Alternative Assessment Guide, p. 40

ZWEITE STUFE

Teaching Resources
pp. 248–251

PRINT
- Lesson Planner, p. 44
- TPR Storytelling Book, pp. 66–67
- Listening Activities, pp. 67–68, 72
- Activities for Communication, pp. 49–50, 107–108, 109, 139–140
- Grammatikheft, pp. 75–78
- Grammar Tutor for Students of German, Chapter 9
- Übungsheft, pp. 102–104
- Testing Program, pp. 227–230
- Alternative Assessment Guide, p. 40
- Student Make-Up Assignments, Chapter 9

MEDIA
- One-Stop Planner
- Audio Compact Discs, CD9, Trs. 8–9, 13, 19–20
- Teaching Transparencies
  Situation 9-1
  Vocabulary 9-B, 9-C
  Mehr Grammatikübungen Answers
  Grammatikheft Answers
- Interactive CD-ROM Tutor, Disc 3
- DVD Tutor, Disc 2

PAGE 248

Bell Work
Ask students to describe the type of activities they like to do on vacation. Do they prefer quiet activities, such as reading, sunbathing, and fishing, or more active things like tennis, running, and hiking?

Group work
Divide the class into groups of three and assign each group one of the interviews on p. 248. After groups have read their paragraph, they should study the text to find out:
  a) what the original travel plans were,
  b) why the person(s) cannot go,
  c) what alternate plans are being considered.
Each group should make a list of words or phrases that support each of the three answers. Call on groups and ask them to share their ideas with the class.

PAGE 249

PRESENTING: Wortschatz
- Have students think of all the water sports they can do at the following locations:
  am/im Meer
  am/im See
  am/auf dem Fluss
  Have students write the names of the activities from the **Wortschatz** under the appropriate headings. They should also include other vocabulary they have already learned. (Examples: **baden, schwimmen**)

- After introducing the hotel vocabulary, ask individual students to describe an ideal hotel, one they would like to stay in for a week-long vacation.

PRESENTING: So sagt man das!
Before introducing the new expressions, ask students what they would say in English to convey doubt, conviction, and resignation. Then go over the German expressions in **So sagt man das!** Demonstrate to students that intonation plays a big role in the perception of what is being said. Ask students to look back at **Los geht's!** on pp. 240–241 and determine where and how the functions listed in **So sagt man das!** are modeled. Have students make a list of the statements they find.

Communication for All Students

For Additional Practice
Give students several different statements to which they have to react, expressing either doubt, conviction, or resignation. Use situations from this chapter or previous chapters. Examples:

In Tirol hat es Hochwasser gegeben.
Drei Tage mit dem Bus fahren? Das ist sehr lange!

A Slower Pace
14 In order for students to follow the conversations, play each conversation several times. Have students listen for the main idea expressed by each speaker. To check students' comprehension, make a chart on the board and elicit students' responses to complete it.

STANDARDS: 1.2

PAGE 250

PRESENTING: Ein wenig Grammatik

The conjunction ob Divide students into groups of three or four, and ask them to give you several examples of English sentences that use "whether." Explain that the German equivalent of this word is **ob**, which, like **weil** and **dass**, requires verb-last position. Then allow the groups ten minutes to come up with four or five sentences that begin with **Ich weiß nicht, ob ...**, after which they should read their results to the class. You may want to award prizes for the most imaginative sentences.

Teaching Suggestion

15 Ask students to incorporate in their conversation as many of the new vocabulary items from the **Wortschatz** on p. 249 as possible. To make the role-playing situation more authentic, students can use a map to choose an interesting **Reiseziel**.

PRESENTING: Grammatik

Expressing direction and location To teach the difference between expressing direction and location, ask students if they can think of other verbs to replace the ones in the **Grammatik**. Here are some examples:

gehen	leben
reisen	wohnen
ziehen	sitzen
besuchen	zelten
sich befinden	

Ask students to rephrase the sentences in the **Grammatik**, replacing each verb with one of their own.

Connections and Comparisons

Music Connection

Refer students to the folk song *Der Mai ist gekommen,* Level 1 *Listening Activities,* p. 86, for additional reading. Have them find the examples of direction (**in die weite, weite Welt**) and location (**am himmlischen Zelt**) used in the song. The song's lyrics were written by Emanuel Geibel and the melody by Justus Wilhelm Lyra. You may also want to play the song. (See Level 1 CD 11, Tr. 31.)

PAGE 251

Communication for All Students

Auditory Learners

18 As an alternative, students could use a tape recorder and record their description on audiocassette, rather than writing in their **Notizbuch.**

Writing Assessment

19 You might want to assess this activity using the following rubric for evaluation.

Writing Rubric	Points			
	4	3	2	1
Content (Complete – Incomplete)				
Comprehensibility (Comprehensible – Seldom comprehensible)				
Accuracy (Accurate – Seldom accurate)				
Organization (Well-organized – Poorly organized)				
Effort (Excellent – Minimal)				

18–20: A 16–17: B 14–15: C 12–13: D Under 12: F

Additional Vocabulary

20 You may want to provide students with some additional vocabulary to help them role-play this situation:

vorschlagen to suggest
übernachten to spend the night
reservieren to reserve
abfahren to depart
ankommen to arrive
erste und zweite Klasse 1st and 2nd class

 **Game**

The game **Kofferpacken** will help auditory learners review vocabulary. Begin the game with the phrase: **Wenn ich diesen Sommer nach … reise, nehme ich … mit.** The first student repeats your sentence and adds another item he or she will take along. If a student misses a previously mentioned word, he or she drops out of the game. The game continues until only one student is left or time is called.

Prepare a class set of index cards. On each card write the name of a travel destination, preferably one by a lake or ocean so that students can use a good portion of the vocabulary from the **Zweite Stufe.** Give each student one of the cards. Then, tell students to take 5–10 minutes to prepare a convincing argument (using expressions of conviction as well as vocabulary from the **Wortschatz**) explaining why this particular location is worth a visit.
Example:
Es lohnt sich, San Francisco zu besuchen, weil …
Additional locations might include **Cancún, Acapulco, Ibiza, die italienische Riviera, die Côte d'Azur, Santa Barbara,** or **Miami.**

Assess
- Testing Program, pp. 227–230
  Quiz 9-2A, Quiz 9-2B
  Audio CD9, Tr. 13
- Student Make-Up Assignments
  Chapter 9, Alternative Quiz
- Alternative Assessment Guide, p. 40

DRITTE STUFE

Teaching Resources
pp. 252–255

PRINT
- Lesson Planner, p. 45
- TPR Storytelling Book, pp. 68–69
- Listening Activities, pp. 68, 73–74
- Activities for Communication, pp. 51–54, 139–140
- Grammatikheft, pp. 79–81
- Grammar Tutor for Students of German, Chapter 9
- Übungsheft, pp. 105–107
- Testing Program, pp. 231–234
- Alternative Assessment Guide, p. 40
- Student Make-Up Assignments, Chapter 9

MEDIA
- One-Stop Planner
- Audio Compact Discs, CD9, Trs. 10, 14, 21–22
- Teaching Transparencies
  Situation 9-2
  Mehr Grammatikübungen Answers
  Grammatikheft Answers
- Interactive CD-ROM Tutor, Disc 3
- DVD Tutor, Disc 2

 **PAGE 252**

Bell Work
In pairs, have students suggest free time activities they want to do this weekend. Then, they should tell each other that none of the activities will be good because of reasons they come up with. Example: **In die Disko gehen. Ich bezweifele, dass die Disko auf hat.**

Communication for All Students

Tactile Learners
On the day you plan to do this activity, bring a large piece of construction paper, rulers, and markers to class. Ask students to work together to create a map of a fictitious city, including at least ten different stores, sights, parks, street names, and street signs. Once the city plan (**Stadtplan**) has been designed, students should come up with a name for their city. You will be able to use this map as you teach the objectives of the **Dritte Stufe.**

Teaching Suggestion

Before students read about the **Stadtrundgang durch Bietigheim,** have them familiarize themselves with the map by locating all the numbered items.

Teacher Note

Posthalterei is a word that dates back to the 18th century. It referred to the building where mail horses were changed and packages were loaded and unloaded.

Cultures and Communities

Background Information

Suffixes of German town names often tell a great deal about a town's origin. Bietigheim, for example, is said to have been founded by Frankish settlers, as have other towns with the **-heim** suffix.

Geography Connection

Ask students to look on a map for other German towns with names ending in **-heim.** (Examples: Mannheim, Heppenheim, Bad Mergentheim, Tauberbischofsheim, Rüsselsheim)

Thinking Critically

Drawing Inferences There is almost always a **Tor** *(gate)* and a **Brunnen** *(well)* in the old parts of German towns. Can students think of the significance of these two landmarks? (A **Tor** and a surrounding wall were usually built to protect a town from invaders. The **Brunnen** supplied water to the population.)

Connections and Comparisons

Language-to-Language

You may want to explain that the German **seit** *(since, for)* is used in a manner similar to the French **depuis** and the Spanish **desde. Seit, depuis,** and **desde** are used to indicate a duration of time (English uses *for*) as well as a point in time (English uses *since*.)
Examples:
English: *I have been working for three days.* (duration)
German: Ich arbeite *seit* drei Tagen.
French: Je travaille *depuis* trois jours.
Spanish: Trabajo *desde* hace tres días.

English: *I have not worked* since *Friday.* (point in time)
German: Ich habe *seit* Freitag nicht gearbeitet.
French: Je n'ai pas travaillé *depuis* vendredi.
Spanish: No he trabajado *desde* el viernes.

▶ **PAGE 254**

PRESENTING: Grammatik

Dative prepositions Write the dative prepositions **mit, zu, aus, bei, nach, von,** and **gegenüber** on the board or a transparency. Then ask students to turn to the description of Bietigheim on p. 252. Have students scan the text and make a list of all phrases that include these prepositions. Students can come up to the board and write each phrase next to the appropriate preposition. Discuss contractions and lead students to discover what each contraction is composed of.

Connections and Comparisons

Music Connection

Refer students to the folksong *Nun ade, du mein lieb Heimatland* (lyrics by August Dischoff), Level 2 *Listening Activities,* p. 46, for additional reading. What prepositions can they find that take only dative objects? **(zu, mit, von)** What two-way preposition appears in the song? **(an)** What case does it take in this instance, and why? (dative; it indicates location.) Can students explain why the adjective endings following these prepositions are as they are? You may also want to play the song, Level 2 CD 6, Tr. 25.

▶ **PAGE 253**

PRESENTING: Wortschatz

To teach the new expressions, use the fictitious map students designed at the beginning of the **Dritte Stufe.** Use the new words and prepositional phrases along with words that students already know. (Example: **Die Schule befindet sich in der Hauptstraße.**) Repeat the new phrases several times, giving directions to different places.

PRESENTING: Ein wenig Grammatik

Accusative prepositions Have the class brainstorm phrases (other than the two in this **Grammatik**) that would use **durch** and **um**. (Examples: **durch die Luft fliegen, durch die Stadt fahren, um den See schwimmen**)

PRESENTING: So sagt man das!

Introduce the expressions to the class. Then have students role-play them with a partner. To provide further practice, ask students to use the map of Bietigheim on p. 252 to review the new functions.

> **PAGE 255**

Communication for All Students

Challenge

24 After the "tourists" have received directions, the "local" should ask them what they plan to do or see at each place. Example: **Was möchten Sie denn dort sehen?**

PRESENTING: Ein wenig Grammatik

Two-way prepositions Prepare on a transparency a list of incomplete sentences such as **Auf diesem Foto steht mein Bruder neben _____ . (das Rathaus)**. Each sentence should include the preposition **vor, neben,** or **zwischen,** and there should be at least one sentence for each member of your class. On the day you present this material, divide the class into two teams. Alternating between the two groups, show the class one sentence at a time and ask a student to complete it using the appropriate case. When a student completes a statement correctly, his or her team wins a point. Everyone should take at least one turn. The team with the greatest number of points at the end of the activity wins.

Connections and Comparisons

Thinking Critically

29 Comparing and Contrasting After students have completed the project, ask them to compare the layout of their town to that of Bietigheim.

Cultures and Communities

Background Information

Finding your way around a German town or city is a challenge. The American-style checkerboard city would be hard to find in Germany. German cities grew and expanded in an irregular pattern over the centuries. Any **Altstadt** in a German town or city is a great model. Typically, the demands of the different historical periods shaped towns into patterns of interlaced streets, alleys, lanes, and squares. The **Tor(e), Brunnen, Marktplatz, Rathaus,** and **Kirche** can usually be found in a central location.

TPR Total Physical Response

Practice the expressions in the **Wortschatz** on p. 253 and the prepositions by asking individual students to follow your directions around the classroom. Examples:

Michael, geh bitte am Tisch von der Karen vorbei, und stell dich gegenüber von Thomas hin!

Maria, geh bitte zwischen den Stühlen von Robert und Susan durch, dann geh an der Tafel entlang!

Assess
▶ Testing Program, pp. 231–234
  Quiz 9-3A, Quiz 9-3B
  Audio CD9, Tr. 14

▶ Student Make-Up Assignments
  Chapter 9, Alternative Quiz

▶ Alternative Assessment Guide, p. 40

STANDARDS: 1.2, 4.2

PAGES 256–257

ZUM LESEN

Teaching Resources
pp. 256–257

PRINT
- Lesson Planner, p. 46
- Übungsheft, p. 108
- Reading Strategies and Skills, Chapter 9
- Lies mit mir! 2, Chapter 9

MEDIA
- One-Stop Planner

Prereading

Building Context
Take a survey in class asking students to talk about the best vacation they have had. Where was it? What did they do there? Compile a list of students' responses on a transparency and keep it for a later activity.

Teacher Note
Activity 1 is a prereading activity.

Reading

Communication for All Students

A Slower Pace

 Ask students to read the girl's interview again to find three facts that she gives to support her vacation paradise.

Connections and Comparisons

Geography Connection
Ask students to read the description made by the fifteen-year-old **Realschüler.** Have students look on a map to find out where he wants to take a bicycle trip. Using the scale on the map, can students tell approximately how far apart Passau and Vienna are? (476 km/295 miles) This student would be riding his bicycle along what river if he went from Passau to Vienna? (Danube)

Post-Reading

Teacher Note
Activity 10 is a post-reading task that will show whether students can apply what they have learned.

Cultures and Communities

Background Information
The fourteen-year-old **Gymnasiastin** talks about her family's **Ferienhaus** in the **Lüneburger Heide.** The **Lüneburger Heide** is a large national park located between the rivers Elbe and Aller and the towns of Lüneburg and Celle. It encompasses an area of 720 square kilometers (278 square miles) and consists mainly of fertile ground. To control the growth of heather, heath-sheep continually graze the area. The **Heide** is considered to be one of the most popular and tranquil areas in northern Germany.

Teaching Suggestion
Put up the transparency of the survey results from the Motivating Activity for students to review. Ask students to compare it to the top ten **Ferienparadiese** in the **Eltern-Umfrage.** How do the two surveys differ? Why are they different?

Zum Lesen Answers
Answers to Activity 1 a. opinion; b. fact; c. fact; d. opinion
Answers to Activity 2 Students are being interviewed about where they like to spend their vacation best; the results of a survey.
Answers to Activity 3 See **"Tiere sind Trumpf"** box on p. 256.
Answers to Activity 4 opinions; facts
Answers to Activity 6 Hawaii; She likes the village where her grandmother lives.
Answers to Activity 7 cycling along a river and on forest paths; Both the first and the last sentences are opinions; the second sentence is a fact.
Answers to Activity 8 Her parents like to go to tourist spots like Mallorca and Gran Canaria; She would like to spend her vacation at a small lake, camping in a tent and having a paddle boat; She has neither a boat nor a tent; fact.
Answers to Activity 9 in the Lüneburg Heath; Sometimes it is a little boring.
Answers to Activity 10 Answers will vary; 5/5, may be subject to discussion; Answers will vary.

PAGES 258–261

MEHR GRAMMATIKÜBUNGEN

The **Mehr Grammatikübungen** activities are designed as supplemental activities for the grammatical concepts presented in the chapter. You might use them as additional practice, for review, or for assessment.

For more grammar presentations, review, and practice, refer to the following:
- Grammatikheft
- Grammar Tutor for Students of German
- Grammar Summary on pp. R20–R36
- Übungsheft
- Grammar and Vocabulary quizzes (Testing Program)
- Test Generator
- Interactive CD-ROM Tutor
- **Interaktive Spiele** at go.hrw.com

> **PAGES 262–263**

ANWENDUNG

Video Wrap-up
Videocassette 3, 36:27–50:45
Videocassette 5 (captioned version),
51:18–55:41
DVD Tutor, Disc 2

At this time, you might want to use the video resources for additional review and enrichment. These resources are also available via the Enhanced Online Student Edition.
See *Video Guide* for suggestions regarding:

- *Verpatzte Ferien* (Dramatic episode)
- **Landeskunde** Interviews
- **Videoclips** (Authentic footage)

Apply and Assess

Challenge

1 After students have completed the listening activity and taken notes, ask them to restate the exchange student's report, using third person conjugations. This can be done orally or in writing. Remind students to use phrases that state facts and opinions in their reports.

Teaching Suggestion

2/3 Make a mini-lesson out of these two activities. Remind students of the **Lesestrategie** in Chapter 6 to help them decipher charts and graphs. Then, brainstorm with students about what they expect to find out in the article. Take down a few of their suggestions. Have students take turns reading the article aloud and remind them not to get distracted by words they don't understand. Rather, they should concentrate on what they can understand. If you need to give students additional vocabulary for clarification, try to give German definitions.

Process Writing

5 Have students work in pairs. They should pretend that they traveled to their various destinations in each other's company, but parted ways once they had arrived in a particular part of town or a specific rural area, in order to explore different aspects of the place. You may want to allow your students to modify this activity slightly, and write a report describing a tour they took of an urban rather than a rural area.

Portfolio Assessment

6 You might want to suggest this activity as an oral portfolio item for your students. See *Alternative Assessment Guide*, p. 26.

> **PAGE 264**

KANN ICH'S WIRKLICH?

This page helps students prepare for the test. It is a brief checklist of the major points covered in the chapter. The students should be reminded that it is only a checklist and not necessarily everything that will appear on the test.

For additional self check options, refer students to the *Grammar Tutor*, the *Interactive CD-ROM Tutor*, and the Online self-test for this chapter.

> **PAGE 265**

WORTSCHATZ

Teacher to Teacher

Paula Bernard
Sandy Creek High School
Fayette County, GA

Paula uses this fast-paced activity to review vocabulary.

"Write *many* chapter vocabulary words or verb conjugations in German on a sheet of paper - some should be at angles, some upside-down. Make copies, one for each pair of students. Each student has a different color pen. Then call out words in English and have students try to circle each word before his or her partner. The students who circle the most correct words win a prize or extra points."

Review and Assess

Circumlocution

To use the circumlocution game, **Das treffende Wort suchen,** as a vocabulary review, ask students to describe what it feels like to do each sport listed in the **Zweite Stufe,** to describe what one wears doing the sport, or to describe what one can do in a particular area at a vacation resort. See p. 3C for procedures.

Teacher Note

Give the **Kapitel 9** Chapter Test: *Testing Program,* pp. 235–240
Audio CD 9, Trs. 15–16.

STANDARDS: 1.1

KAPITEL 9
Wohin in die Ferien?

Objectives

In this chapter you will learn to

Erste Stufe
- express indecision
- ask for and make suggestions

Zweite Stufe
- express doubt, conviction, and resignation

Dritte Stufe
- ask for and give directions

Visit Holt Online
go.hrw.com
KEYWORD: WK3 STUTTGART-9
Online Edition

◀ Ich schlage vor, wir fahren nach Seefeld in Tirol.

Los geht's! · *Verpatzte Ferien*

Los geht's!

CD 9
Trs. 1–2

Strategie Verstehen
Look at the images for the story. Judging by Katrin's expressions, what might be happening in this story? Who do you think are all the characters in the story?

Los geht's! is an abridged version of the video episode.

Katrin   **Judith**   **Roland**   **Boris**   **Mutter**   **Vater**

1
Katrin: Ja, was macht ihr denn? Ihr seht fern so früh am Nachmittag!
Mutter: Wir haben eben den österreichischen Wetterbericht gesehen. Unsere Reise nach Tirol ist wahrscheinlich ins Wasser gefallen.
Katrin: Bist du sicher? Warum? Was ist passiert?

2
Vater: Die hatten ein Hochwasser, und die Brücke auf der Straße nach Mittersill ist kaputt.
Katrin: Da gibt's doch bestimmt eine andere Straße.
Vater: Eben nicht.
Katrin: Ruf doch mal an!
Vater: Das hab ich schon zweimal probiert. Ich glaube nicht, dass ich jetzt durchkomme.

3
Katrin: Katrin Simon. Ja, der ist da. Einen Moment!

4
Vater: Simon. Ja. Ja. Ja, das haben wir eben zufällig im Fernsehen gesehen. Glauben Sie, dass bis Freitag … Ja, das ist sehr schade. Wir sind alle sehr enttäuscht. Aber da kann man nichts machen … Gut! Vielleicht klappt's im nächsten Jahr … Gut, Herr Mooslechner. Ade!

Katrin mit ihren Freunden

Boris: Ja, was machen wir jetzt? Jetzt musst auch du die Pfingstferien zu Hause verbringen.
Judith: Ich bin dafür, dass wir einmal zusammen nach Ulm fahren.
Boris: Blödsinn! Das kennen wir doch schon alle.
Katrin: Dann schlage ich vor, wir fahren nach Würzburg. Wir können uns dort die Stadt anschauen.
Judith: Das kostet zu viel Geld mit der Bahn.
Roland: Ich habe eine bessere Idee! Wir spielen Touristen in einer Stadt. In Bietigheim!
Alle: Spitze! Aber wie?

Als „Touristen" in Bietigheim

Roland: Entschuldigung! Wo ist bitte das Rathaus?
Mann: Da geht ihr diese Straße entlang bis zur nächsten Ecke, nach rechts in die Hauptstraße, und dann seht ihr es schon.

Boris: Entschuldigung! Wissen Sie vielleicht, wo das Kronenzentrum ist?
Frau: Ja, da geht ihr gleich links um die Ecke und dann die erste Straße rechts, und dann steht ihr direkt vorm Kronenzentrum.

1 Was passiert hier?

These activities check for global comprehension only. Students should not yet be expected to produce language modeled in *Los geht's!*

Verstehst du alles in der Fotostory? Beantworte die Fragen!
1. Why is Katrin surprised when she comes home? 1. Because her parents are watching TV in the early afternoon.
2. Why do her parents feel disappointed? 2. Because their vacation "fell through."
3. Why can't the family go where it wanted to go? 3. There is a flood in Tirol and a bridge collapsed.
4. Why doesn't Katrin's father call Austria again? 4. He already tried twice and did not get through.
5. Who is calling and why? 5. the landlord; to cancel their booking
6. What are Katrin and her three friends talking about? 6. about their vacation plans
7. What idea does one of her friends come up with? 7. to play tourists in Bietigheim

2 Stimmt oder stimmt nicht?

Wenn der Satz nicht stimmt, schreib die richtige Antwort!
1. Katrin wollte mit ihrer Familie nach Österreich fahren. 1. Stimmt.
2. Aber Österreich hatte furchtbar viel Regen. 2. Stimmt.
3. Es gibt viele Straßen nach Mittersill. 3. Stimmt nicht. Es gibt nur eine.
4. Katrins Vater hat Herrn Mooslechner angerufen. 4. Stimmt nicht. The other way around.
5. Die vier Freunde fahren jetzt nach Würzburg. 5. Stimmt nicht. Es kostet zu viel Geld mit der Bahn.
6. Am Ende spielen sie Touristen in einer kleinen Stadt in der Nähe von Stuttgart. 6. Stimmt.

3 Was passt zusammen?

Welche Ausdrücke auf der rechten Seite passen zu den Satzanfängen auf der linken Seite?

1. Die Reise nach Tirol — 1. b — a. Hochwasser.
2. Die Brücke nach Mittersill — 2. c — b. kann nicht stattfinden.
3. Österreich hatte — 3. a — c. ist kaputt.
4. Katrin und ihre Eltern — 4. g — d. kostet zu viel Geld.
5. Aber da kann man nichts — 5. e — e. machen.
6. Katrin will die Pfingstferien — 6. f — f. nicht zu Hause verbringen.
7. Nach Würzburg fahren — 7. d — g. sind enttäuscht.
8. Jetzt spielen die Freunde — 8. h — h. Touristen in Bietigheim.

4 Genauer lesen

Lies den Text noch einmal und beantworte diese Fragen!
1. Which word in the text expresses "probability"? 1. wahrscheinlich
2. Which word expresses "doubt"? 2. bezweifle
3. Which words and phrases express "disappointment"? 3. Das ist schade; ... enttäuscht
4. Which phrase expresses "resignation"? 4. ... da kann man nichts machen.
5. Which phrases are used to "make a proposal"? 5. Ich bin dafür, dass ... ; Ich schlage vor, daß ... ; Ich hab eine bessere Idee.

5 Welche Wörter passen in die Lücken?

Welches Wort aus dem Kasten passt in welche Lücke?
1. Katrins Eltern haben früh am Nachmittag __1__.
2. Im Wetterbericht haben sie __2__, dass Österreich Hochwasser __3__.
3. Katrin fragt, was __4__ ist.
4. Ihr Vater sagt, die Reise ist ins Wasser __5__.
5. Die Familie ist __6__, aber vielleicht __7__ die Reise im nächsten Jahr.

Wohin fährst du in den nächsten Ferien? CD 9 Tr. 3

We asked students from around Germany where they were planning to go during their next school holidays. Before you read their answers, think about where students in the United States usually go or what they like to do during summer vacation. Come up with a list of the top ten most popular vacation spots for U.S. teenagers. Then listen to the interviews and read the texts.

Paolo, Stuttgart CD 9 Tr. 4

„Also meistens verbring ich meine Ferien in Italien aufgrund dessen, dass ich selber Italiener bin, aus Salerno komm, die Amalfiküste gerne besuch, zum Beispiel Capri oder Pompeji, Paestum, das gehört ja alles dazu, sehr schöne Gegend."

Gerd, Bietigheim CD 9 Tr. 5

„Also meistens fahr ich in den Ferien überhaupt nicht in Urlaub. Ich mach halt dann Ferienjob und verdien mir 'n bisschen Geld dazu. Da kann ich mir halt auch entweder 'ne neue Gitarre oder 'nen neuen Verstärker, oder halt irgendwas kaufen, was ich halt haben möchte."

Gabi und Anja, München

Gabi: „Also ich, wir fahren in den Ferien zusammen eine Woche zum Reiten auf einen Bauernhof in Niederbayern, ja, in den Urlaub."

Anja: „Ja, weil wir beide sehr gern reiten. Jetzt fahren wir zusammen weg."

Gabi: „Genau. Und ich fahr dann noch zwei Wochen nach Bad Gastein, in Österreich, auch Wandern und Schwimmen, ja."

Anja: „Und ich fahr 'n bissel vielleicht auch noch mit 'ner anderen Freundin auch noch nach Österreich, auch auf 'n Dorf, auch zum Wandern, Schwimmen."

Gabi: „Und nach den Ferien fahr ich acht Wochen nach Washington D.C. Genau. — Ein Schüleraustausch, Englisch lernen." CD 9 Tr. 6

A. 1. Italy, Niederbayern, Bad Gastein, Austria, Washington; Gabi; two of them are vacation, one is a student exchange program; does not go anywhere for vacation, but works.

A. 1. Three of these students mention specific places where they are going. What are they? Which of these students mentions three different trips? Are all three trips vacations? What does the fourth student say she is going to do during vacation?

2. What do each of these students plan to do in each of the places they talked about?

3. How do their plans compare to what you thought most teenagers in the United States would do for summer vacation? Did any German teenagers mention something that was on your list of most popular vacation spots? A. 2. enjoy the landscape; work; ride horses, hike, swim, study English

B. High school students in Germany attend school year round. Although each **Bundesland** has its own schedule, students typically have one or two weeks off for fall holidays, two weeks for Christmas, two weeks in the spring, and six weeks off during the summer. The summer vacation dates for **Bundesländer** are staggered, with the beginning dates about one week apart. Knowing that Germany is very densely populated, can you guess why this is done? How does this vacation schedule compare with your schedule? Who has more vacation time? What do you think the advantages and disadvantages of year-round school might be?

STANDARDS: 1.2, 2.1, 2.2, 3.2, 4.2

Storytelling Book
pp. 64–65

Erste Stufe

Objective Expressing indecision, asking for and making suggestions

WK3 STUTTGART-9

6 Sieben Ferienangebote Script and answers on p. 237G (answers also in box below)

Zuhören Hör dir die Beschreibung von jedem der sieben Ferienangebote an! Welches Angebot passt zu welchem Foto? Trag die Lösung in den Rabattcoupon rechts unten ein!

CD 9 Tr. 7

URLAUB IN LETZTER MINUTE
Unsere heißen Reisetipps

Für diese Kurzreisen sind noch Plätze erhältlich. Rufen Sie an und kommen Sie dann persönlich vorbei, um sich Ihren Platz zu sichern! Mit einem richtig ausgefüllten Coupon erhalten Sie **10% Rabatt**:

1. Mit der Bahn drei Tage an die Nordsee in das kleine Fischerdorf Benserseil. In diesem Dorf direkt an der Küste sind noch Zimmer frei. Entspannen Sie im Hallenbad, beim Reiten und Strandwandern. Ein Besuch im Buddelschiffmuseum lohnt sich!

2. Einmalig preiswert! Eine Drei-Tage-Busfahrt nach Dresden und in die Sächsische Schweiz. In Dresden besuchen Sie den berühmten Zwinger, und Sie erleben die einmalig schönen Sandsteinfelsen der Bastei.

3. Eine Tagesfahrt an den Bodensee nach Unteruhldingen und weiter mit dem Schiff auf die Insel Mainau, wo Sie unter Palmen spazieren und die Blumenwelt bewundern können. Abfahrt: 6.00.

4. Eine Wochenendfahrt (Sa/So) in die Schweiz. Übernachtung in Brienz. Am nächsten Vormittag mit der Bergbahn aufs Brienzer Rothorn, die Schweizer Bergwelt genießen. Ein Superangebot!

5. Sonderfahrt mit dem Bus nach Ulm zum bekannten Fischerstechen auf der Donau. Am Vormittag Gelegenheit zum Messebesuch im Dom. Mittagessen in einem soliden Gasthaus. Das Fischerstechen beginnt um 14 h. Rückkehr gegen 19.30 h.

6. Drei Tage mit dem Bus durch die schönsten Täler in der Schweiz. Im Emmental Besichtigung eines typischen Bauernhauses und Besuch einer Käserei.

7. Drei Tage (Di. - Do.) mit dem Bus nach Österreich, nach Alpbach in Tirol. Sehr preisgünstig. Ideal für Bergwanderer und solche, die's noch werden wollen!

10% RABATT!
1. f
2. b
3. d
4. e
5. g
6. c
7. a

7 Wohin geht's?

Lesen/Sprechen Lies die Reisetipps und beantworte die Fragen!

1. Schreib auf, wohin diese sieben Reisen gehen!
2. Für wie viele Tage ist jede Reise?
3. Welche Reisen führen ans Meer oder an einen See? Welche in die Berge? Welche sind Stadtbesichtigungen?
4. Für welche Reise interessierst du dich? Warum?

For answers, see p. 237P.

Wortschatz

Beliebte Verkehrsmittel:

die Bahn — das Flugzeug — das Schiff

Wohin gehst du in den Ferien?

auf den Tennisplatz — ins Hallenbad — Wer steigt auf einen Berg? Aufs Brienzer Rothorn? Auf die Zugspitze?

Mit welchem Verkehrsmittel fährst du gewöhnlich in die Ferien? Und was machst du in den Ferien? Wohin gehst du?

Übungsheft, S. 99, Ü. 1   Grammatikheft, S. 73, Ü. 1

So sagt man das!

Expressing indecision, asking for and making suggestions

When expressing indecision about your plans, you could say:

> Was machen wir im Urlaub?
> Was sollen wir bloß machen?

If you need specific suggestions, you might ask:

> **Wohin fahren wir? Hast du eine Idee?**
or **Was schlägst du vor?**

When making suggestions, you might say:

> **Wir können mal an die Nordsee fahren.**
or **Fahren wir mal in die Schweiz!**
or **Ich schlage vor, dass wir mal in die Schweiz fahren.**
or **Ich bin dafür, dass wir an den Rhein fahren.**

Which of these expressions are new to you?

Grammatikheft, S. 73, Ü. 2

Ein wenig Grammatik

Many mountains in the German-speaking countries are named (**das**) **Horn** or (**die**) **Spitze**, as in **Matterhorn** and **Zugspitze**. Sometimes mountains are also named for nearby towns. In this case, the ending **-er** is added to the name of the town. For example, near the town of **Brienz** is the **Brienzer Rothorn**.

8 Wohin jetzt?

Sprechen Katrins Familie kann nicht nach Mittersill fahren. Katrin hat die Reisetipps gelesen und schlägt den Eltern ein paar Kurzreisen vor. Die Eltern haben keine große Lust dazu. Spiel die Rolle von Katrin, und such dir einen Partner für die Rolle von Katrins Vater oder Mutter!

ERSTE STUFE   STANDARDS: 1.1   zweihundertfünfundvierzig

Grammatik

Expressing direction: the prepositions **nach, in, an,** and **auf**

To express directions toward a place, German uses different prepositions depending on the nature of the place. The prepositions **nach, in, an,** and **auf** all convey here the meaning of "to a place."

1. The preposition **nach** is used with names of cities, states, countries, and islands that are not preceded by an article (such as **die Schweiz**).

   Wohin fahren wir?
   - **Nach** Ulm. *(city)*
   - Fahren wir mal **nach** Bayern! *(state)*
   - Ich fahre **nach** Österreich. *(country)*
   - Fahren wir heute **nach** Mainau! *(island)*

2. The preposition **in** is used with the names of countries and geographic areas that require the use of the definite article.

   Wohin fahrt ihr?
   - Ich fahre mal **in die** Schweiz.
   - Wir fliegen **in die** Vereinigten Staaten. *(countries)*
   - Wir fahren **in die** Berge, **in die** Alpen. *(areas)*
   - Ihr fahrt **in den** Schwarzwald?

3. The preposition **an** is used when referring to bodies of water.

   Wohin fahrt ihr?
   - Ich fahre **an die** Nordsee.
   - Wir fahren **an den** Rhein.
   - Wir fahren **an den** Bodensee.
   (bodies of water)

4. The preposition **auf** is used when referring to heights or flat surfaces.

   Was macht ihr?   Wir steigen **auf einen** Berg, **aufs** Brienzer Rothorn.
   Wohin geht ihr jetzt?   **Auf den** Tennisplatz.

5. The prepositions **an, auf,** and **in** form contractions with the definite article **das**.

   an + das = **ans**   auf + das = **aufs**   in + das = **ins**

Which case is used with noun phrases following **in, an,** and **auf** to express going somewhere?[1]

Mehr Grammatikübungen, S. 258, Ü. 1–2

9 Grammatik im Kontext

a. **Schreiben** Schreib fünf Reiseziele auf einen Zettel! Diese Ziele können in Deutschland, in den Vereinigten Staaten oder irgendwo anders sein! Schreib auch auf, was du an jedem Ziel machen möchtest! Danach ordne deine Reiseziele! Wohin fährst du zuerst? Danach? Zuletzt? Mit wem fährst du? Im Kasten stehen ein paar Reiseziele in den Vereinigten Staaten.

b. **Sprechen** Such dir eine Partnerin! Frag sie über ihre Reisepläne für den nächsten Sommer! Frag sie, wohin sie fährt und mit wem, und ob sie mit dem Auto fährt oder fliegt! Frag sie auch, was sie überall macht!

nach (Kalifornien)

an den (Michigansee)

in die (Blue Ridge) Mountains

an den Strand in (Mississippi)

auf den (Pikes) Peak

---
1. the accusative case

10 Franks Reisepläne

9–A

E.g.: **Frank fährt zuerst nach München und schaut sich dort bestimmt die Stadt an. Dann fährt er an den Starnberger See und geht bestimmt schwimmen.** Etc.

Lesen/Sprechen Frank und seine Familie (sie wohnen in Stuttgart) haben für die großen Ferien eine lange Reise geplant. Schau auf diese Karte, auf der Frank die Reiseziele eingetragen hat! Sag, wohin er fährt, und was er an jedem Ort bestimmt macht!

Die Reiseroute

1. München
2. Starnberger See
3. Garmisch
4. Tirol/Innsbruck
5. Zürich/Zürichsee
6. Bodensee
7. Schwarzwald
8. Frankfurt/Main
9. Hamburg
10. Lübeck/Ostsee
11. Insel Rügen
12. Potsdam
13. nach Hause

11 Meine Sommerreise

a. **Schreiben** Plane deine Sommerreise! Schreib auf, wohin du fahren möchtest, und was du dort machen möchtest!

b. **Sprechen** Dann erzähle deinen Klassenkameraden von deiner geplanten Reise! Zeig ihnen deine Reiseroute auf einer Landkarte!

Ein wenig Landeskunde

Die Deutschen machen gerne Urlaub. Sie sind viel und gewöhnlich sehr lange unterwegs. Wie fahren die Deutschen in den Urlaub? Hier ist eine kleine Statistik darüber.

mit dem Auto	62,6%
mit dem Flugzeug	17,6%
mit der Bahn	8,6%
mit dem Bus	11,2%

12 Im Reisebüro

Sprechen Du arbeitest in einem Reisebüro. Dein Partner ist ein Kunde. Er ist sehr enttäuscht, denn er kann nicht dorthin fahren, wohin er fahren wollte. Du schlägst ihm ein anderes Reiseziel vor und erzählst ihm, was er dort alles machen kann! Gefällt ihm dein Vorschlag? Wenn nicht, schlag etwas anderes vor! Bring Reisebroschüren mit in die Klasse, die du den Kunden zeigen kannst! — Tauscht dann die Rollen aus!

ERSTE STUFE STANDARDS: 1.1, 1.3, 2.1, 3.1, 3.2, 5.1 zweihundertsiebenundvierzig

Storytelling Book
pp. 66–67

Zweite Stufe

Objectives Expressing doubt, conviction, and resignation

13 Warum so unsicher?

Lesen/Sprechen Lies den Text und beantworte die folgenden Fragen!

1. Warum kann Boris vielleicht nicht nach Italien fahren?
2. Warum hat es Nadine dieses Jahr schwer, sich für einen Ferienort zu entscheiden?
3. Warum fliegt Katrins Familie gern nach Spanien?

1. Er und seine Eltern haben noch keine preiswerte Unterkunft gefunden.
2. Sie kann einen Segelkurs am Gardasee machen oder mit ihren Eltern nach Südfrankreich fahren.
3. Dort gibt es viel Sonne.

WEISST DU SCHON,

BORIS

„Ja, das ist so 'ne Sache. Wir wollen nach Italien, an die Adria. Aber meine Eltern haben zu spät gebucht, und wir glauben nicht, dass wir noch eine Unterkunft bekommen, also etwas, was einigermaßen preiswert ist. In teuren Hotels, da bin ich sicher, gibt's bestimmt noch Zimmer. Aber so viel Geld wollen wir auch wieder nicht ausgeben."

WO DU DIE FERIEN

NADINE

„Also ich hab's dieses Jahr sehr schwer. Ich kann von der Schule aus einen Segelkurs am Gardasee, also in Italien, mitmachen. Aber ich weiß nicht, ob das so eine gute Idee ist. Im Kurs sprechen alle Deutsch, und ich bezweifle, dass ich dort mein Italienisch verbessern kann. Also, ich fahr wohl lieber mit meinen Eltern nach Südfrankreich. Dort kann ich auch segeln, und ich kann ganz bestimmt mein Französisch verbessern. Ich hab in Französisch bloß 'ne Vier. Schlecht, was?"

VERBRINGST?

KATRIN

„Ja, wie ihr wisst, ist unsere Reise ins Wasser gefallen. Ins Hochwasser! Ich bezweifle, dass meine Eltern in den Bergen Urlaub machen wollen. Das Wetter ist eben zu unsicher. Ich bin nicht sicher, ob wir wieder in die Staaten fliegen, wie letztes Jahr. Das war eine sehr teure Reise. Aber vielleicht geht's nach Spanien. Dort gibt's viel Sonne, das könnt ihr mir glauben! Wir waren schon zweimal dort. Wir fahren immer ans Meer, an die Costa Brava und so. Echt super-toll!"

Wortschatz

Ich fahr ans Meer, denn dort kann ich … Übungsheft, S. 102, Ü. 1   Grammatikheft, S. 75, Ü. 5–7

segeln   windsurfen   tauchen   angeln   Boot fahren

In unserm Hotel gibt es …

einen Pool   einen Golfplatz   einen Sandstrand   einen Fitnessraum   eine Diskothek

einen Tennisplatz   eine Liegewiese   eine Sauna   einen Whirlpool   einen Fernsehraum

1. Wo übernachtest du gewöhnlich, wenn du mit deinen Eltern in die Ferien fährst?
2. Was gibt es gewöhnlich in dem Hotel oder Motel, wo ihr übernachtet?
3. Was machst du, wenn du an einem See oder am Meer Ferien machst?

Und dann noch…

rudern	Tretboot fahren
schnorcheln	River Rafting machen
Kajak fahren	Motorboot fahren

So sagt man das!

Expressing doubt, conviction, and resignation

When expressing doubt, you might say:

Ich weiß nicht, ob (wir die Reise schon gebucht haben).
Ich bezweifle, dass (es dort einen Golfplatz gibt).
Ich bin nicht sicher, dass (wir dort surfen können).

When expressing conviction, you might say:

Du kannst mir glauben, dass (es dort einen Golfplatz gibt).
Ich bin sicher, dass (wir dort surfen können).

When expressing resignation, you might say:

Da kann man nichts machen.   or   **Das ist leider so.**

What do you think the conjunction **ob** means in the first sentence?

Mehr Grammatikübungen, S. 259, Ü. 3

Grammatikheft, S. 76, Ü. 8–9

14 Pläne für die Ferien   Script and answers on p. 237G

Zuhören Einige Leute unterhalten sich über ihre Pläne für die Ferien und drücken dabei Zweifel *(doubts)* aus. Schreib zuerst auf, woran sie zweifeln und danach, ob ihre Gesprächspartner zustimmen oder eine andere Meinung haben!

CD 9 Tr. 8

15 Grammatik im Kontext

a. Sprechen Du und deine Partnerin, ihr streitet euch *(argue)* über eure Reiseziele. Sie bezweifelt, was du ihr sagst, aber du bist sicher, dass es an dem Ferienort alles gibt, was sie gern möchte. — Tauscht dann die Rollen aus!

DU **Wohin fährst du denn?**
PARTNERIN **Wir …**
DU **Dort kannst du/gibt es bestimmt …**
PARTNERIN **Ich weiß nicht, ob …**
DU **Aber ich bin sicher, dass …**
PARTNERIN **…**

Was?

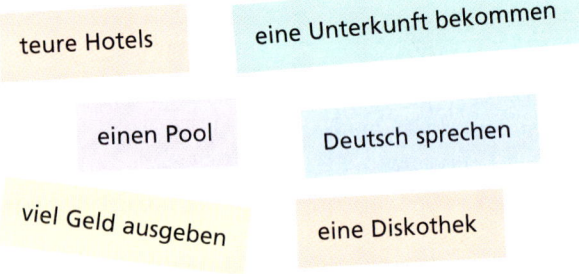

teure Hotels · eine Unterkunft bekommen · einen Pool · Deutsch sprechen · viel Geld ausgeben · eine Diskothek · segeln/tauchen

Ein wenig Grammatik

The conjunction **ob** means *if* or *whether*. Look at the **So sagt man das!** box. What do you notice about the position of the verb in **ob**-clauses? What other conjunctions require verb-last position?[1]

b. Schreiben Schreib mit deiner Partnerin zwei Gespräche wie in dem Beispiel.

Grammatik

Expressing direction and location (Summary)

Read these two blocks of sentences carefully. Which group refers to location? Which to direction? Which question word is used to elicit responses like the ones on the left? And on the right?

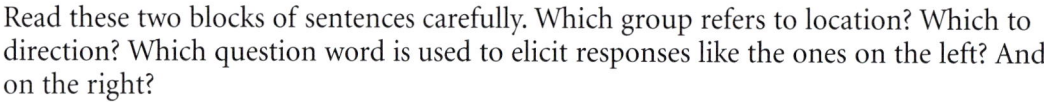

Wir fahren **nach** Frankfurt.
Roland fährt **in die** Schweiz.
Boris fliegt **in die** Vereinigten Staaten.

Katrin fährt **an die** Nordsee.*
Wir fahren morgen **an den** Bodensee.*

Roland fährt **aufs** Brienzer Rothorn.

Ich war auch schon mal **in** Frankfurt.
Ich war auch schon **in der** Schweiz.
Ich war letztes Jahr **in den** Vereinigten Staaten.

Ich war auch schon **an der** Nordsee.
Ich bin auch schon **am** Bodensee gewesen.

Ich war auch schon mal **auf dem** Brienzer Rothorn.

*Note the two meanings of the word **See**: **die See** means *sea*, **der See** means *lake*.

1. To answer a **wo**-question (a question that asks about location), dative-case forms are used after the prepositions **an, in, auf,** and some others.

   Wo warst du in den Ferien? Ich war **an der Nordsee.**

2. To answer a **wohin**-question (a question that asks about direction), accusative-case forms are used after these prepositions.

   Wohin fährst du? Ich fahre **an die Nordsee.**

Mehr Grammatikübungen, S. 259, Ü. 4–5

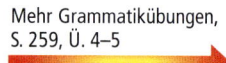

Übungsheft, S. 102–104, Ü. 2–6

Grammatikheft, S. 77–78, Ü. 10–13

---

1. **weil** and **dass**

16 Anrufe. Von wo? Script and answers on p. 237G

Zuhören Einige Freunde haben angerufen und eine Nachricht auf dem Anrufbeantworter hinterlassen. Rufen sie aus dem Ferienort an oder auf dem Weg dahin? Mach dir Notizen!

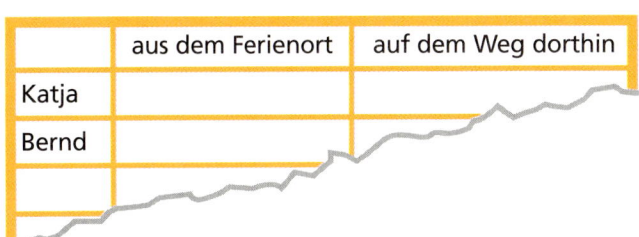

	aus dem Ferienort	auf dem Weg dorthin
Katja		
Bernd		

CD 9 Tr. 9

17 Grammatik im Kontext E.g.: Frank war in München und hat sich dort wahrscheinlich die Stadt angeschaut. Etc.

Sprechen/Schreiben Frank ist von seiner Reise zurück. Er war mit seinen Eltern an allen Orten, die er auf der Landkarte eingetragen hat. — Schau auf die Karte auf Seite 247 und erzähle oder schreibe, wo Frank überall gewesen ist und was er wahrscheinlich dort gemacht hat!

18 Für mein Notizbuch

Schreiben Wohin fährst du mit deinen Eltern oder Verwandten in den nächsten Ferien, oder wohin möchtest du mal fahren? — Beschreibe eine kurze Reise, die drei verschiedene Reiseziele hat! Erwähne:

a. mit wem du fährst
b. wohin ihr fahrt
c. wie ihr dorthin kommt
d. wo ihr übernachtet
e. was ihr dort alles tun könnt

19 Deine Pläne diskutieren

Sprechen Such dir einen Partner! Erzähle ihm von deiner Reise!

20 Du arbeitest als Reiseberater

Schreiben/Sprechen Du arbeitest in einem Reisebüro. Deine Partnerin, eine Kundin, möchte mit dir ihre Ferienpläne besprechen, eine Reise planen und bei dir buchen. Sie hat Fragen über verschiedene Reiseziele. Sie möchte zum Beispiel wissen, was sie an jedem Reiseort unternehmen kann. Als Reiseberater bist du bestens informiert, denn du bist schon überall gewesen und kannst deshalb ihre Fragen beantworten. Schreibt ein Rollenspiel und führt es der Klasse vor!

ZWEITE STUFE   STANDARDS: 1.1, 1.2, 1.3, 5.1   zweihunderteinundfünfzig

Dritte Stufe

Objective Asking for and giving directions

Stadtrundgang durch Bietigheim

Parken Sie Ihren Wagen auf dem Parkplatz am Japangarten. Von hier aus sind es nur zwei Gehminuten in die Stadt.

Vom Parkplatz gehen Sie auf der Holzgartenstraße über unser kleines Flüsschen, die Metter, und Sie kommen direkt in die Hauptstraße und damit in die Fußgängerzone in der Innenstadt.

An der Hauptstraße gehen Sie nach links. Vor Ihnen sehen Sie jetzt das einzige noch gut erhaltene Stadttor. (Es hat einmal vier davon gegeben.) Das imposante Mauerwerk stammt aus dem Ende des 14. Jahrhunderts.

Sie gehen jetzt weiter durch dieses Tor, immer die Hauptstraße entlang bis zur Fräuleinstraße, wo Sie rechts in die Fräuleinstraße einbiegen. An der Ecke Schieringsbrunnerstraße sehen Sie das alte Backhaus auf der rechten Seite. Früher war dieses Haus außerhalb der Stadt.

Nach etwa 60 Metern kommen Sie zur Schieringerstraße. Hier biegen Sie links ein. Auf der linken Seite, Nr. 20, ist das stattliche Bürgerhaus, ein Fachwerkhaus aus dem 17. Jahrhundert.

Neben dem Bürgerhaus befindet sich das Kachelsche Haus, ein repräsentatives Wohnhaus aus dem 16. Jahrhundert.

Schräg gegenüber vom Kachelschen Haus ist die alte Posthalterei, ein schönes Fachwerkhaus aus dem 18. Jahrhundert.

Jetzt kommen Sie bald wieder auf die Hauptstraße. Sie gehen nach rechts, und gleich ein paar Schritte weiter kommen Sie zum Bietigheimer Rathaus mit dem schönen Marktbrunnen davor.

1. Parkplatz
2. Stadttor
3. Backhaus
4. Bürgerhaus
5. Kachelsches Haus
6. Posthalterei
7. Marktbrunnen
8. Rathaus
9. Hormoldhaus
10. Evangelische Stadtkirche
11. Kleines Bürgerhaus
12. Bietigheimer Schloss

KAPITEL 9 Wohin in die Ferien?

21 In Bietigheim

Lesen/Sprechen Lies zuerst den Text auf Seite 252! Dann such dir einen Partner, und beantwortet dann zusammen diese Fragen! Seht euch dabei den Stadtplan von Bietigheim an!

1. Wo kann man den Wagen parken, wenn man die Innenstadt von Bietigheim besuchen will?
2. Wie kommt man vom Parkplatz in die Hauptstraße?
3. Wie kommt man jetzt zum Stadttor?
4. Wie kommt man vom Stadttor in die Fräuleinstraße?
5. Wo steht das Alte Backhaus?
6. Wo ist das Bürgerhaus?
7. Wo befindet sich das Kachelsche Haus?
8. Wo ist die Posthalterei?
9. Wohin kommt man, wenn man wieder rechts in die Hauptstraße einbiegt?

in der ... straße   bis zum ... platz
am ... platz   bis zur ... straße
nach rechts   nach links   dann geradeaus
die erste (zweite) Straße nach rechts   und dann wieder nach links

1. auf dem Parkplatz am Japangarten; 2. auf der Holzgartenstraße über die Metter gehen; 3. an der Hauptstraße nach links gehen; 4. durch das Stadttor, die Hauptstraße entlang, dann rechts einbiegen; 5. an der Ecke Schieringsbrunnerstraße auf der rechten Seite; 6. Schieringerstraße Nr. 20; 7. neben dem Bürgerhaus auf der Schieringerstraße; 8. schräg gegenüber vom Kachelschen Haus auf der Schieringerstraße; 9. zum Bietigheimer Rathaus

Wortschatz

Übungsheft, S. 105–106, Ü. 1–4   Grammatikheft, S. 79, Ü. 14

Der Parkplatz befindet sich an der Holzgartenstraße.

Die Metter läuft zwischen der Innenstadt und dem Palmengarten entlang.

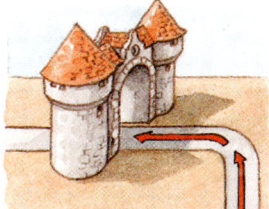

Gehen Sie links um die Ecke; dann kommen Sie zum Stadttor!

Die Hauptstraße führt durch das Stadttor.

Das Rathaus steht hier schon seit dem 16. Jahrhundert.

Vor dem Rathaus steht der Ulrichsbrunnen.

Dieses Fachwerkhaus stammt aus dem 17. Jahrhundert.

Dieses Wohnhaus ist beim Rathaus.

Can you identify the prepositions above? What do you think they mean and how would you express them in English? What case follows each of these prepositions?

22 Wo ist der Tourist jetzt?   Script and answers on p. 237H

Zuhören Du hörst drei Kurzbeschreibungen von einem Rundgang durch Bietigheim. Schau auf die Stadtkarte und schreib auf, wo sich der Tourist am Ende der Beschreibung befindet!
CD 9 Tr. 10

DRITTE STUFE   STANDARDS: 1.2   zweihundertdreiundfünfzig   253

Grammatik

Prepositions followed by dative-case forms

Mehr Grammatikübungen, S. 260, Ü. 6–7

1. The prepositions **mit** and **zu** are always followed by dative-case forms:

   Jens kommt **mit dem Moped zur Schule**. Ich muss jetzt **zum Bäcker** gehen.

Grammatikheft, S. 80, Ü. 15

2. There are other prepositions that must be used with dative-case forms.

aus	*from*	Das Tor ist **aus dem** 14. Jahrhundert.
bei	*by, near*	Das Hormoldhaus ist **beim** Rathaus.
nach	*after*	**Nach** 60 Metern ist man **am** Brunnen.
von	*from*	**Vom Parkplatz** sind es nur zwei Gehminuten.
seit	*since*	Es steht hier **seit dem** 16. Jahrhundert.
gegenüber	*across from*	**Gegenüber dem** Kachelschen Haus ist die Posthalterei.

3. Like **zu**, the prepositions **bei** and **von** also form contractions.

   bei + dem = **beim**   von + dem = **vom**

23 Grammatik im Kontext

Schreiben Your German pen pal is coming to visit. Send him a short description of your town. Rewrite your note with dative prepositions and the correct articles.

… Also, die Amtrakstation ist gar nicht weit vom Stadtzentrum. <u>Von</u> d<u>er</u> Station bis zur Innenstadt sind es nur zehn Minuten zu Fuß. Da ist das alte Rathaus. Es stammt <u>aus</u> d<u>em</u> neunzehnten Jahrhundert. Das ist schon alt in den Vereinigten Staaten! <u>Neben</u> d<u>em</u> Rathaus siehst du das alte Postgebäude. Auf der anderen Straßenseite, <u>gegenüber</u> d<u>em</u> Rathaus, ist ein schöner Park. Dort spiele ich Baseball <u>vor</u> d<u>er</u> Schule.

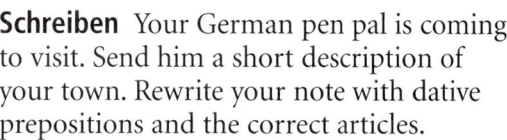

Ein wenig Grammatik

The prepositions **durch**, *through*, and **um**, *around*, are always followed by accusative-case forms.

Wir gehen **durch das Stadttor**.
Das Rathaus ist **um die Ecke**.

Which other two prepositions do you know that are always followed by the accusative case?[1]

Grammatikheft, S. 80, Ü. 16

So sagt man das!

Asking for and giving directions

When asking for directions, you might ask:

Entschuldigung! Wo ist bitte das Rathaus?
or
Wie komme ich bitte zum Stadttor? *or*
Verzeihung! Wissen Sie vielleicht, wie ich zur Post komme?

When giving directions, you might say:

Sie biegen hier rechts ein. Dann kommen Sie zum Rathaus.
Das ist hier rechts um die Ecke.
Tut mir Leid. Ich weiß es leider nicht. Ich bin nicht von hier.

What do the prepositions **zum** and **zur** indicate? Look at the responses on the right. How would you say them in English?

Grammatikheft, S. 81, Ü. 17

1. **für** and **gegen**

24 Verzeihung! Wissen Sie, wo …?

Sprechen Zwei Partner sind Touristen. Du kennst dich in Bietigheim aus, und gibst ihnen Auskunft.

Hier sind die Partner: Sie wollen dorthin:
1. am Rathaus Evangelische Stadtkirche
2. auf dem Parkplatz Fußgängerzone
3. in der Fräuleinstraße Marktbrunnen
4. bei der Stadtkirche Hormoldhaus

25 Touristen in der Stadt

Sprechen Zwei verschiedene Gruppen von Touristen sprechen dich auf dem Parkplatz in Bietigheim an. Eine Gruppe möchte zur Evangelischen Stadtkirche, die andere zum Bietigheimer Schloss. Sag ihnen, wie man dahin kommt!

26 Für mein Notizbuch

Schreiben Schreib in dein Notizbuch
a. wie du mit dem Rad von zu Hause zur Schule kommst!
b. wie du von zu Hause zu einem Freund kommst!

> **Ein wenig Grammatik**
>
> In this chapter you learned that the prepositions **in**, **an** and **auf** can be followed by either accusative or dative noun phrases. Do you remember in which instances the accusative forms are used? And the dative forms? Here are three other prepositions that also follow this rule:
>
> **vor** *in front of*
> **neben** *next to*
> **zwischen** *between*
>
> Like **in**, **an**, and **auf**, these prepositions must be used with the accusative case when indicating direction and with the dative case when indicating location.
>
> Übungsheft, S. 107, Ü. 5–6
> Grammatikheft, S. 81, Ü. 18
> Mehr Grammatikübungen, S. 261, Ü. 8–10

27 Geh vor den Schreibtisch!

Sprechen Take turns with your classmates giving different students commands to move around your classroom. Use the prepositions **an, vor, zwischen,** and **neben**. Each student will do what you tell him or her. When he or she is in the proper place, that student will tell the class where he or she is now located using these same prepositions.

BEISPIEL Du Geh an die Tafel! *(classmate walks to the chalkboard)*
 MITSCHÜLER Ich stehe an der Tafel.

28 So kommst du zu mir!

Sprechen Du machst eine Party und lädst ein paar Klassenkameraden ein. Zwei Klassenkameraden wissen gar nicht, wo du wohnst. Du hast für sie auf einem Zettel eine Route vorbereitet, wie sie am besten zu dir kommen. Gib ihnen den Zettel und erklär es ihnen persönlich!

29 Von der Schule zum Beruf

Du arbeitest im Vermessungsamt *(surveyor's office)* in deiner Stadt. Du musst ein Layout deiner Stadt erstellen, das die wichtigsten Straßen und Gebäude zeigt.

Zum Lesen

Was ist dein Lieblingsreiseziel?

Lesestrategie

Distinguishing between fact and opinion. It is important to notice when an author is expressing a personal opinion or value as opposed to conveying facts. Understanding the values held by a group of people is a key to getting along in that culture. Here are some expressions that indicate when an author is giving a personal opinion:

Ich finde …
Ich glaube …
Für mich …
Es soll … sein.
Ich meine …

For answers, see p. 237W

Getting Started

1. Read the following sentences and determine which ones are fact and which are opinion.
   a. Solche Ferien sind besser als nach Mallorca zu fahren.
   b. Nachts machen wir Waldspiele.
   c. Keine Autos fahren vorbei.
   d. Ein Ferienparadies soll ein Urlaub mit Freunden sein.

2. Look at the title, subtitle, and drawings on these two pages. What is the article about? Scan the article. What kind of information is summarized here?

3. Now read the summary of results **Tiere sind Trumpf**. What are the ten most popular vacations for German teenagers?

4. Does this survey focus on facts or opinions? If the question were **Wo warst du in den**

Eltern — UMFRAGE

Gesucht: Bauernhof zum Ausschlafen

Realschüler, 14 Jahre
Wo Mädchen und Jungen am liebsten Ferien machen

„Für die meisten Menschen ist wohl Hawaii der Urlaubstraum. Für mich ist es das Dorf, wo meine Großmutter wohnt. Da ist ein See mit dem Paddelboot von meinem Opa. Ich habe dort mehrere Freunde. Und Großmutter kocht nur, was mir wirklich schmeckt."
Realschülerin, 13 Jahre

„Es ist und bleibt ein Bauernhof. Es soll ein Urlaub mit Freunden, ohne Eltern sein. Man kann bei der Arbeit freiwillig helfen. Alles, was ich nicht muß wie in der Schule, macht mir Freude. Nachts darf ich mit Freunden schon mal auf dem Heuboden schlafen. Dann hört man plötzlich was. Ist es eine Maus oder ein Siebenschläfer oder ein Marder oder eine der vielen Katzen vom Hof? Dann wird's einem ganz gruselig. Solche Ferien sind besser als nach Mallorca zu müssen in den Ölsardinensitzen."
Realschüler, 13 Jahre

„Mein Ideal ist ein Pfadfinderlager. Nachts machen wir Waldspiele mit

Tiere sind Trumpf

Eltern fragte 2220 Schülerinnen und Schüler acht bis 16 Jahre alt. Was ist für dich ein Ferienparadies? Am häufigsten genannt wurden:
1. Bauernhof, Reiterhof
2. bei Großeltern oder anderen Verwandten
3. Zelten, Jugendlager, Wohnmobil
4. Trampen
5. Strand an südlichen Meeren
6. zu Hause (Ausschlafen)
7. Bergtour
8. Aktivferien (Surfen, Klettern, Angeln)
9. USA/Kanada (Nationalparks, Disney World)
10. Abenteuerreise (Dschungel, Wüste, Vulkane)

Rund zehn Prozent der Befragten bringen zum Ausdruck, daß für sie der Ferienort eigentlich Nebensache ist—sie empfinden es als viel wichtiger, daß die Eltern Zeit haben, entspannt und gutgelaunt sind.

Taschenlampen. Wir haben ein Lagerfeuer. Wenn der Wind ums Zelt heult, kuschelt man sich in seinen Schlafsack."
Realschüler, 14 Jahre

„Für mich muß es ganz, ganz weit weg sein. Wenn ich wieder zu Hause bin, kann ich allen meinen Freunden erzählen, wie weit weg ich war."
Hauptschüler, 14 Jahre

„Meine Eltern gehen immer ins Reisebüro und suchen sich was Tolles aus. Meistens Urlaubsziele, wo sich Menschenmassen

zusammenballen: Mallorca, Gran Canaria, Italien, Kreta, Meran usw. Mein Urlaubstraum aber ist ein kleiner See mit nettem Strand und dahinter etwas weg ein Dorf. Auf dem Strand steht mein Zelt, und daneben liegt mein Paddelboot. Leider habe ich weder ein Boot noch ein Zelt. Nur Träume."

Gymnasiastin, 15 Jahre

„Für mich sind die schönsten Ferien, wenn wir eine Fahrradtour machen. An einem Fluß vorbei und über Waldwege. Daran sieht man, daß es im Urlaub nicht die Super-Luxus-Hotels machen, um echte Freude zu kriegen."

Gymnasiast, 13 Jahre

„Wo keine Abgase sind. Wo man nachts schlafen kann, weil keine Autos und Lastwagen vorbeidonnern."

Realschüler, 13 Jahre

„Viele Urlaubsparadiese kann man erleben, wenn man eine Radtour macht. Am schönsten war für mich der Weg von Passau nach Wien. Im Flugzeug, im Auto, im Bus sieht man doch alles nur hinter Glasscheiben. Aber auf dem Fahrrad ist alles ganz nahe. Die wunderbarsten Waldwege kann man fahren, und an Flüssen und Bächen vorbei."

Realschüler, 15 Jahre

„Wir haben in der Lüneburger Heide ein kleines Ferienhaus. Das ist unser Urlaubsparadies. Wir wandern oder fahren mit einem Pferdewagen durch die Heide. Meine Eltern, meine Schwester und ich, wir fühlen uns dort sehr wohl. Nur manchmal ist es ein bißchen langweilig. Aber diese Stille ist am besten für die Erholung, für mich vom Schulstreß, für meine Eltern von der Firma."

Gymnasiastin, 14 Jahre

„Ein Bauernhof wie in dem Roman ‚Herbstmilch!' So ganz urgemütlich. Betten mit karierten hohen Plümos in einem ganz kleinen Zimmer mit zwei ganz kleinen Fenstern. Aus den Ställen hört man das Vieh brüllen. Pferde sind da und Schafe. Es ist einfach wunderbar, mitten in der Landwirtschaft zu leben. Abends sitzen alle an einem langen Holztisch und essen aus einem Topf und aus einer Pfanne. Es gibt herrliche Suppe, leckere Braten, feine Nachtische und viel Obst. Alles ist deftig gekocht. Und abends sitzen wir an einem alten Kamin. Ja, so erträume ich mir das."

Gymnasiastin, 15 Jahre

letzten Ferien? would the answers be facts or opinions?

5. Skim the interviews. For each interview, jot down the student's age, the main idea (in this case, usually the vacation place or the people with whom the vacation is spent), and one specific fact supporting that person's opinion.

A Closer Look

6. What does the thirteen-year-old **Realschülerin** think most people would describe as a vacation paradise? How does her own opinion differ?

7. What does the thirteen-year-old **Gymnasiast** like about bicycle tours? Which parts of his response are opinion and which are fact?

> **Tipp:** You may not know the expression **weder … noch,** but you can guess its meaning from context because you know the word **leider.**

8. How does the fifteen-year-old **Gymnasiastin**'s idea differ from her parents' idea about a vacation paradise? What does she say about a boat and tent? Is this a fact or opinion?

9. Where does the fourteen-year-old **Gymnasiastin**'s family have a vacation house? What is the only drawback, in her opinion?

10. You have probably formed some impressions and opinions of your own about the readings on these pages. How many of these students do you think are city-dwellers? (Why do you think so?) How many of them are describing vacations they have actually taken, and how many are describing a "daydream?" Which tells you more about a person: his or her real life or his or her hopes and dreams?

Übungsheft, S. 108

Mehr Grammatikübungen

Erste Stufe

Objective Expressing indecision, asking for and making suggestions

1 Du und deine Freunde, ihr wisst nicht, wo ihr eure Ferien verbringen wollt. Du fragst sie um Rat, und sie machen Vorschläge. Schreib die folgenden Sätze ab, und schreib dabei die richtige Präposition und, wenn nötig, den richtigen bestimmten *(definite)* Artikel in die Lücken. Wenn möglich, verwende Kurzformen *(contractions)*. **(S. 246)**

1. Sollen wir mal _____ Ostsee fahren? Was meinst du? — Ich schlage vor, dass wir mal _____ Rhein fahren.

   an die
   an den

2. Wir können mal _____ Schweiz fahren, _____ Zürich. — Der Boris ist dafür, dass wir _____ Schwarzwald fahren, _____ Freiburg.

   in die; nach
   in den; nach

3. Oder sollen wir _____ Berge fahren? Vielleicht _____ Alpen? — Ach, fahren wir doch mal _____ Nordsee, _____ Sylt.

   in die; in die
   an die; nach

4. Sollen wir mal _____ Österreich fahren, _____ Wien? — Ich bin dafür, dass wir _____ Schweiz fahren und _____ Brienzer Rothorn steigen.

   nach; nach
   in die; aufs

5. Fahren wir doch mal _____ Bayern, _____ Starnberger See. — Ja, du, dann bin ich aber dafür, dass wir _____ Garmisch und _____ Zugspitze fahren.

   nach; an den
   nach; auf die

2 Du willst nicht dorthin fahren, wohin dein Freund oder deine Freundin fährt. – Schreib **wenn**-Sätze, wie in dem Beispiel. Verwende dabei die gegebenen Orte mit der richtigen Präposition und dem richtigen Artikel, wenn nötig. **(S. 246)**

BEISPIEL Berlin / München
Ich fahre nach Berlin, wenn du nach München fährst.

1. Deutschland / Schweiz   … nach Deutschland, … in die Schweiz
2. Nordsee / Rhein   … an die Nordsee, … an den Rhein
3. Alpen / Bodensee   … in die Alpen, … an den Bodensee
4. Mexiko / Vereinigte Staaten   … nach Mexiko, … in die Vereinigten Staaten
5. Berge / Ostsee   … in die Berge, … an die Ostsee
6. Schwarzwald / Bayern   … in den Schwarzwald, … nach Bayern

Zweite Stufe

Objectives Expressing doubt, conviction, and resignation

3 Du planst mit deinen Eltern die kommenden Ferien. Du bezweifelst aber, dass euer Ferienort all die Einrichtungen hat, die du dir wünschst. Ergänze die folgenden Sätze, und schreib die in Klammern gegebene Information in die Lücken. (S. 249)

1. (Wir können dort segeln.)   Ich weiß nicht, ob _____ .   *wir dort segeln können*
2. (Es gibt dort einen Golfplatz.)   Ich bezweifle, dass _____ .   *es dort einen Golfplatz gibt*
3. (Es gibt einen Fitnessraum.)   Ich bin nicht sicher, dass _____ .   *es einen Fitnessraum gibt*
4. (Du kannst dort Boot fahren.)   Ich weiß nicht, ob _____ .   *du dort Boot fahren kannst*
5. (Es gibt dort einen Pool.)   Ich weiß nicht, ob _____ .   *es dort einen Pool gibt*
6. (Es gibt dort eine Disko.)   Ich weiß nicht, ob _____ .   *es dort eine Disko gibt*

4 Du erzählst, wo du die letzten Ferien verbracht hast, und du drückst mit Sicherheit aus, wo du die kommenden Ferien verbringen wirst. Schreib die folgenden Sätze ab, und schreib die richtige Präposition und, wenn nötig, den richtigen bestimmten *(definite)* Artikel in die Lücken. Wenn möglich, verwende Kurzformen *(contractions)*. (S. 250)

1. Letztes Jahr waren wir _____ Schweiz, und ich bin sicher, dass wir diesen Urlaub   *in der*
   nicht wieder _____ Schweiz fahren.   *in die*
2. Den letzten Urlaub haben wir _____ Ostsee verbracht, und du kannst mir glauben,   *an der*
   dass wir in diesem Urlaub nicht wieder _____ Ostsee fahren.   *an die*
3. Wir waren letztes Jahr _____ Alpen, und ich bin sicher, dass wir in diesem Jahr nicht   *in den*
   wieder _____ Alpen fahren.   *in die*
4. Den letzten Urlaub haben wir _____ Schwarzwald verbracht, und du kannst mir   *im*
   glauben, dass wir diesen Urlaub nicht wieder _____ Schwarzwald fahren.   *in den*
5. Letztes Jahr waren wir _____ Vereinigten Staaten, und ich bin sicher, dass meine   *in den*
   Eltern dieses Jahr wieder _____ Vereinigten Staaten fliegen.   *in die*
6. Die letzten Ferien habe ich bei meiner Tante _____ Frankfurt verbracht, und ich bin   *in*
   sicher, dass ich die nächsten Ferien wieder _____ Frankfurt fahre.   *nach*

5 Eine Bekannte fragt dich, wohin du gehst, und du sagst ihr, dass du schon dort warst. Schreib die folgenden Fragen und Antworten ab, und schreib die richtige Präposition und, wenn nötig, den richtigen bestimmten *(definite)* Artikel in die Lücken. Wenn möglich, verwende Kurzformen *(contractions)*. (S. 250)

1. Gehst du _____ Golfplatz? — Du, ich war heute schon _____ Golfplatz.   *auf den; auf dem*
2. Gehst du _____ Fitnessraum? — Ich war heute schon _____ Fitnessraum.   *in den; im*
3. Gehst du heute _____ Sauna? — Ich war heute schon _____ Sauna.   *in die; in der*
4. Gehst du _____ Tennisplatz? — Ich war heute schon _____ Tennisplatz.   *auf den; auf dem*
5. Gehst du jetzt _____ Strand? — Ich war heute schon _____ Strand.   *an den; am*
6. Gehst du _____ Liegewiese? — Ich war den ganzen Tag _____ Liegewiese.   *auf die; auf der*
7. Gehst du jetzt _____ Pool? — Ich war heute schon _____ Pool.   *in den; im*

MEHR GRAMMATIKÜBUNGEN   STANDARDS: 1.2

Mehr Grammatikübungen

Dritte Stufe
Objective Asking for and giving directions

6 Eine Freundin fragt dich, wo du warst und du sagst es ihr. – Schau dir das Piktogramm an, und schreibe den Satz zu Ende. Gebrauche die richtige Präposition, den richtigen bestimmten Artikel und den Namen des Piktogramms. (S. 254)

Wo warst du?
Ich war _____ _____ .   im Fitnessraum

Ich war _____ _____ _____ .   in der Diskothek

Ich war _____ _____ _____ .   auf dem Tennisplatz

Ich war _____ _____ .   im Pool

Ich war _____ _____ _____ .   auf dem Golfplatz

Ich war _____ _____ _____ .   in der Sauna

Ich war _____ _____ .   im Fernsehraum

7 Du gibst verschiedenen Leuten Auskunft. Schreib die folgenden Sätze ab, und schreib dabei den richtigen bestimmten Artikel in die Lücken. Gebrauche die üblichen Kurzformen! (S. 254)

1. Wenn Sie aus _____ Rathaus kommen, gehen Sie rechts um _____ Ecke!   **dem; die**
2. Sie gehen durch _____ Stadttor, und der Brunnen ist gleich bei _____ Rathaus!   **durchs; beim**
3. Dieses Fachwerkhaus ist aus _____ 17. Jahrhundert; es ist gegenüber _____ Post.   **dem; der**
4. Von _____ Kirche bis zu _____ Rathaus sind es nur zwei Minuten.   **der; zum**
5. Von _____ Parkplatz bis zu _____ Kirche sind es nur drei Gehminuten.   **Vom; zur**
6. Sie wollen zu _____ Stadttor? Es ist in der Nähe von _____ Parkplatz.   **zum; vom**

8 Welche Präposition passt? Such dir die richtige Präposition aus dem Kasten aus und schreib sie in die Lücke. (S. 255)

| aus | zu | um | von | vor | neben | seit |

1. Geh hier rechts _____ die Ecke, und da siehst du das Rathaus _____ dir. *um; vor*
2. Dieses Rathaus stammt _____ dem 17. Jahrhundert. *aus*
3. Es steht also _____ über 300 Jahren hier. *seit*
4. Ein schöner Brunnen steht _____ dem Rathaus. *neben (vor)*
5. Wie weit ist es _____ der Kirche bis _____ dem Parkplatz? *von; zu*
6. Das Rathaus ist gleich hier _____ die Ecke. *um*

9 Du gibst weitere Auskünfte, besonders übers Parken. Schreib die folgenden Sätze ab, und schreib dabei den richtigen bestimmten Artikel in die Lücken. (S. 255)

1. Zwischen _____ Rathaus und _____ Schloss ist das Hormoldhaus. *dem; dem*
2. Der Brunnen steht auf _____ Marktplatz vor _____ Rathaus. *dem; dem*
3. Ein kleiner Parkplatz ist neben _____ Kirche und neben _____ Rathaus. *der; dem*
4. Ein großer Parkplatz ist vor _____ Innenstadt, an _____ Holzgartenstraße. *der, der*
5. Neben _____ Kirche kann man nicht parken, aber neben _____ Post. *der; der*
6. Neben _____ alten Schloss und vor _____ Kirche kann man auch nicht parken. *dem; der*

10 Schreib Sätze mit den Begriffen (expressions), die in Klammern stehen. (S. 254)

(through)   1. Wir gehen _____ _____ Stadttor. *durch das*
(around)   2. Geh hier _____ _____ Ecke. *um die*
(next to me)   3. Robert sitzt _____ _____ und Gitta. *neben mir*
(between us)   4. Er sitzt _____ _____ . *zwischen uns*
(in front of) 5. Der Brunnen steht _____ _____ Rathaus. *vor dem*
(in front of) 6. Fahr das Auto _____ _____ Rathaus. *vor das*

Storytelling Book pp. 70–71

Anwendung

The **CD-ROM Tutor** offers guided recording and writing activities to accompany the **Anwendung**. These activities are designed to practice students' oral and written communication skills and to review material from each chapter.

1 The German exchange student who lived with your family last summer calls you early one morning and tells you about her trip to Austria. Take notes so that you can tell the rest of your family about her vacation. Script and answers on p. 237H
CD 9 Tr. 11

2 Schau die Tabelle unten an und dann diese Aussagen! Wenn eine Aussage nicht stimmt, ändere sie so, damit sie stimmt!

1. Die deutschen Jugendlichen fahren am liebsten nach Frankreich.   1. ... Spanien
2. Die 17-19-Jährigen fahren nicht so oft nach Portugal wie die 14-16-Jährigen.   2. Die 17-19-Jährigen fahren nach Portugal; die 14-16-Jährigen nicht.
3. Die Niederlande sind ein sehr beliebtes Reiseziel.   3. Die Niederlande sind ein nicht sehr beliebtes Reiseziel.
4. Deutsche Jugendliche fahren lieber nach Jugoslawien als nach Spanien.
5. Nicht sehr viele Jugendliche fahren nach London.   4. Deutsche Jugendliche fahren lieber nach Spanien als nach Jugoslawien.
6. Die 14-28-Jährigen fahren genauso oft nach Dänemark wie nach Griechenland.

5. Stimmt.   6. Die 14-28–Jährigen fahren genauso oft nach Dänemark wie nach Portugal.

Das Ausland steht an erster Stelle

Wohin geht die Haupturlaubsreise der Jugendlichen? Im Inland bleibt nur jeder fünfte. Hier sind vor allem die Küsten von Schleswig-Holstein attraktiv.

Renner sind die Auslandsreisen. Spanien, Frankreich und Italien stehen an den ersten Stellen (siehe Tabelle).

In Spanien ist „schwer was los"

Die Niederlande, Italien, Jugoslawien und die Türkei sind für Deutsche preisgünstig. Großbritannien, Österreich, Italien, Griechenland und die USA bieten nach Ansicht von deutschen Jugendlichen gute Möglichkeiten, neue Leute kennen zu lernen. Die Inseln Spaniens, Italiens, Jugoslawiens, Griechenland und die Türkei bieten eine prima Urlaubsatmosphäre. In Großbritannien, Spanien und Italien ist „schwer was los".

Die wichtigsten Reiseziele der deutschen Jugendlichen im Ausland (2000)

	14-28 Jahre	14-16 Jahre	17-19 Jahre
Spanien (Inseln und Festland):	17,9	12	20
Frankreich:	11,4	7	12
Italien (mit Inseln):	10,8	7	13
Jugoslawien:	5,9	5	6
Griechenland:	5,4	3	3
Österreich:	5,4	7	6
Dänemark:	4,0	6	5
Portugal:	4,0	-	2
Niederlande:	3,7	2	6
Großbritannien:	3,5	7	6

(alle Angaben in Prozent; durch andere Reiseziele und Mehrfachnennungen ergeben sich keine 100 Prozent)

3 Lies den obigen (*above*) Artikel und beantworte die Fragen auf Englisch!

1. What is the topic of the article?   1. where young people from Germany spend their vacation
2. According to the report, what are the different advantages each country has to offer as a vacation spot?   2. The Netherlands, Italy, Yugoslavia, Turkey: inexpensive; Great Britain, Austria, Italy, Greece, USA: best to get to know new people; Islands of Spain, Italy, Yugoslavia, Greece, Turkey: great vacation atmosphere; Great Britain, Spain, Italy: a lot going on
3. Do more German young people choose to travel to another country or to stay within Germany for their vacations? What statistics support your answer?
3. They travel to other countries; only every 5th stays in Germany

4  Get together with three other classmates. Each of you chooses (without telling others) one place to go or thing to do in your hometown. Each begins by suggesting to the others his or her desire and tries to persuade them to come along. The other two should try to express some reservation about the idea. Everyone gets a turn to suggest and persuade. In the end, all of you must agree on one thing to do together.

5

Zum Schreiben

You took a bicycle tour of a small mountainous area in the US or in a German-speaking country and are now writing a short informative piece about your adventures for a high school German club newspaper.

Schreibtipp Organize your thoughts around a main idea, then choose details that support your point of view and that appeal to your audience. This focuses your writing, keeps you on track, and aids you in persuading someone to see your point of view.

Vorbereiten

Keeping a **writer's journal** is an excellent technique to organize information. By keeping a journal of daily observations, thoughts, and feelings, you can organize your ideas in order to write an article that contains lots of interesting details about your trip. Write daily entries that include what you did, how you felt, and observations about the areas you visited.

Ausführen

In this case, your **main idea** could be that the place you visited is well worth the trip. **Es gibt in dieser Gegend viele Jugendherbergen, wo man billig übernachten kann,** might be a detail that would convince some of your readers that this is a type of vacation they could actually afford.

Überarbeiten

- Reread your paper, checking for good details and descriptions. Have you given facts about the area, included humorous anecdotes, and adequately expressed your feelings about the area you visited?
- Exchange papers with a partner and check each other's paper for details, descriptions, facts, anecdotes, and feelings.
- Proofread, make corrections and changes, and read your paper to the class.

6 ## Rollenspiel

With two partners, pick a vacation spot in the United States that you will have to present to a group of German students who are prospective travelers to the United States. Market and "sell" the spot, making it as attractive as possible. Get photos of the area and find out the main attractions and conveniences. Orient your presentation to the interests of German students. Then make your presentation to the class.

ANWENDUNG STANDARDS: 1.1, 1.3, 5.1, 5.2 zweihundertdreiundsechzig **263**

Kann ich's wirklich?

WK3 STUTTGART-9

Can you express indecision? (p. 245)

1 How would you ask someone what you should do?
E.g.: Was soll ich bloß machen?

Can you ask for and make suggestions? (p. 245)

2 How would you ask your friends for specific suggestions on what you all could do this evening?   E.g.: Was machen wir? Hast du eine Idee? Was schlägst du vor?

3 How would your friend suggest that you go to these places?
  a. to Switzerland   a. E.g.: Ich schlage vor, dass wir mal in die Schweiz fahren.
  b. to New York   b. E.g.: Fahren wir mal nach New York!
  c. to Lake Constance (**der Bodensee**)   c. E.g.: Wir können mal an den Bodensee fahren.

4 How might your friends respond if
  a. they like the idea   a. E.g.: Ja, Spitze! Das ist eine gute Idee.
  b. they do not like the idea   b. E.g.: Ich bin nicht dafür.

Can you express doubt, conviction, and resignation? (p. 249)

5 How would you convey to a friend
  a. that you doubt you will be able to go on vacation?   a. E.g.: Ich bezweifle, dass ich in die Ferien fahre.
  b. that you are sure you will go to Florida?   b. E.g.: Ich bin sicher, dass ich nach Florida fahre.

6 How would you say to someone that it will rain all summer and that unfortunately nothing can be done about it?
E.g.: Ich bin sicher, dass es den ganzen Sommer regnet. Da kann man nichts machen. Das ist leider so.

Can you ask for and give directions? (p. 254)

7 How would you ask your teacher how to get to the post office?
E.g.: Entschuldigung! Wie komme ich bitte zur Post?

8 How would you give directions to someone
  a. who needs to go to the post office from your school?   a. E.g.: Gehen Sie von der Schule geradeaus und dann rechts um die Ecke. Dort ist die Post.
  b. who is looking for the shopping center?
  b. Various possibilities. E.g.: Biegen Sie hier rechts in die Hauptstraße ein. Auf der linken Seite ist das Einkaufszentrum.

9 How would you answer if someone asked you for directions, but you were new in town?   E.g.: Tut mir Leid. Ich weiß es leider nicht. Ich bin neu in der Stadt.

Wortschatz

Erste Stufe

Expressing indecision

Was machen wir jetzt?	What are we going to do now?
Was soll ich bloß machen?	Well, what am I supposed to do?

Talking about going on vacation

die Bahn, -en	train
das Flugzeug, -e	airplane
das Schiff, -e	ship
der Urlaub, -e	vacation (time off from work)
die See, -n	ocean, sea
die Nordsee	the North Sea

das Hallenbad, ¨-er	indoor pool
der Tennisplatz, ¨-e	tennis court
steigen	to climb
beliebt	popular

Asking for and making suggestions

Wohin fahren wir?	Where are we going?
Hast du eine Idee?	Do you have an idea?
Was schlägst du vor?	What do you suggest?

Ich schlage vor, dass …	I suggest that …
Ich bin dafür, dass …	I am for doing …
Fahren wir nach … !	Let's go to … !

Useful prepositions for expressing direction

nach	to, toward
an	to, at
in	in, into
auf	to, onto

p. 237X

Zweite Stufe

Words for describing a vacation by the water

das Meer, -e	ocean
segeln	to sail
windsurfen	to windsurf
tauchen	to dive
angeln	to fish
Boot fahren	to go for a boat ride
das Boot, -e	boat

Hotel activities

die Liegewiese, -n	lawn for relaxing and sunning
der Golfplatz, ¨-e	golf course
der Strand, ¨-e	beach

der Sandstrand, ¨-e	sand beach
die Sauna, -s	sauna
der Fitnessraum, ¨-e	training and weight room
der Whirlpool, -s	whirlpool
die Diskothek, -en	discotheque
der Fernsehraum, ¨-e	TV room

Expressing doubt

Ich weiß nicht, ob …	I don't know whether …
Ich bezweifle, dass …	I doubt that …

Ich bin nicht sicher, dass/ob …	I'm not sure that/whether …

Expressing conviction

Ich bin sicher, dass …	I am certain that …
Das kannst du mir glauben!	You can believe me on that!

Expressing resignation

Da kann man nichts machen.	There's nothing you can do.
Das ist leider so.	That's the way it is, unfortunately.

Dritte Stufe

Asking for and giving directions

Entschuldigung!	Excuse me!
Verzeihung!	Pardon me!
Das ist hier um die Ecke.	That's right around the corner.
die Ecke, -n	corner
Biegen Sie hier ein!	Turn in here!
Tut mir Leid. Ich bin nicht von hier.	I'm sorry. I'm not from here.

Describing a city

der Parkplatz, ¨-e	parking lot
das Stadttor, -e	city gate
die Hauptstraße, -n	main street

aus dem (16.) Jahrhundert	from the (16th) century
der Brunnen, -	fountain
das Wohnhaus, ¨-er	residence
Das Fachwerkhaus ist aus dem fünfzehnten Jahrhundert.	The half-timbered house is from the fifteenth century.
aus	from, out of
bei	by, near
nach	after
von	from, of
seit	since, for
gegenüber	across from
durch	through

um	around
neben	next to
vor	in front of
zwischen	between

Other useful words and expressions

Das ist gerade passiert.	That just happened.
kaputt	ruined, broken
eine andere, ein anderer, ein anderes	another (a different) one
eben nicht	actually not
das Jahrhundert, -e	century

KAPITEL 10, 11, 12

Berlin

Teaching Resources
pp. 266–269

PRINT
- Lesson Planner, p. 47
- Video Guide, pp. 61–62

MEDIA
- One-Stop Planner
- Video Program
  Videocassette 4, 01:17–09:58
- DVD Tutor, Disc 2
- Interactive CD-ROM Tutor, Disc 3
- Map Transparency

go.hrw.com
WK3 BERLIN

PAGES 266–267

THE PHOTOGRAPH
Background Information

The **Reichstagsgebäude,** located on the **Platz der Republik,** was built between 1884 and 1894 following the plans of the architect Paul Wallot. The building was severely damaged by a mysterious fire in 1933 and then by heavy bombing at the end of World War II. It was slowly rebuilt between 1957 and 1970 without its original glass dome. A new glass dome, different in style from the original dome, was added to the **Reichstag** as part of the major renovation work undertaken following the decision to move the German Parliament back to Berlin.

THE ALMANAC AND MAP

The coat of arms of Berlin depicts a black bear on a white background. **Der Berliner Bär** originally symbolized the struggle for freedom by the people of Berlin from the rulers of Brandenburg. During the postwar era, both East Berlin and West Berlin kept the same flag, with one difference—a slight variation in the crown above the bear. Since the unification, the crest of West Berlin has become the coat of arms for the united city of Berlin.

Terms in the Almanac

- **Spree:** The Spree river is a tributary of the Havel river. It is 403 kilometers (250 miles) long, and 180 kilometers (112 miles) of the river can be navigated by ships. In the city of Berlin, where the river runs through various lakes, the river is a popular site for boat rides and water sports.

- **Schloss Charlottenburg:** The original castle was commissioned by King Friedrich I in 1695 for his wife Sophie Charlotte. Between 1701 and 1707 the two wings and the tower with its crown-like roof were added. The castle burned almost completely in 1943, but most of the furnishings and art were saved. When the castle was rebuilt, most of the original structure was reconstructed and its contents returned.

- **Pergamonmuseum:** This museum is considered one of the finest museums of ancient art in the world. Its treasures include the Market Gate of Miletus and the celebrated Altar of Athena (180-160 B.C.) from the ancient city of Pergamon, founded by Greek colonists on the Aegean coast of Anatolia, modern Turkey. The altar's elaborate carvings represent a high point in Hellenic sculpture.

- **Wilhelm von Humboldt:** He was a close friend of Schiller and Goethe. He founded the University of Berlin when he was the head of the department of education and arts at the Home Office in Berlin.

- **Alexander von Humboldt:** He was one of the foremost scientists in Germany and the brother of Wilhelm von Humboldt. He traveled extensively in South America and Asia for his scientific studies.

- **Marlene Dietrich:** She was an actress who became famous for her dramatic films in the 1930s. In 1939 she became a U.S. citizen and used her influence to work against Nazi Germany during World War II. She is buried in Berlin.

- **Werner von Siemens:** He was an engineer, inventor, and industrialist who founded one of the major electrical manufacturing companies in Europe.

- **Berliner Pfannkuchen:** The famous **Pfannkuchen** are not pancakes as the name might suggest; rather, they are made from yeast dough, deep-fried, and filled with jam. They are similar to jelly doughnuts, but heavier.

265A   LOCATION OPENER   KAPITEL 10, 11, 12   STANDARDS: 2.2

- **Eisbein:** pig's shanks cooked in boiling water with a variety of spices and served on sauerkraut
- **Buletten:** breaded meat patties served as a main dish or as a cold appetizer

Using the Map
- Have students locate and trace the path of the Havel and Spree rivers on the map on p. xxiv. You may also want to use *Map Transparency* 1.
- Ask students to compare the population of Berlin to a U.S. city or to any other city in the world of similar size. (Examples: Washington, D.C.: 3.2 million; Montreal: 2.9 million)

> **PAGES 268–269**

THE PHOTO ESSAY

① **Das Mahnmal für die Opfer der Berliner Mauer** is one of the many memorials commemorating those who tried unsuccessfully to flee from the East across the Wall to the West. The Wall was first erected on the night of August 12-13, 1961, by the communist government of East Germany, ostensibly to protect East Berliners from the influence of the West. The Wall, which divided the city for 28 years, was 45 kilometers (28 miles) long and stood 3 meters high (10 feet). It was dismantled in 1989; only a few sections remain standing today.

② The **Brandenburger Tor,** the only remaining gate in Berlin, was designed by the German architect Carl Gotthard Langhans and built between 1788 and 1791. It was modeled after the Propylaea of the Acropolis in Athens, Greece. The gate was built as an imperial entrance to Berlin and was originally called the **Friedenstor.** It is crowned by Gottfried von Schadow's bronze Quadriga, showing the goddess of victory, **Viktoria,** in a chariot drawn by four horses. In 1807, Napoleon captured and moved the Quadriga to Paris. It was triumphantly returned to Berlin eight years later by Marshall Blücher. In November of 1989 the gate became the new symbol of freedom when Berliners began tearing down the Wall at the Brandenburg Gate.

③ **Die Kaiser-Wilhelm-Gedächtniskirche** was built between 1891 and 1895. It stands in ruins as a reminder of the destruction caused during World War II. The ruins of the 68-meter high West Tower are all that remain of the original church. Between 1959 and 1961 a new flat-roofed, octagon-shaped church was built adjacent to the ruins by Egon Eiermann. The church is located on the **Kurfürstendamm,** or **Ku'damm,** a boulevard that dates back to the 16th century when it was referred to as the **Knüppeldamm.** It was then used as a hunting trail. In 1871, Chancellor Bismarck was inspired by the Champs-Elysées in Paris and decided to have the boulevard expanded.

④ The **Potsdamer Platz** is located between the districts of **Berlin Mitte** and **Tiergarten** in the center of Berlin. The city square, a former park, was named after the **Potsdamer Tor,** built in 1824. By the 1920s, **Potsdamer Platz** had become a vital traffic intersection in Berlin.

In the 19th century, many hotels and cafés of international importance sprang up around the square. Among the more famous ones were the **Grand-Hotel Bellevue,** the **Palast Hotel,** and the **Café Josty** where politicians, authors, and artists met. In 1923, the **VOX-Haus** became the birthplace of German radio. The **Columbushaus,** a ten-story skeleton-like steel construction, was built by architect Erich Mendelsohn.

During WWII, **Potsdamer Platz** was almost completely destroyed and became an empty, almost forgotten piece of land between the East and West sectors of the city. During the workers' riot of 1953, the **Columbushaus** burned and was demolished in 1961 along with other remaining buildings. After the fall of the Wall in 1990, the square began its slow revival, initiated by enterprises like Daimler-Benz AG who built **the debis-Haus** and Sony. Today, **Potsdamer Platz** has regained most of its status and splendor as one of Berlin's most famous squares.

⑤ The **Leierkastenmann,** here **Orgel-Hermi,** typically strolls along busy pedestrian zones, playing popular tunes on his mechanical organ. The organ-grinder accepts gratuities for the entertainment.

⑥ These six students all belong to a theater group at the Max-Beckmann-Gymnasium, through which they have become close friends. Thieu-Binh Hoang's parents are from Vietnam, but she was born in Berlin. Ismar Hadziefendic was born in Bosnia, but has lived in Berlin most of his life.

- **Thinking Critically** Ask the class why the students in Photo 6 and their families may have come to Berlin to live.

KAPITEL 10, 11, 12

Komm mit nach Berlin!

Map of Germany

Einwohner: 3,5 Millionen

Flüsse: Spree, Havel

Berühmte Gebäude: Kaiser-Wilhelm-Gedächtniskirche, Schloss Charlottenburg, Pergamonmuseum, Brandenburger Tor, Reichstag, Kongresshalle, Nationalgalerie

Bedeutende Berliner: Wilhelm von Humboldt (1767-1835, Diplomat und Linguist), Alexander von Humboldt (1769-1859, Naturforscher), Rahel Varnhagen (1771-1833, Schriftstellerin), Karl Friedrich Schinkel (1781-1841, Architekt), Werner von Siemens (1816-1892, Erfinder), George Grosz (1893-1959, Maler), Marlene Dietrich (1901-1992, Schauspielerin)

Industrie: Elektrotechnik, Textilindustrie, Metallindustrie, Verlage, Pharmazeutische Industrie

Beliebte Gerichte: Berliner Pfannkuchen, Eisbein, Buletten, Grüner Aal

WK3 BERLIN

STANDARDS: 2.2, 3.1

▶ **Das wieder aufgebaute Reichstagsgebäude mit der neuen Glaskuppel von Sir Norman Foster**

Berlin

Berlin ist eine Kulturmetropole von Weltrang, in der alle Künste blühen: Literatur, Musik, Malerei, Theater, Baukunst. Die multikulturelle Bevölkerung verleiht Berlin eine Vitalität, die das Stadtbild prägt. Die interessante Architektur vieler neuer Bauwerke zeigt ein neues Berlin, in dem der letzte Weltkrieg, die Mauer und die Trennung langsam zur Vergangenheit werden. Berlin ist auch die größte deutsche Stadt und seit 1990 wieder die Hauptstadt des vereinten Deutschlands.

Visit Holt Online
go.hrw.com
KEYWORD: WK3 BERLIN
Internet Aktivitäten

1 Maueropfer
Dieses Mahnmal ist den Menschen gewidmet, die an der ehemaligen Berliner Mauer erschossen wurden, als sie versuchten in den Westen zu gelangen.

2 Brandenburger Tor
Das Brandenburger Tor wurde in den Jahren 1788 bis 1791 von Carl Gotthard Langhans errichtet und ist eines der bedeutendsten Bauwerke des deutschen Klassizismus. Auf dem Dach steht die Quadriga von Gottfried Schadow.

3 Kaiser-Wilhelm Gedächtniskirche
Die Kirche, im neoromanischen Stil erbaut, wurde im zweiten Weltkrieg zerstört. Der zerstörte Turm steht heute als symbolisches Kriegsmahnmal. Daneben steht die neue Kirche, die 1961 nach Plänen von Egon Eiermann errichtet wurde.

4 Am Potsdamer Platz: Debis-Haus und Berliner Volksbank
Neue Gebäude wie das Debis-Haus und die Berliner Volksbank bilden nur einen kleinen Teil des ganzen Areals am Potsdamer Platz, das aus Hotels, Restaurants, Theatern, Kinos, Einkaufszentren, Büros und Wohnungen besteht.

5 Ein Leierkastenmann
Leierkastenspieler, wie der „Orgel-Hermi" hier, sieht und hört man überall in Berlin. Sie geben der Stadt einen besonderen Charm.

Kapitel 10, 11, 12
Die letzten Kapitel in unserem Buch zeigen uns Berlin, die alte und neue deutsche Hauptstadt. Die sechs Schüler in diesen Kapiteln gehen aufs Max-Beckmann-Gymnasium in Reinickendorf.

6 Sandra, Astrid, Andreas, Binh, Ismar und Lars

Kapitel 10: Viele Interessen!
Chapter Overview

Los geht's! pp. 272–274	*Mensch, zieh die Handbremse an!* p. 272			
	FUNCTIONS	**GRAMMAR**	**VOCABULARY**	**RE-ENTRY**
Erste Stufe pp. 275–279	• Asking about and expressing interest, p. 276	• Verbs with prepositions; **wo-** and **da-**compounds, p. 277	• Television shows, p. 276	Expressing interest, p. 275 (**Kap. 8, II**); reflexive verbs, p. 275 (**Kap. 4, II**); types of movies, p. 276 (**Kap. 10, I**); giving reasons, p. 276 (**Kap. 8, I**); **weil**, p. 276 (**Kap. 8, I**); saying how often you do things, p. 277 (**Kap. 7, I**); **auf** and **für**, p. 277 (**Kap. 7, I** and **Kap. 5, II**)
Zweite Stufe pp. 282–285	• Asking for and giving permission, p. 283 • Asking for information and expressing an assumption, p. 284	• The verb **lassen**, p. 283 • The verb **laufen**, p. 285	• Television equipment, p. 282 • Days of the week, p. 285	**Dürfen**, p. 283 (**Kap. 4, II**); **können**, p. 283 (**Kap. 7, I**); word order with modals, p. 283 (**Kap. 3, I**); clauses following **wissen**, p. 284 (**Kap. 9, I**); yes/no question, p. 284 (**Kap. 1, I**); **dass**, p. 284 (**Kap. 9, I**); expressing wishes when buying, p. 284 (**Kap. 5, I**); time expressions, p. 284 (**Kap. 3, II**)
Dritte Stufe pp. 286–289	• Expressing surprise, agreement, and disagreement, p. 287 • Talking about plans, p. 288	• **Kein** used to negate a noun, p. 287 • The future tense with **werden**, p. 289	• Auto parts and options, p. 286	**Was für**, p. 287 (**Kap. 10, I**); agreeing and disagreeing, p. 287 (**Kap. 2, I**); **kein**, p. 287 (**Kap. 9, I**); **möchte**, p. 287 (**Kap. 3, I**); giving reasons, p. 287 (**Kap. 8, I**); expressing future events with present tense, p. 288 (**Kap. 7, I**); making plans, p. 288 (**Kap. 6, I**)

Zum Lesen pp. 280–281	Was läuft im Fernsehen?	**Reading Strategy** Predicting the content of a text

Mehr Grammatikübungen	**pp. 290–293**		
	Erste Stufe, pp. 290–291	Zweite Stufe, p. 292	Dritte Stufe, pp. 292–293

Review pp. 294–297	Anwendung, pp. 294–295 Zum Schreiben: Backing up opinions with facts (Writing a persuasive letter)	Kann ich's wirklich?, p. 296	Wortschatz, p. 297

CULTURE

- **Ein wenig Landeskunde:** Television companies in Germany, p. 278
- **Landeskunde:** Was machst du, um zu relaxen? p. 279
- Statistics on television programs and viewing habits, p. 282
- **Ein wenig Landeskunde:** Getting a driver's license in Germany, p. 288

Kapitel 10: Viele Interessen!
Chapter Resources

Lesson Planning
One-Stop Planner
Lesson Planner with Substitute Teacher Lesson Plans, pp. 47–51, 74
Student Make-Up Assignments
- Make-Up Assignment Copying Masters, Chapter 10

Listening and Speaking
TPR Storytelling Book, pp. 72–79
Listening Activities
- Student Response Forms for Listening Activities, pp. 75–77
- Additional Listening Activities 10-1 to 10-6, pp. 79–82
- Additional Listening Activities (song), p. 78
- Scripts and Answers, pp. 157–162

Video Guide
- Teaching Suggestions, pp. 64–65
- Activity Masters, pp. 66–68
- Scripts and Answers, pp. 102–105

Activities for Communication
- Communicative Activities, pp. 55–60
- Realia and Teaching Suggestions, pp. 110–113
- Situation Cards, pp. 141–142

Reading and Writing
Reading Strategies and Skills Handbook, Chapter 10
Lies mit mir! 2, Chapter 10
Übungsheft, pp. 109–120

Grammar
Grammatikheft, pp. 82–90
Grammar Tutor for Students of German, Chapter 10

Assessment
Testing Program
- Grammar and Vocabulary Quizzes, **Stufe** Quizzes, and Chapter Test, pp. 249–266
- Score Sheet, Scripts and Answers, pp. 267–274

Alternative Assessment Guide
- Portfolio Assessment, p. 27
- Performance Assessment, p. 41
- CD-ROM Assessment, p. 55

Student Make-Up Assignments
- Alternative Quizzes, Chapter 10

Online Activities
- Interaktive Spiele
- Internet Aktivitäten

Video Program
- Videocassette 4
- Videocassette 5 (captioned version)
- DVD Tutor, Disc 2

Audio Compact Discs
- Textbook Listening Activities, CD 10, Tracks 1–11
- Additional Listening Activities, CD 10, Tracks 17–23
- Assessment Items, CD 10, Tracks 12–16

Interactive CD-ROM Tutor, Disc 3

Teaching Transparencies
- Situations 10-1 to 10-2
- Vocabulary 10-A to 10-B
- Los geht's!
- Mehr Grammatikübungen Answers
- Grammatikheft Answers

Use the **One-Stop Planner CD-ROM** with Test Generator to aid in lesson planning and pacing.

For each chapter, the **One-Stop Planner** includes:
- Editable lesson plans with direct links to teaching resources
- Printable worksheets from resource books
- Direct launches to the HRW Internet activities
- Video and audio segments
- Test Generator
- Clip Art for vocabulary items

Kapitel 10: Viele Interessen!

Projects

Unsere Infomauer

Students will create a "wall of information" about the city of Berlin. The project should be done in English soon after you've begun Chapter 10 to allow the students time for research and revision. This project can be done individually or in pairs, depending on the number of topics and the size of your class. Final projects should be presented, collected, and attached to the "wall."

MATERIALS
✂ Students may need
- posterboard
- dictionaries
- travel books
- paper
- pencils
- encyclopedia

SUGGESTED TOPICS

Brandenburg Gate	Berlin Wall
Pergamonmuseum	Schloss Charlottenburg
Reichstag	Berlin Airlift
Kurfürstendamm	History of Berlin

SUGGESTED SEQUENCE

1. Students research the history of the topic of their choice using resources such as world reference books, guidebooks, periodicals, and almanacs.
2. Students give their project a title and begin compiling their materials.
3. Students organize their notes, materials, and any illustrations they want to use.
4. Students present their final project to the class.
5. All projects become part of the "wall," a piece of butcher paper long enough to display all projects.

GRADING THE PROJECT
Suggested point distribution (**total = 100 points**)
- Content (accuracy of information)......40
- Appearance (neatness and design).......30
- Correct language usage 30

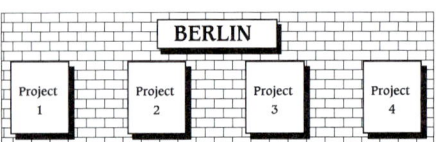

Games

Beschriftungen

This game will help students review automobile vocabulary.

Preparation Prepare a handout of a car with all the parts visible, but without labels.

Procedure Students may not use their books for this game, but may work with a partner. Give each pair a handout. When you give the signal, students begin to identify and label as many parts as they can. The team that first labels all the parts correctly wins.

Heiße Kartoffel

This game is a good vocabulary review for auditory learners.

Procedure Divide the class into small groups of three to five students. Have each group form a circle with their chairs. Provide each group with a potato or a small ball: **die heiße Kartoffel.** Start the game by calling out a word or expression from the **Wortschatz** on p. 297. The student in each group with the **Kartoffel** in his or her hand calls out a word that is associated with the one you just called out. For example, you call out "**Fernsehen,**" and the student answers "**die Sendung**" or "**das Programm.**" He or she then throws the **Kartoffel** to another member of his or her group. The person who catches the potato also has to think of a related word, and so on. If a student cannot think of another word or uses one inappropriately, he or she drops out of the game. The last person remaining in each group wins.

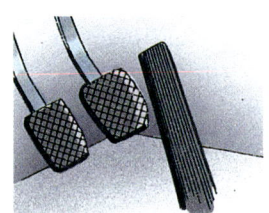

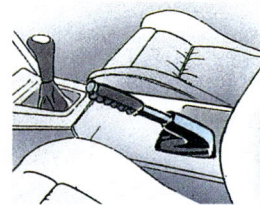

Storytelling

Mini-Geschichte

This story accompanies Teaching Transparency 10-1. Read the Mini-Geschichte to your students, or have them read the story using proper pronunciation and intonation. Using correct word order and punctuation, students should convert the story into a conversation to be role-played.

Mein Fernsehprofil

Ich sehe jeden Tag ungefähr zwei Stunden fern. Ich interessiere mich für Nachrichtensendungen und Diskussionen über Politik. Sportsendungen und Komödien sehe ich mir sehr selten an. Ich interessiere mich halt nicht für Sport, und Komödien finde ich langweilig. Manchmal schau ich mir Abenteuerfilme an, wenn sie spannend sind. So hab ich alle *Indiana Jones* Filme gesehen. Aber am liebsten schau ich mir Tiersendungen an, weil ich Tiere furchtbar gern mag.

Traditions

Hotel Adlon

Lorenz Adlon eröffnete 1907 am Pariser Platz das damals luxuriöseste Hotel der Welt. Kaiser Wilhelm II. floh von seinem Stadtschloss, um den Luxus im Hotel Adlon zu genießen: Elektrizität und fließendes warmes und kaltes Wasser. Zu den Gästen des Hotels gehörten Europas Könige, der Zar, der Maharadscha von Patiala, Edison, Ford, Rockefeller, Einstein und Charlie Chaplin. Marlene Dietrich soll hier entdeckt worden sein. Das Adlon wurde zum „offiziellen Hotel" der Olympischen Spiele von 1936. Ein Brand im Mai 1945 zerstörte das Hotel größtenteils. Als am 9. November 1989 die Mauer fiel, erhielt die Hotelkette Kempinski die Genehmigung für den Bau eines neuen Hotel Adlon an dem gleichen Ort, an dem das legendäre Hotel Adlon gestanden hatte. 1997 eröffnete Roman Herzog, der Bundespräsident Deutschlands, das neue Hotel. Zu den Gästen gehören Europas Adelige, Helmut Kohl, Gerhard Schröder, Bill Clinton, Henry Kissinger, Placido Domingo, Genesis, Claudia Schiffer usw. Die Übernachtung in der Brandenburger Tor Suite kostet ungefähr 3800 Euro.

*Ask students to research in the library or on the Internet the life and politics of **Kaiser Wilhelm II**. Students should present their research to the class.*

Rezept

Berliner Buletten
Für 4 Personen

Zutaten

g=Gramm

- 250 g Rinderhackfleisch, mager (Beefsteakhack, Tatar)
- 250 g Schweinemett
- 1 Brötchen, im Wasser eingeweicht, gut ausgedrückt (ersatzweise 50 g altbackenes Weißbrot)
- 1 Ei
- 1 große Zwiebel, gewürfelt, in Butter leicht angedünstet)
- Salz
- Pfeffer
- Butterschmalz zum Braten (oder Schweineschmalz oder Öl)

Zubereitung

Das Hackfleisch mit dem zerpflückten Brötchen, dem Ei, der Zwiebel und den Gewürzen gut mischen und daraus 8 gleichgroße Kugeln formen. Die Kugel etwas flachdrücken und dann in heißem Butterschmalz auf beiden Seiten langsam auf mittlerer Hitze braun und knusprig braten. Sie können heiß oder kalt serviert werden.

Wenn sie heiß zu Kartoffeln und Gemüse serviert werden, läßt man im Bratfett noch Ringe von 1 bis 2 Zwiebeln goldbraun werden. Kalt isst man sie mit Brötchen ("Knüppel") und Mostrich. Durch die Verwendung von magerem (schierem) Rindfleisch und fettem Schweinefleisch ("Pastetenmischung" aus Frankreich, von den Hugenotten mitgebracht!) bleiben die Buletten besonderes saftig, auch wenn sie kalt sind.

Kapitel 10: Viele Interessen!
Technology

Videocassette 4, 5 (captioned version)
DVD Tutor, Disc 2
See Video Guide, pages 63–68

DVD/Video

Los geht's! • Mensch, zieh die Handbremse an!

Andreas and his friend Ismar are doing their homework. Andreas's mother reminds him that he has to clean out the car today, and so the boys take the vacuum cleaner to do that. Ismar admires the car, checks the oil, and generally expresses his interest in cars. Andreas gets behind the wheel, and the car starts to roll forward.

Landeskunde

Was machst du, um zu relaxen?
People of various ages from various parts of Germany discuss what they do to relax.

Interactive CD-ROM Tutor

Activity	Activity Type	Pupil's Edition Reference
1. Wortschatz	Wort und Bild Erfahren/Wählen	p. 276
2. Grammatik	Was fehlt?	p. 277
3. Wortschatz	Merkspiel	p. 282
4. Wortschatz	Merkspiel	p. 286
5. So sagt man das!	Was ist richtig?	pp. 283, 284, 287, 288
6. Grammatik	Was fehlt?	p. 289
Landeskunde	Was machst du, um zu relaxen? Was ist richtig?	p. 279
Zum Sprechen	Guided recording	pp. 294-295
Zum Schreiben	Guided writing	pp. 294-295

Teacher Management System

Launch the program, type "admin" in the password area, and press RETURN. Log on to www.hrw.com/CDROMTUTOR for a detailed explanation of the Teacher Management System.

Fortsetzung

It turns out that there was a small disaster when the car rolled forward; it rolled over the vacuum cleaner hose, and the plastic attachment was broken. Andreas doesn't know what to tell his mother, but Ismar offers to run home and get the attachment from their vacuum cleaner at home, because they have the same model.

Videoclips
- **The new Opel Corsa®** (passenger car)
- **SFB1** (radio station)
- **SFB1** (radio station)
- **Sat 1 TV for Nature** (television program)

DVD Tutor

The *DVD Tutor* contains all material from the *Video Program* as described above. German captions are available for use at your discretion for all sections of the video. The *DVD Tutor* also provides a variety of video-based activities that assess students' understanding of **Los geht's!, Fortsetzung,** and **Landeskunde,** as well as the new **Grammatik im Kontext** presentations.

> The *DVD Tutor* may be used on any DVD video player connected to a television or video monitor.

Go.Online!

Premier Online Edition

The Premier Online Edition for Komm mit! allows students access to their textbooks anytime, anywhere.
- Audio at point of use
- Additional practice activities
- Self-test activities
- Online reference tools
- Entire Video Program
- Interactive Notebook

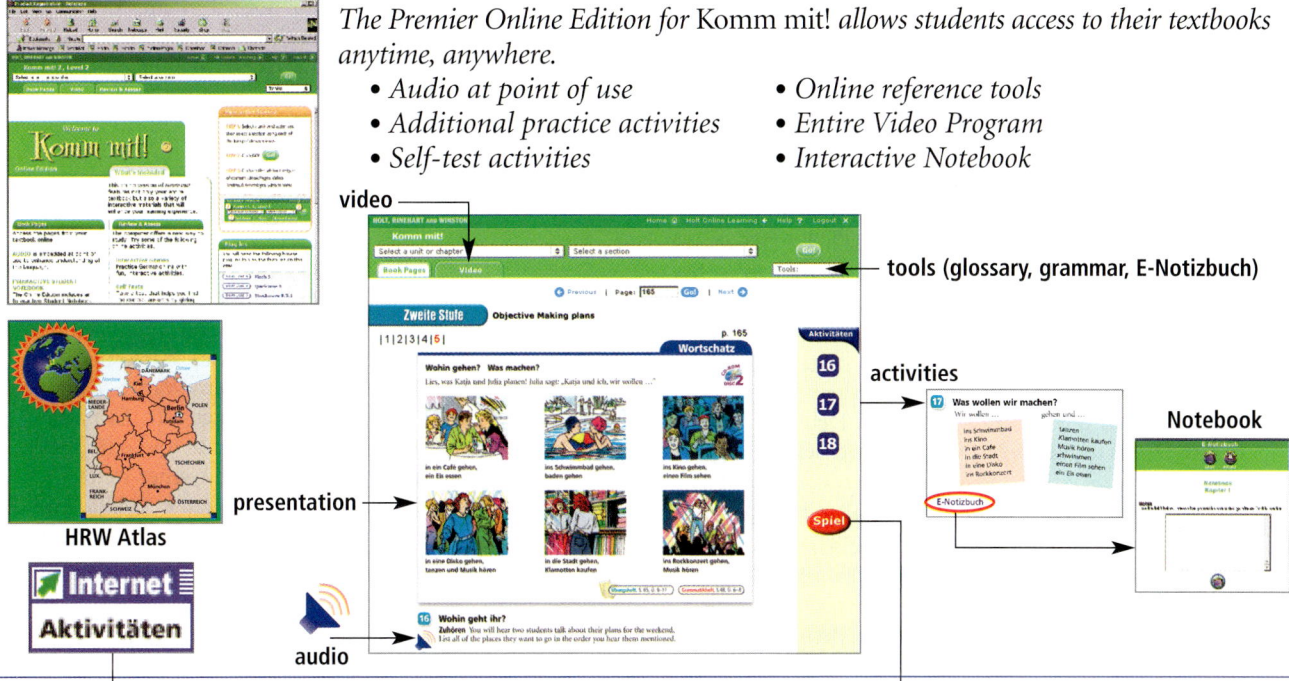

HRW Atlas

Internet Aktivitäten

These guided internet activities include a worksheet and pre-selected and pre-screened authentic web sites from the German-speaking countries. You can use these activities

- to help students develop research skills in the target language
- to introduce students to authentic cultural information
- as a project

Interaktive Spiele

You can use the interactive activities in this chapter
- to practice grammar, vocabulary, and chapter functions
- as homework
- as an assessment option
- as a self-test
- to prepare for the Chapter Test

Webprojekt Have students visit the site of an electronics shop in Germany and choose a TV. They should report on the brand name of the TV and its accessories, technical data, and price. Encourage students to exchange useful Web sites with their classmates. Have students document their sources by referencing the names and URLs of all the sites they consulted.

STANDARDS: 1.2, 1.3, 3.2, 5.1   KAPITEL 10   TECHNOLOGY   269F

Kapitel 10: Viele Interessen!
Textbook Listening Activities Scripts

Erste Stufe

6 p. 275

VERONIKA Welche Sendungen ich sehe? Tja, eigentlich gucke ich außer Sportsendungen fast gar nichts. Für Tennis interessiere ich mich am meisten. Bei den Australian Open habe ich sogar ganz früh morgens vor dem Fernseher gesessen, um ja nichts zu verpassen. Ich spiel selber Tennis im Verein, hier bei uns in Leimen. Das ist übrigens der gleiche Club, in dem auch Boris Becker angefangen hat.

AXEL Ich guck mir zwar auch mal ab und zu Sportsendungen an, weil ich mich für Fußball interessiere, aber eigentlich sehe ich am liebsten spannende Krimis. Am besten gefallen mir die alten Filme mit Sherlock Holmes. Es macht mir total Spaß, selbst Detektiv zu spielen und die Fälle vor dem Fernseher zu lösen.

PATRICK Also, wenn ich Fernsehen gucke, dann will ich mich in erster Linie informieren. Deswegen gucke ich am liebsten die Nachrichten und das Auslandsmagazin. Ich seh auch gern mal eine Talkshow, in der Politiker über verschiedene aktuelle Themen diskutieren. Besonders vor den Bundestagswahlen! Der Meinungsaustausch ist dann fast so spannend wie ein Krimi!

TINA Ja, also die Nachrichten schau ich mir natürlich auch fast jeden Tag an, aber eigentlich nur wegen dem Wetterbericht. Ich fahr nämlich jeden Tag mit dem Rad zur Schule, und deswegen interessiert es mich, wie das Wetter jeden Tag wird. Na ja, und außer dem Wetterbericht schaue ich auch unheimlich gern Tier- und Natursendungen an. Wir wohnen ja hier mitten im Industriegebiet, da ist nicht viel los mit Natur und so. Deswegen gefallen mir alle Sendungen, die mit der Natur oder mit Tieren zu tun haben.

Answers to Activity 6
1. Veronika: Sportsendungen/Tennis, weil sie selber Tennis spielt
2. Axel: Sportsendungen, weil er sich für Fußball interessiert; Kriminalfilme, weil er selber gern Detektiv spielt
3. Patrick: Nachrichten/Auslandsmagazin, weil er sich informieren will; Talkshow/Politikerdiskussionen, weil er sie spannend findet
4. Tina: Nachrichten, weil sie den Wetterbericht sehen will; Tier- und Natursendungen, weil es nicht viel Natur in ihrer Umgebung gibt

Zweite Stufe

15 p. 283

ROLF Also, ich bin total begeistert von meiner neuen Anlage. Du musst sie dir so vorstellen: die komplette Anlage ist in einem ganz tollen Fernseh- und Videowagen im Wohnzimmer untergebracht. Der Fernseh- und Videowagen hat vier Ablagefächer. Also, auf dem Regalfach ganz unten ist das Videogerät. Direkt darüber, also im zweiten Regalfach von unten, da stehen links alle meine Videokassetten und auf der rechten Seite die CDs. Auf dem zweiten Ablagefach von oben stehen der CD-Spieler und über dem CD-Spieler das Radio mit doppeltem Kassettendeck, alles Stereo natürlich! Ja, und ganz oben auf dem Wagen, da habe ich das Farbfernsehgerät hingestellt. Es hat achtundvierzig Programme und eine super Bildqualität! Auf dem Fernseher steht natürlich die Zimmerantenne. Ach ja, und links außen am Fernseh- und Videowagen, da ist ein Haken für den Kopfhörer. Also, meine neue Anlage sieht einfach phantastisch aus!

Answers to Activity 15
bottom shelf: video
second shelf from bottom: videocassettes on left side; CDs on right side
second shelf from top: CD player and radio/cassette deck
top shelf: TV
on top of TV: antenna

Dritte Stufe

24 p. 287

TILL Hallo Silke! Komm steig ein!

SILKE Ach, hallo Till! Das ist ja nett von dir, dass du angehalten hast. Kannst du mich ein Stück mitnehmen?

TILL Ja klar! Wo musst du denn hin?

SILKE Ich muss in die Werkstatt, mein Auto abholen. Es war kaputt. Hoffentlich läuft es jetzt wieder!

TILL Was war denn kaputt?

SILKE Ach, irgendwas am Motor! Und die Scheibenwischer haben auch nicht mehr funktioniert. Na ja. — Aber sag mal, das ist ja ein toller Wagen, den du hier fährst. Ist der neu?

TILL Ja, ich hab ihn erst letzte Woche bekommen. Schau mal, er hat ganz tolle Extras: Automatik und Klimaanlage …

The following scripts are for the listening activities found in the *Pupil's Edition*. For Student Response Forms, see *Listening Activities,* pages 75–78. To provide students with additional listening practice, see *Listening Activities,* pages 79–82.

For resource information, see the **One-Stop Planner CD-ROM,** Disc 3.

SILKE Eine Klimaanlage hätte ich auch gern! Aber dafür hat mein Auto wenigstens ein Schiebedach.

TILL Hier, Silke, hör dir mal den Sound von meinem Stereo-Radio an! Toll, was?

SILKE Spitze! Der Sound ist viel besser als bei meinem Stereo. Du, Till, die Sitzschoner sehen ja toll aus! Gehören die zur Grundausstattung?

TILL Nee! Die hab ich extra dazubestellt, genauso wie die Rallyestreifen außen. Hast du nicht auch Rallyestreifen an deinem Auto?

SILKE Nee! Nur so'n paar blöde Aufkleber hinten. Aber mein Bruder hat mir vor ein paar Tagen ganz tolle Breitreifen ans Auto gemacht. Sieht echt super aus!

TILL Ja, Breitreifen find ich auch toll! Aber die waren so teuer. Da hab ich lieber die Servolenkung als Extra genommen.

SILKE Was? Auch noch Servolenkung? Du, lässt du mich mal mit deinem Auto fahren?

TILL Ja, gern! Ich halte gleich da drüben an der Ecke an!

Answers to Activity 24
Stereo-Radio; Tills Auto: Automatik, Klimaanlage, Sitzschoner, Rallyestreifen, Servolenkung; Silkes Auto: Schiebedach, Aufkleber, Breitreifen

27 p. 288

SVEN Du, Jürgen, gestern habe ich einen tollen Abenteuerfilm im Fernsehen gesehen! Der Film hat von einem Rennfahrer gehandelt, der sich auf den Grand Prix in Monte Carlo vorbereitet hat. Der Film war echt super! Nächste Woche kommt der zweite Teil. Den werde ich mir bestimmt ansehen.

JÜRGEN Ja, genau! Den Film hab ich gestern auch gesehen. Der war echt Klasse! Hast du die tollen Autos im Film gesehen? Super Sportflitzer mit 5-Gang-Getriebe, Breitreifen und Rallyestreifen! Einfach sagenhaft! So ein Auto zu haben, Mensch, Sven, das wäre mein Traum!

SVEN Hm, nicht schlecht. Aber damit kann man ja nicht im normalen Straßenverkehr rumfahren!

JÜRGEN Da hast du Recht! Aber ich werde mir trotzdem einen ganz tollen Sportwagen mit Schiebedach kaufen, wenn ich 'nen Job habe und Geld verdiene.

SVEN Hast du gestern in den Nachrichten dieses neue Solarmobil gesehen? Find ich echt stark, so ein Auto, das nur mit Sonnenenergie betrieben wird!

JÜRGEN Ja, Autos mit Sonnenenergie — das ist ein tolles Konzept, was?

SVEN Also, ich find das echt super! Nur leider gibt es noch nicht so viele Autos damit! Aber in ein paar Jahren ist die Technologie bestimmt so weit. Dann werde ich mir ein Solarmobil kaufen.

Answers to Activity 27
Sven: nächste Woche den zweiten Teil des Films gucken; ein Solarmobil kaufen
Jürgen: einen Sportwagen kaufen

Anwendung

3 p. 294

PETER Klasse! Heute kann sich jeder Krimi-Fan freuen! Es kommen gleich zwei Krimis heute Abend!

FRAU BAUER So? Was kommt denn?

PETER Also, wir können erstmal um sechs Uhr *Mord ist ihr Hobby* mit Angela Lansbury sehen und später dann um acht Uhr den Agatha Christie-Film. Heute soll er besonders spannend sein!

HERR BAUER Ja, will denn keiner heute die Nachrichten sehen?

ANKE Doch, na klar, Vati! Aber die kommen doch genau dazwischen, um sieben Uhr! Das passt doch prima!

FRAU BAUER Ja, heißt das etwa, dass wir heute den ganzen Abend vor dem Fernseher verbringen? Das kann doch nicht euer Ernst sein! Lasst uns lieber mal was anderes zusammen unternehmen!

ANKE Was schlägst du denn vor, Mutti?

FRAU BAUER Lasst uns doch mal wieder einen Spaziergang machen und zum See runter gehen.

HERR BAUER Ja, das ist eine gute Idee! Gleich nach dem Agatha-Christie-Krimi um neun können wir doch einen schönen Abendspaziergang machen!

PETER Ja, aber spätestens um halb elf müssen wir wieder zu Hause sein!

ANKE Wieso das denn?

PETER Weil ich dann unbedingt die Fußballberichte aus der ersten Liga sehen will!

Answers to Activity 3
18 Uhr: RTL; 19 Uhr: 3SAT; 20 Uhr: SW3; 22.30 Uhr: SAT1

Kapitel 10: Viele Interessen!
Suggested Lesson Plans 50-Minute Schedule

Day 1

LOCATION OPENER 15 min.
- Present Location Opener, pp. 266–269
- Using the Almanac and Map, ATE, p. 265A
- Show **Berlin** Video
- Do Viewing and Post-viewing Activities, Video Guide, p. 62

CHAPTER OPENER 5 min.
- Building Context, ATE, p. 269M
- Background Information, ATE, p. 269M

LOS GEHT'S! 25 min.
- Preteaching Vocabulary, ATE, p. 269N
- Teaching Suggestions, ATE, p. 269N
- Have students read **Los geht's!**, pp. 272–273
- Teaching Suggestions, Video Guide, p. 64
- Show **Los geht's!** Video

Wrap-Up 5 min.
- Students respond to questions about getting a driver's license

Homework Options
Pupil's Edition, p. 274, Comprehension Acts. 1–5
Übungsheft, p. 109, Act. 1

Day 2

ERSTE STUFE
Quick Review 10 min.
- Bell Work, ATE, p. 269O
- Check homework, Übungsheft, p. 109, Act. 1

Reading Selection, p. 275 10 min.
- Language Note, ATE, p. 269O
- Read **Wer guckt was?**, p. 275
- Answer questions 1–6, p. 275
- Play Audio CD for Activity 6, p. 275

Wortschatz, p. 276 15 min.
- Presenting **Wortschatz**, ATE, p. 269O
- Teaching Transparency 10-1
- Do Activity 7, p. 276

So sagt man das!, p. 276 10 min.
- Presenting **So sagt man das!**, ATE, p. 269O
- Do Activity 8, p. 276

Wrap-Up 5 min.
- Students respond to questions about what kinds of TV programs interest them

Homework Options
Grammatikheft, p. 82, Act. 1
Übungsheft, p. 110, Acts. 1–2

Day 3

ERSTE STUFE
Quick Review 10 min.
- Check homework, Übungsheft, p. 110, Acts. 1–2

Grammatik, p. 277 25 min.
- Presenting **Grammatik**, ATE, p. 269P
- Do Activities 9 and 10, p. 277
- Do Activities 2–4, pp. 82–83, Grammatikheft
- Do Activities 11, 12, and 13, p. 278

Ein wenig Landeskunde, p. 278 10 min.
- Presenting **Ein wenig Landeskunde**, ATE, p. 269P

Wrap-Up 5 min.
- Students respond to questions about German TV and TV channels

Homework Options
Übungsheft, pp. 111–112, Acts. 3–6

Day 4

ERSTE STUFE
Quick Review 10 min.
- Check homework, Übungsheft, pp. 111–112, Acts. 3–6

LANDESKUNDE 20 min.
- Pre-viewing Suggestion, Video Guide, p. 64
- Teaching Suggestion, ATE, p. 269Q
- Show **Landeskunde** Video
- Do Activities A and B, p. 279
- Do **Landeskunde** Activity, Interactive CD-ROM

Quiz Review 15 min.
- Do Additional Listening Activities 10-1 and 10-2, p. 79
- Do Communicative Activity 10-1, pp. 55–56

Wrap-Up 5 min.
- Students respond to questions about what they do to relax

Homework Options
Übungsheft, p. 113, Acts. 1–3
Mehr Grammatikübungen, Erste Stufe

Day 5

ERSTE STUFE
Quick Review 10 min.
- Check homework, **Mehr Grammatikübungen, Erste Stufe**

Quiz 20 min.
- Quiz 10-1A or 10-1B

ZUM LESEN 15 min.
- Language Notes, ATE, p. 269R
- Career Path, ATE, p. 269S
- Present **Lesestrategie**, p. 280
- Do Activities 1–3, pp. 280–281

Wrap-Up 5 min.
- Students respond to questions about what programs are on German TV

Homework Options
Pupil's Edition, p. 281, Acts. 4–8
Übungsheft, p. 114, Acts. 1–6

Day 6

ZWEITE STUFE
Quick Review 10 min.
- Return and review Quiz 10-1
- Bell Work, ATE, p. 269S
- Check homework, Übungsheft, p. 114, Acts. 1–6

Reading Selection, p. 282 15 min.
- Teacher Notes, ATE, p. 269T
- Do Activity 14, p. 282

Wortschatz, p. 282 10 min.
- Presenting **Wortschatz**, ATE, p. 269T
- Teaching Transparency 10-A
- Play Audio CD for Activity 15, p. 283

So sagt man das!, p. 283 10 min.
- Presenting **So sagt man das!**, ATE, p. 269T
- Do Activity 17, p. 283

Wrap-Up 5 min.
- Students respond to questions about asking for and giving permission

Homework Options
Pupil's Edition, p. 283, Act. 16
Grammatikheft, p. 84, Acts. 5–6
Übungsheft, p. 115, Act. 1

One-Stop Planner CD-ROM

For alternative lesson plans by chapter section, to create your own customized plans, or to preview all resources available for this chapter, use the **One-Stop Planner CD-ROM**, Disc 3.

 For additional homework suggestions, see activities accompanied by this symbol throughout the chapter.

Day 7
ZWEITE STUFE
Quick Review 10 min.
- Check homework, Pupil's Edition, p. 283, Act. 16

Ein wenig Grammatik / So sagt man das!, pp. 283–284 20 min.
- Presenting **Ein wenig Grammatik**, ATE, p. 269T
- Do Activity 7, p. 85, Grammatikheft
- Presenting **So sagt man das!**, ATE, p. 269T
- Do Activities 18, 19, and 20, p. 284

Wortschatz / Ein wenig Grammatik, p. 285 15 min.
- Presenting **Wortschatz / Ein wenig Grammatik**, ATE, p. 269U
- Do Activities 21, 22, and 23, p. 285

Wrap-Up 5 min.
- Students respond to questions about what programs are on German TV on different days of the week

Homework Options
Grammatikheft, pp. 85–86, Acts. 8–11
Übungsheft, pp. 115–117, Acts. 2–6

Day 8
ZWEITE STUFE
Quick Review 10 min.
- Check homework, Grammatikheft, pp. 85–86, Acts. 8–11

Quiz Review 20 min.
- Do **Mehr Grammatikübungen, Zweite Stufe**
- Do Additional Listening Activities 10-3 and 10-4, pp. 80–81

Quiz 20 min.
- Quiz 10-2A or 10-2B

Homework Options
Internet Aktivitäten, see ATE, p. 269F

Day 9
DRITTE STUFE
Quick Review 10 min.
- Return and review Quiz 10-2
- Bell Work, ATE, p. 269V

Reading Selection, p. 286 10 min.
- Language Notes, ATE, p. 269V
- Read **Autofahren kostet viel Geld!**, p. 286

Wortschatz, p. 286 15 min.
- Presenting **Wortschatz**, ATE, p. 269V
- Teaching Transparencies 10-2, 10-B
- Play Audio CD for Activity 24, p. 287
- Do Activity 25, p. 287

So sagt man das! / Ein wenig Grammatik, p. 287 10 min.
- Presenting **So sagt man das!**, ATE, p. 269V
- Present **Ein wenig Grammatik**, p. 287
- Do Activity 26, p. 287

Wrap-Up 5 min.
- Students respond to questions about car parts and accessories

Homework Options
Grammatikheft, pp. 87–88, Acts. 12–16
Übungsheft, p. 118, Acts. 1–2

Day 10
DRITTE STUFE
Quick Review 10 min.
- Check homework, Grammatikheft, pp. 87–88, Acts. 12–16

Ein wenig Landeskunde / So sagt man das!, p. 288 15 min.
- Presenting **Ein wenig Landeskunde**, ATE, p. 269W
- Presenting **So sagt man das!**, ATE, p. 269W
- Play Audio CD for Activity 27, p. 288
- Do Activity 28, p. 288

Grammatik, p. 289 20 min.
- Presenting **Grammatik**, ATE, p. 269W
- Do Activities 29, 30, and 31, p. 289

Wrap-Up 5 min.
- Students respond to questions about what they will do in the future

Homework Options
Übungsheft, pp. 119–120, Acts. 3–7
Grammatikheft, pp. 89–90, Acts. 17–19

Day 11
DRITTE STUFE
Quick Review 10 min.
- Check homework, Übungsheft, pp. 119–120, Acts. 3–7

Quiz Review 15 min.
- Do **Mehr Grammatikübungen, Dritte Stufe**
- Do Communicative Activity 10-3, pp. 59–60
- Do Additional Listening Activity 10-6, p. 82

Quiz 20 min.
- Quiz 10-3A or 10-3B

Wrap-Up 5 min.
- Students respond to **Kann ich's wirklich?** questions

Homework Options
Pupil's Edition, p. 295, Act. 5, **Zum Schreiben**

Day 12
ANWENDUNG
Quick Review 15 min.
- Return and review Quiz 10-3
- Students present **Zum Schreiben** compositions

ANWENDUNG 15 min.
- Do **Anwendung** Activities 1–4 and 6, pp. 294–295

Chapter Review 20 min.
- Review chapter functions, vocabulary, and grammar; choose from **Mehr Grammatikübungen,** Grammar Tutor for Students of German, Activities for Communication, Listening Activities, Interactive CD-ROM Tutor, or **Interaktive Spiele**

Homework Options
Study for Chapter Test

Assessment
Test, Chapter 10 45 min.
- Administer Chapter 10 Test. Select from Testing Program, Alternative Assessment Guide, or Test Generator.

KAPITEL 10 SUGGESTED LESSON PLANS • 50-MINUTE SCHEDULE

Kapitel 10: Viele Interessen!
Suggested Lesson Plans 90-Minute Schedule

Block 1

LOCATION OPENER 15 min.
- Present Location Opener, pp. 266–269
- Using the Almanac and Map, ATE, p. 265A
- Show **Berlin** Video
- Do Viewing and Post-viewing Activities, Video Guide, p. 62

CHAPTER OPENER 10 min.
- Building Context, ATE, p. 269M
- Background Information, ATE, p. 269M

LOS GEHT'S! 25 min.
- Preteaching Vocabulary, ATE, p. 269N
- Teaching Suggestions, ATE, p. 269N
- Have students read **Los geht's!**, pp. 272–273
- Teaching Suggestions, Video Guide, p. 64
- Show **Los geht's!** Video
- Do Activity 1, p. 109, Übungsheft

ERSTE STUFE

Reading Selection, p. 275 15 min.
- Language Note, ATE, p. 269O
- Read **Wer guckt was?**, p. 275
- Answer questions 1–6, p. 275
- Play Audio CD for Activity 6, p. 275

Wortschatz, p. 276 10 min.
- Presenting **Wortschatz**, ATE, p. 269O
- Teaching Transparency 10-1
- Do Activity 7, p. 276

So sagt man das!, p. 276 10 min.
- Presenting **So sagt man das!**, ATE p. 269O
- Do Activity 8, p. 276

Wrap-Up 5 min.
- Students respond to questions about what kinds of TV programs interest them

Homework Options
Pupil's Edition, p. 274, Comprehension Acts. 1–5
Grammatikheft, p. 82, Act. 1
Übungsheft, p. 110, Acts. 1–2

Block 2

ERSTE STUFE
Quick Review 10 min.
- Check homework, Übungsheft, p. 110, Acts. 1–2

Grammatik, p. 277 30 min.
- Presenting **Grammatik**, ATE, p. 269P
- Do Activities 9 and 10, p. 277
- Do Activities 2–4, pp. 82–83, Grammatikheft
- Do Activities 11, 12, and 13, p. 278

Ein wenig Landeskunde, p. 278 10 min.
- Presenting **Ein wenig Landeskunde**, ATE, p. 269P

LANDESKUNDE 20 min.
- Pre-viewing Suggestion, Video Guide, p. 64
- Teaching Suggestion, ATE, p. 269Q
- Show **Landeskunde** Video
- Do Activities A and B, p. 279
- Do **Landeskunde** Activity, Interactive CD-ROM

Quiz Review 15 min.
- Do Additional Listening Activities 10-1 and 10-2, p. 79
- Do Communicative Activity 10-1, pp. 55–56

Wrap-Up 5 min.
- Students respond to questions about what they do to relax

Homework Options
Übungsheft, pp. 111–112, Acts. 3–6; p. 113, Acts. 1–3
Mehr Grammatikübungen, Erste Stufe

Block 3

ERSTE STUFE
Quick Review 10 min.
- Check homework, **Mehr Grammatikübungen**, Erste Stufe

Quiz 20 min.
- Quiz 10-1A or 10-1B

ZUM LESEN 15 min.
- Language Notes, ATE, p. 269R
- Career Path, ATE, p. 269S
- Present **Lesestrategie**, p. 280
- Do Activities 1–3, pp. 280–281

ZWEITE STUFE
Reading Selection, p. 282 20 min.
- Teacher Notes, ATE, p. 269T
- Do Activity 14, p. 282

Wortschatz, p. 282 10 min.
- Presenting **Wortschatz**, ATE, p. 269T
- Teaching Transparency 10-A
- Play Audio CD for Activity 15, p. 283

So sagt man das!, p. 283 10 min.
- Presenting **So sagt man das!**, ATE, p. 269T
- Do Activity 17, p. 283

Wrap-Up 5 min.
- Students respond to questions about asking for and giving permission

Homework Options
Pupil's Edition, p. 281, Acts. 4–8; p. 283, Act. 16
Grammatikheft, p. 84, Acts. 5–6

One-Stop Planner CD-ROM

For alternative lesson plans by chapter section, to create your own customized plans, or to preview all resources available for this chapter, use the **One-Stop Planner CD-ROM**, Disc 3.

 For additional homework suggestions, see activities accompanied by this symbol throughout the chapter.

Block 4

ZWEITE STUFE

Quick Review 15 min.
- Check homework, Pupil's Edition, p. 281, Acts. 4–8

Ein wenig Grammatik / So sagt man das!, pp. 283–284 25 min.
- Presenting **Ein wenig Grammatik**, ATE, p. 269T
- Do Activity 7, p. 85, Grammatikheft
- Presenting **So sagt man das!**, ATE, p. 269T
- Do Activities 18, 19, and 20, p. 248
- Do Activity 8, p. 85, Grammatikheft

Wortschatz / Ein wenig Grammatik, p. 285 25 min.
- Presenting **Wortschatz / Ein wenig Grammatik**, ATE, p. 269U
- Do Activities 21, 22, and 23, p. 285
- Do Activities 10-11, p. 86, Grammatikheft

Quiz Review 20 min.
- Do **Mehr Grammatikübungen**, Zweite Stufe
- Do Additional Listening Activities 10-3 and 10-4, pp. 80–81

Wrap-Up 5 min.
- Students respond to questions about what programs are on German TV on different days of the week

Homework Options
Grammatikheft, p. 86, Act. 9
Übungsheft, pp. 115–117, Acts. 1–6
Internet Aktivitäten, see ATE, p. 269F

Block 5

ZWEITE STUFE

Quick Review 10 min.
- Check homework, Übungsheft, pp. 115–117, Acts. 1–6

Quiz 20 min.
- Quiz 10-2A or 10-2B

DRITTE STUFE

Reading Selection, p. 286 10 min.
- Language Notes, ATE, p. 269V
- Read **Autofahren kostet viel Geld!**, p. 286

Wortschatz, p. 286 15 min.
- Presenting **Wortschatz**, ATE, p. 269V
- Teaching Transparencies 10-2, 10-B
- Play Audio CD for Activity 24, p. 287
- Do Activity 25, p. 287

So sagt man das! / Ein wenig Grammatik, p. 287 10 min.
- Presenting **So sagt man das!**, ATE, p. 269V
- Present **Ein wenig Grammatik**, p. 287
- Do Activity 26, p. 287

Ein wenig Landeskunde / So sagt man das!, p. 288 20 min.
- Presenting **Ein wenig Landeskunde**, ATE, p. 269W
- Presenting **So sagt man das!**, ATE, p. 269W
- Play Audio CD for Activity 27, p. 288
- Do Activity 28, p. 288

Wrap-Up 5 min.
- Students respond to questions about car parts and accessories

Homework Options
Grammatikheft, pp. 87–88, Acts. 12–16
Übungsheft, p. 118, Acts. 1–2
Interaktive Spiele, see ATE, p. 269F

Block 6

DRITTE STUFE

Quick Review 15 min.
- Return and review Quiz 10-2
- Check homework, Übungsheft, p. 118, Acts. 1–2

Grammatik, p. 289 25 min.
- Presenting **Grammatik**, ATE, p. 269W
- Do Activities 17–19, pp. 89–90, Grammatikheft
- Do Activities 29, 30 and 31, p. 289

Quiz Review 10 min.
- Do **Mehr Grammatikübungen**, Dritte Stufe
- Do Communicative Activity 10-3, pp. 59–60

Quiz 20 min.
- Quiz 10-3A or 10-3B

ANWENDUNG 15 min.
- Do **Anwendung** Activities 1–6, pp. 294–295

Wrap-Up 5 min.
- Students respond to **Kann ich's wirklich?** questions

Homework Options
Pupil's Edition, p. 296, **Kann ich's wirklich?**
Übungsheft, pp. 119–120, Acts. 3–7
Study for Chapter Test

Block 7

ANWENDUNG

Quick Review 15 min.
- Return and review Quiz 10-3
- Check homework, **Kann ich's wirklich?**, p. 296

Chapter Review 30 min.
- Review chapter functions, vocabulary, and grammar; choose from **Mehr Grammatikübungen**, Grammar Tutor for Students of German, Activities for Communication, Listening Activities, Interactive CD-ROM Tutor, or **Interaktive Spiele**
- Review test format and provide sample test items for students

Test, Chapter 10 45 min.
- Administer Chapter 10 Test. Select from Testing Program, Alternative Assessment Guide, or Test Generator.

KAPITEL 10 SUGGESTED LESSON PLANS • 90-MINUTE SCHEDULE

Kapitel 10: Viele Interessen!
Teaching Suggestions, pages 270–297

PAGES 270–271

CHAPTER OPENER

Pacing Tips
The **Erste Stufe** focuses on German television. Students learn about **wo-** and **da-** compounds on p. 277. In the **Zweite Stufe**, the functions of 'asking for and giving permission' and 'asking for information and expressing an assumption' are introduced, again in conjunction with television. The **Dritte Stufe** centers around cars and car parts. The future tense with **werden** occurs on p. 289. Because the three **Stufen** are similar in length and the amount of material presented, you will probably spend about the same amount of time teaching each one. For Lesson Plans and timing suggestions, see pages 269I–269L.

Meeting the Standards
Communication
- Asking about and expressing interest, p. 276
- Asking for and giving permission, p. 283
- Asking for information and expressing an assumption, p. 284
- Expressing surprise, agreement, and disagreement, p. 287
- Taking about plans, p. 288

Cultures
- Ein wenig Landeskunde, p. 278
- Landeskunde, p. 279
- Ein wenig Landeskunde, p. 288
- Language Note, p. 269O
- Language Notes, p. 269V

Connections
- Music Connection, p. 269P
- Language Note, p. 269R
- Music Connection, p. 269T

Comparisons
- Language-to-Language, p. 269Q
- Multicultural Connection, p. 269Q
- Background Information, p. 269W

Communities
- Background Information, p. 269M
- Family Link, p. 269Q
- Career Path, p. 269S

For resource information, see the **One-Stop Planner CD-ROM**, Disc 3.

Building Context
Conduct a survey in German on your students' television viewing habits. Find out approximately how many hours per day or per week they watch TV. Write the information on the board and discuss it with students.

Cultures and Communities
Background Information
Students already know from Level 1 that the German school day is shorter than the American school day. Most German students are home by 12:30 or 1:00. Since after-school activities are not part of the school curriculum in Germany, students participate in a variety of other leisure time activities and often join clubs or organizations.

Communication for All Students
Visual Learners
Ask students to create a mini-story surrounding the photo. Have one student begin with what he or she thinks the boys are talking about and what their plan might be. Let other students build on what the previous student said. Students should not repeat any information, but rather try to add to the story in a creative way.

CHAPTER SEQUENCE

Los geht's!	p. 272
Erste Stufe	p. 275
Landeskunde	p. 279
Zum Lesen	p. 280
Zweite Stufe	p. 282
Dritte Stufe	p. 286
Mehr Grammatikübungen	p. 290
Anwendung	p. 294
Kann ich's wirklich?	p. 296
Wortschatz	p. 297

269M   CHAPTER OPENER   KAPITEL 10   STANDARDS: 1.3

LOS GEHT'S!

Teaching Resources
pp. 272–274

PRINT
- Lesson Planner, p. 47
- Video Guide, pp. 63–64, 66
- Übungsheft, p. 109

MEDIA
- One-Stop Planner
- Video Program
  Los geht's!
  Videocassette 4, 10:32–17:04
  Videocassette 5 (captioned version),
  56:20–1:02:51
  Fortsetzung
  Videocassette 4, 17:07–18:50
  Videocassette 5 (captioned version),
  1:02:42–1:04:36
- DVD Tutor, Disc 2
- Audio Compact Discs, CD10, Trs. 1–2
- Los geht's! Transparencies

PAGES 272–273

Los geht's! Transparencies

Preteaching Vocabulary

Activating Prior Knowledge
Have students identify the setting for **Los geht's!** and what Andreas and Ismar are doing. Why does Ismar say: ❷ Ich meine, wir sind müde. Machen wir mal eine kleine Pause!? Ask students if they remember a similar situation from a previous chapter (**Los geht's!** of **Kapitel 6**). Then ask students for the meaning of the word **Fernseher** and have them list related compound words that occur (❷❸❺ im Fernsehen, Fernsehmagazin, Fernbedienung, Fernsehsendungen). What do these compound words mean? Finally, have students locate and guess the meaning of the word ❽ **Führerschein**. Do they remember the word **Abholschein** from **Kapitel 6**? Remind them of other words they may know that end in **–schein** (**Gutschein, Geldschein,** etc.).

Advance Organizer
Ask students to name their favorite television program and say why they enjoy watching it. In addition, you might ask which type of program they like least and have them explain their answers.

STANDARDS: 1.3

Teaching Suggestion
Play the video segment of *Mensch, zieh die Handbremse an!* with the sound turned off. Pause the tape occasionally and have students comment on what might be happening in the story. Write down students' ideas. Then replay the video segment with sound. Have students compare their ideas with what actually happened in the segment.

Fortsetzung
You may choose to continue with the Fortsetzung of *Mensch, zieh die Handbremse an!* now or wait until later in the chapter. For a synopsis of the **Los geht's!** and **Fortsetzung** episodes, see p. 269E.

Teacher Note
The verb **dahinflitzen** is a colloquial expression that means **schnell fahren**.

PAGE 274

Using the Captioned Video/DVD

If students have trouble understanding, you may want to play the captioned version of *Mensch, zieh die Handbremse an!* on Videocassette 5. Ask students to use vocabulary and expressions they know to write two or three sentences in German to describe some of the things Ismar and Andreas did in the video episode.
Note: The *DVD Tutor* contains captions for all sections of the *Video Program*.

Comprehension Check

Challenge
❶ Ask students to answer the questions in German and summarize **Los geht's!** on pp. 272–273. The summary could be done orally or in writing.

Building on Previous Skills
❷ Before students scan the text for phrases, have them think of constructions from previous chapters that could be used to express the six functions. Put the responses on a transparency. After students have read **Los geht's!** again, ask them to point out which expressions were familiar to them and which were new.

Challenge
❸ Have students replace the conjunction **denn** with **weil** and change the word order accordingly.

KAPITEL 10   LOS GEHT'S!

ERSTE STUFE

Teaching Resources
pp. 275–279

PRINT
- Lesson Planner, p. 48
- TPR Storytelling Book, pp. 72–73
- Listening Activities, pp. 75, 79
- Activities for Communication, pp. 55–56, 110, 113 141–142
- Grammatikheft, pp. 82–83
- Grammar Tutor for Students of German, Chapter 10
- Übungsheft, pp. 110–112
- Testing Program, pp. 249–252
- Alternative Assessment Guide, p. 41
- Student Make-Up Assignments, Chapter 10

MEDIA
- One-Stop Planner
- Audio Compact Discs, CD10, Trs. 3, 12, 17–18
- Teaching Transparencies Situation 10-1
- **Mehr Grammatikübungen** Answers
- Grammatikheft Answers
- Interactive CD-ROM Tutor, Disc 3
- DVD Tutor, Disc 2

PAGE 275

Bell Work
Have students make a list in English of the types of programs that are on American television. Then, give students a list of program types in German. Ask them to try to match the German with the English.

Teaching Suggestions

- The conversation on p. 275 contains several new vocabulary items. You might want to introduce some of the vocabulary before students read the text or after they have read it once. Give examples and use synonyms or descriptions.

- Have students role-play the conversation with a partner, then elicit responses from several students to the questions that follow.

Cultures and Communities

Language Note
The German language has several words or phrases meaning *to watch television*. **Gucken** is a colloquial expression which could be replaced with verbs such as **sehen**, **ansehen**, and **anschauen**. **Glotzen** is a slang word meaning *to stare*. **Die Glotzkiste** or **die Glotze** is a humorous slang word for *television set*.

Communication for All Students

Auditory Learners
6 After students have taken notes, play the compact disc again and ask students to listen specifically for words that the speakers use to preface a clause giving reasons. (Examples: **weil**, **deswegen**)

PAGE 276

PRESENTING: Wortschatz
To give students an opportunity to practice the names of different types of TV programs, prepare a list of popular shows on a transparency. You might want to translate some of the names into German. Ask students to classify the programs according to the categories in the **Wortschatz**. Then ask students to give additional examples of shows in each category.

Communication for All Students

Challenge
7 Ask students to give at least one additional reason why Ismar might be interested in each type of program.

PRESENTING: So sagt man das!
To review and practice the expressions in **So sagt man das!**, ask students about the interests of various family members or friends.
Examples:
Wofür interessiert sich deine Mutter?
Was für Interessen hat dein bester Freund?

Building on Previous Skills
8 Ask students to incorporate previously learned functions to elaborate on their reasons for being interested in certain programs. (Example: **Ich interessiere mich für Kriminalfilme, weil sie so spannend sind.**)

PAGE 277

PRESENTING: Grammatik

Verbs with prepositions; **wo-** and **da-**compounds

- Have students scan **Los geht's!** on pp. 272–273 and make a list of all the verbs that are followed by a preposition. Then ask students for the meaning of each verb with and without the preposition.

- To teach the usage of **wo-** and **da-**compounds, show students several examples, such as the ones listed below, and have them try to infer the rules of how and when they are used before you go over the explanation in **So sagt man das!**
  Examples:
  Peter und ich sprechen über Mark.
  Peter und ich sprechen über ihn.

  Peter und ich sprechen oft über Sport.
  Peter und ich sprechen oft darüber.

- After students have learned about the **r** inserted in **darüber,** ask them if they can think of other such compounds that require that insertion. (Examples: **daraus, woraus, darum, worum**)

For Additional Practice

9 To provide students with additional practice of **da-** and **wo-**compounds, ask them to rephrase their sentences by replacing the object with the appropriate compound.

Connections and Comparisons

Music Connection

Refer students to the Moravian folksong *Jetzt kommen die lustigen Tage,* Level 2 *Listening Activities,* p. 93, for additional reading. Have them circle the **da-**compound they find. (**davon**) To what does this compound refer? (**der rote, rote Mohn**) You might also want to play the song, Level 2 CD 12, Tr. 26.

PAGE 278

Reteaching: The 24-hour clock

Before doing Activity 11, you may want to review the 24-hour clock with students. You could do this by asking them when their favorite programs are shown.

Teacher Note

The letters **SO** in the program overview stand for **Sonntag.**

Communication for All Students

Challenge

11 To expand the activity, have partners exchange specific information about the programs they like to watch. On which day does the show air? At what time? What is the name of the program? What is it about?

Thinking Critically

11 **Drawing Inferences** After students have completed the partner activity, ask them to scan the listing again. Based on the title, can students tell what type of program each one is? (Example: **Das Programm um 20 Uhr im BR3 ist eine Natursendung.**)

13 **Analyzing** Since most students are familiar with television commercials, ask them to come up with some reasons the type of products being advertised varies according to the time of day. (Advertisers target different viewing audiences depending on the product they are selling.)

PRESENTING: Ein wenig Landeskunde

Based on what students have read, ask them to compare the television systems in Germany and in the United States. What are the main networks on American television and what are their logos? (NBC: peacock; CBS: eye; ABC: letters a, b, and c in a circle)

Teacher Note

The Culture portion of Quiz 10-1B is based on **Ein wenig Landeskunde** on p. 278.

Reteaching: *Wo-* and *da-*compounds

Ask students to create at least three sentences from the sentence fragments in the following chart. Then have students rephrase their sentences using appropriate compounds.

Er	sich interessieren	über	Politik
Wir	sprechen	für	Mode
Ich	sich unterhalten	auf	die neue
Sie	sich freuen		Fernsehsendung
Die Mädchen	diskutieren		seinen Besuch
			die Sommerferien
			Sport

STANDARDS: 1.1, 2.2, 3.2

PAGE 279

LANDESKUNDE

Teaching Resources
p. 279

PRINT
- Video Guide, pp. 63–64, 66–67
- Übungsheft, p. 113

MEDIA
- One-Stop Planner
- Video Program
  Videocassette 4, 19:28–25:53
- DVD Tutor, Disc 2
- Audio Compact Discs, CD10, Trs. 4–7
- Interactive CD-ROM Tutor, Chapter 10

Teaching Suggestion
Based on students' knowledge of Berlin, Hamburg, and Stuttgart, ask students what types of outdoor activities people might enjoy in those three cities. You might want to introduce the following vocabulary to help students understand the interviews:

Fallschirm springen	parachuting
Tandemsprung	paired parachute jump
vor allen Dingen	above all
dazwischen	in between
mitkriegen	to learn, to find out
beruflich einsteigen	to get into a line of work

Connections and Comparisons

 Multicultural Connection
Ask students to interview anyone they know from a different country about what people in that country typically enjoy doing to relax in their free time.

Group Work
Ask students to work in groups of three. Have each group do Activities A1 through A4 in writing. When students have finished, ask the spokesperson from each group to share his or her answers with the rest of the class.

Teaching Activity
As a final activity, have students scan the three interviews for all the activities mentioned and list them with their infinitive form.

Thinking Critically
A5 **Synthesizing** To expand further on this question, have students come up with reasons so many of these trends are similar. (Examples: exposure to American films; television and music.)

FAMILY LINK
Have students interview their family members about their free time interests and what they do to relax after work or school.

Teaching Suggestion
B2 Help students prepare for this writing assignment by reviewing phrases from previous chapters that they can use to state their opinion. Examples:
Ich finde, dass …
Ich glaube, dass …
Ich meine, dass …

Connections and Comparisons

Language-to-Language
You might want to tell your students that a large number of German loanwords come from the American entertainment and high-tech industries. (Examples: **Sciencefiction, Actionfilm, Musical, Videokassette, CD-ROM, Computer**) Ask your students if they can think of other German high-tech terms that have been adopted from English. (You might have students look at the list of computer terms in the Additional Vocabulary section.)

Teaching Suggestion
Ask students on which current television show they would like to guest star and why. (In welcher Fernsehsendung würdest du gern mitspielen? Und warum?)

Assess
- Testing Program, pp. 249–252
  Quiz 10-1A, Quiz 10-1B
  Audio CD10, Tr. 12
- Student Make-Up Assignments
  Chapter 10, Alternative Quiz
- Alternative Assessment Guide, p. 41

▶ **PAGES 280–281**

ZUM LESEN

> ### Teaching Resources
> pp. 280–281
>
> PRINT
> ▸ Lesson Planner, p. 51
> ▸ Übungsheft, p. 114
> ▸ Reading Strategies and Skills, Chapter 10
> ▸ Lies mit mir! 2, Chapter 10
>
> MEDIA
> ▸ One-Stop Planner

Prereading
Building Context
Go around the classroom and ask several students how they find out what is on TV. How do they decide whether or not to watch a particular program?

Teaching Suggestion
Ask students where one would find program announcements such as the ones in this reading selection. (Examples: newspaper entertainment section, TV program guides)

Connections and Comparisons
Language Note
ARD is the acronym for **Arbeitsgemeinschaft der öffentlich-rechtlichen Rundfunkanstalten der Bundesrepublik Deutschland**. RTL stands for **Radio-Télévision Luxembourg**.

Teacher Note
Activities 1 and 2 are prereading activities

Reading
Building on Previous Skills
Based on the vocabulary students learned in the **Wortschatz** on p. 276, have them classify the six programs described in the reading. (Example: **Die Eishockey WM ist eine Sportsendung.**)

Connections and Comparisons
Language Note
WM stands for **Weltmeisterschaft**. This acronym is used with other sports as well, for example, **Leichtathletik WM, Fußball WM,** and **Gymnastik WM**.

Communication for All Students
Thinking Critically
Synthesizing Students can gather from these pages that Germans can see many American shows on television. Can students think of reasons to explain the fact that American shows are available on German TV, but German shows are rarely shown on American TV? (The German broadcasting industry is smaller than its American counterpart and often imports foreign programs to fill program demands. The American broadcasting industry is large enough to fill program demands without having to import much foreign programming.)

Post-Reading
Teacher Note
Activities 7 and 8 are post-reading tasks that will show whether students can apply what they have learned.

Teaching Suggestion
7 After students have written their preview, have them read it to the rest of the class. The reader should not mention the name of the program so that the class can try to guess what it is.

13.15 PRO 7 Doku — Im Reich der wilden Tiere Auf Flußpferdfang in Afrika und Karibus in Kanada

Flußpferden sieht man nicht an, wie gefährlich sie werden können. Die Wildhüter des Krüger-Nationalparks haben eine spezielle Fangmethode entwickelt: Eine schwere Straßenbaumaschine schützt die Männer bei ihrem gefährlichen Job. Bei den kanadischen Karibus versuchen die Wissenschaftler, der hohen Sterblichkeit unter den Jungtieren auf die Spur zu kommen. **55 Min.**

Hippopotamus amphibius – das Flußpferd und seine Drohgebärde

Cultures and Communities

Multicultural Connection

Have students ask anybody they know from another country about television programming in their country. Then have students report their findings to the rest of the class.

Career Path
Have students come up with scenarios in which someone working in broadcast journalism would benefit from a knowledge of German. (Suggestions: They might be sent to a German-speaking country to cover a breaking story; they could be put in charge of gleaning important news items from German-language sources.)

Zum Lesen Answers
Answers to Activity 1 TV previews
Answers to Activity 2 Answers will vary.
Answers to Activity 3 a. upper left hand corner of each review, first line of little box
b. upper left-hand corner of each review, second line of little box
c. upper left-hand corner of each review, third line of little box
d. at the end of each review text
e. at the very top
The initials refer to the stations/channels; **Praxis Bülowbogen, Eishockey WM, Raumschiff Enterprise**
Answers to Activity 4 Raumschiff Enterprise, Der Prinz von Bel-Air, Im Reich der wilden Tiere, Der Junge mit dem großen schwarzen Hund; predictions will vary.

ZWEITE STUFE

Teaching Resources
pp. 282–285

PRINT
- Lesson Planner, p. 49
- TPR Storytelling Book, pp. 74–75
- Listening Activities, pp. 75, 80–81
- Activities for Communication, pp. 110–112, 113, 141–142
- Grammatikheft, pp. 84–86
- Grammar Tutor for Students of German, Chapter 10
- Übungsheft, pp. 115–117
- Testing Program, pp. 253–256
- Alternative Assessment Guide, p. 41
- Student Make-Up Assignments, Chapter 10

MEDIA
- One-Stop Planner
- Audio Compact Discs, CD10, Trs. 8, 13, 19–20
- Teaching Transparencies
  Vocabulary 10-A
  Mehr Grammatikübungen Answers
  Grammatikheft Answers
- Interactive CD-ROM Tutor, Disc 3
- DVD Tutor, Disc 2

 **PAGE 282**

Bell Work

Ask students to make a list of television programs they would recommend to an exchange student who is new to American television.

Cooperative Learning
14 Divide the class into groups of three students. Each group should have a writer, a discussion leader, and a reporter. Before groups begin to read the two articles and the chart, you might want to introduce the vocabulary and give the information from the following Teacher Notes. Then ask each group to read the articles, examine the chart, and answer the questions. When students have finished, ask each group reporter to share the group's responses to Questions 1–4 with the rest of the class.

269S ZWEITE STUFE KAPITEL 10 STANDARDS: 2.2, 5.1

Teacher Notes

- Here are synonyms and explanations you might want to use to introduce some of the unfamiliar terms in the reading:
  die Fernsehanstalt: ARD, ZDF, RTL sind Fernsehanstalten.
  die Einschaltquote: Statistiken darüber, wie viele Leute den Fernseher anmachen
  unentbehrlich: Für viele Leute ist der Fernseher unentbehrlich geworden. Sie *müssen* unbedingt Fernsehen schauen.
  Vorsicht!: Achtung! Aufpassen!

- Help students interpret the chart "**Hitparade der jüngsten**". Tell students that the percentages indicate the two age groups of viewers who watch a particular channel, those under fifty and those over fifty.

Connections and Comparisons

Thinking Critically

Comparing and Contrasting Ask students what the American equivalent to the German **GfK** in **Nürnberg** is. (A.C. Nielsen Company)

PRESENTING: Wortschatz

Use a TV or VCR cart and equipment from your school's media department or library to introduce the **Wortschatz**. Have students gather around the equipment while you present the various items to them.

▶ **PAGE 283**

Communication for All Students

Challenge

16 Encourage students to elaborate on each question. You might have them work with a partner. Use the first question as a model and direct it to a student. Ask additional questions based on the student's response.

PRESENTING: So sagt man das!

Have students give examples of how they ask their parents for permission to have or do something. What do they say? Write down the different ways students ask for permission and underline the verbs in these questions. Then go over the expressions in **So sagt man das!** with students.

PRESENTING: Ein wenig Grammatik

The verb lassen As you introduce the verb **lassen**, tell students that it has the same stem-vowel change as do **fahren** and **schlafen**. Have them use those verbs as a model to tell you how **lassen** should be conjugated; write the forms on the board as students supply them. Then ask them what they think the **du**-command form would be. (**lass**) Allow students a few minutes to formulate a statement asking for permission to do something, based on the models in this box. When they have finished, ask them to read their sentences to the class.

Connections and Comparisons

Music Connection

For additional reading, refer students to the song *Komm, lieber Mai* (lyrics by Christian Adolph Overbeck; music by Wolfgang Amadeus Mozart), Level 2 *Listening Activities*, p. 70, and ask them if they can spot a form of **lassen**. (**lass**) How is it being used here? (**du**-command form) Have students give you a rough translation of the first sentence. You may also want to play the song, Level 2 CD 9, Tr. 23.

▶ **PAGE 284**

PRESENTING: So sagt man das!

Ask several yes/no questions with **ob**-clauses about school matters to which students can easily respond. Examples:
Weißt du, ob Herr (Smith) heute in der Schule ist?
Wisst ihr, ob (John) noch krank ist?
Könnt ihr mir sagen, ob unsere (Fußball)mannschaft am Samstag spielt?
Next, ask students if they noticed how you formulated your questions. You might have to repeat some of the questions for students to really notice the **ob**-clauses. In order to make the word order more obvious, ask a few questions in two different ways. Examples:
Braucht das Gerät eine Zimmerantenne?
Kannst du mir sagen, ob das Gerät eine Zimmerantenne braucht?
Finally, introduce **So sagt man das!** by going over all the phrases.

STANDARDS: 1.1, 3.2, 4.2

KAPITEL 10   ZWEITE STUFE

> **Communication for All Students**
>
> **Visual Learners**
> 18 Bring a TV or VCR cart to your classroom. Call on pairs to role-play this situation in front of the class, using the television set or the videorecorder (**Videogerät**) as the item to be purchased.

PAGE 285

Writing Assessment

22 You may choose to collect this activity for assessment. The following rubric may help you with evaluation of the written assignments.

Writing Rubric	Points			
	4	3	2	1
Content (Complete – Incomplete)				
Comprehensibility (Comprehensible – Seldom comprehensible)				
Accuracy (Accurate – Seldom accurate)				
Organization (Well-organized – Poorly organized)				
Effort (Excellent – Minimal)				

18–20: A   16–17: B   14–15: C   12–13: D   Under 12: F

PRESENTING: Wortschatz

To practice the vocabulary, provide students with a copy of a television schedule for one week. Students should work in pairs and ask each other what programs are shown and at what times.
Example: **Was gibt's im ZDF** (or ABC if you give them an American schedule) **montags um 15 Uhr?**

PRESENTING: Ein wenig Grammatik

The verb laufen Inform students that **laufen** has the same stem-vowel change as **lassen**, and have the class tell you how the verb should be conjugated. Write down the forms on the board as students guess them correctly. Then explain the new meaning of **laufen** to the class (to be showing on TV or at the movie theater), and reinforce this usage by asking several students questions such as **Was läuft freitags im Fernsehen? Was läuft diese Woche im Kino?**

Teaching Suggestion

22 Encourage students to go beyond the A/B dialogue pattern and continue their conversation for at least one more exchange. They can ask for more information or comment on what their partner says.

TPR **Total Physical Response**

Plan to have a TV/VCR cart in your classroom on the day you plan to do this activity. Ask individual students to follow your directions.
Examples:
Nimm die Fernbedienung und schalte den Fernseher ein!
Setz dir bitte diesen Kopfhörer auf!
Könntest du bitte messen, wie breit dieser Fernseher ist? Schreib die Größe an die Tafel!
Leg bitte diese Kassetten auf das untere Ablagefach des Videowagens!

> **Assess**
> ▸ Testing Program, pp. 253–256
>   Quiz 10-2A, Quiz 10-2B
>   Audio CD10, Tr. 13
>
> ▸ Student Make-Up Assignments
>   Chapter 10, Alternative Quiz
>
> ▸ Alternative Assessment Guide, p. 41

DRITTE STUFE

Teaching Resources
pp. 286–289

PRINT
- Lesson Planner, p. 50
- TPR Storytelling Book, pp. 76–77
- Listening Activities, pp. 76, 81–82
- Activities for Communication, pp. 57–60, 141–142
- Grammatikheft, pp. 87–90
- Grammar Tutor for Students of German, Chapter 10
- Übungsheft, pp. 118–120
- Testing Program, pp. 257–260
- Alternative Assessment Guide, p. 41
- Student Make-Up Assignments, Chapter 10

MEDIA
- One-Stop Planner
- Audio Compact Discs, CD10, Trs. 9–10, 14, 21–22
- Teaching Transparencies
  Situation 10-2
  Vocabulary 10-B
  Mehr Grammatikübungen Answers
  Grammatikheft Answers
- Interactive CD-ROM Tutor, Disc 3
- DVD Tutor, Disc 2

PAGE 286

Bell Work
Ask students if they can recall makes of cars that are manufactured in Germany. Examples: Mercedes (built by DaimlerChrysler), Porsche, Audi, VW (Volkswagen), BMW (**Bayerische Motorenwerke**), and Opel (**Adam Opel AG,** a General Motors group).

Thinking Critically
Analyzing Based on the information in the reading, ask students if they can think of reasons why people in German-speaking countries tend to drive smaller cars than people in the United States. (Examples: Fuel in Europe is very expensive; people in the German-speaking countries tend to be concerned about the environment, roads are more narrow, parking is more limited in inner cities.)

Connections and Comparisons

Language Notes
- **Geld auf den Tisch legen** is a colloquial expression. Here, it could be translated as *to come up with the money.*
- **PKW** is the common acronym for **Personenkraftwagen. LKW** stands for **Lastkraftwagen.**

PRESENTING: Wortschatz
To present the new vocabulary you may want to obtain a car brochure from an auto dealer that has close-up shots of auto parts, such as lights and windshield wipers. After you have gone over the new vocabulary, ask students to list the features of their own car, their parent's car, or a car they would like to have.

PAGE 287

Communication for All Students

Tactile Learners
24 While students listen to the two descriptions, have them draw a sketch of the options (**Extras**) that the car owners mention. Then have students go back to the **Wortschatz** and write the corresponding word beside each sketch.

Visual Learners
25 Ask students to bring a picture of their dream car that they have cut out of a magazine. Students can use these pictures as they exchange information with their partners. Students should take turns labeling the features.

PRESENTING: So sagt man das!
- Ask students to work with a partner and have them write a statement to precede each functional expression. Call on several pairs to role-play what they came up with, using the expressions in **So sagt man das!** as responses.
- Prepare a list of additional statements for students to react to by showing surprise, agreement, or disagreement, depending on the situation. Examples:
  Autofahren ist sehr teuer!
  Ich finde, man braucht keine Klimaanlage.
  　Das ist Luxus.

PAGE 288

PRESENTING: Ein wenig Landeskunde

- Ask students if they can recall the required driving age in Germany for a **Moped.** (16)

- Ask students to compare the age requirements for mopeds and cars in their own state with the requirements in Germany.

- If any of your students are or were enrolled in a driving school, ask them what they learn there.

- After students read the text, ask them questions to assure full understanding. Next, have students list all the requirements that trainees must fulfill to get a driver's license in Germany. Remind them to include costs and hours behind the wheel.

Cultures and Communities

Background Information

In contrast to state procedures in the United States, once a driver's license is issued in Germany, it is valid for life and in all areas of Germany. If a person relocates to another **Bundesland,** for example, he or she does not have to obtain another driver's license.

PRESENTING: So sagt man das!

Ask students to list all the time expressions they have learned so far that can be used to refer to the future. (Examples: **morgen; am 3. Juli; nächsten Sommer; im April; in zwei Wochen; später; morgen Abend**) Ask students to study the examples in **So sagt man das!**, and lead them to discover the similarities between the use of **werden** and the modal verbs. Finally, give students several pairs of sentences that use both **wollen** and **werden,** two verbs that are frequently mixed up. Ask students to explain the difference in meanings of the sentences.
Example: Ich *will* das machen.
　　　　　Ich *werde* das machen.

PAGE 289

PRESENTING: Grammatik

- **The future tense with werden** Ask students to look at the forms of **werden** and examine how **werden** can be used as an auxiliary verb with another verb in the infinitive.

- Have students compare the two ways future can be expressed in German with the way future is expressed in English.

Teaching Suggestion

 Make sure students take notes on the information their partners share with them. Students should be prepared to share their partners' information with the rest of the class.

Connections and Comparisons

Thinking Critically

Comparing and Contrasting The German language has proverbs related to the future: **Morgen, morgen, nur nicht heute, sagen alle faulen Leute. Was du heute kannst besorgen, das verschiebe nicht auf morgen.** Ask students if they know similar proverbs in English. (Example: *Don't put off until tomorrow what can be done today.*)

Game

Play the game **Beschriftungen** to review the vocabulary of auto parts. See p. 269C for the procedure.

Teacher to Teacher

Alisa Glick
Greenwich Country Day School
Greenwich, Connecticut

Alisa teaches both listening skills and current events with this video activity.

"Videotape a segment of the German news for the class. Play it two times. During the first playing, have students watch and listen. On second playing, have students write down all words they recognize in the order said. Elicit words from students and write them on the board, again in order they were said. Based on the words and their order, have students guess what the story is about. You can also ask simple questions in German to guide them."

Assess

- Testing Program, pp. 257–260
  Quiz 10-3A, Quiz 10-3B
  Audio CD10, Tr. 14

- Student Make-Up Assignments
  Chapter 10, Alternative Quiz

- Alternative Assessment Guide, p. 41

> **PAGES 290–293**

MEHR GRAMMATIKÜBUNGEN

The **Mehr Grammatikübungen** activities are designed as supplemental activities for the grammatical concepts presented in the chapter. You might use them as additional practice, for review, or for assessment.

For more grammar presentations, review, and practice, refer to the following:
- Grammatikheft
- Grammar Tutor for Students of German
- Grammar Summary on pp. R20–R36
- Übungsheft
- Grammar and Vocabulary quizzes (Testing Program)
- Test Generator
- Interactive CD-ROM Tutor
- **Interaktive Spiele** at go.hrw.com

> **PAGES 294–295**

ANWENDUNG

Video Wrap-up
Videocassette 4, 10:32–29:52
Videocassette 5 (captioned version), 56:20–1:04:36
DVD Tutor, Disc 2

At this time, you might want to use the video resources for additional review and enrichment. These resources are also available via the Enhanced Online Student Edition.
See *Video Guide* for suggestions regarding:
- *Mensch, zieh die Handbremse an!* Dramatic episode
- **Landeskunde** Interviews
- **Videoclips** Authentic footage

Apply and Assess

Family Link

1 Ask students to expand their polling market by asking members of their family some of the same questions. Remind them that the larger the number of people being surveyed, the more accurate the results will be.

Portfolio Assessment

1 You might want to suggest this activity as a written and oral portfolio item for your students. See *Alternative Assessment Guide*, p. 27.

A Slower Pace

3 Make the listening script available to students as they listen to the activity a second time. Have them identify the name and type of each program the Bauer family plans to watch.

Process Writing

5 You might suggest that your students use comparative adjectives in order to describe the differences between the show they're trying to save and another show they would prefer to see canceled instead.

STANDARDS: 1.1, 5.1

Apply and Assess

5 Allow those students who like to use humor in their writing to make the bulk of their letter a 'testimonial' from a fan of the show. In this testimonial, they should list various ways in which this program has changed their lives, and describe the injurious consequences that will result from the show's cancellation.

> **PAGE 296**

KANN ICH'S WIRKLICH?

This page helps students prepare for the test. It is a brief checklist of the major points covered in the chapter. The students should be reminded that it is only a checklist and not necessarily everything that will appear on the test.

For additional self check options, refer students to the *Grammar Tutor*, the *Interactive CD-ROM Tutor*, and the Online self-test for this chapter.

> **PAGE 297**

WORTSCHATZ

Review and Assess

Visual Learners

Number each program on an overview page from a TV program guide. To review the vocabulary of the **Erste Stufe**, ask students to identify the type of program of the number you call out.

Circumlocution

Play **Das treffende Wort suchen** to review the vocabulary in all three **Stufen** in this chapter. For the **Erste Stufe** vocabulary, ask students to describe what one would see on a particular type of TV show. To review **Zweite Stufe** or **Dritte Stufe** vocabulary, students could describe what a certain object is used for or what it looks like. See p. 3C for procedures.

Game

Play the game **Heiße Kartoffel** to review the vocabulary of this chapter. See p. 269C for the procedure.

Teacher Note

Give the **Kapitel 10** Chapter Test: *Testing Program*, pp. 261–266
Audio CD 10, Trs. 15–16.

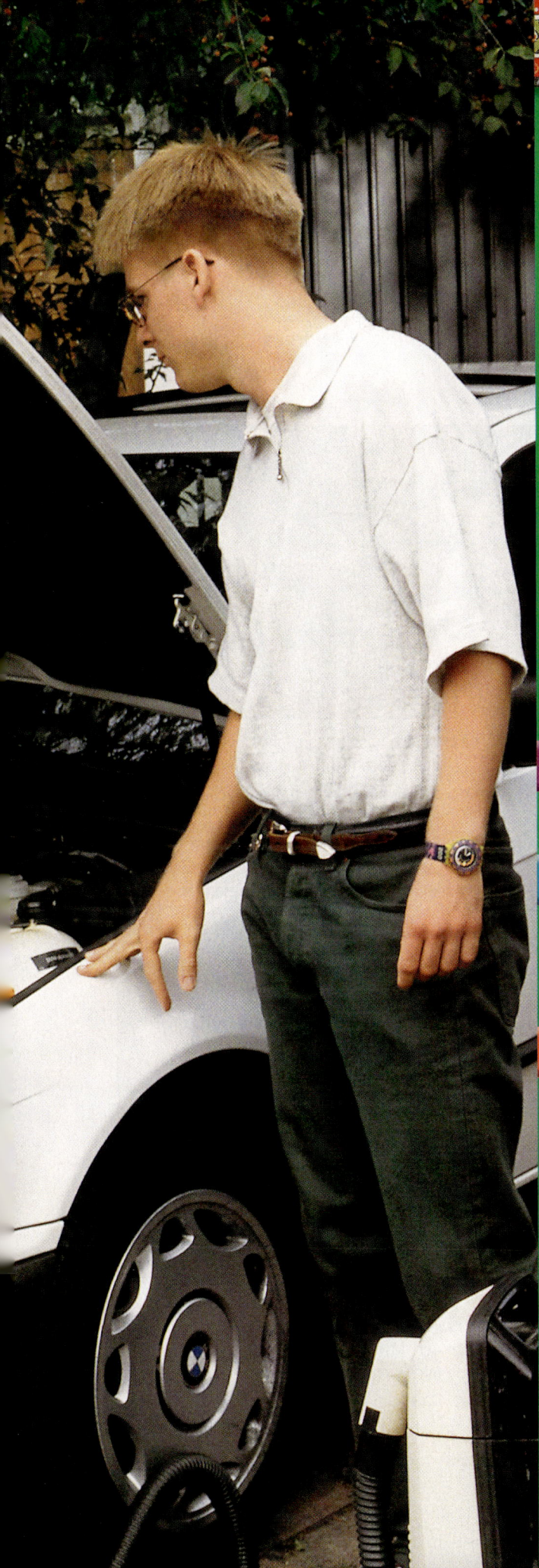

KAPITEL

10 Viele Interessen!

Objectives
In this chapter you will learn to

Erste Stufe
- ask about and express interest

Zweite Stufe
- ask for and give permission
- ask for information and express an assumption

Dritte Stufe
- express surprise, agreement, and disagreement
- talk about plans

Visit Holt Online
go.hrw.com
KEYWORD: WK3 BERLIN-10
Online Edition

◀ Du interessierst dich für Autos, Ismar?

Los geht's! — Mensch, zieh die Handbremse an!

Los geht's! is an abridged version of the video episode.

Strategie Verstehen
Look at the images for the story. What are the boys doing at first? What do you think they are talking about? What do you think is happening with the car?

Ismar

Andreas

1
Andreas: Du, Ismar, lass mal sehen! Das kann doch nicht stimmen. Du hast dich ganz bestimmt verrechnet. Ich meine …
Ismar: Hier, du darfst nachrechnen.

2
Andreas: Du, ich hab ein ganz anderes Ergebnis. Das gibt's doch nicht! Was machen wir jetzt?
Ismar: Ich meine, wir sind müde. Machen wir mal eine kleine Pause!
Andreas: Einverstanden! – Schauen wir mal, was es jetzt im Fernsehen gibt! Um diese Zeit kommt gewöhnlich nichts Besonderes.

3
Ismar: Du hast bestimmt Recht, aber schauen wir mal! – Habt ihr ein Fernsehmagazin?
Andreas: Ja schon. Aber ich weiß nicht, wo es liegt. Gib mir lieber mal die Fernbedienung rüber!
Ismar: Hier!
Andreas: Danke! Schauen wir mal, was es im Ersten Programm gibt!

4
Ismar: Ach, etwas über die Umwelt. Normalerweise interessiert mich so was, aber nicht jetzt. Mach weiter!
Andreas: Ach, Mensch, Politik! Politik interessiert mich wenig.
Ismar: Da stimm ich dir zu.

Andreas' Mutter kommt nach Hause.

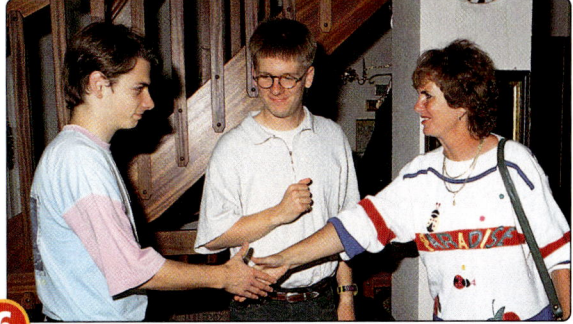

5
- **Andreas:** Und für welche Fernsehsendungen interessierst du dich am meisten?
- **Ismar:** Ich? Ich interessiere mich für Actionfilme und Sport. Und du?
- **Andreas:** Bei mir steht Sport ganz oben. Und dann mag ich eigentlich so ältere Spielfilme ganz gerne, so richtig lustige Filme, so wie mit Peter Sellers.

6
- **Andreas:** Mutti, das ist Ismar, ein Klassenkamerad!
- **Mutter:** Hallo, Ismar!
- **Ismar:** Hallo!
- **Mutter:** Andreas, du musst mir heute noch das Auto sauber machen, ja?

Ismar hilft Andreas das Auto sauber zu machen.

7
- **Ismar:** Der Ölstand ist gut, aber ich meine ... das Öl müsst ihr bald mal wechseln, das sieht alt aus.
- **Andreas:** Du interessierst dich für Autos?
- **Ismar:** Und wie! – Toller Wagen! Da ist keine Klimaanlage eingebaut.
- **Andreas:** Die brauchen wir nicht. Die Mutti kann Klimaanlagen sowieso nicht leiden.

8
- **Ismar:** Echt super. Mit dem möcht ich mal auf der Autobahn dahinflitzen, wenn ich den Führerschein habe.
- **Andreas:** Da musst du noch lange warten!
- **Ismar:** In einem halben Jahr kann ich den Führerschein machen.
- **Andreas:** Ich spar jetzt schon auf meinen Führerschein, aber ich muss noch fast ein Jahr darauf warten, bis ich ihn machen kann.

9
- **Ismar:** Was machst du denn, Andreas? Zieh die Handbremse an!

KNACKS!

Übungsheft, S. 109

1 Was passiert hier?

These activities check for global comprehension only. Students should not yet be expected to produce language modeled in **Los geht's!**

Verstehst du alles, was die Leute in **Los geht's!** sagen? Beantworte die Fragen!

1. What are Andreas and Ismar doing at the beginning? 1. They are doing their math homework.
2. Why do they take a break? What do they do during the break? 2. because they are tired; they watch TV
3. What do you find out about Andreas and Ismar's interests in television? 3. Ismar likes action movies and sports shows; Andreas likes sports shows and old movies
4. Who interrupts them? What does Andreas get reminded of? 4. Andreas's mother; to clean her car
5. Does Ismar know a lot about cars? How do you know? 5. yes; he checks the oil in Andreas's mother's car
6. What happens at the end? What do you think is going to happen next? 6. the car starts moving; it is going to roll over something (the nozzle of the vacuum cleaner)

2 Genauer lesen

Lies den Text noch einmal und beantworte diese Fragen!

1. Which phrases express compliments? Interest? Permission? Surprise? Agreement? Making suggestions? 1. Toller Wagen!; Echt super! / Lass mal sehen!; Ich interessiere mich … / Du darfst … / Das gibt's doch nicht! / Einverstanden!; Da stimm ich dir zu.; Du hast bestimmt Recht.; Ja schon / Machen wir mal … ; Schauen wir mal …

3 Was passt zusammen?

Welche Ausdrücke auf der rechten Seite beenden die Satzanfänge auf der linken Seite?

1. Du hast dich verrechnet, denn … 1. b
2. Andreas will die Fernbedienung, denn … 2. e
3. Ismar braucht das Fernsehmagazin, denn … 3. d
4. Andreas interessiert sich für ältere Spielfilme, denn … 4. a
5. Ismar darf bald Auto fahren, denn … 5. c

a. sie sind oft sehr lustig.
b. ich habe ein anderes Ergebnis.
c. in einem halben Jahr kann er den Führerschein machen.
d. er will wissen, was jetzt am Nachmittag kommt.
e. er will das Fernsehgerät einschalten.

4 Stimmt oder stimmt nicht?

Wenn der Satz nicht stimmt, schreib die richtige Antwort!

1. Die Jungen haben das gleiche Ergebnis in den Matheaufgaben. 1. Stimmt nicht. Sie haben beide ein anderes Ergebnis.
2. Am Nachmittag kommen Sendungen im Fernsehen, für die sie sich interessieren. 2. Stimmt nicht. Sie interessieren sich nicht für die Sendungen am Nachmittag.
3. Ismar schaut im Fernsehmagazin nach, um zu sehen, was am Nachmittag läuft. 3. Stimmt nicht. Andreas nimmt die Fernbedienung.
4. Normalerweise interessiert sich Ismar für Umweltprobleme. 4. Stimmt.
5. Ismar und Andreas sehen die gleichen Filme gern. 5. Stimmt nicht. Ismar sieht gern Actionfilme, und Andreas mag ältere Spielfilme.
6. Ismar versteht viel von Autos. 6. Stimmt.
7. Er hat auch schon seinen Führerschein. 7. Stimmt nicht. Er kann ihn in einem halben Jahr machen.

5 Welche Wörter passen?

Welche Wörter aus dem Kasten passen in die Zusammenfassung von **Los geht's!**?

Andreas und Ismar machen __1__ in Mathe zusammen. Sie machen __2__, weil sie müde sind. Sie wollen __3__ schauen, aber finden __4__ nicht und versuchen mit der __5__ herauszufinden, was es im Ersten Programm gibt. Normalerweise interessieren sie sich für __6__, die mit der Umwelt zu tun haben, aber heute nicht. Sie wollen lieber einen __7__ oder Sport schauen. Die Mutter kommt und erinnert (*reminds*) Andreas daran, __8__ heute noch sauber zu machen. Sie machen das zusammen und sprechen über Autos, Autofahren und __9__.

8 das Auto
7 Actionfilm
4 das Fernsehmagazin
9 den Führerschein
2 eine Pause
3 Fernsehen
5 Fernbedienung
6 Sendungen
1 Hausaufgaben

Storytelling Book pp. 72–73

Erste Stufe

Objective Asking about and expressing interest

WK3 BERLIN-10

Wer guckt was?

Lies, worüber sich Ismar und Andreas unterhalten und beantworte die Fragen!

ISMAR Für welche Sendungen interessierst du dich am meisten?

ANDREAS Das ist leicht zu sagen, wofür ich mich interessiere: für Nachrichtensendungen und ab und zu vielleicht mal für einen tollen Krimi.

ISMAR Dann bist du ein wirklich typischer Fernsehgucker. — Schau, hier ist eine Statistik über die beliebtesten Fernsehsendungen der Deutschen.

ANDREAS Das gibt's doch nicht! — Interessant! Und wofür interessierst du dich?

ISMAR Wir sehen uns zu Hause Nachrichten, Sport und Politik an. Und danach diskutieren wir immer heftig über alles …

ANDREAS Das find ich toll! — Aber jetzt checken wir schnell mal das Nachmittagsprogramm durch!

Ich freu mich schon immer auf ‚Tatort'. Der läuft sonntags um 20 Uhr 15 im Ersten Programm.

1. Wofür interessiert sich Andreas? Worauf freut sich Ismar?
2. Warum ist Andreas ein typischer Fernsehzuschauer?
3. Für welche Sendungen interessiert sich Ismars Familie?
4. Was passiert gewöhnlich nach einer Sendung bei ihm zu Hause?
5. Für welche Sendungen interessieren sich die Deutschen am meisten? Am wenigsten?
6. Welche amerikanischen Sendungen passen in diese Kategorien?

Die TV-Hits der Deutschen

Sendung	%
Nachrichtensendungen	74%
Kriminalfilme	57%
Wetterbericht	50%
Ratesendungen/Spielshows	43%
Sportübertragungen	43%
Tier-/Natursendungen	42%
Familiensendungen	42%
Lustspiele/Komödien	39%
Wildwest-/Abenteuerfilme	37%
Gesundheits-/Medizinthemen	37%
Talkshows	36%
Politikerdiskussionen	36%

---

6 **Wer interessiert sich für was?** Script and answers on p. 269G

Für welche Fernsehsendungen interessieren sich diese Leute und warum? Mach dir Notizen! Vergleiche dann deine Notizen mit den Notizen deiner Mitschüler!

CD 10 Tr. 3

Wortschatz

Was läuft im Fernsehen?
Für welche Sendungen interessierst du dich?
Sag es deinen Klassenkameraden!

die Nachrichten, Nachrichtensendungen

der Wetterbericht

Sportsendungen, Sportübertragungen

Natursendungen

Ratesendungen

Diskussionen über Politik

Und dann noch...

Familiensendungen	Tiersendungen
Kriminalfilme	Lustspiele
Wildwestfilme	Komödien
Abenteuerfilme	Sendungen über
Spielshows	Gesundheit
Talkshows	Werbesendungen

Übungsheft, S. 110, Ü. 1–2   Grammatikheft, S. 82, Ü. 1

7 Grammatik im Kontext

Schreiben Schreib **weil**-Sätze, die zusammen passen.

E.g.: **Ismar interessiert sich für Kriminalfilme, weil er sie sehr spannend findet.**

Ismar interessiert sich für ...

- Sportsendungen
- den Wetterbericht
- die Nachrichten
- Natursendungen
- Komödien
- Kriminalfilme

weil er ...

- gern lustige Sachen sieht
- Tiere furchtbar gern hat
- sie sehr spannend findet
- wissen möchte, was in der Welt passiert
- nur bei gutem Wetter im Gebirge wandert
- selbst gern Sport macht

So sagt man das!

Asking about and expressing interest   *Schon bekannt*

You already know several ways of asking someone about his or her interests:

   Was für Interessen hast du?
   Wofür interessierst du dich?

and of expressing your interests:

   Ich interessiere mich für Sport.

8 Wofür interessierst du dich und warum?

Sprechen Bevor du mit deinem Partner die vielen Sendungen durchcheckst, frag ihn, wofür er sich besonders interessiert und warum! Danach sag ihm, wofür du dich interessierst und warum!

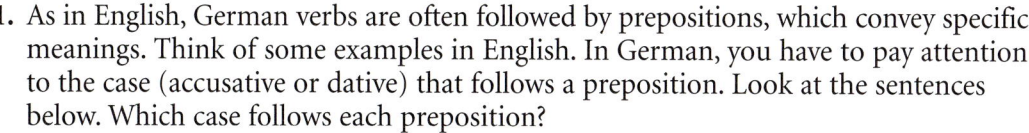

Grammatik

Verbs with prepositions; wo- and da-compounds

1. As in English, German verbs are often followed by prepositions, which convey specific meanings. Think of some examples in English. In German, you have to pay attention to the case (accusative or dative) that follows a preposition. Look at the sentences below. Which case follows each preposition?

   > **sprechen über:** Die Jungen sprechen über das Ergebnis.
   > **sich freuen auf:** Andreas freut sich auf den Krimi.
   > **sich interessieren für:** Er interessiert sich für lustige Filme.

2. When using verbs with prepositions in a question or response, you must do the following:

   a. When referring to people, use the preposition plus the question word **wen** in your questions:

   > **Für wen** interessierst du dich?
   > Ich interessiere mich **für ihn**, den Ralph.

   b. When referring to things or ideas, you use a **wo**-compound (**wo** + preposition) in your question:

   > **Wofür** interessierst du dich?   Ich interessiere mich **für Politik**.

   If you want to refer to the thing or idea in a statement using a pronoun (*it*), you have to use a **da**-compound (**da** + preposition):

   > Ich interessiere mich **für Politik**. — Ja? Ich interessiere mich auch **dafür**.
   > Er freut sich **auf den Krimi**. — Ich freue mich auch **darauf**.

3. If a preposition begins with a vowel, an **r** is inserted between **wo** and **da** and the preposition to facilitate pronunciation:

   > **auf**: worauf, darauf   **über**: worüber, darüber

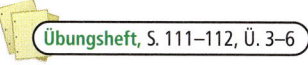

Mehr Grammatikübungen, S. 290–291, Ü. 1–5

---

 9 **Grammatik im Kontext**   Various possibilities. E.g.: **Ich diskutiere immer über Problemfilme.**

Schreiben Schreib mindestens acht Sätze mit den Wörtern in den Kästen.

| ich
meine Freunde und ich, wir
meine Eltern
mein Freund | sprechen
diskutieren
s. freuen
s. interessieren | gewöhnlich
immer
ab und zu
ganz selten | auf
für
über | die Nachrichten
Sportsendungen
Natursendungen
Ratesendungen
Krimis
Kultursendungen
Problemfilme
Kindersendungen
Werbung |

 10 **Wofür interessierst du dich?**

 Sprechen Frag deine Partnerin, wofür sie sich interessiert! Sag ihr, ob du dich auch dafür interessierst oder nicht!

ERSTE STUFE   STANDARDS: 1.1, 4.1   zweihundertsiebenundsiebzig   **277**

11 Was gucken wir?

Sprechen Du möchtest mit deiner Partnerin heute Abend Fernsehen gucken. Du weißt aber nicht genau, wofür sie sich interessiert. Habt ihr die gleichen Interessen? Auf welches Programm freust du dich? Und sie?

12 Für mein Notizbuch

Schreiben Schreib in dein Notizbuch, für welche Sendungen du dich interessierst und was du gewöhnlich guckst! Wann kommen deine Lieblingssendungen? Auf welchem Fernsehsender (*channel*)? Gibt es eine Sendung, auf die du dich besonders freust?

13 Werbung im Fernsehen

Schreiben/Sprechen Guck dir mal die Werbesendungen im Fernsehen an! Für welche Artikel werben die Sender am meisten? —Mach eine Rangliste mit Werbeartikeln, wie im Beispiel unten! Erwähne auch deine Lieblingswerbung und beschreibe sie! Berichte deiner Klasse über dein Ergebnis!

SO	ÜBERSICHT	
18.00 ZDF	Ein Heim für Tiere — Bobby hat zwei Zuhause.	60 Min.
18.00 RTL	Mord ist ihr Hobby mit Angela Lansbury	45 Min.
19.00 3SAT	heute	30 Min.
19.00 RTL	Hans Meiser — Audience Participation Show	70 Min.
20.00 BR3	Die Sterngucker — Sind wir allein im Universum?	45 Min.
20.00 N3	Der amerikan. Bürgerkrieg — Letzter Teil: Robert E. Lee	60 Min.
20.00 SW3	Agatha Christie — Krimiserie: Hercule Poirot	60 Min.
20.00 PRO 7	Matlock — Krimiserie	45 Min.
22.15 ZDF	Die Sport-Reportage	30 Min.
22.30 SAT1	Fußball — Berichte der 1. Liga	30 Min.

Rang	Werbeartikel
1	Fast-foods
2	Geschirrspülmittel
3	Waschpulver
4	Kaffee
5	Video-Spiele
6	Textilien
7	Rasierklingen

Ein wenig Landeskunde

ARD

ZDF

RTL

SAT.1

In Germany there are public and private television companies. The public companies are financed by a monthly viewing fee based upon the number of TV sets in use in each household.

The programming of public companies is scrutinized by a quasi-governmental agency, the **Rundfunk- und Fernsehrat,** that is composed of various interest groups. The two public television companies are **ARD,** producing the **Erstes Programm,** and the **ZDF,** producing the **Zweites Programm.** The **ARD** also produces regional programming, the **Regionalprogramm,** or the **Drittes Programm.** Advertising on these stations is restricted to two 15-minute periods a day.

A number of private TV companies that emerged in the eighties are financed by commercials. The most prominent companies are **RTL** and **SAT 1.** These private stations transmit, above all, sports, entertainment programs, and often controversial series. Other popular private companies are **PRO 7, n-tv, MTV,** and **Eurosport.**

In 2001 the top five TV networks were RTL (1), ZDF (2), ARD (3), SAT 1 (4), and PRO 7 (5).

PRO 7

3 SAT

RTL 2

VOX

Was machst du, um zu relaxen?

You've learned a lot already about the way German-speaking students like to spend their free time. Now we've asked people from around Germany what they do after school or work in order to relax and unwind. Think about what you've learned so far about Germans' free time interests. Then think about what you and your friends do after school or after work to relax. Afterwards, listen to the interviews, then read the text. CD 10 Tr. 4

Sabine, Berlin CD 10 Tr. 5

„In der Freizeit viel lesen, schwimmen gehen, Sport, und ich würde gerne mal Fallschirm springen, diese Tandemsprünge würde ich gerne mal machen. Und was ich vor allen Dingen in der Freizeit mache, ist Schlafen, das finde ich ganz besonders schön."

Uwe, Hamburg CD 10 Tr. 6

„So, ich mach Hausaufgaben, mit sehr viel Musik dazwischen, und, ja dann entweder treff ich mich mit meinen Freunden und spiel Basketball oder Fußball, oder etliches, ja, oder ich faulenze einfach, leg mich aufs Bett und schlafe."

Philipp, Stuttgart

„In der Freizeit, also da fahr ich speziell … fahr Rollerblade und mal fahr … Mountainbike, und das hab ich mitgekriegt, weil mal welche aus Amerika da waren — von dem Film ‚Rollerboys', und dann hab ich das angefangen. Rollerblade fahren, es macht mir ziemlich viel Spaß, ich finde das irgendwie … andere Welt für mich und macht mir sehr viel Spaß. Und mit ihm [meinem Freund] speziell mach ich hobbymäßig noch Computer, und da möchten wir dann später auch mal beruflich einsteigen." CD 10, Tr. 7

A. 1. Write the names of the people interviewed on a piece of paper and next to each the activities or hobbies that he or she talks about.

2. What does Sabine like to do best? What phrase does she use to describe that? Name one thing Sabine would like to do, but has not yet done.

3. What else does Uwe like to do when he's doing homework?

4. When did Philipp first become interested in in-line skating?

5. Scan through the activities again. Which other activities are mentioned that are also popular in the United States? Based on what you already knew about German culture, were you surprised that so many trends popular in the United States are also popular in Germany?

B. 1. People often think the habits of other cultures are somewhat "strange" and difficult to understand. At some time in your life, you may have heard this about German culture. However, once people get to know the other culture (as you've gotten to know German culture) they find it's not so very different from their own. What's your impression? Think about everything you've learned about Germany so far. Are there more similarities between our two cultures or are there more differences?

2. Write an essay in German stating your own opinion. Be sure to support your opinion with several examples based on what you've learned in the **Landeskunde** sections.

STANDARDS: 1.2, 2.1, 2.2, 3.2, 4.2

Zum Lesen

Was läuft im Fernsehen?

> **Lesestrategie** Predicting the content of a text. You're likely to read more quickly and more easily if you are able to make some predictions ahead of time about the content of a text. You have already learned how to predict using pictures, format, titles, and subtitles as clues. In this lesson you will continue to practice predicting using pictures and titles, but you will also develop your ability to predict *while* reading a text.

Getting Started   For answers, see p. 269S.

1. Judging by their format, what kind of texts are these?
2. With your classmates, think of five different kinds of information that you would usually find in a TV schedule at home and list these on the board.

> **Lesetipp:** When reading a schedule, you are usually looking for specific information, for instance, dates or times. To orient yourself, you need to scan the schedule to find out what kind of information is given and where it is located.

3. Locate the following kinds of information in the **Fernsehprogramm** excerpts:
   a. times
   b. channels
   c. types of shows
   d. length of shows
   e. day/date

SAMSTAG 10-20 UHR

 **Der Prinz von Bel-Air**
13.20 RTL Serie
Ist die Katze unterwegs, tanzten die Mäuse auf den Tischen – da macht Bel-Air keine Ausnahme

Will (M. hinten) sitzt ganz schön in der Klemme: Phil muß helfen

Vivian und Phil sind für zwei Tage unterwegs. Hilary übernimmt in ihrer Abwesenheit die Aufsicht über die Kinder. Will nutzt die Gelegenheit für einen Abstecher in die Stadt, läßt sich zu einem Billardspiel mit Einsatz überreden – und verliert prompt 500 Dollar. **25 Min.**

 Praxis Bülowbogen
17.25 ARD Serie
„Schuldgefühle" plagen Thomas: Nach dem Autounfall bleibt Freundin Susanne gelähmt

Behandeln Thomas: Dr. Katrin (l.) und Peter Brockmann (M.)

Seit Susanne durch seine Schuld im Rollstuhl sitzen muß, hat sich Thomas' ganzes Leben verändert. Er kümmert sich rührend um seine Freundin. Doch sie ist überzeugt, daß er sie eines Tags verlassen wird. **65 Min.**

70 TV GUIDE   FILMBE

 **Im Reich der wilden Tiere**
13.15 PRO 7 Doku
Auf Flußpferdfang in Afrika und Karibus in Kanada

Flußpferden sieht man nicht an, wie gefährlich sie werden können. Die Wildhüter des Krüger-Nationalparks haben eine spezielle Fangmethode entwickelt: Eine schwere Straßenbaumaschine schützt die Männer bei ihrem gefährlichen Job. Bei den kanadischen Karibus versuchen die Wissenschaftler, der hohen Sterblichkeit unter den Jungtieren auf die Spur zu kommen. **55 Min.**

Hippopotamus amphibius – das Flußpferd und seine Drohgebärde

10–20 PIC 24. APRIL

15.00 EURO Sport — Eishockey WM *live!*

Aus der Olympiahalle, München: Zweiter der Gruppe B gegen den Dritten der Gruppe A

Die Vorrunde ist ausgespielt. Nun werden im K.O.-System die Endspielgegner ermittelt: Die ersten vier Teams der beiden Vorrundengruppen kommen weiter. Die Deutschen haben bei dieser WM mit Heimvorteil gute Chancen. **180 Min.**

Eine Spielszene der Begegnung BRD – Kanada

16.09 ZDF Serie — Raumschiff Enterprise

„Illusion oder Wirklichkeit": Ein schwarzes Loch im Universum zieht die Enterprise magisch an

Opfer einer fremden Geisteskraft: Picard, Haskell, Data (o.)

Bei dem Versuch, ein Schwarzes Loch im All näher zu untersuchen, wird die Enterprise verschlungen. Gleich darauf kommt es zu seltsamen Sinnestäuschungen: Die Mannschaft kämpft gegen ein romulanisches Kriegsschiff, das gar nicht existiert! **51 Min.**

11.30 ZDF Kinder — Der Junge mit dem großen schwarzen Hund

Ulf und der Neufundländer – eine schwierige Freundschaft

Im Schrebergarten von Oskar hat Nepomuk genug Auslauf

Ulf ist zehn und will schon lange einen eigenen Hund. Eines Tages läuft ihm ein schwarzer Neufundländer hinterher. Ulf gibt ihm den Namen Nepomuk und nimmt ihn mit nach Hause. Seine Eltern sind nicht gerade begeistert, aber für eine Nacht darf er bleiben. **75 Min.**

To what do the initials **ARD**, **ZDF**, etc. refer? If you had time between 3:00 P.M. and 5:30 P.M. on Saturday, what could you watch on German TV?

A Closer Look

4. If you're reading this section of the TV guide, you probably want to figure out what these shows are about or if you've already seen them. For the following shows, look at the photos and read the captions, titles, and subtitles: a science fiction series, an American sitcom, a documentary, and a children's TV show. Then, based on this information alone, predict what each show or episode is about.

5. Read the previews of these shows to confirm or adapt your original prediction. How close were you in predicting the content of the show?

6. Previews of TV shows never give the ending away. However, based on everything you know about the shows so far and on your own knowledge of different kinds of shows, predict the endings for the following shows. Then write, in German, one or two concluding sentences for each summary.

   a. *Raumschiff Enterprise*
   b. *Der Junge mit …*
   c. *Praxis Bülowbogen*
   d. *Der Prinz von Bel-Air*

7. Write a preview for one episode of your favorite show. Write one sentence about the main idea of the episode and four sentences that develop the main idea. Use connecting words such as those in the texts on these pages. Be sure not to give away the ending!

8. Write a movie and TV trivia quiz. Everyone will write three trivia questions in German on three separate cards and then put all the cards in a container. Divide up into two teams and play trivia.

Übungsheft, S. 114

Storytelling Book pp. 74–75

Zweite Stufe

Objectives Asking for and giving permission; asking for information and expressing an assumption

WK3 BERLIN-10

Rang	Sendung	Datum	Anstalt	Zuschauer (Mio)
	Fernseh-Hits in Deutschland 2000			
1	Wetten daß..?	13. 4.	ZDF	17,56
2	Wetten daß..?	2. 3.	ZDF	17,50
3	Die Rudi Carrell Show	26. 1.	ARD	16,60
4	ARD-Sport Extra: EM-Qualifikation Deutschland–Wales	16. 10.	ARD	16,43
5	Die Rudi Carrell Show	26. 10.	ARD	16,12
6	Die Rudi Carrell Show	20. 4.	ARD	15,90
7	Wetten daß..?	14. 12.	ZDF	15,89
8	Wetten daß..?	2. 11.	ZDF	15,72
9	Das Traumschiff	1. 1.	ZDF	15,57
10	Die Rudi Carrell Show	7. 12.	ARD	15,51
11	ZDF-Sport Extra: Fußball Belgien – BRD	20. 11.	ZDF	15,38
12	Tagesschau	3. 2.	ARD	15,35
13	Tagesschau	20. 1.	ARD	15,25
14	Derrick	15. 3.	ZDF	15,09
15	Ein Fall für zwei	25. 1.	ZDF	14,76

Die erfolgreichsten Sendungen

In den Fernsehanstalten weiß man morgens ganz genau, für welche Fernsehprogramme sich die meisten Haushalte am Abend zuvor interessiert haben, denn für alle Sendungen werden die Einschaltquoten gemessen.

Solche Statistiken sind heutzutage für alle Fernsehanstalten für die Planung von neuen Programmen unentbehrlich. Auch wollen die Werbesponsoren diese Einschaltquoten wissen.

Die Gesellschaft für Konsum-, Markt- und Absatzforschung (GfK) in Nürnberg ermittelt diese Einschaltquoten. Fernsehgeräte von ausgewählten Haushalten werden mit kleinen Computern versehen, die der Zentrale sekundengenau anzeigen, wann und wie viele Haushalte die verschiedenen Fernsehprogramme eingeschaltet haben.

PRO 7 und RTL haben das jüngste Publikum

Wenn im Vorabendprogramm die „Real Ghostbusters" oder „Lassie", die „Little Wizards" oder „Doogie Howser" auftauchen, dann ist entweder PRO 7, RTL 2 oder der Kabelkanal eingeschaltet, die Sender mit dem „jüngsten" Publikum (siehe Tabelle rechts). Vor allem Kinder und Jugendliche sehen sich die US-Produktionen an — und die Werbespots für „McDonald's", „Murmel-Mikado" und das Elektronikspiel „Super Nintendo".

Aber Vorsicht mit diesen Zahlen! Die „jüngsten" TV-Sender haben zwar die meisten Zuschauer unter 50 Jahren, doch ist ihr Marktanteil wesentlich geringer als der von ARD und ZDF.

	HITPARADE der „jüngsten" TV-Sender im Juni 2000	
RANG	SENDER	ZUSCHAUER
		unter 50 Jahre / über 50 Jahre
1	PRO 7	76,6% / 23,3%
2	RTL 2	74,4% / 25,6%
3	KABK	65,1% / 34,9%
4	VOX	56,1% / 43,9%
5	RTL	56,1% / 44,0%
6	DSF	54,5% / 45,5%
7	SAT.1	51,2% / 48,8%
8	NTV	45,8% / 58,3%
9	ARD	43,7% / 56,3%
10	ZDF	35,4% / 64,6%

14 Beliebte Sendungen

Lesen/Sprechen Lies die beiden Artikel und beantworte die Fragen!

1. Was haben beide Artikel gemeinsam (*in common*)? *1. sie handeln von Einschaltquoten*
2. Für wen sind die Einschaltquoten von Interesse und warum? *2. für die Fernsehanstalten; zur Planung von neuen Programmen*
3. Welche Sendungen sehen sich die jüngeren Zuschauer an? Auf welchen TV-Sendern kommen diese Sendungen? *3. US-Produktionen; PRO 7, RTL 2, Kabelkanal*
4. Welche sind die beiden größten deutschen Fernsehanstalten? *4. ARD und ZDF*

Wortschatz

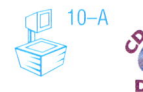 p. 269X 10–A

- 68 cm, 2X30 Watt
- Kabeltuner für 39 Programme
- LED-Programmanzeige
- Kopfhöreranschluss
- Fernbedienung
- mit Videotext

Stereo-Farbfernsehgerät

Diese Fernbedienung steuert bequem Ihr Gerät.

Dieser Fernseh- und Videowagen kommt mit zwei Ablagefächern für Ihre Videocassetten.

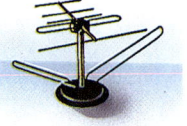

Dieser Stereo-Kopfhörer kommt mit einem Lautstärkeregler.

Eine Zimmerantenne für UHF und VHF

Übungsheft, S. 115, Ü. 1   Grammatikheft, S. 84, Ü. 5

15 Rolfs Fernseh- und Videowagen Script and answers on p. 269G

CD 10 Tr. 8

Zuhören Rolf has just bought himself a new entertainment system with all the latest features. On a piece of paper, draw the outlines of a **Fernseh- und Videowagen.** Then listen to Rolf's description and sketch what you hear. Draw in all the equipment and features he mentions and pay attention to where the features are located.

 16 Und du?

Sprechen Beantworte die Fragen!
1. Was für ein Fernsehgerät habt ihr? Wie groß ist es?
2. Wie viele Programme könnt ihr empfangen (*receive*)?
3. Welche Ausstattung (*features*) hat euer Fernsehgerät?
4. Habt ihr Kabelfernsehen oder eine Zimmerantenne?
5. Wie steuert ihr euer Fernsehgerät?
6. Wie viele Fernsehgeräte habt ihr? Wo stehen sie?
7. Wann gebrauchst du einen Kopfhörer?
8. Hast du einen eigenen Fernseher? Wenn ja, was für einen?

So sagt man das!

Asking for and giving permission

You have been using the helping verbs **dürfen** and **können** in questions such as:

> Warum darfst du keine Bananen essen?
> Kann ich bitte Andrea sprechen?

When asking for permission, you could say:

> Darf ich (bitte) das Fernsehgerät einschalten?
> Kann ich bitte mal die Fernbedienung haben?
> He, du! Lass mich mal das Fernsehmagazin sehen!

When giving permission, you may say:

> Ja, natürlich! Bitte schön!
> Bitte! Hier!
> Gern! Hier ist es!

Which one of these questions seems to be the most formal or polite?

 Grammatikheft, S. 84, Ü. 6

 17 Lass mal ...!

Sprechen Frag deinen Partner, ob du die folgenden Sachen sehen oder haben darfst! Er erlaubt es dir.

Fernbedienung Zimmerantenne
Wetterbericht
Kopfhörer Fernsehmagazin
Fernsehgerät
Sportsendung Programmanzeige

Ein wenig Grammatik

One of the many meanings of the verb **lassen** is *to let*, in questions and statements asking for permission.

> **Lass mich bitte mal sehen!**
> **Lässt du mich bitte fernsehen?**

The verb **lassen** has a stem-vowel change in the **du-** and **er/sie-**forms.

 Übungsheft, S. 115, Ü. 2

 Grammatikheft, S. 85, Ü. 7

Mehr Grammatikübungen, S. 292, Ü. 6

ZWEITE STUFE STANDARDS: 1.1, 1.2, 5.1 *zweihundertdreiundachtzig*

So sagt man das!

Asking for information and expressing an assumption

You already know one way of asking for information using *yes/no* questions:

> **Hat das Gerät eine Fernbedienung?**

Here is another way of asking a *yes/no* question, using an **ob**-clause:

> **Wissen Sie, ob das Gerät eine LED-Programmanzeige hat?**
> **Können Sie mir sagen, ob das Gerät einen Kopfhöreranschluss hat?**

As a response, you may express an assumption by saying:

> **Ich glaube schon, dass** (er eine LED-Programmanzeige hat).
> **Ich meine doch, dass** (das Gerät einen Kopfhöreranschluss hat).

What position does the conjugated verb occupy in the **dass**-clause? And in the **ob**-clause? How would you ask a friend the above questions, using **ob**-clauses? What about asking two friends?

Grammatikheft, S. 85, Ü. 8

18 Du brauchst Information

Sprechen Du brauchst einen neuen Fernseher*, aber bevor du ihn kaufst, hast du viele Fragen. Spiel die Rollen von Kunde und Verkäufer mit einem Klassenkameraden und frag, welche Ausstattung der Fernseher hat!

BEISPIEL   KUNDE   Können Sie mir sagen, ob …

19 Weißt du, ob …?

Sprechen Die neue Fernsehsaison beginnt bald. Du möchtest etwas über deine Lieblingssendung wissen. Dein Partner hat ein Fernsehprogramm von zu Hause mitgebracht. Du möchtest Folgendes wissen (verwende dabei **ob-Sätze**, *if-clauses*):

a. wann die Sendung kommt
b. um welche Zeit sie kommt
c. wer wieder mitspielt

Ausstattung
Farbfernsehgerät
Stereogerät
Kabelfernsehen
LED-Programmanzeige
Fernbedienung
Kopfhöreranschluss

BEISPIEL   DU   Weißt du, ob … noch am Samstag kommt?

20 Und du?

Sprechen/Schreiben Eure Schule macht eine Umfrage über die Fernsehgewohnheiten *(viewing habits)* von Schülern! Beantworte die Fragen des Reporters der Schülerzeitung! Such dir einen Partner und spielt die Rollen von Reporter und Schüler! Mach dir Notizen!

1. Wie viel Zeit verbringst du vor dem Fernsehgerät?
2. Welches Programm siehst du dir am meisten an?
3. Zu welcher Zeit siehst du fern?
4. Welches sind deine Lieblingssendungen? Warum?
5. Welche Sendungen siehst du dir nur ab und zu an? Warum?
6. Wofür interessierst du dich überhaupt nicht?
7. Schaust du dir die Werbespots an? Warum? Warum nicht?

---

*__Fernseher__ is a popular way of referring to a **Fernsehgerät**.

21 Was steht im Fernsehprogramm?

Lesen/Sprechen Lies, was Andreas über das Fernsehprogramm sagt! Was bedeuten die Wörter **montags, dienstags,** usw.?

Montags läuft immer eine Krimiserie. Die kommt abends im ARD. Dienstags kommt auf SAT 1 das „Glücksrad" ... und samstags kommt im ZDF immer „Das aktuelle Sport-Studio."

Wortschatz

montags	freitags
dienstags	samstags
mittwochs	sonntags
donnerstags	

Grammatikheft, S. 86, Ü. 9
Übungsheft, S. 117, Ü. 5–6

22 Grammatik im Kontext

a. Lesen/Sprechen Dein Partner, ein deutscher Austauschschüler, möchte wissen, wann in der Woche im Fernsehen etwas läuft, wofür er sich vielleicht interessiert. Sieh in deinem Fernsehmagazin nach und sag es ihm! Tauscht dann die Rollen aus!

b. Schreiben Schreib mindestens sechs kurze Gespräche, wie im Beispiel.

BEISPIEL   PARTNER Was läuft denn samstags so im Fernsehen?
               DU Samstags läuft fast nie etwas Besonderes. Aber sonntags läuft immer …

Ein wenig Grammatik

The verb **laufen,** *to walk* or *run,* is also used to talk about what *is on* TV. How would you say the following sentence in English?

   Läuft *60 Minutes* **noch am Sonntag?**

Laufen has a stem-vowel change in the **du** and **er/sie**-forms:

   Läufst du schnell zum Zeitungsstand?
   Ich will sehen, was im Fernsehen läuft.

Übungsheft, S. 116, Ü. 3–4
Grammatikheft, S.86, Ü. 10–11

Mehr Grammatikübungen, S. 292, Ü. 7

Wann?

montags
dienstags
mittwochs
donnerstags
freitags
samstags
sonntags

Wie oft?

immer   regelmäßig
fast immer   manchmal
meistens   kaum
    fast nie
häufig   selten
    nie
sehr oft   oft

Was?

etwas/nichts Besonderes
etwas ganz Tolles: …
eine super Sendung: …
ein ganz gutes Programm: …
ein toller Film

23 Eine Reportage

Schreiben Du musst jetzt einen kurzen Bericht über die Fernsehgewohnheiten von deinem Partner, einem typischen Schüler, für deine Schülerzeitung schreiben. Schau auf deine Notizen von Übung 20, und schreib einen kurzen Bericht über ihn!

Dritte Stufe

Objectives Expressing surprise, agreement, and disagreement; talking about plans

Autofahren kostet viel Geld!

Für einen neuen Wagen muss man heute so um die 10 000 Euro auf den Tisch legen, und der Preis kann noch höher sein, wenn man sich eine Menge Auto-Extras dazu kauft, wie zum Beispiel eine Servolenkung oder Breitreifen. Auch sind die monatlichen Unterhaltungskosten ziemlich hoch, was die Statistik nebenan beweist.

1. Wie viele Extras haben deutsche PKWs?
2. Wie viel muss der Autofahrer monatlich für sein Auto zahlen?

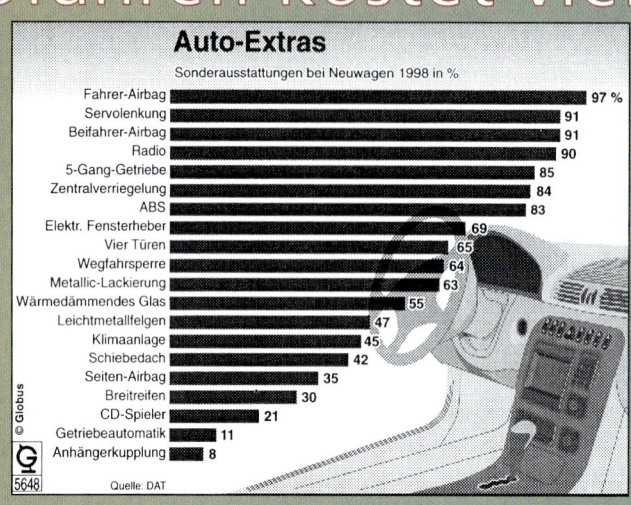

Wortschatz

Jedes Auto hat ...

Übungsheft, S. 118, Ü. 1–2 Grammatikheft, S. 87, Ü. 12

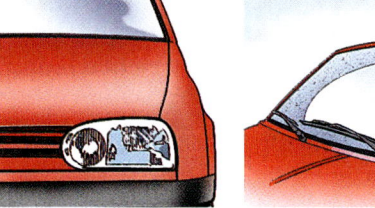

Scheinwerfer   Scheibenwischer   eine Fußbremse   eine Handbremse

Es gibt auch Extras, zum Beispiel ...

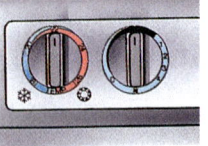  

eine Klimaanlage   ein Schiebedach   Breitreifen

Und dann noch...

ein Stereo-Radio, einen Kassettenspieler
eine Automatik   *automatic transmission*
eine Servolenkung   *power steering*
Servobremsen   *power brakes*
ein 5-Gang Getriebe   *five-speed transmission*
eine Zentralverriegelung   *automatic locks*
eine Alarmanlage   *an alarm system*
Sitzschoner   *seat covers*
Alufelgen   *aluminum rims*
Rallyestreifen   *rally stripes*
Aufkleber   *(bumper) stickers*

KAPITEL 10   Viele Interessen!

24 Welche Extras haben die beiden Autos? Script and answers on p. 269G

Zuhören Zwei Leute beschreiben ihre Autos. Mach dir Notizen! Welche Extras haben beide Autos? Welche Extras hat ein Auto, die das andere nicht hat?
CD 10 Tr. 9

25 Und du?

Sprechen Such dir eine Partnerin und tauscht Informationen zu den folgenden zwei Fragen aus!

1. Welche Ausstattung hat euer Auto zu Hause?
2. Was für ein Auto wünschst du dir einmal? Was für ein Auto muss es sein? Welche Extras muss es haben? Welche Extras brauchst du nicht?

So sagt man das!

Expressing surprise, agreement, and disagreement

You already know many expressions to express surprise, such as:

Was? Wirklich?

Here are some others:

Das ist ja unglaublich! or **Das ist nicht möglich!** or **Das gibt's doch nicht!**

You also know many expressions for expressing agreement, such as:

Gut! Na klar! Gern! Ja, das stimmt!

Here are some others:

Da stimm ich dir zu! or **Da hast du (bestimmt) Recht!** or **Einverstanden!**

When expressing disagreement, you may say:

Das finde ich nicht. or **Das stimmt (überhaupt) nicht!**

Grammatikheft, S. 87–88, Ü. 13–16

---

26 Ja, das gibt's doch nicht!

Sprechen Bring Werbung für Autos mit in die Deutschstunde! Zeig deinem Partner, welches Auto du dir gern kaufen möchtest und warum! Dein Partner ist überrascht, dass dieses Auto nicht viele Extras hat. Du sagst ihm, dass du das nicht brauchst und nennst einen Grund dafür. Dein Partner stimmt dir zu oder auch nicht.

Ein wenig Grammatik

Schon bekannt

Remember to use **kein**, *not, not any, no,* to negate a noun rather than an entire sentence.

Es hat **keine** Klimaanlage.
Ich brauche **kein** Schiebedach.

Mehr Grammatikübungen,
S. 292, Ü. 8

BEISPIEL
DU   Ich möchte mir gern dieses Auto kaufen; es sieht toll aus und ist nicht so teuer.
PARTNER   Aber schau! Es hat keine (Klimaanlage). Das gibt's doch nicht!
DU   Ich brauch keine. Es ist nicht so heiß bei uns.
PARTNER   Da hast du Recht. *oder* Das finde ich nicht. Ich …

DRITTE STUFE   STANDARDS: 1.1, 1.2   *zweihundertsiebenundachtzig*

Ein wenig Landeskunde

In Deutschland muss man 18 Jahre alt sein, um den Führerschein für einen PKW machen zu können. Jeder Bewerber muss erst einmal eine Fahrschule besuchen. Der theoretische Unterricht besteht aus mindestens zehn Doppelstunden zu je 90 Minuten. Für die Fahrpraxis sind heute 20 normale Fahrstunden vorgeschrieben und zehn Sonderfahrten — auf Landstraßen, auf der Autobahn, auch Fahrten bei Regen und in der Nacht. Um den Führerschein zu bekommen, braucht man also ziemlich viel Zeit — und auch viel Geld. Die Durchschnittskosten für einen PKW-Führerschein liegen heute bei EUR 1500. — Wie bekommt man einen Führerschein in den Vereinigten Staaten?

So sagt man das!

Talking about plans

You have been talking about plans in sentences that contain a word referring to future time, such as:

Morgen gehe ich schwimmen. *or* **Wir gehen am Samstag ins Kino.**

If you want to express your future plans in a very definite manner, you can say:

Ich werde mir einmal einen tollen Wagen kaufen.
In einem halben Jahr werde ich den Führerschein machen.

Name the verbs used in each of these two sentences. Which one is the conjugated verb? The infinitive? How would you say these sentences in English?

27 Über Fernsehen und Autos   Script and answers on p. 269H

Zuhören Zwei Schüler unterhalten sich übers Fernsehen und über Autos. Hör ihrem Gespräch gut zu, und schreib nur die Dinge auf, die jeder ganz bestimmt machen wird!

CD 10 Tr. 10

28 Was wirst du dir kaufen?

Du sagst einem Partner, was du dir ganz bestimmt kaufen wirst. Er ist überrascht, aber du gibst ihm einen guten Grund.

Beispiel
Du Ich werde mir mal ein Auto mit einem Schiebedach kaufen.
Partner Wirklich? Was willst du denn mit einem Schiebedach?
Du Ein Schiebedach ist sehr praktisch — Luft und Sonne können ins Auto!
Partner Das finde ich nicht. Ich meine, dass …

Was?
ein Auto

mit einem Schiebedach
mit einer Klimaanlage
mit Zentralverriegelung
mit einer Alarmanlage
mit …

einen Fernseher

mit einer Fernbedienung
mit einem Kabeltuner
mit einer LED-Anzeige
mit …

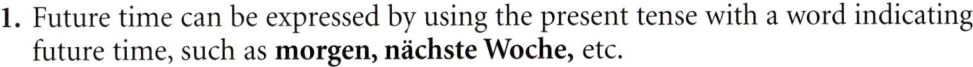

Grammatik

The future tense with **werden**

1. Future time can be expressed by using the present tense with a word indicating future time, such as **morgen, nächste Woche,** etc.

    Morgen gehen wir schwimmen.

2. Another way to express future events is to use the verb **werden** as an auxiliary verb together with another verb in the infinitive.

    In einem halben Jahr **werde** ich den Führerschein **machen.**

3. The present tense forms of **werden** are:

ich	werde	wir	werden
du	wirst	ihr	werdet
er, sie, es, man	wird	sie, Sie	werden

4. In clauses beginning with **dass, ob, wenn,** or **weil,** the conjugated form of **werden** is in last position, preceded by the infinitive.

    Ich weiß nicht, ob ich mir diesen Wagen kaufen **werde.**

Übungsheft, S. 119–120, Ü. 3–7   Grammatikheft, S. 89–90, Ü. 17–19

Mehr Grammatikübungen, S. 293, Ü. 9–11

29 Grammatik im Kontext

a. **Sprechen** Dein Partner macht eine Bemerkung, oder er fragt dich etwas. Du sagst ihm, was du tun wirst. Denk an so viele Antworten wie möglich!

   PARTNER **Du bist wirklich sehr müde.**
   DU **Das stimmt! Und ich werde gleich mal eine kleine Pause machen.**

b. **Schreiben** Schreib mindestens sechs Antworten zu den Bemerkungen, die dein Partner gemacht hat.

30 Du und dein Partner

1. **Sprechen** Frag deinen Partner, was er sich dieses Wochenende im Fernsehen ganz bestimmt ansehen wird! Er nennt dir mindestens drei Sendungen, und er sagt dir auch, warum er sich diese Programme ansehen wird.

2. **Sprechen** Dein Partner fragt dich, was für ein Auto du dir einmal kaufen wirst. Du sagst es ihm, und du sagst ihm auch, was für eine Ausstattung und welche Extras es haben wird und warum.

3. **Sprechen** Frag deine Partnerin, ob sie schon ihren Führerschein hat oder wann sie ihn machen wird! Frag sie auch, wie man sich auf den amerikanischen Führerschein vorbereiten muss! Würdest du lieber den deutschen Führerschein machen? Warum oder warum nicht?

31

Du arbeitest in der Sportabteilung für ein TV-Magazin. Deine Aufgabe ist, Reklame für eine kommende Sportübertragung zu schreiben.

Mehr Grammatikübungen

Erste Stufe Objective Asking about and expressing interest

1 Sieh dir die Illustrationen an und schreib, für welche Sendungen du dich interessierst und wofür sich deine Freunde interessieren. Schreib die richtigen Formen des Verbs und des Reflexivpronomens in den Fragesatz, und die richtige Form des Verbs und des Reflexivpronomens in die Antwort. Schreib auch die Antwort auf die Frage. (S. 277)

BEISPIEL

Wofür _____ du _____ ?
Wofür **interessierst** du **dich**?
Ich _____ _____ für _____ .
Ich **interessiere mich** für **Ratesendungen**.

Wofür _____ ihr _____ ?
Wir _____ _____ für _____ .
interessiert; euch
interessieren; uns; Sportsendungen

Wofür _____ Sie _____ ?
Ich _____ _____ für _____ .
interessieren; sich
interessiere; mich; die Nachrichten

Wofür _____ er _____ ?
Er _____ _____ für _____ .
interessiert; sich
interessiert; sich; Natursendungen

Wofür _____ du _____ ?
Ich _____ _____ für _____ .
interessierst; dich
interessiere; mich; den Wetterbericht

2 Du drückst deine eigenen Interessen und die deiner Freunde aus, und du fragst andere, was für Interessen sie haben. Schreib die folgenden Sätze und Fragen ab, und schreib dabei in zwei Lücken das richtige Reflexivpronomen und in die andere Lücke das richtige **wo**-Adverb (**wo**-compound). (S. 277)

1. Ja, ich interessiere _____ für Sport. Und du, _____ interessierst du _____ ? *mich; wofür; dich*
2. Wir interessieren _____ für Politik. Und ihr, _____ interessiert ihr _____ ? *uns; wofür; euch*
3. Ismar interessiert _____ für Autos. Und _____ interessiert _____ Andreas? *sich; wofür; sich*
4. Astrid interessiert _____ für Mode. Und _____ interessiert _____ Antja? *sich; wofür; sich*
5. Ich interessiere _____ für Filme. Und ihr, _____ interessiert ihr _____ ? *mich; wofür; euch*
6. Wir interessieren _____ für CDs. Und du, _____ interessierst du _____ ? *uns; wofür; dich*

3 Du sprichst über deine eigenen Interessen, und du fragst Freunde nach ihren Interessen. Schreib die folgenden Sätze und Fragen ab, und schreib dabei die fehlenden Reflexivpronomen und **wo**-Adverbien (*wo*-compounds) in die Lücken. (S. 277)

1. Ich freue _____ auf den Krimi. Und _____ freust du _____ ? — mich; worauf; dich
2. Ismar spricht über seinen Führerschein. Und _____ spricht Andreas? — worüber
3. Andreas interessiert _____ für CDs. Und _____ interessierst du _____ ? — sich; wofür; dich
4. Wir freuen _____ auf die Ferien. Und _____ freut ihr _____ ? — uns; worauf; euch
5. Ich spreche heute über Politik. Und _____ sprichst du heute? — worüber
6. Ich interessiere _____ für Sport. Und _____ interessierst du _____ ? — mich; wofür; dich

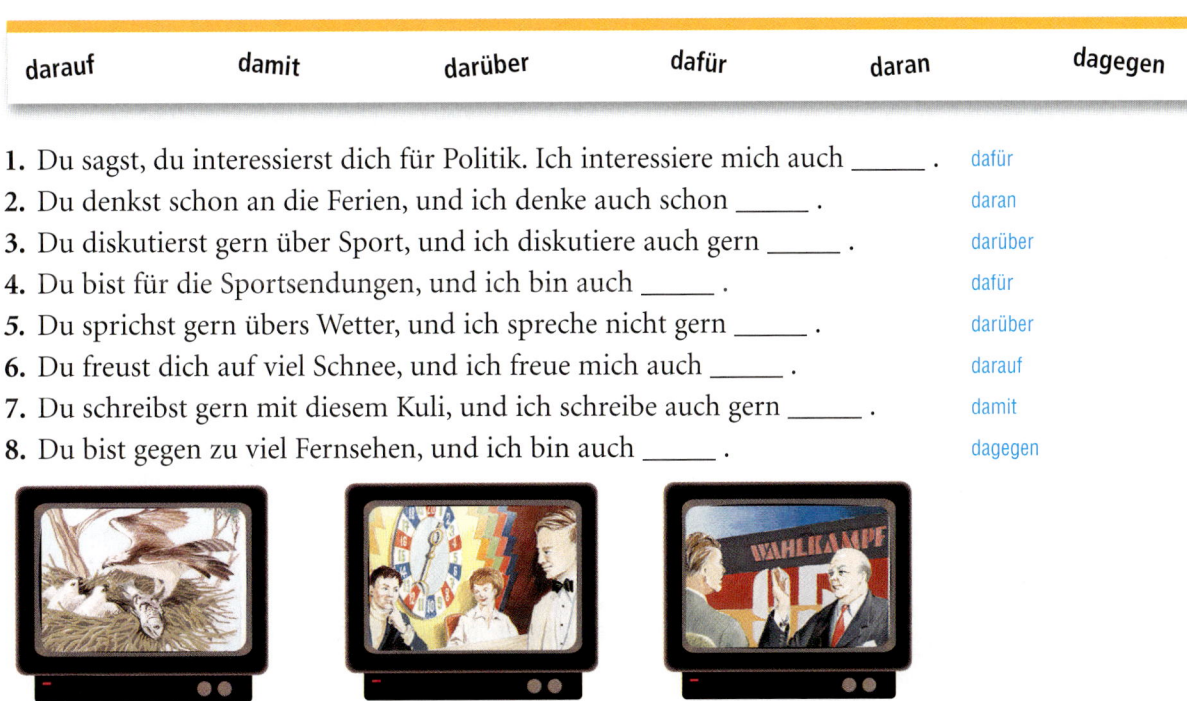

4 Welches **da**-Wort passt? Such dir das richtige **da**-Adverb im Kasten aus und schreib es in die Lücken. (S. 277)

| darauf | damit | darüber | dafür | daran | dagegen |

1. Du sagst, du interessierst dich für Politik. Ich interessiere mich auch _____ . — dafür
2. Du denkst schon an die Ferien, und ich denke auch schon _____ . — daran
3. Du diskutierst gern über Sport, und ich diskutiere auch gern _____ . — darüber
4. Du bist für die Sportsendungen, und ich bin auch _____ . — dafür
5. Du sprichst gern übers Wetter, und ich spreche nicht gern _____ . — darüber
6. Du freust dich auf viel Schnee, und ich freue mich auch _____ . — darauf
7. Du schreibst gern mit diesem Kuli, und ich schreibe auch gern _____ . — damit
8. Du bist gegen zu viel Fernsehen, und ich bin auch _____ . — dagegen

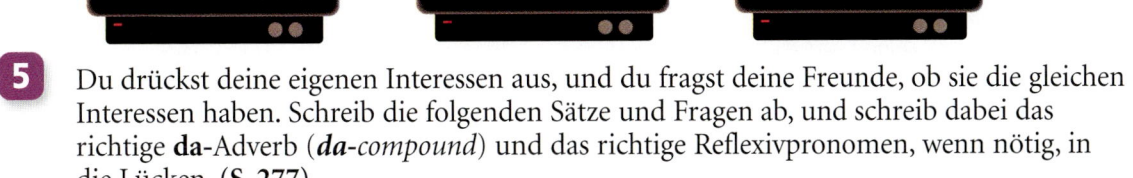

5 Du drückst deine eigenen Interessen aus, und du fragst deine Freunde, ob sie die gleichen Interessen haben. Schreib die folgenden Sätze und Fragen ab, und schreib dabei das richtige **da**-Adverb (*da*-compound) und das richtige Reflexivpronomen, wenn nötig, in die Lücken. (S. 277)

1. Ich freue _____ auf den Krimi. Freust du _____ auch _____ ? — mich; dich; darauf
2. Ich spreche über die Umwelt. Sprichst du auch _____ ? — darüber
3. Ich interessiere _____ für Politik. Interessierst du _____ auch _____ ? — mich; dich; dafür
4. Wir freuen _____ auf die Ferien. Freut ihr _____ auch _____ ? — uns; euch; darauf
5. Wir sprechen über die Talkshow. Sprecht ihr auch _____ ? — darüber
6. Wir interessieren _____ für Mode. Interessiert ihr _____ auch _____ ? — uns; euch; dafür

MEHR GRAMMATIKÜBUNGEN   STANDARDS: 1.2   *zweihunderteinundneunzig*   **291**

Mehr Grammatikübungen

Zweite Stufe
Objectives Asking for and giving permission; asking for information and expressing an assumption

6 Du fragst, ob du fernsehen darfst. Schreib den folgenden Absatz ab, und schreib dabei die richtigen Formen des Verbs **lassen** in die Lücken! (S. 283)

„Mutti, _____ du mich jetzt fernsehen?" — „Ich _____ dich fernsehen,   lässt; lasse

wenn du mir heute Abend hilfst." Viele Eltern _____ ihre Kinder   lassen

immer fernsehen, aber es gibt Eltern, die ihre Kinder nur bestimmte

Programme sehen _____ . Mein Großvater _____ mich alle   lassen; lässt

Programme sehen, aber der Opa hat kein Kabelfernsehen.

7 Du brauchst Informationen übers Fernsehen. Schreib den folgenden Absatz ab, und schreib dabei die richtigen Formen des Verbs **laufen** in die Lücken! (S. 285)

Weißt du, was heute Abend im Fernsehen _____ ? Ich glaube, dass um   läuft

acht Uhr ein Krimi _____ . Heute _____ gleich zwei Krimis, und ich   läuft; laufen

weiß nicht, welchen ich mir ansehen soll. Schau mal nach, was im

ZDF _____ . Ich habe mein Programmheft nicht; _____ doch mal in   läuft; lauf

den Garten, Peter! Es liegt auf dem Gartentisch.

Dritte Stufe
Objectives Expressing surprise, agreement, and disagreement; talking about plans

8 Du bist überrascht, dass eine bestimmte Automarke oder ein bestimmtes Fernsehgerät nicht die Ausrüstung hat, die du erwartest. Schreib die folgenden Sätze ab, und ergänze dabei die Lücken mit der richtigen Form von **kein**! (S. 287)

1. Es ist unglaublich, dass dieses Auto _____ Schiebedach hat.   kein
2. Es ist nicht möglich, dass dieser Wagen _____ Breitreifen hat.   keine
3. Das gibt's doch nicht, dass dieses Modell _____ Klimaanlage hat.   keine
4. Ich kann es nicht glauben, dass du _____ Farbfernseher hast.   keinen
5. Es ist nicht möglich, dass der Fernseher _____ Fernbedienung hat.   keine
6. Es ist unglaublich, dass dieses Gerät _____ Lautstärkeregler hat.   keinen

9 Du sprichst mit verschiedenen Leuten über Dinge, die in der Zukunft liegen. Schreib die folgenden Sätze ab, und ergänze dabei die Lücken mit der richtigen Form des Verbs **werden**! (S. 289)

1. Andreas, was für einen Wagen _____ du dir einmal kaufen? — Ja, ich _____ mir bestimmt mal einen deutschen Wagen kaufen. *wirst; werde*
2. Was _____ ihr einmal tun, wenn ihr aus der Schule kommt? — Ja, wir _____ zuerst einmal an einer Universität studieren. *werdet; werden*
3. Weißt du vielleicht, was der Ismar einmal machen _____ ? — Ich glaube, dass der Ismar für seinen Vater arbeiten _____ . *wird / wird*
4. Frau Wagner, wissen Sie, was Sie machen _____ , wenn die Schule aus ist? — Ich _____ Urlaub machen. *werden / werde*

10 Du bist dir nicht ganz sicher über deine Pläne. Schreib die folgenden Sätze ab und ergänze sie mit der Information, die in Klammern steht. Gebrauche das Futur! (S. 289)

1. (einen Wagen kaufen) Ich weiß nicht, ob ich mir _____ . *einen Wagen kaufen werde*
2. (den Führerschein machen) Ich weiß nicht, ob ich _____ . *den Führerschein machen werde*
3. (heute Abend fernsehen) Ich weiß nicht, ob ich _____ . *heute Abend fernsehen werde*
4. (morgen Fußball spielen) Ich weiß nicht, ob ich _____ . *morgen Fußball spielen werde*
5. (in die Schweiz fahren) Ich weiß nicht, ob ich _____ . *in die Schweiz fahren werde*
6. (morgen ins Kino gehen) Ich weiß nicht, ob ich _____ . *morgen ins Kino gehen werde*

11 Worauf freuen sich diese Leute? Vervollständige diese Sätze und schreib dabei das richtige Reflexivpronomen in die erste Lücke, den abgebildeten Gegenstand in die zweite Lücke und die richtige Form von **werden** in die dritte Lücke. (S. 289)

BEISPIEL

1. Ich freue _____ , dass du dir _____ kaufen _____ .
Ich freue **mich,** dass du dir **ein Auto** kaufen **wirst.**

2. Er freut _____ , dass ich mir _____ kaufen _____ . *sich; einen Fernseher; werde*

3. Wir freuen _____ , dass ihr euch _____ kaufen _____ . *uns; einen Kühlschrank; werdet*

4. Sie freut _____ , dass sie sich _____ kaufen _____ . *sich; ein Rad; wird*

5. Ich freue _____ , dass du dir _____ kaufen _____ . *mich; ein Motorrad; wirst*

Storytelling Book pp. 78–79

Anwendung

Visit Holt Online
go.hrw.com
KEYWORD: WK3 BERLIN-10
Self-Test

The *CD-ROM Tutor* offers guided recording and writing activities to accompany the **Anwendung**. These activities are designed to practice students' oral and written communication skills and to review material from each chapter.

1 **Umfrage halten!** The German channel ZDF is planning a satellite feed into German classes across the United States, and they have hired you to do market research of TV viewing habits. In groups of three, choose one of the categories below and design a questionnaire with at least three questions relating to your topic. Poll the class, tally your results in the group, and present them (in German) to the class.

- **Fernsehkonsum (wie viele Stunden? an welchen Tagen?** usw.**)**
- **beliebte und unbeliebte Programme**
- **beliebte Werbesendungen**
- **Sportsendungen**
- **Musiksendungen**
- **Spielfilme**
- **Serien** (*sitcoms*)
- **Spielshows**

E.g.: Welche Serien schaust du gerne? Wie oft schaust du amerikanische Serien? Wann kommt deine Lieblingsserie? etc.

2 Your partner will describe to you the dream car he or she will one day buy (using **werden**). As your partner describes it, draw a picture according to his or her description. When you're finished, find out if you understood everything by describing the drawing in front of you back to your partner. Then switch roles. Below are types of cars and features your dream car might have.

3 Listen to the Bauer family discuss the evening lineup on TV. As you listen, look at the schedule on page 278 and fill in a chart like the one on the right. For each time slot write the channel the family decides to watch.

CD 10 Tr. 11   Script and answers on p. 269H

18.00	
19.00	
20.00	

4 Schreib in dein Notizbuch deine eigene Meinung zum Thema: Was sind die Vorteile und Nachteile vom Kabelfernsehen?

5 Zum Schreiben

ZDF plans to cancel your favorite television show! You have written a petition and it has been signed by hundreds of people. Now you need to write a persuasive letter to the network convincing them to leave the show on its program schedule.

Schreibtipp The purpose of a **persuasive letter** is not just to inform, but also to convince someone to do or think about something from a different perspective. Consider the person or persons to whom you are writing; what would make them change their minds? What are their expectations, goals, concerns? Your letter should be logical and serious and have a rather formal tone. If you write that the TV show should not be cancelled because it is "way cool," the network might not take your opinion very seriously and would probably not be persuaded.

Vorbereiten

First you need to choose a "favorite show." There are a number of programs listed in this chapter, or you could make up your own program. Then **brainstorm** reasons why people would like this program and use this list to write your letter.

Ausführen

Begin your letter with a sentence that clearly states your reason for writing. Back up your opinion with some facts and good reasons why it is in the best interest of the network to leave your favorite show on the program schedule. One of the facts you could mention is the number of people who signed the petition. You might include "testimonials" by these people. You might also mention any good media reviews the show has received.

Überarbeiten

- Exchange your letter with a partner who should read it and determine whether you have been convincing with your arguments. Have you used strong, clear reasons and believable facts?
- Make changes, proofread for spelling and punctuation errors, revise, print a final copy, and submit it to your teacher.

6 Rollenspiel

In groups of three, pick any product and produce your own commercial for German TV. Try to sell your product to your German audience using the phrases you've learned in this chapter. Be sure to use props or glossy photos!

Kann ich's wirklich?

WK3 BERLIN-10

Can you ask about and express interests? (p. 276)

1 How would you ask a friend, using a **wo**-compound,
a. what his or her interests are? a. Wofür interessierst du dich?
b. what he or she is talking about? b. Worüber sprichst du?
c. what he or she is looking forward to? c. Worauf freust du dich?

2 How would you ask your friend whom he or she is interested in?
2. Für wen interessierst du dich?

3 How would you say, using a **da**-compound, that
a. something interests you? a. Ich interessiere mich dafür.
b. you don't talk about that? b. Ich spreche nicht darüber.
c. you are looking forward to that? c. Ich freue mich darauf.

Can you ask for and give permission? (p. 283)

4 How would you politely ask someone if you may turn on the TV? How might that person respond?
4. Darf (Kann) ich bitte das Fernsehgerät einschalten? — Ja natürlich! Bitte schön!

5 How might you be less polite when asking to have the headphones?
5. He, du! Lass mich mal den Kopfhörer haben!

Can you ask for information and express an assumption? (p. 284)

6 How would you ask
a. a classmate if he or she knows whether you have German today, using an **ob**-clause? How would that person answer that he or she thinks you have class, using a **dass**-clause? a. Weißt du, ob wir heute Deutsch haben? — Ich glaube schon, dass wir heute Deutsch haben.
b. a salesman if a particular car has a lot of extras? How would he respond?
b. Wissen Sie, ob dieses Auto (dieser Wagen) viele Extras hat? — Ich meine doch, dass das Auto viele Extras hat.

Can you express surprise, agreement, and disagreement? (p. 287)

7 How would you respond if someone told you that
a. he or she won $10,000,000 in a sweepstakes? a. E.g.: Was? Wirklich? Das ist ja unglaublich!
b. winning $10,000,000 is difficult? b. E.g.: Da stimm ich dir zu! Da hast du Recht!
c. winning $10,000,000 is very easy?
c. E.g.: Das finde ich nicht. Das stimmt (überhaupt) nicht!

Can you talk about plans? (p. 288)

8 How would you say that a. In einem Jahr werde ich den Führerschein machen.
a. you will get your driver's license in a year?
b. your sister will travel to Berlin soon?
b. Meine Schwester wird bald nach Berlin fahren.

9 How would you ask a friend if he will buy himself a color TV-set?
9. Wirst du dir mal ein Farbfernsehgerät kaufen?

Wortschatz

Erste Stufe

 p. 269X

Talking about television programs

Sehen wir nachher fern?	Are we going to watch TV later?	
fernsehen (sep)	to watch TV	
s. freuen auf (acc)	to look forward to	
Fernseh gucken	to watch TV (colloquial)	
die Sendung, -en	show, program	
das Programm, -e	schedule of shows	
der Sender, -	station, transmitter, channel	
die Nachrichten (pl)	the news	
der Wetterbericht, -e	weather report	
die Sportübertragung, -en	sport telecast	
die Übertragung, -en	telecast, transmission	
die Natursendung, -en	nature program	
die Ratesendung, -en	quiz show	
eine Diskussion über Politik	political discussion	
die Diskussion, -en	discussion	
wo- and da-	compounds (see page 277)	

Zweite Stufe

Talking about a TV set

Habt ihr ein Farbfernsehgerät zu Hause?	Do you have a color television set at home?
das Stereo-Farbfernsehgerät, -e	color stereo television set
der Fernseher, -	television set
die Fernbedienung, -en	remote control
der (Stereo-) Kopfhörer, -	(stereo) headphones
die Zimmerantenne, -n	indoor antenna
der Lautstärkeregler, -	volume control
der Fernseh- und Videowagen, -	TV and video cart
das Ablagefach, ⸚er	storage shelf
die Videocassette, -n	videocassette

Asking for and giving permission

Darf ich (bitte) …?	May I (please) …?
einschalten (sep)	to turn on
Kann ich bitte …?	Can I (please) …?
Lass mich mal …	Let me …
Ja, natürlich!	Yes, of course!
Bitte! Hier!	Here you go!
Gern! Hier ist es!	Here! I insist!
lassen	to let, allow
er/sie lässt	he/she lets, allows

Asking for information

Weißt du, ob …?	Do you know whether …?
Können Sie mir sagen, ob …?	Can you tell me whether …?
Was läuft im Fernsehen?	What's on TV?

Expressing an assumption

Ich glaube schon, dass …	I do believe that …
Ich meine doch, dass …	I really think that …

Expressing recurring time: days of the week

montags	Mondays
dienstags	Tuesdays
mittwochs	Wednesdays
donnerstags	Thursdays
freitags	Fridays
samstags	Saturdays
sonntags	Sundays

Dritte Stufe

Talking about cars

der Scheinwerfer, -	headlight
der Scheibenwischer, -	windshield wiper
die (Fuß-, Hand-) Bremse, -n	(foot, hand) brake
die Klimaanlage, -n	air conditioning
das Schiebedach, ⸚er	sunroof
der Breitreifen, -	wide tire
der Führerschein, -e	driver's license

Expressing surprise

Das ist ja unglaublich!	That's really unbelievable!

Expressing agreement and disagreement

Da stimm ich dir zu!	I agree with you on that!
Da hast du (bestimmt) Recht!	You're right about that!
Einverstanden!	Agreed!
(Das ist) nicht möglich!	(That's) impossible!
Das gibt's doch nicht!	There's just no way!
Das finde ich nicht.	I don't think so.
Das stimmt (überhaupt) nicht!	That's not right (at all)!

Talking about plans

Ich werde mir einen tollen Wagen kaufen.	I'm going to buy myself a great car.
werden	will
du wirst	you will
er/sie/es wird	he/she will

Kapitel 11: Mit Oma ins Restaurant
Chapter Overview

Los geht's! pp. 300–302	*Pläne für Omas Geburtstag,* p. 300			

	FUNCTIONS	**GRAMMAR**	**VOCABULARY**	**RE-ENTRY**
Erste Stufe pp. 303–307	• Asking for, making, and responding to suggestions, p. 306	• The **würde**-forms, p. 307	• Things to see in Berlin, p. 305	Cultural activities and sights in a large city, p. 305 (**Kap. 9, I**); **können**, p. 305 (**Kap. 7, I**); **man**, p. 305 (**Kap. 9, I**); talking about interests, p. 305 (**Kap. 8, II**); making suggestions, p. 306 (**Kap. 6/9, II**)
Zweite Stufe pp. 308–311	• Expressing hearsay, p. 310	• Unpreceded adjectives, p. 311	• German and international cuisine, p. 309 • Words to describe food, p. 310	Eating opportunities, pp. 308 and 310 (**Kap. 6, I**); talking about favorites, p. 310 (**Kap. 10, I**); **dass**, p. 310 (**Kap. 9, I**); **sollen**, p. 310 (**Kap. 8, I**); giving reasons, p. 310 (**Kap. 8, I**); **weil/denn**, p. 310 (**Kap. 8, I**)
Dritte Stufe pp. 312–315	• Ordering in a restaurant, p. 314 • Expressing good wishes, p. 315	• The **hätte**-forms, p. 314	• Things to order in a German restaurant, p. 313	**was für**, p. 313 (**Kap. 10, I**); saying what's available, p. 313 (**Kap. 9, I**); talking about favorites, p. 313 (**Kap. 4, I**); giving reasons, p. 313 (**Kap. 8, I**); ordering in a restaurant, p. 314 (**Kap. 6, I**); ways of addressing people, p. 315 (**Kap. 2, I**); asking for the bill, p. 315 (**Kap. 6, I**)

Zum Lesen pp. 316–317	Das Leben im fremden Land	**Reading Strategy** Reading for comprehension

Mehr Grammatikübungen	**pp. 318–321** Erste Stufe, p. 318	Zweite Stufe, pp. 319–320	Dritte Stufe, pp. 320-321
Review pp. 322–325	Anwendung, pp. 322–323 **Zum Schreiben:** Using all five senses (Writing an advertisement for a restaurant)	Kann ich's wirklich?, p. 324	Wortschatz, p. 325

CULTURE

- Landeskunde: Für welche kulturellen Veranstaltungen interessierst du dich? p. 303
- Ein wenig Landeskunde: State-supported arts, p. 307
- Ein wenig Landeskunde: International cuisine, p. 310
- Menu from **Haus Dannenberg am See**, p. 312

Kapitel 11: Mit Oma ins Restaurant
Chapter Resources

Lesson Planning
One-Stop Planner
Lesson Planner with Substitute Teacher Lesson Plans, pp. 52–56, 75
Student Make-Up Assignments
- Make-Up Assignment Copying Masters, Chapter 11

Listening and Speaking
TPR Storytelling Book, pp. 80–87
Listening Activities
- Student Response Forms for Listening Activities, pp. 83–86
- Additional Listening Activities 11-1 to 11-6, pp. 87–90
- Additional Listening Activities (song), p. 86
- Scripts and Answers, pp. 163–168

Video Guide
- Teaching Suggestions, pp. 70–71
- Activity Masters, pp. 72–74
- Scripts and Answers, pp. 105–107

Activities for Communication
- Communicative Activities, pp. 61–66
- Realia and Teaching Suggestions, pp. 114–117
- Situation Cards, pp. 143–144

Reading and Writing
Reading Strategies and Skills Handbook, Chapter 11
Lies mit mir! 2, Chapter 11
Übungsheft, pp. 121–132

Grammar
Grammatikheft, pp. 91–99
Grammar Tutor for Students of German, Chapter 11

Assessment
Testing Program
- Grammar and Vocabulary Quizzes, **Stufe** Quizzes, and Chapter Test, pp. 275–292
- Score Sheet, Scripts and Answers, pp. 293–300

Alternative Assessment Guide
- Portfolio Assessment, p. 28
- Performance Assessment, p. 42
- CD-ROM Assessment, p. 56

Student Make-Up Assignments
- Alternative Quizzes, Chapter 11

Online Activities
- Interaktive Spiele
- Internet Aktivitäten

Video Program
- Videocassette 4
- Videocassette 5 (captioned version)
- DVD Tutor, Disc 2

Audio Compact Discs
- Textbook Listening Activities, CD 11, Tracks 1–13
- Additional Listening Activities, CD 11, Tracks 19–25
- Assessment Items, CD 11, Tracks 14–18

Interactive CD-ROM Tutor, Disc 3

Teaching Transparencies
- Situations 11-1 to 11-2
- Vocabulary 11-A to 11-B
- Los geht's!
- Mehr Grammatikübungen Answers
- Grammatikheft Answers

Use the **One-Stop Planner CD-ROM** with Test Generator to aid in lesson planning and pacing.

For each chapter, the **One-Stop Planner** includes:
- Editable lesson plans with direct links to teaching resources
- Printable worksheets from resource books
- Direct launches to the HRW Internet activities
- Video and audio segments
- Test Generator
- Clip Art for vocabulary items

Kapitel 11: Mit Oma ins Restaurant

Projects

Berühmte Leute

In this activity students will do a report about a famous German-speaking person. Begin this project before you start Chapter 11, allowing students time for research and revision of their projects. This project is designed for students to do individually. The final project should consist of a written report and a brief oral presentation.

MATERIALS

Students may need

encyclopedias and other reference materials. They should also be encouraged to do research online, providing adequate documentation of all sources.

SUGGESTED SEQUENCE

1. Students do research at a library on the person they choose.
2. Students compile and organize their notes and materials.
3. Students find one piece of realia to support their reports. For example, if the subject of the report is an author, the student might want to bring in a book that the author wrote. For a report on a composer, the student might bring a recording of one of the composer's works, or even try to play part of a piece.
4. Students prepare their written reports and oral presentations.
5. After the oral presentation, students turn in their final projects, which can then be displayed in class.

GRADING THE PROJECT

Suggested point distribution (**total = 100 points**)
Written report (content, correct
usage, appearance) 60
Oral presentation (including realia) 40

Games

Was wird beschrieben?

This game is a good way to review the vocabulary for cultural events.

Preparation Write the names of famous pieces of music, operas, and plays on index cards.

Procedure Have one student at a time come to the front of the room to draw from the stack of index cards. The student looks at the card and then describes the piece without giving away the title. The rest of the class may then ask yes/no questions to which the student responds with **ja** or **nein**. The student who guesses the name of the piece correctly wins a point. This game can also be played in teams, in which case the person who guesses correctly scores a point for his or her team.

Storytelling

Mini-Geschichte

*This story accompanies Teaching Transparency 11-1. Read the **Mini-Geschichte** to your students, or have them role-play the conversation using proper pronunciation and intonation and appropriate facial expressions. Ask students to write possible replies by Erika and Ingrid to Hans's suggestion to go to a restaurant. Do students think that Erika, Ingrid, and Hans will have a good time in Berlin? Why or why not?*

Was machen wir?

ERIKA Endlich sind wir in Berlin! Was wollen wir machen?

INGRID Ich bin dafür, dass wir eine Stadtrundfahrt machen.

HANS Aber es ist doch schon zu spät dafür.

ERIKA Ich würde gern ins Ballett gehen.

HANS Aber das ist doch langweilig! Ich bin total allergisch gegen Ballettröckchen (tutu).

INGRID Ich würde am liebsten in die Oper gehen.

HANS Die Oper? Die ist ja furchtbar und so ungesund für die Ohren.

INGRID Also, Hans, du willst wohl überhaupt nichts machen?

HANS Doch! Wie wär's mit einem Restaurant? Ich bin wahnsinnig hungrig.

Traditions

Die Rosinenbomber

Wenige Tage nach der Währungsreform 1948 sperrten sowjetische Truppen alle Zufahrtswege nach West-Berlin. Durch die Blockade wollte die Sowjetunion die Westmächte zwingen, auf die geplante Gründung eines Weststaates zu verzichten. Daraufhin stellten die Westmächte die Versorgung West-Berlins über eine Luftbrücke sicher. Mit 280 000 Flügen wurden die 2,1 Millionen Einwohner Berlins mit über zwei Millionen Tonnen lebenswichtiger Ware versorgt. Alle zwei bis drei Minuten landete eine Maschine, im Volksmunde „Rosinenbomber" genannt, auf einem der drei West-Berliner Flughäfen. Die Summe aller Flugstunden ergibt eine Flugzeit von mehr als 35 Jahren! Eine besondere Bedeutung für die Kinder Berlins erlangte der US-Pilot Gail Halvorsen. Er warf zu Weihnachten winzige Fallschirme mit Schokolade und Süßigkeiten ab. Bald warteten Tausende von Kindern am Flugfeld Tempelhof auf den „Schokoladenflieger". Obwohl die Sowjets nach 322 Tagen schließlich einlenkten und die Land- und Wasserwege nach Berlin wieder öffneten, brach eine neue Epoche an, die 40 Jahre lang die Weltgeschichte beherrschen sollte: der Kalte Krieg zwischen Ost und West.

Ask students to research in the library or on the Internet the Berlin blockade of 1948. Have students present their research to the class.

Rezept

Eisbein mit Sauerkraut

Für 4 Personen

Zutaten
g=Gramm, EL = Esslöffel, l = Liter

- 4 Portionen Eisbein (Zusammen etwa 1 kg)
- 2 Zwiebeln
- 1 Bund Suppengrün
- 2 Lorbeerblätter
- 3 Gewürzkörner
- 8 Pfefferkörner
- 750 g Sauerkraut
- 50 g Schmalz
- 5 Wacholderbeeren
- 1 Prise Zucker
- 1 Kartoffel
- evtl. etwas Fleischextrakt

Zubereitung
Das Eisbein in reichlich kaltem Wasser aufsetzen, aufkochen, und abschäumen. Dann mit 1 Zwiebel, geputztem, nicht zerkleinertem Suppengrün, 1 Lorbeerblatt, den Gewürz- und Pfefferkörnern etwa 2½ Stunden langsam weich kochen.

Zur gleichen Zeit das Sauerkraut zubereiten: Die zweite Zwiebel würfeln, im Schmalz anbraten. Das Sauerkraut etwas auseinanderzupfen, dann mit dem zweiten Lorbeerblatt, den Wacholderbeeren und 1 Prise Zucker im Schmalz schmoren. Bei Bedarf etwas durchgesiebte Eisbeinbrühe angießen. Das Sauerkraut zum Schluss mit der roh gegriebenen Kartoffel binden und noch einmal 5 Minuten durchkochen lassen.

Kapitel 11: Mit Oma ins Restaurant
Technology

Videocassette 4, 5 (captioned version)
DVD Tutor, Disc 2
See Video Guide, pages 69–74

DVD/Video

Los geht's! • Pläne für Omas Geburtstag

Andreas and Astrid are discussing possible surprises for Oma for her birthday. Finally, Andreas asks Oma what she would like to do. She decides on going to a local restaurant for lunch. Andreas makes reservations at a restaurant right on the river. The entire family goes to the restaurant, they all order drinks and lunch, they discuss the beautiful weather, and they toast Oma.

Landeskunde

Für welche kulturellen Veranstaltungen interessierst du dich?
People discuss cultural events they like to attend.

Fortsetzung

The scene at the restaurant continues. Their food comes, they talk about how they like their food, they watch a boat go by, and they say they would like to come back to this restaurant next year.

Videoclips
- **C&A**® (department store)
- **Brossard Torten**® (cakes)
- **Leibnitz Kekse**® (cookies)

Interactive CD-ROM Tutor

Activity	Activity Type	Pupil's Edition Reference
1. Wortschatz	Merkspiel	p. 305
2. Wortschatz	Was ist richtig?	pp. 309, 310
3. Grammatik	Was fehlt?	p. 311
4. Wortschatz	Wort und Bild Erfahren/Wählen	p. 313
5. Grammatik	Was fehlt?	pp. 307, 314
6. So sagt man das!	Wozu gehört's?	pp. 314, 315
Landeskunde	Für welche kulturellen Veranstaltungen interessierst du dich? Was ist richtig?	p. 303
Zum Sprechen	*Guided recording*	pp. 322–323
Zum Schreiben	*Guided writing*	pp. 322–323

Teacher Management System
Launch the program, type "admin" in the password area, and press RETURN. Log on to **www.hrw.com/CDROMTUTOR** for a detailed explanation of the Teacher Management System.

DVD Tutor

The *DVD Tutor* contains all material from the *Video Program* as described above. German captions are available for use at your discretion for all sections of the video. The *DVD Tutor* also provides a variety of video-based activities that assess students' understanding of **Los geht's!, Fortsetzung,** and **Landeskunde,** as well as the new **Grammatik im Kontext** presentations.

The *DVD Tutor* may be used on any DVD video player connected to a television or video monitor.

One-Stop Planner CD-ROM

To preview all resources available for this chapter, use the **One-Stop Planner CD-ROM**, Disc 3.

Visit Holt Online
go.hrw.com
KEYWORD: WK3 BERLIN-11
Online Edition

Go.Online!

Premier Online Edition

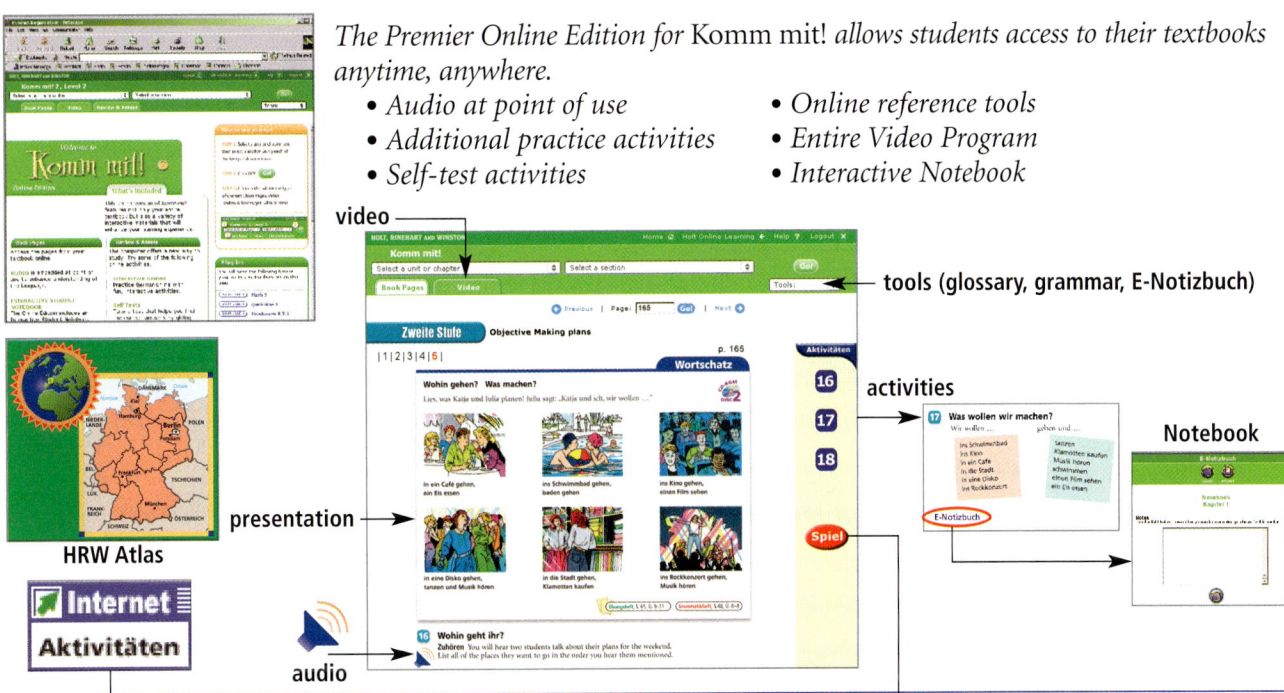

The Premier Online Edition for *Komm mit!* allows students access to their textbooks anytime, anywhere.

- Audio at point of use
- Additional practice activities
- Self-test activities
- Online reference tools
- Entire Video Program
- Interactive Notebook

HRW Atlas — presentation — audio — video — tools (glossary, grammar, E-Notizbuch) — activities — Notebook

Internet Aktivitäten

These guided internet activities include a worksheet and pre-selected and pre-screened authentic web sites from the German-speaking countries. You can use these activities

- to help students develop research skills in the target language
- to introduce students to authentic cultural information
- as a project

Interaktive Spiele

You can use the interactive activities in this chapter

- to practice grammar, vocabulary, and chapter functions
- as homework
- as an assessment option
- as a self-test
- to prepare for the Chapter Test

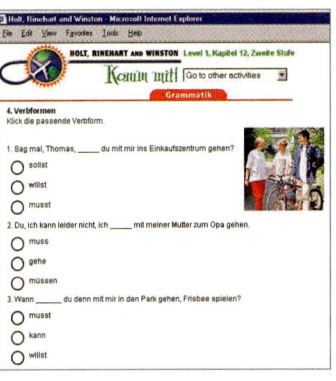

Webprojekt Have students find the recipe for a German or an international dish. Have them list the ingredients and quantities needed for four people. You may also want to have them describe the preparation of the dish. Encourage students to exchange useful Web sites with their classmates. Have students document their sources by referencing the names and URLs of all the sites they consulted.

STANDARDS: 1.2, 3.2, 5.1, 5.2   KAPITEL 11   TECHNOLOGY   297F

Kapitel 11: Mit Oma ins Restaurant
Textbook Listening Activities Scripts

Erste Stufe

7 p. 306

SIMONE Ich gehe sehr gerne ins Theater. Zum Geburtstag habe ich von meinen Großeltern ein Abonnement für das Landestheater in unserer Stadt bekommen. Es gefällt mir sehr, ganz vorne in einer der ersten Reihen im Theater zu sitzen und die Schauspieler aus der Nähe zu sehen. Letzte Woche habe ich eine bayerische Bauernkomödie gesehen. Das Publikum hat Tränen gelacht. Also, ich finde die Atmosphäre in einem Theater tausendmal besser als zu Hause vor dem Fernseher zu sitzen.

ARNO Also, wenn ich mal am Wochenende was ganz Besonderes machen will, dann geh ich in ein Musical. Vor ein paar Monaten habe ich „Das Phantom der Oper" gesehen. Einfach sagenhaft! Ich hab mir sofort danach die CD gekauft! Leider werden bei uns in der Stadt keine Musicals aufgeführt. Da muss man schon bis nach Hamburg reinfahren. Das dauert so ungefähr zwei Stunden, bis man dort ist. Aber der weite Weg lohnt sich auf jeden Fall! Ich finde Musicals einfach toll!

JUTTA Ich liebe Opern! Wagner, Mozart, Verdi … ich höre alles gern. Am liebsten mag ich es, wenn die Oper in Italienisch gesungen wird. Die italienische Sprache ist so temperamentvoll und dramatisch! Aber an einer Oper gefällt mir nicht nur der Gesang, mich faszinieren auch die schönen Kostüme der Sänger. Leider sind Opernkarten so teuer, und deswegen gehe ich nur selten ins Opernhaus. Die meisten Opern hab ich im Fernsehen gesehen.

Answers to Activity 7 Simone: Theaterstück „Andorra" von Max Frisch; Arno: Musical „Oklahoma" von Hammerstein; Jutta: Oper „Die Zauberflöte" von Mozart

10 p. 307

1. PAUL Was sollen wir denn heute unternehmen, Thomas? Hast du Lust, in den Stadtpark zu gehen und Frisbee zu spielen? Oder wir können auch einfach nur so in den Park gehen, uns auf die Wiese legen und faulenzen.

   THOMAS Nee, das ist mir zu langweilig! Hast du keine andere Idee?

   PAUL Ja, also gehen wir doch wieder zum Hafen runter und gucken, welche Schiffe dort liegen.

   THOMAS Mensch, Paul! Das haben wir doch erst letzte Woche gemacht. Ich bin nicht dafür, dass wir schon wieder dorthin gehen.

2. KARSTEN He, Dominik! Sollen wir mal das neue argentinische Steakhaus an der Ecke ausprobieren? Hast du am Samstag Zeit? Danach können wir uns den neuen Action Thriller mit Mel Gibson im Cinemax ansehen. Also, was meinst du?

   DOMINIK Ja, das wär' nicht schlecht!

3. ULRIKE Hi, Moni! Du, mein Opa hat mir zwei Karten für „Cats" geschenkt. Wie wär's? Willst du mitkommen?

   MONI Ach, ich weiß nicht. Ich interessiere mich nicht so sehr für Musicals. Frag doch mal die Alexandra! Ich glaube, die mag so was. Ich bin dafür, dass wir lieber mal zusammen ins Theater gehen.

Answers to Activity 10 1. nicht einverstanden; 2. einverstanden; 3. nicht einverstanden

Zweite Stufe

16 p. 310

MARITA Du, Beate, wo wollen wir denn heute Abend hin? Ich hätte Lust, essen zu gehen.

BEATE Ja, lass uns doch mal wieder zu dem Türken an der Kreuzberger Straße gehen. Weißt du noch, der hat diese tolle Joghurtsoße zu dem gebratenen Lammfleisch!

MARITA Ja, stimmt! Dort ist das Essen wirklich schön würzig, und viel Knoblauch ist überall drin! Aber könnten wir nicht mal was Neues ausprobieren? Wie wäre es zum Beispiel mit dem mexikanischen Restaurant, das vor kurzem auf der Bismarckstraße aufgemacht hat? Acapulco heißt das oder so!

BEATE Ach, Marita, ich weiß nicht. Mexikanisch hab ich noch nie probiert. Das soll doch ziemlich scharf sein, oder?

MARITA Ja, ich glaub schon. Aber vielleicht gibt es dort auch milde Gerichte. Was meinst du?

BEATE Ja, bestimmt. Aber heute möchte ich eigentlich lieber zum Türken. Ich habe dort noch nie den gegrillten Fisch gegessen.

MARITA Also gut, gehen wir halt dorthin. Bis jetzt hat es mir dort immer gut geschmeckt. Ich glaub, ich weiß auch schon, was ich nehme.

BEATE Was denn?

MARITA Ich probiere mal den gebratenen Reis mit den kleinen deftigen Fleischbällchen, die der Johannes hatte, als wir das letzte Mal dort waren.

BEATE Ja, prima! Komm, wir gehen los!

Answers to Activity 16 türkisch und mexikanisch; Sie gehen türkisch essen, weil …; … das Essen dort würzig ist.; … Beate noch nie den gegrillten Fisch; gegessen hat.; … es Marita bis jetzt immer gut dort; geschmeckt hat.

18 p. 311

OLIVER Na endlich sind wir in Berlin! Du, ich freue mich schon auf die Stadtrundfahrt. Oder sag mal, Kati, sollen wir zuerst etwas essen gehen?

KATI Also, weißt du, Oliver, eigentlich würde ich lieber zuerst die Stadtrundfahrt machen, um halt so viel wie möglich von Berlin zu sehen. Hunger hab ich noch keinen.

OLIVER Also gut! Dann gehen wir erst heute Abend essen. Die Manuela hat mir zwei Restaurants empfohlen, die sie ziemlich gut fand, als sie hier in Berlin war. Das eine heißt „Zum Anker". Dort gibt es hauptsächlich Fischgerichte. Es soll ganz toll eingerichtet sein. Sie hat gesagt, dass an der Eingangstür ein richtig schwerer Anker befestigt ist, und an der Decke sollen Fischernetze hängen. Also, eine richtige Seemannsatmosphäre.

KATI Hat Manuela auch etwas über die Preise und die Bedienung gesagt?

OLIVER Ja, also über die Preise weiß ich nichts. Ach ja, über die Bedienung hat sie auch etwas gesagt. Und zwar kommt der Chef persönlich an den Tisch, um das Tagesgericht zu empfehlen.

KATI Und welches Restaurant hat Manuela dir noch empfohlen?

OLIVER Ja, warte mal, das heißt „Schanghai", ein Chinese natürlich. Dort soll es die beste Pekingente geben, die Manuela jemals gegessen hat. Und die Preise sollen völlig okay sein.

KATI Und was ist mit der Bedienung?

OLIVER Ja, also die Bedienung soll nicht so gut sein. Manuela hat erzählt, dass alle Kellner unfreundlich sind.

KATI Ach, du meine Güte!—Du, der Tobias hat mir hier ein Restaurant empfohlen, das ausschließlich hausgemachte, ostdeutsche Spezialitäten serviert. Also zum Beispiel Thüringer Rostbratwurst oder Leipziger Allerlei. Ist übrigens mein Lieblingsgericht! Tobias hat gesagt, dass man dort ziemlich große Portionen für wenig Geld bekommt!

OLIVER Mhm. Nicht schlecht! Richtig gute Hausmannskost! Wie ist es mit der Atmosphäre? Hat Tobias auch etwas über die Einrichtung gesagt? Wie heißt das Restaurant überhaupt?

KATI Ja, also das Restaurant heißt „Ossi", ist rustikal eingerichtet mit alten Holztischen und Bänken. Ziemlich einfach, aber dafür urgemütlich!

OLIVER Du, Kati, ich glaub, da würd ich gern mal hingehen. Das scheint genau das Richtige für heute Abend zu sein, wenn wir von der Besichtigungstour zurückkommen.

KATI Ja, das find ich auch. Aber nun mal los, auf in die Stadt!

Answers to Activity 18 Zum Anker — Essen: Fischgerichte; Bedienung: Chef; Atmosphäre: Seemannsatmosphäre; Preise: (Oliver doesn't know anything about the prices.); Schanghai — Essen: beste Pekingente; Bedienung: unfreundlich; Atmosphäre: (not mentioned); Preise: okay; Ossi — Essen: hausgemachte, ostdeutsche Spezialitäten, große Portionen; Bedienung: (not mentioned); Atmosphäre: rustikal, einfach, urgemütlich; Preise: nicht teuer

Dritte Stufe

24 p. 314

DAGMAR	Mhm! Seebarschfilet! Hast du das hier schon mal gegessen, Lutz?
LUTZ	Nein, ich bin kein Fischfan! Ich esse lieber Fleisch! Aber Manuela, du magst doch gerne Fisch, oder?
MANUELA	Ja schon, aber ich war vorher noch nie im Haus Dannenberg. Also, ich weiß nicht, wie es hier schmeckt.
KELLNER	Guten Tag! Haben Sie schon gewählt?
DAGMAR	Ja, ich hätte gerne das gegrillte Seebarschfilet mit Salzkartoffeln und gemischtem Gemüse. Und bringen Sie mir bitte auch einen Salatteller dazu!
KELLNER	Gern! Was möchten Sie trinken?
DAGMAR	Ein Mineralwasser, bitte!
KELLNER	Möchten Sie auch einen Nachtisch bestellen?
DAGMAR	Ach ja, ich nehme zum Nachtisch die frischen Erdbeeren mit Sahne. Und du Lutz, nimmst du auch die Erdbeeren zum Nachtisch?
LUTZ	Nein, ich nehme nur das Wiener Schnitzel, ohne Beilage bitte, und einen Apfelsaft dazu!
KELLNER	Apfelsaft und Wiener Schnitzel ohne Beilage.—Und was darf ich Ihnen bringen?
MANUELA	Ich bekomme die Seezunge nach Art des Hauses. Und bringen Sie mir doch bitte eine Scheibe Brot dazu!
KELLNER	Ja, unsere Seezunge ist ausgezeichnet. Was hätten Sie gern zu trinken?
MANUELA	Also, ich nehme eine Fruchtlimo, bitte!
KELLNER	Zum Nachtisch kann ich Ihnen die Rote Grütze sehr empfehlen. Sie ist hausgemacht und wird mit feiner Vanillesoße serviert.
MANUELA	Für mich keinen Nachtisch, bitte!
KELLNER	Sehr wohl!—Die Getränke kommen sofort.

Answers to Activity 24 1. Lutz: Wiener Schnitzel; 2. Dagmar: Seebarschfilet mit Salatteller; Manuela: Seezunge mit einer Scheibe Brot; 3. Lutz und Manuela

27 p. 315

Gruppe 1

HERR GÖTZ	Na, wo bleibt denn der Herr Neumann? Wissen Sie, ob er noch kommt, Frau Jäger? Schließlich haben wir es ja vor allem ihm zu verdanken, dass wir heute den Abschluss unseres Projektes hier feiern! Da sollte er doch auf keinen Fall fehlen, finden Sie nicht?
FRAU JÄGER	Ach, der Herr Neumann wird bestimmt in einer halben Stunde hier sein. Er kommt doch direkt vom Flughafen hierher.
HERR GÖTZ	Wieso Flughafen? War er denn heute noch auf einer Geschäftsreise?
FRAU JÄGER	Ja, natürlich! Heute Morgen ist er doch nach Hamburg geflogen, um den neuen Vertrag zu unterschreiben. Wir können gleich am Montag mit der Planung anfangen.
HERR GÖTZ	Ja, dann können wir ja schon mal auf das nächste Projekt anstoßen. Zum Wohl, Frau Jäger!
FRAU JÄGER	Prost, Herr Götz!

Gruppe 2

ARNO	Achtung! Alle mal aufpassen! Hier kommt die Torte mit den Kerzen drauf! Susi, zähl mal, ob es auch wirklich sechzehn sind!
SUSI	Zwei, vier, sechs … vierzehn, fünfzehn, sechzehn! Stimmt genau! Find ich ja super von euch, dass ihr mir eine Torte bestellt habt. Also, wer will das erste Stück?
ANITA	Mensch, Susi, das erste Stück ist doch für dich! Komm, gib mal das Messer her! Ich schneide die Stücke für die anderen ab.—Hier, Arno, probier mal! Volker und Andrea, gebt mir mal eure Teller rüber!
ARNO	Mhm, echt lecker! Schokolade mit Erdbeeren und Vanillecreme!—Also, herzlichen Glückwunsch, Susi! Ach, da kommen ja auch schon die Getränke!
ANITA	Ja, also dann … auf dein Wohl, Susi!
ARNO	Prost, Susi!
SUSI	Danke! Prost alle zusammen!

Gruppe 3

ONKEL NORBERT	Also, weil's so schön ist, wollen wir doch noch einmal einen Toast auf das neue Ehepaar aussprechen! Auf eine glückliche Zukunft, Kinder! Prost!
CLAUDIA	Ach, Onkel Norbert. Nun hast du uns schon zum dritten Mal gratuliert! Komm, Stefan, sprich du doch mal einen Toast auf unsere Gäste aus! Vati hat doch auch schon seine Rede gehalten. Jetzt bist du dran!
STEFAN	Äh, also, vielen Dank, dass Ihr heute alle ins Haus Dannenberg gekommen seid. Claudia und ich, äh, wir freuen uns, dass alle die Einladung zu unserer Hochzeitsfeier angenommen haben. Äh, und ganz besonders möchten wir uns bei Onkel Norbert und Tante Hiltrud bedanken, die die weite Reise aus Österreich gemacht haben, nur um heute mit uns zu feiern. Also, äh, auf das Wohl unserer Gäste!
ONKEL NORBERT	Prost!
TANTE HILTRUD	Danke! Zum Wohl!—Claudia und Stefan, ihr müsst uns recht bald in Salzburg besuchen kommen!
CLAUDIA	Versprochen, Tante Hiltrud!

Answers to Activity 27 Gruppe 1: Abschluss eines Projektes; Geschäftsleute; Gruppe 2: Geburtstag; Freunde; Gruppe 3: Hochzeit; Familienmitglieder

Anwendung

1 p. 322

OLIVER	Also, ich bin dafür, dass wir zuerst einmal eine Stadtrundfahrt durch Berlin machen. Ich finde, dass man so die Stadt ziemlich gut kennen lernen kann. Und man sieht eine ganze Menge.
LARS	Ja, da hast du Recht. Nur leider hält so ein Bus nicht überall an. Ich möchte zum Beispiel unheimlich gerne die Nationalgalerie sehen — aber nicht nur von außen! Ich glaube, dass der Bus bei einer Stadtrundfahrt einfach nur an dem Gebäude vorbeifährt. Also, ich fahr dann schon lieber selbst mit der U-Bahn zur Museumsinsel, wo die Nationalgalerie ist.
JUTTA	Ich will unbedingt zum Ku'damm! Dort gibt es tolle Geschäfte, und ich möchte ein paar Souvenirs einkaufen.
SILKE	Zum Ku'damm? Nee, da ist es mir zu voll! Hat denn keiner von euch Lust, Schloss Charlottenburg zu besichtigen? Ich möchte da auf jeden Fall hingehen!
OLIVER	Also, es scheint, als ob jeder etwas anderes machen will. Ich habe einen Vorschlag. Jeder sieht sich das an, wofür er sich interessiert, und am Abend, wenn wir alle wieder zurück sind, gehen wir zusammen essen. Einverstanden?
LARS	Ja! Das ist eine prima Idee! Also, treffen wir uns dann um halb sieben in dem kleinen Café neben dem Hotel!
JUTTA	Gut! Ich bin auch dafür! Also, dann, bis um halb sieben!
SILKE	Tschüs, und viel Spaß!

Answers for Activity 1 Oliver: Stadtrundfahrt; Lars: Nationalgalerie; Jutta: Ku'damm; Silke: Schloss Charlottenburg / Jeder macht, was er will. Am Abend gehen sie dann zusammen essen.

Kapitel 11: Mit Oma ins Restaurant
Suggested Lesson Plans 50-Minute Schedule

Day 1

CHAPTER OPENER 10 min.
- Building Context, ATE, p. 297M
- Building on Previous Skills, ATE, p. 297M
- Visual Learners, ATE, p. 297M

LOS GEHT'S! 20 min.
- Preteaching Vocabulary, ATE, p. 297N
- Have students read Los geht's!, pp. 300–301
- Teaching Suggestions, Video Guide, p. 70
- Show Los geht's! Video

LANDESKUNDE 15 MIN.
- Pre-viewing Suggestion, Video Guide, p. 70
- Teaching Suggestion, ATE, p. 297N
- Show Landeskunde Video

Wrap-Up 5 min.
- Students respond to questions about which cultural activities interest them

Homework Options
Pupil's Edition, p. 302, Comprehension Acts. 1–4; p. 303, Acts. A and B
Übungsheft, p. 121, Act. 1; p. 122, Acts. 1–3
Interactive CD-ROM, Landeskunde Activity

Day 2

ERSTE STUFE
Quick Review 10 min.
- Check homework, p. 302, Comprehension Acts. 1–4

Reading Selection, p. 304 15 min.
- Do Activity 5, p. 304

Wortschatz, p. 305 20 min.
- Presenting Wortschatz, ATE, p. 297P
- Teaching Transparency 11-1
- Do Activity 6, p. 305
- Do Activity 1, p. 91, Grammatikheft
- Play Audio CD for Activity 7, p. 306
- Do Activities 8 and 9, p. 306

Wrap-Up 5 min.
- Students respond to questions about what one could do on a visit to Berlin

Homework Options
Übungsheft, p. 123, Acts. 1–2

Day 3

ERSTE STUFE
Quick Review 10 min.
- Check homework, Übungsheft, p. 123, Acts. 1–2

So sagt man das!, p. 306 10 min.
- Presenting So sagt man das!, ATE, p. 297Q
- Play Audio CD for Activity 10, p. 307

Grammatik, p. 307 15 min.
- Presenting Grammatik, ATE, p. 297Q
- Do Activity 11, p. 307
- Do Activity 4, p. 124, Übungsheft

Ein wenig Landeskunde, p. 307 10 min.
- Presenting Ein wenig Landeskunde, ATE, p. 297Q
- Do Activity 12, p. 307

Wrap-Up 5 min.
- Students respond to questions about what they would like to do in Berlin

Homework Options
Mehr Grammatikübungen, Erste Stufe
Grammatikheft, pp. 92–93, Acts. 2–5
Übungsheft, p. 124, Act. 3; p. 125, Acts. 5–7

Day 4

ERSTE STUFE
Quick Review 10 min.
- Check homework, Grammatikheft, pp. 92–93, Acts. 2–5

Quiz Review 20 min.
- Do Additional Listening Activities 11-1 and 11-2, pp. 87–88
- Do Erste Stufe Activities, Interactive CD-ROM

Quiz 20 min.
- Quiz 11-1A or 11-1B

Homework Options
Activities for Communication, p. 115, Realia 11-2, write two questions and two answers for each ad (see p. 117)

Day 5

ZWEITE STUFE
Quick Review 15 min.
- Return and review Quiz 11-1
- Bell Work, ATE, p. 297R
- Check homework, Realia 11-2

Reading Selection, p. 308 15 min.
- Teaching Suggestions, ATE, p. 297R
- Do Activity 13, p. 308

Wortschatz, p. 309 15 min.
- Presenting Wortschatz, ATE, p. 297R
- Teaching Transparency 11-A
- Do Activities 14 and 15, p. 309
- Play Audio CD for Activity 16, p. 310

Wrap-Up 5 min.
- Students respond to questions about the food in various ethnic restaurants

Homework Options
Übungsheft, p. 126, Act. 1

Day 6

ZWEITE STUFE
Quick Review 10 min.
- Check homework, Übungsheft, p. 126, Act. 1

Wortschatz, p. 310 10 min.
- Presenting Wortschatz, ATE, p. 297S
- Do Activity 17, p. 310

So sagt man das!/Ein wenig Landeskunde, p. 310 15 min.
- Presenting So sagt man das!, ATE, p. 297S
- Present Ein wenig Landeskunde, p. 310
- Play Audio CD for Activity 18, p. 311
- Do Activity 19, p. 311

Grammatik, p. 311 10 min.
- Presenting Grammatik, ATE, p. 297S
- Do Activities 10–11, p. 96, Grammatikheft

Wrap-Up 5 min.
- Students respond to questions about what they have heard about food in various restaurants

Homework Options
Pupil's Edition, p. 311, Acts. 20–21
Grammatikheft, pp. 94–95, Acts. 6–9
Internet Aktivitäten, see ATE, p. 297F

One-Stop Planner CD-ROM

For alternative lesson plans by chapter section, to create your own customized plans, or to preview all resources available for this chapter, use the **One-Stop Planner CD-ROM**, Disc 3.

 For additional homework suggestions, see activities accompanied by this symbol throughout the chapter.

Day 7

ZWEITE STUFE
Quick Review 15 min.
- Check homework, Grammatikheft, pp. 94–95, Acts. 6–9

Quiz Review 15 min.
- Do **Mehr Grammatikübungen, Zweite Stufe**
- Do Activities 2–7, pp. 126–128, Übungsheft

Quiz
- Quiz 11-2A or 11-2B 20 min.

Homework Options
Prepare Communicative Activity 11-3, pp. 65–66

Day 8

DRITTE STUFE
Quick Review 15 min.
- Return and review Quiz 11-2
- Bell Work, ATE, p. 297T
- Do Communicative Activity 11-3

Reading Selection, p. 312 15 min.
- Teaching Suggestions, ATE, p. 297U
- Do Activity 22, p. 313

Wortschatz, p. 313 15 min.
- Presenting **Wortschatz**, ATE, p. 297U
- Teaching Transparency 11-B
- Do Activity 23, p. 313
- Do Activity 12, p. 97, Grammatikheft

Wrap-Up 5 min.
- Students respond to questions about what they would like to order in a German restaurant

Homework Options
Grammatikheft, p. 97, Act. 13
Übungsheft, pp. 129–130, Acts. 1–3

Day 9

DRITTE STUFE
Quick Review 10 min.
- Check homework, Übungsheft, pp. 129–130, Acts. 1–3

So sagt man das!, p. 314 10 min
- Presenting **So sagt man das!**, ATE, p. 297U
- Present **Sprachtipp**, p. 314
- Play Audio CD for Activity 24, p. 314

Grammatik, p. 314 15 min
- Presenting **Grammatik**, ATE, p. 297U
- Do Activity 25, p. 314
- Do Activity 26, p. 315
- Play Audio CD for Activity 27, p. 315

So sagt man das!, p. 315 10 min.
- Presenting **So sagt man das!**, ATE, p. 297U
- Do Activities 28 and 29, p. 315

Wrap-Up 5 min.
- Students respond to a waiter's questions about what they would like to order

Homework Options
Grammatikheft, pp. 98–99, Acts. 14–18
Übungsheft, pp. 130–131, Acts. 4–6

Day 10

DRITTE STUFE
Quick Review 10 min.
- Check homework, Grammatikheft, pp. 98–99, Acts. 14–18

ZUM LESEN 20 min.
- Present **Lesestrategie**, p. 316
- Do Activities 1–8, pp. 316–317

Quiz Review 20 min.
- Do **Mehr Grammatikübungen, Dritte Stufe**
- Do Additional Listening Activities 11-5 and 11-6, pp. 89–90

Homework Options
Übungsheft, p. 132, Acts. 1–4
Interaktive Spiele, see ATE, p. 297F

Day 11

DRITTE STUFE
Quick Review 10 min.
- Check homework, Übungsheft, p. 132, Acts. 1–4

Quiz 20 min.
- Quiz 11-3A or 11-3B

ANWENDUNG 15 min.
- Do **Anwendung** Activities 1–4 and 6, pp. 322–323

Wrap-Up 5 min.
- Students respond to questions about their plans for next week

Homework Options
Pupil's Edition, p. 323, Act. 5, **Zum Schreiben**

Day 12

ANWENDUNG
Quick Review 15 min.
- Return and review Quiz 11–3
- Students read **Zum Schreiben** compositions

Kann ich's wirklich?, p. 324 15 min.
- Do Activities 1–9, p. 324

Chapter Review 20 min.
- Review chapter functions, vocabulary, and grammar; choose from **Mehr Grammatikübungen,** Grammar Tutor for Students of German, Activities for Communication, Listening Activities, Interactive CD-ROM Tutor, or **Interaktive Spiele.**
- Review test format and provide sample test items for students

Homework Options
Study for Chapter Test

Assessment

Test, Chapter 11 45 min.
- Administer Chapter 11 Test. Select from Testing Program, Alternative Assessment Guide, or Test Generator.

KAPITEL 11 • SUGGESTED LESSON PLANS • 50-MINUTE SCHEDULE

Kapitel 11: Mit Oma ins Restaurant
Suggested Lesson Plans 90-Minute Schedule

Block 1

CHAPTER OPENER
Chapter Opener 10 min.
- Building Context, ATE, p. 297M
- Building on Previous Skills, ATE, p. 297M
- Visual Learners, ATE, p. 297M

LOS GEHT'S! 20 min.
- Preteaching Vocabulary, ATE, p. 297N
- Have students read **Los geht's!**, pp. 300–301
- Teaching Suggestions, Video Guide, p. 70
- Show **Los geht's!** Video

LANDESKUNDE 15 min.
- Pre-viewing Suggestion, Video Guide, p. 70
- Teaching Suggestion, ATE, p. 297N
- Show **Landeskunde** Video

ERSTE STUFE
Reading Selection, p. 304 15 min.
- Do Activity 5, p. 304

Wortschatz, p. 305 25 min.
- Presenting **Wortschatz**, ATE, p. 297P
- Teaching Transparency 11-1
- Do Activity 6, p. 305
- Do Activity 1, p. 91, Grammatikheft
- Play Audio CD for Activity 7, p. 306
- Do Activities 8 and 9, p. 306

Wrap-Up 5 min.
- Students respond to questions about what one could do on a visit to Berlin

Homework Options
Pupil's Edition, p. 302, Comprehension Acts. 1–4; p. 303, Acts. A and B
Übungsheft, p. 121, Act. 1; p. 122, Acts. 1–3; pp. 123–124, Acts. 1–3
Interactive CD-ROM, **Landeskunde** Activity

Block 2

ERSTE STUFE
Quick Review 15 min.
- Check homework, Übungsheft, p. 121, Act. 1; p. 122, Acts. 1–3; pp. 123–124, Acts. 1–3

So sagt man das!, p. 306 10 min.
- Presenting **So sagt man das!**, ATE, p. 297Q
- Play Audio CD for Activity 10, p. 307

Grammatik, p. 307 25 min.
- Presenting **Grammatik**, ATE, p. 297Q
- Do Activity 11, p. 307
- Do Activities 4–7, pp. 124–125, Übungsheft

Ein wenig Landeskunde, p. 307 10 min.
- Presenting **Ein wenig Landeskunde**, ATE, p. 297Q
- Do Activity 12, p. 307

Quiz Review 10 min.
- Do Activities 2–5, pp. 92–93, Grammatikheft
- Do **Erste Stufe** Activities, Interactive CD-ROM

Quiz 20 min.
- Quiz 11-1A or 11-1B

Homework Options
Activities for Communication, p. 115, Realia 11-2, write two questions and two answers for each ad (see p. 117)

Block 3

ZWEITE STUFE
Quick Review 15 min.
- Return and review Quiz 11-1
- Bell Work, ATE, p. 297R
- Check homework, Realia 11-2

Reading Selection, p. 308 15 min.
- Teaching Suggestions, ATE, p. 297R
- Do Activity 13, p. 308

Wortschatz, p. 309 15 min.
- Presenting **Wortschatz**, ATE, p. 297R
- Teaching Transparency 11-A
- Do Activities 14 and 15, p. 309
- Play Audio CD for Activity 16, p. 310

Wortschatz, p. 310 10 min.
- Presenting **Wortschatz**, ATE, p. 297S
- Do Activity 17, p. 310

So sagt man das!/Ein wenig Landeskunde, p. 310 20 min.
- Presenting **So sagt man das!**, ATE, p. 297S
- Present **Ein wenig Landeskunde**, p. 310
- Play Audio CD for Activity 18, p. 311
- Do Activity 19, p. 311

Grammatik, p. 311 10 min.
- Presenting **Grammatik**, ATE, p. 297S
- Do Activities 10–11, p. 96, Grammatikheft

Wrap-Up 5 min.
- Students respond to questions about what they have heard about food in various restaurants

Homework Options
Pupil's Edition, p. 311, Acts. 20–21
Grammatikheft, pp. 94–95, Acts. 6–9
Übungsheft, pp. 126–128, Acts. 1–7
Internet Aktivitäten, see ATE, p. 297F

One-Stop Planner CD-ROM

For alternative lesson plans by chapter section, to create your own customized plans, or to preview all resources available for this chapter, use the **One-Stop Planner CD-ROM, Disc 3**.

 For additional homework suggestions, see activities accompanied by this symbol throughout the chapter.

Block 4

ZWEITE STUFE

Quick Review 15 min.
- Check homework, Übungsheft, pp. 126–128, Acts. 1–7

Quiz Review 15 min.
- Do **Mehr Grammatikübungen, Zweite Stufe**
- Do Additional Listening Activities 11-3 and 11-4, pp. 88–89
- Do **Zweite Stufe** Activities, Interactive CD-ROM

Quiz 20 min.
- Quiz 11-2A or 11-2B

DRITTE STUFE

Reading Selection, p. 312 15 min.
- Teaching Suggestions, ATE, p. 297U
- Do Activity 22, p. 313

Wortschatz, p. 313 20 min.
- Presenting **Wortschatz**, ATE, p. 297U
- Teaching Transparency 11-B
- Do Activity 23, p. 313
- Do Activity 12, p. 97, Grammatikheft

Wrap-Up 5 min.
- Students respond to questions about what they would like to order in a German restaurant

Homework Options
Grammatikheft, p. 97, Act. 13
Übungsheft, pp. 129–130, Acts. 1–3

Block 5

DRITTE STUFE

Quick Review 10 min.
- Check homework, Übungsheft, pp. 129–130, Acts. 1–3

So sagt man das!, p. 314 10 min
- Presenting **So sagt man das!**, ATE, p. 297U
- Present **Sprachtipp**, p. 314
- Play Audio CD for Activity 24, p. 314

Grammatik, p. 314 20 min
- Presenting **Grammatik**, ATE, p. 297U
- Do Activity 25, p. 314
- Do Activity 26, p. 315
- Play Audio CD for Activity 27, p. 315

So sagt man das!, p. 315 10 min.
- Presenting **So sagt man das!**, ATE, p. 297U
- Do Activities 28 and 29, p. 315

ZUM LESEN 20 min.
- Present **Lesestrategie**, p. 316
- Do Activities 1–8, pp. 316–317

Quiz Review 15 min.
- Do **Mehr Grammatikübungen, Dritte Stufe**
- Do Additional Listening Activities 11-5 and 11-6, pp. 89–90

Wrap-Up 5 min.
- Students respond to a waiter's questions about what they would like to order

Homework Options
Pupil's Edition, p. 323, Act. 5, **Zum Schreiben**
Grammatikheft, pp. 98–99, Acts. 14–18
Übungsheft, pp. 130–131, Acts. 4–6; p. 132, Acts. 1–4

Block 6

DRITTE STUFE

Quick Review 15 min.
- Students read **Zum Schreiben** compositions

Quiz 20 min.
- Quiz 11-3A or 11-3B

ANWENDUNG 30 min.
- Do **Anwendung** Activities 1–4 and 6, pp. 322–323

Kann ich's wirklich?, p. 324 20 min.
- Do Activities 1–9, p. 324

Wrap-Up 5 min.
- Students respond to questions about restaurant meals, choosing, ordering, and toasting

Homework Options
Interaktive Spiele, see ATE, p. 297F
Study for Chapter Test

Block 7

ANWENDUNG

Quick Review 10 min.
- Return and review Quiz 11-3

Chapter Review 35 min.
- Review chapter functions, vocabulary, and grammar; choose from **Mehr Grammatikübungen**, Grammar Tutor for Students of German, Activities for Communication, Listening Activities, Interactive CD-ROM Tutor, or **Interaktive Spiele.**
- Review test format and provide sample test items for students

Test, Chapter 11 45 min.
- Administer Chapter 11 Test. Select from Testing Program, Alternative Assessment Guide, or Test Generator.

Kapitel 11: Mit Oma ins Restaurant
Teaching Suggestions, pages 298–325

PAGES 298–299

CHAPTER OPENER

Pacing Tips
The **Erste Stufe** focuses on things to do in Berlin. The **würde**-forms are introduced on p. 307. German and international cuisine is the topic of the **Zweite Stufe** and the **Dritte Stufe**. The **Zweite Stufe** includes the function of 'expressing hearsay' and the concept of unpreceded adjectives. The **Dritte Stufe** covers the functions of 'ordering in a restaurant' using the **hätte**-forms and 'expressing good wishes' during a meal or toast. Because the three **Stufen** are similar in length and the amount of material presented, you will probably spend about the same amount of time teaching each one. For Lesson Plans and timing suggestions, see pages 297I–297L.

Meeting the Standards
Communication
- Asking for, making, and responding to suggestions, p. 306
- Expressing hearsay, p. 310
- Ordering in a restaurant, p. 314
- Expressing good wishes, p. 315

Cultures
- Landeskunde, p. 303
- Ein wenig Landeskunde, p. 307
- Ein wenig Landeskunde, p. 310
- Background Information, p. 297P
- Culture Note, p. 297S
- Culture Note, p. 297U

Comparisons
- Language-to-Language, p. 297R

Communities
- Background Information, p. 297O
- Background Information, p. 297R
- Background Information, p. 297S
- Career Path, p. 237Q

Building Context
- In German, ask students if their family has a favorite restaurant that they like to go to when they eat out. How often do they eat there and for what type of food is the restaurant known?
- Ask students how their family typically celebrates a grandparent's or other older person's birthday.

For resource information, see the **One-Stop Planner CD-ROM**, Disc 3.

Building on Previous Skills
Ask students what dishes the grandmother (**Oma**) could order in a typical **Berliner Lokal** based on what they learned about specialties of Berlin in the Location Opener on p. 267. (Berliner Pfannkuchen, Eisbein, Buletten, Grüner Aal)

Communication for All Students

Visual Learners
Ask students to take a closer look at the photograph and describe what the people are eating. Have them make a list of the foods they see.

Chapter Sequence
Los geht's! . . . . .p. 300
Landeskunde . . . . .p. 303
Erste Stufe . . . . .p. 304
Zweite Stufe . . . . .p. 308
Dritte Stufe . . . . .p. 312
Zum Lesen . . . . .p. 316
Mehr Grammatikübungen . . . . .p. 318
Anwendung . . . . .p. 322
Kann ich's wirklich? . . . . .p. 324
Wortschatz . . . . .p. 325

LOS GEHT'S!

Teaching Resources
pp. 300–302

PRINT
- Lesson Planner, p. 52
- Video Guide, pp. 69–70, 72
- Übungsheft, p. 121

MEDIA
- One-Stop Planner
- Video Program
  Los geht's!
  Videocassette 4, 30:44–36:36
  Videocassette 5 (captioned version),
  1:05:16–1:11:08
  Fortsetzung
  Videocassette 4, 36:40-38:18
  Videocassette 5 (captioned version),
  1:11:11–1:12:50
- DVD Tutor, Disc 2
- Audio Compact Discs, CD11, Trs. 1–2
- Los geht's! Transparencies

PAGES 300–301

Los geht's! Transparencies

Preteaching Vocabulary

Recognizing Cognates

Los geht's! contains several words that students will be able to recognize as cognates. Some are compound words in which only part of the word is a cognate. What does **Seezunge** really mean? Ask students if they can think of the Spanish cognate for **Käse** (**queso**).

1. Sommerkonzert
2. Dinge
3. griechisches, typischen
4. Speisekarte, Weißwein, alkoholfreies
5. Käse, Seezunge, Seebarschfilet

Fortsetzung

You may choose to continue with the Fortsetzung of *Pläne für Omas Geburtstag* now or wait until later in the chapter. For a synopsis of the Los geht's! and Fortsetzung episodes, see p. 297E.

STANDARDS: 1.3, 2.1

Advance Organizer

Ask students about the last birthday celebration they planned or helped to plan for a family member. Whose birthday was it, and what did they do to celebrate?

Teaching Suggestion

After students have read, watched, or listened to *Pläne für Omas Geburtstag*, ask them where the Schmidt family took **Oma** on her birthday. Where is the restaurant located? (on a lake) What is the name of the restaurant? (**Haus Dannenberg am See**) How can someone who does not have a car get to the restaurant? (buses number 13 and 14) Why did they choose that restaurant? (**Oma** wanted to sit on an outside terrace.)

Thinking Critically

- **Analyzing** After students have watched the video, ask them to look at the fifth and seventh frames of Los geht's!. What can students say about the etiquette of ordering in a restaurant? How do Germans order in a restaurant?

Using the Captioned Video/DVD

As an alternative to reading the conversations in the book, you might want to show the captioned version of *Pläne für Omas Geburtstag* available on Videocassette 5.
Note: The *DVD Tutor* contains captions for all sections of the *Video Program*.

PAGE 302

Comprehension Check

Challenge

1. Ask students to work in pairs and take notes as they answer the questions. Based on the notes and the storyline in the video, students should summarize the events in German. This can be done orally or in writing.

A Slower Pace

2. For each of the eight statements, ask students to look back at Los geht's! on pp. 300–301 and point out the specific frame to which each statement refers.

Challenge

4. After students have matched the phrases correctly, ask them to use these expressions in a story entitled **Die Überraschung**. Students can work on an outline in class and then complete the final draft as written homework.

▶ PAGE 303

LANDESKUNDE

Teaching Resources
p. 303

PRINT
- Video Guide, pp. 69–70, 72–73
- Übungsheft, p. 122

MEDIA
- One-Stop Planner
- Video Program
  Videocassette 4, 38:58–41:50
- DVD Tutor, Disc 2
- Audio Compact Discs, CD11, Trs. 3–6
- Interactive CD-ROM Tutor, Disc 3

Communication for All Students

Auditory Learners
A1 Before students look at the text on p. 303, play the compact disc or have them watch the interviews on video. Ask students to make a list of all the cultural events that are mentioned. As students tell you the cultural events they've identified, make a list on the board or on a transparency.

Cultures and Communities

Music Connection
Herr and **Frau Heine** referred to the **Philharmonie** in their interview. Have students do some research to find out more about the famous Berlin Philharmonic Orchestra.

Background Information
Berlin has more than 50 museums and almost 100 public and private galleries. Several of these museums and galleries are located on the **Museumsinsel** in the center of Berlin. The **Pergamonmuseum** is one of the most famous museums.

Teacher Note
Mention to your students that the **Landeskunde** will also be included in Quiz 11-1B given at the end of the **Erste Stufe.**

Connections and Comparisons

Thinking Critically
Comparing and Contrasting Ask students to identify a city in the United States that offers a similar concentration of major museums and galleries in a central area. (Example: The Mall in downtown Washington, D.C., has an impressive variety of museums, such as the Smithsonian Institution, the National Gallery of Art, the National Air and Space Museum, and the National Museum of American History.)

ERSTE STUFE

Teaching Resources
pp. 304–307

PRINT
- Lesson Planner, p. 53
- TPR Storytelling Book, pp. 80–81
- Listening Activities, pp. 83, 87–88
- Activities for Communication, pp. 61–62, 114, 117, 143–144
- Grammatikheft, pp. 91–93
- Grammar Tutor for Students of German, Chapter 11
- Übungsheft, pp. 123–125
- Testing Program, pp. 275–278
- Alternative Assessment Guide, p. 42
- Student Make-Up Assignments, Chapter 11

MEDIA
- One-Stop Planner
- Audio Compact Discs, CD11, Trs. 7–8, 14, 19–20
- Teaching Transparencies
  Situation 11-1
  Mehr Grammatikübungen Answers
  Grammatikheft Answers
- Interactive CD-ROM Tutor, Disc 3
- DVD Tutor, Disc 2

▶ PAGE 304

Bell Work
• Ask students to list the different cultural activities that are available in their area.

• Ask students to recall the last play their school put on. What was the name of it, who wrote it, and which students played the leading roles?

Cultures and Communities

Background Information
Berlin offers a rich variety of entertainment, including theater, opera, operetta, orchestra, chamber music, jazz, and film. The city's architecture further enhances the elegant atmosphere in the staging of these performances. Orchestral and chamber music concerts, including performances of the world-renowned Berlin Philharmonic Orchestra, take place in Philharmonic Hall (**Die Philharmonie**) and at **Schloss Charlottenburg**. Operas and operettas are performed in three opera houses (**Deutsche Oper, Staatsoper, Komische Oper**) and theatrical productions are staged at theaters such as the **Renaissance-Theater, Volksbühne, Schiller Theater, Hansa Theater,** and the **Deutsches Theater,** to name a few.

Group Work
5 Ask students to work on this activity in groups of three. They should first look over the opera and theater program listings and then read the excerpt *Berlin ist eine Reise wert.* Remind students that they are not expected to know every word, but should make use of previously learned reading strategies such as scanning for information. One of the group members should record the responses to the questions. If you feel some vocabulary explanations are necessary, clarify them with synonyms and paraphrasing whenever possible. When groups have completed the activity, call on individual students to share their group's answers with the class.

Thinking Critically
5 Drawing Inferences Can students identify the two operas that will be performed in Italian? *(Aida; Romeo und Julia)*

▶ **PAGE 305**

PRESENTING: Wortschatz
- To introduce the different types of musical and theatrical productions, play excerpts from these musical scores and have a copy of Max Frisch's play on hand.
- To explore the **Und dann noch ...** expressions, ask students about the last time they visited one of the venues listed.

Connections and Comparisons

Geography Connection
Ask students if they can recall another German city where sightseeing by boat is very popular among tourists. (Hamburg) Ask students to look at a map of Germany to find other cities in which boat tours are likely to be of interest to visitors. (Examples: Kiel, Lübeck, Bremerhaven, Wilhelmshaven)

Cultures and Communities

Background Information
The synagogue pictured in the **Wortschatz** (**Neue Jüdische Synagoge**) was first built in the 1860s, and then set on fire during **Kristallnacht** in November 1938. Restoration work began in 1988, and the **Synagoge** was reopened in 1995.

Communication for All Students

Challenge
6 To expand the activity, ask students to choose from the list four activities that they would like to do while visiting Berlin. Have students also explain why they are interested in each sight or activity.

▶ **PAGE 306**

Communication for All Students

A Slower Pace
8 Play the role of Ulf and give students a chance to respond. Repeat several times, each time changing your questions in order to show students a range of possible stimuli. This will prepare students to develop the dialogue on their own.

STANDARDS: 1.1, 1.2, 3.1

Speaking Assessment

9 You might want to use this activity for speaking assessment with the following rubric.

Speaking Rubric

	Points			
	4	3	2	1
Content (Complete – Incomplete)				
Comprehension (Total – Little)				
Comprehensibility (Comprehensible – Incomprehensible)				
Accuracy (Accurate – Seldom accurate)				
Fluency (Fluent – Not fluent)				

18–20: A   16–17: B   14–15: C   12–13: D   Under 12: F

PRESENTING: So sagt man das!

Use the three different ways of making suggestions with the **Wortschatz** on p. 305. Have students respond in any way they wish using one of the functional expressions.

 Total Physical Response

Review the functions with this TPR activity. Have all students stand, then give commands using the functions from **So sagt man das!** on p. 306. At the end of the activity, all students should be seated.
Examples:
Setz dich, wenn du gern in einem italienischen Restaurant essen würdest!
Setz dich, wenn du dafür bist, dass wir alle nach Berlin fliegen!

PAGE 307

Communication for All Students

A Slower Pace

10 Inform students that they will hear the conversation twice. During the first listening, ask them to listen for the suggestions that students make and only take notes on that information. When the conversation is played a second time, students should listen for the friend's responses. Finally, ask students to identify the phrase or expression that showed whether or not the friend liked the suggestion.

PRESENTING: Grammatik

- **The würde forms** Würde, like möchte, is a subjunctive verb form. Using würde-forms is the most polite way to express what you would like to do. Show students the following sentences for contrast:
Ich würde gern mal das Pergamonmuseum besuchen.
Ich möchte das Pergamonmuseum besuchen.
Ich will das Pergamonmuseum besuchen.

- Ask third person questions to give students practice using würde.
Example:
Wohin würde deine Familie gern mal reisen?

Communication for All Students

Challenge

11 Ask students to combine their sentences into a cohesive paragraph in which they describe their friend's interests in Berlin. This can be done orally or in writing.

PRESENTING: Ein wenig Landeskunde

Students may be interested to know that German classes often attend a performance of a literary or musical piece after having studied it in school. **Schülerkarten** are at greatly reduced prices.

Reteaching: Vocabulary

Ask students to look back at the opera and theater programs at the top of p. 304. Tell students that they will be in charge of evening entertainment for their family on a visit to Berlin. For each of the four nights, they should choose a program. Students should then share the suggestions with the rest of the class.

 **Game**

Play the game **Was wird beschrieben?** See p. 297C for the procedure.

Assess

▸ Testing Program, pp. 275–278
Quiz 11-1A, Quiz 11-1B
Audio CD11, Tr. 14

▸ Student Make-Up Assignments
Chapter 11, Alternative Quiz

▸ Alternative Assessment Guide, p. 42

ZWEITE STUFE

Teaching Resources
pp. 308–311

PRINT
- Lesson Planner, p. 54
- TPR Storytelling Book, pp. 82–83
- Listening Activities, pp. 84, 88–89
- Activities for Communication, pp. 115, 117, 143–144
- Grammatikheft, pp. 94–96
- Grammar Tutor for Students of German, Chapter 11
- Übungsheft, pp. 126–128
- Testing Program, pp. 279–282
- Alternative Assessment Guide, p. 42
- Student Make-Up Assignments, Chapter 11

MEDIA
- One-Stop Planner
- Audio Compact Discs, CD11, Trs. 9–10, 15, 21–22
- Teaching Transparencies
  Vocabulary 11-A
  Mehr Grammatikübungen Answers
  Grammatikheft Answers
- Interactive CD-ROM Tutor, Disc 3
- DVD Tutor, Disc 2

PAGE 308

Bell Work
Ask students to list their interest in ethnic foods. What type of foods do they like to eat? Where do they go to eat ethnic foods?

Thinking Critically
Drawing Inferences Ask students how they would find out about the different ethnic restaurants located in their area.

Cultures and Communities
Background Information
Berlin has more than 7,000 cafés, restaurants, and bars, thus offering the greatest variety in culinary tastes of all the German cities.

Teaching Suggestion
13 Since the advertisements include many unfamiliar words and abbreviations, you may want to have students use the questions as an advance organizer to help them focus only on the information in each restaurant description.

PAGE 309

PRESENTING: Wortschatz
- As you introduce and practice the new vocabulary, have students concentrate on the correct pronunciation of the names of various dishes.
- Ask students to recall from previous chapters one additional dish for each category (**chinesisch, ägyptisch, mediterran, gutbürgerlich**).

Connections and Comparisons
Language-to-Language
As was mentioned in Chapter 5, names of different types of foods make up one of the largest categories of loanwords. This is especially true in Germany, which is home to a large population of former **Gastarbeiter** (also called **Arbeitsemigranten**) — workers who originally came from countries such as Greece, Italy, the former Yugoslavia, Spain, Portugal, and Turkey to meet the growing demand for labor created by the economic boom in postwar Germany. Many of these workers opted to stay in Germany and enriched German cuisine with their national dishes. Ask your students to think of dishes that might have been introduced to the German cuisine by former **Arbeitsemigranten**.

Teaching Suggestion
14 On the day you plan to do this activity, you could bring to class several cookbooks on ethnic cooking from your school or local library. This will help students explore the foods of the various countries listed.

> **PAGE 310**

Communication for All Students

Visual Learners

16 For this activity, you could provide students with a copy of restaurant listings featuring ethnic cooking from your local newspaper. Students can use the listings to describe their culinary tastes and reasons for them. Take a survey of the most popular of the listed restaurants at the conclusion of the activity.

PRESENTING: Wortschatz

To introduce these descriptive adjectives you could have a sample tasting of different foods with the characteristics described. Write each adjective on an index card and label each food with the appropriate adjective. You could also review and add other adjectives such as **süß, sauer, salzig, bitter,** and **saftig**.

PRESENTING: So sagt man das!

- Ask students to look back at the the fourth frame of **Los geht's!**. Have them scan the dialogue to find the statement that is used to express hearsay.

- To practice the new expressions, ask students to tell what they have heard about a movie that just came out or the latest CD from a popular singer or group.

- Make up some rumors or hearsay about people and events in your school and present it to the class. Have students react to what you tell them and either agree that they also heard it or disagree, telling you what they know.

> **PAGE 311**

PRESENTING: Grammatik

Unpreceded adjectives The students have already learned to use adjectives following **der-** and **ein-** words. Tell them that unpreceded adjectives have to assume the role of an article: their endings must signal the gender, number, and case of the noun that follows.

Thinking Critically

Analyzing Have students deduce the gender of each of the nouns in the **Grammatik** from the descriptive adjective.

Connections and Comparisons

Music Connection

For additional reading, refer students to Heinrich Heine's poem *Die Lorelei* (music by Friedrich Silcher), Level 2 *Listening Activities,* p. 62. Ask them to underline all the adjective endings they find. Can they explain the reasons for these endings? You may also want to play the song, Level 2 CD 8, Tr. 25.

Social Studies Connection

Ask students to identify cities, streets, schools, and public institutions named after German Americans.

History Connection

Ask students to research the history of German immigrants to their state.

Building on Previous Skills

Ask students when the first German immigrants came to the United States and where they settled. (See *Komm mit!* Level 1, **Vorschau,** p.10 and the following Culture Note.)

Cultures and Communities

Background Information

20 German-American Day, usually celebrated on October 6, was first officially proclaimed and signed into law on October 2, 1987, by President Ronald Reagan. The day honors all Americans of German descent and their contributions to life and culture in the United States.

Culture Note

The first German immigrants arrived at Penn's Landing in Philadelphia in 1683. They had been invited to the New World by the Quaker William Penn. Their first settlement was Germantown, Pennsylvania, northwest of Philadelphia.

Cultures and Communities

Career Path
Have students pair up to think of reasons a corporate lawyer working for an American company might find it helpful to have a background in German. (Suggestions: A corporate lawyer whose client had branches in a German-speaking country would have to be familiar with both the language and the intricacies of its laws; if a company had no such branches, but wanted to begin importing certain types of German goods, it would need lawyers fluent in German to help work out a trade agreement.)

Communication for All Students

Kinesthetic Learners
To review the adjectives from p. 310 (**scharf, würzig,** and so on), prepare the following activity. Bring sample foods that have the characteristics of each of the adjectives. Ask a volunteer to come up to the board, blindfold the volunteer, then ask him or her to sample various foods and comment on how they taste, using the new adjectives.

Assess
▶ Testing Program, pp. 279–282
  Quiz 11-2A, Quiz 11-2B
  Audio CD11, Tr. 15

▶ Student Make-Up Assignments
  Chapter 11, Alternative Quiz

▶ Alternative Assessment Guide, p. 42

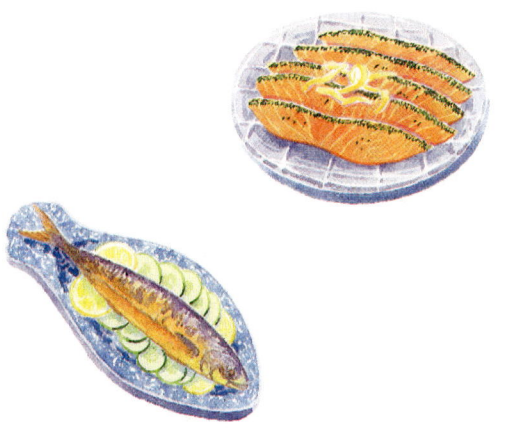

DRITTE STUFE

Teaching Resources
pp. 312–315

PRINT
▶ Lesson Planner, p. 55
▶ TPR Storytelling Book, pp. 84–85
▶ Listening Activities, pp. 85, 89–90
▶ Activities for Communication, pp. 63–66, 116, 117, 143–144
▶ Grammatikheft, pp. 97–99
▶ Grammar Tutor for Students of German, Chapter 11
▶ Übungsheft, pp. 129–131
▶ Testing Program, pp. 283–286
▶ Alternative Assessment Guide, p. 42
▶ Student Make-Up Assignments, Chapter 11

MEDIA
▶ One-Stop Planner
▶ Audio Compact Discs, CD11, Trs. 11-12, 16, 23–24
▶ Teaching Transparencies
  Situation 11-2
  Vocabulary 11-B
  Mehr Grammatikübungen Answers
  Grammatikheft Answers
▶ Interactive CD-ROM Tutor, Disc 3
▶ DVD Tutor, Disc 2

PAGE 312

Bell Work
Have students list all the foreign dishes they have eaten. They should label each dish with the country it came from and whether it was an appetizer, entrée, side dish, or dessert.

Communication for All Students

Visual Learners
To prepare for this activity, gather photos of various food items (appetizers, main dishes, side dishes, and desserts) from magazines. Select dishes that students will be able to talk about in German. Stack the pictures in categories on a table in the front of the class. Ask students to work in pairs or groups of three. Let each group come up to the front and choose a picture from each stack. They should take these back to their desks and use them to organize an original menu. When groups have finished ask them what they will be serving, using the following vocabulary: **Vorspeise, Hauptgericht, Beilage, Nachtisch, Getränke.**

STANDARDS: 5.1

KAPITEL 11   DRITTE STUFE   **297T**

Teaching Suggestions

- Have students look at the **Speisekarte** from **Haus Dannenberg am See** while you replay the video segment of the **Los geht's!** episode. Have students listen for and identify the dishes the family ordered. Then have students make out the bill (**die Rechnung**), listing all the items and prices based on what the family ordered.

- Help students with the pronunciation of the various dishes, especially the names of the main dishes.

Using the Captioned Video/DVD

As an alternative, you may want to play the captioned version of the **Los geht's!** episode, *Pläne für Omas Geburtstag*, on Videocassette 5. Note: The *DVD Tutor* contains captions for all sections of the *Video Program*.

PAGE 313

Communication for All Students

Challenge

 After students have completed this activity, ask them to look at the **Speisekarte** again, this time choosing what they would like to eat. Students should be prepared to share their choices with the rest of the class. Remind students to use sequencing words as they describe their elaborate meal.

PRESENTING: Wortschatz

To practice the vocabulary, ask students to name their favorite item for each of the categories listed. Which ones are their least favorite?

Cultures and Communities

Culture Note

Bratkartoffeln are similar to hash browns, except that they are sliced instead of grated. They are usually served at lunchtime or in the evening.

PAGE 314

PRESENTING: So sagt man das!

After you have introduced the new expressions, replay the video segment that corresponds to Frames 4 and 5 of **Los geht's!** with the sound turned off. Ask several students to take on the roles of the people in the story and to ad-lib the conversation, incorporating the new functions. Students should not try to remember what each person actually ordered; they should make up the storyline as they go along.

Teaching Suggestion

Have students think of all the things a waiter or waitress might say in the following situations. Get several expressions for each of the following functions:

- to greet people
- to ask for the drink order
- to ask for the main order
- to make suggestions
- to serve the food
- to ask if people want dessert
- to bring the bill
- to end the service

PRESENTING: Grammatik

The hätte-forms Explain to students that the addition of an **Umlaut** to the vowel of a past-tense verb signals the subjunctive. Remind them also of the forms of **würde** presented in the **Erste Stufe**. The students should recall that **würde** was used to express what one would like to do.

PAGE 315

Communication for All Students

Visual Learners

 Ask each group to design a **Speisekarte** for the restaurant, including a name for the establishment and prices for each item. Students should use the **Speisekarte** in their skits.

PRESENTING: So sagt man das!

Have students practice toasting each other. Have plastic cups available and juice or water. Students walk around the classroom with their cup in hand, toasting the health of another student.

Connections and Comparisons

Thinking Critically

Comparing and Contrasting Ask students how Americans express good wishes at the table. How is the ritual of toasting used? Do Americans wish the English equivalent of **Guten Appetit!** before a meal? Ask students about their customs at home.

Teaching Suggestion

29 You might want to pick up a menu from a favorite German restaurant in your area. Copy it for students and have them use it to practice the functions in this activity, or use the menu students made for Activity 26.

Reteaching: The *hätte*-forms

Ask students to tell you one thing that they, their best friend, a parent, and a sibling would like to have for their next birthday.

Teaching Suggestion

To review the vocabulary and expressions presented in the **Dritte Stufe,** design a crossword puzzle that contains enough spaces for the words to complete the expressions listed below:

Erdbeeren mit Sahne isst man als … (Nachspeise)
Nenne ein warmes Getränk. (Tee)
Seezunge ist ein … (Fischgericht)
Antwort auf "Guten Appetit!" (Danke!)
Nenne eine typische deutsche Beilage. (Kloß/Klöße)

Teacher to Teacher

Judy Pyne
Homewood-Flossmoor High School
Flossmoor, Illinois

Judy has students request information by writing letters to companies.

"To practice requesting information, I have my class write a formal letter in German to the company of their choice. In the body of the letter, the student must: a) identify him/herself and say that the letter is an actual assignment, b) mention at least one of the company's products that the student really likes, and c) request information from the company about a product. The hidden agenda in this assignment is to find out if the company employs someone who can translate and respond to the letter. It is a lot of fun when the responses start rolling in!"

Assess

- Testing Program, pp. 283–286
  Quiz 11-3A, Quiz 11-3B
  Audio CD11, Tr. 16

- Student Make-Up Assignments
  Chapter 11, Alternative Quiz

- Alternative Assessment Guide, p. 42

PAGES 316–317

ZUM LESEN

Teaching Resources
pp. 316–317

PRINT
- Lesson Planner, p. 56
- Übungsheft, p. 132
- Reading Strategies and Skills, Chapter 11
- Lies mit mir! 2, Chapter 11

MEDIA
- One-Stop Planner

Prereading

Building Context

Ask students if they know of any people from other countries—in their school, in their neighborhood, and maybe even in their family. Where are these people from and what languages do they speak? How do others react to their accents? How are they treated in general?

Building on Previous Skills

Ask students to recall the word **Gastarbeiter** and the more recent term **Arbeitsemigranten** from Level 1. Ask someone to explain what it means. Point out to students that the term **Gastarbeiter** is often derogatory and that **Arbeitsemigranten** is more politically correct.

Teacher Note

Activities 1 and 2 are prereading activities.

STANDARDS: 1.3, 4.2

Reading
Thinking Critically
3 Drawing Inferences After completing this activity, ask students to name the role of each person in the conversation. (taxi driver; passenger)

Teaching Suggestion
You might want to go over the following vocabulary to help students understand the story:

der Kollege *co-worker*
der Kanacke (also spelled **Kanake**) *derogatory slang word often used to refer to a Turkish person; uneducated, unrefined person*
etwas gestehen *to admit something*
ausprobieren *to try out*
danebengehen *to go amiss*

Cooperative Learning
Once students feel comfortable with the text, assign small groups of students to complete Activities 5 through 7 within a set amount of time. Each group member should have a specific task (reader, recorder, or reporter). Call on two or three groups to share their answers and ideas with the class.

Connections and Comparisons
Thinking Critically
Comparing and Contrasting Emigration occurs for various reasons. In the case of the **Gastarbeiter** or **Arbeitsemigranten** in Germany, ethnic groups left their home countries to fill a labor shortage in postwar Germany. Today many people go to Germany to escape persecution or economic hardship in their home countries. Based on what students learn through the news media, what are some of the reasons people want to immigrate to the United States?

Post-Reading
Teacher Note
Activity 8 is a post-reading task that will show whether students can apply what they have learned.

Communication for All Students
Auditory Learners
8 You might ask students to record their summary on a tape recorder. Remind students to use connecting words when appropriate.

Teaching Suggestion
Ask students to share their impressions about some of the misconceptions Turkish and German people seem to have about each other.

Zum Lesen Answers
Answers to Activity 1 a German and a Turk; **Seltsam** and **komisch** both mean *strange, odd, peculiar,* or *weird;* Dashes indicate a change of speaker.
Answers to Activity 2 Answers will vary.
Answers to Activity 3 It is a conversation between a German and a Turk; in a taxi; most likely assumption: Turk—passenger, German—taxi driver
Answers to Activity 4 Examples: car, work, colleagues at work, weather, relationship between Germans and Turks in Germany
Answers to Activity 5 The taxi driver answers the passenger in Turkish; The passenger is a German pretending to be a Turk so that he can find out how a German taxi driver would treat a Turkish passenger.
Answers to Activity 6 It fails because the taxi driver is not a German but a Turk; The passenger is confused and embarrassed; He is surprised that the Turkish taxi driver speaks excellent German.
Answers to Activity 7 One should not be too quick to judge people by their appearances, for appearances are often deceiving; After the German passenger gets out of the taxi, another German gets in. When the Turkish driver makes a comment about the "strange Turk" he has just had as a passenger, the German (not realizing the driver is a Turk) uses the derogatory term **Kanacken** to refer to the Turks. The author does not need to state explicitly that prejudice is bad.

PAGES 318–321

MEHR GRAMMATIKÜBUNGEN

The **Mehr Grammatikübungen** activities were designed as supplemental activities for the grammatical concepts presented in the chapter. You might use them as additional practice, for review, or for assessment.

For more grammar presentations, review, and practice, refer to the following:
- Grammatikheft
- Grammar Tutor for Students of German
- Grammar Summary on pp. R20-R36
- Übungsheft
- Grammar and Vocabulary quizzes (Testing Program)
- Test Generator
- Interactive CD-ROM Tutor
- **Interaktive Spiele** at go.hrw.com

> **PAGES 322–323**

ANWENDUNG

Video Wrap-up
Videocassette 4, 30:44–44:00
Videocassette 5 (captioned version),
1:05:16–1:12:50
DVD Tutor, Disc 2

At this time, you might want to use the video resources for additional review and enrichment. These resources are also available via the Enhanced Online Student Edition.
See *Video Guide* for suggestions regarding:
- **Pläne für Omas Geburtstag** (Dramatic episode)
- **Landeskunde** Interviews
- **Videoclips** (Authentic footage)

Apply and Assess

Teaching Suggestion
1 As an advance organizer for the listening activity, ask students to list at least eight points of interest in Berlin.

Portfolio Assessment
2 You might want to suggest this activity as a written portfolio item for your students. See *Alternative Assessment Guide*, p. 28.

4 You might want to suggest this activity as an oral portfolio item for your students. See *Alternative Assessment Guide*, p. 28.

Process Writing
5 Have students work in groups to go back through the book and find all the adjectives that could be used to describe food. Encourage them to consult a dictionary in order to find others. When your students have finished with this activity, you may want to have each of them read his or her favorite description aloud to the class. Once they have all had a chance to present their favorite dish, take a straw poll (using the question **Welches Gericht hättet ihr am liebsten?**) to find out which one sounded the most appetizing to the class as a whole.

> **PAGE 324**

KANN ICH'S WIRKLICH?

This page helps students prepare for the test. It is a brief checklist of the major points covered in the chapter. The students should be reminded that it is only a checklist and not necessarily everything that will appear on the test.

For additional self check options, refer students to the *Grammar Tutor*, the *Interactive CD-ROM Tutor*, and the Online self-test for this chapter.

> **PAGE 325**

WORTSCHATZ

Review and Assess

Circumlocution
To review, play the circumlocution game with **Erste Stufe** vocabulary indicating places to see and to go that are cognates of their English equivalents. Foods in the **Zweite Stufe** and **Dritte Stufe** vocabularies, which can be easily described according to taste, texture, color, appearance, or when they are served during the meal, lend themselves well to circumlocution. In the **Zweite Stufe** vocabulary there are also many adjectives that describe the countries in which many of the foods in this vocabulary originated. Saying "**Das Gericht ist aus einem Land, wo man mit viel Tomatensauce kocht.**" might elicit either "**Es ist aus Italien.**" or "**Es ist italienisch.**" as a response. See p. 3C for procedures.

Teaching Suggestion
To further practice the vocabulary of cultural events, ask students to categorize the titles of plays or music scores that you call out.
Example:
— Was ist *Carmen*?
— *Carmen* ist eine Oper.

Teacher Note
Give the **Kapitel 11** Chapter Test: *Testing Program*, pp. 287–292
Audio CD 11, Trs. 17–18.

KAPITEL 11
Mit Oma ins Restaurant

Objectives

In this chapter you will learn to

Erste Stufe
- ask for, make, and respond to suggestions

Zweite Stufe
- express hearsay

Dritte Stufe
- order in a restaurant
- express good wishes

Visit Holt Online
go.hrw.com
KEYWORD: WK3 BERLIN-11
Online Edition

◀ Guten Appetit, Oma!

Los geht's! · Pläne für Omas Geburtstag

Strategie Verstehen
Look at the images for the story. Who do you think these people are, and what do you think they are doing?

Andreas   Astrid   Oma   Bedienung   Mutter   Vater

Los geht's! is an abridged version of the video episode.

1

Astrid: Hier ist etwas, was Oma vielleicht gefallen würde, ein Sommerkonzert in der Philharmonie.
Andreas: Ja, Musik mag sie gerne. Vati möchte ja am liebsten nach Schwerin fahren, um dort essen zu gehen.
Astrid: Wirklich? Bei diesem Verkehr? Ich bin dafür, dass wir hier etwas unternehmen.
Andreas: Ich schlage vor, dass ich die Oma mal fragen werde, was sie am liebsten machen möchte.
Astrid: Na, das ist doch keine Überraschung mehr!
Andreas: Das weiß ich.
Astrid: Na gut! Wie du meinst.

2
Andreas: Hallo, Omi! Ich hab dir ein paar Blumen mitgebracht, aus unserm Garten.
Oma: Hallo, Andreas! Schön, dass du mich besuchst.
Andreas: Du hast doch Geburtstag, Omi. Astrid und ich, wir möchten wissen, was du am liebsten machen möchtest. Aber es läuft so viel.
Oma: Ach, ich liebe so viele Dinge.
Andreas: Eben! Nun, Omi, sag schon! Möchtest du vielleicht ein Konzert besuchen, oder möchtest du in eine Oper oder Operette gehen?
Oma: Ich möchte gern ins Theater gehen, aber nicht im Sommer, sondern später, wenn es kühler ist.

3
Andreas: Möchtest du vielleicht in ein griechisches oder italienisches Restaurant? Oder wie wär's mit einem typischen Berliner Lokal?
Oma: Ich würde am liebsten in ein Lokal gehen, wo wir draußen sitzen können.
Andreas: Prima, Oma! Aber, sag nichts dem Vati, dass ich dich gefragt habe! Tschüs!
Oma: Auf Wiedersehen, Andreas! Und noch mal vielen Dank für die Blumen!

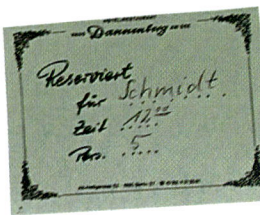

Andreas: Ja, hier ist Schmidt. Ich möchte einen Tisch bestellen, beziehungsweise reservieren, für Samstag, für 12 Uhr 30, und wir sind fünf Personen …Ja, der Name ist Schmidt, mit d-t. Danke! Tschüs!

300   *dreihundert*   STANDARDS: 1.2, 2.2   KAPITEL 11   Mit Oma ins Restaurant

4
- **Bedienung:** So, bitte, die Speisekarte! Möchten Sie zuerst etwas trinken?
- **Mutter:** Ich hätte gern einen Weißwein, aber trocken.
- **Oma:** Ich auch.
- **Astrid:** Ein Mineralwasser, bitte!
- **Andreas:** Und ich hätte gern einen Apfelsaft.
- **Vater:** Für mich ein Bier, ein alkoholfreies, bitte!
- **Vater:** Der Fisch hier soll sehr gut sein, hab ich gehört. Worauf hättest du denn Appetit, Mutter?
- **Oma:** Ich nehme mal die Seezunge.
- **Andreas:** Ich würde gern das Wiener Schnitzel essen, aber ich weiß nicht, ob ich Salzkartoffeln oder Pommes frites dazu bestellen soll.
- **Astrid:** Ich würde die Salzkartoffeln nehmen.
- **Andreas:** Ja, du!

5
- **Bedienung:** Haben Sie schon gewählt?
- **Vater:** Ja, ich denke, wir sind so weit.
- **Mutter:** Ja, ich hätte gern ein Schweinerückensteak, mit Käse überbacken.
- **Oma:** Ich nehme die Seezunge mit Salzkartoffeln und Salat.
- **Vater:** Bringen Sie mir bitte das Seebarschfilet mit Salzkartoffeln und einem kleinen Salat!
- **Astrid:** Ich hätte gerne … Königsberger Klopse und einen kleinen gemischten Salat.
- **Andreas:** Und ich hätte gern das Wiener Schnitzel, aber mit Pommes, bitte!

6
- **Vater:** Also, jetzt trinken wir erst einmal auf dein Wohl, Mutter. Alles Gute!
- **Mutter:** Zum Wohl! Und bleib uns recht lange gesund!
- **Oma:** Zum Wohle, meine Lieben!
- **Astrid:** Prost, Oma! Alles Gute!
- **Andreas:** Alles Gute, Oma! Prost!

Übungsheft, S. 121

1 Was passiert hier?

These activities check for global comprehension only. Students should not yet be expected to produce language modeled in **Los geht's!**

Verstehst du alles, was diese Leute sagen? Beantworte die Fragen!

1. For whom are Astrid and Andreas making plans? 1. grandmother
2. What does their father want to do? What does Astrid suggest? 2. go to a restaurant in Schwerin; concert
3. Why does Andreas go to Oma's? 3. to find out what she wants to do for her birthday
4. What does Oma like to do on her birthday? 4. go to a restaurant where one can sit outside
5. Why is Oma not to say anything about Andreas' visit? 5. it is supposed to be a surprise for her
6. What does Andreas do after he gets home from Oma's? 6. reserves a table in a restaurant
7. What does the family order first in the restaurant? 7. beverages
8. What has the father heard about this place? 8. fish is supposed to be good
9. What does Andreas have trouble deciding about? 9. whether to order potatoes or French fries
10. What kinds of side dishes do they order? 10. potatoes, salad, French fries
11. What happens at the end of the story? 11. they drink to grandmother's health

2 Stimmt oder stimmt nicht?

Wenn der Satz nicht stimmt, schreib die richtige Antwort!

1. Der Vater würde am liebsten zu Omas Geburtstag nach Schwerin fahren. 1. Stimmt.
2. Astrid möchte lieber etwas in Berlin unternehmen. 2. Stimmt.
3. Die Oma würde gern mal in eine Oper gehen. 3. Stimmt nicht. Sie würde gern mal ins Theater gehen.
4. Sie würde aber auch gern in ein griechisches Lokal gehen. 4. Stimmt nicht. Sie möchte in ein typisches Berliner Lokal.
5. Andreas bestellt einen Tisch für vier Personen. 5. Stimmt nicht. Er bestellt ihn für fünf Personen.
6. Andreas' Vater trinkt im Restaurant ein alkoholfreies Bier. 6. Stimmt.
7. Als Hauptgericht bestellt sich die Oma Königsberger Klopse. 7. Stimmt nicht. Sie bestellt Seezunge.
8. Alle trinken auf Vaters Wohl. 8. Stimmt nicht. Alle trinken auf Omas Wohl.

3 Welche Sätze passen zusammen?

Welche Satzteile auf der rechten Seite passen zu den Satzteilen auf der linken Seite?

1. Die beiden Geschwister planen etwas Besonderes, f
2. Ihr Vater möchte nach Schwerin fahren e
3. Andreas schlägt vor, b
4. Die Oma freut sich sehr, a
5. Andreas möchte die Omi fragen, was sie zum Geburtstag tun will, d
6. Am liebsten möchte die Oma in ein Lokal gehen, g
7. Die Oma soll dem Vater nichts von Andreas' Besuch bei ihr sagen, c

a. dass Andreas sie besucht und ihr Blumen mitbringt.
b. dass er die Oma besucht und sie fragt, was sie tun will.
c. denn die Geburtstagsfeier soll eine Überraschung sein.
d. denn in Berlin läuft so viel.
e. und dort ins Restaurant gehen.
f. weil ihre Oma bald Geburtstag hat.
g. wo sie alle draußen sitzen können.

4 Was passt?

Welches Wort im Kasten passt zu welchem Ausdruck unten?

1. Musik
2. eine Operette
3. den Geburtstag
4. mit dem Auto
5. in ein Konzert
6. einen Tisch
7. Appetit
8. auf das Wohl
9. Blumen

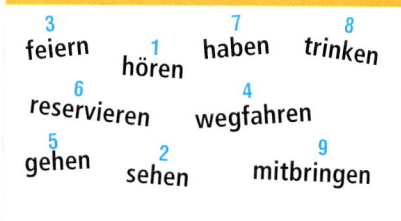

3 feiern   1 hören   7 haben   8 trinken
6 reservieren   4 wegfahren
5 gehen   2 sehen   9 mitbringen

LANDESKUNDE

Für welche kulturellen Veranstaltungen interessierst du dich?

We asked people from around Germany what kinds of cultural interests they have. Listen to the interviews, then read the texts.

Herr und Frau Heine, Goslar

„Ja, als Kultur … wir gehen ganz gern nun mal ins Konzert, ins Theater … und das ist natürlich etwas, was man in der Kleinstadt nicht so hat, das ist ganz klar. In der Kleinstadt müssen wir ungefähr so eine Fahrzeit von ein bis anderthalb Stunden rechnen, um in die nächstgrößere Stadt zu kommen, die dann etwa so 250- bis 500 000 Einwohner hat. In der Großstadt Berlin, oder in 'ner anderen Stadt der Größe oder ähnlicher Größe, wär es natürlich so, dass man ein sehr viel höheres Angebot in der Stadt an Kultur angeboten bekommt — da sind Museen, Theater, Schauspielhäuser, Konzerte. Die Philharmonie hier, die hab ich vor einigen Monaten das erste Mal besuchen können. Das ist schon sehr beeindruckend, überwältigend, auch vom Klang her."

Günther, Berlin

„Zu Konzerten und Ausstellungseröffnungen, und zwar Martin-Gropius-Bau ,Amerikanische Kunst im zwanzigsten Jahrhundert'. Zu so was. Ab und zu Musical, aber eher selten, eigentlich Konzerte mehr."

Claudia und Ursel, Düsseldorf

Claudia: „Also, wir zeigen da eigentlich sehr vielseitige Interessen, zum Beispiel auch Kino oder Theater, und …"

Ursel: „Samstags abends gehen wir auch ganz mal gern in die Disko zum Beispiel."

Claudia: „Oder wir sind ja hier nach Hamburg gekommen, um uns das *Phantom der Oper* anzuschauen, also Musicals auch, also das ist eigentlich sehr weit gefächert."

A. 1. Kino, Theater, Disko, Musicals, Konzerte, Ausstellungen
A. 2. Konzert, Theater; Museen, Theater, Schauspielhäuser, Konzerte; höheres Angebot an Kultur in Großstadt.

A. 1. What different kinds of cultural events do these people mention?

2. Reread Mr. Heine's interview. To what is he referring when he says **Das ist etwas, was man in einer Kleinstadt nicht hat?** What does a city like Berlin have to offer? What phrase does he use to sum this up and make a comparison?

B. Berlin has always been a diverse city with something exciting for everyone. Since unification there is more to see in Berlin than ever. How many of the places below do you recognize? Test your cultural and geographic savvy by matching each name with a photo.

Das Pergamonmuseum

Schloss Charlottenburg

Die Weltzeituhr am Alexanderplatz

Mahnmal (Opfer der Mauer)

STANDARDS: 1.2, 2.2, 3.2, 4.2

TPR Storytelling Book
pp. 80–81

Erste Stufe

Objectives Asking for, making, and responding to suggestions

WK3 BERLIN-11

Berlin ist eine Reise wert. Ein deutsches Sprichwort heißt: „Wer die Wahl hat, hat die Qual." Das trifft besonders auf Berlin zu, denn die neue Metropole Deutschlands macht es den Berlinern selbst und den vielen Besuchern nicht leicht, sich für einige von den vielen kulturellen Möglichkeiten zu entscheiden, die diese Stadt bietet. Sie wollen Berlin ja nicht nur sehen, sondern es auch wirklich erleben.
Ein kleiner Auszug aus dem kulturellen Programm:

KONZERTE

Sonntag, 26. Januar, 16 Uhr
Philharmonie
Konzert für die ganze Familie in Zusammenarbeit mit der Seehausverwaltung für Schule, Jugend und Sport sowie dem JugendKulturService (GmbH).

Dirigent: Niels Muus — Moderator: Otto Sander — Entezami: "Die Maus und der Löwe". Ein musikalisches Märchen für Erzähler und Orchester (Uraufführung)
—**Wüsthoff:** "Das Kuscheltierkonzert" für großes Orchester und Sprecher (Uraufführung)

Karten an den bekannten Vorverkaufskassen, an den jeweiligen Veranstaltungsorten sowie Berliner Symphoniker.
Telefon 325 55 62 Mo. - Fr. 10-14 Uhr.

Sa, 4.9., Deutschlandhalle, 20 Uhr Berlin 88,8 präsentiert
«Das Phantom Traumpaar ist zurück»
Peter Hofmann
Anna Maria Kaufmann
singen
Musical Classics
mit Mitgliedern des
NDR-Sinfonieorchesters
Leitung:
Carl Robert Helg

 **BERLINER DOM**

Sonnabend, 4. August, 19.30 Uhr
Streichkonzert
Israel Camerata
Women's String Orchestra
Werke von Bach u.a.

Sonntag, 5. August, 17 Uhr
Orgelkonzert
Dr. Dieter Hiller (Berlin)
Werke von Schumann, Liszt, Guilmant u.a.

OPER & THEATER

		Deutsche Oper Berlin	Staatsoper Unter den Linden	Theater am Kurfürstendamm	Komödie	Hansa Theater	Berliner Kammerspiele
		Charlottenburg, Bismarckstr. 35, ☎ 3 41 02 49, ☎ 34 38-1 (Zentrale); Ⓤ Dt. Oper; Bus: 101	Mitte, Unter den Linden 7, ☎ 2 00 47 62; Ⓤ Ⓢ Friedrichstraße; Bus: 100, 157	Charlottenburg, Kurfürstendamm 206, ☎ 8 82 78 93; Ⓤ Uhlandstraße; Bus: 119, 129	Charlottenburg, Kurfürstendamm 206, ☎ 8 82 78 93; Ⓤ Uhlandstraße; Bus: 119, 129	Tiergarten, Alt-Moabit 48, ☎ 3 91 44 60; Ⓤ Turmstraße; Bus: 101, 123, 245	Tiergarten, Alt-Moabit 99, ☎ 3 91 55 43; Ⓤ Turmstraße; Bus: 123, 245
2.	Do	19.30 Aida (in ital. Sprache)	20.00 Romeo und Julia (in ital. Sprache)		20.00 Ausreißer	20.00 Don Camillo und Peppone	19.00 Andorra
3.	Fr	19.30 Ballett: Dornröschen	19.30 Hoffmanns Erzählungen	Keine Vorstellung		20.00 Don Camillo und Peppone	19.00 Andorra
4.	Sa	18.30 Liederabend (siehe 'Konzerte')	19.30 Ballett: Nacht/Verklärte Nacht/Der wunderbare Mandarin	20.00 Herr im Haus bin ich (Premiere)	20.00 Ausreißer	19.00 Don Camillo und Peppone	19.00 Andorra
5.	So	17.00: Der Ring des Nibelungen: Götterdämmerung	19.00: Ballett: Nacht/Verklärte Nacht/Der wunderbare Mandarin	20.00 Herr im Haus bin ich	18.00 Ausreißer	15.30 Don Camillo und Peppone	Keine Vorstellung

5 Viel zu tun in Berlin!

Lesen/Sprechen Lies den Text „Berlin ist eine Reise wert", und beantworte die folgenden Fragen!

1. Was bedeutet das Sprichwort „Wer die Wahl hat, hat die Qual"?   *1. It's difficult to choose when the options are equally good.*
2. In welcher Weise passt das Sprichwort zu Berlin?   *2. In Berlin gibt es ein großes kulturelles Angebot.*
3. Für welche kulturellen Veranstaltungen ist dieser Auszug aus dem Berlin Programm?
4. Wohin musst du gehen, wenn du Folgendes sehen oder hören willst?   *3. Konzerte, Oper & Theater*
   a. am Sonnabend „Herr im Haus bin ich"   *a. Theater am Kurfürstendamm*
   b. am Donnerstag „Romeo und Julia"   *b. Staatsoper*
   c. am Sonntag das Orgelkonzert   *c. Berliner Dom*

Wortschatz

Was kann man in Berlin alles sehen?

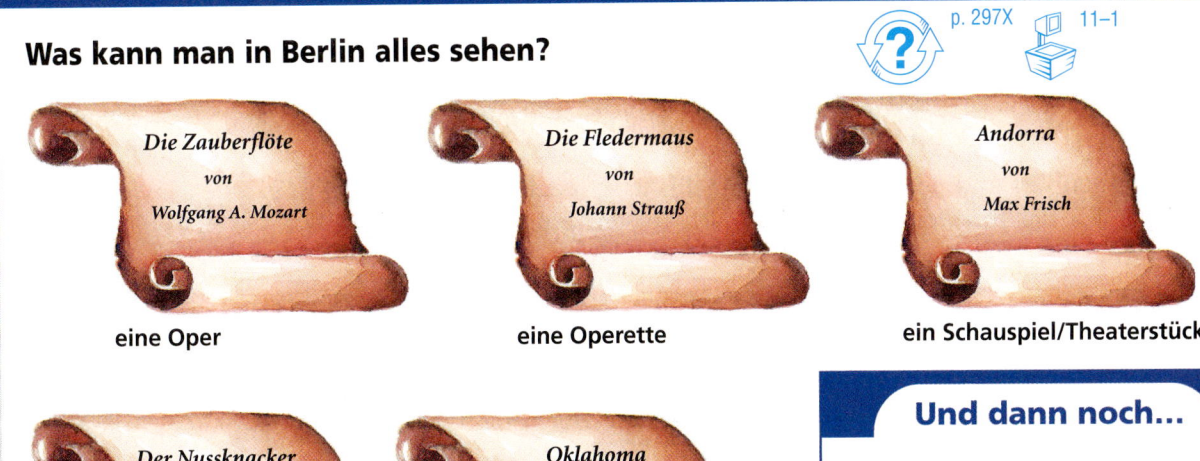

eine Oper eine Operette ein Schauspiel/Theaterstück

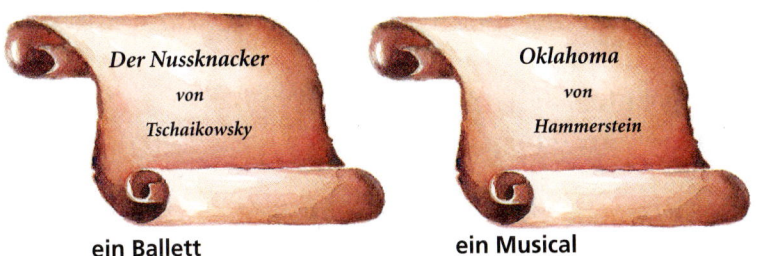

ein Ballett ein Musical

Und dann noch...

in den Zoo gehen
in den Zirkus gehen
ein Symphoniekonzert hören
ein Chorkonzert hören
ins Kabarett gehen

Und man kann **Stadtrundfahrten** machen — mit dem Bus oder mit dem Schiff — und sich die vielen kulturellen **Baudenkmäler** Berlins ansehen.

Busausflug **Ausflugsschiff** **Anschlag für Ausflüge** **Berliner Synagoge**

6 Was kann man alles machen?

Sprechen Erzähl deinen Freunden alles, was man in Berlin machen kann, indem du die Verben mit den richtigen Hauptwörtern verbindest (*by connecting*).

Man kann ...

in den Zoo	gehen
den Dom	machen
eine Stadtrundfahrt	besichtigen
ein Symphoniekonzert	besuchen
ein Schauspiel	sehen
ins Kabarett	hören
Baudenkmäler	
eine Kunstausstellung	
ein Schloss	

ERSTE STUFE   dreihundertfünf 305

7 Für welche Veranstaltungen interessieren sich diese Schüler?

Zuhören Einige Schüler erzählen, für welche kulturellen Veranstaltungen sie sich interessieren und warum. Wähle für jede Beschreibung eine Aktivität aus dem Wortschatzkasten auf Seite 305 aus, die dieser Person besonders gefallen würde!

Script and answers on p. 297G

CD 11 Tr. 7

8 Hast du einen Vorschlag?

Schreiben Ulf und Beate machen gerade Pläne für heute Abend, aber Ulf ist gar nicht sicher, wie das ablaufen soll und fragt nach Vorschlägen. Für jede Antwort schreib eine passende Frage!

ULF	Was sollen wir heute Abend machen?
BEATE	Gehen wir ins Konzert!
ULF	Was kann ich tun?
BEATE	Du kannst schon die Konzertkarten abholen.
ULF	Wo soll ich sie kaufen?
BEATE	Tja, kauf sie am besten im Musikgeschäft!
ULF	Wann fahren wir? Was schlägst du vor?
BEATE	Na, ich schlage vor, dass wir um sechs dahin fahren.
ULF	Und was möchtest du jetzt machen?
BEATE	Ich? Ich möchte mal einfach nach Hause fahren. Also, bis dann!

9 Ich schlage vor, …

Sprechen Du bist mit deiner Familie und einigen Freunden in Berlin, und alle wollen etwas Tolles unternehmen. Als einziger, der Deutsch spricht, musst du eurem Reiseleiter Vorschläge machen. Schau den Wortschatzkasten auf Seite 305 an, und sage, für welche Veranstaltungen sich deine Eltern interessieren und für welche sich deine Freunde interessieren! Teile deine Ideen deinen Mitschülern mit! Danach mach dem Reiseleiter vier Vorschläge, und schreib sie auf ein Blatt Papier!

So sagt man das!

Asking for, making, and responding to suggestions

Here are some new ways of asking for, making, and responding to suggestions:

You could ask for a suggestion by saying:

> Was sollen wir mit der Oma machen? Wofür bist du?

And you could make a suggestion by saying:

> Ich bin dafür, dass wir in Berlin etwas unternehmen.

When making suggestions, you might say:

> Würdest du gern mal in ein italienisches Restaurant gehen?
> Wie wär's mit einem typischen Berliner Lokal?

When responding to suggestions, you might say:

> Nein, ich würde am liebsten in ein deutsches Lokal gehen.
> Das wär' nicht schlecht.

The apostrophe can be dropped **only** in the first person. In the sentence above, **wär'** must retain its apostrophe.

Identify the verb forms in the second and third questions and answers. Of what do these constructions remind you? How would you express these in English? Which case always follows the preposition **mit**?[1]

Übungsheft, S. 124, Ü. 3

Grammatikheft, S. 92–93, Ü. 2–4

---

1. **Mit** is always followed by the dative case.

STANDARDS: 1.2, 1.3   KAPITEL 11   Mit Oma ins Restaurant

10 **Einverstanden?** Scripts and answers on p. 297G

Zuhören Verschiedene Schüler versuchen, mit Freunden Pläne zu machen. Die Schüler machen einige Vorschläge. Für jedes Gespräch, das du hörst, entscheide dich, ob der Freund mit dem Vorschlag einverstanden ist oder nicht.

CD 11 Tr. 8

Grammatik

The würde-forms

1. Using a form of **würde** followed by **gern, lieber,** or **am liebsten** and an infinitive lets you make suggestions and express wishes in a new way.

    Würdest du gern mal in ein italienisches Restaurant **gehen?**
    Ich würde gern mal wieder eine Scholle **essen.**

2. Here are the **würde**-forms:

ich	würde	wir	würden
du	würdest	ihr	würdet
er, sie, es	würde	sie, Sie	würden

Mehr Grammatikübungen, S. 318, Ü. 1–2

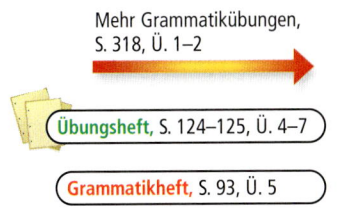

Übungsheft, S. 124–125, Ü. 4–7

Grammatikheft, S. 93, Ü. 5

---

11 **Grammatik im Kontext** E.g.: Ich würde gern mal die Mauerreste sehen.

a. Sprechen Wofür würdet ihr euch (du, deine Familie und Freunde) in Berlin interessieren?

| Meine Eltern
Mein Bruder
Meine Schwester
Ich
Meine Freunde
und ich, wir | bin dafür
ist dafür
sind dafür
würde
würden | dass wir
gern mal
am liebsten | eine Stadtrundfahrt machen
ein Konzert im Berliner Dom hören
eine Ausstellung besuchen
die Mauerreste sehen
einen Ausflug nach Potsdam machen
Schloss Sanssouci besichtigen
in den Zirkus gehen
in ein typisches Berliner Restaurant gehen |

b. Schreiben Schreib, wofür ihr euch (du, deine Familie und Freunde) in Berlin interessieren würdet.

Ein wenig Landeskunde

In Germany the arts are state supported. This enables most cities and even smaller towns to offer most cultural events at reasonable prices. The arts receive such generous support due to a long tradition of art patronage in German-speaking countries. High school students can also take advantage of inexpensive tickets that schools acquire to performances that are not sold out, and university students can make use of sharply reduced tickets at the box office just prior to performances.

---

12 **Was würdest du gern mal tun?**

Sprechen Frag deinen Partner, was er mal gern in Berlin tun würde und warum! Er muss dir drei verschiedene Dinge aufzählen! — Danach fragt er dich.

ERSTE STUFE   STANDARDS: 1.1, 1.2, 2.1, 3.2, 4.1, 5.1   dreihundertsieben

Zweite Stufe

Objective Expressing hearsay

WK3 BERLIN-11

Berliner und ausländische Küche

Friedrich
Altberliner Restaurant
Neue deutsche & vegetarische Küche
Büffet & Veranstaltungsservice
auch außer Haus
Täglich 16-1 Uhr·Küche 16-24 Uhr
Tel.: 421 65 27
Sophie-Charlotten-Str. 80
1000 Berlin 19

SURYA
INDISCHES RESTAURANT
Genießen Sie in indischer Atmosphäre unsere Spezialitäten, Huhn, Lamm, vegetarische Speisen zu kleinen Preisen.
Grolmanstr. 22 · 10623 Berlin-Charlottenbg. (am Savignyplatz) ☎ 312 91 23
täglich geöffnet 12.00 - 1.00 Uhr

CHINA RESTAURANT »HO LIN WAH«
Chinesische Spezialitäten und »DIM SAM«-Köstlichkeiten.
Auch außer Haus Verkauf.
Täglich von 12 bis 24 Uhr geöffnet.
Kurfürstendamm 218 Tel. 8 82 11 71
(in der Passage) 8 82 32 71

RESTAURANTS

… von 11-24 (außer montags; Küche bis 23 Uhr): Folgen Sie einer Empfehlung: Schisch-Kebab - Lammlachs, 24 Stunden in einer Spezialmarinade eingelegt, die einen besonderen Geschmack verspricht. Er wird auf Lavastein gegrillt und mit gebratenen Kartoffeln oder Reis, dazu Sesamsauce und gemischter frischer Salat auf ägyptische Art, serviert für EUR 14,-. Restaurant El Pharao-Wiesenbaude, Steglitz, Goerzallee 1 ☎ 8 33 78 74.

… von 11-24 Uhr: Ausgewählte Köstlichkeiten, mediterrane Delikatessen, Vollwertkost und vegetarische Speisen erwarten Sie im Restaurant Seaside, Reinickendorf, An der Mühle 5-9, Reservierung ☎ 3 61 90 27.

… von 12-24 Uhr: (Küche bis 22 Uhr): deutsche und internationale Spezialitäten sowie zahlreiche Fischgerichte im gepflegten Restaurant mit maritimer Einrichtung. Yachthafen-Restaurant Blau-Rot, das Restaurant mit Terrasse direkt an der Havel. Spandau, Scharfe Lanke 103-107, Reservierung: ☎ 3 61 90 21.

… von 12-24 Uhr: türkische Köstlichkeiten in Berlins erstem türkischen Speiserestaurant Istanbul. Charlottenburg, Knesebeckstr. 77 ☎ 8 83 27 77.

… von 12-1 Uhr: gutbürgerliche Küche und vorzügliche Pfannengerichte, z.B.: 1/2 Bauernente mit Rotkohl und Kartoffelkloß für EUR 13,60. Restaurant Hardtke, Wilmersdorf, Hubertusallee 48 ☎ 8 92 58 48.

… ab 18 Uhr: herzhafte Spezialitäten im rustikalen Pferdestall im Haus Dannenberg am See. Reinickendorf, Alt-Heiligensee 52-54 ☎ 4 31 30 91.

… von 9-14 Uhr: Brunch im Sommergarten (nur bei schönem Wetter) - warme Braten, deftige Wurst- und Käsespezialitäten, Schinken, Lachs, Eier, Rollmops, Salate, dazu süßer Aufstrich und Obst, außerdem Cornflakes oder Müsli und Rote Grütze, Kaffee, Tee oder Fruchtsaft für EUR 8,65, 1/2 Portion EUR 5,10. Britzer Mühle, Neukölln, Buckower Damm 130, neben der restaurierten Mühle am Britzer Garten ☎ 6 04 10 05.

13 Berliner und ausländische Küche

Lesen/Sprechen Lies diese Anzeigen und beantworte die Fragen!
1. Wohin kann man gehen, wenn man chinesisch essen will? **1. Ho Lin Wah**
2. Wo bekommt man neue deutsche und vegetarische Küche? **2. Friedrich**
3. Was bekommt man alles im Restaurant „Blau-Rot"? **3. deutsche und internationale Spezialitäten, Fischgerichte**
4. Was bekommt man zum Brunch im Sommergarten? Nenne fünf Gerichte!
5. Was für ein Restaurant ist „Istanbul"? Was gibt es dort? **5. türkisches Restaurant; türkische Köstlichkeiten**
6. Wo kann man indische Atmosphäre genießen und indisch essen? **6. Surya**

4. E.g.: **Braten, Schinken, Lachs, Eier, Rollmops**

Wortschatz

p. 297X 11–A CD-ROM DISC 3

Ausländische und deutsche Spezialitäten:

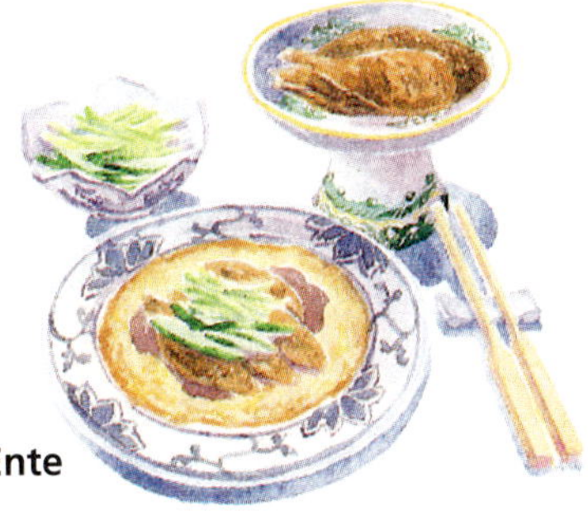

eine chinesische Spezialität: Peking Ente

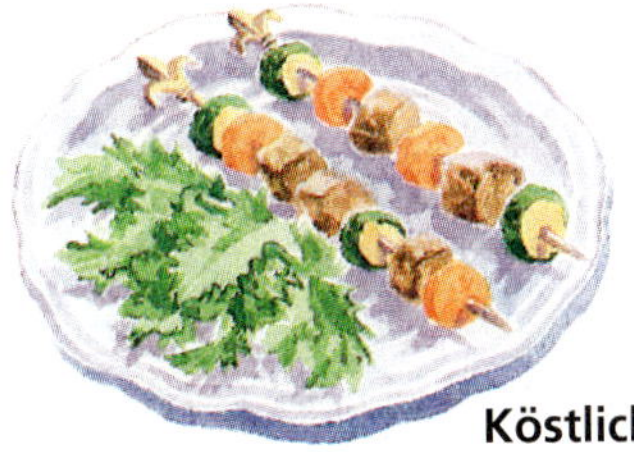

eine ägyptische Köstlichkeit: Schisch-Kebab

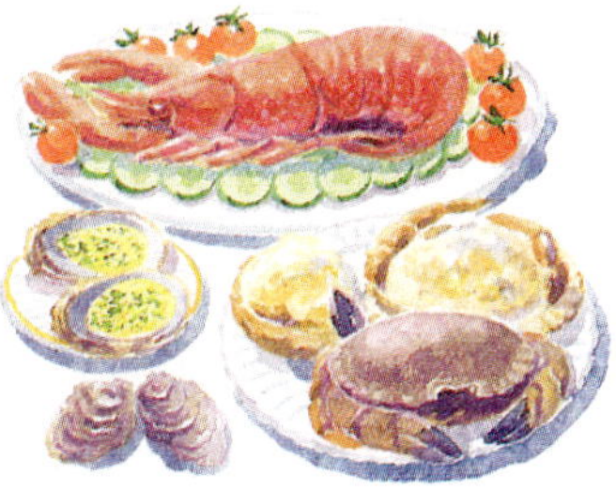

mediterrane Delikatessen: Hummer, Austern, Krabben

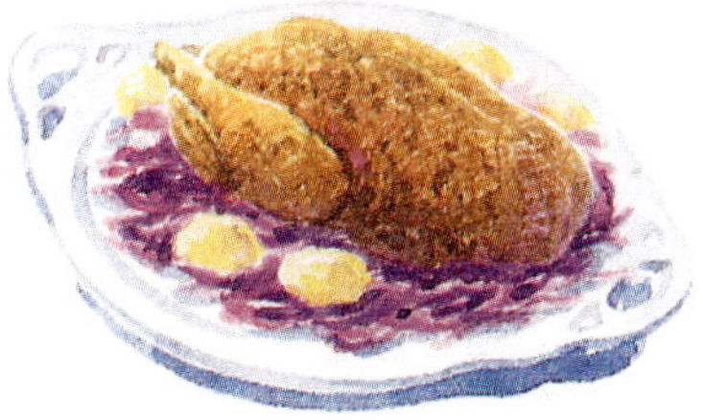

eine gutbürgerliche Küche: Pfannengerichte, z.B. Mastente mit Rotkohl und Kartoffelkloß

Was gibt's zum Brunch?

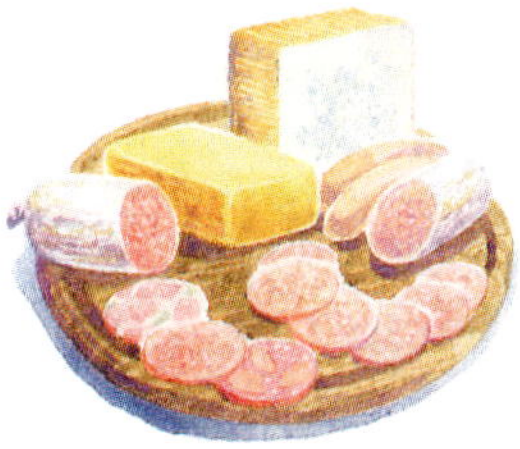

deftige Wurst- und Käsespezialitäten

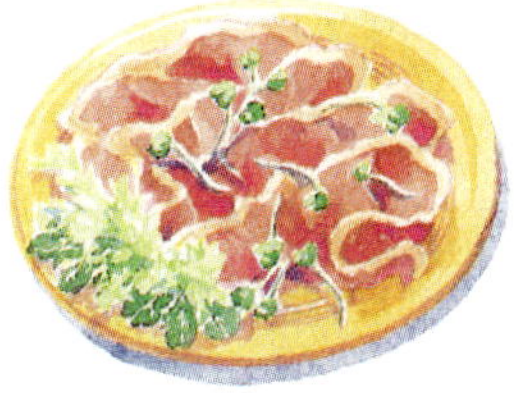

rohen Schinken

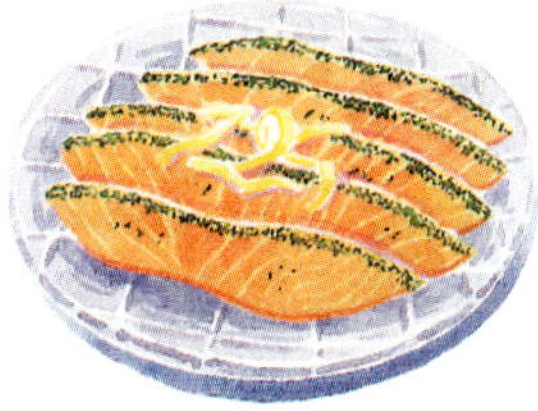

marinierten Lachs

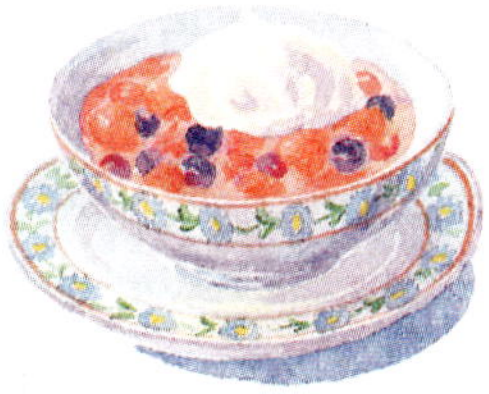

Rote Grütze

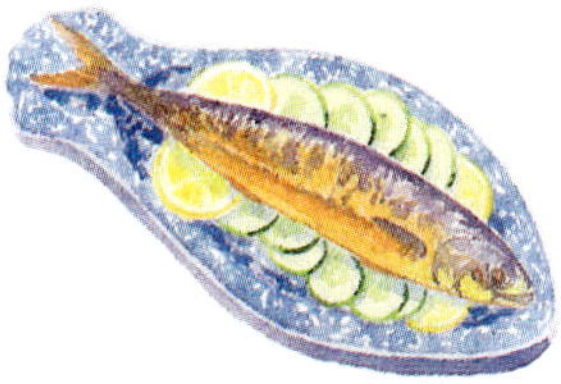

geräucherten Fisch

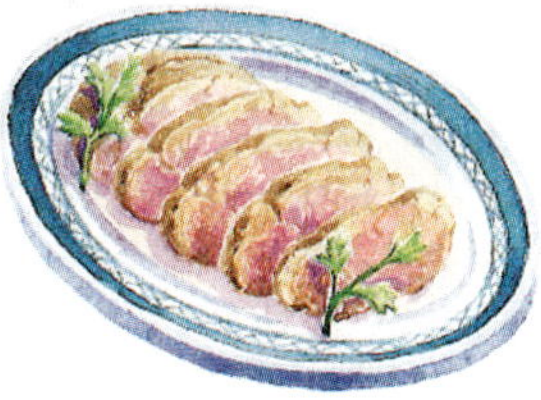

kalten Braten

ägyptisch	italienisch
chinesisch	mexikanisch
deutsch	russisch
französisch	spanisch
griechisch	türkisch
indisch	typisch Berlin

Übungsheft, S. 126, Ü. 1

14 Typische Gerichte

Sprechen Nenne drei typische Gerichte der Länder, für die im Kasten ein Adjektiv steht!

Beispiel **Ein typisches französisches Gericht ist …**

15 Worauf hast du Appetit?

Sprechen Ihr seid den ganzen Tag in Berlin herumgelaufen und habt viel gesehen. Ihr habt großen Hunger und wollt essen gehen. Aber wohin? Die Auswahl ist so furchtbar groß! Mach deinem Partner einen Vorschlag von den Restaurants auf Seite 308! Akzeptiert er ihn? Oder würde er lieber woanders essen? Warum oder warum nicht? Frag ihn mal!

16 Script and answers on p. 297G

In welches Lokal gehen diese Schüler?

Zuhören Zwei Berliner Schüler unterhalten sich darüber, in welches Lokal sie zum Essen gehen wollen. Schreib die verschiedenen Möglichkeiten auf, über die sie sprechen! Wohin gehen sie schließlich und warum?

17

Isst du mal gern ein ausländisches Gericht?

Sprechen Frag deinen Partner, welche ausländische Küche er am liebsten mag und warum! Schau in den Kasten rechts als Hilfe! Dann soll er dich fragen!

Wortschatz

So kann man verschiedene Küchen beschreiben:

scharf *hot, spicy*
würzig *spicy*
herzhaft *hearty*
gegrillt *grilled*
viel Knoblauch *lots of garlic*
mild *mild*
deftig *robust*
gebraten *fried*

Grammatikheft, S. 94, Ü. 6–7

Expressing hearsay

To pass on something that you have heard, you may say in informal conversation:

Ich habe gehört, dass das Essen dort sehr gut ist.
Man hat mir gesagt, dass die Musik dort toll sein soll.
Der Fisch **soll** dort ausgezeichnet **sein**.

How would you express these ideas in English?

Grammatikheft, S. 95, Ü. 8–9

Ein wenig Landeskunde

In den deutschen Großstädten hat es schon immer eine große Anzahl von ausländischen Restaurants gegeben. Ausländische Besucher sollen sich wie zu Hause fühlen, und die Deutschen wollen die internationale Küche genießen.

Heute kann man auch sehr viele ausländische Restaurants und Lokale in kleinen Städten und Dörfern finden, besonders italienische, griechische und türkische Lokale. Und diese findet man sogar in Häusern, die typisch deutsch aussehen, und wo früher mal ein deutsches Lokal war.

18 Welches Restaurant? Script and answers on p. 297G

CD 11
Tr. 10

Zuhören Two students from Potsdam are visiting Berlin. Listen as they discuss three restaurants where they might go for dinner and what they have heard about it from their friends. For each category, write what they heard from their friends about each restaurant.

Essen	Bedienung	Atmosphäre	Preise

19 Wo sollen wir heute Abend hingehen?

Sprechen Together with your partner, decide where you might take a German visitor out for dinner in your town or a large city nearby. Make a suggestion and tell him or her the things you have heard about the restaurant. Your partner will also make a suggestion and say what he or she has heard. Come to a consensus and share your results with your classmates. Ask them if they have heard anything about the restaurant you decided on.

Grammatik

Unprecedent adjectives

1. When an adjective is not preceded by an article (**ein, der, dieser,** etc.), the adjective must show gender and case. Such adjectives get the same endings as the **der** and **dieser-** words would in their place.

> **Der** Salat schmeckt prima.   Griechisch**er** Salat schmeckt prima.
> Ich mag **den** Käse nicht.   Ich mag französisch**en** Käse nicht.
> Dies**e** Milch schmeckt gut.   Kalt**e** Milch schmeckt gut.
> Dies**es** Obst ist gesund.   Frisch**es** Obst ist gesund.
> Wir empfehlen dies**e** Wurstspezialitäten. Wir empfehlen deftig**e** Wurstspezialitäten.

2. When there are two or more adjectives in a series, they both share the same ending.

   Ich esse gern frisch**en** grün**en** Salat.

Übungsheft, S. 126–128, Ü. 2–7   Grammatikheft, S. 96, Ü. 11–11   Mehr Grammatikübungen, S. 319–320, Ü. 3–5

Grammatik im Kontext

20 a. Sprechen It's German-American Day and the German chancellor's personal chef is coming to your class to cook an international meal. Tell him one thing you like and one thing you don't like from the list of possibilities. (Be sure to use the correct adjective endings!)

  b. Schreiben Schreib vier Gerichte auf, die dir schmecken und zwei Gerichte, die dir nicht schmecken. E.g.: **Ich mag italienisches Eis gern. Norwegischer Lachs schmeckt mir nicht.**

bulgarisch	Schisch-Kebab	
kalifornisch	Salat	
italienisch	Eis	
hausgemacht	Wurst	
polnisch	Lachs	schmeckt mir
griechisch	Brot	(nicht).
norwegisch	Käse	
französisch	Spezialitäten	
deutsch	Gulasch	
türkisch	Trauben	
ungarisch	Kuchen	

21 Für mein Notizbuch

Schreib auf, was für Spezialitäten du am liebsten isst, was du gewöhnlich zum Brunch isst und welche Spezialitäten du nicht gern isst!

Dritte Stufe

Objectives Ordering in a restaurant; expressing good wishes

HOTEL-RESTAURANT
HAUS *Dannenberg* AM SEE
Speisenkarte

VORSPEISEN
Gefülltes Ei auf Gemüsesalat	2,70
Geräuchertes Forellenfilet	3,25

SUPPEN
Nudelsuppe mit Huhn	2,10
Frische Gemüsesuppe	2,00

BEILAGEN
Portion Sauerkraut	1,90
Portion Pommes frites	1,75
Portion Gemüse	2,10
Salatteller	2,25
Kloß	1,50
Scheibe Brot	0,35

HAUPTGERICHTE

FISCHGERICHTE
Mit Lachs gefüllte Seezungenröllchen mit Brokkoli-Rahmsauce	12,50
Filets vom Babysteinbutt mit Walnusssauce auf einem Gemüsebett serviert	11,25
Gegrilltes Seebarschfilet m. Salzkartoffeln und gemischtem Gemüse	12,30
Frische Seezunge nach Art des Hauses m. Salzkartoffeln u. gem. Salat	13,25

FLEISCHGERICHTE
Wiener Schnitzel m. Salzkartoffeln oder Pommes frites	11,25
Königsberger Klopse m. Nudeln und gemischtem Salat	8,40
Ungarisches Gulasch mit Kloß	5,95
Frische mecklenburgische Mastente mit Kartoffelkloß	9,25
Schweinerückensteak mit Kräuterbutter u. Pommes frites	10,65

NACHSPEISEN
Rote Grütze mit Vanillesauce	2,30
Apfelstrudel	1,90
Frische Erdbeeren mit Sahne	3,45

GETRÄNKE

WARME GETRÄNKE
1 Tasse Kaffee	1,90
1 Kännchen Kaffee	3,00
1 Tasse Tee	1,90
1 Tasse Kaffee Hag	2,15

ALKOHOLFREIE GETRÄNKE
Mineralwasser	0,3 l	1,90
Apfelsaft	0,4 l	1,80
Orangensaft	0,3 l	1,50
Fruchtlimo	0,3 l	1,50

ALKOHOLISCHE GETRÄNKE
Verlangen Sie bitte unsere Getränkekarte

22 Was steht auf der Speisekarte?

Sprechen Such dir einen Partner! Stellt euch gegenseitig Fragen über die Speisekarte* von „Haus Dannenberg am See"!

1. Was für ein Gericht ist (Seezunge)?
2. Was für Suppen gibt es?
3. Was für Hauptgerichte gibt es?
4. Welche Fischgerichte gibt es? Welche Fleischgerichte?
5. Welche Beilagen gibt es? Und was für Getränke? Nenne drei!
6. Welche Vor- und Nachspeisen gibt es? Nenne eine Vorspeise und eine Nachspeise!

Wortschatz

Was bestellt man gewöhnlich in einem Restaurant?

eine Vorspeise	ein Hauptgericht	eine Beilage
gefülltes Ei	Schweinerückensteak mit Kroketten	Klöße

eine Nachspeise	ein Getränk
Erdbeeren mit Sahne	Spezi

Und dann noch…

Bratkartoffeln
gemischter Salat
eine Scheibe Brot

Was bestellst du gewöhnlich?

Übungsheft, S. 129–130, Ü. 1–3   Grammatikheft, S. 97, Ü. 12–13

23 Beantworte die Fragen!

Sprechen Such dir einen anderen Partner und beantwortet abwechselnd diese Fragen!

1. Was möchtest du dir bestellen? Welche Vorspeise? Eine Suppe? Welches Gericht? Eine Beilage dazu? Welche Nachspeise? Welches Getränk?
2. Welches von diesen Gerichten möchtest du am liebsten essen? Warum? Welches möchtest du nicht essen? Warum nicht?

---

*Both words **Speisenkarte** (usually printed on a German menu) and **Speisekarte** are acceptable, the latter being used in everyday speech.

DRITTE STUFE   STANDARDS: 1.1, 5.1

So sagt man das!

Ordering in a restaurant

Grammatikheft, S. 98, Ü. 14

You have been using various expressions to order food in a restaurant.

Here are some other ways to order:

The waitperson may ask:

Haben Sie schon gewählt?
Und was hätten Sie gern?

You could order by saying:

Ja, bringen Sie mir bitte das Seebarschfilet!
Ich hätte gern das Wiener Schnitzel.

Identify the verb forms in the last question and response. What do these verb forms remind you of? Do these statements refer to the past? What do you think these forms express? How would the waitperson ask several customers at the same time for their order?

24 Was bestellen die Schüler? Script and answers on p. 297H

CD 11
Tr. 11

Zuhören Die Schüler aus der Beckmann-Oberschule machen heute ihre Schulfeier und fahren zum Haus Dannenberg am See. Hör zu, wie sie ihr Essen und ihre Getränke bestellen! Schreib auf, was drei Schüler bestellen, und dann beantworte diese Fragen!

1. Wer bestellt nur ein Hauptgericht?
2. Wer möchte auch eine Beilage zum Hauptgericht?
3. Wer bestellt keinen Nachtisch?

SPRACHTIPP

When ordering from a menu, Germans normally use the definite article before the name of the dish, even though the item may not be listed with an article.
Here is how the dish may be listed on the menu:

Geräuchertes Forellenfilet
Gegrilltes Seebarschfilet
Frische Erdbeeren

Here is how you would order that dish:
Ich hätte gern das geräucherte Filet.
Das gegrillte Seebarschfilet, bitte!
Ich nehme die frischen Erdbeeren.

Mehr Grammatikübungen, S. 320, Ü. 5

Grammatik

The hätte-forms

When ordering a meal you can use the **hätte**-forms together with **gern** or **lieber**.

Ich **hätte gern** eine Suppe.
Was **hättest** du denn **gern**?
Andreas **hätte gern** Rote Grütze.
Wir **hätten gern** Bratkartoffeln.
Und was **hättet** ihr **gern** dazu?
Die Kinder **hätten lieber** einen Salat.

From what verb are the **hätte**-forms derived? How are they like the imperfect form of this verb? What is different? How would you express **hätte gern** in English?

Übungsheft, S. 130, Ü. 4

Grammatikheft, S. 98, Ü. 15

Mehr Grammatikübungen, S. 320–321, Ü. 6–8

25 Grammatik im Kontext

a. **Sprechen** Such dir vier Partner! Frag drei von ihnen, was jeder gern zu essen oder zu trinken hätte! Jeder Partner wählt etwas auf der Speisekarte aus. Du gibst die Bestellung weiter an den vierten Partner. — Tauscht dann die Rollen aus!

b. **Schreiben** Du hast Geburtstag und deine Eltern gehen mit dir in ein Restaurant. Schreib auf, was für Gerichte du gern hättest.

26 Und was hätten Sie gern?

Sprechen Du bist mit deinem Partner in einem guten Restaurant in Berlin. Du feierst deinen Geburtstag und bestellst dir deshalb ein großes Essen, mit Vorspeise, Hauptgericht, Beilage, Nachspeise und Getränk. Ein dritter Schüler übernimmt die Rolle der Bedienung. Was bestellst du alles? Was bestellt dein Partner? Entwickelt ein Rollenspiel und spielt die Szene der Klasse vor!

27 Wer sind diese Leute? Script and answers on p. 297H

Zuhören Einige Gruppen feiern heute im Haus Dannenberg am See. Als Kellner hörst du verschiedene Gespräche. Was feiert jede Gruppe, und was ist das Verhältnis der Leute in jeder Gruppe zueinander? Sind es Familienmitglieder, Freunde oder Geschäftsleute?

CD 11 Tr. 12

So sagt man das!

Expressing good wishes

When toasting someone, you say:

Zum Wohl! *oder* **Auf dein Wohl!**
Prost! *oder* **Auf euer Wohl!**

In response to a toast you say:

Prost! *oder* **Zum Wohl!**
Auf Ihr Wohl! *oder* **Danke! Zum Wohl!**

Before beginning your meal, you say:

Guten Appetit!
Mahlzeit!

In response you can say:

Danke! Dir auch! *oder* **Danke, gleichfalls!**
oder **Mahlzeit! Guten Appetit!**

Which of these expressions would you use with an older person whom you do not know well? Which ones would you use with friends and family?

Übungsheft, S. 131, Ü. 5–6
Grammatikheft, S. 99, Ü. 16–18

---

28 Zum Wohl!

Sprechen Du bist mit verschiedenen Leuten in einem Restaurant. Du trinkst auf ihr Wohl. Was sagst du zu ihnen? Was sagst du …

a. zu einem Freund?
b. zu deinen Eltern?
c. zu zwei Klassenkameraden?
d. zu deiner Deutschlehrerin?

a. Auf dein Wohl!
b. Auf euer Wohl!
c. Auf euer Wohl!
d. Auf Ihr Wohl!

29 Wir gehen zusammen aus

Sprechen At the end of the school year, you and your classmates and German teacher go out to a German restaurant where the waitstaff speaks German. With the people at your table and/or the waiter

— discuss what you will order and why
— suggest to your friends what they should order
— order your food and drink
— toast each other
— begin the meal with good wishes
— talk about how the food tastes
— order dessert and more drinks
— ask for and pay the bill
— arrange for a decent tip

30 Von der Schule zum Beruf

Du arbeitest für das Stadt-Magazin deiner Stadt. Du lernst alle Resorts kennen—du hast schon in der Sportabteilung und in der Fitnessabteilung gearbeitet. Jetzt bist du in der Restaurant-Abteilung gelandet. Deine Aufgabe ist es, für zwei neue Restaurants in der Stadt die Reklame zu schreiben.

Zum Lesen

Das Leben im fremden Land

Lesestrategie **Reading for comprehension.** When reading a short story in German, you need to focus on understanding ideas rather than isolated words. You'll be surprised to find out how much you can understand if you use the following strategy: 1) read at least one-third of the text without looking up any words; 2) reread the same passage and ask yourself what you *do* understand; 3) if you have a general idea of what is happening, read to the end without stopping; and 4) read the story a third time, pausing at intervals to see if you can summarize what you have read.

Getting Started   For answers, see p. 297W.

Weißt du noch? Always look at the title before you begin to read a story or poem.

1. Who are the two people in the title of this story? What does **seltsam** mean? And **komisch**? Knowing that there are two people in the story, can you guess the purpose of the dashes?
2. Use your background knowledge about ethnic groups in Germany and the United States to come up with three possible characteristics of life for Turks in Germany. How do you think they fit into society?
3. Complete steps 1 and 2 of the strategy outlined in the **Lesestrategie** box. In one sentence, summarize what the story is

Seltsamer Deutscher, komischer Türke

- Grüßgott! Du fahren mich das Adresse?
- Ja mei, wozu sind wir denn da, geben's mir mal den Zettel her …(halblaut) Mehmet Öztürk. Klugstr. 19. (laut) Aha, die Klugstraße, in Neuhausen ist die. Steigen S' ein, ich bring Sie hin! (abgewendet) Also, Sepp, Servus. Ich fahr' grad mal nach Neuhausen rüber, vielleicht sehn wir uns noch, die Nacht …
- (Sepp: Wenn nicht, funk mich halt an!)

- Dein Auto gutes Auto. Ich arbeite auch in der BMW. Schichtarbeit. Nach der Arbeit mit Kollegen Bier trinken gehen. Jetzt Alkohol trinken, nix Auto fahren.
- Mit wem sind Sie denn zum Biertrinken gegangen — mit deutschen oder türkischen Kollegen?
- Türkische Kollegen. Deutsche Kollegen sagen immer: Keine Zeit, keine Zeit! Meine alte Freunde erzählen, 1960, 1965, 1968 Deutsche immer freundlich; aber jetzt nix freundlich, immer schimpfen, immer sagen „Kanacke" …
- Tja, schön ist das nicht, wie sich manche Deutsche im Alltag gegenüber Türken benehmen … (Pause)
- Die ganze Nacht regnet's schon! Würden Sie mal bitte mit dem Tuch hier das Fenster abwischen. Damit ich an der Kreuzung die rechte Seite sehen kann. So, es reicht schon, danke schön.
- In Türkei jetzt sehr heiß, sehr schön, immer Sonne.
- Jaja, das glaube ich Ihnen schon, daß in der Türkei sehr schönes Wetter ist …
- Deutschland immer Regen, kalt. Die Deutsche sagen immer „Türken raus!" — Warum? Wir keine schlechte Menschen. Wir immer arbeiten.
- Tja, wissen Sie, die Frage kann ich auch nicht so recht beantworten. Wir sind alle Menschen, da mach' ich überhaupt keinen Unterschied, ob einer Türke ist, Grieche oder Deutscher …
- Sie sind aber ein guter deutsche Mensch. Du sagen nicht, Ausländer nehmen mir Arbeit weg.
- Ja mei, es gibt halt solche und solche …Wir alle versuchen eben, irgendwie über die Runden zu kommen. So, jetzt sind wir gleich da!
- Du sehr gut fahren Auto!
- Danke für das Kompliment!
- Was muß ich bezahlen?
- Yediseksen ediyor arkadasim?

316   *dreihundertsechzehn*   STANDARDS: 1.2, 3.1   KAPITEL 11   Mit Oma ins Restaurant

- Was bitte?
- Dedim ya yediseksen ediyor.
- Hier nehmen Sie, 10 Mark, reicht es?
- Moment mal, ich hab's Ihnen doch schon auf türkisch gesagt. Sagen Sie, sind Sie jetzt eigentlich Türke, oder was!
- Hm, um ehrlich zu sein …Ich muß Ihnen gestehen, ich bin gar kein Türke, äh, ich bin Deutscher, also ich meine …
- Ja um Gottes willen, wieso haben Sie dann die ganze Zeit dieses Theater gespielt?
- Tja, ich wollt' eben mal ausprobieren, wie ein deutscher Taxifahrer einen türkischen Fahrgast behandelt und wollt' mal wissen, wie Sie auf mein Verhalten reagieren würden. Aber sagen Sie mal, was haben Sie da gerade zu mir gesagt? War das tatsächlich Türkisch? Jetzt sagen Sie bloß, Sie sind wirklich Türke!
- Ja, ja, ich bin ein Türke.
- Aber warum sprechen Sie denn so ausgezeichnet Deutsch?
- Tja, ganz einfach. Ich lebe seit 23 Jahren hier in Deutschland, beziehungsweise, ich bin hier geboren.
- Ja! Da mußte mein Versuch ja danebengehen! Es war trotzdem eine lustige Fahrt, oder?
- Jaja, kann man wohl sagen.
- Hier, das Geld. Stimmt schon so! Also dann — Viel Glück noch heut nacht! Wiedersehen!
- Ja, danke, danke! Wiederschaun!

- (aus dem Hintergrund) Hallo, sind Sie frei?
- Ja freilich. Steigen Sie ein!
  Hab gerade so einen „komischen Türken" gefahren …
- Jaja. Unsere Kanacken sind halt so komisch!

Cengiz Kip

about thus far. Where is it taking place? Which character do you think is the Turk? Which is the German?

A Closer Look

> **Tipp:** Summarizing the action of a story every paragraph or so will help you determine how much you understand and what you might need to read again.

4. Complete steps 3 and 4 of the reading strategy. As you read through the third time, try to summarize the action or topics of the dialogue at regular intervals. What are some of the topics of conversation between the German and the Turk?

5. What is the sudden twist in the dialogue? Who is the passenger really and why is he riding in a taxi?

6. Why does the passenger's experiment fail? How does the passenger react when he finds out who the driver really is? What is he so surprised about?

7. What do you think the point of this story is? That is, what message is the author trying to get across? What happens in the final scene to illustrate the author's point?

8. Schreib eine Zusammenfassung (*summary*) von der Geschichte, die du gerade gelesen hast, mit sieben bis acht Sätzen! Verwende dabei so viele Bindewörter (*connecting words*) wie möglich, zum Beispiel Pronomen (er, sie, es usw.) und Zeitausdrücke (zuerst, dann, zuletzt usw.)!

Mehr Grammatikübungen

Erste Stufe

Objectives Asking for, making, and responding to suggestions

1 Du machst verschiedenen Leuten Vorschläge. Sie reagieren darauf und sagen dir, dass sie lieber etwas anderes tun wollen. Schreib die folgenden Fragen und Sätze ab, und schreib dabei in eine Lücke die richtige **würde**-Form und in die andere ein passendes Verb! (S. 307)

1. Du, Astrid, _____ du gern mal in den Zoo _____ ? — Das wäre toll, aber ich _____ lieber mal in den Zirkus _____ .
   würdest; gehen
   würde; gehen

2. Ismar und Andreas, _____ ihr gern mal ein Musical _____ ? — Ja klar, aber wir _____ lieber mal eine Oper _____ , nicht wahr, Ismar?
   würdet; sehen
   würden; sehen

3. Herr Schmidt, _____ Sie gern mal ein Symphoniekonzert _____ ? — Ja, natürlich, aber ich _____ lieber mal ein Chorkonzert _____ .
   würden; hören
   würde; hören

2 Du sagst, was du und deine Freunde **am liebsten** tun würdet. Ergänze die folgenden Satzanfänge mit der in Klammern stehenden Information! (S. 307)

1. (eine Stadtrundfahrt machen)   Also, ich _____ .   würde am liebsten eine Stadtrundfahrt machen
2. (einen Ausflug machen)   Ja, wir _____ .   würden am liebsten einen Ausflug machen
3. (in den Zoo gehen)   Ismar _____ .   würde am liebsten in den Zoo gehen
4. (in ein Museum gehen)   Nun, ich _____ .   würde am liebsten in ein Museum gehen
5. (ein Musical sehen)   Und wir _____ .   würden am liebsten ein Musical sehen
6. (ein Chorkonzert hören)   Astrid _____ .   würde am liebsten ein Chorkonzert hören

Zweite Stufe

Objective Expressing hearsay

3 Du sagst einem Freund, was du über verschiedene Lebensmittel gehört hast. Schreib die folgenden Sätze ab, und schreib dabei die richtige Form des Adjektivs, das in Klammern steht! **(S. 311)**

1. (geräuchert)   Der _____ Fisch soll hier ausgezeichnet sein. — Sag mal, magst du denn überhaupt _____ Fisch?   geräucherte / geräucherten

2. (hausgemacht)   Die _____ Wurst soll hier sehr gut sein. — Sag mal, magst du denn überhaupt _____ Wurst?   hausgemachte / hausgemachte

3. (italienisch)   Das _____ Eis soll in diesem Café am besten schmecken. Sag mal, magst du denn überhaupt _____ Eis?   italienische / italienisches

4. (dunkel)   Das _____ Brot soll gut für die Gesundheit sein. — Sag, magst du denn überhaupt _____ Brot?   dunkle / dunkles

5. (mariniert)   Der _____ Lachs soll in diesem Delikatessenladen viel besser sein. — Magst du denn überhaupt _____ Lachs?   marinierte / marinierten

6. (griechisch)   Die _____ Spezialitäten sollen in diesem Restaurant am besten sein. — Magst du denn _____ Spezialitäten?   griechischen / griechische

7. (roh)   Der _____ Schinken soll in diesem Lokal furchtbar gut sein. — Magst du denn überhaupt _____ Schinken?   rohe / rohen

4 Was würdest du und was würden deine Freunde gern mal essen? Schreib die richtige **würde**-Form in die Fragesätze und die richtige **würde**-Form und das abgebildete Gericht in die Lücken der Antworten. **(S. 311)**

BEISPIEL

Was _____ Maria gern mal essen?
Sie _____ gern mal _____ _____ essen.
Was **würde** Maria gern mal essen?
Sie **würde** gern mal **kalten Braten** essen.

1. Was _____ du gern mal essen?   würdest
   Ich _____ gern mal _____ _____ essen.   würde; geräucherten; Fisch

2. Was _____ Andreas gern mal essen?   würde
   Er _____ gern mal _____ _____ essen.   würde; Rote; Grütze

3. Was _____ ihr gern mal essen?   würdet
   Wir _____ gern mal _____ _____ essen.   würden; marinierten; Lachs

4. Was _____ Astrid gern mal essen?   würde
   Sie _____ gern mal _____ _____ essen.   würde; rohen; Schinken

5. Und was _____ ich gern mal essen?   würde
   Ich _____ gern mal _____ _____ essen.   würde; grüne; Bohnen

MEHR GRAMMATIKÜBUNGEN   STANDARDS: 1.2   *dreihundertneunzehn* **319**

Mehr Grammatikübungen

5 Du hast gehört, dass das Essen in einem gewissen Restaurant ausgezeichnet sein soll. Auf der Speisekarte stehen folgende Gerichte. Schreib diese Gerichte ab, und schreib dabei die richtige Form des Adjektivs vor den Namen jedes Gerichtes! (S. 311)

1. (geräuchert) _____ Forellenfilet
2. (gekocht) _____ Schinken
3. (frisch) _____ Gemüsesuppe
4. (gefüllt) _____ Ei
5. (gemischt) _____ Salat
6. (bayrisch) _____ Sauerkraut
7. (griechisch) _____ Käse
8. (süß) _____ Trauben
9. (indisch) _____ Reis
10. (frisch) _____ Obst
11. (deutsch) _____ Eis
12. (heiß) _____ Tee
13. (kalt) _____ Milch
14. (rot) _____ Grütze
15. (roh) _____ Eier
16. (kalt) _____ Braten
17. (italienisch) _____ Pizza
18. (gebraten) _____ Fisch

Answers: Geräuchertes; Frisches | Gekochter; Deutsches | Frische; Heißer | Gefülltes; Kalte | Gemischter; Rote | Bayrisches; Rohe | Griechischer; Kalter | Süße; Italienische | Indischer; Gebratener

Dritte Stufe

Objectives Ordering in a restaurant; expressing good wishes

6 Wenn du in einem Restaurant ein Gericht bestellst, so kannst du das mit verschiedenen Ausdrücken tun. Schreib die folgenden Sätze ab, und ergänze die Lücken mit der richtigen Endung des Adjektivs! (S. 314)

1. Ich hätte gern die frisch_____ Gemüsesuppe und den roh_____ Schinken. — e; en
2. Ich nehme das gegrillt_____ Seebarschfilet und den gemischt_____ Salat. — e; en
3. Ich hätte gern die hausgemacht_____ Nudelsuppe und den geräuchert_____ Lachs. — e; en
4. Bringen Sie mir bitte den kalt_____ Braten mit einem gemischt_____ Salat. — en; en
5. Und für mich den griechisch_____ Salat und danach das italienisch_____ Eis. — en; e
6. Und ich möchte das Wien_____ Schnitzel und danach frisch_____ Erdbeeren. — er; e

7 Deine Klasse geht zum Abendessen in ein gutes Restaurant. Du fragst deine Klassenkameraden und deinen Lehrer, was sie essen möchten. Schreib die folgenden Fragen und Sätze ab, und schreib dabei die richtige **hätte**-Form in die Lücken! (S. 314)

1. John, was _____ du denn gern? _____ du lieber Bratkartoffeln oder Kroketten? — Ja, ich _____ lieber Bratkartoffeln. — hättest; Hättest; hätte
2. Und ihr beiden? Was _____ ihr denn lieber? _____ ihr lieber das Seebarschfilet oder das Schnitzel? — Wir _____ lieber ein Steak! — hättet; Hättet; hätten
3. Herr Balcke, was _____ Sie denn gern? _____ Sie lieber Fleisch oder Fisch? — Ja, ich _____ lieber Fisch, die frische Seezunge. — hätten; Hätten; hätte
4. Wo ist denn der Mark? Weißt du, was er gern _____ ? _____ er lieber Huhn oder Fisch? — Ich glaube, er _____ lieber Huhn. — hätte; Hätte; hätte
5. Wer von euch _____ lieber eine Vorspeise oder eine Nachspeise? —Du, wir _____ alle lieber eine Nachspeise als eine Vorspeise. — hätte; hätten

8 Was hätten diese Leute gern mal zu essen oder zu trinken? Schreib die richtige **hätte**-Form in die erste Lücke, die richtige Form eines passenden Adjektivs aus dem Kasten in die zweite Lücke und den Namen des abgebildeten Artikels in die dritte Lücke. (S. 314)

deutsch	gefüllt	französisch	grün
hausgemacht	kalt	roh	schwarz

1. Du, ich _____ gern mal _____ _____.   hätte; grünen; Salat

2. Andreas _____ gern mal _____ _____ mit Tofu.   hätte; schwarzes; Brot

3. Oma _____ gern mal _____ _____.   hätte; gefüllte; Eier

4. Opa _____ gern mal _____ _____.   hätte; hausgemachte; Klöße

5. Wir _____ gern mal _____ _____.   hätten; rohen; Schinken

6. Ihr _____ doch gern mal _____ _____.   hättet; deutsche; Marmelade

7. Herr Mai _____ gern mal _____ _____.   hätte; französischen; Käse

8. Ich _____ gern mal _____ _____.   hätte; kalte; Milch

Storytelling Book pp. 86–87

Anwendung

Visit Holt Online
go.hrw.com
KEYWORD: WK3 BERLIN-11
Self-Test

The *CD-ROM Tutor* offers guided recording and writing activities to accompany the **Anwendung**. These activities are designed to practice students' oral and written communication skills and to review material from each chapter.

1 Einige Touristen sprechen über ihre Pläne für Berlin. Hör gut zu! Was wollen sie sich ansehen? Was schlagen sie vor? — Schreib auf, wo jeder gern mal hingehen würde! Aber was tun sie wirklich? *For script and answers, see p. 297H.*

CD 11 Tr. 13

2 Ein Slogan heißt: Berlin ist eine Reise wert! Sieh dir diesen Auszug für Stadtrundfahrten aus dem Berlin Programm an! Welche Sehenswürdigkeiten kennst du schon? Schlag deinem Partner vor, was du dir gern mit ihm ansehen würdest! Was meint er dazu? Hat er bessere Vorschläge?

3 Schreib drei Sehenswürdigkeiten auf, die du dir gern einmal ansehen würdest! Schreib auch auf, warum du daran interessiert bist!

4 Such dir eine Partnerin! Schlag ihr vor, dass sie sich mit dir die Sehenswürdigkeiten ansieht, die du dir ausgesucht hast! Sag ihr auch, was du darüber schon gehört hast! Geht sie mit dir mit? Sie muss ihre Antwort begründen.

5 Zum Schreiben

Your friend has just opened a restaurant and has asked you, the editor of a gourmet magazine, to advertise the restaurant in your magazine by vividly describing five special dishes offered by the restaurant.

Schreibtipp If you focus on **all five senses**, instead of just the sense of sight as we usually do, you will have a wide variety of specific details for your writing. Food can be experienced through all five senses (sight, smell, hearing, taste, and touch), and can therefore be described using a wide variety of adjectives.

Vorbereiten

Make a **list** of adjectives that can be used to indicate taste. **Salzig** and **scharf** are adjectives you could use. In describing aromas you might write that **es riecht nach frischem Kaffee.** The sound of a sizzling steak or of crisp lettuce being cut could be mentioned. You may want to describe the green of lettuce against the red of a tomato. What would the food feel like on your tongue? Ice cream could be described as **kremig** or **kalt.**

Ausführen

Decide on the menu you would like to recommend, and using your list of adjectives, match the foods on your menu with adjectives that describe them. Be sure to make your descriptions as complete and as enticing as possible.

Überarbeiten

- Ask another student to close his or her eyes and listen as you read your descriptions. Can this student visualize your dish? Are your descriptions pleasing to him or her?

- After getting input from your classmate, make corrections, proofread for errors in spelling and grammar, and present your menu to the class.

6 Rollenspiel

Groups of six split into pairs of three: travelers and travel agents. Both groups should review by themselves what they know about famous Berlin places and reasons they have heard for going there.
Set up rows of desks to simulate a travel agency. The travelers then have to go to the agents and ask about some sights they have heard of. The agents should corroborate that information, urging the travelers to go there (or not) and make suggestions of their own. The travel agents tell the travelers which of the city tours listed on page 322 they should take in order to see those sights, what time the tours are, and how much they cost.

ANWENDUNG   STANDARDS: 1.1, 1.3, 5.1, 5.2   *dreihundertdreiundzwanzig*

Kann ich's wirklich?

WK3 BERLIN-11

Can you ask for, make, and respond to suggestions? (p. 306)

1 How would you ask a friend what he or she would like to do? Think of three different ways! *1. Was möchtest du machen? Was würdest du gerne machen? Was möchtest du tun?*

2 How would you tell a friend you are in favor of eating Chinese food? How would you ask your friend if he or she would like that, using **würde**?
2. Ich bin dafür, dass wir chinesisch essen gehen. Würdest du gern mal chinesisch essen gehen?

3 How would your friend respond that it wouldn't be bad, but that he or she would rather eat at a Mexican restaurant? How would you then say: "What about 'Los Compadres'?"   *3. Das wär nicht schlecht. Aber ich würde lieber in einem mexikanischen Restaurant essen. — Wie wär's mit „Los Compadres"?*

Can you express hearsay? (p. 310)

4 How would you say   *4. a. Ich habe gehört, dass das Essen bei Hardtke sehr gut sein soll.*
   a. that you heard the food is very good at Hardtke's?
   b. that Klaus told you the pizza is excellent at "La Bussola"?   *b. Klaus hat mir gesagt, dass die Pizza im „La Bussola" ausgezeichnet sein soll.*
   c. that the service is supposed to be very bad at "Jean-Marc's"?
   c. Der Service bei „Jean Marc" soll sehr schlecht sein.

Can you order in a restaurant? (p. 314)

5 How would a waiter ask you
   a. if you have made your choice?   *a. Haben Sie schon gewählt?*
   b. what you would like?   *b. Was hätten Sie gern?*

6 How would you say
   a. that you would like a bottle of mineral water?   *a. Ich hätte gern eine Flasche Mineralwasser.*
   b. "Please bring me the goulash!"?   *b. Bringen Sie mir bitte das Gulasch!*

7 How would you ask your sister if she would prefer French fries?
7. Möchtest du lieber Pommes frites?

Can you express good wishes? (p. 315)

8 How would you say "Enjoy your meal!" to someone? How would that person respond?   *8. Guten Appetit! Mahlzeit! — Danke, gleichfalls!*

9 How would you toast
   a. a friend?   *a. Prost! Auf dein Wohl!*
   b. a group of friends?   *b. Auf euer Wohl!*
   c. a teacher?   *c. Auf Ihr Wohl!*

   How would those persons respond?
   Prost!; Danke, gleichfalls!; Zum Wohl!

324   *dreihundertvierundzwanzig*   STANDARDS: 1.2   KAPITEL 11   Mit Oma ins Restaurant

Wortschatz

Erste Stufe

 p. 297X

Asking for, making, and responding to suggestions

Würdest du gern mal …?	Wouldn't you like to …?	Das wär' nicht schlecht.	That wouldn't be bad.	die Stadtrundfahrt, -en	city tour
Wie wär's mit …?	How about …?			das Baudenkmal, ¨er	monument
Ich bin dafür, dass …	I'm for … (in favor of)	**Talking about cultural events**		die Synagoge, -n	synagogue
		die Operette, -n	operetta	der Ausflug, ¨e	excursion
Nein, ich würde am liebsten …	No, I would rather …	das Schauspiel, -e	play	der Anschlag, ¨e	announcement
		das Theaterstück, -e	play	würde	would
		das Ballett, -e	ballet	du würdest	
		das Musical, -s	musical	er/sie/es würde	

Zweite Stufe

Expressing hearsay

Ich habe gehört, dass …	I heard that …	türkisch	Turkish	das Pfannengericht, -e	pan-cooked entrée
Man hat mir gesagt, dass …	Someone told me that …	ausländisch	foreign	der Braten, -	roast
		Talking about German and international foods		der Rotkohl	red cabbage
Der Fisch soll prima sein.	The fish is supposed to be great.	die Köstlichkeit, -en	delicacy	der Kloß, ¨e	dumpling
		die Spezialität, -en	specialty	der Knoblauch	garlic
Describing international foods		die Delikatesse, -n	delicacy	Rote Grütze	red berry dessert
chinesisch	Chinese	die Peking Ente, -n	Peking duck	**Ways to describe food**	
mediterran	Mediterranean	die Mastente, -n	fattened duck	deftig	robust
ägyptisch	Egyptian	das Schisch-Kebab	shish kebab	herzhaft	hearty
italienisch	Italian	der Hummer, -	lobster	roh	raw
französisch	French	die Auster, -n	oyster	mariniert	marinated
griechisch	Greek	die Krabbe, -n	crab	würzig	spicy
indisch	(Asian) Indian	der Lachs, -e	salmon	scharf	spicy, hot
mexikanisch	Mexican	gutbürgerliche Küche	good home-cooked cuisine	mild	mild
russisch	Russian			gebraten	fried
spanisch	Spanish	die Küche	cuisine	gegrillt	grilled
		der Schinken	ham	geräuchert	smoked

Dritte Stufe

Ordering in a restaurant

Haben Sie schon gewählt?	Have you decided? Are you ready to order?	Erdbeeren mit Sahne	strawberries with whipped cream	das Spezi, -s	mix of cola and lime soda
wählen	to choose, select	das Getränk, -e	drink	**Expressing good wishes**	
Bringen Sie mir bitte …	Please bring me …	**More German specialties**		Zum Wohl!	To your health!
		das Schweinerücken-steak, -s	pork loin steak	Auf dein/Ihr/euer Wohl!	To your health!
Ich hätte gern …	I would like …	das Wiener Schnitzel, -	veal cutlet	Prost!	Cheers!
Ordering from food categories		das Seebarschfilet, -s	fillet of perch	Guten Appetit!	Bon appétit!
die Vorspeise, -n	appetizer	die Kroketten (pl)	potato croquettes	Mahlzeit!	Bon appétit!
die Beilage, -n	side dish			Danke! Dir/Ihnen auch!	Thank you! The same to you!
das Hauptgericht, -e	main dish	die Bratkartoffeln (pl)	fried potatoes		
die Nachspeise, -n	dessert	das gefüllte Ei, -er	deviled egg	Danke, gleichfalls!	Thank you and the same to you!

Kapitel 12: Die Reinickendorfer Clique *Review Chapter*

Chapter Overview

Los geht's! pp. 328–330
Echt toll, Ismar! p. 328

	FUNCTIONS	GRAMMAR	VOCABULARY	RE-ENTRY
Erste Stufe pp. 331–336	• Reporting past events, p. 334 • Asking for, making, and responding to suggestions, p. 335	• The past tense, p. 333 • Two-way prepositions, pp. 335, 336 • The verb **sollen**, p. 335 • The **würde**-forms, p. 335	• Words used in an article about travel, p. 333	• Chapter 12 is a global review of *Komm mit!* Level 2
Zweite Stufe pp. 337–340	• Ordering food, expressing hearsay and regret, p. 339 • Persuading and dissuading, p. 340	• The command forms of strong verbs, p. 340	• International cuisine, p. 338	• Chapter 12 is a global review of *Komm mit!* Level 2
Dritte Stufe pp. 341–345	• Asking for and giving advice, p. 343 • Expressing preference, p. 343 • Expressing interest, disinterest, and indifference, p. 344	• Adjective endings, p. 341 • More adjective endings, p. 343 • Comparative adjectives, p. 344	• Clothing, p. 342	• Chapter 12 is a global review of *Komm mit!* Level 2

Zum Lesen pp. 346–347
Nach dem Krieg

Reading Strategy
Note-taking

Mehr Grammatikübungen pp. 348–351
Erste Stufe, pp. 348–350   Zweite Stufe, p. 351   Dritte Stufe, p. 351

Review pp. 352–353
Kann ich's wirklich?, p. 352   Wortschatz, p. 353

CULTURE

- **Landeskunde:** Welche ausländische Küche hast du gern? p. 331
- German vacation habits, p. 332
- Report on a popular vacation resort, p. 332
- **Ein wenig Landeskunde:** Etiquette in German restaurants, p. 339
- Franziska van Almsick, p. 341

Kapitel 12: Die Reinickendorfer Clique *Review Chapter*
Chapter Resources

Lesson Planning
One-Stop Planner
Lesson Planner with Substitute Teacher Lesson Plans, pp. 57–61, 76
Student Make-Up Assignments
- Make-Up Assignment Copying Masters, Chapter 12

Listening and Speaking
TPR Storytelling Book, pp. 88–95
Listening Activities
- Student Response Forms for Listening Activities, pp. 91–92
- Additional Listening Activities 12-1 to 12-6, pp. 95–98
- Additional Listening Activities (songs), p. 93
- Scripts and Answers, pp. 169–174

Video Guide
- Teaching Suggestions, pp. 76–77
- Activity Masters, pp. 78–80
- Scripts and Answers, pp. 107–110

Activities for Communication
- Communicative Activities, pp. 67–72
- Realia and Teaching Suggestions, pp. 118–121
- Situation Cards, pp. 145–146

Reading and Writing
Reading Strategies and Skills Handbook, Chapter 12
Lies mit mir! 2, Chapter 12
Übungsheft, pp. 133–144

Grammar
Grammatikheft, pp. 100–108
Grammar Tutor for Students of German, Chapter 12

Assessment
Testing Program
- Grammar and Vocabulary Quizzes, **Stufe** Quizzes, and Chapter Test, pp. 301–318
- Score Sheet, Scripts and Answers, pp. 319–326
- Final Exam, pp. 327–334
- Final Exam Score Sheets, Scripts and Answers, pp. 335–340

Alternative Assessment Guide
- Portfolio Assessment, p. 29
- Performance Assessment, p. 43
- CD-ROM Assessment, p. 57

Student Make-Up Assignments
- Alternative Quizzes, Chapter 12

Online Activities
- Interaktive Spiele
- Internet Aktivitäten

Video Program
- Videocassette 4
- Videocassette 5 (captioned version)
- DVD Tutor, Disc 2

Audio Compact Discs
- Textbook Listening Activities, CD 12, Tracks 1–11
- Additional Listening Activities, CD 12, Tracks 20–26
- Assessment Items, CD 12, Tracks 12–19

Interactive CD-ROM Tutor, Disc 3

Teaching Transparencies
- Situations 12-1 to 12-2
- Vocabulary 12-A to 12-C
- Los geht's!
- Mehr Grammatikübungen Answers
- Grammatikheft Answers

Use the **One-Stop Planner CD-ROM with Test Generator** to aid in lesson planning and pacing.

For each chapter, the **One-Stop Planner** includes:
- Editable lesson plans with direct links to teaching resources
- Printable worksheets from resource books
- Direct launches to the HRW Internet activities
- Video and audio segments
- Test Generator
- Clip Art for vocabulary items

Kapitel 12: Die Reinickendorfer Clique *Review Chapter*

Projects

Ein Reiseführer

Students will compile and design a **Reiseführer** for a city which has not been previously studied in Levels 1 or 2. Students may choose a city in Germany, Austria, Switzerland, or Liechtenstein.

OUTLINE

This project should be started as soon as you begin Chapter 12. Students can work in pairs or individually. The project should be written completely in German and should include the following:

- a brief history of the city,
- an overview of interesting and noteworthy landmarks, including background information,
- typical food and drinks served in this city, including some popular restaurants,
- other significant information that would be of interest to the class.

MATERIALS

Students may need
- posterboard
- glue or masking tape
- scissors
- markers
- travel brochures

SUGGESTED SEQUENCE

1. Once students have decided on a city they would like to research, they should begin to gather materials for their **Reiseführer.**
2. Students prepare an outline of their **Reiseführer** to show you for approval.
3. Students begin their final draft using all gathered information, including visuals.
4. Students give a short presentation on the city they chose and present their **Reiseführer** to the class.

GRADING THE PROJECT

Suggested point distribution (**total = 100 points**)
 Appearance/originality............................25
 Completion of assignment 25
 Correct language usage 25
 Oral presentation..................................25

Games

Bildkarten

In this game students practice the articles **der, die,** and **das** as they apply to the nouns to be reviewed.

Preparation Write nouns from a particular vocabulary group on small index cards. (Examples: foods, clothing) You could also glue or tape pictures of the objects on index cards instead of writing the words. You will need a set of at least twelve cards for each group.

Procedure Students play in groups of five; four students will play, while the fifth student is the leader. Each of the four players receives a blank sheet of paper on which he or she writes the three definite articles.

der	die	das

The leader receives a list with all the nouns, including the corresponding articles, as well as a set of index cards that show the picture or word. The leader places the deck of cards face down. Students take turns drawing a card from the top of the deck. Each student tries to name the correct definite article for the noun written on the card he or she has drawn. If he or she is correct, the card is placed on the sheet in front of him or her under the corresponding article. If the student names the wrong article, the leader receives the card. Once all cards in the deck have been used, the leader reshuffles the remaining cards and continues until all articles have been named correctly. The student with the most cards on his or her sheet (**der-die-das**) wins. To expand this activity, students could also be required to create a complete sentence using each of the nouns. Play the game several times to help students learn all the vocabulary with the correct articles.

Storytelling

Mini-Geschichte

This story accompanies Teaching Transparency 12-C. Read the Mini-Geschichte to students, or have them read the advertisement using proper pronunciation, intonation, and cadence. Ask students if they would enjoy shopping in the Boutique Eleganz. Why or why not?

Boutique Eleganz

Welches Hemd finden Sie eleganter, ein kariertes Hemd mit roter Krawatte oder ein weißes Hemd mit schwarzer Fliege? Was gefällt Ihnen besser, eine braune Lederjacke und Jeans oder ein dunkelblauer Smoking? Wenn Sie sich in saloppen Klamotten nicht wohl fühlen, dann besuchen Sie uns. Wenn Sie gute Qualität suchen, dann haben wir das Richtige für Sie. Wir freuen uns darauf, Sie elegant zu kleiden. Wir haben an Wochentagen bis 20.00 Uhr geöffnet.

Traditions

Der Berliner Bär

Der Berliner Bär hat eine über siebenhundertfünfzigjährige Geschichte. Das erste Siegel Berlins mit der Abbildung eines Bären stammt aus dem Jahre 1280. Dieses Siegel, auf dem zwei aufrecht stehende Bären sind, trägt die Inschrift: „Ich bin das Siegel der Bürger von Berlin". Ein Siegel aus dem Jahre 1338 zeigt einen Adler über dem Bären, was die Vereinigung von Berlin und Cölln symbolisieren sollte. Mit der Gründung des Königreiches Preußen im Jahre 1701 bekam der Bär ein Halsband und stand unter den Wappen mit dem preußischen und dem roten märkischen Adler.

Erst im Jahre 1875 wurde der Berliner Bär von seinem Halsband befreit. Aber nicht nur auf Siegeln, Urkunden, Fahnentüchern und Wappen lebte der Bär, sondern auch im Bärenzwinger im Köllnischen Park, der 1939 eröffnet wurde. Manche Wissenschaftler behaupten sogar, dass Berlin seinen Namen den Bären zu verdanken hat, d. h. das „Ber" in Berlin soll von „Bär" abgeleitet worden sein. Die enge Verbundenheit der Berliner mit ihrem Wappentier zeigt sich in Hunderten von Gedichten und Liedern und in den Namen von Hotels, Restaurants, Geschäften, Sportvereinen, usw.

Have students research in the library or on the Internet the significance of the bear to the history of Berlin. Students should present their research to the class.

Rezept

Bollenfleisch
Für 4 Personen

Zutaten
g= Gramm, EL = Esslöffel, l = Liter

1,2 kg Zwiebel	1 EL Kümmel
1,2 kg Lamm - oder Hammelfleisch	1-2 Lorbeerblätter
	1-2 Knoblauchzehen
Salz	

Zubereitung

Die Zwiebeln schälen und im ganzen zusammen mit dem Fleisch in einen großen Topf geben. Soviel Wasser zugießen, daß das Fleisch und die Zwiebeln knapp bedeckt sind. Kräftig salzen und pfeffern. Kümmel, Lorbeerblätter und geschälte ganze oder durchgedrükte Knoblauchzehen zugeben. Einmal kurz aufkochen lassen, dann herunterschalten und auf kleinerer Hitze in 1 bis 1 1/2 Stunden gar kochen. Das Fleisch herausnehmen, vom Knochen lösen und klein schneiden. Wieder in die Brühe geben und noch einmal erhitzen. Die Lorbeerblätter herausnehmen. Das Bollenfleisch noch einmal abschmecken und vor dem Servieren in einer vorgewärmte Terrine umfüllen. Dazu gibt es Quetschkartoffeln.

Kapitel 12: Die Reinickendorfer Clique *Review Chapter*
Technology

Videocassette 4, 5 (captioned version)
DVD Tutor, Disc 2
See Video Guide, pages 75–80

DVD/Video

Los geht's! • Echt toll, Ismar!

Astrid is complimenting Ismar on his food preparation abilities; the clique is meeting at Andreas and Astrid's house. Sandra calls for directions. Lars arrives with Binh on the moped. Andreas admires it. Binh admires the food, and she and Astrid discuss her eating habits. Ismar teases Lars because he's so well dressed, and Astrid asks if she can try Binh's jacket. Binh has a bandage on her arm.

Landeskunde
Welche ausländische Küche hast du gern?
People discuss their favorite international cuisines.

Fortsetzung

As they sit at the table in the garden, Sandra admires how much quieter this neighborhood is than the one where she lives. Lars tells a little bit about his trip to America, and all the others say where they went for their vacations. Andreas takes everybody in to show them a video of his trip to St. Ulrich in Tirol.

Videoclips
- Kräuterklößchen Suppe® (soup)
- Krönung Kaffee von Jacobs® (coffee)
- Unox Schlemmersoßen® (cooking sauce)
- TUI Ferienwohnungen® (vacation housing)

Interactive CD-ROM Tutor

Activity	Activity Type	Pupil's Edition Reference
1. So sagt man das!	Was kommt dann?	p. 334
2. Grammatik	Was fehlt?	pp. 333, 335, 336
3. Wortschatz	Wort und Bild Erfahren/Wählen	p. 338
4. Wortschatz	Merkspiel	p. 342
5. Grammatik	Was fehlt?	p. 343
6. So sagt man das! Landeskunde	Was ist richtig? Welche ausländische Kuche hast du gern? Was ist richtig?	pp. 335, 343, 344 p. 331
Zum Sprechen	Guided recording	p. 352
Zum Schreiben	Guided writing	p. 352

Teacher Management System
Launch the program, type "admin" in the password area, and press RETURN. Log on to **www.hrw.com/CDROMTUTOR** for a detailed explanation of the Teacher Management System.

DVD Tutor

The *DVD Tutor* contains all material from the *Video Program* as described above. German captions are available for use at your discretion for all sections of the video. The *DVD Tutor* also provides a variety of video-based activities that assess students' understanding of **Los geht's!**, **Fortsetzung**, and **Landeskunde**, as well as the new **Grammatik im Kontext** presentations.

The *DVD Tutor* may be used on any DVD video player connected to a television or video monitor.

One-Stop Planner CD-ROM

To preview all resources available for this chapter, use the **One-Stop Planner CD-ROM**, Disc 3.

Visit Holt Online
go.hrw.com
KEYWORD: WK3 BERLIN-12
Online Edition

Go.Online!

Premier Online Edition

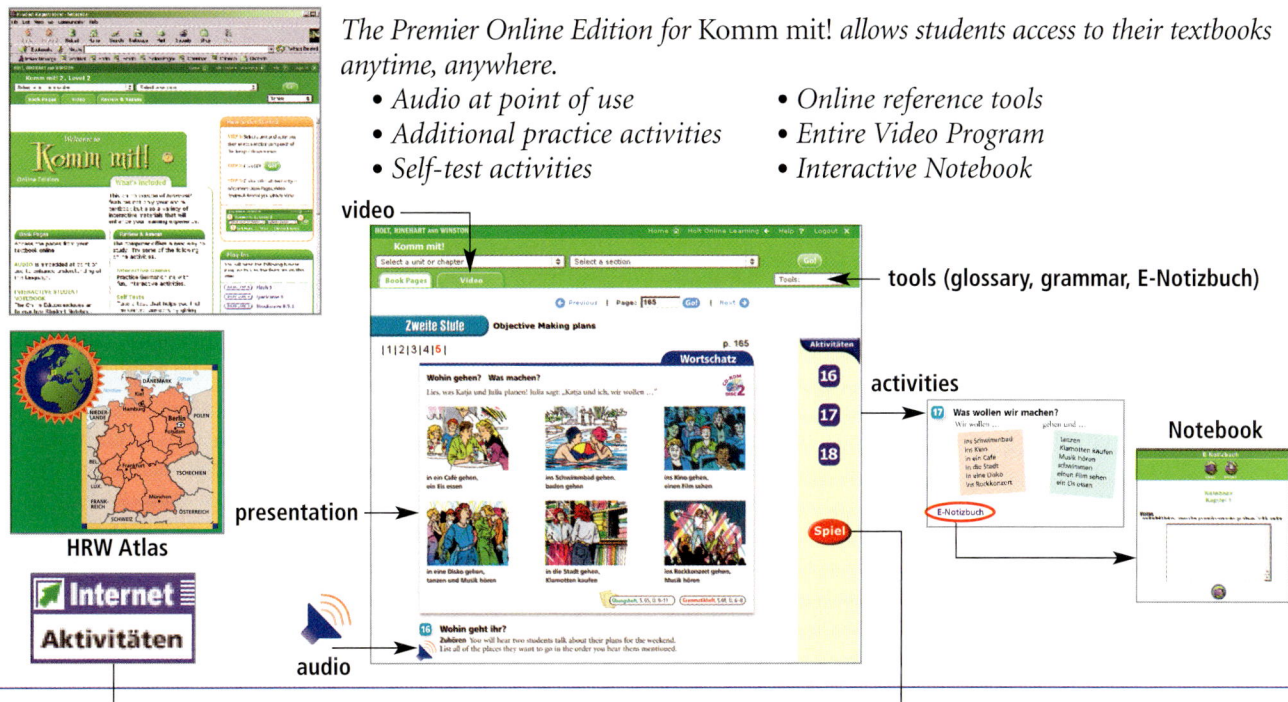

The Premier Online Edition for *Komm mit!* allows students access to their textbooks anytime, anywhere.
- Audio at point of use
- Additional practice activities
- Self-test activities
- Online reference tools
- Entire Video Program
- Interactive Notebook

Internet Aktivitäten

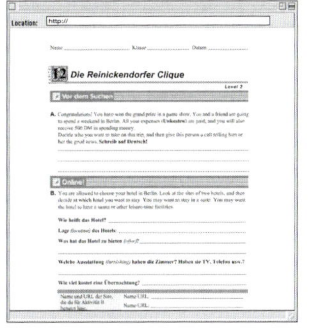

These guided internet activities include a worksheet and pre-selected and pre-screened authentic web sites from the German-speaking countries. You can use these activities
- to help students develop research skills in the target language
- to introduce students to authentic cultural information
- as a project

Interaktive Spiele

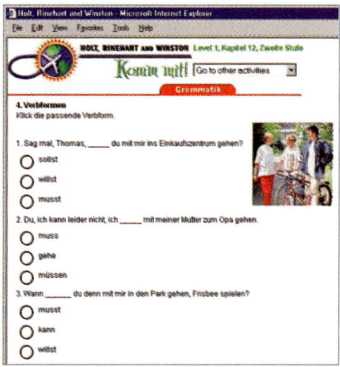

You can use the interactive activities in this chapter
- to practice grammar, vocabulary, and chapter functions
- as homework
- as an assessment option
- as a self-test
- to prepare for the Chapter Test

Webprojekt Have students visit the site of a travel agency in Germany and find information about adventure tours offered by the travel agency. They should report on the destination, the activities offered, the price, dates, and other pertinent information. Encourage students to exchange useful Web sites with their classmates. Have students document their sources by referencing the names and URLs of all the sites they consulted.

STANDARDS: 1.2, 1.3, 2.2, 3.2, 5.1, 5.2   KAPITEL 12   TECHNOLOGY   **325F**

Kapitel 12: Die Reinickendorfer Clique *Review Chapter*
Textbook Listening Activities Scripts

Erste Stufe

6 p. 333

MIRIAM Ach, war die Reise phantastisch! Die fünf Tage sind so schnell vergangen. Das war wirklich ein toller Geheimtipp von meiner Tante. Das nächste Mal müssen wir unbedingt länger dort bleiben. Ich hab echt nicht gewusst, dass Schweden so ein tolles Land ist. Das Meer, der Strand, ach ja, und die steilen Klippen direkt am Wasser …

GABI Ja, stimmt! Schweden hat mir auch wahnsinnig gut gefallen. Die Ostsee ist viel sauberer an den skandinavischen Küsten als hier bei uns. Ich wäre so gern dort segeln gegangen. Aber, na ja, das Segelboot, das wir gemietet hatten, war halt zu klein für uns alle.

MIRIAM Ach, Gabi, es war doch nicht so schlimm. Der Lars und du, ihr seid dann doch zu der kleinen Insel hingeschwommen. Das war doch gar nicht so weit. Dafür brauchte man nun wirklich extra kein Boot mieten, um dahin zu kommen.

GABI Ja, es war zwar nicht weit, aber das Wasser war doch ziemlich kalt! Und außerdem gehe ich nun mal gern segeln. Du hast echt Glück gehabt, dass du noch einen Platz im Boot bekommen hast! Aber, na ja, ist ja jetzt auch egal. Warum bist du eigentlich keinmal mit uns schwimmen gegangen?

MIRIAM Tja, ich war halt lieber auf dem Tennisplatz. Das macht mir mehr Spaß als schwimmen zu gehen. Und gewandert bin ich auch einmal, weißt du, zusammen mit den Engländern, die auch in unserer Pension waren.

GABI Ach, das wusste ich gar nicht. Da wär ich aber auch gern mitgekommen. Warum hast du denn nichts gesagt?

MIRIAM Ganz einfach! Du warst ja nie da, sondern hast nur den ganzen Tag am Strand gelegen. Ach, schau mal! Jetzt sind wir an der Reihe! Komm, gib mir auch dein schwedisches Geld, damit wir gleich alles zusammen umtauschen können.

Answers to Activity 6
Sie haben eine Reise nach Schweden unternommen; Miriam hat am meisten Spaß gehabt; Sie tauschen ihr schwedisches Geld um.

10 p. 335

MUTTER Also, Markus und Annette, Vati und ich haben uns gestern Abend mal die Urlaubsbilder vom letzten Jahr angesehen. Vati meint, dass es schön wäre, wieder in die Schweiz zu fahren …

MARKUS Oh nein, nicht schon wieder!

ANNETTE Ja, ich finde, der Markus hat Recht. Nur weil ihr gern in den Bergen wandern geht, heißt das noch lange nicht, dass wir das auch gern machen! Können wir nicht mal was anderes machen?

VATER Also, dann sagt doch mal, wohin ihr gern fahren möchtet!

ANNETTE Nach Griechenland!

VATER Also, ich weiß nicht. Wir fahren doch jedes Jahr nach Interlaken in die Schweiz, und jedes Mal verbringen wir eine herrliche Zeit in den Bergen und am See. Dieses Jahr wird es auch nicht anders sein.

MARKUS Ja eben! Jedes Jahr das Gleiche! Ich bin echt dafür, dass wir mal woanders hinfahren. In Griechenland gibt es tolle Strände, klares blaues Wasser … ideal zum Surfen. Das würd ich gern mal machen! Wir könnten doch auf einer Insel Urlaub machen, auf Kreta zum Beispiel!

ANNETTE Ja, oder auf Rhodos! Eine Insel mit wahnsinnig viel Kultur und wunderschönen alten Tempelruinen. Ach, das wäre schön, wenn ich die mal besichtigen könnte. In unserem Geschichtsbuch sind sie alle abgebildet! Und Vati, außerdem gibt es in Griechenland auch Berge, wenn du unbedingt wandern willst!

VATER Hmm! Also, ich befürchte, dass mir in Griechenland das Essen bestimmt nicht schmecken wird. Außerdem spricht keiner von uns Griechisch! Was meinst du denn dazu, Helga?

MUTTER Ja also, Günther, ich finde, die Kinder haben Recht! Wir fahren immer nur in die Schweiz! Es wird langsam mal Zeit, dass wir uns was anderes anschauen!

VATER Und was schlägst du vor?

MUTTER Wie wäre es mit … Afrika? Eine richtig abenteuerliche Safari in Kenia, das ist mein Traum!

ANNETTE Ui, Mutti, was für eine super Idee!

VATER Ja, wenn das so ist, dann gehe ich morgen mal ins Reisebüro und hole uns die neuesten Sommerkataloge für Kenia und Griechenland.

MARKUS Prima, Vati! Ich komm mit!

Answers to Activity 10
Vater: Interlaken, Schweiz; wandert gern in den Bergen und am See
Markus: Kreta, Griechenland; will an den Strand gehen und im Meer surfen
Annette: Rhodos, Griechenland; interessiert sich für Kultur und die Tempelruinen
Mutter: Kenia, Afrika; möchte auf eine abenteuerliche Safari

The following scripts are for the listening activities found in the *Pupil's Edition.* For Student Response Forms, see *Listening Activities,* pages 91–93. To provide students with additional listening practice, see *Listening Activities,* pages 95–98.

For resource information, see the **One-Stop Planner CD-ROM**, Disc 3.

Zweite Stufe

19 p. 339

KARSTEN	Find ich echt super von dir, Jutta, dass du mich heute Abend einlädst! Guck dir nur mal diese Speisekarte an! Die haben hier echt alles Mögliche! Du, das meiste kenn ich überhaupt nicht.
JUTTA	Ja, genau deswegen hab ich dieses Restaurant ja ausgesucht. Ich möchte gern mal was völlig Neues ausprobieren. Schau mal, Karsten, die Gerichte auf der Karte sind alle aus Ländern am Mittelmeer. Griechenland, Türkei, Italien, Spanien und sogar Portugal!
KARSTEN	Aha! Jetzt weiß ich auch, warum das Restaurant „Mediterraneo" heißt!
KELLNER	Guten Abend! Haben Sie schon etwas ausgewählt?
KARSTEN	Wir sind gerade dabei! Ich möchte gerne wissen, was Moussaka ist.
KELLNER	Moussaka ist unser beliebtestes griechisches Gericht. Es besteht aus Kartoffeln und Auberginen und wird im Ofen mit Käse überbacken. Sehr zu empfehlen!
JUTTA	Und was ist Calzone?
KELLNER	Calzone ist eine zusammengeklappte Pizza mit verschiedenen Füllungen, ganz nach Ihrem Geschmack!
JUTTA	Ach so! So ähnlich wie 'ne Pizza ... also, nee, was Italienisches esse ich eigentlich öfters, also Pizza und Spaghetti und so ... Heute möchte ich lieber etwas anderes ausprobieren. Was ist denn alles in der Paella drin?
KELLNER	Paella ist ein köstliches spanisches Reisgericht aus der Pfanne. Es wird mit Hähnchen, Krabben, Muscheln und Gemüse zubereitet.
JUTTA	Mhm! Das hört sich lecker an. Ich mag Reis sehr gern. Also, ich nehme dann die Paella. Und du, Karsten, was nimmst du?
KARSTEN	Ich probiere lieber mal die Moussaka. Was Griechisches hab ich noch nie gegessen!
KELLNER	Und was hätten Sie gern zu trinken?
JUTTA	Ein Mineralwasser für mich, bitte.
KARSTEN	Und ich nehme eine Limo.
KELLNER	Kommt sofort!

Answers to Activity 19
Jutta: Paella, spanisches Gericht; Sie mag Reis.
Karsten: Moussaka, griechisches Gericht; Er hat noch nie was Griechisches gegessen.

Dritte Stufe

24 p. 342

ROLAND	Also, heut Abend ziehe ich ein echt klassisches Outfit an, das heißt: weiße Shorts, weißes T-Shirt, weiße Socken und ... ach so, meine Schuhe, die sind natürlich auch weiß. Halt! Ich zieh auch noch ein neues Stirnband an. Es ist total bunt und sieht völlig flippig aus! Das gibt einen tollen Kontrast zum traditionellen Weiß! Das Stirnband hat mir die Silke geschenkt, um mir Glück zu wünschen für das Doppel heute Abend mit Klaus, Andreas und Ralf.
KATJA	Ich ziehe eine saloppe Hose, bequeme Schuhe und eine kurzärmelige Baumwollbluse an. Ja, ach so, einen Pulli nehm ich halt auch noch mit, denn es wird manchmal ganz schön kalt im Flugzeug. Den Rest meiner Klamotten hab ich schon in den Koffer gepackt. Alles nur leichte Sommersachen, genau richtig für den Strand.
AXEL	Meine Schwester will, dass ich einen schwarzen Smoking anziehe, mit weißem Hemd und auch noch 'ne passende Weste dazu! Also, echt schick und elegant. Ist eigentlich überhaupt nicht mein Stil, aber es ist nun mal ein ganz besonderer Tag für meine Schwester und ihren zukünftigen Mann! Da trag ich dann halt ausnahmsweise mal diese edlen Klamotten!
BÄRBEL	Zuerst wollte ich ja mein neues gepunktetes Kleid anziehen, aber dann hat mir der Martin erzählt, dass die ganze Sache draußen im Garten stattfindet! Also, das Barbecue und das Buffet, alles draußen auf der Terrasse! Ja, da ziehe ich lieber meine Jeans an und meine gestreifte Bluse, die mit den kurzen Ärmeln. Ach so, meine Wildlederjacke nehm ich auch noch mit, falls es dann später kalt wird, wenn der Martin dann um Mitternacht seine Geschenke aufmacht.

Answers to Activity 24
Roland: zum Tennis; Katja: in die Ferien;
Axel: zur Hochzeit seiner Schwester; Bärbel: zur Geburtstagsfete von Martin

Kapitel 12: Die Reinickendorfer Clique *Review Chapter*

Suggested Lesson Plans 50-Minute Schedule

Day 1

CHAPTER OPENER 10 min.
- Building Context, ATE, p. 325M
- Challenge, ATE, p. 325M

LOS GEHT'S! 20 min.
- Preteaching Vocabulary, ATE, p. 325N
- Have students read **Los geht's!**, pp. 328–329
- Teaching Suggestions, Video Guide, p. 76
- Show **Los geht's!** Video

LANDESKUNDE 15 min.
- Pre-viewing Suggestion, Video Guide, p. 76
- Teaching Suggestions, ATE, p. 325O
- Show **Landeskunde** Video

Wrap-Up 5 min.
- Students respond to questions about what kinds of ethnic foods they like

Homework Options
Pupil's Edition, p. 330, Comprehension Acts. 1–4; p. 331, Acts. A and B
Übungsheft, p. 133, Act. 1; p. 134, Acts. 1–2

Day 2

ERSTE STUFE
Quick Review 10 min.
- Check homework, p. 330, Comprehension Acts. 1–4

Reading Selection, p. 332 20 min.
- Read **Die Deutschen–die Europameister im Reisen**, p. 332

Wortschatz/Ein wenig Grammatik, p. 333 15 min.
- Presenting **Wortschatz/Ein wenig Grammatik**, ATE, p. 325P
- Teaching Transparency 12-A
- Do Activity 5, p. 333
- Play Audio CD for Activity 6, p. 333

Wrap-Up 5 min.
- Students respond to questions about where they were and what they did on their last vacation

Homework Options
Grammatikheft, pp. 100–101, Acts. 1–2
Übungsheft, p. 135, Act. 1

Day 3

ERSTE STUFE
Quick Review 10 min.
- Check homework, Übungsheft, p. 135, Act. 1

So sagt man das!, p. 334 10 min.
- Presenting **So sagt man das!**, ATE, p. 325P
- Teaching Transparency 12-1
- Do Activities 7 and 8, p. 334

Ein wenig Grammatik, p. 335 10 min.
- Presenting **Ein wenig Grammatik**, ATE, p. 325P
- Do Activity 9, p. 335
- Play Audio CD for Activity 10, p. 335

So sagt man das!/Ein wenig Grammatik, p. 335 15 min.
- Presenting **So sagt man das!**, ATE, p. 325P
- Presenting **Ein wenig Grammatik**, ATE, p. 325Q
- Do Activities 11 and 12, pp. 335–336

Wrap-Up 5 min.
- Students respond to questions about their next vacation

Homework Options
Grammatikheft, p. 102, Act. 3
Übungsheft, pp. 135–137, Acts. 2–6

Day 4

ERSTE STUFE
Quick Review 15 min.
- Check homework, Übungsheft, pp. 135–137, Acts. 2–6

Ein wenig Grammatik, p. 336 15 min.
- Presenting **Ein wenig Grammatik**, ATE, p. 325Q
- Do Activities 13, 14, and 15, p. 336

Quiz Review 20 min.
- Do Additional Listening Activities 12-1 and 12-2, p. 95
- Do Communicative Activity 12-1, pp. 67–68
- Do **Erste Stufe** Activities, Interactive CD-ROM

Homework Options
Mehr Grammatikübungen, Erste Stufe
Grammatikheft, p. 103, Act. 4

Day 5

ERSTE STUFE
Quick Review 10 min.
- Check homework, **Mehr Grammatikübungen, Erste Stufe**

Quiz 20 min.
- Quiz 12-1A or 12-1B

ZWEITE STUFE
Reading Selection, p. 337 15 min.
- Teaching Suggestions, ATE, p. 325R
- Do Activity 16, p. 338

Wrap-Up 5 min.
- Students respond to questions about their favorite ethnic food recipes

Homework Options
Activities for Communication, p. 119, Realia 12-2, students write two questions about each ad to ask classmates (see p. 121)

Day 6

ZWEITE STUFE
Quick Review 10 min.
- Bell Work, ATE, p. 325R
- Check homework, Realia 12-2

Wortschatz, p. 338 15 min.
- Presenting **Wortschatz**, ATE, p. 325R
- Teaching Transparency 12-B
- Do Circumlocution Activity, ATE, p. 325X
- Do Activities 17 and 18, p. 338

So sagt man das!, p. 339 10 min.
- Presenting **So sagt man das!**, ATE, p. 325R
- Play Audio CD for Activity 19, p. 339

Ein wenig Landeskunde, p. 339 10 min.
- Present **Ein wenig Landeskunde**, p. 339
- Do Activity 20, p. 339

Wrap-Up 5 min.
- Students respond to questions about what they have heard about food in various ethnic restaurants

Homework Options
Grammatikheft, p. 104, Act. 5
Übungsheft, pp. 138–140, Acts. 1–6

One-Stop Planner CD-ROM

For alternative lesson plans by chapter section, to create your own customized plans, or to preview all resources available for this chapter, use the **One-Stop Planner CD-ROM**, Disc 3.

 For additional homework suggestions, see activities accompanied by this symbol throughout the chapter.

Day 7

ZWEITE STUFE

Quick Review 15 min.
- Check homework, Übungsheft, pp. 138–140, Acts. 1–6

So sagt man das!/Ein wenig Grammatik, p. 340 15 min.
- Presenting **So sagt man das!/Ein wenig Grammatik**, ATE, p. 325S
- Do Activities 21 and 22, p. 340
- Do Activity 6, p. 105, Grammatikheft

Quiz Review 20 min.
- Do Additional Listening Activities 12-3 and 12-4, pp. 96–97
- Do Communicative Activity 12-2, pp. 69–70
- Do **Zweite Stufe** Activities, Interactive CD-ROM

Homework Options
Mehr Grammatikübungen, Zweite Stufe

Day 8

ZWEITE STUFE

Quick Review 10 min.
- Check homework, **Mehr Grammatikübungen, Zweite Stufe**

Quiz 20 min.
- Quiz 12-2A or 12-2B

DRITTE STUFE

Reading Selection/Ein wenig Grammatik, p. 341 15 min.
- Teaching Suggestion, ATE, p. 325T
- Presenting **Ein wenig Grammatik**, ATE, p. 325T
- Do Activity 23, p. 341

Wrap-Up 5 min.
- Students respond to questions about what their clothing tells other people about them

Homework Options
Übungsheft, p. 141, Act. 1

Day 9

DRITTE STUFE

Quick Review 10 min.
- Return and review Quiz 12-2
- Check homework, Übungsheft, p. 141, Act. 1

Wortschatz, p. 342 15 min.
- Presenting **Wortschatz**, ATE, p. 325U
- Teaching Transparencies 12-2, 12-C
- Play Audio CD for Activity 24, p. 342
- Do Activity 25, p. 342
- Do Activity 26, p. 343

So sagt man das!/Ein wenig Grammatik, p. 343 10 min.
- Presenting **So sagt man das!/Ein wenig Grammatik**, ATE, p. 325U
- Do Activity 27, p. 343

So sagt man das!, p. 343 10 min.
- Presenting **So sagt man das!**, ATE, p. 325U
- Do Activity 28, p. 344

Wrap-Up 5 min.
- Students respond to questions about two articles of clothing they prefer

Homework Options
Grammatikheft, pp. 106–107, Acts. 7–9
Übungsheft, pp. 141–142, Acts. 2–4

Day 10

DRITTE STUFE

Quick Review 10 min.
- Check homework, Übungsheft, pp. 141–142, Acts. 2–4

Ein wenig Grammatik, p. 344 10 min.
- Presenting **Ein wenig Grammatik**, ATE, p. 325V
- Do Activity 29, p. 344

So sagt man das!, p. 344 15 min.
- Presenting **So sagt man das!**, ATE, p. 325V
- Do Activity 30, p. 344
- Do Activities 31 and 32, p. 345

Quiz Review 15 min.
- Do **Mehr Grammatikübungen, Dritte Stufe**
- Do Additional Listening Activities 12-5 and 12-6, pp. 97–98

Homework Options
Grammatikheft, p. 108, Act. 10
Übungsheft, p. 143, Acts. 5–6
Interaktive Spiele, see ATE, p. 325F

Day 11

DRITTE STUFE

Quick Review 10 min.
- Check homework, Übungsheft, p. 143, Acts. 5–6

Quiz 20 min.
- Quiz 12-3A or 12-3B

ZUM LESEN 20 min.
- Present **Lesestrategie**, p. 346
- Do Activities 1–9, pp. 346–347

Homework Options
Übungsheft, p. 144, Acts. 1–3
Internet Aktivitäten, see ATE, p. 325F

Day 12

REVIEW

Quick Review 10 min.
- Return and review Quiz 12-3
- Check homework, Übungsheft, p. 144, Acts. 1–3

Kann ich's wirklich?, p. 352 20 min.
- Do Activities 1–12, p. 352

Chapter Review 20 min.
- Review chapter functions, vocabulary, and grammar; choose from **Mehr Grammatikübungen**, Grammar Tutor for Students of German, Activities for Communication, Listening Activities, Interactive CD-ROM Tutor, or **Interaktive Spiele**

Homework Options
Study for Chapter Test

Assessment

Test, Chapter 12 45 min.
- Administer Chapter 12 Test. Select from Testing Program, Alternative Assessment Guide, or Test Generator.

KAPITEL 12   SUGGESTED LESSON PLANS • 50-MINUTE SCHEDULE   **325J**

Kapitel 12: Die Reinickendorfer Clique *Review Chapter*
Suggested Lesson Plans 90-Minute Schedule

Block 1

CHAPTER OPENER 10 min.
- Building Context, ATE, p. 325M
- Challenge, ATE, p. 325M

LOS GEHT'S! 20 min.
- Preteaching Vocabulary, ATE, p. 325N
- Have students read **Los geht's!**, pp. 328–329
- Teaching Suggestions, Video Guide, p. 76
- Show **Los geht's!** Video

LANDESKUNDE 15 min.
- Pre-viewing Suggestion, Video Guide, p. 76
- Teaching Suggestions, ATE, p. 325O
- Show **Landeskunde** Video

ERSTE STUFE
Reading Selection p. 332 20 min.
- Read **Die Deutschen–die Europameister im Reisen**, p. 332

Wortschatz/Ein wenig Grammatik, p. 333 20 min.
- Presenting **Wortschatz/Ein wenig Grammatik**, ATE, p. 325P
- Teaching Transparency 12-A
- Do Activity 5, p. 333
- Play Audio CD for Activity 6, p. 333

Wrap-Up 5 min.
- Students respond to questions about where they were and what they did on their last vacation

Homework Options
Pupil's Edition, p. 330, Comprehension Acts. 1–4; p. 331, Acts. A and B
Grammatikheft, pp. 100–101, Acts. 1–2
Übungsheft, p. 133, Act. 1; p. 134, Acts. 1–2; p. 135, Act. 1

Block 2

ERSTE STUFE
Quick Review 15 min.
- Check homework, Übungsheft, p. 133, Act. 1; p. 134, Acts. 1–2; p. 135, Act. 1

So sagt man das!, p. 334 10 min.
- Presenting **So sagt man das!**, ATE, p. 325P
- Teaching Transparency 12-1
- Do Activities 7 and 8, p. 334

Ein wenig Grammatik, p. 335 10 min.
- Presenting **Ein wenig Grammatik**, ATE, p. 325P
- Do Activity 9, p. 335
- Play Audio CD for Activity 10, p. 335

So sagt man das!/Ein wenig Grammatik, p. 335 20 min.
- Presenting **So sagt man das!**, ATE, p. 325P
- Presenting **Ein wenig Grammatik**, ATE, p. 325Q
- Do Activity 11, p. 335
- Do Activity 12, p. 336
- Do Activity 3, p. 102, Grammatikheft

Ein wenig Grammatik, p. 336 15 min.
- Presenting **Ein wenig Grammatik**, ATE, p. 325Q
- Do Activities 13, 14, and 15, p. 336

Quiz Review 20 min.
- Do Additional Listening Activities 12-1 and 12-2, p. 95
- Do Communicative Activity 12-1, pp. 67–68
- Do **Mehr Grammatikübungen, Erste Stufe**

Homework Options
Grammatikheft, p. 103, Act. 4
Übungsheft, pp. 135–137, Acts. 2–6

Block 3

ERSTE STUFE
Quick Review 10 min.
- Check homework, Übungsheft, pp. 135–137, Acts. 2–6

Quiz 20 min.
- Quiz 12-1A or 12-1B

ZWEITE STUFE
Reading Selection, p. 337 15 min.
- Teaching Suggestions, ATE, p. 325R
- Do Activity 16, p. 338

Wortschatz, p. 338 20 min.
- Presenting **Wortschatz**, ATE, p. 325R
- Teaching Transparency 12-B
- Do Circumlocution Activity, ATE, p. 325X
- Do Activities 17 and 18, p. 338

So sagt man das!, p. 339 10 min.
- Presenting **So sagt man das!**, ATE, p. 325R
- Play Audio CD for Activity 19, p. 339

Ein wenig Landeskunde, p. 339 10 min.
- Present **Ein wenig Landeskunde**, p. 339
- Do Activity 20, p. 339

Wrap-Up 5 min.
- Students respond to questions about what they have heard about food in various ethnic restaurants

Homework Options
Grammatikheft, p. 104, Act. 5
Übungsheft, pp. 138–140, Acts. 1–6

One-Stop Planner CD-ROM

For alternative lesson plans by chapter section, to create your own customized plans, or to preview all resources available for this chapter, use the **One-Stop Planner CD-ROM**, Disc 3.

 For additional homework suggestions, see activities accompanied by this symbol throughout the chapter.

Block 4

ZWEITE STUFE

Quick Review 15 min.
- Check homework, Übungsheft, pp. 138–140, Acts. 1–6

So sagt man das!/Ein wenig Grammatik, p. 340 20 min.
- Presenting **So sagt man das!/Ein wenig Grammatik,** ATE, p. 325S
- Do Activities 21 and 22, p. 340
- Do Activity 6, p. 105, Grammatikheft

Quiz Review 15 min.
- Do Additional Listening Activities 12-3 and 12-4, pp. 96–97
- Do **Mehr Grammatikübungen, Zweite Stufe**

Quiz 20 min.
- Quiz 12-2A or 12-2B

DRITTE STUFE

Reading Selection/Ein wenig Grammatik, p. 341 15 min.
- Teaching Suggestion, ATE, p. 325T
- Presenting **Ein wenig Grammatik,** ATE, p. 325T
- Do Activity 23, p. 341

Wrap-Up 5 min.
- Students respond to questions about what their clothing tells other people about them

Homework Options
Übungsheft, p. 141, Act. 1
Internet Aktivitäten, see ATE, p. 325F

Block 5

DRITTE STUFE

Quick Review 10 min.
- Return and review Quiz 12-2
- Check homework, Übungsheft, p. 141, Act. 1

Wortschatz, p. 342 15 min.
- Presenting **Wortschatz,** ATE, p. 325U
- Teaching Transparencies 12-2, 12-C
- Play Audio CD for Activity 24, p. 342
- Do Activity 25, p. 342
- Do Activity 26, p. 343

So sagt man das!/Ein wenig Grammatik, p. 343 10 min.
- Presenting **So sagt man das!/Ein wenig Grammatik,** ATE, p. 325U
- Do Activity 27, p. 343

So sagt man das!, p. 343 10 min.
- Presenting **So sagt man das!,** ATE, p. 325U
- Do Activity 28, p. 344

Ein wenig Grammatik, p. 344 10 min.
- Presenting **Ein wenig Grammatik,** ATE, p. 325V
- Do Activity 29, p. 344

So sagt man das!, p. 344 20 min.
- Presenting **So sagt man das!,** ATE, p. 325V
- Do Activity 30, p. 344
- Do Activities 31 and 32, p. 345

Quiz Review 15 min.
- Do **Mehr Grammatikübungen, Dritte Stufe**
- Do Additional Listening Activities 12-5 and 12-6, pp. 97–98

Homework Options
Grammatikheft, pp. 106–108, Acts. 7–10
Übungsheft, pp. 141–143, Acts. 2–6

Block 6

DRITTE STUFE

Quick Review 15 min.
- Check homework, Grammatikheft, pp. 106–108, Acts. 7–10

Quiz 20 min.
- Quiz 12-3A or 12-3B

ZUM LESEN 30 min.
- Present **Lesestrategie,** p. 346
- Do Activities 1–9, pp. 346–347
- Do Activities 1–3, p. 144, Übungsheft

Kann ich's wirklich?, p. 352 20 min.
- Do Activities 1–12, p. 352

Wrap-Up 5 min.
- Students respond to questions about their interest in clothing and their clothing preferences

Homework Options
Interaktive Spiele, see ATE, p. 325F
Study for Chapter Test

Block 7

REVIEW

Quick Review 10 min.
- Return and review Quiz 12-3

Chapter Review 35 min.
- Review chapter functions, vocabulary, and grammar; choose from **Mehr Grammatikübungen,** Grammar Tutor for Students of German, Activities for Communication, Listening Activities, Interactive CD-ROM Tutor, or **Interaktive Spiele**
- Review test format and provide sample test items for students

Test, Chapter 12 45 min.
- Administer Chapter 12 Test. Select from Testing Program, Alternative Assessment Guide or Test Generator.

Kapitel 12: Die Reinickendorfer Clique *Review Chapter*
Teaching Suggestions, pages 326–353

PAGES 326–327

CHAPTER OPENER

Pacing Tips
Chapter 12 is a review chapter. The **Erste Stufe** begins with a reading about vacations and includes the functions of 'reporting past events' and 'asking for, making, and responding to suggestions.' The **Zweite Stufe** centers around international cuisine. The **Dritte Stufe** covers the functions of 'asking for and giving advice,' 'expressing preference,' and 'expressing interest, disinterest, and indifference.' Because this is a review chapter, you should spend more time on whichever **Stufe** your class needs to review the most in preparation for the Final Exam. For Lesson Plans and timing suggestions, see pages 325I–325L.

Meeting the Standards
Communication
- Reporting past events, p. 245
- Asking for, making, and responding to suggestions, p. 335
- Ordering food, expressing hearsay and regret, p. 339
- Persuading and dissuading, p. 340
- Asking for and giving advice, p. 343
- Expressing preference, p. 343
- Expressing interest, disinterest, and indifference, p. 344

Cultures
- **Landeskunde**, p. 331
- **Ein wenig Landeskunde**, p. 339
- Background Information, p. 325P
- Background Information, p. 325W

Connections
- Physical Education Connection, p. 325P
- Geography Connection, p. 325P
- Language Note, p. 325U
- Literature Connection, p. 325W
- History Connection, p. 325W

Comparisons
- Language Note, p. 325S
- Language-to-Language, p. 325U
- Thinking Critically, p. 325S

Communities
- Career Path, p. 325X

For resource information, see the **One-Stop Planner CD-ROM**, Disc 3.

Building Context
Prior to the activity, set up your classroom to look like a travel agency. Write **REISEBÜRO WALTER** (or use your own last name) on the board, along with instructions such as **Nehmen Sie sich bitte eine Nummer! Man wird Ihnen schnellstens behilflich sein.** Set up the chairs along the walls. As students enter the classroom, point to the board to suggest that they are not sitting in a classroom, but are waiting to speak to a travel agent. You play the role of the travel agent. Call on the students by number and ask each a few questions to help them plan their upcoming summer vacation.

Communication for All Students

Challenge
After students have shared their plans for summer vacation with the class, have them get into pairs. Using their notes from the previous activity, students should try to persuade their partners to join them on their trips.

Chapter Sequence
Los geht's!	p. 328
Landeskunde	p. 331
Erste Stufe	p. 332
Zweite Stufe	p. 337
Dritte Stufe	p. 341
Zum Lesen	p. 346
Mehr Grammatikübungen	p. 348
Kann ich's wirklich?	p. 352
Wortschatz	p. 353

LOS GEHT'S!

Teaching Resources
pp. 328–330

PRINT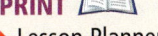
- Lesson Planner, p. 57
- Video Guide, pp. 75–76, 78
- Übungsheft, p. 133

MEDIA
- One-Stop Planner
- Video Program
  Los geht's!
  Videocassette 4, 44:49:38
  Videocassette 5 (captioned version), 1:13:33–1:15:18
  Fortsetzung
  Videocassette 4, 49;42–54:15
  Videocassette 5 (captioned version), 1:18:22–1:22:52
- DVD Tutor, Disc 2
- Audio Compact Discs, CD12, Trs. 1–2
- Los geht's! Transparencies

PAGES 328–329

 Los geht's! Transparencies

Preteaching Vocabulary

Activating Prior Knowledge
Point out that the setting for **Los geht's!** is a party at Andreas and Astrid's house. As a review, have students list topics of conversation that occur in the photo spread. Then ask students to look for the sentences that are in the past or future tense. Finally, ask students to identify the one sentence that is subjunctive (**9 So eine würde ich auch gern mal haben.**).

 **Fortsetzung**
You may choose to continue with the Fortsetzung of *Echt toll, Ismar!* now or wait until later in the chapter. For a synopsis of the **Los geht's!** and **Fortsetzung** episodes, see p. 325E.

Advance Organizer
As an advance organizer for the storyline of the **Los geht's!**, ask students what they usually talk about when they get together with their friends for a party.

Teaching Suggestion
After students have read and watched or listened to *Echt toll, Ismar!*, ask them if they can determine from the context what the expression **Schwirr ab!** in Frame 3 could mean. *(Get lost! Take a hike!)*

Background Information
In Frame 5 Andreas is telling his friends that he will **den Vierer machen**. Tell students that he is referring to the moped license he is planning to get.

PAGE 330

Using the Captioned Video/DVD
 As an alternative to reading the conversations in the book, you might want to show the captioned version of *Echt toll, Ismar!* available on Videocassette 5.
Note: The *DVD Tutor* contains captions for all sections of the *Video Program*.

Comprehension Check

Group Work
1 Ask students to work in groups of three as they answer Questions 1–10. Call on several groups to have them read their answers to the rest of the class.

Auditory Learners
2 Instead of rereading **Los geht's!**, you might want to replay the video segment and have students listen for the four expressions. Students can call out the number (1–4) when they hear the corresponding expression.

Challenge
3 Have students come up with an alternative coordinating or subordinating clause to complete each sentence.

Teaching Suggestion
Play the video episode without sound. Have students take turns playing the roles of the five German teenagers ad-libbing the storyline as best they can.

STANDARDS: 1.1   KAPITEL 12   LOS GEHT'S!   **325N**

> **PAGE 331**

LANDESKUNDE

Teaching Resources
p. 331

PRINT
- Video Guide, pp. 75–76, 78–79
- Übungsheft, p. 134

MEDIA
- One-Stop Planner
- Video Program
  Videocassette 4, 54:52–1:00:30
- DVD Tutor, Disc 2
- Audio Compact Discs, CD12, Trs. 3–7
- Interactive CD-ROM Tutor, Disc 3

Thinking Critically
Drawing Inferences Ask students to name some of their favorite and least-favorite ethnic foods. Which of those would they most likely recommend for the rest of the class to try?

Teaching Suggestion
You might want to introduce this additional vocabulary to help students with the four interviews:
dazugehören *to belong to*
schmackhaft *tasty*
variationsreich *diverse*
drin = darin *in it*
ab und zu *now and then*

Building on Previous Skills
Ask students if they can recall some of the **beliebte Gerichte** from Stuttgart, Hamburg, and Berlin in the Location Openers of this book.

Communication for All Students

Challenge
Ask students to explain the difference between the following groups of words:
die Gaststätte/die Imbissstube/das Restaurant/der Biergarten/das Café

Teacher Note
Mention to your students that the **Landeskunde** will also be included in Quiz 12-1B given at the end of the **Erste Stufe.**

ERSTE STUFE

Teaching Resources
pp. 332–336

PRINT
- Lesson Planner, p. 58
- TPR Storytelling Book, pp. 88–89
- Listening Activities, pp. 91, 95
- Activities for Communication, pp. 67–68, 118, 121, 145–146
- Grammatikheft, pp. 100–103
- Grammar Tutor for Students of German, Chapter 12
- Übungsheft, pp. 135–137
- Testing Program, pp. 301–304
- Alternative Assessment Guide, p. 43
- Student Make-Up Assignments, Chapter 12

MEDIA
- One-Stop Planner
- Audio Compact Discs, CD12, Trs. 8–9, 12, 20–21
- Teaching Transparencies
  Situation 12-1
  Vocabulary 12-A
  Mehr Grammatikübungen Answers
  Grammatikheft Answers
- Interactive CD-ROM Tutor, Disc 3
- DVD Tutor, Disc 2

> **PAGE 332**

 Bell Work
Give a slip of paper to each student as he or she enters the classroom. Each slip of paper should have the name of a domestic or foreign travel destination on it. Students should use the destination on their paper to suggest to their neighbor where he or she should go for his or her next vacation.

Teaching Suggestion
Remind students to use the various reading skills they have been taught throughout the school year as they work through this reading selection.

Connections and Comparisons

Physical Education Connection
Ask students to name the ten events that make up a decathlon. (100-meter run, 400-meter run, 1500-meter run, 110-meter high hurdles, javelin throw, discus throw, shot put, pole vault, high jump, long jump)

Cultures and Communities

Background Information
Ulrike Meifarth was one of Germany's best high-jumpers. She won the gold medal at the age of 16 in the 1972 Olympic Games in Munich and at the age of 28 in the 1984 Olympic Games in Los Angeles. Guido Kratschmer and Jürgen Hingsen were world-class decathlon athletes in the 1980s.

PAGE 333

PRESENTING: Wortschatz
If possible, bring pictures that show the expressions featured in this **Wortschatz**. Introduce the vocabulary by holding up the pictures as you pronounce the words.

Group Work
5 Divide your class into five groups and assign each group two questions. Group members should share the responsibility of reading the text and helping each other as needed. One member of each group assumes responsibility for writing down the responses to the questions the group has been assigned. Call on groups to share their responses with the rest of the class.

PRESENTING: Ein wenig Grammatik
The past tense Write on slips of paper a number of verbs whose past participle forms students have learned. (You may want to consult the Grammar Summary in order to do this.) Give students one slip each and go down the rows, asking them to formulate sentences in the past using the verbs they drew.

Communication for All Students

A Slower Pace
6 After students have listened to the activity once, provide them with a copy of the listening script. Have them underline all verb forms and expressions that indicate the past tense.

PAGE 334

PRESENTING: So sagt man das!
Ask students to read the excerpt in **So sagt man das!** and then make a list of all the verb phrases. There is one verb that uses **sein** as an auxiliary. Did students find it? (**sind gewandert**)

Connections and Comparisons

Geography Connection
7 Before students begin with the activity, have them locate the Canary Islands on a map.

Communication for All Students

Challenge
8 Ask students to assume the role of a reporter for travel brochures and magazines. How would a favorable review of *La Santa* sound? Have students write a review from a travel agent's point of view.

PAGE 335

PRESENTING: Ein wenig Grammatik
Two-way prepositions Divide students into groups of three or four, and ask each group to write a brief travel narrative using the nine two-way prepositions (see the Grammar Summary). You may want to specify regions or cities upon which the groups should base their reports. When students have finished, ask them to read their work aloud to the class.

Teaching Suggestion
9 Ask students to retell the events in a postcard to their best friend back home. They should emphasize all the wonderful things they did in *La Santa*.

PRESENTING: So sagt man das!
Review these expressions with students. Then have students look back at the plans of *La Santa* on p. 334. Pairs of students should take turns making and responding to a least five suggestions based on the activities and facilities that are available there.

STANDARDS: 1.3, 3.1

PRESENTING: Ein wenig Grammatik

Sollen- and würde-forms Divide the class into two teams, and ask one member at a time from each to go to the board. When the two students are ready, read an English sentence whose German equivalent utilizes a form of **sollen** or a **würde**-form. (You may want to base your sentences on those found in **So sagt man das!** on p. 335.) The team whose member first writes a correct translation on the board wins a point. Once all students have had at least one chance to play, tally up the points; the team with the most points wins the game.

Communication for All Students

Visual Learners

⑪ Before students begin working with their partners, you may want to review the sports that are featured in this activity. Enlarge the symbols to a size that can be seen by all students. Show each symbol to the class and ask for the name of the sport it represents. See the following Teacher Note.

Teacher Note

⑪ The sports and activities represented by the symbols are as follows:

1. Reiten
2. Volleyball
3. Handball
4. Fußball
5. Eishockey
6. Hockey
7. Basketball
8. Skilaufen
9. Langlauf
10. Diskuswerfen
11. Speerwerfen
12. Kugelstoßen
13. Fechten
14. Tennis
15. Golf
16. Wasserski
17. Segeln
18. Schach

PAGE 336

PRESENTING: Ein wenig Grammatik

Prepositions and case Write all the prepositions students have learned on the board (see the Grammar Summary). Tell students that, as a class, they are going to compose a short story using these prepositions. Specify a setting for the story or allow the students to decide on one. Then, beginning in one corner of the room, ask a student to generate a sentence using one or more of the prepositions. The next student in line should formulate a second sentence (also utilizing a preposition) that builds on the information supplied by the first student. Keep going until all students have contributed at least one sentence to the story. Write it down as it unfolds and make copies for the class.

Teaching Suggestion

⑭ To review adverbial expressions, ask students to use some of the following time adverbs in their reports:

| regelmäßig | fast nie | häufig |
| sehr oft | manchmal | meistens |

Speaking Assessment

⑮ You may choose to evaluate students' dialogues using the following rubric.

Speaking Rubric	Points			
	4	3	2	1
Content (Complete – Incomplete)				
Comprehension (Total – Little)				
Comprehensibility (Comprehensible – Incomprehensible)				
Accuracy (Accurate – Seldom accurate)				
Fluency (Fluent – Not fluent)				

18–20: A   16–17: B   14–15: C   12–13: D   Under 12: F

Teaching Suggestion

Ask students to complete the following statement. Wenn ihr im kommenden Sommer nach (Hamburg) fahrt, vergesst nicht, …

Assess

▸ Testing Program, pp. 301–304
  Quiz 12-1A, Quiz 12-1B
  Audio CD12, Tr. 12

▸ Student Make-Up Assignments
  Chapter 12, Alternative Quiz

▸ Alternative Assessment Guide, p. 43

ZWEITE STUFE

Teaching Resources
pp. 337–340

PRINT
- Lesson Planner, p. 59
- TPR Storytelling Book, pp. 90–91
- Listening Activities, pp. 92, 96–97
- Activities for Communication, pp. 69–70, 119–120, 121, 145–146
- Grammatikheft, pp. 104–105
- Grammar Tutor for Students of German, Chapter 12
- Übungsheft, pp. 138–140
- Testing Program, pp. 305–308
- Alternative Assessment Guide, p. 43
- Student Make-Up Assignments, Chapter 12

MEDIA
- One-Stop Planner
- Audio Compact Discs, CD12, Trs. 10, 13, 22–23
- Teaching Transparencies Vocabulary 12-B
  Mehr Grammatikübungen Answers
  Grammatikheft Answers
- Interactive CD-ROM Tutor, Disc 3
- DVD Tutor, Disc 2

PAGE 337

Bell Work
Ask students what foods come to mind that start with **F, M, K, S, E**. Use different letters as needed.

Communication for All Students

Tactile Learners
Some students might want to prepare Andreas's spaghetti recipe at home. Have them follow up by writing a brief review of his recipe using the vocabulary on p. 310 (Chapter 11) to describe how the dish tasted.

Teaching Suggestion
Once students have read the article on p. 337, help them discover that the text is written in the narrative past. Next, have students identify at least five verbs in the narrative past and ask them to give the corresponding present tense forms for each.

PAGE 338

PRESENTING: Wortschatz
Teach the vocabulary of **internationale Gerichte** by asking students questions such as **Was für ein Gericht ist denn Paella?** Students should respond with the appropriate category: **Paella ist ein spanisches Gericht.**

Teacher Note
These are active vocabulary words that do not appear in the vocabulary list at the end of the chapter because their English names are the same as their German names. However, you might want to give students their genders:
die Moussaka
die Cevapcici (*pl*)
die Paella
das/der Couscous (*also* Kuskus)
die Fettucine (*pl*)
die Crêpes Suzette (*pl*); die Crêpe (*sing.*) (*also* Krepp)
der Taco
das Steak
das Wiener Schnitzel

For Additional Practice
17 To review the dative preposition in adjective endings and the impersonal pronoun **man,** have students ask each other where one could find the ethnic dishes listed. Students should answer with statements such as **Man kann Tacos in ein*em* mexikanisch*en* Restaurant essen.**

Portfolio Assessment
18 You might want to suggest this activity as a written and oral portfolio item for your students. See *Alternative Assessment Guide*, p. 29.

PAGE 339

PRESENTING: So sagt man das!
To practice the expressions in **So sagt man das!**, ask pairs of students to role-play a restaurant scene using the vocabulary from the **Wortschatz** on p. 338. One partner should play the role of the waiter while the other partner plays the customer.

STANDARDS: 5.1

Communication for All Students

Visual Learners
19 Try to find pictures in food magazines to represent each of the dishes mentioned. Display the pictures in random order at the front of the class. Allow students to look at the pictures as they listen to the recording.

Thinking Critically
Drawing Inferences After students have read **Ein wenig Landeskunde,** ask them in what type of restaurant one would typically find a **Stammtisch.** (**Gaststätte, Lokal**) Once students understand the meaning of **Stammtisch,** ask them to infer the meaning of other related nouns such as **Stammkunde** (regular patron or customer) and **Stammlokal** (regularly frequented bar or restaurant). Encourage students to give a definition or description in German.

PAGE 340

PRESENTING: So sagt man das!
To practice the functions in **So sagt man das!,** give each student a slip of paper and have them write the name of a local restaurant, diner, cafeteria, or fast food chain on it. Put all the slips in a hat and have each student take one. Call on students to persuade someone else in the class to eat at the place written on their slip of paper. The other students should respond favorably or unfavorably, depending on their own opinions of the food offered at that particular establishment. Use the same slips of paper to have students dissuade each other from going there or from eating a certain type of food there.

PRESENTING: Ein wenig Grammatik
Command forms To reteach various command forms, ask students to look back at the plan of *La Santa* (or the Location Opener for Berlin) and come up with suggestions of what to do there, following the example:
Wenn du Berlin besuchst, iss im Café Kranzler am Kurfürstendamm!

21 Teaching Suggestion
If you feel students also need writing practice, you could have them convey their suggestions in the form of a letter to the cousin. This could be assigned as written homework.

Connections and Comparisons

Language Note
22 The German language has a saying related to hunger: **Ich habe einen Bärenhunger.** (*I'm as hungry as a bear.*) Ask students if they know any English sayings related to being hungry. (Example: *I am so hungry I could eat a horse.*)

 Game

Play the game *Tic Tac Toe*. In each of the nine squares of the *Tic Tac Toe* grid, write an adjective that refers to a nationality. Divide the class into teams. In order to get an X or O in a square, team members must come up with a sentence using the adjective in that square. The first team to get three in a row wins.

französisch	italienisch	mexikanisch
spanisch	chinesisch	deutsch
~~griechisch~~ X	bosnisch O	amerikanisch

X: Moussaka ist ein griechisches Gericht.
O: Cevapcici ist ein bosnisches Gericht.

Assess
▶ Testing Program, pp. 305–308
   Quiz 12-2A, Quiz 12-2B
   Audio CD12, Tr. 13

▶ Student Make-Up Assignments
   Chapter12, Alternative Quiz

▶ Alternative Assessment Guide, p. 43

DRITTE STUFE

Teaching Resources
pp. 341–345

PRINT
- Lesson Planner, p. 60
- TPR Storytelling Book, pp. 92–93
- Listening Activities, pp. 92, 97–98
- Activities for Communication, pp. 71–72, 145–146
- Grammatikheft, pp. 106–108
- Grammar Tutor for Students of German, Chapter 12
- Übungsheft, pp. 141–143
- Testing Program, pp. 309–312
- Alternative Assessment Guide, p. 43
- Student Make-Up Assignments, Chapter 12

MEDIA
- One-Stop Planner
- Audio Compact Discs, CD12, Trs. 11, 14, 24–25
- Teaching Transparencies
  Situation 12-2
  Vocabulary 12-C
  Mehr Grammatikübungen Answers
  Grammatikheft Answers
- Interactive CD-ROM Tutor, Disc 3
- DVD Tutor, Disc 2

PAGE 341

Bell Work
Ask students to list as many German-speaking athletes (or athletes from other countries) as they can think of. Also have them say in which sport the athlete participates. (Examples: Katharina Witt—**Eiskunstlauf**, Boris Becker—**Tennis**, Steffi Graf, Martina Hingis—**Tennis**, Guido Kratschmer—**Zehnkampf**, Franz Beckenbauer—**Fußball**, Georg Hackl—**Rodeln**, Katja Seizinger—**Skilaufen**, Hermann Maier—**Skilaufen**, Jan Ullrich—**Radsport**)

Teaching Suggestion
Instead of having students use their books to work on the reading selection *Ich bin kein Wunderkind!*, photocopy the text and white out a number of words to create a **Lückentext**. Distribute copies of the skeletal text to students, then write the missing words in random order on a transparency or on the board. Give students three to five minutes to read through the **Lückentext** and complete it by filling in the corresponding words from the transparency. Have students check their text against the article on p. 341.

Teacher Note
Swimmer Franziska van Almsick is from Berlin. In 1993, she was voted "Athlete of the Year" by the world association of sports journalists. She won four medals in the 1992 Olympic Games in Barcelona, and three medals in the 1996 Olympic Games in Atlanta. Students may be interested to look at her official Web site to get updates about her athletic career.

Communication for All Students

Challenge
23 Ask students to use their answers to the four questions as the basis for a summary of this article. The summary can be done orally or in writing.

Cultures and Communities

Language Note
The German language has a colloquial expression referring to having fun which is used in this article. The expression is **Jux machen** or **herumjuxen**.

PRESENTING: Ein wenig Grammatik

Adjective endings Have students reread *Ich bin kein Wunderkind!* and list all the adjectives they find, as well as the nouns they modify (with the exception of those in the genitive case). Students should then explain why the adjective endings are as they are. (Example: **mit zerissenem Saum: mit** takes dative case; **Saum** is masculine; masculine dative ending of unpreceded adjective is **-em**.)

PAGE 342

PRESENTING: Wortschatz

After introducing the new expressions, provide each student or pair with a picture of a person cut out of a magazine or catalog. Ask each student to study the outfit the person is wearing and then describe it to the rest of the class. In addition, each student should come up with one piece of advice for the person pictured on how the outfit or his or her appearance could be improved.

Connections and Comparisons

Language-to-Language
You might want to tell your students that words may sometimes appear to have been adopted from another language, though they are not actually used or have a completely different meaning in the language of origin. A good example might be **Fahrvergnügen**, which became a household word in the United States in the early nineties but is not used in the German-speaking world. Another example is **Smoking** *(tuxedo)*, adopted from the English by many languages, such as German, Spanish, and French, but not used in English to denote an article of clothing. Ask students if they can think of other such pseudo-loanwords. (Examples: **der Sender, die Sendung, das Handy, das Cordon bleu**)

Communication for All Students

A Slower Pace
24 As an advance organizer for the listening activity, ask students to go over the list of occasions and suggest one outfit for each.

PAGE 343

Communication for All Students

Tactile Learners
26 Once students are seated with a partner, provide each pair with several colored markers and two blank pieces of paper. As one student describes the clothing he or she likes to wear around the house, the other student should sketch it on the paper. After the student is done with the drawing, he or she should show it to his or her partner to see if it resembles the outfit described. Then students switch roles.

PRESENTING: So sagt man das!

To review the expressions in the first **So sagt man das!** box, bring several pieces of clothing to class and ask students to give you advice on what to wear.

PRESENTING: Ein wenig Grammatik

Adjective endings Divide students into groups of four or five. Allow each group to pick its own topic, such as a favorite place, the ideal outfit, the best meal they ever ate, and have each group write a descriptive paragraph about it. Students should use as many adjectives as possible in their work. (You may want to make dictionaries available to students for this activity.) When they have finished, have them read their paragraphs to the class.

For Additional Practice

27 Have students continue practicing the functions of asking and giving advice by changing the occasion. Suggest occasions such as **Strandfete, Maskenball,** or **das Hochzeitsjubiläum der Eltern.** Students should give additional suggestions for appropriate outfits.

PRESENTING: So sagt man das!

Prior to reviewing the functions in the second **So sagt man das!** box, compile a list of contrasting topics. Review the expressions in this box before students start working in pairs. They should use the examples from a list that you have prepared on a transparency or a handout. Examples are ethnic foods (**chinesisch** vs. **mexikanisch**), art (**moderne** vs. **traditionelle Kunst**), and music (**Rock** vs. **klassische Musik**).

PAGE 344

Communication for All Students

A Slower Pace
28 Before students begin the activity, brainstorm with them all the different types of fabrics they have learned. Make a list of the fabrics on the board or on a transparency for students to use when describing their outfits. It might also help students to review colors and patterns before starting the activity.

PRESENTING: Ein wenig Grammatik

Comparative adjectives Have students pair up. Each partner should formulate three sentences describing something of which he or she is particularly proud. (Example: **Ich habe ein schönes Haus mit einem großen Garten.**) Partners should then trade papers and follow the model provided by their counterparts' sentences to boast about their own possessions, which are even better: **Aber ich habe ein schöneres Haus mit einem größeren Garten.** When all students have finished, have the partners read their statements aloud to the class. You may want to give a prize to the pair with the most imaginative sentences.

PRESENTING: So sagt man das!

Ask students to think of some typical questions a salesperson in the following stores might ask a customer to find out what he or she is looking for: **Buchhandlung, Schuhgeschäft, Geschenkwarenladen, Schreibwarenladen,** and **Musikgeschäft.** Once students have compiled a list of questions, have them come up with possible responses using expressions of interest, disinterest, and indifference when possible.

PAGE 345

Cooperative Learning

31 Divide students into groups as suggested and have each group member take the role of reader, writer, proofreader, discussion leader, or reporter. Since this is an extensive activity, you might want to break it into a two- or three-day assignment using some class time each day. Groups work together to answer the questions, and the writer takes notes for the group. On the last day of the activity, the proofreader checks the assignment for accuracy. Once all groups have completed Questions a-j, they should continue with Activity 32 in which the reporter tells about his or her group's plans.

TPR Total Physical Response

Prior to this activity you may want to ask the home economics teacher if you could use the mannequin that is often used in sewing classes to fit clothing. Also bring a bag of clothing and some accessories that represent all the clothing vocabulary students have learned so far. Call on students to come to the front of the class. Give them specific instructions on what to pick from the bag of clothing to dress the mannequin. Once the mannequin is completely dressed, ask students to give each other specific directions to undress the mannequin again.

Von der Schule zum Beruf

You might assign this activity after students have completed the **Webprojekt** on p. 325F in which they are asked to research adventure tours offered by a German travel agency.

Teacher Note

For additional open-ended activities, see **Zum Sprechen** and **Zum Schreiben** suggestions on the **Komm mit!** Interactive CD-ROM Tutor and in the Alternative Assessment Guide.

Teacher to Teacher

Jim Garland
Henry Clay High School
Lexington, Kentucky

Jim uses technology to put a new twist on a popular game.

"A computerized Jeopardy!® board can be made using PowerPoint. Construct the game board like the TV version. Save this as a template. Each game should be saved under a different name so that the template can be reused for future games. Type in an answer or question on each of the PowerPoint slides. This computerized version can be projected with a multimedia projector onto a screen or smart board. Divide the class into three teams and appoint a captain to give the official response. Prizes may be given to the winning team at the end of the game. The technology holds the students' interest, and it's a great way to review for a chapter test while having fun at the same time!"

Assess

- Testing Program, pp. 309–312
  Quiz 12-3A, Quiz 12-3B
  Audio CD12, Tr. 14
- Student Make-Up Assignments
  Chapter 12, Alternative Quiz
- Alternative Assessment Guide, p. 43

▶ PAGES 346–347

ZUM LESEN

> **Teaching Resources**
> pp. 346–347
>
> **PRINT**
> ▶ Lesson Planner, p. 61
> ▶ Übungsheft, p. 144
> ▶ Reading Strategies and Skills, Chapter 12
> ▶ Lies mit mir! 2, Chapter 12
>
> **MEDIA**
> ▶ One-Stop Planner

Prereading

Building Context
Ask students the following questions. What kinds of sounds wake you up at night? How do you react when you are awakened? Have you ever gotten out of bed to go to the kitchen in the middle of the night? Were you hungry or just restless? Did you try to hide what you were doing? Why do you think someone might try to hide doing this?

Teaching Suggestion
Ask students to think about the words they would need to know in order to read a story involving the scenario discussed in the Building Context activity. Have them work in pairs to make a list of words they already know in German and a list in English of words they might need to know but don't already know.

Thinking Critically
Drawing Inferences Tell students that the author of this story does not state the main point directly. Ask them what they need to do or look at to infer what the author is implying. (word choice and arrangement of ideas)

> **Connections and Comparisons**
>
> **Literature Connection**
> Ask students to name the literary era that occurred during the lifetime of Wolfgang Borchert (1921–1947). (Expressionism)

> **Cultures and Communities**
>
> **Background Information**
> Wolfgang Borchert was a German poet and short-story writer. He was born on May 20, 1921 in Hamburg. He published newspaper articles while still in high school, then worked in a bookstore to support himself while studying drama. At age twenty he was drafted and sent to the eastern front, where he was twice arrested and imprisoned on suspicion of "malingering," and for making fun of the Nazis. He is known for portraying the devastation and absurdity of war. He died shortly after World War II of wounds he suffered during the war. Today he remains one of the most read and celebrated writers in German literature.

Teacher Note
Activity 1 is a prereading activity.

Reading

> **Connections and Comparisons**
>
> **History Connection**
> To help students gain a better understanding of the story, you may want to have them do some research about the time during which Borchert lived. Have students check their history books for relevant dates, political figures, and events that occurred during that time period.

> **Communication for All Students**
>
> **A Slower Pace**
> ④ To help students better understand the text, break it into sections and have them try to briefly summarize each section.

Teaching Suggestion
While students read the story, ask them to make notes of words or phrases they might want to know. If available, provide students with a German-English dictionary.

Post-Reading

Teacher Note
Activity 9 is a post-reading task that will show whether students can apply what they have learned.

REVIEW

Cultures and Communities

Career Path
Have students think of scenarios in which someone working for an American software company would find it advantageous to possess a knowledge of German. (Suggestions: Software companies frequently sell their products in other countries, leading to a demand for people to translate the text appearing in the program, as well as the instruction manuals; these companies also need employees who can interact with the foreign firms that distribute their software overseas.)

KANN ICH'S WIRKLICH?

This page helps students prepare for the test. It is a brief checklist of the major points covered in the chapter. The students should be reminded that it is only a checklist and not necessarily everything that will appear on the test.

For additional self check options, refer students to the *Grammar Tutor*, the *Interactive CD-ROM Tutor*, and the Online self-test for this chapter.

PAGE 353

WORTSCHATZ

Review and Assess

Circumlocution

To review, play *Das treffende Wort suchen* with the different sports from the *Erste Stufe* or with the articles of clothing from the *Zweite Stufe*. Both categories lend themselves well to circumlocution because the nouns in these categories can be easily described. See p. 3C for procedures.

Game

Play the games *Wörter kreuz und quer*, *Anziehwettbewerb*, and *Bildkarten*. See pp. 121C, 209C, and 325C for the procedures.

Teacher Note

Give the Kapitel 12 Chapter Test: *Testing Program*, pp. 313–318 Audio CD 12, Trs. 15–16.

Give the Final Exam: *Testing Program*, pp. 327–334 Audio CD 12, Trs. 17–19.

Teaching Suggestion
Ask students to come up with one question they would like to ask the male character and one question they would like to ask the female character in this story. Ask students to take a few moments to write down their questions, then read them aloud in class. Encourage others to come up with possible answers from both the man's and the woman's perspective.

Zum Lesen Answers
Answers to Activity 1 The traditional German dinner, *das Abendbrot*, consists of bread and cold cuts. The title suggests simplicity, sparseness.
Answers to Activity 2 Summaries will vary; The story takes place in the kitchen (of an apartment) at 2:30 A.M.; There are two characters: *sie* and *er* (no names are given).
Answers to Activity 3 1. g; 2. b; 3. f; 4. h; 5. a; 6. e; 7. c; 8. d
Answers to Activity 6 The noise must have come from outside; it must have been the wind against the gutter; He was lying to her.
Answers to Activity 7 She heard his chewing; She realized he was hungry, so the next night she gave him part of her portion of the bread.
Answers to Activity 8 The woman's (third person partially omniscient); The bread (or lack of it) was the source of the conflict, and it was also the resolution; He was hungry; They may have been poor for a long time, but more likely the story reflects the immediate postwar era when food was scarce.

PAGES 348–351

MEHR GRAMMATIKÜBUNGEN

The Mehr Grammatikübungen activities were designed as supplemental activities for the grammatical concepts presented in the chapter. You might use them as additional practice, for review, or for assessment.

For more grammar presentations, review, and practice, refer to the following:
- Grammatikheft
- Grammar Tutor for Students of German
- Grammar Summary on pp. R20–R36
- Übungsheft
- Grammar and Vocabulary quizzes (Testing Program)
- Test Generator
- Interactive CD-ROM Tutor
- Interaktive Spiele at go.hrw.com

PAGE 352

Video Wrap-up

Videocassette 4, 44:54–1:03:30
Videocassette 5 (captioned version), 1:13:33–1:22:52
DVD Tutor, Disc 2

At this time, you might want to use the video resources for additional review and enrichment. These resources are also available via the Enhanced Online Student Edition.
See *Video Guide* for suggestions regarding:
- *Echt toll, Ismar!* Dramatic episode
- Landeskunde Interviews
- Videoclips Authentic footage

STANDARDS: 1.1, 5.1

KAPITEL

12

Die Reinickendorfer Clique

Objectives

In this chapter you will review and practice how to

Erste Stufe

- report past events
- ask for, make, and respond to suggestions

Zweite Stufe

- order food, express hearsay and regret
- persuade and dissuade

Dritte Stufe

- ask for and give advice
- express preference
- express interest, disinterest, and indifference

Visit Holt Online
go.hrw.com
KEYWORD: WK3 BERLIN-12
Online Edition

◀ Echt super! Lässt du mich mal fahren? Absolute Spitze!

dreihundertsiebenundzwanzig **327**

Los geht's! · *Echt toll, Ismar!*

Strategie Verstehen
Look at the images for the story. Where are the students? What are they doing? What do you think they are talking about?

Andreas **Astrid** **Ismar** **Lars** **Binh**

①

Astrid: Das machst du echt toll, Ismar! Du wirst bestimmt mal ein bekannter Chefkoch werden!
Ismar: Du wirst es mir nicht glauben, aber Kochen macht mir großen Spaß. Du musst mal zu uns kommen, dann mach ich für dich ein bosnisches Gericht, Cevapcici. Echt super!
Astrid: Du musst mich eben mal einladen.
Ismar: Mach ich!

②

Andreas: Hm, prima! Das sieht echt lecker aus.
Astrid: Hat Ismar gemacht. — He, Finger weg! Du darfst dir nichts vom Teller nehmen.
Andreas: Ich hab aber Hunger.
Astrid: Pech gehabt! Na gut! Ich mach dir ein belegtes Brot. Was willst du denn drauf haben?
Andreas: Käse und Schinken! Doppelt gemoppelt hält besser.
Astrid: So, hier! Schwirr ab!

③

Andreas: Hallo, Sandra! Was, du weißt nicht, wie du herkommst? … Ach so, du kommst mit dem Rad. Ja, du biegst von der Müllerstraße rechts in die Ungarnstraße rein … fährst diese geradeaus bis zur Basler Straße. Ja … da biegst du links hinein … fährst diese weiter geradeaus …

④ **⑤**

Andreas: Hallo! — Das ist also dein neues Moped. Echt super! Wie lange hast du es jetzt schon?
Lars: Seit ich den Führerschein hab, also seit Anfang der Ferien. Gefällt dir, was?
Andreas: Ich mach den Vierer in sechs Monaten. Du lässt mich doch dann mal fahren, oder?
Lars: Na klar!
Andreas: So, kommt rein! Ismar ist auch schon da, schwer am Arbeiten, und Sandra wird auch gleich da sein.

dreihundertachtundzwanzig   STANDARDS: 1.2   KAPITEL 12   Die Reinickendorfer Clique

Binh: Rohes Gemüse, hm! Wohl für mich?
Astrid: Warum? Bist du etwa Vegetarierin? Das ist mir neu.
Binh: Nein, so schlimm ist das nicht. Ich esse eben gern Obst und Gemüse. Nur Bananen kann ich nicht essen.
Astrid: Warum nicht?
Binh: Ich bin allergisch gegen Bananen.
Astrid: Echt? Das hab ich nicht gewusst.

Binh: Hm, super! Die hast du aber mit viel Liebe vorbereitet.
Astrid: Ehrlich gesagt hab ich gar nichts gemacht. Das hat alles Ismar gemacht — und so schön dekoriert!—Greif zu!

Ismar: Mensch, Lars, du siehst heute so anders aus. Ich erkenn dich kaum wieder: weißes Hemd, schwarze Hosen …
Lars: Tja, ich hatte es einfach satt, in Jeans und T-Shirt rumzurennen.
Ismar: Wirklich? Das soll ich dir glauben?

Astrid: Mensch, Binh, deine Jacke gefällt mir. Die sieht echt toll aus. Und die steht dir auch. Ist sie neu?
Binh: Die hab ich mir vor den Ferien gekauft.
Astrid: Super, echt super! So eine würde ich auch gern mal haben. Darf ich sie mal anprobieren?
Binh: Natürlich! Hier, probier sie an!

Andreas: Was hast du denn mit deinem Arm? Hast du dich verletzt?
Binh: Ich bin vom Fahrrad gefallen.
Andreas: Das hat wohl wehgetan.
Binh: Am Anfang schon. Aber jetzt geht's.

Übungsheft, S.133

1 **Was passiert hier?** 3. because he can't have the food they prepared; prepare a sandwich

Verstehst du alles, was diese Schüler sagen? Beantworte die folgenden Fragen!

1. Why are these students getting together? Where is the story taking place? 1. to eat at Astrid's
2. What are Astrid and Ismar discussing in the opening scene? 2. Ismar's cooking talents
3. Why does Astrid say **Pech gehabt** to Andreas? What does Astrid do for him instead?
4. Why is Sandra calling? What kind of information does Andreas give her?
5. What do Andreas and Lars discuss when Lars and Binh arrive? What kind of deal does Andreas make with Lars? 4. She doesn't know how to get there. Directions 5. They talk about the moped. When Andreas gets his license, Lars will let him ride his moped.
6. Why does Binh mention bananas? 6. She is allergic to them.
7. In what way does Lars look different today? Does Ismar believe the reason Lars gives for the change? 7. He is dressed up. He does not really believe it.
8. What does Astrid say to Binh about her jacket? 8. Astrid says that she likes the jacket.
9. Why does Andreas ask Binh about her arm? What happened to her? 9. Binh has a bandage on her arm. She fell off her bike.
10. In what way does Astrid compliment Ismar at the end of the story?
10. She says that Ismar has prepared all the food.

2 **Genauer Lesen**

a. Lies den Text noch einmal! Such die Wörter oder Ausdrücke aus, die das Folgende ausdrücken! 1. E.g.: Echt toll! 2. E.g.: Finger weg! 3. E.g.: Echt? 4. E.g.: Das hat wohl wehgetan.

1. compliments or praise
2. a warning or reprimand
3. surprise
4. concern for someone else

b. Beantworte die folgenden Fragen!
1. Astrid makes a prediction. What is it? 1. Ismar will become a famous chef.
2. What wish does Astrid express? What words does she use to say this? 2. She would like to be invited by Ismar. Du musst mich eben mal einladen.
3. Several people instruct others to do something. Find at least three examples. 3. E.g.: Kommt rein! Probier sie an! Schwirr ab!
4. Find three instances in which people ask for specific information. Which phrases do they use to do this? 4. E.g.: Ist sie (die Jacke) neu? Was willst du drauf? Wie lange hast du es schon?

3 **Welche Sätze passen zusammen?**

Welche Nebensätze auf der rechten Seite passen zu den Satzanfängen auf der linken Seite?

1. Du darfst dir nichts vom Teller nehmen, d
2. Du darfst noch nicht Moped fahren, e
3. Ich darf das nicht essen, c
4. Ich trage heute mal etwas anderes, f
5. Der Arm tut mir weh, a
6. Das schmeckt echt gut, b

a. denn ich bin vom Rad gefallen.
b. weil du alles mit viel Liebe vorbereitet hast.
c. denn ich bin dagegen allergisch.
d. denn das ist für unsere Gäste.
e. weil du noch keinen Führerschein hast.
f. weil ich es satt habe, immer in denselben Klamotten herumzulaufen.

4 **Nacherzählung**

Erzähl die Geschichte nach, indem du die folgenden Sätze in die richtige Reihenfolge bringst! Zuerst hilft Ismar der Astrid in der Küche.

8 Am Ende sitzen alle am Tisch und essen.
3 Danach ruft die Sandra an.
6 Andreas findet es toll und möchte bald damit fahren.
4 Andreas sagt Sandra, wie man zu ihm kommt.
7 Später sprechen die Schüler über das Essen, Klamotten, und wie Binh sich verletzt hat.
1 Dann kommt der Andreas und will schon ein Sandwich probieren.
5 Kurz danach kommen Lars und Binh mit dem Moped an.
2 Das geht aber nicht. Astrid macht ihm aber schnell ein belegtes Brot.

330 dreihundertdreißig STANDARDS: 1.2 KAPITEL 12 Die Reinickendorfer Clique

Welche ausländische Küche hast du gern?

What kinds of ethnic cuisine do Germans enjoy? Before you read the responses below, think about what you know about popular foods in Germany. Which foreign cuisine do you think is the most popular among German teenagers? CD 12 Tr. 3

Werner, Berlin CD 12 Tr. 4

„Ja, ausländische Küche … würd ich sagen mit Vorliebe italienisch, Spaghetti in jeder Variante, mit Tomatensoße, mit Cremesoßen, Joghurtsoßen, und alles, was zur italienischen Küche dazugehört."

Monika, Hamburg CD 12 Tr. 5

„Ich ess gerne chinesisch, griechisch, ja auch italienisch, weil es ist halt…es schmeckt halt gut. Und Fastfood ess ich auch gerne, weil so schön viele Kalorien drin sind. Wenn du richtig gut Fastfood essen willst, musst du nach Berlin, und dann gehst du ins Hard Rock Café, und dann bestellst du dir 'nen Hamburger."

Margit, Stuttgart CD 12 Tr. 6

„Ich interessier mich am meisten für die italienische Küche, koch das auch sehr gerne, les gerne viel darüber. Am meisten eigentlich Nudelgerichte oder auch spezielle Nachtische von dort, weil ich's sehr schmackhaft finde und sehr variationsreich auch."

Hans, Hamburg CD 12 Tr. 7

„Amerikanische Küche mag ich eigentlich nicht, kein Fastfood, kein Big Mac, mal ab und zu. Aber so, eben so typisch deutsche Gerichte mag ich auch eigentlich gerne, Kartoffeln mit 'nem Steak und Bohnen…und, ja, das ist eigentlich alles."

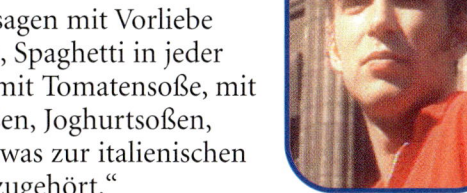

A.
1. Which ethnic cuisines do these people say they like? Which is the most popular cuisine? Is this what you guessed beforehand? A. 1. Italian, Chinese, Greek, American; most popular: Italian
2. What does Hans think of as American food? Why might he think this? How do you feel about this stereotype? A. 2. Fast food
3. What other foreign cuisines popular in Germany were not mentioned by these particular people? A. 3. E.g.: Spanish, Yugoslav, Japanese, Turkish

B.
1. There are many different kinds of eateries in Germany, and you are already familiar with some of them. Which ones can you recall and what are their characteristics? You already know about **Fastfood Restaurants** from your own experience, and there are many American franchises now in Germany. Germany also has some of its own chains, for example, **Nordsee.** Can you guess what kind of food they serve?
2. In addition to fast food, you'll find in every village and town at least one **Gaststätte. Gaststätten** reflect the local color and traditions of the region they are in, both in terms of decor and the type of food served. When the weather is good, Germans flock to the outdoors and often congregate in **Biergärten.** These have a definite family atmosphere, much like the English pub. By custom, patrons can buy food there or bring their own, but must purchase beverages from the establishment.

STANDARDS: 1.2, 2.1, 2.2, 3.2, 4.2

Erste Stufe

Objectives Reporting past events; asking for, making, and responding to suggestions

Die Deutschen – die Europameister im Reisen

DIE DEUTSCHEN SIND ein reiselustiges Volk. Allein im Jahr 1996 gaben sie bei Auslandsreisen $25 Milliarden aus. Damit stehen sie mit weitem Abstand an der Spitze der Europäer. Das liegt wohl zum einen daran, daß die Deutschen ein wohlhabendes Volk sind und über viel Freizeit verfügen. Zum andern suchen sie ihr Urlaubsglück häufiger jenseits der Grenzen als daheim. Andere Europäer verbringen ihre Ferien bevorzugt im eigenen Land.

Spanien   Kanarische Inseln   Lanzarote

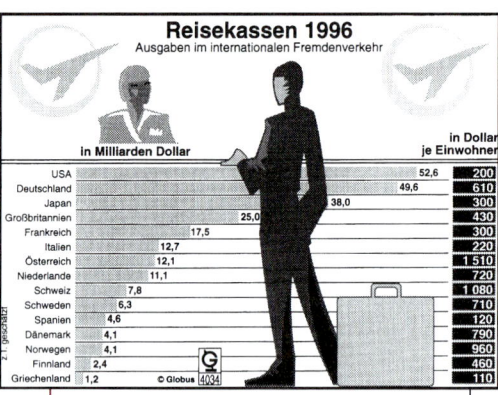

Sport, Spaß und Erholung

Eine Entdeckungsreise auf der ca. 795 Quadratkilometer großen Insel führt Sie vorbei an kleinen, sauberen Dörfern mit weißen Häusern, abwechslungsreichen Stränden mit hellem oder dunklem Sand, Klippen und einsamen Buchten.

Club „La Santa"

Unter Insidern und Top-Athleten gilt er längst als Geheimtip. Jetzt steht der exklusive Club „La Santa", auf der schwarzen Insel Lanzarote, nur etwa 4 Flugstunden von Deutschland entfernt und ca. 150 km vor der afrikanischen Küste, auch den Gästen von Sport-Scheck Reisen offen. Werfen Sie einen Blick hinein in die Traumanlage der fast unbegrenzten Sportmöglichkeiten, wo sich Olympiasieger wie Claudia Losch, Ulrike Meifarth, die Zehnkämpfer Guido Kratschmer, Jürgen Hingsen und ganze Bundesligateams erholen und auf neue Erfolge vorbereiten — Sie werden begeistert sein.
Um den Club „La Santa" zu besuchen, müssen Sie aber kein Spitzensportler sein — Kinder, Erholungssuchende, Aktive, Familien, Gruppen ... im „Club La Santa" ist jeder herzlich willkommen.

Das „Grüne Team"

Junge, profitrainierte Sportleute (vorwiegend englischsprechend) stehen im „Club La Santa" den Gästen mit Rat und Tat zur Seite. Angeboten wird Unterricht im Squash, Badminton, Tennis, Schwimmen, Schnorcheln, Windsurfen, sowie Fitneß-Test und Gewichttraining — je nach Programm unterteilt in Gruppen für Anfänger, Fortgeschrittene, Erfahrene und Kinder.

Weltklasse Einrichtungen für mehr als 20 Sportarten

„La Santa" ist ausgerüstet wie eine kleine Olympiastadt: Mit Fußball- und Leichtathletikstadion, 50-Meter-Swimmingpool, Badminton- und Handballhalle, Squashcourts, Tauchschule, Surfstation, Tennisplätzen, Fitneß-Studio, Tischtennisräumen, Basketballplatz, großes Fahrrad-Depot. Oft beginnen Fitneß und Entspannung auf Lanzarote mit Entdeckungstouren auf Rennrad oder Mountainbike.

Wohnen im Club „La Santa"

Sämtliche Sportanlagen und Einrichtungen sind um das gepflegte Appartement-Dorf, etwa 250 Meter vom offenen Meer entfernt, gruppiert. Obwohl die 400 Wohnungen Platz für mehr als tausend Gäste bieten, entsteht nie der Eindruck von Enge. Restaurants, Bars, Disco, Shops, Video-Kino, Friseur ... sorgen für eine dörfliche Atmosphäre. Der Supermarkt in der Anlage ist sehr gut sortiert — auch die verwöhnten Genießer und ernährungsbewußten Sportler können dort gut einkaufen.
Die Appartements (Varianten von 1 bis 3 Personen) sind einfach und zweckmäßig eingerichtet. Sie verfügen über Bad/WC, Kitchenette mit Kühlschrank, Schlafraum und Wohnraum sowie Patio (keine Aussicht). Ganz nach Lust und Laune wird selbst gekocht oder in einem der zahlreichen Restaurants innerhalb oder außerhalb des Clubs gespeist. Oder aber Sie nehmen die Halb- bzw. Vollpension, die aus europäischem Frühstücksbuffet und wahlweise Mittag- oder Abendbuffet besteht, in Anspruch. Auch am Abend braucht „Jung und Alt" sich nicht zu langweilen. Grill- und Strandfeste, Kinoabende und Kinder-Bühnen-Show, Ausflüge und Turniere verschiedenster Art erwarten Sie. Das „Grüne Team" stellt sich zweimal wöchentlich einmal ganz anders vor — lassen Sie sich überraschen. Selbstverständlich ist auch in den Bars und in der Club-Disco immer was los.

Wortschatz

das Meer und der Strand   die Küste und die Klippen   eine Insel   eine Bucht   eine Oase

auf Deutsch erklärt:

der Anfänger = Schüler, Greenhorn
der Fortgeschrittene = weiß mehr als ein Anfänger
der Erfahrene = Experte
der Olympiasieger = hat in der Olympiade gewonnen
der Zehnkämpfer = kämpft in zehn verschiedenen Sportarten
der Geheimtipp = nicht alle sollen das wissen
abwechslungsreich = nicht langweilig
s. langweilen = nichts zu tun haben
zahlreiche = viele

Sportanlagen
der Court
der Platz
der Pool
die Anlage
die Halle
das Fahrrad-Depot

p. 325X   12–A

Was würdest du auf dieser Insel tun? Welche Sportanlagen würdest du benutzen und warum?

Übungsheft, S. 135, Ü. 1   Grammatikheft, S. 100–101, Ü. 1

5 Der Ferien Club

Lesen/Schreiben/Sprechen Lies den Artikel auf Seite 332! Schreib die Antworten zu den folgenden Fragen auf ein Blatt Papier! Such dir dann einen Partner! Stellt euch abwechselnd diese Fragen und beantwortet sie!

1. Wer gibt am meisten für Auslandsreisen aus?
2. Wo verbringen die meisten Deutschen ihren Urlaub?
3. Warum können die Deutschen so viel Geld für ihren Urlaub ausgeben?
4. Warum besuchen sie gern den Club „La Santa"?
5. Was kann man beim „grünen Team" lernen?
6. Welche Einrichtungen gibt es im Club „La Santa"?
7. Was gibt es alles im Appartement-Dorf?
8. Wie sind die Appartements eingerichtet?
9. Warum braucht sich niemand im Club zu langweilen?

Ein wenig Grammatik

Schon bekannt

When talking about the past, you generally use two verb forms, a helping verb and a past participle.

Wo **bist** du **gewesen**?
Wir **haben** Tennis **gespielt**.

For past participles of verbs that you should know, see the Grammar Summary. You know two verbs that also have a single verb form to refer to the past. What are these verbs? And their forms?

Grammatikheft, S. 101, Ü. 2

Mehr Grammatikübungen, S. 348–349, Ü. 1–4

6 Überhört

Script and answers on p. 325G

Zuhören Du stehst in der Schlange vor dem Bankschalter und hörst, wie sich zwei junge Leute über ihr letztes Wochenende unterhalten. Sind sie in der Stadt geblieben, oder haben sie eine längere Reise unternommen? Wer hat am meisten Spaß gehabt? Warum müssen sie jetzt auf die Bank?

CD 12 Tr. 8

ERSTE STUFE   STANDARDS: 1.2   *dreihundertdreiunddreißig*   **333**

So sagt man das!

Reporting past events

When reporting past events, you use special verb forms. Pay special attention to the verbs here:

Die Osterferien habe ich mit meinen Eltern in der Schweiz verbracht. Wir waren in Brienz, in den Bergen. Wir hatten wunderschönes Wetter und haben viel unternommen. Nach dem Frühstück sind wir gewöhnlich ein paar Stunden gewandert und haben irgendwo zu Mittag gegessen. Nach dem Essen haben wir ein bisschen gefaulenzt, und dann …

When would you use **haben** with the past tense? And **sein**?

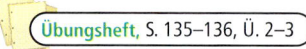

7 Andreas' und Astrids Ferien

Sprechen Die letzten Weihnachtsferien haben Astrid und Andreas mit ihren Eltern auf den Kanarischen Inseln verbracht. Du willst von ihnen wissen, wie es war und was sie dort alles gemacht haben. — Such dir zwei Partner, die die Rollen von Astrid und Andreas spielen!

Du willst folgendes wissen:

a. wo sie waren
b. wo das liegt
c. wo sie gewohnt haben
d. wie das Appartement eingerichtet war
e. welche Sporteinrichtungen es gibt
f. was sie neu gelernt haben
g. welche Spitzensportler sie kennen gelernt haben
h. wie sie ihre Abende verbracht haben

8 Ein großes Angebot

Schreiben „La Santa" ist ausgerüstet wie eine kleine Olympiastadt, und für mehr als 20 Sportarten gibt es Weltklasse Einrichtungen. Sieh dir diesen Plan von „La Santa" an, und schreib sechs Sportarten auf, die du dort gern machen würdest!

9 Grammatik im Kontext

a. Sprechen Erzähl deinem Partner, wo du überall im Club gewesen bist und was du dort alles gemacht hast und wie oft!

Wo? in der Minigolfanlage · in der Pizzeria · am Meer · am Strand · am Pool · im Kraftstudio · in der Diskothek · im Beach Club · im Stadion · im Squashcourt · im Supermarkt · in der Sauna · in der Bucht · in der Basketballhalle · auf dem Tennisplatz

Ein wenig Grammatik

Schon bekannt

You have used questions and statements such as:

**Wart ihr am Pool?
Nein, in der Minigolfanlage.**

What case follows these two prepositions? Why? For more on two-way prepositions, see the Grammar Summary.

Übungsheft, S. 136–137, Ü. 4–6
Grammatikheft, S.102, Ü. 3

b. Schreiben Schreib in dein Tagebuch, was du alles an einem Wochenende im Club gemacht hast.

10 Wohin im Urlaub? Script and answers on p. 325G

CD 12 Tr. 9

Zuhören Die Familie Kohl bespricht ihren kommenden Urlaub. Leider würden die Kinder, Markus und Annette, lieber ganz andere Dinge machen als ihre Eltern. Schreib auf, welche Vorschläge die Eltern und die Kinder machen. Welche Gründe geben sie an?

So sagt man das!

Asking for, making, and responding to suggestions *Schon bekannt*

When asking for suggestions, you could say:

Wohin sollen wir fahren? Was schlägst du vor?

When making suggestions, you could say:

**Würdest du gern mal an die Küste fahren?
Wie wär's denn mit einem Flug nach Spanien?**

And you could respond by saying:

**Eine gute Idee!
Das wäre toll! Super!**

Ein wenig Grammatik

Schon bekannt

For the forms of **sollen** and the **würde**-forms, see the Grammar Summary.

Mehr Grammatikübungen, S. 349, Ü. 5

11 Grammatik im Kontext

Sprechen/Schreiben Erzähl deinem Partner, was du gern mal in den kommenden Ferien tun würdest. Schreib es dann auf.

ERSTE STUFE STANDARDS: 1.1, 1.2, 5.1 dreihundertfünfunddreißig **335**

12 Auf in die Ferien!

Deine Eltern haben dich und deine Schwester gebeten, zahlreiche Reiseprospekte zu besorgen, damit ihr zusammen am Wochenende eure Pläne für die kommenden Ferien machen könnt.

a. **Schreiben** Schreib drei Ferienziele auf ein Blatt Papier!

b. **Schreiben** Schreib daneben ein oder zwei Gründe, warum du gern dorthin fahren würdest!

c. **Sprechen** Such dir jetzt drei Partner für die Rollen von deinen Eltern und deiner Schwester! Schlag den Eltern einen Ferienort vor und begründe deinen Vorschlag! Was meinen die Eltern dazu?

Ein wenig Grammatik

Schon bekannt

Read these questions and statements:

Fahrt ihr wieder ans Meer?
Wir waren im Juli am Meer.
Fahren wir heute in die Berge?
In den Bergen regnet es.
Fliegst du nach Österreich?
Ich war schon in Österreich.

What case follows these prepositions and why? What kind of preposition is **nach?** For more on prepositions, see the Grammar Summary.

 Grammatikheft, S. 103, Ü. 4

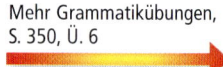 Mehr Grammatikübungen, S. 350, Ü. 6

13 Im Reisebüro

Ihr habt euch in der Familie auf drei Reiseziele geeinigt, aber bevor ihr euch endgültig für einen Ferienort entscheidet, braucht ihr noch mehr Information. Du sollst diese Information besorgen.

a. **Schreiben** Schreib die drei Reiseziele auf eine Liste und trag die Sehenswürdigkeiten (*sights*) ein, die ihr an jedem Ziel besuchen wollt!

b. **Schreiben** Schreib mindestens acht Dinge auf, über die du Auskunft möchtest, zum Beispiel, ob der Ferienort einen großen Swimmingpool hat oder ob die Pension einen schönen Tennisplatz hat!

c. **Sprechen** Such dir jetzt einen Partner! Er übernimmt die Rolle von einem Angestellten im Reisebüro. Er fragt dich, wofür du dich interessierst, und du sagst es ihm. Leider muss der Angestellte dir sagen, dass es nicht alles gibt, was du willst.

BEISPIEL **ANGESTELLTER** Ja, wofür interessieren Sie sich denn?
DU Ich interessiere mich für eine Reise nach …und ich möchte wissen, ob …

14 Für mein Notizbuch

Schreiben Du warst mit deiner Familie in einem schönen Ferienort. Schreib einen Bericht über deine Ferien in dein Notizbuch! Er muss Antworten zu folgenden Fragen enthalten (*include*):

1. Wo wart ihr und wie lange?
2. Wo habt ihr gewohnt, und wie waren die Zimmer?
3. Was für Sportarten habt ihr dort ausgeübt?
4. Wo habt ihr gegessen, und wie hat es euch geschmeckt?
5. Wie habt ihr die Abende verbracht?
6. Was hat euch gefallen und was nicht?
7. Würdet ihr gern noch einmal dorthin fahren oder fliegen? Warum? Warum nicht?

15 Und wo bist du gewesen?

Sprechen Frag deine Partnerin über ihre letzten Ferien! Wo ist sie gewesen, und was hat sie alles gemacht? Danach erzählst du ihr von deinen Ferien.

336 dreihundertsechsunddreißig STANDARDS: 1.1, 1.3 KAPITEL 12 Die Reinickendorfer Clique

Zweite Stufe

Objectives Ordering food, expressing hearsay and regret; persuading and dissuading

Andreas Elsholz präsentiert sein bestes Spaghettirezept!

Man nehme 300 Gramm italienische Nudeln, ein halbes Pfund Hackfleisch, einen großen Topf und — natürlich einen begabten Koch …

Seit ich in meiner eigenen Bude in Berlin-Köpenick wohne, bin ich der perfekte Koch geworden", erzählt Andreas Elsholz (21) stolz beim POP/Rocky-Interview. „Spaghetti sind meine besondere Stärke." Das wollten wir genauer wissen — und stellten Andreas mit einem Kochtest auf die Probe. Null problemo für Andi, der sich beim Nobel-Italiener „La Locanda" in München-Giesing sofort begeistert in die Küche verdrückte. Chefkoch Nicola staunte nicht schlecht, als Andreas ganz fachmännisch zunächst einige Spritzer Olivenöl in das Spaghettiwasser tat. „Nudeln dürfen nicht zu lange kochen, müssen „al dente" sein, das heißt, sie müssen noch Biss haben", erklärt Andreas seine Nudelphilosophie. Und dann legte er wie ein Wirbelwind los: Er hackte die Zwiebeln und den Paprika für die Sauce, rührte zwischendrin die Nudeln um, würzte den Tomatenfond — so, als wäre er in einer Restaurantküche groß geworden. Nach zwanzig Minuten stand das Gourmetgericht dampfend auf dem Tisch. Koch Nicola durfte als erster kosten. Sein Urteil: „Molto bene, grandioso!" Doch das Jobangebot als Koch musste der „Heiko" aus „Gute Zeiten — schlechte Zeiten" leider ablehnen. „Ich präsentiere meinen Fans dafür einen Ohrenschmaus mit meinem ersten Hit, „Immer noch verrückt nach dir …"

SPAGHETTI MIT PAPRIKA UND PILZEN

❋ ✺ ❋

- 225 g Pilze, in Scheiben geschnitten
- 115 g kleingeschnittene Paprika
- 60 g Butter oder Margarine
- 300 g Spaghetti
- Salz und Pfeffer
- 1 EL gehackte Petersilie
- 60 g geriebener Parmesan

Die Pilze und die Paprika in der Hälfte der Butter anbraten. Inzwischen die Spaghetti in reichlich Salzwasser zehn Minuten kochen. Dann ablaufen lassen und zurück in den Topf geben. Den Rest der Butter, Salz, reichlich frisch gemahlenen schwarzen Pfeffer, die Pilze und den Paprika zugeben. Alles gut vermengen. Anschließend die gehackte Petersilie darüberstreuen und geriebenen Parmesan dazu servieren.

Die Rezeptmenge reicht für vier Personen.

16 Beantwortet diese Fragen!

Lesen/Sprechen Lies den Artikel auf Seite 337! Dann such dir einen Partner! Stellt euch abwechselnd diese Fragen und beantwortet sie!

1. Wo wohnt Andreas, und was tut er besonders gern? 1. in Berlin; kochen
2. Wo hat Andis Kochtest stattgefunden? 2. im „La Locanda"
3. Was ist Andis „Nudelphilosophie"?
4. Woraus besteht sein Gourmetgericht?
5. Wie beurteilt Chefkoch Nicola das Gericht? 3. Nudeln müssen „al dente" sein.
   4. Paprika, Pilze, usw.
6. Warum hat Andi das Jobangebot als Koch nicht angenommen? 5. ausgezeichnet
   6. er singt lieber

17 Ausländische Gerichte

Sprechen Such dir eine Partnerin und stell ihr folgende Fragen!

1. Was für ein Gericht ist (Paella)?
2. Welches ist ein (griechisches) Gericht?
3. Welche von diesen Gerichten hast du schon gegessen?
4. Welches Gericht würdest du gern einmal probieren? Warum?
5. Welches Gericht wirst du dir bestimmt bestellen, wenn du einmal nach (Griechenland) kommst?

18 Gerichte beschreiben

Sprechen Alle sollen ein internationales Kochbuch zur Schule mitbringen. Jeder von euch sucht sich ein Gericht aus, das er den Mitschülern genauer beschreiben soll. Ihr müsst euch Fragen ausdenken, um herauszufinden, was das ist.

BEISPIEL	FRAGE	Was ist Paella?
	ANTWORT	Paella ist ein spanisches Reisgericht.
	FRAGE	Woraus besteht dieses Gericht?
	ANTWORT	Aus Huhn, Wurst, Krabben, Muscheln …
	FRAGE	Wie macht (kocht) man das?
	ANTWORT	Man …

Wortschatz

Internationale Gerichte

Moussaka

Cevapcici

Paella

Fettucine

Crêpes Suzette

Tacos

Wiener Schnitzel

Steak

Couscous

In was für ein Lokal würdest du gern einmal gehen? Was würdest du dir dort bestellen? Welche Gerichte kennst du? Welche hast du schon gegessen?

Übungsheft, S. 138–139, Ü. 1–3

So sagt man das!

Ordering food, expressing hearsay and regret *Schon bekannt*

When you order food, you may say:

   Ich hätte gern die Paella.

You might tell your friend what you heard about it:

   Ich habe gehört, die Paella soll hier ausgezeichnet sein.

But the waiter may have bad news:

   Tut mir Leid. Die Paella ist heute schon alle.

Übungsheft, S. 139–140, Ü. 4–6

Grammatikheft, S.104, Ü. 5

19 Wer bestellt was? *Script and answers on p. 325H*

Zuhören Zwei Leute sind in einem Restaurant, wo es viele internationale Gerichte gibt. Sie kennen einige Gerichte überhaupt nicht und unterhalten sich mit der Bedienung darüber. Schreib auf, welches Gericht sich jeder am Ende bestellt, was für ein Gericht das ist und warum sich jeder dieses Gericht bestellt hat!

CD 12 Tr. 10

20 Macht nichts! Dann nehme ich eben …

Zu deinem Geburtstag gehen deine Eltern mit dir in ein nettes Restaurant, wo du schon ab und zu warst. Du erinnerst dich (*recall*) an ein Gericht, das dir besonders gut geschmeckt hat, und du möchtest es wieder bestellen.

   a. Schreiben Schreib auf einen Zettel, was du damals gegessen und getrunken hast! (Vorspeise, Hauptgericht, Beilage, Nachspeise, Getränk.)

   b. Sprechen Such dir einen Partner, der die Rolle der Bedienung übernimmt! Du bestellst das Gericht, das dir so gut geschmeckt hat, aber leider ist es schon alle. Deshalb bestellst du dir eben ein anderes Gericht, das auch sehr gut sein soll.

Ein wenig Landeskunde

In den meisten deutschen Lokalen sucht man sich selbst den Tisch aus. Man muss nur darauf achten, dass man sich nicht an einen reservierten Tisch setzt oder an einen „Stammtisch", der immer für eine bestimmte Gruppe reserviert ist. Wenn man keinen leeren Tisch findet, dann setzt man sich eben zu anderen Leuten, nachdem man vorher höflich gefragt hat: „Ist hier noch frei?" Es ist daher nicht ungewöhnlich, dass drei oder vier verschiedene Gruppen am gleichen Tisch essen und sich miteinander unterhalten. Und unter dem Tisch liegt oft ganz friedlich des Menschen „bester Freund", der Hund, denn in den meisten Lokalen ist es gestattet, seinen Vierbeiner mitzubringen. Gastwirte sind hundelieb. Im Sommer, wenn es sehr heiß ist, stellen viele Wirte einen Wassernapf neben die Eingangstür, damit sich Hunde erfrischen können.

So sagt man das!

Persuading and dissuading *Schon bekannt*

When trying to persuade someone, you might say:

> Geh doch einmal griechisch essen!
> Iss doch mal etwas, was du
>   noch nie gegessen hast!

The response might be:

> Du, die griechische Küche ist mir zu scharf.
> Das ist ein guter Vorschlag.

When trying to dissuade someone, you might say:

> Iss dort ja keinen Fisch!
> Trink dort ja kein ungekochtes Wasser!

The response might be:

> Warum nicht?
> Gut! Mach ich nicht!

Grammatikheft, S. 105, Ü. 6

21 Grammatik im Kontext

a. Sprechen Deine Verwandten fahren in Urlaub. Sie fahren dorthin, wo du mit deinen Eltern letztes Jahr warst. Such dir eine Partnerin, die die Rolle von deiner Kusine übernimmt! — Sag ihr zwei Dinge, die sie am Ferienort unbedingt tun soll und zwei, die sie nicht tun soll! Begründe deine Aussagen! Einige Ideen stehen im Kasten unten. — Tauscht dann die Rollen aus!

Ein wenig Grammatik

Schon bekannt

Do you remember the command forms of various strong verbs? Here are some you should recognize: **Iss! Lies! Nimm! Vergiss!** For command forms, see the Grammar Summary.

Mehr Grammatikübungen
S. 351, Ü. 8

Einige Ideen

ja:
- sich richtig ausruhen
- etwas Sport machen
- in die Disko gehen
- Sonnenschutz nicht vergessen
- die tollen Fischgerichte essen

nein:
- nicht zu viele Klamotten mitnehmen
- nicht zu lange in der Sonne liegen
- kein ungekochtes Wasser trinken

b. Schreiben Schreib deinem Freund drei Dinge auf, die er in den Ferien machen soll, und drei Dinge, die er nicht machen soll!

22 Mensch, hab ich einen Bärenhunger!

Schreiben Deine Eltern haben am Ferienort ein Appartement gemietet, und ihr bereitet euer eigenes Frühstück und Abendessen vor.

a. Schreib mindestens zehn Lebensmittel auf, die deine Familie im Kühlschrank haben würde! Zum Beispiel: frisches Obst, geräucherten Fisch, usw.

b. Sprechen Du bringst einen Freund mit nach Hause ins Appartement. Ihr habt Basketball gespielt, und ihr seid jetzt hungrig und durstig. Du schlägst vor, ein paar belegte Brote zu machen, und du fragst deinen Freund, was er gern drauf hätte. Er sagt dir, was er gern mag und was nicht. Frag ihn, ob es etwas gibt, was er nicht essen darf! Er sagt es dir. — Tauscht dann die Rollen aus!

Dritte Stufe

Objectives Asking for and giving advice; expressing preference; expressing interest, disinterest, and indifference

ICH BIN KEIN WUNDERKIND!

Ihr Hippie-Outfit soll beweisen, daß sie auch als Schwimmstar auf dem Boden bleibt . . .

In Action: Franzi ist im Wasser nicht zu bremsen

Supercool: Franziska van Almsick beim Jux mit Bruder Sebastian

„Peace"— nein, mit dem Hippie-Gruß aus den sechziger Jahren, der prima zu ihrem Outfit passen würde, empfängt Franzi unseren Fotografen nicht. Die vierfache Medaillengewinnerin der Olympischen Spiele von Barcelona 1992 fährt neuerdings völlig auf Kluft à la Woodstock ab. Strickstirnband, Schlabberpulli im Ringelmuster, John-Lennon-Sonnenbrille, Schlaghosen-Jeans mit zerissenem Saum, die eher einer Patchworkdecke gleichen: der Jungstar des deutschen Schwimmsports (geboren am 5. April 1978), der bereits im zarten Alter von fünf Jahren mit dem Hochgeschwindigkeitsbaden begann, zeigt allen Beobachtern sein wahres Ich. Viele haben versucht, ihr das Image eines Nesthäkchens und Wunderkindes anzuhängen. „Alles Quatsch", meint Franzi ganz cool dazu. Und unsere Bilder beweisen es. Franziska ist ein ganz normales Mädchen — und dazu noch total süß und natürlich. Sie kann halt nur ein bisschen schneller schwimmen als die meisten anderen . . .

1. von Franziska   2. Schwimmerin u. Medaillengewinnerin bei der Olympiade '92
3. Hippie-Klamotten   4. „Alles Quatsch."

Übungsheft, S. 141, Ü. 1

23 Habt ihr alles verstanden?

Lesen/Sprechen Lies den obigen Artikel und beantworte die Fragen!

1. Wovon handelt dieser Artikel?
2. Wer ist die Franziska, auch Franzi genannt?
3. Was für Klamotten trägt Franzi zur Zeit?
4. Manche Leute nennen sie ein Wunderkind. Was meint sie dazu?

Ein wenig Grammatik

Schon bekannt

Be careful to watch the adjective endings! Can you explain why these endings are correct?

Kalt**er** Kaffee schmeckt mir nicht!
Ich mag dies**es** frisch**e** Brot.

For adjective endings, see the Grammar Summary.

Mehr Grammatikübungen, S. 351, Ü. 9

Wortschatz

Wie bist du gekleidet? Bist du ...

salopp angezogen, mit Pulli und Jeans, die Löcher haben?

gut angezogen, mit weißem Hemd, schwarzer Hose?

elegant angezogen, mit weißem Hemd und Fliege?

Was ziehst du gern an? Vielleicht ...

einen Pulli mit Ringelmuster?

ein Hemd mit großen Karos?

eine braune Wildlederjacke?

eine Bluse mit Streifen?

Was ziehst du zu Festlichkeiten an?

schwarze Lackschuhe?

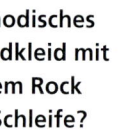
ein modisches Abendkleid mit weitem Rock und Schleife?

einen dunkelblauen Smoking, mit weißem Hemd, Fliege und Kummerbund?

Wie kleidest du dich gewöhnlich?
Was ziehst du zu Festlichkeiten an?

Übungsheft, S. 141–142, Ü. 2–4   Grammatikheft, S. 106, Ü. 7

---

24 Was wir heute Abend anziehen! *Script and answers on p. 325H*

Zuhören Schüler erzählen, was sie sich heute Abend anziehen. Rate, für welchen Anlass sich jeder anzieht! Anlässe stehen in den beiden Kästen unten.
CD 12 Tr. 11

25 Was trägst du gern?

Schreiben Mach eine Liste mit den Kleidungsstücken, die du gern zu drei verschiedenen Anlässen anziehst! Schreib daneben, warum du dir diese Sachen anziehst!

Anlässe

zu Hause
in der Schule
zum Sport
in den Ferien
zum Einkaufen
zu einer Geburtstagsfete

zu Festlichkeiten, wie:
zu einer Hochzeit
zu einem Ball
zu einer Schulfeier

26 Was ziehst du dir gern an?

Sprechen Frag deine Partnerin, was sie gern anzieht, wenn sie zu Hause ist und wenn sie zu einer Geburtstagsfete geht! Was zieht sie an und warum? Danach fragt sie dich.

So sagt man das!

Asking for and giving advice *Schon bekannt*

When asking for advice, you might say:

> Welchen Pulli soll ich mir zur Fete anziehen, diesen roten Pulli oder den blauen?

When giving advice, you may say:

> Zieh doch deinen blauen Pulli an! *or* Ich würde mir diesen blauen Pulli anziehen. Der passt besser zu deiner weißen Jeans.

Grammatikheft, S. 107, Ü. 8

27 Was soll ich mir anziehen?

Sprechen A classmate has invited you to his birthday. Ask your partner which of the different clothing items or styles you should wear to the party. He or she will advise you and say why you should choose one or the other. To get an idea of how the whole outfit will look, sketch a picture as your partner advises you. Then switch roles. Afterwards, share your pictures with the class. Who has given the best advice, judging by the pictures?

— saloppe Kleidung oder gut angezogen?
— Jeans oder dunkle Hose?
— Hemd: einfarbig, gestreift oder kariert?
— bunte Krawatte oder (rote) Fliege?
— T-Shirt: einfach oder modisch?
— hübsches Kleid oder Rock und Bluse?
— Bluse: lange oder kurze Ärmel?
— Lackschuhe oder einfache Sneakers?

Ein wenig Grammatik

Schon bekannt

Look at the adjectives in these sentences. What are their endings? What do these endings indicate?

> Zieh doch den blauen Pulli an!
> Der blaue Pulli ist schöner.
> Ich zieh das grüne Hemd an.
> Ein grünes Hemd passt gut zu dieser bunten Hose.

For adjective endings, see the Grammar Summary.

Mehr Grammatikübungen, S. 351, Ü. 10

So sagt man das!

Expressing preference *Schon bekannt* *Grammatikheft, S. 107, Ü. 9*

When asking what someone prefers, you might say:

> Welches Hemd findest du schöner, dieses weiße Hemd oder das gestreifte?
> Welche Schuhe gefallen dir besser?
>
> Welches Muster ziehst du vor?
> Was soll ich anziehen? Jeans oder ein Kleid? Was meinst du?

When expressing preference, you might say:

> Ich finde das gestreifte Hemd schöner.
>
> Also, mir gefallen eigentlich diese schwarzen Schuhe besser.
> Du, ich ziehe den Pulli mit dem Karomuster vor.
> Also, ich würde mir ein Kleid anziehen.

28 Wer die Wahl hat ...

Schreiben/Sprechen Du hast einfach zu viele Klamotten und weißt nicht, welches Outfit du zum Sting-Konzert anziehen sollst. — Zeichne drei Outfits, die dir gefallen, auf ein Blatt Papier! Beschreibe jedes Outfit und notiere den Namen, Farbe und Stoff von jedem Kleidungsstück! Zeig deinen Mitschülern die Zeichnungen!

Ein wenig Grammatik

Schon bekannt

How would you compare two things in German? Is it the same as in English? Some adjectives are irregular. Can you name some? For comparative adjectives, see the Grammar Summary.

29 Was findest du schöner?

Sprechen Du hast dich noch nicht entschieden, was du zur Fete anziehst. Du beschreibst deinem Partner die drei Outfits, die du dir in Übung 28 ausgesucht hast und fragst ihn, welches Outfit er schöner findet. Dein Partner vergleicht die Outfits. Stimmst du ihm zu? Warum? Warum nicht? — Tauscht dann die Rollen aus!

So sagt man das!

Expressing interest, disinterest, and indifference

Schon bekannt

When asking about someone's interests, you might say:

Wofür interessieren Sie sich?

When expressing interest, you might say:

Ich interessiere mich für nette Klamotten, nicht zu salopp, nicht zu fein.

When expressing disinterest, you might say:

Soll die Bluse aus Acryl sein?

Nein, ich interessier mich nicht für Acryl.

When expressing indifference, you might say:

Welche Farbe soll es sein?

Ach, das ist mir eigentlich egal.

Grammatikheft, S. 108, Ü. 10

30 Also doch etwas Neues kaufen!

Du hast beschlossen, dass du wirklich kein flottes Outfit für die Fete hast und dass du dir lieber ein neues Kleidungsstück kaufen möchtest.

a. Schreiben Schreib dir zwei Kleidungsstücke auf, die du dir kaufen möchtest! Welche Farbe? Welches Material? Welche Accessoires?

b. Sprechen Deine Partnerin ist Verkäuferin in einem Bekleidungsgeschäft. Sie fragt dich, wofür du dich interessierst. Sag es ihr! Sag ihr auch, wofür du dich nicht interessierst!

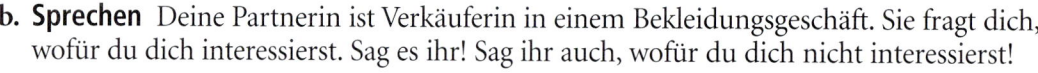

Für eine lange Reise planen

 Schreiben/Sprechen Nächsten Sommer darfst du mit deiner Klasse und deiner Deutschlehrerin vier Wochen lang die deutschsprachigen Länder besuchen. Aber bevor ihr fliegt, müsst ihr gemeinsam die Reise planen, und jeder von euch muss sich individuell auf diese Reise vorbereiten. Setzt euch in Gruppen von vier oder fünf Personen zusammen, und arbeitet gemeinsam einen detaillierten Reiseplan aus, den ihr aufschreibt und später der ganzen Klasse vortragt! Euer Plan muss Folgendes enthalten:

a. Wie sieht eure Reiseroute aus? Welche Orte wollt ihr besuchen, und was würdet ihr dort machen?

b. Würdet ihr nur Städte besuchen, oder möchtet ihr auch viel von der schönen deutschen Landschaft sehen? Was interessiert euch am meisten und warum?

c. Was für Kleidung müsst ihr mitnehmen, denn es kann ziemlich kühl oder auch sehr warm sein?

d. Wo würdet ihr wohnen? Bei deutschen Familien? In Jugendherbergen oder Pensionen?

e. Wie würdet ihr euch ernähren? Möchtet ihr immer nur in Gasthäusern essen, oder würdet ihr euch auch oft Lebensmittel in Läden und Supermärkten kaufen? Warum?

f. Welche einheimischen Gerichte möchtet ihr unbedingt einmal probieren? Habt ihr von diesen Gerichten gehört oder gelesen?

g. Wie würdet ihr euch auf der Reise fit halten?

h. Was würdet ihr tun, wenn ihr euch in Deutschland plötzlich nicht wohl fühlt?

i. Welche Fernsehsendungen würdet ihr euch in Deutschland ansehen?

j. Welche sportlichen oder kulturellen Veranstaltungen würdet ihr gern besuchen? In welchen Städten? Welche Gründe habt ihr für den Besuch von solchen Veranstaltungen?

 Reisebericht an die Klasse

 Sprechen Nun tragen abwechselnd die einzelnen Mitglieder jeder Gruppe ihren detaillierten Reiseplan der ganzen Klasse vor. Ist der Rest der Klasse mit dem Plan einverstanden? Welche Teile des Plans gefallen oder missfallen den andern in der Klasse? Diskutiert dann über die einzelnen Teile des Plans! — Nachdem jede Gruppe ihren Plan vorgetragen hat, muss ein gemeinsamer Plan von allen Schülern ausgearbeitet (*worked out*) werden!

  **Von der Schule zum Beruf**

Du arbeitest für ein Reise-Magazin. Nach 3-jähriger guter Arbeit hat man dich befördert (*you advanced*), und du hast jetzt einen ganz tollen Job. Du musst für deine Firma im Inland und im Ausland neue Reiseziele finden und diese genau fürs Reise-Magazin beschreiben: Lage, Angebot, Essen und Trinken, Klima, Kosten und Kleidung, die für dieses Reiseziel geeignet sind.

Zum Lesen

Nach dem Krieg

> **Lesestrategie** Note-taking. In this chapter you will practice taking notes that summarize a short story. Note-taking is a strategy that you can use in all of your classes. When you take summarizing notes as you read, you can gauge whether or not you understand what is going on, and you'll remember the content better and longer. You can also use those same notes to save time when studying for a test.

Getting Started   For answers, see p. 325X

> **Tipp:** The title of a short story often holds the key to what the story is about. If the title refers to an object, the key is usually the relationship of the object to the main character(s).

1. Another word for **Abendessen** is **Abendbrot**. Does this tell you anything about the role of **das tägliche Brot** in German life? If the title were *Der Apfelkuchen* or *Die Pommes frites,* you might expect certain kinds of characters or a certain atmosphere. What kind of atmosphere does *Das Brot* suggest?
2. Use the reading strategy you learned in **Kapitel 11** (p. 316) to get a general idea of what the story is about. On your third reading, try to summarize the story in three or four sentences. Where and when is the action taking place? How many characters are there?

Das Brot
von Wolfgang Borchert

Plötzlich wachte sie auf. Es war halb drei. Sie überlegte, warum sie aufgewacht war. Ach so! In der Küche hatte jemand gegen einen Stuhl gestoßen. Sie horchte nach der Küche. Es war still. Es war zu still und als sie mit der Hand über das Bett neben sich fuhr, fand sie es leer. Das war es, was es so besonders still gemacht hatte: sein Atem fehlte. Sie stand auf und tappte durch die dunkle Wohnung zur Küche. In der Küche trafen sie sich. Die Uhr war halb drei. Sie sah etwas Weißes am Küchenschrank stehen. Sie machte Licht. Sie standen sich im Hemd gegenüber. Nachts. Um halb drei. In der Küche.

Auf dem Küchentisch stand der Brotteller. Sie sah, daß er sich Brot abgeschnitten hatte. Das Messer lag noch neben dem Teller. Und auf der Decke lagen Brotkrümel. Wenn sie abends zu Bett gingen, machte sie immer das Tischtuch sauber. Jeden Abend. Aber nun lagen Krümel auf dem Tuch. Und das Messer lag da. Sie fühlte, wie die Kälte der Fliesen langsam an ihr hochkroch. Und sie sah von dem Teller weg.

„Ich dachte, hier wär was", sagte er und sah in der Küche umher.

„Ich habe auch was gehört", antwortete sie und dabei fand sie, daß er nachts im Hemd doch schon recht alt aussah. So alt wie er war. Dreiundsechzig. Tagsüber sah er manchmal jünger aus. Sie sieht doch schon alt aus, dachte er, im Hemd sieht sie doch ziemlich alt aus. Aber das liegt vielleicht an den Haaren. Bei den Frauen liegt das nachts immer an den Haaren. Die machen dann auf einmal so alt.

„Du hättest Schuhe anziehen sollen. So barfuß auf den kalten Fliesen. Du erkältest dich noch."

Sie sah ihn nicht an, weil sie nicht ertragen konnte, daß er log. Daß er log, nachdem sie neununddreißig Jahre verheiratet waren.

„Ich dachte, hier wäre was", sagte er noch einmal und sah wieder so sinnlos von einer Ecke in die andere, „ich hörte hier was. Da dachte ich, hier wäre was."

„Ich hab auch was gehört. Aber es war wohl nichts." Sie stellte den Teller vom Tisch und schnippte die Krümel von der Decke.

„Nein, es war wohl nichts", echote er unsicher.

Sie kam ihm zu Hilfe. „Komm man. Das war wohl draußen. Komm man zu Bett. Du erkältest dich noch. Auf den kalten Fliesen."

Er sah zum Fenster hin. „Ja, das muß wohl draußen gewesen sein. Ich dachte, es wäre hier."

Sie hob die Hand zum Lichtschalter. Ich muß das Licht jetzt ausmachen, sonst muß ich nach dem Teller sehen, dachte sie. Ich darf doch nicht nach dem Teller sehen. „Komm man", sagte sie und machte das Licht aus, „das war wohl draußen. Die

Dachrinne schlägt immer bei Wind gegen die Wand. Es war sicher die Dachrinne. Bei Wind klappert sie immer."

Sie tappten sich beide über den dunklen Korridor zum Schlafzimmer. Ihre nackten Füße platschten auf den Fußboden.

„Wind ist ja", meinte er. „Wind war schon die ganze Nacht."

Als sie im Bett lagen, sagte sie: „Ja, Wind war schon die ganze Nacht. Es war wohl die Dachrinne."

„Ja, ich dachte, es wäre in der Küche. Es war wohl die Dachrinne." Er sagte das, als ob er schon halb im Schlaf wäre.

Aber sie merkte, wie unecht seine Stimme klang, wenn er log.

„Es ist kalt", sagte sie und gähnte leise, „ich krieche unter die Decke. Gute Nacht."

„Nacht", antwortete er und noch: „Ja, kalt ist es schon ganz schön."

Dann war es still. Nach vielen Minuten hörte sie, daß er leise und vorsichtig kaute. Sie atmete absichtlich tief und gleichmäßig, damit er nicht merken sollte, daß sie noch wach war. Aber sein Kauen war so regelmäßig, daß sie davon langsam einschlief.

Als er am nächsten Abend nach Hause kam, schob sie ihm vier Scheiben Brot hin. Sonst hatte er immer nur drei essen können.

„Du kannst ruhig vier essen", sagte sie und ging von der Lampe weg. „Ich kann dieses Brot nicht so recht vertragen. Iß du man eine mehr. Ich vertrag es nicht so gut."

Sie sah, wie er sich über den Teller beugte. Er sah nicht auf. In diesem Augenblick tat er ihr leid.

„Du kannst doch nicht nur zwei Scheiben essen", sagte er auf seinen Teller.

„Doch. Abends vertrag ich das Brot nicht gut. Iß man. Iß man."

Erst nach einer Weile setzte sie sich unter die Lampe an den Tisch.

(published posthumously in 1949)

3. Using context as a clue, determine the meaning of the words below.
   1. überlegen
   2. Atem
   3. verheiratet
   4. ertragen
   5. lügen
   6. horchen nach
   7. Dachrinne
   8. kauen

   a. *to lie*
   b. *breath*
   c. *gutter*
   d. *to chew*
   e. *to listen to*
   f. *married*
   g. *to think about*
   h. *to endure*

A Closer Look

4. Read the story again. As you read, you and your partner will take summarizing notes in English, jotting down the main points under these categories: Actions/Dialogues and Thoughts.

5. Compare your summary chart (**Zusammenstellung**) with those of your classmates. Did you understand, in general, the sequence of events and the thoughts of the woman?

6. What excuse did the woman make up for coming down to the kitchen? Why was she upset with her husband?

7. After they went back to bed, what did she hear? What did she seem to have realized by the next day?

8. From whose perspective is the story told? What is the significance of the title? What is implied about the man's motives, but never stated? What kind of social conditions might give rise to the kind of conflict portrayed in this story?

9. Schau noch einmal auf deine Zusammenstellung und stell fest, was durch die Gedanken der Frau erzählt wurde! Rekonstruiere jetzt die Erzählung aus der Perspektive des Mannes! (Vergiss nicht, Zeitausdrücke, wo nötig, zu verwenden!)

Übungsheft, S. 144

Mehr Grammatikübungen

Erste Stufe

Objectives Reporting past events; asking for, making, and responding to suggestions

1 Ein Bericht aus den Ferien: Schreib die richtigen Partizipien aus dem Kasten in die Lücken. (S. 333)

gefahren	gefallen	gegessen	gelaufen	gelesen
geschwommen	gesehen	gespielt	getrunken	
gewesen	gewohnt			

1. Sag mal, wo bist du denn in den Ferien _____ ? — gewesen
2. Ich bin mit meinen Eltern an die Norsee _____ . — gefahren
3. Das kleine Dorf an der Nordsee hat mir gut _____ . — gefallen
4. Ich bin viel am Strand _____ , und ich habe Tennis _____ . — gelaufen; gespielt
5. An warmen Tagen bin ich in der Nordsee _____ . — geschwommen
6. An schlechten Tagen habe ich Bücher _____ . — gelesen
7. Wir haben in einem schönen Gasthaus _____ . — gewohnt
8. Wir haben viel Fisch _____ und Tee _____ . — gegessen; getrunken
9. Im Hafen haben wir viele Segelschiffe _____ . — gesehen

2 Du möchtest wissen, wo deine Freunde während der Ferien waren. Schreib die folgenden Fragen und Antworten ab, und schreib dabei die richtigen Vergangenheitsformen des Verbs **sein** in die Lücken! (S. 333)

1. Mark, wo _____ du denn in den Ferien? — Ich _____ in den Bergen. warst; war
2. Wie _____ denn das Wetter? — Es _____ eigentlich immer schön. war; war
3. Und ihr beiden, wo _____ ihr denn? — Wir _____ in der Schweiz. wart; waren
4. _____ ihr allein oder mit den Eltern? — Wir _____ mit den Eltern dort. Wart; waren
5. Wo _____ Sie, Herr Strom? — Ich _____ in Bayern beim Wandern. waren; war
6. Weiß jemand, wo der Mark _____ ? — Ich glaube, er _____ in Berlin. war; war

3 Du erzählst, wo verschiedene Freunde gestern waren. Ergänze jeden der folgenden Satzanfänge mit der Information, die in Klammern steht, und mit der richtigen Vergangenheitsform des Verbs **sein**! (S. 333)

1. (Astrid; Tennisplatz)   Die Astrid _____ .   war auf dem Tennisplatz
2. (Andreas; Kraftstudio)   Der Andreas _____ .   war im Kraftstudio
3. (Mark und Uwe; Kino)   Mark und Uwe _____ . waren im Kino
4. (ich; Pizzeria)   Ich _____ .   war in der Pizzeria
5. (wir; Diskothek)   Wir _____ .   waren in der Diskothek
6. (ihr; am Meer)   Ihr _____ , nicht?   wart am Meer

348   dreihundertachtundvierzig   STANDARDS: 1.2   KAPITEL 12   Die Reinickendorfer Clique

4 Du erzählst, was du während der Ferien alles getan hast. Schreib die folgenden Absätze ab, und schreib dabei die richtige Vergangenheitsform des Verbs, das in Klammern steht, in die Lücken! Achte dabei auf die richtige Form von **haben** oder **sein**! (S. 333)

1. (verbringen) Die Sommerferien _____ ich mit den Eltern in Bayern _____ . — habe; verbracht
   (wohnen) Wir _____ in einer Pension in einem kleinen Dorf _____ . — haben; gewohnt
   (wandern) Jeden Tag _____ wir viele Stunden in den Bergen _____. — sind; gewandert
   (bleiben) Bei schlechtem Wetter _____ wir in der Pension _____ , — sind; geblieben
   (spielen) und wir _____ dort mit anderen Besuchern Karten _____ . — haben; gespielt

2. (fahren) Ja, ich _____ mit meinen Freunden an die Nordsee _____ . — bin; gefahren
   (übernachten) Wir _____ dort in einer ganz tollen Jugendherberge _____ , — haben; übernachtet
   (wandern) wir _____ viele Kilometer den Sandstrand entlang _____ und — sind; gewandert
   (schwimmen) wir _____ im kalten Nordseewasser _____ . Am Nachmittag — sind; geschwommen
   (gehen) _____ wir oft in ein kleines Dorf _____ . Das war ganz toll! — sind; gegangen

3. (sein) Ich _____ in den Osterferien bei meinen Großeltern _____ . — bin; gewesen
   (faulenzen) Die meiste Zeit _____ ich in Opas Garten _____ . Manchmal — habe; gefaulenzt
   (helfen) _____ ich meinem Opa im Garten _____ . Einmal in der — habe; geholfen
   (mähen) Woche _____ ich für meinen Opa den Rasen _____ , und ich — habe; gemäht
   (gießen) _____ die vielen Blumen und Sträucher im Garten _____ . — habe; gegossen

4. (besuchen) Meine Schwester _____ unsere Tante in Frankfurt _____ . — hat; besucht
   (sehen) Die Astrid _____ in Frankfurt wirklich sehr viel _____ . Sie — hat; gesehen
   (spazieren) _____ mit meiner Tante durch die Zeil _____ , aber die beiden — ist; spaziert
   (kaufen) _____ nichts _____ . In Frankfurt kann man so viel sehen, — haben; gekauft
   (gefallen) und ich glaube, dass es meiner Schwester gut _____ _____ . — gefallen; hat

5 Du bittest um Vorschläge, und du machst selbst Vorschläge, bestimmte Ferienorte zu besuchen. Schreib die folgenden Fragen und Sätze ab, und schreib dabei die richtige **würde**-Form in die erste Lücke und eine Präposition mit dem richtigen bestimmten Artikel in die zweite! Gebrauche Kurzformen, wenn möglich! (S. 335)

1. Peter, _____ du gern mal _____ Nordsee fahren? — würdest; an die
2. Astrid und Katja, _____ ihr gern mal _____ Schwarzwald fahren? — würdet; in den
3. Wir _____ wirklich gern mal _____ Berge fahren. — würden; in die
4. Und ich _____ gern mal _____ Vereinigten Staaten fliegen. — würde; in die
5. Meine Geschwister _____ gern _____ Küste fahren, _____ Sylt. — würden; an die; nach
6. Und wohin _____ ihr gern fahren? _____ Ostsee vielleicht? — würdet; An die

MEHR GRAMMATIKÜBUNGEN STANDARDS: 1.2 *dreihundertneunundvierzig* **349**

Mehr Grammatikübungen

6 Du schlägst einem Freund verschiedene Ferienorte vor, und er sagt, dass er bald dorthin fahren wird. Schreib die folgenden Fragen und Sätze ab, und schreib dabei die richtigen Präpositionen und, wenn nötig, die richtige Form des bestimmten Artikels (*definite article*) in die Lücken! Gebrauche Kurzformen, wenn möglich! (S. 336)

1. Warst du schon mal _____ Meer? — Ich fahre diesen Sommer _____ Meer.   am; ans
2. Warst du mal _____ Schwarzwald? — Ich fahre heute _____ Schwarzwald.   im; in den
3. Warst du mal _____ Bayern? — Ich fahre im Winter _____ Bayern.   in; nach
4. Warst du mal _____ Bergen? — Ich fahre im Herbst _____ Berge.   in den; in die
5. Warst du mal _____ Ostsee? — Ich fahre in den Ferien _____ Ostsee.   an der; an die
6. Warst du mal _____ Schweiz? — Ich fahre im Frühjahr _____ Schweiz.   in der; in die
7. Warst du schon mal _____ Rhein? — Ich fahre nächste Woche _____ Rhein.   am; an den

7 Wie heißen diese Gerichte? Schreib den Namen des Gerichts in die erste Lücke und woher dieser Gericht kommt in die zweite Lücke. (S. 338)

Das ist ___ , ein ___ Gericht.
Das ist **Couscous**, ein **marokkanisches** Gericht.

1. Das ist ___ , ein ___ Gericht.   Paella; spanisches
2. Das ist ___ , ein ___ Gericht.   Steak; amerikanisches
3. Das sind ___ , ein ___ Gericht.   Tacos; mexikanisches
4. Das sind ___ , ein ___ Gericht.   Fettucine; italienisches
5. Das sind ___ ___ , ein ___ Gericht.   Crêpes Suzette; französisches
6. Das ist ein ___ ___ , ein ___ Gericht.   Wiener Schnitzel; österreichisches

Zweite Stufe

Objectives Ordering food, expressing hearsay and regret; persuading and dissuading

8 Du bist mit Freunden in einem Restaurant. Du empfiehlst erst einem Freund und dann zwei Freunden, gewisse Gerichte zu bestellen. Schreib die folgenden Empfehlungen zweimal ab, und schreib dabei die Befehlsformen des Verbs, das in Klammern steht, in die Lücken! (S. 340)

1. (gehen)	_____ doch einmal griechisch essen!	Geh	Geht
2. (essen)	_____ doch lieber Fisch als Fleisch!	Iss	Esst
3. (bestellen)	_____ doch mal ein Wiener Schnitzel!	Bestell	Bestellt
4. (trinken)	_____ doch ein kühles Spezi dazu!	Trink	Trinkt
5. (geben)	_____ mir doch mal den Kartoffelsalat!	Gib	Gebt
6. (nehmen)	_____ doch noch eine Portion Fleisch!	Nimm	Nehmt
7. (sagen)	_____ mir, was ich hier noch bekommen kann!	Sag	Sagt
8. (vergessen)	_____ nicht, dem Kellner ein Trinkgeld zu geben!	Vergiss	Vergesst

Dritte Stufe

Objectives Asking for and giving advice; expressing preference; expressing interest, disinterest, and indifference

9 Du erzählst, was für Getränke und Gerichte du nicht so gern hast und was du lieber magst. Schreib die folgenden Sätze ab, und schreib dabei die richtige Adjektivendung in die Lücken! (S. 341)

1. Kalt_____ Kaffee schmeckt mir nicht; ich trinke heiß_____ Kaffee lieber.   er; en
2. Alt_____ Brot ist nicht so gut; ich esse frisch_____ Brot viel lieber.   es; es
3. Warm_____ Getränke mag ich nicht; ich habe kalt_____ Getränke lieber.   e; e
4. Mild_____ Käse mag ich nicht so gern, ich habe scharf_____ Käse lieber.   en; en
5. Griechisch_____ Käse schmeckt mir nicht; ich habe deutsch_____ Käse lieber.   er; en
6. Gebraten_____ Fisch schmeckt mir nicht, ich esse gegrillt_____ Fisch lieber.   er; en
7. Roh_____ Schinken mag ich nicht; mir schmeckt gekocht_____ Schinken besser.   en; er
8. Geräuchert_____ Fisch mag ich nicht, mariniert_____ Fisch mag ich lieber.   en; en

10 Du berätst deine Freunde welche Klamotten sie tragen sollen. Schreib die folgenden Sätze ab, und schreib dabei die richtige Adjektivendung in die Lücken! (S. 343)

1. Zieh doch dies_____ blau_____ Pulli an; dies_____ blau_____ Pulli ist schöner!   en; en; er; e
2. Kauf doch dies_____ grün_____ Hemd; dies_____ grün_____ Hemd ist schöner!   es; e; es; e
3. Kauf dies_____ rot_____ Fliege; dies_____ rot_____ Fliege sieht besser aus!   e; e; e; e
4. Nimm dies_____ schwarz_____ Anzug; dies_____ schwarz_____ Anzug ist toll!   en; en; er; e
5. Nimm dies_____ klein_____ Schleife; dies_____ klein_____ Schleife ist schön!   e; e; e; e
6. Kauf dies_____ gelb_____ T-Shirt; dies_____ gelb_____ T-Shirt passt besser!   es; e; es; e
7. Nimm dies_____ braun_____ Schuhe; dies_____ braun_____ Schuhe sind toll!   e; en; e; en
8. Kauf dies_____ blau_____ Smoking; blau_____ Smokings sind in Mode!   en; en; e

Storytelling Book pp. 94–95

Kann ich's wirklich?

WK3 BERLIN-12

Can you report past events? (p. 334)

1 How would you tell a friend what you did yesterday after school? How would you tell someone about the last vacation you enjoyed?
1. E.g.: Gestern nach der Schule habe ich … ; In den letzten Ferien war ich …

Can you ask for, make, and respond to suggestions? (p. 335)

2 How would you ask your father to suggest a place to go on vacation? How would you suggest that you would like to fly to Austria? How could your father respond positively? 2. E.g.: Wo sollen wir in den Ferien hinfahren? Was schlägst du vor?; Ich würde gern mal nach Österreich fliegen.; Eine gute Idee!

3 How would you say that you would like to order a veal cutlet and a glass of mineral water?
3. Ich würde gern ein Wiener Schnitzel und ein Glas Mineralwasser bestellen.

Can you order food, and express hearsay and regret? (p. 339)

4 How would you say that you heard
a. that the French fries are very spicy?   a. Ich habe gehört, die Pommes frites sollen sehr scharf sein.
b. that the shish kebab at "The Slovenia" is excellent?
b. Ich habe gehört, das Schisch-Kebab im „Slovenia" soll ausgezeichnet sein.

5 How would a waiter say that there are no dumplings?
5. Tut mir Leid. Die Klöße sind schon alle.

Can you persuade and dissuade someone? (p. 340)

6 How would you persuade someone to go eat Mexican food? How would a friend dissuade you from eating a salad?
6. Geh doch einmal mexikanisch essen!; Iss ja keinen Salat!

Can you ask for and give advice? (p. 343)

7 How would you ask a friend's advice on what to wear
a. to a birthday party?   a. E.g.: Welche Bluse soll ich mir zur Geburtstagsparty anziehen, die rote oder die blaue?
b. for a day at the beach?
b. E.g.: Welches T-Shirt soll ich für einen Tag am Strand anziehen, das kurze oder das lange?

8 How would you suggest the same things to your friend?
8. Zieh doch die rote Bluse an!; Ich würde das kurze T-Shirt anziehen.

Can you express preference? (p. 343)

9 How would you ask a friend if she prefers
a. the blue blouse or the green one?   a. Welche Bluse findest du schöner, die blaue oder die grüne?
b. the striped pants or the checkered ones?
b. Welche Hose ziehst du vor, die gestreifte oder die karierte?

10 How would you say that
a. you really prefer the brown leather shoes?   a. Mir gefallen eigentlich die braunen Lederschuhe besser.
b. you prefer the T-shirt with the Germany motif?
b. Ich ziehe das T-Shirt mit dem Deutschland-Motiv vor.

Can you express interest, disinterest, and indifference? (p. 344)

11 How would you ask someone what he or she is interested in? How would you say you're interested in colorful clothes, but don't care for sweaters made of wool?
11. Wofür interessierst du dich?; Ich interessiere mich für bunte Klamotten, aber ich interessiere mich nicht für Pullover aus Wolle.

12 How would you say to your friend that it doesn't really matter to you which shoes he or she wears?   12. Es ist mir eigentlich egal, was für Schuhe du trägst.

352   dreihundertzweiundfünfzig   KAPITEL 12   Die Reinickendorfer Clique

Wortschatz

Erste Stufe  p. 325X

Reporting past events

Ich bin gern im Mittelmeer geschwommen.	I enjoyed swimming in the Mediterranean Sea.
Ich habe auch viel gesehen.	I saw a lot, too.

Talking about travel

Ich war (in, an, auf) …	I was (in, at, on) …
die Küste, -n	coast
die Klippe, -n	cliff
die Insel, -n	island
die Bucht, -en	bay
die Oase, -n	oasis
die Sportanlage, -n	sport facility
die Anlage, -n	grounds, site
der Court, -s	court
der Platz, ¨e	place
der Pool, -s	swimming pool
die Halle, -n	hall
das Fahrrad-Depot, -s	bicycle shed
der Flug, ¨e	flight

Other useful words

der Anfänger, -	beginner
der Fortgeschrittene, -n	advanced (person)
der Erfahrene, -n	experienced (person)
der Olympiasieger, -	olympic champion
der Zehnkämpfer, -	decathlete
der Geheimtipp, -s	secret tip
abwechslungsreich	varied, diversified
sich langweilen	to be bored
zahlreich	numerous

Responding to suggestions

Gute Idee!	Good idea!
Das wäre toll!	That would be great!

Zweite Stufe

Talking about international foods

see page 338

Expressing regret

Tut mir Leid, aber der Couscous ist leider schon alle.	Sorry, but unfortunately we're all out of couscous.

Responding to persuasion

Das ist ein guter Vorschlag.	That's a good suggestion.
der Vorschlag, ¨e	suggestion
ungekocht	unboiled

Dritte Stufe

Talking about clothing

gekleidet sein	to be dressed
salopp	casual
elegant	elegant
weit	big, broad
fein	fine, exquisite
der Ringel, -	ringlet
das Muster, -	pattern
das Karo, -s	check, diamonds
der Streifen, -	stripe
das Loch, ¨er	hole
die Schleife, -n	loop, bow
die Fliege, -n	bow tie
die Wildlederjacke, -n	suede jacket
das Abendkleid, -er	evening gown
der Smoking, -s	tuxedo
der Kummerbund, -e	cummerbund
der Lackschuh, -e	patent-leather shoe

Reference Section

- Summary of Functions R2
- Additional Vocabulary R12
- Grammar Summary R20
- German-English Vocabulary R38
- English-German Vocabulary R64
- Grammar Index R78
- Acknowledgments and Credits R83

Summary of Functions

Functions are probably best defined as the ways in which you use a language for specific purposes. When you find yourself in specific situations, such as in a restaurant, in a grocery store, or at school, you will want to communicate with those around you. In order to do that, you have to "function" in the language so that you can be understood: you place an order, make a purchase, or talk about your class schedule.

Such functions form the core of this book. They are easily identified by the boxes in each chapter that are labeled SO SAGT MAN DAS! These functions are the building blocks you need to become a speaker of German. All the other features in the chapter—the grammar, the vocabulary, even the culture notes—are there to support the functions you are learning.

Here is a list of the functions presented in this book and the German expressions you will need in order to communicate in a wide range of situations. Following each function is the chapter and page number where it was introduced.

Socializing

Saying hello
I, Ch. 1, p. 21
    Guten Morgen!
    Guten Tag!
    Morgen!
    Tag!   } *shortened forms*
    Hallo!
    Grüß dich! } *informal*

Saying goodbye
I, Ch. 1, p. 21
    Auf Wiedersehen!
    Wiedersehen! *shortened form*
    Tschüs!
    Tschau! } *informal*
    Bis dann!

Offering something to eat and drink
I, Ch. 3, p. 74
    Was möchtest du trinken?
    Was möchte *(name)* trinken?
    Was möchtet ihr essen?

Responding to an offer
I, Ch. 3, p. 74
    Ich möchte *(beverage)* trinken.
    Er/Sie möchte im Moment gar nichts.
    Wir möchten *(food/beverage)*, bitte.

Saying please
I, Ch. 3, p. 76
    Bitte!

Saying thank you
I, Ch. 3, p. 76
    Danke!
    Danke schön!
    Danke sehr!

Saying you're welcome
I, Ch. 3, p. 76
    Bitte!
    Bitte schön!
    Bitte sehr!

Giving compliments
I, Ch. 5, p. 139
    Der/Die/Das *(thing)* sieht *(adjective)* aus!
    Der/Die/Das *(thing)* gefällt mir.
II, Ch. 8, p. 222
    Dein/Deine *(clothing item)* sieht echt fetzig aus.
    Sie/Er/Es passt dir auch echt gut.
    Und dieser/diese/dieses *(clothing item)* passt dir prima!
    Sie/Er/Es passt gut zu deiner/deinem *(clothing item)*.

Responding to compliments
I, Ch. 5, p. 139
    Ehrlich?
    Wirklich?
    Nicht zu *(adjective)*?
    Meinst du?
II, Ch. 8, p. 222
    Meinst du wirklich?
    Ist er/sie/es mir nicht zu *(adjective)*?

Das ist auch mein/meine Lieblings *(clothing item)*.
Echt?

Starting a conversation
I, Ch. 6, p. 161

Wie geht's?	} *Asking how someone is doing*
Wie geht's denn?	
Sehr gut!	
Prima!	
Danke, gut!	
Gut!	
Danke, es geht.	
So lala.	} *Responding to* **Wie geht's?**
Nicht schlecht.	
Nicht so gut.	
Schlecht.	
Sehr schlecht.	
Miserabel.	

Making plans
I, Ch. 6, p. 166

Was willst du machen?   Ich will *(activity)*.
Wohin will *(person)* gehen?   Er/Sie will in/ins *(place)* gehen.

Ordering food and beverages
I, Ch. 6, p. 170

Was bekommen Sie?   Ich bekomme *(food/beverage)*.

Ja, bitte?
Was essen Sie?   Ein(e)(n) *(food)*, bitte.

Was möchten Sie?   Ich möchte *(food/beverage)*, bitte.

Was trinken Sie?   Ich trinke *(beverage)*.

Was nimmst du?   Ich nehme *(food/beverage)*.

Was isst du?   Ich esse *(food)*.

II, Ch. 11, p. 314

Haben Sie schon gewählt?   Ja, bringen Sie mir bitte den/die/das *(menu item)*.

Und was hätten Sie gern?   Ich hätte gern den/die/das *(menu item)*.

Talking about how something tastes
I, Ch. 6, p. 172

Wie schmeckt's?   Gut!
   Prima!
   Sagenhaft!
   Der/die/das *(food/beverage)* schmeckt lecker!

Schmeckt's?   Der/die/das *(food/beverage)* schmeckt nicht.
   Ja, gut!
   Nein, nicht so gut.
   Nicht besonders.

Paying the check
I, Ch. 6, p. 172

Hallo! Ich will/möchte zahlen.
Stimmt schon!   Das macht (zusammen) *(total)*.

Extending an invitation
I, Ch. 7, p. 194; Ch. 11, p. 313

Willst du *(activity)*?
Wir wollen *(activity)*. Komm doch mit!
Möchtest du mitkommen?
Ich habe am *(day/date)* eine Party. Ich lade dich ein. Kannst du kommen?

Responding to an invitation
I, Ch. 7, p. 194; Ch. 11, p. 313

Ja, gern!	
Toll!	
Ich komme gern mit.	} *accepting*
Aber sicher!	
Natürlich!	
Das geht nicht.	} *declining*
Ich kann leider nicht.	

Expressing obligations
I, Ch. 7, p. 195

Ich habe keine Zeit. Ich muss *(activity)*.

Offering help
I, Ch. 7, p. 199

Was kann ich für dich tun?	
Kann ich etwas für dich tun?	} *asking*
Brauchst du Hilfe?	
Gut! Mach ich!	*agreeing*

Asking what you should do
I, Ch. 8, p. 222

Was soll ich für dich tun?   Du kannst für mich *(chore)*.

Wo soll ich *(thing/things)* kaufen?   Beim (Metzger/Bäcker). In der/Im *(store)*.

Soll ich *(thing/things)* in der/im *(store)* kaufen?   Nein, das kannst du besser in der/im *(store)* kaufen.

Getting someone's attention
I, Ch. 9, p. 250

Verzeihung!
Entschuldigung!

Summary of Functions

Summary of Functions

Offering more
I, Ch. 9, p. 258
   Möchtest du noch etwas?
   Möchtest du noch ein(e)(n) *(food/beverage)*?
   Noch ein(e)(n) *(food/beverage)*?

Saying you want more
I, Ch. 9, p. 258
   Ja, bitte. Ich nehme noch ein(e)(n) *(food/beverage)*.
   Ja, bitte. Noch ein(e)(n) *(food/beverage)*.
   Ja, gern.

Saying you don't want more
I, Ch. 9, p. 258
   Nein, danke! Ich habe keinen Hunger mehr.
   Nein, danke! Ich habe genug.
   Danke, nichts mehr für mich.
   Nein, danke, kein(e)(n) *(food/beverage)* mehr.

Using the telephone
I, Ch. 11, p. 310
   Hier *(name)*.
   Hier ist *(name)*.
   Ich möchte bitte *(name)* sprechen.
   Kann ich bitte *(name)* sprechen?
   Tag! Hier ist *(name)*.
      } *starting a conversation*
   Wiederhören!
   Auf Wiederhören!
   Tschüs!
      } *ending a conversation*

Talking about birthdays
I, Ch. 11, p. 314
   Wann hast du Geburtstag?   Ich habe am *(date)* Geburtstag.
      Am *(date)*.

Expressing good wishes
I, Ch. 11, p. 314
   Alles Gute zu(m)(r)*(occasion)*!
   Herzlichen Glückwunsch zu(m)(r)*(occasion)*!
II, Ch. 11, p. 315
   Zum Wohl!
   Prost!
   Auf dein/euer/Ihr Wohl!
   Guten Appetit!
   Mahlzeit!

Exchanging Information

Asking someone his or her name and giving yours
I, Ch. 1, p. 22
   Wie heißt du?   Ich heiße *(name)*.
   Heißt du *(name)*?   Ja, ich heiße *(name)*.

Asking and giving someone else's name
I, Ch. 1, p. 22
   Wie heißt der Junge?   Der Junge heißt *(name)*.
   Heißt der Junge *(name)*?   Ja, er heißt *(name)*.
   Wie heißt das Mädchen?   Das Mädchen heißt *(name)*.
   Heißt das Mädchen *(name)*?   Nein, sie heißt *(name)*.

Asking and telling who someone is
I, Ch. 1, p. 23
   Wer ist das?   Das ist der/die *(name)*.

Asking someone his or her age and giving yours
I, Ch. 1, p. 25
   Wie alt bist du?   Ich bin *(number)* Jahre alt.
      Ich bin *(number)*.
      (Number).
   Bist du schon *(number)*?   Nein, ich bin *(number)*.

Asking and giving someone else's age
I, Ch. 1, p. 25
   Wie alt ist der Peter?   Er ist *(number)*.
   Und die Monika? Ist sie auch *(number)*?   Ja, sie ist auch *(number)*.

Asking someone where he or she is from and telling where you are from
I, Ch. 1, p. 28
   Woher kommst du?   Ich komme aus *(place)*.
   Woher bist du?   Ich bin aus *(place)*.
   Bist du aus *(place)*?   Nein, ich bin aus *(place)*.

Asking and telling where someone else is from
I, Ch. 1, p. 28
   Woher ist *(person)*?   Er/sie ist aus *(place)*.
   Kommt *(person)* aus *(place)*?   Nein, sie kommt aus *(place)*.

Talking about how someone gets to school
I, Ch. 1, p. 31
   Wie kommst du zur Schule?   Ich komme mit der/dem *(mode of transportation)*.
   Kommt Ahmet zu Fuß zur Schule?   Nein, er kommt auch mit der/dem *(mode of transportation)*.
   Wie kommt Ayla zur Schule?   Sie kommt mit der/dem *(mode of transportation)*.

Talking about interests
I, Ch. 2, p. 48

Was machst du in
deiner Freizeit? — Ich *(activity)*.
Spielst du *(sport/
instrument/game)*? — Ja, ich spiele *(sport/
instrument/game)*.
Nein, *(sport/
instrument/
game)* spiele ich
nicht.
Was macht *(name)*? — Er/Sie spielt *(sport/
instrument/game)*.

Asking about interests
II, Ch. 8, p. 221; Ch. 10, p. 276

Interessierst du dich für *(thing)*?
Wofür interessierst du dich?
Was für Interessen hast du?

Expressing interest
II, Ch. 8, p. 221; Ch. 10, p. 276

Ja, *(thing)* interessiert mich.
Ich interessiere mich für *(thing)*.

Expressing disinterest
II, Ch. 8, p. 221

(Thing) interessiert mich nicht.
Ich hab kein Interesse an *(thing)*.

Expressing indifference
II, Ch. 8, p. 221

(Thing) ist mir egal.

Saying when you do various activities
I, Ch. 2, p. 55

Was machst du nach
der Schule? — Am Nachmittag
(activity).
Am Abend *(activity)*.
Und am Wochenende? — Am Wochenende
(activity).
Was machst du im
Sommer? — Im Sommer *(activity)*.

Talking about where you and others live
I, Ch. 3, p. 73

Wo wohnst du? — Ich wohne in
(place).
In *(place)*.
Wo wohnt der/die *(name)*? — Er/Sie wohnt in
(place).
In *(place)*.

Describing a room
I, Ch. 3, p. 79

Der/Die/Das *(thing)* ist alt.
Der/Die/Das *(thing)* ist kaputt.
Der/Die/Das *(thing)* ist klein, aber ganz bequem.
Ist *(thing)* neu? — Ja, er/sie/es ist neu.

Talking about family members
I, Ch. 3, p. 82

Ist das dein(e)
(family member)? — Ja, das ist mein(e)
(family member).
Und dein(e) *(family
member)*? Wie
heißt er/sie? — Er/Sie heißt *(name)*.
Wo wohnen deine
(family members)? — In *(place)*.

Describing people
I, Ch. 3, p. 84

Wie sieht *(person)* aus? — Er/sie hat *(color)* Haare
und *(color)* Augen.

Talking about class schedules
I, Ch. 4, p. 106

Welche Fächer hast du? — Ich habe *(classes)*.
Was hast du am *(day)*? — *(Classes)*.
Was hat die Katja am *(day)*? — Sie hat *(classes)*.
Welche Fächer habt ihr? — Wir haben
(classes).
Was habt ihr nach der
Pause? — Wir haben
(classes).
Und was habt ihr am
Samstag? — Wir haben frei!

Using a schedule to talk about time
I, Ch. 4, p. 107

Wann hast du *(class)*? — Um *(hour)* Uhr
(minutes).
Was hast du um
(hour) Uhr? — *(Class)*.
Was hast du von *(time)*
bis *(time)*? — Ich habe *(class)*.

Sequencing events
I, Ch. 4, p. 109

Welche Fächer
hast du am *(day)*? — Zuerst hab ich
(class), dann
(class), danach
(class) und
zuletzt *(class)*.

Talking about prices
I, Ch. 4, p. 115

Was kostet *(thing)*? — Er/Sie kostet nur
(price).
Was kosten *(things)*? — Sie kosten *(price)*.
Das ist (ziemlich) teuer!
Das ist (sehr) billig!
Das ist (sehr) preiswert!

Summary of Functions

Pointing things out
I, Ch. 4, p. 116

Wo sind die *(things)*?   Schauen Sie! Dort!
Sie sind dort drüben!
Sie sind da hinten.
Sie sind da vorn.

Expressing wishes when shopping
I, Ch. 5, p. 134

Was möchten Sie?	Ich möchte ein(e)(n) *(thing)* sehen, bitte.
	Ich brauche ein(e)(n) *(thing)*.
Was bekommen Sie?	Ein(e)(n) *(thing)*, bitte.
Haben Sie einen Wunsch?	Ich suche ein(e)(n) *(thing)*.

Describing how clothes fit
I, Ch. 5, p. 137

Es passt prima.
Es passt nicht.

Talking about trying on clothes
I, Ch. 5, p. 143

Ich probiere den/die/das *(item of clothing)* an.
Ich ziehe den/die/das *(item of clothing)* an.

If you buy it:	*If you don't:*
Ich nehme es.	Ich nehme es nicht.
Ich kaufe es.	Ich kaufe es nicht.

Telling time
I, Ch. 6, p. 162

Wie spät ist es jetzt?	Es ist *(time)*.
Wie viel Uhr ist es?	Es ist *(time)*.

Talking about when you do things
I, Ch. 6, p. 162

Wann gehst du *(activity)*?	Um *(time)*.
Um wie viel Uhr *(action)* du?	Um *(time)*.
Und du? Wann *(action)* du?	Um *(time)*.

Talking about how often you do things
I, Ch. 7, p. 198

Wie oft *(action)* du?	(Einmal) in der Woche.
Und wie oft musst du *(action)*?	Jeden Tag.
	Ungefähr (zweimal) im Monat.

Explaining what to do
I, Ch. 7, p. 190

Du kannst für mich *(action)*.

Talking about the weather
I, Ch. 7, p. 203

Wie ist das Wetter heute?	Heute regnet es. Wolkig und kühl.
Wie ist das Wetter morgen?	Sonnig, aber kalt.
Regnet es heute?	Ich glaube schon.
Schneit es am Abend?	Nein, es schneit nicht.
Wie viel Grad haben wir heute?	Ungefähr 10 Grad.

Talking about quantities
I, Ch. 8, p. 226

Wie viel *(food item)* bekommen Sie?	500 Gramm *(food item)*.
	100 Gramm, bitte.

Asking if someone wants anything else
I, Ch. 8, p. 227

Sonst noch etwas?
Was bekommen Sie noch?
Haben Sie noch einen Wunsch?

Saying that you want something else
I, Ch. 8, p. 227

Ich brauche noch ein(e)(n) *(food/beverage/thing)*.
Ich bekomme noch ein(e)(n) *(food/beverage/thing)*.

Telling someone you don't need anything else
I, Ch. 8, p. 227

Nein, danke.
Danke, das ist alles.

Giving a reason
I, Ch. 8, p. 230

Jetzt kann ich nicht, weil …
Es geht nicht, denn …

Saying where you were
I, Ch. 8, p. 231

Wo warst du heute Morgen?	Ich war in/im/an/am *(place)*.
Wo warst du gestern?	Ich war war in/im/an/am *(place)*.

Saying what you bought
I, Ch. 8, p. 231

Was hast du gekauft?	Ich habe *(thing)* gekauft.

Talking about where something is located
I, Ch. 9, p. 250

Verzeihung, wissen Sie, wo der/die/das *(place)* ist?	In der Innenstadt.
	Am *(place name)*.
	In der *(street name)*.

Wo ist der/die/das *(place)*? Es tut mir Leid. Das weiß ich nicht.

Entschuldigung! Weißt du, wo der/die/das *(place)* ist? Keine Ahnung! Ich bin nicht von hier.

Asking for directions
I, Ch. 9, p. 254
 Wie komme ich zu(m)(r) *(place)*?
 Wie kommt man zu(m)(r) *(place)*?
II, Ch. 9, p. 254
 Entschuldigung! Wo ist bitte *(place)*.
 Verzeihung! Wissen Sie vielleicht, wie ich zum/zur *(place)* komme?

Giving directions
I, Ch. 9, p. 254
 Gehen Sie geradeaus bis zu(m)(r) *(place)*.
 Nach rechts/links.
 Hier rechts/links.
II, Ch. 9, p. 254
 Sie biegen hier *(direction)* in die *(streetname)* ein. Dann kommen Sie zum/zur *(place)*.
 Das ist hier *(direction)* um die Ecke.
 Ich weiß es leider nicht. Ich bin nicht von hier.

Talking about what there is to eat and drink
I, Ch. 9, p. 257
 Was gibt es hier
  zu essen? Es gibt *(foods)*.
 Und zu trinken? Es gibt *(beverage)* und auch *(beverage)*.

Talking about what you did in your free time
I, Ch. 10, p. 292
 Was hast du *(time phrase)* gemacht? Ich habe …
  (person/thing) gesehen.
  (book, magazine, etc.) gelesen.
  mit *(person)* über *(subject)* gesprochen.

Discussing gift ideas,
I, Ch. 11, p. 318
 Schenkst du *(person)* ein(e)(n) *(thing)* zu(m)(r) *(occasion)*? Nein, ich schenke ihm/ihr ein(e)(n) *(thing)*.
 Was schenkst du *(person)* zu(m)(r) *(occasion)*? Ich weiß noch nicht. Hast du eine Idee?
 Wem schenkst du den/die/das *(thing)*? Ich schenke *(person)* den/die/das *(thing)*.

Asking about past events
II, Ch. 3, p. 65; Ch. 3, p. 71
 Was hast du *(time phrase)* gemacht?
 Was hat *(person)* *(time phrase)* gemacht?

Asking what someone did
II, Ch. 3, p. 65
 Was hast du *(time phrase)* gemacht?
 Was hat *(person)* *(time phrase)* gemacht?

Telling what someone did
II, Ch. 3, p. 65
 Ich habe *(activity + past participle)*.
 Er/Sie hat *(activity + past participle)*.

Asking where someone was
II, Ch. 3, p. 71
 Wo bist du gewesen?
 Und wo warst du?

Telling where you were
II, Ch. 3, p. 71
 Ich bin in/im/an/am *(place)* gewesen.
 Ich war in/im/an/am *(place)*.
 Ich war mit *(person)* in/im/an/am *(place)*.

Asking for information
II, Ch. 4, p. 107; Ch. 10, p. 284
 Ich habe eine Frage: …?
 Sag mal, …?
 Wie steht's mit *(thing)*?
 Darf ich dich etwas fragen? …?
 Wissen Sie, ob …?
 Können Sie mir sagen, ob …?

Stating information
II, Ch. 10, p. 284
 Ich glaube schon, dass …
 Ich meine doch, dass …

Responding emphatically
II, Ch. 4, p. 107
 Ja, natürlich!
 Na klar!
 Aber sicher!

Agreeing, with reservations
II, Ch. 4, p. 107
 Ja, das kann sein, aber …
 Das stimmt, aber …
 Eigentlich schon, aber …

Asking what someone may or may not do
II, Ch. 4, p. 110
 Was darfst du (nicht) tun?
 Was darfst du (nicht) essen/trinken?
 Darfst du *(activity)*?

Telling what you may or may not do
II, Ch. 4, p. 110
 Ich darf (nicht) *(activity)*.
 Ich darf *(food/drink)* (nicht) essen/trinken.

Expressing skepticism
II, Ch. 5, p. 130
    Was soll denn das sein, dieser/diese/dieses *(thing)*?

Making certain
II, Ch. 5, p. 130
    Du isst nur vegetarisch, was?   Ja/Nein.
    Du isst wohl viel Fleisch, ja?   Nicht unbedingt!
    Du magst Joghurt, oder?   Na klar!
    Du magst doch Quark, nicht wahr?   Sicher!

Calling someone's attention to something and responding
II, Ch. 5, p. 134
    Schau mal!   Ja, was denn?
    Guck mal!   Ja, was bitte?
    Sieh mal!   Was ist denn los?
    Hör mal!   Was ist?
    Hör mal zu!   Was gibt's?

Inquiring about someone's health
II, Ch. 6, p. 157
    Wie fühlst du dich?
    Wie geht es dir?
    Ist dir nicht gut?
    Ist was mit dir?
    Was fehlt dir?

Responding to questions about your health
II, Ch. 6, p. 157
    Ich fühl mich wohl!
    Es geht mir (nicht) gut!
    Mir ist schlecht.
    Mir ist nicht gut.

Responding to statements about someone's health
II, Ch. 6, p. 157
    Ach schade!
    Gute Besserung!
    Hoffentlich geht es dir bald besser!

Asking about pain
II, Ch. 6, p. 163
    Tut's weh?
    Was tut dir weh?
    Tut dir was weh?
    Tut dir *(body part)* weh?

Expressing pain
II, Ch. 6, p. 163
    Au!
    Aua!
    Es tut weh!
    Der/Die/Das *(body part)* tut mir weh.
    Ja, ich hab *(body part)* Schmerzen.

Expressing wishes
II, Ch. 7, p. 192
    Was möchtest du gern mal haben?   Ich möchte gern mal einen/eine/ein *(thing)*!
    Was wünschst du dir mal?   Ich wünsche mir mal …
    Und was wünscht ihr euch?   Wir wünschen uns …

Talking about plans
II, Ch. 10, p. 288
    Ich werde *(activity)*.
    (Time phrase) werde ich *(activity)*.

Expressing hearsay
II, Ch. 11, p. 310
    Ich habe gehört, dass …
    Man hat mir gesagt, dass …
    (Thing) soll *(adjective)* sein.

Expressing Attitudes and Opinions

Asking for an opinion
I, Ch. 2, p. 57; Ch. 9, p. 260
    Wie findest du *(thing/activity/place)*?

Expressing your opinion
I, Ch. 2, p. 57; Ch. 9, p. 260
    Ich finde *(thing/activity/place)* langweilig.
    (Thing/Activity/Place) ist Spitze!
    (Activity) macht Spaß!
    Ich finde es toll, dass …
    Ich glaube, dass …

Agreeing
I, Ch. 2, p. 58
    Ich auch!
    Das finde ich auch!
    Stimmt!
II, Ch. 10, p. 287
    Da stimm ich dir zu!
    Da hast du (bestimmt) recht!
    Einverstanden!

Disagreeing
I, Ch. 2, p. 58
    Ich nicht!
    Das finde ich nicht!
    Stimmt nicht!
II, Ch. 10, p. 287
    Das stimmt (überhaupt) nicht!

Agreeing, with reservations
II, Ch. 7, p. 199
    Ja, schon, aber …

Ja, aber …
Eigentlich schon, aber …
Ja, ich stimme dir zwar zu, aber …

Commenting on clothes
I, Ch. 5, p. 137
Wie findest du den/die/das *(clothing item)*?
Ich finde ihn/sie/es *(adjective)*.
Er/Sie/Es gefällt mir (nicht).

Expressing uncertainty, not knowing
I, Ch. 5, p. 137; Ch. 9, p. 250
Ich bin nicht sicher.
Ich weiß nicht.
Keine Ahnung!

Expressing regret
I, Ch. 9, p. 250
Es tut mir Leid.
II, Ch. 5, p. 129
Ich bedaure, …
Was für ein Pech, …
Leider, …

Downplaying
II, Ch. 5, p. 129
Das macht nichts!
Schon gut!
Nicht so schlimm!
Dann *(action)* ich eben *(alternative)*.
Dann *(action)* ich halt *(alternative)*.

Asking how someone liked something
II, Ch. 3, p. 76
Wie war's?
Wie hat dir Dresden gefallen?
Wie hat es dir gefallen?
Hat es dir gefallen?

Responding enthusiastically
II, Ch. 3, p. 76
Na, prima!
Ja, Spitze!
Das freut mich!

Responding sympathetically
II, Ch. 3, p. 76
Schade!
Tut mir Leid!
Das tut mir aber Leid!

Expressing enthusiasm
II, Ch. 3, p. 76
Phantastisch!
Es war echt super!
Es hat mir gut gefallen.
Wahnsinnig gut!

Expressing disappointment
II, Ch. 3, p. 76
Na ja, soso!
Nicht besonders.
Es hat mir nicht gefallen.
Es war furchtbar!

Expressing approval
II, Ch. 4, p. 100
Es ist prima, dass …
Ich finde es toll, dass …
Ich freue mich, dass …
Ich bin froh, dass …

Expressing disapproval
II, Ch. 4, p. 100
Es ist schade, dass …
Ich finde es nicht gut, dass …

Expressing indecision
II, Ch. 9, p. 245
Was machen wir jetzt?
Was sollen wir bloß machen?

Asking for suggestions
II, Ch. 9, p. 245; Ch. 11, p. 306
Hast du eine Idee?
Was schlägst du vor?
Was sollen wir machen?
Wofür bist du?

Making suggestions
II, Ch. 9, p. 245; Ch. 11, p. 306
Wir können mal *(activity)*.
Ich schlage vor, …
Ich schlage vor, dass …
Ich bin dafür, dass …
Wie wär's mit *(activity/place)*?

Responding to suggestions
II, Ch. 11, p. 306
Das wäre nicht schlecht.

Expressing Feelings and Emotions

Asking about likes and dislikes
I, Ch. 2, p. 50; Ch. 4, p. 110; Ch. 10, p. 282
Was *(action)* du gern?
(Action) du gern?
Magst du *(things/activities)*?
Was für *(things/activities)* magst du?

Expressing likes
I, Ch. 2, p. 50; Ch. 4, p. 110; Ch. 10, p. 282
Ich *(action)* gern.
Ich mag *(things/activities)*.
(Thing/Activities) mag ich (sehr/furchtbar) gern.

Summary of Functions

Expressing dislikes
I, Ch. 2, p. 50; Ch. 10, p. 282
Ich *(action)* nicht so gern.
Ich mag *(things/action)* (überhaupt) nicht.

Talking about favorites
I, Ch. 4, p. 110
Was ist dein
Lieblings*(category)*?
Mein Lieblings*(category)*
ist *(thing)*.

Responding to good news
I, Ch. 4, p. 112
Toll!
Das ist prima!
Nicht schlecht.

Responding to bad news
I, Ch. 4, p. 112
Schade!
So ein Pech!
So ein Mist!
Das ist sehr schlecht!

Expressing familiarity
I, Ch. 10, p. 284
Kennst du
(person/place/thing)?
Ja, sicher!
Ja, klar! or
Nein, den/die/das kenne
ich nicht.
Nein, überhaupt nicht.

Expressing preferences
I, Ch. 10, p. 285
(Siehst) du gern …?
Ja, aber … (sehe) ich
lieber.
Und am liebsten (sehe)
ich …

(Siehst) du lieber …
oder …?
Lieber …

II, Ch. 5, p. 139; Ch. 7, p. 189
Welche *(thing)* magst
du lieber? *(Thing)*
oder *(thing)*?
Welcher/Welche/Welches
(food item) schmeckt
dir besser? *(Food item)*
oder *(food item)*?

(Thing) mag ich lieber.

(Food item) schmeckt
mir besser.

Mir gefällt *(person/
place/thing)* besser als
(person/place/thing).
Ich finde die *(person/
place/thing)* schöner.
Ich ziehe *(person/place/
thing)* vor.

Expressing strong preference and favorites
I, Ch. 10, p. 285
Was (siehst) du am
liebsten?
Am liebsten (sehe) ich …

II, Ch. 5, p. 139
Welches *(thing)* magst
du am liebsten?
Welche *(food item)*
schmeckt dir am besten?
Am liebsten mag
ich *(thing)*.
(Food item) schmeckt
mir am besten.

Expressing hope
II, Ch. 6, p. 168
Ich hoffe, …
Wir hoffen, …
Hoffentlich …

Expressing doubt
II, Ch. 9, p. 249
Ich weiß nicht, ob …
Ich bezweifle, dass …
Ich bin nicht sicher, ob …

Expressing resignation
II, Ch. 9, p. 249
Da kann man nichts machen.
Das ist leider so.

Expressing conviction
II, Ch. 9, p. 249
Du kannst mir glauben: …
Ich bin sicher, dass …

Expressing surprise
II, Ch. 10, p. 287
Das ist ja unglaublich!
(Das ist) nicht möglich!
Das gibt's doch nicht!

PERSUADING

Telling someone what to do
I, Ch. 8, p. 223
Geh bitte *(action)*!
(Thing/Things) holen, bitte!

Making suggestions
II, Ch. 6, p. 158
Möchtest du *(activity)*?
Willst du *(activity)*?
Du kannst für mich *(activity)*.
(Activity) wir mal!
Sollen wir mal *(activity)*?

Asking for advice
II, Ch. 6, p. 167
    Was soll ich machen?
    Was soll ich bloß tun?

Giving advice
II, Ch. 6, p. 167
    Am besten …
    Du musst unbedingt …

Persuading
II, Ch. 8, p. 226
    Warum kaufst du dir keinen/keine/kein *(thing)*?
    Kauf dir doch diesen/diese/diese *(thing)*!
    Trag doch mal etwas *(adjective)*!

Dissuading
II, Ch. 8, p. 226
    Kauf dir ja keinen/keine/kein *(thing)*!
    Trag ja nichts aus *(material)*!

Asking for permission
II, Ch. 10, p. 283
    Darf ich (bitte) *(activity)*?
    Kann ich bitte mal *(activity)*?
    He, du! Lass mich mal *(activity)*!

Giving permission
II, Ch. 10, p. 283
    Ja, natürlich!
    Bitte schön!
    Bitte!
    Gern!

Additional Vocabulary

This list includes additional vocabulary that you may want to use to personalize activities. If you can't find the words you need here, try the German–English and English–German vocabulary sections beginning on page R38 and R64 respectively.

Sport und Interessen
(Sports and Interests)

angeln	to fish
Baseball spielen	to play baseball
Bodybuilding machen	to lift weights
Brettspiele spielen	to play board games
fotografieren	to take photographs
Gewichtheben	lift weights
Handball spielen	to play handball
joggen	to jog
Kajak fahren	to kayak
kochen	to cook
malen	to paint
Münzen sammeln	to collect coins
nähen	to sew
Rad fahren	to ride a bike
reiten	to ride (a horse)
Rollschuh laufen	to roller skate
rudern	to row
schnorcheln	to snorkel
segeln	to sail
Skateboard laufen	to ride a skateboard
Ski laufen	to (snow) ski
stricken	to knit
Tischtennis spielen	to play table tennis
Videospiele spielen	to play video games

Familie *(Family)*

der Halbbruder, ⸚	halfbrother
die Halbschwester, -n	halfsister
der Stiefbruder, ⸚	stepbrother
die Stiefmutter, ⸚	stepmother
die Stiefschwester, -n	stepsister
der Stiefvater, ⸚	stepfather

Zum Diskutieren *(Topics to Discuss)*

die Armut	poverty
die Gesundheit	health
der Präsident	the president
die Politik	politics
die Reklame	advertising
die Umwelt	the environment
das Verbrechen	crime
der Wehrdienst	military service
der Zivildienst	alternate service

Haustiere *(Pets)*

die Eidechse, -n	lizard
der Fisch, -e	fish
der Frosch, ⸚e	frog
der Hamster, -	hamster
der Hase, -n	hare
der Kanarienvogel, ⸚	canary
das Kaninchen, -	rabbit
die Maus, ⸚e	mouse
das Meerschweinchen, -	guinea pig
der Papagei, -en	parrot
das Pferd, -e	horse

die Schildkröte, -n	turtle
die Schlange, -n	snake
das Schwein, -e	pig
der Vogel, ¨	bird

Getränke (Beverages)

die Limo, -s	lemon-flavored drink
ein Glas Milch	a glass of milk
ein Glas Tee	a glass of tea
eine Tasse, -n Kaffee	a cup of coffee

Speisen (Foods)

die Ananas, -	pineapple
der Apfelstrudel, -	apple strudel
die Banane, -n	banana
die Birne, -n	pear
die Bratkartoffeln (pl)	pan-fried potatoes
der Chip, -s	potato chip
das Ei, -er	egg
der Eintopf	stew
die Erdbeere, -n	strawberry
die Erdnussbutter	peanut butter
das Gebäck	baked goods
der gemischte Salat	tossed salad
das Gulasch, -e	gulash
die Gurke, -n	cucumber
die Himbeere, -n	raspberry
der Joghurt	yogurt
die Karotte, -n	carrot
die Magermilch	low-fat milk
die Marmelade, -n	jam, jelly
die Mayonnaise	mayonnaise
die Melone, -n	melon
die Möhre, -n	carrot
das Müsli	muesli (cereal)
die Nuss, ¨e	nut
die Orange, -n	orange
das Plätzchen, -	cookie
die Pommes frites (pl)	french fries
der Pudding, -s	pudding
die Sahne	cream
der Spinat	spinach
die Vollmilch	whole milk
die Zwiebel, -n	onion

Farben (Colors)

beige	beige
bunt	colorful
gepunktet	polka-dotted
gestreift	striped
golden	gold
lila	purple
orange	orange
rosa	pink
silbern	silver
türkis	turquoise

Kleidungsstücke (Clothing)

der Anzug, ¨e	suit
der Badeanzug, ¨e	swimsuit
der Blazer, -	blazer
das Halstuch, ¨er	scarf
der Handschuh, -e	glove
der Hut, ¨e	hat
die Krawatte, -n	tie
der Mantel, ¨	coat
der Minirock, ¨e	miniskirt
die Mütze, -n	cap
der Parka, -s	parka
der Rollkragenpullover, -	turtleneck sweater
die Sandalen (pl)	sandals
der Schal, -s	shawl
die Steghose, -n	stirrup pants
die Strumpfhose, -n	panty hose
die Weste, -n	vest

Stoffe (Materials)

Acryl	acrylic
Kunstfasern	synthetic fibers
Kunstseide	rayon
Nylon	nylon
Polyacryl	acrylic
Polyester	polyester
Viskose	viscose

Fächer (School Subjects)

Algebra	algebra
Band	band
Chemie	chemistry
Chor	chorus
Französisch	French
Hauswirtschaft	home economics
Informatik	computer science
Italienisch	Italian
Japanisch	Japanese
Latein	Latin
Orchester	orchestra
Physik	physics
Russisch	Russian
Spanisch	Spanish
Sozialkunde	social studies
Werken	shop
Wirtschaftskunde	economics

Körperteile (Parts of the body)

das Auge, -n	eye
die Augenbraue, -n	eyebrow
das Augenlid, -er	eyelid
die Faust, ⸚e	fist
die Ferse, -n	heel
das Gesicht, -er	face
der Kiefer, -	jaw
das Kinn, -e	chin
der Nacken, -	neck
der Oberschenkel, -	thigh
die Stirn, -en	forehead
der Unterschenkel, -	shin
die Wade, -n	calf
die Wange, -n	cheek
die Wimper, -n	eyelash

Labels: die Stirn, die Wange, das Kinn, der Oberschenkel, der Unterschenkel

Instrumente (Instruments)

die Blockflöte, -n	recorder
die Bratsche, -n	viola
das Cello (Violoncello), -s	cello
die Flöte, -n	flute
die Geige, -n	violin
die Harfe, -n	harp
die Klarinette, -n	clarinet
der Kontrabass, ⸚e	double bass
die Mandoline, -n	mandolin
die Mundharmonika, -s	harmonica
die Oboe, -n	oboe
die Posaune, -n	trombone
das Saxophon, -e	saxophone
das Schlagzeug, -e	drums
die Trompete, -n	trumpet
die Tuba, (pl) Tuben	tuba

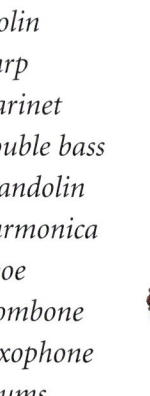
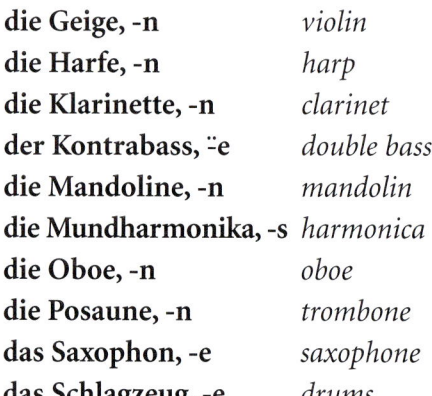

Wetter (Weather)

feucht	damp
gewittrig	stormy
halbbedeckt	partly cloudy
heiter	bright
kühl	cool
neblig	foggy
nieslig	drizzly
trüb	murky
windig	windy

Computer (Computer)

die Anzeige	prompt
das Bedienungsfeld, -er	control panel
der Benutzer, -	user

der Bildschirm, -e	screen
der Browser	browser
CD-ROM	CD-ROM
die CD-ROM	CD-ROM disc
das CD-ROM Laufwerk, -e	CD-ROM drive
der Computer, -	computer

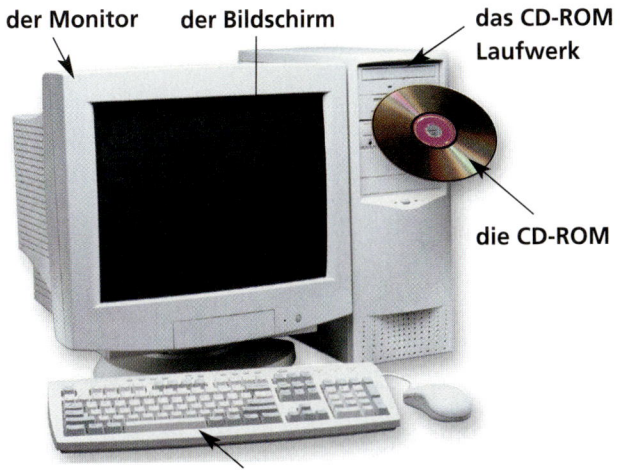

der Monitor — der Bildschirm — das CD-ROM Laufwerk — die CD-ROM — die Tastatur

der Crash	crash
die Datei, -en	(data)file
die Diskette, -n	diskette, floppy disk
die E-Mail	e-mail
die E-Mailadresse	e-mail address
der Cursor	cursor
die Entferntaste, -n	delete key
das Feedback	feedback
die Festplatte, -n	hard drive
die Feststelltaste, -n	caps lock
die Hardware	hardware
die Homepage	homepage
das Internet	internet
das Kennwort, ¨er	password
das Laufwerk, -e	disc drive
das Lesezeichen, -	bookmark
der Link, -s	link
die Löschtaste, -n	delete key
die Maus	mouse

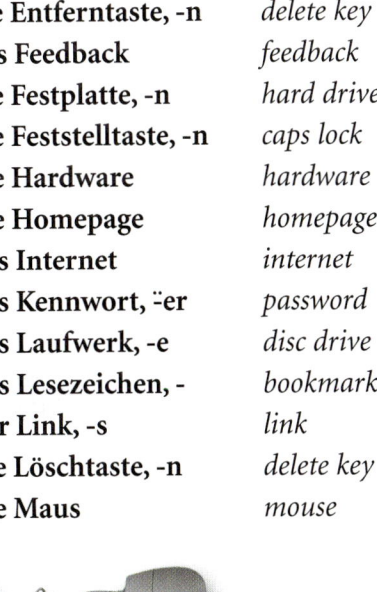

der Mausklick	click
das Modem	modem
der Monitor, -e	monitor
das Netz (das Internet)	internet
das Netzwerk, -e	network
der Papierkorb, ¨e	trash
die Pfeiltaste, -n	arrow key
die Rücktaste, -n	back space
das Schlüsselwort, ¨er	keyword
die Schnittstelle, -n	interface
der Server	server
die Steuerung	control
die Software	software
die Suchmaschine, -n	search engine
das Symbol, -e	icon
der Tabulator	tab
die Textverarbeitung	word processing
die Umschalttaste, -n	shift
das Verzeichnis, -se	directory
die Webpage	Web site
der Zeilenschalter	return key
die Zentraleinheit (auch: der Prozessor)	central processing unit
abbrechen	to cancel/abort
abrufen (die E-Mail abrufen)	to check the e-mail
anklicken	to click
bearbeiten	edit
beenden	to close
bei (auch: at)	at (@)
Bild ⇓ (Bild runter)	page down
Bild ⇑ (Bild rauf)	page up
blättern	to scroll
drucken	to print
drücken auf	to press
eingeben (Daten)	enter (data)
einfügen	to insert
einladen (sep)	to upload
einloggen (sep)	to log on

ADDITIONAL VOCABULARY

Additional Vocabulary

entfernen	to delete
erstellen	to create
formatieren	to format
herunterladen (sep)	to download
kopieren	to copy
löschen	to cancel
neu starten	to reboot, restart
öffnen	to open
online	online
senden	to send
speichern	save
suchen	to search
surfen	to surf
versenden	to post
ziehen (auf ein Symbol)	to drag (to an icon)

Hausarbeit (Housework)

das Auto polieren	to polish the car
das Auto waschen	to wash the car
den Fußboden kehren	to sweep the floor
den Müll wegtragen	to take out the trash
putzen	to clean
Staub wischen	to dust
sauber machen	to clean
die Wäsche waschen	to do the laundry
trocknen	to dry
aufhängen	to hang
zusammenlegen	to fold
bügeln	to iron
einräumen	to put away

Fernsehen (Television)

der Abenteuerfilm, -e	adventure film
die Familiensendung, -en	family program
die Komödie, -n	comedy
der Kriminalfilm, -e	detective film
das Lustspiel, -e	comedy
die Sendung, -en (über Gesundheit)	program (about health)
die Spielshow, -s	game show
die Talkshow, -s	talk show
die Tiersendung, -en	animal program
der Wildwestfilm, -e	western
die Werbesendung, -en	commercial, advertisement

Möbel (Furniture)

das Bett, -en	bed
das Bild, -er	picture
der Computer, -	computer
die Couch, -s or -en	couch
der Kleiderschrank, ⸚	wardrobe
die Kommode, -n	chest of drawers
die Lampe, -n	lamp
der Nachttisch, -e	night stand
das Regal, -e	bookshelf
der Sessel, -	armchair
der Schreibtisch, -e	desk
das Sofa, -s	sofa
der Stuhl, ⸚e	chair
der Teppich, -e	carpet, rug
der Tisch, -e	table
der Vorhang, ⸚e	curtain

In der Stadt (Places around Town)

die Brücke, -n	bridge
die Bücherei, -en	library
die Diskothek, -en	dance club
der Flughafen, (pl) Flughäfen	airport
das Fremdenverkehrsamt, ⸚er	tourist office
der Frisiersalon, -s	beauty shop
das Krankenhaus, ⸚er	hospital
der Kreis, -e	district; county
die Minigolfanlage, -n	mini-golf course
der Park, -s	park
die Polizei	police station
das Stadion, (pl) Stadien	stadium

der Stadtrand	outskirts
der Stadtteil, -e	urban district

das Stadtzentrum, (pl) Stadtzentren	downtown
der Tennisplatz, ⸚e	tennis court
der Zoo, -s	zoo

Kulturelle Veranstaltungen (Cultural Events)

die Ausstellung, -en	exhibit
das Chorkonzert, -e	choir concert
das Kabarett, -e	cabaret
das Symphoniekonzert, -e	symphony
der Zirkus	circus

Geographische Adjektive (Geographic Adjectives)

amerikanisch	American
ägyptisch	Egyptian
chinesisch	Chinese
deutsch	German
englisch	English
französisch	French
griechisch	Greek
indisch	Indian
italienisch	Italian
japanisch	Japanese
mexikanisch	Mexican
österreichisch	Austrian
polnisch	Polish
russisch	Russian
Schweizer	Swiss
spanisch	Spanisch
türkisch	Turkish

Geschenkideen (Gift Ideas)

das Bild, -er	picture
die Kette, -n	chain, necklace
der Ohrring, -e	earring
die Puppe, -n	doll
das Puppenhaus, ⸚er	dollhouse
der Ring, -e	ring
aus Silber	made of silver
aus Gold	made of gold
die Schokolade	chocolate
das Spielzeug, -e	toy

Auto (Automobiles)

die Alarmanlage, -n	alarm system
die Alufelge, -n	aluminum rims, mag wheels
der Aufkleber, -	(bumper) sticker
die Automatik, -en	automatic transmission
die Lautsprecherbox, -en	speaker

das 5-Gang Getriebe	five-speed (standard) transmission
das Kabriolett, -s	convertible
der Kassettenspieler	cassette player
der Kombiwagen, -	station wagon
der Rallyestreifen, -	racing stripes
die Servolenkung, -en	power steering
die Servobremsen (pl)	power brakes
der Sitzschoner, -	seat cover
das Stereo-Radio, -s	stereo
die Zentralverriegelung, -en	automatic locks

ADDITIONAL VOCABULARY

ERDKUNDE (GEOGRAPHY)

Here are some terms you will find on German-language maps:

Länder (States)

Most of the states in the United States (**die Vereinigten Staaten**) have the same spelling in German that they have in English. Listed below are those states that have a different spelling.

Kalifornien	*California*
Neumexiko	*New Mexico*
Nordkarolina	*North Carolina*
Norddakota	*North Dakota*
Südkarolina	*South Carolina*
Süddakota	*South Dakota*

Staaten (Countries)

Ägypten	*Egypt*
Argentinien	*Argentina*
Brasilien	*Brazil*
China	*China*
England	*England*
Frankreich	*France*
Griechenland	*Greece*
Indien	*India*
Indonesien	*Indonesia*
Italien	*Italy*
Japan	*Japan*
Kanada	*Canada*
Mexiko	*Mexico*
Polen	*Poland*
Russland	*Russia*
Spanien	*Spain*
Türkei	*Turkey*
die Vereinigten Staaten	*The United States*

Kontinente (Continents)

Afrika	*Africa*
die Antarktis	*Antarctica*
Asien	*Asia*
Australien	*Australia*
Europa	*Europe*
Nordamerika	*North America*
Südamerika	*South America*

Meere (Bodies of Water)

der Atlantik	*the Atlantic*
der Golf von Mexiko	*the Gulf of Mexico*
der Indische Ozean	*the Indian Ocean*
das Mittelmeer	*the Mediterranean*
der Pazifik	*the Pacific*
das Rote Meer	*the Red Sea*
das Schwarze Meer	*the Black Sea*

Geographical terms

der Breitengrad	*latitude*
die Ebene, -n	*plain*
der Fluss, ¨e	*river*
das ... Gebirge	*the ... mountains*
die Grenze, -n	*border*
die Hauptstadt, ¨e	*capital*
der Kontinent, -e	*continent*
das Land, ¨er	*state*
der Längengrad	*longitude*
das Meer, -e	*ocean, sea*
der Nordpol	*the North Pole*
der See, -n	*lake*
der Staat, -en	*country*
der Südpol	*the South Pole*
das Tal, ¨er	*valley*

DEUTSCHE NAMEN (GERMAN NAMES)

Here are some names that you will hear when you visit a German-speaking country.

Mädchen (girls)

Andrea
Angela, Angelika
Anja
Anna/Anne
Anneliese
Annette
Antje
Barbara
Bärbel
Beate
Birgit
Brigitte
Britta
Christa
Christiane
Christine
Claudia
Connie
Cordula
Danielle
Dorothea
Dorothee
Elfriede
Elisabeth (Lisa)
Elke
Erika
Eva
Gabriele (Gabi)
Gertrud (Trudi(e))
Gisela
Grete
Gudrun
Hannelore
Heidi/Heidemarie
Heike
Helga
Hilde
Hildegard
Ilse
Ina
Inge
Ingrid
Irmgard
Jennifer
Julie
Jutta
Karin
Katharina
Katja
Katrin
Kirstin
Liselotte (Lotte)
Marie
Marta
Martina
Meike
Michaela
Monika
Nicole
Petra
Regina
Renate
Roswitha
Rotraud
Sabine
Sara
Silke
Simone
Sonja
Stephanie
Susanne
Susie
Silvia
Tanja
Ulrike (Uli)
Ursel
Ursula (Uschi)
Ute
Veronika
Waltraud

Jungen (boys)

Adam
Alexander
Andreas
Axel
Bastian
Bernd(t)
Bernhard
Bruno
Christian
Christoph
Daniel
David
Detlev
Dieter
Dietmar
Dirk
Eberhard
Erik
Felix
Frank
Franz
Friedrich
Fritz
Georg
Gerd
Gerhard
Gottfried
Gregor
Günter
Gustav
Hannes
Hans
Hans-Georg
Hans-Jürgen
Harald
Hartmut
Hauke
Heinrich
Heinz
Heinz-Dieter
Helmar
Helmut
Ingo
Jan
Jens
Joachim
Jochen
Johann
Johannes
Jörg
Josef
Jürgen
Karl
Karl-Heinz
Klaus
Konrad
Kurt
Lars
Lothar
Lutz
Manfred
Markus
Martin
Mathias
Max
Michael
Norbert
Oskar
Otto
Patrick
Paul
Peter
Philipp
Rainer (Reiner)
Ralf
Reinhard
Reinhold
Robert
Rolf
Rudi
Rüdiger
Rudolf
Sebastian
Stefan (Stephan)
Thomas
Udo
Ulf
Ulrich (Uli)
Uwe
Volker
Werner
Wilhelm (Willi)
Wolfgang

Grammar Summary

NOUNS AND THEIR MODIFIERS

In German, nouns (words that name a person, place, or thing) are grouped into three classes or genders: masculine, feminine, and neuter. All nouns, both persons and objects, fall into one of these groups. There are words used with nouns that signal the class of the noun. One of these is the definite article. In English there is one definite article: *the*. In German, there are three, one for each class: **der, die,** and **das**.

THE DEFINITE ARTICLE

SUMMARY OF DEFINITE ARTICLES

	Nominative	Accusative	Dative
Masculine	der	den	dem
Feminine	die	die	der
Neuter	das	das	dem
Plural	die	die	den

When the definite article is used with a noun, a noun phrase is formed. Noun phrases that are used as subjects are in the nominative case. Nouns that are used as direct objects or the objects of certain prepositions (such as **für**) are in the accusative case. Nouns that are indirect objects, the objects of certain prepositions (such as **mit, bei**), or the objects of special verbs (see page R30) are in the dative case. Below is a summary of the definite articles combined with nouns to form noun phrases.

SUMMARY OF NOUN PHRASES

	Nominative	Accusative	Dative
Masculine	der Vater der Ball	den Vater den Ball	dem Vater dem Ball
Feminine	die Mutter die Kassette	die Mutter die Kassette	der Mutter der Kassette
Neuter	das Mädchen das Haus	das Mädchen das Haus	dem Mädchen dem Haus
Plural	die Kassetten die Häuser	die Kassetten die Häuser	den Kassetten den Häusern

DIESER-WORDS

The determiners **dieser, jeder, welcher,** and **alle** are called **dieser**-words. Their endings are similar to those of the definite articles. Note that the endings of the **dieser**-words are very similar to the definite articles.

SUMMARY OF DIESER-WORDS

dieser	this, that, these
jeder	each, every
alle	all
welcher	which, what

	Nominative			Accusative			Dative		
Masculine	dieser	jeder	welcher	diesen	jeden	welchen	diesem	jedem	welchem
Feminine	diese	jede	welche	diese	jede	welche	dieser	jeder	welcher
Neuter	dieses	jedes	welches	dieses	jedes	welches	diesem	jedem	welchem
Plural	diese	alle	welche	diese	alle	welche	diesen	allen	welchen

THE INDEFINITE ARTICLE

Another type of word that is used with nouns is the *indefinite article*: **ein, eine, ein** in German, *a, an* in English. There is no plural form of **ein**.

SUMMARY OF INDEFINITE ARTICLES

	Nominative	Accusative	Dative
Masculine	ein	einen	einem
Feminine	eine	eine	einer
Neuter	ein	ein	einem
Plural	—	—	—

THE NEGATING WORD KEIN

The word **kein** is also used with nouns and means *no, not,* or *not any*. Unlike the **ein-** words, **kein** has a plural form.

	Nominative	Accusative	Dative
Masculine	kein	keinen	keinem
Feminine	keine	keine	keiner
Neuter	kein	kein	keinem
Plural	keine	keine	keinen

THE POSSESSIVES

These words also modify nouns and tell you *whose* object or person is being referred to (*my* car, *his* book, *her* mother). These words have the same endings as **kein**.

SUMMARY OF POSSESSIVES

	Before Masculine Nouns			Before Feminine Nouns		Before Neuter Nouns		Before Plural Nouns	
	Nom	Acc	Dat	Nom & Acc	Dat	Nom & Acc	Dat	Nom & Acc	Dat
my	mein	meinen	meinem	meine	meiner	mein	meinem	meine	meinen
your	dein	deinen	deinem	deine	deiner	dein	deinem	deine	deinen
his	sein	seinen	seinem	seine	seiner	sein	seinem	seine	seinen
her	ihr	ihren	ihrem	ihre	ihrer	ihr	ihrem	ihre	ihren
our	unser	unseren	unserem	usere	unserer	unser	unserem	unsere	unseren
your	euer	eueren	euerem	euere	euerer	euer	euerem	euere	eueren
their	ihr	ihren	ihrem	ihre	ihrer	ihr	ihrem	ihre	ihren
your	Ihr	Ihren	Ihrem	Ihre	Ihrer	Ihr	Ihrem	Ihre	Ihren

Commonly used short forms for **unseren**: unsren *or* unsern   *for* **unsere**: unsre
                   eueren: euren *or* euern   **euere**: eure
           for **unserem**: unsrem *or* unserm   *for* **unserer**: unsrer
                 euerem: eurem *or* euerm   **euerer**: eurer

NOUN PLURALS

Noun class and plural forms are not always predictable. Therefore, you must learn each noun together with its article (**der, die, das**) and with its plural form. As you learn more nouns, however, you will discover certain patterns. Although there are always exceptions to these patterns, you may find them helpful in remembering the plural forms of many nouns.

Most German nouns form their plurals in one of two ways: some nouns add endings in the plural; some add endings and/or change the sound of the stem vowel in the plural, indicating the sound change with the umlaut (¨). Only the vowels **a, o, u**, and the diphthong **au** can take the umlaut. If a noun has an umlaut in the singular, it keeps the umlaut in the plural. Most German nouns fit into one of the following five plural groups.

1. Nouns that do not have any ending in the plural. Sometimes they take an umlaut.
   NOTE: There are only two feminine nouns in this group: **die Mutter** and **die Tochter**.

der Bruder, die Brüder	**der Schüler, die Schüler**	**das Fräulein, die Fräulein**
der Lehrer, die Lehrer	**der Vater, die Väter**	**das Mädchen, die Mädchen**
der Onkel, die Onkel	**die Mutter, die Mütter**	**das Poster, die Poster**
der Mantel, die Mäntel	**die Tochter, die Töchter**	**das Zimmer, die Zimmer**

2. Nouns that add the ending **-e** in the plural. Sometimes they also take an umlaut.
   NOTE: There are many one-syllable words in this group.

der Bleistift, die Bleistifte	**der Sohn, die Söhne**	**das Jahr, die Jahre**
der Freund, die Freunde	**die Stadt, die Städte**	**das Spiel, die Spiele**

3. Nouns that add the ending **-er** in the plural. Whenever possible, they take an umlaut, i.e., when the noun contains the vowels **a, o**, or **u**, or the diphthong **au**. **NOTE:** There are no feminine nouns in this group. There are many one-syllable words in this group.

das Buch, die Bücher	**das Haus, die Häuser**
das Fach, die Fächer	**das Land, die Länder**

4. Nouns that add the ending **-en** or **-n** in the plural. These nouns never add an umlaut.
   NOTE: There are many feminine nouns in this group.

der Herr, die Herren	**die Klasse, die Klassen**	**die Tante, die Tanten**
der Junge, die Jungen	**die Karte, die Karten**	**die Wohnung, die Wohnungen**
die Briefmarke, die Briefmarken	**der Name, die Namen**	**die Zahl, die Zahlen**
die Familie, die Familien	**der Vetter, die Vettern**	**die Zeitung, die Zeitungen**
die Farbe, die Farben	**die Küche, die Küchen**	
die Frau, die Frauen	**die Schwester, die Schwestern**	

   Feminine nouns ending in **-in** add the ending **-nen** in the plural.

die Freundin, die Freundinnen	**die Verkäuferin, die Verkäuferinnen**
die Lehrerin, die Lehrerinnen	

5. Nouns that add the ending **-s** in the plural. These nouns never add an umlaut.
   NOTE: There are many words of foreign origin in this group.

der Kuli, die Kulis	**das Auto, die Autos**
die Kamera, die Kameras	**das Hobby, die Hobbys**

SUMMARY OF PLURAL ENDINGS

Group	1	2	3	4	5
Ending:	-	-e	-er	-(e)n	-s
Umlaut:	sometimes	sometimes	always	never	never

PRONOUNS

PERSONAL PRONOUNS | REFLEXIVE

	Nominative	Accusative	Dative	Accusative	Dative
Singular					
1st person	ich	mich	mir	mich	mir
2nd person	du	dich	dir	dich	dir
3rd person m.	er	ihn	ihm	sich	sich
3rd person f.	sie	sie	ihr	sich	sich
3rd person n.	es	es	ihm	sich	sich
Plural					
1st person	wir	uns	uns	uns	uns
2nd person	ihr	euch	euch	euch	euch
3rd person	sie	sie	ihnen	sich	sich
you (formal, sing. & pl.)	Sie	Sie	Ihnen	sich	sich

DEFINITE ARTICLES AS DEMONSTRATIVE PRONOUNS

The definite articles can be used as demonstrative pronouns, giving more emphasis to the sentences than the personal pronouns **er, sie, es.** Note that these demonstrative pronouns have the same forms as the definite articles: An exception is **denen**.

Wer bekommt *den* Cappuccino? *Der* ist für mich.

	Nominative	Accusative	Dative
Masculine	der	den	dem
Feminine	die	die	der
Neuter	das	das	dem
Plural	die	die	denen

INTERROGATIVES

INTERROGATIVE PRONOUNS

	People	Things
Nominative	**wer?** *who?*	**was?** *what?*
Accusative	**wen?** *whom?*	**was?** *what?*
Dative	**wem?** *to, for whom?*	

OTHER INTERROGATIVES

wann? *when?* **warum?** *why?* **wie?** *how?* **wie viel?** *how much? how many?*	**wie viele?** *how many?* **wo?** *where?* **woher?** *from where?* **wohin?** *to where?*	**welche?** *which?* **was für (ein)?** *what kind of (a)?*

PREPOSITIONS

Accusative	durch, für, gegen, ohne, um
Dative	aus, bei, mit, nach, seit, von, zu, gegenüber

Two-Way:
    *Dative–**wo?***
    *Accusative–**wohin?***
	an, auf, hinter, in, neben, über, unter, vor, zwischen

WORD ORDER

POSITION OF VERBS IN A SENTENCE

*The conjugated verb is in **first** position in:*	yes/no questions (questions that do not begin with an interrogative)
	   Trinkst du Kaffee?
	   Spielst du Tennis?
	   Möchtest du ins Konzert gehen?
	
	both formal and informal commands
	   Kommen Sie bitte um 2 Uhr!
	   Geh doch mit ins Kino!

*The conjugated verb is in **second** position in:*	statements with normal word order
	   Wir spielen heute Volleyball.
	statements with inverted word order
	   Heute spielen wir Volleyball.
	questions that begin with an interrogative
	   Wohin gehst du?
	   Woher kommst du?
	   Was macht er?
	sentences connected by **und, oder, aber, denn**
	   Ich komme nicht, denn ich habe keine Zeit.

*The conjugated verb is in **second** position and the infinitive or past participle is **final** in:*	statements with modals
	   Ich möchte heute ins Kino gehen.
	statements in conversational past
	   Ich habe das Buch gelesen.
	statements with **werde** and **würde**
	   Ich werde im Mai nach Berlin fliegen.
	   Die Oma würde gern ins Theater gehen.

*The conjugated verb is in **final** position in:*	clauses that begin with interrogatives (**wo, wann, warum,** etc.)
	   Ich weiß, wo das Hotel ist.
	   Ich weiß nicht, wer heute Morgen angerufen hat.
	clauses that begin with **weil, dass,** or **ob**
	   Ich gehe nicht ins Kino, weil ich kein Geld habe.
	   Ich glaube, dass er Rockmusik gern hört.
	   Ich komme morgen nicht, weil ich zu Hause helfen muss.
	   Ich weiß nicht, ob er den Film schon gesehen hat.

POSITION OF NICHT IN A SENTENCE

To negate the entire sentence, as close to end of sentence as possible:	Er fragt seinen Vater	nicht.	
Before a separable prefix:	Ich rufe ihn	nicht	an.
Before any part of a sentence you want to negate, contrast, or emphasize:	Er kommt	nicht	heute. (Er kommt morgen.)
Before part of a sentence that answers the questions *wo?*	Ich wohne	nicht	in Berlin.

ADJECTIVES

ENDINGS OF ADJECTIVES AFTER DER- AND DIESER- WORDS

	Nominative	Accusative	Dative
Masculine	der -e Vorort	den -en Vorort	dem -en Vorort
Feminine	die -e Stadt	die -e Stadt	der -en Stadt
Neuter	das -e Dorf	das -e Dorf	dem -en Dorf
Plural	die -en Vororte	die -en Vororte	den -en Vororten

NOTE: Names of cities used as adjectives always have the ending **-er: der Frankfurter Zoo, das Münchner Oktoberfest**

ENDINGS OF ADJECTIVES AFTER EIN

	Nominative	Accusative	Dative
Masculine	ein -er Vorort	einen -en Vorort	einem -en Vorort
Feminine	eine -e Stadt	eine -e Stadt	einer -en Stadt
Neuter	ein -es Dorf	ein -es Dorf	einem -en Dorf

ENDINGS OF ADJECTIVES AFTER KEIN AND THE POSSESSIVES

	Nominative	Accusative	Dative
Masculine	kein -er Vorort	keinen -en Vorort	keinem -en Vorort
Feminine	keine -e Stadt	keine -e Stadt	keiner -en Stadt
Neuter	kein -es Dorf	kein -es Dorf	keinem -en Dorf
Plural	keine -en Vororte	keine -en Vororte	keinen -en Vororten

ENDINGS OF UNPRECEDED ADJECTIVES

	Nominative	Accusative	Dative
Masculine	-er Salat	-en Salat	-em Salat
Feminine	-e Suppe	-e Suppe	-er Suppe
Neuter	-es Eis	-es Eis	-em Eis
Plural	-e Getränke	-e Getränke	-en Getränken

MAKING COMPARISONS

	Positive	Comparative
1. All comparative forms end in -**er.**	schnell	schneller
2. Most one-syllable forms have an umlaut.	alt	älter
3. Exceptions must be learned as they appear.	dunkel gut	dunkler besser

Equal Comparisons:	Er spielt **so gut wie** ich (spiele). *He plays as well as I (do).*
Unequal Comparisons:	Sie spielt **besser als** ich (spiele). *She plays better than I (do).*
Comparative adjectives before nouns:	der **bessere** Wagen ein **schöneres** Auto

NOTE: Comparative adjectives before nouns have the same endings as descriptive adjectives (see page R27).

VERBS

PRESENT TENSE VERB FORMS

		Regular	-eln Verbs	Stem Ending with t/d	Stem Ending with s/ß
INFINITIVES		spiel -en	bastel -n	find -en	heiß -en
PRONOUNS		stem + ending	stem + ending	stem + ending	stem + ending
I	ich	spiel -e	bastl -e	find -e	heiß -e
you	du	spiel -st	bastel -st	find -est	heiß -t
he she it	er sie es	spiel -t	bastel -t	find -et	heiß -t
we	wir	spiel -en	bastel -n	find -en	heiß -en
you (plural)	ihr	spiel -t	bastel -t	find -et	heiß -t
they	sie	spiel -en	bastel -n	find -en	heiß -en
you (formal)	Sie	spiel -en	bastel -n	find -en	heiß -en

NOTE: There are important differences between the verbs in the above chart:

1. Verbs ending in -eln (**basteln, segeln**) drop the **e** of the ending -eln in the **ich**-form: **ich bastle, ich segle** and add only -n in the **wir-, sie-,** and **Sie**-forms. These forms are always identical to the infinitive: **basteln, wir basteln, sie basteln, Sie basteln.** Verbs ending in -ern (**wandern**) sometimes drop the **e** of the ending -ern in the **ich**-form: **ich wandre** and add only -n in the **wir-, sie-,** and **Sie**-forms. These forms are always identical to the infinitive: **wandern.**

2. Verbs with a stem ending in **d** or **t**, such as **finden,** add an **e** before the ending in the **du**-form (**du findest**) and the **er**- and **ihr**-forms (**er findet, ihr findet**).

3. All verbs with stems ending in an **s**-sound (**heißen**) add only -t in the **du**-form: **du heißt.**

VERBS WITH A STEM-VOWEL CHANGE

There are a number of verbs in German that change their stem vowel in the **du**- and **er/sie**-forms. A few verbs, such as **nehmen** (*to take*), have a change in the consonant as well. You cannot predict these verbs, so it is best to learn each one individually. They are usually irregular only in the **du**- and **er/sie**- forms.

	e → i			e → ie		a → ä	
	essen	geben	nehmen	lesen	sehen	fahren	einladen
ich	esse	gebe	nehme	lese	sehe	fahre	lade ein
du	isst	gibst	nimmst	liest	siehst	fährst	lädst ein
er, sie	isst	gibt	nimmt	liest	sieht	fährt	lädt ein
wir	essen	geben	nehmen	lesen	sehen	fahren	laden ein
ihr	esst	gebt	nehmt	lest	seht	fahrt	ladet ein
sie	essen	geben	nehmen	lesen	sehen	fahren	laden ein
Sie	essen	geben	nehmen	lesen	sehen	fahren	laden ein

SOME IMPORTANT IRREGULAR VERBS: HABEN, SEIN, WISSEN, AND WERDEN

	haben	sein	wissen	werden
ich	habe	bin	weiß	werde
du	hast	bist	weißt	wirst
er, sie	hat	ist	weiß	wird
wir	haben	sind	wissen	werden
ihr	habt	seid	wisst	werdet
sie	haben	sind	wissen	werden
Sie	haben	sind	wissen	werden

VERBS FOLLOWED BY AN OBJECT IN THE DATIVE CASE

antworten, *to answer*	**gratulieren,** *to congratulate*
danken, *to thank*	**helfen,** *to help*
gefallen, *to like*	**passen,** *to fit*
glauben, *to believe*	

Es geht (mir) gut.	Es steht (dir) gut.
Es schmeckt (mir) nicht.	Es macht (mir) Spaß.
Es tut (mir) Leid.	Es tut (mir) weh.
Was fehlt (dir)?	

MODAL (AUXILIARY) VERBS

The verbs **dürfen, können, müssen, sollen, wollen, mögen** (and the **möchte**-forms) are usually used with an infinitive at the end of the sentence. If the meaning of that infinitive is clear, it can be left out: **Du musst sofort nach Hause!** (**Gehen** is understood and omitted.)

	dürfen	können	müssen	sollen	wollen	mögen	möchte
ich	darf	kann	muss	soll	will	mag	möchte
du	darfst	kannst	musst	sollst	willst	magst	möchtest
er, sie	darf	kann	muss	soll	will	mag	möchte
wir	dürfen	können	müssen	sollen	wollen	mögen	möchten
ihr	dürft	könnt	müsst	sollt	wollt	mögt	möchtet
sie	dürfen	können	müssen	sollen	wollen	mögen	möchten
Sie	dürfen	können	müssen	sollen	wollen	mögen	möchten

VERBS WITH SEPARABLE PREFIXES

Some verbs have separable prefixes: prefixes that separate from the conjugated verbs and are moved to the end of the sentence.

	Infinitive: aussehen
ich sehe ... aus	Ich sehe heute aber sehr schick aus!
du siehst ... aus	Du siehst heute sehr fesch aus!
er/sie/es sieht ... aus	Sieht sie immer so modern aus?
	Sieht dein Zimmer immer so unordentlich aus?
wir sehen ... aus	Wir sehen heute sehr lustig aus.
ihr seht ... aus	Ihr seht alle so traurig aus.
sie sehen ... aus	Sie sehen sehr schön aus.
Sie sehen ... aus	Sie sehen immer so ernst aus.

Here are the separable-prefix verbs you learned in Level 1 and Level 2.

abheben	aufräumen	fernsehen	weggeben
abräumen	ausgehen	herausnehmen	wegtragen
anprobieren	aussehen	mitkommen	wegwerfen
anrufen	einkaufen	vorschlagen	wehtun
anziehen	einladen	vorziehen	zustimmen
auflegen	einstecken		

COMMAND FORMS

Regular Verbs	gehen	spielen
Persons you address with **du** (singular)	Geh!	Spiel!
with **ihr** (plural)	Geht!	Spielt!
with **Sie** (sing & pl)	Gehen Sie!	Spielen Sie!
"let's" form	Gehen wir!	Spielen wir!

Separable-prefix Verbs	mitkommen	anrufen	aufräumen	anziehen	ausgehen
	Komm mit!	Ruf an!	Räum auf!	Zieh an!	Geh aus!
	Kommt mit!	Ruft an!	Räumt auf!	Zieht an!	Geht aus!
	Kommen Sie mit!	Rufen Sie an!	Räumen Sie auf!	Ziehen Sie an!	Gehen Sie aus!
	Kommen wir mit!	Rufen wir an!	Räumen wir auf!	Ziehen wir an!	Gehen wir aus!

Stem-changing Verbs	essen	nehmen	geben	sehen	fahren
	Iss!	Nimm!	Gib!	Sieh!	Fahr!
	Esst!	Nehmt!	Gebt!	Seht!	Fahrt!
	Essen Sie!	Nehmen Sie!	Geben Sie!	Sehen Sie!	Fahren Sie!
	Essen wir!	Nehmen wir!	Geben wir!	Sehen wir!	Fahren wir!

Note: The vowel changes **e → i** and **e → ie** are maintained in the **du-** form of the command. The vowel change **a → ä** does not occur in the command form.

EXPRESSING FUTURE TIME

In German, there are three ways to express future time:

1. present tense verb forms	Ich **kaufe** eine Jeans. Ich **finde** bestimmt etwas.	I'm going to buy a pair of jeans. I will surely find something.
2. present tense verb forms with words like **morgen, später**	Er kommt **morgen**. Elke ruft **später** an.	He's coming tomorrow. Elke will call later.
3. **werden**, *will*, plus infinitive	Ich **werde** ein Hemd **kaufen**. Er **wird** bald **gehen**.	I'll buy a shirt. He'll go soon.

SUBJUNCTIVE FORMS

THE FORMS HÄTTE, WÄRE, KÖNNTE, AND WÜRDE

ich	hätte	wäre	könnte	würde
du	hättest	wärest	könntest	würdest
er, sie, es	hätte	wäre	könnte	würde
wir	hätten	wären	könnten	würden
ihr	hättet	wäret	könntet	würdet
sie, Sie	hätten	wären	könnten	würden

NOTE: In spoken German the forms **wärest** and **wäret** are often shortened to **wärst** and **wärt**.

PAST TENSE VERB FORMS

In this book, you learned the simple past of **haben** and **sein**:

THE SIMPLE PAST OF HABEN AND SEIN

	haben	sein
ich	hatte	war
du	hattest	warst
er, sie	hatte	war
wir	hatten	waren
ihr	hattet	wart
sie	hatten	waren
Sie (formal)	hatten	waren

THE CONVERSATIONAL PAST

German verbs are divided into two groups: weak verbs and strong verbs. Weak verbs usually follow a regular pattern, such as the English verb forms *play — played — has played*. Strong verbs usually have irregularities, like the English verb forms *run — ran — has run* or *go — went — has gone*.

The conversational past tense of weak and strong verbs consists of the present tense of **haben** or **sein** and a form called the past participle, which is usually in last position in the clause or sentence.

Die Schüler	**haben**	ihre Hausaufgaben schon	**gemacht.**
Sabine	**ist**	gestern zu Hause	**geblieben.**

Formation of Past Participles				
Weak Verbs	spielen	(er) spielt	gespielt	Er hat gespielt.
with inseparable prefixes	besuchen	(er) besucht	besucht	Er hat ihn besucht.
with separable prefixes	aufräumen	(er) räumt auf	aufgeräumt	Er hat aufgeräumt.
Strong Verbs	kommen	(er) kommt	gekommen	Er ist gekommen
with inseparable prefixes	bekommen	(er) bekommt	bekommen	Er hat es bekommen.
with separable prefixes	mitkommen	(er) kommt mit	mitgekommen	Er ist mitgekommen.

NOTE: For past participles of strong verbs and irregular verbs, see pages R34–R36.

WEAK VERBS FORMING THE PAST PARTICIPLE WITH SEIN

bummeln, *to stroll*	ist gebummelt	**surfen,** *to surf*	ist gesurft
reisen, *to travel*	ist gereist	**wandern,** *to hike*	ist gewandert

PRINCIPAL PARTS OF THE VERBS PRESENTED IN LEVELS 1 AND 2

This list includes all verbs included in the **Wortschatz** sections of Level 1 and Level 2. Both strong and weak verbs, including verbs with separable prefixes, stem-vowel changes, and other irregularities are listed. Though most of the verbs in this list form the conversational past with **haben**, a few of the verbs you have learned take **sein** in the present perfect tense.

STRONG VERBS

Infinitive	Present (stem-vowel change and/or separable prefix)	Past Participle	Meaning
abheben	hebt ab	abgehoben	to lift (the receiver)
anrufen	ruft an	angerufen	to call up
anziehen	zieht an	angezogen	to put on (clothes)
aussehen	sieht aus	ausgesehen	to look, appear
bekommen	bekommt	bekommen	to get, receive
beschreiben	beschreibt	beschrieben	to describe
bleiben	bleibt	(ist) geblieben	to stay
brechen	bricht	gebrochen	to break
einladen	lädt ein	eingeladen	to invite
essen	isst	gegessen	to eat
fahren	fährt	(ist) gefahren	to drive, ride
fernsehen	sieht fern	ferngesehen	to watch tv
finden	findet	gefunden	to find
geben	gibt	gegeben	to give
gefallen	gefällt	gefallen	to like, be pleasing to
gehen	geht	(ist) gegangen	to go
gießen	gießt	gegossen	to pour; to water
haben	hat	gehabt	to have
halten	hält	gehalten	to keep
heißen	heißt	geheißen	to be called
helfen	hilft	geholfen	to help
herausnehmen	nimmt heraus	herausgenommen	to take out
kommen	kommt	(ist) gekommen	to come
lassen	lässt	gelassen	to let
laufen	läuft	(ist) gelaufen	to run
lesen	liest	gelesen	to read
messen	misst	gemessen	to measure
nehmen	nimmt	genommen	to take
Rad fahren	fährt Rad	(ist) Rad gefahren	to bicycle
scheinen	scheint	geschienen	to shine
schlafen	schläft	geschlafen	to sleep
schlagen	schlägt	geschlagen	to slam
schreiben	schreibt	geschrieben	to write
schwimmen	schwimmt	(ist) geschwommen	to swim
sehen	sieht	gesehen	to see
sein	ist	(ist) gewesen	to be
sprechen	spricht	gesprochen	to speak
tragen	trägt	getragen	to wear
trinken	trinkt	getrunken	to drink
tun	tut	getan	to do

Infinitive	Present (stem-vowel change and/or separable prefix)	Past Participle	Meaning
vermeiden	vermeidet	vermieden	to avoid
vorschlagen	schlägt vor	vorgeschlagen	to suggest
vorziehen	zieht vor	*vorgezogen	to prefer
waschen	wäscht	gewaschen	to wash
weggeben	gibt weg	weggegeben	to give away
wegtragen	trägt weg	weggetragen	to take away
wegwerfen	wirft weg	weggeworfen	to throw away
wehtun	tut weh	wehgetan	to hurt
wissen	weiß	gewusst	to know

*These verbs have a consonant change in the past participle.

WEAK VERBS

Infinitive	Present (stem-vowel change and/or separable prefix)	Past Participle	Meaning
abräumen	räumt ab	abgeräumt	to clear away
angeln	angelt	geangelt	to fish
anprobieren	probiert an	anprobiert	to try on
arbeiten	arbeitet	gearbeitet	to work
auflegen	legt auf	aufgelegt	to hang up (receiver)
aufräumen	räumt auf	aufgeräumt	to pick up/clean room
basteln	bastelt	gebastelt	to do arts and crafts
bedauern	bedauert	bedauert	to be sorry about
bedienen	bedient	bedient	to serve
besichtigen	besichtigt	besichtigt	to sight see
besuchen	besucht	besucht	to visit
bezweifeln	bezweifelt	bezweifelt	to doubt
brauchen	braucht	gebraucht	to need
bringen	bringt	**gebracht	to bring
bügeln	bügelt	gebügelt	to iron
decken	deckt	gedeckt	to set (the table)
einkaufen	kauft ein	eingekauft	to shop
einlegen	legt ein	eingelegt	to insert
einstecken	steckt ein	eingesteckt	to insert (coin)
ernähren	ernährt	ernährt	to nourish
faulenzen	faulenzt	gefaulenzt	to be lazy
fotografieren	fotografiert	fotografiert	to photograph
s. freuen	freut s.	gefreut	to be happy about
s. fühlen	fühlt s.	gefühlt	to feel
füttern	füttert	gefüttert	to feed
glauben	glaubt	geglaubt	to believe
gucken	guckt	geguckt	to look
hoffen	hofft	gehofft	to hope
holen	holt	geholt	to get
hören	hört	gehört	to hear

Infinitive	Present (stem-vowel change and/or separable prefix)	Past Participle	Meaning
s. interessieren	interessiert s.	interessiert	to be interested in
kämmen	kämmt	gekämmt	to comb
kaufen	kauft	gekauft	to buy
kennen	kennt	**gekannt	to know
kosten	kostet	gekostet	to cost
leben	lebt	gelebt	to live
machen	macht	gemacht	to do or make
mähen	mäht	gemäht	to mow
meinen	meint	gemeint	to think, be of the opinion
passen	passt	gepasst	to fit
polieren	poliert	poliert	to polish
putzen	putzt	geputzt	to clean
rauchen	raucht	geraucht	to smoke
regnen	regnet	geregnet	to rain
sagen	sagt	gesagt	to say
sammeln	sammelt	gesammelt	to collect
schauen	schaut	geschaut	to look (at)
schenken	schenkt	geschenkt	to give (a gift)
schmecken	schmeckt	geschmeckt	to taste
segeln	segelt	(ist) gesegelt	to sail
sortieren	sortiert	sortiert	to sort
spielen	spielt	gespielt	to play
spülen	spült	gespült	to wash dishes
suchen	sucht	gesucht	to look for
tanzen	tanzt	getanzt	to dance
tauchen	taucht	getaucht	to dive
telefonieren	telefoniert	telefoniert	to call (on the phone)
trocknen	trocknet	getrocknet	to dry
verbringen	verbringt	**verbracht	to spend time
s. verletzen	verletzt s.	verletzt	to injure
s. verstauchen	verstaucht s.	verstaucht	to sprain
wählen	wählt	gewählt	to dial
wandern	wandert	(ist) gewandert	to hike
wischen	wischt	gewischt	to dust
wohnen	wohnt	gewohnt	to live
wünschen	wünscht	gewünscht	to wish
zahlen	zahlt	gezahlt	to pay
zeichnen	zeichnet	gezeichnet	to draw
zustimmen	stimmt zu	zugestimmt	to agree

**Although weak, these verbs have a vowel and/or consonant change in the past participle.

German-English Vocabulary

German-English Vocabulary

This vocabulary includes almost all words in this textbook, both active (for production) and passive (for recognition only). Active words and phrases are practiced in the chapter and are listed in the Wortschatz section at the end of each chapter. You are expected to know and be able to use active vocabulary. An entry in black, heavy type indicates that the word or phrase is active. All other words—some in the opening dialogs, in exercises, in optional and visual material, in the Landeskunde, Zum Lesen and Kann ich's wirklich? sections—are for recognition only. The meaning of these words and phrases can usually be understood from the context or may be looked up in this vocabulary.

With some exceptions, the following are not included: proper nouns, verb conjugations, and forms of determiners.

Nouns are listed with definite article and plural form, when applicable. The numbers in the entries refer to the level and chapter where the word or phrase first appears or where it becomes an active vocabulary word. Vocabulary from the location openers is followed by a Loc and the chapter number directly following the location spread.

The following abbreviations are used in this vocabulary: adj (adjective), pl (plural), prep (preposition), sep (separable-prefix verb), poss adj (possessive adjective), sing (singular), dat (dative), acc (accusative), s. (*sich*, or reflexive), and conj (conjunction).

der Aal, -e *eel*, Loc 10
die Aalsuppe, -n *eel soup*, Loc 4
ab (prep) *down, off*, II1
ab und zu *now and then*, II4
der Abend, -e *evening*, I; **am Abend** *in the evening*, I
das Abendbrot, -e *dinner*, II12
das Abendbuffet, -s *dinner buffet*, II12
das Abendessen, - *dinner, evening meal*, II5
das Abendkleid, -er *evening gown*, II12
abends *evenings*, II1
das Abenteuer, - *adventure*, II11
der Abenteuerfilm, -e *adventure movie*, I
die Abenteuerreise, -n *exotic vacation*, II9
aber (conj) *but*, I; **aber sicher!** *but of course!*, I
die Abfahrt, -en *departure*, II9
das Abgas, -e *exhaust*, II9
abgebildet *depicted*, II2
abgehakt *crossed off*, II3
abgelegen *remote*, II5
abgeschnitten *cut-off*, II8
abgestanden *stale, flat*, II2
abgewendet *turned away*, II11
abheben (sep) *to pick up*, I; **den Hörer abheben** *to pick up the receiver*, I

abholen (sep) *to come for, pick up*, II11
der Abholschein, -e *receipt to pick up a prescription*, II6
abladen (sep) *to unload*, II2
das Ablagefach, ̈-er *storage shelf*, II10
ablaufen (sep) *to flow or run off; to elapse, expire*, II11
ablehnen (sep) *to decline, turn down*, II12
abräumen (sep) *to clean up, clear off*, I
der Absatz, ̈-e *shoe heel*, II8
die Absatzforschung, -en *marketing research*, II10
abschaffen (sep) *to abolish*, II10
abschneiden (sep) *to cut off*, II5
abschreiben (sep) *to copy*, II5
abschwirren (sep) *to buzz off*, II12
absichtlich *on purpose*, II12
absolut *absolute(ly), unconditional(ly)*, II6
der Abstand, ̈-e *distance, gap*, II12
der Abstecher, - *detour*, II10
abstellen (sep) *to switch off*, II7
die Abteilung, -en *division, department*, II1
abtrocknen (sep) *to dry off*, II5
abwechselnd *alternating, one after the other*, II3
die Abwechslung, -en *change, variety*, II3
abwechslungsreich *varied, diverse*, II12
die Abwesenheit *absence*, II10

abwischen (sep) *to erase, wipe up*, II11
Ach *Oh!*, I; **Ach ja!** *Oh yeah!*, I
Ach schade! *That's too bad.*, II6
achten auf (acc) *to pay attention to*, II12
das Acryl *acrylic*, II8
der Actionfilm, -e *action movie*, I
das Adjektiv, -e *adjective*, II8
die Adresse, -n *address*, II11
afrikanisch (adj) *African*, II12
die Agentur, -en *agency*, II8
ägyptisch (adj) *Egyptian*, II11
ähnlich *similar*, II1
die Ahnung, -en *idea, notion*, II8; **Keine Ahnung!** *I have no idea!*, I
die Aktie, -n *share, stock*, II8
aktiv *active*, II8
die Aktivität, -en *activity*, II4
aktuell *current, contemporary*, II1
akzeptiert *accepted*, II11
die Alarmanlage, -n *alarm system*, II10
der Alkohol, -e *alcohol*, II4
alkoholfrei *non-alcoholic*, II11
all- *all*, II8
allein *alone*, II2
allerbesten: am allerbesten *best of all*, II8
die Allergie, -n *allergy*, II4
allergisch (gegen) *allergic (to)*, II4
alles *everything*, II4
der Alltag, -e *weekday, workday routine*, II9

allzu *much too, far too,* II7
als *than,* II7
also (conj) *so, therefore,* II6; (particle) *well, okay;* II1
alt *old,* I
älter *older,* II7
die **Alterserscheinung, -en** *sign of old age,* II6
die **Alufelge, -n** *aluminum rim,* II10
am=an dem *at the,* I; **am …platz** *on … Square,* I; **am Abend** *in the evening,* I; **am ersten (Juli)** *on the first (of July),* I; **am letzten Tag** *on the last day,* II3; **am liebsten** *most of all,* I; **am Tag** *during the day,* II4; **an der Schule** *at school,* II4; **am besten** *best (of all),* II5
der **Amerikaner, -** *American,* II4
amerikanisch (adj) *American,* II1
die **Ampel, -n** *traffic light,* I; **bis zur Ampel** *until you get to the traffic light,* I
an *to, at,* II9
anbieten (sep) *to offer,* II7
anbraten (sep) *to grill, roast,* II12
ander- *other,* I; **ein(-) ander- another (a different) one,* II9
andererseits *on the other hand,* II7
ändern *o change,* II9
der **Anfang, ̈e** *beginning,* II8
der **Anfänger, -** *beginner,* II12
die **Angabe, -en** *information,* II6
angeben (sep) *to indicate, state,* II2
das **Angebot, -e** *offer,* I; **Angebot der Woche** *weekly special,* I
angeboten *offered,* II12
angeln *to fish,* II9
angenommen *accepted, assumed,* II12
angeregt *lively,* II3
angeschlossen *joined,* II3
angestarrt werden *to be stared at,* II8
der **Angestellte, -n** *employee,* II4
angezogen *dressed,* II8
angucken (sep) *to look at,* II10
anhaben (sep) *to have on,* II1
anhören (sep) *to listen to,* II6
ankommen (sep) *to arrive,* II12
ankreuzen (sep) *to cross, mark off,* II3
die **Anlage, -n** *grounds, site,* II12; *system, installation,* II2
der **Anlass, ̈e** *occasion,* II2
die **Anleitung, -en** *instruction,* II6
der **Anorak, -s** *parka,* II8
anprobieren (sep) *to try on,* I
anregen (sep) *stimulate,* II4
die **Anregung, -en** *stimulation, incitement,* II1; **zur Anregung** *as a start,* II1
der **Anrufbeantworter, -** *answering machine,* II9

anrufen (sep) *to call (on the phone),* I
anschauen (sep) *to look at,* II7
der **Anschlag, ̈e** *announcement,* II11
die **Anschlagtafel, -n** *bulletin board,* II2
anschließend *following, adjacent,* II12
s. **ansehen** (sep) *to have a look at,* II2
die **Ansicht, -en** *view, point of view,* II9; **nach Ansicht von** *in the opinion of,* II9
ansonsten *otherwise,* II3
die **Ansprache, -n** *speech, address,* II3
ansprechen (sep) *to talk to,* II9
der **Anspruch, ̈e** *claim; right,* II12
die **Anstalt, -en** *institute, establishment,* Loc 7
die **Anstrengung, -en** *exertion, effort, strain,* II6
die **Antwort, -en** *answer,* II2
antworten (dat) *to answer,* II2
die **Anwendung, -en** *application, use,* II3
die **Anzahl, -en** *number, quantity,* II8
die **Anzeige, -n** *ad,* II10
anzeigen (sep) *to show, indicate or record,* II10
anziehen (sep) *to put on, wear,* I
der **Anzug, ̈e** *suit,* II8
der **Apfel, ̈** *apple,* I
der **Apfelkuchen, -** *apple cake,* I
der **Apfelsaft, ̈e** *apple juice,* I; **ein Glas Apfelsaft** *a glass of apple juice,* I
die **Apotheke, -n** *pharmacy,* II6
der **Apotheker, -** *pharmacist,* II6
der **Apparat, -e** *telephone,* I
das **Appartement, -s** *apartment,* II12
der **Appetit: Guten Appetit!** *Bon appétit!,* II11
die **Aprikose, -n** *apricot,* II4
der **April** *April,* I
die **Arbeit, -en** *work,* II2
arbeiten *to work,* II3
die **Arbeitsklamotte, -n** *work clothes,* II8
die **Architektur** *architecture,* II3
arg *very; annoying,* II4
ärgerlich *annoying,* II3
der **Arm, -e** *arm,* II6
das **Armband, ̈er** *bracelet,* II1
die **Armbanduhr, -en** *wristwatch,* I
der **Ärmel, -** *sleeve,* II1
ärmellos *sleeveless,* II8
die **Armut** *poverty,* II7
der **Artikel, -** *article, commodity,* II2
der **Arzt, ̈e** *doctor,* II6
assoziieren *to associate,* II3
der **Atem** *breath, breathing,* II12
der **Athlet, -en** *athlete,* II12
atmen *to breathe,* II12
die **Atmosphäre, -n** *atmosphere, environment,* II11
attraktiv *attractive,* II1

Au!, Aua! *Ouch!,* II6
auch *also,* I; **Ich auch.** *Me too.,* I; **auch noch** *also,* II9; **auch schon** *also, already,* II3
aufliegen (sep) *lie (on),* II1
auf (prep) *on, onto, to,* II1; **Auf dein/Ihr/euer Wohl!** *To your health!,* II11; **auf dem Land** *in the country,* I; **Auf Wiederhören!** *Goodbye!,* I; **auf einer Fete** *at a party,* II8
aufdrehen (sep) *to turn up,* II2
der **Aufdruck** *print impression,* II1
die **Aufgabe, -n** *assignment,* II3
aufgeben (sep) *to give up,* II4
aufgelistet *listed,* II4
aufgeschnitten *cut open,* II5
aufgießen (sep) *to brew a drink (tea, coffee),* II5
aufgrund dessen *because of that,* II9
aufhängen (sep) *to hang out, up,* II4
aufheben (sep) *to lift or raise,* II2
aufhören (sep) *to stop,* II6
der **Aufkleber, -** *sticker,* II10
aufkommen (sep) *to get up; to arise,* II5
der **Auflauf, ̈e** *soufflé,* II5
auflegen (sep) *to hang up (the telephone),* I
aufliegen (sep) *lie (on),* II1
aufräumen (sep) *to clean up,* I
der **Aufsatz, ̈e** *essay,* II12
der **Aufschnitt** *cold cuts,* I
aufschreiben (sep) *to write down,* II12
aufsetzen (sep) *to put or place on,* II5
die **Aufsicht, -en** *supervision,* II10
aufstehen (sep) *to get up,* II6
der **Aufstrich, -e** *spread,* II11
auftauchen (sep) *to turn up, arise,* II10
auftreten (sep) *to appear,* II6
aufwachen (sep) *to wake up,* II12
aufwachsen (sep) *to grow up,* II7
aufwärmen (sep) *to warm up,* II5
aufzählen (sep) *to enumerate,* II11
das **Auge, -n** *eye,* I
der **Augenblick, -e** *moment,* II12
die **Augenfarbe, -n** *eye color,* II1
der **August** *August,* I
aus (prep) *from, out of,* II1; **aus Baumwolle** *made of cotton,* I; **aus dem (16.) Jahrhundert** *from the (16th) century,* II9; **aus den 60er Jahren** *from the sixties,* II8; **aus welchen Gründen** *for what reasons,* II8
die **Ausbildung, -en** *education,* II7
der **Ausdruck, ̈e** *expression,* II2
ausdrücken (sep) *to express,* II6

GERMAN-ENGLISH VOCABULARY

der **Ausflug**, ⸚e *excursion*, II11
das Ausflugsschiff, -e *excursion boat*, II11
das Ausflugsziel, -e *destination*, II9
das **Ausführen**, *developing*, II9
ausfüllen *to fill out*, II4
ausgeben (sep) *to give out; to spend (money)*, II12
ausgehen (sep) *to go out*, II1
ausgeschnitten *low-cut*, II8
ausgewählt *chosen*, II11
ausgezeichnet *excellent, outstanding*, II1
aushöhlen (sep) *to hollow out*, II5
s. auskennen (sep) *to know all about*, II9
die Auskunft, ⸚e *information*, II3
der Ausländer, - *foreigner*, II11
das Ausland *foreign country*, II9
ausländisch *foreign*, II11
die Auslandsreise, -n *foreign travel, trip*, II9
der Auslauf *run*, II10
auslegen (sep) *to lay out (money, etc.)*, II5
ausmachen (sep) *to make up, constitute*, II12
die Ausnahme, -n *exception*, II8
ausprobieren (sep) *to try out*, II5
ausquatschen (sep) *to have a good chat*, II2
ausrechnen (sep) *to calculate; to figure out*, II8
die Ausrede, -n *excuse*, II6
ausreden (sep) *to finish speaking*, II2
der Ausreißer, - *deserter, runaway*, II11
ausrufen (sep) *to call out*, II2
s. ausruhen (sep) *to relax, rest*, II5
die Ausrüstung, -en *equipment, outfit*, II10
die Aussage, -n *statement*, II7
aussagen (sep) *to state, express*, II9
s. ausschlafen *to sleep one's fill*, II9
der Ausschnitt, -e *excerpt*, II4
aussehen (sep) *to look like, to appear*, I; **der Rock sieht … aus.** *The skirt looks …*, I; **Wie sieht er aus?** *What does he look like?*, I
außerdem *besides*, II5
die Aussicht, -en *view*, II12
die Ausstattung, -en *equipment, furnishing*, II10
die Ausstellung, -en *exhibition*, II11
die Ausstellungseröffnung, -en *opening of an exhibition*, II11
aussuchen (sep) *to choose*, II7
austauschen (sep) *to exchange*, II2
der Austauschschüler, - *exchange student (male)*, II4
die Austauschwoche, -n *exchange week*, II2
die **Auster**, -n *oyster*, II11

die Auswahl, -en *choice, selection*, II8
auswählen (sep) *to choose from*, II5
s. ausdenken (sep) *to think up*, II5
ausfüllen (sep) *to fill in (a form)*, II8
außer (prep) *except for*, II11
außerdem *besides*, II5
außereuropäisch *outside of Europe*, II12
außerhalb (prep) *outside of*, II3
der Auszug, ⸚e *excerpt*, II11
das **Auto**, -s *car*, I; **mit dem Auto** *by car*, I
die Autobahn, -en *highway*, II10
der Autofahrer, - *driver*, II10
der Automat, -en *vending machine; robot*, II2
die Automatik *automatic transmission*, II10
die Automobilindustrie, -n *automobile industry*, Loc 1
die Autotür, -en *car door*, II7
der Autounfall, ⸚e *car accident*, II10

der Bach, ⸚e *creek*, II9
der **Bäcker**, - *baker*, I
die **Bäckerei**, -en *bakery*, I
das Backhaus, ⸚er *bakehouse*, II9
das Bad, ⸚er *bath*, II6
baden *to swim*, I; **baden gehen** *to go swimming*, I
der Badestrand, ⸚e *beach*, II3
das **Badezimmer**, - *bathroom*, II7
die **Bahn**, -en *train*, II9
der **Bahnhof**, ⸚e *train station*, I
der Bahnübergang, ⸚e *train crossing*, II7
das **Ballett**, -e *ballet*, II11
die **Banane**, -n *banana*, II2
die **Bank**, -en *bank*, I
der Bankschalter, - *bank counter*, II12
der Bärenhunger *hungry as a bear*, II12
barfuß *barefoot*, II12
die Barockstadt, ⸚e *baroque city*, II3
Basketball *basketball*, I
die Basketballhalle, -n *basketball gym*, II12
der Basketballplatz, ⸚e *basketball court*, II12
basteln *to do crafts*, I
der Bau *construction*, II3
der **Bauch**, ⸚e *stomach*, II6
die **Bauchschmerzen** (pl) *stomach-ache*, II6
das **Baudenkmal**, ⸚er *monument*, II11
bauen *to build*, II2
der Bauer, -n *farmer*, II10

die Bauernente, -n *farm-raised duck*, II11
das Bauernhaus, ⸚er *farm house*, II9
der Bauernhof, ⸚e *farm*, II3
der **Baum**, ⸚e *tree*, II7
die **Baumwolle**, *cotton*, I
bayerisch (adj) *Bavarian*, II1
Bayern (das) *Bavaria*, II4
beachten *to notice, heed, regard*, II7
beantworten *to answer*, II2
der Becher, - *cup*, II2
bedauern *to be sorry about*, II5
bedeuten *to mean*, II1
bedeutend *meaningful*, Loc 1
bedienen *to serve*, II 3; **die Kamera bedienen** *to operate the camera*, II 3
die Bedienung, -en *wait person*, II1
bedruckt *printed*, II8
beeindruckend *impressive*, II11
beenden *to end*, II10
die Beere, -n *berry*, II4
s. **befinden** *to find oneself, to be*, II9
befragen *to ask questions*, II9
begabt *talented*, II12
begeistert *enthusiastic*, II1
beginnen *to begin*, II12
begleiten *to accompany*, II4
begründen *to found; to give a reason for*, II2
beherbergt *given shelter*, II3
bei (prep) *by, near, at*, II9; **bei uns** *with us at home*, II10; **beim Bäcker** *at the baker's*, I
beide *both*, II2
die **Beilage**, -n *side dish*, II11
das **Bein**, -e *leg*, II6
das Beispiel, -e *example*, II1
beitragen zu (sep) *to contribute to*, II7
bekannt *known*, II3
der Bekannte, -n *acquaintance (male)*, II7
die Bekleidungsabteilung, -en *clothing department*, II1
das Bekleidungsgeschäft, -e *clothing store*, II12
bekommen *to get, receive*, I
belästigen *to annoy*, II7
belegen *to cover; to register for*, II5
beliebt *popular*, II9
beliefern *to supply (with)*, II7
bemerken *to notice*, II7
die Bemerkung, -en *comment, remark*, II10
s. benehmen *to behave*, II11
benutzen *to use*, II6
das Benzin *gasoline, fuel*, II10
der Beobachter, - *observer*, II12
bequem *comfortable*, I
beraten *to advise*, II8
der Bereich, -e *area*, Loc 7
bereit *willing; prepared*, II5
bereits *already*, II12
der **Berg**, -e *mountain*, II7

die Bergbahn, -en *mountain or alpine railway*, II9
das Bergsteigen *mountain climbing*, II3
die Bergtour, -en *tour or trip in the mountains*, II9
der Bergwanderer, - *mountain hiker*, II9
berichten (über) *to report on*, Loc 1
beruflich *professional(ly)*, II10
die Berufsschule, -n *vocational school*, II5
berühmt *famous*, II3
beschäftigt *busy*, II3
die Bescheidenheit, -en *modesty*, II8
beschlossen *decided*, II12
beschreiben *to describe*, II1
die Beschreibung, -en *description*, II1
beschrieben *described*, II1
beschriften *to inscribe*, II8
die Beschwerde, -n *trouble, complaint*, II6
beseitigen *to remove, abolish*, II7
besetzt *busy (telephone)*, I
besichtigen *to sightsee, visit a place*, II3
die Besichtigung, -en *sightseeing, visit*, II9
der Besitz, -e *ownership*, II1
besonders *especially*, I
besorgen *to provide*, II12
besprechen *to discuss*, II9
besser *better*, I
die Besserung, -en *improvement*, II6; **Gute Besserung!** *Get well soon!*, II6
bestehen *to pass*, II2
bestehen aus *to consist of*, II2
bestellen *to order*, II1
die Bestellkarte, -n *order form*, II8
die Bestellnummer, -n *order number*, II8
die Bestellung, -en *order*, II11
besten: **am besten** *the best*, II5
bestens *very well, best*, II1
bestimmt *certainly, definitely*, I
bestreuen *to sprinkle*, II5
der Besuch, -e *visit*, II2
besuchen *to visit*, I
der Besucher, - *visitor*, II11
betreten *to step on; to enter*, II8
der Betrieb, -e *business, firm*, Loc 10
das Bett, -en *bed*, I
beugen *to bend*, II12
beurteilen *to judge*, II12
die Bevölkerung *population, inhabitants*, II4
bevor (conj) *before*, II2
bevorzugen *to prefer, to favor*, II12
beweisen *to prove*, II12
der Bewerber, - *applicant*, II10
bewundern *to admire*, II9
bewusst *conscious*, II6
bezahlen *to pay*, II11
bezahlt *paid for*, II1
bezeugen *to testify to*, Loc 10

beziehungsweise=bzw. *respectively, that is to say*, II11
das Bezirksamt, -̈er *local government office*, II11
bezweifeln *to doubt*, II9
die Bibliothek, -en *library*, II5
biegen *to bend, turn*, II9; einbiegen (sep): **Biegen Sie hier ein!** *Turn here!*, II9
der Biergarten, -̈ *open-air restaurant, beer garden*, II12
das Biertrinken *drinking beer*, II11
bieten *to offer*, II7
das Bild, -er *picture*, II5
bilden *to form, shape, construct*, II1
billig *cheap*, I
der Bioladen, -̈ *natural foods store*, II4
die Biologie=Bio *biology*, I
die Biologielehrerin, -nen *biology teacher (female)*, I
die Birne, -n *pear*, II5
bis (prep) *until*, II1; bis auf *except for, all but*, II5; **Bis dann!** *Till then! See you later!*, I; bis zu *up to*, II9
der Bischof, -̈e *bishop*, II3
der Biss, -e *bite, sting*, II12
bisschen: **ein bisschen** *a little*, I
bissel=bisschen *a little*, II4
bitte *please*, I; **Bitte (sehr/schön)!** *You're (very) welcome!*, I; **Bitte! Hier!** *Here you go!*, II10
bitter *bitter*, II1
das Blatt, -̈er *leaf; page*, II12
blau *blue*, I
die Blaubeere, -n *blueberry*, II4
der Blazer, - *blazer*, II8
bleiben *to stay, remain*, II3
bleich *pale*, II6
der Bleistift, -e *pencil*, I
der Blick, -e *glance, view*, II3
blöd *dumb*, I
der Blödsinn *nonsense*, II9
blond *blonde*, I
bloß *only*, I; **Was soll ich bloß tun?** *What should I do?*, II6
der Blouson, -s *bomber jacket*, II8
die Blume, -n *flower*, I
das Blumenbeet, -e *flower bed*, II7
der Blumenkohl *cauliflower*, II4
der Blumenmarkt, -̈e *flower market*, Loc 7
der Blumenstrauß, -̈e *flower bouquet*, I
die Bluse, -n *blouse*, I
der Boden *floor, ground*, II12
das Bogenschießen *archery*, II1
die Bohne, -n *bean*, II2
das Boot, -e *boat*, II9; **Boot fahren** *to go for a boat ride*, II9
botanisch *botanical*, II3
boxen *to box, punch*, II10
braten *to roast, bake*, II9
der Braten *roast*, II11
die Bratkartoffeln (pl) *fried potatoes*, II11

die Bratwurst, -̈e *fried sausage*, II2
brauchen *to need*, I
braun *brown*, I
bräunen *to dye brown; to tan*, II8
s. **brechen (etwas)** *to break (something)*, II6; **er/sie bricht** *he/she breaks*, II6
breit *large, wide*, II1
die Bremse, -n *brake*, II10
bremsen *to brake*, II12
das Brettspiel, -e *board game*, I; **ein Brettspiel spielen** *to play a board game*, I
die Brezel, -n *pretzel*, I
der Brieffreund, -e *pen pal*, II6
die Briefmarke, -n *stamp*, I
der Briefpartner, - *pen pal*, II7
die Brille, -n *a pair of glasses*, I
bringen *to bring*, II8; zum Ausdruck bringen *to express*, II9; etwas in Ordnung bringen *to get something in order*, II8
der Brokkoli *broccoli*, II4
die Bronzefigur, -en *bronze figure*, Loc 7
das Brot, -e *bread*, I
das Brötchen, - *breakfast roll*, II5
der Brotkrümel, - *bread crumb*, II12
der Brotteller, - *bread plate*, II12
die Brücke, -n *bridge*, II9
der Bruder, -̈ *brother*, I
brüllen *to shout, holler*, II9
der Brunnen, - *fountain*, II9
die Brusttasche, -n *breast pocket*, II8
brutal *brutal, violent*, I
das Buch, -̈er *book*, I
buchen *to book, reserve*, II9
der Buchstabe, -n *letter (of the alphabet)*, II1
die Bucht, -en *bay*, II12
das Buddelschiffmuseum, -museen *museum of bottled boats*, II9
die Bude, -n *hut, room*, II12
bügeln *to iron*, II2
die Bühne, -n *stage*, II12
die Bulette, -n *meatball*, Loc 10
bulgarisch (adj) *Bulgarian*, II11
der Bummel *stroll*, II1
bummeln *to stroll*, II1
das Bund *bunch*, II2
der Bund *waistband*, II8
das Bundesland, -̈er *(German or Austrian) federal state*, I
das Bundesligateam, -s *team in the federal league*, II12
die Bundfalte, -n *pleat*, II8
die Bundfaltenhose, -n *pleated pants*, II8
bunt *colorful*, II8
das Bürgerhaus, -̈er *home of a prosperous citizen*, II9
der Bürgerkrieg, -e *civil war*, II10
bürgerlich *civic, civil*, II11; **gut-bürgerliche Küche** *good home-cooked food*, II11
der Bürgermeister, - *mayor*, II3
das Büro, -s *office*, II3

GERMAN-ENGLISH VOCABULARY

der Bus, -se *bus*, I
der Busausflug, ⸚e *bus excursion*, II11
die Busfahrt, -en *bus trip*, II9
die **Butter** *butter*, I
die Buttermilch *buttermilk*, II2
das **Butterschmalz** *shortening*, I
bzw.=beziehungsweise *respectively, that is to say*, II12

das Café, -s *café*, I
der **Camembert Käse,** - *Camembert cheese*, II5
der Cappuccino, -s *cappuccino coffee*, II2
die CD, -s *compact disc*, I
der Cent, - *cent*, (smallest unit of the euro; 1/100th of a euro), I
Cevapcici (Serbocroat: *rolled spicy ground meat*), II12
Chanukka *Hanukkah*, I; **Frohes Chanukka-Fest!** *Happy Hanukkah!*, I
der Charakter *character, personality, quality*, II8
charakterisieren *to characterize*, II1
checken *to check*, II10
der Chefkoch, ⸚e *head chef*, II12
die Chemie *chemistry*, I
chemisch *chemical*, II4
chic *smart (looking)*, I
der Chinese, -n *Chinese (male)*, II12
chinesisch (adj) *Chinese*, II11
das Chorkonzert, -e *choir concert*, II11
die Clique, -n *clique*, II4
das Cola, -s *cola* (also: die Cola), I
die Comics (pl) *comic books*, I
der Computer, - *computer*, I
cool (adj) *cool*, II8
die Couch, -en *couch*, I
der Court, -s *court*, II12
der Couscous=Kuskus *couscous*, II12
der Cousin, -s *cousin (male)*, I
die Creme, -s *cream*, II6
die Cremesoße, -n *cream sauce*, II6
die Crêpes (pl) *crepes*, II12

da *there*, II1; **Da hast du (bestimmt) Recht!** *You're right about that!*, II10; **da hinten** *there in the back*, I; **da vorn** *there in the front*, I; **Da stimm ich dir zu!** *I agree with you about that!*, II10
dabei *by it; near it; beside it, with it*, II2
die Dachrinne, -n *rain gutter*, II12
dafür *for it*, II10; **Ich bin dafür, dass …** *I am for doing …*, II11; *I prefer that …*, II12
daheim *at home, in one's own country*, II12
daher *from there*; (conj) *for that reason*, II7
dahin *to that place*, II9
dahinflitzen (sep) *to speed along*, II10
dahinter *behind it*, II9
damals *then, in those days*, II12
damit *with it*; (conj) *so that*, II1
der Damm, ⸚e *dam, dike*, II7
dampfend *steaming*, II12
danach *after that*, I
daneben *next to it*, II1
danebengehen (sep) *to be way off, miss the mark*, II11
Dänemark (das) *Denmark*, II9
Danke! *Thank you!*, I; **Danke (sehr/schön)!** *Thank you (very much)!*, I; **Danke! Dir/Ihnen auch!** *Thank you! Same to you!*, II11; **Danke gleichfalls!** *Thank you and the same to you!*, II11
danken (dat) *to thank*, II1
dann *then*, II1; **Dann nehm ich eben …** *In that case I'll take …*, II5; **Dann trink ich halt …** *I'll drink instead …*, II5
daran *at it; on it*, II4
darauf *on it; to it*, II3
Darf ich (bitte) …? *May I (please) …?*, II10
darin *in it*, II8
darüber *over it*, II8
darüberstreuen (sep) *to sprinkle over something*, II12
darunter *under it, underneath*, II8
dass (conj) *that*, I
der Dativ *dative case*, II6
die Datscha, (pl) Datschen (*Russian*) *garden house*, II11
die Dauer *duration*, II6
der Daumen, - *thumb*, II6
davon *away from it; of it*, II7
davor *in front of it*, II9
dazu *for it; with it*, II2
dazwischen *between it*, II10
der Decathlet, -en *decathlete (male)*, II12
die Decke, -n *blanket, cover*, II2
der Deckel, - *lid*, II5
decken *to cover*, II2; **den Tisch decken** *to set the table*, I
deftig *hearty*, II11
dein (poss adj) *your*, I
dekoriert *decorated*, II12
die Delikatesse, -n *delicacy*, II11
denken *to think*, II2
das Denkmal, ⸚er *monument*, Loc 1
denn (particle), I, (conj) *because, for*, I
derselbe *the same*, II3
des *of the*, II1
deshalb (conj) *for this reason*, II2
desinfizieren *to disinfect*, II7
das Desinteresse *disinterest*, II8
dessen *of him, it; of whose*, II9
deswegen (conj) *because of that, for this reason*, II1
detailliert *detailed*, II12
das **Deutsch** *German (language)*, I; *(school subject)*, I
die Deutschklasse, -n *German class*, II2
Deutschland (das) *Germany*, I
der **Deutschlehrer,** - *German teacher (male)*, I
die **Deutschlehrerin, -nen** *German teacher (female)*, I
der Deutschschüler, - *German student (male)*, II5
deutschsprachig *German-speaking*, II12
der **Dezember** *December*, I
das Dia, -s *slide*, II3
die Diätmargarine *diet margarine*, II2
der Dichter, - *writer, poet*, II3
dick (adj) *fat*, II4; **dick machen** *to be fattening*, II4
der **Dienstag** *Tuesday*, I
dienstags *Tuesdays*, II10
dies- *this*, II5
dieselbe *the same*, II6
diesmal *this time*, II3
das Diktatschreiben, - *dictation*, II2
das Ding, -e *thing*, II1; vor allen Dingen *especially*, II10
dir *to you*, II3
direkt *direct*, II9
die Dirigentin, -nen *conductor (of an orchestra) (female)*, II11
die **Disko, -s** *disco*, I; **in eine Disko gehen** *to go to a disco*, I
die Diskothek, -en *discothek*, II9
die Diskussion, -en *discussion*, II10
das Diskuswerfen *discus throw*, II1
diskutieren *to discuss*, II7
DM=Deutsche Mark *German mark (former German monetary unit)*, I
doch (particle) *yes, it is!*, I; **Ich meine doch, dass …**, *I really think that …*, II10
der Doktor, -en *doctor*, II8
der **Dom, -e** *cathedral*, II3
der **Donnerstag** *Thursday*, I
donnerstags *Thursdays*, II10
doof *dumb*, I
die Doppelstunde, -n *two-hour block*, II10
doppelt gemoppelt *something done twice*, II12
das **Dorf,** ⸚er *village*, II7
die Dorfgemeinde, -n *village community*, II3
die Dorfkirche, -n *village church*, II3
dörflich *rural*, II12

der Dorfplatz, ⸚e *village square*, II3
die Dorfplatzeinweihung, -en *village square dedication*, II3
dort *there*, I; **dort drüben** *over there*, I
dorthin *to there*, II9
das Drahtbett, -en *wire-frame bed*, II7
drauf=darauf *on top of it*, II5
draußen *outside*, II5
der Dreck *dirt*, II2
dreckig *dirty*, II7
drehen *to turn*, II7
das Dreikörnerbrot *three-grain bread*, II2
drin=darin *in it*, II8
dringend *urgent*, II7
dritt- *third*, II1
die Drogerie, -n *drugstore*, II6
der Drogist, -en *druggist (male)*, II6
die Drogistin, -nen *druggist (female)*, II6
drücken *to press, squeeze*, II6
der Druckfehler, - *printing error*, II2
der Druckknopf, ⸚e *snap*, II8
drunter=darunter *underneath it*, II5
der Dschungel, - *jungle*, II9
der Duft, ⸚e *scent, perfume*, II2
dumm *dumb, stupid*, I
dummerweise *stupidly*, II3
das Düngemittel, - *fertilizer*, II4
dunkel *dark*, II1
dunkelgrau *dark gray*, II8
durch (prep) *through*, II9
durchchecken (sep) *to check through*, II10
durchkommen (sep) *to get through*, II9
durchschnittlich *average*, II5
die Durchschnittskosten (pl) *average cost*, II10
dürfen *to be allowed to*, II4; **er/sie/es darf** *he/she/it is allowed to*, II4
der Durst *thirst*, II2; **Durst haben** *to be thirsty*, II2

eben (particle), II5; **Dann nehm ich eben …** *In that case I'll take …*, II5; **eben nicht** *actually not*, II9
ebenfalls *likewise*, II5
echt *real(ly)*, I; *genuine*, II1
die Ecke, -n *corner*, II9
eckig *with corners*, I
egal *alike, equal*, II5; **egal sein: Mode ist mir egal.** *I don't care about fashion.*, II8
eher *sooner; rather*, II3
ehrlich *honestly*, I
das Ei, -er *egg*, I

der Eifer *enthusiasm*, II7
eigen *(one's) own*, II7
die Eigenschaft, -en *quality, property, attribute*, II1
eigentlich *actual(ly)*, II1; **Eigentlich schon, aber …** *Well yes, but …*, II4
ein(-) ander- *another (a different) one*, II9
einander *one another*, II7
einbiegen (sep) *to turn*, II9
der Eindruck, ⸚e *impression*, II12
Einfach! *That's easy!*, I
einfarbig *one-colored*, II8
einfüllen (sep) *to fill in*, II5
der Eingang, ⸚e *entrance*, II1
die Eingangstür, -en *entrance door*, II12
eingebildet *arrogant*, II8
eingeweiht *dedicated*, II3
einheimisch *local, native*, II9
einige *some*, II2
s. einigen auf (acc) *to agree on*, II12
einigermaßen *to a certain extent*, II4
der Einkauf, ⸚e *purchase*, II8
einkaufen (sep) *to shop*, I; **einkaufen gehen** *to go shopping*, I, II5
der Einkaufsbummel *window shopping*, II9
die Einkaufsliste, -n *shopping list*, II5
das Einkaufszentrum *shopping center*, II2
der Einkaufszettel, - *shopping list*, II2
das Einkommen, - *income*, II7
einladen (sep) *to invite*, I; **er/sie lädt … ein** *he/she invites*, I
die Einladung, -en *invitation*, II1
einlegen (sep): **ein Video einlegen** *to insert a video*, II3
einmal *once*, I; **einmal am Tag** *once a day*, II4
einmalig *unique*, II9
einnehmen (sep) *to take*, II6
der Einreiher, - *coat with one row of buttons*, II8
einrichten (sep) *to arrange*, II7
die Einrichtung, -en *arrangement*, II11
einsam *lonely*, II12
der Einsatz, ⸚e *stake*, II10
einschalten (sep) *turn on*, II10
die Einschaltquote, -n *number of viewers*, II10
einschlafen (sep) *to fall asleep*, II12
einschüchtern (sep) *to intimidate*, II7
einsetzen (sep) *to put, fill in*, II7
einsteigen (sep) *to get into, onto a vehicle*, II10
die Einstellung, -en *attitude, outlook*, II8
eintragen (sep) *to record (an entry)*, II2

eintreten (sep) *to enter*, II6
Einverstanden! *Agreed!*, II10
die Einweihung, -en *(formal) opening*, II3
der Einwohner, - *resident*, Loc 1
einzeln *single, individual, solitary*, II2
einzig *only; unique*, II9
das Eis *ice cream*, I
der Eisbecher, - *a dish of ice cream*, I
das Eisbein *pickled knuckle of pork*, Loc 10
die Eischeibe, -n *slice of egg*, II5
der Eistee *iced tea*, II5
elastisch *elastic*, II8
elegant *elegant*, II12
die Elektroindustrie, -n *electrical appliances industry*, Loc 1
die Elektrotechnik *electrical engineering*, Loc 4
der Ellbogen, - *elbow*, II6
die Eltern (pl) *parents*, I
empfangen *to greet, receive*, II10
empfehlen *to recommend*, II11
die Empfehlung, -en *recommendation*, II11
empfinden *to feel*, II9
das Ende, -n *end*, II2
endgültig *final(ly), last(ly)*, II12
endlich *at last*, II8
die Endung, -en *ending*, II5
die Energie, -n *energy*, II4
eng *tight*, I
englisch (adj) *English*, II1
das Englisch *English (school subject)*, I; *(language)*, I
das Englischlernen *learning English*, II6
englischsprechend *English-speaking*, II12
die Englischvokabel, -n *English vocabulary word*, II6
die Entdeckungsreise, -n *voyage of discovery or exploration*, II12
die Entdeckungstour, -en *discovery tour*, II12
die Ente, -n *duck*, II11
entfernt *far-off, distant*, II3
enthalten *to contain*, II2
entlang *along*, II9
s. entscheiden *to decide*, II9
entscheidend sein *to be crucial*, II9
Entschuldigung! *Excuse me!*, I
s. entspannen *to relax*, II9
die Entspannung, -en *relaxation*, II12
entsprechen (dat) *to correspond to, to agree with*, II2
entstehen *to come into existence*, II12
enttäuscht *disappointed*, II9
entweder: **entweder … oder** *either … or*, II3
entwerfen *to draw up, draft, design*, II2
entwickeln *to develop*, II11
die Epoche, -n *epoch*, II3
er *he*, I; *it*, I

German-English Vocabulary

erarbeiten *to get or gain by working for*, II7
erbaut *built, constructed*, Loc 1
die **Erbse, -n** *pea*, II2
die **Erdbeere, -n** *strawberry*, II4; **Erdbeeren mit Sahne** *strawberries with whipped cream*, II11
die **Erdkunde** *geography*, I
die **Erdnussbutter** *peanut butter*, II5
erfahren *to experience*, II3
der **Erfahrene, -n** *experienced (person)*, II12
erfinden *to invent*, II3
der **Erfolg, -e** *success*, II12
erfolgreich *successful*, II10
erfragen *to ascertain by questioning*, II3
erfrischen *to refresh, revive*, II12
erfüllen *to fulfill*, II7
ergänzen *to add to, complete*, II4
ergeben *to produce, yield*, II9
das **Ergebnis, -se** *result*, II2
erhalten: gut erhalten *well maintained*, II9
erhältlich *obtainable*, II9
erhöht *raised*, II6
s. **erholen** *to recover*, II12
die **Erholung, -en** *recovery*, II9
der **Erholungssuchende, -n** *person looking to recuperate*, II12
s. **erinnern an** (acc) *to remember, to remind one of*, II3
s. **erkälten** *to catch cold*, II12
die **Erkältung, -en** *cold* (illness), II6
erkennen *to recognize*, II3
erklären *to explain*, II5
erlaubt *permitted*, II10
erleben *to experience*, II9
das **Erlebnis, -se** *experience*, II5
ermitteln *to find out*, II10
s. **ernähren** *to feed, nourish*, II4
die **Ernährung** *food*, II4
der **Ernährungsbewusste, -n** *person conscious of his diet*, II12
erraten *solve a riddle, guess correctly*, II1
erscheinen *to appear*, II4
erst *first*, II1
erstaunlich *astonishing*, II5
erstellen *to make available*, II9
ersten: am ersten *on the first*, I
erstens *first of all*, II4
ersticken *to suffocate*, II8
ertragen *to bear*, II12
erträumen *to dream of or about, imagine*, II9
erwachsen (pp) *grown up*, II5
erwähnen *to mention*, II3
erwarten *to expect*, II11
erzählen *to tell* (a story), II1
die **Erzählung, -en** *story*, II12
essen *to eat*, I; **er/sie isst** *he/she eats*, I
der **Esslöffel=EL** *tablespoon*, II5
der **Esstisch, -e** *dining table*, I
das **Esszimmer, -** *dining room*, II7
etlich- *some, a certain*, II10

das **Etui, -s** *case*, II1
etwa *about, more or less*, II4
etwas *something*, I; **Sonst noch etwas?** *Anything else?*, I
euch (pl, acc case) *you*, I; (pl, dat case) *to you*, II3; (reflexive) *yourselves*, II4
euer (poss adj) *your*, II3
der **Euro, -** *euro* (the national currency of most European countries), I
der **Europäer, -** *European*, II12
europäisch (adj) *European*, II12
evangelisch *Protestant*, II9
exklusiv *exclusive*, II12
experimentieren *to experiment*, II8
der **Experte, -n** *expert*, II12

die **Fabrik, -en** *factory*, II8
das **Fach, ⸚er** *school subject*, I
fachmännisch (adj) *expert, competent*, II12
das **Fachwerkhaus, ⸚er** *cross-timbered house*, II3
fahren *to go, ride, drive* (using a vehicle), I; **er/sie fährt** *he/she drives*, I; **Fahren wir mal nach … !** *Let's go to … !*, II9
der **Fahrgast, -e** *passenger*, II11
die **Fahrpraxis** *driving experience*, II10
das **Fahrrad, ⸚er** *bicycle*, II4
das **Fahrrad-Depot, -s** *bicycle shed*, II12
die **Fahrradclique, -n** *bicycle group*, II1
die **Fahrradtour, -en** *tour by bicycle*, II9
die **Fahrschule, -n** *driving school*, II10
die **Fahrstunde, -n** *driving lesson*, II10
die **Fahrt, -en** *ride, drive, journey*, II2
die **Fahrzeit, -en** *travel time*, II11
das **Fahrzeug, -e** *vehicle*, II7
der **Fakir, -e** *fakir*, II7
der **Fall, ⸚e** *case*, II3
das **Fallschirmspringen** *skydiving*, II10
der **Faltenrock, ⸚e** *pleated skirt*, II8
die **Familie, -n** *family*, I
das **Familienmitglied, -er** *family member*, II5
die **Familiensendung, -en** *family program*, II10
der **Fantasyroman, -e** *fantasy novel*, I
das **Farbbild, -er** *color photograph*, II3
die **Farbe, -n** *color*, I
das **Farbfernsehgerät, -e** *color TV set*, II10
farblich *colorful*, II8
die **Faser, -n** *thread, material*, II8
faszinierend *fascinating*, Loc 10
faul *lazy*, II1

faulenzen *to be lazy*, II3
der **Februar** *February*, I
fechten *to fence*, II1
fehlen: Was fehlt dir? *What's wrong with you?*, II6
der **Fehler, -** *mistake*, II2
die **Feier, -n** *celebration, party*, II2
der **Feiertag, -e** *holiday*, I
fein *fine, exquisite*, II12
der **Feind, -e** *enemy*, II4
die **Feinmechanik** *precision tool mechanics*, Loc 7
der **Fels, -en** *boulder*, II9
feminin *feminine*, II5
das **Fenster, -** *window*, I
die **Ferien** (pl) *vacation* (from school), II3
das **Ferienangebot, -e** *special vacation offer*, II9
der **Ferienjob** *summer job*, II9
der **Ferienort, -e** *resort*, II3
das **Ferienparadies, -e** *vacation paradise*, II9
der **Ferienplan, ⸚e** *vacation plan*, II9
das **Ferienziel, -e** *vacation destination*, II12
die **Fernbedienung, -en** *remote control*, II10
Fernseh gucken *to watch TV* (colloquial), II10
der **Fernseh- und Videowagen** *TV and video cart*, II10
die **Fernsehanstalt, -en** *TV station*, II10
fernsehen (sep) *to watch TV*, II10
Fernsehen schauen *to watch TV*, I
der **Fernseher, -** *television set*, II10
das **Fernsehgerät, -e** *television set*, II10
die **Fernsehgewohnheit, -en** *TV viewing habit*, II10
der **Fernsehgucker, -** *TV viewer*, II10
der **Fernsehkonsum** *time spent watching television*, II10
das **Fernsehmagazin, -e** *TV magazine*, II10
das **Fernsehprogramm, -e** *TV schedule*, II10
der **Fernsehrat** *TV advisory board*, II10
der **Fernsehraum, ⸚e** *TV room*, II9
die **Fernsehsaison, -s** *programming season*, II10
die **Fernsehsendung, -en** *TV program, show*, II12
der **Fernsehzuschauer, -** *TV viewer*, II10
fertigen *to finish*, II9
das **Fertiggericht, -e** *frozen food*, II5
fesch *stylish, smart*, I
fest *firm*, II12
das **Festland** *mainland*, II9
die **Festlichkeit, -en** *party, celebration*, II12
feststellen (sep) *determine*, II6
der **Festtag, -e** *holiday, festival*, II8
fett *fat, greasy*, II6

das Fett: **hat zu viel Fett** *has too much fat*, II4
die **Fettucine**, (pl) *fettucine*, II12
fetzig *really sharp (looking)*, II8
feuerrot *bright red*, II8
das **Fieber**, - *fever*, II6
der **Film, -e** *movie*, I; *roll of film*, II3
filmen *to film, videotape*, II3
der **Filzstift**, -e *felt-tip pen*, II1
die **Finanzmetropole**, -n *financial center*, II3
finden *to think about, to find*, I; **Das finde ich auch.** *I think so, too.*, I; **Das finde ich nicht.** *I disagree.*, I; *I don't think so.*, II10; **Ich finde es gut/schlecht, dass …** *I think it's good/bad that …*, I; **Ich finde den Pulli stark!** *The sweater is awesome!*, I; **Wie findest du (Tennis)?** *What do you think of (tennis)?*, I
die **Firma**, (pl) Firmen *company*, II3
der **Fisch, -e** *fish*, I
das **Fischerdorf**, ¨-er *fishing village*, II9
die **Fischerhose**, -n *pedal pushers*, II8
das **Fischgericht**, -e *fish entrée*, II11
das **Fischstäbchen**, - *fish stick*, II5
s. **fit halten** *to stay fit*, II4
die **Fitness** *fitness*, II12
die **Fitnessgewohnheit**, -en *fitness habit*, II4
der **Fitnessraum**, ¨-e *training and weight room*, II9
flach *flat*, II8
die **Fläche**, -n *flat area, surface*, Loc 1
die **Flasche**, -n *bottle*, II5
die **Fledermaus**, ¨-e *bat*, II11
das **Fleisch** *meat*, I
das **Fleischgericht**, -e *meat dish*, II11
der **Fleischsalat**, -e *meat salad*, II5
der **Fleiß** *diligence*, II7
fleißig *hard-working*, II1
die **Fliege**, -n *bow tie*, II12
fliegen *to fly*, II9
die **Fliese**, -n *tile*, II12
der **Flohmarkt**, ¨-e *flea market*, II1
flott *lively, brisk*, II12
der **Flug**, ¨-e *flight*, II12
der **Flughafen**, ¨ *airport*, II3
die **Flugstunde**, -n *hour of flying time*, II12
das **Flugzeug**, -e *airplane*, II7
der **Flur**, -e *hallway*, II7
der **Fluss**, ¨-e *river*, II7
das **Flüsschen**, - *streamlet*, II9
das **Flusspferd**, -e *hippopotamus*, II10
folgen (dat) *to follow*, II8
folgend- *following*, II2
fordern *to demand*, II5
die **Forelle**, -n *trout*, II4
das **Forellenfilet**, -s *trout fillet*, II11
die **Forstwirtschaft** *forestry*, Loc 1
der **Fortgeschrittene**, -n *advanced (person)*, II12
das **Foto**, -s *photo*, II1
die **Fotogeschichte**, -n *photo story*, II6

der **Fotograf**, -en *photographer*, II12
fotografieren *to photograph*, II3
die **Frage**, -n *question*, II4
der **Fragebogen**, ¨ *questionnaire*, II3
fragen *to ask*, II4
(das) **Frankreich** *France*, II4
fransig *frayed*, II8
französisch (adj) *French*, II11
die **Frau**, -en *woman; Ms.*, I
die **Frauenrechtlerin**, -nen *supporter of equal rights for women (female)*, Loc 7
frei *free*, II9; **Wir haben frei.** *We have off (from school).*, I
freilich *to be sure, quite so*, II11
der **Freitag** *Friday*, I
freitags *Fridays*, II10
freiwillig *voluntary*, II9
die **Freizeit** *free time, leisure time*, I
die **Freizeitbeschäftigung**, -en *free time activity*, II3
das **Freizeitzentrum**, (pl) -zentren *leisure time meeting area*, II1
fremd *foreign; strange*, II11
der **Fremdenverkehrsverein**, -e *tourist bureau*, II3
das **Fremdwort**, ¨-er *foreign word*, II2
die **Freude** *happiness*, II9
s. **freuen auf** (acc) *to look forward to*, II10
s. **freuen über** (acc) *to be happy about*, II4; **Ich freue mich, dass …** *I am happy that …*, II4
der **Freund**, -e *friend (male)*, I
die **Freundin**, -nen *friend (female)*, II1
freundlich *friendly*, II1
die **Freundschaft**, -en *friendship*, II10
friedlich *peaceful*, II7
frisch *fresh*, I
der **Friseur**, -e *hair stylist*, II12
froh *happy*, II4
fröhlich *cheerful, happy*, II2
der **Froschschenkel**, - *frog's leg*, II5
die **Frucht**, ¨-e *fruit*, II5
das **Fruchtfleisch** *fruit pulp*, II5
der **Fruchtsaft**, ¨-e *fruit juice*, II11
früh *early*, II6
früher *former, earlier*, II7
der **Frühling** *spring (season)*, I
das **Frühstück**, -e *breakfast*, II5
s. **fühlen** *to feel*, II4; **Ich fühle mich wohl!** *I feel great!*, II6
führen *to lead*, II9
der **Führerschein**, -e *driver's license*, II10
die **Fülle**, -n *fullness, abundance*, II4
fünft- *fifth*, II9
fünftgrößt- *fifth biggest*, II3
fünfzeilig *five line*, II7
funken *to radio*, II11
für (prep) *for*, I
furchtbar *terrible, awful*, I; **furchtbar gern haben** *to like a lot*, I
fürs=für das *for it*, II1
der **Fuß**, ¨-e *foot*, II6

der **Fußball** *soccer*, I
der **Fußboden**, ¨ *floor*, II12
die **Fußbremse**, -n *foot brake*, II10
die **Fußgängerzone**, -n *pedestrian zone*, II9
füttern *to feed*, I

gähnen *to yawn*, II12
ganz *really, quite*, I; *all, whole*, II1; **Ganz klar!** *Of course!*, I; **ganz wohl** *extremely well*, II4
ganz schön eng *quite narrow*, II5
gar nicht gern haben *not to like at all*, I
die **Garage**, -n *garage*, II2; **die Garage aufräumen** *to clean the garage*, II2
die **Gardine**, -n *curtain*, II7
der **Garten**, ¨ *garden, yard*, I
die **Gartenarbeit**, -en *yard work*, II2
der **Gast**, ¨-e *guest*, II3
der **Gastgeber**, - *host*, II2
das **Gasthaus**, ¨-er *hotel, bed and breakfast*, II3
der **Gasthof**, ¨-e *restaurant, inn*, II3
das **Gastland**, ¨-er *host country*, II9
die **Gastronomie** *gastronomy*, II3
die **Gaststätte**, -n *restaurant, coffee house*, II12
der **Gastwirt**, -e *owner of a restaurant, hotel*, II12
der **Gaumen**, - *palate*, II4
das **Gebäude**, - *building*, Loc 4
geben *to give*, I; **er/sie gibt** *he/she gives*, I; **es gibt** *there is, there are*; **Das gibt's doch nicht!** *There's just no way!*, II10
gebeten *asked*, II12
das **Gebirge**, - *mountains*, II3
geblieben *remained, stayed*, II3
geblümt *flowery*, II8
geboren *born*, II3
das **Gebot**, -e *commandment*, II4
gebracht *brought*, 8
gebraten *fried*, II11
gebrauchen *to use*, II1
gebrochen *broken*, II6
der **Geburtstag**, -e *birthday*, I; **Alles Gute zum Geburtstag!** *Best wishes on your birthday!*, I; **Herzlichen Glückwunsch zum Geburtstag!** *Best wishes on your birthday!*, I; **Ich habe am … Geburtstag.** *My birthday is on …*, I
die **Geburtstagsfeier**, -n *birthday celebration*, II11
die **Geburtstagsfete**, -n *birthday party*, II2

die **Gedächtniskirche** *Memorial Church*, Loc 10
gedämpft *subdued*, II5
der **Gedanke, -n** *thought, idea*, II5
das **Gedicht, -e** *poem*, II7
gefächert *varied*, II11
gefährlich *dangerous*, II10
gefallen *to like;* **Hat es dir gefallen?** *Did you like it?*, II3; **Wie hat es dir gefallen?** *How did you like it?*, II3
das **Gefäß, -e** *container for liquid*, II3
gefüllt: das gefüllte Ei, -er *deviled egg*, II11
gefüttert *padded*, II8
gegangen *gone*, II3
gegen (prep) *against*, II1
die **Gegend, -en** *area*, II7
gegenseitig *mutual(ly)*, II1
gegenüber (prep) *across from*, II9
gegessen *eaten*, II3
der **Gegner, -** *opponent*, II1
gegrillt *grilled*, II11
gehackt *chopped*, II12
der **Geheimtipp, -s** *secret tip*, II12
gehen *to go*, I; **Das geht nicht.** *That won't work*, I; **Es geht.** *It's okay*, I; **Wie geht's (denn)?** *How are you?*, I; **Gehen wir mal auf den Golfplatz!** *Let's go to the golf course!*, II9
geholfen *helped*, II3
der **Geigenbau** *violin making*, Loc 1
gekauft *bought*, I; **Was hast du gekauft?** *What did you buy?*, I
gekleidet *dressed*, II12
geknotet *knotted, tied*, II1
gekrönt *crowned*, II3
gekühlt *cooled*, II5
gekürzt *shortened, abbreviated*, II3
gelähmt *paralyzed*, II10
gelaunt: gut gelaunt *in a good mood*, II1; **schlecht gelaunt** *in a bad mood*, II1
gelb *yellow*, I
das **Geld** *money*, I
die **Gelegenheit, -en** *opportunity*, II2
gelesen (pp) *read*, I; **Was hast du gelesen?** *What did you read?*, I
gemacht *done*, I; **Was hast du am Wochenende gemacht?** *What did you do on the weekend?*, I
gemahlen (pp) *milled, ground*, II12
das **Gemälde, -** *painting*, II2
die **Gemäldegalerie, -n** *gallery*, II3
gemeinsam *in common; joint, together*, II3
die **Gemeinschaft, -en** *community*, II3
gemietet *rented*, II12
gemischt *mixed*, II11
das **Gemüse** *vegetables*, I; **im Obst- und Gemüseladen** *at the produce store*, I
die **Gemüsefrau** *produce vendor (female)*, II2
der **Gemüseladen, -̈** *produce store*, I

der **Gemüsemann** *produce vendor (male)*, II2
die **Gemüsesuppe, -n** *vegetable soup*, II5
gemustert *patterned*, II8
gemütlich *comfortable*, II7
genannt *named*, II3
genau *exact(ly)*, II4
genauso wie *just as …*, II8
das **Genie, -s** *genius*, II12
genießen *to enjoy*, II9
genossen *enjoyed*, II3
genug *enough*, I; **Ich habe genug.** *I have enough.*, I
genügend *enough*, II4; **genügend schlafen** *to get enough sleep*, II4
der **Genuss, -̈e** *pleasure*, II6
die **Geografie** *geography*, I
gepflegt *well cared for, well groomed*, II12
gepunktet *polka-dotted*, I
gerade *straight*, II2; *precisely, just*, II9; **Das ist gerade passiert.** *It just happened.*, II9
geradeaus *straight ahead*, I
das **Gerät, -e** *appliance*, II10
geraten: in Schwierigkeiten geraten *to get into trouble*, II4
geräuchert *smoked*, II11
das **Gericht, -e** *meal, entrée*, II11
gerieben *grated*, II12
gering *small, unimportant*, II7
die **Germanistik** (sing) *German studies*, II4
gern (machen) *to like (to do)*, I; **gern haben** *to like*, I; **Gern geschehen!** *My pleasure!*, I; **besonders gern** *especially like*, I; **Gern! Hier ist es!** *Here! I insist!*, II10
gerne=gern, II2
der **Gesamtpreis, -e** *total price*, II8
der **Gesamtschüler, -** *student at a comprehensive school*, II8
die **Gesäßtasche, -n** *back pocket*, II8
das **Geschäft, -e** *store; business*, I
die **Geschäftsleute** (pl) *business people*, II11
gescheit *intelligent*, II8
das **Geschenk, -e** *gift*, I
die **Geschenkidee, -n** *gift idea*, I
die **Geschichte** *history*, I
das **Geschirr** *dishes*, I; **Geschirr spülen** *to wash the dishes*, I
das **Geschirrspülmittel, -** *dishwashing detergent*, II10
geschlossen *closed*, II7
der **Geschmack, -̈e** *taste*, II5
geschnitten (pp) *cut*, II12
geschrieben *written*, II2
die **Geschwindigkeitsbeschränkung, -en** *speed limit*, II7
die **Geschwister** (pl) *brothers and sisters*, I
geschwommen *swum*, II3
die **Gesellenprüfung, -en** *apprentice's final exam*, II7

die **Gesellschaft, -en** *social group; society*, II10
das **Gespräch, -e** *conversation*, II1
gesprochen *spoken*, I; **Worüber habt ihr gesprochen?** *What did you (pl) talk about?*, I
gestatten *to allow, permit*, II12
gestehen *to admit*, II11
gestern *yesterday*, I; **gestern Abend** *yesterday evening*, I
gestiegen *climbed*, II3
gestoßen *shoved*, II12
gestreift *striped*, I
gesund *healthy*, II4
die **Gesundheit** *health*, II4
der **Gesundheitsfanatiker, -** *health fanatic*, II4
der **Gesundheitstipp, -s** *health tip*, II4
gesüßt *sweetened*, II5
das **Getränk, -e** *drink*, II11
die **Getränkekarte, -n** *beverage menu*, II11
das **Getriebe, -** *transmission*, II10
gewesen (pp) *been*, II3
das **Gewichttraining** *weight training*, II12
das **Gewissen, -** *conscience*, II4
das **Gewitter, -** *thunderstorm*, I
die **Gewohnheit, -en** *habit*, II4
gewöhnlich *usually*, II3
das **Gewölbe, -** *archway, vault*, II3
gewonnen *won*, II8
geworden (pp) *became*, II12; **er ist groß geworden** *he got big, grew up*, II12
gezeigt *shown*, II2
gießen *to water*, I; **Blumen gießen** *to water the flowers*, I
giftfrei *non-toxic*, II7
die **Gitarre, -n** *guitar*, I
glänzen *to shine*, II3
das **Glas, -̈er** *glass*, I; **ein Glas Apfelsaft** *a glass of apple juice*, I
die **Glasscheibe, -n** *pane of glass*, II9
glauben *to believe*, I; **ich glaube** *I think*, I; **Ich glaube nicht, dass …** *I don't think that …*, II9
gleich *immediately; equal*, II9
gleichaltrig *of the same age*, II9
das **Gleiche** *the same*, II7
gleichfalls: Danke, gleichfalls! *Thank you and the same to you!*, II11
gleichmäßig *even, symmetrical*, II5
glotzen *to stare*, II10; **Fernseh glotzen** *to watch TV*, II10
das **Glück** *luck*, I; **So ein Glück!** *What luck!*, I
das **Glücksrad, -̈er** *lotto wheel, wheel of fortune*, II10
das **Goethehaus** *(Goethe's birthplace)*, II3
Golf *golf*, I
der **Golfplatz, -̈e** *golf course*, II9
der **Gott, -̈er** *God*, II1; **um Gottes willen** *for God's sake*, II11

die Götterdämmerung, -en *twilight of the gods*, II11
der Grad *degree(s)*, I; **zwei Grad** *two degrees*, I; **Wie viel Grad haben wir?** *What's the temperature?*, I
das Gramm *gram*, I
das Gras, ¨-er *grass* II4
grau *gray*, I; **in Grau** *in gray*, I
grausam *cruel*, I
die Grenze, -n *border*, II12
der Grieche -n *Greek*, II9
Griechenland (das) *Greece* II9
griechisch (adj) *Greek*, II11
groß *big*, I
großartig *wonderful*, II4
Großbritannien (das) *Great Britain*, II9
die Größe, -n *size*, I
die Großeltern (pl) *grandparents*, I
größer *bigger*, II7
die Großmutter, ¨- *grandmother*, I
der Großraum, ¨-e *metropolitan area*, Loc 10
die Großstadt, ¨-e *big city*, II7
der Großvater, ¨- *grandfather*, I
die Großzügigkeit, -en *generosity*, II8
gruftimäßig *grunge*, II8
grün *green*, I; **in Grün** *in green*, I
der Grund *reason*, II2
der Grundriss, -e *framework*, II7
der Grundschüler, - *elementary school student*, II2
die Gruppe, -n *group*, I
gruselig *horrible, frightening*, II9
der Gruselroman, -e *horror novel*, I
der Gruß, ¨-e *greeting*, II7; **grüßen** *to greet*, II1; **Grüß dich!** *Hi!*, I; **Grüß Gott!** *Hello!*, II1
die Grütze: **Rote Grütze** (name of a dessert), II11
gucken *to look*, II5; **Guck mal!** *Look!*, II5; **Fernseh gucken** *to watch TV* (colloquial), II10
das Gulasch, -e *goulash*, II11
das Gummiband, ¨-er *rubber band*, II8
günstig *favorable*, II9
die Gurke, -n *cucumber*, II2
die Gurkenscheibe, -n *cucumber slice*, II2
der Gürtel, - *belt*, I
gut *good*, I; **Gut!** *Good! Well!*, I; **gut gelaunt** *in a good mood*, II1; **Gut! Mach ich!** *Okay, I'll do that!*, I; **gut sein: Ist dir nicht gut?** *Are you not feeling well?*, II6
die Gürtelschlaufe, -n *belt loop*, II8
guterhalten *well-preserved*, II9
der Gymnasiast, -en *student in Gymnasium (male)*, II2
die Gymnasiastin, -nen *student in Gymnasium (female)*, II2
die Gymnastik *exercise, calisthenics*, II4; **Gymnastik machen** *to exercise*, II4
das Gyros *gyros*, I

H

das Haar, -e *hair*, I
die Haarfarbe *hair color*, II1
die Haarlänge *hair length*, II1
haben *to have*, I; **er/sie hat** *he/she has*, I; **Haben Sie das auch in Rot?** *Do you also have that in red?*, I
die Hacke, -n *hoe*, II7
der Hacken, - *heel*, II8
das Hackfleisch *ground meat*, I
die Haftung, -en *liability*, II2
das Hähnchen, - *chicken*, I
halb *half*, I; **halb (eins, zwei, usw.)** *half past (twelve, one, etc.)*, I
halblaut (adj) *whispering*, II11
die Hälfte, -n *half*, II12
die Halle, -n *hall*, II12
das Hallenbad, ¨-er *indoor pool*, II9
Hallo! *Hi! Hello!*, I
der Hals, ¨-e *throat*, II6
die Halskette, -n *necklace*, II1
die Halsschmerzen (pl) *sore throat*, II6
das Halstuch, ¨-er *kerchief*, II1
das Halsweh *sore throat*, II6
halt (particle), I; **Die Kleinstadt gefällt mir gut, weil es da halt ruhiger ist.** *I like a small town because it's just quieter there.*, II7
halten *to stop, hold*, II4; **(für)** *to consider as*, II9; **s. fit halten** *to keep fit*, II4
der Hamster, - *hamster*, II7
die Hand, ¨-e *hand*, II6
die Handbremse, -n *emergency brake*, II10
die Handcreme *hand cream*, II6
der Handel *business, trade*, Loc 7
handeln von *to be about*, II12
der Handelsplatz, ¨-e *trading center*, Loc 4
die Handtasche, -n *handbag*, II1
das Handy, -s *cell phone*, I
hängen *to hang*, II3
hart *hard, tough*, II6; **hart gekocht** *hard-boiled*, II5
hassen *to hate*, II5
hässlich *ugly*, I
hätte: **Ich hätte gern …** *I would like …*, II11
der Haufen, - *pile*, II7
häufig *frequent(ly)*, II6
das Hauptgericht, -e *main dish*, II11
der Hauptpunkt, -e *main point*, II3
der Hauptschüler, - *(male) student at the Hauptschule*, II8
die Hauptschülerin, -nen *(female) student at the Hauptschule*, II8
die Hauptstadt, ¨-e *capital*, I
die Hauptstraße, -n *main street*, II9
die Haupturlaubsreise, -n *main vacation trip*, II9
das Hauptwort, ¨-er *noun*, II11

das Haus, ¨-er *house*, II7; **zu Hause bleiben** *to stay at home*, II6
Haus halten *to keep house*, II10
die Hausarbeit, -en *housework*, II2
die Hausaufgaben (pl) *homework*, I; **Hausaufgaben machen** *to do homework*, I
hausgemacht *home-made*, II11
der Haushalt, -e *household*, II10
die Hausmannskost *simple, hearty food*, II5
das Haustier, -e *pet*, I
die Haut, ¨-e *skin*, II6
die Heckenschere, -n *pruning shears*, II7
das Heft, -e *notebook*, I
heftig *intense*, II10
die Heide *heath*, II7
der Heilbutt *halibut*, II5
das Heim, -e *home; institute*, II10
der Heimatort, -e *native place*, II7
die Heimatstadt, ¨-e *native city*, II7
die Heimfahrt *trip home*, II2
das Heimweh *homesickness*, II4
heiß *hot*, I
heißen *to be called*, I; **er heißt** *his name is*, I
helfen (dat) *to help*, I; **zu Hause helfen** *to help at home*, I
hell *bright*, II7
hellbraun *light brown*, II1
das Hemd, -en *shirt*, I
die Hemdbluse, -n *shirt*, II8
heraus *out*, II3
herausfinden (sep) *to find out*, II5
herauslösen (sep) *to filter out, to remove*, II5
herausnehmen (sep) *to take out*, II3
herausschneiden (sep) *to cut out*, II5
heraussuchen (sep) *to pick out, select*, II8
der Herbst *fall (season)*, I; **im Herbst** *in the fall*, I
der Herd, -e *stove*, I
herstellen (sep) *to manufacture, produce*, II5
der Herr *Mr.*, I
herrlich *fantastic*, II9
die Herrschaft, -en *rule, dominion; person*, II3
herumlaufen (sep) *to run around*, II11
das Herz, -en *heart*, II6
herzhaft *hearty*, II11
herzlich *heartfelt*, II12; **Herzlichen Glückwunsch zum Geburtstag!** *Best wishes on your birthday!*, I
der Herzog, ¨-e *duke*, II1
das Heu *hay*, II 4
der Heuboden, ¨- *hayloft*, II9
heulen *to cry*, II9
heute *today*, I; **heute Morgen** *this morning*, I; **heute Nachmittag**

GERMAN-ENGLISH VOCABULARY R47

this afternoon, I; **heute Abend** *tonight, this evening*, I
heutzutage *nowadays*, II8
hier *here*, I; **Hier bei …** *The … residence.*, I; **Hier ist … This is …*, I
die **Hilfe, -n** *help*, II11
die **Hilfsbereitschaft** *cooperation*, II8
die **Himbeere, -n** *raspberry*, II2
die **Himbeermarmelade, -n** *raspberry marmalade*, II5
die **Himbeertorte, -n** *raspberry cake*, II1
der **Himmel, -** *sky, heaven*, II6
das **Himmelbett, -en** *canopy bed*, II7
hin *to*, II1
hinaus *out*, II7
hinausziehen (sep) *to go outside*, II7
hinein *into*, II12
hineinwerfen (sep) *to throw into*, II12
hingehen (sep) *to go to*, II2
hinten *at the back*, II1; **da hinten** *there in the back*, I
der **Hintergrund, ⸚e** *background*, II11
hinterlassen *to leave behind*, II9
der **Hinweis, -e** *hint, direction*, II4
historisch *historical*, II1
die **Hitze** *heat*, II6
der **Hitzschlag, ⸚e** *heat stroke*, II6
hob (past) *lifted*, II12
das **Hobby, -s** *hobby*, II1
hobbymäßig *for a hobby*, II10
hoch *high*, II6
hochkriechen (sep) *to creep up*, II12
hochrot *deep red, crimson*, II6
das **Hochwasser, ⸚** *flood*, II9
die **Hochzeit, -en** *wedding*, II12
der **Hof, ⸚e** *court, courtyard*, II9
hoffen *to hope*, II6
hoffentlich … *hopefully …*, II6; **Hoffentlich geht es dir bald besser!** *I hope you'll get better soon.*, II6
die **Hoffnung, -en** *hope*, II6
höflich *polite, courteous*, II12
hoh- *high*, II1
höher: noch höher *still higher*, II10
holen *to get, fetch*, I
holländisch *Dutch*, II5
das **Holz, ⸚er** *wood*, I; **aus Holz** *out of wood*, I
der **Holztisch, -e** *wooden table*, II9
der **Honig** *honey*, II5
hören: Hör mal zu! *Listen to this!*, II5; **Hör mal!** *Listen!*, II5; **Musik hören** *to listen to music*, I; **Hör gut zu!** *Listen carefully.*, I
horchen *to listen carefully*, II12
der **Hörer, -** *listener; receiver*, I; **den Hörer abheben** *to pick up the receiver*, I; **den Hörer auflegen** *to hang up (the telephone)*, I

der **Horrorfilm, -e** *horror movie*, I
die **Hose, -n** *pants*, I
das **Hotel, -s** *hotel*, I
hübsch *pretty*, I
die **Hüfte, -n** *hip*, II6
das **Huhn, ⸚er** *chicken*, II4
der **Hummer, -** *lobster*, II11
humorvoll *humorous*, II8
der **Hund, -e** *dog*, I
hundelieb *fond of dogs*, II12
der **Hunger** *hunger*, I; **Ich habe Hunger.** *I am hungry*, II6
hungrig *hungry*, II12
hupen *to honk the horn*, II7
der **Hürdenlauf, ⸚e** *hurdling*, II1
der **Husten, -** *cough*, II6
der **Hut, ⸚e** *hat*, II1

ich *I*, I; **Ich auch.** *Me too.*, I; **Ich nicht.** *I don't.*, I
die **Idee, -n** *idea*, II9; **Gute Idee!** *Good idea!*, II12; **Hast du eine Idee?** *Do you have an idea?*, II9
identifizieren *to identify*, II1
s. **identifizieren mit** *to identify yourself with*, II7
das **Idol, -e** *idol*, II1
ihm *to, for him*, I
ihn *it, him*, I
ihnen *to them*, II3
Ihnen (formal) *to you*, II3
ihr (poss adj) *her, their*, I; *to, for her*, I; (pl) *you*, I
Ihr (poss adj, formal, pl, sing) *your*, II5
die **Illustration, -en** *illustration*, II7
die **Illustrierte, -n** *magazine*, II5
im=in dem; im Frühling *in the spring*, I; **im Januar** *in January*, I; **(einmal) im Monat** *(once) a month*, I; **im Wohnzimmer** *in the living room*, I
der **Imbissstand, ⸚e** *fast-food stand*, II2
die **Imbissstube, -n** *snack bar*, I
immer *always*, I
das **Imperfekt** *past tense*, II3
imposant *impressive, majestic*, II9
in (prep) *in, into*, II9; **in Blau** *in blue*, I; **in der (Basketball) Mannschaft** *on the (basketball) team*, II4; **in die Apotheke gehen** *to go to the pharmacy*, II6
indem (conj) *in that*, II11
indisch (adj) *Indian*, II11
individuell (adj) *individual*, II12
die **Industrie, -n** *industry*, Loc 1
der **Industriestandort, -e** *industrial location*, Loc 7
das **Infoblatt, ⸚er** *information brochure*, II4

die **Informatik, ⸚e** *computer science*, I
die **Information, -en** *information*, II4
der **Innenraum, ⸚e** *interior, inside*, II5
die **Innenstadt, ⸚e** *downtown*, II9
die **Innentasche, -n** *inside pocket*, II8
die **Innereien** (pl) *innards*, II5
innerhalb (prep) *within, on the inside*, II12
die **Insel, -n** *island*, II12
insgesamt *altogether*, II5
das **Instrument, -e** *instrument*, I
intelligent *intelligent*, II1
intensiv *intensive*, II6
interessant *interesting*, I
das **Interesse, -n** *interest*, I; **Hast du andere Interessen?** *Do you have any other interests?*, I; **Ich habe kein Interesse an Mode.** *I am not interested in fashion.*, II8
s. **interessieren für** *to be interested in*, I18; **Interessierst du dich für Mode?** *Are you interested in fashion?*, II8
international *international*, II7
das **Internet** *Internet*, I
interviewen *to interview*, II7
inzwischen *in the meantime*, II12
irgendein- *someone, something*, II2
irgendwas *anything, something*, II2
irgendwelch- *some, any*, II2
irgendwie *somehow*, II1
irgendwo *somewhere*, II2
irgendwohin *to somewhere*, II1
das **Islandpferd, -e** *Iceland pony*, II3
ist: er/sie/es ist *he/she/it is*, I; **sie ist aus** *she's from*, I; **Ist was mit dir?** *Is something wrong?*, II6
Italien (das) *Italy*, II9
der **Italiener, -** *Italian*, II9
italienisch (adj) *Italian*, II11

ja *yes*, I; **Ja klar!** *Of course!*, I; **Das ist ja unglaublich!** *That's really unbelievable!*, II10; **Ja, kann sein, aber …** *Yes, maybe, but …*, II4; **Ja, natürlich!** *Certainly!*, II4; **Ja, of course!**, II10; **Ja, schon, aber …** *Well yes, but …*, II7; **Ja? Was denn?** *Okay, what is it?*, II5
die **Jacke, -n** *jacket*, I
das **Jahr, -e** *year*, I; **Ich bin … Jahre alt.** *I am …years old.*, I
der **Jahrestil, -e** *year's style*, II8
die **Jahreszeit, -en** *season*, II5
das **Jahrhundert, -e** *century*, II9; **aus dem 17. Jahrhundert** *from the 17th century*, II9
jährig *year-old*, II9
jahrzehntelang *for decades*, Loc 4

der **Januar** *January*, I; **im Januar** *in January*, I
der **Japangarten** *Japanese garden*, II9
je *each, every*, II8; **je nach Gelegenheit** *according to the occasion*, II8
die **Jeans** (mostly sing) *jeans*, I
die **Jeansjacke, -n** *jeans jacket*, II1
die **Jeansweste, -n** *jeans vest*, II8
jed- *every*, II2; **jede Woche** *every week*, II4; **jeden Tag** *every day*, I; **jedes Wochenende** *every weekend*, II4
jemand *someone, somebody*, II6
jenseits (prep) *on the other side, beyond*, II12
jetzt *at present, now*, I
der **Job, -s** *job*, II7
das **Jobangebot, -e** *job offer*, II12
joggen *to jog*, I
der **Jogging-Anzug, ̈-e** *jogging suit*, I
der **Joghurt, -s** (or **das**) *yogurt*, I
die **Jugend** *youth*, II3
die **Jugendherberge, -n** *youth hostel*, II3
das **Jugendlager, -** *youth camp*, II9
der **Jugendliche, -n** *teenager (male)*, II8
die **Jugendliche, -n** *teenager (female)*, II8
die **Jugendpflege, -n** *youth welfare*, II11
der **Juli** *July*, I
jung *young*, II7
der **Junge, -n** *boy*, I
jünger *younger*, II7
der **Juni** *June*, I
der **Jux** *practical joke*, II12

das **Kabarett, -e** *cabaret*, II11
das **Kabelfernsehen** *cable TV*, II10
der **Kabeltuner, -** *cable tuner*, II10
das **Kabriolett, -s** *convertible, cabriolet*, II10
der **Kaffee** *coffee*, I
der **Kajak, -s** *canoe, kayak*, II7
der **Kakao** *chocolate milk*, II5
der **Kalender, -** *calendar*, I
kalifornisch (adj) *Californian*, II11
die **Kalorie, -n** *calorie*, II1
kalt (adj) *cold*, I
die **Kälte, -n** *cold, coldness*, II12
die **Kamera, -s** *camera*, II3
der **Kamin, -e** *fireplace, chimney*, II9
s. **kämmen** *to comb*, II6
die **Kammerspiele** (pl) *(small) theater*, II11

kämpfen *to fight*, II12
der **Kanake -n**, also der **Kanacke, -n**, *derogatory term for foreigner*, II11
der **Kanal, ̈-e** *canal*, II1
das **Kapitel, -** *chapter*, II1
das **Käppi, -s** *(baseball) cap*, II8
kaputt *ruined, broken*, I, II9
die **Kapuze, -n** *hood*, II8
kariert *checked*, II8
das **Karo, -s** *(pattern) check, diamond*, II12
die **Karotte, -n** *carrot*, II7
der **Karpfen, -** *carp*, II4
die **Karte, -n** *card; ticket*, I
die **Karteikarte, -n** *index card*, II7
die **Kartoffel, -n** *potato*, I
der **Käse, -** *cheese*, I
das **Käsebrot, -e** *cheese sandwich*, I
der **Käsekuchen, -** *cheese cake*, II5
die **Käserei, -en** *cheese dairy*, II9
die **Kasse, -n** *cash register*, II8
die **Kassette, -n** *cassette*, I
der **Kassettenspieler, -** *cassette deck*, II10
der **Kasten, ̈** *box*, II1
der **Katalog, -e** *catalogue*, II8
die **Kategorie, -n** *category*, II1
der **Katholik, -en** *Catholic*, II3
die **Katze, -n** *cat*, I
das **Kaubonbon, -s** *chewy candy*, II7
kauen *to chew*, II4
kaufen *to buy*, I
das **Kaufhaus, ̈-er** *department store*, II2
der **Kaufmann**, (pl) **Kaufleute** *salesman*, II11
der **Kaugummi, -s** *chewing gum*, II1
kaum *barely, hardly*, II6
der **Kavalierstart, -s** *jack-rabbit start*, II7
die **Kegelbahn, -en** *bowling alley*, II3
kegeln *to bowl*, II3
kein *no, none, not any*, I; **Ich habe keine Zeit.** *I don't have time.*, I; **Ich habe keinen Hunger mehr.** *I'm not hungry any more.*, I; **Keine Ahnung!** *I have no idea!*, I
der **Keks, -e** *cookie*, I
der **Keller, -** *cellar*, II7
der **Kellner, -** *waiter*, II11
kennen *to know, be familiar or acquainted with*, I
kennen lernen (sep) *to get to know*, II12
das **Kilo=Kilogramm, -** *kilogram*, I
das **Kind, -er** *child*, II1
die **Kinderermäßigung, -en** *discount for children*, II11
kinderlieb *fond of children*, II1
das **Kinderzimmer, -** *nursery, playroom*, II7
die **Kindheit** *childhood*, II3
das **Kinn, -e** *chin*, II3
das **Kino, -s** *cinema*, I; **ins Kino gehen** *to go to the movies*, I
die **Kirche, -n** *church*, I
die **Kirsche, -n** *cherry*, II4

die **Klamotten** (pl) *casual term for clothes*, I
der **Klang, ̈-e** *sound, ring*, II11; **vom Klang her** *as far as the sound goes*, II11
klappen *to go smoothly, work*, II9
klappern *to rattle, clatter*, II12
klar *clear*, II2
Klasse! *Great!; Terrific!*, I
die **Klasse, -n** *grade level*, I; *class*, II4
die **Klassenarbeit, -en** *(written) class test*, II6
der **Klassenkamerad, -en** *classmate (male)*, II2
die **Klassenkameradin, -nen** *classmate (female)*, II2
das **Klassenzimmer, -** *classroom*, II2
klassisch *classic(al)*, I
das **Klavier, -e** *piano*, I; **Ich spiele Klavier.** *I play the piano.*, I
kleben *to glue, stick*, II8
das **Kleid, -er** *dress*, I
die **Kleidung** *clothing*, II1
der **Kleidungsartikel, -** *article of clothing*, II8
die **Kleidungsreklame, -n** *clothing ad*, II8
der **Kleidungsstil, -e** *clothing style*, II8
das **Kleidungsstück, -e** *piece of clothing*, II12
klein *small*, I; **klein geschnitten** *cut small*, II12
die **Kleinstadt, ̈-e** *town*, II7
klettern *to climb*, II9
die **Klimaanlage, -n** *air conditioning*, II10
klingeln *to ring (the bell)*, II7
klingen *to sound*, II5
die **Klippe, -n** *cliff*, II12
der **Klops, -e** *meat ball*, II11
der **Kloß, ̈-e** *dumpling*, II11
das **Kloster, ̈** *monastery*, Loc 1
der **Klub, -s** *club*, II3
das **Klubmitglied, -er** *club member*, II3
die **Kluft** *gap, crevice*, II12
klug *intelligent*, II8
knabbern *to gnaw, nibble*, II2
knackig *crispy*, II4
knallgelb *glaring yellow*, II8
das **Knie, -** *knee*, II6
knien *to kneel*, II1
der **Knoblauch** *garlic*, II11
der **Knöchel, -** *ankle*, II6
der **Knochen, -** *bone*, II2
der **Knopf, ̈-e** *button*, II8
der **Koch, ̈-e** *cook (male)*, II12
das **Kochbuch, ̈-er** *cookbook*, II2
kochen *to cook*, II1
die **Köchin, -nen** *cook (female)*, II8
der **Kofferraumdeckel, -** *trunk lid*, II7
der **Kohl** *cabbage*, II12
der **Kollege, -n** *colleague*, II11
der **Kombi, -s** (**Kombiwagen**) *station wagon*, II2
kombinieren *to combine*, II8
komisch *funny; strange*, II11

kommen *to come,* I; **er kommt aus** *he's from,* I; **Komm doch mit!** *Why don't you come along?,* I; **Wie komme ich zum (zur) … ?** *How do I get to …?,* I
die **Komödie, -n** *comedy,* I
das **Kompliment, -e** *compliment,* II1
der **Komponist, -en** *composer,* Loc 1
die **Kondition, -en** *condition, shape,* II4
der **König, -e** *king,* II3
königlich *royal,* II3
können *to be able to,* I; **Kann ich bitte Andrea sprechen?** *Could I please speak with Andrea?,* I; **Was kann ich für dich tun?** *What can I do for you?,* I
konservativ *conservative,* II8
der **Konsum** *consumption,* II10
die **Kontaktlinse, -n** *contact lens,* II1
konvertiert *converted,* II3
das **Konzert, -e** *concert,* I; **ins Konzert gehen** *to go to a concert,* I
konzertmäßig *as far as concerts go,* II7
der **Kopf, ⸚e** *head,* II6
der **Kopfhörer, -** *headphones,* II10
der **Kopfhöreranschluss, ⸚e** *headphone outlet,* II10
der **Kopfsalat, -e** *head of lettuce,* II2
die **Kopfschmerzen** (pl) *headache,* II6
kopieren *to copy,* II1
körperlich *physical(ly),* II6
die **Körpertemperatur, -en** *body temperature,* II6
der **Korridor, -e** *hallway,* II12
die **Kost** *food, board,* II4
kosten *to cost,* I; *to taste,* II4
köstlich *delicious, charming,* II2
die **Köstlichkeit, -en** *delicacy,* II11
die **Krabbe, -n** *crab,* II11
der **Kraftfahrer, -** *driver,* II7
das **Kraftstudio, -s** *weight gym,* II12
der **Kraftwagen, -** *motor vehicle,* II7
krank *sick,* II5
das **Krankenhaus, ⸚er** *hospital,* II4
das **Kraut, ⸚er** *herb,* II5
der **Kräutergarten, ⸚** *herb garden,* II7
die **Krawatte, -n** *tie,* II8
der **Kreis, -e** *circle; district,* II7
der **Kreislauf** *circulation (of the blood),* II6
die **Kreuzung, -en** *crossing, junction,* II11
kriechen *to crawl,* II12
der **Krieg, -e** *war,* II7
kriegen *to get, receive,* II9
der **Kriegsfilm, -e** *war movie,* I
das **Kriegsschiff, -e** *battleship,* II10
die **Kriegszerstörung** *war destruction,* II1
der **Krimi, -s** *detective movie,* I
der **Kriminalfilm, -e** *detective film,* II10

die **Krimiserie, -n** *detective series,* II10
kritisieren *to criticize,* II7
die **Kroketten** (pl) *potato croquettes,* II11
der **Krümel, -** *crumb,* II12
die **Küche, -n** *kitchen; cuisine,* I, II7
der **Kuchen, -** *cake,* I
der **Küchendienst, -e** *kitchen duty,* II2
die **Kuchenschlacht, -en** *run for the cake,* II5
der **Küchenschrank, ⸚e** *kitchen cabinet,* II12
der **Kugelschreiber, -** *ballpoint pen,* II1
das **Kugelstoßen** *shot put,* II1
kühl *cool,* I
kühlen *to cool,* II7
der **Kühlschrank, ⸚e** *refrigerator,* I
der **Kuli, -s** *ballpoint pen,* I
die **Kultur, -en** *culture,* II9
kulturell *cultural,* II3
die **Kulturmetropole, -n** *cultural metropolis,* II1
die **Kultursendung, -en** *cultural program,* II10
die **Kulturstadt, ⸚e** *city of great cultural significance,* II3
der **Kummerbund, -e** *cummerbund,* II12
der **Kunde, -n** *customer (male),* II1
die **Kundin, -nen** *customer (female),* II9
die **Kunst, ⸚e** *art,* I
die **Kunstausstellung, -en** *art exhibition,* II11
die **Kunstfaser, -n** *synthetic fabric,* II8
die **Kunstsammlung, -en** *art collection,* II8
die **Kunstseide, -n** *synthetic silk, rayon,* II8
der **Kunststoff, -e: aus Kunststoff** *made of plastic,* I
die **Kur, -en** *(course of) treatment,* II6
der **Kurfürst, -en** *Elector (of a king),* II3
der **Kurs, -e** *course,* II9
die **Kurve, -n** *curve,* II7
kurz *short,* I
kürzer *shorter,* II8
die **Kuschelecke, -n** *a place to cuddle,* II7
kuscheln *to cuddle,* II9
die **Kusine, -n** *cousin (female),* I
die **Küste, -n** *coast,* II12

lachen *to laugh,* II2
lachend *laughing,* II2
der **Lachs, -e** *salmon,* II11
der **Lackschuh, -e** *patent leather shoe,* II12

der **Laden, ⸚** *store,* I
die **Lage, -n** *setting, place,* II12
das **Lagerfeuer, -** *campfire,* II9
das **Lammfleisch** *lamb,* II5
die **Lampe, -n** *lamp,* I
das **Land, ⸚er** *country,* I; **auf dem Land** *in the country,* I
die **Land- und Forstwirtschaft** *agriculture and forestry,* II1
der **Landesfürst, -en** *sovereign, prince,* II3
die **Landeshauptstadt, ⸚e** *state capital,* II1
die **Landeskunde** *culture,* II3
die **Landeszeitung, -en** *newspaper (distributed statewide),* II3
die **Landkarte, -n** *map of the country,* II9
die **Landschaft, -en** *countryside,* II9
die **Landstraße, -n** *highway,* II10
die **Landwirtschaft** *agriculture,* II9
lang *long,* I
länger *longer,* II8
der **Langlauf** *cross-country skiing,* II4
langsam *slow(ly),* II7
längst *long ago, since,* II12
der **Langstreckenlauf, ⸚e** *long distance run,* II1
s. **langweilen** *to be bored,* II12
langweilig *boring,* I
der **Lärm** *noise,* II7
lärmbewusst *conscious of noise,* II7
die **Lärmminderung, -en** *lessening of noise,* II7
der **Lärmschutz** *noise protection,* II7
Lärmschutzgründe: aus Lärmschutzgründen *for noise protection,* II7
lassen *to let, allow;* **er/sie lässt** *he/she lets,* II10; **Lass mich mal …** *Let me …,* II10
lässig *casual,* I
das **Laster, -** *vice,* II4
lästig *bothersome,* II8
der **Lastkraftwagen (Lkw), -** *truck,* II7
das **Latein** *Latin,* I
der **Lauf, ⸚e** *run,* II1; **der 100-Meter-Lauf** *the 100 meter dash,* II1
laufen *to run,* II3; **er/sie läuft** *he/she runs,* II3; **Was läuft im Fernsehen?** *What's on TV?,* II10
die **Laune, -n** *temper, mood,* II12
laut *loud,* II2
lauten *to sound, read,* II2
der **Lautstärkeregler, -** *volume control,* II10
leben *to live,* II2
das **Leben** *life,* II7
die **Lebensmittel** (pl) *groceries,* I
die **Leber** *liver,* II2
der **Leberkäs** *(a Bavarian specialty),* I
lecker *tasty, delicious,* I

das **Leder** *leather,* I
die **Lederjacke, -n** *leather jacket,* II8
leer *empty,* II3
legen *to lay,* II2
der **Lehrer, -** *teacher (male),* I
die **Lehrerin, -nen** *teacher (female),* I
das **Lehrjahr, -e** *apprenticeship year,* II7
der **Lehrplan, ⸚e** *teaching curriculum,* II2
die **Lehrstelle, -n** *apprenticeship,* II7
leicht *easy, simple,* II1; *light,* II6
die **Leichtathletik** *track and field,* II1
das **Leichtkraftrad, ⸚er** *motorbike,* II7
Leid: Es tut mir Leid. *I'm sorry.,* I
leiden: Ich kann dich nicht leiden. *I can't stand you.,* II10
leider *unfortunately,* I; **Ich kann leider nicht.** *Sorry, I can't.,* I; **Das ist leider so.** *That's the way it is unfortunately.,* II10; **Ich hab leider nur …** *I only have …,* II5
der **Leierkastenmann** *organ grinder,* II1, Loc 1
das **Leinen, -** *linen,* II8
leise *soft, lightly,* II12
leiten *to direct,* II3
die **Leitung, -en** *direction, conduit,* II3
lesen *to read,* I; **er/sie liest** *he/she reads,* I
letzt- *last,* I; **letzte Woche** *last week,* I; **letztes Wochenende** *last weekend,* I
die **Leute** (pl) *people,* I
das **Licht, -er** *light, lamp,* II12
der **Lichtschalter, -** *light switch,* II12
der **Lichtschutzfaktor, -en** *sun protection factor,* II6
die **Liebe** *love,* II1
lieber: lieber mögen *to prefer,* I
der **Liebesfilm, -e** *romance,* I
der **Liebesroman, -e** *romance novel,* I
liebevoll *loving, caring,* II8
Lieblings- *favorite,* I
liebst: Ich würde am liebsten … *I would rather …,* II11
das **Lied, -er** *song,* I
der **Liederabend, -e** *evening of songs,* II11
liegen *to lie on,* II6; **das liegt an dir** *it's your fault,* II12
die **Liegewiese, -n** *lawn for relaxing and sunning,* II9
die **Liga, (pl) Ligen** *league,* II10
die **Limo, -s (Limonade, -n)** *lemon drink,* I
die **Linie, -n** *line,* II8; **in erster Linie** *first of all,* II8
die **Liste, -n** *list,* II1
der **Liter, -** *liter,* I
der **Lkw=Lastkraftwagen, -** *truck,* II7
das **Loch, ⸚er** *hole,* II12
locker *loose,* II8
logisch *logical,* II4
s. **lohnen** *to be worth it,* II9
das **Lokal, -e** *small restaurant,* II3

los *detached,* II3
lösen *to solve,* II7
die **Lücke, -n** *blank,* II9
die **Luft** *air,* II7
der **Luftballon, -s** *air-balloon,* II7
die **Lüftlmalerei, -en** *frescoes on houses (in Bavaria),* Loc 1
die **Luftverschmutzung** *air pollution,* II7
lügen *to tell a lie,* II11
lustig *funny,* I
das **Lustspiel, -e** *comedy,* II10
der **Luxus** *luxury,* II8
die **Luxusgüter** (pl) *luxury items,* II8

machen *to do,* I; **Das macht (zusammen) …** *That comes to …,* I; **Gut! Mach ich!** *Okay, I'll do that!,* I; **Machst du Sport?** *Do you play sports?,* I; **Hausaufgaben machen** *to do homework,* I; **macht dick** *is fattening,* II4; **Macht nichts!** *That's all right,* II5
das **Mädchen, -** *girl,* I
mag: *see* **mögen**
das **Magazin, -e** *journal,* II10
der **Magenkrampf, ⸚e** *stomach cramp,* II6
die **Magenschmerzen** (pl) *stomach pains,* II4
mager *lean,* II4
die **Magermilch** *skim milk,* II4
mähen *to mow,* I
Mahlzeit! *Bon appétit!* II11
die **Mahlzeit, -en** *meal,* II6
das **Mahnmal, -e** *memorial,* Loc 10
die **Mahnung, -en** *warning,* II7
der **Mai** *May,* I; **im Mai** *in May,* I
mal (particle), I
malen *to paint,* II1
der **Maler, -** *painter,* II1
malerisch *picturesque,* II1
man *one, you (in general), people,* I; **Man hat mir gesagt, dass …** *Someone told me that …,* II11
manche *some,* II4
manchmal *sometimes,* I
der **Mann, ⸚er** *man,* I
die **Mannschaft, -en** *team,* II4
der **Marder, -** *marten,* II9
die **Margarine** *margarine,* II5
mariniert *marinated,* II11
die **Mark, -** *mark (former German monetary unit),* I
die **Markenbutter** *brand-name butter,* II2
der **Markt, ⸚e** *market,* II10
der **Marktanteil** *market share,* II10

der **Marktbrunnen, -** *market fountain,* II9
der **Marktplatz, ⸚e** *market square,* I, II3
die **Marmelade** *marmalade,* II5
marschieren *to march,* II3
der **März** *March,* I
das **Marzipan, -e** *marzipan,* II7
der **Maschinenbau** *mechanical engineering,* II1
die **Mastente, -n** *fattened duck,* II11
materiell (adj) *material,* II7
die **Mathematik=Mathe** *math,* I
die **Mauer, -n** *wall,* II11
der **Mauerrest, -e** *remnant of wall,* II11
das **Mauerwerk** *masonry,* II9
die **Maus, ⸚e** *mouse,* II9
die **Mayonnaise** *mayonnaise,* II5
die **Medaillengewinnerin, -nen** *medal winner (female),* II12
mediterran *Mediterranean,* II11
die **Medizin** *medicine,* II6
das **Meer, -e** *ocean,* II9
die **Meeresfrüchte** (pl) *seafood,* II5
das **Mehl** *flour,* I
die **Mehlspeise, -n** *food made of flour,* II5
mehr *more,* I; **Ich habe keinen Hunger mehr.** *I'm not hungry anymore.,* I
die **Mehrfachnennung, -en** *repeated reference,* II9
mehrfarbig *many-colored,* II8
meiden *to avoid,* II4
mein (poss adj) *my,* I
meinen: Meinst du? *Do you think so?,* I
die **Meinung, -en** *opinion,* II8
meist *most,* II9
meistens *most of the time,* II4
der **Meister, -** *master, champion,* II3
das **Meisterstück, -e** *masterpiece,* II3
die **Melone, -n** *melon,* II5
die **Menge, -n** *quantity, heap,* II8
die **Mensa** *student cafeteria,* II4
der **Mensch, -en** *human, person,* II1; **mehr Menschen** *more people,* II7
die **Menschenmasse, -n** *mass of people,* II9
merken *to notice, pay attention to,* II12
die **Messe, -n** *fair,* II3; *Catholic Mass,* II9
messen: Fieber messen *to take someone's temperature,* II6; **er/sie misst** *he/she measures,* II6
das **Messer, -** *knife,* II12
die **Metallkette, -n** *metal chain,* II1
der **Meter, -** *meter,* II9
die **Metropole, -n** *metropolis,* II11
der **Metzger, -** *butcher,* I
die **Metzgerei, -en** *butcher shop,* I
mexikanisch (adj) *Mexican,* II11
mich *me, myself,* I
miesest *the worst,* II2

GERMAN-ENGLISH VOCABULARY

die Miete, -n *rent*, II7
das Mietshaus, ¨-er *rental house*, II7
die Mietwohnung, -en *apartment*, II7
die Milch *milk*, I
mild *mild*, II11
die Milliarde, -n *billion*, II12
mindern *to lessen*, II7
mindestens *at least*, II3
das Mineralwasser *mineral water*, I
mir *to, for me*, II3; **Mir gefällt … besser als …** *I like … better than …*, II7
die Mischfasern (pl) *blended fibers*, II8
miserabel *miserable*, I
missfallen (dat) *to displease, offend*, II12
Mist: So ein Mist! *Darn it!*, I
mit (prep) *with, by*, I; **mit Brot** *with bread*, I; **mit dem Auto** *by car*, I
mitbringen (sep) *to bring along*, II9
miteinander *with one another*, II5
mitgebracht *brought along*, II5
mitgehen (sep) *to go along*, II1
mitgekommen (pp) *come along*, II3
mitgekriegt *understood*, II10
mitgenommen *took along*, II3
das Mitglied, -er *member*, II9
mitkommen (sep) *to come along*, I
mitmachen (sep) *to take part*, II1
der Mitmensch, en *fellow-being*, II7
mitnehmen (sep) *to take along*, II2
der Mitschüler, - *schoolmate (male)*, II1
die Mitschülerin, -nen *schoolmate (female)*, II1
der Mittag *noon*, II1
das Mittagessen *lunch*, II3
die Mitte *middle*, II11
mitteilen (sep) *to communicate; to share*, II4
das Mittelalter *the Middle Ages*, Loc 7
mittelgroß *middle-sized*, II5
mittellang *medium-length*, II1
der Mittwoch *Wednesday*, I; **am Mittwoch** *on Wednesday*, I
mittwochs *Wednesdays*, II10
die Möbel (pl) *furniture*, I
möchten *would like to*, I; **Ich möchte … sehen.** *I would like to see …*, I; **Ich möchte noch ein …** *I'd like another …*, I; **Ich möchte kein … mehr.** *I don't want another …*, I
die Mode, -n *fashion*, I
die Modefachfrau, -en *fashion consultant (female)*, II8
der Modefachmann, ¨-er *fashion consultant (male)*, II8

das Modell, -e *model*, II8
die Modenschau, -en *fashion show*, II8
die Moderatorin, -nen *moderator (female)*, II11
modern *modern*, I
modisch *fashionable*, II8
das Mofa, -s *moped*, II7
mögen *to like, care for*, I; **Ich mag kein …** *I don't like …*, II4
möglich *possible*, II10
die Möglichkeit, -en *possibility*, II9
möglichst *as … as possible*, II8
die Möhre, -n *carrot*, II4
der Moment, -e *moment*, I; **Einen Moment, bitte!** *Just a minute, please.*, I; **im Moment gar nichts** *nothing at the moment*, I
der Monat, -e *month*, I; **einmal im Monat** *once a month*, I
monatlich *monthly*, II10
die Monatsausgabe, -n *monthly expenditure*, II10
monoton *monotonous*, II8
der Montag *Monday*, I; **am Montag** *on Monday*, I
montags *Mondays*, II10
das Moor(bad) *mud-bath*, II6
das Moped, -s *moped*, I; **mit dem Moped** *by moped*, I
der Mord, -e *murder*, II10
morgen *tomorrow*, I
der Morgen, - *morning*, I; **Guten Morgen!** *Good morning!*, I; **Morgen!** *Morning!*, I
morgens *in the mornings*, II2
das Motiv, -e *motif*, II3
der Motor, -en *motor*, II7
das Motorboot, -e *motorboat*, II9
motorisiert *motorized*, II7
das Motorrad, ¨-er *motorcycle*, II7
die Moussaka *moussaka*, II12
müde *tired*, II6
der Muffel, - *a person not interested in something*, II4
die Mühle, -n *mill*, II11
der Müll *trash*, I; **den Müll sortieren** *to sort the trash*, I
der Müllhaufen, - *pile of trash*, II2
die Münze, -n *coin*, I; **Münzen einstecken** *to insert coins*, I
murmeln *to murmur, to mutter*, II10
die Muschel, -n *mussel*, II5
das Museum, (pl) Museen *museum*, I
das Musical, -s *musical*, II11
die Musik *music*, I; **klassische Musik** *classical music*, I
das Musikgeschäft, -e *music shop*, II11
die Musikkapelle, -n *musical band*, II3
der Musikkapellmeister, - *band-leader*, II3
der Musikraum, ¨-e *music room*, II2
das Müsli *grain cereal*, II11
müssen *to have to*, I; **ich muss** *I have to*, I

das Muster, - *pattern*, II12
die Mutter, ¨- *mother*, I
der Muttertag *Mother's Day*, I; **Alles Gute zum Muttertag!** *Happy Mother's Day!*, I
die Mütze, -n *cap*, II1

Na ja, soso. *Oh, all right.*, II3
Na klar! *Of course!*, II4
nach (prep) *after*, I; **nach der Schule** *after school*, I; **nach links** *to the left*, I; **nach rechts** *to the right*, I; **nach Hause gehen** *to go home*, I; **nach dem Mittagessen** *after lunch*, II3
der Nachbarort, -e *neighboring town*, II7
nachdem (conj) *after*, II12
nachdenken (sep) *to think, to reflect*, II5
nachdenkenswert *worthy of reflection*, II8
nacherzählen (sep) *to retell*, II6
die Nacherzählung, -en *retelling*, II12
nachher *afterwards*, II10
der Nachmittag, -e *afternoon*, I
das Nachmittagsprogramm, e *afternoon program*, II10
der Nachnahmekauf *collect on delivery (COD)*, II8
der Nachname, -n *last name*, II7
nachrechnen (sep) *check*, II10
die Nachricht, -en *message*, II9
die Nachrichten (pl) *the news*, II10
nachsehen (sep) *to look up, look again*, II10
die Nachspeise, -n *dessert*, II11
nächst- *next*, II2; **die nächste Straße** *the next street*, I
nächstgrößer- *next-largest*, II11
die Nacht, ¨-e *night*, II10
der Nachteil, -e *disadvantage*, II7
der Nachtisch, -e *dessert*, II5
nachts *nights, at night*, II9
der Nachtzug, ¨-e *overnight train*, II2
nackt *bare, naked*, II12
das Nagelbett, -en *bed of nails*, II7
nah *near*, II9
die Nähe *vicinity*, II3; in der Nähe von *near to*, II9
die Nahrungsmittel (pl) *food*, II5
der Name, -n *name*, II4
nämlich *namely*, II2
die Nase, -n *nose*, II6
nass *wet*, I
die Nationalversammlung, -en *National Assembly*, II3
die Natur *nature*, II3
der Naturforscher, - *natural scientist (male)*, Loc 4
Natürlich! *Certainly!*, I

die **Natursendung**, -en *nature program*, II10
neben (prep) *next to*, II9
nebenan *close by*, II10
der **Nebenjob**, -s *second job*, II8
die **Nebensache**, -n *matter of minor importance*, II9
der **Nebensatz**, ⸚e *dependent clause*, II12
negativ *negative*, II4
nehmen *to take*, I; **er/sie nimmt** *he/she takes*, I; **Ich nehme …** *I'll take …*, I
neidisch *envious*, II8
nein *no*, I
nennen *to name*, II2
nervös *nervous*, II1
das **Nesthäkchen**, - *baby of the family*, II12
nett *nice*, II1
neu *new*, I
neuerdings *recently*, II12
neuest *newest*, II8
der **Neufundländer**, - *Newfoundland dog*, II10
neugierig *curious*, II1
nicht *not*, I; **Nicht besonders.** *Not really.*, I; *Not especially.*, II3; **nicht gern haben** *to dislike*, I; **nicht schlecht** *not bad*, I; **Ich nicht.** *I don't.*, I
der **Nichtraucher**, - *non-smoker*, II4
nichts *nothing*, I; **Nichts mehr, danke!** *Nothing else, thanks!*, I
nie *never*, I
die **Niederlande** *Netherlands*, II9
niemand *no one*, II12
nix=nichts II8
noch *yet, still*, I; **Haben Sie noch einen Wunsch?** *Would you like anything else?*, I; **Ich brauche noch …** *I also need …*, I; **Möchtest du noch etwas?** *Would you like something else?*, I; **Noch einen Saft?** *Another glass of juice?*, I; **noch höher** *still higher*, II10; **noch nie** *not yet, never*, II3
normal *normal*, II2
normalerweise *normally, usually*, II4
die **Normalstärke** *normal volume*, II7
norwegisch *Norwegian*, II11
die **Not**, ⸚e *need, want*, II5
die **Note**, -n *grade*, I
notieren *to note, jot down*, II12
nötig *necessary*, II4
die **Notiz**, -en *note*, II1
der **Notizblock**, ⸚e *note pad*, II9
das **Notizbuch**, ⸚er *notebook*, II1
notwendig *necessary*, II7
der **November** *November*, I
die **Nudel**, -n *noodle*, II5
das **Nudelgericht**, -e *noodle dish*, II5
die **Nudelsuppe**, -n *noodle soup*, I
null *zero*, I

die **Nummer**, -n *number*, II8
nur *only*, II1; **nicht nur … sondern auch** *not only … but also*, II3
der **Nussknacker**, - *nutcracker*, II11

die **Oase**, -n *oasis*, II12
ob (conj) *whether*, II9
oben *above*, II2
ober- *upper*, II3
die **Oberschule**, -n (same as Gymnasium), II7
das **Objekt**, -e *project*, II7
das Obst *fruit*, I
der **Obst- und Gemüseladen**, ⸚ *fresh produce store*, I
der **Obstgarten**, ⸚e *orchard*, Loc 7
obwohl (conj) *although*, II7
oder (conj) *or*, I
der **Ofen**, ⸚ *oven*, I
offen *open*, II8
öffentliche Verkehrsmittel (pl) *public transportation*, II7
offiziell *official*, II3
die **Öffnungszeiten** (pl) *opening hours*, II2
oft *often*, I
öfters *quite often*, II6
ohne (prep) *without*, II2
ohne … zu *without …*; ohne zu schlafen *without sleeping*, II4
das **Ohrensausen** *ringing in the ears*, II6
der **Ohrenschmaus** *musical treat*, II12
die **Ohrenschmerzen** (pl) *earache*, II6
der **Ohrring**, -e *earring*, II1
der **Oktober** *October*, I
das **Olivenöl**, -e *olive oil*, II12
olivgrün *olive green*, II8
der **Ölstand**, ⸚e *oil level*, II10
die **Olympiade** *Olympiad*, II12
der **Olympiasieger**, - *olympic champion*, II12
olympisch *olympic*, II12
die **Oma**, -s *grandmother*, I
der **Onkel**, - *uncle*, I
der **Opa**, -s *grandfather*, I
die **Oper**, -n *opera*, I
die **Operette**, -n *operetta*, II11
das **Opfer**, - *victim*, Loc 10
der **Optimist**, -en *optimist*, II9
die **Orange**, -n *orange*, II5
der **Orangensaft** *orange juice*, I
die **Ordnung** *order*, II8
die **Organisation**, -en *organization*, II9
organisieren *to organize*, II1
das **Orgelkonzert**, -e *organ concert*, II11

die **Orientierungsstufenschülerin**, -nen (student in the beginning years of Gymnasium) (female), II8
der **Ort**, -e *place; location*, II3
die **Osterferien** (pl) *Easter vacation*, II12
das Ostern *Easter*, I; **Frohe Ostern!** *Happy Easter*, I
Österreich (**das**) *Austria*, I
österreichisch (adj) *Austrian*, II3
die **Ostküste** *east coast*, II3

paar: **ein paar**, *a few*, I
das **Päckchen**, - *small package*, II5
das **Paddelboot**, -e *paddle boat*, II9
die **Paella**, -s *paella*, II12
die **Palme**, -n *palm tree*, II9
der **Palmengarten**, ⸚ *garden of palm trees*, II9
der **Pantoffel**, -n *slipper*, II2
das **Papier**, -e *paper*, II1
die **Paradejacke**, -n *marching band uniform*, II1
das **Parfüm**, -e *perfume*, I
parfümiert *perfumed*, II6
der **Park**, -s *park*, I; **in den Park gehen** *to go to the park*, I
parken *to park*, II9
der **Parkplatz**, ⸚e *parking spot, lot*, II9
der **Partner**, - *partner (male)*, I
die **Partnerin**, -nen *partner (female)*, I
die **Party**, -s *party*, I
partymäßig *for parties*, II7
passen *to fit*, I; **Der Rock passt prima!** *The skirt fits great!*, I
passend *fitting*, II11
passieren *to occur*, II1; **Das ist gerade passiert.** *It just happened.*, II9
Passt auf! *Pay attention!*, I
die **Patchworkdecke**, -n *quilt*, II12
der **Patient**, -en *patient*, II6
die **Pause**, -n *break*, I
das **Pausenbrot**, -e *sandwich* (made especially for class break), II5
das **Pausenklingeln** *recess bell*, II2
das **Pech** *bad luck*, I; **So ein Pech!** *Bad luck!*, I; **Was für ein Pech!** *That's too bad!*, II5
der **Pegel**, - *level*, II5
die **Peking Ente**, -n *Peking duck*, II11
die **Penne** (casual term for) *school*, II7
die **Pension**, -en *inn, bed and breakfast*, II3
pensioniert *retired*, II4
perfekt *perfect*, II12
die **Person**, -en *person*, II1
die **Personenbeschreibung**, -en *personal description*, II7

GERMAN-ENGLISH VOCABULARY

der Personenkraftwagen, - (Pkw) *car*, II7
persönlich *personal(ly)*, II7
die Persönlichkeit, -en *personality*, II8
die Perspektive, -n *perspective*, II12
der Pessimist, -en *pessimist*, II9
das Pestizid, -e *pesticide*, II4
die Petersilie *parsley*, II12
das Pfadfinderlager, - *boy scout camp*, II9
die Pfanne, -n *pan*, II9
das **Pfannengericht, -e** *pan-cooked entrée*, II11
der Pfannkuchen, - *pancake*, Loc 10
das **Pfd.=Pfund** *pound*, I
der Pfeffer, *pepper*, II5
der Pfennig, - *(smallest unit of former German currency; 1/100 of a mark)*, I
das Pferd, -e *horse*, II9
der Pferdestall, ⸚e *stable*, II11
der Pferdewagen, - *horse-drawn carriage*, II9
die Pfingstferien (pl) *Pentecost vacation*, II9
der **Pfirsich, -e** *peach*, II2
die Pflanze, -n *plant*, II2
die Pflaume, -n *plum*, II2
das **Pfund, - (Pfd.)** *pound*, I
das Phänomen, -e *phenomenon*, II6
phantasievoll *imaginative*, I
Phantastisch! *Fantastic!*, II3
pharmazeutisch *pharmaceutical*, II10
piekfein *very fine*, II7
der **Pilz, -e** *mushroom*, II4
die **Pizza, -s** *pizza*, I
der **Pkw, -s** *car*, II7
plagen *to bother*, II10
der Plan, ⸚e *plan*, II1
planen *to plan*, II5
die Planung, -en *planning*, II10
platschen *to make a flapping sound*, II12
der **Platz, ⸚e** *place, site*, II12
plötzlich *sudden(ly)*, II9
das Plumeau, -s *comforter*, II9
der Pokal, -e *trophy*, II1
polieren *to polish*, II2
die **Politik** (sing) *politics*, I
polnisch *Polish*, II11
die **Pommes (frites)** (pl) *French fries*, II5
das Ponyreiten *pony ride*, II3
der **Pool, -s** *swimming pool*, II7
der Popstar, -s *pop star*, II1
populär *popular*, Loc 7
positiv *positive*, II4
die **Post** *post office*, I
der Posten, - *place, position*, II2
das **Poster, -** *poster*, I
die Posthalterei, -en *stable for post horses*, II9
die Pracht *splendor*, II3
prächtig *magnificent*, II6
praktisch *practical*, II10

die **Praline, -n** *fancy chocolate*, I
präsentieren *to present*, II12
die Praxis *practice; doctor's office*, II10
der Preis, -e *price*, II1
preisgünstig *cheap*, II9
preiswert *reasonably priced*, I;
Das ist preiswert. *That's a bargain.*, I
Prima! *Great!* I
der Prinz, -en *prince*, II10
das **Privathaus, ⸚er** *private home*, II3
das Privatquartier, -e *private accommodation*, II3
die Probe, -n: auf die Probe stellen *to test*, II12
probieren *to try*, I
das Problem, -e *problem*, II7
die Produktion, -en *production*, II10
produzieren *to produce*, II7
profitrainiert *trained by a professional*, II12
das **Programm, -e** *schedule of shows*, II10
die Programmanzeige, -n *listing of shows*, II10
das Projekt, -e *project*, II8
das Pronomen, - *pronoun*, II6
der Prospekt, -e *brochure*, II12
Prost! *Cheers!*, II11
das Prozent *percent*, II4
das Publikum *public; audience*, II10
der Pudding, -e *pudding*, II4
der **Pulli, -s** *pullover, sweater*, I
der **Pullover, -** *sweater*, I
der Puls *pulse*, II6
der Punker, - *punker*, II1
putzen *to clean*, I; **Fenster putzen** *to wash the windows*, I

der Quadratkilometer, - *square kilometer*, II1
die Qual, -en *pain*, II11
die Qualität *quality*, II3
der **Quark** *(a soft cheese similar to ricotta or cream cheese)*, II5
das Quartier, -e *quarter, accommodation* II3
der Quatsch *nonsense*, II12
die Quelle, -n *source, (underground) spring*, II9

der Rabatt, -e *discount*, II9
das **Rad, ⸚er** *bike; wheel*, II1; **mit dem Rad** *by bike*, I; **Rad fahren** (sep) *to ride a bike*, II4

die Radfahrgruppe, -n *group of bicycle riders*, II3
der **Radiergummi, -s** *eraser*, I
das Radieschen *radish*, II5
das **Radio, -s** *radio*, II2
die Radiosendung, -en *radio show*, II7
die Radtour, -en *bicycle tour*, II1
der Rang, ⸚e *rank*, Loc 7
die Rangliste, -n *ranking chart*, II10
der Rallyestreifen, - *rally stripe*, II10
das Rascheln *rustle*, II5
der **Rasen, -** *lawn*, I; **den Rasen mähen** *to mow the lawn*, I
die Rasierklinge, -n *razor blade*, II10
raten *to guess*, II1
die **Ratesendung, -en** *quiz show*, II10
das Ratespiel, -e *quiz game*, II1
das **Rathaus, ⸚er** *city hall*, I
der Ratschlag, ⸚e *advice*, II6
rauchen *to smoke*, II4
der Raucherfeind, -e *person who dislikes smokers*, II4
der Raum, ⸚e *room*, II4
das Raumschiff, -e *spacecraft*, II10
raus=heraus *out, away*, II11
reagieren auf (acc) *to react to*, II3
der Realschüler, - *student at a Realschule*, II2
die Rebe, -n *vine*, Loc 7
rechnen *to tabulate, calculate*, II11
die Rechnung, -en *bill, check*, II1
das Recht, -e *law; right*, II1; **Recht haben** *to be right*, II10
recht- *right, right-hand*, I; **nach rechts** *to the right*, I
reden *to talk, speak*, II4
das Reformhaus, ⸚er *natural food store*, II4
das **Regal, -e** *bookcase*, I
die Regel, -n *rule*, II4
regelmäßig *regularly*, II4
der **Regen** *rain*, I
regnen: Es regnet. *It's raining.*, I
reiben *to rub, grate*, II10
das Reich, -e *empire*, II1
reichlich *plenty*, II12
reicht: Es reicht. *That's enough.*, II11
der Reifen, - *tire*, II10
die Reihe, -n *row; line*, II1
die Reihenfolge, -n *succession, sequence*, II12
die Reihenwörter (pl) *sequencing words*, II3
der Reim, -e *rhyme*, II2
rein *pure*, II8
die **Reinigung, -en** *cleaners*, II8
reinkommen=hereinkommen (sep) *to come in*, II2
reinschauen=hereinschauen (sep) *to look in*, II1
der **Reis** *rice*, II4
die Reise, -n *trip, voyage*, II3
der Reiseberater, - *travel agent*, II9
der Reisebericht, -e *travel report*, II12

das **Reisebüro**, -s *travel agency*, II9
der **Reiseleiter**, - *tour guide (person)*, II11
reiselustig *wanting to travel*, II12
reisen *to travel, take a trip*, II1
der **Reiseort**, -e *vacation spot*, II9
die **Reiseroute**, -n *itinerary*, II9
das **Reiseziel**, -e *travel destination*, II9
das **Reisgericht**, -e *rice dish*, II12
der **Reißverschluss**, ⸚e *zipper*, II8
reiten *to ride a horse*, II3
der **Reiterhof**, ⸚e *horse farm*, II9
die **Reithalle**, -n *riding court*, II3
die **Reithose**, -n *riding breeches*, II8
die **Reklame**, -n *advertisement*, II8
die **Reklameabteilung**, -en *advertising department*, II8
die **Reklameseite**, -n *page of advertising*, II8
rekonstruieren *to reconstruct*, II12
die **Religion**, -en *religion (school subject)*, I
der **Renner**, - *runner; top product*, II9
das **Rennrad**, ⸚er *racing bicycle*, II12
renoviert *renovated*, II3
die **Reparatur**, -en *repair*, II10
repräsentativ *representative*, II9
reservieren *to reserve*, II11
die **Reservierung**, -en *reservation*, II11
das **Restaurant**, -s *restaurant*, II3
restauriert *restored*, II11
das **Resultat**, -e *result*, II4
der **Rettungswagen**, ⸚ *ambulance*, II6
die **Reue** *remorse, regret*, II4
das **Rezept**, -e *recipe*, II12; *prescription*, II6
die **Rezeptmenge**, -n *amount in a recipe*, II12
s. **richten nach** *to conform to*, II2
richtig *proper(ly)*, II4
riechen nach *to smell like*, II2
das **Rindfleisch** *beef*, II4; **Rind schmeckt mir besser.** *Beef tastes better to me.*, II5
der **Ring**, -e *ring*, II2
der **Ringel**, - *ringlet*, II12
das **Rindersteak** *(beef) steak*, II5
der **Rock**, ⸚e *skirt*, I
rodeln *to sled*, II1
roh *raw*, II11
das **Rohr**, -e *pipe*, II8
die **Rolle**, -n *role*, II1
der **Rollkragen**, - *turtle-neck*, II8
der **Rollschuh**, -e *roller skate*, II9
Rollschuh laufen (sep) *to roller-skate*, II1
der **Rollstuhl**, ⸚e *wheelchair*, II10
der **Roman**, -e *novel*, I
der **Römer** *(name of the city hall in Frankfurt)*, II3
die **Rosine**, -n *raisin*, II7
rot *red*, I; **in Rot** *in red*, I
Rote Grütze *(red berry dessert)*, II11

der **Rotkohl** *red cabbage*, II11
rötlich *reddish*, II1
rüber=herüber *from there to here*, II3
der **Rücken**, - *back*, II6
die **Rückkehr** *return*, II9
das **Ruderboot**, -e *row boat*, II3
rudern *to row*, II9
die **Ruhe** *calm*, II5; **in Ruhe lassen** *to leave alone*, II1
ruhig *calm(ly)*, II5
rund *round*, I
die **Runde: über die Runden kommen** *to make ends meet*, II11
runden *to round*, II11
die **Rundfunk -und Fernsehanstalt**, -en *television and radio communications*, Loc 4
der **Rundgang**, ⸚e *tour, walk*, II9
runter=herunter *from there down here*, II3
das **Rüschenhemd**, -en *frilled shirt*, II1
russisch (adj) *Russian*, II11
rustikal *rustic*, II11

das **Sachbuch**, ⸚er *non-fiction book*, I
die **Sache**, -n *thing; matter*, II9
sächsisch (adj) *Saxon*, II9
der **Saft**, ⸚e *juice*, I
sagen *to say*, I; **Sag mal …** *Tell me …*, II4; **Was sagt der Wetterbericht?** *What does the weather report say?*, I
sagenhaft *great*, I
die **Sahne**, -n *(whipped) cream*, II11
der **Sakko**, -s *business jacket*, II8
der **Salat**, -e *lettuce; salad*, I
das **Salatblatt**, ⸚er *lettuce leaf*, II5
die **Salatgurke**, -n *cucumber*, II5
salopp *casual*, II12
das **Salz** *salt*, I
salzig *salty*, II1
sammeln *to collect*, I
die **Sammlung**, -en *collection*, II3
der **Samstag** *Saturday*, I
samstags *Saturdays*, II10
sämtlich *entire*, II12
der **Sandstrand**, ⸚e *sand beach*, II9
der **Sänger**, - *singer (male)*, I
die **Sängerin**, -nen *singer (female)*, I
satt *full*, II7; **satt haben** *to be fed up with*, II12
der **Satz**, ⸚e *sentence*, II2
der **Satzanfang**, ⸚e *beginning of a sentence*, II10
die **Satzlücke**, -n *blank*, II2
der **Satzteil**, -e *part of a sentence*, II11
sauber *clean*, II7; **sauber machen** *to clean*, II10

das **Sauerkraut** *sauerkraut*, II5
saugen: Staub saugen *to vacuum*, I
saumäßig *filthy, lousy*, II2
die **Sauna**, -s *sauna*, II9
saure Gurken *pickled cucumbers*, II5
sauwohl *great*, II8
das **Schach** *chess*, I
Schade! *Too bad!*, I
schaden (dat) *to harm*, II6
schädlich *harmful*, II7
der **Schal**, -s *scarf*, II1
schälen *to peel*, II5
scharf *sharp*, II8; *spicy, hot*, II11
schauen *to look*, I; **Schau mal!** *Look!*, II5
der **Schaukelstuhl**, ⸚e *rocking chair*, II7
der **Schaumstoff**, -e *foam rubber*, II4
das **Schauspiel**, -e *play*, II11
der **Schauspieler**, - *actor*, I
die **Schauspielerin**, -nen *actress*, I
das **Schauspielhaus**, ⸚er *playhouse*, II11
die **Scheibe**, -n *slice*, II5
der **Scheibenwischer**, - *windshield wiper*, II10
der **Schein**, -e *bill*, II2
scheinen *to shine*, I; **Die Sonne scheint.** *The sun is shining.*, I
der **Scheinwerfer**, - *headlight*, II10
schenken *to give (a gift)*, I; **Was schenkst du deiner Mutter?** *What are you giving your mother?*, I
scheußlich *hideous*, I
die **Schichtarbeit** *shift work*, II11
schick *smart (looking)*, I
das **Schiebedach**, ⸚er *sun roof*, II10
das **Schiff**, -e *ship*, II9
der **Schimmel** *molds*, II4
schimpfen *to scold*, II11
der **Schinken**, - *ham*, II11
das **Schisch-Kebab** *shish kebab*, II11
der **Schlabberpulli**, -s *baggy sweater*, II12
schlafen *to sleep*, II4
der **Schlafsack**, ⸚e *sleeping bag*, II9
das **Schlafzimmer**, - *bedroom*, II7
die **Schlaghose**, -n *bell bottoms*, II12
die **Schlange**, -n *line*, II12
schlank *slim*, II1
die **Schlaufe**, -n *belt loop*, II8
schlecht *bad(ly)*, I; **schlecht gelaunt** *in a bad mood*, II1; **Mir ist schlecht.** *I feel sick.*, II6
die **Schleife**, -n *loop, bow*, II2
schließlich *at the end, after all*, II4
schlimm *bad*, II5
Schlittschuh laufen *to ice skate*, I
das **Schlitzohr**, -en *rascal*, II2
das **Schloss**, ⸚er *castle*, II3
schlucken *to swallow*, II6; **Ich kann kaum schlucken.** *I can barely swallow.*, II6

schmackhaft *tasty*, II12
schmalzig *corny, mushy*, I
schmecken *to taste*, II5; **Schmeckt's?** *Does it taste good?*, I; **Wie schmeckt's?** *How does it taste?*, I; **schmeckt mir nicht** *doesn't taste good*, II4; **schmeckt mir am besten** *tastes best to me*, II5
der **Schmerz, -en** *pain*, II6
der **Schmuck** *jewelry*, I
der **Schmuse-Typ, -en** *cuddly type*, II7
schmutzig *dirty*, II7
die **Schnecke, -n** *snail*, II5
der **Schnee** *snow*, I
schneiden *to cut*, II5
schneien: Es schneit. *It's snowing.*, I
schnell *fast*, II7
schnippen *whisk off*, II12
der **Schnittkäse** *cheese for slicing*, II2
der **Schnittlauch** (sing) *chives*, II5
das **Schnitzel, -** *cutlet (pork or veal)*, II5
schnorcheln *to snorkel*, II9
der **Schnupfen** *runny nose*, II6
die **Schokolade, -n** *chocolate*, II2
die **Scholle, -n** *plaice (type of flounder)*, Loc 4
schon *already*, I; **Schon gut!** *It's okay!*, II5; **schon oft** *a lot, often*, II3; **Ich glaube schon, dass …** *I do believe that …*, II10
schön *pretty, beautiful*, I
die **Schönheit, -en** *beauty*, II8
der **Schönheitswettbewerb, -e** *beauty competition*, II8
schräg *diagonal*, II9
der **Schrank, ⸚e** *cabinet*, I
die **Schranke, -n** *barrier*, II7
schreiben *to write*, I
der **Schreibtisch, -e** *desk*, I
der **Schreiner, -** *cabinet-maker*, II7
der **Schriftsteller, -** *author (male)*, Loc 1
der **Schritt, -e** *step*, II9
der **Schubkarren, -** *wheelbarrow*, II7
der **Schuh, -e** *shoe*, II8
das **Schuhwerk, -e** *footwear*, II4
die **Schulaula, Schulaulen** *school auditorium*, II5
die **Schuld** *guilt, fault*, II10
das **Schuldgefühl, -e** *feeling of guilt*, II10
schuldig sein *to owe*, II6
die **Schule, -n** *school*, I
der **Schüler, -** *student, pupil (male)*, I
der **Schüleraustausch** *exchange student program*, II3
die **Schülerin, -nen** *student, pupil (female)*, I
die **Schülerzeitung, -en** *school newspaper*, II10
die **Schulfeier, -n** *school celebration*, II11
der **Schulhof, ⸚e** *schoolyard*, II2

das **Schuljahrbuch, ⸚er** *school yearbook*, II7
die **Schulsachen** (pl) *school supplies*, I
die **Schultasche, -n** *schoolbag*, I
die **Schulter, -n** *shoulder*, II6
schützen *to protect*, II6
der **Schutzfaktor, -en** *protection factor*, II6
schwarz *black*, I
das **Schwein, -e** *pig, pork*, II5
der **Schweinebraten, -** *pork roast*, II2
das **Schweinefleisch** *pork*, II5
das **Schweinekotelett, -s** *pork chop*, II5
das **Schweinerückensteak, -s** *pork loin steak*, II1
der **Schweizer, -** *Swiss (male)*, II5
der **Schweizer Käse** *Swiss cheese*, II5
schwer *heavy; difficult*, II4; **schwer haben** (sep) *to have a hard time*, II9
die **Schwester, -n** *sister*, I
die **Schwierigkeit, -en** *difficulty, problem*, II4
das **Schwimmbad, ⸚er** *swimming pool*, I
das **Schwimmbecken, -** *pool*, II7
schwimmen *to swim*, I
schwitzen *to sweat*, II2
schwören *to swear*, II7
der **Sciencefictionfilm, -e** *science fiction movie*, I
der **Sciencefictionroman, -e** *science fiction novel*, I
der **See, -n** *lake*, II7
die **See, -n** *ocean, sea*, II9
das **Seebarschfilet, -s** *fillet of perch*, II11
die **Seezunge, -n** *sole*, II11
das **Segel, -** *sail*, Loc 7
der **Segelkurs, -e** *sailing class*, II9
segeln *to sail*, II9
das **Segelschiff, -e** *sailboat*, Loc 4
sehen *to see*, I; **er/sie sieht** *he/she sees*, I
die **Sehenswürdigkeit, -en** *place of interest*, II1
sehr *very*, I; **Sehr gut!** *Very well!*, I; **sehr gesund leben** *to live in a very healthy way*, II4
sei: Sei … ! *Be …!*, II5
seicht *shallow*, II9
seid: ihr seid *you* (pl) *are*, I
die **Seide, -n** *silk*, I
das **Seidenhemd, -en** *silk shirt*, II8
der **Seidenschal, -s** *silk scarf*, II8
die **Seife, -n** *soap*, II6
sein (poss adj) *his*, I
sein *to be*, I; **er ist** *he is*, I
seit (prep) *since, for*, II9
die **Seite, -n** *page*, II1
sekundengenau *accurate within a second*, II10
selber *self*, II9
selbst *self*, II1
selbstverständlich *of course*, II12

die **Selbstverteidigung** *self-defense*, II1
selten *seldom*, II4
seltsam *strange*, II1
die **Semmel, -n** *roll*, I
der **Sender, -** *station, transmitter, channel*, II10
der **Sendesaal**, (pl) **Sendesäle** *broadcasting studio*, II11
die **Sendung, -en** *show, program*, II10
der **Senf** *mustard*, I
sensationell *sensational*, I
der **September** *September*, I
die **Serie, -n** *series*, II10
servieren *to serve*, II5
die **Servobremsen** (pl) *power brakes*, II10
die **Servolenkung, -en** *power steering*, II10
Servus! *Hello!; So long!*, II1
der **Sessel, -** *armchair*, I
setzen *to put*, II6
s.setzen *to sit down*, II12
das **Shampoo, -s** *shampoo*, II6
die **Shorts** (sing or pl) *pair of shorts*, I
sich *herself, himself, itself, yourself, themselves, yourselves*, II4
Sicher! *Certainly!*, I; **Ich bin nicht sicher.** *I'm not sure.*, I; **Aber sicher!** *But of course!*, II4; **Ich bin sicher, dass …** *I'm certain that …*, II9
sicher *secure*, II7
sichern *to secure*, II9
sie *she; it; they; them*, I
Sie *you* (formal), I
der **Siebenschläfer, -** *dormouse*, II9
das **Silber** *silver*, II2; **aus Silber** *made of silver*, II6
sind: sie sind *they are*, I; **Sie** (formal) **sind** *you are*, I; **wir sind** *we are*, I
singen *to sing*, II3
die **Sinnestäuschung, -en** *hallucination*, II10
sinnlos *senseless*, II12
der **Sitz, -e** *place*, II3
sitzen *to be sitting*, II1
der **Sitzschoner, -** *seat cover*, II10
skeptisch *skeptical*, II5
das **Skifahren** *skiing*, II4
Ski laufen *to ski*, II1
die **Skizze, -n** *sketch*, II8
der **Smoking, -s** *tuxedo*, II12
so *so, well, then*, I; **so lala** *so so*, I; **So sagt man das!** *Here's how to say it!*, I; **so viel** *so much*, II6; **so was** *the like, like that*, II11
so genannt *so-called*, II3
so … wie *as … as*, II7
die **Socke, -n** *sock*, I
das **Sofa, -s** *sofa*, I
sofort *immediately*, II6
sogar *even*, II2
der **Sohn, ⸚e** *son*, II1
die **Sojasprossen** (pl) *bean sprouts*, II5

das Solarmobil, -e *solar-powered car*, II10
solch- *such*, II9
solid *solid*, II9
sollen *should, to be supposed to*, I
der Sommer, - *summer*, I
die Sonderfahrt, -en *chartered tour*, II9
sondern: nicht nur … sondern auch *not only … but also*, II3
der Sonnabend, -e *Saturday*, I
die Sonne *sun*, I
s. sonnen *to sunbathe*, II9
die Sonnenallergie, -n *sun allergy*, II3
das Sonnenbad, ⸚er *sunbathing*, II6
die Sonnenbrille, -n *sunglasses*, II12
die Sonnencreme *suntan lotion*, II6
die Sonneneinstrahlung, -en *solar radiation*, II6
die Sonnenmilch *suntan lotion*, II6
der Sonnenschutz *sun protection*, II6
der Sonnenstich, -e *sunstroke*, II6
der Sonnenstrahl, -en *sun ray*, II6
sonnig *sunny*, I
der Sonntag, -e *Sunday*, I
sonntags *Sundays*, II10
sonst: Sonst noch etwas? *Anything else?*, II2
sonstig- *other*, II8
sorgen für *to take care of*, II5
die Sorte, -n *kind, type*, II2
sortieren *to sort*, I
die Soße, -n *sauce*, II5
sowie *and*, II7
sowohl … als auch … *…as well as …*, II7
sozial *social*, II8
Spanien (das) *Spain*, II9
spanisch (adj) *Spanish*, II11
spannend *exciting, thrilling*, I
die Spannung, -en *suspense*, II10
sparen auf (acc) *to save for*, II10
der Spaß *fun*, I; (Tennis) macht keinen Spaß *(Tennis) is no fun*, I
spät *late*, II4
der Spaten, - *spade*, II7
später *later*, II10
spazieren *to walk, stroll*, II3; spazieren gehen (sep) *to go for a walk*, II3
das Speerwerfen *javelin throw*, II1
die Speise, -n *food*, II4
die Speisekarte, -n *menu*, II5
speisen *to eat, dine*, II11
die Spezialität, -en *specialty*, II11
speziell *especially*, II10
das Spiegelei, -er *fried egg*, II3
das Spiel, -e *game*, II3
spielen *to play*, I
der Spielfilm, -e *feature film*, II10
die Spielshow, -s *game show*, II10
der Spinat *spinach*, II2
Spitze! *Super!*, I
die Spitzenqualität *top quality*, II2
der Spitzensportler, - *top athlete*, II12

der Spitzer, - *pencil sharpener*, II5
der Sport *sports; physical education*, I
die Sportanlage, -n *sport facility*, II12
die Sportart, -en *kind of sport*, II1
der Sportartikel, - *sporting equipment*, II2
die Sporteinrichtung, -en *sport facility*, II12
der Sportler, - *athlete*, II12
sportlich *sporty*, II8
die Sportsendung, -en *sports show*, II10
die Sportübertragung, -en *sports telecast*, II10
der Sportwagen, - *sports car*, II10
die Sprache, -n *language*, II4
der Sprachkurs, -e *language course*, II3
die Sprechblase, -n *speech bubble*, II5
sprechen *to speak*, I; sprechen über *to talk about, discuss*, I; er/sie spricht über *he/she talks about*, I; Kann ich bitte Andrea sprechen? *Could I please speak with Andrea?*, I
das Sprichwort, ⸚er *saying*, II11
spritzen *to spray*, II4
der Spritzer, - *splash*, II12
das Spülbecken, - *sink*, I
spülen *to wash*, I
der Staat, -en *country, state*, II3
die Staatssammlung, -en *state collection*, II1
der Stabhochsprung *pole vault*, II1
stabilisieren *to stabilize*, II6
das Stadion, (pl) Stadien *stadium*, II3
die Stadt, ⸚e *city*, I; in der Stadt *in the city*, I; in die Stadt gehen *to go downtown*, I
die Stadtbesichtigung, -en *city tour*, II3
der Stadtbummel *stroll downtown*, II1
die Stadtkarte, -n *city map*, II9
der Stadtplan, ⸚e *city map*, II9
der Stadtrand, ⸚er *edge of the city*, II7
die Stadtrundfahrt, -en *city sightseeing tour*, II11
der Stadtrundgang, ⸚e *city walking tour, stroll around town*, II9
der Stadtteil, -e *neighborhood in a city*, II3
das Stadttor, -e *city gate*, II9
das Stadtzentrum, (pl) Stadtzentren *downtown*, II7
stammen aus *to come from*, II1
der Stammtisch, -e *(table reserved for regular guests)*, II12
der Stand, ⸚e *stand*, II5
das Stangenbrot, -e *bread stick*, II5
der Stapel, - *pile*, II7
stark *great; strong*, I
die Stärke *strength*, II12
die Statistik, -en *statistics*, II10
stattfinden (sep) *to take place*, II9
stattgefunden *taken place*, II3
stattlich *stately; imposing*, II9

der Staub *dust*, I; Staub saugen *to vacuum*, I; Staub wischen *to dust*, II2
staunen *to be surprised*, er staunte nicht schlecht *he was quite surprised*, II12
das Steak, -s *steak*, II12
der Steckbrief, -e *(here:) personal profile*, II1
die Steghose, -n *stirrup pants*, II8
stehen: auf etwas stehen *to swear by*, II2; Das steht dir prima! *That looks great on you!*, II8; Wie steht's mit …? *So what about …?*, II4
steigen *to climb*, II9
die Stelle, -n *position; job*, II7
stellen *to put*, II1; Stell deinem Partner Fragen! *Ask your partner questions.*, II5
die Sterblichkeit *mortality*, II10
das Stereo-Farbfernsehgerät, -e *color stereo television set*, II10
die Stereoanlage, -n *stereo*, I
das Stereogerät, -e *stereo*, II10
der Sterngucker, - *stargazer*, II10
der Steuerberater, - *tax advisor*, II8
steuern *to steer, operate*, II10
das Stichwort, ⸚er *key word*, II3
stickig *stuffy, suffocating*, II7
der Stiefel, - *boot*, I
der Stift, -e *pencil*, II9
der Stil, -e *style*, II8
still *quiet*, II9
stimmen *to be correct*, II2; Stimmt (schon)! *Keep the change.*, I; Stimmt! *That's right! True!*, I; Stimmt nicht! *Not true!; False!*, I; Stimmt (überhaupt) nicht! *That's not right (at all)!*, II10; Stimmt, aber … *That's true, but …*, II4
die Stimmung, -en *mood*, II3
die Stirn, -en *forehead*, II6
das Stirnband, ⸚er *head band*, II1
der Stock, ⸚e *floor*, II1
der Stoff, -e *material*, II12
das Stofftier, -e *stuffed animal*, II7
der Stolz *pride*, II3
stolz auf (acc) *proud of*, II3; stören *to disturb*, II5
die Strafe, -n *punishment*, II2
der Strahl, -en *ray*, II6
der Strand, ⸚e *beach*, II9
die Straße, -n *street*, I; bis zur …straße *until you get to … Street*, I; in der …straße *on … Street*, I
der Strauch, ⸚er *bush*, II7
der Strauß, ⸚e *bouquet*, I
das Streichkonzert, -e *concert for strings*, II11
der Streifen, - *stripe*, II12
streiten *to argue*, II9
der Stress *stress*, II7
stricken *to knit*, II7

GERMAN-ENGLISH VOCABULARY

der **Strumpf**, ⸚e *stocking*, II8
das **Stück**, -e *piece*, I; **ein Stück Kuchen** *a piece of cake*, I
stückeln *to cut into pieces*, II5
der **Student**, -en *(college) student (male)*, II4
die **Studentin**, -nen *(college) student (female)*, II4
der **Studienkreis**, -e *study circle*, II9
studieren *to study*, II4
die **Stufe**, -n *step, level*, II1
der **Stuhl**, ⸚e *chair*, I
die **Stunde**, -n *hour*, II3
stundenlang *for hours*, II2
der **Stundenplan**, ⸚e *class schedule*, I
suchen *to look for, search for*, I
südlich *southern*, II9
super *super*, I
das **Superangebot**, -e *special offer*, II2
der **Supermarkt**, ⸚e *supermarket*, I
supertoll *really great*, II4
die **Suppe**, -n *soup*, II1
surfen *to surf*, I
süß *sweet*, II6
süßsauer *sweet and sour*, II1
der **Süßstoff**, -e *sweetener*, II5
sympathisch *nice, pleasant*, II1
das **Symphoniekonzert**, -e *orchestral concert*, II11
das **Symphonieorchester**, - *symphony orchestra*, II11
die **Symphoniker** (pl) *members of a symphony orchestra*, II11
das **Symptom**, -e *symptom*, II6
die **Synagoge**, -n *synagogue*, II11
die **Szene**, -n *scene*, II2

die Tabelle, -n *table, grid*, II4
die Tablette, -n *pill*, II6
die **Tacos** (pl) *tacos*, II12
die Tafel, -n *table, blackboard*, II1
der **Tag**, -e *day*, I; **eines Tages** *one day*, I
die Tagesfahrt, -en *day trip*, II9
täglich *daily*, II2
tagsüber *during the day, in the daytime*, II12
der Tagungsort, -e *conference site*, II3
das Tal, ⸚er *valley*, II9
der Talkessel, - *basin of the valley*, Loc 10
die **Talkshow**, -s *talk show*, II10
der Tandemsprung, ⸚e *tandem jump*, II10
die **Tante**, -n *aunt*, I
tanzen *to dance*, I; **tanzen gehen** *to go dancing*, I
die Tanzveranstaltung, -en *dance*, II3
tappen *to fumble about, to grope*, II12

die **Tasche**, -n *bag; pocket*, II8
die Taschenlampe, -n *flashlight*, II9
der Taschenrechner, - *pocket calculator*, I
das Taschenwörterbuch, ⸚er *pocket dictionary*, II1
die Tätigkeit, -en *activity*, II6
der Tatort, -e *scene of a crime*, II10
tatsächlich *really, actually*, II11
tauchen *to dive*, II9
die Tauchschule, -n *diving school*, II12
tauschen *to trade*, II2
tausend *thousand*, II12
der Taxifahrer, - *taxi driver*, II11
der **Tee** *tea*, I; **ein Glas Tee** *a glass of tea*, I
der Teelöffel, - *teaspoon*, II5
der Teil, -e *part*, II1
teilen *to divide, share*, II3
teilnehmen an (sep, dat) *to participate in*, II4
teilweise *partly*, II4
das **Telefon**, -e *telephone*, I
telefonieren *to call*, I
die **Telefonkarte**, -n *phone card*, I
die **Telefonnummer**, -n *telephone number*, I
die **Telefonzelle**, -n *telephone booth*, I
die **Temperatur**, -en *temperature*, II6
das **Tennis** *tennis*, I
der **Tennisplatz**, ⸚e *tennis court*, II9
der **Tennisschläger**, - *tennis racket*, II2
der Tennisspieler, - *tennis player*, II1
das Tennisturnier, -e *tennis tournament*, II1
der **Teppich**, -e *carpet*, I
die **Terrasse**, -n *terrace, porch*, II7
testen *to test*, II2
teuer *expensive*, I
die Textilindustrie, -n *textile industry*, Loc 1
das **Theater**, - *theater*, I; **ins Theater gehen** *to go to the theater*, I
die Theateraufführung, -en *theatrical performance*, II3
das **Theaterstück**, -e *play*, II11
die Theke, -n *bar, counter*, II4
das Thema, (pl) Themen *subject, topic*, II2
theoretisch *theoretical(ly)*, II10
der Thunfischsalat *tuna salad*, II5
tief *deep*, II12
die Tiefkühlerdbeere, -n *frozen strawberry*, II5
die Tiefkühlkost *frozen food*, II5
tiefschwarz *jet black*, II8
das Tier, -e *animal*, II2
der Tierarzt, ⸚e *veterinarian*, II3
der Tiergarten, ⸚ *zoo*, II11
tierlieb *fond of animals*, II1
die Tierliebe *love of animals*, II5
die **Tiersendung**, -en *animal documentary*, II10
der Tilsiter Käse *Tilsiter cheese*, II5
das Tirol *Tyrol*, II3

der **Tisch**, -e *table*, I
das Tischtennis *table tennis*, II3
das Tischtuch, ⸚er *tablecloth*, II12
der Titel, - *title*, I
Tja … *Well …*, I
die **Tochter**, ⸚ *daughter*, II1
todlangweilig *extremely boring*, II7
der Tofu *tofu*, II5
die Toilette, -n *bathroom, toilet*, II7
toll *great, terrific*, I
die **Tomate**, -n *tomato*, I
die Tomatensoße, -n *tomato sauce*, II12
der Topf, ⸚e *pot*, II9
das Tor, -e *gate*, Loc 4
die **Torte**, -n *layer cake*, I
die Tour, -en *tour, trip*, II4
der Tourismus *tourism*, Loc 1
der Tourist, -en *tourist*, II9
die Tracht, -en *ethnic costume*, II8
tragen *to wear; carry*, II8; **er/sie trägt** *he/she wears*, II8; **tragen zu** *to wear with*, II8
der Träger, - *strap*, II8
das **Trägerhemd**, -en *camisole*, II8
trainiert *trained*, II3
das Training *training*, II3
trampen *to hitchhike*, II9
die Träne, -n *tear*, II7
die **Traube**, -n *grape*, I
der Traubenzucker *glucose*, II5
der Traum, ⸚e *dream*, II9
die Traumanlage, -n *dream spot*, II12
das Traumhaus, ⸚er *dream house*, II7
traurig *sad*, I
der Treff, -s *meeting, rendezvous*, II9
s. treffen *to meet*, II3
treiben: Sport treiben *to play sports*, II4
die Treppe, -n *staircase*, II7
das Tretboot, -e *pedal boat*, II9
treten *to step on; to pedal*, II6
trinken *to drink*, I
trocken *dry*, I
trocknen *to dry*, II2
der Trödelmarkt, ⸚e *second-hand or flea market*, II8
der Troll, -e *troll*, II11
trollen *to trot, to troddle*, II11
trotz (prep) *in spite of, despite*, II8
trotzdem *nevertheless*, II3
der Trumpf, ⸚e *trump (card)*, II9
Tschau! *Bye! So long!*, I
Tschüs! *Bye! So long!*, I
das **T-Shirt**, -s *T-shirt*, I
die Tube, -n *tube*, II6
das **Tuch**, ⸚er *scarf*, II1
tun *to do*, I; **Leid tun: Es tut mir Leid.** *I'm sorry.*, I; **Tut mir Leid. Ich bin nicht von hier.** *I'm sorry. I'm not from here.*, II9; **weh tun: Tut dir … weh?** *Does your … hurt?*, II6; **Tut dir was weh?** *Does something hurt?*, II6; **Tut's weh?** *Does it hurt?*, II6
die Türkei *Turkey*, II9

türkisblau *turquoise*, II8
türkisch (adj) *Turkish*, II11
der Turm, -̈e *tower*, II11
turnen *to do gymnastics*, II2
das Turnier, -e *tournament*, II12
der Turnschuh, -e *sneaker, athletic shoe*, I
das Tüteneis, - *ice cream bar*, II2
der Typ, -en *guy; type*, II8
typisch *typical*, II1

die U-Bahn=Untergrundbahn, -en *subway*, I
die U-Bahnstation, -en *subway station*, I
über (prep) *over; about; above*, II1
überall *everywhere; all over*, II3
das **Überarbeiten**, *revising*, II9
überbacken *au gratin*, II11
überhaupt *generally; absolutely*, II2; **überhaupt nicht** *not at all*, I; **überhaupt nicht gern haben** *to strongly dislike*, I; **überhaupt nicht wohl** *not well at all*, II4
s. überlegen *to consider, reflect*, II7
übernachten *to spend the night*, II3
die Übernachtung, -en *overnight stay*, II9
übernehmen *to take over*, II1
überraschen *to surprise*, II12
die Überraschung, -en *surprise*, II11
die Überschrift, -en *title*, II6
überstand (past) *overcame*, Loc 4
die Übertragung, -en *telecast, transmission*, II10
übertreiben *to exaggerate*, II7
überwältigend *overwhelming*, II11
überzeugt *convinced, persuaded*, II8
das Übliche *the usual*, II3
übrig bleiben *to be left over*, II7
übrigens *by the way*, II6
die Übung, -en *exercise*, II2
die Uhr, -en *watch, clock*, II1
die Uhrzeit, -en *time of the day*, II3
um (prep) *at; around*, II9; **um 8 Uhr** *at 8 o'clock*, I; **um ein Uhr** *at one o'clock*, I; **Wie viel Uhr ist es?** *What time is it?*, I; **Um wie viel Uhr?** *At what time?*, I
um … zu *in order to …*, II4
die Umfrage, -n *survey, poll*, II2
die Umgebung, -en *surrounding area*, II7
umher *around, on all sides*, II12
umrahmen *to frame*, Loc 10
umrühren (sep) *to stir*, II12
umschreiben (sep) *to rewrite*, II4
die Umwelt *environment*, I

das Umweltbewusstsein *environmental consciousness*, II4
der Umzug, -̈e *change of residence, move*, II7
unbedingt *absolutely, by all means*, II6; **Nicht unbedingt!** *Not entirely! Not necessarily!*, II5
unbegrenzt *boundless, limitless*, II12
unbequem *uncomfortable*, I
und (conj) *and*, I
unecht *not genuine*, II12
unentbehrlich *indispensable, absolutely necessary*, II10
unfreundlich *unfriendly*, II1
ungarisch *Hungarian*, II11
ungefähr *about, approximately*, I
ungekocht *unboiled*, II12
ungestört *undisturbed*, II5
ungesund *unhealthy*, II4
ungewöhnlich *unusual*, II12
unglaublich *unbelievable*, II10
die Uni, -s=Universität *university*, II3
die Universität, -en *university*, II3
das Universum *universe*, II10
unmöglich *impossible*, II8
unnötig *unnecessary*, II7
unpraktisch *impractical*, II8
uns *us*, I; *ourselves*, II4; *to us*, II3
unser (poss adj) *our*, II5
unsicher *unsure*, II9
unsportlich *unathletic*, II1
unsympathisch *unfriendly, unpleasant*, II1
unten *underneath, below*, II2
s. unterhalten *to chat, converse*, II2
die Unterhaltung, -en *conversation; entertainment*, II3
die Unterhaltungskosten (pl) *cost of upkeep*, II10
die Unterhaltungsmöglichkeit, -en *entertainment option*, II3
die Unterkunft, -̈e *accommodation*, II3
unternehmen *to undertake, to attempt*, II1
unternommen *undertaken, attempted*, II12
der Unterricht *class, lesson*, II2
unterscheiden *to distinguish*, II8
der Unterschied, -e *difference*, II11
untersuchen *to examine*, II10
die Untersuchung, -en *examination*, II6
unterteilt *subdivided*, II12
unterwegs *on the way, underway*, II3
unwohl *unwell*, II6
der Urlaub, -e *vacation* (time off from work), II3
der Urlauber, - *person on vacation*, II12
das Urlaubsglück *vacation happiness*, II12
der Urlaubsort, -e *vacation site*, II9

das Urlaubsparadies, -e *vacation paradise*, II9
das Urlaubsziel, -e *vacation destination*, II9
das Urteil, -e *verdict, judgment*, II12
usw.=und so weiter *et cetera, and so on*, II1

die Vanille *vanilla*, II5
das Vanilleeis *vanilla-flavored ice cream*, II5
die Vanillemilch *vanilla-flavored milk*, II5
die Variante, -n *variant*, II12
variationsreich *full of variations*, II12
der Vater, -̈ *father*, I
der Vatertag *Father's Day*, I; **Alles Gute zum Vatertag!** *Happy Father's Day!*, I
der Vati=Vater *father*, II1
der Vegetarier, - *vegetarian*, II5
vegetarisch (adj) *vegetarian*, II5
verändern *to modify, change*, II8
die Veranstaltung, -en *performance, show, arrangement*, II11
das Verb, -en *verb*, II11
verbessern *to improve, to correct*, II1
der Verbesserungsvorschlag, -̈e *suggestion for improvement*, II7
verbieten *to forbid*, II7
das Verbot, -e *prohibition*, II4
verbracht (pp) *spent*, II3
verbreitet *spread, disseminated*, II2
verbringen *to spend* (time), I
s. verdrücken *to slip away*, II12
der Verein, -e *association, club*, II9
vereinigt *unified*, II3
vereint *united*, Loc 4
verfügen über (acc) *to have something at one's disposal*, II12
die Verfügung: zur Verfügung stehen *to be available*, II7
die Vergangenheit *past*, II3
vergessen *to forget*, II1
vergiftet *poisoned, contaminated*, II7
vergleichen *to compare*, II7
das Verhalten, - *behavior*, II7
s. verhalten *to behave*, II7
das Verhältnis, -se *situation, circumstance; relationship*, II11
verheiratet *married*, II12
verhindern *to prevent*, II4
verkaufen *to sell*, II7
der Verkäufer, - *salesman*, II1
der Verkehr *traffic*, II7
der Verkehrslärm *traffic noise*, II7

das **Verkehrsmittel,** - *transportation,* II9; **öffentliche Verkehrsmittel** *public transportation* II9
verklärt *transfigured, radiant,* II11
der Verlag, -e *publishing house,* Loc 4
verlassen *to leave,* II2; *(adj, pp) deserted, abandoned,* II2
verlegen *embarrassed, self-conscious,* II1
s. **verletzen** *to injure (oneself),* II6
die Verletzung, -en *injury,* II4
verlieren *to lose,* II10
verlockend *tempting,* II4
verloren *lost,* II3
vermeiden *to avoid,* II4
vermengen *to mix,* II12
der Vermieter, - *landlord,* II7
vernünftig *reasonable, sensible,* II4; **vernünftig essen** *to eat sensibly,* II4
verpatzt *bungled,* II9
verrechnen *to miscalculate,* II10
verreisen *to leave on a trip,* II8
verrückt *crazy,* II5
verrühren *to mix, stir,* II5
verschieden *different,* I
verschlingen *to devour,* II10
der Verschluss, ⸚e *lock, clasp, seal,* II8
versehen *to provide,* II5; *(pp) provided,* II5
das Versehen, - *oversight, error,* II5
die Versicherung, -en *insurance,* II10
versprechen *to promise,* II11
verstanden *understood,* II3
verständigen *to communicate,* II1
das Verständnis, -se *comprehension; sympathy,* II2
der Verstärker, - *amplifier,* II9
s. **verstauchen** *to sprain,* II6
verstehen *to understand,* II4
verstellbar *movable, adjustable,* II8
der Versuch, -e *attempt,* II3
versuchen *to try,* II10
der Vertrag, ⸚e *contract, agreement,* II12
vertragen: **Ich kann das Brot nicht vertragen.** *The bread doesn't agree with me.,* II12
vertreiben *to banish, expel,* II7
vertun *to squander, waste,* II2
verursachen *to cause,* II6
verwandelt *transformed,* II3
der Verwandte, -n *relative,* II7
verwenden *to make use of, use,* II4
verwöhnen *to spoil, pamper,* II12
Verzeihung! *Excuse me!,* I; *Pardon me!,* II9
verzichten auf (acc) *to do without,* II4
das **Video, -s** *video cassette,* I
die **Videocassette, -n** *video cassette,* II10
die **Videokamera, -s** *camcorder,* II3
der **Videorecorder,** - *video cassette recorder,* II3

der Videotext, -e *videotext,* II10
der Videowagen, - *VCR cart,* II10
das Vieh *cattle,* II9
viel *a lot,* I; **viel zu** *much too,* I; **viel Obst essen** *to eat lots of fruit,* II4
viele *many,* I; **Vielen Dank!** *Thank you very much!,* I
vielleicht *maybe, perhaps,* I
vielseitig *versatile,* II11
die Vielzahl, -en *multitude,* II10
der Vierbeiner, - *four-legged animal,* II12
der Vierer, - *driver's license for a moped,* II12
vierfach- *quadruple,* II12
viert- *fourth,* II11
das **Viertel: Viertel nach** *a quarter after,* I; **Viertel vor** *a quarter till,* I
die Viskose *viscose,* II8
die Vitalität *vitality,* Loc 10
das Volk, ⸚er *people,* II12
das Volksfest, -e *festival,* II8
voll *full,* II5
Volleyball *volleyball,* I
völlig *completely,* II3
der Vollkontakt *full contact,* II1
das Vollkornbrötchen, - *whole grain roll,* II5
die Vollkornsemmel, -n *whole grain roll,* I
die Vollmilch *whole milk,* II4
die Vollpension *all meals included,* II12
vollschlank *not-so-slim,* II1
vollwaschbar *fully-washable,* II8
die Vollwertkost *highly nutritional food,* II4
vom=von dem
von (prep) *from, of,* II9; **von 8 Uhr bis 8 Uhr 45** *from 8:00 until 8:45,* I; **von daher** *for this reason,* II7; **von hier aus** *from here,* II9; **von hinten** *from behind,* II8; **von vorn** *from the beginning,* II8; **von zu Hause** *from home,* II9
vor (prep) *before, in front of,* II9; **vor allem** *most importantly,* II8; **vor allen Dingen** *especially,* II10; **zehn vor ...** *ten till ...,* I
das Vorabendprogramm, -e *schedule for the early evening,* II10
der Vorbehalt, -e *reservations,* II7
vorbei *along, by, past,* II3
vorbeidonnern (sep) *to roar past,* II9
vorbeiführen (sep) *to lead past,* II12
vorbeikommen (sep) *to pass by, drop by,* II9
das **Vorbereiten,** *to prepare,* II9
vorbereiten auf (sep, acc) *to prepare for,* II5

die Vorführung, -en *production, performance,* II3
vorgehen (sep) *to go before; to take action,* II5
vorgeschrieben *prescribed,* II10
vorgestern *day before yesterday,* I
vorhaben (sep) *to intend, plan,* II1
vorher *before, previously,* II12
vorkommen (sep) *to happen,* II4
vorlesen (sep) *to read aloud,* II4
die Vorliebe, -n *preference,* II12
der Vormittag, -e *morning,* II1
der Vorort, -e *suburb,* I
der Vorschlag, ⸚e *suggestion, proposition, proposal,* II12; **Das ist ein guter Vorschlag.** *That's a good suggestion.,* II12
vorschlagen (sep) *to suggest,* II9
vorschreiben (sep) *prescribe,* II10
die Vorsicht *caution,* II6
vorsichtig *cautious,* II5
die Vorspeise, -n *appetizer,* II11
vorspielen (sep) *to act out,* II5
die Vorstadt, ⸚e *suburb,* Loc 1
s. vorstellen (sep) *to present, introduce; to imagine,* II7
die Vorstellung, -en *presentation; idea,* II11
der Vorteil, -e *advantage,* II7
der Vortrag, ⸚e *lecture, presentation,* II3
vortragen (sep) *to report,* II5
vorüber *past, beyond,* II2
das Vorurteil, -e *prejudice,* II8
die Vorverkaufskasse, -n *advance booking office,* II11
vorwiegend *primarily, prevailing,* II12
vorziehen (sep) *to prefer,* II7
vorzüglich *superior, excellent,* II11
der Vulkan, -e *volcano,* II9

W

wachsen *to grow,* II7
die Waffe, -n *weapon,* II3
die Waffel, -n *waffle,* II2
der Wagen, - *car, truck, wagon,* II10
die Wahl, -en *choice; election,* II9
wählen *to choose; select,* II11
wahlweise *by choice,* II12
wahnsinnig *insanely, extremely,* II3; **Wahnsinnig gut!** *Extremely well!,* II3
wahr *true,* II3
während (conj, prep) *during,* II3
wahrscheinlich *probably,* I
das Wahrzeichen, - *landmark, symbol,* Loc 4
das Waldspiel, -e *forest game,* II9
der Waldweg, -e *forest path,* II9

die Wand, ⸚e *wall*, II8
die Wanderhose, -n *hiking breeches*, II8
wandern *to hike*, I
der Wanderweg, -e *hiking trail*, II3
wann? *when?*, I
das Wappen, - *coat of arms*, II1
war: ich war *I was*, I
wäre *would be*, II2; **Das wäre toll!** *That would be great!*, II12; **Das wär' nicht schlecht.** *That wouldn't be bad.*, II11
das Warenhaus, ⸚er *department store*, II1
warm *warm*, I
warten auf (acc) *to wait for*, II2
warum? *why?*, I
was? *what?*, I; **Was noch?** *What else?*, I; **Was gibt's** *What is it?*, II5; **Was ist?** *What is it?*, II5
was=etwas *something*, II6; **Ist was mit dir?** *Is something wrong?*, II6
was für *what kind of?*, I; **Was für ein Pech!** *That's too bad!*, II5
die Wäsche *laundry, clothes*, II2
waschen *to wash*, II6
s. waschen *to wash oneself*, II6
das Waschpulver, - *laundry detergent*, II10
das Wasser *water*, I
der Wasserhaushalt *water conservation*, II5
der Wassernapf, ⸚e *water bowl*, II12
das Wechselgeld *change*, II2
wechseln *to change*, II10
der Wecker, - *alarm clock*, II2
weder ... noch *neither ... nor*, II9
wegfahren (sep) *to drive away*, II11
weggeben (sep) *to give away*, II8
weggehen (sep) *to go away*, II8
wegwerfen (sep) *to throw out*, II8
wehtun (sep) *to hurt*, II6
weich *soft*, II8
Weihnachten *Christmas*, I; **Fröhliche Weihnachten!** *Merry Christmas!*, I
weil (conj) *because*, I
die Weile *while*, II7
der Wein, -e *wine*, II2
der Weinberg, -e *vineyard*, Loc 7
weiß *white*, I
die Weißwurst, ⸚e *(southern German sausage specialty)*, I
weit *far; wide*, I; *big, broad*, II12; **Wir sind so weit.** *We're ready.*, II11; **weit von hier** *far from here*, I
weiter *further*, II3
weitergeben (sep) *to pass on*, II11
weithin *far and wide*, II3
der Weitsprung *long jump*, II1
welch-? *which?*, I; **Welche Fächer hast du?** *Which subjects do you have?*, I
die Welt, -en *world*, II10

der Weltmeister, - *world champion*, II12
der Weltruf *international reputation*, Loc 10
wem? *whom, to whom?, for whom?*, I
wen? *whom?*, I
wenig *little*, II4
wenigstens *at least*, II4
wenn (conj) *whenever*, II8
wer? *who?*, I; **Wer ist das?** *Who is that?*, I
werben *to advertise*, II10
die Werbesendung, -en *commercial*, II10
die Werbung, -en *advertisement*, II8
werden *will*, II10; **er/sie wird** *he/she will*, II10; **Ich werde mir ... kaufen.** *I'll buy myself ...*, II10
werfen *to throw*, II12
das Werk, -e *work; factory*, II11
der Wert *worth, value*, II8
wert sein *to be worth*, II11
wesentlich *substantial(ly)*, II10
der Westen *west*, II7
der Western, - *western (movie)*, I
wetten *to bet*, II5
das Wetter *weather*, I
der Wetterbericht, -e *weather report*, II10
die Wetterjacke, -n *rain jacket*, II8
der Whirlpool, -s *whirlpool*, II9
wichtig *important*, II4
wie? *how?*, I; **wie oft?** *how often?*, I; **Wie spät ist es?** *What time is it?*, I; **Wie steht's mit ...?** *So what about ...?*, II4; **Wie wär's mit ...?** *How would ... be?*, II11; **Wie war's?** *How was it?*, II3; **wie lange?** *how long?*, II6; **wie viel?** *how much?*, I; **Wie viel Grad haben wir?** *What's the temperature?*, I; **Wie viel Uhr ist es?** *What time is it?*, I
wieder *again*, I; **wieder aufgebaut** *rebuilt*, Loc 10
wiedergeben (sep) *to repeat*, II9
wiederholen *to repeat*, II2
Wiederhören! *Bye!* (on the telephone), I; **Auf Wiederhören!** *Goodbye!* (on the telephone), I
Wiederschaun! *Goodbye!*, II11
Wiedersehen! *Bye!*, I; **Auf Wiedersehen!** *Goodbye!*, I;
wiegen *to weigh*, I
das Wiener Schnitzel, - *veal cutlet*, II11
die Wiese, -n *meadow*, II3
wieso *why?; how?*, II11
wievielmal *how many times, how often*, II6
der Wildhüter, - *gamekeeper*, II10
die Wildlederjacke, -n *suede jacket*, II12
die Wildspezialität, -en *game

specialty*, II11
der Wildwestfilm, -e *wild west film*, II10
willkommen *welcome*, II12
die Windjacke, -n *windbreaker*, II8
windsurfen *to wind surf*, II9
der Winter *winter*, I
wir *we*, I
der Wirbelwind, -e *whirlwind*, II12
wirklich *really*, I
der Wirt, -e *proprietor*, II12
die Wirtschaft *business, economy*, Loc 7
wischen *to wipe*, II2
wissen *to know* (a fact, information, etc.), I; **Das weiß ich nicht.** *That I don't know.*, I; **Ich weiß nicht, ob ...** *I don't know whether ...*, II9
witzig *fun, witty*, II8
wo? *where?*, I
woanders *somewhere else*, II2
wobei *whereby*, II4
die Woche, -n *week*, I; **(einmal) in der Woche** *(once) a week*, I
das Wochenende, -n *weekend*, I
die Wochenendfahrt, -en *weekend trip*, II9
wochentags *on weekdays*, II5
wöchentlich *weekly*, II12
wofür? *for what?*, II7; **Wofür interessierst du dich?** *What are you interested in?*, II8
woher? *from where?*, I; **Woher bist du?** *Where are you from?*, I; **Woher kommst du?** *Where are you from?*, I
wohin? *where (to)?*, I; **Wohin fahren wir?** *Where are we going?*, II9
wohl *well*, II1; **Ich fühle mich wohl.** *I feel great.*, II6
wohlhabend *well-to-do*, II12
wohnen *to live*, I
das Wohngebiet, -e *residential area*, II7
die Wohngegend, -en *residential area*, II7
das Wohnhaus, ⸚er *residence*, II9
das Wohnmobil, -e *mobile home*, II9
der Wohnort, -e *residence*, II1
der Wohnraum, ⸚e *living space*, II12
die Wohnung, -en *apartment*, II7
das Wohnzimmer, - *living room*, II7
wolkig *cloudy*, I
die Wolle *wool*, II8
wollen *to want (to)*, I
das Wollhemd, -en *wool shirt*, II8
wollweiß *off-white*, II8
woran? *at, on what?*, II9
worauf? *on, to what?*, II10
woraus? *out of, from what?*, II12
das Wort, ⸚er *word*, II2
das Wörterbuch, ⸚er *dictionary*, I
der Wortschatz, ⸚e *vocabulary*, II1

worüber? *about, over what?*, I; **Worüber habt ihr gesprochen?** *What did you talk about?*, I
Worum geht's? *What's it about?*, II6
wovon? *of what?*, II12
wozu? *why?; to what purpose?*, II11
wunderbar *wonderful*, II8
das Wunderkind, -er *prodigy*, II12
wunderschön *incredibly beautiful*, II12
wundervoll *wonderful, full of wonder*, II3
der Wunsch, ̈-e *wish*, I; **Haben Sie einen Wunsch?** *May I help you?*, I; **Haben Sie noch einen Wunsch?** *Would you like anything else?*, I
s. **wünschen** *to wish*, II5; **Ich wünsche mir …** *I wish for …*, II7
der Wunschtraum, ̈-e *wish-dream*, II7
wurde (past) *became*, II3
würde *would*, II11; **Würdest du gern mal …?** *Wouldn't you like to …?*, II11
die Wurst, ̈-e *sausage*, I
das Wurstbrot, -e *bologna sandwich*, I
würzen *to spice*, II5
würzig *spicy*, II11
die Wüste, -n *desert*, II3

z. B. (zum Beispiel) *for example*, II1
die Zahl, -en *number*, II1
zahlreich *countless*, II12
der Zahn, ̈-e *tooth*, II6
die Zahnbürste, -n *toothbrush*, II7
die Zahnpasta *toothpaste*, II6
die Zahnschmerzen (pl) *toothache*, II6
zart *tender*, II2
die Zauberflöte *magic flute*, II11
zeckig *hip* (with clothing), II8
der Zehnkämpfer, - *decathlete*, II12
zeichnen *to draw*, I

die Zeichnung, -en *drawing*, II5
zeigen *to show*, II3
die Zeit *time*, I; **zur Zeit** *right now*, II8
die Zeitausdrücke (pl) *time expressions*, II3
die Zeitschrift, -en *magazine*, I
die Zeitung, -en *newspaper*, I
der Zeitungsstand, ̈-e *newsstand*, II10
das Zelt, -e *tent*, II9
die Zentrale, -n *center*, II10
die Zentralverriegelung, -en *central locking system*, II10
zerrissen *torn*, II12
zerstört *destroyed*, II3
die Zerstörung, -en *destruction*, II3
der Zettel, - *note*, II2
das Zeug, -e *stuff*, II8
ziehen *to pull*, II5
das Ziel, -e *goal*, II9
zielen *to aim*, II9
ziemlich *rather*, I
die Zigarette, -n *cigarette*, II4
das Zimmer, - *room*, I; **mein Zimmer aufräumen** *to clean my room*, I
die Zimmerantenne, -n *indoor antenna*, II10
der Zimt *cinnamon*, I
der Zirkus, -se *circus*, II11
die Zitrone, -n *lemon*, I
zögern *to hesitate*, II9
der Zoo, -s *zoo*, I
zu *too; to*, I; **zu Fuß** *on foot*, I; **zu Hause helfen** *to help at home*, I; **zu bitter** *too bitter*, II1; **zu viel** *too much*, II4; **zu viele** *too many*, II4
das Zuhause, - *home*, II4
zuallererst *first of all*, II4
die Zubereitung, -en *preparation*, II5
der Zucker *sugar*, I
zueinander *to one another*, II11
zuerst *first*, I
zufällig *coincidentally, by accident*, II9
zufrieden *satisfied*, II7
die Zufriedenheit, -en *satisfaction*, II8
der Zug, ̈-e *train*, II1
zugeben (sep) *to admit*, II12
zugleich *at the same time*, Loc 4
zugreifen (sep) *to grab, take*, II12
zuhören (sep) *to listen to*, II6; **Hör gut zu!** *Listen carefully!*, I
der Zuhörer, - *listener*, II7
die Zukunft *future*, II3

zuletzt *last of all*, I
zum=zu dem: **zum Abendessen** *for dinner*, II5; **Zum Wohl!** *To your health!*, II11
zumachen (sep) *to close*, II5
zunächst *for the time being*, II12
zunehmend *increasingly*, Loc 1
die Zunge, -n *tongue*, II2
zur=zu der: **zur Anregung** *as a start*, II1; **zur Zeit** *right now*, II8
zurechtkommen (sep) *to get on well*, II6
zurück *back*, II1
zurückkommen (sep) *to return, come back*, II1
zurückziehen (sep) *withdraw*, II5
zusammen *together*, II1
die Zusammenarbeit *cooperation*, II11
zusammenballen (sep) *to conglomerate*, II9
die Zusammenfassung, -en *synopsis*, II11
zusammenkommen (sep) *to come together*, II3
zusammenpassen (sep) *to match*, II8
zusammensetzen (sep) *to put together*, II4
zusammenstellen (sep) *to put together*, II5
die Zusammenstellung, -en *combination*, II1
zusammentreffen (sep) *to meet*, II1
zusätzlich *additional*, II4
der Zuschauer, - *viewer*, II10
zuschlagen (sep) *to slam*, II7
zustimmen (sep) *to agree*, II7
die Zutaten (pl) *ingredients*, II5
zutreffen (sep) *to be correct*, II6
zuvor *before*, II10
zwar *indeed*, II7
zweckmäßig *appropriate, suitable*, II12
der Zweifel, - *doubt*, II9
zweimal *twice*, I
das Zweirad, ̈-er *bicycle*, II7
zweisprachig *bilingual*, Loc 4
zweit- *second*, II1
die Zwetschge, -n *plum*, II2
die Zwiebel, -n *onion*, I
der Zwiebelturm, ̈-e *tower with onion-shaped dome*, Loc 1
der Zwilling, -e *twin*, II1
zwischen (prep) *between*, II9
zwischendrin *in between*, II12

English-German Vocabulary

English-German Vocabulary

This vocabulary includes all of the words in the **Wortschatz** sections of the chapters. These words are considered active—you are expected to know them and be able to use them.

Idioms are listed under the English word you would be most likely to look up. German nouns are listed with definite article and plural ending, when applicable. The number after each German word or phrase refers to the chapter in which it becomes active vocabulary. To be sure you are using the German words and phrases in the correct context, refer to the chapters in which they appear.

The following abbreviations are used in the vocabulary: sep (separable-prefix verb), pl (plural), acc (accusative), dat (dative), masc (masculine), and poss adj (possessive adjective).

a, an *ein(e),* I
about *ungefähr,* I
across from *gegenüber,* II9
action movie *der Actionfilm, -e,* I
actor *der Schauspieler, -,* I
actress *die Schauspielerin, -nen,* I
advanced: to be advanced (person) *der Fortgeschrittene, -n,* II12
advantage *der Vorteil, -e,* II7
after *nach,* I; **after school** *nach der Schule,* I; **after the break** *nach der Pause,* I; **after lunch** *nach dem Mittagessen,* II3
after that *danach,* I
afternoon *der Nachmittag, -e,* I; **in the afternoon** *am Nachmittag,* I
afterward *nachher,* II10
again *wieder,* I
agree: I agree with you on that! *Da stimm ich dir zu!,* II10; **Yes, I do agree with you, but...** *Ja, ich stimme dir zwar zu, aber ...,* II7
Agreed! *Einverstanden!,* II10
air *die Luft,* II7; **air conditioning** *die Klimaanlage, -n,* II10
airplane *das Flugzeug, -e,* II7
alarm clock *der Wecker, -,* II2
alcohol: to not drink alcohol *keinen Alkohol trinken,* II4
all *all-,* II8
all right: Oh, (I'm) all right. *Na ja, soso!,* II3
allergic: I am allergic to... *Ich bin allergisch gegen ...,* II4
allowed: to be allowed to *dürfen,* II4
along: Why don't you come along! *Komm doch mit!,* I
already *schon,* I; *auch schon,* II3

also *auch,* I; *auch schon,* II3; **I also need...** *Ich brauche noch ...,* I
always *immer,* I
am: I am *ich bin,* I
and *und,* I
ankle *der Knöchel, -,* II6
announcement *der Anschlag, ⸚e,* II11
another *noch ein,* I; **I don't want any more...** *Ich möchte kein(e)(en) ... mehr.,* I; **I'd like another...** *Ich möchte noch ein(e)(en) ...,* I
another (a different) one *ein(-) ander-,* II9
antenna: indoor antenna *die Zimmerantenne, -n,* II10
anything: Anything else? *Sonst noch etwas?,* I, II2
apartment *die Wohnung, -en,* II7
appear *aussehen (sep),* I
appetizer *die Vorspeise, -n,* II11
apple *der Apfel, ⸚,* I
apple cake *der Apfelkuchen, -,* I
apple juice *der Apfelsaft, ⸚e,* I; **a glass of apple juice** *ein Glas Apfelsaft,* I
approximately *ungefähr,* I
apricot *die Aprikose, -n,* II4
April *der April,* I
archery *das Bogenschießen,* II1
are: you are *du bist,* I; (formal) *Sie sind,* I; (pl) *ihr seid,* I; **we are** *wir sind,* I
arm *der Arm, -e,* II6
armchair *der Sessel, -,* I
around *um,* II9
art *die Kunst,* I
as ... as *so ... wie,* II7
at: at 8 o'clock *um 8 Uhr,* I; **at one o'clock** *um ein Uhr,* I; **at the baker's** *beim Bäcker,* I; **At what time?** *Um wie viel Uhr?,* I
at *an, in,* II3
athletic *sportlich,* II8
August *der August,* I

aunt *die Tante -n,* I
Austria *Österreich,* I
avoid (the sun) *(die Sonne) vermeiden,* II4
awesome *stark,* I; **The sweater is awesome!** *Ich finde den Pulli stark!,* I
awful *furchtbar,* I

back *der Rücken, -,* II6
bad *schlecht,* I; **badly** *schlecht,* I; **Bad luck!** *So ein Pech!,* I; **It's too bad that...** *Es ist schade, dass ...,* II4; **That's not so bad.** *Nicht so schlimm!,* II5; **That's too bad!** *Was für ein Pech!,* II5; *Ach schade!,* II6
baker *der Bäcker, -,* I; **at the baker's** *beim Bäcker,* I
bakery *die Bäckerei, -en,* I
bald: to be bald *eine Glatze haben,* I
ballet *das Ballett, -e,* II11
ballpoint pen *der Kuli, -s,* I
banana *die Banane, -n,* II2
bank *die Bank, -en,* I
bargain: That's a bargain. *Das ist preiswert.,* I
basketball *Basketball,* I
bathroom *das Badezimmer, -,* II7; **toilet** *die Toilette, -n,* II7
bay *die Bucht, -en,* II12
be *sein,* I; **I am** *ich bin,* I; **you are** *du bist,* I; **he/she is** *er/sie ist,* I; **we are** *wir sind,* I; (pl) **you are** *ihr seid,* I; (formal) **you are** *Sie sind,* I; **they are** *sie sind,* I

R64 ENGLISH-GERMAN VOCABULARY

be able to können, I
be called heißen, I
beach der Strand, ⸚e, II9; **sand beach** der Sandstrand, ⸚e, II9
bean (green) die (grüne) Bohne, -n, II2
beautiful schön, I
because denn, weil, I
become werden, II10; **he/she becomes** er/sie wird, II10
bed das Bett, -en, I; **to make the bed** das Bett machen, I
bed and breakfast die Pension, -en, II3
bedroom das Schlafzimmer, -, II7
beef das Rindfleisch, II4
beginner der Anfänger, -, II12
behind: from behind von hinten, II8
believe glauben, I; **You can believe me on that!** Das kannst du mir glauben!, II9; **I do believe that...** Ich glaube schon, dass ..., II10
belt der Gürtel, -, I; **belt loop** die Schlaufe, -n, II8
best: Best wishes on your birthday! Herzlichen Glückwunsch zum Geburtstag!, I
better besser, I, II5
between zwischen, II9
bicycle Rad fahren, II4; das Fahrrad, ⸚er, I; **by bike** mit dem Rad, I
bicycle racks das Fahrrad-Depot, -s, II12
big groß, I; weit, II12
bigger größer, II7
biology Bio (die Biologie), I
biology teacher (female) die Biologielehrerin, -nen, I
birthday der Geburtstag, -e, I; **Best wishes on your birthday!** Herzlichen Glückwunsch zum Geburtstag!, I; **Happy Birthday!** Alles Gute zum Geburtstag!, I; **My birthday is on...** Ich habe am ... Geburtstag., I; **When is your birthday?** Wann hast du Geburtstag?, I
bitter: too bitter zu bitter, I
black schwarz, I; **in black** in Schwarz, I
blazer der Blazer, -, II8
blond blond, I
blouse die Bluse, -n, I
blue blau, I; **blue (green, brown) eyes** blaue (grüne, braune) Augen, I; **in blue** in Blau, I
blueberry die Blaubeere, -n, II4
board game das Brettspiel, -e, I
boat das Boot, -e, II9; **to go for a boat ride** Boot fahren, II9
bologna sandwich das Wurstbrot, -e, I
bomber jacket der Blouson, -s, II8
Bon appétit Mahlzeit!, II11; Guten Appetit!, II11
book das Buch, ⸚er, I
bookcase das Regal -e, I
boot der Stiefel, -, I, II8
bored: to be bored sich langweilen, II12

boring langweilig, I; **extremely boring**, todlangweilig, II7
bought gekauft, I; **I bought bread.** Ich habe Brot gekauft., I
bouquet of flowers der Blumenstrauß, ⸚e, I
bow die Schleife, -n, II12
bow tie die Fliege, -n, II12
boy der Junge, -n, I
bracelet das Armband, ⸚er, II1
brake: (foot, hand) brake die (Fuß, Hand)bremse, -n, II10
bread das Brot, -e, I
break die Pause, -n, I; **after the break** nach der Pause, I; **to break something** sich etwas brechen, II6; **he/she/it breaks something** er/sie/es bricht sich etwas, II6
breakfast das Frühstück, II5; **For breakfast I eat...** Zum Frühstück ess ich ..., II5
bright hell, II7
bring: Please bring me... Bringen Sie mir bitte ..., II11
broad weit, II12
broccoli der Brokkoli, -, II4
broken kaputt, I, II9
brother der Bruder, ⸚, I; **brothers and sisters** die Geschwister (pl), I
brown braun, I; **in brown** in Braun, I
brush one's teeth sich die Zähne putzen, II6
brutal brutal, I
bus der Bus, -se, I; **by bus** mit dem Bus, I
bush der Strauch, ⸚er, II7
business das Geschäft, -e, I
busy (telephone) besetzt, I
but aber, I
butcher der Metzger, -, I
butcher shop die Metzgerei, -en, I; **at the butcher's** beim Metzger, I
butter die Butter, I
button der Knopf, ⸚e, II8
buy kaufen, I; **What did you buy?** Was hast du gekauft?, I; **Why don't you just buy...** Kauf dir doch ...!, I, II8
by bei, II9; **by bike** mit dem Rad, I; **by bus** mit dem Bus, I; **by car** mit dem Auto, I; **by moped** mit dem Moped, I; **by subway** mit der U-Bahn, I
Bye! Wiedersehen! Tschau! Tschüs!, I; (on the telephone) Wiederhören!, I

cabinet der Schrank, ⸚e, I
café das Café, -s, I; **to the café** ins Café, I

cake der Kuchen, -, I; **a piece of cake** ein Stück Kuchen, I
calendar der Kalender, -, I
call anrufen (sep), telefonieren, I
calm ruhig, II7
calories: has too many calories hat zu viele Kalorien, II4
camcorder die Videokamera, -s, II3
Camembert cheese der Camembert Käse, II5
camera die Kamera, -s, II3
camisole das Trägerhemd, -en, II8
can können, I; **Can I please...?** Kann ich bitte ...?, II10; **Can I ask (you pl) something?** Kann ich (euch) etwas fragen?, II4; **Can you tell me whether...?** Können Sie mir sagen, ob ...?, II10
cap die Mütze, -n, II1; **(baseball) cap** das Käppi, -s, II8
capital die Hauptstadt, ⸚e, I
car das Auto, -s, I; der Wagen, -, II10; **by car** mit dem Auto, I; **He's slamming the car door (the trunk)!** Er schlägt die Autotür (den Kofferraumdeckel) zu!, II7; **to polish the car** das Auto polieren, II2
card die Karte, -n, I
care: I don't care about fashion. Mode ist mir egal., II8
care for mögen, I
carp der Karpfen, -, II5
carpet der Teppich, -e, I
carrot die Möhre, -n, II4
cassette die Kassette, -n, I
casual lässig, I; salopp, II12
cat die Katze, -n, I; **to feed the cat** die Katze füttern, I
cathedral der Dom, -e, II3
cauliflower der Blumenkohl, II4
cell phone das Handy, -s, I
cellar der Keller, -, II7
cent der Cent, -, I
century das Jahrhundert, -e, II9
certain: I am certain that... Ich bin sicher, dass ..., II9
Certainly! Natürlich!, I; Sicher!, I; Ja, natürlich!, II4
chair der Stuhl, ⸚e, I
change: Keep the change! Stimmt (schon)!, I
channel der Sender, -; das Programm, -e, II10
cheap billig, I
check: The check please! Hallo! Ich möchte/will zahlen!, I
checked kariert, II8
Cheers! Prost!, II11
cheese der Käse, -, I; **Swiss cheese** der Schweizer Käse, II5
cheese sandwich das Käsebrot, -e, I
chemistry (die) Chemie, I
chess Schach, I
cherry die Kirsche, -n, II4

chicken das Hähnchen, -, I; *das Huhn, ̈er*, II4
child das Kind, -er, II1
Chinese chinesisch (adj), II11
chives der Schnittlauch, II5
chocolate die Schokolade, II2; **chocolate milk** der Kakao, II5; **fancy chocolate** die Praline, -n, I
choose wählen, II11
Christmas das Weihnachten, -, I; **Merry Christmas!** Fröhliche Weihnachten!, I
church die Kirche, -n, I
cinema das Kino, -s, I
cinnamon der Zimt, I
city die Stadt, ̈e, I; **in the city** in der Stadt, I; **city gate** das Stadttor, -e, II9; **in a big city** in einer Großstadt, II7; **in this city** in dieser Stadt, II4
city hall das Rathaus, ̈er, I
class die Klasse, -n; **in class** in der Klasse, II4
class schedule der Stundenplan, ̈e, I
classical klassisch, I
classical music klassische Musik, I
clean (sich) putzen, II2; **to clean the windows** die Fenster putzen, I; **to clean up my room** mein Zimmer aufräumen (sep), I
clean sauber (adj), II7
clear: to clear the table den Tisch abräumen (sep), I
clever(ly) witzig, II8
cliff die Klippe, -n, II12
climb steigen, II9
clique: in the clique in der Clique, II4
clothes (casual term for) *die Klamotten* (pl), I; **to pick up my clothes** meine Klamotten aufräumen (sep), I
cloudy wolkig, I
coast die Küste, -n, II12
coffee der Kaffee, I; **a cup of coffee** eine Tasse Kaffee, I
coin die Münze, -n, I
cold kalt, I
cold cuts der Aufschnitt, I
collect sammeln, I; **to collect comics** Comics sammeln, I; **to collect stamps** Briefmarken sammeln, I
color die Farbe, -n, I
colorful bunt, II8
comb (sich) kämmen, II6
come kommen, I; **That comes to...** Das macht (zusammen) ..., I; **to come along** mitkommen (sep), I
comedy die Komödie, -n, I
comfortable bequem, I; gemütlich, II7
comics die Comics, I; **to collect comics** Comics sammeln, I
compact disc die CD, -s, I
computer der Computer, -, I
computer science die Informatik, I

concert das Konzert, -e, I; **to go to a concert** ins Konzert gehen, I
conservative konservativ, II8
cook kochen, II1
cookie der Keks, -e, I; **a few cookies** ein paar Kekse, I
cool kühl, I, II8
corner die Ecke, -n, II9; **That's right around the corner.** Das ist hier um die Ecke., II9
corners: with corners eckig, I
corny schmalzig, I
cost kosten, I; **How much does… cost?** Was kostet ...?, I
cotton die Baumwolle, I; **made of cotton** aus Baumwolle, I
couch die Couch, -en, I
cough: I have a cough and runny nose. Ich habe Husten und Schnupfen., II6
countless zahlreich, II12
country das Land, ̈er, I; **in the country** auf dem Land, I
court der Court, -s, II12
cousin (female) die Kusine, -n, I; **cousin (male)** der Cousin, -s, I
cozy gemütlich, II7
crab die Krabbe, -n, II11
cream: hand cream die Handcreme, II6
crime drama der Krimi, -s, I
cross-timbered house das Fachwerkhaus, ̈er, II3
cruel grausam, I
cucumber die Gurke, -n, II2
cummerbund der Kummerbund, -e, II12
curious neugierig, II1
curve: You're taking the curve too fast! Du fährst zu schnell in die Kurve!, II7
cut off abgeschnitten, II8
cutlet das Schnitzel, -, II5

dance tanzen, I; **to go dancing** tanzen gehen, I
dancing das Tanzen, I
dark dunkel, II1
dark blue dunkelblau, I; **in dark blue** in Dunkelblau, I
Darn it! So ein Mist!, I
dash: 100 meter dash der 100-Meter-Lauf, II1
daughter die Tochter, ̈, II1
day der Tag, -e, I; **day before yesterday** vorgestern, I; **every day** jeden Tag, I; **on the last day** am letzten Tag, II3

decathlete der Zehnkämpfer, -, II12
December der Dezember, I
definitely bestimmt, I
degree der Grad, -, I
delicacy die Delikatesse, -n, II11; die Köstlichkeit, -en, II11
Delicious! Lecker!, I
describe beschreiben, II1
desk der Schreibtisch, -e, I
dessert die Nachspeise, -n, II11
detective movie der Krimi, -s, I
detective novel der Krimi, -s, I
dial wählen, I; **to dial the number** die Nummer wählen, I
diamonds: check, diamond (pattern) das Karo, -s, II12
dictionary das Wörterbuch, ̈er, I
different verschieden, II1
dining room das Esszimmer, -, II7
dining table der Esstisch, -e, I
dinner das Abendessen, II5; **For dinner we are having...** Zum Abendessen haben wir ..., II5
directly direkt, I
dirty schmutzig, II7
disadvantage der Nachteil, -e, II7
disagree: I disagree. Das finde ich nicht., I
disco die Disko, -s, I; **to go to a disco** in eine Disko gehen, I
discothek die Diskothek, -en, II9
discus throw das Diskuswerfen, II1
discussion die Diskussion, -en, II10
dish: main dish das Hauptgericht, -e, II11
dishes das Geschirr, I; **to wash the dishes** das Geschirr spülen, I
dislike nicht gern haben, I; **strongly dislike** überhaupt nicht gern haben, I
diverse abwechslungsreich, II12
dive tauchen, II9
do machen, I; tun, I; **do crafts** basteln, I; **do homework** die Hausaufgaben machen, I
doctor der Arzt, ̈e, II6
documentary: animal documentary die Tiersendung, -en, II10
dog der Hund, -e, I
done gemacht (pp), I
don't you: You like quark, don't you? Du magst doch Quark, nicht wahr?, II5; **You like yogurt, don't you?** Du magst Joghurt, oder?, II5
doubt: I doubt that... Ich bezweifle, dass ..., II9
downtown die Innenstadt, ̈e, I, II9; **to go downtown** in die Stadt gehen, I
draw zeichnen, I
dress das Kleid, -er, I
dressed gekleidet, II12
drink trinken, I; **drink** das Getränk, -e, II11

drive *fahren,* I; **he/she drives** *er/sie fährt,* I
drugstore *die Drogerie, -n,* II6
dry *trocken,* I
dry clothes *die Wäsche trocknen,* II2
duck: fattened duck *die Mastente, -n,* II11; **Peking duck** *die Peking Ente, -n,* II11
dumb *blöd,* I; *doof, dumm,* I
dumpling *der Kloß, ¨-e,* II10
dust *Staub wischen,* II2

each, every *jed-,* II3
earache *die Ohrenschmerzen (pl),* II6
earring *der Ohrring, -e,* II1; **a pair of earrings** *ein Paar Ohrringe,* II1
Easter *das Ostern, -,* I; **Happy Easter!** *Frohe Ostern!,* I
easy *einfach,* I; **That's easy!** *Also, einfach!,* I
eat *essen,* I; **he/she eats** *er/sie isst,* I; **to eat ice cream** *ein Eis essen,* I; **to eat sensibly** *vernünftig essen,* II4
eat and drink *sich ernähren,* II4
education *die Ausbildung, -en,* II7
egg *das Ei, -er,* I; **deviled egg** *das gefüllte Ei, -er,* II11
Egyptian *ägyptisch (adj),* II11
elegant *elegant,* II12
enough *genug,* I
environment *die Umwelt,* I, II7
eraser *der Radiergummi, -s,* I
especially *besonders,* I; **especially like** *besonders gern,* I; **Not especially.** *Nicht besonders.,* II3
euro *der Euro, -,* I
evening *der Abend, -e,* I; **in the evening** *am Abend,* I
every: every day *jeden Tag,* I; **every evening** *jeden Abend,* II3; **every morning** *jeden Morgen,* II3
everything *alles,* II4
excellent *ausgezeichnet,* II1
exciting *spannend,* I
excursion *der Ausflug, ¨-e,* II11
Excuse me! *Entschuldigung!, Verzeihung!,* I, II9
exercise *Gymnastik machen,* II4
expensive *teuer,* I
experienced (person) *der, die Erfahrene, -n,* II12
exquisite *fein,* II12
eye *das Auge, -n,* I; **blue (green, brown) eyes** *blaue (grüne, braune) Augen,* I

F

fall *der Herbst,* I; **in the fall** *im Herbst,* I
family *die Familie, -n,* I
fancy chocolate *die Praline, -n,* I
Fantastic! *Phantastisch!,* II3
fantasy novel *der Fantasyroman, -e,* I
far *weit,* I; **far from here** *weit von hier,* I
fashion *die Mode,* I
fashionable *modisch,* II8
fast *schnell,* II7
fat: has too much fat *hat zu viel Fett,* II4; **It is fattening.** *Es macht dick.,* II4
father *der Vater, ¨-,* I
Father's Day *der Vatertag,* I; **Happy Father's Day!** *Alles Gute zum Vatertag!,* I
favorite *Lieblings-,* I; **Which vegetable is your favorite?** *Welches Gemüse magst du am liebsten?,* II5
February *der Februar,* I
feed *füttern,* I; **to feed the cat** *die Katze füttern,* I
feel *sich fühlen,* II4; **How do you feel?** *Wie fühlst du dich?,* II6; **I feel great!** *Ich fühle mich wohl!,* II6; **Are you not feeling well?** *Ist dir nicht gut?,* II6
fence *fechten,* II1
fetch *holen,* I
fettucine *die Fettucine (pl),* II12
fever *das Fieber,* II6; **to take one's temperature** *Fieber messen,* II6
few: a few *ein paar,* I; **a few cookies** *ein paar Kekse,* I
fibers: made from natural fibers *aus Naturfasern,* II8
film, videotape *filmen,* II3; **adventure film** *der Abenteuerfilm, -e,* II10
fine *fein,* II12
first *erst-,* I; **first of all** *zuerst,* I; **on the first of July** *am ersten Juli,* I; **the first street** *die erste Straße,* I
fish *angeln,* II9; **fish stick** *das Fischstäbchen, -,* II5
fit *passen,* I; **The skirt fits great!** *Der Rock passt prima!,* I; **to keep fit** *sich fit halten,* II4
flats *Schuhe mit flachen Absätzen,* II8
flight *der Flug, ¨-e,* II12
flower *die Blume, -n,* I; **to water the flowers** *die Blumen gießen,* I
flowery *geblümt,* II8
food *die Speise, -n,* II4
foods: to only eat light foods *nur leichte Speisen essen,* II6
foot: to walk on foot *zu Fuß gehen,* I, II6
for *für,* I; *denn (conj),* I; **I am for doing...** *Ich bin dafür, dass ...,* II9; **for whom?** *für wen?,* II1

foreign *ausländisch,* II11
fountain *der Brunnen, -,* II9
free time *die Freizeit,* I
French *französisch (adj),* II11
fresh *frisch,* I
fresh produce store *der Obst- und Gemüseladen, ¨-,* I
Friday *der Freitag,* I; **Fridays** *freitags,* II10
fried *gebraten,* II11; **fried potatoes** *die Bratkartoffeln (pl),* II11
friend (male) *der Freund, -e,* I; **(female)** *die Freundin, -nen,* I; **to visit friends** *Freunde besuchen,* I
friendly *freundlich,* II1
fries: French fries *die Pommes frites (pl),* II5
from *aus,* I; *von,* I; **from 8 until 8:45** *von 8 Uhr bis 8 Uhr 45,* I; **from the fifteenth century** *aus dem fünfzehnten Jahrhundert,* II9
from where? *woher?,* I; **I'm from** *ich bin (komme) aus,* I; **Where are you from?** *Woher bist (kommst) du?,* I
front: in front of *vor,* II9; **there in the front** *da vorn,* I
fruit *das Obst,* I, II4; **a piece of fruit** *ein Stück Obst,* I; **to eat lots of fruit** *viel Obst essen,* II4
fun *der Spaß,* I; **(Tennis) is fun.** *(Tennis) macht Spaß.,* I; **(Tennis) is no fun.** *(Tennis) macht keinen Spaß.,* I
funny *lustig,* I, II1
furniture *die Möbel (pl),* I

garage *die Garage, -n,* II2
garbage *der Müll,* II2
garden(s) *der Garten, ¨-,* I, II7
garlic *der Knoblauch,* II11
geography *die Erdkunde,* I
German mark (German monetary unit) *DM = die Deutsche Mark,* I
German teacher (male) *der Deutschlehrer, -,* I; **(female)** *die Deutschlehrerin, -nen,* I
Germany *Deutschland,* I
get *bekommen,* I; *holen,* I; **Get well soon!** *Gute Besserung!,* II6
gift *das Geschenk, -e,* I
gift idea *die Geschenkidee, -n,* I
girl *das Mädchen, -,* I
give *geben,* I; **he/she gives** *er/sie gibt,* I
give (a gift) *schenken,* I
glad: I'm really glad! *Das freut mich!,* II3
glass *das Glas, ¨-er,* I; **a glass of tea** *ein Glas Tee,* I; **a glass of (mineral) water** *ein Glas (Mineral)Wasser,* I

ENGLISH-GERMAN VOCABULARY

glasses: a pair of glasses *eine Brille, -n,* I
go *gehen,* I; **to go home** *nach Hause gehen,* I; **goes with: The pretty blouse goes (really) well with the blue skirt.** *Die schöne Bluse passt (toll) zu dem blauen Rock.,* II8
Goethe's birthplace *das Goethehaus,* II3
gold: made of gold *aus Gold,* II2
golf *Golf,* I; **golf course** *der Golfplatz, ⸚e,* II9
good *gut,* I; **Good!** *Gut!,* I
Good morning! *Guten Morgen!, Morgen!,* I
Goodbye! *Auf Wiedersehen!,* I; (on the telephone) *Auf Wiederhören!,* I
gown: evening gown *das Abendkleid, -er,* II12
grade *die Note, -n,* I
grade level *die Klasse, -n,* I
grades: a 1, 2, 3, 4, 5, 6 *eine Eins, Zwei, Drei, Vier, Fünf, Sechs,* I
gram *das Gramm, -,* I
grandfather *der Großvater, ⸚,* I; *Opa, -s,* I
grandmother *die Großmutter, ⸚,* I; *Oma, -s,* I
grandparents *die Großeltern* (pl), I
grape *die Traube, -n,* I, II5
gray *grau,* I; **in gray** *in Grau,* I
great: It's great that... *Es ist prima, dass ...,* II4; **really great** *supertoll,* II4; *Echt super!,* II3; **Great!** *Prima!,* I; *Sagenhaft!,* I; *Klasse!, Toll!,* I
Greek *griechisch* (adj), II11
green *grün,* I; **in green** *in Grün,* I
grilled *gegrillt,* II11
groceries *die Lebensmittel* (pl), I
ground meat *das Hackfleisch,* I
grounds *die Anlage, -n,* II12
group *die Gruppe, -n,* I
guitar *die Gitarre, -n,* I
guy *der Typ, -en,* II8
gyros *das Gyros, -,* I

hair *die Haare* (pl), I
half *halb,* I; **half past (twelve, one, etc.)** *halb (eins, zwei, usw.),* I
halibut *der Heilbutt,* II5
hall *die Halle, -n,* II12
hallway *der Flur, -e,* II7
ham *der Schinken, -,* II11
hand cream *die Handcreme,* II6
handbag *die Handtasche, -n,* II1
hang up (the telephone) *auflegen* (sep), I
Hanukka *Chanukka,* I; **Happy Hanukka!** *Frohes Chanukka Fest!,* I
happy: I am happy that... *Ich freue mich, dass ...,* II4; *Ich bin froh, dass ...,* II4
hard-working *fleißig,* II1
hat *der Hut, ⸚e,* II1
have *haben,* I; **he/she has English** *er/sie hat Englisch,* I; **I have German.** *Ich habe Deutsch.,* I; **I have no classes on Saturday.** *Am Samstag habe ich frei.,* I; **I'll have...** *Ich bekomme ...,* I
have to *müssen,* I; **I have to** *ich muss,* I
he *er,* I; **he is** *er ist,* I; **he's from** *er ist (kommt) aus,* I
head *der Kopf, ⸚e,* II6; **headband** *das Stirnband, ⸚er,* II1; **headache** *die Kopfschmerzen* (pl), II6
headlight *der Scheinwerfer, -,* II10
headphones (stereo) *der (Stereo) Kopfhörer, -,* II10
health: To your health! *Auf dein/Ihr/ euer Wohl!, Zum Wohl!,* II11; **to do a lot for your health** *viel für die Gesundheit tun,* II4
hear *hören,* I
heard: I heard that... *Ich habe gehört, dass ...,* II11
hearty *herzhaft, deftig,* II11
heel *der Absatz, ⸚e,* II8; **flats** *Schuhe mit flachen Absätzen,* II8; **high heels** *hohe Absätze,* II8
Hello! *Guten Tag!, Tag!, Hallo!, Grüß dich!,* I
help *helfen,* I; **to help at home** *zu Hause helfen,* I
her *ihr* (poss adj), I; **her name is** *sie heißt,* I
Here you go! *Bitte! Hier!,* II10; **Here! I insist!** *Gern! Hier ist es!,* II10
herself *sich,* II4
hideous *scheußlich,* I
high heels *hohe Absätze,* II8
hike *wandern,* I
him *ihn,* I
himself *sich,* II4
hip *die Hüfte, -n,* II6
his *sein* (poss adj), I; **his name is** *er heißt,* I
history *die Geschichte,* I
hobby *das Hobby, -s,* II1
hobby book *das Hobbybuch, ⸚er,* II1
hole *das Loch, ⸚er,* II12
holiday *der Feiertag, -e,* I
home: good home cooked food *gut- bürgerliche Küche, -n,* II11; **private home** *das Privathaus, ⸚er,* II3; **to stay at home** *zu Hause bleiben,* II6

homework *die Hausaufgabe, -n,* I; **to do homework** *Hausaufgaben machen,* I
honestly *ehrlich,* I
honk (the horn) *hupen,* II7
hood *die Kapuze, -n,* II8
hope: I hope that... *Ich hoffe, dass ...,* II6; **I hope you'll get better soon.** *Hoffentlich geht es dir bald besser!,* II6
Hopefully... *Hoffentlich ...,* II6
horror movie *der Horrorfilm, -e,* I
horror novel *der Gruselroman, -e,* I
hot *heiß,* I
hot (spicy) *scharf,* II11
hotel *das Hotel, -s,* I, II7
house *das Haus, ⸚er,* II7
how? *wie?,* I; **How are you?** *Wie geht es dir?,* I, II6; **How do I get to...?** *Wie komme ich zum (zur) ...?,* I; **How does it taste?** *Wie schmeckt's?,* I; **How's the weather?** *Wie ist das Wetter?,* I; **How was it?** *Wie war's?,* II3; **How about...?** *Wie wär's mit ...?,* II11
how much? *wie viel?,* I; **How much does... cost?** *Was kostet ...?,* I
how often? *wie oft?,* I
hunger *der Hunger,* I
hungry: I'm hungry. *Ich habe Hunger.,* I, II6; **I'm not hungry any more.** *Ich habe keinen Hunger mehr.,* I
hurdling *der Hürdenlauf,* II1
hurt: Does it hurt? *Tut's weh?,* II6; **Does your... hurt?** *Tut dir ... weh?,* II6; **It hurts!** *Es tut weh!,* II6; **My... hurts.** *... tut mir weh.,* II6; **What hurts?** *Was tut dir weh?,* II6

I *ich,* I; **I don't.** *Ich nicht.,* I
ice cream *das Eis,* I; **a dish of ice cream** *ein Eisbecher,* I
ice skate *Schlittschuh laufen,* I
idea: I have no idea! *Keine Ahnung!,* I; **Do you have an idea?** *Hast du eine Idee?,* II9; **Good idea!** *Gute Idee!,* II12
imaginative *phantasievoll,* I
impossible: (That's) impossible! *(Das ist) nicht möglich!,* II10
in *in,* I; **in the afternoon** *am Nachmittag,* I; **in the city** *in der Stadt,* I; **in the country** *auf dem Land,* I; **in the evening** *am Abend,* I; **in the fall** *im Herbst,* I; **in the kitchen** *in der Küche,* I

income *das Einkommen,* II7
Indian: (Asian) Indian *indisch (adj),* II11
injure (oneself) *sich verletzen,* II6
inn *die Pension, -en,* II3
insert *einstecken (sep),* I; **to insert coins** *Münzen einstecken,* I
instead: I'll drink...instead *Dann trink ich halt ...,* II5
instrument *das Instrument, -e,* I; **Do you play an instrument?** *Spielst du ein Instrument?,* I
intelligent *intelligent,* II1
interest *das Interesse, -n,* I; **Do you have any other interests?** *Hast du andere Interessen?,* I; **I'm not interested in fashion.** *Ich hab kein Interesse an Mode.,* II8; **to be interested in** *s. interessieren für; Fashion doesn't interest me. Mode interessiert mich nicht.,* II8; **Are you interested in fashion?** *Interessierst du dich für Mode?,* II8; **What are you interested in?** *Wofür interessierst du dich?,* II8
interesting *interessant,* I
Internet *das Internet,* I
into *in,* II9
invite *einladen (sep),* I; **he/she invites** *er/sie lädt ... ein,* I
is: he/she is *er/sie ist,* I
island *die Insel, -n,* II12
it *er, sie, es,* I; *ihn,* I
Italian *italienisch (adj),* II11

jacket *die Jacke, -n,* I; **business jacket** *der Sakko, -s,* II8; **leather jacket** *die Lederjacke, -n,* II8; **bomber jacket** *der Blouson, -s,* II8
January *der Januar,* I; **in January** *im Januar,* I
javelin throw *das Speerwerfen,* II1
jeans *die Jeans, -,* I
jewelry *der Schmuck,* I
job *der Job, -s,* II7
jog *joggen,* I, II4
jogging suit *der Jogging-Anzug, ˝e,* I
juice *der Saft, ˝e,* I
July *der Juli,* I
jump: long jump *der Weitsprung,* II1
June *der Juni,* I
just: Just a minute, please. *Einen Moment, bitte!,* I; **Just don't buy...** *Kauf dir ja kein ...!,* II8; **That just happened.** *Das ist gerade passiert.,* II9

keep: Keep the change! *Stimmt (schon)!,* I
kilogram *das Kilo, -,* I
kitchen *die Küche, -n,* I, II7; **in the kitchen** *in der Küche,* I; **to help in the kitchen** *in der Küche helfen,* II2
knee *das Knie, -,* II6
know (a fact, information, etc.) *wissen,* I; **Do you know whether...?** *Weißt du, ob ...?,* II10; **I don't know whether...** *Ich weiß nicht, ob ...,* I, II9
know (be familiar or acquainted with) *kennen,* I

L

lake *der See, -n,* II7
lamb *das Lammfleisch,* II5
lamp *die Lampe, -n,* I
last *letzt-,* I; **last of all** *zuletzt,* I; **last week** *letzte Woche,* I; **last weekend** *letztes Wochenende,* I
Latin *Latein,* I
laundry *die Wäsche,* II2
lawn *der Rasen, -,* I; **to mow the lawn** *den Rasen mähen,* I; **lawn for relaxing and sunning** *die Liegewiese, -n,* II9
layer cake *die Torte, -n,* I
lazy *faul,* II1; **to be lazy** *faulenzen,* II3; **I want to be lazy!** *Ich will faulenzen!,* II1
leather *das Leder,* I; **made of leather** *aus Leder,* I
left: to the left *nach links,* I
leg *das Bein, -e,* II6
lemon *die Zitrone, -n,* I
lemon drink *die Limo, -s,* I
let, allow *lassen,* II10; **he/she lets, allows** *er/sie lässt,* II10; **Let me...** *Lass mich mal ...,* II10; **Let's go to the golf course!** *Gehen wir mal auf den Golfplatz!,* II9; **Let's go to...!** *Fahren wir mal nach ...!,* II9
lettuce *der Salat, -e,* I
license: driver's license *der Führerschein, -e,* II10
life *das Leben,* II7
light blue *hellblau,* I; **in light blue** *in Hellblau,* I
like *gefallen, mögen, gern haben,* I, II7; **I like it.** *Er/Sie/Es gefällt mir.,* I; **I like them.** *Sie gefallen mir.,* I; **Did you like it?** *Hat es dir gefallen?,* II3; **to like an awful lot** *furchtbar gern haben,* I; **to not like at all** *gar nicht gern haben,* I; **to not like very much** *nicht so gern haben,* I; **I don't like...** *Ich mag kein ...,* II4; **I like to go to the ocean.** *Ich fahre gern ans Meer.,* II9; **I would like...** *Ich hätte gern ...,* II11
like (to do) *gern (machen),* I; **to not like (to do)** *nicht gern (machen),* I
linen *das Leinen,* II8
listen (to) *hören,* I; *zuhören,* I; **Listen!** *Hör mal!,* II5; **Listen to this!** *Hör mal zu!,* II5
liter *der Liter, -,* I
little *klein,* I; *wenig,* II4; **a little** *ein bisschen,* I; **a little more** *ein bisschen mehr,* I
live *wohnen,* I; *leben,* II4
living room *das Wohnzimmer, -,* II7; **in the living room** *im Wohnzimmer,* I
lobster *der Hummer, -,* II11
long *lang,* I
look *schauen,* I; **Look!** *Schauen Sie!,* I; *Guck mal!, Schau mal!, Sieh mal!,* II5; **That looks great on you!** *Das steht dir prima!,* II8
look for *suchen,* I; **I'm looking for** *ich suche,* I
look forward to *s. freuen auf (acc),* II10
look like *aussehen (sep),* I; **he/she looks like** *er/sie sieht ... aus,* I; **The skirt looks...** *Der Rock sieht ... aus.,* I
lot: a lot *viel,* I; **I saw a lot, too.** *Ich habe auch viel gesehen.,* II12
luck: Bad luck! *So ein Pech!,* I; **What luck!** *So ein Glück!,* I
lunch *das Mittagessen;* **For lunch there is...** *Zum Mittagessen gibt es ...,* II5

made: made of cotton *aus Baumwolle,* I; **made of leather** *aus Leder,* I
magazine *die Zeitschrift, -en,* I
make *machen,* I; **to make the bed** *das Bett machen,* I
man *der Mann, ˝er,* I
many *viele,* I
March *der März,* I
margarine *die Margarine,* II5
marinated *mariniert,* II11
market square *der Marktplatz, ˝e,* I

marmalade *die Marmelade, -n*, II5
math *Mathe (die Mathematik)*, I
May *der Mai*, I
may: May I help you? *Haben Sie einen Wunsch?*, I; May I (please)...? *Darf ich (bitte) ...?*, II10; he/she may *er/sie darf*, II4
maybe *vielleicht*, I; Yes, maybe, but... *Ja, das kann sein, aber ...*, II4
me *mich, mir*, I, II3; Me too! *Ich auch!*, I, II12
measure *messen*, II6; he/she measures *er/sie misst*, II6
meat *das Fleisch*, I; You eat a lot of meat, right? *Du isst wohl viel Fleisch, ja?*, II5
Mediterranean *mediterran* (adj), II11
mess: What a mess! *So ein Mist!*, I
Mexican *mexikanisch* (adj), II11
mild *mild*, II11
milk *die Milch*, I, II5
mineral water *das Mineralwasser*, I
minute: Just a minute, please. *Einen Moment, bitte!*, I
miserable *miserabel*, I
modern *modern*, I
moment *der Moment, -e*, I
Monday *der Montag*, I; Mondays *montags*, II10
money *das Geld*, I
month *der Monat, -e*, I
monument *das Baudenkmal, ̈-er*, II11
mood: in a bad mood *schlecht gelaunt*, II1; in a good mood *gut gelaunt*, II1
moped *das Moped, -s*, I; by moped *mit dem Moped*, I
more *mehr*, I
morning *der Morgen*, I; Morning! *Morgen!*, I
most of all *am liebsten*, I
most of the time *meistens*, II4
mother *die Mutter, ̈-*, I
Mother's Day *der Muttertag*, I; Happy Mother's Day! *Alles Gute zum Muttertag!*, I
motor *der Motor, -en*, II7
motorcycle *das Motorrad, ̈-er*, II7
mountain *der Berg, -e*, II7; in the mountains *in den Bergen*, II7
moussaka *die Moussaka*, II12
movie *der Film, -e*, I; to go to the movies *ins Kino gehen*, I
movie theater *das Kino, -s*, I
mow *mähen*, I; to mow the lawn *den Rasen mähen*, I
Mr. *Herr*, I
Ms. *Frau*, I
much *viel*, I; much too *viel zu*, I
museum *das Museum*, (pl) *Museen*, I, II3
mushroom *der Pilz, -e*, II4
music *die Musik*, I; to listen to music *Musik hören*, I
musical *das Musical, -s*, II11
mustard *der Senf*, I; with mustard *mit Senf*, I
my *mein* (poss adj), I; my name is *ich heiße*, I
myself *mich*, II4

name *der Name, -n*, I; her name is *sie heißt*, I; What's the boy's name? *Wie heißt der Junge?*, I
nauseous: I'm nauseous. *Mir ist schlecht.*, II6
nearby *in der Nähe*, I
necklace *die Halskette, -n*, II1
need *brauchen*, I; I need *ich brauche*, I
never *nie*, I; not yet, never *noch nie*, II3
new *neu*, I
news: the news *die Nachrichten* (pl), II10
newspaper *die Zeitung, -en*, I
next: next week *nächste Woche*, I; the next street *die nächste Straße*, I
next to *neben*, II9
night: to spend the night *übernachten*, II3
no *kein*, I; No more, thanks! *Nichts mehr, danke!*, I
no way: There's just no way! *Das gibt's doch nicht!*, II10
noise *der Lärm*, II7
non-fiction book *das Sachbuch, ̈-er*, I
none *kein*, I
noodle soup *die Nudelsuppe, -n*, I
normally *normalerweise*, II4
North: the North Sea *die Nordsee*, II9
not *nicht*, I; not at all *überhaupt nicht*, I; to not like at all *gar nicht gern haben*, I; Not really. *Nicht besonders.*, I
not any *kein*, I
Not entirely!/Not necessarily! *Nicht unbedingt!*, II5; actually not *eben nicht*, II9
notebook *das Notizbuch, ̈-er*, I; *das Heft, -e*, I
nothing *nichts*, I, II9; nothing at the moment *im Moment gar nichts*, I; Nothing, thank you! *Nichts, danke!*, I; There's nothing you can do. *Da kann man nichts machen.*, II9
novel *der Roman, -e*, I
November *der November*, I
now *jetzt*, I
number *die (Telefon)nummer*, I; to dial the number *die Nummer wählen*, I

oasis *die Oase, -n*, II12
ocean *das Meer, -e*; *die See, -n*, II9
o'clock: at 1 o'clock *um 1 Uhr*, I
October *der Oktober*, I
of *von*, II9; made of wool *aus Wolle*, II8
Of course! *Ja klar!*, I; *Ganz klar!*, I; *Na klar!*, II4; Yes, of course! *Ja, natürlich!*, II10
offer *das Angebot, -e*, I
often *oft*, I; *schon oft*, I, II3
Oh! *Ach!*, I; Oh yeah! *Ach ja!*, I
oil *das Öl*, I
Okay! I'll do that! *Gut! Mach ich!*, I; It's okay. *Es geht.*, I; *Schon gut!*, II5
old *alt*, I; How old are you? *Wie alt bist du?*, I
older *älter*, II7
olympic champion *der Olympiasieger, -*, II12
on: on ... Square *am ...platz*, I; on ... Street *in der ...straße*, I; to walk on foot *zu Fuß gehen*, I; on Monday *am Montag*, I; on the first of July *am ersten Juli*, I; on a lake *an einem See*, II7; on a river *an einem Fluss*, II7
once *einmal*, I; once a month *einmal im Monat*, I; once a week *einmal in der Woche*, I; once a day *einmal am Tag*, II4
onion *die Zwiebel, -n*, I
only *bloß*, I; *nur*, II5
onto *auf*, II9
opera *die Oper, -n*, I
opera house *die Oper, -n*, II3
operetta *die Operette, -n*, II11
or *oder*, I
orange juice *der Orangensaft*, I
order *bestellen*, II1
other *andere*, I
Ouch! *Au!, Aua!*, II6
ourselves *uns*, II4
out of *aus*, II9
outstanding *ausgezeichnet*, II5
oven *der Ofen, ̈-*, I
over it *darüber*, II8
over there *dort drüben*, I; over there in the back *da hinten*, I
overcast *trüb*, I
own: (one's) own *eigen-* (adj), II7
oyster *die Auster, -n*, II11

padded *gefüttert*, II8
paella *die Paella*, II12
pain *der Schmerz, -en*, II6
painting *das Gemälde, -*, II2
pair *das Paar, -e*, II1
pan dish *das Pfannengericht, -e*, II11
pants *die Hose, -n*, I
Pardon me! *Verzeihung!*, II9
parents *die Eltern* (pl), I
park *der Park, -s*, I, II9; **to go to the park** *in den Park gehen*, I
parka *der Anorak, -s*, II8
parking place/lot *der Parkplatz, ⸚e*, II9
party *die Party, -s*, I
pattern *das Muster, -*, II12
pea *die Erbse, -n*, II2
peaceful *friedlich*, 7
peach *der Pfirsich, -e*, II2
pear *die Birne, -n*, II5
pencil *der Bleistift, -e*, I
people *die Leute* (pl), I; **more people** *mehr Menschen*, II7
perch: fillet of perch *das Seebarschfilet, -s*, II11
perfume *das Parfüm, -e or -s*, I
perfumed *parfümiert*, II6
pet *das Haustier, -e*, I
pharmacy *die Apotheke, -n*, II6
phone card *die Telefonkarte, -n*, I
photograph *fotografieren*, II3; **color photograph** *das Farbbild, -er*, II3; **I took pictures.** *Ich habe fotografiert.*, II3
physical education *der Sport*, I
physics *(die) Physik*, I
piano *das Klavier, -e*, I; **I play the piano.** *Ich spiele Klavier.*, I
pick up *aufräumen* (sep), I; **to pick up my clothes** *meine Klamotten aufräumen*, I; **to pick up the telephone** *den Hörer abheben* (sep), I
piece *das Stück, -e*, I; **a piece of cake** *ein Stück Kuchen*, I; **a piece of fruit** *ein Stück Obst*, I
pizza *die Pizza, -s*, I
place *der Platz, ⸚e*, II12
plastic *der Kunststoff, -e*, I; **made of plastic** *aus Kunststoff*, I
play *spielen*, I; **I play the piano.** *Ich spiele Klavier.*, I; **to play a board game** *ein Brettspiel spielen*, I; *das Schauspiel, -e*, II11; *das Theaterstück, -e*, II11
pleasant *sympathisch*, II1
please *bitte*, I

pleasure: My pleasure! *Gern geschehen!*, I
plum *die Zwetschge, -n*, II2
pocket *die Tasche, -n*, II8; **back pocket** *die Gesäßtasche, -n*, II8
pocket calculator *der Taschenrechner, -*, I
pole vault *der Stabhochsprung*, II1
political discussion *eine Diskussion über Politik*, II10
politics *die Politik* (sing), I
polka-dotted *gepunktet*, I
pool *der Pool, -s*, II7; **indoor pool** *das Hallenbad, ⸚er*, II9
popular *beliebt*, II9
porch *die Terrasse, -n*, II7
pork chop *das Schweinekotelett, -s*, II5; **pork loin steak** *das Schweinerückensteak, -s*, II11
possible *möglich*, II10
post office *die Post*, I
poster *das Poster, -*, I
potato *die Kartoffel, -n*, I; **fried potatoes** *die Bratkartoffeln* (pl), II11; **potato croquettes** *die Kroketten* (pl), II11
pound *das Pfund, -*, I
poverty *die Armut*, II7
prefer *lieber (mögen)*, I; *vorziehen*, II7; **I prefer...** *Ich ziehe ... vor*, II7; **I prefer noodle soup.** *Nudelsuppe mag ich lieber.*, II5; **I prefer that...** *Ich bin dafür, dass ...*, II11
pretty *hübsch*, I; *schön*, I
pretzel *die Brezel, -n*, I
probably *wahrscheinlich*, I
produce *produzieren*, II7
produce store *der Obst- und Gemüseladen, ⸚*, I; **at the produce store** *im Obst- und Gemüseladen*, I
program (TV) *die Sendung, -en*, II10; **family program** *die Familiensendung, -en*, II10; **nature program** *die Natursendung, -en*, II10
proper(ly) *richtig*, II4
Pullover *der Pulli, -s*, I
put on *anziehen* (sep), I

quark *der Quark*, II5
quarter: a quarter after *Viertel nach*, I; **a quarter to** *Viertel vor*, I
question *die Frage, -n*, II4
quiz show *die Ratesendung, -en*, II10

radio *das Radio, -s*, II2
railroad station *der Bahnhof, ⸚e*, I
rain *der Regen*, I; **It's raining.** *Es regnet.*, I
rainy *regnerisch*, I
raspberry marmalade *die Himbeermarmelade, -n*, II5
rather *ziemlich*, I
raw *roh*, II11
read *lesen*, I; **he/she reads** *er/sie liest*, I; **What did you read?** *Was hast du gelesen?*, I
really *ganz*, I; *wirklich*, I; *echt*, II1; **Not really.** *Nicht besonders.*, II1
receive *bekommen*, I
receiver *der Hörer, -*, I
red *rot*, I; **in red** *in Rot*, I
red berry dessert *Rote Grütze*, II11
red cabbage *der Rotkohl*, II11
refrigerator *der Kühlschrank, ⸚e*, I
religion *die Religion, -en*, I
remote control *die Fernbedienung, -en*, II10
report card *das Zeugnis*, I
residence *das Wohnhaus, ⸚er*, II9; **the ... residence** *Hier bei ...*, I
restaurant *das Restaurant, -s*, II3; *der Gasthof, ⸚e*, II3; **small restaurant** *das Lokal, -e*, II3
rice *der Reis*, II4
right: That's all right. *Macht nichts!*, II5; **That's not right (at all)!** *Das stimmt (überhaupt) nicht!*, II10
right: to be right *Recht haben*, II10; **You're right about that!** *Da hast du Recht!*, II10
right: to the right *nach rechts*, I
ring *der Ring, -e*, II2
ringlet *der Ringel, -*, II12
river *der Fluss, ⸚e*, II7; **on a river** *an einem Fluss*, II7
roast *der Braten*, II11
roll *die Semmel, -n*, I
roll of film *der Film, -e*, II3
romance *der Liebesfilm, -e*, I; **romance novel** *der Liebesroman, -e*, I
room *das Zimmer, -*, I; **to clean up my room** *mein Zimmer aufräumen* (sep), I
round *rund*, I
ruined *kaputt*, I, II9
run *laufen*, II3; **he/she runs** *er/sie läuft*, II3; **long distance run** *der Langstreckenlauf*, II1
Russian *russisch* (adj), II11

S

sad *traurig*, I
sail *segeln*, II9
salad *der Salat, -e*, I
salmon *der Lachs, -e*, II11
salt *das Salz*, I
salty: too salty *zu salzig*, II1
sandwich *das Sandwich, -es*, II5; *das Pausenbrot*, II5; **What do you have on your sandwich?** *Was hast du denn auf dem Brot?*, II5
Saturday *der Samstag*, I; *der Sonnabend*, I; **Saturdays** *samstags*, II10
sauerkraut *das Sauerkraut*, II5
sauna *die Sauna, -s*, II9
sausage *die Wurst, ⸚e*, I
say *sagen*, I; **Say!** *Sag mal!*, I; **What does the weather report say?** *Was sagt der Wetterbericht?*, I
scarf *der Schal, -s, das Tuch, ⸚er*, II1
schedule of shows *das Programm, -e*, II10
school *die Schule, -n*, I; **after school** *nach der Schule*, I; **How do you get to school?** *Wie kommst du zur Schule?*, I; **at school** *an der Schule*, II4
school subject *das Fach, ⸚er*, I
school supplies *die Schulsachen (pl)*, I
schoolbag *die Schultasche, -n*, I
science fiction movie *der Science-fictionfilm, -e*, I
science fiction novel *der Sciencefictionroman, -e*, I
sea *die See, -n; das Meer, -e*, II9
search (for) *suchen*, I
second *zweit-*, I; **the second street** *die zweite Straße*, I
secret tip *der Geheimtip, -s*, II12
secure *sicher*, II7
see *sehen*, I; **he/she sees** *er/sie sieht*, I; **See you later!** *Bis dann!*, I; **to see a movie** *einen Film sehen*, I; **What did you see?** *Was hast du gesehen?*, I
seldom *selten*, II4
sensational *sensationell*, I
September *der September*, I
set *decken*, I; **to set the table** *den Tisch decken*, I
shampoo *das Shampoo, -s*, II6
sharp (clothing) *scharf*, II8; **really sharp** *fetzig*, II8
she *sie*, I; **she is** *sie ist*, I; **she's from** *sie ist (kommt) aus*, I
shine: the sun is shining *die Sonne scheint*, I
ship *das Schiff, -e*, II9
shirt *das Hemd, -en*, I

shish kebab *das Schisch Kebab*, 11
shoe *der Schuh, -e*, II8; **patent leather shoe** *der Lackschuh, -e*, II12
shop *einkaufen (sep)*, I; **to go shopping** *einkaufen gehen*, I
short *kurz*, I
shortening *das Butterschmalz*, I
shorts: pair of shorts *die Shorts, -*, I
shot put *das Kugelstoßen*, II1
should *sollen*, I
shoulder *die Schulter, -n*, II6
show *die Sendung, -en*, II10
sick *krank*, II6
side dish *die Beilage, -n*, II11
sightsee *etwas besichtigen*, II3
silk *die Seide*, I; **made of silk** *aus Seide*, I; **silk shirt** *das Seidenhemd, -en*, II8; **real silk** *echte Seide*, II8
silver: made of silver *aus Silber*, II2
since *seit*, II9
singer (female) *die Sängerin, -nen*, I; **singer (male)** *der Sänger, -*, I
sink *das Spülbecken, -*, I
sister *die Schwester, -n*, I; **brothers and sisters** *die Geschwister (pl)*, I
site *die Anlage, -n*, II12
size *die Größe, -n*, I
skin *die Haut*, II6
skirt *der Rock, ⸚e*, I; **pleated skirt** *der Faltenrock, ⸚e*, II8
sledding *rodeln*, II1
sleep: to get enough sleep *genügend schlafen*, II4; **he/she sleeps** *er/sie schläft*, II4
sleeveless *ärmellos*, II8
sleeves: with long sleeves *mit langen Ärmeln*, II8; **with short sleeves** *mit kurzen Ärmeln*, II8
slender *schlank*, II1
slide *das Dia, -s*, II3
slow(ly) *langsam*, II7
small *klein*, I
smart (looking) *fesch, schick, chic*, I
smoke *rauchen*, II4
smoked *geräuchert*, II11
snack bar, stand *die Imbissstube, -n*, I, II3
snap *der Druckknopf, ⸚e*, II8
sneaker *der Turnschuh, -e*, I
snow *der Schnee*, I; **It's snowing.** *Es schneit.*, I
so *so*, I; **So long!** *Tschau! Tschüs!*, I; **so so** *so lala*, I
soap *die Seife, -n*, II6
soccer *Fußball*, I; **I play soccer.** *Ich spiele Fußball.*, I
sock *die Socke, -n*, I, II8
soda: lemon-flavored soda *die Limo, -s (die Limonade, -n)*, I; **cola and lemon soda** *das Spezi, -s*, II11
sofa *das Sofa, -s*, I
soft *weich*, II8
someone: Someone told me that... *Man hat mir gesagt, dass ...*, II11
something *etwas*, I

sometimes *manchmal*, I
son *der Sohn, ⸚e*, II1
song *das Lied, -er*, I
soon *bald*, I
sorry: to be sorry *bedauern*, II5; *Leid tun*, II3; **I'm sorry.** *Es tut mir Leid.*, I, II3; **Sorry, I can't.** *Ich kann leider nicht.*, I; **Sorry, but unfortunately we're all out of couscous.** *Tut mir Leid, aber der Couscous ist leider schon alle.*, II12; **I'm so sorry.** *Das tut mir aber Leid!*, II3; **I'm sorry. I'm not from here.** *Tut mir Leid. Ich bin nicht von hier.*, II9
sort *sortieren*, I; **to sort the trash** *den Müll sortieren*, I
soup *die Suppe, -n*, II1
Spanish *spanisch (adj)*, II11
specialty *die Spezialität, -en*, II11
spend (time) *verbringen*, I
spend: to spend the night *übernachten*, II3
spicy *würzig*, II11; **spicy, hot** *scharf*, II11
spinach *der Spinat*, II2
sport(s) *der Sport*, I, II1; **sport facility** *die Sportanlage, -n*, II12; **sports telecast** *die Sportübertragung, -en*, II10; **Do you play sports?** *Machst du Sport?*, I
sporty *sportlich*, II8
sprain (something) *sich (etwas) verstauchen*, II6
spring *der Frühling*, I; **in the spring** *im Frühling*, I
sprouts (bean) *die Sojasprossen*, II5
square *der Platz, ⸚e*, I; **on ... Square** *am ...platz*, I
stamp *die Briefmarke, -n*, I; **to collect stamps** *Briefmarken sammeln*, I
state: German federal state *das Bundesland, ⸚er*, I
station *der Sender, -*, II10
stay, remain *bleiben*, II3
steak *das steak, -s*, II12
steak (beef) *das Rindersteak, -s*, II5
stereo *die Stereoanlage -n*, I
stinks: That stinks! *So ein Mist!*, I
stirrup pants *die Steghose, -n*, II8
stocking *der Strumpf, ⸚e*, II8
stomach *der Bauch, ⸚e*, II6; **stomachache** *die Bauchschmerzen (pl)*, II6
storage shelf *das Ablagefach, ⸚er*, II10
store *der Laden, ⸚, das Geschäft, -e*, I; **fewer stores** *weniger Geschäfte*, II7
storm *das Gewitter, -*, I
stove *der Herd, -e*, I
straight ahead *geradeaus*, I
strawberry *die Erdbeere, -n*, II4; **strawberry marmalade** *die Erdbeermarmelade*, II5;

strawberries with whipped cream *Erdbeeren mit Sahne*, II11
street *die Straße, -n*, I; **on ... Street** *in der ...straße*, I; **main street** *die Hauptstraße, -n*, II9
stripe *der Streifen, -*, II12
striped *gestreift*, I
stroll *spazieren*, II3
strong *stark*, I
stupid *blöd*, I
style *der Stil, -e*, II8
subject (school) *das Fach, ⸚er*, I; **Which subjects do you have?** *Welche Fächer hast du?*, I
suburb *der Vorort, -e*, I, II7; **a suburb of** *ein Vorort von*, I; **in a suburb** *in einem Vorort*, II7
subway *die U-Bahn*, I; **by subway** *mit der U-Bahn*, I
subway station *die U-Bahnstation, -en*, I
suede jacket *die Wildlederjacke, -n*, II12
sugar *der Zucker*, I, II4
suggest *vorschlagen*, II9; **I suggest that...** *Ich schlage vor, dass ...*, II9; **What do you suggest?** *Was schlägst du vor?*, II9
suggestion *der Vorschlag, ⸚e*, II12
suit *der Anzug, ⸚e*, II8
summer *der Sommer*, I; **in the summer** *im Sommer*, I
sun *die Sonne*, I; **the sun is shining** *die Sonne scheint*, I
sun protection factor *der Lichtschutzfaktor, -en*, II6
sun tan lotion *die Sonnenmilch*, II6; *die Sonnencreme*, II6
Sunday *der Sonntag*, I; **Sundays** *sonntags*, II10
sunny *sonnig*, I
sunroof *das Schiebedach, ⸚er*, II10
sunstroke *der Sonnenstich, -e*, II6
Super! *Spitze!, Super!*, I
supermarket *der Supermarkt, ⸚e*, I; **at the supermarket** *im Supermarkt*, I
suppose: I suppose so, but... *Eigentlich schon, aber ...*, II7
supposed to *sollen*, I; **The fish is supposed to be great.** *Der Fisch soll prima sein.*, II11; **Well, what am I supposed to do?** *Was soll ich bloß machen?*, II9; **What's that supposed to be?** *Was soll denn das sein?*, II5
Sure! *Aber sicher!, Ja, gern!*, I
sure: I'm not sure. *Ich bin nicht sicher.*, I; **I'm not sure that/whether...** *Ich bin nicht sicher, dass/ob ...*, II9
surf *surfen*, I
surrounding area *die Umgebung, -en*, II7
swallow: I can hardly swallow. *Ich kann kaum schlucken.*, II6
sweater *der Pulli, -s*, I
sweet *süß*, II6

swim *schwimmen*, I; **to go swimming** *baden gehen*, I
swimming: I enjoyed swimming in the Mediterranean Sea. *Ich bin gern im Mittelmeer geschwommen.*, II12
swimming pool *das Schwimmbad, ⸚er*, I; *der Pool, -s*, II12; **to go to the (swimming) pool** *ins Schwimmbad gehen*, I
switch off *abstellen* (sep), II7
synagogue *die Synagoge, -n*, II11

table *der Tisch, -e*, I; **to clear the table** *den Tisch abräumen* (sep), I; **to set the table** *den Tisch decken*, I
tacos *die Tacos*, II12
take *nehmen*, I, II5; **he/she takes** *er/sie nimmt*, I; **I'll take** *ich nehme*, I
talk about *sprechen über*, I; **he/she talks about** *er/sie spricht über*, I; **What did you (pl) talk about?** *Worüber habt ihr gesprochen?*, I
taste *schmecken*, I, II4; **Does it taste good?** *Schmeckt's?*, I; **How does it taste?** *Wie schmeckt's?*, I, II1; **doesn't taste good** *schmeckt mir nicht*, II4; **Beef tastes better to me.** *Rind schmeckt mir besser.*, II5; **Which soup tastes best to you?** *Welche Suppe schmeckt dir am besten?*, II5
Tasty! *Lecker!*, I
tea *der Tee*, I; **a glass of tea** *ein Glas Tee*, I
teacher (male) *der Lehrer, -*, I; **(female)** *die Lehrerin, -nen*, I
team *die Mannschaft, -en*, II4; **on the (basketball) team** *in der (Basketball)mannschaft*, II4
telecast, transmission *die Übertragung, -en*, II10
telephone *das Telefon, -e, der Apparat, -e*, I; **to pick up the telephone** *den Hörer abheben* (sep), I
telephone booth *die Telefonzelle, -n*, I
telephone number *die Telefonnummer, -n*, I
television (medium of) *das Fernsehen*, I; **TV set** *der Fernseher, -*, II10; **to watch TV** *Fernsehen schauen*, I; *fernsehen* (sep), *Fernseh gucken*, II10; **color stereo television set** *das Stereo Farbfernsehgerät, -e*, II10; **TV and video cart** *der Fernseh- und Videowagen, -*, II10; **TV room** *der Fernsehraum, ⸚e*, II9; **What's on TV?** *Was läuft im Fernsehen?*, II10

Tell me,... *Sag mal, ...*, II4
temperature: What's the temperature? *Wie viel Grad haben wir?*, I; **to take someone's temperature** *die Temperatur messen*, II6; **he/she takes someone's temperature** *er/sie misst die Temperatur*, II6
tennis *Tennis*, I
tennis court *der Tennisplatz, ⸚e*, II9
tennis racket *der Tennisschläger, -*, II2
terrace *die Terrasse, -n*, II7
terrible *furchtbar*, I
terrific *Klasse, prima, toll*, I;
than *als*, II7
thank *danken*, I; **Thank you (very much)!** *Danke (sehr/schön)!*, I; *Vielen Dank!*, I; **Thank you and the same to you!** *Danke gleichfalls!*, II11; *Danke! Dir/Ihnen auch!*, II11
that *dass* (conj), I; **That's all.** *Das ist alles.*, I; **That's...** *Das ist ...*, I
theater *das Theater, -*, I
them *sie, ihnen*, II3
then *dann*, I
there *dort*, I
There is/are... *Es gibt...*, I
they *sie*, I; **they are** *sie sind*, I; **they're from** *sie sind (kommen) aus*, I
think *denken*, I
think: Do you think so? *Meinst du?*, I; **I think** *ich glaube*, I; **I think (tennis) is...** *Ich finde (Tennis) ...*, I; **I think so too.** *Das finde ich auch.*, I; **What do you think of (tennis)?** *Wie findest du (Tennis)?*, I; **I don't think so.** *Das finde ich nicht.*, II10; **I don't think that...** *Ich glaube nicht, dass ...*, II9; **I really think that...** *Ich meine doch, dass ...*, II10; **I think I'm sick.** *Ich glaube, ich bin krank.*, II6; **I think it's bad that...** *Ich finde es nicht gut, dass ...*, II4; **I think it's great that...** *Ich finde es toll, dass ...*, II4
third *dritte*, I
thirst *der Durst*, II2; **to be thirsty** *Durst haben*, II2
this *dies-*, II5; **this afternoon** *heute Nachmittag*, I; **This is...(on the telephone)** *Hier ist ...*, I; **this morning** *heute Morgen*, I
three times *dreimal*, I
thrilling *spannend*, I
throat *der Hals, ⸚e*, II6; **sore throat** *die Halsschmerzen* (pl), II6
through *durch*, II9
Thursday *der Donnerstag*, I; **Thursdays** *donnerstags*, II10
tie *die Krawatte, -n*, II8; **bow tie** *die Fliege, -n*, II12
tight *eng*, I; **It's too tight on you.** *Es ist dir zu eng.*, II8
till: ten till two *zehn vor zwei*, I

Tilsiter cheese *der Tilsiter Käse*, II5
time *die Zeit*, I; **At what time?** *Um wie viel Uhr?*, I; **I don't have time.** *Ich habe keine Zeit.*, I; **What time is it?** *Wie spät ist es?, Wie viel Uhr ist es?*, I
tire: wide tire *der Breitreifen, -*, II10
tired *müde*, II6
to *an, auf, nach*, II9; **Let's drive to the ocean.** *Fahren wir ans Meer!*, I; **Are you going to the golf course?** *Gehst du auf den Golfplatz?*; **We're going to Austria.** *Wir fahren nach Österreich.*, II9
to, for her *ihr*, I
to, for him *ihm*, I
today *heute*, I
tofu *der Tofu*, II5
toilet *die Toilette, -n*, II7
tomato *die Tomate, -n*, I
tomorrow *morgen*, I
tonight *heute Abend*, I
too *zu*, I; **Too bad!** *Schade!*, I
toothache *die Zahnschmerzen (pl)*, II6
toothpaste *die Zahnpasta*, II6
tour *besichtigen*, I; **to tour the city** *die Stadt besichtigen*, I; **city tour** *die Stadrundfahrt, -en*, II11
toward *nach*, II9
town *die Kleinstadt, ⸚e*, II7; **in a town** *in einer Kleinstadt*, II7
traffic *der Verkehr*, II7
train *die Bahn, -en*, II9
train station *der Bahnhof, ⸚e*, I
training and weight room *der Fitnessraum, ⸚e*, II9
transmitter *der Sender, -*, II10
transportation *das Verkehrsmittel, -*, II9; **public transportation** *öffentliche Verkehrsmittel (pl)*, II7
trash *der Müll*, I; **to sort the trash** *den Müll sortieren*, I
tree *der Baum, ⸚e*, II7
trout *die Forelle, -n*, II4
truck *der Lastkraftwagen, -, (LKW, -s)* II7
true: Not true! *Stimmt nicht!*, I; **That's right! True!** *Stimmt!*, I; **That's true, but...** *Das stimmt, aber ...*, II4
try *probieren*, I
try on *anprobieren (sep)*, I
T-shirt *das T-Shirt, -s*, I
Tuesday *der Dienstag*, I; **Tuesdays** *dienstags*, II10
Turkish *türkisch (adj)*, II11
turn *einbiegen (sep)*; **Turn in here!** *Biegen Sie hier ein!*, II9
tuxedo *der Smoking, -s*, II12
twice *zweimal*, I
twin *der Zwilling, -e*, II1
type *der Typ, -en*, II8

ugly *hässlich*, I
unbelievable *unglaublich*; **That's really unbelievable!** *Das ist ja unglaublich!*, II10
unboiled *ungekocht*, II12
uncle *der Onkel, -*, I
uncomfortable *unbequem*, I
under it, underneath *darunter*, II8
unfortunately *leider*, I; **Unfortunately I can't.** *Leider kann ich nicht.*, I; **That's the way it is, unfortunately.** *Das ist leider so.*, II9
unfriendly *unsympathisch*, II1
unhealthy *ungesund*, II4; *nicht gut für die Gesundheit*, II4
unpleasant *unsympathisch*, II1
until: from 8 until 8:45 *von 8 Uhr bis 8 Uhr 45*, I; **until you get to ... Square** *bis zum ...platz*, I; **until you get to ... Street** *bis zur ...straße*, I; **until you get to the traffic light** *bis zur Ampel*, I
us *uns*, I, II3
use *benutzen*, II6
usually *gewöhnlich*, II3

vacation (from school) *die Ferien (pl)*, II3; **vacation (from work)** *der Urlaub, -e*, II9; **What did you do on your vacation?** *Was hast du in den Ferien gemacht?*, II3
vacuum *Staub saugen*, I
vanilla-flavored milk *die Vanillemilch*, II5
varied *abwechslungsreich*, II12
vegetables *das Gemüse*, I
vegetarian *vegetarisch*; **You're vegetarian, right?** *Du isst wohl vegetarisch, was?*, II5
very *sehr*, I, II4; **Very well!** *Sehr gut!*, I
vest: jeans vest *die Jeansweste, -n*, II8
video: use a video camera/a camera *die Videokamera/die Kamera bedienen*, II3
video cassette *das Video, -s*, I, II3; *die Videocassette, -n*, II10; **insert a video cassette** *ein Video einlegen (sep)*, II3; **take out the video cassette** *das Video herausnehmen (sep)*, II3

village *das Dorf, ⸚er*, II7; **in a village** *in einem Dorf*, II7
violent *brutal*, I
visit *besuchen*, I; **to visit friends** *Freunde besuchen*, I
visit (a place) *besuchen, besichtigen*, II3; **I visited (the cathedral).** *Ich habe (den Dom) besichtigt.*, II3
volleyball *Volleyball*, I
volume control *der Lautstärkeregler*, II10

walk *spazieren*, II3
want (to) *wollen*, I, II1; **What do you want to do?** *Was willst du machen?*, II1
war *der Krieg, -e*, II7; **war movie** *der Kriegsfilm, -e*, I
warm *warm*, I
was: I was (in, at, on)... *ich war (in an, auf) ...*, I, II12; **I was at the baker's.** *Ich war beim Bäcker.*, I; **he/she was** *er/sie war*, I
wash *spülen*, I; **to wash the dishes** *das Geschirr spülen*, I; **to wash** *(sich) waschen*, II6; **to wash clothes** *die Wäsche waschen*, II2; **he/she/it washes** *er/sie/es wäscht (sich)*, II6
watch *schauen*, I; **to watch TV** *Fernsehen schauen*, I; *fernsehen (sep)*, II10; (colloquial) *Fernsehen gucken*, II10
water *das Wasser*, I; **a glass of (mineral) water** *ein Glas (Mineral) Wasser*, I
water: to water the flowers *die Blumen gießen*, I
we *wir*, I
wear *anziehen (sep)*, I; *tragen*, II8; **Don't wear anything made of...** *Trag ja nichts aus ...!*, II8; **Go ahead and wear...** *Trag doch mal ...!*, II8
weather *das Wetter*, I; **How's the weather?** *Wie ist das Wetter?*, I
weather report *der Wetterbericht, -e*, II10; **What does the weather report say?** *Was sagt der Wetterbericht?*, I
Wednesday *der Mittwoch*, I; **Wednesdays** *mittwochs*, II10
week *die Woche, -n*, I; **every week** *jede Woche*, II4
weekend *das Wochenende, -n*, I; **on the weekend** *am Wochenende*, I; **every weekend** *jedes Wochenende*, II4

weekly special *das Angebot der Woche*, I
weigh *wiegen*, I
well: Well yes, but... *Eigentlich schon, aber ...*, II4; *Ja, schon, aber ...*, II7; **extremely well** *ganz wohl*, II4; **Get well soon!** *Gute Besserung!*, II6; **I'm (not) doing well.** *Es geht mir (nicht) gut!*, II6; *Mir ist (nicht) gut.*, II6; **not well at all** *überhaupt nicht wohl*, II4
were: Where were you? *Wo bist du gewesen?*, I, II3; **we were** *wir waren*, I; **they were** *sie waren*, I; **(pl) you were** *ihr wart*, I; **(formal) you were** *Sie waren*, I
western (movie) *der Western, -*, I
wet *nass*, I
what *was*; **What are we going to do now?** *Was machen wir jetzt?*, II9; **What is it?** *Was gibt's?*, II5; *Was ist?*, II5; **Okay, what is it?** *Ja? Was denn?*, II5; **So what about...?** *Wie steht's mit ...?*, II4; **Yes, what?** *Ja, was bitte?*, II5; **What can I do for you?** *Was kann ich für dich tun?*, I; **What did you talk about?** *Worüber habt ihr gesprochen?*, I; **What else?** *Noch etwas?*, I; **what kind of?** *was für?*, I; **What kinds of music do you like?** *Was für Musik hörst du gern?*, I; **What's there to eat** *Was gibt's zu essen?*, I
when? *wann?*, I
whenever *wenn (conj)*, II8
where? *wo?*, I
where (from)? *woher?*, I; **Where are you from?** *Woher bist (kommst) du?*, I
where (to)? *wohin?*, I; **Where are we going?** *Wohin fahren wir?*, II9
whether *ob (conj)*, II9
which *welch–*, I, II8; **Which soup do you prefer?** *Welche Suppe magst du lieber?*, II5
whirlpool *der Whirlpool, -s*, II9
white *weiß*, I; **in white** *in Weiß*, I
who? *wer?*, I; **Who is that?** *Wer ist das?*, I

whole wheat roll *die Vollkornsemmel, -n*, I
whom? *wen?*, I; **to, for whom?**, *wem?*, I
why? *warum?*, I; **Why don't you come along!** *Komm doch mit!*, I
wide *weit*, I
will *werden*; **you will** *du wirst*; **he/she will** *er/sie wird*, II10; **I'm going to buy myself a great car.** *Ich werde mir einen tollen Wagen kaufen.*, II10
wind surf *windsurfen*, II9
windbreaker *die Wind-, Wetterjacke, -n*, II8
window *das Fenster, -*, I; **to clean the windows** *die Fenster putzen*, I
windshield wiper *der Scheibenwischer, -*, II10
winter *der Winter*, I; **in the winter** *im Winter*, I
wish *sich wünschen*; **I wish for...** *Ich wünsche mir ...*, II7; **What would you wish for?** *Was wünschst du dir (mal)?*, II7
with *mit*, I; **with bread** *mit Brot*, I; **with corners** *eckig*, I
witty *witzig*, II8
woman *die Frau, -en*, I
wonderful *großartig*, II4
wood: made of wood *aus Holz*, I
wool *die Wolle*, II8
wool shirt *das Wollhemd, -en*, II8; **made of wool** *aus Wolle*, II1
work *arbeiten*, II3; **That won't work.** *Das geht nicht.*, I
worse than *schlechter als*, II7
would: No, I would rather... *Nein, ich würde lieber ...*, II11; **That would be great!** *Das wäre toll!*, II12; **Wouldn't you like to...?** *Würdest du gern mal ...?*, II11; **That wouldn't be bad.** *Das wär' nicht schlecht.*, II11
would like (to) *möchten*, I; **I would like to see...** *Ich möchte ... sehen.*, I; **What would you like to eat?** *Was möchtest du essen?*, I; **What would you like?** *Was bekommen Sie?*, I;

Would you like anything else? *Haben Sie noch einen Wunsch?*, I
wristwatch *die Armbanduhr, -en*, I
write *schreiben*, I
wrong: Is something wrong? *Ist was mit dir?*, II6; **What's wrong with you?** *Was fehlt dir?*, II6

yard *der Garten, ⸚*, II7
year *das Jahr, -e*, I; **I am...years old.** *Ich bin ... Jahre alt.*, I
yellow *gelb*, I; **in yellow** *in Gelb*, I
yes *ja*, I; **Yes?** *Bitte?*, I; **Yes, I do!** *Doch!*, II4
yesterday *gestern*, I; **yesterday evening** *gestern Abend*, I; **the day before yesterday** *vorgestern*, I
yogurt *der Joghurt, -*, II5
you *du, Sie, ihr*, I
you're (very) welcome! *Bitte (sehr/schön)!*, I
younger *jünger*, II7
your *dein (poss adj)*, I; *Ihr*, II5
yourself *dich, sich*, II4
yourselves *euch*, II4
youth hostel *die Jugendherberge, -n*, II3

zero *null*, I
zipper *der Reißverschluss, ⸚e*, II8
zoo *der Zoo, -s*, I; **to go to the zoo** *in den Zoo gehen*, I

Grammar Index

Grammar Index

This grammar index includes grammar topics introduced in **Komm mit!** Levels 1 and 2. The Roman numeral I preceding the page number(s) indicates Level 1; the Roman numeral II indicates Level 2. Page numbers beginning with R refer to the Grammar Summary in this reference section.

aber: I: 79 *see also* conjunctions
accusative case: definite article I: **135**; indefinite article I: **135, 258**; noun phrase in I: **135**; third person pronoun, singular I: **140; 171**; third person pronoun, plural I: **200**; first and second person pronoun I: **200**; following **für** I: **200**; the interogative pronoun **wen** I: **200, 337**; following **es gibt** I: **257**; of reflexive pronouns II: **102, 222**; of **jeder** II: **106**; of **kein** I: **259**; II: **110**; of possessives II: **136**; following **in, an, auf** to express going somewhere II: **246, 250**; following **durch** and **um** II: **254**; *see also* direct object
adjectives: I: 57, 79, 84, 202, 288; comparative forms of II: 190; endings following **ein**-words II: 194; endings of comparatives II: 200; endings following **der**- and **dieser**-words II: 217; endings of unpreceded adjectives II: 311; *see also* R27
adjective endings: *see* adjectives
als: in a comparison II: 190, R28
am: contraction of **an dem** II: 73
am liebsten: I: **285** use of, with **würde** II: 307
an: followed by dative (location) II: 73; followed by accusative (direction) II: 246; *see also* R25
anprobieren: I: 143; *see also* separable prefix verbs, R31
ans: contraction of **an das** II: 246
anziehen: present tense forms of I: 143; *see also* separable-prefix verbs, R31
article: *see* definite article, indefinite article
auf: followed by dative (location) II: 135; followed by accusative (direction) II: 246; use of, with **s. freuen**, II. 277, R25
aufs: contraction of **auf das** II: 246
aus: followed by dative II: 254, R25
aussehen: present tense forms of I: **144**; *see also* separable-prefix verbs; R31
auxiliary: *see* modal auxiliary verbs

bei: followed by dative II: 254, R25
beim: contraction of **bei dem** II: 254
s. brechen: present tense of II: 165

case: I: **135, 319** *see also* nominative case, accusative case, dative case
class: definition of I: 24; R20

clauses: I: 230, 250; *see also* dependent clauses
command forms: du-commands I: 223, **224, 255**, 337; **ihr**-commands I: 223, 224; **Sie**-commands I: **255**; inclusive commands II: 159; R31
comparatives: *see* adjectives
conjugations: *see* present tense; present perfect
conjunctions: und I: 29; **aber** I: 79; **denn** and **weil** I: **230**, II: 39; **dass** I: **260**; **wenn** II: 227; **ob** II: 250
connecting words: *see* conjunctions
contractions: of **in dem, im** II: 73; of **an dem, am** I: 55, 106; II: 73; of **zu dem, zum** I: 30, 254; II: 141; of **zu der, zur** II: 141; of **an das, ans** II: 246; of **auf das, aufs** II: 246; of **in das, ins** I: 162, 165; II: 246; of **bei dem, beim** II: 254; of **von dem, vom** II: 254
conversational past: *see* past participle

da-compounds: II: 277
dass-clauses: I: **260**; verb in final position II: 101, R26; with reflex verbs II: 102
dative case: introduction to I: **319**; following **mit** I: **319**; interrogative pronoun **wem** I: **319**; word order with I: **320**; following **in** and **an** when expressing location II: 73; with **gefallen** II: 77; of personal pronouns II: 77; plural of definite article II: 77; of **ein**- words II: 79; following **auf** when expressing location II: 135, 250; of possessives II: 136; verbs used with dative forms, **gefallen, schmecken** II: 139; following **zu** II: 141, 223; use of, to talk about how you feel II: 157; verbs requiring dative forms II: 163; reflexive verbs requiring dative forms II: 164, 192, 226; reflexive pronouns II: 164; use of, to express idea of something being too expensive/large/small II: 169; plural endings of adjectives II: 194; endings of adjectives II: 217; further uses of II: 223; prepositions followed by II: 254; *see also* indirect object
definite article: I: **24, 78; 135,** 128; II: 164; dative I: **319**; dative summary II: 77; dative plural II: 77; *see also* R20; R24
demonstratives: II: 130, R24
den: dative plural of definite article II: 77, R20
denn: I: **230**; *see also* conjunctions
dependent clauses: wo I: **250**; *see also* word order for **denn, weil,** and **dass**-clauses; *see also* clauses
dich: as a reflexive pronoun II: 102, R24
dieser-words: demonstratives II: 130; adj following **dieser**-words II: 217, R21; *see also* **jeder**

dir: dative personal pronouns II: 77; reflexive personal pronouns II: 164, R24
direct object: definition I: **135;** dative II: **163;** noun phrases as I: **135;** *see also* accusative case
direct object pronouns: I: **140; 200;** R24
direction: expressed by **nach, an, in** and **auf** II: 246; use of prepositions to express II: 250, R25
du-commands: I: 223, **224;** II: R31; of **messen** II: 168; of **tragen** II: 222; *see also* command forms
durch: followed by accusative II: 254, R25
dürfen: present tense of II: 102, R30

ein: nominative I: **76;** accusative I: **135, 171, 258;** dative I: **319;** II: 79; *see also* R21
ein-words: **mein(e), dein(e)** I: **82; sein(e), ihr(e)** I: **83;** accusative I: **258; kein** I: **259;** dative I: **319;** adjective endings following II: **194;** *see also* R21–R22
emphasis words: denn, mal, halt, doch I: 50; for **denn** *see also* conjunctions
endings: *see* plural formation of nouns, possessives, present tense verb endings, past tense, and infinitive
-er: ending in place names II: 245
es gibt: I: **257**
essen: present tense forms of I: **171,** R25; *see also* stem-changing verbs
euch: dative personal pronouns II: 77; as a reflexive pronoun II: 102; *see also* R24

fahren: present tense forms of I: 254; **fahren** vs. **gehen** I: 255; R34
fehlen: use of dative with II: 163, R30
first person: ich, wir; *see* subject pronouns
s. fit halten: reflexive verb II: 102
formal form of address: I: 52
s. freuen: reflexive verb II: 102, R35; **s. freuen auf** II: 277
s. fühlen: reflexive verb II: 102, R35
für: followed by accusative I: **200, 337,** II: 101; use of with **s. interessieren** II: 222, R25
future: use of **morgen** and present tense for I: 203; **werden** II: 289; *see also* R32

gefallen: I: **137;** use of dative with II: 77, 139, 163, R30
gegenüber: followed by dative II: 254
gehen: use of, with dative forms II: 159, R30
gender: *see* class
gern: I: 50, 282, 285; use of, with **würde** II: 307; use of, with **hätte** II: 314

haben: present tense forms of I: **108;** use of, in conversational past II: 66; past participle of II: 67; simple past tense forms of II: 72; *see also* R30; R32–R34
hätte: forms of II: 314; R32
helfen: use of dative with II: 163, R30
helping verbs: *see* **haben** and **sein**

ihm: dative personal pronoun II: 77, R24
Ihnen, ihnen: dative personal pronoun II: 77, R24
ihr: dative personal pronoun, dative case II: 77, R24
ihr-commands: I: 223, **224,** 255, 337
im: contraction of **in dem** II: 73
imperatives: *see* command forms
imperfect: simple past of **haben** and **sein** II: 72, R32
in: followed by dative (location) II: 73; followed by accusative (direction) II: 246; R25
inclusive commands: *see* command forms
indefinite articles: ein, nominative I: **76;** accusative I: **135, 258;** dative II: 79
indirect object: definition of I: **319;** word order I: **320;** *see also* R21; dative case
indirect object pronouns: definition of I: **319**
infinitive: definition of I: **52;** use of, with modals I: **166, 195, 196, 342;** with **werden** II: 289; with **würde** II: 307; *see also* R29–R36; word order
ins: contraction of **in das** II: 246
s. interessieren: R35; **s. interessieren für** II: 277
interrogative pronouns: nominative form **wer** I: **23; was:** I: 50; accusative form **wen** I: **200;** dative form **wem** I: **319;** *see also* R25
interrogatives: *see* questions and question words
irregular verbs: *see* present tense, past participle, and stem-changing verbs

jeder: II: **106;** accusative of II: 106

kaufen: with dative reflexive pronoun II: 224
kein: I: **259;** accusative forms II: 110, 287; *see also* R21, R27
können: present tense of I: **199;** R30; *see also* modal auxiliary verbs

lassen: present tense of II: 283, R34; *see also* stem changing verbs
laufen: present tense of II: 285, R34; *see also* stem changing verbs

lieber: I: **285;** use of, with **würde** II: **307;** use of, with **hätte** II: **314**
Lieblings-: I: **110**
location: use of prepositions to express II: 250, R25

mich: as a reflexive pronoun II: 102, R24
mir: dative personal pronouns II: 77; reflexive personal pronouns II: 164, R24
mit: followed by dative II: 254, R25
möchte-forms: present tense I: **75, 171,** R30; *see also* modal auxiliary verbs
modal auxiliary verbs: möchte-forms I: **75; wollen** I: **166; müssen** I: **195; können** I: **199; sollen** I: **223** II: **159; mögen** I: **282; dürfen** II: **111,** R30
mögen: present tense forms of I: **282,** R30; *see also* modal auxiliary verbs
morgen: I: **203;** *see also* future
müssen: present tense forms of I: **195,** R30; *see also* modal auxiliary verbs

nach: use of to express direction II: 246; followed by dative (location) II: 254, R25
neben: followed by accusative (direction) or dative (location) II: 255, R25
nehmen: present tense forms of I: **144;** *see also* stem-changing verbs
nicht: I: 58; with **besonders** II: 76; position of, in a sentence R26
noch ein: I: **258,** R29
nominative case: definition of I: **135;** interrogative pronouns **wer** I: **23; dein** and **mein** I: **82;** noun phrase in I: **135;** indefinite article I: **135, 140;** *see also* R25; subject
noun phrases: masculine, feminine, neuter I: **24;** definition of I: **135;** *see also* R20; definite article, accusative, dative, nominative
nouns: classes of I: **24;** plural of I: **114,** R23
numbers: I: 25, 83

ob-clause: verb in final position II: 250, R26
object pronouns: *see* direct object pronouns and indirect object pronouns

past participle: II: 66-67, R34
past tense of: sein I: **231; haben** and **sein** II: 72, R34
personal pronouns: *see* pronouns
plural formation of nouns: I: **114;** dative plural II: 136, R23
possessives: mein(e), dein(e), nominative I: **82; sein(e), ihr(e),**
nominative I: **83;** accusative I: **258;** dative I: **345;** summary II: 136, 194, R22
prefix: Lieblings-: I: **110;** *see also* separable prefixes
prepositions: für I: **200; über,** use of with **sprechen** I: **291; mit** I: **319** II: 254; dative with **in** and **an** when expressing location II: 73; dative with **auf** when expressing location II: 135; **zu** II: 141, 254; use of, to express direction, **nach, an, in,** and **auf** II: 246; expressing direction and location, summary II: 250; followed by dative forms, **aus, bei, nach, von, gegenüber** II: 254; followed by accusative forms, **durch, um** II: 254; followed by accusative or dative forms, **vor, neben, zwischen** II: 255; verbs requiring prepositional phrase **sprechen über, s. freuen auf, s. interessieren für** II: 277; R25
present perfect: I: 292–293
present tense: definition of I: **52;** of **sein** I: **26;** of **spielen** I: **52;** of the **möchte**-forms I: **75;** of **haben** I: **108;** of **anziehen** I: **143;** of **nehmen, aussehen** I: **144;** of **wollen** I: **166;** of **essen** I: **171;** of **müssen** I: **195;** of **können** I: **199;** of **sollen** I: **223;** of **wissen** I: **250;** of **mögen** I: **282;** of **sehen** I: **285;** of **lesen, sprechen** I: **291;** of **schlafen** II: **100;** of s. **fühlen** II: **102;** of **dürfen** II: **111;** of **s. brechen** II: **165;** of **tragen** II: **222;** *see also* R29–R35
present tense verb endings: definition I: **52;** verbs with stems ending in **d, t,** or **n** I: **57;** verbs with stems ending in **-eln** I: **58;** *see also* present tense; stem-changing verbs; verbs
pronouns: personal pronouns singular I: **26;** personal pronouns plural I: **50;** class/gender, **er, sie, es, sie** (pl) I: **79, 115;** third person singular, accusative I: **140;** third person, plural I: **200;** first and second person I: **200;** dative I: **319, 345;** dative summary II: **77;** accusative reflexive forms II: 102; dative reflexive forms II: 164; *see also* R24; direct object pronouns; indirect object pronouns; subject pronouns; personal pronouns

question words/interrogatives: wer, wo, woher, wie I: **23; was** I: **50; worüber** I: **291; wann** I: **107; wem** I: **319; warum** II: **39; welcher** II: **140; wofür** II: **277; worauf** II: **277;** *see also* R25
questions: asking and answering questions I: **23;** questions beginning with a verb I: **23;** questions beginning with a question word I: **23;** word order of question with reflexive verbs II: 102; *see also* R26; word order

reflexive pronouns: II: 102; dative forms II: 164; accusative forms II: 222; *see also* R24
reflexive verbs: II: 102, 157; used with dative case forms II: 164, used with accusative case forms II: 222; *see also* R30
regular verbs: II: 12, R35

schlafen: present tense of II: 100; *see also* R34; stem changing verbs
schmecken: use of, with or without dative II: 139; use of with dative II: 163, R30

second person: **du, ihr, Sie** (formal singular and plural), *see* subject pronouns
sehen: present tense forms of I: **285**, R24
sein: present tense forms of I: **26**; R30; simple past tense forms of I: **231**; use of, in conversational past II: 66, R33; past participle of verbs with II: 67, R33
separable prefixes: an, aus I: **143–144**; **auf, ab, mit** I: **196**; **ein** I: 313; placement of I: **143, 196**
separable-prefix verbs: definition of I: **143**; **anziehen, anprobieren, aussehen** I: **143**; **aufräumen, abräumen, mitkommen** I: **196**; use of in conversational past II: 67; inclusive commands with II: 159; **wehtun** as a separable prefix verb II: 163; R31
sich: reflexive pronoun II: 102, R24
s. interessieren: reflexive verb II: 222
Sie-commands: I: **255**, R23; *see also* command forms
so ... wie: used in comparison II: 186, R28
sollen: present tense forms of I: **223**; use of to make a suggestion II: 159; *see also* R30; modal auxiliary verbs
sprechen: present tense forms of I: **291**; R34; **sprechen über** I: **291**; II: 277
stem-changing verbs: nehmen, aussehen I: 144; **essen** I: **171**; **fahren** I: **255**; **sehen** I: **285**; **lesen, sprechen** I: **291** II: 12; **schlafen** II: **100**; **brechen** II: 167; **waschen** II: 167; **messen** II: 168; **tragen** II: 222; **lassen** II: 283; *see also* R35–R36; present tense verb endings
subject: definition of I: **135**; *see also* nominative case
subject pronouns: I: 26 plurals I: **50, 79**; as opposed to direct object pronouns I: **140**
subjunctive forms: würde II: 307; **hätte** II: 314; *see also* R32
subordinating conjunctions: denn, weil, *see* word order
superlatives: suffix -**ste** I: 287

third person: **er, sie, sie** (plural), **Sie** (plural formal), *see* subject pronouns
time expressions: I: 55, 106, 107, 198; **morgen** I: **203**
tragen: present tense of II: 222, R34

über: following **sprechen** II: 277, R25
um: followed by accusative II: 254, R25
unpreceded adjectives: endings of II: 311, R27
uns: dative personal pronouns II: 77; as a reflexive pronoun II: 102; *see also* R24

verbs: with separable prefixes, **anziehen, anprobieren, aussehen** I: **143; aufräumen, abräumen, mitkommen** I: **196**; with vowel change in the **du-** and **er/sie-**form, **nehmen, aussehen** I: **144**; **essen** I: **171**; **fahren** I: **255**; **sehen** I: **285**; **lesen, sprechen** I: **291**; **schlafen** II: **100**; **brechen** II: 165; **waschen** II: 165; **messen** II: 168; **tragen** II: 222; **lassen** II: 283; conversational past tense II: 66–67; reflexive verbs: II: 102; used with dative, **gefallen, schmecken** II: 139; verbs requiring dative case forms II: 163–164; **s. wünschen** II: 192; **passen** and **stehen** with dative II: 223; verbs requiring prepositional phrase, **sprechen über, s. freuen auf, s. interessieren für** II: 277; *see also* R29–R36; present tense and present tense verb endings
verb-final position: in **weil-**clauses I: 230 II: 189; in clauses following **wissen** I: **250**; in **dass-** clauses I: **260** II: 101; in **wenn-**clauses II: 227; in **ob-**clauses II: 250; with **werden** in clauses beginning with **dass, ob, wenn, weil** II: 289; *see also* R26
verb-second position: I: **56, 167**, R20
vom: contraction of **von dem** II: 254
von: followed by dative II, 254, R25
vor: followed by accusative (direction) or dative (location) II: 255, R25

was: I: 50; R25
waschen: present tense of II: 165, R31, R35
wehtun: as a separable prefix verb II: 163, R31; use of dative with II: 163, R30
weil: *see* conjunctions
weil-clause: verb in final position II: 189, R26
welcher: forms of II: 140; *see also* **dieser**
wenn: *see* conjunctions
wenn-clauses: verb in final position II: 227, R26
werden: use of to express future, forms of II: 289, R32, R36
wissen: present tense forms of I: **250, wissen** vs. **kennen** I: **284**, R25
wo: questions beginning with I: **23**; II: 73; location questions II: 250
wo-compounds: I: **291**; II: 277
wollen: present tense forms of I: **166**, R22; *see also* modal auxiliary verbs
word order: questions beginning with a verb I: **23**; questions beginning with a question word I: **23**; verb in second position I: **56, 167**; with separable prefix verbs I: **143**; using modals I: **166, 167**; in **denn-** and **weil-**clauses I: **230**; verb-final in clauses following **wissen** I: **250**; verb-final in **dass-**clauses I: **260**; with dative case I: **320**; inclusive commands II: 159; with **wehtun** II: 163; **weil** clauses II: 189; in **wenn-**clauses II: 227; in **ob-**clauses II: 250; with **werden** in clauses beginning with **dass, ob, wenn, weil** II: 289, R26; *see also* infinititve; questions, separable prefixes
worüber: I: 291
s. wünschen: with dative reflexive pronouns II: 192
würde: forms of II: 307, R32

zu: II: 141; preposition followed by dative II: 223, R25
zum: contraction of **zu dem** II: 141
zur: contraction of **zu der** II: 141
zwischen: followed by accusative (direction) or dative (location) II: 255, R25

Credits

ACKNOWLEDGMENTS (continued from page ii)

Berliner Bären Stadtrundfahrt GmbH: Logo for Berliner Bären Stadtrundfahrt GmbH and "Tägliche Stadtrundfahrten Daily Sightseeingtours + Potsdam" advertisement from *Berlin Programm,* September 1993, p. 58.

Berliner Dom: From advertisement, "Berliner Dom" from *Berlin Programm,* September 1993, p. 41.

Berliner Symphoniker: Advertisement, "Berliner Symphoniker," concert information for January 26, 1997.

Burda Publications: "Sechs Tips, die für Sie so wichtig sind wie für Boris" with photographs from "Warum ist Dr. Müller-Wohlfahrt nie krank?" from *BUNTE,* no. 22, May 27, 1993, p. 40. "Jetzt ein Eis!" from *BUNTE,* no. 33, August 12, 1993, p. 83.

China-Restaurant Ho-Lin-Wah: Advertisement, "Ho-Lin-Wah" from *Berlin Programm,* September 1993.

Club La Santa: Photograph of "Club La Santa auf Lanzarote" from *Sport-Scheck Reisen,* Summer 1993, pp. 172–173.

Concert Concept GmbH: Advertisement, "Peter Hofmann, Anna Maria Kaufman singen Musical Classics" from *Berlin Programm,* September 1993, p. 39.

Deutscher Taschenbuch Verlag GmbH & Co. KG: From "Seltsamer Deutscher, komischer Türke" by Cengiz Kip from *Türken deutscher Sprache.* Copyright © 1984 by Deutscher Taschenbuch Verlag, München.

Focus Syndication: "Der neue Trend: 'Bleich ist beautiful'" from *Focus-Das moderne Nachrichtenmagazin,* no. 28, 1993, p. 81.

Alexander Fuhrmann: From "Wenn Kinder feiern …" by Alexander Fuhrmann from *Neue Apotheken Illustrierte,* 6/93, p. 28.

GLOBUS-Kartendienst GmbH: Graphs no. 5648, no. 6809, and no. 4034. "Die Deutschen sind," from *Süddeutsche Zeitung,* no. 44, 1992. p. 36. Copyright © 1992 by GLOBUS-Kartendienst GmbH.

Kartographischer Verlag Busche GmbH: "Baden-Baden" from *Aral Auto-Reisebuch,* 1994/95.

Picture Press Bild-und Textagentur GmbH: "Das Pausenklingeln ist die schönste Musik!" from *Eltern,* October 1990, pp. 208–211. Copyright © 1990 by Gruner + Jahr AG & Co. From "Reich ist, wer nix mehr lernen muß!" from *Eltern,* July 1991, pp. 168, 169, 171. Copyright © 1991 by Gruner + Jahr AG & Co. "Gesucht: Bauernhof zum Ausschlafen!" from *Eltern,* August 1991, pp. 146–148. Copyright © 1991 by Gruner + Jahr AG & Co.

Pop/Rocky: From "Ich bin kein Wunderkind!" and from "Nudeln mit Biss" from *Pop/Rocky,* no. 18, 1993, pp. 42, 49.

Redaktion Pierzel: "Kuren und Bäder" from *Neue Gesundheit,* January 1, 1994, pp. 20–21.

Rowohlt Verlag GmbH: "Das Brot" by Wolfgang Borchert from *Das Gesamtwerk.* Copyright © 1949 by Rowohlt Verlag GmbH, Reinbek.

Severin + Kühn: From advertisement, "8-sprachige City-Tour/multilingual City-Tour" from *Berlin Programm,* September 1993, p. 59.

Sport-Scheck Reisen GmbH: "Club La Santa auf Lanzarote" from *Sport-Scheck Reisen,* Summer 1993, pp. 172–173.

Surya Indisches Restaurant: Advertisement, "Surya Indisches Restaurant" from *Berlin Programm,* September 1993.

Tiefdruck Schwann-Bagel GmbH: "100 Mark für Nichtraucher," from *JUMA: Das Jugendmagazin,* 2/91, p. 4, April 1991. "Mein Traumhaus ist aus Schokolade" from *JUMA: Das Jugendmagazin,* 1/92, pp. 16–19, January 1992. From "Tina-das Mädchen aus dem Katalog" from *JUMA: Das Jugendmagazin,* 3/92, pp. 1, 10–11, July 1992. Text from "Hier hab ich meine Ruhe" from *JUMA: Das Jugendmagazin,* 3/93, pp. 6–10, July 1993. From "Schule im Garten" from *JUMA: Das Jugendmagazin,* 4/93, pp. 32 & 35, October 1993.

TV Spielfilm Verlag GmbH: Reviews for "Der Junge mit dem großen schwarzen Hund," "Der Prinz von Bel-Air," "Eishockey WM," "Im Reich der wilden Tiere," "Praxis Bülowbogen," and "Raumschiff Enterprise," from *TV Spielfilm/TV Guide,* 9/93, pp. 36–37, 70–71. Copyright © 1993 by TV Spielfilm Verlag GmbH.

Josef Witt GmbH: "Persönliche Bestellkarte" from Kaufen + Sparen.

PHOTOGRAPHY CREDITS

Abbreviations used: (t) top, (c) center, (b), bottom, (l) left, (r) right, (i) inset

TABLE OF CONTENTS: Page vi, viii, (tl), ix, (br), x, (tl), xi, (bl), xii, (tl), xiii, (br), xiv, (tl), xv, (br), George Winkler, other images are HRW Photos/Sam Dudgeon

Chapter Opener Backgrounds: Scott Van Osdol

All photographs by George Winkler/Holt, Rinehart and Winston, Inc. except:

UNIT ONE: Chapter One: Page 11, HRW Photo/Sam Dudgeon. **Chapter Two:** Page 32, 37(top row), HRW Photo/Sam Dudgeon; 44(tr), Edge Video Productions; 45, HRW Photo/Sam Dudgeon; 48(tl), Michelle Bridwell/Frontera Fotos; 48(cl), HRW/Sam Dudgeon; 48(bl), (cr), (br), Michelle Bridwell/Frontera Fotos. **Chapter Three:** Page 53(b),55(br), HRW Photo/Ken Karp; 57(clockwise, l to r), David Frazier Photolibrary; Robert Brenner/PhotoEdit; HRW Photo/Sam Dugeon; Michelle Bridwell/Frontera Fotos, (remaining four), 59 HRW Photo/Sam Dudgeon; 63(bcr), Merten/ZEFA; 63(bl), E. Estenfelder/Helga Lade/Peter Arnold, Inc.; 64, HRW Photo/Sam Dudgeon; 65, Courtesy Zie L. Smith/Smith Productions 1992, from JUMA: Das Jugendmagazin, April 1993, pg. 47.

UNIT TWO: Page 78-79, ZEFA/Waldkirch/The Stock Market. **Chapter Four:** Page 82, HRW Photo/Lisa Davis; 83(b), HRW Photo/Sam Dudgeon; 85(tr), HRW Photo; 86, HRW Photo/Sam Dudgeon; 92, Edge Video Productions. **Chapter Five:** Page 110, HRW Photo/Sam Dudgeon; 111, 135, Edge Video Productions.

UNIT THREE: Page 154-155, W.H. Mueller/ZEFA; 157 (t), (c), (b), Werner H. Muller/Peter Arnold, Inc. **Chapter Seven:** Page 167, Edge Video Productions; 172–173, Pädagogische Aktion E.V.; **Chapter Eight:** Page 187, Edgeo Video Productions; 192(cr), (tr), (bl), Michelle Bridwell/Frontera Fotos. **Chapter Nine:** Page 211(tl), (b), Edge Video Productions.

UNIT FOUR: Chapter Ten: Page 243, Edge Video Productions; 263 (tl), (tr), Edge Video Productions; 273 (tl),(tr), Michelle Bridwell/Frontera Fotos. **Chapter Twelve:** Page 287 (br), (tl), Edge Video Productions.

ILLUSTRATION AND CARTOGRAPHY CREDITS

Unit One: Page 1, GeoSystems.

Chapter 1: Page 10 (t), Michael Krone; 10 (b), George McLeod; 17, Eduard Böhm; 19, Eduard Böhm. **Chapter 2:** Page 38, Paul Hess; 39, Paul Hess; 40, Paul Hess. **Chapter 3:** Page 74, Michael Krone.

Unit Two: Page 79, GeoSystems.

Chapter 4: Page 87, Giorgio Mizzi; 89, Ully Arndt; 95, Giorgio Mizzi; 97, Giorgio Mizzi; 98, Eduard Böhm. **Chapter 5:** Page 112 (l), Eduard Böhm; 112 (r), Maria Lyle; 118, Eduard Böhm; 121, Eduard Böhm. **Chapter 6:** Page 136, Giorgio Mizzi; 137 (l), Giorgio Mizzi; 137 (r), Eduard Böhm; 142, Giorgio Mizzi; 145, Giorgio Mizzi; 146, Eduard Böhm; 147, Giorgio Mizzi; 149, Giorgio Mizzi; 150, Giorgio Mizzi; 152, Giorgio Mizzi.

Unit Three: Page 155, GeoSystems.

Chapter 7: Page 169, Jutta Tillmann; 174, Jutta Tillmann; 178, Jutta Tillmann.

Chapter 8: Page 188, Jutta Tillmann; 190, Eduard Böhm; 193, Biruta Schööl; 195, Tom Rummonds; 196, Antonia Enthoven; 197, Antonia Enthoven. **Chapter 9:** Page 213, George McLeod; 215, Susan Carlson; 217 (t), George McLeod; 217 (b), Aletha Reppel; 220, Michael Krone; 221, Michael Krone.

Unit Four: Page 231, GeoSystems.

Chapter 10 Page 240, George McLeod; 246, Jutta Tillmann; 247, Jutta Tillmann; 250, Jutta Tillmann; 252, Eduard Böhm. **Chapter 11:** Page 265, Maria Lyle; 269, Antonia Enthoven; 273, Camille Meyer. **Chapter 12:** Page 289, Antonia Enthoven; 294, Eduard Böhm; 298, Eduard Böhm; 301, Giorgio Mizzi. **Back Matter:** Page 394, Susan Carlson; 395, Susan Carlson.